UNIX®
for the
Impatient

Second Edition

*

Paul W. Abrahams
Bruce R. Larson

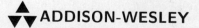
ADDISON-WESLEY

An imprint of Addison Wesley Longman, Inc.

Reading, Massachusetts • Harlow, England • Menlo Park, California • Berkeley, California
Don Mills, Ontario • Sydney • Bonn • Amsterdam • Tokyo • Mexico City

This book was designed and composed by Paul Abrahams. It was typeset using TeX, supplemented by the `eplain` macro package and an extensive set of customized macros. The `eplain` package was written primarily by Karl Berry. The index was prepared with the help of an auxiliary program written in Icon. The cover was designed by Eileen R. Hoff and drawn by Toni St. Regis. The book was phototypeset by Pure Imaging of Watertown, Massachusetts, and printed and bound by Maple Press using Saimamatt 45-lb. paper.

The main text was set in Bitstream Baskerville. Examples and other program text were set in Computer Modern Typewriter with the hard-to-read hat and tilde characters of that font replaced by larger and clearer typeforms. Section and chapter heads were set in Zapf Humanist (the Bitstream version of Optima) and sans-serif material such as keycaps in Bitstream News Gothic.

The companion CD-ROM, included in the CD-ROM version of the book and also available separately, was designed and prepared by QuickScan Electronic Publishing of Marlow, New Hampshire. The *Dyna*Text software was provided by Electronic Book Technologies, Inc., of Providence, Rhode Island.

The quotation on the back cover is reprinted, with permission, from *IEEE Software* **10**(1), January 1993, p. 123.

Access the latest information about Addison-Wesley titles from our World Wide Web site: `http://www.awl.com/cseng`

The Library of Congress has cataloged the second edition of this title as follows:

Abrahams, Paul W.
Unix for the impatient / Paul W. Abrahams, Bruce R. Larson. – 2nd ed.
p. cm.
Includes bibliographical references and index.

1. Operating systems (Computers)   2. UNIX (Computer file)
I. Larson, Bruce R.   II. Title.
QA76.76.063A27   1995
005.4'3–dc20
95-14174
CIP

ISBN 0-201-82376-4
ISBN 0-201-41979-3   Book/CD-ROM

5 6 7 8 9 10 MA   01 00 99 98

5th Printing September, 1998

Preface

UNIX for the Impatient is a UNIX handbook—a detailed, comprehensive guide to the UNIX system that can serve both as a ready reference and as a means of learning UNIX. We've consciously aimed the book at readers who are comfortable with technical material, presenting the subject as concisely as possible rather than in gentle but lengthy tutorial steps and covering in a section what other authors cover in a volume. We achieve that not by omitting details but by omitting long explanations and numerous examples that illustrate a single point. Though the tutorial approach may be less demanding, ours is faster; thus the title of our book.

The UNIX Operating System

UNIX has become the standard operating system for computers in scientific, engineering, and research environments. Designed to be used interactively, UNIX is not bound by inherent memory constraints, handles multiple processes and users easily and naturally, and is well suited as a platform for networking and graphical environments. As the only major operating system not irrevocably tied to a specific hardware architecture, UNIX is particularly well adapted to use in networks of heterogeneous computers. Most UNIX systems now support the graphical user interface provided by the X Window System and most UNIX users use that interface. The result is that UNIX is now as easy and comfortable to use as any of the other graphics-based systems such as Microsoft Windows that are available on workstations and personal computers.

Commercially supported versions of UNIX have long been available for most computers, but their price has usually been prohibitive for individual

iii

users. High-quality free systems that run on personal computers are now widely available as well. The advent of those free systems, Linux in particular, has enormously broadened the population of UNIX users.

The POSIX.1 standard for UNIX-like system calls has been widely accepted for several years and has enabled programmers to write portable UNIX programs. The newer POSIX.2 standard for user commands, the standard on which this book is based, has meant that UNIX systems from different sources and on different computers have become more consistent with one another. Additional POSIX standards under development promise to make it even easier to move among UNIX systems.

But UNIX is not an easy system to learn. In the early days of UNIX when it was still a research project, one person could master all its details and even a casual user could master most of them. That is true no longer. Today's UNIX user faces great obstacles: the profusion of commands and their options, variables, and subcommands; the differences among implementations; the rapid pace of change; the proliferation of related subsystems such as the Network File System and the X Window System; the sheer volume of material to be assimilated; the historical accretions; and the assumption all too prevalent in UNIX documentation that the reader is already familiar with what is being described.

Technically sophisticated people often prefer to learn new programs and computer systems by reading the reference manuals, but it's hard to learn UNIX that way. The traditional UNIX reference manual consists of an alphabetical list of command descriptions called "manual pages". Many manual pages are cryptic, misleading, poorly organized, or erroneous in subtle ways. UNIX-specific terminology is often used without being defined; terminology is often used inconsistently from one command to another. The customary alphabetical list of options makes it difficult to see how the options relate to one another. Few manuals provide an overview or explanation of the basic UNIX concepts, and those that do often rely on early technical papers that are now about two decades old and cannot reflect what has happened since they were written.

Overview of the Book

The central purpose of *UNIX for the Impatient* is to serve as a better manual for people who like to learn from manuals. We tell you about those undocumented, confusing, or subtle aspects of UNIX commands that a reading of the manual pages is unlikely to reveal. Rather than lead you by the hand through UNIX, we assist you in finding your own way. If you're seeking an easier but slower route to learning how to use UNIX, we suggest getting started with tutorial books (you may need several) and then turning to *UNIX for the Impatient* as you progress.

We describe UNIX from the standpoint of a user; that is, a person primarily interested in it as a tool rather than as an object of study for its own sake. Much of the book consists of command descriptions, usually as detailed as the ones in your system's manual. An important difference between our book and your manual is that we've organized the book and its parts, including the descriptions of the commands, logically by function rather than alphabetically. The functional arrangement enables you to see how different commands and options relate to one another, making it easier to find the right tools for a particular task. We include an alphabetical summary of commands and their options cross-referenced to the pages where you'll find the full descriptions. You can use the alphabetical summary both to get a quick reminder of what a particular command or option does and to retrieve the full description. The synopsis preceding the table of contents provides a fast overview of everything in the book and we have paid particular attention to providing a thorough index.

In the second chapter of the book we cover the essential concepts of UNIX such as processes, files, shells, regular expressions, pipes, and redirection. These concepts underly the detailed descriptions in the rest of the book. We also provide a glossary containing concise definitions of UNIX terminology. When you encounter a technical term that you haven't seen before, you can easily find out what it means. We provide abundant cross-references to help you through the thicket of dependencies among different UNIX commands and concepts. To get you oriented, we provide a discussion of how to use this book in Section 1.3.

In keeping with our orientation of *UNIX for the Impatient* as a book primarily for users, we don't generally say much about UNIX internals—those aspects of UNIX mainly of interest to system programmers—although if you're a system programmer, this book can still be helpful for dealing with the external aspects of UNIX. Nor do we attempt to describe the programming facilities of UNIX such as the C compiler, `lex`, and `yacc`. How to use these tools, particularly C, can occupy a book by itself.

We do, however, describe `awk`, which is relatively easy to learn and which provides an easy way of transforming and filtering data while enabling you to carry out fairly complex programming tasks. In a few places, such as our discussions of `awk` and of shell scripts, we assume some familiarity with programming methods and terminology—we couldn't avoid it—but most of the book can be understood even if you aren't familiar with programming.

Why UNIX Is Hard to Describe

UNIX has become what it is today more through accretion than through conscious planning. There's a principle of programming language design called "orthogonality"—the idea that different aspects of the language interact as little as possible and can be treated independently. UNIX, unfortunately, violates that principle egregiously. Programs are sensitive to the conventions of other programs and interact with each other in complex ways. For example, the `vi` visual editor was built on top of the `ex` extended line editor, so-called because it extended the earlier `ed` editor. Thus to understand `vi` fully you also must know `ex` even though you have no interest in `ex` for its own sake.

Moreover, many UNIX facilities are someone's improvement or elaboration on an existing facility. The old version persists even when the new version is indisputably better. Programs with overlapping functions are common. Thus there are three data compression programs, `pack`, `compress`, and `gzip`; at least two different mail programs that call themselves `mail`; and several programs for splitting files into segments, `head`, `tail`, `split`, `csplit`, and `dd`. There are at least four widely used shells for managing interaction with your terminal: the KornShell `ksh`, the Bourne shell `sh`, the C shell `csh`, and Bash, the GNU "Bourne-again Shell".

This profusion of similar facilities created a dilemma for us. How many of these programs should we try to cover? We have chosen to describe nearly all the utility commands despite their overlapping functions. On the other hand, we have based our discussion of shells in general on the KornShell, since that shell includes nearly all the facilities found in the others. We supplement that discussion by a description of the features of the other shells where they differ from the KornShell.

British lorries roll on tyres, while American trucks roll on tires. Just as there are many dialects of English, there are many versions of UNIX. Fortunately the POSIX.2 standard has brought a measure of consistency to the UNIX world; most implementors now adhere to it. But major differences among systems persist, particularly between System V-based systems and BSD-based systems. The POSIX specifications for some commands such as `man` and `ps` are deliberately skeletal, recognizing that the differences among existing implementations are too great to be bridged. Most systems provide additional commands beyond those specified by POSIX and additional options for the commands that are specified by POSIX. Pre-POSIX systems such as Solaris 1.x are still widely used, and pre-POSIX commands are still often found in otherwise POSIX-conforming systems.

The command descriptions in the Second Edition of *UNIX for the Impatient* follow the POSIX standard. However, we note many important variations and include a number of commands that are not part of POSIX. For example, we describe both the POSIX `lp` command for sending files to a line printer, derived from the System V command of the same name, and the BSD `lpr` command that does nearly the same thing but does it differently. You may find that some commands don't work on *your* system exactly as we describe them, but the differences will usually be minor.

Our Approach

You'll find topics covered in this book that don't make it into most UNIX books. Some examples are the X Window System, the `emacs` editor, communications programs such as `telnet` and `ftp`, the addressing conventions used for Internet and UUCP electronic mail, and popular but nonstandard utilities such as the `gzip` compression program and the `shar` archiver for sending files via electronic mail. Although we hope this book is the first one you take off the shelf, we realize it may not be the last, so we provide a list of printed and electronic resources you can use for additional information or for another view of the same material.

Our approach to UNIX is like Albert Einstein's approach to physics: make it as simple as possible, but no simpler. We explain UNIX as clearly as we can without neglecting difficult or complicated, but nevertheless essential, details. While some of these details may not seem important when you first see them, you're likely to find them indispensable as you read the manuals supplied with your system.

For those who notice such things, we mention that we've adopted the British (logical) treatment of punctuation at the end of a sentence: when a quotation ends a sentence, we place the period outside the quotation. We consider this policy necessary for any book whose subject matter demands great orthographic precision. We appreciate the indulgence of our editors.

Some people use UNIX by choice, others by necessity. We hope *UNIX for the Impatient* will be useful to you whatever your view of UNIX may be.

About the Second Edition	The Second Edition of *UNIX for the Impatient* reflects both the dramatic changes in the UNIX world from 1991 to 1995 and changes in our own understanding of how we as authors can best meet the needs of our readers. The world of commercial UNIX has been profoundly affected by AT&T's sale of UNIX Systems Laboratories (USL) to Novell, Inc., and by the refinement and general acceptance of the POSIX standards. High-quality free systems such as Linux and FreeBSD, complete with source code unaffected by USL licensing restrictions, have appeared, at last making UNIX affordable and available to individual users. The scope of the software components found in the GNU collection from the Free Software Foundation has broadened and the components themselves have matured; some of these components are now used in nearly every UNIX installation. The number of Internet users, the services available through the Internet, and the number of Internet service providers have all multiplied prodigiously to the point where "Internet" is now a household term and great numbers of people access the Internet as individuals, not as members of some organization.

In the First Edition we used System V as the base for our description of UNIX's facilities; in the Second Edition we use the POSIX.2 standard. This shift has led us to introduce descriptions of additional commands and has brought about many and pervasive textual revisions, including changes in terminology to be consistent with POSIX. Following the practice in the POSIX standard, we have replaced most generalized references to "*options*" in the syntax of commands with lists of the specific options each command accepts.

Because POSIX has already been widely adopted and POSIX conformance by UNIX vendors is increasing, you are now likely to find fewer differences between the features we describe and the ones you find in your particular version of UNIX. Nearly all the purely syntactic changes specified by POSIX are for the sake of greater uniformity and consistency. These changes have made the UNIX command interface much easier to use.

We have greatly expanded the number of commands we cover. The Second Edition describes all the POSIX user-level commands except for a few specifically intended for programmers: `ctags` and `nm` from the User Portability Utilities and `ar`, `make`, and `strip` from the Software Development Utilities. We have, however, retained our brief discussion of tag tables from the First Edition, and the material on software installation includes a discussion of makefiles from the user's viewpoint. We have also added some widely used non-POSIX commands such as `gzip` and `shar`.

It would take a separate book to provide anything like an adequate guide to the Internet, and indeed a number of such books have already been written. In this book we have expanded our Internet coverage to include the World Wide Web and other tools for exploring the riches of the Internet. We also include an explanation of USENET newsgroups and the newsreader programs used to access them.

Version 19 of Emacs is fully integrated with the X Window System and has many new and enhanced features. We have expanded our coverage of Emacs and have divided our treatment into two parts: a chapter on the editing facilities proper and another on Emacs's rich set of utilities, utilities such as the Directory Editor, the Mailer, and the Outliner.

The Bourne shell `sh` has largely been superseded as a user-level shell, even though it still provides a base set of facilities useful for writing shell scripts intended for general distribution. We have replaced its description by a description of the KornShell `ksh`, which provides a superset of the shell facilities specified by POSIX and also of those in the Bourne shell. We note those features of the KornShell that are not supported by the POSIX shell or the Bourne shell. We have folded our description of the C shell into the description of the KornShell and have added material on Bash.

As use of UNIX has spread beyond its American origins, internationalization has become essential to many UNIX users. The POSIX standard provides locales and other features that make UNIX suitable for international use. We have added a section on internationalization to the Concepts chapter and have modified the descriptions of UNIX facilities to account for the new POSIX features.

The brief section on "System Administration for Single-User Systems" has been moved and expanded into a full chapter, "Managing Your System". The new chapter covers important system files such as those usually found in the `/etc` directory and programs such as `mount`, `lpd`, and `init` that provide administrative services. It also explains how to install new software, particularly in the usual case where the software has been distributed in the form of source code. While intended primarily for readers who are running single-user systems for themselves, the new chapter should be helpful to users of larger systems who wish to understand what is going on within those systems or need to install software from an outside source. It will also assist anyone attempting to decode the frequent references to these files and programs in the UNIX literature.

About the CD-ROM

UNIX for the Hyper-Impatient is a hypertext version of *UNIX for the Impatient*, distributed on a CD-ROM. The idea of it came from Lisa Richards of QuickScan Electronic Publishing, who pointed out that a book such as this one is a natural candidate for a hypertext form because there are so many cross-references from one part to another. *UNIX for the Hyper-Impatient* is included in the CD-ROM version of this book and is also available separately.

UNIX for the Hyper-Impatient contains the entire text of *UNIX for the Impatient*, together with the *Dyna*Text browser developed by Electronic Book Technologies of Providence, Rhode Island. The primary view of the book contains two windows, one showing the Table of Contents and the other the text of the book. Using the Table of Contents, which you can expand or collapse, you can select any part of the book and scroll through the text starting there.

Wherever there's a cross-reference in the printed book, there's a hyperlink in the hypertext version. By clicking your mouse on that hyperlink, you can jump directly to the cross-referenced text, then easily return to where you were before. You can also check out all the index references to a topic by going to the index entry, then looking at the references one by one. Footnotes and figures don't interrupt the flow of the text; you view them by clicking on an icon that appears where the footnote or figure is referenced. You can also search either the entire book or just the headings, using a variety of search specifications.

Information about the features of the *Dyna*Text browser and how to use the CD-ROM is provided in the shaded pages at the end of the CD-ROM version of the printed book and in the booklet that accompanies the separately packaged version of *UNIX for the Hyper-Impatient*.

Acknowledgments

We wish to thank our colleagues at Addison-Wesley who made this book possible, especially Peter Gordon, our editor, who conceived the idea of the book and whose encouragement and helpful suggestions were invaluable, and Helen Goldstein, his associate editor, who patiently and unfailingly navigated the book past many obstacles. We are grateful to our production supervisors, Loren Hilgenhurst Stevens for the First Edition and Nancy Fenton for the Second Edition, whose skill and patience contributed so much to turning a manuscript into a book; and to Karen Wernholm and Patricia Unubun, the production supervisors of the CD-ROM version, for their help in dealing with all the novel problems of this type of production. We thank Lorraine Ferrier, the able proofreader of the First Edition, for an exceptionally thorough job performed under stringent time constraints. To Constance G. Burt, the proofreader of the Second Edition, we pay the ultimate compliment a fastidious author can offer: we agreed with practically all her corrections.

We also wish to thank George Lukas, who helped refine the original plan of the book; Bob Morris, Betty O'Neil, and Rick Martin of the Computer Science Department at the University of Massachusetts, Boston, who generously provided us with access to the Department's computing facilities; Karl Berry, who provided us with access to several UNIX systems and patiently answered many of our questions, both about UNIX and about TₑX; Keith Bostic of UC Berkeley for his assistance in interpreting the POSIX standard and figuring out how the bugs in it might be fixed; Jack Dwyer of the Open Software Foundation for answering many questions about the role of OSF in UNIX development; Paul English, who provided us with access to a variety of other UNIX systems; Rob Kolstad of Berkeley Software Design for providing information about recent BSD systems and their derivatives; Michael Larson, who carefully checked and critiqued much of the First Edition and the Emacs chapters in the Second Edition; Don Libes for his valuable explanation of the mystical behavior of 'cat -u'; Jared P. Martin of the Shell Oil Company for his many small but essential corrections; Sandra O'Donnell of the Open Software Foundation for her enlightening explanation of the subtler aspects of POSIX locales; Frank and Lisa Richards of QuickScan Electronic Publishing for suggesting the CD-ROM version and for their skill and hard work in developing it; Peter Weidner for his comments on the First Edition, which we've gratefully applied to the Second Edition; Dick Wood and Jeff Hanson of X/Open for clarifying to us the new role of X/Open as custodian of the UNIX trademark; and Jerry Nowlin of Iconic Software, Inc., John Norden of Amdahl, and John Chambers and Dick Muldoon of USL, who answered some of our more exotic questions.

We especially thank the reviewers of both editions, whose comments and feedback made the book far better than it would have been otherwise: Manuel Bermudez, Don Bolinger, Lyn Dupré, Jennifer Knuth, Alan Langerman, George Leach, Thomas F. Reid, Bjorn Satdeva, Steven Stepanek, Gregory Tucker, and Gerald Weiss. Of course, the responsibility for any improvements we should have made but didn't remains our own.

Then there are our individual debts of gratitude to those who provided us with support and encouragement and were so patient and understanding with us: from Bruce to his friends and colleagues Susan Kubany, Bob Heinmiller, and Dave Curado of Omnet, Inc., and Mike Gauthier and Henry McAvoy of Artis, Ltd., and to his wife, Cathy, and his children, Elsa and Eric; and from Paul to his daughter, Jodi, his sister, Nan Rubin, his parents, Al and Evelyn Abrahams, and his companion during the development of the CD-ROM version, Roberta B. Morris.

Bruce wishes to express his personal gratitude to Tom Wester and Ted Treibick of Vianet, Larry Conway and Larry Cudlitz of Epsilon, and Karl Berry for the support they gave him during the preparation of the Second Edition.

Deerfield, Massachusetts   P. W. A.
Milton, Massachusetts   B. R. L.

Synopsis

1 Introduction • 1

UNIX Background ∘ The POSIX.2 Standard ∘ How to Use This Book ∘ Typographical Conventions ∘ Syntactic Conventions ∘ Getting Started

2 Concepts • 24

The UNIX Manual ∘ System Administration and the Superuser ∘ Users and Groups ∘ What the Shell Does ∘ The UNIX Kernel ∘ Processes ∘ The UNIX File System ∘ File Permissions ∘ Conventions for Using Files ∘ Standard Files and Redirection ∘ Other Facilities for Interprocess Communication ∘ UNIX Commands ∘ Local Variables ∘ Initialization Files ∘ Terminal Descriptions ∘ Locales, Code Sets, and Internationalization ∘ Regular Expressions ∘ Devices

3 Operations on Files • 92

Operations on Directories ∘ Listing Files with `ls` ∘ Displaying and Concatenating Files with `cat` ∘ Linking, Moving, and Copying Files with `ln`, `mv`, and `cp` ∘ Removing Files ∘ Examining Files or Output with a Pager ∘ Printing Files ∘ Finding Files with `find` ∘ Locating, Classifying, and Checking Files ∘ Comparing Files ∘ Controlling File Access and Ownership ∘ Miscellaneous File Utilities ∘ Data Compression and Encoding ∘ Archiving Sets of Files ∘ Examining Files with `od` ∘ Copying and Converting Data with `dd` ∘ Updating Files with `patch` ∘ Creating Special Files

4   Data Manipulation Using Filters   •   170

Sorting Files with `sort` ∘ Finding Patterns with `grep` ∘ Simple Data Transformations ∘ Extracting Parts of Files ∘ Combining Files ∘ Using `sed` to Edit from a Script ∘ The `awk` Programming Language ∘ Other Data Manipulation Languages

5   Utility Programs   •   226

Information Services ∘ Reporting on the Status of Processes ∘ Managing Processes ∘ Commands Related to Logging In ∘ Controlling Your Terminal ∘ On-Line Communication with Other Users ∘ Disk Usage Statistics ∘ Writing and Reading Strings ∘ Evaluating Expressions ∘ Special Invocation of Commands ∘ Querying Your UNIX Environment ∘ Miscellaneous Services ∘ Producing Locale Information and Defining a Locale ∘ Document Processing ∘ Version Control

6   The Korn and POSIX Shells   •   307

Overview of the KornShell ∘ Interacting with the Shell ∘ Editing an Input Line ∘ Calling the Shell Directly ∘ Shell Scripts ∘ Syntax of Shell Input ∘ Patterns ∘ Simple Commands ∘ Linking Commands with Operators ∘ Redirection ∘ Here-Documents ∘ The `test`, `true`, and `false` Commands ∘ Compound Commands ∘ How Commands Are Executed ∘ Parameters ∘ Parameter Expansions ∘ Quotation ∘ Substitutions ∘ Aliases ∘ Commands for Job Control ∘ The Command History and the `fc` Command ∘ Intrinsic Commands and Predefined Aliases ∘ Predefined Variables Used by the Shell ∘ Execution Options ∘ Initialization Files for the Shell ∘ Parsing Command Lines with `getopts` ∘ A Sample Shell Script

7   Other Shells   •   381

The C Shell `csh` ∘ Bash, the "Bourne-again Shell"

8   Standard Editors   •   411

The `vi` Visual Editor ∘ Local Variables for `vi` and `ex` ∘ The Extended Editor `ex` ∘ The `ed` Line Editor ∘ Tag Files

9   The GNU Emacs Editor   •   467

Calling and Terminating Emacs ∘ Conventions for Typing Input ∘ Getting Acquainted with Emacs ∘ Emacs Concepts ∘ How to Issue Commands ∘ Getting Help ∘ Exiting from or Suspending Emacs ∘ Basic Editing Commands ∘ Mouse Operations on Text ∘ Additional Editing Commands ∘ Indentation ∘ Operations on Rectangles ∘ Operations on Windows ∘ Operations on Frames ∘ Operations on Files ∘ Explicit Operations on Buffers ∘ The Buffer Menu ∘ Printing ∘ Registers and Their Operations ∘ Searching and Replacing ∘ Operations on Variables ∘ Evaluating LISP Expressions ∘ Executing UNIX Commands from Emacs ∘ Environmental Inquiries ∘ Customizing Emacs

10   Emacs Utilities   •   550

Directory Operations with Dired ∘ Composing and Editing Pictures ∘ Tags and Tag Tables ∘ The Emacs Mailer ∘ The GNUS Newsreader ∘ The Calendar ∘ The Diary ∘ The Version Control Interface ∘ Amusements

11   Mailers and Newsreaders • 582

What's in a Message? ○ Recipients ○ Mailboxes ○ Forwarding Mail ○ The `mailx` (Berkeley `Mail`) Mailer ○ Other Mailers ○ Archiving Files for Mailing with `shar` ○ Newsgroups and Newsreaders ○ UNIX Newsreaders

12   Communicating with Remote Computers • 617

Network Addresses ○ Local-Area Networks ○ Distributing Files Over Networks ○ Internet Resources ○ Programs for Remote Communications ○ Remote Operations on "Nearby" Computers ○ Calling a Remote Computer with `telnet` ○ Transferring Files Between Computers with `ftp` ○ File Transfers Based on `uucp` ○ Connecting to Remote Computers with `cu`

13   The X Window System • 670

The X Screen ○ Getting Started and Quitting ○ Window Managers ○ Servers, Displays, and Display Specifications ○ Widgets ○ Properties ○ Command-Line Options for X Applications ○ Resources and Their Specifications ○ The Resource Database ○ Geometry Specifications ○ Fonts ○ Colors ○ Initialization Files for X ○ The `xterm` Terminal Emulator ○ Informational Displays for X ○ Color and Font Information for X ○ Clients for Initializing and Customizing X ○ Killing an X Client with `xkill` ○ Viewing Manual Pages with `xman`

14   Managing Your System • 689

Running with Superuser Privileges ○ System Administration Programs ○ Explicit System Administration ○ Software Installation ○ File System Maintenance ○ Startup and Shutdown

Appendixes

A   Alphabetical Summary of Commands • 708

List of Commands ○ Summary of Commands and Features

B   Comparison of MS-DOS and UNIX • 784

Treatment of Files ○ MS-DOS Commands and Their UNIX Equivalents ○ Other Related Features

C   Resources • 789

Books ○ CD-ROMs

D   Glossary • 796

Index • 808

Using the CD-ROM   (CD-ROM version only) • **CD-1**

Directory Structure ○ Available DynaText Browsers ○ Installing the DynaText Software ○ Using the DynaText Software ○ Installing the Emacs Editor ○ Installing and Using Slackware Linux

Contents

1   Introduction • 1

1.1   UNIX Background • 1

1.1.1   Early History ∘ 1
1.1.2   System V ∘ 2
1.1.3   The BSD Systems ∘ 3
1.1.4   The X Window System ∘ 5
1.1.5   Licensing and Its Effects ∘ 5
1.1.6   Non-AT&T Commercial Systems ∘ 6
1.1.7   Free UNIX Systems ∘ 7
1.1.8   UNIX Then and Now ∘ 9
1.1.9   UNIX Standards ∘ 9
1.1.10   The Role of C in UNIX ∘ 11

1.2   The POSIX.2 Standard • 11

1.2.1   Goals of POSIX.2 ∘ 11
1.2.2   Components of POSIX.2 ∘ 12

1.3   How to Use This Book • 13

1.4   Typographical Conventions • 15

1.5   Syntactic Conventions • 16

1.6   Getting Started • 18

1.6.1   Logging In for the First Time ∘ 19
1.6.2   Installing a New System ∘ 21
1.6.3   Ten Particularly Useful Commands and Constructs ∘ 22

2 Concepts • 24

2.1	The UNIX Manual • 24	
	2.1.1	Viewing Manual Pages with **man** ○ 25
	2.1.2	Viewing Manual Pages Under X ○ 26
	2.1.3	Other Sources of UNIX Documentation ○ 26
2.2	System Administration and the Superuser • 26	
2.3	Users and Groups • 27	
2.4	What the Shell Does • 28	
2.5	The UNIX Kernel • 29	
2.6	Processes • 30	
	2.6.1	Signals ○ 31
	2.6.2	Exit Status of a Process ○ 32
	2.6.3	Job Control ○ 33
	2.6.4	Process Groups ○ 35
	2.6.5	Environment Variables ○ 35
	2.6.6	Real and Effective Users and Groups ○ 36
2.7	The UNIX File System • 36	
	2.7.1	Filenames ○ 37
	2.7.2	Pathnames ○ 38
	2.7.3	Home Directories ○ 39
	2.7.4	Subsidiary File Systems ○ 40
	2.7.5	Links ○ 41
	2.7.6	Symbolic Links ○ 41
	2.7.7	How Files Are Stored ○ 42
	2.7.8	Space Limitations on Files ○ 43
	2.7.9	Buffers ○ 43
2.8	File Permissions • 44	
	2.8.1	Permissions for Basic Operations ○ 44
	2.8.2	Other File Permissions ○ 46
	2.8.3	Constructing Permission Sets Symbolically ○ 48
	2.8.4	Octal Representation of Permissions ○ 50
	2.8.5	Permissions for Newly Created Files ○ 50
2.9	Conventions for Using Files • 51	
	2.9.1	Wildcards in Pathnames ○ 51
	2.9.2	The **PATH** Environment Variable ○ 52
	2.9.3	Conventions for Naming Directories ○ 53
	2.9.4	The Linux File System Standard ○ 55
	2.9.5	Compressed Files ○ 55
2.10	Standard Files and Redirection • 56	
	2.10.1	Pipes and Filters ○ 57
	2.10.2	File Descriptors ○ 58
2.11	Other Facilities for Interprocess Communication • 58	
	2.11.1	FIFO Special Files (Named Pipes) ○ 59
	2.11.2	Sockets ○ 59
	2.11.3	Streams ○ 60

2.12   UNIX Commands • 60
        2.12.1   Standard Syntax of Commands   ∘   60
        2.12.2   Quotation   ∘   63
        2.12.3   Command Substitution   ∘   63
        2.12.4   Other Common Conventions   ∘   64

2.13   Local Variables • 65

2.14   Initialization Files • 66

2.15   Terminal Descriptions • 68
        2.15.1   Codes and Control Sequences   ∘   68
        2.15.2   The `termcap` and `terminfo` Databases   ∘   69
        2.15.3   Examining `terminfo`   ∘   70
        2.15.4   Initialization and Reset   ∘   70
        2.15.5   Designating Your Terminal Type   ∘   70
        2.15.6   Terminal Emulation   ∘   71
        2.15.7   Setting Your Terminal Type   ∘   72

2.16   Locales, Code Sets, and Internationalization • 72
        2.16.1   Code Sets   ∘   73
        2.16.2   Character Maps   ∘   74
        2.16.3   Locale Categories   ∘   75
        2.16.4   Environment Variables for Locales   ∘   80

2.17   Regular Expressions • 81
        2.17.1   Basic Regular Expressions   ∘   81
        2.17.2   Extended Regular Expressions   ∘   84
        2.17.3   Precedence for Regular Expressions   ∘   85
        2.17.4   Replacements for Regular Expressions   ∘   85
        2.17.5   Multiple Matches   ∘   86

2.18   Devices • 86
        2.18.1   Character Devices and Block Devices   ∘   87
        2.18.2   Special Files and Their Interfaces   ∘   88
        2.18.3   Interfaces for Terminals   ∘   89
        2.18.4   Device Numbers   ∘   90
        2.18.5   Device Names for Hardware Devices   ∘   90
        2.18.6   Other Devices   ∘   91

3   **Operations on Files • 92**

3.1   Operations on Directories • 92
        3.1.1   Changing Directories with `cd`   ∘   92
        3.1.2   Showing the Working Directory with `pwd`   ∘   93
        3.1.3   Creating a Directory with `mkdir`   ∘   93

3.2   Listing Files with `ls` • 94
        3.2.1   Command-Line Options   ∘   95
        3.2.2   Interpreting the Long Format   ∘   97

3.3   Displaying and Concatenating Files with `cat` • 98

3.4   Linking, Moving, and Copying Files with `ln`, `mv`, and `cp` • 100
        3.4.1   Linking Files with `ln`   ∘   101
        3.4.2   Moving Files with `mv`   ∘   102
        3.4.3   Copying Files with `cp`   ∘   103

3.5　　Removing Files　•　105
　　　3.5.1　Removing Links with `rm`　○　105
　　　3.5.2　Removing Links to Directories with `rmdir`　○　106
　　　3.5.3　Removing Files with Unusual Names　○　106

3.6　　Examining Files or Output with a Pager　•　107
　　　3.6.1　The `more` Pager　○　108
　　　3.6.2　The Model of the Screen　○　108
　　　3.6.3　Interactive Commands for `more`　○　109
　　　3.6.4　Command-Line Options for `more`　○　112
　　　3.6.5　Environment Variables for `more`　○　113

3.7　　Printing Files　•　113
　　　3.7.1　Printing Files with `lp`　○　114
　　　3.7.2　Printing Files Under BSD with `lpr`　○　115
　　　3.7.3　Displaying Printer Status with `lpstat`　○　117
　　　3.7.4　Cancelling Printer Requests with `cancel`　○　118
　　　3.7.5　Formatting Files for Printing with `pr`　○　118

3.8　　Finding Files with `find`　•　121
　　　3.8.1　Primary Tests for `find`　○　122
　　　3.8.2　Logical Combinations of Tests　○　126
　　　3.8.3　Examples　○　127

3.9　　Locating, Classifying, and Checking Files　•　127
　　　3.9.1　Locating Programs with `which`　○　128
　　　3.9.2　Classifying Files with `file`　○　128
　　　3.9.3　Checksumming Files with `cksum`　○　129
　　　3.9.4　Checking Pathnames with `pathchk`　○　129

3.10　Comparing Files　•　129
　　　3.10.1　Comparing Files with `cmp`　○　130
　　　3.10.2　Finding Differences Between Files with `diff`　○　130

3.11　Controlling File Access and Ownership　•　134
　　　3.11.1　Setting Access Permissions with `chmod`　○　134
　　　3.11.2　Reducing Default File Permissions with `umask`　○　135
　　　3.11.3　Setting Ownership with `chown` and `chgrp`　○　136

3.12　Miscellaneous File Utilities　•　137
　　　3.12.1　Counting Words, Lines, or Characters with `wc`　○　137
　　　3.12.2　Touching a File with `touch`　○　138
　　　3.12.3　Duplicating Input with `tee`　○　139

3.13　Data Compression and Encoding　•　139
　　　3.13.1　Compression with `compress`　○　140
　　　3.13.2　Compression with `gzip` and `gunzip`　○　141
　　　3.13.3　Encoding and Decoding with `uuencode` and `uudecode`　○　143

3.14　Archiving Sets of Files　•　144
　　　3.14.1　The `pax` Portable Archiver　○　145
　　　3.14.2　The `tar` Tape Archiver　○　151
　　　3.14.3　Copying Archives with `cpio`　○　154

3.15　Examining Files with `od`　•　158
　　　3.15.1　Type Specifications　○　158
　　　3.15.2　Command-Line Options　○　159
　　　3.15.3　An Example　○　159
　　　3.15.4　Older System V Syntax of `od`　○　160

3.16   Copying and Converting Data with `dd` • 160

        3.16.1   How the Files Are Processed   ○   161
        3.16.2   Operands   ○   161
        3.16.3   Keywords for Data Conversions   ○   162
        3.16.4   Examples   ○   164

3.17   Updating Files with `patch` • 164

        3.17.1   Determining the Files to be Patched   ○   165
        3.17.2   Command-Line Options   ○   166
        3.17.3   Examples   ○   167

3.18   Creating Special Files • 168

        3.18.1   Making FIFO Special Files with `mkfifo`   ○   168
        3.18.2   Making Special Files with `mknod`   ○   169

4   Data Manipulation Using Filters • 170

4.1   Sorting Files with `sort` • 170

        4.1.1   Key Specifications   ○   171
        4.1.2   Options Affecting the Entire Sort   ○   173
        4.1.3   Flags Applying to Individual Keys   ○   174

4.2   Finding Patterns with `grep` • 175

4.3   Simple Data Transformations • 177

        4.3.1   Translating or Deleting Characters with `tr`   ○   177
        4.3.2   Extracting Portions of Input Lines with `cut`   ○   179
        4.3.3   Folding Long Lines with `fold`   ○   181
        4.3.4   Transforming Spaces to Tabs and Vice Versa   ○   181
        4.3.5   Eliminating Repeated Lines with `uniq`   ○   183
        4.3.6   Listing Common Lines with `comm`   ○   184

4.4   Extracting Parts of Files • 184

        4.4.1   Extracting the Beginning of a File with `head`   ○   184
        4.4.2   Extracting the End of a File with `tail`   ○   184
        4.4.3   Splitting Files by Context with `csplit`   ○   186
        4.4.4   Splitting Files by Counts with `split`   ○   188

4.5   Combining Files • 189

        4.5.1   Pasting Fields from Several Files with `paste`   ○   189
        4.5.2   Joining Two Database Files with `join`   ○   190

4.6   Using `sed` to Edit from a Script • 192

        4.6.1   Command-Line Options   ○   193
        4.6.2   The Editing Cycle   ○   193
        4.6.3   Form of an Editing Script   ○   194
        4.6.4   Commands   ○   195

4.7   The `awk` Programming Language • 199

        4.7.1   Calling `awk`   ○   199
        4.7.2   Simple `awk` Programs   ○   200
        4.7.3   Form of an `awk` Program   ○   201
        4.7.4   Regular Expressions in `awk`   ○   202
        4.7.5   Program Format   ○   203
        4.7.6   Values and Expressions   ○   203

4.7.7   Constants and Variables   ○   205
4.7.8   Type of an Expression   ○   206
4.7.9   Fields and Field Variables   ○   206
4.7.10   Arrays   ○   207
4.7.11   Operators   ○   208
4.7.12   Function Calls   ○   212
4.7.13   Predefined String Functions   ○   213
4.7.14   Predefined Numerical Functions   ○   215
4.7.15   Reading Input Explicitly   ○   216
4.7.16   Producing Output   ○   217
4.7.17   Closing Files and Pipes   ○   219
4.7.18   Executing System Commands   ○   220
4.7.19   Predefined Variables   ○   220
4.7.20   Expressions as Statements   ○   221
4.7.21   Control-Flow Statements   ○   222
4.7.22   User-Defined Functions   ○   223

4.8   Other Data Manipulation Languages   •   224

4.8.1   The Icon Programming Language   ○   224
4.8.2   The `perl` Language   ○   225

5   Utility Programs   •   226

5.1   Information Services   •   226

5.1.1   Viewing Manual Pages with `man`   ○   226
5.1.2   Who's Using the System: `who`   ○   228
5.1.3   Looking Up User Information with `finger`   ○   230
5.1.4   Getting Terminal Information with `tty`   ○   232
5.1.5   Showing the Date and Time with `date`   ○   232
5.1.6   Displaying a Calendar with `cal`   ○   234

5.2   Reporting on the Status of Processes   •   235

5.2.1   Showing Processes with `ps` (System V Version)   ○   235
5.2.2   Showing Processes with `ps` (BSD Version)   ○   237
5.2.3   Showing Processes with `ps` (POSIX Version)   ○   240

5.3   Managing Processes   •   242

5.3.1   Signalling Processes with `kill`   ○   242
5.3.2   Ignoring Hangups with `nohup`   ○   243
5.3.3   Scheduling Future Activities with `at` and `batch`   ○   243
5.3.4   Scheduling Periodic Jobs with `crontab`   ○   246
5.3.5   Running a Command at Low Priority with `nice`   ○   248
5.3.6   Adjusting Process Priorities with `renice`   ○   248
5.3.7   Suspending Execution with `sleep`   ○   249
5.3.8   Waiting for a Process with `wait`   ○   249

5.4   Commands Related to Logging In   •   250

5.4.1   Logging In with `login`   ○   250
5.4.2   Changing User Identity with `su`   ○   252
5.4.3   Changing Your Group with `newgrp`   ○   253
5.4.4   Changing Your Password with `passwd`   ○   254
5.4.5   Changing Your Login Shell with `chsh`   ○   254
5.4.6   Returning Your Login Name with `logname`   ○   255
5.4.7   Showing User and Group IDs with `id`   ○   255

5.5   Controlling Your Terminal   •   256
         5.5.1   Preparing Your Terminal with `tset`   ○   256
         5.5.2   Setting Your Terminal Characteristics with `stty`   ○   260
         5.5.3   Sending Instructions to Your Terminal with `tput`   ○   265
         5.5.4   Setting Tabs with `tabs`   ○   267

5.6   On-Line Communication with Other Users   •   269
         5.6.1   Talking to Another User with `talk`   ○   269
         5.6.2   Sending Messages with `write`   ○   270
         5.6.3   Turning Messages On and Off with `mesg`   ○   270

5.7   Disk Usage Statistics   •   270
         5.7.1   Reporting Free Disk Space with `df`   ○   271
         5.7.2   Reporting Disk Space in Use with `du`   ○   271

5.8   Writing and Reading Strings   •   272
         5.8.1   Echoing a String with `echo`   ○   272
         5.8.2   Producing Output with `printf`   ○   274
         5.8.3   Producing KornShell Output with `print`   ○   278
         5.8.4   Reading an Input Line with `read`   ○   279

5.9   Evaluating Expressions   •   280
         5.9.1   The `bc` Calculator   ○   280
         5.9.2   The `expr` Evaluator   ○   286

5.10   Special Invocation of Commands   •   287
         5.10.1   Invoking a Program with `command`   ○   288
         5.10.2   Constructing Command Arguments with `xargs`   ○   289

5.11   Querying Your UNIX Environment   •   290
         5.11.1   Producing System Information with `uname`   ○   291
         5.11.2   Getting Configuration Values with `getconf`   ○   291

5.12   Miscellaneous Services   •   292
         5.12.1   Classifying Commands with `type`   ○   292
         5.12.2   Timing a Command with `time`   ○   292
         5.12.3   Locating Strings in Files with `strings`   ○   293
         5.12.4   Parsing Pathnames   ○   294
         5.12.5   Recording Errors in the System Log   ○   295

5.13   Producing Locale Information and Defining a Locale   •   295
         5.13.1   Displaying Locale Information with `locale`   ○   296
         5.13.2   Defining a New Locale with `localedef`   ○   297

5.14   Document Processing   •   298
         5.14.1   The `nroff` and `troff` Formatters   ○   298
         5.14.2   Preprocessors for `nroff` and `troff`   ○   299
         5.14.3   TeX and LaTeX   ○   301

5.15   Version Control   •   302
         5.15.1   RCS Functions   ○   302
         5.15.2   Basic Concepts of RCS   ○   303
         5.15.3   Version Numbering and Naming   ○   305
         5.15.4   The RCS Utilities Set   ○   305

6   The Korn and POSIX Shells • 307

6.1   Overview of the KornShell • 308

6.2   Interacting with the Shell • 310
  6.2.1   Quick Exit   ○   310
  6.2.2   Running as a Restricted Shell   ○   310

6.3   Editing an Input Line • 311
  6.3.1   Choosing the Editor   ○   311
  6.3.2   The emacs Editor   ○   312
  6.3.3   The vi Editor   ○   314

6.4   Calling the Shell Directly • 317
  6.4.1   Calling ksh   ○   317
  6.4.2   Calling a POSIX Shell   ○   318

6.5   Shell Scripts • 318

6.6   Syntax of Shell Input • 320
  6.6.1   Effects of Quotation   ○   321
  6.6.2   Effects of Substitutions   ○   321
  6.6.3   Comments   ○   321

6.7   Patterns • 322

6.8   Simple Commands • 322
  6.8.1   Interpretation of Command Names   ○   323
  6.8.2   Executing a Utility in a Modified Environment with env   ○   326

6.9   Linking Commands with Operators • 326
  6.9.1   Combinations of Operators   ○   328
  6.9.2   Uses of Background Execution   ○   328
  6.9.3   Coprocesses   ○   329

6.10   Redirection • 330

6.11   Here-Documents • 332

6.12   The test, true, and false Commands • 333
  6.12.1   String Comparisons   ○   333
  6.12.2   Numerical Comparisons   ○   334
  6.12.3   File Tests   ○   334
  6.12.4   Option Test   ○   335
  6.12.5   Combinations of Tests   ○   335
  6.12.6   The true and false Commands   ○   335

6.13   Compound Commands • 335
  6.13.1   Conditional Commands   ○   336
  6.13.2   Iteration   ○   338
  6.13.3   Execution of Command Lists   ○   339
  6.13.4   Function Definitions   ○   340
  6.13.5   Menu Selection   ○   341

6.14   How Commands Are Executed • 342
  6.14.1   Example of Execution Methods   ○   343
  6.14.2   Indirectly Executing Commands in a Subshell   ○   344

6.15   Parameters • 344

6.15.1   Positional Parameters ○ 344
6.15.2   Variables ○ 345
6.15.3   Exporting Variables to a Subshell ○ 345
6.15.4   Array Variables ○ 346
6.15.5   Attributes of Variables ○ 347
6.15.6   Assignments to Variables ○ 348
6.15.7   Special Parameters ○ 349

6.16   Parameter Expansions • 349

6.17   Quotation • 352

6.18   Substitutions • 354

6.18.1   Command Substitution ○ 354
6.18.2   Arithmetic Evaluation ○ 355
6.18.3   Nested Substitutions and Quotations ○ 356

6.19   Aliases • 358

6.19.1   Defining or Displaying Aliases with `alias` ○ 358
6.19.2   Removing Aliases with `unalias` ○ 358
6.19.3   Examples ○ 359
6.19.4   Tracked Aliases ○ 359

6.20   Commands for Job Control • 359

6.20.1   Activating Jobs with `fg` and `bg` ○ 359
6.20.2   Listing Jobs with `jobs` ○ 360
6.20.3   Form of the `jobs` Output ○ 360

6.21   The Command History and the `fc` Command • 360

6.21.1   Editing and Executing Commands ○ 361
6.21.2   Listing Commands ○ 362
6.21.3   Modifying and Executing a Single Command ○ 362
6.21.4   Command-Line Options ○ 363

6.22   Intrinsic Commands and Predefined Aliases • 363

6.22.1   Special Forms of Command Execution ○ 363
6.22.2   Exiting from the Shell ○ 363
6.22.3   Exiting from Shell Functions ○ 364
6.22.4   Exiting from an Iteration ○ 364
6.22.5   Null Command ○ 364
6.22.6   Catching Signals ○ 364
6.22.7   Operations Pertaining to Variables ○ 365
6.22.8   Setting Options and Parameters ○ 367
6.22.9   Evaluations ○ 367
6.22.10   Process Monitoring and Control ○ 368
6.22.11   Utility Commands ○ 368

6.23   Predefined Variables Used by the Shell • 369

6.23.1   Predefined Variables Set by the Shell ○ 370
6.23.2   Directory Operations ○ 370
6.23.3   Prompts and Separators ○ 371
6.23.4   Mail Notification ○ 372
6.23.5   Other Variables ○ 373

6.24   Execution Options • 374

    6.24.1   Process-Related Options ○ 374
    6.24.2   Debugging Options ○ 375
    6.24.3   Options Affecting Names ○ 375
    6.24.4   Editor-Related Options ○ 375
    6.24.5   Miscellaneous Options ○ 376

6.25   Initialization Files for the Shell • 376

6.26   Parsing Command Lines with `getopts` • 377

    6.26.1   Using `getopts` ○ 378
    6.26.2   Example of `getopts` ○ 378

6.27   A Sample Shell Script • 379

7   Other Shells • 381

7.1   The C Shell `csh` • 381

    7.1.1   Summary of Differences ○ 382
    7.1.2   History Substitutions ○ 384
    7.1.3   Command Lookup ○ 387
    7.1.4   Interpretation of Aliases ○ 388
    7.1.5   Command Completion ○ 388
    7.1.6   File Name Expansions ○ 389
    7.1.7   Variables ○ 389
    7.1.8   Parameter Expansions ○ 389
    7.1.9   Quotation ○ 391
    7.1.10   Command Substitutions ○ 391
    7.1.11   Expressions ○ 392
    7.1.12   Predefined Variables ○ 393
    7.1.13   Simple Intrinsic Commands ○ 395
    7.1.14   Compound Commands (Statements) ○ 399
    7.1.15   Calling `csh` ○ 400

7.2   Bash, the "Bourne-again Shell" • 401

    7.2.1   Invoking Bash ○ 401
    7.2.2   Command-Line Editing ○ 402
    7.2.3   Syntax of Bash Input ○ 402
    7.2.4   Commands, Redirections, and Parameters ○ 403
    7.2.5   Substitutions and Expansions ○ 404
    7.2.6   Predefined Variables Used by Bash ○ 405
    7.2.7   Intrinsic Commands ○ 407
    7.2.8   Execution Options ○ 409
    7.2.9   Initialization Files ○ 410

8   Standard Editors • 411

8.1   The `vi` Visual Editor • 412

    8.1.1   Organization of the Screen ○ 413
    8.1.2   Meanings of Keys ○ 413

8.1.3   Modes ○ 414
8.1.4   Commands ○ 414
8.1.5   Cancelling and Interrupting Commands ○ 416
8.1.6   Typing Text in Input Mode ○ 416
8.1.7   Typing Text in Status-Line Mode ○ 416
8.1.8   Using **ex** Commands ○ 417
8.1.9   Autoindent Mode ○ 417
8.1.10   The Screen Window ○ 418
8.1.11   Regular Expressions in **vi** and **ex** ○ 418
8.1.12   Calling **vi** ○ 419
8.1.13   Command-Line Options ○ 419
8.1.14   Quick Exit ○ 420
8.1.15   Initializing **vi** or **ex** ○ 420
8.1.16   Adjusting the Screen ○ 420
8.1.17   Moving by Direction ○ 422
8.1.18   Moving by Syntactic Units ○ 423
8.1.19   Searching ○ 424
8.1.20   Setting and Moving to Placemarks ○ 426
8.1.21   Inserting Text ○ 426
8.1.22   Deleting and Altering Text ○ 427
8.1.23   Moving and Copying Text ○ 430
8.1.24   Named Buffers ○ 430
8.1.25   Undoing or Repeating Actions ○ 432
8.1.26   Checking the Status ○ 432
8.1.27   Reading Files, Writing Files, and Exiting ○ 432
8.1.28   Setting Local Variables ○ 433
8.1.29   Defining Macros ○ 433
8.1.30   Switching to **ex** ○ 435

8.2   Local Variables for **vi** and **ex** • 435

8.2.1   Search Control ○ 435
8.2.2   Read-Only Mode and Automatic Writing ○ 436
8.2.3   Warnings and Status Information ○ 437
8.2.4   Tabbing and Word Wrap ○ 438
8.2.5   Input Interpretation ○ 438
8.2.6   Macro Expansion and Definition ○ 439
8.2.7   Display Control ○ 440
8.2.8   Editor Commands in Documents ○ 441
8.2.9   Inhibiting Messages ○ 441
8.2.10   Environmental Information ○ 441

8.3   The Extended Editor **ex** • 442

8.3.1   Calling **ex** ○ 442
8.3.2   Initializing **ex** ○ 443
8.3.3   The Main Buffer ○ 443
8.3.4   Form of a Command ○ 443
8.3.5   Line Addresses and Line Ranges ○ 445
8.3.6   Specifying Groups of Lines ○ 446
8.3.7   Command Flags ○ 446
8.3.8   Abbreviations ○ 447
8.3.9   Comments ○ 447
8.3.10   Typing Conventions ○ 447
8.3.11   Special Buffers ○ 447
8.3.12   Producing Lines ○ 448
8.3.13   Status Information ○ 449
8.3.14   Inserting Text ○ 449

8.3.15   Modifying Text ○ 449
8.3.16   Moving and Copying Text ○ 450
8.3.17   Substitutions ○ 451
8.3.18   Marking Lines ○ 452
8.3.19   File Operations ○ 452
8.3.20   Exiting from the Editor ○ 455
8.3.21   Setting Local Variables ○ 455
8.3.22   Abbreviations and Macros ○ 456
8.3.23   Performing Commands Globally ○ 456
8.3.24   Calling Programs from Within the Editor ○ 457
8.3.25   Saving and Recovering ○ 457
8.3.26   Entering Visual Mode ○ 457
8.3.27   Undoing the Previous Action ○ 458
8.3.28   Executing Commands from a File ○ 458
8.3.29   Executing Commands in a Buffer ○ 458

8.4   The `ed` Line Editor • 458
8.4.1   The Command Line ○ 459
8.4.2   The Buffer ○ 459
8.4.3   Form of a Command ○ 459
8.4.4   Producing Lines ○ 461
8.4.5   Showing the Line Number ○ 462
8.4.6   Inserting Text ○ 462
8.4.7   Modifying Text ○ 462
8.4.8   Moving and Copying Text ○ 462
8.4.9   Substitutions ○ 462
8.4.10   Marking Lines ○ 463
8.4.11   File Operations ○ 463
8.4.12   Exiting from the Editor ○ 464
8.4.13   Performing Commands Globally ○ 464
8.4.14   Calling Programs from Within the Editor ○ 465
8.4.15   Undoing the Previous Action ○ 466
8.4.16   Prompts and Error Messages ○ 466

8.5   Tag Files • 466

9   The GNU Emacs Editor • 467

9.1   Calling and Terminating Emacs • 468
9.1.1   Command-Line Options ○ 468
9.1.2   Quick Exit ○ 470

9.2   Conventions for Typing Input • 470

9.3   Getting Acquainted with Emacs • 471

9.4   Emacs Concepts • 472
9.4.1   Buffers ○ 472
9.4.2   Treatment of Newlines ○ 473
9.4.3   Typing Special Characters ○ 473
9.4.4   Major and Minor Modes ○ 473
9.4.5   Windows ○ 475
9.4.6   Frames ○ 476
9.4.7   The Point, the Cursor, the Mark, and the Region ○ 476
9.4.8   Variables ○ 477
9.4.9   Faces, Fonts, and Colors ○ 478
9.4.10   The Syntax Table ○ 478

9.5   How to Issue Commands   •   479

    9.5.1   The Minibuffer   ○   479
    9.5.2   Cancelling Commands   ○   480
    9.5.3   Command Completion   ○   480
    9.5.4   Arguments to Commands   ○   480
    9.5.5   Recalling Complex Commands   ○   481
    9.5.6   Recursive Editing   ○   482
    9.5.7   Disabling Commands   ○   482
    9.5.8   Undoing Changes   ○   483

9.6   Getting Help   •   484

    9.6.1   Information About Commands and Key Bindings   ○   484
    9.6.2   Information About LISP Symbols   ○   485
    9.6.3   Information About Recently Executed Commands   ○   485
    9.6.4   Tutorial and On-Line Manual   ○   485
    9.6.5   Information About Emacs Itself   ○   485
    9.6.6   Other Help Commands   ○   486
    9.6.7   Command Continuations   ○   486

9.7   Exiting from or Suspending Emacs   •   486

9.8   Basic Editing Commands   •   487

    9.8.1   Moving the Point   ○   487
    9.8.2   Positioning and Scrolling the Window   ○   489
    9.8.3   Erasing, Moving, and Copying Text   ○   489
    9.8.4   Setting the Mark   ○   493

9.9   Mouse Operations on Text   •   494

    9.9.1   Operations on the Mark and the Region   ○   494
    9.9.2   Operations on the Secondary Selection   ○   495

9.10   Additional Editing Commands   •   496

    9.10.1   Filling Regions   ○   496
    9.10.2   Auto Fill Mode   ○   497
    9.10.3   Transposing Textual Units   ○   497
    9.10.4   Changing the Case of Text   ○   498
    9.10.5   Commands for Inserting Newlines   ○   498
    9.10.6   Operations on Lists   ○   499
    9.10.7   Sorting   ○   500
    9.10.8   Checking and Correcting Spelling   ○   501
    9.10.9   Working with Outlines   ○   502

9.11   Indentation   •   502

9.12   Operations on Rectangles   •   504

9.13   Operations on Windows   •   505

    9.13.1   Splitting Windows   ○   505
    9.13.2   Operations on Other Windows   ○   506
    9.13.3   Deleting and Resizing Windows   ○   507
    9.13.4   Mouse Actions for Rearranging Windows   ○   507

9.14   Operations on Frames   •   507

    9.14.1   Opening a New Frame   ○   508
    9.14.2   Other Operations on Frames   ○   508

9.15   Operations on Files   •   508
    9.15.1   Specifying File Names   ○   508
    9.15.2   Visiting Files   ○   509
    9.15.3   Saving Regions and Buffers to Files   ○   510
    9.15.4   Inserting a File   ○   511
    9.15.5   Miscellaneous File Operations   ○   511
    9.15.6   Automatically Saving, Recovering, and Backing Up Files   ○   512

9.16   Explicit Operations on Buffers   •   513
    9.16.1   Specifying a Buffer Name   ○   514
    9.16.2   Bringing a Buffer into a Window   ○   514
    9.16.3   Killing Buffers   ○   514
    9.16.4   Positions and Counts   ○   514
    9.16.5   Selective Display   ○   515
    9.16.6   Narrowing a Buffer   ○   515
    9.16.7   Displaying Line Numbers   ○   515
    9.16.8   Modifying Read-Only Status   ○   516
    9.16.9   Other Operations   ○   516

9.17   The Buffer Menu   •   516
    9.17.1   Creating or Selecting a Buffer Menu   ○   517
    9.17.2   Operations on a Buffer Menu   ○   517
    9.17.3   The Electric Buffer List   ○   518

9.18   Printing   •   519

9.19   Registers and Their Operations   •   519
    9.19.1   Viewing Register Contents   ○   519
    9.19.2   Saving and Retrieving Positions   ○   520
    9.19.3   Saving and Retrieving Text Using Registers   ○   520
    9.19.4   Quick File Access with Registers   ○   520

9.20   Searching and Replacing   •   520
    9.20.1   Incremental Search   ○   521
    9.20.2   Nonincremental Search   ○   522
    9.20.3   Word Search   ○   523
    9.20.4   Regular Expression Search   ○   523
    9.20.5   Replacement   ○   525
    9.20.6   Searching for Matching Lines   ○   527

9.21   Operations on Variables   •   527
    9.21.1   Examining and Setting Variables   ○   527
    9.21.2   Creating and Removing Local Variables   ○   528

9.22   Evaluating LISP Expressions   •   528
    9.22.1   LISP Expressions   ○   528
    9.22.2   Commands for Evaluating LISP Expressions   ○   529

9.23   Executing UNIX Commands from Emacs   •   530
    9.23.1   Executing a Single Command   ○   530
    9.23.2   Running a Subshell in a Buffer   ○   530
    9.23.3   Initiating a Subshell   ○   531
    9.23.4   Executing and Editing Subshell Commands   ○   531
    9.23.5   Using the Command History   ○   532
    9.23.6   Subshell Control Characters   ○   533
    9.23.7   Other Subshell Operations   ○   534

9.24   Environmental Inquiries • 534
9.25   Customizing Emacs • 534
         9.25.1   Key Bindings ○ 535
         9.25.2   Keyboard Macros ○ 538
         9.25.3   Abbreviations ○ 541
         9.25.4   Customizations for X Operations ○ 543
         9.25.5   The `.emacs` Initialization File ○ 545

10   Emacs Utilities • 550

10.1   Directory Operations with Dired • 550
         10.1.1   Starting Dired ○ 551
         10.1.2   Getting Help ○ 551
         10.1.3   Marks and Flags ○ 551
         10.1.4   Moving Around the Listing ○ 552
         10.1.5   Visiting and Viewing Files ○ 553
         10.1.6   Deleting Files ○ 554
         10.1.7   Other Operations on Files ○ 554
         10.1.8   Directory Operations ○ 556
         10.1.9   Modifying the Display ○ 556
         10.1.10   Finding Files ○ 557

10.2   Composing and Editing Pictures • 557
         10.2.1   Entering and Leaving Picture Mode ○ 558
         10.2.2   Moving Around a Picture ○ 558
         10.2.3   Inserting New Lines ○ 558
         10.2.4   Erasing Parts of a Picture ○ 559
         10.2.5   Linear Motions ○ 559
         10.2.6   Tab-Based Operations ○ 560
         10.2.7   Rectangle-Based Operations ○ 560

10.3   Tags and Tag Tables • 561
         10.3.1   Selecting a Tag Table ○ 561
         10.3.2   Finding a Definition ○ 561
         10.3.3   Regular Expression Search and Replace ○ 562
         10.3.4   Visiting Files Containing Definitions ○ 562
         10.3.5   Information About Tags ○ 562

10.4   The Emacs Mailer • 562
         10.4.1   Sending Mail with Smail ○ 563
         10.4.2   Receiving Mail with Rmail ○ 565
         10.4.3   Rmail Summary Commands ○ 570

10.5   The GNUS Newsreader • 571

10.6   The Calendar • 572
         10.6.1   Moving Around the Calendar ○ 573
         10.6.2   Other Calendar Operations ○ 574

10.7   The Diary • 575
         10.7.1   The Diary File ○ 575
         10.7.2   Diary Operations ○ 576

10.8   The Version Control Interface • 578
         10.8.1   Checking Files In and Out ○ 578
         10.8.2   Other Version Control Commands ○ 579

10.9   Amusements • 580

11   Mailers and Newsreaders • 582

11.1   What's in a Message? • 583

11.2   Recipients • 584

11.3   Mailboxes • 585

11.4   Forwarding Mail • 586

11.5   The `mailx` (Berkeley `Mail`) Mailer • 587

11.5.1   Sending a Message ○ 587
11.5.2   Reading Your Mail ○ 587
11.5.3   Quick Exit ○ 588
11.5.4   Recipients for `mailx` Messages ○ 588
11.5.5   Naming Files After Recipients ○ 589
11.5.6   Command-Line Options ○ 589
11.5.7   Initialization Files for `mailx` ○ 591
11.5.8   Using a Folder Directory ○ 592
11.5.9   Message Lists ○ 592
11.5.10   Header Summary and Status Codes ○ 593
11.5.11   Command Mode ○ 594
11.5.12   Commands for General Information ○ 594
11.5.13   Showing Messages ○ 595
11.5.14   Responding to Messages ○ 596
11.5.15   Saving and Deleting Messages ○ 598
11.5.16   Editing Messages ○ 599
11.5.17   Switching Files and Directories ○ 600
11.5.18   Quitting `mailx` ○ 600
11.5.19   Shells and Pipes ○ 600
11.5.20   Commands Useful for Initialization ○ 601
11.5.21   Input Mode ○ 602
11.5.22   Getting Help ○ 603
11.5.23   Showing or Saving the Message ○ 603
11.5.24   Editing the Message ○ 603
11.5.25   Inserting Text ○ 604
11.5.26   Specifying Header Fields ○ 605
11.5.27   Issuing Other Commands ○ 605
11.5.28   Quitting `mailx` ○ 605
11.5.29   Local and Imported Variables ○ 606
11.5.30   Controlling What `mailx` Shows You ○ 606
11.5.31   Input Interpretation ○ 607
11.5.32   Message Processing ○ 608
11.5.33   Mailbox Locations ○ 609
11.5.34   Command Interpreters ○ 609
11.5.35   Network Addressing ○ 610

11.6   Other Mailers • 610

11.6.1   The MH Message Handling System ○ 610
11.6.2   The `elm` Mailer ○ 612

11.7   Archiving Files for Mailing with `shar` • 612

11.8   Newsgroups and Newsreaders • 614

11.9   UNIX Newsreaders • 615

12 **Communicating with Remote Computers** • 617

12.1   Network Addresses • 618
  12.1.1   Domain-Style (Internet) Addresses ∘ 619
  12.1.2   Path-Style (UUCP Network) Addresses ∘ 622
  12.1.3   Addresses Involving More Than One Network ∘ 624
  12.1.4   When Messages Go Astray ∘ 625
  12.1.5   Addressing Considerations for File Transmission ∘ 627

12.2   Local-Area Networks • 627

12.3   Distributing Files Over Networks • 628

12.4   Internet Resources • 629
  12.4.1   Exploring the World Wide Web ∘ 629
  12.4.2   Browsing Menus with a Gopher ∘ 630
  12.4.3   Locating Files with Archie ∘ 630

12.5   Programs for Remote Communications • 631

12.6   Remote Operations on "Nearby" Computers • 632
  12.6.1   Files Used for Remote Operations ∘ 632
  12.6.2   Remote Login with `rlogin` ∘ 634
  12.6.3   Executing a Shell Command Remotely with `rsh` ∘ 635
  12.6.4   Remote Copying with `rcp` ∘ 636
  12.6.5   Listing Users on the Local Network with `rwho` ∘ 636

12.7   Calling a Remote Computer with `telnet` • 637
  12.7.1   Quick Exit ∘ 638
  12.7.2   Commands ∘ 638
  12.7.3   Variables with Values ∘ 640
  12.7.4   Toggles ∘ 640

12.8   Transferring Files Between Computers with `ftp` • 642
  12.8.1   Anonymous `ftp` ∘ 643
  12.8.2   Quick Exit ∘ 643
  12.8.3   Auto-Login ∘ 644
  12.8.4   Opening, Closing, and Controlling Remote Connections ∘ 644
  12.8.5   Getting Help ∘ 645
  12.8.6   Remote File Operations ∘ 646
  12.8.7   Transmitting Files ∘ 648
  12.8.8   Translating File Names ∘ 649
  12.8.9   Interpretation of Transmitted Files ∘ 651
  12.8.10   Local Operations ∘ 653
  12.8.11   Controlling Feedback from `ftp` ∘ 653
  12.8.12   Linking Two Remote Computers ∘ 654
  12.8.13   Defining and Using Macros ∘ 654
  12.8.14   The `.netrc` File ∘ 655
  12.8.15   Special Forms of File Names ∘ 657
  12.8.16   Command-Line Options ∘ 657

12.9   File Transfers Based on `uucp` • 658
  12.9.1   Sending Files with `uuto` ∘ 659
  12.9.2   Retrieving Files with `uupick` ∘ 659
  12.9.3   UNIX to UNIX Copying with `uucp` ∘ 660
  12.9.4   Controlling and Querying `uucp` with `uustat` ∘ 663
  12.9.5   The `Systems` File ∘ 665
  12.9.6   Identifying Remote Computers with `uuname` ∘ 665

12.10 Connecting to Remote Computers with `cu` • 666

    12.10.1   Quick Exit ○ 667
    12.10.2   Command-Line Options ○ 667
    12.10.3   Tilde Commands for `cu` ○ 667
    12.10.4   Output Diversions ○ 669

13   The X Window System • 670

13.1   The X Screen • 670

13.2   Getting Started and Quitting • 671

13.3   Window Managers • 671

13.4   Servers, Displays, and Display Specifications • 672

13.5   Widgets • 673

13.6   Properties • 673

13.7   Command-Line Options for X Applications • 673

13.8   Resources and Their Specifications • 675

13.9   The Resource Database • 677

13.10   Geometry Specifications • 677

13.11   Fonts • 678

13.12   Colors • 679

    13.12.1   Color Names ○ 679
    13.12.2   Color Numbers ○ 679

13.13   Initialization Files for X • 680

13.14   The `xterm` Terminal Emulator • 680

    13.14.1   Emulations ○ 681
    13.14.2   Using the Mouse ○ 681

13.15   Informational Displays for X • 683

    13.15.1   Displaying a Clock with `xclock` ○ 683
    13.15.2   Flagging Mail with `xbiff` ○ 683

13.16   Color and Font Information for X • 684

    13.16.1   Displaying Colors with `xcolors` ○ 684
    13.16.2   Displaying a Font with `xfd` ○ 684
    13.16.3   Listing Fonts with `xlsfonts` ○ 684
    13.16.4   Selecting and Displaying Fonts with `xfontsel` ○ 684

13.17   Clients for Initializing and Customizing X • 685

    13.17.1   Initiating X with `xinit` ○ 685
    13.17.2   Specifying Global Resources with `xrdb` ○ 686
    13.17.3   Setting User Preferences for X ○ 686
    13.17.4   Setting the Root Window Appearance with `xsetroot` ○ 686

13.18   Killing an X Client with `xkill` • 687

13.19   Viewing Manual Pages with `xman` • 687

14   Managing Your System   •   689

14.1   Running with Superuser Privileges   •   689

14.2   System Administration Programs   •   691

14.3   Explicit System Administration   •   691

14.3.1   User and Group Information   ○   691
14.3.2   Printers   ○   692
14.3.3   Terminals   ○   692
14.3.4   Reconfiguring the Kernel   ○   692

14.4   Software Installation   •   693

14.4.1   Using `make` and Makefiles   ○   694
14.4.2   Manual Pages   ○   694

14.5   File System Maintenance   •   696

14.5.1   Mounting a File System with `mount`   ○   696
14.5.2   Unmounting a File System with `umount`   ○   698
14.5.3   The Mounting Tables   ○   698
14.5.4   Creating a File System   ○   699
14.5.5   Checking a File System with `fsck`   ○   700
14.5.6   Backup   ○   701

14.6   Startup and Shutdown   •   702

14.6.1   Boot and Recovery Procedures   ○   702
14.6.2   Initializing the System   ○   704
14.6.3   Shutting Down   ○   705
14.6.4   Single-User Mode   ○   707

Appendixes

A   Alphabetical Summary of Commands   •   708

A.1   List of Commands   •   708

A.2   Summary of Commands and Features   •   711

A.2.1   `alias` (Define or Display Aliases)   ○   711
A.2.2   `at` (Schedule a Job at a Future Time)   ○   711
A.2.3   `awk` (Programming Language for Data Manipulation)   ○   712
A.2.4   `basename` (Extract Base of Pathname)   ○   714
A.2.5   `batch` (Schedule a Batch Job)   ○   715
A.2.6   `bc` (Arbitrary Precision Calculator)   ○   715
A.2.7   `bg` (Run Jobs in Background)   ○   716
A.2.8   `cal` (Show a Calendar)   ○   716
A.2.9   `cancel` (Cancel Printer Requests)   ○   716
A.2.10   `cat` (Concatenate Files)   ○   716
A.2.11   `cd` (Change Directory)   ○   717
A.2.12   `chgrp` (Change File Group)   ○   717
A.2.13   `chmod` (Change File Permissions)   ○   717
A.2.14   `chown` (Change File Owner)   ○   717
A.2.15   `chsh` (Change Your Login Shell)   ○   717
A.2.16   `cksum` (Calculate Checksums of Files)   ○   718
A.2.17   `cmp` (Compare Files)   ○   718

A.2.18   comm (List Lines Common to Two Sorted Files) ○ 718
A.2.19   command (Execute a Simple Command) ○ 718
A.2.20   compress (Compress a File) ○ 718
A.2.21   cp (Copy Files) ○ 718
A.2.22   cpio (Copy File Archives) ○ 719
A.2.23   crontab (Define Schedule of Background Jobs) ○ 719
A.2.24   csplit (Split File by Context) ○ 720
A.2.25   cu (Connect to a UNIX System) ○ 720
A.2.26   cut (Extract Fields from Lines) ○ 721
A.2.27   date (Display the Date and Time) ○ 721
A.2.28   dd (Convert and Copy a File) ○ 722
A.2.29   df (Report Free Disk Space) ○ 722
A.2.30   diff (Find File Differences) ○ 723
A.2.31   dirname (Extract Directory from Pathname) ○ 723
A.2.32   du (Report Disk Space in Use) ○ 723
A.2.33   echo (Echo Arguments) ○ 723
A.2.34   ed (Line Editor) ○ 723
A.2.35   egrep (Find Regular Expression, Extended Version) ○ 725
A.2.36   emacs (Emacs Extensible Text Editor) ○ 725
A.2.37   env (Set Environment for Command Invocation) ○ 736
A.2.38   ex (Extended Editor) ○ 736
A.2.39   expand (Convert Tabs to Spaces) ○ 738
A.2.40   expr (Evaluate an Expression) ○ 739
A.2.41   false (Return False) ○ 739
A.2.42   fc (Processing the Command History with fc) ○ 739
A.2.43   fg (Run a Job in Foreground) ○ 739
A.2.44   fgrep (Find Regular Expression, Fast Version) ○ 739
A.2.45   file (Classify Files) ○ 739
A.2.46   find (Find Files) ○ 740
A.2.47   finger (Look Up Information About a User) ○ 741
A.2.48   fold (Fold Input Lines) ○ 741
A.2.49   ftp (Transfer Files with File Transfer Protocol) ○ 741
A.2.50   getconf (Get Configuration Values) ○ 743
A.2.51   grep (Find Regular Expression) ○ 743
A.2.52   gunzip (Expand Zip-Encoded Files) ○ 743
A.2.53   gzcat (Expand and Concatenate Zip-Encoded Files) ○ 743
A.2.54   gzip (Compress Files Using Zip Encoding) ○ 744
A.2.55   halt (Shut Down the System and Halt) ○ 744
A.2.56   head (Copy Beginning of Files) ○ 744
A.2.57   id (Show User and Group IDs) ○ 744
A.2.58   jobs (Show Job Status) ○ 745
A.2.59   join (Database Join on Two Files) ○ 745
A.2.60   kill (Signal a Process) ○ 745
A.2.61   ksh (The KornShell) ○ 745
A.2.62   ln (Link Pathnames) ○ 749
A.2.63   locale (Get Locale Information) ○ 750
A.2.64   localedef (Define a New Locale) ○ 750
A.2.65   logger (Save Message for Administrator) ○ 750
A.2.66   login (Log In) ○ 750
A.2.67   logname (Return User's Login Name) ○ 750
A.2.68   lp (Send Files to a Printer) ○ 751
A.2.69   lpr (Berkeley Print Spooler) ○ 751
A.2.70   lpstat (Show Printer Status) ○ 751
A.2.71   ls (File Lister) ○ 752
A.2.72   mailx (Send and Receive Mail) ○ 752

A.2.73   `man` (Display Manual Pages) ∘ 755
A.2.74   `mesg` (Lock Out Messages) ∘ 756
A.2.75   `mkdir` (Make a Directory) ∘ 756
A.2.76   `mkfifo` (Make a FIFO Special File) ∘ 756
A.2.77   `mknod` (Make a Special File) ∘ 756
A.2.78   `more` (Page Through Files Interactively) ∘ 756
A.2.79   `mount` (Mount a File System) ∘ 757
A.2.80   `mv` (Move Files) ∘ 758
A.2.81   `newgrp` (Change Your Current Group) ∘ 758
A.2.82   `nice` (Run a Command at Low Priority) ∘ 758
A.2.83   `nohup` (Ignore Hangups) ∘ 758
A.2.84   `od` (Octal Dump) ∘ 758
A.2.85   `paste` (Paste Input Fields) ∘ 759
A.2.86   `patch` (Apply Changes to Files) ∘ 759
A.2.87   `pathchk` (Check Validity of Pathnames) ∘ 760
A.2.88   `pax` (Portable Archive Interchange) ∘ 760
A.2.89   `pr` (Format Files for Printing) ∘ 761
A.2.90   `print` (Write Output Arguments under `ksh`) ∘ 761
A.2.91   `printf` (Write Formatted Output) ∘ 761
A.2.92   `ps` (List Processes, BSD Version) ∘ 762
A.2.93   `ps` (List Processes, POSIX Version) ∘ 763
A.2.94   `ps` (List Processes, System V Version) ∘ 763
A.2.95   `pwd` (Show Working Directory) ∘ 763
A.2.96   `rcp` (Remote Copy) ∘ 763
A.2.97   `read` (Read an Input Line) ∘ 763
A.2.98   `reboot` (Shut Down the System and Reboot) ∘ 764
A.2.99   `renice` (Set Priorities of Processes) ∘ 764
A.2.100   `rlogin` (Remote Login) ∘ 764
A.2.101   `rm` (Remove Files or Directories) ∘ 764
A.2.102   `rmdir` (Remove Directories) ∘ 765
A.2.103   `rsh` (Remote Execution of a Shell Command) ∘ 765
A.2.104   `rwho` (List Users on the Local Network) ∘ 765
A.2.105   `sed` (Edit from a Script) ∘ 765
A.2.106   `sh` (POSIX Shell) ∘ 766
A.2.107   `shar` (Create a Shell Archive) ∘ 766
A.2.108   `shutdown` (Shut Down the System) ∘ 767
A.2.109   `sleep` (Suspend Execution) ∘ 767
A.2.110   `sort` (Sort Files) ∘ 767
A.2.111   `split` (Split Files into Pieces) ∘ 767
A.2.112   `strings` (Find Printable Strings in Files) ∘ 768
A.2.113   `stty` (Set Terminal Characteristics) ∘ 768
A.2.114   `su` (Substitute User) ∘ 769
A.2.115   `tabs` (Set Tabs on Your Terminal) ∘ 769
A.2.116   `tail` (Extract the End of a File) ∘ 769
A.2.117   `talk` (Talk to Another User) ∘ 770
A.2.118   `tar` (Tape Archiver) ∘ 770
A.2.119   `tee` (Duplicate Input) ∘ 770
A.2.120   `telnet` (Call a Remote System Over a Network) ∘ 770
A.2.121   `test` (Compare Values, Test File Properties) ∘ 771
A.2.122   `time` (Time a Command) ∘ 772
A.2.123   `touch` (Touch a File) ∘ 773
A.2.124   `tput` (Send Setup Instructions to a Terminal) ∘ 773
A.2.125   `tr` (Translate or Delete Characters) ∘ 773
A.2.126   `true` (Return True) ∘ 773
A.2.127   `tset` (Set Terminal Information) ∘ 773

A.2.128   **tty** (Get the Terminal Name) ○ 774
A.2.129   **type** (Show Interpretation of a Command) ○ 774
A.2.130   **umask** (Mask Default File Permissions) ○ 774
A.2.131   **umount** (Unmount a File System) ○ 774
A.2.132   **unalias** (Remove Alias Definitions) ○ 774
A.2.133   **uname** (Produce System Information) ○ 775
A.2.134   **uncompress** (Uncompress a File) ○ 775
A.2.135   **unexpand** (Convert Spaces to Tabs) ○ 775
A.2.136   **uniq** (Eliminate Adjacent Repeated Lines) ○ 775
A.2.137   **uucp** (UNIX to UNIX Copy) ○ 775
A.2.138   **uudecode** (Decode a Binary File) ○ 776
A.2.139   **uuencode** (Encode a Binary File) ○ 776
A.2.140   **uuname** (Get Names of Remote UNIX Systems) ○ 776
A.2.141   **uupick** (Pick Up Files from UNIX to UNIX Transfer) ○ 776
A.2.142   **uustat** (Check **uucp** Status) ○ 776
A.2.143   **uuto** (Send Files UNIX to UNIX) ○ 777
A.2.144   **vi** (Visual Editor) ○ 777
A.2.145   **wait** (Wait for a Process to Finish) ○ 781
A.2.146   **wc** (Count Words, Lines, or Characters) ○ 781
A.2.147   **which** (Show Pathname of Command) ○ 781
A.2.148   **who** (List Users and Processes) ○ 781
A.2.149   **write** (Write to Terminal) ○ 781
A.2.150   **xargs** (Call a Utility with Constructed Arguments) ○ 782
A.2.151   **xbiff** (Mailbox Flag for X) ○ 782
A.2.152   **xclock** (Analog/Digital Clock for X) ○ 782
A.2.153   **xcolors** (Display the X Colors) ○ 782
A.2.154   **xfd** (Display an X Font) ○ 782
A.2.155   **xfontsel** (Select and Display X Fonts) ○ 782
A.2.156   **xinit** (Start the X Server) ○ 782
A.2.157   **xkill** (Kill an X Client) ○ 782
A.2.158   **xlsfonts** (Display a List of X Fonts) ○ 783
A.2.159   **xman** (Display Manual Pages Under X) ○ 783
A.2.160   **xrdb** (Resource Database Utility for X) ○ 783
A.2.161   **xset** (Set User Preferences for X) ○ 783
A.2.162   **xsetroot** (Set Root Window Appearance for X) ○ 783
A.2.163   **xterm** (Terminal Emulator for X) ○ 783
A.2.164   **zcat** (Uncompress and Concatenate Files) ○ 783

B   Comparison of MS-DOS and UNIX • 784

B.1   Treatment of Files • 784
B.2   MS-DOS Commands and Their UNIX Equivalents • 786
B.3   Other Related Features • 787

C   Resources • 789

C.1   Books • 789
C.2   CD-ROMs • 794

D   Glossary • 796

Index • 808

Using the CD-ROM   (CD-ROM version only)   •   **CD-1**

CD.1   Directory Structure   •   CD-2

CD.2   Available DynaText Browsers   •   CD-3

    CD.2.1   Browsers for UNIX   ○   CD-4
    CD.2.2   Browsers for Windows   ○   CD-4
    CD.2.3   Browsers for the Macintosh   ○   CD-4
    CD.2.4   Obtaining Updated Browsers   ○   CD-5

CD.3   Installing the DynaText Software   •   CD-5

    CD.3.1   Installation of the UNIX Browsers   ○   CD-5
    CD.3.2   Installation of the Windows Browsers   ○   CD-6
    CD.3.3   Installation on the Macintosh   ○   CD-8
    CD.3.4   Using Other DynaText Documents   ○   CD-8

CD.4   Using the DynaText Software   •   CD-9

    CD.4.1   Help Facilities   ○   CD-12
    CD.4.2   The Menu and the Button Bar   ○   CD-12
    CD.4.3   Enlarging or Reducing the View   ○   CD-13
    CD.4.4   Moving Through the Text   ○   CD-13
    CD.4.5   Using the Table of Contents   ○   CD-13
    CD.4.6   Multiple Windows   ○   CD-14
    CD.4.7   Hypertext Facilities   ○   CD-14
    CD.4.8   Searching   ○   CD-16
    CD.4.9   Printing Excerpts of a Book   ○   CD-18
    CD.4.10   Adding Your Own Annotations   ○   CD-18
    CD.4.11   Creating and Using Journals   ○   CD-19

CD.5   Installing the Emacs Editor   •   CD-20

    CD.5.1   Installation Procedures   ○   CD-21
    CD.5.2   Updating the Distribution   ○   CD-24

CD.6   Installing and Using Slackware Linux   •   CD-25

    CD.6.1   Hardware Requirements   ○   CD-26
    CD.6.2   Installation Procedures   ○   CD-26
    CD.6.3   Post-Installation Procedures   ○   CD-28
    CD.6.4   Useful Documentation   ○   CD-30

1

Introduction

In this chapter we discuss the background of UNIX and offer some advice on how to use this book. We present a summary of the typographical conventions we follow for displaying UNIX syntax and propose a list of the 10 most useful UNIX commands and constructs.

1.1 UNIX Background

In this section we describe the history of UNIX and other aspects of its background.

1.1.1
Early History

The first version of UNIX, called Unics, was written in 1969 by Ken Thompson at Bell Laboratories, Murray Hill, New Jersey. It ran on a Digital Equipment PDP-7 computer. Bell Laboratories had been involved, together with MIT and General Electric, in the development of the Multics system, a large, highly capable time-sharing system that embodied a number of pioneering ideas about operating systems design. Thompson and his colleagues admired the capabilities of Multics but felt it was far too complicated. They set out to prove it was possible to build an operating system that provided a comfortable working environment in a much simpler way. In this they succeeded admirably—though UNIX today, ironically, is far more complex than Multics ever was.

In 1970 Thompson, together with Dennis Ritchie, moved Unics to a PDP-11/20. Ritchie also designed and wrote the first C compiler in order to provide a language that could be used to write a portable version of the system. In 1973 Ritchie and Thompson rewrote the UNIX kernel, the heart of the operating system, in C.

UNIX was first licensed to universities for educational purposes in 1974 in a version known as the Fifth Edition. (The "editions" refer to editions of the UNIX reference manual.) The Sixth Edition, also known as V6, was released in 1975 and distributed far more widely than the Fifth Edition. The Seventh Edition, released by Bell Laboratories in 1979, was the first to have portability as a specific goal. Implemented on the DEC PDP-11, the Interdata 8/32, and the VAX, the Seventh Edition served as a common starting point for the entire UNIX world. If there is a single version of UNIX that defines "classical" UNIX, the Seventh Edition is it. The two most influential offshoots of the Seventh Edition were System V (not to be confused with the Fifth Edition) and the various Berkeley Software Distribution (BSD) systems.

Although System V and the BSD systems greatly influenced each other and shared many of their newer features, the two systems developed different personalities. System V was more conservative and solid; BSD systems were more innovative and experimental. System V was a commercial product; BSD was not (although some systems based on it were). These different personalities were reflected in their progeny. The two threads of evolution eventually reunited with the release of System V Release 4 (SVR4).

After releasing the Seventh Edition, Bell Laboratories, later to become AT&T Bell Laboratories, continued to develop new versions of UNIX as research projects. These included the Ninth Edition (1987) and the Tenth Edition (1990), neither widely distributed. The Tenth Edition was the last version of UNIX developed by the Labs.

1.1.2
System V

System V was developed by AT&T as a commercial version of the Seventh Edition and first released in 1983. In 1984, a famous court decree ordered AT&T to divest itself of its operating companies but freed AT&T to enter the computer business and to sell both hardware and software. As a result, AT&T Information Systems began to market UNIX aggressively. The first release of System V was followed by Release 2 in 1984, Release 3 in 1986, and Release 4 in 1989. Release 4 (SVR4) was largely written by Sun Microsystems and included many features taken from the BSD systems. SVR4 marked the reunion of the two diverging threads of UNIX development.

In 1990 AT&T established UNIX Systems Laboratories (USL) as a wholly owned subsidiary that would market System V and also handle licensing and further development. USL was acquired by Novell in 1993. The acquisition was particularly appropriate because of Novell's history of developing networking software. Later that year Novell gave the UNIX trademark to the X/Open standards organization (see Section 1.1.9) with the intent that the future definition of UNIX be in the hands of that group. Novell added NetWare support and other features to System V and now markets the enhanced system under the name UnixWare, though System V without the enhancements is also available. In 1995, SCO announced that it had agreed to acquire UnixWare from Novell and was planning to merge UnixWare with SCO's Open Server by 1997.

In 1987 AT&T and Sun Microsystems entered into a joint agreement on UNIX development that led to a partial unification of the System V and BSD approaches to UNIX. Though the agreement was dissolved by mutual consent in 1991, its unifying effects on System V have survived and are evident in the many systems based on SVR4.

Besides UnixWare, major commercial systems based on System V include SunOS $5.x$ (also known as Solaris 2), Hewlett-Packard's HP-UX, Amdahl's UTS, IBM's AIX, SCO's Open Server Release 5, and Silicon Graphics's IRIX. Two older System V–based systems that deserve to be mentioned are Interactive's System V/386[1] and SCO's Xenix. Xenix, sublicensed from Microsoft by SCO and based on the Seventh Edition, was at one time said to account for more installations than any other version of UNIX, probably because for a while it was the only AT&T–based version that would run on the Intel 80286 family of computers.[2]

The 1987 alliance between AT&T and Sun Microsystems led a group of System V licensees to establish UNIX International as an organization independent of AT&T in 1988. The purpose of UNIX International was to influence the direction of System V development. It appears the licensees felt they needed a counterweight to OSF, formed by AT&T's and Sun's competitors as a reaction to the alliance, and also needed to address their own worries about the competitive advantages AT&T and Sun might be gaining in the UNIX marketplace. The evolution of X/Open as the body defining UNIX eventually removed much of the reason for UNIX International's existence, and UNIX International was dissolved at the end of 1993.

1.1.3
The BSD Systems

The first version of BSD was built by Bill Joy at the University of California, Berkeley (UCB), in 1978.[3] In 1980 he ported the 32V version of UNIX, obtained from Bell Laboratories, to Digital Equipment Corporation's VAX computer.

At that time Robert Fabry was the faculty advisor to the Computer Science Research Group (CSRG) at UCB. The success of the port to the VAX helped Fabry convince the Defense Advanced Research Projects Agency (DARPA[4]) to provide a major grant in support of the Berkeley developments that same year. A major goal of the BSD project was to support

---

1. Interactive Systems Corporation (ISC) was designated the "Principal Publisher" of SVR4 by USL in 1990. A year later, ISC was purchased by Sun Microsystems and incorporated into its SunSoft division.

2. While Xenix would run on the 80286, all recent versions of UNIX require at least an 80386.

3. After his work at UCB, Joy went on to become a founder of Sun Microsystems.

4. DARPA is now ARPA, which is what it was before it became DARPA.

communication over networks using a variety of protocols, not just the direct-line communication provided by the Seventh Edition. DARPA found the Berkeley work attractive because it was immediately applicable to communications over the DARPA-sponsored Arpanet, which later became the Internet. DARPA also saw BSD as potentially becoming the standard operating system for research projects using the VAX, at that time the most popular computer in research institutions. UNIX had the further advantage for DARPA of not being tied to a particular architecture.

The first VAX version of BSD was 3BSD, released late in 1979. It was followed by 4BSD (1980), 4.1BSD (1981), 4.2BSD (1983), 4.3BSD (1987), and BSD Networking Release 1 (1988). The BSD systems prior to Networking Release 1 were built under AT&T license, but Networking Release 1 was distributed without any requirement that the recipient have a prior license either from AT&T or from the University of California itself. BSD Networking Release 2 (1991), also known as Net/2, was a sanitized version of 4.3BSD with the AT&T code removed. It led to 386BSD, a version developed by Bill Jolitz that would run on the Intel i386 architecture. That architecture includes the Intel 80386, the 80486, and the Pentium processors. 386BSD was described in a series of articles in *Dr. Dobb's Journal*. A commercial version of 386BSD, BSD/386, was released in 1993 by Berkeley Software Design, Inc. (BSDI) following the resolution of a lawsuit initiated by USL that affected Net/2 and all of its descendents.

UCB's involvement with the BSD releases ended in 1993, when 4.4BSD was released and the CSRG was dissolved. Unlike Net/2, 4.4BSD retained some vestigial AT&T code and thus required the appropriate (expensive) license for the source code. A version stripped of the AT&T code was made available under the name 4.4BSD Lite. However, 4.4BSD Lite would not run as distributed; it was necessary to replace the missing components. The 4.4BSD Lite version served as the base for BSD/OS (1995), FreeBSD (1994), and NetBSD (1994).

A major BSD contribution was the `vi` visual text editor, written by Bill Joy, which subsequently became the primary text editor for System V. Other major contributions included the `C` shell, the support for the TCP/IP communications protocols, a virtual memory system, device drivers for many kinds of peripheral equipment, and libraries of terminal-independent subroutines for screen-based applications.

Major descendents of BSD are the 4.1.x versions of Sun Microsystems's SunOS, also known as Solaris 1, and Digital Equipment Corporation's (DEC's) Ultrix. However, both these systems are gradually being phased out by their vendors—SunOS in favor of Solaris 2 and Ultrix in favor of Digital UNIX, the DEC implementation of OSF/1 (see p. 6). BSD/OS, 4.4BSD Lite, FreeBSD, and NetBSD are thus, as of early 1995, the only active direct descendents of the BSD line.

**1.1.4
The X Window
System**

The late 1980's saw a major change in the UNIX world as the introduction into the UNIX environment of the X Window System, called X for short, led to a shift from character-based working environments to graphical user interfaces. X was developed at MIT in 1984 as part of Project Athena, a project to create a first-rate computing facility for the entire student body. X works particularly well in networked environments, allowing a user to run a program on a remote computer and display it in a window on the user's local computer. Most UNIX workstations nowadays run X, though Solaris 1 systems may still be running NeWS, the Network/ extensible Window System once offered by Sun Microsystems. The most recent version is Release 6 of X Version 11 (X11R6), which has been adopted as an industry-wide standard.

In 1988 MIT formed the X Consortium to further the development of the X Window System. The X Consortium is now an independent organization that formulates the generally accepted standards for X.

The two best-known graphical user interfaces for X are OPEN LOOK and Motif. OPEN LOOK was developed by Sun with help from AT&T and industry reviewers; Motif was developed by OSF. The software for these interfaces includes window managers that handle the user-level inter-action with application programs and toolkits for building application programs.

**1.1.5
Licensing and Its
Effects**

Just about all commercial UNIX systems have included some AT&T–derived code and therefore have required an AT&T source license, which in 1990 became a USL license. That includes all the Berkeley-derived systems (up to the Net/1 release, that is). Legally speaking, this source code has been unpublished and proprietary—an AT&T trade secret, in fact—ever since the inception of UNIX. Only AT&T licensees have been permitted to look at it. Yet this code has been examined, analyzed, and modified by thousands of computer science researchers and students. How did this apparently contradictory state of affairs come to be?

On the one hand, the early AT&T UNIX licenses given to universities explicitly permitted staff and students to examine the source code for educational purposes. For a long time, in fact, AT&T sold educational licenses for little more than the cost of distributing the UNIX media. On the other hand, AT&T has always been zealous in enforcing its intellectual property rights when necessary.[5] The threat of action by a large corporation with such an awe-inspiring legal staff was quite sufficient to prevent

---

5. Whether a trade secret is legally defensible when it has been so widely distributed is questionable. However, the UNIX source code is protected by copyright as well, and that protection is probably what really counts.

any significant breaches of AT&T's licensing terms.[6] In any event, AT&T changed its policy when it released the Seventh Edition; from then on, source licenses prohibited the code from being studied in courses.

Making UNIX and its sources available to students during the formative years of UNIX was very much in AT&T's interest. For a long time, computer manufacturers had provided hardware to universities on easy terms, thus ensuring that generations of students—future corporate decision-makers—would become proselytizers for their equipment. Much the same happened with low-cost UNIX software as those who had used UNIX as students became some of its most enthusiastic and influential supporters.

1.1.6
Non-AT&T
Commercial
Systems

Concerned about the competitive effects of the AT&T-Sun agreement, a number of other vendors including IBM, Digital, and Hewlett-Packard established the Open Software Foundation in 1988 with the announced aim of developing an alternative to the AT&T-Sun version of UNIX, one that would fulfill the promise of open systems and conform to all major UNIX-related standards. The first version of this system, OSF/1, was released in 1991, using the Mach kernel developed at Carnegie-Mellon University from earlier BSD code.

This release was in the form of source code, but it still included some vestigial AT&T code and thus required the AT&T license. Though technically that makes OSF/1 an AT&T–based system, OSF has pursued an independent line of development. The OSF/1 code has been incorporated into systems released by OSF members, notably DEC, Hewlett-Packard, and IBM. One particularly important OSF/1 product is the Motif window manager that provides a graphical user interface to X.

An early commercial UNIX clone was IDRIS, built by Whitesmiths Ltd. in the late seventies. A principal of Whitesmiths was P.J. (Bill) Plauger, co-author with Brian Kernighan of the well-known book *Software Tools*. A more recent clone is Coherent, developed by Mark Williams Company, that runs on Intel 8086-family processors. Mortice Kern Systems (MKS) sells an extensive and very popular package of UNIX tools that runs under both MS-DOS and OS/2. It includes the usual file utilities as well as ksh, vi, awk, and make.

BSDI now markets BSD/OS, a POSIX.1-compliant derivative of 4.4BSD Lite for the i386 architecture, as a replacement for BSD/386. BSD/OS's

---

6. At one time a message was jokingly posted on a public network containing a universal shell script for clearing the screen of a terminal. It consisted of the text

```
#    Copyright (c) 1984 AT&T
#      All Rights Reserved

#    THIS IS UNPUBLISHED PROPRIETARY SOURCE CODE OF AT&T
#    The copyright notice above does not evidence any
#    actual or intended publication of such source code.
```

followed by a line that simply echoed a form feed. Presumably the notice itself wasn't proprietary, or at least AT&T didn't care if it was.

claimed advantages over free BSD versions include its ability to act as a gateway to the Internet without an external router, its more extensive and highly tuned collection of drivers and other supporting software, and the user support BSDI provides for it.

1.1.7
Free UNIX Systems

Free UNIX–compatible systems for the i386 architecture, notably Linux, FreeBSD, and NetBSD, have at last made UNIX accessible and affordable to individuals. These systems provide excellent performance and come with a full set of UNIX utilities and other features. They are robust enough that many organizations are using them.

Since these systems contain no proprietary code, they are unaffected by USL or Berkeley licensing restrictions and can be used, copied, and distributed by anyone free of charge. Copies are easily obtained either on CD-ROM or by file transfer over the Internet. Both Linux and FreeBSD use software from the GNU and XFree86 projects.

Linux. Linux is a freely distributable version of UNIX originated by Linus Torvalds at the University of Helsinki in Finland. It was inspired by MINIX, a Seventh Edition–compatible UNIX written by Andrew Tanenbaum and generally follows System V conventions. Its further development has been helped by UNIX programmers and wizards across the Internet. It includes a great deal of code developed by the GNU project as well as the XFree86 version of X, and it generally conforms to the POSIX standards. Linux also includes an emulator, `dosemu`, for MS-DOS programs, and an emulator for Microsoft Windows is reportedly being worked on. Several different distributions of Linux are available, the best known being Yggdrasil and Slackware. Linux is covered by the GNU General Public License, discussed below. The Slackware distribution along with a large collection of other Linux-related material is available on CD-ROM (reference [C4]). The Yggdrasil distribution is also available on CD-ROM (reference [C10]).

FreeBSD and NetBSD. FreeBSD is a derivative of 4.4BSD for the i386 architecture whose purpose is to develop a stable working environment for that architecture, with an emphasis on stability and upgraded utility programs. The current version of FreeBSD is built from the 4.4BSD Lite code; an earlier version was based on 386BSD. It is supported by an international team of volunteers. Documentation is available in the 4.4BSD Manual Set (reference [B6]). Information and complete distributions are available over the Internet from `ftp.FreeBSD.org`, with information also available from `info@FreeBSD.org` (general questions to `questions@FreeBSD.org`). The complete distribution is also available on CD-ROMs (references [C1] and [C2]). Most of FreeBSD, unlike Linux, is governed by a Berkeley-style license that permits redistribution as long as the code includes a notice acknowledging the copyright of the Regents of the University of California and the FreeBSD Project. A few parts of

FreeBSD include GNU software and are therefore covered by the GPL, however. These are kept in a different part of the source tree.

NetBSD is another descendent of Net/2, 386BSD, and 4.4BSD Lite, created by the members of the network community. Compared with FreeBSD, it is more experimental and innovative, with an emphasis on multiple platform support. Unlike FreeBSD, therefore, NetBSD has been ported to non-Intel architectures. The system is available over the Internet from `ftp.netbsd.org` and on CD-ROM (reference [C2]).

The GNU Project. The GNU project aims to develop a complete UNIX–compatible software system. It is operated by the Free Software Foundation, an organization founded by Richard Stallman. Stallman has written much of the GNU software himself. GNU stands for "GNU's Not UNIX". (The 'G' in GNU should be pronounced.) Software developed and distributed by the GNU project includes the Emacs editor, the GNU C Compiler `gcc`, the `gdb` debugger, and versions of nearly all the UNIX utilities. These versions conform to the POSIX standards but also provide many useful enhancements and extensions. Because of its high quality, the GNU software is widely used even at installations that are running commercial UNIX systems.

All GNU software is covered by the GNU General Public License (GPL). According to the terms of that license, anyone can modify the software and distribute his or her own version of it. The essential constraint is that no one can prevent a recipient of the software from further distributing it for free. This right attaches not just to the original software but to all modified derivatives of it. Anyone who distributes the software or a derivative, whether free or for a fee, is also obligated to make the source code available for no more than the cost of copying it. The license does not prevent a vendor from making a handsome profit from distributing GNU software—it only ensures that anyone else can distribute the same software at a lower price or at no price at all. Software covered by the GPL is often said to be *copylefted*.

XFree86. Linux and FreeBSD also include XFree86, a port of the X Window System to the i386 architecture, that includes drivers for a great many i386 video cards. XFree86 was developed and is being maintained by a group known as the XFree86 Core Team. The XFree86 Core Team formed a corporation, The XFree86 Project, Inc., to provide a way that the XFree86 Project could be represented within the X Consortium and also to provide a structure for funding ongoing XFree86 development. XFree86 can be copied and redistributed freely and is not constrained by the GNU GPL.

The `emx` Package for MS-DOS and OS/2. A great deal of GNU software, including a fine implementation of Emacs, has been ported to MS-DOS and to the OS/2 operating system by Eberhard Mattes. The port is based on a runtime package called `emx` and includes `gcc`, the GNU C compiler.

Mattes has also developed a version of TₑX called emTeX that runs under MS-DOS and OS/2. This software is available over the Internet from node `ftp.uni-stuttgart.de`, directory `/pub/systems`, and from other sources as well.

1.1.8 UNIX Then and Now

UNIX today is a very different system than it was in the early seventies. The typical system then was a single processor serving a set of teletypewriter-like terminals with the terminals connected to the processor by direct or dial-up phone lines. The typical system now is a workstation with a high-resolution bitmapped display, running a windowing system and actively participating in an extensive network of computers. UNIX then was small, simple, and aimed at a small and select audience. UNIX now is large, complicated, and used in a wide variety of applications, often by people with no programming experience. UNIX then was a research project. UNIX now is a major commercial product and also available in highly sophisticated free versions.

An interesting example that shows how UNIX has changed as it grew, often contrary to its original philosophy, is the System V version of the `who` command. In the Seventh Edition,[7] it had two forms, `who` and `who am i` (plus `who are you` and `who am I`, which meant the same thing) and no options. The System V version of `who` sported no fewer than 12 options, including such exotica as when the system clock was last changed and which processes were started by `init` but are now dead.

1.1.9 UNIX Standards

The variations among UNIX systems and the problems those variations caused have led to a strong interest in developing standards for what a UNIX system should be.

The POSIX Standards. At the level of the user-oriented commands that are the primary subject of this book, the most important standard has been POSIX.2, Part 2 of the Portable Operating System Interface developed by the Institute of Electrical and Electronics Engineers (IEEE) and the American National Standards Institute (ANSI). POSIX is intended to define an operating system that *behaves* like UNIX whether or not it really *is* UNIX.

Each of the POSIX standards defines a particular aspect of such an operating system. POSIX.1, IEEE 1003.1-1990, defines the System Application Program Interface—in other words, the C procedure calls to be used in writing programs for UNIX. POSIX.1 has been accepted as the basis of a Federal Information Processing Standard. POSIX.2, which we discuss in more detail below, defines the Shell and Utilities and is formally known as IEEE Standard 1003.2–1992. The POSIX.2 standard depends heavily on the POSIX.1 standard since it assumes that many of those procedure calls

---

7. As documented in the version of the UNIX *Programmer's Manual* published by Bell Laboratories in 1983.

are available. Additional POSIX standards, still under development, are expected to cover system administration, real-time processing, and other topics.

The X/Open Standards.   In 1984 a group of European computer vendors formed the X/Open organization. Its goal was to establish international standards for "open systems", systems not bound to any particular computer architecture. UNIX just happened to be the particular open system with which X/Open was most concerned. The X/Open standards became particularly important when Novell in 1993 transferred the UNIX trademark, and with it all rights to the name "UNIX", to X/Open. Now any implementation that passes X/Open's verification suite can legally be called a UNIX system.

X/Open formulates packages of standards but does not, in general, formulate standards of its own. The X/Open standards are intended to encourage vendors to provide a minimum set of compatible facilities so that applications can easily be moved from one system to another and users can move among systems without needing a lot of retraining. X/Open does, however, work with other standards organizations to create standards for functions that have none. The X/Open standards for UNIX incorporate the corresponding POSIX standards but extend them to include specifications for other topics.

The X/Open strategy has been to formulate a series of standards called the XPG (X/Open Portability Guide) standards. The XPG standards include a portfolio of application programming interfaces (APIs) intended to make application programs more portable. The XPG standards collectively are called the Common Application Environment (CAE). To encourage conformance to the CAE, X/Open has also created a trademark, the XPG brand, that can be applied to products meeting the CAE specifications. The X/Open standard for UNIX is a superset of the XPG4 Base standard (Version 2); that is, it includes the XPG4 base requirements plus certain optional parts: UNIX extensions, networking, and the `curses` package.[8]

The AT&T SVID Standard.   As part of its UNIX activities, AT&T produced its own UNIX standard called SVID (System V Interface Definition). SVID, while enormously influential, was totally under AT&T's control—a condition that prevented its adoption as a standard by accredited standards organizations such as ANSI. The last version of SVID, published in 1989 and amended in 1990, was based on Release 4 of System V and published by USL.

---

8. The two systems we know of as of mid-1995 that have been granted the X/Open UNIX brand are Digital UNIX and SCO Open Server Release 5, but branded UNIX products from other vendors are sure to be added to the list.

**1.1.10
The Role of C
in UNIX**

The C programming language is often mentioned in the same breath as UNIX, yet it is often unclear to users who don't intend to do any programming why this relationship is important.

- Most publicly available UNIX software is distributed in the form of C programs that must be compiled before they can be used. This UNIX tradition arose from the need to distribute programs in a portable form that would work on many different kinds of computers.

- UNIX system calls, which programs use to request services from the kernel, have historically been defined as C functions.[9] Although these system calls are primarily of interest to programmers, references to them often appear in user documentation. Sometimes the only way to understand how a user-level program really works is to see what the underlying system calls do.

- Most UNIX system code is written in C, both in AT&T–based and non-AT&T–based systems. An organization running a commercial UNIX system and holding the appropriate source license can alter the behavior of the system by modifying and then recompiling source programs. Users of public systems can do the same without such licensing concerns and indeed are encouraged to do so by the authors of those systems.

- Some important UNIX programs follow C's syntactic conventions. For instance, the `awk` programming language (see Section 4.7) uses many of the same operators and control structures that C does.

1.2   The POSIX.2 Standard

The POSIX.2 working group was formed in 1986 as work on the POSIX.1 standard for system calls and library functions neared completion and the importance of creating a further standard for the utilities and shell became apparent. POSIX.2 promises to be the document that implementors will conform to when providing user-level commands, which is why we have adopted it as the basis of our descriptions in this edition of *UNIX for the Impatient*. In the rest of this book, references to POSIX are references to the POSIX.2 standard.

**1.2.1
Goals of POSIX.2**

The first priority of the POSIX.2 committee was to ensure that insofar as possible, existing applications would continue to run on conforming implementations. The committee took its model from four sources: the

---

9. Definitions for other programming languages have also become available, however.

SVID, the BSD User Manual, the Bolsky and Korn book on the KornShell, and the X/Open Portability Guide. The second priority was to improve the interfaces of the utilities, particularly the command-line interface. That goal led to the following modifications to often inconsistent historical practices:

- The utilities were extended to account for internationalization, including differences in character sets, collating sequences, and cultural conventions.

- The command-line syntax of nearly every utility was modified to conform to the Utility Syntax Guidelines, thus rationalizing one of the most confusing and frustrating aspects of working with UNIX. Older forms were included but labeled as "obsolescent".

- Features not portable across implementations were replaced by new, more portable versions, with the old versions marked as obsolescent.

- Features found useful in particular UNIX systems but not yet in wide use were adopted.

- Unreasonable inconsistencies among otherwise similar interfaces were reconciled; when the inconsistencies could not be reconciled, new interfaces with new names were defined.

- Arbitrary limits on sizes and capacities were removed.

- Syntactic and semantic restrictions that would preclude popular but nonstandard extensions were removed.

- Input and output formats were in many cases specified in detail so that programs could more easily process the input and output of utilities mechanically.

What was *not* given much priority by the committee was enabling existing implementations (as contrasted with applications) to conform to the standard with little modification.

1.2.2 Components of POSIX.2

These are the major aspects of UNIX (or a UNIX-like system) defined by the POSIX.2 standard that we cover in this book:

- **The Execution Environment Utilities.** These utilities are the ones that don't require user interaction and are therefore useful in shell scripts and application programs (though they are also often useful interactively). Examples are `cat`, `find`, `kill`, and `sort`.

- **The User Portability Utilities.** These utilities, which are actually an optional extension of POSIX.2, are generally useful only when run in an interactive environment. Examples are `more`, `vi`, `who`, and `jobs`. In this book we don't distinguish between the two groups of utilities.

- **The shell command language.** The shell command language defines the nature of user interaction with the system, assuming the user is working at a character-oriented display terminal connected to a multi-user time-sharing system. It also defines the programming language used for shell scripts.

- **Definitions, general requirements, and the** UNIX **environment.** These topics cover such important aspects of UNIX as locales, guidelines for utility command-line syntax, system-wide environment variables, and regular expressions. We cover much of this material in Chapter 2.

Aspects of POSIX.2 that we don't cover are the Software Development Utilities, the C Development Utilities, and the language-independent interfaces for high-level programming languages. These aspects are important to programmers but not very important to users who are not actually writing UNIX programs.

Some important issues were considered to be outside the scope of POSIX.2 and thus intentionally were not covered by it:

- System administration, installation, configuration, and maintenance
- Networking commands
- Terminal control and user interface programs such as visual shells
- Graphics programs and their interfaces
- Text formatting and database programs

1.3   How to Use This Book

UNIX for the Impatient is both an introduction to and a handbook for UNIX. To gain the most benefit from it, you need to know what is in it and how to find what you're looking for. These are the first steps we recommend:

- Scan the Synopsis that precedes the Table of Contents to get an overview of the material that we cover.

- If you're new to UNIX, start by reading Chapter 2. It explains the concepts and terminology that are essential to any discussion of UNIX.

- Skim one of the main chapters to become familiar with the way that the material in the book is organized.

- Look at the Alphabetic Summary of Commands in Appendix A and at the Index to see how these parts of the book can help you retrieve information.

Don't feel that you have to read the book in order from front to back or that you have to read everything in it. You'll find it easier and more productive to pick and choose your way through it.

UNIX systems have many minor and some not-so-minor variations from one vendor to another. Even systems from a single vendor change significantly from one release to the next. We usually note when a command behaves differently in different systems, but we don't attempt to catalog all the variations. We urge you to experiment to discover the peculiarities of your own environment.

As you work with UNIX you'll have two kinds of questions:

- Here's what I want to do. How do I do it?
- How does this command work?

The first kind of question is best answered by a *functional* organization, the second by an *alphabetical* organization. We provide both kinds of organization, but in different parts of the book.

The body of the book is organized functionally. Commands that do similar or related things are described together; descriptions of the facilities of individual commands are organized similarly. For instance, when we describe the `ftp` file transfer program, we collect all the commands that pertain to transmitting files in one subsection. The UNIX manual pages for `ftp` list the `ftp` subcommands alphabetically, making it difficult to locate and compare those that pertain to transmitting files.

If you have a particular task to perform and you're looking for the command that will help you do it, here are a few ways to find that command:

- Look in the Synopsis to find the chapter that deals with such tasks. Then use the Table of Contents to narrow down your search.

- Look in the Index to see if the task is listed there.

- If you know of a command that does something similar or related to the task, locate its description. The command you're really looking for may be nearby.

- Check the beginning of the chapter or section that addresses your task for a summary that might direct you to what you want.

On the other hand, you may need to know how a particular command, option, or subcommand works. Appendix A contains an alphabetical list of commands and brief descriptions of what they do, followed by a list, also alphabetical, of the subcommands, options, and other features of each command. Each brief description contains a phrase or sentence to remind you of what the facility does and a cross-reference to the page where you'll find the full description. Appendix A is particularly useful when you encounter an unfamiliar construct or command in a shell script or in some other set of UNIX instructions that someone else wrote. Generally you won't find the details of commands listed in the Index, since listing every option and subcommand there would be redundant and lead to distracting clutter.

Often you'll encounter a term or concept that you don't understand, particularly if you haven't used UNIX before. The Glossary defines most of the technical terms that appear in the book. The Index can also help you locate information about particular terms or concepts. Pages where terms are defined are printed in italics in the Index.

Occasionally you'll encounter forward references—references to topics discussed later in the book. We've tried to minimize them, but in the interest of keeping all the information about a topic in one place, we haven't tried to eliminate them altogether. By skimming the material at a forward reference you can gain a general understanding of it, returning to it later when convenient.

We recognize that *UNIX for the Impatient* is unlikely to be your only source of UNIX information. To help you find information elsewhere, we've included lists of printed and electronic resources in Appendix C. In addition to anything you'll find in this book, the online manual pages and printed documentation that come with your system provide essential information.

1.4   Typographical Conventions

In this book we observe the following typographical conventions, which correspond to those typically used in UNIX documentation:

- UNIX entities such as commands and file names appear in typewriter type; for example, `grep` and `/dev/null`. Within running text, command fragments and examples of explicit input and output also appear in typewriter type and are often enclosed in single quotes, like this: '.'. We omit the quotes when the context makes it clear just which characters are being quoted.[10] When a long keyword must be hyphenated at the end of a line, the hyphen appears in ordinary type (-) rather than in typewriter type (-) to indicate that the hyphen is *not* part of the keyword. On the other hand, the hyphens in the names of Emacs commands appear in typewriter type and are actually part of the commands.

- When a sentence starts with the name of a UNIX command, its first letter is capitalized even if the actual name of the command starts with a lowercase letter. `Vi` is an example. Since virtually all UNIX commands have strictly lowercase names, this practice should cause no confusion once you're aware of it.[11]

- Names of special keys on your keyboard are enclosed in boxes:
  - The keys used for certain UNIX functions are shown by using the name of the function as the name of the key. For example,

---

10. Devising consistent rules for when to use single quotes and when not to was one of the more difficult typographical quandaries we encountered in preparing this book.

11. Some BSD systems call their mail program '`Mail`'; that is the only exception we are aware of.

we indicate the "enter" key by `Enter`. The actual key you
would use for some functions (such as `EOF`) depends on the
settings of your keyboard parameters (see Section 1.6).

○ Control keys such as control-D are shown like this: `Ctrl` D. You
  get this key by holding down the control key on your terminal
  and pressing 'D'.

○ The Emacs editor uses "meta" keys, which are shown like this:
  `Meta` X. The method of typing a meta key depends on your
  keyboard and system.

○ Mouse clicks (for programs running under X) are shown similarly. For instance, the action of clicking on mouse button 2 is
  shown as `Mouse-2`.

• Character names in sans-serif font and angle brackets such as ⟨return⟩
  represent ASCII control characters.

• Sometimes we refer to special characters by their names. The names
  we have chosen correspond to the most common colloquial UNIX
  usage, but aren't necessarily the same as those used either in POSIX
  documents or in books on English usage and punctuation. Here are
  the names in alphabetical order:

&	ampersand	:	colon	(	parenthesis, left
'	apostrophe	,	comma	)	parenthesis, right
@	at	–	hyphen	%	percent
`	backquote	$	dollar sign	+	plus
\	backslash	.	dot	?	question mark
!	bang	"	double quote	;	semicolon
|	bar	=	equals	/	slash
{	brace, left	>	greater than	*	star
}	brace, right	#	hash mark	~	tilde
[	bracket, left	∧	hat	_	underscore
]	bracket, right	<	less than		

• Spaces in samples of input and output are usually shown just as
  that—spaces. But for the sake of clarity we sometimes use the displayed character ␣, known as a *visible space*, to represent a space
  explicitly.

1.5   Syntactic Conventions

We use the following conventions for describing the forms of commands
and constructs, which agree with those commonly used in UNIX documentation:

- A word in italic type, like *this*, represents a variable part of a construct. Usually the word describes the information that you must provide. For instance, in the construct

      source *file*

  the variable *file* indicates the pathname of a file.

- Square brackets around a construct indicate that the construct is optional, as in

      cd [*dir*]

  The form of the cd command indicates that you can either specify the directory *dir* or omit it. Square brackets are sometimes supposed to be taken literally. The typeface indicates which sense is intended—literal brackets look like this: '[ ]' rather than like this: '[ ]'.

- Three dots indicate that the immediately preceding construct can be repeated one or more times. If the construct is in square brackets, however, it can be repeated zero or more times. For example, the form

      file ...

  denotes one or more *file*s, while the form

      [*file* ...]

  denotes zero or more *file*s. The form

      [*name=value*] ...

  denotes zero or more repetitions of '*name=value*'. Were the dots to be within the square brackets, a single *name* could have one or more *value*s.

    When you type a repeated construct as input, you should ordinarily separate its elements with whitespace (a sequence of one or more spaces or tabs). We don't show that whitespace when we give the syntax of a command.

- A vertical bar between constructs indicates that the constructs are alternatives. For example, the syntax of the tail command is

      tail [-f][-c *number* | -n *number*] [*file*]

  The vertical bar indicates that you can specify either the -c option or the -n option. Since the alternatives appear within square brackets, you can also omit them both.

- Braces around a construct indicate grouping.[12] For example, the notation

      {+|-}

---

12. Unlike the other syntactic conventions here, this one is not used in the POSIX standard.

indicates an entity that can be either '+' or '-'. Literal braces are shown in typewriter font, like this: { }.

- When a command recognizes several single-letter options, we usually show them as a single option. For example, the `rm` command recognizes the options `-f`, `-i`, `-R`, and `-r`. The rules for command syntax permit them to appear in any order and to be grouped, so the following commands are all equivalent:

```
rm -i -R junque
rm -R -i junque
rm -iR junque
rm -Ri junque
```

We indicate the form of this command as

```
rm -firR file ...
```

1.6   Getting Started

We assume for now that you're using a UNIX system that was set up by someone else; Section 1.6.2 explains what to do if that's not the case. To get started you'll need instructions on how to connect to the system (either by dialing into it or by turning on your workstation or terminal), a user name, and an initial password.

When the system detects that you've established a new connection to it, it issues a '`login:`' prompt.[13] To respond, type your user name followed by ⌊Enter⌋.[14] (UNIX is case-sensitive, so '`KEVIN`', '`Kevin`', and '`kevin`' are three different users.) The system then prompts you for your password; type it followed by another ⌊Enter⌋. Your password doesn't appear on your screen as you type it, so type it carefully.

After you've successfully logged in, you'll receive a confirmation message. You may also see a "message of the day" containing information about the status of the system and newly installed software. Following that, depending on how your system has been set up, you may see some "welcoming mail". You can usually escape from the mailer by typing '`q`'.

At this point your interaction with UNIX is controlled by a program called a *shell*. To issue a command to the shell, type the command followed by ⌊Enter⌋. The shell will execute the command and send its output to your terminal (see Chapter 6).

---

13. If you're running under a non-USA environment, you might see the equivalent of `login:` in your own language.

14. Although UNIX systems often vary in their use of terminal keys, you can almost always count on ⌊Enter⌋ (or ⌊Return⌋ on some terminals) terminating a line by sending a ⟨newline⟩ character.

To terminate your session and log out, type 'exit', 'logout', or [Ctrl]D. Typing exit will work on nearly any system. Exiting via [Ctrl]D is often disabled as a safeguard against logging out unintentionally. You may also be able to log out by breaking the connection with the computer, but this is *not* recommended. Some older systems are set up in such a way that the next person to come in on the same phone line will take over your session where you abandoned it, and such rogue access to your account is a serious security hazard.

1.6.1
Logging In for the First Time

When you log in for the first time, you should go through the following three steps:

(1)   Check that your terminal type is correct.
(2)   See how the control characters for your terminal have been assigned.
(3)   Change your password if it was assigned by a system administrator.

Checking Your Terminal Type.   To check your terminal type, type the command

```
echo $TERM
```

If the value indicated for TERM doesn't seem to correspond to the kind of terminal you have, either ask your system administrator to change your terminal type or change it yourself using the methods described in Section 2.15.7.

Viewing the Control Character Assignments.   The UNIX *control characters* are characters that, when sent from your terminal, perform control functions such as interrupting a program or erasing the previously typed character. To view the control character assigned to each such function, type

```
stty -a
```

On some older systems you may instead have to type

```
stty all
```

The relevant portion of the output will look something like this:

```
intr = ^C; quit = ^\; erase = ^H; kill = ^U; eof = ^D;
eol = <undef>; eol2 = <undef>; start = ^Q; stop = ^S;
susp = ^Z; rprnt = ^R; werase = ^W; lnext = ^V; flush = ^O;
```

The first entry, 'intr = ^C', indicates that the "interrupt" control character is [Ctrl]C; that is, the character that you produce by holding down the control key on your keyboard while pressing the C key. The other entries are similar. These assignments are typical of what you're likely to encounter.

The key or key combination that you press to erase the previous character is often called the "erase key", which we denote by [Erase]. Key combinations for other functions are named similarly. In a typical UNIX system, keys for the following functions have control characters assigned to them:

Erase   Deletes the most recently typed character. This key is usually assigned to Delete or Backspace.

Kill   Cancels the line you're typing. This key is usually assigned to Ctrl U.

Intr (interrupt)
        Interrupts the program currently executing. The interrupt key may not work if the program you're executing uses the interrupt key for a special purpose.[15] This key is usually assigned to Ctrl C.

Quit   Provides a stronger form of interrupt. Quit often works when Intr doesn't, but it also produces a (usually useless) file named `core` that records the contents of computer memory. This key is usually assigned to Ctrl \ .

EOF (end-of-file)
        Indicates the end of typed input. EOF may log you out if you type it as a command to the shell that controls your terminal interactions.[16] Normally this key is assigned to Ctrl D, which is also used for other purposes by a number of programs. Changing the end-of-file key doesn't change these other interpretations of Ctrl D.[17]

Flush   Causes output from the currently running program to be discarded but does not stop that program from executing. Flush is useful when a program is producing a file in addition to its normal output and you want to ignore the rest of the displayed output while still producing the entire file. Not all systems provide a flush key. This key is usually assigned to Ctrl O.

Suspend   Enables you to suspend the program you're running and do something else. The suspended program is not destroyed, so you can resume it later. Only systems that support job control (see Section 2.6.3) provide this key. This key is usually assigned to Ctrl Z.

WdErase (word erase)
        Erases the previous word on the line you just typed. This key is a feature of BSD. This key is usually assigned to Ctrl W.

---

15. A program can do this by intercepting the interrupt.

16. If you're in a shell within a shell, only the inner shell is terminated.

17. Some shells provide an `ignoreeof` variable (see p. 376) as a safety measure. If you set this variable within a copy of such a shell, EOF won't log you out of that copy.

⟨Stop⟩ ("Xoff ")
⟨Start⟩ ("Xon")

> Controls output sent to your terminal. The stop key stops output and the start key restarts it. When you press ⟨Stop⟩ the program sending the output waits in suspension, holding its output, until you restart it with ⟨Start⟩. ⟨Stop⟩ is usually assigned to ⟨Ctrl⟩S and ⟨Start⟩ to ⟨Ctrl⟩Q. These assignments correspond to the ASCII control functions ⟨DC3⟩ and ⟨DC1⟩. On some systems these keys cannot be reassigned.

Some systems may provide additional functions such as eol for an alternate end-of-line character, lnext for quoting the next character literally, or rprnt for redrawing the current line. See "Settings for Control Characters" on page 262 for further discussion of these and other special keys.

Verifying the Rows and Columns.   Many programs need to know how many rows and how many columns your terminal has. If the stty -a command indicates that rows and columns are 0, which can happen when you log in remotely to some systems, you'll need to use stty to set those values correctly (see "Settings for Screen Dimensions" on p. 265).

Changing Your Password.   You can change your password by issuing the passwd command. You'll be asked for your current password once and then for your new password twice—the second time to verify that you entered it correctly, since it won't be visible on your screen.[18]

1.6.2
Installing a
New System

You may be in the awkward situation of having to install a UNIX system without yet knowing how to use UNIX. Most modern UNIX systems include a menu-driven installation program that guides you through the installation process. Very few of the decisions you make during installation are irrevocable, although you can't alter the size of the disk partition allocated to the entire UNIX system without rebuilding the system. Once your system is up and running and you know more about what you're doing, you can modify it to suit your needs (see Chapter 14).

After completing the installation, your first step should be to register yourself as a user if you didn't already do so during the installation:

(1)   Log in as root, using the root password you specified (or were given by default) during the installation.

(2)   Use your system administration program to register yourself.

---

18. On some networked systems there are two passwd files that store password information—a local one on your workstation and a global one. The passwd command on these systems might affect only the local file, thus denying you access to the rest of the network with your new password. In this case you'll need to use the yppasswd command instead to set the global password file. You can check for this by typing

    ypmatch *logname* passwd

where *logname* is your login name. If you see a line from the passwd file that lists your name along with other information separated by colons, then you'll need to use yppasswd. If you get any other response, you won't.

As a general rule you should not use the `root` identity unless you need the special privileges it confers. Using `root` only when necessary is a safeguard against accidental damage to your system.

<table>
<tr><td>

**1.6.3
Ten Particularly
Useful Commands
and Constructs**

</td><td>

Newcomers to UNIX are often bewildered by the great number of its commands and constructs. Where do you begin?

In this section we provide a list of 10 useful commands and constructs that we hope will help, although these are certainly not the only ones you'll need or want. If you're a UNIX aficionado, your list will probably differ from ours.

</td></tr>
</table>

`ls -aCF`   This form of the `ls` (list) command lists all the files in your current directory in a convenient format (see Section 3.2). The 'CF' must be in uppercase as shown. On some systems you'll obtain the same result if you type `ls` by itself. For more details on the files, use '`ls -l | more`'.

`cat`   The `cat` (concatenate) command, among its other functions, displays the contents of a file—just type '`cat` *file*'. You can also use it to build a short file; type '`cat >`*file*' followed by the text of the file and EOF.[19] See Sections 1.6 and 3.3. If a file you're viewing is too long for your screen, use '`more` *file*' to view it a screenful at a time.

`pwd`   This command prints your current (working) directory (see Section 3.1.2).

`cd [`*dir*`]`   This command moves you to the directory *dir*. If you omit *dir*, it returns you to your home directory (see Section 3.1.1).

c1 `|` *c2* `,` `>` *file*`,` `<` *file*
         The form '*c1* `|` *c2*' connects the standard output of the command *c1* to the standard input of the command *c2* through a pipeline, thus combining their effects. The form '`>` *file*' following a command redirects its standard output to *file*; the form '`<` *file*' following a command redirects its standard input from *file* (see Section 2.10).

`*`   The character '`*`', used in a file name, acts as a "wildcard" that stands for any sequence of characters. For instance, '`x*c`' includes the files `xc`, `xotic`, and `xebec` (if they exist) (see Section 2.9.1).

`cp`   This command copies the contents of one file into another file. For example, typing '`cp banana aper`' copies the contents of the file `banana` into the file `aper` (see Section 3.4.3).

---

19. Watch out—the previous contents of the file, if any, will be lost.

rm   This command deletes a file.[20]   For example, typing 'rm junque' deletes (removes) the file junque from the current directory (see Section 3.5.1).

mv   This command moves a file from one directory to another. For example, typing 'mv hobo Greece' moves the file named hobo from the current directory to the directory Greece, here assumed to be a subdirectory of the current directory (see Section 3.4.2).   You can also use mv to rename a file within a directory.

grep   The grep command extracts from its input the lines containing a specified string.[21]   It is often useful in conjunction with the '|' operator. For example, typing '| grep thelma' after a command filters the output of the command and extracts just those lines containing the string 'thelma'.[22]   The name grep stands for "global regular expression print" (see Section 4.2).

---

20. More accurately, it deletes a link.

21. This is really a special case; in general, grep extracts the lines containing a regular expression (see Section 2.17).

22. On many keyboards the '|' character has a little break in the middle.

2

Concepts

In this chapter we explain the underlying concepts of the UNIX system and the terminology associated with these concepts. We also discuss a number of conventions, such as the definition of a regular expression, that are common to many UNIX commands. The rest of the book relies on your understanding of the information contained in this chapter. Nevertheless, since some of the material discussed in this chapter is highly technical, you may wish to postpone reading advanced topics in detail until the need for them arises.

2.1   The UNIX Manual

UNIX documentation is published in a standard format established by the earliest versions of the UNIX *Programmer's Manual*. Most UNIX systems provide the "manual pages" on-line as well as in printed form. The description of each command, C function, etc., has its own manual page (which may actually be several pages long), divided into more or less standardized sections: "Name", "Synopsis", "Description", "Files", etc. The manual as a whole has a major division for each category of manual pages. The original AT&T numbering is still used widely but not universally. It is as follows:

1   Commands available to users at the shell level
2   System calls in the C library

3   Other functions in the C library
4   Devices and device drivers, sometimes called "special files"
5   File formats and file conventions
6   Games
7   Miscellaneous
8   System maintenance programs and information

You'll often see references of the form "*stty* (1)" in UNIX literature. The "(1)" indicates that *stty* is in Section 1 of the manual and is therefore a shell-level command. In this book we omit the numbers for two reasons: we find them distracting and usually redundant, and nearly everything we refer to is in Section 1. In a few cases, however, the same name appears in several sections. In these cases you'll need to specify the section number to get the item you want.

2.1.1 Viewing Manual Pages with man

The tool for looking at manual pages is the `man` utility, described in detail in Section 5.1.1. To see the manual page for a particular topic, type

```
man topic
```

where *topic* is the name of the topic. For example, to see the manual page for the `grep` utility, type

```
man grep
```

In some cases the same topic may appear in several categories. To select a particular category, type

```
man cat topic
```

where *cat* is the category. Most of the time you'll want category 1. For example, `mkdir` is the name both of a user command (category 1) and a system call (category 2). To see the manual page for the `mkdir` user command, type

```
man 1 mkdir
```

Man uses a pager (see Section 3.6) to display the manual pages one screenful at a time.[1] Manual pages include page headers and are traditionally formatted for a line printer having 66 lines per page—not a convenient format for viewing.[2]

---

1. You can get an even more readable display by filtering out the internal page headers. The following cryptic shell script (see Section 6.5) does both the paging and the filtering:

```
man $1 | awk 'NR<=8||(NR%66>=8&&NR%66<=60)' | more
```

It deletes lines 61–66 on the first page and lines 1–7 and 61–66 on all subsequent pages. To use this script, store it in a file `mypager` and specify the option '`-P mypager`' when you call `man`. You can cause this option to be inserted automatically by defining an alias for `man` with the command

```
alias man="\man -P mypager"
```

2. UNIX software distributed in source form usually includes manual pages in the form of input for the `nroff` formatter (see Section 5.14.1).

You can also do a keyword search on either topic names or their descriptions by typing

    man -k *keyword*

For example, typing

    man -k director

shows you a list of all manual pages whose titles or descriptions include 'directory' or 'directories'. In some systems such as BSD, the functionality of 'man -k' is provided by a separate command, apropos.

2.1.2
Viewing Manual
Pages Under X

If you are using X, there's a particularly useful program for viewing manual pages on-line called xman (see Section 13.19). You can display several manual pages at once in separate windows, look at all the manual pages in a section, or perform an apropos-style search. When a manual page is displayed in a window, you can easily scroll through it and look at any part of it.

2.1.3
Other Sources of
UNIX
Documentation

Other sources of UNIX documentation are often available, either as files accompanying a software distribution or over the Internet:

- Your system may include a directory such as /usr/doc that includes useful documents in various forms. Many of these documents are in the form of a PostScript file that can be printed on an appropriately equipped printer or viewed on-line. Such files usually have names ending in '.ps'.

- A UNIX software distribution often includes a file called README that gives an overview of the distribution.

- Many major UNIX software packages have files of frequently asked questions, called FAQs. These files are usually updated periodically and can be retrieved from many Internet sites. A large collection of them can be found at the Internet node rtfm.mit.edu.

- The Usenet newsgroups, which are accessible over the Internet (see Section 11.8), offer a forum for answering questions you can't answer otherwise.

2.2   System Administration and the Superuser

System administration refers to a collection of tasks whose purpose is to make the UNIX system available to its users in an orderly and secure manner. These tasks include registering and deleting users, configuring the kernel, controlling access to parts of the file system, backing up and restoring files, and installing new software packages. If you're setting up a UNIX system for yourself, you'll need to perform these tasks both when you install the system and later as you use it. We briefly discuss system administration from the standpoint of an individual system proprietor in Chapter 14.

The design of UNIX reflects the belief that any facility accessible to users should be protected from accidental or malicious modification by users and that users should be protected from each other. Therefore the programs and files for system administration are accessible only to a specially designated user called the *superuser*. The superuser has a special user name, `root`; whoever knows the password for `root` can act as the superuser.

The initial password for `root` is set as part of the process of installing the system; like other passwords, it can be changed at any time thereafter. The person who installs the system chooses the initial `root` password, so that person necessarily can become the superuser. Thereafter the ability to become the superuser is inherited by those who learn the password from someone who already knows it.[3]

Some versions of UNIX restrict the ability to log in as the superuser. For example, they only accept superuser logins from the console or require that a superuser not at the console belong to a special group, often named 'wheel'.

Anyone who can log in as `root` should have an ordinary user name as well and should avoid using the superuser privileges except when necessary. Security considerations aside, it is all too easy to make a costly mistake in superuser mode, such as deleting a critical system file by accident.

2.3   Users and Groups

In order to use a UNIX system, you must be registered as one of its users. Each user has a login name, a password, and an area of the file system reserved for storing his or her files. In addition, each user belongs to a *group*. Most systems allow a user to belong to more than one group.[4] A group can have just one user in it or can even be empty. Your groups are established when your UNIX account is created and can be changed at any time by the system administrator. You can specify group permissions for a file that you own (see Section 2.8), thus controlling what kinds of access members of your groups have to it.

At any moment, just one of your groups is active; that one determines your group permissions. You can change your active group with the

---

3. An intruder who obtains the password for `root` can lock out the legitimate superuser by changing the password.

4. The file `/etc/group` lists the groups and the users in each group.

newgrp command (see Section 5.4.3). Your active group on login is your *primary group*; the others are your *supplementary groups*.

Information about your user account is stored in a file named /etc/passwd. This file, despite its name, does *not* contain your password, although in most older systems it contains your password in an encrypted form. It does contain your user number, primary group number, and full name—information that is not considered privileged and is often useful to other users. Except on enhanced-security systems, anyone can read the /etc/passwd file, but only the superuser can modify it (see "The /etc/passwd File" on p. 251).

On most systems the id command shows you your user number, your user name, and the numbers and names of the groups you belong to. On older BSD systems that don't have the id command, the groups command shows the groups you belong to.

2.4   What the Shell Does

When you log into UNIX, your interaction with the system is managed by a program called a *shell* or *command interpreter*. In this book we generally assume you're using a POSIX-compliant shell such as the KornShell (see Chapter 6), but all shells in common use follow similar conventions. When we make a statement about "the shell" without further qualification, it applies to a POSIX-compliant shell at least.

When the shell is waiting for input, it produces a prompt on your terminal, typically '$'. Usually, you'll respond by typing a command that tells UNIX to do something. A command consists of the name of the command followed by options, pathnames of files, or other information that affects the command's behavior. The general conventions that govern commands are discussed in Section 2.12.

The shell called on your behalf when you log in is called your *login shell*. Your /etc/passwd entry (see "The /etc/passwd File" on p. 251) can contain a field that specifies your login shell. If this field is missing from your /etc/passwd entry, your login shell is determined by a system-wide default. The system administrator who sets up your user account establishes your login shell, though on most systems you can change it with the chsh command (see Section 5.4.5). (Recent Berkeley systems instead have a more general command, chpass, for changing your entry in /etc/passwd.) Alternatively, you can switch to a different shell once you're logged in by placing the command

```
exec shell
```

at the end of your login initialization file (see Section 2.14). This command transfers control of your terminal to the shell *shell*.[5]

In addition to its role as an interactive command interpreter, a shell also provides a programming language for writing programs called *shell scripts* or *shell procedures*. You can store these programs and call them just as you would call any other program; the shell then interprets them. The main application of shell scripts is writing short programs for combinations of commands that you use often, but it's possible to write quite complex shell scripts. The main advantage of shell scripts is that they are easy to write and easy to install. Their disadvantages are (a) they lack both low-level programming features such as pointers and high-level features such as modularization and user-definable data types, and (b) they are not particularly efficient since they are interpreted rather than compiled. Most UNIX systems include quite a number of commands defined by shell scripts.

2.5   The UNIX Kernel

The UNIX kernel is the heart of the operating system. It controls access to the computer and its files, allocates resources among the various activities taking place within the computer, maintains the file system, and manages the computer's memory. Although ordinary users rarely have any explicit interaction with the kernel, the kernel is central to UNIX and is often referred to elsewhere in this book and in UNIX documentation.

A system administrator (see Section 2.2) can adjust the system's operating characteristics by *configuring* the kernel. Configuring the kernel chiefly involves specifying whether certain features of the system should be included, tuning certain internal parameters, and for some systems, specifying which versions of device drivers should be used. Even a system administrator cannot modify the *structure* of the kernel, since that would entail rewriting the UNIX system itself.

---

5. In this case, *shell* won't appear to be a login shell and will behave somewhat differently. For instance, the login initialization file for *shell* won't be executed.

2.6   Processes

When UNIX is running, many activities are underway at the same time. These activities are called *processes*.[6] You can think of processes as working in parallel, although most computers that run UNIX can only support true parallelism for a few specialized activities, such as printing.

Minimally, there is one process for the kernel and one process for each user logged into the system. In normal operation the kernel always has several processes running and any user may also have several processes running. The `ps` (process status) command lists the running processes (see Section 5.2.1). To call it, type either

        ps -ef

or

        ps -ag

or

        ps -A

depending on your system.

The kernel manages the processes, switching back and forth among them according to their needs and priorities. A process can create other processes; the creator is the *parent process* and the processes thus created are *child processes*. Certain system processes called *dæmons* reside in the system more or less permanently and perform ongoing tasks such as handling mail, scheduling tasks that should be performed at regular intervals, and transferring files from the print queue to printers.

By creating multiple processes, you can run several programs at once. For example, suppose you want to execute a program that takes a long time to complete. You can run the program at a low priority in the background and do something else at the terminal while it is running. All modern shells provide a facility called *job control* that lets you switch back and forth among processes (see Section 2.6.3). Even the older Bourne shell enables you to run a process in the background and to lower its priority with the `nice` command (see Section 5.3.5).

Sometimes one of your processes may get stuck and you'll need to kill it. If the stuck process is not in control of your terminal, you can use the `ps` command to get its process ID and the `kill` command to remove it (see Section 5.3.1). Otherwise you may be able to regain control by using

---

6. The sequence of actions that takes place as a process executes is called a *thread*. On a machine with multiple processors, a process may have more than one thread associated with it if the UNIX system supports that capability. Threads are sometimes called *lightweight processes* because, unlike full-fledged processes, they share an execution environment.

Intr or, if necessary, Quit. If neither key works, you'll need to kill the process from another terminal if you can or, as a last resort, ask someone with superuser privileges to kill it for you.[7]

**2.6.1
Signals**

A *signal* notifies a process of an abnormal external event, such as disconnection of the terminal. With few exceptions, a process has the option of *catching* any signal sent to it. The information associated with a process includes a list of signals that it catches and an action to be taken for each one.

When a signal is sent to a process, the kernel performs the specified action if the signal is caught and a default action (which usually includes killing the process) if it is not. Killing a process causes it to terminate abnormally (see Section 2.6.2). The `trap` command of `ksh` (see p. 364) is an example of how a process can catch signals. You can use the `kill` program (see Section 5.3.1) to send a signal to another process provided that the process is one of yours or you are the superuser.

Signals and Their Codes. The following signals are implemented on nearly all systems. Each signal is preceded by its numerical code and its name. Both the numerical codes and the names are used in UNIX documentation. For most signals, the default action is to terminate the process (and in some cases to produce a memory dump, storing it in a file named `core`); for the others, the default action is to suspend the process or to do nothing at all.

The following signals are recognized by all systems:

1	`SIGHUP`	Terminal hangup
2	`SIGINT`	Terminal interrupt
3	`SIGQUIT`	Terminal quit (with a memory dump)
9	`SIGKILL`	Process killed
13	`SIGPIPE`	Broken pipe (writing when the reader has terminated)
14	`SIGALRM`	Alarm clock interrupt
15	`SIGTERM`	Software termination

Programs such as `kill` normally use `TERM` to kill another process (see Section 5.3.1). The receiving process can catch it and choose to continue. `KILL` cannot be caught; a process receiving that signal is always killed, although the kill may not always work.[8] Signals 4–8 and 10–12 indicate various kinds of machine errors, which are usually caused by program misbehavior rather than a computer malfunction.

The `WINCH` signal is used in windowing systems such as X; the other signals in the following group are used only in systems that support job

---

7. For a single-user system, the ultimate recourse is to reboot the computer.

8. That can happen, for instance, if the process invoked a device driver that is stuck waiting for a response from the device. In that case the signal will wait indefinitely for recognition with no indication of what is happening.

control (see Section 2.6.3). Systems vary in how they number these signals, but the names have the same meanings for all systems.

20	SIGWINCH	Window size has changed
23	SIGCONT	Continue job if stopped
24	SIGSTOP	Noninteractive stop signal
25	SIGTSTP	Interactive stop signal
26	SIGTTIN	Read attempted by a background job
27	SIGTTOU	Write attempted by a background job

Stopping a job suspends its activity but does not terminate it. A stopped job can be resumed later. By default, CONT has no effect unless it's sent to a stopped job, in which case it reactivates the job and brings it to the foreground. STOP, like KILL above, cannot be caught; it provides a reliable way of stopping a job. By default, TTIN and TTOU stop a job that is running in the background.

Under most systems, the command kill -1 will produce a list of all signals known to your system, showing both their symbolic names and numerical codes.

2.6.2
Exit Status of
a Process

Calling a process has three possible outcomes: the process can succeed, fail, or terminate abnormally. The *exit status* of the process is a number that reveals this outcome.

A process can terminate normally of its own accord, returning an exit status to its parent process. By convention, an exit status of zero indicates success—the process has accomplished its assigned task. Any other exit status indicates failure; the actual value acts as a code that indicates the nature of the failure. Failure does not necessarily indicate that the process failed altogether to accomplish its task, though. A nonzero exit status may merely warn of an unexpected condition or outcome. Ordinarily a normal exit status is less than 128 to avoid confusion with an exit status resulting from abnormal termination.[9]

A process can terminate abnormally—for example, if you interrupt it—because of a signal sent to it (see Section 2.6.1). In this case the process itself can't return an exit status because it has lost control, so the kernel returns an exit status on behalf of the process indicating why it terminated. The exit status in this case is 128 plus the signal code number; for example, 137 if you kill the process with SIGKILL (see "Signals and Their Codes" on p. 31).

---

9. A C program can distinguish between normal and abnormal termination by examining the value returned by the *wait* function. This value stores normal and abnormal termination codes separately; for example, in the upper and lower bytes of a 16-bit word. Only one of the codes can be nonzero. But at the shell level, the two codes are merged; the value of the '$?' shell variable, which indicates the exit status of the previous shell command, is effectively the logical "or" of the two codes. At the shell level you can't distinguish between a command that exited normally with an 'exit 137' command and one that was externally terminated by a 'KILL' signal.

You can test the exit status of a process and choose what to do next according to the result of the test. You don't have to be a C programmer to do this; for instance, you can test the status in a shell script with `if` (p. 336) or any other shell construct that does numeric comparisons.

2.6.3
Job Control

Job control is a shell facility, introduced by BSD and standardized by POSIX, that enables you to create groups of processes called *jobs* and control them from your terminal using shell commands. For example, you might wish to carry on two activities more or less in parallel: editing a file and communicating interactively with a remote system. At the same time you might be sorting a large file. By making each activity a job, you can easily switch back and forth between editing and remote communication, all the time having the sort going on as a low-priority activity in the background.

Whenever you are logged in, your shell is in one of two states: at a shell prompt waiting for input, or executing a command that has control of your terminal. If it is executing a command, then the processes entailed in that execution constitute the *foreground job*. Thus there is either one foreground job or none.

In addition, any number of jobs can be running in the background or stopped (suspended). A *background job* is a job that is running but is not the foreground job. A stopped job is in a state of suspense; it remains dormant until you take action to resume it. If there are any stopped jobs, the *current job* is the one that was stopped most recently; otherwise the current job, if any, is the background job most recently suspended or initiated. So in deciding which job is the current one, the shell gives priority to stopped jobs over jobs running in the background.[10] If there are no background jobs or stopped jobs, then the current job is undefined. You can view the status of all your jobs with the `jobs` command (see Section 6.20.2).

When you start a background job, the shell displays the job number and the process number associated with the job. A background pipeline (see Section 2.10.1) containing several processes shows a process number for each one. A sample message is

```
[2]      470 471
```

Here the job number is 2 and the process numbers are 470 and 471. When a job terminates or changes status in some other way, the shell notifies you of the change just before it issues the next command prompt.

If a background job should attempt to read from the terminal, it simply waits until it becomes the foreground job. If a background job should attempt to write to a terminal, the result depends on the value of the terminal setting `tostop` (p. 264). If the setting is enabled, the write is held up until the job is moved to the foreground; if the setting is disabled, the

---

10. The POSIX standard is contradictory on this point, but this is how most shells seem to behave.

output from the background job is intermingled with the output from the foreground job.[11]

Job Identifiers.   Several commands use a *job identifier* to refer to a job. A job identifier has the following forms:

%*n*   Job number *n*.

%*str*   The unique job whose name begins with *str*. If there is only one background job, *str* may be empty and '%' by itself refers to the current job.

%?*str*   The unique job whose name contains the string *str*.

%+
%%   The current job.

%−   The previous job.

The C shell and Bash also interpret '%' as referring to the current job. Some versions of the KornShell interpret '%' as referring to the current job only if there is just a single background or stopped job.

Changing the Status of a Job.   There are several ways you can change the status of a job:

- You can stop the foreground job if there is one by sending it a STOP signal, thereby making that job a background job and changing its status to 'Stopped'. The usual way to send the signal is to type the suspend character, normally Ctrl Z (see "Viewing the Control Character Assignments" on p. 19). To restart a stopped job as a background job, use the `bg` command.

- You can bring a background job '%*job*' to the foreground, giving it control of your terminal, by typing '`fg` %*job*' at a shell prompt (or just '%*job*' for some shells).

- You can cause a stopped job '%*job*' to execute in the background by typing '`bg` %*job*' at a shell prompt, provided that the stopped job is not waiting for terminal input. If you try to restart in the background a job that is waiting for terminal input, it becomes the current job but remains stopped.

- You can kill a job '%*job*' by typing '`kill` %*job*' at a shell prompt, provided that the job does not catch and then ignore the signal (see Section 5.3.1). Killing a job kills all of its processes. You can also use `kill` to send other signals to a job.

---

11. If a background job attempts to read from the terminal, it is sent the TTIN signal. Similarly, if a background job attempts to write to the terminal but `tostop` is enabled, it is sent the TTOU signal. A program can adjust its behavior in the background by trapping these signals and responding to them.

The `fg` and `bg` commands are described in Section 6.20.1.

Alternatives to Job Control.   Job control is not the only way to manage multiple processes:

- The X Window System (see Chapter 13) enables you to run multiple processes in a graphical environment by creating several pseudo-terminals in separate windows and running a different program in each one.

- Many versions of UNIX that run on the i386 architecture, including Linux and UnixWare, provide a *virtual terminal* facility that does not require windowing support. On these systems, pressing a special key combination switches you to a different virtual terminal. For example, pressing [Alt] [Sysreq] followed by [F1] (or [Alt] [F1] for some systems) switches you to virtual terminal #1. The virtual terminals behave logically as independent connections to your computer, but physically they share the same keyboard and screen. Switching to a different virtual terminal restores the contents of your screen to what they were when you previously were using that virtual terminal.

2.6.4
Process Groups

A *process group* is a set of processes that can be signalled together. In other words, sending a signal to a process group sends that signal to each process in the group. In particular, you can kill all the processes in a process group by sending a `KILL` signal to the group.

In the absence of job control, the processes associated with each logged-in terminal form a process group—in effect, a single job. Every process belongs to a process group. As a user, you can't do much with process groups—they're mainly a convenience for systems programmers—but they're often referred to in UNIX documentation.

The first process to enter a process group becomes the *process group leader*. For example, the processes in a pipeline (see Section 2.10.1) form a process group whose leader is the first process in the pipeline. The leader's process number becomes the process group number and identifies the entire group.

2.6.5
Environment
Variables

Each process has a collection of *environment variables* associated with it. These variables can be queried or set by the process and are inherited by its subprocesses. An example of an environment variable is `TERM`, which contains your terminal type. You can see the values of the environment variables currently in effect by issuing the `env` command (see Section 6.8.2), or for some non-POSIX shells, the `printenv` command. In addition, most UNIX programs that accept commands interactively (including shells) have a set of local variables that help define the program's behavior. The relationship between environment variables and local variables can be confusing; we discuss it on page 66.

Whenever you start a new process as a child of another, UNIX sets the environment variables of the child process to a copy of those of its parent. Thereafter the environment variables of the child and the parent are independent, since one process cannot examine or modify the environment variables of another. When a process terminates, its environment variables disappear and any changes to these variables are lost.

Some systems enable you to set environment variables by specifying them after your name when you log in (see "Environment Variables on Login" on p. 251). This facility provides a powerful and convenient method of customizing your environment since the commands in your login initialization file (see Section 2.14) can test the values of these variables.

2.6.6
Real and Effective
Users and Groups

The *real user ID* of a process ordinarily identifies the user who created that process. When a process spawns a child process, the child process inherits the real user ID of its parent.[12]

In addition, each process also has an *effective user ID* that determines the process's privileges. The effective user ID provides a mechanism for a program to carry out privileged operations on your behalf. For instance, the `passwd` program that sets or changes your password needs full access to the password files, but it would be unsafe to allow any user to modify those files directly. Therefore `passwd` runs with the real user ID of the user who called it but with an effective user ID of `root`, the superuser. The mechanism that allows you to call a program that runs under its own effective user ID is described in "The Set-uid Bit" on page 46.

In addition, each process has a *real group ID* and an *effective group ID*. These are handled in essentially the same way as the user IDs.

2.7   The UNIX File System

The UNIX file system consists of a set of *files*. Each file has one or more names, called *file names*. There are three kinds of files:

- *Regular files*, which contain stored data
- *Directories*, which contain information about a set of files and are used to locate a file by its name

---

12. Only a process with appropriate privileges, such as a superuser process, can change its real user ID. The C system call for doing that is called *setuid*. An example of its use is the process for handling logins, whose real user ID is `root`. When you log in, that supervisory process creates a process *P* for you, still with real user ID `root`. But before giving you control, *P* changes its real user ID to your own user ID. Process *P* then no longer has the privileges needed to change the user ID back to `root`.

- Special files of several kinds:
  - *Device special files*, which provide access to devices such as terminals and printers (see Section 2.18.2)
  - *FIFO special files*, sometimes called *named pipes*, which provide a channel for communication between independent processes (see Section 2.11.1)
  - Implementation-specific varieties of special files provided by particular versions of UNIX

Like most modern operating systems, UNIX organizes its file system as a hierarchy of directories. The directory hierarchy is often called a *tree*, although it's almost always drawn as an upside-down tree. A special directory, `root`, sits at the top of the hierarchy. Commands for navigating and modifying the directory tree are described in Section 3.1.

A directory can include subdirectories as well as regular files and special files. UNIX treats a subdirectory as just a particular kind of file. If you display the contents of a directory, the subdirectories are listed along with the other files.

UNIX views a file, no matter what its type, as a sequence of bytes. Whatever internal structure a file might have affects only those programs that care about it. Most published descriptions of UNIX make much of this, a viewpoint that can confuse newcomers since they naturally assume that files have no predefined internal structure. Historically, the mainframe operating systems that were dominant when UNIX was first built did have file types with different internal structures—regional, indexed sequential, and so forth—but most current operating systems, MS-DOS in particular, treat files with the same uniformity that UNIX does.

Whenever possible, UNIX programs have been designed to operate on text files; that is, files that can sensibly be printed. Within these files a *newline* character, represented as the ASCII ⟨linefeed⟩ character,[13] indicates the end of one line and the beginning of the next. Text files can include any character except the null character, the character whose binary representation is all zeros. Because C interprets a null character as indicating the end of a string and most UNIX programs are written in C, null characters in text files give many UNIX programs severe indigestion. Implementations may also limit the number of bytes in a line; files that violate that constraint will also break many programs.

2.7.1
Filenames

A filename[14] names a file in a directory. A filename consists of up to 255 characters in most systems, though some older systems may limit it to 14.[15]

---

13. Some locales might represent a newline differently, but the convention is nearly universal.

14. In the first edition of this book we used the term "file identifier" to denote a filename because of the inconsistency in UNIX literature at that time as to what a file name (or filename) really is. POSIX has straightened out the confusion so we no longer use that term.

15. For collections of files to be sent to other systems, it is wise to limit filenames to 14 characters. POSIX allows an implementation to set the limit that low.

A filename can include any character other than '/' or the null character, although some characters such as '&' and ⟨space⟩ can be troublesome because of their special meanings on command lines.[16] If your system uses a code set (see Section 2.16.1) that includes non-ASCII characters, such as letters from other alphabets, you can use those characters in filenames also. Letters (either uppercase or lowercase), digits, dots, and underscores are usually safe. Hyphens are also safe except as the first character. By convention, a dot at the start of a filename identifies an initialization file or other supporting file for a particular program. Directory listings don't normally include files whose identifiers start with a dot. "Dot files" are also treated specially during wildcard expansion (see Section 2.9.1).

Filenames are case-sensitive, so `psaltery`, `Psaltery`, and `PSALTERY` name three different files. Some UNIX programs expect the identifiers of their input and output files to consist of a name part followed by a dot and an extension. For example, when the `compress` program compresses a file *file*, the resulting compressed file has the name *file*.`Z`. As another example, the `C` compiler expects its input files to have filenames of the form *file*.`c`.

2.7.2 Pathnames

A *pathname* is a name that designates a file. A pathname consists of a sequence of filenames separated by slashes (/). Multiple successive slashes are considered to be the same as one slash.[17] However, POSIX allows a system to give a different interpretation to '//' at the beginning of a pathname (or as a pathname by itself), and some systems adopt the convention that a path beginning with '//*host*/' designates the root directory of the networked host *host*.

The filenames are the *components* of the pathname. The last filename is called the *basename* and the portion of the pathname preceding the last filename is called the *path prefix*. When you write a path prefix to designate a directory, the trailing slash is optional.

There are two kinds of pathnames: absolute and relative. An absolute pathname starts with a slash; a relative pathname does not.

Absolute Pathnames. You can refer to a file anywhere in the tree by giving its *absolute pathname*. The absolute pathname specifies the sequence of subdirectories you must traverse in order to get from the root to the file. The '/' that always begins an absolute pathname designates the root directory. For instance, UNIX interprets the pathname `/home/humbert/toads` as follows:

(1)   From the root, go to the subdirectory named `home`.

---

16. A filename can even contain nonprinting characters such as ⟨backspace⟩. Only under very unusual circumstances would anyone deliberately create a file with a name containing nonprinting characters, but files with such names are sometimes created by accident. These files are difficult to get rid of—see Section 3.5.3 for instructions on how to do it.

17. Emacs does not follow this convention—in Emacs, multiple slashes begin an absolute pathname.

(2)   From this subdirectory, go to the subdirectory named `humbert`.

(3)   From this subdirectory, pick the file named `toads` (which could itself
be a directory).

Relative Pathnames.   Each process has a directory called the *current directory* or *working directory* that can serve as a starting point for pathnames.
The `pwd` command displays ("prints") your working directory (i.e., the
working directory of your shell process). A pathname that does not start
with '`/`' is called a *relative pathname* and is taken as relative to your working
directory unless it (a) is a command to execute a program and (b) contains no slashes. In that case the rules for searching your path given in
Section 2.9.2 apply. Thus if your working directory is `/home/humbert`, the
relative pathname

```
travel/city.data/jakarta
```

corresponds to the full pathname

```
/home/humbert/travel/city.data/jakarta
```

The simplest and most common case of a relative pathname is a single
filename *file* used as a pathname. Such a pathname refers to the file *file*
in your current directory.

The '`.`' and '`..`' Notations.   The *parent* of a directory *d* (other than the
root) is the directory just above *d* in the hierarchy. The current directory
is named '`.`' and its parent is named '`..`', so you can use paths to go up
the hierarchy as well as down it. For example, if the current directory is
`/home/humbert` as above, '`..`' refers to `/home`, '`../..`' refers to the root,
and '`../tinkerbell`' refers to `/home/tinkerbell`. The root is a special
case in that its parent is itself; thus '`/..`' refers to the root just as '`/`' does.[18]

**2.7.3
Home Directories**

Each user has a *home directory*. The pathname for this directory varies
according to the system, but its last component is usually the user's name.
In the first UNIX systems, a user's home directory was an immediate
descendant of the root directory; a user named `zsazsa` had a home directory named `/zsazsa`. That convention soon became untenable, however,
and all modern systems place home directories at a lower level than the
root, usually but not always within a single subdirectory of the root. For
different systems the home directory for user *user* might variously be `/`
`home/`*u*, `/usr/`*user*, `/u/`*user*, or `/u/`*site*`/u`, where *site* is the computer's
host name; other locations are possible. In this book we follow the convention that *user*'s home directory is `/home/`*user*.

Because home directories are so important, there's a special notation
for them recognized by every UNIX shell except the Bourne shell: the

---

18.   POSIX allows an implementation to give a different interpretation to '`/..`', just as it does
for a leading '`//`' in a pathname. On some systems, '`/../`*host*`/`' refers to the root directory
of networked host *host*.

character '~' at the start of a pathname refers to the home directory of the current user, while '~*user*' refers to the home directory of user *user*. We use that notation throughout this book. Thus for user `humbert`, '~/ice.cream' refers to /home/humbert/ice.cream and '~zelda/cookies' refers to /home/zelda/cookies. Referring to other people's directories is often useful when you're working on a cooperative project or just accessing information that someone has made publicly available, and the '~*user*' notation makes it easy.

A less convenient notation for referring to your home directory is `$HOME`, which yields the value of the variable `HOME` that every shell, including the Bourne shell, supports. Thus `$HOME/oldcars` refers to the file `oldcars` in your home directory. This notation has no provision for simplifying references to the home directory of another user.

2.7.4 Subsidiary File Systems

UNIX allows parts of the directory hierarchy, called *file systems* (as distinct from *the* UNIX file system), to reside on separate storage devices or in separate disk partitions. There are several reasons why:

- The disks or other devices that hold the directories and their files may not be large enough to hold the entire hierarchy, so it may be necessary to distribute the hierarchy among several devices.

- For administrative convenience, it may be helpful to break up a very large disk into partitions.

- The storage devices may not be permanently attached to the computer. A floppy disk that contains its own directory structure is an example of such a file system. The Network File System (see p. 628) enables computers on a network to have their own file systems; by linking these file systems together, it causes files distributed over the network to appear as though they were all in the same computer.

UNIX accommodates file systems by associating them with *mount points*. A mount point is a directory in a file system that corresponds to the root directory of some other file system. The primary file system is the one emanating from the true root directory and is named '/'. A secondary file system is linked into the primary system by the `mount` command, which is given the pathname of the mount point and the location of the secondary file system. Its effect is to make the root of the secondary file system correspond to the mount point. Once a file system has been mounted, you can refer to any file or directory within it by using a path that passes through the mount point. Unmounting a file system invalidates all the paths that pass through its mount point.

As a user, you need to be aware of file system boundaries for two reasons. First, there are restrictions on connections across file system boundaries (see Section 2.7.5). Second, when a file system is unmounted, you lose all access to its files until it is remounted.[19]

---

19. The kernel does not allow a file system to be unmounted if any of its files are in use.

UNIX literature, including this book, refers both to "the UNIX file system" and to "file systems". When we talk about "the UNIX file system", we're referring to how UNIX generally handles files. When we use the term "file system" without qualification, we're using it in the sense of this section.

2.7.5
Links

A *link* to a file is a directory entry for that file, consisting of a filename that names the file within the directory and an i-node number (see Section 2.7.7).[20] A UNIX file can have multiple links. The links to a file have the same i-node number but different names. The links can reside in different directories provided that they are all within the same file system.

The `ln` command (see Section 3.4.1) creates a link to an existing file. Because there is only one copy of a file, a change made to a file through one of its links becomes visible through all of its other links. The `rm` command (see Section 3.5.1) removes a link to a file, not the file itself. A file is not deleted from the file system until its last link is removed. Properly speaking, every file is a linked file because every file has at least one link. Unfortunately the term "link" is not always used correctly in UNIX documentation—sometimes you'll see a reference to a "linked file" when what is really meant is a file with *multiple* links.

2.7.6
Symbolic Links

Modern UNIX systems provide another form of link, a *symbolic link*, that references a file indirectly. Symbolic links are sometimes called *soft links* to distinguish them from the more traditional links, *hard links*. When we use the term "link" without qualification, we mean a hard link.

As of this writing, symbolic links are not included in POSIX, though it's likely they will be included in the future. You should bear that in mind when reading a command description that refers to symbolic links.

A symbolic link specifies a pathname. If that pathname designates an actual file, then the symbolic link refers to that file. If it designates another symbolic link, then that link is followed in turn. A symbolic link can specify a pathname for which no file at all exists; in that case a reference to the link is treated like a reference to any other nonexistent file.

You can create a symbolic link by issuing the command

```
ln -s target source
```

where *target* is the pathname of the file you wish to reference with the symbolic link and *source* is the pathname of the symbolic link itself.

Symbolic links behave differently than you might expect in certain situations:

- When you list a directory containing a symbolic link using `ls`, the listing indicates information about the link itself (with `l` as the file type) rather than about the linked-to file. The `ls -R` command (see p. 95), which descends recursively through subdirectories, does not

---

20. The official POSIX term for an i-node number is a *file serial number*, but most people still use the "i-node number" term.

treat a symbolic link as a directory even if it points to a directory, so it doesn't descend through the linked-to directory.

- If you use the `cd` command (see Section 3.1.1) to transfer to a directory via a symbolic link *l*, the target directory *td* of the link *l* will be made the current directory. The parent of the current directory will then be the parent of *td*, not the parent of the directory where *l* is located.

Hard Links versus Symbolic Links. Symbolic links have certain advantages over hard links:

- A symbolic link, unlike an ordinary link, can refer to a file in another file system.
- A symbolic link can refer to any kind of file, even a directory or a special file.

But there are also some hazards in using symbolic links:

- Symbolic links can create circular references. A program that attempts to access a pathname defined by a circular reference will abort when the kernel detects the circularity.

- If you delete or rename the target of a symbolic link, the pathname defined by that symbolic reference will become undefined. On the other hand, if you delete or rename the target of a hard link, the link will remain valid.

So if you need to link to anything other than a regular file in the same file system, your only choice is to use a symbolic link. In other cases, the choice is probably a matter of taste.

2.7.7
How Files Are Stored

We generally don't discuss the details of the UNIX implementation in this book. Nevertheless, we make an exception in this section, where we discuss how files are stored in the UNIX file system. UNIX documentation frequently makes reference to this subject, and an understanding of it can help in understanding other aspects of the file system and the UNIX utilities.

The file system stores the essential information about a file in an *i-node* (information node): where the file's actual contents are stored, how long the file is, how many links there are to it, when it was created, and so on. Each i-node has an *i-number* that identifies it. I-numbers are unique *within* file systems but not *among* file systems, which is why links across file systems must be treated specially. In this discussion we consider only hard links; that is, links within a single file system.

Examine a directory with the `od` command (see Section 3.15) and you'll see the i-number as the first few bytes (usually two) of the entry for each file in the directory, followed by the name. The same i-number can (and usually does) refer to different files in different file systems. For this reason and because file systems can be dismounted, UNIX doesn't allow a link from a directory in one file system to a file in another unless the file is a mount point.

The actual data in a file is stored as a sequence of blocks. A typical block size for a modern system is 4096 bytes, though some programs still assume the block size of 512 bytes used in elderly UNIX implementations. The file system stores files longer than one block in scattered data blocks and uses a smaller set of blocks to keep track of where the data blocks are. The blocks in this smaller set contain pointers to the data blocks and are called *indirect blocks* because they provide access to the data indirectly. For small files, all the pointers can be stored in the i-node. For very large files there may be a second level of indirect blocks that point to the first-level blocks or even, in some cases, a third level. The UNIX utilities that show the number of blocks in a file count indirect blocks, as well as the blocks containing the actual data of the file.

2.7.8
Space Limitations on Files

The space available in any real UNIX system is limited and fills up faster than most people would expect. Most modern UNIX systems therefore place limits on the file space allocated to users, using one or both of two different mechanisms (neither covered by POSIX):

- The maximum size of a file is limited by a parameter called `ULIMIT` that is part of the configuration of the kernel. Several shells, including the KornShell, provide a `ulimit` command (see p. 368) for seeing what the limit is, although only the superuser can raise it. The C shell provides `limit` for examining the limit and `unlimit` for removing the limit (see p. 398). Some systems such as Linux recognize the limit but give it a default value of "unlimited".

- The superuser may impose a quota of the total file space a user's files can occupy. The quota may be different for different users and may vary from one file system to another, even for the same user (depending on the particular implementation).

Programs that write large files may occasionally behave strangely when they encounter one of these limits. For example, some programs will not be aware that the end of the file has been truncated and will simply produce a defective file—leaving it to the next program that uses the file to discover that something has gone wrong.

2.7.9
Buffers

A *buffer* is a region of computer memory that holds a portion of the data in a file after that portion has been read from the file or before that portion is written to the file. The term is used in two very different contexts.

Buffered Input and Output.   When a program reads a file using *buffered input*, it reads the file in chunks of, say, 1024 bytes. Each chunk constitutes a buffer. When the program asks for a certain number of bytes from the file, the supporting software takes those bytes from the buffer rather than directly from the file as it would were it using unbuffered input. If there aren't enough bytes in the buffer, the supporting software brings in another bufferload of data from the file. Buffering has two efficiency advantages: it reduces the number of separate reading operations required, and it enables the reading to take place in parallel with other operations. Its disadvantage for some applications is that it provides less control over the reading action.

Buffered output is analogous to buffered input. When a program using buffered output sends bytes to a file, those bytes are put into a buffer rather than written out immediately. When the buffer is full, the supporting software writes its contents to the file.

Editor Buffers.   Editors such as `vi`, `ed`, and `emacs` use a buffer to hold the contents of a file while it is being edited. The basic editing cycle is as follows:

(1)   Read a file into the buffer.
(2)   Edit the file.
(3)   Write the contents of the buffer back to the file.

There's lots of room for variation in this cycle—for instance, when you create a file the first step is omitted.

2.8   File Permissions

The *file access permissions* of a file, more commonly called its *permissions* or its *protection mode*, specify who can do what to a file. A file's permissions are set by its owner. You can view the permissions of a file with '`ls -l`' (see Section 3.2.2 for a sample output) and specify them with the `chmod` command (see Section 3.11.1).

Since the permissions of a file are a property of the file itself, all links to a file (see Section 2.7.5) have the same permissions. Changing the permissions of a file via one hard link therefore changes the permissions as seen by the other hard links automatically. In many systems a symbolic link appears to have all permissions granted, but the effect of that is merely to cause the link to take on the permissions of the target of the symbolic link.

**2.8.1
Permissions for
Basic Operations**

The three basic operations on a file are "read", "write", and "execute". The permissions required to perform these operations are denoted by '`r`', '`w`', and '`x`'. The `x` permission is needed for compiled programs and for any shell script that you intend to use directly as a command. For instance, if the file `yodel` contains a shell script but lacks the `x` (execute) permission, you can't give the command

```
yodel
```

by itself. If you try it, you'll get an error message such as

```
yodel: not found
```

Nevertheless, you can execute `yodel` with the command

```
sh yodel
```

even if `yodel` doesn't have execute permission since this command explicitly passes `yodel` to the Bourne shell `sh`. You also need the `r` permission for a shell script in order to execute the script either directly or indirectly, but you don't need `r` to execute a compiled program.

The `r`, `w`, and `x` permissions can be specified independently for the owner of a file, for those in the owner's group, and for all others. POSIX calls these sets of permissions the *file owner class*, the *file group class*, and the *file other class*. They are represented symbolically as `u`, `g`, and `o`. UNIX always checks permissions for the smallest category that applies. For instance, a user in the owner's group (other than the owner) is always given the group permissions even if the permissions for "others" are broader. It doesn't make sense to provide a permission to a category of users but deny it to a smaller category (e.g., to make it available to others but deny it to your group), but UNIX won't stop you from doing that.

The permissions you assign to a file can protect it not just from unwanted access but also from your own errors. For instance, you can protect a file from accidental modification or deletion by cancelling its `w` permission. Cancelling the `w` permission doesn't actually prevent the file from being deleted but does usually trigger a warning if you attempt to delete it. Similarly, a file that you don't intend to execute should not have its `x` permission turned on.

Permissions for Directories.   File permissions also apply to directories.

- The `r` permission for a directory lets you find out what is in the directory, but is insufficient for accessing the files whose names appear in it. For instance, you can't read the contents of files in a directory if you only have `r` access to the directory.

- The `w` permission for a directory is required in order to add files to it or delete files from it. However, `w` permission for a directory is not required in order to modify a file listed in the directory or delete its contents.

- The `x` permission for a directory lets you operate on the names in that directory if you know them, but does not let you find out what they are if you don't. Normally `r` is granted whenever `x` is; you can get some strange effects if a directory has `x` but not `r`. For instance, if a directory has `x` turned on but not `r`, you can't list its contents—but if you already know its contents, you can delete or copy its files.[21]

---

21. Some organizations use this peculiarity when making files available for transfer over the Internet. Certain files and directories are made known only to those outsiders who are supposed to be able to retrieve them.

When you specify a permission using chmod, you can use X rather than x to denote an x permission that applies only to directories or to files that already have the x permission set for at least one category. That convention is particularly useful when you want to provide x permission for all subdirectories in a directory *D* without making all the regular files in *D* look like executable programs. Some older systems may not recognize the X permission.

**2.8.2
Other File
Permissions**

In addition to the rwx permissions, UNIX has other kinds of file permissions used primarily (but not exclusively) by system programmers. We describe these next.

The Set-uid Bit.   The *set-uid bit* enables a program to run with the permissions of its owner rather than with the permissions of the user who called it. You specify the set-uid bit with s when you use the chmod command. In a listing, it is indicated by an s replacing the x in the owner's permissions.

Normally, when you call a program and that program accesses a file, the program's access privileges for the file are the ones associated with your own user ID. As an example, suppose the following:

- User adlai owns the executable file ouija.
- The ouija program uses adlai's private data file tarot.
- User ike executes the program ouija.

The permissions that apply to tarot during this execution are those of "others" (since ike doesn't own tarot) rather than those of the owner adlai. Unless adlai grants read permission for tarot to "others", the ouija program can't access it. Yet were that read permission to be granted, ike would be able to read tarot directly and do whatever he liked with the information contained there, even using it in ways not intended by adlai.

The set-uid bit provides a way around this. When a process executes a program, it first retrieves the program's code from an executable file *progfile*.[22] If the permissions of *progfile* include the set-uid bit, then the effective user ID (see Section 2.6.6) of the process becomes that of the owner of *progfile*, so the program executes with the owner's privileges. The real user ID of the process remains that of the user who initiated the process.

In effect, the set-uid bit enables a user to access a file such as tarot indirectly—with ouija as the agent—but not directly. For instance, suppose the following additions to the example above:

- The owner permissions for tarot are rw.
- The "others" permissions for tarot are all turned off.
- The set-uid bit of the ouija file is turned on.

---

22. More precisely, the process invokes the system function *exec*, specifying to *exec* the pathname of the program to be called.

Now when `ike` executes `ouija`, the executing process has `adlai` as its effective user ID. Since `adlai` owns `tarot`, the process therefore has the necessary read permission for `tarot`. Yet `ike` cannot get at `tarot` by reading or writing it directly.

The classic example of the use of the set-uid bit is the `passwd` command (see Section 5.4.4). The password file `/etc/passwd` is owned by `root` (the superuser) and must be written by the `passwd` program.[23] Ordinary users must be able to execute the `passwd` program, yet they must not be allowed to modify the password file. Therefore the set-uid bit is turned on for the `passwd` program, enabling it to write to `/etc/passwd` while that ability remains denied to ordinary users.

You might at first think that the set-uid bit creates an obvious security hole. To gain system privileges, all you'd need do is set the set-uid bit of an executable file. But in fact, if that file isn't owned by `root`, you won't gain those privileges; if it is owned by `root`, you won't (or shouldn't) have write access to the directory containing the file and therefore won't have the power to change the set-uid bit.[24]

Some systems recognize the set-uid bit only when it appears among the permissions of a compiled program and ignore it when it appears among the permissions of a shell script. However, use of the set-uid bit is not restricted to the superuser.[25]

The Set-Gid Bit.   The *set-gid bit* is like the set-uid bit except that it applies to group permissions rather than owner permissions. When a process retrieves the contents of an executable file in order to execute the program it contains, the set-gid bit is checked. If it is turned on, the effective group ID of the process becomes the group of the owner of the executable file and the program thus executes with the permissions of that group. The real group ID of the process remains that of the user who initiated the process. The set-gid bit is specified by `s` in the `x` position of the group permissions.

---

23.   That the file and the program are both named '`passwd`' is not significant.

24.   Programs that rely on the set-uid bit are essential to a UNIX system. However, the set-uid bit, if set improperly, can expose a system to security hazards. UNIX security experts therefore pay a lot of attention to the conditions under which this bit can be set and who is permitted to set it (at least for files owned by `root`).

25.   If you are able to log in under two different user IDs, say `mark` and `maggie`, you can see the effect of the set-uid bit:

    (1)   Log in as `mark`.

    (2)   Copy the `id` program (see Section 5.4.7), typically stored as `/usr/bin/id`, to your home directory. (Some tightly secured systems might disallow that, however.)

    (3)   Execute the command

```
chmod u+s id
```

    to turn on the set-uid bit in this copy of `id`.

    (4)   Log out and log in again as `maggie`.

    (5)   Execute the command `~mark/id`. You'll get an output that will show `uid` (the real user ID) as `maggie` but `euid` (the effective user ID) as `mark`.

The Locking Bit.   System V-based systems provide a *locking bit.* If a file's locking bit is on, a program that is reading or writing a file can lock out other attempts to access that file at the same time. Turning on this bit prevents nearly simultaneous accesses to the file that could corrupt its meaning or leave it in an inconsistent state. The locking bit and the set-gid bit are actually the same bit; if a group-executable file has this bit turned on, the bit is interpreted as the set-gid bit rather than as the locking bit. The locking bit is indicated by a `l` replacing the `x` in the group permissions.

The Sticky Bit.   Applied to a directory, the *sticky bit* prevents files in that directory from being deleted or renamed by anyone other than their owner (or the superuser). Applied to an executable program, it provides a means of retaining that program in memory when that program can be shared among many users.[26] A program can be loaded from disk to main memory in shared mode, allowing any number of users to share the memory copy. If the sticky bit of the program's file is set, the text of the program remains in memory (or in a swap area) even when it is no longer in use. When another user later executes the program, it need not be reloaded. Only the owner of a file, or the superuser, can set the sticky bit. The sticky bit is indicated by a `t` replacing the `x` in the others permissions.

**2.8.3
Constructing
Permission Sets
Symbolically**

The `chmod`, `umask`, and `find` commands all make use of the ability to construct a set of permissions symbolically. You do that by specifying a *symbolic mode* that specifies how to modify an existing, possibly empty, set of permissions.

A symbolic mode consists of one or more clauses separated by commas. Each clause, in turn, consists of zero or more "who" letters followed by a sequence of one or more actions to be applied to the categories designated by the "who" letters. Each action consists of an operator followed either by one or more permission letters, by a "who" letter, or by nothing at all. The effect of a symbolic mode is achieved by executing in sequence the actions of each clause.

These are the "who" letters:

u   Permissions for the file's user
g   Permissions for the file's group
o   Permissions for others (i.e., the rest of the world)
a   Permissions for everyone (equivalent to `ugo`)

If you omit the "who" letters preceding the operator, then `a` is assumed and the file creation mask (see Section 2.8.5) is applied to reduce the permissions as they would be reduced for a newly created file.

---

26. Historically, the use of the sticky bit for executable programs preceded its use for directories, even though the latter is now the more important application.

These are the operators:

+ Add these permissions
- Take away these permissions
= Set exactly these permissions, removing any others for the indicated
  "who" letters

These are the permission letters:

r   Read
w   Write
x   Execute
X   Execute only if file is a directory or some x permission is already set
s   Set user or group ID
t   Sticky bit
l   Lock during access (System V only)

If you specify a "who" letter after an operator, then a copy of the permissions currently associated with that letter is used. A '+' or '–' operator followed by nothing has no effect, but an '=' operator followed by nothing has the effect of clearing the permissions for those sets specified by the "who" letters. A permission change can be affected by the file creation mask (see Section 2.8.5).

Here are some examples showing the effect of symbolic modes:

Starting Permissions	Symbolic Mode	Final Permissions	
u= g= o=	a=rw	u=rw g=rw o=rw	
u=rw g= o=	go+r	u=rw g=r o=r	
u=rwx g=rwx o=rwx	a-x	u=rw g=rw o=rw	
u=rwx g=rwx o=rwx	g-w,o-wx	u=rwx g=rx o=r	
u=rwx g=rwx o=	o=g	u=rwx g=rwx o=rwx	
u=rwx g=rwx o=	o=g-xw	u=rwx g=rwx o=r	
u=rwx g=rw o=rw	g+X	u=rwx g=rwx o=rw	
u=rw g=rw o=rw	a+X	u=rwx g=rwx o=rwx	(file is a directory)
u=rw g=rw o=rw	a+X	u=rw g=rw o=rw	(file is not a directory)
u=rw g=rwx o=rw	a+X	u=rwx g=rwx o=rwx	(file is not a directory)
u=r g=r o=r	+w	u=rw g=r o=r	(mask is ----w--w-)

Note: If you use a symbolic mode starting with '–' as part of a command, you may need to precede it with '--' to ensure that it is not interpreted as a command option (see p. 62).

2.8.4
Octal
Representation of
Permissions

The permissions of a file can also be given as an octal number. This form is obsolescent and not recommended, but older UNIX documentation often uses the octal form and some systems do not yet support the symbolic form in all contexts. The octal number is obtained as the logical sum of numbers from the following list:

4000	Set user ID on execution.
$20d0$	Set group ID on execution if d is 7, 5, 3, or 1 (execute permission granted); enable locking otherwise.
1000	Turn on the sticky bit.
0400	Set read permission for owner.
0200	Set write permission for owner.
0100	Set execute permission for owner.
0040, 0020, 0010	
	Set read, write, or execute permission for group.
0004, 0002, 0001	
	Set read, write, or execute permission for others.

2.8.5
Permissions for
Newly Created Files

When a program creates a file, it specifies a set of permissions for that file. Typical sets are u=rw g=rw o=rw (rw-rw-rw-, or octal 666) for data files and u=rwx g=rwx o=rwx (rwxrwxrwx, or octal 777) for executable files. The permissions in this initial set are then reduced by the *file creation mask*, also known as the *umask* ("user mask") *value* because you can change it with the umask command (see Section 3.11.2). In other words, the bits in the file creation mask represent permissions to be *denied* to newly created files.

The permissions of a newly created file are calculated by logically subtracting the bits in the file creation mask from the permission bits specified by the program creating the file. Thus if your umask value is rwxrwxr-x (octal 002), which excludes write permission for others, those outside of your group will not be able to write to files that you create unless you later change the mode of those files with chmod or change your umask value.

A typical default umask value is rwxr-xr-x (octal 022), which denies write permission to everyone but you. With this umask value, a file created with permissions specified as u=rw g=rw o=rw is actually created with permissions u=rw g=r o=r. The reduction of permissions by the umask value applies to newly created directories as well as to newly created ordinary files.

The file creation mask is also applied when you change permissions with chmod but don't specify any who letters. In this case it inhibits any change (either positive or negative) to the permissions in the mask. For instance, suppose the file creation mask is 022 and the file nebbish has permissions u=rw g=rw o=rw. If you issue the command

```
chmod = nebbish
```

with the intent of clearing all the permissions, you'll find that the new permissions are g=w o=w. However, if you instead issue the command

```
chmod a= nebbish
```

all the permissions will be cleared.

In most systems you can use the command 'umask -S' to produce the file creation mask in symbolic form. The symbolic form, however, is the *inverse* of the octal form; it shows the permissions that can be included rather than those that are excluded. For example, octal 022 corresponds to the symbolic permissions u=rwx g=rx o=rx.

2.9   Conventions for Using Files

All shells and other UNIX programs follow certain conventions for referring to files. We describe these conventions in the following subsections.

2.9.1
Wildcards in
Pathnames

You can refer to a set of files by using a pathname containing one or more *wildcards*. A wildcard matches an arbitrary character or sequence of characters. There are three notations for wildcards:

- The character * denotes any sequence of zero or more characters.
- The character ? denotes a single character.
- The construct [*cset*] denotes any single character in the set *cset*. The set *cset* is written using the bracket expression notation described on page 82, except that '!' rather than '∧' is used as the negation character.[27]   (Older shells may not support bracket expressions in their full generality.) For example, the bracket expression '[[:digits:]]', which can also be written as '[0-9]', denotes a decimal digit.

  Wildcards are usually interpreted by the shell, not by individual programs. A filename containing wildcards is expanded by the shell into a sequence of individual filenames (or left alone if it can't be matched). For those programs that interpret wildcards themselves, you have to quote the filenames so that the shell won't interpret them first (see Section 2.12.2).

  A '/' in the actual pathname must always be matched by an explicit '/' in the pattern, not by a wildcard. Furthermore, a '.' in the actual pathname that comes at the beginning or follows a '/' must similarly be matched by an explicit '.' in the pattern.

---

27. One peculiarity is that a collating element such as '[.ch.]' matches two characters, not one.

Here are some examples of wildcards and the files they can refer to:

Name	*Files*
`gn*.1`	`gnu.1, gneiss.1, gn.1`
	but not `gn/x.1`
`~/.[[:alpha:]]*`	`~/.login, ~/.mailrc`
	but not `~/login`
`~/.[A-Za-z]*`	the same (in the POSIX locale)
`*/doit*`	`one/doit, two/doit.c, three/doit.h`
	but not `doit`
`zz?`	`zz1, zza`
	but not `zz12`
`[[:upper:]]*[![:digit:]]`	`BAGEL, Bagel#, Bagel37X`
	but not `bagel, Bagel7`
`*.[acAC]`	`file.a, file.C`
	but not `.a`

The wildcard notation is recognized by the various shells rather than being built into the UNIX file mechanism. When a shell sees a pathname containing wildcards, it translates it into a sequence of specific pathnames, one after another. This process is called *pathname expansion* in the KornShell and *globbing* in the C shell. For example, if you write the filename 'byron?', your shell turns it into something like this:

```
byron1 byron2 byrons
```

assuming that these are the pathnames that match. Most UNIX programs accept sequences of pathnames in this form.

2.9.2 The PATH Environment Variable

Programs and other executable files can reside in many different directories. UNIX therefore provides a search path for executable files so that you don't need to remember (and type) the pathname of each command that you execute. The search path is recorded in the environment variable PATH (see Section 2.6.5), which you can examine by typing

```
echo $PATH
```

For example, the typical path

```
~/bin:/usr/local/bin:/bin:/usr/bin:.
```

indicates that the shell looks first in your personal `bin` directory, then in various public `bin` directories, and finally in your current (working) directory. You could also write this path as

```
~/bin:/usr/local/bin:/bin:/usr/bin:
```

with the final dot omitted, since by convention an empty directory name refers to your current directory.[28] If the command you type is 'hoptoit',

---

28. Your default path may have the current directory first. We recommend against this practice for security reasons—if your current directory happens to be one created by someone else and it contains a Trojan horse version of a common utility, you'll end up executing the Trojan rather than the utility.

the shell examines each directory of the search path in turn, looking for an executable file named 'hoptoit'. It pays no attention to files that are not executable (i.e., files whose x permission is not turned on), even if they have the right name.[29]

You can set PATH to any search sequence you wish, using the facilities in your shell for assigning values to variables; see, for example, Section 6.15.6. Under the C shell csh, PATH is also available as a shell variable, path; csh ensures that any change to one of these variables is reflected in the other.

**2.9.3
Conventions for
Naming Directories**

In theory, UNIX directories could be named anything. In practice, the names and usage of several top-level and second-level directories of UNIX systems are firmly established by tradition. However, some of the directories in the following list might not be included with your system.

/usr   Contains subdirectories of interest to users, which, especially in modern UNIX systems, includes almost everything. In older UNIX systems, /usr contains subdirectories for individual users, but now these are more often found in /home or /u. The subdirectory structure of /usr partly imitates the directory structure of root and contains the important subdirectories listed below. On some systems, /usr is read-only and anything that might need to be writable is moved to the /var directory or elsewhere. The advantages of making /usr read-only are that it protects those files from corruption and also makes it easier to share the files among machines on a network.

/bin
/usr/bin   Contain executable versions of system utilities and other user commands. These directories are usually linked together to make them synonymous. If they happen to be separate on your system, /bin probably contains programs, such as ls, that are essential to starting a system and repairing it when it is broken.[30] Executable files that are local to your installation might be kept in /usr/bin but are more likely to be found in another directory, such as /usr/local/bin. Specialized executable files may be found in other directories, most of which have 'bin' in their names.

/sbin   On System V-style systems, contains executable programs used when your system starts up and for manual recovery from a system failure—the same kinds of programs that are in /bin or /etc on older systems.

---

29. Under csh, if you add new commands to any of the directories in the path, you'll need to use the command rehash (p. 398) to make the shell aware of them.

30. The reason for the distinction between /bin and /usr/bin appears to go back to early UNIX systems, for which a single disk could not hold all of the executable files.

`/dev`	Contains files that correspond to external devices such as printers.
`/etc`	Contains installation-specific files, such as the password file `/etc/passwd`, that are required for system administration. Both data files and programs may be kept in this directory, though recent systems have tended to move most or all programs either to `/sbin` or to `/usr/sbin`, leaving a symbolic link behind.
`/home`	Often used for the home directories of individual users (see Section 2.7.3), with user *u*'s home directory at `/home/`*u*. The location of these home directories is up to the system administrator and varies greatly. Other common locations for users' home directories are `/u` and `/usr`.
`/lib` `/usr/lib`	Contain compiled C subprogram libraries ('`.a`' and '`.sa`' files) for linkage by C programs, architecture-dependent databases, executable dæmon programs, and subdirectories of specialized libraries for facilities such as X or the programming language Lisp. Like `bin` and `/usr/bin`, these directories are usually linked together to make them synonymous.
`/usr/local`	Contains a collection of subdirectories that partially mirror the top-level structure and contain installation-specific files. For instance, `/usr/local/bin` contains executable programs provided by your particular UNIX installation.
`/usr/src`	Contains UNIX source files; that is, the text of the C programs that come with your system. For commercial systems, these files are available only if your system is covered by a UNIX source license; access to them is restricted (see Section 1.1.5). On some systems this directory is located at `/usr/share/src`.
`/usr/include`	Contains header files for C programs.
`/usr/share`	Contains platform-independent textual information such as manual pages, run-time databases, and source files.
`/usr/sbin`	Contains executable programs used for system administration in a system that is running normally.
`/usr/tmp`	An alternative to `/tmp`, described below.
`/usr/ucb`	Contains Berkeley-specific versions of programs such as `vi` and `Mail` (even on some non-Berkeley systems).
`/tmp`	Contains temporary files created by various programs as they are operating. In some systems the contents of `/tmp` are lost when the system is shut down.

/var   Contains administrative files that often change or are in transit, such as files awaiting printing, mail messages, and log files.

/var/adm
/usr/adm Contain accounting information, diagnostic files generated at the time of system crashes, and similar information needed by system administrators. These directories are usually linked together to make them synonymous.

/var/spool
/usr/spool
          Contains spool files; that is, temporary files awaiting processing. These include files to be printed, administrative logs, files to be sent to other computers, and files received from other computers that are waiting to be picked up by users. These directories are usually linked together to make them synonymous. The files in /var/spool, unlike those in /tmp, are always preserved, even when the system is shut down.

/proc   Contains active system processes by number, a memory image of the machine, and other "pseudo-files" that don't represent stored information but are usefully treated as though they did.

/stand
/kernel   Contains the system kernel.

Parts of this directory structure are often replicated within other directories. For instance, a user named zachary might keep his personal programs in /home/zachary/bin and the sources for these programs in /home/zachary/src.

**2.9.4
The Linux
File System
Standard**

A standard for naming files and directories has recently been developed for Linux, with the overall goal of establishing the location where commonly used files can be found. The standard was deliberately formulated to be consonant with existing practice not just for Linux but for other flavors of UNIX as well. It therefore can serve as a useful guide for almost any system. You can obtain a copy of it by FTP from tsx11.mit.edu, document pub/linux/docs/linux-standards/fsstnd.

**2.9.5
Compressed Files**

To save space, files are often kept in a compressed form. Two programs are commonly used to compress files: compress, a System V program widely available elsewhere (see Section 3.13.1), and gzip, a program produced by the GNU project (see Section 3.13.2). Both programs use forms of Lempel-Ziv compression, though gzip usually achieves better compression ratios. A much older compression program based on Huffman coding, pack, is rarely used any more.

A particular naming convention is used for files compressed by these programs: a suffix of '.Z' indicates a file compressed by compress and a suffix of '.gz' indicates a file compressed by gzip. For instance, bundle.gz

indicates the compressed form of the file `bundle` as compressed by `gzip`.
Some UNIX programs recognize these suffixes and automatically decompress a file if necessary. If you specify a file `bundle` to such a program but
only the file `bundle.gz` is present, the program decompresses `bundle.gz`
on the fly using `gzip` with the decompression option `-d`, and then uses
the resulting copy of `bundle` as its input.

2.10   Standard Files and Redirection

Many UNIX commands read their input from *standard input* unless you
specify input files explicitly, and write their output to *standard output*.
By default, standard input and standard output are associated with your
terminal. Thus, when a program looks for input from standard input,
it reads that input from your terminal; when it sends output to standard
output, it writes that output to your terminal. Another standard file,
standard error, is used for error messages and other information about the
operation of a command. Information sent to standard error is also sent
to your terminal. Standard input, standard output, and standard error
are all file descriptors associated with each process (see Section 2.10.2).

   This convention works well because you can *redirect* standard input and
standard output. When you redirect standard input to come from a file
named *ifile*, the program reading standard input takes the input from *ifile*
instead of from your terminal; when you redirect standard output to go to
a file *ofile*, the program writing standard output writes the output to *ofile*
instead of to your terminal. Input redirection is indicated by '<' in front
of a pathname, while output redirection is indicated by '>' in front of a
pathname. The space that we use after a redirection operator is optional.

   For example, the `cat` command copies standard input to standard output if it is called with no files specified, so the command

```
cat < felix > fido
```

causes the file `felix` to be copied to the file `fido`. Putting `>>` in front of
a pathname causes output to be appended to the file rather than written
directly. In the previous example the contents of `fido` are overwritten by
the contents of `felix`; but if you instead write

```
cat < felix >> fido
```

the contents of `felix` are put after whatever is already in `fido`. Other
forms of redirection are discussed in Sections 2.10.1 and 6.10.

   You can redirect standard error as well as standard input and output;
the method is different for different shells.

- For the Bourne shell and the KornShell, the construct '2> *file*' specifies that anything sent to standard error should be redirected to *file*.
  For example,

  ```
  diff yin yang 2> yerror
  ```

compares the files `yin` and `yang` with the `diff` command, sending
the error output to the file `yerror`. (Do *not* put a space between the
'2' and the '>'.)

- For the C shell, the construct '`>&` *file*' sends both standard output
  and standard error to *file*. The C shell does not provide an explicit
  construct for redirecting standard output to one file and standard
  error to a different file.[31]

A valuable and important property of redirection is that a program
whose input or output is redirected does not need to know about it.[32] In
other words, a program written under the assumption that it reads from
standard input and writes to standard output also works for reading from
files and writing to files, provided only that the files are specified through
redirection. The same property applies to shell scripts. It is because of
this property that so many programs are written to use standard input
and standard output.

Note: In this book we say that a program *produces* a result when it
sends that result to standard output. The traditional UNIX terminology
is to say that the program "prints" the result. That terminology comes
from the days when most UNIX systems used printing terminals rather
than display screens. It is now thoroughly out of date. It is also confusing,
since "print" has the additional meaning of sending a file to an off-line
printer. We also sometimes use the term *list* to describe the action of a
program in producing descriptive information on standard output.

2.10.1
Pipes and Filters

You can use the output of one command as the input of another by
connecting the two commands with a *pipe*. The construct that results is a
pipeline. As with the forms of redirection discussed earlier, the connected
programs don't need to know about the connection.

Syntactically, you create a pipeline by writing two commands with a pipe
symbol (|) between them. For example, the command line

```
grep "pest" phones | sort
```

calls the program `grep` (see Section 4.2), which extracts from the file
`phones` all lines containing the string 'pest' and produces these lines as
its standard output. This output is then piped to `sort`, which sees that
output as its standard input. The output of the entire command line is a
sorted list of the lines in `phone` containing 'pest'.

In a line containing both redirections and pipes, the redirections have
higher precedence: first the redirections are associated with commands

---

31. You can redirect the standard output of *cmd* to *file₁* and its standard error to *file₂* with
the command line

$$(cmd \ > \ file_1) \ >\& \ file_2$$

32. The `tty` command (see Section 5.1.4) reveals whether standard input is coming from a
terminal, however.

and then the commands with their redirections are passed through the pipes. For example, the command line

```
grep "pest" phones | sort > hangups
```

extracts lines from the file `phones` as above, sorts them, and stores the sorted lines in the file `hangups`.

Creation of a pipeline implies creation of a pair of processes, one for the command producing the piped information and one for the command consuming the piped information. These processes are created by the shell that interprets the command line.

A *filter* is a program that reads data from standard input, transforms it in some way, and writes the transformed data to standard output. You can construct a pipeline as a sequence of filters; such sequences provide a powerful and flexible way of using simple programs in combination to accomplish many different tasks and are often cited as examples of the UNIX philosophy.

2.10.2
File Descriptors

Each process has a numbered set of *file descriptors* associated with it. When a program reads from or writes to a file, it refers to that file by its file descriptor. Three file descriptors are created when the process starts up:

    0   standard input
    1   standard output
    2   standard error

Every file descriptor is associated with a file; file descriptors 0, 1, and 2 are by default associated with the file `/dev/tty`, which is your terminal. These associations can be modified by redirection (see Section 2.10).

A program can read or write additional files by asking the kernel to open them (the standard files are opened automatically). When the kernel opens a file, it provides the program with a file descriptor for the file and also associates the file descriptor with the program's process. These additional file descriptors have numbers greater than 2, although ordinarily you never see them.

Although you'll rarely need to do it, you can create file descriptors with numbers greater than 2 and associate them with files using the extended forms of redirection provided by the shell (see Section 6.10).

2.11   Other Facilities for Interprocess Communication

We now describe three facilities that provide more general forms of pipes: FIFO special files, sockets, and Streams. Sockets and Streams provide more disciplined and sophisticated interprocess communication than FIFO special files, but FIFO special files do have one advantage: they are easily constructed at the user level and require no programming.

2.11.1
FIFO Special Files (Named Pipes)

A *FIFO special file*, also known as a *named pipe*, is a kind of file that behaves much like a pipe but exists independently of any process. If you look at the entry for a FIFO special file in a directory listing produced by the 'ls -l' command (see Section 3.2), you'll see that the first letter in its permissions is p (for pipe).

FIFO special files are called that because the data passed through them follows a first-in, first-out discipline. A FIFO special file can be used to connect two processes that are running on different terminals or to implement a dæmon (see p. 30) that collects error notices from any process that issues them. The input processes and the output processes can be completely unrelated.

You can create a FIFO special file corncob with the command

```
mkfifo corncob p
```

Now suppose that devour is a program that waits for input to appear in corncob and processes that input whenever it appears. The command to start up devour would be

```
devour < corncob &
```

The devour command should be run in the background since it will be blocked until it receives input. Another program babble can send input to devour via corncob with the command

```
babble > corncob
```

The devour and babble commands can originate from different terminals as long as both terminals have access to corncob. It might be desirable to run babble in the background as well, since if corncob is full—a FIFO special file usually has a very small capacity—babble has to wait for it to be emptied.[33]

2.11.2
Sockets

A socket is an endpoint for data communication. A pair of sockets provides a generalization of a pipe and resembles a FIFO special file. Data can be sent to a socket or retrieved from a socket just as it can from a file. Sockets were introduced by BSD and are not part of the earlier AT&T–derived UNIX systems. You won't find them mentioned in the older classic books on UNIX.

A socket can transmit data to any process, even one running on a different computer. Moreover, socket pairs are bidirectional; either process can

---

33. A process that opens a FIFO special file, or indeed an ordinary pipe, for writing is blocked until some other process opens that pipe for reading. This is another possible reason for running babble in the background—if devour hasn't started, babble becomes blocked.

send data to the other. Certain types of sockets can exist independently of any particular process.

You can't create a socket or socket pair by issuing shell commands. However, a number of commands such as `telnet` (see p. 637) and `rlogin` (see p. 634) construct sockets implicitly. You can also construct a socket or a socket pair from within a C or Perl program.

Because sockets are so much more general than pipes, they require a more complex underlying mechanism. Communicating data through a socket can require all the facilities of packet-based data transmission over networks.

2.11.3
Streams

Streams, a facility that originated in System V, are communication channels very similar to sockets. Like sockets, they provide a uniform method of communicating over networks and are bidirectional. The principal difference between a socket and a Stream is that a socket connects one process to another while a Stream connects a process to an entity that logically behaves like an input-output device. Streams were designed to be used by programmers, not by end users, so you won't find any commands for working with them.

2.12   UNIX Commands

A *command* is an instruction to UNIX that tells it to do something. The usual way to issue a command is to pass it to a shell by typing it in response to a prompt from the shell.

The term "command" is also used to refer to the instructions expected by programs such as the `vi` editor or the `mailx` mailer. In this context, the term "command" really means "subcommand". You should usually be able to identify the sense in which the term is being used from the context.

2.12.1
Standard Syntax of Commands

POSIX defines a standard syntax for commands but not all commands follow it. Many commands defined by POSIX have both a modern form and an older obsolescent syntactic form "grandfathered" into the standard. Because these obsolescent forms are embedded in widely distributed shell scripts, they may be with us forever. Systems that are not entirely POSIX-conformant may still support only the obsolescent forms, which for commands such as `kill` and `sort` are quite different from the modern forms. In addition, systems may have their own system-specific commands and command forms that don't conform to POSIX standards. In our descriptions of commands we provide both modern and obsolescent forms (as the POSIX standard itself does), but we strongly recommend use of the modern forms whenever possible.

In a few cases such as the `find` utility, even the modern forms don't conform completely to the standard syntax. For instance, the standard syntax allows options (though not necessarily operands) to appear in any order, but some commands may require options to appear in a particular order. Such deviations from standard syntax are often not noted explicitly in the manual page that describes a command. We point out many of them, but you still may need to do some experimenting.

A command consists of a sequence of *words* separated by *whitespace* consisting of one or more spaces, tabs, or (for some shells) escaped new-lines (see Section 2.12.2).[34] The first word is the command name and the remaining words provide the *arguments* of the command. The command name refers to the program or shell script to be executed. Section 6.8.1 describes how the meaning of the command name is determined. Some arguments specify which files the command operates on while others control or modify what the command does. The arguments consist of the command's *options*, if any, followed by its *operands*, if any. The options control or modify what the command does. The operands specify path-names or similar information. Each operand is a single word.

Specifying the Options.   The options are specified by a sequence of words. Each word is either an *option group* or an *option argument*. Options generally are denoted by single letters. You can write them in any order, and you can combine several of them into a single group provided that they don't have any option arguments of their own (see below). Each group of options is preceded by a hyphen (-). For example, the commands

```
ls -al
ls -l -a
```

are equivalent and indicate that the `ls` (list files) command is to be called with the options `a` (all files) and `l` (long listing).

The last (or only) option of an option group can be followed by a word that specifies one or more option arguments for it. For example, the command

```
sed -f bluescript heartthrob
```

causes the `sed` script editor to edit the file `heartthrob` using the script `bluescript`; in this case `bluescript` is an argument to the `-f` option and `heartthrob` is an argument of the `sed` command itself.

Multiple arguments of an option are normally separated by commas, but you can separate them by blanks if you enclose the list of arguments in

---

34. An escaped newline (i.e., one preceded by '\') is treated as whitespace by the C shell but not by the KornShell, which ignores it. Typing

```
echo one two\
three
```

reveals how a shell treats escaped newlines. An unquoted and unescaped newline always terminates a command and therefore can never be interpreted as whitespace.

single or double quotes, or if you put a backslash in front of each blank to escape it. In any event, the multiple arguments must form a single word. The following pair of options shows both conventions:

```
prog -o zed1,zed2 -y "are you with us"
```

or, alternatively,

```
prog -o zed1,zed2 -y are\ you\ with\ us
```

Other Conventions for Arguments.   There are two other common conventions for specifying arguments:

- '--' indicates the end of the options.   When you want to give operands that start with '-' to a command, you can put '--' in front of them to ensure that they are interpreted as operands rather than as options.   For example,

  ```
  rm -- -giraffe
  ```

  is one way to remove the file **-giraffe**. If you had simply written

  ```
  rm -giraffe
  ```

  you'd get an error complaint about an unrecognized g option.

- '-' by itself indicates standard input in a context where the command expects a pathname.   For example, the command

  ```
  diff - quince
  ```

  finds the differences between standard input and the contents of the file **quince**. In a few older BSD systems, however, certain commands such as **rm**, **rmdir**, and **mv** follow the older convention of using '-' to indicate the end of the options.

Signed Options.   Most utilities for X use both '-' and '+' as option indicators, with the convention that '-' turns an option on and '+' turns it off.[35]   For these utilities, options have multicharacter names and cannot be combined. For example, in

```
xterm +sb -j
```

the '+sb' instructs the **xterm** program *not* to attach a scrollbar to the X window that it generates ('+sb'), but to do jump scrolling ('-j').   The KornShell uses '-' and '+' similarly as option indicators, but restricts option names to single letters so that they can be combined. The KornShell also provides a pair of repeatable forms '-o *opt*' and '+o *opt*' for specifying options by their full names. You may encounter other programs that use '-' and '+' similarly.

---

35. It may seem odd that '+' turns an option off rather than on. The reason for that behavior is that options that could be turned either on or off appeared well after the convention of using '-' to introduce options had become solidly established. Using the signs in their more natural sense would have conflicted with that usage.

Options for GNU Utilities.   Many GNU programs use the form '--*string*' to specify options that are not part of POSIX, where *string* is not limited to a single character. Options in this form often duplicate those in the shorter '-*c*' form; the intent is to provide a more mnemonic and self-evident notation. A nearly universal GNU convention is to use the option '--help' to produce an on-line brief description of what a program's options are.

2.12.2
Quotation

All of the standard shells assign special meanings to certain characters, called *metacharacters*. To use these characters as ordinary data characters on a command line, you must quote them. Each shell has its own set of metacharacters and its own quotation conventions, but certain rules generally hold:

- A backslash acts as an *escape* for one or more characters following it, giving those characters a special meaning. If that character is a metacharacter, the special meaning is usually the character itself. For example, '\\' usually stands for a single backslash and '\$' for a dollar sign. In these cases the backslash effectively quotes the character after it, sometimes called an *escaped character*. The backslash itself is called an *escape character*.

- When text is enclosed in double quotes ("), most metacharacters are treated as data characters, but those such as '$' that specify substitutions are interpreted as metacharacters. For instance, in a construct such as

      "<<$1>>"

  the '$' character is interpreted but the '<' and '>' characters are not. (The '$1' refers to the first argument passed to a shell script; see Section 6.5.) If the first argument is 'dhoti', the construct becomes

      <<dhoti>>

- When text is enclosed in apostrophes ('), all characters within the apostrophes are treated as data characters. Quoting with apostrophes is a stronger form of quotation than quoting with double quotes.

Spaces and tabs are always treated as data characters within quoted text, so you can use quotation to create a single command argument that contains these characters.

2.12.3
Command
Substitution

A closely related construct is *command substitution*, which enables you to execute a command and then use its output as part of another command. A command substitution is given by enclosing it in backquotes (' ... ') or by using the notation '$(...)'. The great advantage of the latter notation is that it works easily for nested substitutions, though the older csh and sh shells don't recognize it. The backquote notation is simpler but quickly becomes unreadable and easy to get wrong when you try to use it for nested substitutions.

   For example, if the current directory is /home/jodi, the command

      echo The current directory is `pwd`.

or equivalently, the command

```
echo The current directory is $(pwd).
```

produces the output

```
The current directory is /home/jodi.
```

Three commands that are particularly useful in command substitutions within loops or shell scripts are `expr` (see Section 5.9.2), and `dirname` and `basename` (see "Extracting the Directory Part with `dirname`" on p. 294). For example, the command

```
for fn in *.doc
do
   mv $fn $(basename $fn .doc).txt
done
```

renames each filename in the current directory whose name ends with '`.doc`' to a corresponding filename whose name ends with '`.txt`'.

Another useful command is '`grep -l`' (see Section 4.2), which enables you to select files that contain a particular fragment of text. For example, you can use the command

```
more `grep -l giraffe *`
```

to page through all files in the current directory that contain the string `giraffe`.[36]

Exactly which characters are quoted by the various forms of quotation, the treatment of newlines within quotations, and how the various forms of quotation and command substitution interact depend on which shell you're using.

2.12.4 Other Common Conventions

As we mentioned earlier, many UNIX commands read their input from standard input and write their output to standard output (see Section 2.10). If standard input and standard output have not been redirected, they correspond to your terminal. Redirecting the input or the output is the usual way of applying UNIX commands to particular files.

Some UNIX commands operate on one or more files and expect those files to be specified by a list of pathnames, with the names in the list separated by whitespace. A hyphen in the list indicates standard input, read as though it were a file. If the list is missing, the command takes its input from standard input—so this form includes the previous one. Since this is the form produced by the expansion of wildcards (see Section 2.9.1), you can easily apply these commands to sets of files. For example, the command

```
cat leopard/* > felix
```

---

36. On some systems you may see harmless error complaints like

```
grep: misc: Is a directory
```

You can safely ignore them.

causes all the files in the `leopard` subdirectory to be concatenated into a single file and written to the file `felix`. The fully expanded form of the command might be

```
cat leopard/this leopard/that leopard/file1 > felix
```

The `cat` command also handles the case when no input files are specified, so that

```
cat > felix
```

copies standard input to the file `felix`.

You can use the `echo` command (see Section 5.8.1) to show the files that would be produced by a pathname containing wildcards. For example,

```
echo leopard/a*
```

shows you all the files in the `leopard` directory whose names start with 'a'.

2.13   Local Variables

Most UNIX programs that accept commands interactively have a set of *local variables* whose values help to define the program's behavior. For instance, the `mailx` mailer has a variable `keep` that tells it not to remove a mailbox when it becomes empty. Most programs that provide local variables are either shells, such as `sh` and `csh`, or programs that behave like shells, such as the `mailx` mailer. Some of these programs allow the set of variables to be open-ended, enabling you to define your own variables. These new variables augment the ones defined by the program and can be particularly useful when you're writing shell scripts (see Chapter 6).

A variable can have one of three states:

(1)   It doesn't exist.
(2)   It exists, but has an empty value.
(3)   It exists and has a nonempty value.

A variable that exists is *enabled* or *set*, whether or not it has a value; a variable that doesn't exist is *disabled* or *unset*.

A disabled variable may still have a default value. For example, the `toplines` variable of `mailx` is disabled by default, but it still has a default value of 5 (the value assumed by `mailx` if you don't set `toplines` at all).

The programs that provide variables have a `set` command or something similar to it to set and retrieve the values of those variables. The command usually works as follows:

- The command `set` by itself prints a list of all existing variables.
- The command `set` *v* sets *v* to an empty value.
- The command `set` *v=s* sets *v* to the value *s*.
- The command `set` no*v*, or its equivalent, `unset` *v*, removes *v*.

If a variable has an empty value, you just see its name when you type `set`; if it has a nonempty value, you see its value as well. For example, typing

```
set askcc
```

in the `mailx` program enables the `mailx` variable `askcc`. Typing

```
set SHELL=/bin/csh
```

sets the `SHELL` variable to refer to the C shell. **Note:** The KornShell `sh` has different syntax for these commands.

Don't confuse local variables with environment variables (see Section 2.6.5). Local variables belong to a program and are only visible to that program; environment variables belong to a process and are copied to the environment of any program that executes as part of that process. A local variable named `elliott` can coexist with an environment variable named `elliott`. The difference between the two types of variables is obscured by two facts:

- Most programs that have local variables copy some or all of the environment variables into the local variables. For example, many programs copy the value of the environment variable `HOME` into a local variable named either `home` or `HOME`. The KornShell copies its environment variables into its local variables when it starts up and thereafter provides access only to the local variables.

- Every shell provides some way of exporting its local variables to the environment of commands executed by the shell. Once exported, a local variable becomes part of the environment of all programs you call subsequently from within that shell. But an unexported local variable is not part of the environment of those programs. Modern shells re-export an inherited environment variable or its local counterpart by default.[37]

2.14   Initialization Files

Many UNIX programs are set up to look for *initialization files* in your home directory. These files contain commands that the program executes before it does anything else. The names of these files always start with a dot and often end with `rc` ("run commands"). (The `ls` program for listing the contents of a directory omits such files by default.) Some programs

---

37.   The older Bourne shell doesn't update a re-exported inherited variable with the value of its local counterpart unless you explicitly mark the variable for export. That behavior can lead to unpleasant surprises—the variable is visible but it has the old value, not the new one.

also look for initialization commands in special environment variables (see Section 2.6.5). Here are some examples:

- The login process looks for initialization commands in the `~/ .profile` file if you're using the KornShell, or in the `~/.login` file if you're using the C shell.

- When called as subshells, the KornShell and POSIX-compliant shells more generally look for initialization commands in the file whose name is found as the value of the `ENV` environment variable. If that value doesn't exist or doesn't contain an absolute pathname, no initialization is done when a subshell is started. The C shell looks for subshell initialization commands in the `~/.cshrc` file. The subshell initialization files are also executed after the login initialization files when you first log in, so you can always rely on the commands in those files having been executed when you are at a shell prompt. (For the KornShell, that's the case provided that `$ENV` has an appropriate value.)

- The `vi` and `ex` editors look for initialization commands first in the `EXINIT` environment variable and then (if `EXINIT` is empty) in the `.exrc` file.

- The `mailx` mailer looks for initialization commands in the file whose name is found in the environment variable `MAILRC`. If `MAILRC` has nothing in it, `mailx` looks in the file `.mailrc` in your home directory.

When your login shell starts up, it first looks in your home directory for a login initialization file and executes the commands in it. A "canned" version of this file is usually placed in your home directory when your account is created, which you can modify to suit your needs and tastes. Here are some examples of useful actions you might include in your login initialization file:

- Setting characteristics of your terminal, including the control characters used for functions such as (Erase) and (Kill) (see Section 5.5.2)
- Reading your mail (see Chapter 11)

Useful actions for your subshell initialization file might be these:

- Setting your path (see Section 2.9.2)

- Defining aliases (see Section 6.19.1) and shell functions (see Section 6.13.4)

- Setting environment variables for programs that you often use (see Section 2.6.5)

Some of these may already be in the canned file. It's usually a good idea to put actions you want to execute only once per login in the login initialization file and everything else in the subshell initialization file. That's because the latter file is executed on login anyway and may get executed under circumstances where the login initialization has not been executed.

2.15 Terminal Descriptions

A number of UNIX programs, full-screen editors such as `vi` in particular, assume they are communicating with a classic computer terminal consisting of a keyboard, a display screen,[38] and a connection to a computer, either direct or over a telephone line. Such programs need to know the characteristics of the terminal. You specify your terminal by setting the environment variable `TERM` to the name of your terminal, though usually your login initialization file does it for you. The program then looks up those characteristics in a database of terminal descriptions called either `termcap` or `terminfo`.

Classic terminals are uncommon nowadays, but a workstation operating in text mode (as distinct from the graphics mode used in X) still uses the classic terminal model for the keyboard and display. In this case the terminal and display are individually attached to the workstation as peripheral devices. Programs such as `telnet`, `rlogin`, and `kermit` that enable you to communicate with a remote UNIX system make your computer look like a classic terminal to the remote system, as do the many terminal emulation programs that run on personal computers.

2.15.1 Codes and Control Sequences

When you press a key on the keyboard of a classic terminal, the terminal sends a sequence of ASCII characters to the computer. For a key such as the Y key, it sends either the code for y or for Y. Which code is sent depends on whether the alphabetic shift key is held down and on the state of the Caps Lock key. For an extra key such as a function key, the terminal sends a sequence of several characters called a *control sequence*. For most terminals, the control sequences all start with the ⟨escape⟩ character (ASCII code 27). However, if you type (Esc) at your terminal, it will usually be interpreted by whatever program (editor, etc.) that you're using and never be transmitted to the terminal.[39] Thus the chance of issuing a control sequence by accident is very small.

In the other direction, the computer sends characters back to the terminal, including echoes of the characters you type. Each character sent to the terminal is either a data character such as the letter T, a single control character such as ⟨linefeed⟩ (ASCII code 10), or part of a control sequence—control sequences (though usually different ones) are used for output as well as for input. A data character, which is necessarily a graphic

---

38. In the early days of UNIX most terminals were printing terminals rather than display terminals, but printing terminals are rarely seen nowadays.

39. You can experiment with control sequences by issuing the `cat` command and typing them. Since `cat` transmits its input to the terminal without interpretation (except for newlines), you can see the effect of each one as you type it.

(printable) character, is displayed directly on the screen. A single control character or a control sequence instructs the terminal to carry out an action such as starting a new line, moving the cursor to a particular position, or displaying the following characters in a particular color. For example, if a DEC VT102 terminal receives the control sequence '⟨escape⟩[M', it deletes the line containing the cursor. The second and later characters of a control sequence might be graphic characters, but in this context they aren't displayed.

2.15.2
The `termcap` and `terminfo` Databases

Terminals differ in their features and in the control sequences they use to represent a particular feature. For example, keyboards differ in the keys they provide, some displays show color while others don't, and terminals differ in the control sequence they use to scroll the screen down by one line. To account for these differences, UNIX programs consult the `termcap` or `terminfo` database when they issue or interpret a terminal-dependent control sequence.

Termcap (for "terminal capabilities"), the older of the two databases, was originally developed as part of BSD to support the `vi` editor. Terminfo was derived from `termcap` for use in System V and has now largely replaced `termcap`. The two databases differ in form but resemble each other in content. Older programs compiled to work in the BSD environment refer to `termcap` while programs compiled to work in the System V environment refer to `terminfo`. Many UNIX systems provide both databases. BSD-based systems also provide a separate but similar database, `printcap`, for describing printers. Terminfo includes printer descriptions.

A typical edition of `terminfo` or `termcap` contains descriptions of hundreds of different terminals, though mostly obsolete ones. The main difference between `terminfo` and `termcap` is that `terminfo` is compiled into a compact form while `termcap` is not. Terminfo can only be read by using a special program `infocmp` or `untic` that can decompile a description.[40] Nearly all of the following discussion of `terminfo` applies to `termcap` as well.

The information in `terminfo` specifies the control sequences that a program must send to a particular terminal in order to perform a particular function, such as clearing the screen or displaying the succeeding characters in boldface, as well as the control sequences generated by function keys. Terminfo contains three kinds of items:

- Boolean capabilities, which indicate whether or not the terminal supports some particular feature
- Numeric capabilities, which indicate the size of the terminal or the limits on particular features
- String capabilities, which indicate what control sequence must be sent to the terminal to achieve a particular effect or is sent by a particular key

---

40.   The `tic` program recompiles descriptions.

You'll often see references in UNIX literature to `curses`, a high-level programming interface to `terminfo` developed as part of the BSD project that enables a programmer to control a terminal efficiently without knowing the particular control sequences it expects.

2.15.3
Examining `terminfo`

As a user you'll rarely need to look at the information in `terminfo`, although you might want to look at it to see which terminals it supports. You often can find `terminfo` in the directory `/usr/lib` or `/usr/share/lib`, though the location varies among systems. `Terminfo` is actually a directory, not a regular file, with subdirectories whose names are single characters. The directory `/usr/lib/terminfo/h`, for example, contains the descriptions of terminals whose names start with 'h', such as `hp2621`. On systems that support `terminfo`, you can usually use the command

```
infocmp
```

to see the full description of your terminal, including all the names by which it is known. You can also use the form

```
infocmp term
```

to see the full description of terminal *term*. You can use `untic` the same way. On some systems the command

```
tput -T name longname
```

will produce the full name of the terminal in `terminfo` whose description is named *name* (see Section 5.5.3). These forms can be useful for checking whether a terminal in `terminfo` is the one you think it is.

2.15.4
Initialization and Reset

The information in `terminfo` also includes two special strings, the *initialization string* and the *reset string*. The initialization string, when sent to your terminal, makes it behave as described in `terminfo`, assuming the terminal is in a reasonable state such as its power-on state. The reset string, when sent to your terminal, restores it to sanity if it is in an unusable but unknown state. Normally the reset string does everything that the initialization string does, but it may also produce strange flashes on the screen and other unpleasant side effects—so you should only use the reset string if the initialization string doesn't work. The `tput` and `tset` commands each provide ways to issue these strings and also to perform other useful operations on your terminal, such as changing its mode of operation.

2.15.5
Designating Your Terminal Type

When you log in, you may sometimes get a query

```
TERM=
```

because the port you've logged in on doesn't uniquely determine your terminal type.[41] It's a good idea to know what the "official" name of your terminal is so that you can respond to such a query. You can find it by typing

```
echo $TERM
```

or on some systems

```
tset -r
```

**2.15.6
Terminal Emulation**

If you're working under the X Window System or using a non-UNIX communications program to communicate with a UNIX system, the classic terminal model does not directly apply to your environment. In these and similar situations, your program has to *emulate* a classic terminal. A common choice is the DEC VT100. Under this convention, control sequences sent to your program have the same effect that they would have on a VT100, and function keys send the same sequences of characters that they would on a VT100.[42] If a program such as the vi editor wants to delete a line, it retrieves the appropriate sequence from terminfo, either directly or by using the curses package, and sends it to the virtual terminal. When xterm sees that sequence in the input to the virtual terminal, it deletes the line.

The fact that your program is running in VT100 emulation mode does *not* mean that you need to know anything about the VT100. It just means that your program and the UNIX machine it is connected to have agreed to talk in VT100 language. In fact, even the programmer who wrote the application did not need to know about the VT100, only about curses or the entries available in terminfo. You usually need not be concerned with the language in which the messages are expressed, only with the effect of the messages themselves.

The xterm terminal emulator (see Section 13.14) that runs under X provides two separate emulations: the DEC VT102 (for historical reasons referred to as the VT100) and the Tektronix 4015 graphics terminal. When you're using this program, the TERM environment variable is set to xterm—and if you're using xterm to communicate with a remote UNIX system, you should set TERM on that system to xterm. The terminfo description for xterm assumes VT100 mode. The xterm terminal is not quite the same as the vt100 terminal, since it includes some X-specific extensions and lacks some capabilities that only make sense on an actual VT100.

---

41. The query comes from the default login initialization file, so you can eliminate it by modifying that file.

42. Some control sequences are useful only on a real VT100; for example, the '⟨escape⟩#8' sequence that performs a DEC screen alignment test.

Another common choice for emulation is `ansi`, which designates a terminal that conforms to ANSI Standard X3.64. An important difference between `ansi` and `vt100` is that `ansi` provides for setting colors.

**2.15.7
Setting Your
Terminal Type**

Ordinarily your terminal type is set in your login initialization file (see Section 2.14), but you might need to set it yourself for one of the following reasons:

- For some reason your normal initialization file isn't being called.
- Your original initialization files aren't correct.
- You customarily log in at two different terminals and these terminals have different types.

Setting your terminal entails setting the `TERM` environment variable and initializing the terminal itself. If you're using the KornShell, you can set `TERM` with `export` together with an assignment; if you're using the C shell, you can set it with the `setenv` command. The most convenient way to initialize the terminal is with `tset` (see Section 5.5.1), if it's available; if it isn't, you can use the command 'tput init' or sometimes `reset`.

The login program sets certain characteristics of your terminal, such as whether uppercase characters should be mapped to lowercase ones. If any are set inappropriately, you can use `stty` to change them. You should include the command for making the changes in your login initialization file.

2.16   Locales, Code Sets, and Internationalization

UNIX systems are in use throughout the world. Many UNIX programs depend in both obvious and subtle ways on orthographic, linguistic, and cultural conventions. For instance, Japanese documents should be represented by using Japanese characters, a convention that affects any program that operates on those documents. The appropriate behavior of the `sort` program depends on the letter- and word-ordering conventions of the local language, and that of the `date` program on the local names for the days of the week and the customary form and order of the year, month, and day. When a program issues an error message, that message ought to be in the native language of the person reading it. More subtly, the `rm` command sometimes asks for confirmation that a file should be removed; the appropriate user response is language-dependent. The adaptations of UNIX needed to provide such behaviors are called *internationalization*. The book by O'Donnell (reference [B21]) is a particularly good source of information on the issues raised by internationalization and how they are handled under UNIX.

A *locale* defines those aspects of the UNIX environment that depend on national linguistic and cultural conventions. A locale definition has six categories of information: character attributes, collating rules, monetary formatting, numeric formatting, time and date formatting, and the form of confirmation responses. An auxiliary definition, the *charmap*, associates symbolic names of characters with the numerical codes that represent them within the computer.[43] A single definition of a locale's categories, if properly written, can be used with more than one charmap.

You establish the locale under which you are operating by setting certain environment variables (see Section 2.16.4). In most cases setting `LANG` is sufficient. You can examine a locale definition with `locale` or create a new one with `localedef` (see Section 5.13). An application program adapts to the current locale by calling the C function `setlocale`. To see the definition of your current locale, type `locale`; to see the current charmap, type

```
locale -k charmap
```

A particularly important locale—and the only one on some systems—is the `POSIX` locale, also named the `C` locale. That locale corresponds to the traditional use of the ASCII character set in the UNIX environment and POSIX-conforming systems are required to provide it (though they may of course provide other locales as well).

Locales were originally designed for use by C programs and were later adopted as part of POSIX. Some UNIX systems do not yet support locales or support then only partially. Locale support is more common among systems installed outside the United States.

2.16.1 Code Sets

A *code set* is a mapping or table that lists a set of glyphs—graphical representations of characters—and for each glyph defines how that glyph is represented numerically in computerized text. The usual ASCII table is an example of a code set. Standards documents often use the more formal term "coded character set".

Since different code sets may include different characters, providing an appropriate code set is an important part of internationalization. For instance, a UNIX system adapted to Swedish users should use a code set that includes all the characters of the Swedish alphabet, some of which are not ASCII characters. When you select a locale, you must also select a particular code set to go with that locale, either implicitly or explicitly.

A popular code set for international use is ISO 8859-1. It includes the accented characters, ligatures, and special characters such as the Danish letter 'ø' and the German letter 'ß' needed for Western European languages. It is not adequate for Hungarian or Arabic, say—these and other languages are provided for by other code sets in the ISO 8859 series. All the code sets in the ISO 8859 series use eight-bit codes, one per character.

---

43. The POSIX standard fudges the question of whether a charmap is part of a locale. A careful reading suggests that POSIX views a charmap as being part of a locale but not part of a locale definition.

Japanese and other languages that use ideographs have far too many characters to accommodate within the 255-character limit of an eight-bit code set. A number of different code sets for these languages have been defined, all of which use more than one eight-bit byte to represent a character. Some of them just have a specific multiple-byte representation for each character. Others use shift characters to define an interpretation state, much as pressing but not releasing the shift key on a keyboard causes the following letters to be uppercased. State-dependent representations save space but have the disadvantage that you can't interpret a character code without knowing what shifts have preceded it. POSIX does not yet support state-dependent representations, though particular UNIX implementations may.

The code set in use affects the meaning of what you type at a UNIX terminal. UNIX commands and their options are all constrained to be expressed in pure ASCII—no special characters permitted.[44] However, non-ASCII characters can appear in filenames, in strings within commands, and in fact in any context where an arbitrary character is permitted. For instance, the command

```
grep âne gurus
```

selects from the file gurus all lines containing the French word 'âne'.

In order to understand the role of code sets in UNIX, it helps to remember that *a code set relates numerical character codes to what characters mean, not just to what they look like.* If you press the key on your keyboard labelled 'f' in an ASCII environment, the program on the other end sees not a glyph but the number 38. Its response is linked to that number. If your environment uses a different code set, the number seen by the program when you type an 'f' will in general be different—and unless the program has been set up to recognize that other code set, it will respond differently.

**2.16.2
Character Maps**

A *character map*, or *charmap*, is a file that defines symbolic names for the characters in a code set. These names can then be used in locale definitions. A character map does *not* specify, except perhaps by implication, the relationship between numerical character codes and their corresponding glyphs. As a matter of fact, it would take a bitmap of each glyph to do that.

By choosing a charmap, you effectively specify which code set is to be used for locale-dependent data. Here is a line taken from the charmap for the ISO 8859-1 code set:

```
<a?>    /xe3   LATIN SMALL LETTER A WITH TILDE
```

---

44. This requirement does not preclude code sets such as the IBM EBCDIC set that include the ASCII characters but assign them different numerical codes.

The first item is the symbolic name for the character, the second item is its numeric code (hexadecimal e3), and the third item is a comment that explains what character is defined by this line.

A single set of locale category definitions can be used with different charmaps as long as (a) each character referred to in the category definitions is specified as a symbolic name, and (b) each of those symbolic names is defined in each charmap. The different charmaps do *not* have to specify the same numeric code for each such symbolic name. However, unless all the charmaps provided by a particular implementation are at least in agreement on the encodings of the ASCII characters (called the *portable character set*), UNIX utilities are not guaranteed to work properly. All charmaps are required to include the ASCII characters (though not necessarily with the ASCII encodings), and these are also the characters in the POSIX locale.[45]

**2.16.3
Locale Categories**

A locale definition consists of the five categories of definitions that follow. Each category has a name that is used to designate it in certain contexts. A locale definition usually exists in the form of a file that can be understood by the `localedef` command and can be regurgitated by the `locale` command (see Section 5.13). The rules for defining a category specify the format of that file, and the parameters associated with the category act as keywords in the file. You can usually find information about locales for your system by doing an "apropos" search on the keyword `locale` with the `apropos` or 'man -k' command.

Character Classification and Attributes.   The character classification category is named LC_CTYPE. The definitions in these categories define which characters fall under certain classifications.[46] In some cases, such as the numeric digits (`digit`), the characters are required to be the same for all locales. In others, such as the lowercase letters (`lower`), certain characters are required either to be included or to be excluded but the category is still open-ended. These classifications play an important part in the syntax of regular expressions (see p. 82). The classifications are as follows:

upper   The uppercase letters. These must always include the letters A through Z but may include other letters taken from non-English alphabets. For the POSIX locale these are just A through Z.

lower   Similarly, the lowercase letters (these are a through z for the POSIX locale).

---

45. A UNIX environment may support more than one code set. A UNIX system in Japan, for instance, might support code sets for katakana and Kanji in addition to a roman set. For that to work, there are two requirements: that the supported code sets be disjoint and that at least one of them include the portable code set. Disjointness means that it is possible to scan a string and determine, for each (possibly multi-byte) character, the code set to which it belongs. Without disjointness, it is impossible to interpret a string; without inclusion of the portable code set, it is impossible to type UNIX commands.

46. These classifications are closely related to similarly named C functions such as *isdigit*.

alpha   All letters. These must include the uppercase and lowercase letters but may include others. For the POSIX locale they are just A through Z and a through z.

digit   The digits 0 through 9, precisely.

xdigit   The hexadecimal digits. More than one representation of a digit is permitted. For the POSIX locale these are

         0123456789ABCDEFabcdef

space   The "whitespace" characters, which include at least ⟨space⟩, ⟨formfeed⟩, ⟨newline⟩, ⟨carriage-return⟩, ⟨tab⟩, and ⟨vertical-tab⟩. For the POSIX locale the category consists of exactly those characters.

blank   The characters that produce horizontal whitespace. For the POSIX locale these are ⟨space⟩ and ⟨tab⟩.

cntrl   The control characters, mutually exclusive with the printable characters. The control characters for the POSIX locale are precisely the nonprintable characters; (i.e., the characters with decimal ASCII codes 0–31 and 127).

punct   The punctuation characters, mutually exclusive with alpha, digit, and xdigit. For the POSIX locale these are

         !"#$%&'()*+,-./:;<=>?@[\]^_'{}|~

graph   The "graphic" characters, namely, all the printable characters except ⟨space⟩. For the POSIX locale these are the characters in alpha, digit, and punct.

print   The printable characters, including ⟨space⟩. For the POSIX locale these are the graphic characters plus ⟨space⟩.

The LC_CTYPE category also includes two lists, toupper and tolower, that define the correspondences between uppercase and lowercase characters. These affect the behavior of a number of user-level programs such as awk, dd, and tr.

Collating Rules and Collating Elements. The collating rules category is named LC_COLLATE. The rules in this category answer the question essential to sorting, "When two strings are compared, which one comes first?"

Even for ordinary English text, the answer is not straightforward. A simple algorithm based on the ASCII codes for the letters would mistakenly place Qatar ahead of baseball since all the uppercase letters precede all the lowercase letters in the ASCII ordering. For other languages the requirements can become much more complicated.

One of the complications is that for some languages, certain multicharacter letter sequences behave like single letters for sorting purposes. For instance, in Spanish the sequence ch acts like a single letter that comes between c and d, so the collating rules should place chocolate after curioso, not before it.

Another complication is the treatment of letters with diacritics (accents). For sorting French words, for instance, two passes are required in a comparison. In the first pass the various forms of a letter such as e are treated as equivalent, thus ensuring that `effigie` comes after `éclair` but before `épouiller`.[47] Without the equivalence, all words starting with é would have to either precede or follow all words starting with e. In the second pass ties are broken between words that differ only in the occurrence of diacritics; in this pass the different forms of e are considered to be different letters.

A *collating element* is a sequence of characters that acts as a single character for sorting and collation purposes. A collating element is one of the possible elementary components of a regular expression (see p. 83). The `LC_COLLATE` rules provide for the definition of collating elements; such definitions precede the definition of the collating sequence itself. A sample of such a definition is

```
collating-element <ch> from "<c><h>"
```

This defines the collating element `ch` to consist of the character with symbolic name `<c>` followed by the character with symbolic name `<h>`. These symbolic names are defined by the charmap file associated with the locale definition containing this particular collating rule. Presumably that charmap file defines `<c>` to have the character code for the letter 'c' and similarly defines `<h>`.

The comparison rules themselves are specified by listing all the collating elements in order, together with artificial collating symbols that can be introduced to help the specification. Each collating element is followed by a sequence of weights that determine how the sorting works on successive passes. The details of the comparison rules are beyond the scope of this book, but one aspect of those rules is essential: the use of primary weights to create equivalence classes of collating elements.

An *equivalence class* in this context is a set of characters that all have the same primary weight (and therefore all sort to the same position on the first pass). An equivalence class is another possible elementary component of a regular expression (see p. 83). For English dictionary-order sorting, A and a would belong to an equivalence class; their lines in the collating rules would be

```
<A> <a>
<a> <a>
```

These lines indicate that (a) `<A>` comes before `<a>`, and (b) both `<A>` and `<a>` have the same primary weight, namely, `<a>`. (Both letters implicitly

---

47. But in Danish 'A' and 'Å' are entirely different letters. 'Å' comes at the end of the alphabet, in fact.

have themselves as secondary weights, so on a second pass, <A> comes
before <a>.) For French sorting, similar lines might be the following:

```
<a>              <a>;<a>;<a>
<A>              <a>;<a>;<A>
<a-'>            <a>;<a-'>;<a-'>
<A-'>            <a>;<a-'>;<A-'>
<a-'>            <a>;<a-'>;<a-'>
<A-'>            <a>;<a-'>;<A-'>
<a-^>            <a>;<a-^>;<a-^>
<A-^>            <a>;<a-^>;<A-^>
```

Since all eight letters have the same primary weight, they all belong to
the same equivalence class. The second pass distinguishes diacritics but
ignores case; the third pass considers case (for those strings that are equal
in every respect except case). These lines would be valid only in conjunction with a charmap that defined the symbolic names <a>, <A>, <a-'>,
<A-'>, etc., by specifying the numeric code of each one ('a-' being the
symbolic name for 'á', etc.).[48]

Monetary Quantities.   The category for monetary quantities is named
`LC_MONETARY`. The definitions in this category specify the string to be used
as the local currency symbol, the string to be used as the decimal delimiter, the number of fractional digits that should appear to the right of
that delimiter, and a number of other formatting parameters. None of
the standard UNIX utilities use the information in this category, although
applications such as spreadsheets are likely to. The information in this
category is usually not relevant at the user level.

Other Numeric Quantities.   The category for numeric quantities other
than monetary quantities is named `LC_NUMERIC`. Three parameters specify
how such quantities should be formatted:

`decimal_point`

> The delimiter between the integer part and the fraction part
> of a decimal fraction (a dot in the POSIX locale). Utilities such
> as `awk` and `od` are sensitive to that delimiter.

`thousands_sep`

> The delimiter between groups of digits in the integer part of
> a number (not defined in the POSIX locale, but a comma in
> American usage and a period in European usage).

`grouping` The sizes of the groups of digits separated by `thousands_sep`
> (not defined in the POSIX locale, but usually 3). If this param-
> eter is a single integer, then the groups have that size. If it is

---

48. The POSIX approach confounds two slightly different notions: a natural equivalence
class and a set of characters that sort equally on the first pass. The various forms of 'a'
in French are naturally a different equivalence class than the various forms of 'A', but the
collation rules force the two classes to be combined into one.

a sequence of integers, then the rightmost group has the size of the first integer, the next rightmost the size of the second integer, and so forth. The last integer is used for all remaining groups unless it is −1; in that case the remaining digits in the number are ungrouped.

Dates and Times.   The category for expressing dates and times is named LC_TIME. The parameters in this category define how the field descriptors in the date command (see Section 5.1.5) are to be interpreted:

day   The full names of the days of the week (e.g., Tuesday) as called for by the '%A' field descriptor.

abday   The abbreviated names of the days of the week (e.g., Thu) as called for by the '%a' field descriptor.

mon   The full names of the months (e.g., November) as called for by the '%B' field descriptor.

abmon   The abbreviated names of the months (e.g., Jul) as called for by the '%b' field descriptor.

am_pm   The strings that denote forenoon and afternoon, as called for by the %p field descriptor.

d_t_fm   A string indicating how the date and time are to be formatted, as called for by the %c field descriptor. This string can include both constant characters and other field descriptors. For instance, the POSIX locale defines d_t_fm to be

```
%a %b %e %H:%M:%S %Y
```

A date and time specified by %c under the POSIX locale might be

```
Tue Nov 17 14:32:59 1995
```

d_fmt   A string indicating how the date by itself is to be formatted, as called for by the %x field descriptor. The POSIX locale defines d_fmt to be

```
%m/%d/%y
```

A date specified by %x under the POSIX locale might be

```
11/17/95
```

t_fmt   A string indicating how the time by itself is to be formatted, as called for by the %X field descriptor. The POSIX locale defines t_fmt to be

```
%H:%M:%S
```

A time specified by %X under the POSIX locale might be

```
14:32:59
```

t_fmt_ampm

> Like t_fmt but for a 12-hour clock in the am/pm notation, as called for by the %r field descriptor. The POSIX locale defines t_fmt_ampm to be
>
> > %I:%M:%S %p
>
> A time specified by %r under the POSIX locale might be
>
> > 2:32:59 PM

POSIX defines additional optional keywords for formatting dates in scripts such as Kanji or Hindi and for calendars that use eras other than the Christian era (the one that uses the year of the birth of Christ as Year One). We do not discuss those here.

Form of Confirmations. The category for defining the user inputs that mean "yes" and "no" is named LC_MESSAGES. These user inputs need to be recognized as responses to queries asking for confirmation of an action such as deleting a file. There are two parameters in this category:

yesexpr   An (extended) regular expression that describes an affirmative response to a query such as the ones issued by rm. The POSIX locale specified this regular expression as '∧[yY]' so that any response that starts with y or Y is treated as affirmative.

noexpr   An (extended) regular expression that describes a negative response to a query. The POSIX locale specified this regular expression as '∧[nN]' so that any response that starts with n or N is treated as negative.

Particular systems may include other information in this category to support output messages that are different for different languages or cultures.

**2.16.4
Environment
Variables for Locales**

You select a locale or just certain categories of a locale by setting certain environment variables:

(1) If you set LC_ALL to the name of a locale, then that locale is used for all categories no matter what values the other variables have.

(2) If LC_ALL is not set (or has a null value) and one or more of the category variables LC_CTYPE, LC_COLLATE, LC_MONETARY, LC_NUMERIC, LC_TIME, and LC_MESSAGES is set to the name of a locale, then the designated locale is used for each of those categories.

(3) If LC_ALL is not set but LANG is set to the name of the locale, then that locale is used for any category not specified by one of the LC_* variables.

For each of these variables you can use the pathname of a locale definition instead of a locale name.

The effect of these rules is to create a precedence order among the variables, with LC_ALL taking precedence over all the others and the specific LC_* variables taking precedence over LANG. For instance, the settings

```
LANG=POSIX
LC_TIME=fr_CH.ISO8859-1
```

would cause the French Swiss locale `fr_CH.ISO8859-1` to be used for dates and times and the `POSIX` locale to be used for everything else.

A reasonable way to use these variables is to set `LANG` to your usual locale at the outermost level of your operating environment (say in your login initialization file) and then to override it by setting the other variables in subshells.

2.17   Regular Expressions

A *regular expression* defines a pattern of text to be matched. A number of UNIX utilities, such as `sed`, expect you to specify search patterns as regular expressions. The meaning of a regular expression depends on the current locale (see Section 2.16).

There are two kinds of regular expressions: *basic regular expressions* and *extended regular expressions*. Basic regular expressions are understood by many older UNIX programs such as `ed`, `grep`, and `sed`. In fact, older UNIX documentation usually refers to the manual pages for `ed` as the place to find the definition of a regular expression. Extended regular expressions are a generalization of basic regular expressions recognized by `egrep` (equivalent to `grep` with the `-E` option). Some systems may provide an `-E` option for other utilities such as `sed` to enable them to recognize extended regular expressions.

The `vi` and `ex` editors use basic regular expressions but provide some additional facilities (see Section 8.1.11). The Emacs editor has its own rules for regular expressions, which resemble those for basic regular expressions (see "Regular Expressions in Emacs" on p. 524).

**2.17.1
Basic
Regular Expressions**

In general, any character appearing in a basic regular expression (BRE) matches that character in the text. For example, the BRE `elvis` matches the string `elvis`. However, certain characters are used to specify variable patterns and are therefore special. The following characters are special anywhere in a string:

> `.   *   [ \`

In addition, other characters are special under particular conditions:

- The character '∧' is special at the beginning of a string.
- The character '$' is special at the end of a string.
- The character that terminates a string is special throughout the string. What this character is depends on the context.

If you want to use a special character in a pattern, you must quote it, in effect, by escaping it with a preceding backslash (\). For example, the BRE `cheap at $9\.98` matches the string `cheap at $9.98`. Here the '.' needs to be quoted but the '$' doesn't since it isn't at the end of the string and therefore isn't special.

The character, if any, that terminates a BRE is also special and must be quoted if you want to use it within the string. For example, the BRE '/\//' might be used in `ed` to search for a string consisting of a single '/'. The outer slashes enclose the BRE and aren't actually part of it.

The meanings of the special characters are as follows:

\   The backslash quotes the character after it if that character is special. The behavior of a backslash preceding a nonspecial character is undefined, so you should avoid using backslashes in front of nonspecial characters.

.   The dot matches any single (non-null) character.

*   A single character followed by a star matches zero or more occurrences of that character. Similarly, a pattern that matches a set of characters followed by a star matches zero or more characters from that set. In particular, '.*' matches an arbitrary, possibly empty, string. Note that this use of the star is different from that of the shell, for which '*' rather than '.*' matches zero or more arbitrary characters.

The matching mechanism is clever enough to consider the whole string when testing for a match. For example, it can discover that '^a.*b.c$' matches 'axybbcc', even though this match requires that the '.*' should consume the first 'b' but not the second one. When a BRE can be matched in more than one way, the longest possible matching sequence is always used. See Section 2.17.5 for further discussion of multiple matches.

^   A hat at the beginning of an outermost regular expression matches the beginning of a line. Anywhere else in a regular expression, it matches itself.

$ A dollar sign at the end of an outermost regular expression matches the end of a line. Anywhere else in a regular expression, it matches itself.

[*set*]   A set of characters in square brackets matches any single character from the set. For example, [moxie] matches any of the characters (e i m o x). This form is called a *bracket expression*. The notation for a bracket expression is extended as follows:

- Within the set, the only characters with special meanings are '-', ']', '^', and '['. The '[' is special only when it appears in one of the combinations '[:', '[.', or '[='. All other characters, even '\', stand for themselves.

- The notation '[:*class*:]' designates those characters in the character class *class*. For instance,

  ```
  [[:lower:]]
  ```

is matched by any lowercase letter. The classes are listed in "Character Classification and Attributes" on page 75. The characters in a particular class depend on the current locale. Note that if you're looking for a character that is either '[' or ':', you should use the bracket expression '[:[]' to avoid misinterpretation. This form, unlike the next two, is useful even when you are not using any of UNIX's internationalization features.

- The notation '[.*symb*.]' designates a collating element— that is, a sequence of characters that should be treated as a single character for sorting and collation purposes (see "Collating Rules and Collating Elements" on p. 76). (A single character is a valid collating element but not a particularly useful one in this context.) For instance,

      [.ch.]

  refers to the Spanish-language collating element ch, which behaves like a single letter during a sort. The POSIX locale (the usual default) does not include any nontrivial collating elements, but the locales for languages other than English may. Collating elements are most often used to specify an endpoint of a range.

- The notation '[=*class*=]' designates all collating elements (see "Collating Rules and Collating Elements" on p. 76) that are equivalent to *class*. This notation is useful for retrieving multiple forms of letters in languages other than English, such as 'a', 'à', and 'á' in French. In a French locale the BRE

      [[=a=]]

  or, equivalently,

      [[=á=]]

  would match any of them.[49]

- The notation *c1*-*c2* indicates the set of characters ranging from *c1* to *c2*. For example, '[a-hA-H]' matches any lowercase or uppercase letter between 'A' and 'H'. A minus sign at the beginning or end of the set stands for itself, however; thus '[+-]' matches a plus or a hyphen, as does '[-+]'. A Spanish-language search might use the notation for collating elements to search for strings from ch to f with the BRE

      [[.ch.]-f]

---

49. This expression would also match 'A', which might not be the effect you want.

- The sequence [∧*set*] matches any character that is *not* in *set*. (In this case a '-' or ']' following the initial '∧' stands for itself, as above.) Thus '[∧[:digit:]]' matches any character except a digit.

- A right bracket as the first character of the set or following '∧' represents itself and does not end the set. (Within the set, a left bracket is not special.) Thus '[][]' matches a left bracket or a right bracket.

Note that a set of characters can be followed by an asterisk. Thus '[[:digit:]a-f]*' matches a possibly empty sequence of characters, each of which is either a digit or a letter between a and f.

Subexpressions. You can enclose a portion of a regular expression between the markers '\(' and '\)'. The entire construct is called a *subexpression*.[50] Later in the expression you can match a subexpression by writing a *backreference* '\n', where n is a digit between 1 and 9. Here '\1' denotes the first subexpression, '\2' the second one, and so forth. Thus

$$\texttt{\\([[:lower:]]*\\)\\\&\\1}$$

matches the string 'gnat&gnat'. A subexpression or a backreference can also be followed by an asterisk, indicating an indefinite number of repetitions.

Interval Expressions. You can follow a single character, or a regular expression that denotes a single character, by one of the following forms, called an *interval expression*:

$$\texttt{\\\{}m\texttt{\\\}} \qquad \texttt{\\\{}m\texttt{,\\\}} \qquad \texttt{\\\{}m\texttt{,}n\texttt{\\\}}$$

Here m and n are non-negative integers less than 256. Let S be the set containing either the single character or the characters that match the regular expression.

- The first form denotes exactly m occurrences of characters belonging to S.
- The second form denotes at least m occurrences of characters belonging to S.
- The third form denotes between m and n occurrences of characters belonging to S.

For example, '[[:digit:]]\{2,\}' matches a sequence consisting of two or more digits.

2.17.2 Extended Regular Expressions

An extended regular expression (ERE) follows the rules for a basic regular expression with the following additions and changes:

- *Unquoted* parentheses are used for grouping subexpressions. For example, the pattern '(cat|dog)(fish|fight)' matches any line

---

50. Older UNIX documentation uses the term "bracketed expression", a usage that conflicts with the more modern POSIX terminology.

containing either 'catfish', 'catfight', 'dogfish', or 'dogfight'. (An unquoted parenthesis is an ordinary character in a BRE.)

- Similarly, *unquoted* braces are used for interval expressions.

- The form '*e*+' matches one or more occurrences of the ERE *e*, where *e* must be either a parenthesized subexpression or an ERE that always matches exactly one character. (A bracket expression always matches exactly one character, so it qualifies.) For example, the ERE

      [[:upper:]][[:digit:]]+

  (or '[A-Z][0-9]+') matches strings consisting of an uppercase letter followed by one or more digits.

- The form '*e*?' matches zero or one occurrences of the ERE *e*; that is, an optional occurrence. The requirements for *e* are the same as for '*e*+'.

- Two regular expressions separated by '|' match an occurrence of either of them; that is, the '|' operator acts as an "or".

- Awk also recognizes certain escape sequences that start with a back-slash (see p. 205).

In an ERE, the characters

      + ? | ( ) "

are additional special characters that need to be quoted with a backslash if they are used to stand for themselves.

2.17.3 Precedence for Regular Expressions

When several operators occur in a regular expression, whether a BRE or an ERE, they are interpreted in order of precedence from highest to lowest. In other words, the highest precedence operators are applied first. The precedence of the operators is as follows (highest first):

(1) [ ]
(2) * + ?
(3) |

2.17.4 Replacements for Regular Expressions

In many contexts where regular expressions are used, you can provide a replacement to be substituted for the regular expression. Within a replacement, the following conventions apply:

- A backslash quotes the following character. The special characters within a replacement are '&' and '\'; these are the only characters that need to be quoted. The construct '\&' produces a single '&' and the construct '\\' produces a single backslash.

- As a special case of the quotation convention, a newline is indicated by inserting an actual newline preceded by a backslash. For example, the replacement text

      white\
      rabbit

produces the text

```
white
rabbit
```

- An ampersand (&) indicates the entire matched regular expression. For example, the replacement '&&' would consist of two copies of the matched expression.

- The sequence '\\n', where n is a single digit, indicates the text matching the nth parenthesized component of the regular expression.

2.17.5
Multiple Matches

When a program is searching for strings that match a regular expression, a particular string or substring may match in more than one way, thanks to the '*' and '|' operators. That doesn't affect anything as long as backreferences are not being used to extract all or part of the match. But when such backreferences exist, it's essential to specify which of the possible matches is chosen.

When multiple matches are possible, a particular one is chosen according to the following rules:

(1)   The match that begins earliest in the string is chosen.

(2)   For matches that begin at the same place, the longest one is chosen.

(3)   For matches that begin in the same place and have the same length, the subexpressions, taken from left to right, each match the longest possible string. For this purpose a null string is considered to be longer than no match at all.

For instance, if the ERE

```
((h.*)*hee)|(hohoho(he+)+)
```

is matched against the string

```
hohohoheehehenha
```

the subexpression `(hohoho(he+)+)` matches `hohohoheehehe`.

2.18   Devices

A *device* is a piece of equipment for storing or communicating data. Printers, disks, and terminals are examples of devices.

UNIX provides access to a device by associating one or more files with it. The files associated with devices are called *special files* (see Section 2.18.2).[51]   For example, you can read a line from your terminal

---

51. "Device files" would have been a better name.

by reading from the special file `/dev/tty` associated with your terminal. Similarly, you can print a file on printer 1 (assuming you're entitled to) by sending it to the special file `/dev/lp1` associated with that printer. Operations such as these that involve special files are usually carried out by system programs rather than user-level programs, but since UNIX documentation often refers to devices and special files, it's helpful to know what they are.

Conventionally, special files live in the `/dev` directory, which you can examine to see which devices are attached to your system. When a program performs an operation on a special file, such as asking the kernel to read the file, the operation is actually carried out by a *device driver* associated with the special file. Each kind of special file has its own device driver that translates file-oriented operations into instructions specific to the device's hardware. The device driver is sometimes called an *interface* to its device. A particular device can have several interfaces, each of which treats the device differently.

Device special files, like other files, have read and write permissions. Though execute permission normally has no meaning for a device special file, there are exceptions. For example, Sun Microsystems provides some SunOS programs on compact disks; for these programs to be executable, the disk itself must be made executable by setting the `x` permission.

2.18.1 Character Devices and Block Devices

There are two kinds of devices: character devices and block devices. They differ in how they transfer data between the device and computer memory.

Character Devices.   A *character device* is one that transfers data character by character. A single data transfer can include any number of characters up to some limit that depends on the device. A character device usually produces a stream of characters (like a keyboard), consumes a stream of characters (like a printer), or does both (like a terminal or a phone line). Most character devices are memoryless—you can't write information to the device and get it back later.

Block Devices.   A *block device* transfers data in batches of characters called *blocks*. Disks and tapes are the most common examples of block devices.[52] UNIX can read from or write to a block device at the hardware level only a block at a time, although higher-level software usually conceals that fact.

All blocks on a block device ordinarily have the same size, with the block size depending on the nature of the device. Although much historical UNIX literature suggests a standard block size of 512, a size of 4096 is more typical of modern systems. Some magnetic tape units can read and write variable-sized blocks—but even these units read or write a block all

---

52. A more unusual example in UNIX environments is a block terminal such as the IBM 3270. Such terminals, which transmit a screenful of data at a time, are commonly used with mainframe systems. The Amdahl Universal Timeshare System (UTS) has supported them since the late 1970s.

at once, not a character at a time.[53] It's unlikely that you'll ever need to deal with the individual blocks on a block device since part of a device driver's job is to provide a more convenient interface to the device.

Block devices, unlike character devices, are chiefly used to store information rather than to produce or consume it. File systems can be stored only on block devices; the structure of a file system depends on that assumption and the many references in UNIX utilities to blocks and block counts reflect it. When you operate on a file, the kernel translates that operation into an operation on a block special file, namely, the block special file associated with the device containing the file system that in turn contains the file.

The dd utility (see Section 3.16) is often useful for moving data to or from a block device since it provides control over the block sizes.

2.18.2 Special Files and Their Interfaces

Just as there are two kinds of devices, character devices and block devices, there are two kinds of special files for accessing them, *character special files* and *block special files*. In a long directory listing, the two kinds are indicated by c and b, respectively. Each device special file has a corresponding interface.

The relation between devices and device special files can be confusing. A block device can be accessed via either a block special file or a character special file, as explained below, while a character device is always accessed via a character special file. The device driver associated with a block special file is called a *block interface*, while that associated with a character special file is called a *character interface*.

When a block interface reads a block of data from a device, it attempts to save the contents of that block in a *cache* of buffers. If a program asks to read some data that's already in the cache, the interface can provide the data without having to fetch it from the device again.[54] Caching is particularly efficient when a block interface is performing input/output operations on a file system stored on a block device—the activity that probably affects the performance of a UNIX system more than any other.

A character interface, on the other hand, never saves data in a cache. Although some character interfaces may save data in other types of buffers, these buffers are used only once; after the data in a buffer has been read or written, the buffer is discarded.

Under most circumstances the only difference between using a block interface and using a character interface is efficiency; the actual results

---

53. Although you can read information from anywhere on a magnetic tape, ordinarily you can write information only at the end of the portion already written. This limitation exists because magnetic tape drives can't position the tape precisely enough to ensure that when the desired portion of the tape is written the rest of the tape is left undisturbed.

54. Although the block interface carefully ensures the consistency of the data it works with, it provides no protection against changes to the data on the device that result when the device is accessed through a different interface. A device should *never* be accessed through more than one interface at a time unless all of the accesses are read-only.

are the same. A block interface more efficiently supports operations on a file system; a character interface more efficiently supports operations such as copying the contents of one device to another, since in this case the data is used only once and caching merely adds overhead.

Usually the /dev directory contains two entries for a block device: a block special file and a character special file.[55] For example, /dev/mt1 might be the block special file for magnetic tape unit 1 and /dev/rmt1 might be the character special file for the same unit. The 'r' in 'rmt1' stands for "raw"; the character interface is often called the "raw interface" to signify that it passes data directly between the device and the programs that use it.

2.18.3
Interfaces for
Terminals

A terminal is a kind of character device. As a character device, a terminal has some special properties. When you communicate with UNIX via your terminal, the sequence of characters you type is not necessarily the sequence that you want the program you're running to see. For instance, if you type Erase, you don't want your program to see the character you just erased. The interface for a terminal therefore interprets and transforms both the incoming and outgoing streams of characters. Terminals are the only devices whose interfaces perform this interpretation, which you can specify or deactivate altogether with stty (see Section 5.5.2). When the interpretation is deactivated, the terminal is in *raw mode*; otherwise, it is in *cooked mode*.[56] Although it's rarely useful for a user to operate a terminal in raw mode, it's often useful for a program to do so.

A terminal operating in cooked mode collects characters until it has a complete line. It must work that way for the Kill and Erase characters to be effective; otherwise, a program reading your terminal would see characters that you didn't intend it to. When a terminal is in cooked mode, the terminal interface performs the following important transformations:

- Processing Kill and Erase characters
- Echoing characters back to the terminal
- Expanding output tabs to sequences of spaces
- Generating signals for terminal hangups, end of file, interrupt, etc.
- If necessary, deleting ⟨return⟩ characters in front of ⟨newline⟩s in the input and inserting them into the output

---

55. A disk usually has a pair of entries for each disk partition rather than one pair for the entire disk, making the disk appear to be a set of devices.

56. The word "raw" in this context can be confusing because the same word is used to describe the character interface to a block device. The two usages are related since in each case the device and the program operating on it communicate directly—the transmitted data is not processed in any way. For a raw interface, the omitted processing is the storage of the transmitted data in a cache, while for a terminal operating in raw mode, the omitted processing is the interpretation of the input and output data streams. For a block device, the raw interface and the block interface differ only in efficiency—you get the same computed results except under unusual circumstances. But for a character device, raw mode and cooked mode differ in effect—you get different computed results when you switch a terminal from one mode to the other.

2.18.4
Device Numbers

Each device has two numbers associated with it: a *major number* that specifies the type of the device and a *minor number* that specifies a physical or logical unit within the type. Devices with the same major number use the same device driver. For instance, all terminals might have major number 1. A particular terminal, /dev/tty29, would have minor number 29. If you list the devices with ls (see Section 3.2), the major and minor numbers appear in place of the length for a file.

2.18.5
Device Names for Hardware Devices

Device names for hardware devices vary greatly from one system to another, depending not only on the vendor but also on the system's hardware configuration. Device names usually have the form

> [r]*type* [*unit*] [*attributes*]

where r indicates a raw interface; *type*, the type of unit (corresponding to the major number); *unit*, a unit number (the minor number); and *attributes*, additional properties of the device. We describe the names often used for some common devices.

Hard Disks and Their Partitions. In most systems, hard disks can be divided into partitions. On some systems the device name /dev/dsk/1s3 indicates partition 3 on disk drive 1. On Linux the device name /dev/hda1 indicates all of disk drive 1, /dev/hdb1 indicates all of disk drive 2, etc., while the partitions of disk drive 1 are /dev/hda2, /dev/hda3, etc. SCSI[57] disk drives are named /dev/sda1, /dev/sdb1, etc., with analogous names for their partitions.

Terminals. In most systems the terminals are named '/dev/tty*nn*', where *nn* is a two-digit number. Device names of the form 'pty*nn*' often refer to pseudo-terminals such as those used in X.

Diskettes. In System V, diskettes are accessed via the devices

> /dev/[r]dsk/f*uds*[d][t]
> /dev/[r]dsk/f*uqs*[d][t]

The notations in this form are as follows:

r	If present, this is a raw interface
u	Drive number
d or q	Double density (512 bytes/sector) or quad density (1024 bytes/sector). Double density is used only for 360KB 5$\frac{1}{4}$" diskettes.
s	Sectors per track
d	If present, the disk is double-sided
t	If present, the entire disk, including track 0, can be accessed

For example, a standard 1.44MB 3$\frac{1}{2}$" diskette in drive 1, excluding track 0, is referred to as

> /dev/dsk/f1q18d

---

57. Small Computer System Interface.

while a 360KB 5 ¹/₄" diskette in drive 0, including track 0, is referred to as

```
/dev/dsk/f0d9dt
```

Under Linux, SunOS, and many other systems, however, a diskette in the first drive is accessed simply as `/dev/fd0` since these systems can auto-sense all the other disk characteristics.

Magnetic Tapes.   Magnetic tapes are usually named '`/dev/mt`n', where n is the unit number. Accessing that device implies that the tape is rewound after the corresponding file is closed. The device '`/dev/nmt`n' calls upon an interface that does not rewind the tape after closing its file. The raw interface is named '`/dev/rmt`n'. Most systems include a program called `mt` for performing magnetic tape operations such as rewinding or skipping files.

**2.18.6
Other Devices**

Three particularly useful devices are `/dev/null`, `/dev/tty`, and `/dev/mem`.

- `/dev/null`, the null device, is a "bit bucket". Anything you send to it is simply thrown away; whenever you attempt to read from it, you get an end-of-file. `/dev/null` is sometimes called a pseudo-device because it doesn't correspond to any actual hardware.

- `/dev/tty` refers to your terminal, whichever one it happens to be. Your terminal also has a specific designation (e.g., `/dev/tty03`), which you can find out with the `tty` command (see Section 5.1.4). Only you can read from your terminal, but anyone can write to it using the `write` command (see Section 5.6.2) unless you prevent them from doing so with a command such as `chmod` (see Section 3.11.1) or `mesg` (see Section 5.6.3).

- The special file `/dev/mem` is often supported as an image of computer memory. The nth byte of this file corresponds to the nth byte of memory. This special file is accessible only to the superuser.

3

Operations
on Files

A classic tenet of UNIX philosophy is that the way to get a job done is to use simple tools in combination. UNIX therefore provides a large—for many people, bewilderingly large—collection of simple tools for operating on files and directories. We describe many of these tools in this chapter and others in Chapter 4. If you're using the Emacs editor, you can use its directory editor, Dired, for some of the most frequent operations on files.

3.1   Operations on Directories

In this section we describe a number of commands for operating on directories. The `rm`, `rmdir`, and `ls` commands, which also operate on directories, are described in Sections 3.5.1 and 3.2.

**3.1.1
Changing
Directories with** `cd`

The `cd` command changes your current directory. The form of the command line is

    cd [*dir*]

where *dir* is the pathname of your new current directory (see Section 2.7.2). Your new current directory is determined as follows:

(1)   If *dir* is omitted, it is taken to be your home directory. Typing `cd` by itself is therefore a fast way to get back to your home directory.

92

(2) If *dir* is given as '-' (under the KornShell and many other shells), it is taken to be the previous directory, enabling you to use the form 'cd -' to toggle between two directories.

(3) Otherwise, if *dir* starts with '/' (the root directory), cd interprets *dir* as an absolute pathname.

(4) Otherwise, *dir* is taken to be relative to the first feasible path in the environment variable CDPATH (or cdpath for the C shell csh) if that variable is defined (see p. 371). If CDPATH is not defined, it is taken to be empty and thus equivalent to the current directory, so in this case *dir* is taken as relative to the current directory.

In other words, suppose that $p_1, p_2, \ldots, p_n$ are the paths listed in CDPATH. Then cd tries each of the paths p_1/dir, p_2/dir, $\ldots$, p_n/dir until it finds one that designates a valid directory. It then switches to that directory.

Cd uses neither standard input nor standard output, but it does send error messages to standard error. Because cd wouldn't work properly if it were called as an ordinary program (the effect of the cd call would be lost when its subprocess terminated), cd is an intrinsic command of every shell and also of some other interactive programs such as ftp.

The C shell provides a directory stack that you can use to return to previously active directories easily (see "The Directory Stack" on p. 396). The same feature has been included in Bash and may yet appear in other shells.

3.1.2
Showing the
Working Directory
with pwd

The pwd command sends the full pathname of your current (working) directory to standard output. For instance, if your user name is sissela and your current directory is the subdirectory darts of your home directory, the command

    pwd

produces the output

    /home/sissela/darts

(assuming that your home directory is /home/sissela).

3.1.3
Creating a Directory
with mkdir

The mkdir command creates one or more new directories. The form of the command is

    mkdir [-p] [-m *mode*] *dir* ...

Here each *dir* is the pathname of a directory you want to create. Each newly created directory has two entries: '.' for the directory itself and '..' for its parent directory. The permissions of the directory are set to 777 as modified by the current umask value (see Section 3.11.2), although you can specify different permissions with the -m option. The owner and group of each new directory are set to those of the process under whose auspices the directory was created. Creation of a directory, like creation of a file, requires write permission in the parent directory.

Command-Line Options.   The following command-line options apply to `mkdir`:

-m *n*   Set the permissions of each created directory to *n*.

-p   If a pathname lacks any components, make the necessary intermediate directories. For instance, suppose that `~/yorick` has no subdirectories and user `yorick` issues the command

        mkdir -p ~/gravity/tools

Then `mkdir` creates an intermediate directory `gravity` with the directory `tools` as an initial entry.

Not all systems recognize these options.

3.2   Listing Files with `ls`

The `ls` command lists a set of files, the contents of a directory, the contents of a tree of directories, or any combination of these. You can use it to see if files exist or to examine their characteristics. The form of the `ls` command line is

    ls [-1CFRabcdfgilmnopqrstux] [*pathname* ...]

This command lists the directories and files specified in *pathname* ... , with the style of the listing determined by *options* or by default. If no *pathname*s are given, it lists the current directory. Two particularly useful sets of options are '-CF' and '-l'. The command

    ls -CF *pathname* ...

lists the files in columnar format and indicates which ones are directories, executable files, symbolic links, or FIFO special files. The command

    ls -l *pathname* ...

provides a "long" listing that contains detailed information about the listed files.

Each *pathname* is the pathname of either a directory or a file; successive pathnames are separated by blanks. If you omit the pathnames, `ls` operates on '.' (the current directory). The items to be listed are determined as follows:

- If a name designates a file that is not a directory, that file is listed.
- If a name designates a directory, the files in that directory are listed.
- If there is no file with a particular name, nothing is listed for that name and an error message is sent to standard output.

Files and directories whose names begin with a dot are excluded unless the `-a` option is specified.

An example of the `ls` command is

```
ls -Fl -a .. stuart
```

This command lists two sets of files: those in the parent directory of the current directory and those in `stuart`. If `stuart` is a subdirectory of the current directory, it lists the files in that subdirectory; if `stuart` is a file in the current directory, it lists just that file; and if `stuart` is not in the current directory at all, it lists nothing for `stuart` and issues a diagnostic message. The listing options that apply are `-F`, `-l`, and `-a`.

The command `ls` by itself lists the files in the current directory, omitting those whose names begin with a dot. If there are no qualifying files, it produces no output. Initialization files such as '`.profile`' usually have names that start with a dot. A file whose name starts with a dot is sometimes called a *hidden file*.

3.2.1 Command-Line Options

The `ls` command can produce two kinds of listings: short and long. A short listing, which is the default, includes the name of each file and any other information you ask for explicitly; a long listing includes file permissions and other information (see Section 3.2.2). The `-l`, `-n`, `-o`, and `-g` options all force a long listing; if these are absent, you get a short listing.

The following options affect the set of files included in the listing:

-a   List all files, including those whose names begin with a dot or are contained in a directory whose name begins with a dot.

-d   If a name on the command line designates a directory, list only the name of that directory, not its contents. You can use this option with `-l` to display the status of a directory.

-R   List subdirectories recursively. In other words, for each subdirectory that `ls` encounters, list the files in that subdirectory and in every subdirectory contained in it either directly or indirectly (not counting symbolic links). POSIX does not specify how the combination `-dR` should behave.

-f   This option applies only to directories. It causes `ls` to list all files contained in a directory in the order in which they are actually stored within that directory. This option nullifies the `-l`, `-t`, `-s`, and `-r` options if they are given and implies the `-a` option for the files contained in the directory. The `-f` option is not included in POSIX.

The following options affect the information associated with each file in a listing, either short or long:

-p   Put '`/`' after each file in the listing that is a directory. The `-p` option is not included in POSIX.

-F   Put '/' after each file in the listing that is a directory, a '*' after each file that is executable, an '@' after each file that is a symbolic link, and a '|' after each file that is a FIFO special file (see Section 2.11.1). (A file cannot be more than one of these.)

-i   Show the i-node number of each file.

-s   Show the size of each file in blocks, including indirect blocks (blocks that contain pointers to other blocks). The -s option is not included in POSIX.

The following options control the layout of a short listing:

-C   Produce multicolumn output, with the entries sorted down the columns.

-x   Produce multicolumn output, with the entries sorted across the rows. The -x option is not included in POSIX.

-m   List the files across the page, with successive files separated by commas. The -m option is not included in POSIX.

-1   List exactly one ("1") file per line.

The following options force a long listing, one file per line, in the format described in Section 3.2.2. These options may be used in any combination. By default, the owner name and group name of each file are listed; -n, -o, and -g change the default.

-l   List the files using the long format.

-n   List the files using the long format, replacing the owner name and group name in the listing with the user number and group number. The -n option is not included in POSIX.

-o   List the files in the long format, omitting the group. The -o option is not included in POSIX.

-g   List the files in the long format, omitting the owner. On some systems, the default long listing does not include the group name; the -g option then specifies that the group name should be included. The -g option is not included in POSIX.

The following options affect the order in which files are listed:

-t   List the files in chronological order, newest ones first (unless the order is reversed by the -r option). For sorting purposes, the time of last modification is used unless the -u option is specified.

-r   List the files in reverse alphabetic order if the -t option is absent and in oldest-first time order if the -t option is present.

The following options affect the time listed for each file. The time affects the order of the files if you've specified the -t option; it also shows up in the long listings even if you haven't specified -t. The default time is the time of last modification.

-u   Use the time when the file was last accessed.

-c   Use the time when the file's i-node was last modified, namely,
                when the file was created or its permissions were last modified.
                If -u and -c are both present, -u controls the time.

By default, nonprinting characters in a file name appear without change
in the listing output.[1] The following options provide special treatment for
these characters:

-b   If a file name contains a nonprinting character, show that char-
                acter as an octal number using the notation *ddd*. The -b
                option is not included in POSIX.

-q   If a file name contains a nonprinting character, show '?' in place
                of that character.

**3.2.2
Interpreting the
Long Format**

The `ls` command produces a long listing if you specify the -l option or
another option in the same group. Here is an example of the contents of
a directory listed using the -lF options:

```
total 7
drwxrwxr-x    3 clio      muses   176 Mar 19 12:06 ./
drwxrwxr-x   13 clio      muses   944 Feb 16 19:39 ../
drwxr-xr-x    2 clio      muses    48 Apr  4 11:54 d1/
-rwxr-xr-x    1 root      other     3 Apr 11 12:05 lookup*
lrwxrwxrwx    1 clio      muses     9 Mar 23 09:38 mark -> tmp/marvin
-rw-r--r--    3 clio      mail      4 Apr  3 11:02 news
prw-r--r--    1 euterpe   muses     0 Apr 11 11:09 tube
```

And here is an example of a couple of (nonconsecutive) lines from a similar
listing for /dev, where device files are kept:

```
brw-rw-rw-    1 root      disk      2,  28 Nov 30   1993 fd0H1440
crw-rw-rw-    1 root      root      4, 128 Mar  7 20:24 ptyp0
```

These listings are interpreted as follows:

- The first character on the line indicates the file type:

  -   Ordinary file
  d   Directory
  l   Symbolic link (see p. 41)
  b   Block device (see Section 2.18)
  c   Character device (see Section 2.18)
  p   FIFO special file (named pipe) (see Section 2.11.1)
  s   Socket link (for BSD-like systems)

---

1. The set of nonprinting characters depends on the locale.

The entry for a symbolic link shows both its name in the current directory entry and the pathname to which it is linked.

- The next three groups of three letters indicate the file permissions for the user, the group, and others (see Section 2.8). Other letters besides r, w, and x are possible.

- The next item indicates how many links this file has (see Section 2.7.5). A directory *dir* often has several links, because each of its subdirectories includes an entry for *dir* as the parent directory, and that entry counts as a link to *dir*.

- The next two items indicate the user and group who own the file. The group is usually the user's group, but it need not be.

- The next item indicates the file size in characters. If the listing was created using the -s option, the total number of disk blocks occupied by the listed files is shown at the top; in this case it is 7.

- The next two items indicate the date and time when the file was last modified. If you've used the -u option, the time of last access is shown instead; if you've used the -c option, the time of last i-node modification is shown instead (see the description of these options above).

- The last item indicates the file name. A '/' after the file name indicates a directory; a '*' indicates an executable file (and corresponds to x in the user permissions). These indicators are attached because of the -F option.

3.3   Displaying and Concatenating Files with cat

The cat command gets its name from the fact that it copies and concatenates files. It has some common applications that don't involve concatenation and that make it one of the most useful UNIX commands.

The general form of the cat command line is

```
cat [-estuv] [file] . . .
```

The files designated by the pathnames in *file* . . . are concatenated and copied to standard output. The result is a copy of the first file, followed by a copy of the second file, etc. A '-' in place of a *file* indicates standard input.

For example, the command

```
cat pebbles boulders
```

copies the contents of file pebbles followed by the contents of file boulders to standard output, while the command

```
cat pebbles boulders > rocks
```

copies their successive contents into the file `rocks`.

If only one pathname appears on the command line, that pathname's file is copied to standard output. If no pathnames appear on the command line, standard input is copied to standard output. These rules lead to the following important special cases:

- To list the contents of *file*, use the command

      cat *file*

  For example,

      cat snakes

  displays the contents of the file `snakes` on your terminal.

- To copy one file to another, use the command

      cat *infile* > *outfile*

  or the command

      cat < *infile* > *outfile*

  These commands are ordinarily equivalent to

      cp *infile* *outfile*

  (see Section 3.4.3).

- To place some text in *file*, type

      cat > *file*

  followed by the text and (EOF) . For short text of just a line or two, that is often faster than using an editor. For example, the input

  ```
  cat > list
  echo Listing of file "$1":
  cat $1
  (EOF)
  chmod +x list
  ```

  creates a short executable shell script in the file `list` that lists a file along with its name.

- To append the text of *file*$_1$ followed by *file*$_2$ to the end of *file*$_3$, type

      cat *file*$_1$ *file*$_2$ >> *file*$_3$

  See Section 2.10 for an explanation of '>>'. Be careful when you type this; if you type '>' instead of '>>', you'll clobber *file*$_3$. Some people advise using a temporary file instead to avoid such a mistake.

Command-Line Options.   These are the command line options for `cat`:

-s   Don't complain about nonexistent source files.

-u   Don't buffer the output. With this option set, `cat` writes each byte as soon as it can. When a group of bytes is read in, `cat` writes out all of those bytes before reading any more. Note that input buffering is not affected; even with –u specified, cat may read any number of bytes at a time. Moreover, some systems use unbuffered output in all cases, while others use unbuffered output when certain other options are present even if –u isn't.

Buffered output is usually more efficient because it reduces the number of separate output transmissions, but in some unusual circumstances involving FIFO special files, you may find that your output seems to be blocked unless you specify –u. Some non-POSIX systems use the –u option to distinguish between line buffering (everything up to a ⟨newline⟩ in a batch) and block buffering (a fixed number of bytes in a batch).[2]

–v   Represent nonprinting characters as sequences of printable ones. The nonprinting characters have ASCII codes less than 32 or greater than 126.

- The characters from 0 to 31 are shown as '∧*c*' (control-*c*), where *c* has the character's ASCII code plus 64. For example, the character whose ASCII code is 8 (backspace) is represented as '∧H' since H has ASCII code 72.

- The character 127 (delete) is represented as '∧?'.

- The characters from 128 to 257 are represented as 'M-*c*' (meta-*c*), where *c* has the character's ASCII code minus 128. For example, the character 140 is represented as 'M-∧L' since L has ASCII code 76 and ∧L therefore has ASCII code $76 - 64 = 12$.

The exceptions to this rule are ⟨tab⟩s, ⟨newline⟩s, and ⟨formfeed⟩s, which are sent unchanged to the output of cat (but see the descriptions of the –e and –t options).

–e   Put $ at the end of each line. This option is only valid if the –v option is also present.

–t   Show tabs as ∧I. This option is only valid if the –v option is also present.

3.4   Linking, Moving, and Copying Files with ln, mv, and cp

The commands ln (link), mv (move), and cp (copy) are closely related:
- Linking to a file creates another name for it.
- Moving a file changes one of its names.
- Copying a file replicates its contents under another name.

---

2. Kernighan and Pike (reference [B11]) give an example on pages 44–45 showing the effect of –u. Their example depends on this particular behavior, but they don't say so.

These commands, unlike most, do not use standard input or standard output by default.

3.4.1
Linking Files with ln

The ln command creates links to one or more existing files. The new links provide additional names for the files. Links are discussed in Section 2.7.5.

The forms of the ln command line are

> ln [-fs] *file pathname*
> ln [-fs] *file ... dir*

In the first form, ln links the pathname *pathname* to the file named by the pathname *file*; that is, *pathname* is made to designate *file*. If *pathname* is already linked to a file (i.e., it names an existing file), ln produces an error message and does not replace the existing link.[3] After the new link has been created, both *file* and *pathname* are names of the file previously named by *file*.

In the second form, ln creates a link in *dir* to each file in *file ...* and gives that link the same filename as *file*, provided again that no link with the same name already exists.

For example, suppose mabel and susan are subdirectories of your current directory and mabel contains the two files ron and don. Then the command

> ln mabel/* susan

constructs the links susan/ron and susan/don provided that neither of these names already exists as links within susan. After ln has executed, mabel/ron and susan/ron refer to the same file, as do mabel/don and susan/don.

Linking does not entail any copying of data and does not destroy any existing links unless you force that behavior with the -f option. When ln creates a link, the target pathname has the same set of permissions and the same owner and group as the source pathname.

You are not permitted to create a link from a directory in one file system to a file in another file system (see Section 2.7.4) unless the link is a symbolic link. You can specify a symbolic link with the -s option if your system supports symbolic links.

By default, ln creates hard links and asks for confirmation whenever it overwrites a link to a file lacking write permission. You can change this behavior with the following two command-line options:

-s   Create symbolic (soft) links rather than hard links. See Section 2.7.6 for a discussion of symbolic links. This option is not available on systems that do not support symbolic links.

-f   Don't ask for confirmation when overwriting a link that lacks write permission.

---

3. Older System V-based systems silently replace the existing link.

**3.4.2
Moving Files with** mv

The mv command moves one or more files from one directory, the source directory, to another directory, the target directory. If the source and target directories are both in the same file system, mv merely changes their links and does not move any data. If they are not, mv copies the data in the files from the source file system to the target file system, creates the necessary links in the target file system, and removes the links in the source file system. You can think of moving as a kind of renaming; the standard way to rename a file is to move it.

The POSIX version of mv, unlike some older versions, allows a directory to be moved to a different file system. Moving a file leaves its protection mode and ownership unchanged unless the move is across file systems; in this case, the ownership becomes that of the user who executed the mv command unless that user was the superuser. A file to be moved can itself be a directory; in this case, the entire subtree rooted at the directory is moved.

The forms of the mv command line are

> mv [-if] *file pathname*
> mv [-if] *file ... dir*

In the first form, a link is created from *pathname* to the file named by *file* and the original link from *file* is deleted. If *pathname* already was linked to a file (i.e., was a name of an existing file), the existing link is destroyed when the new link is created.[4]

In the second form, each file in *file ...* is moved to *dir*. The move preserves the filenames of the files that were moved. For example, suppose mabel and susan are subdirectories of your current directory and mabel contains the two files ron and don. Then the command

> mv mabel/* susan

moves mabel/ron to susan/ron and mabel/don to susan/don. After the move, the mabel directory is empty and the susan directory has the two files don and ron. If either don or ron previously existed in susan, the old version is unlinked (and deleted, unless it had other links).

With either form, any of the *file*s to be moved can be a directory rather than a regular file. With the first form, if *file* is a directory, then *pathname*, if it already exists, must name a directory. However, some older systems either don't support the ability to move directories in this manner or support it only for moves within a single file system.

By default, mv asks for confirmation whenever it overwrites a link to a file lacking write permission. You can change this behavior with the following command-line options:

-i   Ask for confirmation when overwriting any link no matter what its permissions (BSD only).

---

4. This is not the same thing as destroying the file itself, since other links to the file may remain.

-f   Don't ask for confirmation even when overwriting a link that lacks write permission.

**3.4.3
Copying Files
with** cp

The cp command copies one or more files. Unlike ln and mv, cp actually copies data and does not just reshuffle directory entries.

The cp command is not the only way to copy files. The cat program (see Section 3.3) is often an alternative to cp. The pax program with the -rw options (see Section 3.14.1) and the cpio program with the -p option (see Section 3.14.3) both copy files and directories from one directory to another, reconstructing the original directory structure at the destination. You can also use the tar archiver for the same purpose, as in the following example:

```
tar cvf - sourcedir | (cd destdir; tar xf -)
```

Here the first call on tar packs up the files in sourcedir. The resulting archive is piped to the second call on tar, which unpacks the files into destdir.

The forms of the cp command line are:

cp [-fip] *ifile ofile*
cp [-fiprR] *iname ... odir*

where *ifile* is the pathname of an input file, *ofile* is the pathname of an output file, each *iname* is the pathname of an input file or directory, and *odir* is the pathname of an output directory. Input items are called "sources"; output items are called "targets".

- The first form applies when the target is a file. In this case there may be only one source, a file. The input file is copied to the output file.

- The second form applies when the target is a directory.

A copy may be recursive or nonrecursive, although System V versions of cp generally support only nonrecursive copying and issue an error message if you attempt a recursive copy. The -r option specifies recursive copying. It affects only the copying of directories.

Nonrecursive Copying.   For a nonrecursive copy, the directory *odir* must already exist and each *iname* must name a file rather than a directory. Each input file is copied to the output directory and given the same base name it had originally. For example, suppose that /home/cathy and fishes are both directories, with /home/cathy containing files trout and pike. Then the command

```
cp /home/cathy/* fishes
```

copies /home/cathy/trout to a file named fishes/trout and /home/cathy/pike to a file named fishes/pike. If a target file does not exist, a file of that name is created. If a target file does exist, then the link specified by the target file is removed and a new link is created. The data is then copied from each source file to its corresponding target file. After the copy, the source and target files are independent—a change to one file does not affect the other.

A file created by cp assumes the owner, mode, and permissions of the target file if that file existed prior to the copy; otherwise, it assumes those of the source file.[5] If a copy operation would destroy an existing link to a file whose write permission is turned off, cp displays the protection mode of that file (as a three-digit octal number) and asks you to confirm the copy. Typing something that starts with 'y' permits the copy; typing anything else cancels it.

Recursive Copying. The behavior of a recursive copy depends on whether the output directory *odir* already exists:

- If *odir* does not already exist, the input must consist of a single directory. After creating *odir*, cp copies all the files and subdirectories of the input directory to *odir*, thereby making *odir* a clone of the input directory.

- If *odir* already exists, each input file is copied to the output directory as it would be for a nonrecursive copy. Each input directory is reproduced as a subdirectory of the output directory, including both its contained files and contained subdirectories.

Command-Line Options. The cp command has the following command-line options:

-i   Ask interactively for confirmation of each copy.

-p   Preserve the permission modes and modification time of the original file.

-R
-r   Copy subdirectories recursively as described previously. The target file must be a directory. The difference between -R and -r is how special files are treated, since such files cannot normally be copied. For -R, the preferred form under most circumstances, FIFO special files are replicated. Other special files cause an error diagnostic to be generated but do not prevent the copy from continuing with the remaining files. For -r, the treatment of special files depends on the implementation.[6]

-f   Force copying if necessary by unlinking the destination file.

---

5. The sticky bit of the target file is not set unless the copying is done by the superuser.

6. Historically, BSD systems just read the files and copy them straightforwardly when -r is specified. Some applications depend on that behavior. That's why POSIX retained the -r option, but with lots of caveats.

3.5   Removing Files

The two commands for removing files are `rm` and `rmdir`. Rm can remove any type of file, while `rmdir` can only remove directories. On the other hand, `rmdir` can delete parent directories that become empty as a result of earlier removals, while `rm` can't.

"Removing" a file, whether an ordinary file or a directory, means removing a filename from a directory rather than removing the file itself. If there are other links to the file, those links remain and the file itself remains. A file is deleted only when its last link is removed. Since a directory is a particular kind of file, the same rule applies to directories.

3.5.1
Removing Links with `rm`

The `rm` command removes links to files, either ordinary files or directories. A file is deleted when all its links have been deleted, so removing the only link to a file deletes the file itself.

The form of the `rm` command line is

> `rm [-firR]` *file* ...

where each file in *file* ... may include links to directories if the `-r` option is present. By default, `rm` asks you for confirmation if you attempt to remove a link to a file that does not have write permission.[7] The confirmation query indicates the file's permissions as a three-digit octal number (see Section 2.8). You can change this behavior with the `-i` and `-f` options described below.

Rm returns a zero exit code if it succeeds in deleting all the specified links and a nonzero exit code otherwise.

Command-Line Options.   These are the command-line options for `rm`:

`-i`   Ask interactively for confirmation of each removal. A response that starts with 'y' or 'Y' indicates that the file should be removed; any other response indicates that it shouldn't. Rm asks for these confirmations even if standard input is not a terminal.

`-R`
`-r`   Remove links to directories recursively; that is, remove links to the directories and to all files and subdirectories contained in them either directly or indirectly. This option in effect lops off an entire branch of the directory tree. Rm still asks you to confirm the removal of links without write permission, but if

---

7. You may remove a link to a file if you have write permission for the directory containing the link (see Section 2.8). The permissions of the file are irrelevant—the confirmation query is just a precaution.

standard input is not from the terminal or if you've specified the -f option, the query is suppressed. If you reject removal of a link, rm won't remove any directory that contains that link either directly or indirectly.

-f   Don't ask for confirmation of removals, even for links that lack write permission. If you specify both -f and -i, -f governs.

Note: You can't remove links from a directory for which you don't have write permission no matter what options you use.

3.5.2
Removing Links to Directories with rmdir

The rmdir command removes links to directories. The form of its command line is

    rmdir [-ps] *dir* ...

where *dir* ... is a list of directory pathnames. For example,

    rmdir denver

causes rmdir to remove the link to the denver subdirectory of the current directory. Unlike rm -r, rmdir won't remove a link to a directory unless the directory is empty.

   Rmdir returns a zero exit code if it succeeds in deleting all the specified links and a nonzero exit code otherwise.

Command-Line Options.   The command-line options for rmdir are as follows:

-p   For each pathname *dir*, remove the link to each empty directory in the pathname as well as to *dir*. For example, suppose you execute the command

          rmdir -p ~/buildings/shacks/doors

          If removing the link to doors leaves its parent directory shacks empty, then the link to ~/buildings/shacks is removed; if that removal leaves buildings empty, the the link to ~/buildings is removed, and so forth. Rmdir sends a message to standard error announcing each link that it removes and each removal attempt that fails.

-s   Suppress the messages generated by rmdir. This option is not included in POSIX.

3.5.3
Removing Files with Unusual Names

Once in a while you may accidentally create a file with a name containing characters meaningful to the shell, such as '|' and ';', or containing other troublesome characters such as spaces, hyphens, backspaces, or newlines. You can't remove these files with rm in the obvious way because you can't type their names on the command line. Sometimes you can remove them by quoting the troublesome characters. For example,

    rm "␣"

removes a file whose name consists of a single space. A more general method is to type

```
rm -i -- *
```

and select just those files you want to delete. The '--' is needed to handle file names that start with '-', since otherwise those names will be misinterpreted as command-line arguments (see Section 2.12.4).[8] Better yet, use wildcards in combination with legitimate parts of the file name. For instance, to remove a file named a Ctrl H b, you could type

```
rm -i a?b
```

The -i in this case is a precaution against unintentionally selecting a different file.

Another method, useful when the file name contains nonprinting characters, is to delete the file by specifying its i-node (see Section 2.7.7). The command 'ls -ib' lists the files in the current directory, showing all the nonprinting characters in octal notation and indicating the i-node number for each one. If the file you want to delete has i-node number n, you can then delete it using the find command (see Section 3.8) as follows:

```
find . -inum n -exec rm {} \;
```

3.6   Examining Files or Output with a Pager

A *pager* is a program for viewing the output of a command at a terminal, one screenful at a time, thereby solving the problem of text flying by on the screen faster than you can read it. For example, you can use the combination 'ls | more' to view the results of ls with the more pager. You can also use a pager to examine a file in the same way.

In this section we describe only one pager, the more pager as defined by POSIX, but other pagers are very similar. All those we know of use the convention that the h command displays a help screen showing what commands are available, and in some cases what command-line options are available.

Another pager of particular interest is less, now available as part of the GNU utilities. We prefer less to more because it is free of several historical anomalies that afflict more, and since it is ordinarily only used interactively, the issue of shell-script compatibility doesn't arise. You can obtain less electronically by FTP from prep.ai.mit.edu, directory /pub/gnu, or from any other location that has the GNU software.

You can also use an editor to examine a file—and a full-screen editor such as vi or emacs (see Chapter 8) provides at least as many conveniences

---

8. Some older versions of rm use '-' to end the arguments.

as does a pager. If you edit in read-only mode, you don't need to worry about modifying the file by accident. However, you generally can't use an editor to view standard input; an editor expects its input to contain editing commands, not the text to be edited.

Finally, we mention the `pg` pager that often comes with System V. While better than old versions of `more`, it really has no advantages over a POSIX-conformant `more` or over `less`.

3.6.1
The `more` Pager

The `more` command enables you to examine one or more files[9] at your terminal a screenful at a time. You can also use `more` to examine standard input, and hence to examine the output of a command by piping it to `more`. Unlike more primitive pagers, `more` allows you to move backward as well as forward through a file. The form of the `more` command line is

> `more [-ceisu] [-n` *number*`] [-t` *tag*`] [-p` *cmd*`] [`*file...* `]`

The files designated by the pathnames *file* ... are displayed in sequence; when you terminate the display of one file, `more` begins the display of the next one or terminates if there aren't any more. The filename '-' designates standard input; if you omit the *file*s, `more` assumes that standard input is what you intend. You control the portion of the input that you see on your screen by issuing interactive commands to `more`. These commands are described below.

There are many versions of `more`. The version you have may not support all of the POSIX commands, but it's likely that the commands it does support have the same meaning as the POSIX ones below. The `h` command will show you what is available.[10] Some common points of difference are:

- ability to scroll backwards
- default action at end-of-file
- different behavior for `s` and `f` commands
- different behavior for `b` and Ctrl B commands

3.6.2
The Model of the Screen

The specifications of `more` assume that a screen contains a certain number of lines, either given explicitly by the `-n` option or obtained from the environment, and similarly, a certain number of columns obtained from the environment. The last line of the screen is reserved for status information and also for a prompt; thus the number of lines containing data is one less than the screen length. If a line to be displayed contains too many characters to fit on a row of the screen, it is wrapped to one or more

---

9. The files can be of any type—even binary programs. In particular, `more` can view files containing null characters.

10. The POSIX description of `more` contains a number of ambiguities and conflicting specifications. We have interpreted these as best we can, but implementors may differ with us and with each other on what they mean.

additional rows. These rows are logically independent; that is, commands pertaining to a single line affect them separately. The file is said to be positioned at end-of-file if the last line of the file is visible on the screen.

A number of commands cause a particular line of the file to be brought to the top of the screen. If the number of lines remaining is less than the screen length, most versions of `more` will indicate in one way or another that the rest of the file is empty, usually by filling out the screen with rows containing a single tilde. You'll get the same effect if you view a file that has fewer lines than there are on the screen.

3.6.3 Interactive Commands for `more`

To advance through a file one page at a time, press ⎵Space⎵ after you've examined each page. If you've specified more than one file, then when `more` reaches end-of-file on a file other than the last, it will prompt you for another action. If you try to advance further, `more` will terminate the display of the file and proceed to the next one. After displaying the last line of the last (or only) file, `more` will exit.[11] (The `-e` option modifies this behavior.) Note that a "goto"-type command, such as a forward search, doesn't cause viewing of a file to be terminated. You can use the commands described below to move around the file in a different order, to examine a later file in the sequence, or to return to a previous file.

Block-mode terminals, which transmit characters a line or a screenful at a time, may not be able to accept commands that don't end with a ⟨newline⟩. If you have such a terminal, `more` will probably accept the usual commands as long as you follow each one with a ⟨newline⟩, with a ⟨newline⟩ by itself having the usual meaning of "advance to the next line".

Many of the commands below are the same as those in the `vi` editor, reflecting the BSD ancestry of `more`.

Help Command. The following command displays a screen that lists the available commands:

h	Display a help list containing an abbreviated summary of the `more` commands.

Command for Quitting. The following command is what you use to terminate `more` at any time:

q	
:q	
ZZ	Quit the program.

Motion Commands. The commands below enable you to move around the file. The variable n denotes a decimal integer. If you give a count n with any of these commands, the command moves or scrolls by n lines

---

11. The behavior at end-of-file is one of the reasons we prefer `less` to `more`. If you invoke `less` without the `-e` option, the only way you can terminate viewing a file is to do so explicitly; viewing the end of the file or even moving forward from the end-of-file doesn't terminate the view. With `-e` specified, viewing is terminated when you specify a forward motion and the last line of the file is already visible. We find that behavior far more sensible and convenient.

(never *n* screenfuls). The difference between moving and scrolling is that moving skips over lines that don't appear in the final screen while scrolling displays all the lines (unless the -c option forces the screen to be redrawn). The end result is the same, but with a scrolling command you can see the lines fly by unless your terminal is too fast for that. You can see the difference between moving and scrolling by comparing the effects of the commands '500f' and '500 Space'.

[*n*] j
[*n*] Space
[*n*] Enter   Scroll forward *n* lines, with a default of one screenful for Space and one line for j or Enter.

[*n*] k   Scroll backward *n* lines, with a default of one line.

[*n*] f
[*n*] Ctrl F   Move forward by *n* lines, with a default of one screenful.

[*n*] b
[*n*] Ctrl B   Move backward by *n* lines, with a default of one screenful.

[*n*] d
[*n*] Ctrl D   Scroll forward (down) by *n* lines, with a default of half a page. However, if you specify *n* explicitly, it becomes the default for subsequent d and u commands.

[*n*] u
[*n*] Ctrl U   Scroll backward (up) by *n* lines, with a default of half a page. However, if you specify *n* explicitly, it becomes the default for subsequent d and u commands.

[*n*] s   Skip forward by *n* lines, with a default of one line. The *n*th line following the last line on the current screen becomes the top line of the new screen.

Positioning Commands.   The following commands move you to a specific location in the file or mark a position in the file. Moving *to* a position *n* causes the screenful of lines beginning with line *n* of the file to be displayed.

[*n*] g   Move to the *n*th line of the file, or to the first line if *n* is not given.

[*n*] G   Move to the *n*th line of the file, or display the last screenful of the file if *n* is not given. Note that G by itself is *not* equivalent to *l*G, where *l* is the last line of the file, since in the latter case only the last line of the file will appear on the screen.

m *letter*   Mark the current position in the file with the lowercase letter *letter*.

' *letter*   Return to the position that was previously marked with the letter *letter*.

''   Return to the position from which the last large movement (any movement of more than a screenful) was executed or to the beginning of the file if no such movement has taken place.

Searching Commands. The following commands enable you to locate a pattern within a file:

[*k*] / [!] *pat* (Enter)
         Move forward to the *k*th instance of a line containing the pattern *pat*, where *pat* is a basic regular expression (see Section 2.17.1) and *k* is an unsigned integer. The default for *k* is 1. If *pat* is preceded by '!', the search is for lines that do *not* contain the pattern. If *pat* is empty, the previous search is repeated.

[*k*] ? [!] *pat* (Enter)
         Move backward to the *k*th instance of a line containing the pattern *pat*, using the same rules that apply to /*pat*/.

[*k*]n   Move to the *k*th instance of a line containing the pattern most recently searched for (default is the first such line). The direction of search is the same as in the previous search.

[*k*]N   Like n, but searches in the direction opposite from the previous search.

:t *tag* (Enter)
         Move to the line located by the tag *tag* (see Section 8.5).

Each of these searches starts at the line after the current position (or, in the case of a backward search, at the line before the current position). The current line does not qualify for the search.

Commands for Refreshing the Screen. The following commands redisplay the current page:

(Ctrl)L

r   Redisplay the current page. This command is useful when your screen has gotten scrambled.

R   Reread the file and redisplay the current page.[12] If the file has changed while you were viewing it, you'll see the modified version.

Commands for Selecting a File. The following commands enable you to move among the files in the file list on the command line.

[*k*]:n   Examine the *k*th next file (default is the immediately next file).

[*k*]:p   Examine the *k*th previous file (default is the immediately previous file).

---

12. If the file being displayed is nonseekable, however, no input is discarded, so r and R behave identically.

:e [*file*] (Enter)
> Examine the file whose pathname is *file*. If *file* is given as '#', reexamine the previous file (like ':p'). If *file* is omitted, reload and reexamine the current file (useful if a file changed while you were examining it). If *file* contains any wildcards, all designated files are examined (using the shell's rules for filename expansion), so a name such as '*.h' causes all files whose names ended in '.h' to be examined.

Miscellaneous Commands.   There are three miscellaneous commands:

v
> Invoke an editor to edit the file being examined. The name of the editor is taken from the environment variable EDITOR if it's defined and otherwise defaults to vi. Generally the editor is initially positioned at the part of the file at which you were looking. When you're done, the file being examined reflects any changes you made.

(Ctrl) G
=
> Show the name of the file being examined, its sequence number among all files to be examined, the current line number, the current byte number, the total number of bytes in the file, and the position as a percentage. The information appears on the status line, usually at the bottom of the screen.

!*cmd*
> Execute the command *cmd* in a subshell. This command is not included in POSIX but is provided by nearly all versions of more.

**3.6.4
Command-Line
Options for** more

The following options enable you to start examining files at a place other than the first line. They affect every file that you display, not just the first one.

-p *cmd*
+*cmd*
> Execute the more interactive command *cmd* before starting to examine each file. The usual purpose of this option is to start looking at the file someplace other than at the beginning. For example, the command line

    more -p /scads plethora surfeit

> causes the display of each of the files plethora and surfeit to begin with the first line containing scads. The '+*cmd*' form is obsolescent.

The following options affect the behavior of more in other ways:

-i
> Ignore case when doing a pattern match.

-n *number*
> Assume *number* lines per screenful, overriding the value obtained from the environment.

-s   Replace consecutive empty lines with a single empty line. This option is useful for viewing output with a lot of empty lines.

-c   If a screen is to be displayed that has no lines in common with the previous screen, bypass scrolling and display the new screen directly. In addition, clear the screen before displaying the first screenful of more's output.

-u   Treat ⟨backspace⟩ as a printable control character. Without this option, backspacing combined with underscoring usually produces underlined or emboldened text on your screen.

-e   If the argument list contained only one file, exit immediately after displaying the last line of that file. Otherwise, exit only after twice reaching the end-of-file of the last file without an intervening operation.

-t *tag*   Identical in effect to

               -p :t *tag*

**3.6.5
Environment
Variables for** more

The following environment variables affect the behavior of more:

LINES   The number of lines in a screen, assumed to be the size of a "screenful". If it isn't set, the number of lines is taken from the description of your terminal (see Section 2.15).

COLUMNS   The number of columns across the screen. If it isn't set, the number of lines is taken from the description of your terminal.

TERM   The name of your terminal type.

EDITOR   The name (not necessarily a full pathname) of the editor to be used when you type the v command.

MORE   A string giving a default set of options to be used when more is called. Any options you provide explicitly override the ones in MORE. A typical value for MORE is -ic.

3.7   Printing Files

The following commands relate to printing files:

- The POSIX and System V command lp requests that files be sent to a printer. The corresponding BSD command is lpr.
- The System V command lpstat provides status information about printers and printer requests. The corresponding BSD command is lpq.
- The System V command cancel cancels a print request. The corresponding BSD command is lprm.
- The pr command formats a file for printing but doesn't actually send the output to a printer. It is intended to be used as a filter.

Of these commands, only `lp` and `pr` are included in POSIX.

A print request may include multiple files. Each request is assigned a request ID that you can use when inquiring about the status of the request or cancelling it.

On a system having several equivalent printers, such printers are usually grouped into a named class of printers. It's usually better to send a request to a class of printers than to a specific printer, since you'll get the results sooner when some printers in the class are available but others are busy.

3.7.1
Printing Files
with `lp`

The `lp` command causes a set of files to be queued for printing. The POSIX version of `lp` supports only the `-c`, `-d`, and `-n` command-line options described below; the others are supported under System V.

The files specified in a single call on `lp` are treated as a single request. When you issue the request, `lp` returns a request ID that you can later use to refer to the request. The `-m` and `-w` options cause a notice to be sent to you when the request has been completed.

The form of the `lp` command line is

   `lp` [-cmsw] [-d *dest*] [-n *n*] [-t *title*] [-o *prinopt*] [*file* ...]

where each *file* is a file to be printed. Some versions of `lp` allow options and files to be intermixed. If you omit the files, standard input is printed; using `lp` at the end of a pipeline is the usual way of printing the output of a command. If '-' appears as a file, the contents of standard input are transcribed and printed.

You can use the '-d' option to specify a particular printer or class of printers. Without that option, `lp` gets the destination as follows:

(1)   From the `LPDEST` environment variable if it exists
(2)   Otherwise, from the `PRINTER` environment variable if it exists
(3)   Otherwise, from a system default

Older System V systems don't recognize the `PRINTER` variable, however. The destination may be either a specific printer or a class of printers.

By default, `lp` does not make copies of files you ask to have printed. Unless you've specified the `-c` option, any changes that you make to those files between the time you issue the request and the time the files are printed appear in the printed version.

Command-Line Options.   The following options affect what is actually printed.

`-n` *n*   Make *n* copies of the output. By default, one copy is printed.

`-t` *title*   Put *title* on the banner page of the output (if there is a banner page). Normally you should enclose *title* in quotes as in the command

            `lp -t "Dining Out in Antarctica" penguins`

         This option is not included in POSIX.

-o *printopt*

> Specify a printer option. The names and effects of printer options available to you depend on your system. A typical option for a dot matrix printer might specify letter- or draft-quality output. You may include more than one -o option; you must specify '-o' for each one. This option is not included in POSIX.

The following options affect how a print request is handled:

-c

> Exit from `lp` only when access to the input files is no longer needed. Under System V, the interpretation of this option is more specific: make copies of the files when the command is executed. Specifying this option ensures that changes to a file between the time you issue the print request and the time it is printed have no effect on the printed output. By default, no safeguard is provided against such changes affecting the output.
>
> If you specify the -c option, it is safe to modify the printed files once the command has terminated no matter whether you're operating under a POSIX system or under a System V system.

-d *dest*

> Send the job to the specific printer or class of printers name by *dest*. If you send a job to a class of printers, it is printed by the first available printer in the class.

The following options affect the information produced by a print request:

-s

> Suppress messages issued by `lp` itself.

-m

> Send a mail message to the requestor when the request has been completed.

-w

> Write a message to the requestor's terminal when all files in a request have been printed. If the requestor isn't logged in, a mail message is sent instead.

None of these options are included in POSIX.

**3.7.2
Printing Files
Under BSD with `lpr`**

Under BSD, the command for sending files to a printer is `lpr`. To examine the printer queue, use `lpq`; to remove a job from the queue, use `lprm`.

  The form of the `lpr` command line is

> lpr [-flpsrmh] [-i [*n*]] [-T *text*] [-w *n*] [-P *printer*]
>   [-#*n*] [-J *text*] [-C *text*] [*file* ...]

where the *files* are the files to be printed. Standard input is printed if you don't specify any files, so `lpr` at the end of a pipeline prints the output of the preceding programs in the pipeline. The options are described below.

Filtering Options. By default, files to be printed are sent to the printer without interpretation. The following options specify filtering to be applied to each file before it is printed:

-i [*n*]   Indent the output by *n* columns. If you don't specify *n*, lpr uses 8 as the default.

-f   Interpret the first character of each line according to the Fortran conventions for carriage control.

-l   Print control characters, suppress page breaks.

-p   Pass the files through pr (see Section 3.7.5).

The following two options are meaningful only if you specify -p:

-T *text*   Use *text* as the title passed to pr.

-w *n*   Pass *n* to pr as the page width.

Most systems provide additional lpr options for filtering the output of specific programs such as TEX and troff.

Job Control Options. The following options enable you to control the printer used for the job, the number of copies printed, and the treatment of the files to be printed. By default, lpr makes its own copy of each file to be printed and saves the copy in a spooling directory until it can be printed; therefore, any changes to the file after lpr has received it do not affect the printed copy.

-P *printer* Print the job on the printer named *printer*.

-#*n*   Print *n* copies.

-s   Use symbolic links for the files to be printed. This option saves storage space, but implies that changes made to the file before it is printed affect the printed copy. If you specify this option, take care not to remove a file before it is printed.

-r   Remove the file after printing it.

-m   Send a mail message to the requestor when all the files in the request have been printed.

Header Page. A header page, called the "burst page" in BSD documents, precedes each print job and contains identifying information for the job. The following options enable you to change the information on the header page or suppress it altogether.

-J *text*   Use *text* as the job name on the header page.

-C *text*   Use *text* as the system name on the header page.

-h   Suppress the header page.

**3.7.3
Displaying Printer
Status with** lpstat

The System V command lpstat displays the status of print requests. It also displays information about the printers attached to your system and what they are doing. The BSD version of this command is lpq.

The form of the lpstat command line is

> lpstat [-drst] [-o [*list*]] [-u [*list*]] [-p [*list*]]
> [-a [*list*]] [-c [*list*]] [-v [*list*]]

If you omit the options, you'll get the status of all print requests, both yours and those of other users; however, on enhanced security systems you may see only your own.

Several options accept a list of items as an argument. You may provide this list either by separating the items by commas with no spaces after the commas or by enclosing the list in quotes and separating the items by spaces. If you omit an optional list, lpstat assumes all applicable items. For instance, the command 'lpstat -o' produces a list of all pending print requests.

Command-Line Options. The following options produce information about the status of print requests.

-o [*list*]   Show the status of each output request in *list*. An item in *list* can be a request ID, a printer, or a printer class. The request IDs are those you receive from lp.

-u [*ulist*]   Show the status of each output request for each user in *ulist*. If you omit *ulist*, the output requests for all users are shown.

-t   Show all status information.

The following options produce information about the status of the printers and the print scheduler.

-p [*list*]   Show the status of each printer in *list*.

-a [*list*]   Show the acceptance status of each printer or printer class in *list*. A printer may be unable to accept requests either because it isn't available or because there isn't enough file space to hold any more print requests.

-s   Show a summary of information about the printers attached to your system. The summary includes the system default destination, the class names and printer names known to your system, and the device associated with each printer.

-r   Show the status of the scheduler that handles print requests.

The -t option described above also shows information about printers and classes.

The following options produce information about the printers themselves.

-d   Show the name of the default printer.

-c [*list*]   Show the names of the printer classes and their members.

-v [*list*]   Show the pathnames of the devices associated with the printers
in *list*.

3.7.4
Cancelling Printer
Requests with
cancel

The System V command cancel enables you to cancel an outstanding
print request. Unless you have superuser privileges, you cannot cancel a
print request issued by another user. The BSD version of this command
is lprm.

The cancel command has two forms:

    cancel [*id...*] [*printer...*]
    cancel -u *login-names* [*printer...*]

In the first form, each *id* identifies a printer request and each *printer* identifies a particular printer. The printer request IDs are those announced
by lp. You can also see the IDs of your pending printer requests by using
lpstat. Cancelling a printer cancels the request that is currently printing
on that printer (assuming it's one of yours).

In the second form, not supported on older systems, all print requests
associated with the users specified by *login-names* are cancelled, except
that if you specify any *printer*s, only requests queued for those printers
are cancelled. Unless you are the superuser, the only valid login name is
your own. If you specify more than one name in *login-names*, the list must
be enclosed in quotes so that it appears as a single argument to cancel.

3.7.5
Formatting Files
for Printing
with pr

The pr command formats files for printing on a line printer. Although pr
behaves like a filter such as cut or sed and is not directly related to the
other programs discussed above, it is rarely useful for any other purpose—
that's why we discuss it here rather than in Chapter 4. It works best when
the destination printer has a single fixed-width font; for other kinds of
printers, the output that it produces is likely to be unreadable. Note that
with the -m option, you can produce side-by-side formatting of two or
more files.

The form of the pr command line is

    pr [+ *bgn*] [- *col*] [-adfFmrt] [-e[*tc*][*k*]] [-h *hdr*] [-i[*tc*][*k*]]
        [-l *lines*] [-n[*tc*][*k*]] [-o *offset*] [-s[*tc*]] [-w *width*] [*file* ...]

If you don't specify any files, pr formats standard input. It sends its
results to standard output, which is usually piped to lp. The pr program,
in violation of the usual conventions for command-line syntax, does not
allow any space between the name of an option and its arguments.

Output consists of a sequence of pages. By default, each page contains
66 lines, but you can change the page length with the -l option.[13] Each
page starts with a five-line header and ends with a five-line trailer, unless
the page length is 10 lines or less, or you inhibit the header and trailer

---

13. Laser printers usually print only 60 or 61 lines on a page at their default settings, so 66
is an inappropriate default for them.

with the -t option. The header and trailer lines are counted as part of the page length. The header consists of two blank lines, a line of text, and two more blank lines; the trailer consists of five blank lines. The default header text contains the page number, the date and time, and the pathname of the file; you can replace the pathname by other text with the -h option.

You can produce either single-column or multicolumn output. For single-column output, lp allows a line to have any length. For multicolumn output, it assumes a fixed total line width. That width is divided by the number of columns to obtain the width of a single column, allowing for at least one space between columns. Lines exceeding this width are truncated unless you specify the -s option. The default total line width is 72 characters, but you can change it with the -w option.

Multicolumn output has three variations:

- If you specify the -m option and provide more than one input file, each input file appears in its own column.

- If you specify the -*col* option but not the -a option, the input text is arranged vertically into *col* columns. Successive lines of text on a page are placed in the first column until it is filled, then in the second column, and so forth.

- If you specify both the -*col* option and the -a option, the input text is arranged horizontally across the page into *col* columns. Successive lines of text on a page are placed into the columns of the first row, then into the columns of the second row, and so forth.

Command-Line Options.   The following options determine the page dimensions:

-l *lines*	Set the page length to *lines* lines. The default is 66 lines (which is also what you get if you set *lines* to 0). If the page length is 10 or less, the header and trailer lines are omitted.
-w *width*	Set the line width to *width* characters. The default line width is 72 characters. This option does not affect single-column output.
-o *offset*	Offset each line by *offset* spaces so as to produce a left margin n spaces wide. The offset is not counted as part of the line width.

The following options define the layout of multicolumn output:

-*col*	Format the output using *col* columns, where n is an integer. This option conflicts with the -m option.
-a	Format columns across the page, with successive input lines filling an output line before proceeding to the next output line. This option conflicts with the -m option.
-m	Merge and format files, one file per column. This option conflicts with the -*col* and -a options.

-s[*tc*]   Use *tc* as the separator character between columns (i.e., place a single *tc* between adjacent columns). You must not leave a space between '-s' and *tc*. The default for *tc* is ⟨tab⟩. If you specify this option, lines within columns are *not* truncated.

The following options affect the header and trailer areas:

-h *hdr*   Use *hdr* as the page header text instead of the pathname. The date, time, and page number still appear.

-t   Don't set aside space for top and bottom margins; that is, omit the header and trailer. This option nullifies the -h option. If the page length is less than 10, the header and trailer are omitted in any case.

The following options affect the treatment of tabs and of consecutive spaces:

-e[*tc*][*k*]   Replace each tab character in the input with spaces, assuming tab stops at positions $1, k + 1, 2 \times k + 1$, etc. If *tc* is specified, it is taken as the tab character. (The character *tc* must not be a digit.) If *k* is omitted or specified as zero, a default tab spacing of 8 is assumed.

-i[*tc*][*k*]   Replace consecutive spaces with tabs wherever possible, assuming tab stops at positions $1, k + 1, 2 \times k + 1$, etc. If *tc* is specified, it is taken as the tab character. (The character *tc* must not be a digit.) If *k* is omitted or specified as zero, a default tab spacing of 8 is assumed. You must not leave a space between '-i' and *tc*.

The following options produce various other effects on the output:

+*bgn*   Start formatted output at page *bgn*. **Note:** This option does not follow the standard rules for options since it does not start with '-'.

-d   Format the output with double spacing.

-n[*tc*][*k*]   Provide *k*-digit line numbers followed by the character *tc*. You must not leave a space between '-n' and *tc*. In the case of multicolumn output, the line numbers appear on each line, not in each column, and are counted as part of the line width. The default for *tc* is ⟨tab⟩; the default for *k* is 5. For example, you could get two-column output of a file, with line numbering corresponding to the input lines, with the command

```
pr -t -n file | pr +2
```

-F   End pages with formfeeds rather than linefeeds. If you specify this option, all trailing empty lines on a page, including the trailer, are deleted.

-f   Like -F, except that there is a pause before beginning the first page if standard output is associated with a terminal. This option is not supported by POSIX but is found on some System V systems.

The following options affect your interaction with pr:

-p   Pause and send an alert to standard error before starting each
            page if the output is being sent to a terminal. This option is
            not included in POSIX.

-r   Don't issue messages about files that can't be opened.

3.8   **Finding Files with** find

The find program searches specified parts of the UNIX file system for files
that match a criterion. The form of the command line is

> find *pathname* ... [*criterion*]

Here *pathname* ... is a list of pathnames of files and directories (usually
just directories). In the simpler case, the search criterion *criterion* is a
sequence of primary tests, each indicated by a hyphen. Each primary
test tests a candidate file for some property, though some primary tests
are always satisfied and are executed just for their side effects. More
generally, *criterion* is an arbitrary logical combination of tests built up
from the primary tests.

The -print primary test is particularly useful. It is always true, and
as a side effect causes the pathname of each located file to be produced
on standard output. If *criterion* contains none of the tests -exec, -ok, or
-print described below (or is omitted altogether), it is treated as though
it were enclosed in parentheses and followed by -print. In other words,
-print is an implicit test in most cases, though some older versions of
find don't support that convention.

The specification *pathname* ... generates a list of files to be tested against
the criterion. That list consists of all files, subdirectories themselves
included, in the directory tree descending from each of the specified
pathnames. A nondirectory pathname is merely included by itself. The
entire criterion is applied to a file before the next file is tested. The tests
in a sequence are "and"ed together and act as filters; if a test fails, the
remaining tests are not executed.

For example, the command

> find /usr -name "v*.h"

sends to standard output a list of all files contained within /usr and its
subdirectories whose names start with 'v' and end with '.h'. The output

action results from the implicit `-print` test. Each file is shown with its entire relative pathname. The list might look like this:

```
/usr/spool/uucppublic/src/vlimit.h
/usr/include/sys/var.h
/usr/include/sys/vt.h
/usr/include/sys/vtoc.h
/usr/include/values.h
/usr/include/varargs.h
```

Quoting 'v*.h' is essential to ensuring that `find`, not the shell, interprets the wildcard '*'.

Some older BSD versions of `find` recognize the simpler form

> `find` *string*

This command produces a list of all known files whose names contain *string* as a substring.[14] For consistency with POSIX, 4.4BSD uses the command `locate` for that purpose.

**3.8.1
Primary Tests
for `find`**

The primary tests described below return "true" or "false", depending on the file to which they are applied.

Meaning of Numerical Values in Tests. A numerical value n appearing in a test may be given in one of three ways:

- n by itself indicates exactly the value n.
- $-n$ indicates a value less than n.
- $+n$ indicates a value greater than n.

For example, the test '`-size +1000c`' is satisfied by files containing more than 1000 characters.

Testing Properties of Files. The following tests test properties of files:

`-name` *file* True if the current file matches *file*, with wildcards taken into consideration (see Section 2.9.1). Be sure to quote *file* if it contains any wildcard characters to ensure that the wildcards are interpreted by `find` rather than by your shell.

`-type` *c* True if the type of the current file is *c*, where *c* is one of the following:

- f   Ordinary file
- d   Directory
- b   Block device (see Section 2.18)
- c   Character device (see Section 2.18)
- p   FIFO special file (named pipe) (see Section 2.11.1)
- l   Symbolic link (see Section 2.7.5)
- s   Socket (see Section 2.11.2)

---

14. The known files are those in a database prepared by the system administrator and typically updated nightly.

Most of these letters are the same ones shown by the long listing format of `ls` (see Section 3.2.2). Some of these file types may not be available on your system.

-links *n* True if the current file has *n* links. For the form and interpretation of *n*, see the explanation of numerical values at the beginning of this section.

-perm [-]*mode*

True if the set of permissions of the current file (see Section 2.8) agrees with a set specified by the symbolic mode *mode* (see Section 2.8.3). The symbolic mode, which must not start with '-' (since that would create an ambiguity) is applied to an empty set of permissions to obtain the set of permissions *p* used for this test.

- If the '-' preceding *mode* is omitted, the test is satisfied when the permissions of the current file match *p* exactly.

- If the '-' is present, the test is satisfied when the permissions of the current file *include* all the permissions in *p*, enabling you to test for the presence of particular bits independently of any others that might be present.

For example, the test

```
-perm =r,u+w
```

is satisfied for files whose permissions are given exactly by `u=rw g=r o=r`, while the test

```
-perm -x
```

is satisfied for files that have execute permission for all, regardless of the other permissions.

-perm [-]*octnum*

True if the permissions of the current file are given by the octal number *octnum* (see Section 2.8.4). As with the previous form, the permissions of *octnum* must be a subset of the permissions of the file if '-' is present; an exact match is required if '-' is not present. This form is obsolescent and not recommended.

-user *uname*

True if the owner of the current file is user *uname*. If *uname* is a number, it is taken as a user number (unless there is a user whose name is that number).

-group *gname*

True if the current file belongs to group *gname*. Like *uname*, a numerical *gname* is taken as a group number unless there is a group whose name is that number.

-size *n*

-size *nc*   True if the current file is *n* units long. The units are bytes if
             c is present and 512-byte blocks otherwise.[15] The comparison
             is with the file size as shown by ls (see Section 3.2). For the
             form and interpretation of *n*, see the explanation of numerical
             values at the beginning of this section.

-atime *n*   True if the current file has been accessed *n* days ago.[16] For the
             form and interpretation of *n*, see the explanation of numerical
             values at the beginning of this section.

-mtime *n*   True if the current file has been modified *n* days ago. For the
             form and interpretation of *n*, see the explanation of numerical
             values at the beginning of this section.

-ctime *n*   True if the i-node information of the current file (creation time
             and permissions) has been modified *n* days ago. For the form
             and interpretation of *n*, see the explanation of numerical values
             at the beginning of this section.

-newer *file*

             True if the current file has been modified more recently than
             a particular file *file*.

-local   True if the current file resides on the local system rather than
             on a remote system. The -local test is not included in POSIX.

-inum *n*   True if the current file starts with i-node *n*. This test is useful
             for locating a file when a diagnostic message identifies it only
             by its i-node. The -inum test is not included in POSIX.

Applying Commands to Files.   The following tests produce their results
by applying a command to a file:

-exec *cmd*

             True if the command *cmd* returns an exit status of 0 (when
             executed as a child process). The end of *cmd* and its arguments
             must be marked with a semicolon, escaped or quoted so the
             shell doesn't interpret it (see Section 2.12.2). Within *cmd* you
             may use the notation '{}' to designate the pathname of the
             current file.

                 The exec criterion is often used for its side effects rather than
             for its result. For example, the command

```
find crud -name "*.bak" -type f -exec rm {} \;
```

---

15. The assumed 512-byte block size reflects the block size used on early UNIX systems.
Block sizes in current systems are far larger.

16. Find itself accesses directories and therefore affects their access times.

removes all files matching '`*.bak`' in the directory `crud` and its subdirectories. Be sure that the '`{}`' and '`;`' appear as separate arguments to `find` after all shell quotation has been removed. For example, this version of the previous command won't work:

```
find crud -name "*.bak" -type f -exec "rm {} ;"
```

The problem is that `find` sees '`rm {} ;`' as a single argument.

-ok *cmd*   Like -exec, except that the generated command is sent to standard error (normally the terminal) with a question mark after it. If you answer 'y', the command is executed; if you answer anything else, it isn't. An unexecuted command yields "false".

Tests Executed for Their Side Effects.   The following tests are always true and are executed only for the sake of their side effects. The side effects take place even if the file being tested is rejected by a subsequent test, so you should usually place these tests at the end of the criterion.

-print   Always true; as a side effect, sends the pathname of the current file (relative to the command-line pathname that contained it) to standard output.[17,18] Note that the command

```
find . -user bin
```

will produce those files in or below the current directory belonging to user `bin`, but the command

```
find . -print -user bin
```

will produce all files in the current directory no matter whom they belong to since -print will be tested before -user.

-cpio *file* Always true, but gives an error if *file* cannot be written to. As a side effect, adds the current file to a cpio-formatted archive in *archive* (see Section 3.14.3). The added files are blocked as they would be with the `cpio` option -B. The output file used here is often a device name.[19] The -cpio test is not included in POSIX.

-depth   Always true; as a side effect, causes `find` to process the entries in a directory before processing the directory itself when descending the directory hierarchy. This "test" bypasses an exotic problem that may occur when `find` is being used to generate

---

17. Since the side effect takes place before the result is returned, '`\! -print`' sends the pathname to standard output and then returns false, bypassing any subsequent tests.

18. The GNU version of `find` includes a -print0 test that is like `print` except that the filename is followed by ⟨null⟩ rather than ⟨newline⟩. The purpose of this test is to allow filenames that contain ⟨newline⟩s to be interpreted correctly by programs that process `find`'s output.

19. In fact, the manual pages for all versions of `find` we've seen that support -cpio refer to *file* as a device file even though our experiments suggest it can be a regular file as well.

pathnames for 'cpio -pd' or '-cpio -o' and some of the directories involved don't have write permission.[20] The 4.4BSD version of find does not provide this test but does provide a -d option with the same effect; older BSD systems don't provide the test at all.

-prune   Always true; as a side effect, if the current pathname refers to a directory, -prune prevents find from looking at its members. If -depth is also present, however, the effect of prune is cancelled.

-mount
-xdev   Always true; as a side effect, causes find to restrict the search to the file system containing the current pathname from *pathlist*. This test is called mount in System V and is gotten by the -x option in 4.4BSD.

Additional Tests. The following tests are not included in POSIX but are nevertheless found on some systems:

-follow   Always true; as a side effect, causes symbolic links to be followed. Find keeps track of the directories it visits while following symbolic links in order to detect infinite loops such as might occur if a symbolic link pointed to one of its ancestors. This test should not be used with the -type l test.

-nouser   True if the current file belongs to a user not listed in the /etc/passwd file. This option and the next one are useful for certain security checks.

-nogroup   True if the current file belongs to a group not listed in the /etc/group file. This option and the previous one are useful for certain security checks.

**3.8.2
Logical
Combinations of
Tests**

You may form logical combinations of tests in the following ways:

(1) Enclose a combination of tests in parentheses. Because find treats these parentheses as arguments, they must be surrounded by whitespace—and because parentheses are meaningful to the shell, they must be quoted either by writing them as '\(' and '\)' or by enclosing them in a quotation.

(2) Negate a test by preceding it with '!'. Only the files that don't satisfy the test are accepted. As with parentheses, the '!' must be surrounded by whitespace.

---

20. When cpio creates an implicit intermediate directory during a pass operation, it always gives that directory write permission so that it may insert files into it. When it copies a directory lacking write permission, however, it is unable to insert anything into that directory. The reordering resulting from the -depth option causes cpio to create intermediate directories implicitly rather than explicitly. When the time later comes to copy them explicitly, cpio changes the permission of the target directory, which by this time already exists, to agree with that of the source directory.

(3)   Write two tests one after the other. In this case, the combination is satisfied only if both individual tests are satisfied ("and"). If the first test is not satisfied, the second test is not performed. You may also put '-a' between the tests (with the same effect).

(4)   Put -o ("or") between two tests, indicating that the combination is satisfied if either test is individually satisfied. If the first test is satisfied, the second is not performed.

These constructs are listed in order of decreasing precedence, so the combinations are interpreted in the order listed (parentheses first and -o last).

**3.8.3
Examples**

Here are some examples of find:

- List all files anywhere in /usr or /lib whose names end in '.1':

  ```
  find /usr /lib -name "*.1"
  ```

- Copy all files within your own directories that have been modified within the last week to the device /dev/mt0 in cpio format:

  ```
  find ~ /dev/mt0 -mtime -8 -cpio
  ```

- Remove all regular files within the directories hold and backup that are larger than 10 blocks (5120 bytes) or have another link somewhere:

```
find hold backup -type f \( -size +10 -o -links +1 \) -exec rm {} \;
```

- List all files within the directories hold and backup, skipping any that are within a subdirectory (at any level) named anathema:

  ```
  find hold backup -name anathema -prune -o -print
  ```

- List all subdirectories of the directory ~/tmp that do not belong to you (assuming your user name is naomi):[21]

  ```
  find ~/tmp ! -user naomi -type d -print
  ```

3.9   Locating, Classifying, and Checking Files

The utilities described here provide facilities for locating executable programs, for classifying files, for checking pathnames for validity, and for

---

21. For the C shell or Bash, the '!' needs to be escaped, so the example becomes
     ```
     find ~/tmp \! -user naomi -type d -print
     ```

calculating the checksum of a file. The `type` command, provided by most shells, is useful for the related purpose of determining how a command name will be interpreted (see Section 5.12.1). The `find` program for finding files is discussed separately in Section 3.8.

3.9.1 Locating Programs with `which`

The `which` command enables you to locate an executable program; that is, to determine its full pathname. Though `which` is not included in POSIX, it is found on many UNIX systems.

The form of the `which` command line is

> `which` *progname* ...

where *progname* ... is a series of programs to be located. For each *progname*, `which` simulates the search that your shell would perform by checking each directory listed in the `PATH` environment variable to see if *progname* is there. If `which` finds the program, it produces its full pathname; if not, it produces a message indicating which directories were searched.

An alternative to `which` is the POSIX command '`command -v`' (see Section 5.10.1).

3.9.2 Classifying Files with `file`

The `file` command attempts to classify a file by examining its first few bytes. The form of the command line is

> `file` [`-cL`] [`-f` *file*] [`-m` *file*] *file* ...

Types of files recognized by `file` include ASCII text, natural language text,[22] executable binary files, C code, shell scripts, and binary data. `File` is not included in POSIX.

The System V version of `file` bases its guesses on a list of "magic numbers" recorded in a "magic file". The usual magic file is stored as `/etc/magic`, but you can use a different magic file by applying the `-m` option.

Command-Line Options. The command-line options for `file` are as follows:

`-f` *lfile*   Read a list of files to be classified from the file *lfile*, and classify these files in addition to any in *file* ....

`-m` *mfile*   Use *mfile* as the magic file instead of the default, `/etc/magic`.

`-c`   Check that the magic file is in the right format.

`-L`   If a file is a symbolic link, test the file that the link refers to rather than the link itself. This option is only available on systems that support symbolic links.

Not all systems support these options.

---

22. If the file appears to contain ASCII text, `file` examines its first 512 bytes and tries to guess what language the text is in.

3.9.3
Checksumming
Files with `cksum`

The `cksum` program calculates the checksums of one or more files. The checksum provides an integrity check on a file and is particularly useful when the file is transmitted over a network.

The form of the `cksum` command line is

    `cksum` [*file* . . .]

For each pathname *file* . . . , or for standard input if no *files* are specified, `cksum` computes a checksum of the designated file according to a standard algorithm. The algorithm is the usual one for cyclic redundancy check (CRC) error checking. The output of `cksum` is a line giving the checksum and also the number of octets (eight-bit bytes) in each file.[23]

3.9.4
Checking
Pathnames with
`pathchk`

The `pathchk` utility checks one or more pathnames for validity. A pathname is valid if these conditions hold:

- Each directory in the pathname has search (execute) permission.
- The string length of the pathname does not exceed your system's limit on the length of a pathname.
- No component of the pathname is longer than your system's limit on the length of a filename.

The form of the `pathchk` command line is

    `pathchk` [-p] *pathname* . . .

where *pathname* . . . are the pathnames to be checked for validity. The `pathchk` utility has one option:

-p   Check that each *pathname* conforms to the POSIX limits on pathname length and filename length and contains only characters in the POSIX character set for portable filenames. This check is completely independent of the limits for your particular system and of the directory structure of your system.

3.10   Comparing Files

The two principal programs for comparing files are `cmp` and `diff`. Cmp quickly determines if files differ but doesn't give you much information about the difference; `diff`, on the other hand, produces a list of instructions for transforming one file into another and tries to make that list as short as possible.

Some other file comparison programs, not discussed here, are `bdiff`, which is designed to compare very big files, and `diff3`, which performs a three-way comparison.

---

23.   The POSIX `cksum` utility computes a 32-bit checksum, while the older BSD and System V `sum` utilities compute only a 16-bit checksum.

3.10.1
Comparing Files
with `cmp`

The `cmp` command compares two files. The form of the `cmp` command line is

> `cmp [-1 | -s]` *file*$_1$ *file*$_2$

The exit status is 0 if the files match, 1 if they differ, and 2 if one or both files could not be accessed. By default `cmp` stops at the first difference and shows the line number and character position of that difference; the `-1` option causes `cmp` to look for all differences. *Cmp* is most useful for determining if two files differ when you don't care what the difference is. It is also useful for comparing binary files.

Command-Line Options. The following command-line options are available:

`-1`   Show the byte number and the differing characters (as octal numbers) for all differences. This option is nearly useless for text files with varying line lengths.

`-s`   Show nothing. This option is useful when you're interested only in the exit status.

3.10.2
Finding Differences
Between Files
with `diff`

The `diff` command analyzes the differences between two files, such as different versions of the same document. The form of the `diff` command line is

> `diff [-bcefhr] [-C` *n*`]` *file*$_1$ *file*$_2$

The `diff` command produces a list of instructions for transforming *file*$_1$ to *file*$_2$, where *file*$_1$ and *file*$_2$ are either pathnames or '-', denoting standard input. *Diff* is cleverly programmed to minimize the list of differences, though it will break down if the differences are too complex.

The form of the messages produced by `diff` has been standardized by POSIX. If you build shell scripts and other programs that analyze these messages, you can use them on any POSIX-compliant system.

The most useful way of calling `diff` is with the `-c` option described below, which shows differences in context. The output is useful both for examining the differences visually and for creating input to the `patch` program for updating a collection of files (see Section 3.17). One way to store a sequence of versions of text files compactly is as a base file together with a set of difference files. The `patch` program then provides a convenient way to retrieve any particular version.

Calling `diff` Without Options. When called without options, `diff` generates a reversible list of instructions for transforming *file*$_1$ to *file*$_2$. A pair of numbers indicates a range of lines. When the range consists of a single line, the pair is replaced by a single number. The kinds of instructions are the following:

n_1,n_2 d n_3
    Delete lines n_1 through n_2 of *file*$_1$.

n_1 a n_3,n_4

> Append lines n_3 through n_4 of *file*$_2$ after line n_1 of *file*$_1$.

n_1,n_2 c n_3,n_4

> Replace (change) lines n_1 through n_2 of *file*$_1$ with lines n_3 through n_4 of *file*$_2$.

The output shows all lines involved in the transformation, with '<' indicating lines deleted from *file*$_1$ and '>' indicating lines taken from the original *file*$_2$. Sample output is shown below.

Directories as Arguments.   Either or both of the pathnames *file*$_1$ and *file*$_2$ can designate a directory. The following option affects the comparison in this case:

-r

> Compare directories recursively. With this option, comparing two directories causes their corresponding subdirectories to be compared also.

Comparing two directories causes corresponding filenames within those directories to be compared as follows:

- If a filename exists in one directory but not the other, a message reporting that fact is produced.
- If a filename exists in both directories:
  - If the files are both regular files, then the files are compared.
  - If the files are both subdirectories, then the subdirectories are compared only if -r is specified. If they are not compared, a message to that effect may or may not be produced—it depends on your system.
  - In all other cases, no comparison is done for that filename and a message to that effect is produced.

If one of the pathnames, say *file*$_1$, designates a directory and the other one doesn't, then a comparison is done between *file*$_1$/*file*$_2$ and *file*$_2$. For example, if you type

```
diff birds pests/sparrow
```

diff will do a comparison between `birds/sparrow` and `pests/sparrow`.

Showing the Context of Differences.   There are two command-line options for showing the context of differences:

-C *n*

> Show *n* lines of context surrounding each difference; that is, the *n* lines preceding the difference and the *n* lines following it. Here *n* is an unsigned integer.

-c

> Show three lines of context surrounding each difference.

These options are useful when you want to analyze the differences visually rather than use them as input to an editing script. If you specify -c or -C, you cannot also specify the -e or -f options described below.

Creating an Editing Script with the -e Option.   When called with the -e option, diff generates a set of instructions for ed to perform the transformation (see Section 8.4). If you execute the command

```
diff -e file1 file2 > df
```

then you can later reproduce file2 with the command

```
(cat df; echo '1,$p') | ed -s file1
```

The instructions work from the end of the file back to the beginning so that early changes won't affect the line numbers appearing in later changes.

The editing scripts produced by older versions of diff don't work correctly if one of the text lines in the script consists of a single dot, since that will signal ed to quit. Newer POSIX-compliant versions turn any such line into a line containing exactly two dots and then include in the script an s (substitute) command that removes the first dot.

Other Command-Line Options.   The diff command has several other options:

-b   When comparing input lines, ignore trailing whitespace and treat sequences of whitespace characters as equivalent to a single blank.

-f   Generate a list of editing instructions like those generated with -e but in forward rather than reverse order. This list is easier to read, but it usually won't work as an edit script because the instructions early in the list change the line numbers required for later instructions. The actual list doesn't account for this effect. The -f option is not included in POSIX.

-h   Do a fast but not as effective ("half-hearted") job. This option works only when the changed areas are short and well-separated from each other, but it enables diff to process longer files than it otherwise could. The -h option conflicts with -e and -f. It is not included in POSIX.

Exit Status.   You can use the exit status returned by diff in a shell script to test whether two files (or sets of files) have differences. The status values are:

0   All compared files were equal.
1   At least one difference was found.
> 1   An error occurred.

Examples of diff Output.   Figure 3-1 shows a sample of the output produced by diff when called with the -c option. Lines labelled with stars refer to the first file, lines labelled with hyphens to the second file. The header lines show the names of the files being compared and their most recent access times. The lines headed by '*** 1,8 ****' show the status of lines 1–8 from numbers1, the first file. Those headed by '--- 1,6 ----' show the status of lines 1–6 from numbers2, the second file, which

File 1	*File 2*	diff -c
one	one	```*** numbers1 Fri Apr 14 10:08:18 1995```
two	TWO	```--- numbers2 Fri Apr 21 15:29:45 1995```
three	THREE	```***************```
four	five	```*** 1,8 ****```
five	eight	``` one```
six	nine	```! two```
seven		```! three```
eight		```! four```
		``` five```
		```- six```
		```- seven```
		``` eight```
		```--- 1,6 ----```
		``` one```
		```! TWO```
		```! THREE```
		``` five```
		``` eight```
		```+ nine```

Fig. 3-1.   Sample output produced by '`diff -c`'.

File 1	*File 2*	diff	diff -e	diff -f
one	one	2,4c2,3	8a	c2 4
two	TWO	< two	nine	TWO
three	THREE	< three	.	THREE
four	five	< four	6,7d	.
five	eight	---	2,4c	d6 7
six	nine	> TWO	TWO	a8
seven		> THREE	THREE	nine
eight		6,7d4	.	.
		< six		
		< seven		
		8a6		
		> nine		

Fig. 3-2.   Sample output produced by `diff` with various options.

correspond to lines 1–8 from the first file. A line prefixed by '+' shows
text in the second file but not in the first one, and vice versa for '-'. A
line prefixed by '!' indicates a changed line; sequences of changed lines
correspond, though they need not have the same length.

Figure 3-2 shows the output when `diff` is called in several other ways: with no options, with the `-e` option, and with the `-f` option. The letters `d`, `a`, and `c` indicate `delete`, `append`, and `change`, respectively. This list of instructions can be changed to one that transforms $file_2$ to $file_1$ by replacing each 'a' with 'd', each 'd' with 'a', and then interchanging the numbers before each instruction letter with those after each instruction letter. For the example in Figure 3-2 of `diff` without options, the reversed instructions (omitting the text) would be

```
2,3c2,4
4a6,7
6,7d8
```

The purpose of the mysterious second number on 'd' is to make this reversal possible.

3.11   Controlling File Access and Ownership

Access to a file is controlled by its permissions (see Section 2.8). You can use the `chmod` command to change file permissions and the `chown` and `chgrp` commands to change the owner or group of a file.

3.11.1
Setting Access
Permissions
with `chmod`

You can change the permissions of a file with the `chmod` command. For this command to work, you need search (`x`) access to the directories containing the files.

The form of the `chmod` ("change mode") command line is

```
chmod [-Rf] perms file ...
```

where each *file* is a pathname and *perms* is either a symbolic mode (see Section 2.8.3) or an octal number of up to four digits. In the first case, the symbolic mode given by *perms* is applied to the current permissions of each file included in *file* ... , changing the permissions accordingly. In the second case, the octal number specifies the entire set of permissions at once. Section 2.8.4 describes how a set of permissions is represented as an octal number. Using octal numbers to specify permissions is an obsolescent practice and not recommended.

Command-Line Options.   `Chmod` recognizes the following command-line options:

-R   If an indicated file is a directory, descend through it recursively and change the permissions of all files encountered.

-f   Suppress complaints that the permissions cannot be changed (BSD-based systems only).

Other systems may recognize additional options.

Restrictions.   The following restrictions apply to chmod:

- Only the owner of a file or the superuser may change a file's permissions.
- Only the superuser may change the sticky bit of a non-directory file.
- You may only turn on the s bit for a group if your own group is the same as that of the file and group execution of the file is permitted. Thus the permission change g=xs is legal (assuming your group agrees with that of the file) but the permission change g=s is not.
- The s bit is not meaningful for o.
- The t bit is not meaningful for g or o.

Examples.   Here are some examples of how to use chmod:

- The command

      chmod ug+wx,o+x erato

  grants write and execute permissions for file erato to the owner and group of erato and grants execute permission to everyone else.

- Suppose your file creation mask (see Section 2.8.5) has the value 027. Then the command

      chmod +x polyhymnia

  grants execute permission for polyhymnia to you and those in your group but not to others, since the file creation mask removes all permissions for others. In contrast,

      chmod a+x polyhymnia

  grants execute permission to everyone, ignoring the mask.

- The command

      chmod o=wx urania

  sets the permissions of urania for others to "write" and "execute". The u and g permissions remain the same.

**3.11.2
Reducing Default
File Permissions
with** umask

The umask command enables you to set or examine your file creation mask, also called your umask value (see Section 2.8.5). The umask command is built into each shell rather than being an independent program.

The umask command has the form:

      umask [-S] [*perm*]

where *perm* specifies a set of permissions, either symbolically or as an octal number. If you omit *perm*, umask produces your current umask value without changing the value. If you specify *perm*, your umask value is set according to these conventions:

- If *perm* is given as a symbolic mode (see Section 2.8.3), then that mode is applied to the current file creation mask to obtain a new one. The symbolic representation of a file creation mask is the *complement* of the bits in the mask. In other words, the symbolic representation specifies the permissions that *are* possible for a newly created file. For example, the command

```
umask u=rwx,g=rx,o=r
```

specifies a file creation mask of octal 023. With this mask in effect, a newly created file cannot have write permission for the group nor write nor execute permission for others. The command

```
umask o+r
```

removes the 004 bit from the file creation mask, thus *permitting* others to read a newly created file. A `chmod` command without any "who" letters (see Section 3.11.1) is affected similarly.

- If *perm* is given as an octal number (see Section 2.8.4), the bits of that number specify the file creation mask explicitly; that is, the permissions to be *removed* from a newly created file. Thus the octal notation has the opposite sense of the symbolic notation. The octal version of the first example above is

  ```
  umask 023
  ```

  The octal form is not only less transparent than the symbolic form; it is also less general since it provides no equivalent of the '+' and '-' operators.

Once set, your umask value remains in effect for the duration of your shell execution or until you change it again.

The `-S` option specifies that the symbolic permissions are to be produced on standard output. In particular, the command 'umask -S' causes the permissions to be produced symbolically rather than as an octal number. According to POSIX, if you specify both `-S` and *perm*, the permissions are set but no output is produced. However, some systems produce the output anyway in this case.

The form of the output produced by `umask` without *perm* may be different for different systems, and POSIX allows it to be an octal number (or a symbolic form, for that matter). Any value produced in this default case is a legitimate input value for a later invocation of `umask`.[24]

3.11.3 Setting Ownership with `chown` and `chgrp`

The `chown` and `chgrp` commands enable you to transfer ownership and group ownership of a set of files and directories to someone else. The forms of the command line for these commands are

```
chown [-R] owner [:group] file ...
chgrp [-R] group file ...
```

---

24. The POSIX standard even goes so far as to say that if this default value is octal, then the use of that value later on is not obsolescent. The intent is that you should be able to call `umask` either by using the output of a previous `umask` or by providing an explicit symbolic value for *perm*.

where *file* . . . is a list of the files and directories whose ownerships you wish to change. For chown, the default *group* is the group to which *file* already belongs. Some older versions of chown don't support -R or :group. The effect of the command-line option -R is as follows:

-R   For each *file* that is a directory, recursively change the ownership and/or group of each file contained in the subtree rooted at that directory.

An example of the chown command is

```
chown genghis pillagings
```

which makes genghis the owner of pillagings. An example of the chgrp command is

```
chgrp ducks pond/*
```

which sets the group of all files in the pond directory to ducks.

You may change the ownership (individual or group) of a file only if you own it or are the superuser. Once you've changed the ownership of a file, you can't change it back (unless you're the superuser) since you no longer own it.[25]

The BSD version of chown won't allow you to change ownership of a file unless you're the superuser. This version requires that at least one of *owner* and *group* be specified. The BSD version of chgrp won't allow you to change the group of a file even if you own it unless you belong to the target group.

3.12 Miscellaneous File Utilities

The utilities in this group enable you to count characters, words, or lines in a file, to mark a file as having been modified, and to duplicate standard output on another file.

**3.12.1
Counting Words,
Lines, or Characters
with wc**

The wc command counts the number of characters, words, or lines in a file or a set of files. A word is considered to be a (nonempty) sequence of characters delimited by whitespace.

The form of the wc command line is

```
wc [-clw] [file ... ]
```

---

25. The new owner can give it back to you, however.

The options are `-c` for characters, `-w` for words, and `-l` for lines, with `-cwl` as the default.

- If no files are specified, `wc` counts items in standard input and sends a list of counts (on a single line) to standard output in the order (lines, words, characters).

- If files are specified, the counts for each file appear on a single line together with the name of the file.

The `wc` command is often useful in conjunction with other commands as a way of counting items in a list. For example, you can display the number of currently logged-in users with the command

```
who | wc -l
```

**3.12.2
Touching a File
with** `touch`

The `touch` command touches a file, updating its access and modification times. If the file does not exist, it is created unless you specify otherwise. Touching a file is an easy way to create an empty file.

The form of the `touch` command line is

```
touch [-acm] [-r ref-file | -t time] file ...
```

where *time* is a sequence of digits of the form

$$[[CC]YY]MMDDhhmm[.ss]$$

and the pairs of digits have the following meanings:

CC	century (first two digits of the year)
YY	year (2000+ assumed for 00–68 if *CC* not given)
MM	month (01-12)
DD	day (01-31)
hh	hour (00-23)
mm	minute (00-59)
ss	second (00-61)[26]

If the time is not specified with the `-t` or `-r` option, it defaults to the current time. For example, the command

```
touch softie
```

causes the file `softie` to be created if it doesn't already exist and in any case causes its access and modification times to be set to the current time.

Command-Line Options.   The following options enable you to specify the times explicitly:

`-t` *time*   Set the access and modification times of the file to *time*.

`-r` *ref-file* Set the access and modification times of the file to those of the pathname *ref-file*.

Some older BSD systems do not support these options.

---

26. The extra two digits allow for leap seconds.

By default, both access and modification times are updated. You can cause only one of those times to be updated by specifying just one of the following options:

-a   Update the access time.

-m   Update the modification time.

It is not an error to specify both -a and -m.

There are two further options:

-c   Don't create the file if it doesn't already exist.

-f   Force the touch no matter what the file permissions (not included in POSIX).

Obsolescent Form of touch.   Some older systems, versions of System V in particular, use an obsolescent syntax for touch:

    touch [-acm] [*time*] *file* ...

The time in this case has the form *MMDDhhmm*[*YY*], where *MM* is the month, *DD* is the day, *hh* is the hour, *mm* is the minute, and *YY* is the year. The value of *YY* here should be in the range 69–99, so *YY* may not be usable after the year 1999.

**3.12.3
Duplicating Input
with** tee

The tee command provides a way to capture the contents of a pipe in a file without disrupting the flow of information through the pipe (see Section 2.10.1). It gets its name from its similarity to a tee joint in a plumbing installation. The form of the command is

    tee [-ai] [*file* ...]

Tee causes standard input to be copied to standard output and also to the files *file* .... For example, if you type

    soundoff | tee transcript | hearken

the standard output of soundoff becomes the standard input of hearken and is also recorded in the file transcript. If you specify no files, tee simply copies standard input to standard output. Tee does not buffer its output, so each output byte is sent to all of the target files before the next byte is sent to any of them. (The input may be buffered, however.) Thus you can be assured that when tee is used in a pipeline and the pipeline terminates because of an interrupt, no data will be lost.

There are two options for tee:

-i   Ignore interrupts.

-a   Append the output to each file instead of overwriting the file.

3.13   Data Compression and Encoding

You can reduce the space occupied by a file by storing the file in compressed form. Data compression programs come in pairs, one for compressing and one for uncompressing. Each pair is associated with a particular compression method. We discuss two of these pairs: `compress–uncompress` and `gzip–gunzip`. Data compression programs are often used in conjunction with archiving programs (see Section 3.14) since file archives tend to be large. We also discuss the encoding and decoding programs `uuencode` and `uudecode`.

3.13.1 Compression with `compress`

The `compress` program compresses a set of files using the Lempel-Ziv coding method; the `uncompress` and `zcat` programs undo the compression. When `compress` compresses a file named *file*, it renames the file to '*file*.Z'.

Calling `compress`.   The form of the command line for `compress` is

>   `compress [-cfv] [-b` *n*`] [`*file*`... ]`

where *file* ... is a list of files to be compressed. Each listed file is replaced by its compressed version *file*.Z. If a file would not be shortened by compression, it is left unchanged. You can force compression in any case by specifying the `-f` option. If no files are given, standard input is compressed to standard output.

These are the command-line options for `compress`:

`-c`   Write the compressed files to standard output, leaving the original files unchanged. If this option is specified, only one file can be compressed.

`-v`   Show the percentage of reduction for each file compressed, sending the report to standard error.

`-f`   Force compression of a file even if nothing is gained.

`-b` *n*   Use *n* bits in the compression algorithm. Higher values of *n* slow down the compression but produce better results. The range for *n* is 9–16, with 16 being the default. Values of *n* above 12 may not work on computers with a small address space.

Calling `uncompress`.   The form of the `uncompress` command line is

>   `uncompress [-cv] [`*file*`... ]`

where *file* ... is a list of files to be uncompressed. Each file is replaced by its uncompressed version. A file to be uncompressed must have a name of the form '*file*.Z', although you may specify it in the file list either as '*file*' or as '*file*.Z'. If no files are given, standard input is uncompressed to standard output. The only meaningful options for `uncompress` are `-v` and `-c`, which have the same meaning that they do for `compress`, and `-f`, which can force overwriting of an existing file with the same name as the target.

Calling `zcat`.   The form of the `zcat` command line is

>   `zcat [`*file*`... ]`

It is equivalent to '`uncompress -c`'. If *file* is absent, `zcat` takes its input from standard input. Otherwise `zcat` doesn't read anything from standard input, although you can specify standard input as a file with '`-`'.

**3.13.2
Compression with**
gzip
and gunzip

The gzip program, one of the GNU utilities, compresses files using Lempel-Ziv compression, the same method used by the well-known PKZIP program. The corresponding expansion program is gunzip. A version of gunzip that concatenates the expanded files is also available. On systems that don't support compress, this version is usually called zcat; on systems that do support compress, it's usually called gzcat to avoid conflict with the older use of zcat as a decompression program for compress. We call it gzcat here. Typical compression ratios for gzip are 60 to 70 percent for natural language text or computer programs in source form.

A great deal of publicly available software is distributed in the form of '.tar.gz' files or (the same thing) '.taz' or '.tgz' files. These are constructed by first archiving the directory containing the software using tar and then compressing the resulting archive using gzip. The directory can then be reconstructed by first expanding the '.taz' file to a tar archive and then unarchiving the directory using tar. A typical command sequence is

```
gzcat gem-of-a-program.tar.gz | (cd progloc; tar xvf -)
```

Alternatively, the GNU version of tar can be used (in either direction) with the z option, which compresses or expands the archive as appropriate. The tar archiving steps are necessary because gzip, unlike PKZIP, cannot combine several files into a single compressed file.

In addition, some systems, such as Linux, keep certain system files in compressed form. Linux compresses the Linux kernel and also optionally compresses manual pages. The GNU man program is able to do on-the-fly expansion if necessary.

The forms of the command lines for gzip, gunzip, and gzcat are

```
gzip [-cdfhlLnNrtvV] [-digit] [-S suffix] [name … ]
gunzip [-cfhlLnNrtvV] [-S suffix] [name … ]
gzcat [-fhLV] [name … ]
```

An additional option, -a, is provided on non-UNIX systems for ASCII conversions. The behavior of the three programs is as follows:

- If no *names* are specified, gzip compresses standard input to standard output. Otherwise, gzip compresses each of the specified files, removing the original file and installing a compressed file named '*name*.gz. You can override this behavior with the -c option, or specify a different suffix with the -S option. Calling gzip with the -d option causes it to do expansion rather than compression.

- If no *names* are specified, gunzip expands standard input to standard output. Gunzip is capable of expanding not just files compressed with gzip, but also those compressed with compress or with the obsolete pack program. Detection of the compression type is automatic. If *name* … is specified and the output is not being sent to standard output, only those files whose names end with '.gz', '-gz', '.z', '-z', '_z', '.Z', '.tgz', or '.taz' are expanded. For '*name*.tgz' or '*name*.taz', the compressed file is assumed to be a tar archive and the expanded file is named '*name*.tar'. For the other suffixes, the expanded file is named *name*. In each case, the original compressed file is deleted if the expansion is successful.

- The gzcat program behaves like gunzip except that the expanded files are concatenated and produced on standard output. The gzcat program is equivalent to 'gunzip -c'.

Command-Line Options. The command-line options have the same or analogous meanings for all three programs. Gzcat recognizes only the -f option and the three display options -hLV.

The following options affect file handling and error checking:

-c   Send the output to standard output, leaving the original file unchanged.

-f   Force compression or decompression even if the file has multiple links, the corresponding file already exists, or the compressed data is being read from or written to a terminal.

-S *suffix*   Use *suffix* in place of .gz.

-n   When compressing, don't save the original name and timestamp. When expanding, don't restore the original pathname and timestamp; just remove the suffix from the compressed file's name. This option is the default for expansion.

-N   When compressing, save the original pathname and timestamp; this option is the default. When expanding, restore the original pathname and timestamp.

-r   Traverse the directory structure recursively.

The following option affects what information is displayed:

-v   Display the name of each file compressed or expanded and the percentage by which its size was reduced.

The following options apply only to gzip:

-d   Do decompression rather than compression.

-*digit*   Adjust the ratio of speed of compression versus compactness. Low numbers favor speed, high numbers compactness. Thus -1 causes gzip to run at maximum speed, while -9 causes it to produce the smallest possible compressed file.

The following options apply only to gunzip or to gzip with the -d option:

-l   List extended information about each compressed file.

-t   Test the compressed file for integrity but don't do any actual restoration.

The following options cause the programs to display information and quit:

-h   Display a help screen and quit.

-L	Display the program license.
-V	Display the version number and compilation options.

3.13.3
Encoding and
Decoding
with uuencode
and uudecode

You can use the uuencode program to encode a binary file into a sequence of lines, each of a convenient length and each consisting entirely of printable ASCII characters. You can include the encoded file in a mail message or use it anywhere else you are restricted to using printable characters. The encoded file includes as well the name of a target file and the file permissions to be used in reconstructing that file.[27] The uudecode program decodes a file encoded by uuencode and stores the decoded data in the specified target file, setting the file permissions as recorded in the encoded file. The encoding method, far from compressing the data, expands it. On the other hand, you can use these programs to encode a binary file that was created by a compression program such as gzip.

The forms of the uuencode and uudecode command lines are

> uuencode [*file*] *tpath*
> uudecode [*file*]

For uuencode, the file to be encoded is read either from standard input or from the file named by the pathname *file* if that has been specified. The target path *tpath* says where the decoded file should be put. The permissions are those of *file*, or a=rw if the input is taken from standard input.

For uudecode, the encoded file is read from the pathname given by *file* or, alternatively, from standard input. It is decoded and copied into the target pathname as determined from the first line of the input, and the permissions of that pathname are set as specified. The location of the decoded file is not and indeed cannot be specified as part of the uudecode command because that information is in the encoded file itself.

---

27. The encoded file has the form

> **begin** *perms tpath*
> . . .
> **end**

Here *tpath* is the path of the target file for decoding and *perms* are the file permissions to be assigned to it (as an octal number). The actual encoding is obtained by taking groups of 24 bits at a time (ordinarily three eight-bit bytes) and encoding them into four characters. Each character is gotten by adding a six-bit number to 32, the ASCII code for ⟨space⟩. (The maximum resulting character is '~', with ASCII code 127.) That process yields a stream of printable characters. The stream is then broken up into lines, where the first character of each line is the length count. POSIX specifies a 45-character maximum for the data on an input line, which can yield up to 60 characters on the output line. The length count is encoded in the same way by adding the code for ⟨space⟩ to it.

3.14   Archiving Sets of Files

An *archive* is a collection of files in which each file is labelled with information about its origin. Archives serve two main purposes: backing up a group of files so that the files can be restored in case they are lost or damaged, and packaging a group of files for transmission to another computer.

UNIX has three main archiving programs: `pax`, `cpio`, and `tar`. Pax, included in POSIX, is the most powerful of the three since it can accept or generate archives in the formats used by `cpio` and `tar`. We generally recommend using either `pax` or the GNU version of `tar`, which has a number of enhancements over the older System V and BSD versions. Advantages of `cpio` over `tar` are that `cpio` can archive device files and create multivolume archives, although some newer versions of `tar` can also create multivolume archives. An advantage of `tar` is that you can archive all the files contained in a directory just by naming the directory on the command line; `cpio` requires that you name all the files explicitly in an input list. You can circumvent this behavior of `cpio` by using `find` with the `-cpio` criterion (see p. 125), or `find` piped to `cpio`. An archive written with one of these programs must be read by the same program or by `pax`. Tar format is by far the most popular format for software distributions, and even some recent versions of `cpio` can read and write archives in this format.

You can use `pax` or `cpio` for another purpose not necessarily connected with archiving: copying a set of files from one directory to another. This capability was probably just an artifact of the way `cpio` was designed and implemented, but it is very convenient. It was retained in `pax`.

None of these programs provide data compression; for that you must use a program such as `compress` or `gzip` (see Section 3.13). The GNU version of `tar` includes a `z` option for compression, but that's just a convenience—its effect is to pipe the output of `tar` into `gzip` or, in the other direction, to pipe the output of `gunzip` into `tar`. A disadvantage of compressing your archives is that if part of the compressed archive becomes corrupted, the entire archive becomes unreadable. Some commercial archivers provide error correction to reduce that hazard.

Several MS-DOS programs such as PKZIP and ARC combine the two functions of collecting files and compressing them. UNIX adaptations of these programs may be available on your system; for example, Linux distributions often include versions of PKZIP and PKUNZIP under the names `zip` and `unzip`.

You can archive a collection of files in order to include them in a mail message with the `shar` utility (see Section 11.7).

3.14.1
The pax **Portable**
Archiver

The pax portable archiver was designed by the POSIX Committee as a "peaceful compromise" between the advocates of tar and those of cpio. It provides both tar-style and cpio-style interfaces and can accept or generate either tar-format or cpio-format archive files. As of this writing, the POSIX Committee is working on a new archive format that will address issues of security and internationalization, to be published as part of a future revision of POSIX.

The operation pax performs depends on what combination of the -r and -w options you specify. The meanings of these options are as follows:

-r   Read and process an archive or, with -w, copy a set of files.

-w   Create (write) an archive or, with -r, copy a set of files.

The possible actions are these:

- **Listing an Archive.** The form for listing an archive is

  pax [-cdnv] [-f *archive*] [-s *repl*] ... [*pattern* ...]

  In this case, when you specify neither -r nor -w, pax reads an archive and produces a list of the files it contains.

- **Reading an Archive.** The form for reading an archive is

  pax -r [-cdiknuv] [-f *archive*] [-o *options*] ... [-p *privs*] ...
    [-s *repl*] ... [*pattern* ...]

  In this case, when you specify -r but not -w, pax reads an archive and extracts its members. Each member has a pathname and an associated file (in the strict sense of a sequence of bytes). When a member is extracted, the file is written to the corresponding pathname, gotten by taking the recorded pathname and modifying it if necessary according to the -s and -i options described below.

  Note: If a file was placed in the archive using a relative pathname, then that file is restored using the same pathname relative to the current directory (see Section 2.7.2). So beware—if the current directory is not the same as what the current directory was when the archive was created, the file will be restored to a different place.

- **Creating or Updating an Archive.** The form for creating or updating an archive is

  pax -w [-dituvX] [-b *blksize*] [-f *archive* [-a]] [-o *options*] ...
    [-s *repl*] ... [-x *fmt*] [*file* ...]

  In this case, when you specify -w but not -r, pax either creates or updates an archive from a set of files, depending on whether or not you also specify -u. Updating makes sense only if you've specified an explicit archive file that already exists, and is controlled by the -u and -a options. The files to be archived are given by *file* .... If you don't specify any *file*s, pax reads a list of files to be archived, one per line, from standard input.

- **Copying Files.** The form for copying files is[28]

      pax -rw [-dikltuvX] [-p *privs*] ... [-s *repl*] ... [*file* ...] *dir*

  In this case, when you specify both -r and -w, pax copies a set of files from one directory to another. The files to be copied are given by *file* ... and the target directory is given by *dir*. If you don't specify any *files*, pax reads a list of files to be copied, one per line, from standard input. No explicit archive is involved, but you can think of this operation as creating a temporary archive from the contents of one directory and extracting the members of that temporary archive into another directory.

The form for each operation indicates which options you can use with it.

By default, an operation on a directory applies to that directory and all files contained directly or indirectly within it. You can override that default with the -d option.

You can use pax to write an archive to a sequence of removable media such as tapes or diskettes. Your system should prompt you when you need to change the media.

Specifying the Archive File Explicitly.   For any operation other than copying files, the convention is that the archive is read from standard input and written to standard output. You can, however specify an archive file explicitly:

-f *archive*
> Use the file *archive* as the archive, where *archive* is a pathname.

You can also indicate that if the archive already exists, the archived files are to be appended to it:

-a
> Append files to the end of the archive. This option is valid only when you are creating or updating an archive and have specified -f. Furthermore, some archive formats may not support appending. This option is only useful if *archive* already exists.

Selecting Files.   When you're listing or reading an archive, you can either operate on all members of the archive (the default) or specify a subset of those members by providing a sequence of patterns *pattern* ... as shown in the forms. Each pattern represents a set of pathnames using the wildcard notation described in Section 2.9.1. If a member name matches any one of the patterns, the member is selected.

The following options modify how *pattern* ... is interpreted:

-c
> Select all members of the archive whose pathnames do not match any of *pattern* ... , ignoring those that do match. You can use this option to specify the members *not* to be read.

---

28. The POSIX standard indicates that the -n option can also be specified, but we believe that to be in error.

-n   Select only the first archive member that matches each *pattern*.
            The remaining archive members are ignored.

These options are meaningful only if you've provided at least one pattern.

General Command-Line Options.   The following options apply to all four
operations:

-v   Produce a verbose list of the files that were processed or, in the
            case of listing an archive, are contained in the archive. Depend-
            ing on the operation, the list may show just the filenames, the
            pathnames, or the filenames and the attributes of each file in
            the format of 'ls -l' (see Section 3.2).

-d   When processing a directory, process the directory itself but
            not the hierarchy beneath it. In other words, when reading a
            directory, just read the directory itself as a file; when creating
            or writing to a directory, don't put any files into that directory.

-s *repl*   Modify the name of each file or archive member according to
            the substitution *repl*. If you're reading an archive, the files
            actually written are determined by applying the substitution
            to the name of each archive member as it is brought in. If a
            substitution results in a null string, nothing is done with the
            file or member; that gives you a convenient way of filtering the
            files or the members.

            The substitution *repl* has the form

            /*old*/*new*/ [gp]

            Here *old* is a basic regular expression (see Section 2.17.1) and
            new is the string to be substituted for *old* in each name. Within
            new, '\n' references the *n*th subexpression of *old* (see p. 84)
            and '&' represents the entire string matched by *old*. Just the
            first occurrence of *old* within the name is replaced unless you
            specify g as shown; if you specify g, then all occurrences are
            replaced. You can replace the '/' in this form by any other
            delimiter character. These are the same conventions used in
            the ed editor. In addition, p specifies that the result of each
            substitution should be written to standard error.

            You can specify more than one substitution by providing
            multiple -s options. If you do, the substitutions are applied
            in sequence to each name, ending with the first substitution (if
            any) that succeeds.

            Note: When pax selects archive members or files for process-
            ing, it makes the selection before applying any substitutions (or
            renamings with the -i option described below).

File Processing Options.   Pax provides a number of options for controlling how files are processed:

-i   Interactively rename files or archive members. For each
            archive member or file to be transferred, pax prompts you

at your terminal with the pathname of the member or file. You can respond by typing a different pathname, a dot, or an empty line.

- If you type a different pathname, that pathname replaces the original one.
- If you type a dot, the member or file is processed as usual.
- If you type an empty (or all-blank) line, the member or file is skipped and not processed at all.

This option applies to all operations except listing an archive. If you specify both -i and -s, the substitutions given with -s are applied first.

-X   Don't cross file system boundaries when creating an archive or copying files. If pax is processing a member of the sequence *file* ... on the command line and encounters a mount point (see p. 40), pax does not process any files in the file system mounted at that point. This option is particularly useful as a way of avoiding an accidental attempt to archive all the files in a network.

-u   When extracting files from an archive or copying files, don't overwrite files with older ones. If you specify -u when writing to an archive (the -w option) and the target archive already exists, it is updated rather than replaced. The update consists of adding files that were not already in the archive and replacing archive members in the case where the file to be archived is newer than the archive member (though some implementations may achieve the replacement by appending the replacement files to the archive). If you are writing to an archive that does not already exist, this option has no effect.

-l   When copying files, install a new file by creating a link to an existing file whenever that is possible.

-k   When reading an archive or copying files, only process files that don't already exist. In other words, files that already exist will not be overwritten if you've specified -k.

-p *privs*   Retain or discard the file characteristics ("privileges") given by *privs* when extracting a file from an archive or when copying a file. Here *privs* is a sequence of specification characters as follows:

e   Preserve the user ID, group ID, permissions (see Section 2.8), access time, and modification time of the file. Your particular system may preserve other file properties as well.

o   Preserve the user ID and group ID.

p   Preserve the file permissions.

a   Discard the file access time.

m   Discard the file modification time.

When a file is placed in an archive, its privileges are stored along with it. By default, when an archive member is extracted its access and modification times are restored to what they were when the archive was created.

Preserving a particular privilege causes that privilege to be assigned to the file created when the member is extracted. If the privileges you specify are in conflict, the one that appears later in *privs* governs. In any event, the privileges of an extracted file are limited by the privileges you have as a user. For example, if you are not the superuser, you cannot assign ownership of an extracted file to someone else.

-t   When writing an archive or copying files, inhibit any change to the access time of the files being transferred. If you don't specify this option, each file that is placed in an archive or copied has its access time set to the time when `pax` processed it.

Specifying the Archive Format.   An archive created by `pax` can be in `cpio` format, `ustar` format (the standard format used by the `tar` archiver), or in a format particular to your system. When you read an archive, you don't need to, and indeed cannot, specify the archive's format since `pax` detects the format automatically. When you create an archive, `pax` uses a default format unless you tell it otherwise. The default format can be any format that your version of `pax` can read.

You use the following options to specify the format explicitly when you create an archive. They do not apply to any other `pax` operations.

-x *fmt*   Specify the output format to be *fmt*. Here *fmt* can be `cpio`, `ustar`, or some other keyword that names a format available on your system.

-b *blksize* Write the archive using blocks of *blksize* bytes. Usually you should not have to specify this value, though it may sometimes be useful to give a value of 32756 (the maximum permitted) if you're archiving to a slow tape device.

The following option applies both when creating an archive and when reading one:

-o *options*

Use *options* to provide additional information that modifies the algorithm used for extracting or writing files. It is likely that in the future, POSIX will use *options* to specify such features as code set translations, security, and accounting in conjunction with additional formats to be added to the -x option.

Examples.   Here are some examples of using `pax`:

- The command line

  ```
  pax -w ~ > /dev/fd0
  ```

creates an archive on diskettes (drive 0) containing all the files in your home directory and its subdirectories. If more than one diskette is needed to accommodate the archive, `pax` will prompt you for the additional ones. The command line

```
pax -v < /dev/fd0
```

produces a verbose listing of that archive, and the command line

```
pax -ru < /dev/fd0
```

restores the files in the archive, leaving any files newer than the corresponding archive members unchanged. The three commands can also be given as

```
pax -wf /dev/fd0 ~
pax -vf /dev/fd0
pax -ruf /dev/fd0
```

- Suppose `kudzu` is a subdirectory of the current directory. The command lines

```
mkdir poison_ivy
pax -rwl kudzu poison_ivy
```

copy all files within `kudzu` to the newly created `poison_ivy` directory, creating hard links from `poison_ivy` to `kudzu` whenever possible. Any necessary subdirectories of `poison_ivy` will be created as though by `mkdir` (see Section 3.1.3), however, since otherwise it would not be possible to add files to those subdirectories later on or remove files from them.

- When executed in superuser mode, the command line

```
pax -rf cistern -p e -s /.tar.gz/.taz/ "*.tar.gz"
```

extracts from the archive file found in pathname `cistern` all files whose names end in '.tar.gz'. The double quotes are needed around `*.tar.gz` so that `pax` rather than the shell does the pattern matching. Only files in the top-level directory of the archive are extracted. Selective extraction of `tar.gz` files at all levels requires two calls on `pax`: one to generate a table of contents for the archive, and a second to do the extraction with a list of pathnames generated from the table of contents by command substitution (see Section 2.12.3). Each file *name*`.tar.gz` is renamed to *name*`.taz` before it is stored. The permissions, access times, and ownership of the archive members are preserved in the stored files. Were this command not to be executed in superuser mode, the restored files would be owned by the user executing this command.

- The command line

```
pax -wvXf /dev/mt2 / /usr
```

creates an archive on tape unit 2 of all the files in the root file system on your computer, together with those in /usr (assuming /usr is on a different file system). It would probably not make sense to execute this command outside of superuser mode, since otherwise files to which you did not have access would have to be left out of the archive. The command line

```
pax -wvXf /dev/mt2 -x cpio / /usr
```

does the same thing, except that the archive is written in cpio format and therefore can be read back using the cpio program. Note that in both of these examples, pax will blithely archive two copies of the contents of /usr if / and /usr happen to reside in the same file system after all.

- The command line

```
pax -rif vault
```

restores the files from the archive vault. As each archive member is read, pax shows its name on your terminal and gives you the opportunity to change the name of the restored file by typing the new name, accept the file as is by typing '.', or skip the file by just typing (Enter).

**3.14.2
The tar
Tape Archiver**

The tar program is primarily intended to read and write archives stored on magnetic tape, although the archives that it works with may also be stored on other media or kept as ordinary files. In fact, a common use of tar nowadays is to package software collections in a form suitable for distribution via the Internet. The details of how to call tar vary greatly, even among System V-style or BSD-style systems. What we describe here is a generic form whose options are common to most implementations. Tar is not included in POSIX because its functions are provided by pax— among its other capabilities, pax is able to create or unpack tar-format archives.

The most common form of the tar command line is

```
tar key [arg... ] [file... ]
```

The *key* consists of a sequence of key letters that play the role of options. Modern versions of tar allow (but don't require) key letters to be preceded by a hyphen, but older versions don't. The number of *args* is equal to the number of letters in *key* that require arguments. The *args* appear in the order of the key letters that require them; as each key letter is processed, it consumes the next unconsumed *arg* if it needs to. The *files* are the files to be written to the archive or extracted. Writing a directory implies writing all its recursively contained subdirectories and files; reading a directory implies restoring all its recursively contained subdirectories and files. For example, the command

```
tar rbf 12 /dev/rdsk/mt3 /home/luigi
```

specifies that an archive should be written (r) with a blocking factor of 12 (b) to the device /dev/rdsk/mt3 (f) containing all the files in the directory /home/luigi and its subdirectories. The conventions for associating key letters with arguments are different from what they are for any other UNIX program that we know of.

Because a magnetic tape cannot be positioned precisely, anything written onto the tape must either be written at the very beginning of the tape (making the rest of it unreadable) or appended to what is already there. The archives created by tar are designed with this fact in mind. They are usually written cumulatively, with new files added at the end of the archive. A particular file may appear in the archive a number of times, the latest version being the last one. When files are extracted from the archive, all the versions of each file are read in. Each version of a file overwrites any older version of that file. The versions that are left are thus the latest ones.

Specifying the Operation.   The following key letters specify the operation to be performed. Exactly one of them must be specified.

r   Append the files to the end of the archive.

x   Extract the files from the archive and restore them. If no files are specified, all files on the archive are extracted. The owner, modification time, and permissions of each file are restored if possible.

t   List the contents of the archive. A file that occurs more than once is listed once for each occurrence.

u   Update the archive by adding only those files that are not already there or that have been modified since the archive was most recently written.

c   Create a new archive containing the files.[29]

In some implementations, if the file list for writing an archive contains a pair

    -C *dir*

then tar changes the current directory to *dir* and writes all of the files in *dir*. Any number of such pairs may appear in the list of files. **Note:** Any wildcards such as '*' in the list of files are interpreted by the shell, not by tar. They therefore are expanded in the context of the directory from which tar was called, not in the context of *dir*. However, '.' is a valid filename, so a command such as

    tar c -C /usr include -C /etc .

---

29. When you create an archive on a magnetic tape, the tape is not automatically rewound before the archive is written (see "Magnetic Tapes" on p. 91). Many systems provide an mt command you can use to rewind the tape.

might be used to archive the `/usr/include` and `/etc` directories.

Archive Characteristics.   The following key letters specify where the archive is to be found and how it is to be written:

n Use drive #n for the archive. The interpretation of n depends on the system.

f   Take the archive pathname from the next argument. If that argument is '`-`', an important special case, the archive is read from standard input or written to standard output.

b   Take the blocking factor for raw magnetic tape from the next argument. The tape consists of a set of records, each record containing some number of blocks. The number of bytes in a block is given by a parameter known to your system; 512 and 1024 are typical values. The blocking factor specifies how many blocks are in a record. The maximum value is usually 20.

k   Take the capacity of the archive device in kilobytes from the next argument. This information enables `tar` to know when the device is nearly full. Not all systems provide this capability.

z   When creating an archive, compress it using `gzip`; when listing an archive or extracting files from it, expand it using `gunzip`. This option is a feature of GNU `tar`.

Z   When creating an archive, compress it using `compress`; when listing an archive or extracting files from it, expand it using `uncompress`. This option is a feature of GNU `tar`.

Status Information and Confirmations.   The following key letters specify where the archive is to be found and what its characteristics are:

v   Show the name of each file processed.

w   Wait for confirmation of each action.

l   Don't complain about files that can't be found.

Attributes of Restored Files.   The following key letters affect the attributes of restored files as indicated in their directory entries:

m   When restoring a file, set its modification time to the current time rather than to the modification time recorded in the archive.

o   Set the owner and group of each restored file to that of the user running the program rather than to that recorded in the archive.

p   Assign the original permissions to restored files rather than the permissions that would be assigned to a newly created file.

Examples.   Here are a few examples of using `tar`:

- To make an archive of the files belonging to `imelda` on device `rst0`, type

```
tar cvbf 20 /dev/rst0 /home/imelda
```

- To list all the files in that archive, type

      tar tf /dev/rst0

- To extract the files from `imelda`'s directory `shoes` within that archive and restore them to their original places, type

      tar xvf /dev/rst0 /home/imelda/shoes

- To extract the contents of the distribution file `wizbang.tar.gz` in such a way that the distribution becomes a subdirectory of `~/local`, type

      tar -xvz -C ~/local -f wizbang.tar.gz

  if you're using GNU `tar`. An alternative, not depending on the GNU options, is

      gunzip -c wizbang.tar.gz | (cd ~/local; tar -xvf -)

3.14.3 Copying Archives with `cpio`

The `cpio` program provides three functions:

- Creating an archive from a list of files (the `-o` option)
- Extracting some or all of the files in an archive (the `-i` option)
- Copying files from one directory to another, recreating the original directory structure at the destination (the `-p` option)

The name 'cpio' stands for "copy in and out". Cpio is not included in POSIX because it has been superseded by `pax`.

The forms of the `cpio` command line are

    cpio -o [-acBLvV] [-C size] [-H hdr] [-O file]
    cpio -i [-BcdkmrtuvVbsS6] [-C size] [-H hdr] [-I file] [[-f] pattern]
    cpio -p [-adlLmuvV] dir

Here *pat* specifies files to be extracted from an archive and is used only with the `-i` option, while *dir* specifies a destination directory and is used only with the `-p` option. The `-o`, `-i`, or `-p` option need not be given first.

An archive created by `cpio` includes a pathname for each file in the archive. The pathname may be either absolute or relative (see Section 2.7.2). Relative pathnames are taken relative to the current directory both when the archive is created and when files are restored from it. The current directory need not be the same at the two times. In fact, reading files from one directory and writing them to another can be a useful operation in its own right and is explicitly supported by the `-p` option.

Selecting the Archive Operation.   The options that follow specify whether `cpio` creates an archive, reads an archive, or copies files from one directory to another. You must specify exactly one of them.

`-i`   Copy in or list the files in an archive. The archive is read from standard input unless the `-I` option is specified. If any patterns are specified by *pat* on the command line, `cpio` extracts the files selected by the patterns; otherwise, it extracts all the files. The patterns are pathnames with wildcards permitted. The pattern matching, unlike that in the shell, treats '/' as an ordinary character.

Cpio will not overwrite a file with an older version unless you explicitly ask it to with the -u option. You can list the contents of an archive without extracting anything by specifying the -t option.

When cpio creates a copy of an archived file, the permissions attached to the copy become whatever they were when the archive was created. The owner and group of the extracted file are those of the user calling cpio.[30]

-o   Copy a set of files out to an archive. The list of files, one per line, is taken from standard input; you can often produce it conveniently by piping the output of ls to cpio.[31] The access times of the copied files are updated unless you specify the -a option.

-p   Copy ("pass") a set of files from one directory to another. The list of files to be copied is taken from standard input as with -o; the destination directory is given on the command line. The -l option, which helps prevent cpio from creating redundant files, is often useful in conjunction with -p.

The following options specify the archive location explicitly instead of using standard input or output:

-I *file*   Read the archive from *file* (with -i only).

-O *file*   Write the archive to *file* (with -o only).

Not all systems provide these options.

File Creation. The following options affect the files that cpio creates when it reads an archive:

-t   Don't create any files, just show a table of contents of the input. If -v is also specified, the listing is in the long format and shows the file attributes.

-f   Copy in those files *not* matching the patterns.

-r   Interactively rename files. As cpio reads a file, it prompts you for the name under which it should be stored. Pressing (Enter) causes that file not to be stored at all.

---

30. If the user is the superuser, however, the owner and group of the extracted files are whatever they were when the archive was created.

31. If your version of ls produces a multicolumn listing because it's been aliased to something like 'ls -CF', you can call up the single-column version by typing '\ls -1'.

The following options affect file creation both for reading an archive and for passing files from one directory to another:

-d   Create subdirectories as needed. Without this option, `cpio` is not able to store files in subdirectories that don't already exist.

-u   Copy unconditionally, replacing newer files. Normally `cpio` will not replace a file with an older version.

-m   Retain the previous file modification time; that is, the one that was stored with the file in the archive.

The following option applies only when files are being passed from one directory to another using the -p option:

-l   Link files when possible rather than copying them.

Directory Entries for Copied or Passed Files. The following option affects the directory entry for a file that `cpio` writes to an archive or passes to another directory:

-a   Leave the access time of a file unchanged when writing it to an archive or passing it to another directory.

Status Information. The following options affect the messages that `cpio` issues as it runs:

-M *msg*   Issue *msg* when switching media.

-v   List all pathnames verbosely; that is, as they would be listed with '`ls -l`'.

-V   Display a dot for each file transferred.

Not all systems provide the -M and -V options.

Treatment of Symbolic Links. The following option affects how symbolic links are handled:

-L   Follow symbolic links and process the files in the directories to which they point. The default is not to follow them. This option is valid only when used together with -o or -p.

Header Information and Error Control. The following option affects the form of headers used in an archive:

-c   Read and write header information in ASCII character form as an aid to portability among different versions of `cpio`. We recommend always using this option. Most versions of `cpio` can read an archive in either format and ignore the -c option on input.

-H *format*

        Read or write header information in the header format *format*. Valid values for *format* are:

        crc   ASCII headers with expanded device numbers and additional checksums

`odc`	ASCII headers with small device numbers (pre-SVR4 format)
`tar`	Tar header and format
`ustar`	IEEE/P1003 Data Interchange Standard header and format

-k   Attempt to get past bad headers and i/o errors when reading an archive instead of stopping. Using this option, you can resume restoring a multivolume option with a volume other than the first one. Not all systems provide this option.

Blocking Factors for Data Transfer.   By default, `cpio` uses a block size of 512 bytes when transferring data to or from an archive. The block size usually affects how fast the transfer proceeds but does not significantly affect the contents or interpretation of the archive itself. You can write an archive with one block size and read it back with another. Increasing the block size usually speeds up the transfer, which is why the -B option is often recommended. The following two options change the block size:

-B   Use 5120-byte blocks for data transfer.

-C *n*   Use *n*-byte blocks for data transfer. Not all systems provide this option.

Data Transformations.   The following options provide data transformations for input. They may only be used with the -i option.

-b   Reverse byte order within each word.

-s   Reverse byte order within each halfword.

-S   Reverse halfword order within each word.

-6   Read archive in Sixth Edition format.

Examples.   Here are some examples of `cpio`:

- The command line

    ```
    /bin/ls | cpio -ocBv > /dev/fd0
    ```

  archives the current directory and its subdirectories onto device `fd0`, presumably a floppy disk. The use of `/bin/ls` avoids the accidental use of a local variant of `ls`, possibly introduced by an alias. It produces a list of the copied files.

- The command line

    ```
    cd wotan; cpio -icdBvm < /dev/fd0
    ```

  reads the archive created in the previous example into the directory `wotan`, unconditionally overwriting any existing file in `wotan` with the same name as one in the archive. A listing of the files is produced on standard output. The modification dates of the restored files are the dates recorded in the archive.

- The command line

    ```
    find . -depth -print | cpio -pvdlum ../galahad
    ```

recursively copies the contents of the current directory and its subdirectories into the parallel directory `galahad`. The use of `find`
in conjunction with `cpio` is typical; see Section 3.8 for a discussion
of `find`. The `l` and `u` options ensure that unnecessary copying is
avoided and that the new directory mirrors the old one even if that
involves replacing newer files by older ones.

3.15   Examining Files with `od`

The `od` command produces a listing of the contents of a file, displaying
the bytes of the file in one or more selected formats. The letters 'od' stand
for "octal dump", although you can use `od` for dumps in several other
representations as well.

Older versions of UNIX vary in their syntax for `od`. The POSIX form of
the command line is

> `od [-v] [-A` *base*`] [-j` *skip*`] [-N` *count*`] [-t` *type-spec* ... `] [`*file* ... `]`

In the default case where you type just `od`, you get an octal dump of
standard input, with each octal number representing two bytes and the
address at the start of each output line also expressed in octal. More
generally, `od` produces an octal dump of each of its input files as given by
the sequence of pathnames *file* . . . .

3.15.1 Type Specifications

A type specification is used with the `-t` option to specify how the bytes of
the input are to be grouped and how each group is to be represented.
It consists of a type character and an optional byte count or input type
descriptor. The type character specifies how each displayed value is to be
represented and is one of the following:

d	Decimal number
u	Unsigned decimal number
o	Octal number
x	Hexadecimal number
f	Floating point number
c	Character
a	Named character (nonprintable characters shown symbolically)

Any of the numerical type characters (`d`, `u`, `o`, `x`, or `f`) can be followed by
a decimal count indicating how many bytes are to be represented. For
example, `x4` indicates that groups of four bytes should be represented by
a single hexadecimal number. Instead of a count, you can use one of the
following letters, corresponding to types in C:

F	*float* (for `f` only)
D	*double* (for `f` only)

L	*long double* (for f only)
C	*char* (for d, u, o, or x)
S	*short* (for d, u, o, or x)
I	*int* (for d, u, o, or x)
L	*long* (for d, u, o, or x)

For example, oI indicates that the input data should be broken up into *int*-sized units and each such unit should be shown as an octal number.

3.15.2
Command-Line
Options

The following options affect the form of the output:

-A *base*   Express the offset location at the beginning of each output line using base *base* (o for octal, d for decimal, x for hexadecimal, and n for "none"). The offset location gives the position in the input stream of the data whose values are shown on the line. A *base* of n means that the offset is to be omitted.

-t *type-spec*

Express the data on each line using the format described by the type specification *type-spec*. You can specify multiple *type-spec*s (with no intervening whitespace), multiple -t options, or both. If you do, the data in its different formats is produced on successive lines in the order of the *type-spec*s.

The following options specify that only a portion of the input stream is to be examined:

-j *skip*   Skip over *skip* bytes, where *skip* is a decimal number unless it starts with 0x or 0X, indicating a hexadecimal number, or with a leading 0 digit, indicating an octal number. You can append one of the characters b, k, or m to the *skip* value to have it interpreted as a multiple of 512, 1024, or 1,048,576 respectively (e.g., 4k to mean 4096 bytes). The displayed data starts with the portion following the skipped data.

-N *count*   Produce output for at most *count* bytes, where *count* is interpreted the same way as *skip* except that the b, k, and m suffixes are not recognized. It is not an error if fewer than *count* bytes are available.

The following option affects how repeated data is shown:

-v   Show repeated data explicitly. Without this option, repeated groups of output lines are indicated by asterisks.

Finally, the -b, -c, d, -o, and -x options recognized by the System V version of od are also often recognized by newer versions as an alternative to certain forms of -t.

3.15.3
An Example

Suppose you use od to examine the short file wabbit:

```
od -t xCc wabbit
```

This command produces the following dump in *char*-sized hexadecimal and in characters:

```
0000000000    54  68  61  74  20  40  5E  25  2A  02  20  77  61  62  62  69
               T   h   a   t       @   ^   %   *  002       w   a   b   b   i
0000000020    74  21  0A
               t   !  \n
0000000023
```

The numbers in the first column are byte offsets in octal. Note the treatment of the nonprintable characters 002 and newline (\n).

3.15.4
Older System V
Syntax of od

Older versions of System V use a somewhat different form of the command line:

> od [-bcdox] [*file*] [*offset*]

The options describe how bytes or groups of bytes are represented:

-b   Interpret each byte as an octal number.

-o   Interpret each word as an octal number.

-c   Interpret each byte as an ASCII character, using the C notations *c* and *ddd* for nonprinting characters (e.g., newline as \n and the octal character 274 as \274).

-d   Interpret each word as an unsigned decimal number.

-x   Interpret each word as a hexadecimal number.

If you specify *offset*, the dump begins at the byte indicated by *offset*, which has the form

> [+] *n* [.] [b]

If only the number *n* is present, the dump starts at byte *n* of the file, and *n* is interpreted in octal. A '.' indicates that *n* is given in decimal rather than octal; a b indicates that the offset is measured in 512-byte blocks, not single bytes. The '+' has no special meaning, but you must supply it if you omit *file* so that od knows what follows is an offset rather than a pathname.

The older BSD version of od is similar but provides several additional options.

3.16   Copying and Converting Data with dd

The dd command has several purposes: copying data to or from a block or character device (see Section 2.18), changing the representation or form of the data, and partitioning a file into smaller files. The name probably stands for "device to device copy".

The form of the dd command line is

> dd [*operand* ...]

This form is *not* consistent with the usual conventions for command options, but it has been retained for the sake of compatibility with existing applications and scripts.[32] If neither the input nor the output file is given explicitly by the *operand*s, standard input is copied and converted to standard output, converted according to the *operand*s.

3.16.1
How the Files Are Processed

You can think of dd as working in three stages:

(1)   Data is read from the input file and short blocks are padded if necessary.
(2)   Any requested data conversions are performed.
(3)   The possibly transformed data is written to the output file.

Although the actual cycle is based on reading a block at a time and processing it, conceptually it's easier to think of all the data as being read in at once.

In the first stage, dd reads the data one block at a time, the block size being determined by the ibs or bs operand and bs taking precedence. If the sync conversion is specified and fewer than the requested number of bytes are read in, the block is padded to the specified size with null bytes or, in the case where the block or unblock conversion was specified, with spaces. Otherwise, any short blocks are used as is. Short blocks ordinarily occur only at the end of a file or when dd is taking its input from your terminal (since a *read* operation in cooked mode terminates when it sees a ⟨newline⟩).

The second stage happens only if a data conversion other than sync, notrunc, or noerror is requested. (The data conversions are specified by the conv operand.) First, bytes are swapped if the swab conversion was specified. Then any remaining conversions (block, unblock, lcase, or ucase) are performed in order to obtain the data to be sent to the output file.

In the third stage, blocks of data are written to the output file. For a block device such as a magnetic tape, the block size actually affects the way the data is stored on the device. The block size is determined by the obs or bs operand, with bs taking precedence. When the data is exhausted, the last block is padded with nulls or spaces (just as for the input) if the sync conversion is specified and written as a short block otherwise. In the case where the bs operand is specified and no actual data transformations are requested, short blocks in the input are preserved in the output.

3.16.2
Operands

The following operands specify the input or output files explicitly, overriding standard input and standard output:

if=*file*   Read input from *file*.

of=*file*   Write output to *file*.

---

32.   The POSIX Committee has indicated it intends to develop a new syntax for dd consistent with standard utility conventions.

The following operands control the block sizes used for input and output:

ibs=*size*   Use *size* as the input block size, with a default of 512 bytes.

obs=*size*   Use *size* as the output block size with a default of 512 bytes.

bs=*size*   Use *size* as both the input and output block size. If this operand is specified, it overrides ibs and obs.

In these three operands as well as in the next one, *size* is one of the following:

- A decimal constant possibly suffixed by k or b
- The product of two such decimal constants, written with an x between them

In this notation, k stands for units of 1024 bytes and b for units of 512 bytes, the traditional UNIX block size.

There's a difference between specifying the block size using ibs and obs versus specifying it with bs, even if the size is the same in every case. With bs specified (and no data transformations on individual bytes), short input blocks are copied as is to the output; with bs not specified, short input blocks are aggregated into full-size output blocks except at the very end of the data transfer.

The following operand controls the block size used with conversion of variable-length records to fixed-length records and vice versa:

cbs=*size*   Use *size* as conversion block size.

The following operands control the initial position in the input and output files and the number of input blocks to be copied:

skip=*n*   Initially skip *n* input blocks.

seek=*n*   Initially skip *n* output blocks. If there aren't already that many output blocks in the output file, either because it doesn't exist or because it's too short, create blocks of nulls to fill the space.

count=*n*   Copy only *n* input blocks. Any skipped blocks are not included in the count.

The following operand specifies data conversions to be performed as the data is read:

conv=*kw-list*

Perform the conversions specified in *kw-list*, where *kw-list* is a list of keywords for data conversion. The keywords are described below.

3.16.3
Keywords for Data Conversions

When you are using dd to transform data rather than just reblock it, the keywords associated with the conv operand specify what conversions are to be done.

The following mutually exclusive keywords specify a change from fixed-length records to variable-length records, with each variable-length record ended by a ⟨newline⟩:

block   Treat the input as a sequence of variable-length records and convert each record to the fixed length given by the cbs operand. The trailing ⟨newline⟩ of each input record is removed; then short records are padded with spaces and long records are truncated.

unblock   Treat the input as a sequence of fixed-length records whose length is given by the cbs operand and convert each record to variable-length form. A record is converted by removing any trailing spaces and then appending a ⟨newline⟩. The last input record may have fewer than the specified number of bytes.

The following mutually exclusive keywords specify case conversions:

lcase   Map each uppercase character to the corresponding lowercase character.

ucase   Map each lowercase character to the corresponding uppercase character.

The correspondence between lowercase and uppercase characters is given by the character classification category of the current locale (see "Character Classification and Attributes" on p. 75); for the default locale, it is the usual mapping between a–z and A–Z.

The following keyword specifies byte interchange:

swab   Group the input bytes into pairs and swap the bytes of each pair. This option is useful because some computers store two-byte words with the high-order byte first ("big-endian form") while others store them with the low-order byte first ("little-endian form").

The following keywords specify aspects of processing that do not require data transformation of individual bytes:

noerror   Continue processing when an error occurs.

notrunc   Don't truncate the output file; that is, start writing new data at the end of the existing file or at the location specified by the seek operand if it was given. The notrunc operand has no effect on some kinds of output devices such as printers.

sync   Pad each input block to the specified block size, using ⟨space⟩ as the padding character if block or noblock was specified and ⟨null⟩ otherwise.

The following conversions, which are not included in POSIX, convert among code sets. They require that a conversion block size be specified with the cbs operand.

ascii   Assume the input is EBCDIC and convert it to ASCII.

ebcdic   Assume the input is ASCII and convert it to standard EBCDIC.

ibm   Assume the input is ASCII and convert it to IBM EBCDIC.

Here are some examples of the use of dd:

- The commands

```
dd if=monster bs=10k count=100 of=monsterlet1
dd if=monster bs=10k count=100 of=monsterlet2 skip=100
```

  breaks the 2-megabyte file `monster` into two 1-megabyte files `monsterlet1` and `monsterlet2` (perhaps so that you can fit them onto diskettes). An alternative to using dd is to use `split` (see Section 4.4.4).

- The command

```
dd if=/dev/mt0 of=/dev/mt2 bs=32k
```

  copies data from magnetic tape unit 0 to magnetic tape unit 1, preserving block sizes for blocks shorter than 32,768 bytes.

- The command

```
dd if=/dev/mt0 conv=noerror | tar -xvf -
```

  reads a `tar` archive from a tape and extracts the files in it. If the tape has errors, much of the archive may still be salvaged.

- The command

```
dd cbs=80 conv=unblock < click > clack
```

  copies data from file `click` to file `clack`, stripping trailing spaces from each 80-character block and appending a ⟨newline⟩.

3.17   Updating Files with patch

The `patch` program, originally written by Larry Wall, is used in conjunction with the `diff` program (see Section 3.10.2) to update a text file to a later version. The text file can be a program, a document, or anything else.

The maintainer of the file uses `diff` to generate a set of differences between an old version and a newer revised one. These differences are the patches. A person who has a copy of the file can then use `patch` to apply the patches in order to get an updated (patched) copy that reflects the newer version.

`Patch` is very clever in how it screens its input. For example, you can use an electronic mail message containing a set of patches as input to `patch`. `Patch` will ignore any extraneous material such as the message header and the explanatory text that precedes or follows the patches themselves. Furthermore, `patch` can understand any one of the three forms of difference listings that the POSIX version of `diff` can generate[33] (though usually a context difference produced by '`diff -c`' is used).

The call on `diff` should have the old file as the first file argument. If it doesn't, however, `patch` can usually figure out how to compensate.

The form of the `patch` command line is

> `patch` [`-bflNRs`] [`-c` | `-e` | `-n`] [`-d` *dir*] [`-D` *def*] [`-F` *ff*] [`-i` *pfile*]
> [`-o` *ofile*] [`-p` *num*] [`-r` *rfile*] [*file*]

where *file* is the file to be patched. If *file* is not specified, the file or files to be patched (there can be more than one) are deduced from the patches themselves. The patches are read from standard input unless a different file *pfile* is specified by the `-i` *pfile* option.

3.17.1
Determining the Files to be Patched

You can explicitly specify the file to be patched by providing *file* in the call on `patch`. If you specify *file* but not the '`-o` *ofile*' option, then *file* is modified in place to reflect the patches. If you do specify '`-o` *ofile*', then *ofile* is used for the revised file.

When the form '`diff -c`' is used to create a patch set, the output of '`diff -c`' includes the name of both the original file and the revised one. The lines containing that information look like this:

> `***` *pathname*₁ *timestamp*₁
> `---` *pathname*₂ *timestamp*₂

where *pathname*$_1$ and *timestamp*$_1$ are the name and modification time of the original file and *pathname*$_2$ and *timestamp*$_2$ are the name and modification time of the revised one. If this information is present but *file* is not specified, then the *pathname*s are used to determine the file to be patched. You can override that choice with *file*. By default, the file is patched in place; you can override that behavior with the `-o` option.

If the material before the beginning of the patches themselves contains a line containing the string '`Index:`' followed by a pathname, then that pathname is assumed to be the location of the file to be patched unless you override it with an explicit *file* or with the `-o` option. If you are creating a set of patches but for some reason you can't or don't wish to use the '`diff -c`' form, then you should prepend an '`Index:`' line to the patches.

A patch file may and often does contain patches that update several different files. Each set of patches is then processed separately. The individual patches within a set are called "hunks".

The *pathname*s derived by either of these procedures can be modified by the `-p` or `-d` options. If you don't specify `-p`, then only the basename of each pertinent pathname is used in order to determine the files.

---

33.   Some non-POSIX versions of `diff` can generate other forms as well.

The command-line options for `patch` are described below.

Locating the Relevant Files. The following options locate files used by
`patch`:

-d *dir*   Change to directory *dir* before processing the patches. The
             effect is to assume that both the starting file and the resulting
             patched file are specified by pathnames relative to *dir*.

-i *pfile*   Read the patches from file *pfile*. The default is standard input.

-o *ofile*   Write the patched file to *ofile*. **Note:** If a series of patches
             is applied to the same file, the intermediate files generated at
             each step will be concatenated onto *ofile*. That is probably not
             what you want.

-b   Save a copy of the original version of each modified file *file*
             in the file *file*.`orig`.[34] If the '.`orig`' file already exists, it will
             be overwritten; if more than one patch is being applied to a
             particular file, only the version before the first patch will be
             written. If you've also specified a particular output file *ofile*
             with the -o option, the *ofile*.`orig` file will be written only if *ofile*
             already exists.

-r *rfile*   Send rejected hunks of patches (i.e., hunks that could not be
             applied) to *rfile*. The default for *rfile* is the output file with
             '.`rej`' appended.

The following option affects how the pathnames derived from the patches
themselves are to be modified:

-p *num*   Delete *num* pathname components from the name of each file
             to be patched, with a leading '/' counted as a component. If
             num is zero, the full pathname is used; if -p is omitted, only the
             basename of the pathname (i.e., its last component) is used.

Interpretation of Patches. The following options force `patch` to assume
that the patches were generated by a particular form of `diff`. They are
useful when for some reason `patch` is not able to determine the form on
its own.

-n   Interpret patches as if they were generated by calling `diff`
             normally—that is, without those options (-e,-c, or -C) that
             change the type of output `diff` produces.

-e   Interpret the patches as if they were generated by '`diff -e`',
             the form used to obtain a script usable by the `ed` editor (see
             Section 8.4).

-c   Interpret the patches as if they were generated by calling `diff`
             with the -c or -C option.

---

34. Some non-POSIX versions of `patch` interpret the -b option differently: -b *sfx* specifies
that a copy is to be saved under the name *file*.*sfx*, *sfx* being the suffix.

The following options adjust how `patch` deduces what the changes are:

`-l`   Treat all sequences of tabs and spaces as equivalent when comparing the patches to the input file. For example, a tab would be equivalent to a sequence of spaces or two spaces would be equivalent to three.

`-F` *ff*   Ignore *ff* (fuzz factor) lines of context. The default fuzz factor is usually 2. Increasing it may enable some files to be updated that could not otherwise be, but also increases the chances of a faulty patch. This option is not included in POSIX.

The following option specifies the direction of the patch:

`-R`   Assume that the patch is being done in reverse, going from the new file to the old one. This option is useful when the old and new files have accidentally been interchanged. If you don't specify this option but `patch` concludes that it is needed, `patch` will prompt you for it.

The following option enables a patch to be applied conditionally to a C program or to a program in any other language with C-like preprocessing.

`-D` *def*   Surround each change with the C preprocessor form

```
#ifdef def
...
#endif def
```

When you compile a program file constructed in this way, you can choose to apply or not to apply the correction set *def* by defining or not defining the preprocessor variable by that name.

User Input and Error Control.   The following options affect whether `patch` queries for user input in cases of doubt:

`-f`   Force processing in cases of doubt; don't ask for user input. This option is not supported by POSIX.

`-N`   Ignore any patches that have already been applied rather than sending them to the reject file. Note that this option affects entire patches, not hunks within patches. A patch is either processed normally or ignored entirely. This option is particularly useful when you are calling `patch` noninteractively and are processing a collection of patches where some of the patches have already been applied.

`-s`   Work silently, issuing no messages. This option is not supported by POSIX.

**3.17.3
Examples**

Here are some examples of how to use `patch`:

- Suppose the file `shards.diff` contains updates to `shards.tex` in ed format; that is, the updates were generated using the `-e` option of `diff`. The command

```
patch -eb shards.tex < shards.diff
```

will update `shards.tex` in place, saving the original contents in the file `shards.tex.orig`.

- Suppose you have a program called `ezex` whose relevant files you keep in a subdirectory `~/ezex`. Your version of `ezex` is at level 15. You obtain patches to bring `ezex` to level 18 in the form of three files `ezex15-16.diff`, `ezex16-17.diff`, and `ezex17-18.diff`. The command

  ```
  cat ezex15-16.diff ezex16-17.diff ezex17-18.diff \
      | patch -bd ~/ezex
  ```

  will cause all of your `ezex` files to be brought up to level 18, with the old files preserved as `.orig` files—an important precaution.

- Suppose you're using the `mailx` mailer and the current message contains a set of patches, generated by `diff -c`, that was sent to you. Suppose also that the files to be patched are in the directory `/usr/local/src/colors`. Then the `mailx` command

  ```
  | "patch -d /usr/local/src/colors"
  ```

  will apply the patches to the proper files, ignoring the extraneous material that is part of the mail message.

3.18   Creating Special Files

You can create an ordinary file just by writing to it, but to create other kinds of files you need special commands: `mkdir` for directories (see Section 3.1.3), `mkfifo` for FIFO special files, and `mknod` for special files in general, including both FIFOs and device files.

**3.18.1
Making FIFO Special
Files with** `mkfifo`

The `mkfifo` command creates one or more FIFO special files. The form of the command is

```
mkfifo [-m mode] pathname ...
```

where *pathname* ... are the pathnames of the files to be created. The default permissions are `a=rw` minus any bits specified in the file creation mask (see Section 2.8.5). If you specify '`-m` *mode*', the default permissions are modified by the symbolic mode *mode* (see Section 2.8.3). For example, the command

```
mkfifo -m go-w fiefdom
```

creates a FIFO special file `fiefdom` whose permissions are `u=rw g=r o=r`. The 4.4BSD version of `mkfifo` doesn't recognize the `-m` option.

3.18.2
Making Special Files
with mknod

Most systems provide a mknod command for creating special files in general, though this command was not included in POSIX because of the system-dependent nature of special files. You can use mknod to create both FIFO special files and device special files (see Sections 2.11.1 and 2.18). The forms of the mknod command line are

> mknod [-m *mode*] *pathname* b *major minor*
> mknod [-m *mode*] *pathname* c *major minor*
> mknod [-m *mode*] *pathname* p

where *pathname* is the pathname of the file to be constructed and the letters b, c, and p specify its type to be a block special file, character special file, or FIFO special file (named pipe), respectively. The numbers *major* and *minor* specify the major and minor numbers of the corresponding device (see Section 2.18.4). If you specify '-m *mode*', the default permissions are modified by the symbolic mode *mode* (see Section 2.8.3). Not all versions of mknod recognize the -m option.

You need superuser privileges to create a block special file or a character special file, but you don't need these privileges to create a FIFO special file.

4

Data Manipulation Using Filters

A *filter* is a program that modifies or transforms its input in order to obtain its output. By convention, a filter reads its input from standard input and writes it to standard output, so it's easy to connect several filters as a pipeline (see Section 2.10.1). Such combinations of filters are one of the best-known and most useful methods of using UNIX effectively, since they enable you to build complex transformations out of simple components. Most filters are also able to take their input from one or more explicitly specified files.

In this chapter we discuss a number of specialized filters such as sort, grep, and join. We also discuss the script editor sed and the programming language awk, which provide programmable filters. We also describe briefly the Icon and perl programming languages, which offer alternatives to awk.

4.1 Sorting Files with sort

The sort command sorts a single file or a sequence of files, either treating each line as a single record or basing the order of the output on keys extracted from each line. Used without any options or file specifications, sort sorts standard input, writes the result to standard output, sorts by lines, and compares individual characters according to their positions in

the collating sequence of the current locale. For the POSIX locale, the
collating sequence is the usual ASCII ordering. Sort is limited to sorting
records that occupy a single line, although the line can be very long if
necessary. You can sort a file in place with the -o command-line option.

The forms of the `sort` command line are

> sort [-m] [-o *ofile*] [-bdfinru] [-t *char*] [-k *keydef*] ... [*file* ...]
> sort -c [-bdfinru] [-t *char*] [-k *keydef*] ... [*file*]

There are also two obsolescent forms:

> sort [-mu] [-o *ofile*] [-bdfinr] [-t *char*] [+pos_1 [-pos_2]] ... [*file* ...]
> sort -c [-u] [-bdfinr] [-t *char*] [+pos_1 [-pos_2]] ... [*file*]

The specified files *file* ... are concatenated and sorted. If no files are
specified, standard input is sorted. Within the list of files, '-' denotes
standard input treated as a file.

The *keydef*s define the sort keys (see below). If no *keydef*s are present,
the entire line is treated as a single sort key. The pos_1 and pos_2 specifications in the obsolescent forms have the same meaning as they do in
a *keydef*, except that in the obsolescent forms the numbering of fields and
characters starts with zero rather than with one.

4.1.1
Key Specifications

By providing *keydef*s on the command line, you can base the order of
sort's output on a sequence of *keys* extracted from each input record
(line). Output records are ordered by the first key; for records having the
same first key, by the second key, and so forth. Records having all keys
equal are further sorted by comparing the records byte for byte.

Each *keydef* specifies the location of a single key within the record and
how that key is to be interpreted. A *keydef* has the form

> pos_1[,pos_2]

where pos_1 indicates where within the line the key starts and pos_2 where it
ends. If pos_2 is missing, the key continues to the end of the line. You can
also include flags in pos_1 or pos_2 that change how the key is interpreted.
By default, the key is treated simply as a sequence of characters, ordered
according to the collating sequence of the current locale.

To define the locations of keys within a record, the record is partitioned
into a sequence of fields bounded by delimiters. By default the delimiters are the space and tab characters; the spaces and tabs are themselves
considered part of the field that they begin. For example, the input record

> cruel␣␣gruel

is partitioned into two fields, 'cruel' and '␣␣gruel'. The second field
begins with two spaces.

You can override the default delimiters by specifying a single delimiter
character with the -t option. In this case the delimiter character is not
considered part of a field, and two delimiter characters in a row define

an empty field.[1] (Although the delimiter set contains two characters by
default, it can only contain one delimiter character if you specify it explicitly.) Fields are always ended by the end of the line, so missing fields are
effectively empty.

Each *pos* in a key specification has the form

$f[.c][\textit{flags}]$

Here f specifies a field and c a character within the field, with fields and
characters numbered starting with one. For the obsolescent forms that use
+pos_1 and −pos_2, the numbering starts with zero.[2] The ending position is
the first position *not* in the key. If you omit '.c', it defaults to one. For
instance, the key specification

```
-k 3.2,6.4
```

specifies a key that starts with the second character of the third field and
is ended by but does not include the fourth character of the sixth field.
The key specification

```
-k 2,3
```

specifies a key that begins with the first character of the second field and
is ended by but does not include the first character of the third field—in
other words, the second field exactly.

The flags, listed in Section 4.1.3, are specified as letters only (no
hyphens). For instance, the key specification

```
-k 3r
```

indicates a key that starts with the third field, runs to the end of the line,
and is to be sorted in reverse order. You can attach flags either to pos_1 or
pos_2. Except for the b flag, it makes no difference where you attach a flag.

An example showing these facilities used in combination is

```
sort -t: -k 3,3.3 -k 1n,2
```

In this case there are two sort keys. The input (taken from standard
input) is first sorted according to the first two characters of the third field.
Within each group of records with identical first keys, the input is sorted
numerically (because of the n) according to the contents of the first field.

---

1.   Thus there is an important difference between the default case and the effect of the
option '-t"␣"', which specifies a space as the delimiter. Aside from the fact that tabs no
longer serve as delimiters with this option, the second field of the record in the example just
above would be empty.

2.   The POSIX Committee introduced this important change for the sake of consistency
with other utilities. It means that you cannot just copy *keyspec*s from the older form to the
newer one.

4.1.2
Options Affecting
the Entire Sort

The following options apply to the entire sort.

General Options. The following options have general effects on how `sort` operates:

-o *outfile* Send the output to *outfile* rather than to standard output. The file *outfile* can be one of the input files; if it is, that input file is replaced by the result of the sort.

-c Check that the input is already sorted. The exit status is 0 if the input is sorted, 1 if it isn't. In either case, no output is produced.

-m Merge the input files, assuming them to be already sorted.

-u Produce unique keys only; that is, when several lines have equal keys, produce only one of the lines. The extra lines are suppressed even when the complete lines are not identical. In conjunction with -c, this option causes `sort` to terminate with exit status 1 if it finds any lines with equal keys.

-t *char* Use *char* as the field delimiter.

Flags Applying to All Keys. The -b, -d, -f, -i, -n, and -r options pertain to how keys are interpreted. Each of these options can also be used as a flag on an individual key as described in Section 4.1.3. These options must precede the -k option.

 The options apply to all keys unless they are overridden by a flag on an individual key. For example, an -r option is equivalent to attaching r to each key specification that does not already have a flag, while a -b option is equivalent to attaching b to *pos*$_1$ and *pos*$_2$ of each key that does not already have a flag.

System V Capacity and Performance Options. System V `sort` provides the following options for tuning its capacity and performance:

-y [*n*] Use *n* kilobytes of main memory, enlarging this space as necessary. If *n* is 0, `sort` starts with a minimum amount of memory; if *n* is omitted, `sort` starts with a maximum amount of memory. Adding memory may reduce sorting time but increases the load on your system.

-z *n* Assume *n* to be the longest record size. If you don't specify *n*, `sort` uses a default value, typically 1024. This option has an effect only if you've specified -c or -m, since otherwise `sort` determines the longest record size when it's first passing through the input. If the longest record is longer than the assumed maximum, `sort` terminates abnormally.

4.1.3
Flags Applying to Individual Keys

The flags described below affect the interpretation of individual keys. As noted previously, these flags can also be used as options. If you specify any flags on an individual key, the global options are ignored. The b flag applies individually to *pos*$_1$ and *pos*$_2$; the other options apply to the key as a whole.

Ignoring Initial Whitespace in Keys.   By default, leading whitespace in a non-numeric key is significant. The following flag enables you to ignore it:

-b   Ignore leading or trailing whitespace in determining character positions within a non-numeric key. Thus if b is attached to *pos*$_1$, the first position of the key is the first *nonwhite* character of the key; if b is attached to *pos*$_2$, whitespace at the end of the key is removed before any comparisons are made.

Reversing the Sort Order.   The following flag reverses the sort order:

-r   Reverse the sense of comparisons for the indicated key, causing keys that would normally come first to come last.

Interpreting Keys.   The following options provide different ways of interpreting keys. By default, the key is treated simply as a sequence of characters, ordered according to the collating sequence of the current locale.

-d   Use dictionary order, ignoring characters other than letters, digits, and whitespace in making comparisons. The characters are classified using the classification rules as given by LC_TYPE (see "Character Classification and Attributes" on p. 75). Note that in the POSIX locale at least, all uppercase letters still precede all lowercase letters, so 'Z' precedes 'a'. This flag should not be used with the -i or -n flags.

-f   Fold lowercase letters to uppercase; that is, convert every lowercase letter to its uppercase counterpart. The conversion is performed according to the current locale's character classification rules as given by LC_TYPE (see "Character Classification and Attributes" on p. 75).

-i   Ignore nonprinting characters. The nonprinting characters are defined by the current locale's character classification rules as given by LC_TYPE (see "Character Classification and Attributes" on p. 75). For ASCII (as in the POSIX locale), the nonprinting characters are those whose decimal values are less than 32 or greater than 126.

-n   Treat the key as a number. If the key contains a number followed by whitespace and other text, sort considers only the number part. The number can include a plus or minus sign and a decimal point. Sort ignores initial whitespace within a numeric key field but does not ignore initial whitespace at the beginning of a line when performing a numeric sort on entire lines. For example, the command 'sort -n' with the input

```
    2
  1
```

produces output consisting of these two lines in the original order. For the command 'sort -k 1n', the whitespace preceding the '2' is ignored and the order of the output lines is reversed.

-M   Treat the key as a three-letter case-insensitive month name. Whitespace preceding the month name is ignored, as is the part of the key after the first three letters. Thus 'jan' precedes 'feb', 'feb' precedes 'MAR', and so forth. A key that is not a month name precedes 'jan'; all such keys compare equal. This option is only supported in System V versions of sort.

4.2 Finding Patterns with grep

The grep utility enables you to search through a set of files for all lines that match a specified pattern. Depending on the options, the pattern may be a BRE, an ERE, or a fixed string (see the discussion of regular expressions in Section 2.17). The name grep stands for "Global Regular Expression Print". You can also use grep as a filter to extract the matching lines from standard input and send those lines to standard output. The POSIX grep provides two options, -E and -F, that cause grep to behave like two older variants, egrep and fgrep. These variants are now considered obsolescent.

The Command Line.   The forms of the grep command line are

```
grep [-E | -F] [-c | -l | -q] [-insvx] -e patlist ...
   [-f patfile] ... [file ...]
grep [-E | -F] [-c | -l | -q] [-insvx] [-e patlist] ...
   -f patfile ... [file ...]
grep [-E | -F] [-c | -l | -q] patlist [file ...]
```

The obsolescent commands egrep and fgrep are equivalent to 'grep -E' and 'grep -F', respectively. In these forms, *patlist* is a list of patterns to be searched for, *patfile* is a file containing a list of patterns, and *file* ... is a list of files to be searched. If no files are specified, the program searches standard input. The results of the search are sent to standard output.

Usually you should quote the pattern in apostrophes in order to prevent any of the characters within it from being interpreted as shell metacharacters (see Section 2.12.2). For example, the command

```
egrep 'idol|adultery' KingJames
```

searches the file `KingJames` for each line containing either the string 'idol' or the string 'adultery' and sends each such line to standard output.

Output of `grep`.   If you don't specify any of the options `-nclq` and provide only a single *file*, the output of `grep` consists of all matching lines. If you provide more than one *file*, each output line is prefixed by the pathname of the file as it was specified on the command line (after shell expansion of wildcards). The following options modify the form of the output:

`-n`	Precede each line by its file name and line number.
`-b`	Precede each line by its disk block number. This option is not included in POSIX.
`-c`	Only show a count of matching lines.
`-l`	Only show the names of files containing matching strings— don't show the strings themselves.
`-s`	Suppress error messages that pertain to nonexistent or unreadable files.
`-q`	Run quietly; don't write anything to standard output, regardless of matching lines. Exit with zero status if any input lines are selected.

Specifying the Search Patterns.   Grep searches for lines that match any pattern in a pattern list. A pattern matches a line if it matches any portion of the line, although you can force it to match an entire line with the `-x` option. The pattern list consists of a sequence of patterns separated by ⟨newline⟩s. Two consecutive ⟨newline⟩s define an empty pattern, which matches every line.

   The following options provide other ways to specify the pattern list:

`-e` *patlist*	Search for the patterns in *patlist*. The purpose of this option is to provide for patterns that begin with '–'.
`-f` *patfile*	Read a pattern list from the file named by the pathname *patfile* and search for the patterns in that list.

You can specify multiple `-e` or multiple `-f` options, but not both. If you specify neither of these options, then you can specify the pattern list directly as in the third form.

Options for Defining the Search Variant.   The `grep` options provide a choice among three search variants that differ in the generality of the expressions that they search for and in the speed of search. The default variant, the original form of `grep`, interprets each pattern as a BRE and uses a compact nondeterministic algorithm for the search. The options for the other two variants are these:

`-F`	Interpret each pattern as a fixed string, using a search algorithm that is both fast and compact. The obsolescent command `fgrep` is equivalent to 'grep `-F`'.

-E
Interpret each pattern as an ERE, using a fast deterministic search algorithm. This algorithm can require huge amounts of space in pathological cases, but these cases almost never arise. The obsolescent command `egrep` is equivalent to 'grep -E'.

Generally you should specify -F to search for a single string and -E otherwise.

Other Command-Line Options.   The following options affect the pattern match itself:

-w
Search for the pattern as a word. Any character other than a letter or digit counts as a word delimiter. This option is only recognized by the BSD version of `grep`.

-x
Accept a match only if the pattern matches the entire line. Some versions of `grep` don't support this option.

-v
Select the lines that *don't* match.

-i
Ignore the case of letters in making comparisons; that is, treat uppercase and lowercase letters as equivalent.

4.3   Simple Data Transformations

The programs described in this section perform relatively simple transformations of their input:

- Tr translates from one character set to another, deletes characters, or eliminates repetitions of certain characters.

- Cut extracts specified portions of each input line.

- Paste pastes together corresponding lines from several files into one long line or concatenates all the lines of a single file into one long line.

- Fold folds long lines into sequences of shorter ones.

- Expand and unexpand transform tabs to spaces and spaces to tabs.

- Uniq eliminates or reports adjacent repeated lines in its input.

- Comm selects or rejects lines that are common to two sorted files.

**4.3.1
Translating or
Deleting Characters
with** tr

The `tr` command enables you to edit a file by replacing certain characters by other characters, by deleting certain characters, or by removing repeated sequences of certain characters. The form of the `tr` command line is

tr [-cds] *str*$_1$ [*str*$_2$]

where *str*$_1$ specifies a string of characters to be replaced or deleted and *str*$_2$ specifies a string of characters to be substituted or condensed. `Tr` reads from standard input and writes to standard output.

Command-Line Options.   The `tr` command has the following options, which can be used in combination:

-d   Delete the characters in *str*$_1$ instead of replacing them. If the
            -s option is also present, *str*$_2$ is required; if the -s option is not
            also present, *str*$_2$ is irrelevant.

-s   Squeeze repetitions of characters in *str*$_2$ (if -d is present) or *str*$_1$
            (if -d is absent) to single characters. For instance, if *str*$_i$ contains
            the space character, sequences of several spaces are condensed
            to a single space (independently of whether substitutions are
            taking place). Sequences of different characters from *str*$_i$ are
            not squeezed.

-c   Use the complement of *str*$_1$ instead of *str*$_1$. The complement
            consists of all non-null characters that are not in *str*$_1$, taken
            in their collating sequence order. This option is usually useful
            only if you also specify -d; in this case the characters in *str*$_1$ are
            retained and all others are deleted.

Interpretation of Translation Strings.   The following conventions apply to the translation strings *str*$_1$ and *str*$_2$:

- The usual escape sequences \b (⟨backspace⟩), \f (⟨formfeed⟩), \n (⟨newline⟩), \r (⟨return⟩), \t (⟨tab⟩), and \v (⟨vertical tab⟩) are recognized within the strings.
- A backslash followed by one, two, or three octal digits represents the character whose numerical code is given by those digits. (If this construct is to be followed by an octal digit that isn't part of it, you should write the octal number using all three digits.)
- The effect of any other backslash is up to the implementation; most versions of `tr` treat such backslashes as illegal characters.
- The notation c_1-c_2 represents the sequence of characters in the collating sequence of the current locale (ASCII for the POSIX locale), starting with the character c_1 and ending with the character c_2.
- The notation [c*[n]] represents n repetitions of the character c. If n starts with 0, it is taken as an octal number; otherwise, as a decimal number. If n is missing or zero, it is taken as indefinitely large.
- The notation [:*class*:] represents all characters belonging to the character class *class* as defined by the LC_TYPE category for the current locale (see "Character Classification and Attributes" on p. 75). The following character-class names are acceptable in *str*$_1$:

      alnum blank digit lower punct upper
      alpha cntrl graph print space xdigit

The same set is acceptable in *str*$_2$ if both -d and -s have been specified. If -d and -s have not both been specified, only [:upper:]

and [:lower:] are acceptable in *str*$_2$. Moreover, [:upper:] and [:lower:] must appear in pairs in corresponding positions of *str*$_1$ and *str*$_2$, denoting the tolower or toupper mappings of the current locale.

- The notation [=*equiv*=] represents all characters or collating elements belonging to the same equivalence class as *equiv* as defined for the current locale (see "Collating Rules and Collating Elements" on p. 76). It is valid only when both -d and -s have been specified.

If no options are specified, tr replaces each occurrence of the *n*th character of *str*$_1$ by the *n*th character of *str*$_2$. If *str*$_1$ is longer than *str*$_2$, the excess characters of *str*$_1$ are ignored. The -d option causes tr to delete the characters in *str*$_1$; the -s option causes it to condense the characters in *str*$_2$ if -d is present and *str*$_1$ if -d is absent.

A simple and useful example of tr is

```
tr "[:lower:]" "[:upper:]"
```

This command replaces each lowercase character in standard input by the corresponding uppercase character and sends the result to standard output.

4.3.2
Extracting Portions
of Input Lines
with cut

The cut command extracts specified portions of each line of its input. You can define the portions either by specifying the positions (byte or character) they occupy or by specifying the fields they occupy and the delimiter character that separates the fields.

The forms of the cut command line are

```
cut -b list [-n] [file... ]
cut -c list [file... ]
cut -f list [-d delim] [-s] [file... ]
```

where the input consists of the concatenation of the files *file* ... . If no files are specified, cut takes its input from standard input. A *file* given by '-' specifies standard input. The -b, -c, and -f options specify extraction by bytes, characters, and fields, respectively. The difference between bytes and characters becomes significant when your locale specifies multibyte characters.

The *list* argument of the command line specifies the portions of each input line to be extracted. A *list* is written as a sequence of single numbers and ranges, with items separated by commas or whitespace.[3] The first character or field is numbered as 1. The numbers should be in increasing order. A range is indicated as a pair of numbers separated by '-'. Within a range, you can omit the first number (implying the first item) or the last number (implying the last item). If all or part of the text selected by a range is missing because an input line is too short, the missing portion

---

3. If you use whitespace as the separator, you need to quote the argument.

is just ignored. Overlapping selections are combined and the resulting selections are then produced in order of their starting positions.[4]

For example, the command

```
cut -c 2,5-8,14-
```

extracts characters 2, 5 through 8, and 14 through l from each line, where l is the line length.

Extracting Characters or Bytes. The following command-line option applies when you are extracting characters:

-c *list*   Extract the characters specified in *list*.

The following command-line options apply when you are extracting bytes:

-b *list*   Extract the bytes specified in *list*.

-n   Don't split multibyte characters. With this option specified, each range is adjusted leftward if necessary so that only entire characters are selected. If the first byte of the range doesn't begin a character, it is decremented until it does begin a character. If the last byte doesn't end a character, it is decremented until it reaches the last byte of the preceding character (or the beginning of the line).

Extracting Delimited Fields. The following command-line options apply when you are extracting fields separated by delimiters. The default delimiter is ⟨tab⟩.

-f *list*   Extract the fields specified in *list*. The fields are concatenated and sent to standard output.

-d *delim*   Use the character *delim* instead of ⟨tab⟩ as the field delimiter.

-s   Suppress lines containing no delimiter characters. By default, such lines are included in the output. The -s option can sometimes be useful for suppressing header lines in a tabular file.

A sequence of several delimiters in a row defines a sequence of several fields; empty fields are permitted and recognized. If the delimiter is a space, this may not be what you want. Cut inserts the delimiter character between consecutive fields of the output, even if they are empty. For example, the command

```
cut -f1,3-4 -d:
```

specifies that fields 1, 3, and 4 should be extracted from each line with ':' as the field delimiter. Applied to the input line

```
I:say::what:I:mean
```

this command yields the output

```
I::what
```

---

4. Specifying the list items in nonincreasing order is permitted but doesn't increase the power of cut—it just creates confusion as to what the output will be.

Note: If the number of fields on an input line is fewer than the largest field number specified on the command line, cut ignores the missing fields and produces no delimiters for them.

4.3.3
Folding Long Lines with fold

The fold program reads input lines and folds each one by breaking it into several lines if necessary to ensure that the output lines are no longer than a specified length. The form of the fold command line is

    fold [-bs] [-w *width*] [*file* ...]

Fold reads lines from the input files or from standard input if no *files* are specified. By default, any line whose length exceeds *width* columns is broken into two lines by inserting a ⟨newline⟩ following column *width*. The second line that results is then folded in the same way if necessary. The default for *width* is 80, and by default each column is occupied by one character (with the exceptions noted below for certain characters). If a break would occur in the middle of a multibyte character, it is moved leftward to the beginning of that character.

Certain characters are treated specially:

- A ⟨return⟩ character resets the column count to zero. Fold never inserts a ⟨newline⟩ just before or just after a ⟨return⟩.
- A ⟨backspace⟩ decrements the column count by one. Fold never inserts a ⟨newline⟩ just before or just after a ⟨backspace⟩.
- A ⟨tab⟩ advances the column position to the next tab stop, assuming tab stops at positions 1, 9, 17, ...

Command-Line Options. The following command-line options apply to fold:

-w *width*   Take *width* as the maximum line length.

-b   Count column positions in bytes rather than characters.

-s   Break each line at the end of the last whitespace that lies entirely within the *width* columns. If no whitespace meets that requirement, then break the line normally.

4.3.4
Transforming Spaces to Tabs and Vice Versa

A pair of utilities, expand and unexpand, transform tab characters to spaces and spaces to tabs. Both utilities assume a model wherein a line has tab positions at various locations just as a typewriter does. The default tab positions are placed every 8 columns starting with positions 1 and 9.[5] A tab is then considered to be equivalent to the sequence of spaces that would advance the column position to the next tab stop.

The forms of the expand and unexpand command lines are

    expand [-t *tablist*] [*file* ...]
    unexpand [-a | -t *tablist*] [*file* ...]

---

5. This default is singularly inappropriate for programming in any modern high-level language since indented code rapidly migrates over to the right margin. It appears to trace back to early DEC assembler language. The default has carried over to other operating systems such as OS/2 and MS-DOS.

In these forms, *tablist* specifies a list of one or more tab positions. The list consists of an increasing sequence of unsigned integers separated by whitespace or commas. (If you use whitespace, you need to quote the list.) An obsolescent form of `expand` is

> `expand` [-*tab*₁, *tab*₂, ... , *tab*ₙ] [*file* ...]

In this form, the sequence of *tab* values specifies the same tab positions as *tablist* does. For either tranformation, the input consists of the concatenation of *file* ..., with '-' representing standard input. The transformation produces its result on standard output.

Defining the Transformations.   The `expand` transformation replaces each tab character in the input with as many spaces as needed to bring the column position up to the next tab position. For instance, if the next tab position is at column 9 and a tab occurs in column 5 (the first character of the line being in column 1), the tab is replaced by four spaces (occupying columns 5–8). A tab following the last tab position is replaced by a single space. A tab is always replaced by at least one character. For example, executing the command

> `expand -t 4`

sets the tab positions at columns 1, 5, 9, ... and causes the input line

> ⟨tab⟩abc⟨tab⟩d

to be transformed to the line

> ␣␣␣␣abc␣d

In the other direction, the `unexpand` transformation replaces whitespace at the beginning of a line by an equivalent sequence of tabs and spaces, using as many tabs as possible. In addition, if either `-a` or `-t` is specified, sequences of two or more spaces preceding a tab position are replaced by a sequence of spaces and tabs, using as many tabs as possible.[6] A ⟨backspace⟩ in the input has the effect of decreasing the column position by 1. For example, executing the command

> `unexpand -t 4`

causes the input line

> ␣␣␣␣␣Y␣␣␣␣␣␣␣␣Z

to be transformed to the line

> ⟨tab⟩␣Y⟨tab⟩⟨tab⟩␣Z

---

6. If neither `-a` nor `-t` is specified, whitespace other than at the beginning of the line is *not* transformed into tabs. This behavior is a historical artifact that the POSIX Committee declined to change. It's easy enough to circumvent.

Command-Line Options.   You specify the tab positions for either expand or unexpand with the following option:

-t *tablist* If *tablist* consists of a single integer k, then the tab positions are assumed to be k columns apart, starting with position 1. Otherwise the tab positions are assumed to be as listed in *tablist*. The default for *tablist* is '8'.

For unexpand you can specify whether internal tabs are also inserted within the line:

-a   Also transform whitespace within a line to tabs. If you specify -t, -a is also assumed.

**4.3.5
Eliminating
Repeated Lines
with** uniq

The uniq command processes a file, eliminating or reporting consecutive lines that are identical. You can optionally cause initial parts of the lines to be ignored in the comparison; in this case, the first line in a group of equal lines is the one that is retained.

The form of the uniq command line is

uniq [-c | -d | -u] [-f *nf*] [-s *nc*] [*infile* [*outfile*]]

where the input comes from *infile* and is written to *outfile*. An obsolescent form is

uniq [-c | -d | -u] [-*nf*] [+*nc*] [*infile* [*outfile*]]

where -*nf* and +*nc* are equivalent to '-f *nf*' and '-s *nc*', respectively. As usual, the files *infile* and *outfile* default to standard input and standard output. If none of the -u, -c, or -d options are specified, uniq produces each nonrepeated line and the first line of each sequence of repeated lines. This effect is equivalent to the -u and -d options together.

Command-Line Options.   The following options affect which lines appear in the output:

-d   Produce just the first copy of each repeated line.

-u   Produce just the lines that are not repeated.

-c   Precede each output line by a count of how many times it occurs. This option implies the -d and -u options.

The following options enable you to ignore initial parts of lines when comparing them:

-*nf*
-f *nf*   Ignore the first *nf* fields. For the purposes of the comparison, fields are assumed to be separated by whitespace (or, more generally, blank characters as defined by the current locale). Whitespace preceding any of the first *nf* fields (but not the $(n + 1)$th field) is ignored.

+*nc*
-s *nc*   Ignore the first *nc* characters.

If both -f and -s are specified, fields are skipped first, then characters. If all of a line is skipped, an empty string is used for the comparison.

**4.3.6
Listing Common
Lines
with** comm

The comm command enables you to compare two *sorted* files, listing the lines that are common to both of them and sending that listing to standard output. The default listing has three columns:

(1)   The lines that only occur in the first file.
(2)   The lines that only occur in the second file.
(3)   The lines that occur in both files.

You can suppress one or more of these columns by specifying flags on the command line, which has the form

comm [-*flags*] *file*$_1$ *file*$_2$

Here *flags* consists of one or more of the digits 123. Each digit in *flags* indicates that the corresponding column of the listing should be suppressed. The command arguments *file*$_1$ and *file*$_2$ are the two files being compared; either one can be given as '-', indicating standard input.

4.4   Extracting Parts of Files

The programs in this section can be used to extract portions of a file, to break a file into pieces, or to join two files together, database-style.

- Head extracts the beginning of a file.
- Tail extracts the end of a file and can also be used to monitor a file as it is being written.
- Split splits a file into smaller pieces.

**4.4.1
Extracting the
Beginning of a File
with** head

The head program extracts the beginning of a file, or several files. The form of the head command line is

head [-n *num*] [*files* ...]

By default, the first 10 lines of each of *files* ... are copied to standard output. You can copy a different number of lines by specifying the -n option:

-n *num*   Copy *num* lines from each file. In an obsolescent form of the command, the -n is omitted and only *num* is specified.

**4.4.2
Extracting the End of
a File with** tail

The tail program extracts the last part of a file. As a special case, you can also use it to monitor what is being added to a file. The form of the command line is

tail [-f][-c *number* | -n *number*] [*file*]

where *number* is an integer *n* optionally preceded by '+' or '−'. Tail copies the contents of *file* to standard output, beginning at a position specified by the -c or -n option.

The particular form

```
tail -c +n
```

starts the copy with the *n*th byte[7] of the file (the first byte being numbered as 1). If *number* is unsigned or starts with '−', the copy starts with the *n*th byte from the end (the last byte being numbered as −1). If you specify -n rather than -c, the starting point is measured in lines rather than in bytes.

If you specify neither -n nor -c, tail assumes an option of '-n 10'; that is, it produces the last 10 lines of the file. If you omit *file*, tail assumes that its input file is standard input. For example,

```
tail -c +200 lariat
```

produces the contents of lariat, beginning with the 200th character, while

```
sort trivia | tail -n 20
```

sorts the file trivia and produces the last 20 lines of the sorted output.

If you specify -f, then tail does not terminate after producing its output. Instead, it awaits further bytes from its input file, reading and producing them as they become available (if they ever do). The only way to terminate it in this case is to interrupt it (or kill its parent process). The -f option is ignored if the input to tail is a pipe.

'Tail -f' is particularly useful for monitoring the output of a background process. For instance, suppose logfile is a file that one or more processes are using to record their activities. Whenever one of the processes does anything notable, it adds a line to logfile. You can see what the processes are doing by issuing the command

```
tail -f logfile
```

Tail immediately produces the last 10 lines of the current contents of logfile; as processes write additional lines to logfile, tail produces those lines. Tail continues to run until you type (Intr) or terminate it some other way.

If you specify -f and omit *file*, tail continues to read from standard input until you interrupt it. However, if standard input is coming from a pipe, tail quits when the process supplying standard input terminates. For instance, suppose you type

```
cat | tail -f
one
two
three
(Ctrl) D
```

---

7. Historically, c stood for "character" in the days when bytes and characters were thought of as equivalent. In modern UNIX systems that can support multiple locales, a character might contain several bytes, but the c notation persists for the sake of compatibility.

When you type Ctrl D , the `cat` process terminates, causing the parent process (the one corresponding to the pipeline) to terminate. That termination in turn causes `tail` to terminate.

The length of a tail at the end of a file is limited to 4096 characters on many systems.

Some systems still use an obsolescent syntax for `tail`:

> `tail` *sign*[*n*][*unit*][`f`] [*file*]

The items in this form, which must be written with no intervening whitespace, are as follows:

sign	'+' or '−'
n	An integer (default is 10)
unit	One of `l` (lines), `b` (1024-byte blocks), or `c` (bytes). The default is `l`.
`f`	Indicator for continuous monitoring of text added to *file*

The meaning of this form is similar to that of the newer one. If *unit* is omitted, lines (`l`) are assumed.

4.4.3
Splitting Files by
Context with `csplit`

The `csplit` utility splits a file into portions according to a sequence of criteria and copies each portion other than the tail into a subfile. The `split` utility (see Section 4.4.4) performs a similar function but provides only one way to split a file: partitioning by size. `Split` creates as many subfiles as needed and copies the tail of the file into a subfile also, while `csplit` in contrast uses only a fixed list of splits and does not copy the rest of the file into a subfile. In addition, `split` can split a file by byte count; `csplit` can't.

The form of the `csplit` command line is

> `csplit` [`-ks`] [`-f` *pfx*] [`-n` *digs*] *file crit* ...

The file *file* is split into portions according to the criteria *crit* ... (see below), and the portions are copied into a sequence of subfiles. By default the subfiles are named `xx00`, `xx01`, ... , `xx99`. More generally, the subfiles are named *pfx.n*, where *pfx* is specified by the `-f` option (default 'xx') and *n* is a *digs*-digit number, where *digs* is specified by the `-n` option (default 2 digits). At least one *crit* must be specified, so there is no default criterion for choosing where to split the file. By default, if an error occurs during the `csplit` operation, any subfiles already created are removed. By default, `csplit` produces a line on standard output giving the name and size of each subfile it created.

Command-Line Options. These are the command-line options for `csplit`:

`-f` *pfx*	Use the prefix *pfx* in forming the names of the subfiles created by `csplit`.
`-n` *digs*	Use *digs* digits in forming the names of the subfiles created by `csplit`.

-k   If an error occurs, don't delete subfiles that have already been created.

-s   Suppress the output of lines describing the subfiles created by `csplit`.

Forms of the Criteria.   The split points are defined by applying the criteria *crit* ... in the order they appear. Each criterion selects a line of the input file *file*. When a criterion is applied, the portion of the input file up to but not including the selected line is either copied to the next subfile or, for one type of criterion, ignored. Then the portion is removed from consideration, so the search for the line selected by the next criterion behaves as though the line just selected was the first line of the file. In effect, each criterion is taken relative to the preceding one. When the last criterion has been applied, the rest of the input file is ignored. If the search for a criterion fails, `csplit` reports an error.

Each criterion has the form

> *locator* [{*num*}]

where *num*, a decimal integer, is a repetition count and *locator* locates the next boundary. Attaching a repetition count *num* to a locator causes that locator to be used *num* times, just as though it had been written out *num* times. For example, the criterion

> `/doggerel/ 4`

is equivalent to the sequence of single locators

> `/doggerel/ /doggerel/ /doggerel/ /doggerel/`

The locator *locator* must be one of the following:

/regexpr/[*offset*]

The line selected for the split is the next line that matches the basic regular expression *regexpr* (see Section 2.17.1), with the selection possibly modified by an offset *offset*. An offset is a decimal integer preceded by '+' or '-'. If an offset is specified, the selected line is that number of lines either before ('-') or after ('+') the line matching the regular expression. The portion of the input file from the previous selection up to but not including this one is copied to the next subfile. For example, the criterion `/kiwi/-2` locates the line that is two lines before the next line (after deleting previously extracted portions) containing the string `kiwi`.

%regexpr%[*offset*]

A line is selected just as with the previous form, but the selected portion of the input file is not copied to a subfile and is effectively skipped.

linenbr

The line selected for the split is line number *linenbr* relative to the previous selection (or the beginning of the input file if no selections have yet been made). The portion of the input file from the previous selection up to but not including this one is copied to the next subfile.

<table>
<tr><td>

4.4.4
Splitting Files by
Counts with `split`

</td><td>

The `split` command splits a file into subfiles of a specified size, naming the subfiles systematically. The `csplit` utility (see Section 4.4.4), which performs a similar function, is more flexible but lacks `split`'s capability of splitting a file by byte count. The `dd` utility (see Section 3.16) can also split a file by byte count but requires a separate command for each subfile to be created.

The forms of the `split` command line are

</td></tr>
</table>

    `split` [`-l` *lines*] [`-a` *len*] [*file* [*name*]]
    `split -b` *n*[k | m] [`-a` *len*] [*file* [*name*]]

An obsolescent form is

    `split` [`-`*lines*] [`-a` *len*] [*file* [*name*]]

This form is equivalent to the first form without the '`-l`'.

The simplest case is when you call `split` with no options whatsoever. In this case, the contents of standard input are split into subfiles of 1000 lines and written to a sequence of files named `xaa`, `xab`, ..., `xaz`, `xba`, ... (The last file may be shorter.) If you specify a pathname *file*, the file designated by that pathname is split instead ('`-`' denotes standard input). By specifying the options described below, you can change the size of the subfiles or the names of the output files.

In general, the names of the split files consist of a prefix followed by a suffix. If you specify *name* on the command line, then that is used as the prefix (which is why specifying *file* as '`-`' can be useful). The suffix is gotten by cycling through sequences of lowercase letters as defined by the current locale, last letter changing most rapidly. (For the case of the POSIX locale and the default suffix length 2, that implies a limit of 626 [26 × 26] output files.)

Command-Line Options.   These are the command-line options for `split`:

`-l` *lines*   Split the file into subfiles of *lines* lines.

`-b` *n*   Split the file into subfiles of *n* bytes. When you specify *n*, a suffix of k signifies kilobytes (1024 bytes) and a suffix of m signifies megabytes (1,048,576 bytes).

`-a` *len*   Use *len* letters rather than two letters to form the suffixes of the split portions.

Examples.   Here are some examples of `split`:

- The command

    `split -l 500 -a 1 - pt.`

  splits the contents of standard input into 500-line subfiles named `pt.a`, `pt.b`, etc. You can reconstruct the subfiles into a file called `recon` with the command

    `cat $(ls -1 pt.* | paste -sd " " -) > recon`

Here's how the reconstruction works:

(1)   The `ls` command generates a one-column list of the `pt.`x files in alphabetical order.

(2)   The `paste` command pastes the lines of the list into one long line with a space as separator, producing a single line that lists the `pt.`x files.

(3)   Using the command substitution '`$(...)`', the result of those two commands is used as the argument list to `cat`, which concatenates the `pt.`x files.

See page 290 for another way to do the reassembly.

● The command

```
split -b 1m -a 3 bigfile f_
```

splits the file `bigfile` into one-megabyte subfiles named `f_aaa`, `f_aab`, etc.

4.5   Combining Files

The commands in this section combine corresponding lines of two or more files. The `paste` program combines lines with the same line number, while the `join` program performs a database-style join.

4.5.1
Pasting Fields from
Several Files
with `paste`

The `paste` command pastes together corresponding lines from several files, sending the result to standard output. If there are just two input files, each output line contains a line from the first file followed by a separator character and a line from the second file. If there are more than two input files, the output is analogous. By default, the separator character is a tab. You can also use `paste` with the `-s` option to paste together the lines of a single file into one long line.

The `paste` command line has the form

```
paste [-d list] [-s] [file... ]
```

The files *file* ... contain the lines that are to be pasted together, with the usual convention that '`-`' indicates standard input. If no files are specified, then '`-`' must be specified if standard input is to be pasted. For example, if the file `beach` contains

```
walrus
oysters
carpenter
```

and the file `party` contains

```
dormouse
hatter
Alice
white rabbit
```

then the result of the command `paste beach party` is

```
walrus       dormouse
oysters      hatter
carpenter    Alice
             white rabbit
```

where the spaces preceding the second column indicate a single tab character.[8]

Paste is sometimes used with `cut` (see Section 4.3.2) to rearrange the fields of a file.

Command-Line Options.   The options for `paste` are as follows:

-d *list*   Use the characters in *list* circularly as separators. Within *list*, four escape sequences are recognized: \n (⟨newline⟩), \t (⟨tab⟩), \\ (backslash), and \0 (empty string).[9]   For instance, if you specify '-d,:' and have four input files, a line might look like this:

```
tweedledum,tweedledee:egg,fall
```

-s   Merge lines serially from one file, combining them into one long line. If you specify more than one input file, you'll get a useless and confusing result.

4.5.2 Joining Two Database Files with `join`

The `join` command performs a database-style join on two input files. The lines of each file are assumed to consist of a sequence of fields, one of which is selected as the join field, and the lines are assumed to be sorted in nondecreasing order of their join fields. Join merges corresponding lines of each file, where lines with the same join field are assumed to correspond, to produce an output line whose fields are selected from the fields of the corresponding input lines.

The form of the `join` command line is

join [-a *fnum* | -v *fnum*] [-e *str*] [-o *list*] [-t *char*]
     [-1 *fdnum*] [-2 *fdnum*] *file*$_1$ *file*$_2$

An obsolescent form is

join [-a *fnum*] [-e *str*] [-j *fdnum*] [-j1 *fdnum*] [-j2 *fdnum*]
     [-o *list* ...] [-t *char*] *file*$_1$ *file*$_2$

The obsolescent options -j1 and -j2 are equivalent to -1 and -2, respectively; -j is equivalent to both of them together.

The join is performed on *file*$_1$ and *file*$_2$. Either *file*$_1$ or *file*$_2$, but not both, can be specified as '-', denoting standard input. By default, input

---

8. If you actually display this result, the columns probably won't line up as neatly as they do here.

9. The empty string is a string with no characters, not the null character.

fields are separated by whitespace, with the first input field taken as the join field. Leading whitespace is ignored.

The default output consists of the join field, then the remaining fields of $file_1$, and then the remaining fields of $file_2$, all separated by spaces. Missing fields are treated as empty strings. By default, lines that don't match don't appear in the output at all.

Command-Line Options.   The following command-line options are provided:

-1 *fdnum*   Use field number *fdnum* of file 1 as the first join field.

-2 *fdnum*   Use field number *fdnum* of file 2 as the second join field.

-o *list*   Construct the output line from the fields in *list*, which must appear as a single command-line argument. Often, therefore, *list* is enclosed in single or double quotes. Each item in *list* is either 0, denoting the join field,[10] or has the form '*fnum.fdnum*', where *fnum* is the file number (1 or 2) and *fdnum* is the field number. Successive items in the list are separated by commas or whitespace. In the obsolescent form of the join command, -o accepts a sequence of field arguments, which need not be quoted.

-e *str*   Replace each empty output field with the string *str*.

-t *char*   Use *char* as the field separator for both input and output. Every occurrence of *char* is significant, including those at the start of an input line. Two consecutive occurrences of *char* define an empty field.

-a *fnum*   Produce a line for each unpairable line in file *fnum*. This option can be specified twice, once for file 1 and once for file 2. The output lines have the same format as for paired lines, except that the fields belonging to the other file are empty.

-v *fnum*   Don't produce output for lines that are joined; just produce lines for unpairable lines in file *fnum*. This option can be specified twice, once for file 1 and once for file 2.

An Example.   Suppose the file `candies` contains the data

```
caramels    New-York  2.37
josephines  Boston    83.12
mints       Beijing   .15
nougats     Cairo     .15
wafers      Toronto   4.98
```

---

10. Many older versions of `join` don't recognize the 0 notation for the join field.

and the file `nibblers` contains

```
Amiri   caramels
Maria   fudge
Lars    josephines
Fahima  mints
Rhonda  nougats
```

Then executing the command

```
join -2 2 -o 2.1,1.2,2.2,1.3 candies nibblers
```

will produce the output

```
Amiri New-York caramels 2.37
Lars Boston josephines 83.12
Fahima Beijing mints .15
Rhonda Cairo nougats .15
```

4.6   Using `sed` to Edit from a Script

The `sed` editor applies a fixed set of editing changes to a file or a sequence of files. A typical application of `sed` is to rearrange the output of a UNIX utility such as `who`. Historically, `sed` is derived from the `ed` editor—but it isn't "just like" ed, despite statements to that effect in the UNIX literature.

Sed is particularly good for simple changes such as uniform substitutions. You can also use it for more complex editing tasks, although its one-pass approach limits what it can do and `awk` is usually easier to use for such tasks (see Section 4.7). Sed almost always runs faster than `awk`.

An application of `sed` consists of applying a fixed "editing script" to a sequence of files. The forms of the `sed` command line are

```
sed [-n] script [file... ]
sed [-n] [-e  script] ... [-f  sfile] [file... ]
```

where *script* is a script of editing commands and *file* ... is a list of files to be edited. You can supply the script by giving it explicitly as part of the command, as in

```
sed -e 's/knave/jack/g' cardgame
```

This command replaces each occurrence of 'knave' in the file `cardgame` by 'jack' and sends the result to standard output. The original `cardgame` file is unaffected. You could also put the text of the script in a file `deknave` and issue the command

```
sed -f deknave cardgame
```

A command equivalent to the first one is

```
sed 's/knave/jack/g' cardgame
```

since if there is just one -e option and there are no -f options, the -e
option is implicit. See Section 4.6.1 for further discussion of these options.

The following options can appear on the command line:

4.6.1
Command-Line
Options

-e *script*   Edit the files according to *script*. The script usually needs to
be enclosed in single quotes so that special characters such as
';' and '\' are interpreted by sed rather than by the shell. If a
command line contains a single -e option and no -f options,
you can omit the -e and provide *script* only. You can provide
a multiple-line script with this option; if you do, pay careful
attention to the shell conventions about quoting ⟨newline⟩s and
backslashes. These conventions are not the same for all shells.

-f *sfile*   Edit the files according to the script found in *sfile*. Since sed
itself reads the script, shell conventions about quoting backslashes and ⟨newline⟩s do not apply.

-n   Don't produce the input buffer after processing a line. You can
also produce the effect of this option by beginning a script with
a line that starts with '#n'.

A command line may contain several -e and -f options—if it does, the various scripts are concatenated, so the order in which these options appear
is significant.

4.6.2
The Editing Cycle

Sed makes use of two buffers that can hold text: the *input buffer* and the
hold buffer. These are called the "pattern space" and "hold space" in the
sed manual pages. For most edits, the hold buffer isn't needed; it only
becomes active if you use a command that refers to it. Initially the hold
buffer contains a single empty line.

Editing proceeds irrevocably in the forward direction—a constraint that
you can often overcome with some cleverness in using the hold buffer.
Sed repeats the following cycle until the input is exhausted. If you specify
several files as input, they are effectively concatenated.

(1)   If the input buffer is empty, sed reads the next input line, removes
its trailing ⟨newline⟩, and places it into the buffer. The input buffer
might not be empty if the previous cycle was terminated by a 'D'
command; in this case, sed doesn't read another line, but it does
perform the rest of the steps below.

(2)   It examines in sequence the commands in the command script, performing those that are currently selected (see Section 4.6.3).

(3)   If the command script wasn't terminated by a 'd' or 'D' command,
and if output hasn't been suppressed by the -n option, it writes
the contents of the input buffer followed by a ⟨newline⟩ to standard
output and empties the input buffer. For some editing tasks it is
convenient to suppress the normal output and to produce the output
explicitly with 'p' or 'P' commands instead.

Note: Every line that `sed` writes is followed by a ⟨newline⟩; there is no way to suppress that ⟨newline⟩.

**4.6.3
Form of an
Editing Script**

An editing script consists of a sequence of commands separated either by ⟨newline⟩s or by semicolons.[11] A script with no commands is acceptable. Each command is denoted by a single letter or other character. Most commands can be preceded by a selector, either an address or a pair of addresses. A command is executed only if it is selected; that is, if its selector is satisfied. Ordinarily, an address selects a set of individual lines, while a pair of addresses selects a set of ranges of lines. For example, the command

```
/jam/,/jelly/d
```

specifies that whenever `sed` finds a line containing the pattern 'jam', it deletes that line and all others up to and including the next line containing the pattern 'jelly'. (If 'jam' and 'jelly' occur on the same line, just that line is deleted.) Any number of line ranges may be deleted in this way. A command without any addresses applies to all lines. This description is a slight oversimplification since patterns are actually matched against the input buffer (see below).

A `sed` script can contain groups of commands enclosed in curly braces. You can label particular points in the script with the ':' command and transfer to a labelled point with the 'b' and 't' commands.

`Sed` recognizes two kinds of addresses: line numbers and BREs (see Section 2.17.1).

- A line number address is a single integer or '$', which denotes the last line. Each time `sed` reads a line, it advances the line number (the first line is line #1). A line number address is satisfied if the line most recently read has that number.

- A BRE address usually has the form

    /*regexpr*/

    Alternatively, you can write such an address as

    \c *regexpr* c

    where *regexpr* is a BRE and *c* is any single character. (The spaces surrounding '*regexpr*' are for clarity only and are not part of the form.) For example, the pattern

    \#quince#

_____

11. Historically, the manual pages for various versions of `sed` have not mentioned that semicolons also work as command separators—but they do in every version we've tried. The rationale of the POSIX standard remarks that this feature was overlooked in the development of the standard because it was never documented, but that it may be introduced in a future revision.

matches any line containing the string 'quince'.

A BRE address is satisfied if it matches the input buffer. Ordinarily, the input buffer contains a single input line, but it can contain additional text as a result of the 'G', 'H', or 'N' commands. In checking for a match, sed assumes '\n' matches a ⟨newline⟩ and dot (.) matches any character except a ⟨newline⟩ at the end of the input buffer.

When a selector is a range (i.e., it consists of a pair of addresses), the first address starts selection and the second one ends it. If the first address is a BRE, it can be reselected any number of times. Here are some examples:

- The range '3,5' selects lines 3 through 5.
- The range '/walrus/,/oyster/' selects groups of lines that start with a line containing 'walrus' and end with the next line containing 'oyster'. A single line containing both 'walrus' and 'oyster' is a group by itself.
- The range '3,/oyster/' selects line 3 and all lines up to and including the next line containing 'oyster', or the rest of the input starting with line 3 if 'oyster' does not appear.
- The range /walrus/,5 consists of the first line containing 'walrus' and continues through line 5. If the first line containing 'walrus' is later than line 5, the range consists of just one line.

You can apply a command to those addresses not in a range with the '!' command (see "Miscellaneous Commands" on p. 198).

**4.6.4
Commands**

In the commands discussed below, *r* indicates an address range and *a* indicates a single address. A range can be replaced by an address or omitted; a single address can also be omitted. A command is executed either if its selector (range or address) applies or if it has no selector.

Textual Substitutions.   The following commands enable you to perform textual substitutions. Many applications of sed use a script consisting of a single 's' command.

r s/*pat*/*repl*/[*flags*]

Substitutes *repl* for the pattern *pat*, where *pat* is an expression having the same form as a BRE used in an address (see Section 4.6.3). By default, sed substitutes for the first occurrence of the pattern in the input buffer only.[12] The following flags modify how sed does the substitution:

g   Substitute for all occurrences rather than for the first occurrence.

---

12. The regular expression notation doesn't provide any way of writing nonprinting characters in a printable notation, either within the pattern or within the replacement. But the following shell script shows how you can sometimes get around this limitation:

```
CR=$(printf "\r")
add_cr () { sed -e "s/${CR}*$//g; s/$/${CR}/"; }
remove_cr () { sed "s/${CR}*$//g"; }
```

The shell functions `add_cr` and `remove_cr` perform the transformations needed to convert UNIX files to MS-DOS files and vice versa.

n	Substitute for the *n*th occurrence rather than for the first occurrence.
p	Produce the input buffer if any substitutions were made.
w *file*	Append the input buffer to *file* if any substitutions were made.

Note carefully that the notation '\n' has different meanings in the pattern and in the replacement. In the pattern, it indicates a ⟨newline⟩; in the replacement, it simply indicates the letter 'n'. To include a ⟨newline⟩ in the replacement, use a backslash at the end of a line, as in the following example:

```
"s/cut here/cut\
here/"
```

This command replaces the blank between cut and here by a ⟨newline⟩. The quotes we show here are not part of the command but are needed for correct parsing by the shell.

r y/*string₁*/*string₂*/

Substitutes characters in *string₂* for the corresponding characters of *string₁*.

Deletions.   The following commands perform deletions:

r d   Deletes the input buffer and starts another cycle, ignoring the rest of the script.

r D   Deletes the first line of the input buffer and starts another cycle, ignoring the rest of the script. This command is unique in that it can leave the input buffer nonempty; if it does leave the input buffer nonempty, a new line is not read in on the next cycle. When you've collected a group of lines in the input buffer—using, for instance, the commands involving the hold buffer—you can use D to process the lines one at a time.

Inserting and Changing Groups of Lines.   The following commands insert and change groups of lines. Their input consists of lines of text, with the command itself and each line other than the last one ended by a backslash. For example, the input

```
$a\
Your manuscript is both good and original,\
but the part that is good is not original,\
and the part that is original is not good.\
\
-- Samuel Johnson
```

appends the indicated five lines of text after the last input line.

a i\⟨newline⟩*text*

Produces *text* immediately ("inserts" it). Although this command and the next one expect at most one address, you can get them to work with a range by enclosing them in braces and applying the range to the braces.

a a\⟨newline⟩*text*

Produces *text* before reading the next line ("appends" it). Note that the effect of this command is postponed until all other commands in the script have been executed. Multiple 'a' commands take effect in the order that they are executed.

r c\⟨newline⟩ *text*

Changes the lines in *r* to *text* and starts another cycle, ignoring the rest of the script. Equivalent to 'a' followed by 'd'.

Note: It is not possible to transfer the text introduced by one of these commands into either the input buffer or the hold buffer.

Using the Hold Buffer.   The hold buffer is useful for accumulating sequences of lines, either to move them to another location later in the input or to compare them to a pattern that spans several lines.   The following commands provide operations that transfer information to or from the hold buffer:

r g   Replaces the input buffer by the hold buffer.

r G   Appends the hold buffer to the input buffer.

r h   Replaces the hold buffer by the input buffer.

r H   Appends the input buffer to the hold buffer.

r x   Exchanges the input buffer with the hold buffer.

The following commands illustrate the use of the hold buffer:

    4h; 5,10H; $G

These commands taken together move lines 4 through 10 of the input file to the end of the file.   The command '4,10H' doesn't work correctly for this purpose because it introduces an extraneous blank line (the original contents of the hold buffer) at the start of the transferred material.

Other Input and Output Operations.   The following commands enable you to produce the contents of the first line of the input buffer or all of it, to read the next line into the input buffer, and to show the contents of the input buffer unambiguously (almost):

r n   Produces the input buffer, then replaces it with the next input line. The line number is advanced. This command does not start a new cycle; after executing it, sed continues with the rest of the script.

r N   Appends the next input line to the input buffer.   The line number is advanced. This command does not start a new cycle; after executing it, sed continues with the rest of the script.

r p   Produces the input buffer followed by a ⟨newline⟩. This command is useful in conjunction with the -n option, since it enables you to replace implicit output (the default action at the end of a cycle) by explicit output. Explicit output is often more convenient than implicit output in complex scripts.

r l   Produces the input buffer, followed by a ⟨newline⟩, in a representation that accounts for control characters and long lines. Lines that exceed the line length of your terminal are folded so that they don't exceed that length, with continued lines indicated by a trailing backslash. The end of each input line is indicated by a '$', thus revealing any trailing spaces. Nonprinting characters are replaced by escape sequences or by '*ddd*', where *ddd* is the octal representation of the character.

r P   Produces the first line of the input buffer along with its ⟨newline⟩. This command is often followed by 'D'.

The following command enables you to produce the line number:

a=   Produces a line containing the current line number. This command does not affect the input buffer.

Reading and Writing Files Explicitly.   The following commands enable you to read from and write to files not named on the command line:

r r *file*   Produces the contents of *file* before reading the next line. Like the 'a' command, this command does not have its effect until the end of the editing cycle.

r w *file*   Appends the input buffer to *file*. This command is like the 'p' command, except that it affects a named file rather than standard output.

Labels and Branches.   The following commands enable you to label a place in the script and to branch to a label either unconditionally or conditionally:

: *label*   Places the label *label*.

r b [*label*]   Branches to the point in the script bearing the label *label*.

r t [*label*]   Branches to the point in the script labelled *label* if any substitutions have been successfully made by an 's' command since sed most recently either read an input line or executed a 't' command.

a q   Quits editing. No more commands are executed, no more lines are read, and no more output is produced.

Miscellaneous Commands.   The following commands don't naturally fall into any of the groups above:

Indicates a comment. The '#' can be preceded by whitespace. If the line starts with '#n', the default output is suppressed just as it is with the -n option. This command enables you to cause output suppression from within a script.

(*empty*)   Does nothing.

r!*cmd*   Applies the command *cmd* to all lines not selected by *r*.

r{ [*cmd*...] }

Executes the commands *cmd* ... . If any commands within the braces have addresses or ranges attached to them, those addresses or ranges act as selectors just as they do outside of braces. Each command, including the last one, must be followed by a ⟨newline⟩ or a semicolon.

4.7 The awk Programming Language

The awk programming language provides a convenient way of doing many data manipulation tasks. Some awk programs are so short and simple that you can easily write them on a single command line, yet awk is expressive enough so that you can use it for general programming. Stylistically, awk is much like C, but it also incorporates ideas from other languages such as Snobol and PL/I. Awk was named after its authors Alfred Aho, Peter Weinberger, and Brian Kernighan.

In presenting awk, we cannot avoid assuming that you have had some programming experience—though not necessarily very much. But even lacking that experience, you can write awk programs for many simple tasks. Awk is thoroughly described in a book by its authors (see reference [B2]).

**4.7.1
Calling** awk

The forms of the awk command line are[13]

```
awk [-F regexpr] [-v asst] ... prog [ arg ... ]
awk [-F regexpr] -f progfile [-v asst] [ arg ... ]
```

You provide the awk program either directly on the command line, as in the first form, or in a file referenced by the -f option, as in the second form. If you provide the program on the command line, you should enclose it in apostrophes (see the discussion of quotation in Section 2.12.2) to prevent metacharacters and whitespace in the program from being misinterpreted as shell metacharacters.

Command-Line Options.   These are the named options that can appear on the awk command line:

-F *regexpr*

Set the field separator to the (extended) regular expression *regexpr* (see "Input Field Separators" on p. 206).

---

13. On some elderly systems the program named awk may be the original version of awk; the current version is then usually named nawk (new awk). If that is the case, we recommend that you either make awk an alias for nawk (if your shell lets you) or create a link to nawk under the name awk, setting your PATH environment variable so that the link to nawk is seen before the link to the older version of awk.

-f *progfile*

> Read the program from the file *file* instead of taking it from the command line. This option is usually the better way to provide awk programs of more than a line or two.

-v *asst*   Carry out the awk assignment *asst* before executing any part of the awk program.

Command-Line Arguments.   Each argument *arg* ... on the command line designates either an assignment or the pathname of a file. In the simplest case, all the *args* are pathnames and the concatenation of the designated files (with '-' designating standard input) constitutes the input to your program. The lines that awk reads in are called *input records*.

More generally, each argument is either a pathname or an assignment of the form '*var=val*'. An assignment assigns the value *val* to the variable *var* using the usual rules for the assignment operator (see "Assignment Operators" on p. 211). Each assignment is executed at the point when awk is ready to read the file designated by the next pathname. In particular, any assignments preceding the first pathname are executed immediately after the BEGIN actions are completed (see p. 201). Assignments following the last pathname are executed just prior to executing the END actions— which you can think of as the time when awk would read another file were it to be specified.[14] If none of the arguments are pathnames, awk reads standard input after executing any assignments that might be present.

A program can access the command-line arguments via the ARGV array (see "Command-Line Arguments" on p. 220) and can even modify an argument before awk gets to interpret it. If an awk program consists only of BEGIN actions, then the only possible use of the arguments is as data to be accessed via ARGV.

4.7.2
Simple awk
Programs

To illustrate how to write simple programs in awk, we assume that the file products contains the following data on products, their prices, and their sales:

```
knapsacks    22.00     11
knickers     44.95      0
knishes       1.29    193
knives       11.98     57
knobs          .27     35
```

By default, an awk program reads its input either from standard input or from a sequence of files specified on the command line. As it reads each input record, it decomposes the record into a sequence of *fields* separated by whitespace. The fields are named $1, $2, etc.; the entire line is named $0. A line of an awk program has the form of a *pattern-action*

---

14. If there are no END actions, it doesn't matter whether those assignments are executed since they cannot have any visible effect—the program is already done.

statement, where the pattern selects some set of input records and the action, enclosed in braces, specifies what is to be done for each of those lines. For example, the command

```
awk '{print $1, $2, $2 * $3}' products
```

produces the following list of products and the amounts of their sales:

```
knapsacks 22.00 242
knickers 44.95 0
knishes 1.29 248.97
knives 11.98 682.86
knobs .27 9.45
```

In the command the '*' indicates multiplication, the pattern is omitted since all input records are selected, and the action is enclosed in braces. Here is a more elaborate version of the same program:

```
awk '$3 > 0 {print $1, $2, $2 * $3; sum += $2 * $3}
    END {print "\nTOTAL:", sum}' products
```

This version omits lines for products with zero sales, thanks to the pattern '$3 > 0', and produces a total after all lines have been read. The 'END' indicates actions to be performed after all input has been read. In this case the action is to produce a total. The variable sum, like all awk variables, is implicitly initialized to the empty string. It is then converted to 0 since the context requires that conversion.

4.7.3
Form of an awk Program

An awk program consists of a sequence of pattern-action statements and user function definitions. User function definitions are discussed in Section 4.7.22. A pattern-action statement may contain a pattern (see "Patterns" on p. 202), an action (see "Actions and Statements" on p. 202), or both. A pattern-action statement has one of the following forms:

BEGIN { *action* }

> Executes *action* once, before any data is read in. If an awk program consists of a single pattern-action statement having this form, the action is executed and no data is read in except as requested explicitly by the action. Awk programs consisting of a single 'BEGIN' action are very useful since you can use them to carry out any computations whatsoever without your being bound by awk's normal method of reading and processing data.

END { *action* }

> Executes *action* once, after awk has read in all the input data and encountered an end of file. If awk never sees an end of file, the 'END' actions are not executed.

{ *action* } Executes *action* for each input record.

pattern [{ *action* }]

> Executes *action* for each input record that satisfies *pattern*. The

default action is 'print $0', so if no action is specified, each input record satisfying *pattern* is shown.

*pattern*₁, *pattern*₂ [{ *action* }]

> Executes *action* for each input record starting with the first one matching *pattern*₁ and continuing through the next one matching *pattern*₂. If a subsequent input record matches *pattern*₁, the process is repeated. If no match is found for *pattern*₂, execution continues to the end of the data. The default action is 'print $0', so if no action is specified, each input record within the pattern range is shown.

Note that several different actions may apply to a single line of input data.

Patterns. A *pattern* is either an expression or an extended regular expression (see Section 4.7.4) enclosed in slashes:

- An ordinary expression used as a pattern is evaluated for its logical value, either truth or falsity (see "Truth Values" on p. 204). Usually a pattern is given by a comparison such as '$2 > 0', which tests if the second field of the input line is greater than zero, or by a combination of such comparisons. Conventionally, a successful comparison returns 1 (true) and an unsuccessful comparison returns 0 (false).

- A regular expression enclosed in slashes and used as a pattern matches an input record if a match for the regular expression can be found within the input record.

For example, a pattern '/unc.+ble/' would match any input record containing the word 'runcible'.

Actions and Statements. An *action* is a sequence of zero or more *statements*. A statement carries out an action such as producing some output text or conditionally executing another statement depending on the result of a test. Since certain kinds of statements contain other statements, a single action can be quite complex. We classify the kinds of statements as follows:

- Expressions as statements (see Section 4.7.20)
- Printing statements (see Section 4.7.16)
- Control-flow statements (see Section 4.7.21)
- Miscellaneous statements: the close statement (see Section 4.7.17), the delete statement (see Section 4.7.10), and the return statement (see "Returning from a Function" on p. 224)

**4.7.4
Regular Expressions
in awk**

The regular expressions recognized by awk are the extended regular expressions described in Section 2.17.2, extended to allow the escape sequences described on page 205 to appear in the regular expression. For example, the regular expression '(\t\n␣)+' matches any nonempty sequence of ⟨tab⟩, ⟨newline⟩, or space characters.

**4.7.5
Program Format**

An awk program is formatted according to the following rules:

- A pattern and the opening left brace of its action must appear on the same line. This rule also applies to BEGIN and END.

- Statements are separated by ⟨newline⟩s or semicolons. A statement can be continued onto additional lines by ending all but the last line with a backslash. A ⟨newline⟩ (with or without a backslash) can be inserted after any of the following elements:

  ```
  ,  {  &&  ||  do  else  if(...)  for(...)
  ```

  A basic awk element such as a number, a string, or a variable, however, must appear entirely on one line.

- Comments start with '#' and extend to the end of a line. Comments and blank lines are ignored.

- Spaces and tabs can be used around basic awk elements but are not required unless running two elements together could cause those elements to be interpreted as a single element. Awk is generally permissive about omitting spaces; for example, the program

  ```
  BEGIN{a=94 + 3;print"abc"2a}
  ```

  produces the output 'abc297'.

- A left parenthesis that introduces an argument list, either for a user-defined function or for a statement such as print or close, must be immediately adjacent to the function or statement name, with no intervening whitespace. For example, you must write

  ```
  print($1, $2)
  ```

  rather than

  ```
  print ($1, $2)
  ```

**4.7.6
Values and
Expressions**

Awk recognizes two kinds of values: numbers and strings.

- Numbers are represented internally in floating-point form. In output, however, integer values normally appear as integers; other numbers normally appear as decimal fractions.

- Strings are sequences of characters.

If you use a number in a context where awk is expecting a string, awk converts the number to a string and vice versa (see "Coercions Between Strings and Numbers" on p. 204).

An *expression* is a formula for computing a value. The awk statement

```
print expr
```

illustrates a particularly simple use of an expression; it sends the value of the expression *expr* to standard output. An expression can be used as a statement by itself.

An expression is built up from three kinds of primary elements: constants (numeric or string), variables (user-defined, predefined, or field), and regular expressions. (Older `awk` documentation uses the term "built-in" rather than "predefined".) Constants and variables are expressions in their own right and are discussed in Section 4.7.7. Regular expressions are used as the right operands of the '~' and '!~' pattern-matching operators and as arguments of certain predefined functions.

Awk also provides three kinds of elements in addition to the primary ones: array elements (see Section 4.7.10), function calls (see Section 4.7.12), and parenthesized expressions. Array elements and function calls can themselves contain expressions.

In general, an expression consists of a sequence of elements and operators (see Section 4.7.11), with the operators specifying how the elements are to be combined. For example, the expression

```
($2 + 17) * saxify(3, a + 9)
```

is formed by combining two elements, a parenthesized expression and a function call, using the multiplication operator '*'.

Truth Values.   Certain `awk` constructs, such as the `if` statement, test the value of an expression for truth or falsity. Awk treats a nonzero numerical value or a nonempty string value as being true and a zero numerical value or an empty string value as being false.

Coercions Between Strings and Numbers.   You can coerce a string to a number in an expression by writing

   $+ \; str$

This expression forces `awk` to treat the string *str* as a number but leaves the numerical value unchanged. When `awk` treats a string as a number, it produces the number represented by the string; if the string does not represent a number, `awk` produces zero. For example, the expression

```
("4." "92") + "abc"
```

evaluates to 4.92. (Juxtaposing two strings causes `awk` to concatenate them.) Similarly, you can coerce a number *n* in an expression to a string by writing

   n `""`

This subexpression concatenates a null string onto *n*, forcing `awk` to convert *n* to a string but leaving the string unchanged.

Awk converts a number to a string by formatting it according to the format specification contained in the `CONVFMT` predefined variable. The default value of `CONVFMT` is '`%.6g`' (see "Output Formats" on p. 218). This format usually yields the most natural representation of a number. However, when the conversion takes place in the context of an output statement, awk uses instead the format specification contained in the OFMT predefined variable.[15]

Note: Coercing the value of a variable from numeric to string or vice versa has no effect on the stored variable (see Section 4.7.8).

**4.7.7
Constants and
Variables**

As mentioned earlier, awk represents numbers internally in floating-point form. A numeric constant can be written as an integer such as '747', a decimal fraction such as '2.718', or a number in scientific notation such as '69e-7' or '6.9E-6'. The last two of these numbers both represent the decimal value 0.0000069; 'e' and 'E' are equivalent here.

You write a string constant by enclosing it in double quotes. Within a string constant, you can use the following escape sequences to denote certain special characters:

\b	⟨backspace⟩
\f	⟨formfeed⟩
\n	⟨newline⟩
\r	⟨return⟩
\t	⟨tab⟩
ddd	Octal number *ddd*, where *ddd* contains one to three digits
c	The character *c*, where *c* is none of the above

If the *ddd* form is followed by a digit, you must provide all three digits of *ddd*, using leading zeros if necessary. You can include a double quote within a string by writing it as '\"'.

Awk provides three kinds of variables: user-defined, predefined, and field:

- A *user-defined variable* is named by a sequence of letters, digits, and underscores starting with a letter. User-defined variables are never declared; they simply come into existence when you start using them. The initial value of a user-defined variable is the null string.

- A *predefined variable* is a variable such as RLENGTH (see p. 213) whose meaning is defined by awk. All predefined variables have names written entirely in upper case.

- A *field variable* is a variable whose value ordinarily is a portion of the text of the current input record. Field variables are discussed in Section 4.7.9.

---

15. The POSIX standard is inconsistent in its view as to whether conversions caused by using the %s format in a printf statement use CONVFMT or OFMT. The descriptions of the CONVFMT and OFMT variables say that OFMT applies to "output statements", but the description of the printf statement suggests that no exception is made to the usual conversion rules—and those rules say that CONVFMT is used for number-to-string conversions. In our description of awk we have assumed the first interpretation.

4.7.8
Type of an
Expression

The type of an expression, and of a variable in particular, is either "numeric" or "string". An uninitialized variable has an ambiguous type; depending on the context where it is used, it either has a numeric value of zero or a string value of the empty string. Once initialized, a variable acquires its type from whatever was assigned to it.[16] A variable may also acquire an ambiguous type as the result of splitting an input line or calling the `split` function (see p. 214). The question of an expression's type is particularly important in understanding how comparison operators are interpreted (see "Comparisons" on p. 209).

4.7.9
Fields and Field
Variables

When `awk` reads an input record, it splits the record into *fields* and assigns the text of those fields to the field variables $1, $2, and so forth. It assigns the entire input record to $0. By default, the fields are separated by whitespace, the same convention used in analyzing arguments to an ordinary command. The predefined variable NF is set to the number of fields; field variables with numbers greater than NF are set to the null string. For example, suppose `awk` reads the input record

    Karl and Groucho Marx

Awk sets the field variables as follows:

```
$0:  Karl and Groucho Marx
$1:  Karl
$2:  and
$3:  Groucho
$4:  Marx
$5, $6, ... :  (empty string)
NF:  4
```

You can change the value of a field variable by assigning something else to it.

A field whose text represents a number is treated as a number rather than as a string in any context where it makes a difference. For instance, in the comparison '$3 < 7', the field $3 is treated as a number rather than as a string if it contains text such as '29'. In this case the comparison yields a false result even though a string comparison would yield a true result.

Input Field Separators. By default, successive input fields are separated by whitespace, a sequence of one or more spaces or tabs. A ⟨newline⟩ is considered to be a whitespace character if it is not a record separator (see "Input Record Separators" on p. 207). You can specify the input field separator by assigning a string value to the predefined variable FS (input

---

16. In older implementations of `awk`, referencing a variable can make its type ambiguous if its value happens to be a numeric string (i.e., a string that represents a number). In POSIX `awk`, referencing a variable has no effect on its value.

field separator). The default value of FS is a single space. If FS has this specific value, awk ignores whitespace at the beginning of a record and treats *both* spaces and tabs as separators. If FS has any other value, a separator at the beginning of an input record indicates that the first field of the record is an empty string. The behavior is virtually identical to that of the shell variable IFS (see p. 372).

If the value of FS is a single character other than a blank, that character acts as the input field separator. Otherwise the value of FS is an extended regular expression that specifies the set of all possible input field separators. Usually you should specify FS either on the command line, using the -F option (see p. 199), or in a BEGIN action. For example, starting an awk program with

```
BEGIN { FS = "[, \t][ \t]*" }
```

causes either a comma, a comma followed by whitespace, or whitespace alone to act as a separator between input fields.

Note: If you want the separator to be a single blank, you must write it as '[ ]' or the equivalent.

Input Record Separators.   Just as you can specify input field separators with the FS predefined variable, you can specify the input record separator with the RS predefined variable. The input record separator marks the boundary between input records. For example, if you set RS to ';', awk finds successive input records by scanning up to the next semicolon. The record separator itself can never be part of a record. The record separator, unlike the field separator, is always either a single character or a null string; if you set RS to a longer string, awk uses only the first character of it.

The default value of RS is '\n'; that is, a single ⟨newline⟩. Setting RS to the empty string causes one or more blank lines to act as the record separator and thus provides one way of treating several lines as a single record. If you change RS, ⟨newline⟩s will act as field separators no matter what value FS has.

**4.7.10
Arrays**

An *array* is a kind of lookup table that consists of a set of *elements*. Each element acts as a variable; you can use its value in an expression or change its value in an assignment. The values you use to look up the elements of an array are its *subscripts*. An array subscript can be either a number or a string, so awk arrays are more like tables in the Snobol and Icon programming languages than they are like arrays in a language such as Pascal or C. If *a* is an array, the element specified by the subscript *sub* is written as '*a*[*sub*]'.

An array comes into existence when you first use it. The same holds true for its individual elements. An array element, like any other variable, has the empty string as its initial value. The statement

```
delete a[sub]
```

deletes the element of the array *a* with subscript *sub*. This is the *only* way to delete an array element.

For example, the effect of the assignment expression

```
pulchritude["brigitte"] = 97
```

is to create a `pulchritude` array if it doesn't already exist and to place an element with subscript 'brigitte' and value 97 in that array. A subsequent use of 'pulchritude["brigitte"]' in an expression yields the value 97 (unless you meanwhile assign a different value to that array element).

There are two special constructs for operating on arrays:

- The `in` operator tests whether an array has an element indexed by a particular subscript (see p. 210).

- The `for` statement has a form that iterates through the subscripts of an array (see p. 223).

Multidimensional Arrays. A multidimensional array is an array with more than one subscript. Although `awk` does not support multidimensional arrays directly, it does provide a method of simulating them. When you write an array reference of the form

$arr[sub_1, sub_2]$

`awk` translates the subscript pair 'sub_1, sub_2' into the string

sub_1 *sep* sub_2

where *sep* is the value of the predefined variable SUBSEP (subscript separator). For example, if you set SUBSEP to ':', the subscript pair

```
"lemur", 17
```

is translated into the string

```
lemur::17
```

The default value of SUBSEP is a one-character string consisting of the character with ASCII code 28, which you obtain by typing Ctrl \.[17] Arrays of more than two dimensions are handled analogously. You can even construct an array that has some one-dimensional and some two-dimensional subscripts. When you iterate through a multidimensional array using a `for` statement (see p. 223), the iteration values are strings that include the subscript separator.

4.7.11 Operators

The following subsections describe the operators you can use to combine elements into larger expressions. Their relative precedence is described in "Precedence of Operators" on page 212. You can use parentheses within expressions to group subexpressions in the usual way, thus overriding the normal precedences.

---

17. This value was chosen because it is relatively unlikely to appear in a subscript string.

Ordinary Arithmetic Operators. The arithmetic operators operate on numbers. A string appearing as an operand of an arithmetic operator is converted to a number (see "Coercions Between Strings and Numbers" on p. 204). The binary arithmetic operators are:

+	Addition.
−	Subtraction.
*	Multiplication.
/	Division. The value of x/y is a decimal fraction if x is not evenly divisible by y.
%	Remainder. The result has the same sign as the first operand.
^	Exponentiation. The value of $x \wedge y$ is x to the power y. If the result is not mathematically well defined, awk issues an error diagnostic.

In addition, the + and − operators can be used as unary operators. The only effect of the unary + operator is to convert its operand to a number if it isn't one already.

Incrementing and Decrementing Operators. The incrementing and decrementing operators can be applied only to a variable. Here they are:

v++	Returns the value of the variable v and then adds 1 to v. For instance, suppose the value of x is 5. Evaluating the expression 'x++' then yields the value 5 and changes the value of x to 6.
++v	Adds 1 to the variable v and returns the result. For instance, suppose the value of x is 5. Evaluating the expression '++x' then yields the value 6 and also changes the value of x to 6.
v−−	Like v++ except that 1 is subtracted from v rather than added to it.
−−v	Like ++v except that 1 is subtracted from v rather than added to it.

Concatenation. Concatenation is an *implicit* operator. You concatenate two strings by writing them one after another. If you concatenate a number with a string or even with another number, the number is converted to a string. For example, evaluating the expression

```
"meow"(2*8)"arf""oink" "moo"
```

yields the value

```
meow16arfoinkmoo
```

Note that the concatenated operands can be written with or without whitespace between them.

Comparisons. You can use the awk comparison operators to compare either numbers or strings. Strings are compared character by character from left to right until a differing character is found or one string is exhausted. If a differing character is found, the string with the lesser character according to the collating sequence of the current locale is the lesser string; if one string is exhausted, that one is the lesser. For the usual POSIX locale, the collating sequence is just the ASCII ordering.

A comparison is done numerically either if both comparands have numeric type (see Section 4.7.8) or if one has numeric type and the other is a string that represents a number. In the latter case, the string operand is converted to the number it represents. In all other cases, each comparand is converted to a string if necessary and a string comparison is done. Note that when a variable has both string type and numeric type, comparing it with a numeric value results in a numeric comparison; comparing it with a string value results in a string comparison. Comparing two such variables results in a numeric comparison.

These are the comparison operators:

`==`	Equal. Don't confuse this with the assignment operator '='.
`!=`	Not equal.
`<`	Less than.
`>`	Greater than.
`<=`	Less than or equal to.
`>=`	Greater than or equal to.

A true comparison yields 1 and a false comparison yields 0.

Pattern-Matching Operators.   The following pattern-matching operators check whether a string contains a match for a regular expression. Using them, you can perform the same kinds of tests within an expression that you can using the pattern part of a pattern-action statement.

`~`	The expression '*str~pat*' is true if the string *str* contains a match for the regular expression *pat* and false otherwise.
`!~`	The expression '*str*!~*pat*' is true if the string *str* does *not* contain a match for the regular expression *pat* and false if it does.

Here as elsewhere, truth is represented by the number 1 and falsity by the number 0.

In expressions using these operators, the second operand of *pat* can be given as a string rather than as a regular expression. Thus you can store the regular expression in a variable. A string used in a pattern match is like a regular expression, but with one critical difference: any backslashes within the string must be quoted with a backslash, even if they are themselves used for quotation. For example, the expressions

```
sep ~ /\.|\?/
sep ~ "\\.|\\?"
```

are equivalent; they both are true if `sep` contains either '.' or '?'.

Array Membership Operator.   The array membership operator `in` tests whether an array contains an element corresponding to a certain subscript (see Section 4.7.10). The form of the test is

```
sub in arr
```

where *arr* is an array and *sub* is a possible subscript for *arr*. If *arr* contains an element with subscript *sub*, the test is true and yields 1; otherwise, it is false and yields 0.

Logical Operators.   The logical operators are usually used to combine the results of comparisons and other tests, although their operands can be any expressions at all. These are the logical operators:

`&&`   The expression '$x \&\& y$' is true and yields 1 if both x and y are true (i.e., have nonzero values). If x is false, however, the expression yields 0 immediately and y is never evaluated. For example, the expression

```
y > 0 && x / y > t
```

does not cause a division by zero even if y is zero. In this case, the logical combination yields false as soon as 'y > 0' is evaluated, so the division 'x / y' is never performed.

`||`   The expression '$x || y$' is true and yields 1 if either x or y is true. If x is true, y is never evaluated.

`!`   The expression '$!x$' yields the logical negation of x: its value is 1 if x is zero or an empty string and 0 otherwise.

Conditional Expressions.   A conditional expression is analogous to a conditional statement. The form of a conditional expression is

$$expr_1 \; ? \; expr_2 \; : \; expr_3$$

It yields the value of $expr_2$ if $expr_1$ is true and the value of $expr_3$ otherwise. Only one of the expressions $expr_2$ and $expr_3$ is ever evaluated.

Field Selection Operator.   The field selection operator '`$`' (see Section 4.7.9) is a unary operator that takes a single numeric operand. Its operand is normally an integer or a variable but can be a more general expression. For example, the expression '`$(NF-1)`' refers to the next to the last field of an input record.

Assignment Operators.   An assignment operator sets a variable to a value. An assignment expression is one whose main operator is an assignment operator. Like any expression, an assignment expression also can be used as a statement.

   The most straightforward kind of assignment expression is a *direct assignment* of the form

$$var = expr$$

where *var* is a variable and *expr* is an expression. The effect of evaluating the assignment expression is to evaluate *expr*, obtaining a value *val*, and then to make the value of *var* be *val*. The value of the assignment expression is *val*.

   If *var* and *expr* have different types (one has a string value and the other a numeric value, for example), the type of *var* is changed to agree with that of *expr*. For example, if the variable `falafel` has the value 7 and the variable `pita` has the value 0, the effect of the assignment

```
pita = (falafel = "hum") "mus"
```

is to set the value of `falafel` to 'hum' and then, since the value of the inner assignment expression is 'hum', to set the value of `pita` to 'hummus'.

The other form of assignment is a *modifying assignment*. There are five modifying assignment operators:

```
+=   -=   *=   /=   %=
```

The effect of the assignment expression

var += *expr*

is to evaluate *expr*, obtaining a value *val*, and then to add *val* to *var*. The value of the entire expression is the new value of *var*. For example, suppose the value of `macaw` is 12. Then the assignment expression

```
macaw += 18
```

sets the value of `macaw` to 30. The value of the expression is also 30. The other modifying assignment operators have analogous meanings.

Precedence of Operators. When several operators appear in an expression, they are grouped according to their relative precedence: an operator with greater precedence is applied before one with lesser precedence, and operators having the same precedence are applied in order from left to right. Here is a list of the `awk` operators in order of decreasing precedence:

(...)	(grouping)
$	(field selection)
++ --	(increment and decrement)
^	(exponentiation)
! + -	(logical "not", unary additive)
* / %	(multiplicative)
+ -	(binary additive)
juxtaposition	(concatenation)
< <= == != > >=	(relational)
~ !~	(pattern matching)
in	(array membership)
&&	(logical "and")
||	(logical "or")
? ... :	(conditional)
= += -= *= /= %= ^=	(assignment)

**4.7.12
Function Calls**

A function call is a type of expression. The value of that expression is determined by the function's definition. If a function does not explicitly return a value when it is called, the value of the function call is undefined.

Most calls on predefined functions and all calls on user-defined functions have the form

$$f(a_1, a_2, \ldots, a_n)$$

where f is the name of the function and the a_i are its *arguments*. No space is permitted between the function name and the left parenthesis that encloses its argument list.

The arguments of an ordinary function call are given by expressions. When the function is called, awk evaluates the expressions and passes their values to the function by assigning them to the function's *parameters*. The argument list can be empty; an empty argument list is written as '()'.

A few predefined functions extend the form of a function call:

- Certain predefined string functions expect one of their arguments to be a regular expression delimited by slashes.

- The getline predefined function does not take an argument list but can have a redirection attached to it (see Section 4.7.15).

4.7.13
Predefined String
Functions

Awk provides a number of predefined functions for operating on strings. They all follow the convention that the first character has position 1 and succeeding characters have successively higher position numbers.

Basic String Analysis.   The following predefined functions perform basic string analysis:

length(s)

   Returns the number of characters in the string s.

index(s,t)

   Returns the position of the first place in the string s where the string t occurs. If t does not occur within s, index returns 0.

substr($s,p[,n]$)

   If n is not specified or if $p + n - 1$ is greater than the length of the string s, returns the substring of s starting with the pth character; otherwise returns the substring of s that starts with the pth character and is n characters long. For example, the value of 'substr("bullock",2,4)' is 'ullo' and the value of 'substr("bullock",4,5)' is 'lock'.

Pattern Matching and Substitution.   The following predefined functions perform pattern matching and substitution. Some of them take a regular expression as an argument; such a regular expression is enclosed in slashes. Alternatively, a string can be provided in place of the regular expression (see p. 202).

match(s,r)

   Tests whether the string s contains a match for the regular expression r.

   - If it does, match returns the position of the character that begins the leftmost matching substring and sets the predefined variable RLENGTH to the length of the longest matching substring that starts at that position.
   - If it does not, match returns 0 and sets RLENGTH to -1.

In either case the predefined variable RSTART is set to the value returned by match. For example, the value of

```
match("sitzmark", /[ratzk]+/)
```

is 3; evaluating this expression sets RSTART to 3 and RLENGTH to 2.

sub(r, s[, t])

If the string t is specified, substitutes the string s for the first occurrence of the regular expression r in t. If t is not specified, it is taken to be $0. An occurrence of '&' within s is replaced by the substring of t that matches r. Sub is usually evaluated for the sake of its side effect, which is to change t; since this side effect is the only way to retrieve the result of the substitution, t is usually a variable. The value returned by sub is the number of substitutions that were made. For example, the output of the program

```
BEGIN {
    var = "chalcedony"
    print sub(/l.*n/, "nc", var), var
    }
```

is

```
1 chancy
```

gsub(r, s[, t])

Like sub, except that the substitution is made globally (i.e., for all occurrences of r in t). Each substitution is made to t as modified by previous substitutions and is made at the first occurrence of r to the right of where the previous substitution (if any) ended. The value returned by gsub is the number of substitutions made.

split(s, a[, fs])

Splits the string s into fields using the separator fs, then puts those fields into elements of the array a with subscripts '1', '2', etc. If fs is not specified, it is taken to be FS. The string s is split in the same way that an input record would be (see Section 4.7.9). Note that the subscripts are strings, not numbers, so the subscript '10' comes before the subscript '2' when you iterate through the subscripts of the array. Each array element has string type; if the string represents a number, it has numeric type as well (see Section 4.7.8).

Case Conversion. The following functions perform case conversion:

tolower(s)

Produces the string obtained by converting each uppercase character in s to lowercase. In general, the conversion is defined by the LC_TYPE category of the current locale.

`toupper(`*s*`)`

>Produces the string obtained by converting each lowercase character in *s* to uppercase. In general, the conversion is defined by the LC_TYPE category of the current locale.

Formatting a Sequence of Values. The following function formats a sequence of values:

`sprintf(`*fmt*`,`*expr*`, ... )`

>Formats *expr* ... according to the format *fmt* and returns the string containing these formatted values. The formatting is done in the same way that it is by the `print` statement (see Section 4.7.16), except that CONVFMT rather than OFMT is used for number-to-string conversions.

4.7.14
Predefined
Numerical
Functions

The following functions provide various numerical operations.

Integer Part. The following awk function provides the integer part of a number:

`int(`*x*`)`   Returns the integer part of *x*; that is, truncates *x* towards zero to an integer. For example, the value of '`int(-2.7)`' is -2.

Elementary Functions. Awk provides the following elementary mathematical functions:

`sin(`*x*`)`   Returns the sine of *x* radians.

`cos(`*x*`)`   Returns the cosine of *x* radians.

`exp(`*x*`)`   Returns e^x, the exponential function of *x*.

`log(`*x*`)`   Returns $\log x$, the natural logarithm of *x*.

`atan2(`*y*`,`*x*`)`

>Returns the arctangent of y/x. The result r is chosen so that $-\pi \le r \le \pi$.

`sqrt(`*x*`)`   Returns the square root of *x*.

Random Number Generation. The following functions support random number generation:

`rand()`   Returns a random number r, $0 \le r < 1$.

`srand([`*x*`])`

>Uses *x* as a new seed for `rand`. The seed provides a starting value for the sequence of random numbers produced by `rand`. If you call `srand` with a particular argument k, then k determines the ensuing sequence of `rand` values. If you later call `srand` again with the same argument k, `rand` will produce the same sequence of values.

The value of the seed x should be a nonzero integer.[18] If you omit x, awk uses the time of day as the seed.

4.7.15
Reading Input Explicitly

The getline predefined function reads an input line from a specified source, either a file or the output of a UNIX command. The getline function provides more precise control over reading than does awk's default reading mechanism and also enables you to read from files other than standard input.

Although getline is considered to be a function, the conventions for calling it are entirely different from those of other functions. A call on getline has one of the following forms:

getline [*var*]

> Reads the next record from standard input into the variable *var* if *var* is specified and into $0 otherwise. As a side effect, the predefined variables NR and FNR (see "Input-Related Variables" on p. 220) are both incremented. If *var* is specified, the input line is not split into fields and the predefined variable NF is left unchanged. If *var* is not specified, the input line is split just as though it had been read implicitly and NF is set to the number of fields. The value returned by getline is 1 if a record was read successfully, 0 if an end of file was encountered, and -1 if an error occurred on the attempted read.

getline [*var*] < *file*

> Like the previous form, except that awk reads the record from *file* instead of from standard input. The variable *file* must be specified as a string-valued expression giving the name of the file. A '<' operator following getline is interpreted as specifying a file rather than as a comparison operator, unless the getline happens to be preceded by '|'. Successive getlines specifying the same file read successive lines of that file unless you close the file with close (see Section 4.7.17).

cmd | getline [*var*]

> Like the first form, except that awk executes the UNIX command *cmd* in a subshell and sends the lines of its standard output to getline. The variable *cmd* must be specified as a string-valued expression giving the name of the command. Repeated calls on getline with the same command do not cause the command to be executed repeatedly. Instead, the command is executed once and its output is passed to getline one line at a time, so successive getline calls retrieve successive output

---

18. Note that although the seed is an integer, the values produced by **rand** are not integers. **Rand** actually computes the random numbers as integers and then converts them to floating-point numbers before returning them. Each integer is derived from the previous one unless it is specified by a call on **srand**.

lines. You can cause *cmd* to be executed again by using the `close` statement (see Section 4.7.17).

Because the `getline` call has such an odd syntax, it's wise to enclose it in parentheses if it's part of a larger expression.

4.7.16
Producing Output

The `print` and `printf` statements produce output. By default this output is sent to standard output, but you can redirect it by attaching a redirection to the statement. A redirection is indicated by *redir* in the statement forms below (see "Redirecting Output" on p. 218).

Here are the forms of the `print` and `printf` statements:

`print`   Sends $0 to standard output.

`print` *expr* [, *expr*...] [*redir*]
`print(`*expr* [, *expr*...]`)` [*redir*]

> Evaluates each expression *expr* in turn, converts its value to a string if necessary, and sends that string to standard output (see "Coercions Between Strings and Numbers" on p. 204). Successive values are separated by the output field separator, whose value is given by the predefined variable `OFS`. The last value is followed by the output record separator, whose value is given by the predefined variable `ORS`. The default value of `OFS` is a single space; the default value of `ORS` is a single ⟨newline⟩.

`printf` *fmt*, *expr* [, *expr*...] [*redir*]
`printf(`*fmt*, *expr* [, *expr*...]`)` [*redir*]

> Evaluates each expression *expr* in turn and sends the values of these expressions to standard output, formatting them according to the output format *fmt* (see "Output Formats" on p. 218). To format a list of expressions and send the result to a string instead of to a file or pipe, use the `sprintf` function (see "Formatting a Sequence of Values" on p. 215).

When `awk` needs to convert a number to a string while executing the output statements `print` or `printf`, it uses the format found as the value of the `OFMT` predefined variable rather than the `CONVFMT` predefined variable otherwise used for such conversions.

A use of '>' in a `print` or `printf` statement is interpreted as a redirection operator rather than as a comparison unless either the '>' and its operands or the expression list of the statement is enclosed in parentheses. In the parenthesized forms of `print` and `printf`, no whitespace is permitted between the left parenthesis and the 'print' or 'printf'.

Note the difference between the following two statements:

```
print 1 2 3
print 1, 2, 3
```

The first one contains a single expression that is the concatenation of three numbers and produces '123'. The second one contains three expressions and therefore produces three numbers separated by the output field separator, namely, '1 2 3'.

Redirecting Output. The *redir* components of the `print` and `printf` statements have one of the following forms:

> `> file`   Sends the output to *file*. The variable *file* is a string that names a file. The first such redirection for a particular file erases the contents of the file; subsequent redirections accumulate output in that file.

> `>> file`   Appends the output to *file*. The variable *file* is a string that names a file. Unlike '> *file*', this form does not erase the previous contents of the file.

> `| cmd`   Pipes the output to the UNIX command *cmd*, making it part of the standard input to *cmd*. The variable *cmd* is a string that names a UNIX command. The command is called only once unless it is closed by a `close` statement (see Section 4.7.17). Successive outputs from `print` and `printf` are passed as successive lines of input to *cmd*.

Output Formats. An output format specifies how a list of values is to be represented as a string. The format is a string that acts as a template, with fixed and variable parts. The fixed parts are reproduced literally; successive variable parts, called *format specifications*, specify how successive values are to be represented. The format specifications are always introduced by '%', with '%%' indicating a literal '%'. For example, the format in the `print` statement

```
printf("The current value of %s is %03d.\n", "lemming", 29)
```

has two format specifications, '%s' and '%03d', that format the values 'lemming' and 29. The '%s' specifies string formatting and the '%03d' specifies three-digit decimal formatting with leading zeros. The resulting output is

```
The current value of lemming is 029.
```

In general, a format specification has three parts: the '%' that introduces the format specification, a sequence of up to three modifiers, and a format character. The format character specifies the general form of the result, called a *field*, while the modifiers provide additional details. The format characters are as follows:

> `c`   The character with this numerical encoding.

> `s`   String.

> `d`   Decimal integer.

> `o`   Octal integer (unsigned).

> `x`   Hexadecimal integer (unsigned).

> `f`   Decimal fraction in the form [-]d ... d.dddddd with as many digits as necessary preceding the decimal point.

> `e`   Scientific notation in the form [-]d.ddddddE[+-]dd.

> `g`   Either `e` or `f` format, whichever is shorter, with extra zeros suppressed.

Format	Value	Result
%c	68	D
%d	-68	-68
%4d	68	␣␣68
%-4d	68	68␣␣
%04d	68	0068
%x	68	44
%f	68.1	68.100000
%7.2f	68.1	␣␣68.10
%e	68.1	6.810000e+01
%g	68.1	68.1
%s	shark	shark
%.4s	shark	shar
%-5.2s	shark	sh␣␣␣

Fig. 4-1.   Values formatted for awk output.

The modifiers, which must appear in the indicated order if they appear at all, are as follows:

- Left-justify the output string within its field.

w If the field is less than *w* characters wide, pad it out to *w* characters. If *w* is written with a leading zero, pad with zeros; otherwise pad with blanks.

.prec For a string, truncate the string after *prec* characters; for a number with a decimal fraction part, use *prec* digits in that part.

When a number is converted to a string by printf, it is treated as though it were processed using the format given by the OFMT predefined variable (default value '%.6g').

The examples in Figure 4-1 show how values are formatted according to various specifications.

4.7.17
Closing Files and Pipes

When output is redirected to a file, the file is ordinarily opened only once. Successive output lines are sent to the file, so its final contents become the concatenation of all the lines sent to it. Similarly, when input is redirected from a file, the file is ordinarily opened only once and successive input lines are read from it. Input and output piped to or from commands behave analogously.

You can in effect reinitialize a file or pipe by closing it with the following command:

close(*str*)

Closes the file or piped command whose name is *str*. Subsequent input from or output to a file causes it to be reopened.

Subsequent reads or writes start again from the beginning. Subsequent input to or output from a piped command causes it to be executed again.

4.7.18 Executing System Commands

The following function enables you to execute a UNIX command from within an `awk` program:

`system(`*cmd*`)`

> Executes the UNIX command *cmd* in a subshell. The value of the function is the exit value of *cmd* (see Section 2.6.2).

4.7.19 Predefined Variables

`Awk` provides a number of predefined special variables.

Input-Related Variables. The following predefined variables are related to reading input records:

FS
: The specification of the input field separator (see "Input Field Separators" on p. 206).

RS
: The specification of the input record separator (see "Input Record Separators" on p. 207).

NF
: The number of fields in the current record (see p. 206).

FNR
: The number of records read so far from the current input file, counting the current one.

NR
: The total number of records read so far from all input files.

FILENAME
: The name of the current input file. If the current file is standard input, the value of FILENAME is '-'.

Command-Line Arguments. You can retrieve the command-line arguments via the following two predefined variables, which are set by `awk` when it starts up:

ARGV
: An array containing the command-line arguments. The first argument, ARGV[0], is the name of the command itself, normally 'awk'.[19] The remaining ones, ARGV[1], ARGV[2], ... , contain the actual arguments *arg* ... (see the form of the `awk` call on p. 199).

ARGC
: The number of command-line arguments, including ARGV[0]. This number is equal to the subscript of the last actual argument.

For example, the command line

```
awk -f kvetch ketch yawl
```

---

19. If `awk` is called via a differently named link, ARGV[0] contains the name of that link.

leads to the following values for ARGV and ARGC:

```
ARGV[0]: awk
ARGV[1]: ketch
ARGV[2]: yawl
ARGC: 3
```

Pattern-Matching Variables.   The following two variables record information about a successful pattern match (see "Pattern Matching and Substitution" on p. 213):

RSTART   The starting position of the string that is matched by the match function.

RLENGTH   The length of the string matched by the match function.

Output-Related Variables.   The following variables affect the form of output:

OFMT   The printf format used when a number is converted to a string by an output statement (see Section 4.7.16). The default format is '%.6g'.

CONVFMT   The printf format used when a number is converted to a string in a context other than an output statement (see "Output Formats" on p. 218). The default format is '%.6g'.

OFS   The separator for the output fields produced by a print statement (see Section 4.7.16).

ORS   The separator for the output records produced by a print statement.

Miscellaneous Variables.   There are a few variables that don't fall into any particular category:

SUBSEP   The string used to separate the indices of a multidimensional array (see "Multidimensional Arrays" on p. 208). The default value depends on your system; a typical value is the nonprintable character ⟨FS⟩, whose numerical code in ASCII is 28 (decimal).

ENVIRON   An array containing the values of all environment variables. The indices of the array are the variable names and the element values are the values of the variables. If a value is a numeric string, then the array element has the numeric value denoted by that string. The contents of this array are determined when awk begins executing, but may be modified by later changes to the environment. Whether those changes are actually visible depends on your system.

**4.7.20
Expressions as
Statements**

An expression can be treated as a statement. An expression appearing in the context of a statement is evaluated and its value discarded. Expressions whose main operator is an assignment operator are often used as statements (see "Assignment Operators" on p. 211).

**4.7.21
Control-Flow
Statements**

The control-flow statements relate to the grouping of statements and to statements that affect what is executed next.

Grouping and Empty Statements.   The following two constructs provide grouping and an empty statement:

{ *stmt* ...}
> Executes a group of statements. A group of statements enclosed in braces can be used in any context requiring a single statement. The statements must be separated by semicolons or ⟨newline⟩s.

;
> Does nothing. This construct is called an *empty statement*. You can provide an empty statement by writing nothing at all in any context where a semicolon would not be required after some other kind of statement. For example, a group containing a single empty statement can be written as '{}'.

Conditional Statement.   Using a conditional statement, you can test the value of an expression and use the result to select a statement to be executed:

if (*expr*) *stmt*₁ [; else *stmt*₂]
> Executes the statement $stmt_1$ if the value of the expression *expr* is true; otherwise executes the statement $stmt_2$. For nested if's, each else is paired with the nearest unpaired if to its left. Although $stmt_1$ and $stmt_2$ are single statements, you can execute any number of statements as $stmt_1$ or $stmt_2$ by making the statements into a group.

Iteration Statements.   The following statements provide various forms of iteration. Wherever a single statement is required, you can put several statements by enclosing those statements in a group.

while (*expr*) *stmt*
> Executes the statement *stmt* while the expression *expr* is true.

do *stmt* while (*expr*)
> Executes the statement *stmt* once, then executes it repeatedly while the expression *expr* is true. The expression *expr* is tested before each execution of *stmt* except the first one.

for (*expr*₁; *expr*₂; *expr*₃) *stmt*
> Evaluates the expression $expr_1$, then performs the following steps repeatedly:
>
> (1) Evaluates $expr_2$. If the value is false, terminates the iteration.
> (2) Executes *stmt*.
> (3) Evaluates $expr_3$.

For example, the awk program

```
BEGIN {
    n = ARGV[1]
    for (i = 1; i <= n; i++)
        print i, sqrt(i)
}
```

produces a sequence of lines listing the integers from 1 to n and their square roots, with n being provided as the command-line argument.

Any of the expressions in a for statement may be omitted; if $expr_2$ is omitted, it is taken to be true. Thus the form

> for (;;) *stmt*

causes awk to execute *stmt* repeatedly until the iteration is somehow interrupted (e.g., by a break statement).

for (*var* in *array*) *stmt*
: Executes the statement *stmt* with *var* set to each subscript of the array *array* in turn.

Breaking Out of Iterations.   The following statements break out of iterations:

break
: Leaves the innermost while, for, or do statement containing the break, then terminates execution of the containing statement.

continue
: Starts the next iteration of the innermost while, for, or do statement containing the continue, skipping any statements remaining in the current iteration.

next
: Reads a new input record and starts the next iteration of the main input loop. The next statement cannot be used within the action of a BEGIN or END statement-action pair.

exit [*expr*]
: If awk is currently executing the action of an END statement-action pair or if there is no END statement-action pair, exits from the program with exit status *expr*. The default for *expr* is 0. Otherwise, goes immediately to the action of the END statement-action pair.

**4.7.22
User-Defined
Functions**

A user-defined function has the form

> function *name*(*param* [, *param*...]) {
>   [*stmt*...]
> }

and may appear wherever a pattern-action statement may. When the function is called, the parameters *param* ... are initialized to the corresponding arguments. The calling protocol passes copies of numerical or string arguments ("call by value") but passes array arguments without copying the array elements ("call by reference"). Therefore, the effect of an assignment to a numerical or string parameter is not visible at the point of call, but an assignment to an element of an array parameter *is* visible at the point of call. The nature of a particular parameter is determined only when the function call actually takes place.

A function call can have fewer arguments than there are parameters in the corresponding function definition. The excess parameters act as local variables for the function definition, and in fact the only way to create local variables is to make them extra parameters. Changes to local variables (aside from changes to array elements) are not visible upon return from a function call. Any variables that are not local are global. Global variables are accessible throughout the `awk` program except when they are obscured by a parameter with the same name. `Awk` functions can be recursive.

Returning from a Function.   You can return from a function to the calling context either by running off the end of the list of statements in the function definition or by executing a `return` statement of the form

        return [*expr*]

If *expr* is given, its value becomes the value of the function at the point of call. If *expr* is not given, the value of the function is undefined—which is not a problem provided that the function call appears in the context of a statement. Running off the end of the list of statements is equivalent to executing `return` without an expression.

4.8   Other Data Manipulation Languages

You may be interested in knowing of two other languages commonly used on UNIX systems for the same purposes as `awk`: Icon and `perl`. Neither is part of any UNIX vendor's standard distribution, but they are widely available nonetheless.

**4.8.1
The Icon
Programming
Language**

Icon is a general-purpose high-level language with a large repertoire of operations for processing strings and other symbolic data. Icon has a C-like syntax and borrows many ideas from C, but its principal ancestor is the string processing language Snobol. Designed by Ralph Griswold at the University of Arizona, Icon is one of the most elegant and powerful programming languages now available. The program used to generate the index of this book was written in Icon.

The Icon language is described in reference [B8]. You can obtain Icon over the Internet via anonymous FTP from `ftp.cs.arizona.edu.` in the directory `/icon` (see Section 12.8). For inquiries, send electronic mail to Internet address `icon-project@cs.arizona.edu`.

Central to Icon is the notion of a *generator*, a procedure that yields a sequence of values rather than a single value. When the generator has no more values to yield, it fails. Control structures are driven by the failure of generators rather than by the more usual true and false boolean values. Generators lead naturally to the notion of goal-directed evaluation, in which alternatives in a pattern match or other similar constructs are tried until a combination is found that succeeds.

Icon provides a variety of high-level data structures including strings of arbitrary length, records, tables (like awk associative arrays), sets, and lists. These are supported by a large collection of useful intrinsic operations. String scanning is provided by string-analysis functions and a pattern-matching operator '?' rather than by regular expression matching. Like awk, Icon uses no declarations; a variable can contain a value of any type. Conversions among data types are automatic but can also be requested explicitly.

Icon has been implemented for UNIX as well as for many other operating systems. The most popular implementation as of this writing is based on an interpreter, but a compiler for Icon has recently been developed. A noteworthy feature of the UNIX version of Icon is its ability to open a UNIX command as a pipe. For example, the Icon expression

```
datfiles := open("ls *.dat", "p")
```

assigns a pipe to the file object datfiles. A subsequent expression

```
while write(read(datfiles))
```

sends the list of the files whose names end with '*.dat' to standard output. Version 9.0 of Icon introduced an extensive set of graphics facilities.

4.8.2
The perl Language

The perl Practical Extraction and Report Language is a language for manipulating text, files, and processes designed by Larry Wall and Randal L. Schwartz. You can obtain perl over the Internet via anonymous FTP from prep.ai.mit.edu in the directory /pub/gnu, file perl*ver*.tar.gz, where *ver* is the latest version number. A CD-ROM version is also available (reference [C5]).

Stylistically eclectic, perl borrows from C, awk, and shell programming. It is free of arbitrary limitations—lines can be of any length, arrays can have any number of elements, variable names can be as long as you wish, and binary data will not cause problems. Perl provides all the capability of awk but in addition provides convenient access to the facilities of UNIX itself. Using perl, you can move files, rename them, change their permissions, and so forth. You can create and destroy processes, control the flow of data among processes, and use sockets to communicate with processes on other machines. Perl has become particularly popular among UNIX system administrators.

5

Utility Programs

In this chapter we discuss an assortment of tools for finding out what's going on in your system, controlling your terminal, and managing other aspects of your working environment. We also discuss some programs that don't fall into any other category.

5.1   Information Services

The commands in this group display manual pages, provide information about users and terminals, and provide other information such as the date, the time, and a calendar. The `ps` command described in Section 5.2.1 provides related information about the processes running in your system.

5.1.1
Viewing Manual
Pages with man

You can use the `man` command to view pages from the UNIX manual (see Section 2.1) on-line. The POSIX form of the `man` command is

    man [-k] *name* ...

where each name in *name* ... is the subject of a manual page. A subject can be the name of a program such as `grep`, the format of a file such as `fstab`, or any other topic. Typing 'man *name*' displays the manual page for *name*. If you specify more than one *name*, the manual pages for all the specified *name*s are displayed.

Most systems, however, provide a more elaborate version of man. The form of the command for a version with typical options looks like one of these:

man [-ahkw] [-M *path*] [-P *pager*] [*section*] *name* ...
man [-ahkw] [-M *path*] [-P *pager*] [-s *section*] *name* ...

In this form the manual pages are restricted to those found in the section *section* (e.g., 1 for user commands). If more than one manual page is found, only the first is shown.

Most versions of man display a manual page by piping it to a pager. The pager is given by the value of the PAGER environment variable if that's defined; otherwise, the pager usually defaults to more (see Section 3.6.1). You can override that variable with the -P option; if no pager is defined explicitly, man uses the more pager (though some systems change this).

If you specify the -k option, each *name* is taken as a keyword rather than as the name of a particular manual page. The man utility searches a database of one-line descriptions of manual pages. Examples of such descriptions are

```
chmod (1)      - Change the access permissions of files
bzero (3)      - Write zeros to a byte string
```

In this example, the chmod entry is for a user utility, the bzero entry for a C library function. A description matches if it contains *name* as a substring. The match can be in either the title or the descriptive text. Man then produces each matching description on standard output. A lookup with the -k option is sometimes called an "apropos search". Many systems provide a command apropos that is equivalent to 'man -k', either in addition to or as a replacement for 'man -k'.

Command-Line Options.   The following is a set of typical options for man:

-a   Display all matching manual pages, not just the first one.

-h   Produce a help message and exit.

-k   Produce all descriptions that match keyword *name* according to a keyword search. Usually the descriptions are just one line long. The descriptions are sent to standard output.

-M *path*   Search for manual pages using the path *path* instead of the usual default path as given by the environment variable MANPATH. This option is useful when you're searching for manual pages on another system.

-P *pager*   Use the pager *pager* for viewing.

-w   Show the locations of the files containing the manual pages, not the pages themselves.

Environment Variables.   Typical environment variables that affect man are the following:

MANPATH   A colon-separated list of directories to search for manual pages.

MANSEC   A colon-separated list of manual sections to search.

PAGER   The pager to use for viewing manual pages.

You can override each of these variables with an appropriate command-line option or by using the `env` command (see Section 6.8.2).

5.1.2
Who's Using the System: who

The `who` command shows who is currently using the system. The System V version of `who` also has options for obtaining information about processes that are running and events of interest since the system was last restarted. Two related commands are `rwho`, which lists users on other computers on a network (see Section 12.6.5),[1] and `finger`, which locates users whether or not they are logged in (see Section 5.1.3).

The POSIX version of `who` provides a minimal set of services. The POSIX form of the command line is

```
who [-mTu]
```

Who sends a list of users to standard output. The form of the output depends on your system unless you specify the `-T` option. Here is an example of the output of `who`, called with the `-T` option:

```
root       - console    Apr 10 09:36
yorick     + tty01      Apr 11 16:59
bottom     + tty04      Apr 11 14:16
quince     ? ttyp1      Apr 11 15:02
```

The first column shows the name of each logged-in user, the second column the write status of the user's terminal (see below), the third column the name of that terminal, and the remaining columns the date and time when each user logged in. Many versions of `who` also show you the network host name from which a remote user has logged in.

A number of systems, including 4.4BSD and Linux, provide a `w` command that displays information similar to what `who` displays. For each user, it shows the login name, the terminal name, the remote host if any where the user is logged in, the idle time, some time usage statistics, and the command the user is currently executing. Generally the output of `w` is more useful than the output of `who`. System V provides a similar but wordier command called `whodo`.

Command-Line Options for POSIX.   The POSIX version of `who` supports these three options:

-m   Show only information about your own terminal; that is, the terminal from which this command was issued. The behavior is the same as for the traditional 'who am i' command.

-T   Show information in a standard form, including the *write state* of each terminal; that is, whether the terminal will accept

---

1. An alternative on some commercial systems is a program called `rusers`, which uses less bandwidth than `rwho`.

write commands (see Section 5.6.2). The possible states are '+' (writable by other users), '-' (not writable by other users), and '?' (cannot be determined). For non-POSIX versions of who, the −T option usually specifies that the listing is to include the write state, but it does not otherwise modify the form of the listing.

−u   Show the idle time for each displayed user following the login time. The idle time is the time since the most recent activity on the user's terminal.

Command-Line Options for System V.   The command-line options listed below apply only to the System V version of who and to its derivatives.

  The following option provides the default explicitly:

−s   List only the name, terminal, and login time of each user. In combination with most other options, −s suppresses additional fields of the listing. In no case does it affect which terminals and processes are listed.

The following options control which terminals are listed:

−u   List the terminals where a user is logged in.

−l   List the terminals where no one is logged in.

The −u and −l options also cause who to include for each terminal the time since it last showed activity and the number of its controlling process.

  The following option provides a quick listing:

−q   Display only the number of users currently logged on and their names. If −q is present, who ignores all other options.

The following option provides column headings:

−H   Put a heading above each column.

The following option causes the write state of each terminal to be shown:

−T   Indicate the *write state* of each terminal; that is, whether the terminal will accept write commands (see Section 5.6.2). The possible states are the same as for the POSIX −T option.

The following options provide information about the state of the system that is usually interesting and meaningful only to those who maintain your system. We mention them for the sake of completeness.

−r   Indicate the current run level of the init process together with its termination status, process ID, and exit status.

−b   Indicate the last time the system was rebooted.

−t   Indicate the last time the system clock was explicitly changed, if it ever was.

-p   List all processes started by the `init` process and still active. The listed information is taken from `/etc/inittab`.[2]

-d   List all processes started by the `init` process that are now dead (i.e., that have terminated). The exit status in the comments field indicates why the process terminated.

The following option shows you almost everything:

-a   Turn on all other options except (on some systems) -T.

Command Form for Other Non-POSIX Versions.   For other non-POSIX versions of `who`, the command line has the form

> who [*options*] [*file* | am i]

where *file*, if given, is the file from which `who` derives its information.[3] The BSD version of `who` recognizes no options at all. The form

> who am i

or equivalently,

> who am I

shows your login name and the name of the terminal you're currently using. BSD also provides a `whoami` command, which produces your effective user name on standard output and is equivalent to 'id -un'.

5.1.3 Looking Up User Information with `finger`

The `finger` command enables you to look up information about a specific user or about all users currently logged in. It is particularly useful for looking up a user when the user is at a remote location or when you only know part of the user's full name. The information that you get is system-dependent but typically includes the user's full name, user name, office location, and telephone number. For logged-in users it also includes the time since the user last typed anything and a '*' indicator if the user's terminal is blocked from receiving messages (see Section 5.6.3). This command is not included in POSIX.

The form of the `finger` command line is

> finger [-lmps] [*name...*]

---

2. The `/etc/inittab` file contains a table listing the processes that should be initiated whenever the system's run state changes. Each process in `/etc/inittab` has a list of states associated with it; it is restarted whenever the run state is changed to one of those states listed. In addition, a process may be marked for "respawning". A respawning process is restarted whenever it is found to have terminated.

3. The default file is named `utmp`. Historically its location was `/etc/utmp`, but modern systems may locate it at `/var/adm/utmp`, `/var/run/utmp` (4.4BSD), or elsewhere. Occasionally you may want to use the file `/etc/wtmp`, which contains all logins since it was created. Common alternate locations for this file are `/usr/adm/wtmp`, `/var/adm/wtmp`, and `/var/run/wtmp`. Any file that you use must be in the same format as the `utmp` file.

where each *name* indicates a user or group of users to be looked up and has one of the following forms:

(empty)   Provide information about all users currently logged in.

word   Provide information about each user on your computer whose name matches *word*.

word@hostname

Provide information about each user at remote computer *hostname* whose name matches *word*.

@hostname

Provide information about all users currently logged in at remote computer *hostname*.

A match succeeds if *word* agrees with a user's user name or with any word in that user's full name (as listed in the /etc/passwd file). For comparison purposes, words are separated by spaces. The comparison is case-insensitive for the full name but not for the user name. For instance, if the user "Hubert van Gogh" has user name 'hvg', you can look him up as 'hvg', 'gogh', or 'Hubert'—but not as 'bert', since 'bert' doesn't match a complete word in the user's name, nor by 'HVG', since the user-name comparison is case-sensitive. If a single *name* matches several users, you see them all.

Finger recognizes two special files if they exist in your home directory: .plan and .project. Any text you put into .plan appears in your finger listing, so .plan is a good place to provide information such as your telephone number, office location, and usual schedule. The .project file is similar. Newer BSD versions of finger also include information from a .forward file if it exists in your home directory.

Output of finger has short and long forms. The short form has one line per user and lists only basic information; the long form has several lines per user. The short form looks like this:

```
Login      Name              TTY Idle      When      Where
operator  Operator on Console   a  2:12 Mon 10:06
felix     Felix the Cat         p2 3:03 Mon 09:32  cinema.com
```

The long form (for one user) looks like this:

```
Login name: felix                    In real life: Felix the Cat
Directory: /home/felix                  Shell: /bin/csh
On since Jun 24 09:56:16 on ttyp2
3 hours 3 minutes Idle Time
No unread mail
Plan:
Try X2378 or
look for me at the nearest mousehole.
```

By default you get the long form for users specified explicitly and the short form for the list of all users at a site, but you can force a particular form with the `-l` or `-s` option.

Command-Line Options.   The command-line options for the `finger` command are as follows:

`-l`   Use the long output format (several lines per user).

`-s`   Use the short output format (one line per user).

`-m`   Match each *name* against user names only (and require an exact match).

`-p`   Don't show the `.plan` or `.project` files (or the `.forward` file if it would have been shown).

**5.1.4
Getting Terminal
Information
with** `tty`

The `tty` command sends the path name of your terminal to standard output. It can also reveal whether standard input is a terminal. The form of the `tty` command line is

        `tty [-ls]`

The form of the output is a string such as '`/dev/tty03`'. The POSIX version does not support any options.

You can use the exit code of `tty` to test if standard input is a terminal. These are the exit codes:

0   Standard input is a terminal.
1   Standard input is not a terminal.
2   Invalid options were specified.

Command-Line Options.   These are the options for the `tty` command line, neither of which is supported by POSIX:

`-l`   Show the line number of the terminal if the terminal is on an active synchronous line. Most UNIX terminals are not on synchronous lines, which are primarily used to connect block-style terminals to mainframe systems. If the terminal is not on an active synchronous line, a message to that effect is added to the output. Not all systems support this option.

`-s`   Don't send the terminal's path name to standard output. This option is useful when you're using `tty` in a shell script to determine whether standard input is indeed a terminal but don't care about its name. Under POSIX systems you can achieve the same effect with the command '`test -t 0`' (see Section 6.12).

**5.1.5
Showing the Date
and Time with** `date`

The `date` command sends the date and time to standard output. In addition, the superuser can use it to set the date and time.[4] The form of the command is

        `date [-u] [+`*format*`]`

---

4. System administrators often use this command indirectly through an administrative interface program such as `admintool`.

The simple command

    date

produces the date and time in a default format, shown by the output

    Sat Apr 13 16:25:00 EDT 1996

The -u option causes the date and time to be calculated using Greenwich Mean Time.

You can specify the format explicitly with the option-argument *format*, a string with interspersed format descriptors. Each format descriptor is preceded by '%'; if you want a '%' in the text, you must write it as '%%'. The strings associated with the format descriptors are affected by the locale (see "Dates and Times" on p. 79). In the description that follows we assume the POSIX locale, which gives the results traditionally produced by American UNIX systems.

The format descriptors vary somewhat from one system to another, and some older systems don't support user-specified formats at all. These are the format descriptors defined by POSIX:[5]

c	Date and time in the default format (as above)
x	Date in the default format
D	Date in the form '*mm/dd/yy*' (e.g., '07/04/96')
C	Century (e.g., '19')
y	Last two digits of the year
Y	Four-digit year
j	Day of year as three digits ('001'–'366')
m	Month as two digits ('01'–'12')
h	Month as three letters ('Jan'–'Dec')
b	Same as h
B	Month spelled in full ('January'–'December')
d	Day of month as two digits ('01'–'31')
e	Day of month as one or two digits with leading ⟨space⟩ for 1–9
w	Day of week as one digit ('0' for Sunday, '6' for Saturday)
u	Day of week as one digit ('1' for Monday, '7' for Sunday)
a	Day of week as three letters ('Sun'–'Sat')
A	Day of week spelled in full ('Sunday'–'Saturday')
U	Week of the year ('00'–'53') with Sunday as the first day of the week and all days in a new year preceding the first Sunday considered to be in week 0
W	Week of the year ('00'–'53') with Monday as the first day of the week and all days in a new year preceding the first Monday considered to be in week 0

---

5. In addition to the descriptors we list here, POSIX provides for alternate methods of numbering years and alternate sets of digits such as those used for Hindi and Kanji. The %Ex descriptor denotes the alternate date representation of the locale, while the %Od descriptor denotes the day of the month using the alternate numeric symbols of the locale. A number of other similar descriptors are provided, with the %E prefix indicating alternate year numbering and the %O prefix indicating alternate digits.

V	Week of the year ('01'–'53') with Monday as the first day of the week and the first week calculated according to standard ISO 8601[6]
X	Time in the default format
T	Time in the form '*hh*:*mm*:*ss*' (e.g., '14:00:00' for 2 PM exactly)
r	Time in AM/PM notation (e.g., '04:45:10 pm')
H	Hour as two digits in a 24-hour clock ('00'–'23')
I	Hour as two digits in a 12-hour clock ('01'–'12')
p	Either 'AM' or 'PM' for forenoon or afternoon
Z	Time zone (e.g., 'EDT')
M	Minute as two digits ('00'–'59')
S	Second as two digits ('00'–'59')
n	⟨newline⟩ character
t	⟨tab⟩ character

For example, the command

```
date '+It is now %T on %h %d, 19%y% (%a).%nThank you for your interest.'
```

produces output like this:

```
        It is now 10:29:42 on Nov 01, 1995 (Wed).
        Thank you for your interest.
```

Note that the format has been quoted so that blanks within it are correctly reproduced (see Section 2.12.2).

Setting the Date.   The superuser may use the `date` command to set the system date. The command

> date *mmddhhmmyy*

sets the system date to month *mm*, day *dd*, hour *hh*, minute *mm*, and year *yy*. You may omit *yy*; if you do, `date` takes it as the current year.

   Note: You must issue this command at an exact minute if you want the time to be correct to the second.

5.1.6
Displaying a
Calendar with `cal`

The `cal` command produces a calendar for a single month or for an entire year and sends it to standard output. It is not included in POSIX.
   The form of the `cal` command line is

> cal [[*month*] *year*]

---

6. The somewhat complicated algorithm used by that standard takes the week containing January 1 to be week 1 of the new year if it has at least four days in the new year. Otherwise, it takes that week to be week 53 of the previous year.

The following rules apply to `cal`:

- If you omit both month and year, you get a calendar for the current month.

- If you specify both a month and a year, you get a calendar just for that month.

- If you specify only a year, you get a calendar for that entire year. Note that 'cal 11' gives you a calendar for the year 11, not for November of the current year.

For example, the command

```
cal 7 1776
```

produces the following calendar:

```
    July 1776
 S  M Tu  W Th  F  S
       1  2  3  4  5  6
 7  8  9 10 11 12 13
14 15 16 17 18 19 20
21 22 23 24 25 26 27
28 29 30 31
```

5.2   Reporting on the Status of Processes

The `ps` command is used for reporting the status of processes, but it varies enormously among systems. We first describe two commonly installed versions of the `ps` (list processes) command: one that is used on System V systems and another that is used on BSD systems. We then describe the POSIX version, which as far as we know has not yet (mid-1995) been fully adopted in practice.

**5.2.1
Showing Processes
with** `ps`
(System V Version)

The System V `ps` command lists processes running on a System V system (see Section 2.6). Using the `ps` options, you can select the processes to be listed and can choose between a brief, full, or extended listing.

The form of the `ps` command line is

```
ps [-adefl] [-g grouplist] [-n name] [-p proclist]
   [-t termlist] [-u userlist]
```

As befits a command that provides information about the inner workings of your system, the options and the information in the listing vary considerably among systems. The simple form 'ps' should work on all systems, however, and should list in abbreviated form the processes running at your own terminal.

Options for Selecting Processes.   The following options specify which processes are listed. By default, the only ones listed are those associated with your terminal. In these options, a *list* is a sequence of items separated by spaces or commas.

-e   Produce information about every process.

-d   Produce information about every process except for process group leaders. A process group leader has a group number identical to its process number. Unfortunately, the information produced by ps does not include group numbers, so the only way to tell which processes are process group leaders is to compare this listing with the one obtained from -e.

-a   Produce information about every process except process group leaders and processes not associated with a terminal.

-u *userlist*

Produce only output pertaining to the specified users. Users are denoted by their user IDs.

-t *termlist*

Produce only output describing processes that are running at the specified terminals. You can identify a terminal by its file-name within the /dev directory (e.g., 'tty02') or by two digits with an assumed prefix of 'tty'.

-p *proclist*

Produce only output pertaining to the specified processes. A process is specified by its process number (which you would normally derive from a previous listing).

-g *grouplist*

Produce only output pertaining to the specified process groups. A process group is denoted by its number, which is the process number of its leader.

The following option enables you to list processes when your system has been started up with a kernel other than /unix. It is useful only if you're maintaining a UNIX system.

-n *name*   Assume that the system has been started from the kernel *name* rather than from the kernel /unix. If that is the case and you don't use this option, you won't get any output from ps.[7] This option requires superuser privileges.

---

7.   The reason is that ps uses information in the kernel file in order to locate the processes.

Options for Specifying What Is Listed.   By default, ps provides only an abbreviated listing, such as the following one:

```
PID TTY      TIME COMMAND
100 console  0:02 csh
236 console  0:00 sh
319 console  0:01 cp
320 console  0:00 ps
```

The options below provide listings with more information.

-f   Produce a full listing, such as the following one:

UID	PID	PPID	C	STIME	TTY	TIME	COMMAND
alice	100	1	1	15:12:57	console	0:02	csh
alice	236	100	10	15:27:09	console	0:00	/bin/sh try
alice	274	236	2	15:28:00	console	0:00	cp king court
alice	272	100	8	15:27:59	console	0:00	ps -f

-l   Produce an extended (long) listing. The additional fields in this listing are usually of interest only to system maintainers.

In the next subsection we indicate the items included in each type of listing.

Interpreting the Output.   Below we describe the items that appear in the listings. A **B** item appears in a brief listing and an **F** item appears in a full listing. Examples of these listings are given above.

UID   **(F)** The user associated with the process.

PID   **(BF)** The process number.

PPID   **(F)** The process number of the process's parent.

C   **(F)** The processor utilization, for scheduling purposes.

STIME   **(F)** The starting time of the process. A process started more than a day ago is given in months and days.

TTY   **(BF)** The controlling terminal for the process. A '?' indicates that the process is not associated with a terminal. System processes almost always have a '?' in this field.

TIME   **(BF)** The cumulative execution time for the process in minutes and seconds of central processor time.

COMMAND   **(BF)** The command being executed by the process. For the -f option, the arguments to the command are shown as well.

**5.2.2
Showing Processes
with ps
(BSD Version)**

The ps command in BSD, like the one in System V, shows processes running on your system. The BSD version of ps is compatible with the Seventh Edition version but extends it significantly. BSD-derived systems are likely to have their own small variations on this command.

The form of the ps command line for BSD is

ps [-][acegklnsuvwx][t *term*] [*pid*]

where *pid* is a process ID. If *pid* is specified, only information about the process with this ID is shown. The command line may contain additional specifications of interest to system maintainers, which we do not describe here. Note that there must not be a space between the '-' and the options that follow, if any options are provided, and that the '-' itself can be omitted.

Options for Selecting Processes. The following options specify which processes are listed. By default, only those processes associated with your terminal are listed.

g   Produce information about all processes.

a   Produce information about all processes that are associated with terminals.

t*term*   Show only processes running on terminal *term*. You should write *term* in the same form as it appears in the ps listing (e.g., 't3' for 'tty3' and 'tco' for the console). This option must appear last.

x   Show information about processes that are not associated with a terminal.

Options for Specifying What Is Listed. By default, ps provides only an abbreviated listing like this one:

```
  PID TT STAT   TIME COMMAND
15345 co IW     0:00 - std.9600 console (getty)
 8181 p0 IW     0:02 -tcsh (tcsh)
12883 q7 IW     0:00 mail
16899 q5 S      0:00 -h -i (tcsh)
12901 q7 Z      0:00 <defunct>
 7895 p2 TW     0:00 emacs assignment
```

The options below provide listings with more information. The recently added -o option provides a way of customizing the listing.

u   Produce information in a user-oriented format. Here is an example of such a listing:

USER	PID	%CPU	%MEM	SZ	RSS	TT	STAT	START	TIME	COMMAND
root	15345	0.0	0.0	56	0	co	IW	20:31	0:00	- std.9600 console (getty)
betsys	12883	0.0	0.0	112	0	q7	IW	17:11	0:00	mail
root	12901	0.0	0.0	0	0	q7	Z	Oct 7	0:00	<defunct>
prancer	16912	7.7	1.7	208	512	q5	R	22:42	0:00	ps -uag
donder	7295	0.0	0.0	152	0	p5	IW	Oct 8	0:00	-tcsh (tcsh)
vixen	5281	0.0	0.0	1248	0	pb	IW	10:19	1:15	emacs

The specific fields may be different on your system.

l   Produce a long listing. This listing is the only one that shows you the parent of each process; the other additional fields in this listing are usually of interest only to system maintainers.

c   Show the internally stored command name rather than the command name gotten from the argument list. The internally stored command name is more reliable but may be less informative.

e   Show the environment of the command.

v   Show virtual memory statistics. These statistics are not likely to be meaningful unless you are familiar with the internals of your system.

w   Use a wide output format of 132 columns rather than 80. Repeating this option causes an arbitrarily wide format to be used.

-o *items* Use the items listed in *items*, a comma- or whitespace-separated list, as the headings for the process listing. The valid items include those listed in "Items for a Customized Listing" on page 241, but others are also available (see your manual page).

Interpreting the Output.   Below we describe the items that appear in the listings. A **B** item appears in a brief listing and a **U** item appears in a full listing. Examples of these listings are given above.

USER   **(U)** The user associated with the process.

PID   **(BU)** The process number.

%CPU   **(U)** The percentage of available central processor time being used by this process within the past minute (approximately).

%MEM   **(U)** The percentage of available real memory being used by this process.

SZ   **(U)** The virtual memory size of the process in 1024-byte units.

RSS   **(U)** The real memory size of the process in 1024-byte units.

TT   **(BU)** The controlling terminal for the process.

STAT   **(BU)** The state of the process (see below).

START   **(U)** The starting time of the process. A process started more than a day ago is given in months and days.

TIME   **(BU)** The cumulative execution time for the process in minutes and seconds of central processor time.

COMMAND   **(BU)** The command being executed by the process. For the -u option, the arguments to the command are shown as well.

Information on the Process State.   Each ps listing contains an indication labelled 'STAT' of the state of each process in the listing. The state is given by four indicators, denoted by *RWNA*:

R   The runnability of the process:

          R   Able to run
          T   Stopped

	P	Waiting for a memory page
	D	Waiting for disk
	S	Sleeping for less than about 20 seconds
	I	Idle (sleeping for more than about 20 seconds)

W   The swapping state of the process:

(blank)	Loaded in memory
W	Swapped out
>	Memory requirements exceeded

N   The niceness of the process:

(blank)	No special treatment
N	Reduced priority
>	Raised priority

A   The treatment of the process for the purpose of virtual memory replacement:

(blank)	No special treatment
A	LISP garbage collection or similar activity
S	Sequentially addressing large volumes of data

Options for System Maintainers.   The following options are likely to be of interest only to system maintainers. We list them for the sake of completeness.

n   Show information numerically rather than symbolically.

s   Show the kernel stack size of each process.

k   Use the /vmcore file.

U   Update the private database of system information.

**5.2.3
Showing Processes
with** ps
(POSIX Version)

The POSIX ps command was designed as a compromise between the System V and BSD versions, whose options have little in common. The POSIX options were specified so that they could be adopted by either version without major difficulty, so it's likely that you will see them appear on your local version of ps sooner or later.

The form of the POSIX ps command line is

>   ps [-aA] [-G *grouplist*] [-o *items*] ...
>   [-p *proclist*] [-t *termlist*] [-U *userlist*]

Command-Line Options.   The following options specify which processes are listed. By default, the only ones listed are those associated with your terminal. In these options, a list such as *userlist* is a sequence of items separated by spaces or commas.

-A   Produce information about every process.

-a   Produce information about every process associated with a terminal except possibly for process group leaders.

-U *userlist*

> Produce only output pertaining to processes whose real user IDs are in *userlist*. Users are denoted by their user IDs or by their login names.

-G *grouplist*

> Produce only output pertaining to processes whose real group IDs are in *grouplist*.

-t *termlist*

> Produce only output describing processes that are running at the specified terminals. You can identify a terminal by its filename (e.g., 'tty02') or by two digits with an assumed prefix of 'tty'.

-p *proclist*

> Produce only output pertaining to the specified processes. A process is specified by its process number (which you would normally derive from a previous listing).

The following option provides a way of customizing the listing produced by ps:

-o *items*   Use the items listed in *items*, a comma- or whitespace-separated list, as the headings for the process listing. The valid items are listed below.

Items for a Customized Listing.   The following items can appear in the list associated with the -o option:

ruser	Real user ID of the process.
user	Effective user ID of the process.
rgroup	Real group ID of the process.
group	Effective group ID of the process.
pid	Decimal value of the process ID.
ppid	Decimal value of the parent process ID.
pgid	Decimal value of the process group ID.
pcpu	CPU utilization of the process (as a percentage).
vsz	Amount of virtual memory (in kilobytes) used by the process.
nice	The scheduling priority of the process.
etime	The elapsed time since the process was started.
time	The accumulated CPU time used by the process.
tty	The name of the process's controlling terminal.
comm	The name of the command the process is executing.
args	That command with all its arguments as a string.

When particular implementations provide the -o option, it's likely they'll add to this list.

5.3   Managing Processes

In the following subsections we describe a number of commands for killing processes, scheduling them, adjusting their priorities, putting them to sleep, and waiting for them to finish.

5.3.1
Signalling Processes with `kill`

The `kill` command sends a signal to a process. Its name is misleading since the "kill" signal is not the only one it can send. The POSIX forms of the `kill` command are

```
kill -s signame pid ...
kill -l [ signum]
```

Two obsolescent forms are also recognized:

```
kill [-signame] pid ...
kill [-signum] pid ...
```

The signal designated by the symbolic name *signame* or by the signal number *signum* is sent to the processes numbered *pid* .... In addition to being a process number, *pid* can be a job identifier if job control is active. The numeric *signum* form is obsolescent and should be avoided. The default signal is SIGTERM (terminate), which usually kills the process receiving it. See Section 2.6.1 for a discussion of signals and a list of available signals.

You can send the null signal to a process to see if it is alive (i.e., if *pid* is valid) by specifying *signame* as 0, which is actually recognized as a valid signal *name*. The null signal isn't a real signal, but `kill` recognizes it.

Command-Line Options.   In the recommended form of `kill`, one or the other of the following two options is specified:

-s   Send the signal named by *signame*, where *signame* is the case-independent name of a signal.

-l   If *signum* is the number of a signal known to your system, produce the signal's name; if *signum* is an exit status, such as might be gotten from the $? shell variable (see p. 349), produce the name of the signal corresponding to that exit status (traditionally the exit status minus 128). If *signum* is omitted, produce the names of all signals known to your particular system.

In all cases, these forms remove the initial SIG from the name of a signal (e.g., they refer to the SIGHUP signal as HUP).

Examples.   Here are some examples of the use of `kill`:

- To kill process 47 (the number 47 presumably having been gotten from a `ps` listing), issue the command

```
kill -s KILL 47
```

- To produce the name of the signal that terminated the previous shell command, issue the command

      kill -l $?

  For instance, if the command terminated because of a SIGQUIT signal, the word QUIT will be produced on standard output.

- To produce the names of all known signals, issue the command

      kill -l

5.3.2
Ignoring Hangups
with nohup

The nohup command executes a command in such a way that the command continues to execute even if you log out or disconnect your terminal (hang up). It is chiefly used to execute a background job that you wish to leave running even after you've ended your session at the terminal.

To execute a command *cmd* in this manner, type

      nohup *cmd* [*argument* ...]

Any hangup signals (see Section 2.6.1) sent to the process are ignored. The following command shows a typical use of nohup:

      nohup quilting patch38 &

The command quilting with argument patch38 is executed in the background and does not terminate when you log out. The '&' at the end of the command is necessary since nohup by itself does not cause a command to be executed in the background.

A job run with nohup should not attempt to read from standard input. Standard output is sent to nohup.out (in the current directory).

5.3.3
Scheduling Future
Activities with at
and batch

The at and batch commands schedule a job to run at a future time.[8] With at, you specify when the job should be run; with batch, you leave it up to the system to decide when to run it, based on the system load. Batch is usually appropriate for long, low-priority jobs. At has options for removing jobs and for listing jobs that you've scheduled (with either at or batch).

Both commands expect the job to appear in standard input. For example, if you type

      at 3:30am tomorrow
      update mailing_list
      gen -y mailing_list >labels.3
      [EOF]

---

8. Under some systems, permission to use at may be restricted to certain users. The files at.allow and at.deny determine who may use at. They typically live in either the /etc/cron.d directory or in the /usr/lib/cron directory. If neither file exists, only root may use at.

the job consisting of the two commands `update` and `gen` will be run at 3:30 AM the day after you typed this. When the job is run, the current directory and environment are made the same as they were at the time you created the job.

You can submit a job from a file by redirecting the input of `at` or `batch` from that file. The standard input of the submitted job is taken from `/dev/null`, the empty file. The standard output and standard error of a submitted job are sent to you in the form of a mail message. When you submit a job, the job number and schedule time are written to standard error.

The forms of the two commands are

> `at [-m] [-f` *file*`] [-q` *queue*`]` *atime* `[`*adate*`] [+` *increment*`]`
> `at [-m] [-f` *file*`] [-q` *queue*`] -t` *time*
> `batch`
> `at -l [`*job* `... ]`
> `at -lq` *queue*
> `at -r` *job* `...`

Here is what these forms do:

- The first three forms submit a job for later execution. The job is taken from standard input unless the `-f` option is specified.

- The form 'at `-l`' lists jobs that you've submitted. If you supply a list of job numbers, you're told about those jobs; if you don't supply that list, you're told about all your jobs.

- The form 'at `-lq`' lists the jobs in queue *queue*.

- The form 'at `-r`' removes jobs that were previously scheduled by `at` or `batch`. You may only remove your own jobs, although the superuser may remove anyone's jobs. The `-r` option doesn't provide a direct way to remove all your jobs, but you can do it with the line

> `at -r ‘at -l | cut -f1‘`

Although both the first and second forms of `at` provide for specifying a time, the syntax of the time is different in each case. We describe the syntax for the first form below; the syntax of the second form is that used by the `touch` command (see Section 3.12.2).

Command-Line Options for `at`. The following command-line options for `at` relate to submitting a job for later execution:

`-m`   Send mail to the invoking user after the scheduled job has run. The contents of standard output and standard error are sent in separate messages if the job writes anything to them.

`-f` *file*   Take the job to be scheduled from file *file*.

`-q` *queue*   Specify the execution queue for the job being submitted, or if used with `-l`, the queue whose jobs are to be listed. The default queue is 'a', except that jobs submitted with the `batch` command are placed in queue 'b'.

The following command-line options specify other operations:

`-l`	List jobs scheduled for the invoking user; if used with `-q`, restrict the list to those jobs in the specified queue.
`-r`	Remove the specified jobs from their queues.
`-t` *time*	Schedule the job for the time given by *time*, where *time* is in the same form as for the `touch` command (see Section 3.12.2).

Specifying the Time and Date for `at` **(First Form).**   You specify *atime* in one of the following ways:

- As a one-digit or two-digit number specifying an hour.
- As a four-digit number specifying an hour and minute.
- As two numbers (hour and minute) separated by a colon.
- As one of these followed by either or both of (a) 'am' or 'pm' and (b) a time zone specification. If neither 'am' nor 'pm' is specified, a 24-hour clock is assumed.[9] The time zone can be given as 'utc' (Coordinated Universal Time, or Greenwich Mean Time). Most systems recognize 'zulu' (Z for zero longitude) as equivalent. Another typical value is 'edt' (Eastern Daylight Time).
- As one of the special times 'noon', 'midnight', or 'now'. 'Now' only makes sense if you also provide an increment.

You specify *adate* in one of the following ways:

- As a month name followed by a day number.
- As above, followed by an optional comma and a two-digit or four-digit year number.
- As a day of the week.
- As one of the special forms 'today' or 'tomorrow'.

You may write a month name either in full or by using its three-letter abbreviation; the same holds for a day of the week. If you omit *adate*, `at` assumes 'today' if the time is later than the present time and 'tomorrow' otherwise. If you specify a date before the current date (and no year), `at` assumes the next year.

The increment specifies an amount of time to be added to the time you specify. It should be given as a number followed by one of the intervals 'minutes', 'hours', 'days', 'weeks', 'months', or 'years'. `At` also recognizes the singular forms of these intervals.

In all of these forms, lowercase and uppercase letters are equivalent. Spaces between elements are permitted but not required.

---

9. For a locale other than `POSIX`, the 'am' and 'pm' strings may have different representations.

Some examples of legitimate `at` calls are the following:

```
at 2200 Sat
at now + 2 days
at now + 1 hour
at 5:50am Feb 28
at 4 AM
at 11
at now+1year
```

**5.3.4
Scheduling Periodic
Jobs with** `crontab`

You can schedule jobs to be run periodically by inserting requests into your `crontab` entry, kept in a `crontab` file. The principal purpose of job scheduling with `crontab` entries is to run administrative jobs such as retrieving system mail, but POSIX provides the same facility for individual users. Most systems keep each user's `crontab` entry in a separate file named for the user. You must use the `crontab` utility to operate on your `crontab` entry; you cannot operate on it directly.[10] The `crontab` file for user *user* is usually located at `/var/spool/cron/crontabs/user` or at a similar location within `/usr/spool`.

The form of the `crontab` command line is

> `crontab [` *file* `| -e | -l | -r]`

Depending on the option you select, your `crontab` entry is either listed, edited, removed, or replaced. The default is to replace it with the contents of standard input. The options are as follows:

file   Read a new `crontab` entry from *file*.

`-e`   Edit a copy of your `crontab` entry using the editor whose name is the value of the `EDITOR` environment variable (default `vi`). Many systems do not support this option.

`-l`   List your `crontab` entry.

`-r`   Remove your `crontab` entry.

`-u` *user*   Operate on the `crontab` entry for user *user*. This option is not included in POSIX.

Contents of a `crontab` **Entry.**   Each line of a `crontab` entry either specifies a job to be scheduled or is a comment. Comment lines either have '#' in column 1 or are all blank. Each specification has the following fields, separated by whitespace:[11]

(1)   Minute (0–59)
(2)   Hour (0–23)

---

10. As of this writing, 4.4BSD does not support the `crontab` command, so there is no way for a user to schedule his or her own jobs through the `crontab` mechanism. BSD systems have a single system-wide `crontab` table at `/etc/crontab` and sometimes a second `crontab` table at `/etc/crontab.local`. The structure of these tables makes it possible to initiate a job on a user's behalf even though a user cannot insert items into the table.

11. BSD systems have a single `crontab` table whose entries contain as their sixth field the name of a user on whose behalf a job is to be initiated, with the command displaced to the seventh field.

(3)   Day of month (1–31)
(4)   Month of year (1–12)
(5)   Day of week (0–6, 0=Sunday)
(6)   Command to execute

A specification must appear entirely on a single line. The interpretation of `crontab` specifications in a locale other than the POSIX locale may be different.

Each of the items 1–5 is either an asterisk (all valid values), an element, or a list of elements separated by commas. Each element is either a number n or a range 'n-m'. The command in item 6[12] is executed whenever your system examines `crontab` (typically once a minute) and the fields all match.[13] However, if both the day of month and day of week are restricted (i.e., are not specified by '*'), the command is executed if *either* day matches. [14] For instance, the schedule

```
30 9 1,11,21 * 1,5
```

would cause the corresponding command to be run at 9:30 AM on the 1st, 11th, and 21st day of every month plus every Monday and Friday. You ordinarily should not specify the minute as a star, since then the job will be executed once a minute during any qualifying day and hour.

The command in item 6 consists of a command line optionally followed by lines that the command is to read from standard input. Although the command must be written on a single line, you can use a percent to represent either the ⟨newline⟩ that separates the command from its input or a ⟨newline⟩ at the end of an input line for the command. In addition, you can use a backslash within the command to cause the next character to be taken literally. In particular, you should use '\%' to represent a percent character within the command.

Authorization to Use `crontab`. Many systems (but not BSD) include a mechanism to either allow or not allow particular users to use `crontab`. In Linux, for example, there are two files, an *allow* file and a *deny* file, kept at `/var/cron/allow` and `/var/cron/deny`. If the *allow* file exists, then you have to be listed in it in order to use `crontab`. If the *allow* file doesn't exist but the *deny* file exists, you can use `crontab` as long as you are *not* listed in the *deny* file. And if neither file exists, `crontab` is either available to everyone or available only to the superuser, depending on how your system has been configured. The mechanism is the same for

---

12. Item 7 for BSD systems.

13. The actual work of starting scheduled tasks is performed by the `cron` (or `crond`) dæmon. This dæmon starts when your system starts up and wakes up once a minute to check the `crontab` files and see what commands need to be activated.

14. Although the behavior we describe matches existing `cron` implementations, the POSIX specification is slightly different and appears to us to be in error. According to POSIX, if you specify a day of the week and a month explicitly, the command is also executed when the month matches, even if neither the day of month nor day of week matches.

other systems, although the names of the *allow* and *deny* files may be different.

An Example.   Suppose you have a program `flypaper` that you use to generate periodic summary reports about how many flies have been caught. The period of the report is specified by an option passed to the program. In addition, you send your grandmother your best wishes every year on her birthday, April 15. Then the following call on `crontab` establishes the necessary `crontab` file:

```
crontab << ender
# Flypaper report at 6pm Monday - Friday
00 18 * * 1-5 flypaper -d
# Flypaper report first day of month at midnight
00 00 1 * * flypaper -m
* Flypaper report for each quarter, also at midnight
00 00 1 1,4,7,10 * flypaper -q
# Grandma's birthday
00 00 15 4 * mailx -s "Happy Birthday"\! granny@oldfolks.org \
 % Congratulations, Grandma!%Love, Hyacinth
ender
```

(In the actual input, the line ending with backslash must be combined with the following one; `crontab` provides no way of concatenating lines.)

5.3.5 Running a Command at Low Priority with `nice`

The `nice` command enables you to execute another command at lower priority. It's called 'nice' because lowering your execution priority is a way of being nice to other users. The form of the `nice` command line is

   `nice` [-n *n*] *cmd* [*arg*...]

An obsolescent equivalent is

   `nice` [-*n*] *cmd* [*arg*...]

The command *cmd* with arguments *arg* ... is executed with a priority *n* lower than it otherwise would be. The default value of *n* is 10; its permissible range is 1 to 19. The superuser may specify a negative value such as -6 for *n*, thereby raising a command's priority. (You would write that as '--6' in the obsolescent syntax.)

   `Nice` does not by itself cause *cmd* to be executed in the background; to do that, you must follow it by '&' or put it in the background by another method. A convention common to many systems is that 0 represents ordinary priority, 20 the lowest possible priority.

5.3.6 Adjusting Process Priorities with `renice`

The `renice` command adjusts the priorities of running processes. It thus differs from `nice`, which adjusts the priority of a process about to run. You can use `renice` to adjust the priority of several processes at once. If you try to execute `renice` but don't have the appropriate privileges to change the priorities of the specified processes, `renice` exits with an error status.

The form of the `renice` command line is

> `renice [-n` *incr*`] [-g | -p | -u]` *id* `...`

Renice adjusts the priorities of the processes designated by *id* up or down
by *incr*, an optionally signed decimal integer. A positive value for *incr*
lowers the priority of a process, giving it less preference, and vice versa
for a negative value. If the change would exceed the priority bounds for
your system, the appropriate bound (upper or lower) is used instead. If
you omit `-n`, the priorities are lowered by a system-dependent amount.

The interpretation of *id* ... depends on the options: `-p` for process IDs
(the default), `-g` for process group IDs, and `-u` for user IDs. A user ID is
interpreted as a user name if possible; otherwise, it must be a user number
as an unsigned decimal integer.

The `renice` command also has these obsolescent forms:

> `renice` *niceval* `[-p]` *id* `...` `[-g` *id* `...] [-p` *id* `...] [-u` *id* `...]`
> `renice` *niceval* `-g` *id* `...` `[-g` *id* `...] [-p` *id* `...] [-u` *id* `...]`
> `renice` *niceval* `-u` *id* `...` `[-g` *id* `...] [-p` *id* `...] [-u` *id* `...]`

In these forms *niceval* is the actual priority value, not the change in priority. The interpretation of an *id* is determined by the preceding option,
with process IDs as the default.

Command-Line Options.   The options (for the modern form of `renice`)
specify the priority adjustment and the interpretation of the *id*'s:

`-n` *incr*	Adjust priorities up or down by *incr*
`-g`	Interpret *id* ... as process group IDs.
`-p`	Interpret *id* ... as process IDs
`-u`	Interpret *id* ... as user IDs

5.3.7 Suspending Execution with `sleep`

The `sleep` command sleeps (i.e., does nothing) for a specified number of
seconds. After that time has elapsed, it terminates. The form of the `sleep`
command line is

> `sleep` *n*

where *n* is the number of seconds for which the process should sleep. You
can use `sleep` to postpone execution of a command until after a certain
amount of time has passed.

5.3.8 Waiting for a Process with `wait`

The `wait` command waits for a specified process to finish. The form of
the `wait` command line is

> `wait [`*n*`]`

where *n* is the number of the process being waited for. If you omit *n*,
`wait` waits until all background processes have finished. The exit code
of `wait` is the same as that of the process for which it's waiting, or zero if
it's waiting for all background processes. `Wait` is an intrinsic command of
every shell.

5.4   Commands Related to Logging In

The commands in this group relate to logging in, controlling your password, and setting your group.

5.4.1
**Logging In
with** `login`

Your first step in logging in is to create a new connection to the system. When UNIX detects your connection,[15] it calls the `login` program on your behalf. After issuing a prompt, the `login` program awaits a response from you of the form

> *name* [*var-setting...*]

where *name* is your user name and the *var-setting*s (recognized only under System V versions) are settings of environment variables as described below. `Login` then asks for your password, which is not echoed to your terminal. After validating your password, `login` executes your login shell, which in turn executes your login initialization file, usually either `.profile` or `.login` (see Section 2.14). Your login shell is either recorded in the `/etc/passwd` file or determined by default.[16] The usual default is `/bin/sh`, which nowadays is most often linked to the KornShell or, on GNU-based systems, to Bash. If you have not successfully logged in within a certain time limit, the system may disconnect you as a security measure.

Calling `login` **Explicitly.**   Once you're logged in, you may call `login` explicitly at any time in order to replace your login identity by a different one or to reinitialize your environment. To do this you must be executing your login process, so you can't call `login` from a subshell. You log in again by typing

> `exec login` [*name* [*var-setting...*]]

If you don't supply a name, `login` asks you for one. Your new login replaces the old one, just as though you had logged in that way originally.

Under BSD and also Solaris 2, you may specify a `-p` option preceding your name when you call `login` explicitly. If this option is specified, `login` preserves your environment variables across the login (see Section 2.6.5).

Explicitly logging in with `login` is not included in POSIX.

---

15. On traditional UNIX systems the connection is ordinarily detected by the `getty` ("get teletypewriter") program, a copy of which monitors each input line. Newer System V–based systems have replaced the multiple copies of `getty` by a single program, `ttymon`, that monitors all terminals at once.

16. The `login` program prefixes the name of the shell with '-' when it calls it; for example, if your shell is `sh`, it is called under the name '`-sh`'. This convention enables a shell to determine if it was called as a login shell.

Environment Variables on Login.   When you log in, `login` automatically sets up certain environment variables for you (see Section 2.6.5):

HOME   The absolute path name of your home directory (see Section 2.7.3).

PATH   The search path for commands, initially '`/bin:/usr/bin`' (see Section 2.9.2).

SHELL   The full name of your login shell as it appears in your `/etc/passwd` entry, or `/bin/sh` if no shell is specified there.

MAIL   The file name of your primary mailbox (see p. 585).

TZ   The time zone in which your system is located.

Assignments to Variables.   Under the System V version of `login`, you may use *var-setting* ... to change the settings of the environment variables listed above, except for PATH and SHELL. You may also assign values to other environment variables. Each *var-setting* has the form

> [*name* =] *value*

Values without names are assigned to the variables L0, L1, and so forth. For example, the login

> `fifi HOME=/home/fifi/startup INIT=qxt 12 b`

changes HOME to `/home/fifi/startup` and sets INIT to `qxt`, L0 to `12`, and L1 to `b`. In this example, INIT is a variable whose name you have chosen for yourself and L0 and L1 are variables whose names are fixed by convention. Setting environment variables on login provides a convenient way to customize the actions taken by your login initialization file (see Section 2.14), since the login initialization file can test the values of these variables.

The `/etc/passwd` File.   The `/etc/passwd` file contains the information required by the `login` program to verify that a login is valid and to initiate the appropriate shell. Other programs also use the information in this file. Since it usually contains no actual passwords, anyone is permitted to read it.[17] A fragment of it looks like this:

> `root:x:0:1:0000-Admin(0000):/:`
> `alice:x:387:108:Alice Liddell:/home/alice:/bin/ksh`
> `qoh:x:389:108:Queen of Hearts:/home/qoh:`

Each line contains information about a single user and consists of the following sequence of fields, with the fields separated by colons:

(1)   The user name as expected by `login`.

(2)   A dummy indicator for the password. The first line represents the superuser, named `root`. In most newer systems, the actual passwords are stored in a different file called the *shadow file*, where

---

17. In older systems, `/etc/passwd` may contain actual passwords, but in an encrypted form. That practice is now viewed as a security hazard.

they are kept in an encrypted form. In older systems, however, the encrypted password is stored here.[18]

(3)   The user's user number.

(4)   The user's group number.

(5)   The user's full name.

(6)   The path name of the user's home directory.

(7)   The path name of the user's login shell. If it is not specified, it defaults to `/bin/sh`.

**5.4.2
Changing User
Identity with** su

The `su` ("substitute user") command enables you to take on the identity of a different user. It is not included in POSIX. The form of the command is

> su [-fl] [-c *cmd*] [-] [*user* [*arg* . . .]]

Here *user* is the name of the user whose identity you wish to assume; if you omit it, `root` (the name of the superuser) is assumed.

Su starts a copy of the new user's login shell, running it under the new user's name with the new user's login shell and privileges. You're prompted for a password unless the new user's login doesn't require one. The new shell becomes a child process of the current process. When you exit from this new shell, the previous context is restored. Note the difference in this respect between `su` and `login`—exiting from the new shell that you get with `login` logs you out altogether. If the new user is the superuser, the shell prompt is changed to '#' to remind you that superuser privileges are in effect.

Unless you specify -1 or '-', you continue working in the same environment as before. In particular, the current directory isn't changed and most environment variables available before the `su` call remain available after it. The exceptions are `HOME` and `SHELL`—and in the case where the new user isn't the superuser, `USER` also.

The principal use of arguments with the `su` command is to execute a single command while assuming the identity of another user. To execute the command *cmd* with arguments *args*, using the permissions and environment of user *user*, type

> su -1 -c "*cmd args*" *user*

The arguments *args* . . . are passed to the new shell when it starts up (see Section 6.15). As seen by the shell, argument 1 is the first argument following *user* and arguments 2, 3, . . . are the following ones. Argument 0 is the name of the shell prefixed by '-' (e.g., '-sh' or '-csh'). The shell can use argument 0 to determine if it was called as a login shell. The quotes around *args* can be omitted if *args* doesn't contain any spaces.

---

18.   The encryption uses a "trapdoor algorithm" that makes it easy to transform the password to its encrypted form but prohibitively time-consuming to transform the encrypted form back to the password. You should avoid using an ordinary word as a password because an intruder can write a program that runs through a dictionary and computes one of 4096 possible passwords that might be generated by each dictionary word. If one of these passwords is found in the `/etc/passwd` file, the intruder has just learned how to impersonate the user with that password.

Command-Line Options.   The command-line options vary from one system to another. The most common ones are as follows:

-f   Fast startup; don't execute the login initialization file of the new shell.

–

-l   Make the new shell a login shell. The environment is the same one you'd get if you logged in as *user*; in particular, you don't see the environment variables from su's calling context and the current directory becomes *user*'s home directory. Some versions of su recognize both '-' and '-l', while others recognize only one or the other.

-c *cmd*   Instead of starting the new shell interactively, cause it to execute *cmd* by passing *cmd* to it using the new shell's -c option.

Examples.   Here are some examples of su:

- Suppose your user name is ishmael. If you issue the command

      su -l ahab

  it will appear that you have just logged in as ahab, with ahab's login shell and initializations. If you now type exit or ⎓EOF⎓, you'll be back to where you were before you issued the su.

- If you know the superuser password, you can use the command

      su - root -c sysadm

  to call the system administration program sysadm. Before running the program, su asks you for the superuser password and verifies it. When sysadm terminates, your normal identity is restored.

5.4.3
Changing Your
Group with newgrp

The newgrp command enables you to change to a group different from the one you logged in with, provided you're listed in the /etc/group file as a member of the new group.[19] You may then access any file belonging to the new group for which the appropriate group permission has been set. Because BSD allows a single user to belong to several groups, it neither needs nor supports this command.

The form of the command is

    newgrp [-l] [*group*]

where *group* is the name of the group you wish to join. An obsolescent form is

    newgrp [-] [*group*]

If you're authorized to join that group, the command changes your group to *group* for the rest of the current session.

- If you omit *group*, your login group (as shown in the password file) is assumed.

---

19. You may also switch to a group, even if you're not a member of it, if the group has a group password and you know that password. Most UNIX experts consider group passwords a security weakness in UNIX and discourage their use.

- If you specify -l (or '-'), the effect is as if you had just logged in as a member of *group*. Any initializations associated with your login shell are performed.

In either case a new copy of your login shell is created and given control of your terminal. Environment variables are preserved across newgrp, but local variables are not. If you specify '-' in the newgrp command, however, you get a fresh environment also, as you would when you log in.

5.4.4
Changing Your Password
with passwd

The passwd command enables you to change your password after you've been registered as a user in your system. For the sake of security, you should change your password periodically; some systems require you to. The passwd command is not included in POSIX.

The form of the passwd command is

    passwd [*name*]

where *name* is a user name. The default for *name* is the name of the user issuing the command. For an ordinary user the default value is the only legal value, so *name* is usually omitted. The superuser, however, may set the password for other values of *name*. Passwd first prompts you for your old password and then prompts you for your new password twice—the second time to make sure that you typed it correctly (since it isn't displayed on your terminal as you type it).

Many systems impose security constraints on passwd, such as the following ones:

- You may not change your password if you've already changed it within the last *n* days.

- Your password has at least six characters.

- Your password includes at least two alphabetic characters and at least one nonalphabetic character.

- Your password is sufficiently different from your login name.

- Your new password differs from your old one by at least three characters.

None of these requirements apply to the superuser, who may construct user accounts having no password at all. Not using passwords is a dangerous security hazard under most conditions, but would be convenient and appropriate for a single-user system in an environment such as a home office where security is not a major concern.

5.4.5
Changing Your Login
Shell with chsh

On many systems you can change your login shell with the chsh command. This command is not supported by POSIX. Though 4.4BSD does not include chsh, it does include a more general command, chpass, that enables you to change more of the information in your /etc/passwd entry.

The form of the chsh command line is

    chsh [*user*]

The command first prompts you for your password and then prompts you for the name of your new shell. The superuser can change the login shell of any user by specifying *user*, but of course no other user can do that.

5.4.6
Returning Your
Login Name with
`logname`

You can use the `logname` command to produce your login name on standard output. This command is a standardized alternative to 'who am i' (see Section 5.1.2). The form of the `logname` command line is simply

```
logname
```

5.4.7
Showing User and
Group IDs with `id`

The `id` command produces user and group IDs on standard output. The forms of the command are

```
id [ user]
id -G [-n] [ user]
id -g [-nr] [ user]
id -u [-nr] [ user]
```

In the simplest case, when the command is simply `id` with no options, the number and name of the user and the group for the invoking process are produced. A typical output is

```
uid=145(felix) gid=117(cats)
```

If *user* is specified and the invoking process has appropriate privileges, which in most cases means root privileges, then information for that user and the user's group are produced.

For a process executing a program for which the set-uid bit is on, both the real user ID and the effective user ID (the one that currently defines file access) are shown (see "The Set-uid Bit" on p. 46). Similarly, when the set-gid bit is on, both the real group ID and the effective group ID are shown. Some older systems don't support the `id` command, or support it only when it is called without options.

Command-Line Options. The command-line options for `id` modify the information produced by `id`:

-g   Produce only the effective group ID (the same as the real ID if the set-uid bit is not on).

-G   Produce all group IDs (real, effective, and supplementary). The supplementary groups are all the other groups to which the user belongs.

-u   Produce only the effective user ID (the same as the real ID if the set-uid bit is not on).

-n   Produce the user or group name rather than the user or group number.

-r   Produce the real ID, not the effective one.

Many older systems support only an -a option, which causes `id` to list all groups a user belongs to.

5.5   Controlling Your Terminal

In order to communicate effectively with your terminal, UNIX has to know
what sequences of characters it should send to produce effects such as
starting a new line or clearing the screen. The commands described in this
section provide UNIX with the information it needs about your terminal.
You can also use them to control the terminal yourself; for example, to
reset it to a sane state when it's become confused by a random sequence
of characters sent by accident.

- The `tset` program determines your terminal type, sends appropriate initialization commands to it, and enables you to define your
  erase and kill characters. Not all systems provide `tset`. For those
  that don't, you can achieve its effects more laboriously with `stty`
  and `tput`.

- The `stty` program defines the meanings of control characters sent
  to your terminal, sets terminal and line characteristics such as the
  communication speed, and provides information about your terminal. Though the erase and kill characters may be defined either
  with `tset` or with `stty`, the other control characters may be defined
  only with `stty`.

- The `tput` program sends the control sequences (sequences of characters) needed to achieve a particular function, such as resetting the
  terminal or clearing the screen. You can also use it to learn what
  those sequences are.

- The `tabs` program sets the positions of the built-in tabs on your
  terminal (provided your terminal has them).

See Section 2.15 for a discussion of terminals, control sequences, and
`terminfo` and `termcap`, the two alternate forms of the database that UNIX
uses to record information about terminals.

5.5.1
**Preparing Your
Terminal with** `tset`

The `tset` command serves several purposes:

- It determines the type of your terminal and transmits the control
  sequences needed to initialize it.

- It can produce a sequence of commands that sets the TERM environment variable to your terminal type (see Section 2.15). You can save
  these commands in a file and issue them later.

- You can use it to set your erase and kill characters.

The form of the `tset` command line is

```
tset [-IQrs] [-] [-e[ c]] [-i[ c]] [-k[ c]]
     [-m [itype][test speed]:[?] type] [ term]
```

where *term* is the name of a terminal type. If the environment variable
TERM contains the name of your terminal, as it usually does, the simple
call 'tset' sends an initialization string to your terminal (see Section 2.15
for a discussion of initialization and reset strings). Your login initialization
file should include a call on tset to initialize your terminal after you have
logged in. The tset command is not included in POSIX.

Some BSD-based systems include a reset program, similar to tset,
that sends the reset string to your terminal. If your terminal gets into
a confused state, typing 'Ctrl J reset Ctrl J' may restore it, though you
may not be able to see what you're typing. The equivalent command for
non-BSD systems is 'tput reset'.

Determining Your Terminal Type.   Tset's first task is to determine your
terminal type. It uses the following decision procedure:

(1)   If you didn't specify any -m options, then

    (a)   If you specified *term*, *term* is the terminal type.

    (b)   Otherwise, if you specified the -h option, the terminal type is
that associated with the port you're using, as recorded in the
file /etc/ttytype or /etc/ttys (depending on your system).

    (c)   Otherwise, if the environment variable TERM is defined, its
value specifies the terminal type.

    (d)   Otherwise, the terminal type is the one associated with your
port, as with the -h option.

(2)   If you specified one or more -m options (see below) and one of them
applies, then that option determines the terminal type.

(3)   If you specified one or more -m options (see below), none of which
apply, then

    (a)   If you specified *term* (not associated with any option) on the
command line, then *term* is the terminal type.

    (b)   Otherwise, the terminal type is the one associated with your
port, as with the -h option.

Two options are relevant to this procedure:

-h   Use the terminal type associated with your port rather than the
one found in TERM. Not all systems provide this option.

-m   Attempt to determine the terminal type by matching its speed
as described below.

Testing Terminal Speed with the -m Option.   The -m option specifies that
tset should attempt to determine the terminal type by testing the terminal
speed. Its syntax is

    -m [*itype*][*test speed*]:[?]*type*

To prevent shell metacharacters in this specification from being misinterpreted, you should enclose it in double quotes.

The items before the colon specify two matching criteria:

- The variable *itype* specifies an "indeterminate" terminal type such as 'dialup' or 'network' that characterizes the line rather than the terminal itself. If your port has that terminal type, the criterion is satisfied. If you omit *itype*, the terminal type of your port does not affect the match.

- If the test and speed are specified, tset compares *speed* with the actual speed (baud rate) of your terminal port. The permissible speeds are the same as those recognized by stty (see p. 263). The criterion is one of the comparison operators

  $$= \quad @ \quad < \quad > \quad <= \quad >= \quad != \quad !@ \quad !< \quad !>$$

  where '@' and '=' both mean equality and '!' in front of an operator negates it (e.g., '!=' means "not equal"). If this criterion is omitted, the port speed does not affect the match.

The type following the colon specifies the terminal type to be used if the criterion is satisfied. A question mark preceding *type* instructs tset to confirm the terminal type. If you press (Enter), *type* is accepted; any other response causes it to be rejected.

For example, the command

```
tset - -m "dialup@2400:?h19" -m "dialup:vt100" ">=9600:sun" AT386
```

---

specifies the following procedure:

(1) If you're coming in on a dialup line at 2400 baud, tset asks if your terminal is of type 'h19'. If you confirm, then tset uses 'h19'; otherwise, it goes on to the next test.

(2) If you're coming in on a dialup line at any speed, tset assumes type 'vt100'.

(3) If you're coming in at 9600 baud or faster, tset assumes type 'sun'.

(4) If none of these tests are satisfied, tset assumes 'AT386'.

The '-' option in the command sends the selected terminal type to standard output, as described below.

Suppressing the Initialization String. The following option suppresses the initialization string:

-I   Don't send the initialization string. Depending on the version of tset you've got, this option may or may not cause the reset string to be sent instead. BSD versions that provide reset usually don't send it.

Setting the Erase, Kill, and Interrupt Characters.   You can use `tset` to specify the erase and kill characters for your terminal by specifying one or more of the following options:

`-e [c]`   Set the erase character to c. The character c is normally a control character, specified with a preceding caret, as in '∧B'. If you omit c, '∧H' is assumed.

`-E [c]`   Set the erase character to c as in the `-e` option, but only if the information in `terminfo` or `termcap` indicates that the terminal can backspace. Not all systems provide this option.

`-k [c]`   Set the kill character to c, using the same notation as in the `-e` option. The default is '∧U'.

`-i [c]`   Set the interrupt character to c, using the same notation as in the `-e` option. The default is '∧C'. Not all systems provide this option.

If the erase and kill characters are anything other than '∧H' and '∧U', `tset` sends to standard error a line such as

```
Kill set to ∧C
```

This line does not appear unless you've explicitly requested output using one of the options described in the next subsection. You can suppress this commentary with the `-Q` option.

Controlling the Output.   The output of `tset` serves two purposes: to inform you of the terminal type `tset` is using and to provide the text of a sequence of commands for setting the `TERM` environment variable. The following options affect the output:

`-`   Produce the terminal type on standard output, followed by a ⟨newline⟩.

`-s`   Produce the shell commands for setting `TERM` on standard output. Tset looks at your login shell to decide which commands to produce. It recognizes just two cases: `csh`, the C shell, and everything else, which it takes to be equivalent to the Bourne shell `sh`. For `csh` the commands are

```
set noglob;
setenv TERM term;
unset noglob;
```

and for everything else,

```
export TERM;
TERM=term;
```

You can then set up your terminal, and set `TERM` as well, with a command such as

```
'tset -s'
```

This command uses the command substitution notation described in Section 6.18.1.[20]

-S   If your login shell is csh, produce the same text as the - option produces, but without the ⟨newline⟩. Otherwise produce the same text as the -s option produces. Not all systems provide the -S option.

-r   Send a message identifying your terminal type to standard error.

-Q   Suppress the 'Erase set to' and 'Kill set to' messages that tset normally sends to standard error whenever the erase or kill character has a nondefault value.

5.5.2 Setting Your Terminal Characteristics with stty

The stty command sets or reports certain characteristics of your terminal. It does not send any data to your terminal. The terminal characteristics serve the following main purposes:

- They instruct the terminal driver[21] how to interpret and modify the characters it receives from or sends to your terminal.

- They describe the commmunications port, if any, that connects your terminal to the computer; for example, by specifying its speed.

- If you're communicating over a phone line, they specify when the terminal driver should disconnect the phone line.

The initial values for these characteristics are set by the system during login.

The usual form of the stty command line is

    stty [-ag] [*setting...*]

These are the POSIX options; in general, the options and settings vary considerably among systems. The options specify what information is reported to standard output; the settings specify what terminal characteristics are to be changed. Ordinarily a single call on stty specifies options or settings but not both.

The command stty without options produces a short listing that shows only the line speed, parity, and settings that differ from their default values. A typical example is

```
speed 9600 baud; evenp
intr = ^c; erase = ^h; kill = ^u; swtch = ^`;
brkint -inpck icrnl onlcr tab3
echo echoe echok
```

20. Be careful of how you do this; if the command is executed in a subshell, its effects are lost when the subshell exits.

21. The terminal driver is the program that handles the communication between your terminal and the programs that read from or write to it.

The POSIX options are as follows:

-a   List all the settings.

-g   List the current settings in a form that can later be used as
           input to stty.

Although some of the settings also start with a hyphen, none of them
consist of single letters.

Below we describe many of the stty settings, including a few that are
not specified by POSIX. We omit those that are obscure or rarely used,
such as the ones needed only for printing terminals.[22]

A number of settings control the interpretation of the ⟨newline⟩ and
⟨return⟩ characters. They are needed because terminals differ in how they
represent and process ⟨newline⟩s. By default, the ⟨newline⟩ character is
taken to be the ASCII ⟨linefeed⟩ character; a terminal needs to accompany
this character by a motion to the left margin in order to achieve the effect
of a ⟨newline⟩. For some terminals this additional motion is automatic,
but for others it isn't. Some terminals use ⟨return⟩ rather than ⟨newline⟩ to
indicate the end of a line. The characters that a terminal emits to indicate
a typed ⟨newline⟩ may also vary.

Other settings are concerned with the interpretation of special control
characters, such as the erase and kill characters. Stty enables you to
specify what those characters are, and, in addition, enables you to turn
the interpretation of those characters on or off.

We discuss the settings in several groups:

- The settings for control characters enable you to specify the characters used for special functions such as Erase and Kill .
- The settings for control modes affect the characteristics of the communications line between your terminal and your computer.
- The settings for interpreting input affect how the stream of input
  characters coming from your terminal is transformed into the stream
  of input characters seen by the program you're running.
- The settings for interpreting output affect how the stream of output
  characters generated by the program you're running is transformed
  to the stream of characters sent to your terminal.
- The composite settings are combinations of the other settings.
- The settings for screen dimensions specify how many rows and how
  many columns your terminal has.

A '-' in front of a setting disables it or reverses its effect. For example,
the command

    stty hup -echoe

specifies that hup should be turned on and echoe should be turned off.

---

22. Printing terminals require that delays be inserted for actions such as returning the
carriage so that the next character doesn't arrive before the action has been completed.

Settings for Control Characters.   The settings below enable you to specify the values of the special control characters. If the character *c* is a control character—as it nearly always is—you indicate it with a caret, as in '∧D' or '∧d'. The uppercase and lowercase forms are equivalent. For each character we indicate the most common defaults.

erase *c*   Set the erase character to *c*. This character erases the previous one typed. Its default is (Ctrl) H or '#'.

kill *c*   Set the kill character to *c*. This character erases the entire current line. Its default is (Ctrl) U or '@'. **Note:** The kill character kills a line of text, not a process.

eof *c*   Set the eof (end-of-file) character to *c*. This character indicates the end of standard input, and also acts as an exit for the shell (unless you inhibit that effect with ignoreeof). Its default value is (Ctrl) D.

intr *c*   Set the interrupt character to *c*. This character interrupts the currently executing process. Its default value is (DEL) or (Ctrl) C.

quit *c*   Set the quit character to *c*. This character also interrupts the currently executing process, but in addition generates a memory dump in a file in your current directory named core.Its default value is (Ctrl) \.

stop *c*   Set the stop character to *c*. This character temporarily stops output to your terminal. You resume the output with the start character. Its default value is (Ctrl) S (ASCII ⟨DC3⟩); many systems won't let you change it.

start *c*   Set the start character to *c*. This character restarts output to your terminal when it's been stopped by the stop character. Its default value is (Ctrl) Q (ASCII ⟨DC1⟩); many systems won't let you change it.

flush *c*   Set the flush character to *c*. This character causes the rest of the output from the currently active process to be discarded but without interrupting the process. Many systems don't provide a flush character. Its default value is (Ctrl) O.

susp *c*   Set the job suspension character to *c*. Typing this character suspends but does not kill the currently active process. Its default value is (Ctrl) Z.

swtch *c*   Set the job switch character to *c*. This character is used by the shell layers facility offered by some versions of System V to switch from one layer to another. Other versions of System V assign it exactly the same function as the job suspension character. Its default value is (Ctrl) ' or (Ctrl) Z.

werase *c*   Set the word erase character to *c*. Typing this character erases the most recently typed word. Its default value is (Ctrl) W. The word erase character is a feature of BSD.

Settings for Control Modes.   The following settings affect the communications line between your terminal and your computer:

speed　　　Set the line to the indicated speed (baud rate). The recognized speeds are 110, 300, 600, 1200, 1800, 2400, 4800, 9600, 19200, and 38400.

0　　　　　Disconnect the phone line immediately.

[-]hup　　Disconnect the phone line when you log out.

cs5 cs6 cs7 cs8
　　　　　Set the character size to 5, 6, 7, or 8 bits.

[-]cstopb Use two stop bits per character (one with -).

[-]parenb Enable parity generation and detection.   If parity is not enabled, no other parity settings have any effect.

[-]parodd Set odd parity (even with -).

[-]cread　Allow the terminal to receive input.

[-]clocal Disable modem control signals.

[-]rtscts Enable RTS/CTS handshaking as a method of modem flow control (non-POSIX).

The composite settings evenp and oddp described below are convenient for the ordinary cases where you want parity checking.

Settings for Interpreting Input.   These settings affect how the terminal driver transforms the stream of characters received from your terminal into the stream of characters seen by the program you're running.

　　The following settings affect the treatment of ⟨newline⟩ and ⟨return⟩:

[-]icrnl　Map ⟨return⟩ to ⟨newline⟩ on input.
[-]igncr　Ignore ⟨return⟩ on input.
[-]inlcr　Map ⟨newline⟩ to ⟨return⟩ on input.

The following settings affect the treatment of control characters:

[-]icanon Enable the use of the erase and kill characters for editing input lines. With this option turned off, the erase and kill characters are treated just like data characters.

[-]isig　Enable the interrupt, quit, switch, and flush characters.

[-]ixon　Enable the start and stop characters.   The negation of this option, -ixon, is necessary with programs such as Emacs that give Ctrl Q and Ctrl S special meanings, although Emacs usually makes the necessary change for you.

[-]istrip Force the high (eighth) bit of each input character to zero. The high bit may be replaced by a parity bit before the character is finally transmitted.

The following settings affect the treatment of lowercase characters:

[-]iuclc　Map uppercase alphabetic characters to lowercase on input (non-POSIX). This option is useful for older (*much* older) terminals that have only uppercase characters.

The following settings affect echoing; that is, sending a copy of a typed character back to the terminal. Most terminals don't display a character as you type it; instead, they expect the computer to send it back. With echoing turned on, each character you type is sent back to your terminal to be displayed; with echoing turned off, it isn't. Echoing is not always desirable—for instance, it should be turned off while you're typing your password.

[-]echo Echo each typed character.

[-]echoe Echo erase characters as ⟨backspace⟩⟨space⟩⟨backspace⟩.

[-]echok Send a ⟨newline⟩ after each kill character.

The following setting affects tab characters in the input:

[-]tabs Replace tabs by spaces when displaying or printing. This setting is effective only if your terminal can interpret tab characters. You can set the positions of the tabs with the `tabs` command (see Section 5.5.4).

Settings for Interpreting Output. The following settings affect how the terminal driver transforms the stream of characters sent by the program you're running to the stream of characters actually sent to your terminal:

[-]opost Post-process the output. If this setting is disabled, no other output setting has any effect.

[-]ocrnl Map ⟨return⟩ to ⟨newline⟩ on output.

[-]onlcr Map ⟨newline⟩ to ⟨return⟩ on output.

[-]olcuc Map lowercase alphabetic characters to uppercase on output. This setting, like `iuclc`, applies to terminals that can't handle lowercase characters.

[-]xcase Indicate uppercase characters with a backslash (i.e, transform 'A' to '\A').

The following setting affects whether a background job can send output to your terminal:

[-]tostop Inhibit background jobs from sending output to your terminal. If a background job is moved to the foreground, any waiting output is sent to the terminal. If this setting is turned off, output from background jobs is intermingled with output from the foreground job.[23] If the current shell does not support job control or has job control turned off, this setting has no effect.

Composite Settings. The following settings produce combinations of effects:

sane Set all settings to reasonable values.

---

23. A background job that attempts to produce output on standard output receives the TTOU signal. The default response to that signal is to suspend the job.

term Set all settings to values appropriate for the terminal *term*. The list of recognized values for *term* depends on your system.

cooked
[-]raw Disable processing of special control characters. Setting cooked is equivalent to setting -raw.

ek Set the erase and kill characters to '#' and '@'. This option is useful for terminals that print rather than display their output.[24]

[-]lcase Enable conversion of lowercase alphabetic characters to uppercase ones. This setting combines the effects of xcase, iuclc, and olcuc.

[-]nl Disable special processing of ⟨newline⟩ and ⟨return⟩. When this setting is enabled, all ⟨newline⟩ and ⟨return⟩ characters are transmitted in either direction exactly as received no matter what other settings are in effect.

[-]evenp
[-]parity Select even parity and assume seven-bit characters. The -evenp setting turns off parity and assumes eight-bit characters.

[-]oddp Select odd parity and assume seven-bit characters. The -oddp setting turns off parity and assumes eight-bit characters.

[-]pass8 Transmit eight-bit input characters literally (a combination of -parenb, -istrip, and cs8). With -, enable parity and send seven-bit characters (a combination of parenb, istrip, and cs7).

[-]litout Transmit eight-bit characters literally for both input and output (a combination of -parenb, -istrip, -opost, and cs8). With -, enable parity and transmit seven-bit characters (a combination of parenb, istrip, opost, and cs7).

Settings for Screen Dimensions. Many programs need to know the number of rows and the number of columns your terminal appears to have. (For programs running under X, these numbers describe the current window, not the entire screen.) The following settings specify these numbers:

rows *n* Specify to the UNIX kernel that your terminal has *n* rows.

columns *n*
cols *n* Specify to the UNIX kernel that your terminal has *n* columns.

**5.5.3
Sending Instructions
to Your Terminal
with tput**

The tput program can retrieve and display the control sequences for a particular terminal, not necessarily the one you're using. These control sequences instruct the terminal to perform operations such as resetting itself or clearing the screen. Tput can also retrieve the full description of a terminal. It extracts all this information from your system's database of terminal descriptions (see Section 2.15). Tput is not available on older BSD-style systems.

---

24. In the early days of UNIX, most terminals were printing terminals.

The form of the `tput` command line is

> `tput [-T term] cmd`

If you specify a particular terminal with `-T`, you get the sequences for that terminal; otherwise, you get the sequences for your terminal type, as recorded in the environment variable `TERM`. If `tput` can't determine the terminal type, it exits with a nonzero exit status (see below). The variable *cmd* specifies the function to be performed:

`clear`   Send the string that clears the screen to standard output.

`init`   Send the terminal initialization string to standard output.

`reset`   Send the terminal reset string to standard output.

`longname` Produce the full name of the terminal on standard output. Each terminal description in the terminal database should include this information. The `longname` option is not included in POSIX.

name [*param...*]

> Retrieve the terminal capability *name* as indicated by the *param*s. The following are the types of capabilities and the result produced by `tput` for each type:
>
> - A boolean capability specifies whether or not the terminal has a particular feature. For a boolean capability, the exit status (see below) indicates the presence or absence of the capability.
>
> - An integer capability specifies a size or capacity of the terminal, such as the number of lines on the screen. For an integer capability, the integer value is sent to standard output.
>
> - A string capability specifies the control sequence needed to accomplish a particular terminal operation. For a string capability, the string value is sent to standard output.
>
> This option is not included in POSIX.
> An example of this form of `tput` is

> `tput cup 2 10`

which moves the cursor to row 2, column 10. To see what characters are sent to your terminal by this sequence, use the command

> `tput cup 2 10 | od`

See Section 3.15 for a discussion of the `od` command. The terminal database defines a large collection of capabilities, further discussion of which is beyond the scope of this book.

In particular, the commands

```
tput init
tput reset
```

initialize and reset the terminal, respectively.

Exit Status.   The `tput` exit status conveys two kinds of information: whether or not a terminal has a particular capability and whether or not the `tput` call itself is in the correct form. The exit status codes are defined as follows:

0   String was produced or capability is present.
1   Capability is absent. (This status does not indicate an error.)
2   Call is incorrect.
3   Terminal type can't be identified.
4   Capability is unknown.

**5.5.4
Setting Tabs
with** `tabs`

If your terminal has tab stops that can be externally set, the `tabs` command sends it a sequence of characters that sets them. The POSIX forms of the `tabs` command line are

```
tabs [-n] [-T term]
tabs [-T term] n₁ [, n₂, ... ]
```

The options for this command vary greatly among non-POSIX versions, though support for the $-n$ option, which sets tab stops every n spaces, is nearly universal. The options we describe below include common ones that are not included in the POSIX syntax given above.

   Other common options are those that specify a left margin or your terminal type. The simple command `tabs` without options sets tab stops every eight spaces. If your terminal type is not specified on the command line with the `-T` option, `tabs` retrieves it from the `TERM` environment variable.

Positioning the Tab Stops.   The following options specify the locations of the tab stops. No more than one of them may be specified. The default for these options is `-8`, which sets tab stops every eight spaces.

$n_1, n_2, \ldots$ Set tab stops at positions n_1, n_2, etc.

$-n$ Set tab stops every n spaces, with the first tab stop at position 1.

$-code$ Use the "canned" tabs for the programming language designated by *code*. For example, `-f` indicates FORTRAN conventions, with tabs at positions 1, 7, 11, 15, 19, and 23. Check your system documentation for the codes recognized by your version of `tabs`. This option is not useful for most modern programming languages (including C) since programs in these languages are usually written with uniformly spaced tab stops. It is not included in POSIX.

--*file*   Use the tab stops given in the format specification in *file* (see "Format Specifications in Files" below). This option is not included in POSIX.

Specifying Your Terminal.   The following option specifies your terminal type, which `tabs` needs in order to issue the correct tab-setting instructions:

-T *term*   Send the tab-setting sequence for a terminal of type *term*.

By default, `tabs` assumes your terminal type is given in the `TERM` environment variable. If `TERM` is not defined and you haven't provided a -T option, `tabs` sends a generic sequence that works on many terminals.

Setting a Left Margin.   The following option specifies a left margin:

+m[*n*]   Use a left margin of *n* spaces. All tab stops are moved right by *n* spaces, with the first tab stop set at column $n + 1$. If you omit *n*, it defaults to 10. `Tabs` applies this option last. This option is not supported by POSIX.

Format Specifications in Files.   Several UNIX programs recognize and use format specifications that appear on the first line of a file.[25] A format specification has the form

    <: *spec* ... :>

where each *spec* consists of a key letter followed by a value. Other material, such as comment indicators for various programming languages, may also appear on the line. Thus you may include a format specification as the first line of a program without having that specification affect the program. Format specifications are not included in POSIX.

The key letter `t` specifies the tab settings for the file that follows. (A format specification may also include several other key letters, not relevant here.) The settings have one of the following forms:

- A list of column numbers separated by commas.
- A '-' followed by an integer *n*, indicating that tab stops should be set every *n*th column, as above.
- A "canned" tab sequence, as defined above.

An example of a first line following these conventions is

    # <: t3 :>

Here the # makes the line a comment for several languages, including the KornShell.

---

25. Except for `tabs`, we don't discuss those programs in this book. An example of such a program is `newform`, which reformats a file.

5.6   On-Line Communication with Other Users

Several utilities are available for on-line communication with other users or, in one case, with your system administrator:

- The `talk` utility enables you to carry on a conversation using a split screen.
- The `write` utility enables you to send a message to another user.
- The `mesg` utility enables you to permit or block out messages sent to you.

5.6.1
Talking to Another
User with `talk`

The `talk` program enables you to carry on an on-line conversation with another user. The form of the `talk` command line is

```
talk user [term]
```

Typing the command initiates on-line conversation with the user *user*. If *user* is logged in at more than one terminal, you can specify the terminal for the conversation with *term*. You can use the `who` command (see Section 5.1.2) to find out who is on-line and what terminal(s) each user is using.

The user name *user* need not be the simple name of a local user. For example, your system is likely to support user names of the form *user@hostname* for talking to users at other network locations.

An Example.   Suppose your user name is `heloise`. Using the `who` command, you discover that `abelard` is on-line and you wish to talk to him, so you type

```
talk abelard
```

Now abelard sees messages similar to

```
Message from Talk_Daemon@russula at 10:54 ...
talk: connection requested by heloise@russula.
talk: respond with:  talk abelard@russula
```

To enter the conversation, abelard types

```
talk heloise
```

Now each of you sees a screen split into two parts. Whatever you type appears in your upper screen; whatever your partner types appears in your lower screen. To refresh your screen if it's become garbled, type Ctrl L . To terminate the conversation, type your Intr or EOF character. Your partner is then notified that the talk session has ended.

5.6.2
Sending Messages
with `write`

You can send messages to other logged-in users (or even to yourself) with the `write` command. Although you can use `write` for interactive conversation, the newer `talk` utility is much easier to use for that purpose.

To use `write`, type

```
write user [line]
... text of the message
EOF
```

Here *user* is the user name of the person to whom you're sending the message, which may contain any number of lines. You need provide *line* only if the person is logged in at more than one terminal, in which case you must specify the terminal as *line* (e.g., 'tty17'). After you type the command line, *user* receives a message at his or her terminal similar to

```
Message from sender (ttynn)
```

followed by the lines of the message as you type them.

If messages from other users are disrupting your output, you may block them with the command 'chmod -w /dev/tty' (see Section 3.11.1) or with the command 'mesg n' (see Section 5.6.3).

5.6.3
Turning Messages
On and Off
with `mesg`

The `mesg` command blocks your terminal to incoming messages or permits your terminal to receive them. The form of the command is

```
mesg [n | y]
```

You can block your terminal to incoming messages with the command

```
mesg n
```

Typing 'mesg n' is useful when you want to prevent your output from being interrupted. Messages from the superuser are never blocked.

To unblock your terminal, issue the command

```
mesg y
```

The command `mesg` by itself simply reports on whether your terminal is currently accepting messages. **Note:** This command does not use the standard command syntax since the options are not preceded by a dash.

You can get the same effect as 'mesg n' with the command

```
chmod -w /dev/tty
```

Note: The superuser may write to your terminal even if you've blocked it.

5.7   Disk Usage Statistics

Two programs provide information about disk usage: `df` reports free disk space and `du` reports disk space in use. They are useful on systems in which disk space is scarce. Disk usage is measured in blocks; the size of a block is system-dependent, with 4096 a typical value.

5.7.1
Reporting Free Disk Space with df

The `df` command reports the number of free blocks and free i-nodes in one or more file systems. The options vary greatly among systems. The main variants of the `df` command line are

df [-kP] [*name* ...]	(POSIX)
df [-lt] [*name*...]	(System V)
df [-in] [-t *type*] [*name* ...]	(4.4BSD, SunOS)

where each *name* refers to a mounted file system (either local or remote) or a directory. If you specify a directory, you'll get the statistics for the file system containing that directory. If you omit the names, you'll get a report on all mounted file systems, whether local or remote.

Command-Line Options for POSIX.   The command-line options for the POSIX version of `df` are as follows:

-k   Use units of 1024 bytes rather than 512 bytes.

-P   Produce one line of output for each file system in a POSIX standard format.

Command-Line Options for System V and Solaris 2.x.   The command-line options for the System V and Solaris 2.*x* versions of `df` are as follows:

-l   Report only on local file systems.

-t   Report the total number of allocated blocks and i-nodes on the device, as well as the number of free ones. The total includes the blocks that contain the i-nodes for the device.

Command-Line Options for SunOS and BSD.   The command-line options for the SunOS and BSD versions of `df` are as follows:

-i   Report the number of free i-nodes.

-t *type*   Report only on file systems of type *type*, such as 'nfs' (Network File System).

-n   Use previously available statistics without recalculating new ones. The purpose of this option is to avoid delay when a file system is in a state where it would take a long time to get up-to-date statistics. This option is supported by 4.4BSD but not by SunOS.

5.7.2
Reporting Disk Space in Use with du

The `du` command reports the number of disk blocks occupied by a file or by the files in a directory and its descendent subdirectories (including the disk blocks occupied by the directories themselves). The form of the `du` command line is

du [-ars] [*name*...]

where each *name* is a directory or a file. If you omit the names, you get a report on the current directory.

Du always shows fewer blocks in use within the root directory of a file system than you obtain by typing 'df -t' and subtracting the free blocks from the total blocks to obtain the blocks in use. That's because df includes i-node blocks in its total while du does not. Du does not count i-node blocks because they are not associated with any particular file.

Command-Line Options.   The du command-line options are as follows:

-a   Produce an output line for each file. Each line contains the block count followed by a tab and the name of the file.

-s   Report only the total usage for each *name*; that is, don't report on the individual files within a directory.

-r   Produce messages about directories that can't be read and files that can't be opened. By default, these messages are not issued. Not all systems recognize this option.

5.8   Writing and Reading Strings

There are two general commands for producing specific strings to be sent to standard output: echo and printf. In addition, the KornShell provides a print command that does much the same thing but includes some KornShell-specific options. The echo command is simple to use in most cases, but different versions of it are utterly incompatible in their treatment of options and escape characters. For that reason the POSIX Committee introduced the printf command, a more general and powerful way of producing strings. Printf is usually preferable to echo in systems that provide it, although the command line may require a little more typing. For example, here's how you would produce the string shuttlecocks as a line by itself on standard output using the two commands:

```
echo shuttlecocks
printf shuttlecocks\\n
```

On the other hand, producing the string *without* the ⟨newline⟩ is easier with printf (just omit the '\\n'), especially since there's no universally valid way to do it with echo.

In the other direction, the read command reads a single line from standard input and stores it in a shell variable.

**5.8.1
Echoing a String
with** echo

The echo command echoes a string to standard output. The echoed string is ordinarily followed by a ⟨newline⟩. The uses of echo include producing error messages in shell scripts, displaying the values of shell or environment variables, and constructing short files.

The form of the echo command is

    echo [-n] *string*

where *string* is the string to be echoed. The *string* part consists of all characters up to the ⟨newline⟩ that terminates the command. For example, the command

    echo $PATH

displays the value of the environment variable PATH. The command

    echo 'find ~ -name $1 -print' >ff

puts the text between the quotes into the file ff; the quotes are necessary to prevent the shell from interpreting the '$1' before the text is stored in the file.

The -n option specifies that the echoed string is *not* to be followed by a ⟨newline⟩. The -n option is not recognized by most System V versions of echo, and POSIX explicitly permits that behavior. In fact, the POSIX standard says that the behavior of -n, if recognized at all, is "implementation defined".

You can simulate the behavior of echo with the printf command. For instance, assuming the System V version of echo, the following two commands are equivalent:

    echo *string*
    printf "%b\n" "*string*"

For versions of echo that recognize -n, the following two commands are also equivalent:

    echo -n *string*
    printf %b "*string*"

The quotes in these examples are necessary so that printf will receive just a single argument.

Escape Sequences in Echoed Strings. The System V version of echo permits certain escape sequences in the echoed string. The 4.4BSD version (but not earlier BSD versions) permits such sequences, but only if an -e option, mutually exclusive with -n, is specified. The POSIX standard waffles, leaving the treatment of escape sequences up to the implementation (a good reason for using printf rather than echo).

The System V version of echo recognizes the following escape sequences in the echoed text:

\c	Cancel output of remaining characters or trailing ⟨newline⟩
\n	⟨newline⟩
\r	⟨return⟩
\f	⟨formfeed⟩ (new page)
\v	⟨vertical tab⟩
\b	⟨backspace⟩
\t	⟨tab⟩

| \\ | Backslash |
| \0*nnn* | Character with ASCII code *nnn* (one to three octal digits) |

The backslashes in these escape characters must be quoted so that `echo` rather than the shell interprets them. By ending the echoed string with \c, you can achieve the effect of -n, namely, cancelling the ⟨newline⟩ after the echoed string. Depending on your system, \c earlier in the string may cancel the rest of the string or cancel only the trailing ⟨newline⟩.

**5.8.2
Producing Output
with** `printf`

The `printf` command provides C-style formatting of strings you wish to produce on standard output. The form of the `printf` command line is

> `printf` *format* [*argument* ...]

The effect of the command is to format the *argument*s according to the format string *format* and produce the result on standard output.

The format string contains a conversion for each argument. `Printf` proceeds by examining the format string, looking for conversions and escape sequences. Everything that is neither a conversion nor an escape sequence is produced literally. Note in particular that a ⟨newline⟩ is *not* attached to the output unless one is specified explicitly. This is an important difference in behavior between `printf` and `echo`. The escape sequences consist of a backslash followed by a single character and are described below.

Each conversion begins with a percent and has the form

> `%` [*flag* ...] [*width*] [. *precision*] *convchar*

where *convchar* is a character specifying the type of conversion, *width* and *precision* are integers giving subfield widths, and each *flag* modifies the meaning of the conversion. When `printf` encounters a conversion, it consumes the next argument and formats that argument as specified by the conversion, producing the result on standard output. In the important special case where there are no conversions at all, the format string is simply copied to standard output (without a following ⟨newline⟩).

For example, suppose the value of the shell variable `TEXTFILE` is `~/roster` and the file `~/roster` contains 83 lines. Then executing the command

```
printf "The file %s contains %i lines.\n" $TEXTFILE `wc -l < $TEXTFILE`
```

produces the output

> `The file /home/vincent/roster contains 83 lines.`

(assuming your user name is `vincent`). The two conversions within the format are `%s` and `%i`.

The number of arguments provided to `printf` need not be the same as the number of conversions within the format string. If there are extra arguments, the format string is reused as many times as necessary; if there are not enough (including the case of a reused format string), missing string arguments are taken to be the null string and missing numerical arguments are taken to be zero.

Numerical arguments generally have the same form that they do in C. However, `printf` provides an extension: if an argument begins with a single or double quote, then the numerical value of the following character, as derived from the underlying code set, is used as the value of the argument. For instance, in the POSIX locale, the value of the argument '"T' is 84 (decimal).

The command-line version of `printf` is simpler than the `printf` of the C language. The command-line version assumes all field widths to be fixed; the C version allows a field width to be given by an additional argument. (But you can usually get the effect of a variable field width by inserting a shell variable into the format string.)[26] The command-line version assumes that all values to be converted are strings (albeit possibly strings that represent numbers); the C version allows them to be actual numbers as well.

Field Width and Precision.   A conversion takes an argument string *arg* as input and produces from *arg* a converted value, also a string, that represents *arg*. By default the converted value occupies no more characters than are needed to represent it. For instance, converting the string 007 using the decimal conversion `%d` produces the string 7, not 007. (The `%i` conversion, however, may add surrounding spaces, as described below.) You can cause the converted value to be padded with extra characters, by default spaces on the left, by providing a field width *width* in the conversion. For instance, the conversion `%5d` would cause the number 17 to be produced as '␣␣␣17'.

If a value to be produced contains more digits or characters than specified by the field width, the extra digits or characters are not truncated. For instance, converting the argument '2874' according to the conversion `%2d` produces the string '2874'; converting it according to the conversion `%6d` produces the string '␣␣2874'.

You can specify the number of digits or characters in a portion of the result of a conversion by giving a precision *prec*. The meaning of the precision depends on the conversion. For instance, for the decimal conversion `%f`, the precision gives the number of digits after the radix point. You can provide a precision even if you don't provide a field width.

Flag Characters.   A conversion specification can include various flag characters (more than one is permitted) that modify the form of the result:

-    Left-justify the converted string within its field. This flag has an effect only if the field width is larger than the number of characters in the converted string.

---

26. Moreover, some implementations may add variable field widths as an enhancement to `printf`.

⟨space⟩ Prefix a space to the result of a signed numeric conversion such as %d or %E if the result is nonnegative. Unsigned and string conversions such as %u and %s are not affected. Using this flag makes the width of the result independent of its sign. This flag is ignored if the + flag also appears.

+ If the conversion is a signed numeric conversion, always start the converted string with a sign (+ or -).

0 If padding is required in front of a numerical value, use zeroes instead of spaces. (The 0 flag has no effect if you also specify an explicit precision.)

Use the alternate form of the requested conversion. The alternate forms vary according to the type of conversion and are described in connection with the individual conversions. If the meaning of # is not mentioned in connection with a particular conversion, then # is not meaningful for that conversion.

Conversion Characters. The following characters specify conversion to an integer:

d Consider the input string as the representation of a decimal number and convert that decimal number back to a string. The output is not necessarily the same as the input; for example, the strings '89', '␣␣89', '+89', and '␣+89', when converted with the %d format, all yield the result '89'. The precision (default value 1) specifies the minimum number of digits in the result, with leading zeroes being attached if necessary. For example, converting the string '␣-13' with the conversion %8.5d yields the result '␣␣-00013'.

i Like d, except that some versions of `printf` might add spaces before or after the result string.[27]

u Like d, except that the number is treated as though it were stored in a machine register and then evaluated as an unsigned integer. For positive numbers, this makes no difference; for negative numbers, you get the two's complement of the number. For example, if your machine has 32-bit integers, converting the string '-9' according to the conversion %u yields the output string '4294967287'.

o Like u, except that the result is expressed as an octal number. The # flag forces the number to have a leading 0.

x Like u, except that the result is expressed as a hexadecimal number using the letters `abcdef` for the digits 10–15. The # flag causes the result to be preceded by 0x.

---

27. POSIX explicitly allows that behavior, although we don't know of any implementations that actually do add the spaces.

X   Like u, except that the result is expressed as a hexadecimal number using the letters ABCDEF for the digits 10–15. The # flag causes the result to be preceded by 0X.

The following characters specify conversion of decimal fractions or floating-point numbers. POSIX does not require an implementation to support them.

f   Convert the input number to a decimal fraction with *prec* digits to the right of the radix point (default is six digits). If *prec* is zero, omit the radix point unless the # flag is present. For example, converting the string '89.5' according to the conversion %f produces the result string '89.500000'.

e   Convert the input number to a floating-point number with one digit to the left of the radix point, *prec* digits to the right of the radix point (default is six digits), and an exponent of at least two digits preceded by the letter e. If *prec* is zero, omit the radix point unless the # flag is present.

E   Like e, except that the exponent letter is E.

g   Like either e or f, depending on the value to be converted. If the exponent *e* resulting from the conversion to a floating-point number is in the range $-4 \le e \le prec$, the f conversion is used and trailing zeroes are removed from the decimal fraction part of the result; otherwise, the e conversion is used. For example, converting the value '0.70' with the %g format produces the result '0.7', but converting the value '.00007' produces the value '7e-05'. You can think of this conversion as using the more readable decimal fraction format if the result is in a reasonable range and the more general floating-point format otherwise.

G   Like g, except that the exponent letter, if used, is E rather than e.

The following two conversions provide for strings and single characters:

s   Treat the input argument as a (null-terminated) string and produce that same string as the result, with spaces prepended if the field width exceeds the length of the string. If a precision *prec* is specified, truncate the string after *prec* characters.

c   Produce just the first character of the input argument.

The following conversion produces echo-style string conversion:

b   Convert the input argument as a string, recognizing the same escape sequences as in the format string, as well as the two additional escape sequences, \0*nnn* and \c.

Finally, the following "conversion" specifies a literal percent character:

%   Produce a literal percent character. Thus, the way to include a percent character in a format string is to write '%%'.

Escape Sequences. The format string can contain escape sequences, each of which starts with a backslash. The escape sequences provide names for common control characters and also provide a way of specifying an arbitrary byte.

\\	Backslash
\a	⟨alert⟩
\b	⟨backspace⟩
\f	⟨formfeed⟩
\n	⟨newline⟩
\r	⟨return⟩
\t	⟨tab⟩
\v	⟨vertical tab⟩

There are two additional escape sequences you can use in an argument to the %b conversion, for consistency with `echo`:

\0*nnn*   The character whose octal code is *nnn*, where *nnn* has from one to three octal digits.

\c   Ignore any characters remaining in this argument string, as well as any characters remaining in the format string.

**5.8.3
Producing
KornShell Output
with** `print`

The KornShell (`ksh`) provides a `print` command that somewhat resembles `echo` but recognizes the same escape sequences that `printf` does. The form of the `print` command is

> `print [-Rnprs] [-u[n]] [arg ... ]`

By default the arguments are sent to standard output, with escape sequences (including \c and \0*nnn*) treated as they are by `printf` and the results followed by a ⟨newline⟩. The command-line options are as follows:

-R   Treat backslashes and hyphens literally. A backslash does not escape the following character and a hyphen does not introduce an option, except for the one special case -n.

-n   Don't add a trailing ⟨newline⟩ to the output.

-p   Redirect the arguments to the coprocess (see Section 6.9.3), which must exist.

-r   Treat backslashes literally, not as escapes.

-s   Redirect the arguments to the history file, where they appear as another command.

-u [n]   Redirect the arguments to file descriptor n, or to file descriptor 1 (standard output) if n is omitted. If file descriptor n does not refer to a file open for writing, n must be 1 (standard input) or 2 (standard error). Unlike an output redirection operator, `print` with the -u option does not cause a file to be opened and closed each time it is called, nor a file descriptor to be duplicated again.

5.8.4
Reading an Input
Line with read

The read command reads a line from standard input and splits that line into fields.[28] The form of the command is

    read [-r] *var* ...

where *var* ... is a list of variables to which successive fields are to be assigned. Read returns an exit status of zero unless it encounters an end-of-file.

The input line is treated as a sequence of fields separated by one or more separator characters. The set of separator characters is given by the IFS environment variable (see p. 372); if that variable is not set, the default separator characters are ⟨space⟩, ⟨tab⟩, and ⟨newline⟩. Successive fields are assigned to the shell variables *var* ....

If there are more variables than fields, the extra variables are set to the empty string. If there are more fields than variables, read assigns the extra fields to the last name, replacing each separator by a single space. For example, if you type

    IFS="; "
    read a b c
    one two; three;;four
    echo [$a] [$b] [$c]

you obtain the output

    echo [one] [two] [three four]

In this example, the input field separators are the semicolon and the space.

Within the input text, lines can be continued with '\ Enter '. Other characters can be quoted by escaping them with backslashes; the backslashes are removed before the fields are assigned to the names. However, the effect of backslashes can be nullified with the -r option:

-r   Treat backslashes as ordinary characters, including any back-
            slashes at the end of a line. Not all systems support this option.

Command-Line Options for ksh. The version of the read command implemented within the KornShell (ksh) provides some additional options:

-p   Read the input line from the coprocess (see Section 6.9.3).

-s   Save a copy of the input line in the history file, where it appears
            as just another command.

-u [*n*]   Read the input line from file descriptor *n*, or from file descrip-
            tor 0 (standard input) if *n* is omitted. If *n* has a value other
            than 0 or 2 (standard error), the file descriptor must refer to
            an open file.

---

28. All known shells implement the read command as an internal command, which is why you'll usually find it described as part of the shell rather than as a command in its own right.

5.9   Evaluating Expressions

There are two commands for evaluating expressions: bc and expr. The bc command is useful mainly as an arbitrary-precision on-line interactive calculator. For programmed calculations of any complexity, awk (see Section 4.7) is often better. The expr command, which handles integers and strings, is important mainly because of its use in existing shell scripts; most uses of expr can be replaced by shell operations.

**5.9.1
The bc Calculator**

The bc program provides an arbitrary-precision desk calculator with additional facilities for composing rudimentary programs. The original version was written by Lorinda Cherry and Robert Morris at Bell Telephone Laboratories as a front end to an older desk calculator program, dc. The bc program can handle integers of arbitrary size and decimal fractions, but not floating-point numbers. It provides input and output in non-decimal bases, control over the precision ("scale") of decimal fractions, user-definable functions, and simple arrays. If you are primarily interested in bc for its ability to handle long integers, however, the Icon language (see Section 4.8.1) is likely to be a better alternative for calculations of any complexity.

The form of the bc command line is

    bc [-l] [*file* ...]

where *file* ... are files containing definitions to be processed before bc requests user input. The purpose of the files is to enable you to build collections of function definitions for use with bc. The -l option, described below, causes a small set of predefined mathematical functions to be loaded and also sets the default precision to 20.

After reading any files you've specified, bc reads "statements" from standard input, normally your terminal. Usually there's just one statement per input line, though you can have more than one by separating the statements with semicolons. Some complex statements themselves permit or require embedded ⟨newline⟩s, so a complex statement may have one or more continuation lines.

The simplest form of statement is an expression to be evaluated. For example, if you type

    38.25*83

bc will respond with the result of the calculation, namely, 3174.75. A statement can also assign a value to a named expression, such as a variable, or define a function. Structured statements such as the if statement provide more complex actions; such statements often occupy several lines. The quit statement causes bc to exit.

After reading a line and its continuations, if any, bc evaluates each statement on the line. If the statement is an expression, bc produces the value of that expression on standard output. Evaluating any other kind of statement produces nothing.

Note: The hexadecimal digits ABCDEF must be written as capital letters (and are also displayed that way). This rule ensures that a single hexadecimal digit such as A can never be confused with the variable named a.

Internal Registers. Bc has three internal registers to which you can assign values:

ibase The base for interpreting input. The default value is 10; permissible values range from 2 to 16. You can specify the base as a single hexadecimal digit; that is particularly useful when the current ibase value is not 10. In particular, setting ibase to A sets it to decimal 10 no matter what its current value is.

obase The base for producing output. The default value is 10; permissible values range from 2 to at least 99, depending on your system. When obase is greater than 16, each "digit" is shown as a *decimal* number, with each digit preceded by a space. For example, if obase is 1000, the decimal number 1234567 appears as '␣001␣234␣567'. Setting obase to 10^k is a handy way to display long numbers readably as groups of k digits.

scale The number of digits to the right of the radix point for the result of certain operations such as division. Not all results are affected by the value of scale; for instance, the number of fractional digits in the result of an addition depends only on the operands. The default for scale is 0 (integer results only); the maximum value is at least 99, depending on your system.

The values of ibase and obase affect input and output only, not the actual result of any computation. Be careful when setting a register—the number you set it to is interpreted according to the current value of ibase. If ibase isn't 10, you may be surprised by the result.[29]

The main purpose of changing ibase or obase, aside from displaying long numbers nicely, is to do conversions from one base to another. For instance, if you set ibase to 16 and obase to A, you can perform hexadecimal to decimal conversions as in the following example (with > used to indicate input lines):

```
> ibase=A
> obase=16
> 82
52
> 255
FF
```

---

29. If the value of obase is 16 or less, it always displays as 10—no matter what its actual value is! And setting ibase to 12 twice in a row actually sets it to decimal 14.

Expressions and Operands.   The usual way to perform a calculation is to type a single expression on an input line. An expression is a particular kind of statement. An expression can be either a single operand or a combination of operands and operators.

An operand can be any of the following:

- A number, either an integer or a decimal fraction. A number can be preceded by a + or – sign.

- A named expression, which is one of the following:
    - A simple variable, denoted by a single lowercase letter.
    - An array reference, denoted by a single letter followed by a subscript expression in square brackets.
    - An internal register (`ibase`, `obase`, or `scale`).

- An expression in parentheses.

- A function call of the form

    $f([expr [, expr] \dots])$

    where f is the function name and *expr* ... are the expressions passed as the function's arguments. A function need not have any arguments at all. Function definitions are described below.

- The form '`length`(*expr*)', whose value is the number of digits in *expr* (counting the digits both before and after the radix point).

- The form '`scale`(*expr*)', whose value is the number of digits in *expr* after the radix point.

- The form '`sqrt`(*expr*)', whose value is the square root of *expr*. The number of fractional digits in the result is given by `scale` or by the number of fractional digits in *expr*, whichever is greater.

Functions, arrays, and simple variables are all denoted by single lowercase letters. The same letter can be used for all three of these since the context always determines which one is intended.

The permissible subscript values for an array range from 0 to some system-dependent upper bound, at least 2048. An example of an array reference is `w[z+2]`.

Operators.   These are the arithmetic operators:

+	Addition. The scale of the result is the larger of the scales of the two operands.
–	Subtraction. The scale of the result is the larger of the scales of the two operands.
*	Multiplication. The scale of the result is given by the formula $$\min(s_a + s_b, \max(s, s_a, s_b))$$ where s_a and s_b are the scales of the operands and s is the value of `scale`.
/	Division. The scale of the result is simply the value of `scale`, no matter what the scales of the operands.

%   Remainder. The value of $a\%b$ is computed as

$$a - (a/b) \times b$$

The scale of the result is

$$\max(s + s_b, s_a)$$

where s_a, s_b, and s denote the scale of a, the scale of b, and the value of scale, respectively.

^   Power. The value of $a\wedge b$ is a raised to the bth power. The exponent b must be an integer, and a must be nonnegative if b is negative. The scale of the result is scale if b is negative and

$$\min(s_a \times s_b, \max(s_a, s))$$

otherwise.

There are two modifying operators for named expressions:

++   Increment by 1 (prefix or postfix). The form e++ retrieves the value of e and then increments e by 1; the form ++e increments e by 1 and returns the incremented value.

--   Decrement by 1, similar to ++.

Assignments can also be embedded in expressions. The expression $a=b$ assigns the value of b to the named expression a and also returns that value. Each of the arithmetic operators has a corresponding assignment form; for instance, the expression $a+=b$ assigns $a+b$ to a and has the sum as its value.

Relational expressions are used within some of the statement forms described below. A relational expression contains a single relational operator. The relational operators are

    ==   !=   <   >   <=   >=

with the customary meanings (note that as in C, the equality comparison is ==, not =). The value of a relational expression is 0 (false) or 1 (true). In general, a numerical expression can be used as a relational expression, with a nonzero result signifying true and a zero result signifying false. It's often useful to set a variable to 0 or 1 and then later use that variable as a relational expression.

When used in combination, the operators have the usual precedence, listed here in order from highest to lowest:

```
++ --
unary -
^        (associate right to left)
* / %       (associate left to right)
+ binary -      (associate left to right)
=   +=   -=   *=   /=   %=   ^=      (associate right to left)
==   !=   <   >   <=   >=
```

Note that bc, unlike C, assigns higher precedence to = than to <.

Statements.   Bc provides a number of programmatic statement forms. In the following forms, *expr* represents an expression with a value, *relexpr* represents a relational expression, and *stmt* represents a statement.

expr   As noted above, an expression by itself constitutes a statement.

string   A character string *string* enclosed in double quotes is a statement. Evaluating it causes *string* (without the double quotes) to be produced on standard output (without a trailing ⟨newline⟩). There is no way to include a double quote as part of a string.

quit   Reading the quit statement causes bc to terminate—even if it occurs in a context where it isn't executed.

{ *stmt* ; ... ; *stmt*}
              A block statement consists of a sequence of statements separated by semicolons and enclosed in braces. Any of the semicolons may be replaced by ⟨newline⟩, and ⟨newline⟩s are also permitted after the opening brace. Once you type the opening brace of a block statement, bc continues to read lines until it encounters the closing brace.

if (*relexpr*) *stmt*
              An if statement tests the relational expression *relexpr* and executes *stmt* if and only if *relexpr* is true (i.e., has a nonzero value). The entire if statement must appear on a single line unless *stmt* is a block statement, in which case the opening brace must appear on the same line as the preceding parts of the statement. A similar rule applies to while and for statements.

while (*relexpr*) *stmt*
              A while statement repeatedly tests *relexpr*. If *relexpr* is true, *stmt* is executed. If not, evaluation of the while statement is complete.

for ($expr_1$; *relexpr*; $expr_2$) *stmt*
              The for statement is equivalent to the sequence

$$\{expr_1$$
$$\text{while } (relexpr) \text{ \{}$$
$$stmt$$
$$expr_2$$
$$\}\}$$

It is useful for iterative loops.

break   The break statement causes evaluation of the innermost enclosing for or while statement to terminate.

return [(*expr*)]
              The return statement is meaningful only within a function definition. Without *expr* it causes the function to return 0; with *expr* it causes the function to return the value of *expr*.

Function Definitions.   A function definition has the form

```
define fn ([arg [, arg] ... ]) {
    [auto var [, var] ... ]
    stmt ...
}
```

where *fn*, *arg*, and *var* are single letters denoting the function name, the argument names, and the automatic variables, respectively, and *stmt* denotes a statement. The statement following the opening brace must be on a new line. A function need not have any arguments and may be executed purely for its side effects. Recursive functions that call themselves directly or indirectly are permitted. Function arguments are passed by value; an assignment to a function argument is legal but has no effect on the surrounding context.

The automatic variables are local to the definition; their values disappear when evaluation of the function is complete, and they have no effect on other variables by the same name. Any variables referenced within the function definition and not declared as automatic are global and are visible outside the function definition. Every function definition has an implicit `return` statement at its end.

Comments.   The input to `bc` may contain comments. As in C, a comment begins with '/*' and ends with '*/', and may extend over several lines. Comments are primarily useful in files of function definitions. Syntactically, a comment is equivalent to a space.

Preloading the Math Library.   `Bc` has a library of math functions that you can preload by specifying the `-l` option. This option has two effects: it makes the functions available just as though you had defined them yourself, and it sets the value of `scale` to 20. The preloaded math functions are the following:

`s(x)`	Sine
`c(x)`	Cosine
`a(x)`	Arctangent
`e(x)`	Exponential
`l(x)`	Natural logarithm
`j(n, x)`	Bessel function

GNU Extensions.   The GNU version of `bc` provides a number of useful extensions:

- The names of variables, arrays, and functions can have any number of letters.

- The register `last` contains the value of the last number that was produced on standard output.

- A relational expression can appear anywhere, not just in a statement that expects one as a test.

- The boolean operations '!' (unary negation), '&&' (and), and '||' (or) are provided.

- The `if` statement can include an `else` clause.

- The `read()` function reads a number from standard input.

- The '`print` *list*' statement produces the sequence of strings and expressions found in *list* on standard output. Escape sequences starting with a backslash are permitted in the strings, though the double-quote characters still cannot be included.

- The `continue` statement causes the nearest enclosing `for` statement to start the next iteration immediately.

- The `halt` statement is like the `quit` statement except that it causes `bc` to exit only if it is actually evaluated.

**5.9.2
The `expr` Evaluator**

The `expr` command evaluates an expression, which may include arithmetic operations, comparisons, logical operations, and pattern matches. The form of the `expr` command line is

    expr *expr*

where *expr* is the expression to be evaluated. The value of the expression, which may be either an integer or a string, is sent to standard output. Under most circumstances, you can replace the use of `expr` by an arithmetic expression recognized by the KornShell; the need for `expr` is the result of limitations in older shells.

Conventions for Writing the Expression.   The expression consists of a sequence of words, each of which is either a value, an operator, or a parenthesis. Words must be separated by whitespace. A number of the operators contain characters such as '<' that are meaningful to various shells; these characters must be quoted. Parentheses, which usually must be quoted, have their usual mathematical meaning. For example, if you type

    expr \(3 + 4 \) * 8

you'll get the output 56. You must also quote null strings and strings containing blanks.

Arithmetic Operators.   An expression may contain the following arithmetic operators:

    + - * / %

The expression 'e_1 % e_2' gives the remainder after dividing e_1 by e_2. The '-' operator may be used either as a unary operator or as a binary operator.

Comparison Operators.   An expression may contain the following comparison operators:

    < > <= >= !=

The operator '!=' indicates inequality. If both arguments to an operator are integers, `expr` compares them numerically; otherwise, it compares them lexicographically (as strings). The result of a comparison is 1 if the comparison succeeds and 0 if it fails.

Logical Operators.   The logical operators '&' and '|' are useful for combining the results of tests:

$expr_1$ | $expr_2$
> If $expr_1$ is neither null nor zero, the result is $expr_1$; otherwise, it is $expr_2$.

$expr_1$ & $expr_2$
> If neither $expr_1$ nor $expr_2$ is null or zero, the result is $expr_1$; otherwise, it is zero.

Pattern-Matching Operator.   The expression '$expr_1$: $expr_2$' yields the result of matching the string $expr_1$ against the BRE $expr_2$ (see Section 2.17). The recognized components of the regular expression are as given in Section 2.17 with one exception: the BRE may contain at most one parenthesized subexpression (although you may still use the '\1' notation to repeat that subexpression).

The value returned by the match is the number of characters matched, or zero if the match failed. If $expr_2$ contains a parenthesized subexpression, however, the result of the entire expression is the substring matched by the parenthesized subexpression. For example, if you type

```
expr Okeefenokee : '.*\(...\).*\1.*'
```

you'll get the output `kee`, representing the first (and only) repeated three-character string in 'Okeefenokee'.

Application to Shell Scripts.   Expr is particularly useful in Bourne-shell scripts as a way of doing internal arithmetic. For instance, the following line in a Bourne-shell script sets the variable `w` to the sum of the variables `w1` and `w2`:

```
w = `expr $w1 + $w2`
```

Most modern shells such as the KornShell or the C shell already include the capability of evaluating arithmetic expressions (see Section 6.18.2). For scripts to be interpreted by those shells, `expr` isn't needed.

5.10   Special Invocation of Commands

You can invoke a command by typing its name and arguments in response to a shell prompt. The utilities in this section provide different ways of invoking a command. The `command` utility always interprets a command name as a program rather than as the name of one of the special shell built-in commands. The xargs utility provides a way of constructing the arguments to a command. The standard syntax of commands and the conventions for calling commands are discussed in Section 2.12.

You can use the command utility for two purposes. First, you can use it to override the rules for the interpretation of command names given in Section 6.8.1 so that user-defined functions are ignored and thus cannot supersede intrinsic commands or user-level utilities of the same name. For instance, if you're writing a shell script and you want to be sure that the standard sort utility is called even though a user-defined sort might also exist, you can call 'command -p sort' rather than just sort. Second, you can use it to determine how your shell interprets a particular command name.

The first form of the command command line is

command [-p] *cmd* [*arg ...*]

Except for the effects of the options and the different rule for command-name interpretation, executing a command with this form of command is just the same as executing the command without it.

The second form of the command command line is

command -v *cmd*

or

command -V *cmd*

This form is used to determine how the shell interprets a command name and can be used in place of the type command (see Section 5.12.1) or the which command (see Section 3.9.1).

Command-Line Options. These are the command-line options for command:

-p   Use a value of PATH that is guaranteed to find all (POSIX) standard utilities. This option is useful as a way of bypassing differences between the default value of PATH and a value you've assigned yourself.

-v   Produce the interpretation given to *cmd*:
          - If *cmd* designates an executable file of any kind, produce the absolute pathname of that file.
          - If *cmd* is an intrinsic shell command, produce the string *cmd*.
          - If *cmd* is an alias (see Section 6.19), produce the definition of the alias.

-V   Like -v, but more verbose: produce in addition an explicit and more detailed indication of how *cmd* is interpreted.

**5.10.2
Constructing
Command
Arguments with**
`xargs`

The `xargs` utility invokes a command repeatedly, each time applying it to a sequence of arguments taken from standard input. The form of the `xargs` command line is

> `xargs [-t] [-n nargs [-x]] [-s size] [ cmd [ arg ... ]]`

In each cycle, `xargs` reads a sequence of extra arguments *xarg ...* from standard input, starting from just after the last argument already extracted. The arguments are assumed to be separated by whitespace and ⟨newline⟩s as described below. Each group of arguments includes as many arguments as possible, subject to the constraints of the command-line options and the maximum line length permitted by your implementation of `xargs`. Some older implementations of `xargs` require that no whitespace be present between an option flag and its operand.

Having retrieved the arguments, `xargs` executes the command

> *cmd arg ... xarg ...*

It then waits for the command to complete, ensuring that two invocations of *cmd* are not active at the same time.

The command *cmd* must not itself read from standard input. If *cmd* is not given, it defaults to `echo` (see Section 5.8.1).

Command-Line Options.   The following `xargs` options jointly constrain the number of arguments supplied to each invocation of *cmd*:

-n *nargs*   When calling *cmd*, extract no more than *nargs* arguments from standard input.

-s *size*   When calling *cmd*, extract no more arguments than will fit within a command line of length *size*.

The following additional options can also be specified:

-t   Enable trace mode, causing each generated command line to be written to standard error.

-x   Terminate the invocation of `xargs` if *nargs* arguments won't fit within a command line. The length can be given explicitly with the -s option or implicitly by the limit imposed by your `xargs` implementation.

Syntax of the Input Arguments.   The arguments that `xargs` reads from standard input don't follow quite the same quoting conventions that shell arguments do. Within the input, arguments are separated by (unescaped) whitespace, with ⟨newline⟩ treated as a whitespace character. A possibly empty sequence of characters can be enclosed either in double quotes if it contains no (unescaped) double quotes itself or in apostrophes if it contains no (unescaped) apostrophes itself. In addition, any character outside of such a quoted sequence can be quoted with a preceding backslash. One sure (if verbose) way to transform any string into a quoted form is to precede every character of the string with a backslash. This method is appropriate for mechanical transformations but for little else.[30]

Exit Codes.   The exit codes resulting from calling `xargs` are often useful. Here they are:

0	All utility invocations completed successfully.
1–125	An error occurred in an attempted exection of *cmd*.
126	The utility specified by *cmd* was found but couldn't be invoked.
127	The utility specified by *cmd* couldn't be located.

Examples.   Here are some examples of `xargs`:

- Assume that `split` (see Section 4.4.4) has been called and has generated the files `pt.aa`, `pt.ab`, etc., that contain consecutive segments of an input file. Then the command line

  ```
  ls -1 pt.* | xargs cat > recon
  ```

  reassembles the segments into a copy `recon` of the original file.

- The command line

  ```
  find jeremiad -type f -name "*.ps" | xargs -n 1 lpr
  ```

  calls `lpr` to print each '.ps' file within the directory tree rooted at `jeremiad`. The input file passed through the pipe is a list of the files, one per line. If there's any possibility that the file names could include spaces or ⟨newline⟩s, you'll have to pass the output of `find` through an additional filter that quotes each such character with a backslash. This example is a classic use of `xargs`, designed to reduce the number of processes launched by the otherwise equivalent command

  ```
  find jeremiad -type f -name "*.ps" -exec lpr {} \;
  ```

5.11   Querying Your UNIX Environment

The commands in this section enable you to get information about your operating system and hardware, as well as about size limits for your particular version of UNIX.

---

30. The GNU version of `xargs` has a `-0` option that causes `xargs` to expect each argument to be terminated by ⟨null⟩. This option complements the `-print0` option of GNU `find`. Using 'find ... -print0' and 'xargs -0 ...' together ensures that a filename with an embedded ⟨newline⟩ passed to `xargs` will be treated correctly.

5.11.1
Producing System Information with uname

You can use the `uname` command to obtain a description of your operating system, network node, and hardware. The form of the `uname` command line is

        uname [-amnrsv]

Information about your system is produced on standard output. The default output is the same as with `-s`. Examples of the output produced by `uname -a` are

        Linux russula 1.1.50 #1 Thu Nov 10 23:37:56 EST 1994 i586
        SunOS equinox 4.1.3_U1 2 sun4c
        SunOS ohm 5.4 generic i86pc
        IRIX world 5.3 11091811 IP19 mips

Command-Line Options.   The command-line options for `uname` specify what information is produced:

-a   Produce the information for all the other options.

-m   Produce the name of the hardware type of your machine.

-n   Produce the name of your network node.

-r   Produce the release level of your operating system.

-s   Produce the name of the implementation of your operating system.

-v   Produce the version level of the current release of your operating system.

5.11.2
Getting Configuration Values with getconf

The `getconf` command retrieves information about various limits built into your version of UNIX. It is mostly useful within shell scripts. The `getconf` command line has two forms:

        getconf *sysvar*
        getconf *pathvar pathname*

The first form retrieves the value of a system-defined value; the second retrieves the value of a configuration variable that depends on a pathname.

Most uses of `getconf` require a more detailed knowledge of the POSIX standard than we can present in this book. However, one simple use is the command

        getconf PATH

which produces the value of the system default for the `PATH` environment variable. That value is not necessarily the same as `PATH` in your own environment because you might have changed it. Another example of the first form is

        getconf LINE_MAX

which produces the maximum length (in bytes) permitted for the input line of a utility intended to process text files. An example of the second form is

```
getconf NAME_MAX /usr
```

which produces the maximum length of a filename in the /usr directory. (The second argument is needed because the maximum length might be different for a different directory.)

5.12   Miscellaneous Services

The commands in this group provide an assortment of convenient services that don't fall into any other category.

5.12.1
Classifying
Commands
with type

Several shells, including the KornShell, provide a type command that indicates how a name would be interpreted if used as a command name, though this command is not included in POSIX. The form of the type command line is

```
type [name ... ]
```

The interpretation of each specified *name* is produced on standard output, showing how the shell would interpret each *name* were it given as a command. For example, the command

```
type cd ps
```

produces the output

```
cd is a shell builtin
ps is /bin/ps
```

If no *name*s appear, the command does nothing. An alternative to type is the POSIX command 'command -v' (see Section 5.10.1).

5.12.2
Timing a Command
with time

The time command enables you to time a command to see how long it takes to execute. The form of the time command line is

```
time [-p] cmd
```

where *cmd* is the command to be timed. The POSIX version of time requires *cmd* to be a simple command (no parentheses). However, the KornShell allows *cmd* to be anything you can enclose in parentheses or braces.[31] The -p option specifies that the output is to be in POSIX standard format rather than in a format chosen by the implementation.

An example of a call on time is

```
time -p tex screed
```

---

31. This is one of the subtle differences between the POSIX shell and the KornShell.

This command times how long it takes `tex` to process the input file `screed.tex` (the '.tex' is implicit). A sample output might be this:

```
real 14.14
user 10.20
sys 0.82
```

The three times shown here are the elapsed time, the time consumed by the user process, and the time consumed by system processes (all in minutes and seconds). The output of `time` follows the output of *cmd* itself and is sent to standard error rather than standard output. The output produced by the C shell's `time` command has a different form (see p. 399). You can also use the C shell's `time` variable to time a complex command (see p. 395).

You can circumvent the requirement that *cmd* be a simple command by calling `sh` explicitly, as in

```
time sh -c 'complex-command-line'
```

The indicated time will include the overhead of creating a subshell to run *complex-command-line*.

5.12.3
Locating Strings in Files with `strings`

The `strings` utility locates printable strings (i.e., strings consisting of a sequence of printable characters) within a set of files. It's most useful for scanning binary files such as program executable files for interesting data such as error messages and program identification. There's not much point in applying `strings` to a text file since such a file consists entirely or almost entirely of printable characters.

The form of the `strings` command line is

```
strings [-a] [-t fchar] [-n len] [file ... ]
```

The files named by the pathnames *file* ... are searched for printable strings. An obsolescent form is

```
strings [-] [-t fchar] [-len] [file ... ]
```

where the '-' has the same meaning as `-a`. The files named by the pathnames *files* ... ('-' for standard input) are scanned for printable strings consisting of *len* or more consecutive printable characters (default 4), and each such string is produced on standard output. The default output shows the strings only; by specifying `-n`, you can see the location of each string as well. `Strings` does not necessarily scan all of a file; for instance, in most systems, it will only scan the text and data segments of object files. You can force it to scan the entire file with the `-a` option.

Command-Line Options. These are the command-line options for `strings`:

`-a`   Scan each file in its entirety.

`-n` *len*   Require a candidate string to have at least *len* consecutive printable characters.

Command	Result
dirname a	.
dirname a/	.
dirname a/b	a
dirname a//b/	a
dirname /a/b	/a
dirname //a//b//	//a
dirname ///	/
dirname //	// or /
dirname //a	// or /

Fig. 5-1. Sample results from `dirname`.

-t *fchar*   Write the byte offset of each string found, representing the number in base *fchar* (d for decimal, o for octal, x for hexadecimal).

**5.12.4
Parsing Pathnames**

The `basename` and `dirname` commands parse pathnames to extract their parts. They are used almost exclusively in shell scripts. If *string* is the pathname of a file *file*, the result of '`basename` *string*' is the filename of *file* in the directory '`dirname` *string*'.

Extracting the Directory Part with `dirname`.   The form of the `dirname` command line is

dirname *string*

where *string* is a string that represents a pathname. The command produces the name of the directory containing that pathname. The precise rules for obtaining the result are a bit complicated:

(1)   If *string* has the form

//[*name*[/ ...]]

where *name* is a string of non-slashes, the result is either '/' or '//', depending on the implementation.

(2)   Otherwise, if *string* is a sequence of slashes, the result is a single slash.

(3)   Otherwise, if *string* ends in one or more slashes, remove them.

(4)   If no slash characters remain, the result is a single dot.

(5)   Otherwise, remove any trailing non-slash characters and then remove any trailing slash characters.

(6)   If no characters remain, the result is a single slash; otherwise, it is the remaining characters.

Some examples of `dirname` are shown in Figure 5-1.

Extracting the Filename Part with `basename`. The form of the `basename` command line is

   `basename` *string₁* [*string₂*]

where *string₁* is a string that represents a file name and *string₂* is an expected suffix of *string₁*. If *string₂* is absent, it is taken to be the null string. The command deletes *string₂* from the end of *string₁* (if it is there) and then produces on standard output the portion that follows the last slash, if any. The basename of '//' is '/' or '//', depending on the implementation. The basename of any other string consisting entirely of slashes is a single slash, though some non-POSIX versions produce a null string in this case.

   For example, the command

   `basename /home/natasha/borscht.Z .Z`

produces the output

   `borscht`

**5.12.5
Recording Errors in
the System Log**

When a noninteractive utility fails, it is often useful to record that fact in the system log. The `logger` command is intended to be used in shell scripts for recording such events.

   The form of the `logger` command line is simply

   `logger` *string* ...

The command causes a message derived from *string* ... to be appended to the system log file. The form of the message depends on your system, and as a user you generally need not be concerned with just what it is.

Command-Line Options for BSD. The 4.4BSD version of `logger`, also found in Linux, provides several command-line options:

`-i`   Include the process ID of the logger process itself in each log message.

`-s`   Send each log message both to the system log and to standard error.

`-f` *file*   Send the contents of *file* to the system log.

`-p` *pri*   Include the priority *pri* in the log message.

`-t` *tag*   Mark each line of the log message with *tag*.

5.13   Producing Locale Information and Defining a Locale

A locale (see Section 2.16) defines those aspects of the UNIX environment that depend on national linguistic and cultural conventions. You can produce information about available locales with the `locale` command or define a new locale with the `localedef` command. Neither of these commands change anything about your current locale; to do that, you have to set one of the environment variables described in Section 2.16.4.

5.13.1 Displaying Locale Information with `locale`

The `locale` command produces information about the current locale or about all publicly known locales, sending the information to standard output. The forms of the `locale` command are

```
locale [-a | -m]
locale [-ck] name ...
```

If you call `locale` without any options, it produces the names and values of the `LANG` environment variable and the various `LC_*` environment variables (see Section 2.16.4). This information defines your current locale and appears in a format suitable for shell input at a later time.

Information About All Locales. The first form of `locale`, with `-a` or `-m` specified, provides information about all publicly known locales:

-a   Produce the names of all publicly known locales.

-m   Produce the names of all known charmaps (see Section 2.16.2). A charmap can be provided to the `localedef` command when that command is used to build a new locale. However, you don't specify a charmap when you are specifying your current locale; the charmap is implicit in the locale definition.

Information About the Current Locale. The second form of `locale` provides information about the current locale. Each *name* is a keyword in a locale category, the name of a locale category, or `charmap`:

- If you specify a keyword, then information about that keyword is produced.

- If you specify a locale category, then information about all keywords belonging to that category is produced. The locale categories are the names of the `LC_*` environment variables such as `LC_TIME`.

- If you specify `charmap`, then what is produced is the name of the charmap that was specified when the locale was created.

By default, only the values of the relevant keywords are produced. You can use the `-c` and `-k` options to see more information:

-k   For each keyword, include the name of that keyword in the output line.

-c   For each keyword, include the name of its category in the output line. The `charmap` keyword does not have a category.

Sample output from `locale` called with various information options is shown in Figure 5-2. For the locale name `fr_FR.iso88591`, the `fr` indicates the French language, the `FR` indicates the country France, and the `iso88591` indicates the ISO 8859-1 codeset.

```
$ locale
LANG=C
LC_CTYPE="en_US.iso88591"
LC_COLLATE="en_US.iso88591"
LC_TIME="en_US.iso88591"
LC_NUMERIC="en_US.iso88591"
LC_MONETARY="en_US.iso88591"
LC_MESSAGES="en_US.iso88591"
LC_ALL=en_US.iso88591
$ locale -a
POSIX
C
en_US.iso88591
en_US.roman8
fr_CA.iso88591
fr_CA.roman8
fr_FR.iso88591
fr_FR.roman8
$ locale -ck digit abday
LC_CTYPE
digit='0';'1';'2';'3';'4';'5';'6';'7';'8';'9'
LC_TIME
abday="Sun";"Mon";"Tue";"Wed";"Thu";"Fri";"Sat"
```

Fig. 5-2.   Sample output from `locale` (input indicated by $).

**5.13.2
Defining a
New Locale with
`localedef`**

The `localedef` command defines a new locale (see Section 2.16). Not all systems, even POSIX-conforming systems, support this command.[32] Its form is

> `localedef` [-c] [-f *charmap*] [-i *source*] *name*

where *name* is the name of the new locale you wish to define. Without any options, `localedef` reads a locale definition from standard input and creates a locale named *name* from it using a default charmap. The input format is defined by the POSIX standard. If anything is wrong with the input, the locale is not created. You can use the `locale` command to see what information needs to be provided, but the output of `locale` is not necessarily in the form required by the input to `localedef`.

If the locale name specified by *name* starts with a slash, it specifies the pathname where the locale is to be stored. Otherwise, *name* specifies the name of a publicly accessible locale—if your system allows you to

---

32. The POSIX standard does not require a conforming implementation to implement `localedef`; it merely says how `localedef` shall behave if it *is* implemented.

create publicly accessible locales in this way. When you create a locale by specifying a pathname, the locale may be public if it is in a location that your system recognizes as public and you have write access to that location.

Command-Line Options.   The `localedef` command has the following options:

`-i` *source* Get the source definitions from file *source* rather than from standard input.

`-f` *charmap*
        Get the charmap from file *charmap* instead of using the default charmap.

`-c`   Create the locale even if `localedef` issued warnings while trying to build it.

5.14   Document Processing

In the following subsections we briefly describe the major document processors available under UNIX. All of them expect their input to be an ordinary text file prepared with a text editor such as `emacs` or `vi`.

5.14.1
The `nroff` and `troff` Formatters

The `nroff` formatter ("New Runoff", pronounced "en-roff") takes as its input a document with interspersed formatting commands and produces a version of that document suitable for printing on a line printer. The `troff` ("Typesetter Runoff", pronounced "tee-roff") formatter is similar, except that its output consists of a set of instructions to a typesetting machine. The original `troff` only worked with a specific typesetter; more recent versions produce device-independent output that may be piped through another program, the postprocessor, to drive a particular typesetter such as a laser printer.[33]   `Nroff` is very close in spirit to the DEC RUNOFF formatter and to the IBM Script formatter; all three formatters share the same input format, as well as a number of specific commands.[34]   `Nroff` and `troff` were written by Joseph Osanna at Bell Telephone Laboratories. Reference [B7] provides a tutorial on `nroff`, `troff`, and the preprocessors described later in this section.

---

33.   Some systems are configured with `troff` linked to the old device-specific formatter and with the newer device-independent formatter available under the name `ditroff`.

34.   The three formatters show unmistakable signs of a common origin. DEC RUNOFF and UNIX `nroff` are both descendents of the RUNOFF program written by Jerry Saltzer for the CTSS system at MIT in the mid-1960s. We assume that Script was derived from RUNOFF also.

A GNU version of `troff`, developed by James Clark, is available under the name `gtroff`. Access to `gtroff` is usually through a front-end program called `groff`. Groff is also capable of simulating `nroff`. Under 4.4BSD, the `troff` and `nroff` commands invoke shell scripts that call `groff` to carry out the appropriate simulations.

Input to `nroff` has the form of a sequence of *text lines* with interspersed directives, also called *control lines*. The directives are one-letter or two-letter instructions preceded by a period and possibly followed by some arguments. For example, the directive '.sp 2' instructs `nroff` to space down by two lines; that is, to insert two blank lines in the output. Text lines may also include *interpolations* that specify text to be substituted; for instance, an occurrence of '*G' in a text line is replaced by the current value of the string named 'G'.

`Nroff` enables you to define *macros*. A macro definition defines a new command as a sequence of input lines. The new command can accept *arguments* on the input line; these are made available to the macro definition and may be retrieved as interpolations. A macro may be called either explicitly or by associating it with a *trap*. A trap is a condition such as the end of a page; when the condition is satisfied, the macro is called. A trap may test for three kinds of conditions: reaching the end of the page, reaching the nth line on the page, or reaching the nth line of a *diversion*. Processed output may be diverted into a macro for such purposes as creating a footnote or measuring the dimensions of the output in order to decide whether it is time to start a new page.

`Nroff` is almost always used with a prepackaged collection of macros. You may specify the macro package with the `-m` option on the command line. Strictly speaking, the option '`-ms`' calls the macro package named '`s`' rather than the macro package named '`-ms`', but the custom is to call the package '`ms`' nevertheless. These are the major macro packages available:

- The `ms` package is the original collection of macros developed at Bell Laboratories early in the history of `nroff`. It is no longer supported by AT&T but is still provided with many UNIX systems.

- The `mm` package is an enhanced version of `ms` for formatting technical documents, memoranda, and letters. The letters 'mm' stand for "Memorandum Macros". This package is provided as part of the AT&T Documenter's Workbench.

- The `me` package is distributed as part of BSD. It is comparable to `ms` and `mm`.

Many specialized packages are also available, such as the `-man` package for preparing pages of the UNIX manual.

**5.14.2
Preprocessors for
nroff and troff**

Three specialized preprocessors are available for `nroff` and `troff`:

- The `eqn` preprocessor typesets mathematical formulas.
- The `tbl` preprocessor lays out tables in a document.
- The `pic` preprocessor draws pictures.

If you use all three of them in a single document, your command line should be something like this:

```
pic file | tbl | eqn | troff -mm | postprocessor
```

It's important to call these preprocessors in the order shown.

Eqn was written by Brian Kernighan and Lorinda Cherry, `tbl` was written by Michael Lesk, and `pic` was written by Brian Kernighan, all at Bell Telephone Laboratories. GNU versions of `eqn`, `tbl`, and `pic` are available under the names `geqn`, `gtbl`, and `gpic`; under 4.4BSD, the names `eqn`, `tbl`, and `pic` are linked to these GNU programs.

Typesetting Formulas with `eqn`. The `eqn` preprocessor takes as its input a `troff` file containing pairs of the special directives '`.eq`' and '`.en`'. The material between these directives describes a mathematical formula to be typeset. The output is a `troff` input file in which this material has been replaced by `troff` instructions for constructing the formula on the printed page. A version of `eqn` called `neqn` works with `nroff` but does not usually produce satisfactory results because of `nroff`'s limitations. Eqn normally places a formula on a line by itself; you may typeset a formula within a line by surrounding the formula with special delimiters. The facilities provided by `eqn` include the following:

- Greek letters and other special symbols
- Subscripts and superscripts
- Summations, integral, products, and limits that contain upper and lower parts
- Enclosing parts of formulas in big brackets, braces, parentheses, or other delimiters
- Fractions, arrays, matrices, and vertical piles of subformulas
- Notations for controlling the amount of space between parts of a formula and for using different fonts within a formula

Formatting Tables with `tbl`. The `tbl` preprocessor takes as its input a `troff` or `nroff` file containing special table-building instructions between the directives '`.ts`' and '`.te`'. Its output contains the necessary instructions for producing the tables. For simple tables, each row of the table is given by a line of input, with '`@`' or some other defined tab character separating the column entries. For more complex tables, the input format is modified appropriately. The facilities provided by `tbl` include the following:

- Left-justifying, right-justifying, or centering data within a column
- Aligning decimal numbers by their decimal points
- Drawing horizontal and vertical rules
- Vertically centering entries that apply to a set of rows
- Allowing entries to span several rows
- Turning blocks of text into table entries

Drawing Pictures with `pic`. The `pic` preprocessor inserts picture-drawing instructions into a document. It requires full typesetting capabilities and cannot be used with `nroff`. Picture-drawing commands are surrounded by the directives '`.ps`' and '`.pe`'. The facilities provided by `pic` include the following:

- Drawing boxes, circles, ellipses, arcs, arrows, lines, and splines
- Placing text within graphical objects
- Connecting objects with various kinds of lines
- Placing objects relative to other objects

The notation for describing pictures is essentially verbal; a typical line of `pic` input would be

```
arrow left down from bottom of last ellipse
```

5.14.3
TEX and LATEX

TEX is a computerized typesetting system that provides nearly everything needed for typesetting mathematics as well as ordinary text. It was written by Donald E. Knuth at Stanford University. TEX is especially notable for its flexibility, its repertoire of mathematical constructs and symbols, its superb hyphenation, and its ability to choose aesthetically satisfying line breaks. It has become quite popular in the UNIX world as an alternative to `nroff` and `troff`. TEX is described in references [B13] and [B1]. An extensive collection of TEX software and other TEX-related materials is available on CD-ROM (reference [C7]). This book was typeset using TEX.

Input to TEX consists of an ordinary text file. The file contains the text of a document augmented by *control sequences* that provide special formatting instructions. A control sequence starts with a backslash and may appear anywhere, not just at the beginning of a line. A number of other notations are also available; for example, a mathematical formula can be specified by enclosing it in dollar signs if it is to appear in running text and in double dollar signs if it is to be displayed on a line by itself. Serious users of TEX almost always use packages of macros, some quite elaborate, to define useful control sequences. The output of TEX is *not* sent to standard output; instead, it is sent to a file named '*file*`.dvi`', where '*file*`.tex`' (or simply '*file*') is the name of the input file.

A disadvantage of TEX is that considerable skill is required to use it effectively. The LATEX document processing system, written by Leslie Lamport of the Digital Equipment Corporation, is a collection of TEX macros that makes TEX easier to use by enabling the user to concentrate on the structure of the text rather than on the particular commands needed to format it (see reference [B15]). LATEX documents are particularly simple to prepare; as a result, LATEX has outstripped TEX in popularity. At the same time, LATEX provides access to all the facilities of TEX. Some notable features provided by LATEX are its sets of commands for drawing diagrams and for referring to citations in a bibliographic database. The bibliographic database is maintained by another program called BIBTEX. The 1994 version of LATEX, LATEX2_ε, contains commands for including graphics and producing colors, as well as an improved method of handling different type styles.

A disadvantage of LaTeX is that it is difficult to customize it except within rather narrow limits. As a result, documents from different sources produced using LaTeX all tend to look the same. Customizing LaTeX is certainly possible but even more difficult than customizing TeX, since to do it, you have to know both TeX and the LaTeX implementation very well.

A number of UNIX vendors include TeX and LaTeX as part of their standard system distributions. A very large collection of public-domain TeX and LaTeX material, including both the programs themselves and related tools, is available through the Comprehensive TeX Archive Network (CTAN). This archive is available via anonymous FTP from `ftp.shsu.edu`, `ftp.tex.ac.uk`, or `ftp.dante.de`. The CTAN material is also available on a CD-ROM published by Prime Time Freeware, which can be purchased from the TeX User Group (reference [C7]). A useful collection of additional TeX-related tools developed or enhanced by Karl Berry can be gotten via anonymous FTP from `ftp.cs.umb.edu`, directory `pub/tex`.

5.15   Version Control

When you or a group of people are developing a document of any kind, be it a textual document or a computer program, it's often valuable to have a history of past changes to the document. When several people are working on the document at once, it's also important to keep the changes made by different people consistent with one another.

The Revision Control System (RCS), originally designed by Walter Tichy, is a collection of utilities that keeps track of multiple versions of a document or a set of documents. A program similar to RCS called Source Code Control System (SCCS) is provided as a standard component of System V. SCCS has fewer capabilities than RCS, but some people still prefer SCCS because it is a component of a supported commercial system. In this section we present an overview of RCS.

5.15.1
RCS Functions

The RCS utilities perform the following functions:

- **Storing and retrieving multiple versions of a document.** Documents are kept in a form that maintains a full history of changes and makes both the current version and all previous versions accessible. You can retrieve a particular version according to its revision number, its revision name, its timestamp, its author, its state (an arbitrary descriptive identifier such as `Released`, `Stable`, or `Experimental`), or a combination of these criteria. Because versions are recorded in terms of their differences from a base version and stores unchanged parts just once, RCS needs far less storage than would be required to store each version in its full textual form.

- **Attaching identifying information to versions.** Whenever you create a new version, RCS prompts you for a log entry to describe that version. In addition, you can get RCS automatically to insert other identifying information into the actual text of each version. The identifying information can include a version name, the author's name, a timestamp, a state, and similar information.

- **Building a release from a set of versions.** You can collect a set of documents into an RCS release. A release is really nothing more than a symbolic name for a snapshot of the revision levels of the documents in the set at a particular moment.

- **Resolving access conflicts.** Through a locking mechanism, RCS ensures that only one person at a time can modify a particular version of a document (though several people can simultaneously generate distinct later versions). However, there are provisions for a user "breaking" a lock under certain circumstances.

- **Maintaining a tree of versions.** You can use RCS to maintain simultaneous parallel revisions of a document. RCS keeps parallel revisions in different branches of the version tree.

- **Merging independently created versions.** You can combine several independently created versions into a single version. If a section of text is modified by more than one version, RCS alerts you to the conflict.

**5.15.2
Basic Concepts
of RCS**

A document to be managed by RCS is stored as an RCS file. The RCS file is an archive that contains both the raw text of the document and its revision history. From the archive file, you can regenerate any particular version of the document and carry out many other useful operations as well. A copy of a particular version of the document is called a working file. The manual page called `rcsintro` provides an overview of RCS.

When a set of documents is being managed by RCS, the usual practice is to keep the working files in a single directory and the RCS files in a subdirectory called RCS. When several people are working on the same set of documents, a mode of operation for which RCS was designed, the RCS directory ordinarily belongs to a user who serves as RCS administrator for the documents but is group-writable for the group of those working on the documents.

Checking In and Out. The two basic RCS commands are `ci` ("check in") and `co` ("check out"), each with a multitude of options. Checking in a document registers it with RCS. The simplest form of the check-in command for a document *doc* is '`ci doc`'. You can check in an initial version or a later version. Unless you specifically indicate otherwise, the working file for a document is deleted when you check it in.

You get the document back by checking it out from RCS, which creates a new working file for it. The command for that purpose is '`co doc`'.

Options for co provide various forms of selective retrieval. In particular, -r*ver* retrieves the version numbered *ver*. By default, the working file is read-only, so you can't modify it. The purpose of that restriction is to prevent unintended simultaneous updates by two or more users.

To edit a document, you lock its RCS file when you check it out by using the command 'co -l *doc*'. Only one person at a time can hold a lock on an RCS file. Once you've checked out a document and locked its RCS file, no one else can lock that file or check in a new version until you release the lock by checking the file in again. Other users, however, can check out a working file in a read-only state.

If you are the only person who is modifying a document, you can simplify the check-in procedure by turning off strict locking. In this case you can check in the file without having checked it out and locked it, so you can continually edit it and check in new edited versions.[35] To turn off strict locking for the document *doc*, issue the command 'rcs -U *doc*'. To turn it on again, issue the command 'rcs -L *doc*'.

Identifying Information. A document can contain RCS identification as part of its text. This identification is automatically updated whenever the document is checked in. You enable this updating action by embedding the marker 'Id' in a document, typically within a comment. RCS then augments the marker with a current identification in the form

$Id: *filename revision date time author state* $

The ident utility can extract RCS identification not just from the document, but also from other files generated from it, provided the identification has somehow been incorporated into the generated file. For example, if you include the marker in an unused string constant of a C program, ident will be able to extract the RCS identification from the compiled version of that program.[36] Other markers besides 'Id' are also available.

Comparing and Merging Versions. You can determine the difference between two versions with the rcsdiff utility. The simple call 'rcsdiff *doc*' compares the working file of the document *doc* with the most recently checked-in version. The options for rcsdiff enable you to specify other versions to compare and to suppress differences due solely to RCS identification strings.

You can merge two versions, or merge an existing version into a working file, with the rcsmerge command. The merging operation is particularly useful for merging changes developed by different people. To merge more than two versions, merge the first two and then merge the resulting

---

35. If you're editing from several locations and have multiple symbolic links pointing to the RCS repository, it's safer to leave strict locking on as a protection against checking in the wrong version of a working file by accident.

36. Provided a clever compiler hasn't optimized the constant away.

working file with the remaining ones. If a merge results in overlapping modifications, `rcsmerge` tells you where they are. As an example, the command

```
rcsmerge -r2.2 -r2.3.1.2 bogify.c
```

creates a working file for the document `bogify.c`, gotten by merging the changes in revision 2.2 (from the original version) with the changes in revision 2.3.1.2.

**5.15.3
Version Numbering
and Naming**

An RCS version number consists of a sequence of pairs of numbers separated by dots (e.g., '2.1.4.2'). The version numbers containing just one pair (e.g., '3.1') form the trunk of the revision tree and represent the main line of evolution, in numerical order. The first number is changed by specifying it explicitly, the second merely by checking in a new version. The newest version in the trunk is called the *head* of the version tree. For example, here is a sequence of check-ins and the corresponding revision numbers:

```
ci          1.1
ci          1.2
ci -r2      2.1
ci -r3.1    3.1
ci          3.2
ci          3.3
```

The head in this case is version 3.3.

Version numbers with more than one pair indicate parallel developments. In each pair, the first number indicates the line of development and the second number the sequence number within the line. For example, versions 1.2.1.1 and 1.2.2.1 would indicate the first versions in two lines of development preceding in parallel from version 1.2. Version 1.2.1.2 would indicate the version after 1.2.1.1 in the same line of development. The command 'ci -r1.2.1' (or 'ci -r1.2.1.1') would initiate this line.

Symbolic Names for Versions. Using the `-N` or `-n` options of `ci`, you can assign a symbolic name to a version when you check it in. For example, the command

```
ci -r2.1.4.1 -Nnuhax llamas.tex
```

assigns the symbolic name `nuhax` to version 2.1.4.1 of the document `llamas.tex`. A subsequent checkout of `nuhax.3.19` would retrieve version 2.1.4.1.3.19.

**5.15.4
The RCS Utilities Set**

Here is a summary of the RCS utilities:

`co`   Checks out a working file derived from a document, optionally locking the RCS file. If the RCS file is not locked, the working file is read-only. Using various options whose names start with -k, you can modify the RCS identification as the file is checked out.

ci   Checks in a working file, provided that the corresponding RCS file is not locked.

rcs   Creates new RCS files or changes attributes of existing ones. The attributes can include non-strict locking, the list of users permitted to check in new versions of the RCS files, and the default treatment of RCS identification when a file is checked out.

rcsdiff   Compares two different versions of a document in an RCS file, or compares a working file with a stored version. Differences are calculated using the diff utility. The -k option can be used to suppress extraneous differences resulting from the RCS identification.

rcsmerge   Combines the changes from different versions of a document into a single version, or combines a stored version with a working file.

rcsfreeze

Creates a "release" by assigning a unique symbolic name, the release name, to the latest version on the trunk of the version tree of each document in the current directory. The default name is C_*num*, where *num* is incremented each time rcsfreeze is run, but you can also provide your own symbolic name. All files to be included must be checked in. Rcsfreeze uses a simple approach that may not give the results you want in complex situations.

rlog   Produces information about a set of RCS files. The information includes the file name, working file name, latest main revision, access list, and other statistics, together with information about each particular version. Options can be used to restrict the output.

ident   Searches for all occurrences of the pattern '$*keyword*:...$' in a set of files, where *keyword* is an RCS marker such as Id used for RCS identification. The search works on object files and dumps as well as on text files.

Note also that the rcsintro manual page provides an overview of RCS and the rcsfile manual page describes the internal format of an RCS file.

6

The Korn and POSIX Shells

A *shell* or *command interpreter* is a program that interprets and executes commands as you issue them from your terminal. A shell requires no special privileges to run; as far as the UNIX kernel is concerned, a shell is just another program. A shell can also interpret *shell scripts*, which are sequences of commands stored in a file. Shell scripts often enable you to customize your working environment without having to do "real" programming.

Because some shell facilities are intrinsic to the UNIX style of working and are common to all shells, we explain them in Chapter 2 (Concepts) rather than in this chapter. Pipelines, the simpler forms of redirection, and quotation are examples. Although in principle someone could write a shell that provided the functionality of these facilities differently or not at all, no one has and no one is likely to.

All shells now in common use are descendents of the Bourne shell, the earliest major UNIX shell. The Bourne shell was written by Steve Bourne in 1979 and was part of Seventh Edition UNIX. Important features provided by the Bourne shell and carried over by its descendents include the following:

- Interpretation of shell scripts.

- Operators for background or conditional execution of commands.

- Statements for repeated execution of commands, including iteration over a sequence of values that can be assigned to an iteration variable.

- Positional, special, and named parameters. Positional parameters contain the arguments to a command, while named parameters act as variables.

- Export of specified variables to child processes.

- Three forms of quotation.

- Substitution of the output of a command into the text of another command.

- Execution of commands in subshells.

- Automatic notification when mail arrives.

- Inclusion of input data for a command in a shell script as part of the script.

- Trapping of signals and execution of specified commands when a specified signal occurs.

- Execution of commands in initialization files before any input is read. These initialization files can be used to customize `sh`.

The Bourne shell is now mostly of historical interest. Any modern UNIX system is sure to include a better shell for interactive use, whether the KornShell, Bash, or the C shell. These newer shells provide conveniences such as command-line editing, recall of previously issued commands, and aliases for often-used commands that the Bourne shell lacks. A modern system should also include a POSIX-compliant shell suitable for interpreting most Bourne shell scripts. The Bourne shell remains useful only as the interpreter of ancient shell scripts whose peculiarities are incompatible with the POSIX shell.

In this chapter we discuss the KornShell, a generally POSIX-compliant extension of the Bourne shell that is also known by its program name, `ksh`. In this discussion we refer to "the shell" when discussing POSIX-compliant features of the KornShell and to `ksh` when discussing KornShell extensions not included in POSIX. In the next chapter we discuss two other shells more briefly, the C shell and Bash, outlining how they differ from the KornShell.

6.1   Overview of the KornShell

The KornShell, `ksh`, was designed as a compatible extension of the Bourne shell, adding features of the C shell as well as a number of useful additions of its own. It was developed by David Korn at AT&T Bell Laboratories in 1982, with major improvements released in 1986, 1988, and 1993. The KornShell is included as a standard feature of System V Release 4 and of some other systems. It can also be purchased separately.

These are the principal features adopted from the C shell:

- History lists for retrieval of previous commands.
- Job control, with the ability to move specific jobs to the foreground or background.
- Aliases for command names.
- Use of '~' to denote the home directory of the current user or, when combined with a user name, of another user.
- Ability to compute general numerical expressions and assign the result of the computation to a variable.

These are some of the features new to `ksh`:

- Interactive editing of the command line, including file name completion and the ability to edit the history list.
- Improved function definitions that provide local variables and the ability to write recursive functions.
- Extended pattern matching for file names and other constructs, similar to that provided by extended regular expressions.
- Ability to extract the portion of a string specified by a pattern.
- Ability to switch easily between two directories.

Relation to the Bourne Shell.   Almost any shell script written for the Bourne shell will also run under the KornShell. Although some Bourne shell constructs are interpreted differently, these constructs usually arise only in obscure cases. Unfortunately, a few of these cases still arise in distributed shell scripts, which is why the Bourne shell is still sometimes needed for interpreting elderly scripts.[1]

Relation to the POSIX Shell.   The POSIX shell, named `sh` in the POSIX standard, is a subset of the KornShell. In fact, the POSIX Committee used the KornShell as its primary model when formulating the POSIX shell. A shell script that is valid according to POSIX should usually behave identically when run under a modern edition of `ksh`, but some features of the KornShell are not included in the POSIX shell. We generally note these in our description.[2]

---

1. Some old Bourne shell scripts use the construct '$(*text*)' in place of the parameter expansion '${*text*}', which conflicts with its POSIX use for command substitution, or use the `echo` utility in incompatible ways. If you have access to the script, you can easily repair it by replacing the parentheses by braces in the first construct and by replacing uses of `echo` by uses of `printf` in the second.

2. While writing this book, we observed some minor deviations from the POSIX standard in the behavior of the `ksh` implementations available to us. These are likely to be corrected in the future.

6.2   Interacting with the Shell

You can run the shell either interactively or noninteractively. In interactive mode, the shell reads input from your terminal and writes output to your terminal; in noninteractive mode, it reads input from a file and writes output to a file.

Input to the shell consists of a sequence of commands. A command may be continued over several input lines and may include input of its own. When the shell is running interactively and expecting input, it displays a prompt: the primary prompt string ('$' by default) when it's expecting a new command and the secondary prompt string ('>' by default) when it's expecting a command continuation. You can change these prompt strings by assigning other values to the variables PS1 and PS2 (see p. 371).

When you're working with the shell interactively, you can edit a command line with an editor built into the shell before you send the command line to the shell for execution. Ksh provides two such built-in editors, one based on vi and the other based on emacs (see Section 6.3). Only the one based on vi is included in POSIX.

6.2.1
Quick Exit

You can interrupt most commands executing under control of the shell by pressing ⟨Intr⟩. A few commands, however, take control of the keyboard and assign their own interpretation to the ⟨Intr⟩ key; for one of those, you'll have to consult the command's description to see how to interrupt it. When you interrupt a command, the shell returns you to its command level and prompts you for another command. You then can exit from the shell by typing either ⟨EOF⟩ or exit.

6.2.2
Running as a
Restricted Shell

Ksh is able to run as a restricted shell, limiting its user to a small, well-understood set of capabilities. This mode is useful for allowing a system to accept logins from unknown or untrustworthy sources.[3] Restricted operation is not included in POSIX.

An invocation of ksh becomes restricted if it is initiated in any of the following ways:

- By a call on ksh with the -r option.

- By a call on ksh when the SHELL environment variable exists and has as its value a pathname whose filename is rsh, rksh, or krsh.

---

3. The restricted mode of the Bourne shell did not live up to its billing since its implementation was not totally secure. We are uncertain as to how secure the restricted mode of the KornShell is.

In restricted mode, the following actions are disallowed:

- Changing the current directory.
- Assigning a value to the PATH, ENV, or SHELL variable.
- Specifying a path name or a command name containing '/' (i.e., one that might not be in the current directory).
- Redirecting output with '>', '>>', '>|', or '<>'.

These restrictions don't apply while the `.profile` initialization file is being executed, nor while the file (if any) defined by the ENV variable (see p. 373) is being executed. Thus the author of `.profile` (which resides in the user's home directory) can perform whatever actions are necessary to set up a controlled environment for the user. Usually these actions include changing the current directory so as to deny the user access to `.profile`, although setting the permissions on `.profile` appropriately can often achieve the same effect. Since the ENV file is available, the user has a convenient way to do other initializations.

6.3   Editing an Input Line

You can edit an input line before you pass it to the shell for execution. Ksh provides two built-in editors for that purpose, emacs and vi. (A third editor, gmacs, differs from emacs only in the interpretation of one editing directive.) These editors enable you to edit any part of a line after you've typed it and to retrieve previously executed commands from the command history (see Section 6.21). An important difference between the editors is that emacs operates on single lines, while vi operates on entire commands. The names emacs and vi should not be taken too literally, since the editing directives differ in detail from the corresponding directives in true Emacs and vi, and some of the ksh editing directives are not present in Emacs and vi at all.

Nevertheless, if you're familiar with Emacs or vi, you'll find it easy to use the corresponding ksh editor. Since we describe both Emacs and vi elsewhere in this book, we just list the ksh editing directives and point out the major differences between the ksh editors and their full-bore counterparts.

Only the vi built-in shell editor is supported by POSIX.

6.3.1
Choosing the Editor

You can activate a shell built-in editor in either of two ways:

- You can issue the command

      set -o *editor*

where *editor* is either emacs, gmacs, or vi (only vi under POSIX).

- You can set either or both of the variables EDITOR and VISUAL to a pathname '... /*editor*'. The assignment of a value to those variables activates the editor *editor*. If they are assigned differently, VISUAL determines the choice.[4] This interpretation of EDITOR and VISUAL is not included in POSIX.

You can deactivate all command-line editing by issuing the command

  set +o *editor*

where *editor* is the current editor.

6.3.2
The emacs Editor

The editing directives provided by the emacs editor are listed in Figure 6-1. Note the following additional points:

- If an editing key also has a meaning as a control key, the control-key meaning takes precedence. For example, if (Ctrl)C is your interrupt key, it will act that way rather than as a capitalization key. The two keys for which that question is likely to arise are (Ctrl)C and (Ctrl)U.

- The (Esc)*n*(Ctrl)K directive does not cause (Ctrl)K to operate on *n* lines. Instead, if the cursor is at or to the right of column *n*, it deletes the characters between the cursor and column *n*, including the endpoints; otherwise, it deletes the characters between the cursor and column *n*, excluding the endpoints.[5]

- The (Esc)p directive saves the region in a buffer and destroys the previous contents of that buffer, so there is nothing corresponding to the Emacs mark ring.

- The gmacs version of (Ctrl)T transposes the two previous characters rather than the current and next character. Neither version agrees exactly with what (Ctrl)T does under true Emacs.

- The use of (Ctrl)C for changing characters to uppercase is unrelated to its use in true Emacs. There is no emacs directive for changing characters to lowercase.

- The (Ctrl)C command moves the cursor one character to the right, while the (Esc)c and (Esc)l commands move it one word to the right.

- Each of the (EOF) and (Ctrl)D directives generates an end-of-file if it is the first character typed on a line. Otherwise, the character has its usual effect. The (EOF) character is determined by your stty settings (see "Viewing the Control Character Assignments" on p. 19). The ignoreeof option (see p. 376) prevents a typed (EOF) from causing the shell to exit.

---

4. Unsetting these variables or assigning them meaningless values has no effect on which editor is active.

5. This is the behavior we've observed; the description in Korn and Bolsky's book treats the endpoints differently.

Key	Description
Ctrl F	Moves cursor right one character
Ctrl B	Moves cursor left one character
Esc f	Moves cursor right one word
Esc b	Moves cursor left one word
Ctrl A	Moves cursor to start of line
Ctrl E	Moves cursor to end of line
Ctrl] *c*	Moves cursor to next character *c*
Erase	Deletes the preceding character
Ctrl K	Deletes to end of line
Esc *n* Ctrl K	Deletes between *n*th character and cursor
Ctrl D	Deletes one character, or signals end-of-file
Esc d	Deletes one word forward
Esc Ctrl H	Deletes one word backward
Esc Ctrl ?	Deletes one word backward
Ctrl W	Deletes from cursor to mark
Esc Space	Sets mark to cursor
Ctrl X Ctrl X	Exchanges mark and cursor
Esc p	Selects region, saves it in buffer
Ctrl Y	Retrieves text from buffer
Ctrl T	Transposes current and next characters
Ctrl C	Changes one character to uppercase
Esc c	Changes one word to uppercase
Esc l	Changes one word to lowercase
Ctrl L	Redisplays current line
EOF	Signals end-of-file or inserts character
Ctrl J	Executes the current line
Enter	Executes the current line
Ctrl M	Executes the current line
Esc =	Lists pathnames matching current word plus *
Esc Esc	Completes pathname
Esc *	Expands current word plus * to pathnames
Ctrl U	Multiplies count of next directive by 4
Ctrl V	Displays version date of the shell
Esc *l*	Inserts value of _*l* alias into input
Esc .	Inserts last word of previous **ksh** command
Esc _	Inserts last word of previous **ksh** command
Ctrl P	Fetches previous line in history list
Esc <	Fetches oldest line in history list
Esc >	Fetches most recent line in history list
Ctrl N	Moves down one item in **ksh** history
[Esc O] Ctrl R [*string*] Enter	Searches history list for a line containing *string*
[Esc O] Ctrl R ^ [*string*] Enter	Searches history list for a line beginning with *string*
Ctrl O	Processes current line, fetches next line from history list

Notes:

(1) Motion and deletion directives, as well as Ctrl P , can be preceded by Esc *n* to cause them to operate on *n* units.

(2) You cannot use Meta *x* in place of Esc *x*.

(3) For editing purposes, a word consists of a sequence of letters, digits, and underscores.

Fig. 6-1. Editing directives for **emacs** mode.

- The Esc Esc directive appends characters to the word under the cursor, attempting to complete the pathname of an existing file. Characters are appended up to the point where there is a unique completion. If a complete pathname results, the editor appends a slash if the pathname designates a directory and a space otherwise.

- The (Esc) * directive generates all pathnames matching the pattern '*word**', where *word* is the word under the cursor. If several pathnames match, they are separated by spaces.

- Unlike true Emacs, you cannot provide a number *n* after the (Ctrl) U directive to cause a directive to be repeated *n* times.

- If you define an alias for _*c*, where *c* is a letter, then typing (Esc) *c* causes the value of the alias to be inserted into the input. Generally, *c* should be an uppercase letter since (Esc) *c* for certain lowercase letters already has a meaning.

- The (Ctrl) R command, which fetches matching lines from the command history, has several variants:

  - If you omit *string*, the most recent value of *string* is reused.
  - If you specify both (Esc) 0 and *string*, the search goes forward through the command history.
  - If you specify neither (Esc) 0 nor *string*, the search goes in the same direction as the previous search.
  - If you specify (Esc) 0 but not *string*, the search goes in the opposite direction from the previous search.
  - If you specify *string* but not (Esc) 0, the search goes backward through the command history.
  - Prefixing *string* by a hat requires *string* to be found at the beginning of a line.

- Since the (Ctrl) 0 directive processes a line and then fetches the following line from the command history, it is useful for editing a multiline command.

6.3.3
The vi Editor

Like the true vi, the vi editor provided by the shell has two modes: input mode and command mode. Editing directives that require input take you into input mode; you end the input and get back to command mode by typing (Esc). Unlike the true vi, the editor starts in input mode rather than in command mode.

When in input mode, the editor can be instructed to use either character input or line input. For character input, each character is interpreted as you type it, just as with the true vi editor. In line input, the editor absorbs input up to the next (Esc) or (Enter) before interpreting any part of that input. Since character input is functionally superior to line input in every way, you should use line input only when you are working over a slow phone line. However, character input isn't the default; to activate it, you need to issue the command

```
set -o viraw
```

which sets the viraw execution option. (You still must select vi as your editor explicitly; viraw merely modifies the way that vi works.) When in command mode, the editor always assumes character input. POSIX leaves it up to the implementation to choose between character input and line input and does not include the viraw option.

The following directives apply to input mode:

(Erase)	Deletes the previous character
(Kill)	Deletes the entire line, goes to the character after the prompt
(Ctrl) V	Causes the next character to be taken literally
\	Causes the next (Erase) or (Kill) to be taken literally, otherwise just \
(EOF)	Signals end-of-file or acts as a normal character
(Ctrl) W	Deletes the previous word

The following directives apply to command mode:

(Enter)	Executes the current line
(Ctrl) L	Redisplays current line
#	Inserts # at beginning of line to make the line a comment
=	Lists pathnames matching current word plus *
\	Completes pathname by extending current Word
*	Expands current Word plus * to pathnames
@c	Inserts value of _l alias into input
[n]~	Reverses the case of the next n characters
[n].	Repeats the most recent modifying directive n times
[n]v	Returns a command that calls the true **vi** with the nth command in the history list
[n]l	Moves cursor right n characters
[n] (Space)	Moves cursor right n characters
[n]h	Moves cursor left n characters
[n]w	Moves cursor right to the start of the nth word
[n]W	Moves cursor right to the start of the nth Word
[n]e	Moves cursor right to the end of the nth word
[n]E	Moves cursor right to the end of the nth Word
[n]b	Moves cursor left to the start of the nth preceding word
[n]B	Moves cursor left to the start of the nth preceding Word
^	Moves cursor left to the first non-whitespace character on the line
0	Moves cursor left to the first character on the line
$	Moves cursor right to the last character on the line
[n]|	Moves cursor to the nth character on the line
[n]fc	Moves cursor right to the nth next occurrence of character c
[n]Fc	Moves cursor left to the nth previous occurrence of character c
[n]tc	Moves cursor right to just before the nth next occurrence of character c
[n]Tc	Moves cursor left to just after the nth next occurrence of character c
[n];	Repeats most recent f, F, t, or T n times
[n],	Repeats most recent f, F, t, or T n times, but in the other direction
a	Appends text at right of cursor

Fig. 6-2, Part 1. Editing directives for **vi** mode.

The editing directives provided by the **vi** editor are listed in Figure 6-2. Note the following additional points:

- A word is a sequence of letters and digits delimited by ⟨newline⟩, space, ⟨tab⟩, or a punctuation mark. A sequence of punctuation marks counts as a single word.

- A Word is a sequence of non-whitespace characters delimited by whitespace characters.

- A command can comprise more than one line, but for editing purposes it appears as a single line with the shell-level lines separated by '^J'.

- The (EOF) directive generates an end-of-file if it is the first character typed on a line. Otherwise, the character has its usual effect.

A	Appends text at end of line
i	Inserts text at left of cursor
I	Inserts text to left of first non-whitespace character on line
R	Replaces text by overwriting
c*n m*	Changes characters between cursor and *n m* by new text
C	Deletes to end of line and inserts text
S	Deletes entire line and inserts text
[*n*]r*c*	Replaces *n* characters with character *c*
[*n*]_	Appends *n*th last Word from previous shell input, then inserts text
[*n*]x	Deletes *n* characters from cursor going right
[*n*]X	Deletes *n* characters from cursor going left
d*n m*	Deletes characters between cursor and *n m*
D	Deletes to end of line
dd	Deletes entire line
y*n m*	Yanks characters between cursor and *n m* to the region buffer, leaving the line unchanged
Y	Yanks characters to end of line to the region buffer, leaving the line unchanged
yy	Yanks entire line to the region buffer, leaving the line unchanged
[*n*]p	Puts *n* copies of region buffer to right of cursor
[*n*]P	Puts *n* copies of region buffer to left of cursor
u	Undoes the previous text modification
U	Undoes all modifications to current line
[*n*]k	Fetches *n*th previous shell command
[*n*]-	Fetches *n*th previous shell command
[*n*]j	Fetches *n*th next shell command
[*n*]+	Fetches *n*th next shell command
*n*G	Fetches *n*th command from command history
G	Fetches oldest command from command history
/*string*	Searches backward through command history for *string*
/^*string*	Searches backward through command history for *string* at start of line
?*string*	Searches forward through command history for *string*
?^*string*	Searches forward through command history for *string* at start of line
n	Repeats most recent / or ? directive
N	Repeats most recent / or ? directive but in the other direction

Notes:

(1) The default for *n* is 1.

(2) For the directives c*n m*, d*n m*, and y*n m*, *n* is a count and *m* is a motion in the vi sense. These directives can also be written as *n*c*m*, *n*d*m*, and *n*y*m*, respectively.

Fig. 6-2, Part 2.   Editing directives for vi mode.

The (EOF) character is determined by your stty settings (see "Viewing the Control Character Assignments" on p. 19). The ignoreeof option (see p. 376) prevents a typed (EOF) from causing the shell to exit.

- The '#' directive is useful for inserting comments into the history list.

- Without a preceding count, the v command calls the true vi with the line you're currently editing as input file. With a preceding count, it takes the *n*th command in the history list as its input file. When you're done editing with true vi, the new contents of the edited file are executed as shell commands. It's possible to turn one input command into several output commands.

- The '\' directive appends characters to the Word under the cursor, attempting to complete the pathname of an existing file. Characters

      are appended up to the point where there is a unique completion.
If a complete pathname results, the editor appends a slash if the
pathname designates a directory, and a space otherwise.

- The '*' directive generates all pathnames matching the pattern
  '*word**', where *word* is the Word under the cursor. If several pathnames match, they are separated by spaces.

- If you define an alias for _*c*, where *c* is a letter, then the @*c* directive
  causes the value of the alias to be inserted into the input.

- The directives such as G and k that fetch lines from the history file
  operate analogously to how they operate on the input buffer in
  true vi.

6.4   Calling the Shell Directly

You can call the shell directly as you would any other command. Unfortunately, the forms for calling ksh and calling a POSIX shell are slightly
different.[6] In either case, you can specify options for the shell when you
invoke it and modify most of them later with the set command (p. 367).

6.4.1
Calling ksh

The form of the command line for calling ksh is

```
ksh [{+|-}Caefhimnoprstuvx] [{+|-}o option]...
    [-c cmds] [arg ... ]
```

You can specify on the command line that an option should be disabled
rather than enabled by replacing its '-' with a '+'. The -v and -x options
are particularly useful for debugging shell scripts.

    Options that can be changed with set are described in Section 6.24.
The following additional options are available only when ksh is invoked:

-c *cmds* Cause ksh to use *cmds* as its input. For example, the call

```
ksh -c 'hem; haw'
```

causes a new ksh process to be initiated that sequentially executes the two commands hem and haw. If *cmds* contains any
commands that operate on standard input or standard output,
those commands use the file descriptors in effect at the point
where ksh was invoked. In particular, if you call ksh with -c
from your terminal to execute *cmds*, any commands in *cmds*
that read standard input read from your terminal and similarly
for standard output.

---

6. If your version of ksh is truly POSIX-conformant, however, it will honor the POSIX
forms.

-s   Cause ksh to read its input from standard input and write its
            own output to standard error (file descriptor 2). Any argu-
            ments on the command line become parameters to ksh. This
            option is set by default if you do not specify -c and do not
            specify any arguments *arg* . . . .

-i   Cause ksh to expect its input to be interactive. This option
            affects the handling of certain signals in ksh (see "Signals and
            Their Codes" on p. 31):

   • SIGTERM and SIGQUIT are ignored.
   • SIGINT is caught but then ignored, so it can be used to
     interrupt a wait.

-r   Invoke ksh in restricted mode (see Section 6.2.2).

6.4.2
Calling a
POSIX Shell

The forms of the command line for calling a POSIX shell are[7]

    sh [-Cabefimnuvx] [-o *option*] . . . [*cmdfile* [*arg* . . .]]
    sh -c [-Cabefimnuvx] [-o *option*] . . . *cmdlist* [*cmdname* [*arg* . . .]]
    sh -s [-Cabefimnuvx] [-o *option*] . . . [*arg* . . .]

On some systems sh is a synonym for ksh, in which case the ksh conventions apply.

   • The first form treats *cmdfile* as the pathname of a file containing
     commands to be read and executed. The file need not have its
     execute permission set. If the pathname contains no slashes and
     cmdfile isn't in the current directory either, the shell uses PATH to
     locate it. (In this case, it must have execute permission.)

   • The second form uses the -c option as described for ksh, except that
     the positional parameter $0 is set to *cmdname*. If *cmdname* is not
     provided, $0 is set to the name under which sh was called.

   • The third form has the same meaning as for ksh.

In all cases when *arg* . . . are supplied, the positional parameters $1, $2, . . .
are set to *arg* . . . in sequence in the environment where the shell commands
are executed.

6.5   Shell Scripts

A *shell script*, also called a *shell procedure*, enables you to customize your
environment by adding your own commands. Although writing a shell

---

7. The POSIX standard does not provide for multiple occurrences of -o, but we believe
that to be an error.

script does call for some simple programming, it's far easier than writing a C program.

Short shell scripts are easy to compose and install. For instance, suppose you wish to define a `dir` command that produces a nicer directory listing than the one you get by default. We assume that you use a `bin` subdirectory of your home directory for storing your personal collection of programs and shell scripts and that this directory is on your search path (see the discussion of `PATH` in Section 2.9.2). You can create such a `dir` command for yourself by typing

```
cat >~/bin/dir
ls -aCF $@
EOF
chmod +rx ~/bin/dir
```

Here the `cat` line copies the second line to the `dir` file; the `ls` line defines the meaning of `dir`; and the `chmod` line makes the `dir` file executable (a precondition to executing a shell script).[8]

Once you've created this command, you obtain your improved listing by typing `dir` followed by a set of file and directory names. The names can include wildcards. The command also works if you type `dir` by itself; in this case, you get the contents of the current directory. A more elaborate version of `dir` might, for example, recognize a variety of options. This particular example can actually be implemented more conveniently using an alias (see Section 6.19), but it nevertheless illustrates the method.

Note: If you use functions within a shell script, each function must be defined before it is actually called. That can lead to an unnatural ordering of the code in which the highest-level functions come last. For a more natural ordering, define a function `main` (local to the script) that handles the top-level actions. Then, at the very end of the script, insert a call on `main`. With this method you can order the functions in whatever way makes the code most transparent.

Interpretation of Shell Scripts. When the shell encounters a command that is not intrinsic (i.e., not recognized and executed directly by the shell itself), the shell calls upon the kernel to execute that command. The command can be either a compiled program or a shell script. If it is a shell script, the kernel must then select a shell to execute the script.

How the kernel makes that selection depends on your system. The default case is usually a POSIX-compliant shell if one is available, otherwise some version of the Bourne shell. Bourne-shell compatibility, which POSIX-compliant shells provide, is essential because, historically, the Bourne shell was the only shell available in the Seventh Edition. Many older shell scripts in common use assume without any explicit indication that they are being interpreted by the Bourne shell.

---

8. A shell script must have read permission as well, but a newly created file normally has read permission by default.

Modern systems honor the convention that if the first line of a shell script has the form

```
#! shell
```

where *shell* is the full path name of a shell, that shell is used to interpret the script. The whitespace after '#!' is optional. For instance, if you write a script using the C shell command set, it should start with

```
#! /bin/csh
```

In fact, you can cause a script to be interpreted by any program at all. For instance, suppose you issue a command naming an executable file whose first line is

```
#!/home/sybil/read.entrails
```

Then the `read.entrails` program in `sybil`'s home directory is given control with the executable file as its input. Naturally, `read.entrails` must be clever enough to recognize the first line as a comment and ignore it.

The shell provides a `-v` option for displaying each input line as it is read and an `-x` option for displaying each command as it is executed. These options are very useful for debugging shell scripts.

6.6   Syntax of Shell Input

The shell processes its input in two stages. First it decomposes its input into a sequence of tokens, a token being a sequence of characters that the shell treats as an elementary syntactic unit. Then it organizes the tokens into commands and their continuations.

There are two kinds of tokens: words and operators. A word is defined by its boundaries: a word is a sequence of characters delimited on each end by a separator character (space, ⟨tab⟩, or ⟨newline⟩) or by an operator. The operators are

```
>   >>   >&  >|   <   <<   <<-   <&   <>
|   &   ;   (  )   ||   &&   ;;   ((  ))   |&
```

The operators on the first line are redirection operators, which can be preceded by a single digit. The digit is part of the operator but must be preceded by a separator, so 'elijah2>' is parsed as the word 'elijah2' followed by the operator '>', while 'elijah␣2>' is parsed as the word 'elijah' followed by the operator '2>'. A double-character operator such as '&&' must be written without an intervening space to distinguish it from two '&' operators in a row.

The effect of a ⟨newline⟩, which you produce by pressing ⟨Enter⟩ on most keyboards, depends on the contents of the line:

(1)   If the line satisfies the syntax of a complete command, the ⟨newline⟩ ends the command (and is equivalent to a semicolon; see below).

(2)   If the line contains no words, the line and the ⟨newline⟩ are ignored.

(3)   Otherwise, the ⟨newline⟩ is ignored and the next line is taken as a continuation of the current line.

In any event, a ⟨newline⟩ acts as a separator in that it ends a word.

6.6.1 Effects of Quotation

The rules for parsing tokens must be modified to account for quotation (see Section 6.17). A character that normally acts as a separator does not act as a separator if quoted. In particular, a quoted blank does not separate words and a quoted ⟨newline⟩ does not end a command. Furthermore, a quotation (either with single or double quotes) acts as a single word or, if immediately adjacent to a word, as part of a word. Thus a quotation immediately following a word (with no separator between) extends the word with the quoted characters, and two successive quotations combine to form a single word. For example, the text

```
abc'$$'de\$fg
```

represents the single word

```
abc$$de$fg
```

6.6.2 Effects of Substitutions

The shell provides three forms of substitution: command substitution (using either of two notations), parameter expansion, and arithmetic evaluation (see Section 6.18). Each of these forms, after evaluation, yields a sequence of characters. These characters are then treated as though they had appeared in the original input. In particular, separators and operators within the evaluated forms have their usual meanings.

Substitutions can be nested within each other and within quotations. Nested forms are interpreted recursively from the inside out (see Section 6.18.3). However, quotation is taken into account in determining where the substitutions are. In other words, a substitution is considered only if the characters that define it aren't already quoted.

6.6.3 Comments

Input to the shell can include comments. A comment starts with a '#' at the beginning of a word and extends to the end of the line. A '#' in the middle of a word does *not* start a comment. The shell ignores anything in a comment. For example, the input

```
echo Greetings from the under#world
#and points beyond
```

produces the output

```
Greetings from the under#world
```

Comments are primarily useful in shell scripts.

6.7   Patterns

The shell provides a generalization of the wildcard notation for pathnames described in Section 2.9.1. This generalization, not included in POSIX, provides the power of regular expression matching, albeit with a slightly different notation. The primitive patterns are the same ones provided by POSIX wildcards:

[...]   A single character matching a bracket expression.[9]

?   An arbitrary single character.

*   An arbitrary, possibly empty, sequence of characters.

The additional patterns are combinations formed as follows:

?(*pat*[|*pat* ...])
           Matches zero or one occurrence of any of the patterns *pat*.

*(*pat*[|*pat* ...])
           Matches zero or more occurrences of any of the patterns *pat*.

+(*pat*[|*pat* ...])
           Matches one or more occurrences of any of the patterns *pat*.

@(*pat*[|*pat* ...])
           Matches a single occurrence of one of the patterns *pat*.

!(*pat*[|*pat* ...])
           Matches any string not matched by one of the patterns *pat*.

For example, the pattern `*.@(gz|taz|z|Z)` matches any pathname ending in '`.gz`', '`.taz`', '`.z`', or '`.Z`'.

6.8   Simple Commands

A *simple command* is either an intrinsic command or a program call. Intrinsic commands are discussed in Section 6.22. Syntactically, a simple command consists of a sequence of words, none of which are among the operators listed below in Section 6.9 or among the keywords listed on page 335. The shell takes the first word as the name of the command and the remaining words as its arguments.

---

9. As noted in Section 2.9.1, there is one anomaly here: a collating element such as '`[.ch.]`' matches two characters, not one.

A program call causes the program to be executed. A program call can be preceded by one or more assignments to variables.[10]   These assignments apply to the environment of the subshell created by the command (see Section 6.15.3) but do not affect any local variables (see Section 6.15.2). For instance, if you type

```
OPS="+-" recalc
```

the `recalc` program (or shell script) is executed with the environment variable OPS set to '+-'. If a local variable OPS exists, it is unaffected; if it does not exist, it is not created.

6.8.1
Interpretation of Command Names

When you type the name of a command *cmd*, the shell determines how *cmd* is to be interpreted by checking the following sequence of possibilities:

(1)   Is *cmd* one of the reserved words

```
!         elif    fi      in       while
case      else    for     then     {
do        esac    if      until    }
done
```

If so, the reserved word defines the interpretation of *cmd*.

(2)   Is *cmd* an unquoted alias? If *cmd* is quoted in any way, then alias testing is not done, so an easy way to cancel the effect of an alias is to put a backslash in front of it. Otherwise, *cmd* is checked to see if it is defined as an alias (see Section 6.19). Ksh also checks for tracked aliases (see Section 6.19.4) at this point, though tracked aliases are not supported by POSIX.

If *cmd* is defined as an alias, the alias is expanded to its defined value *str*. If *str* ends in whitespace, then the next word is also checked for alias substitution, and this process is continued until it no longer applies. After alias substitution, the same sequence of possibilities is rechecked, so it's possible for an alias to expand to a reserved word.

If at any point in alias expansion a name arises that is already being checked for alias expansion, that name is not expanded further. This rule prevents recursive aliasing from creating an infinite loop.

(3)   Is *cmd* one of the special intrinsic commands built into the shell? For a POSIX-conformant shell, those commands are

```
break              exec           set
: (null utility)   exit           shift
continue           export         trap
. file             readonly       unset
eval               return
```

---

10. For compatibility with the Bourne shell, ksh provides a `keyword` option. If this option is set, a word within a simple command that has the form of an assignment is treated as an assignment even if it doesn't precede the command name. You should shun this option unless you really need it.

(4) Is *cmd* a function defined from within the shell by a function definition command? (The shell has a facility for local function definitions.)[11]

(5) Is *cmd* one of the built-in utilities? The built-in utilities are

alias	fg	true
bg	getopts	umask
cd	jobs	unalias
command	kill	wait
false	newgrp	
fc	read	

(6) Is *cmd* some other utility built into the shell?

(7) Is *cmd* the absolute pathname of an executable program? Since an absolute pathname starts with a slash, this possibility excludes all others.

(8) Is *cmd* the name of an executable program that can be found via a search of the directories in the PATH environment variable (see Section 2.9.2)?

If none of these questions can be answered positively, then the command is undefined.

These rules have certain important properties:

- It doesn't matter whether a standard utility is implemented as a freestanding program, a shell script, or a function built into your particular shell implementation. The effect of calling it and the interpretation of its name are the same.

- You can override the interpretation of any standard utility other than one of the special shell built-in utilities of Case (3) by defining a shell function of the same name. You can always access the standard interpretation as a utility by calling the command function (see Section 5.10.1).

Autoloading Function Definitions in ksh.   Ksh provides two ways to import a function definition from a file. First, you can use the dot command (see p. 363) to load the definition explicitly, possibly along with several others. Second, you can predefine the function with typeset (see p. 365) and arrange for it to be loaded when it is first called, thus saving the computational resources needed to load and store function definitions that are never used.

A function predefined in this way is said to be *autoloaded*. For example, to autoload the function bogify, issue the command

```
typeset -fu bogify
```

---

11. As a user you can define local shell functions, but your system may also predefine standard POSIX commands as functions too. Such system functions are not considered in this step.

Ordinarily, commands like this one are included in your shell initialization files (see Section 6.25). When `bogify` is first called, `ksh` searches the paths given in the `FPATH` variable for a file named `bogify`, which must exist and must contain a function definition for `bogify`. Ksh then reads the file, executes its contents in the current environment (which causes the definition of `bogify` to be remembered), and executes the actual call on `bogify`. POSIX does not support autoloading.

Note: When `ksh` reads a file as a result of autoloading, it reads and executes the entire contents of the file, not just the function definition you were referencing. You can utilize this behavior to load a library of function definitions as soon as any member of the library is referenced. To do that, use the `ln` command (see Section 3.4.1) to create links (either hard or symbolic) to the file from each function name in the library. For instance, if the file `bogify` also contains a function `exhume`, you could execute the command '`ln bogify exhume`' to create the link and cause both `bogify` and `exhume` to be loaded as soon as one of them is called.

Attributes of Defined Functions. You can use the `typeset` command (see p. 365) to specify attributes of defined functions. The particular form to use is

> `typeset {+|-}f[tux] [`*name* ... `]`

If you specify attributes, then the hyphen turns them on and the plus sign turns them off. If you don't specify attributes, then `typeset` lists the function definitions for *name* ... , or all function definitions if no *name*s are specified. If you use the form '`-f`", both names and definitions are produced; if you use '`+f`', then only the names are produced.

The following attributes apply to this form of `typeset`:

t
: Turn tracing on or off. Using `typeset` with this option is equivalent to setting or unsetting the `xtrace` option with `set`.

u
: Autoload this function on first use as described above.

x
: Export this function to indirectly executed shell scripts. Without this option, a function is not visible within an indirectly executed shell script.

Note: These attributes have different meanings when they are specified for variables.

Portability Problems with Intrinsic Commands. Non-POSIX shells such as the Bourne shell and the C shell often treat every command built into the shell as intrinsic. A POSIX shell, on the other hand, uses the fixed list of intrinsic commands given on page 323. For example, a non-POSIX shell might treat the `cd` command as intrinsic even though it isn't on the POSIX list. If you define your own version of `cd`, either as a function or as a program, the intrinsic command `cd` will still be called instead of your own version. Consequently, it's not possible to write portable scripts for non-POSIX shells that override system utilities with new functions of the same name.

**6.8.2
Executing a Utility in
a Modified
Environment
with** env

The env utility executes a utility in an environment with modified values of the environment variables. The form of the env command line is

> env [-i] [*name=value*] ... [*cmd* [*arg* ...]]

In the obsolescent form, the -i is written as '-'. The env utility obtains the current shell environment, modifies it by performing the indicated assignments, and then executes the utility *cmd* in the modified environment. If you specify -i, the inherited environment is ignored and *cmd* is executed in an environment containing only the variables you've specified. If no utility *cmd* is specified, the environment as modified by the assignments is produced on standard output. In particular, if you type env by itself, you see your current environment.

Issuing the command

> env *name=value* ... *cmd* [*arg* ...]

is equivalent to issuing the command

> *name=value* ... *cmd* [*arg* ...]

The value of env comes from its ability to display the environment and to limit the environment with the -i option.

Example.   The command line

> env -i PATH=~/bin myproc hobbits

executes the program myproc in an environment in which the only variable available is PATH and the value of PATH is ~/bin.

6.9   Linking Commands with Operators

The shell provides several operators for executing commands either sequentially or in parallel and for connecting the standard output of one command to the standard input of its successor. We first explain what each operator does, assuming that just one operator is being used at a time. We then explain what operator combinations do.

| The '|' operator connects two commands through a *pipe*. The standard output of the first command becomes the standard input of the second. A group of one or more commands connected this way is called a *pipeline*. For example, the pipeline

> ps | sort | lp

causes the output of ps (see Section 5.2.1) to become the input of sort (see Section 4.1) and the output of sort to become the input of lp (see Section 3.7.1). The result is that a sorted list of the currently active processes is sent to the printer. The shell implements a pipeline as a set of processes, one for each command in the pipeline.

|| If c_1 and c_2 are commands, the combination '$c_1 || c_2$' first executes c_1. If the exit status of c_1 is nonzero (see Section 2.6.2), c_2 is executed. A nonzero exit status usually indicates unsuccessful execution. In other words, c_2 is executed only if c_1 fails.

&&   The '&&' operator is like '||' except that it tests for successful execution rather than unsuccessful execution. If c_1 and c_2 are commands, the combination '$c_1 && c_2$' first executes c_1. If the exit status of c_1 is zero, c_2 is executed. In other words, c_2 is executed only if c_1 succeeds.

;   A semicolon marks the end of a command. When the shell sees a semicolon after a command, it executes that command and goes on to the next one. Thus the sequence 'c_1; c_2' has the effect of "execute c_1, then execute c_2". For example,

```
ls; who
```

causes the command `ls` to be executed, followed by the command `who`. A ⟨newline⟩ is equivalent to a semicolon in any context where a semicolon is permitted (see Section 6.6).

&   An ampersand specifies that the preceding command is to be executed as a background process. When the shell sees an ampersand after a command, it initiates the background process and proceeds immediately to the next command, if any. In other words, the sequence 'c_1 & c_2' has the effect of "start c_1 executing in the background, then execute c_2", while the sequence 'c &' has the effect of "execute c in the background". For example, the input line

```
devour & engulf
```

causes the command `devour` to be executed as a background process. As soon as the shell has started this process, it starts executing the `engulf` command. As another example, the input line

```
sort < elephantine > humongous &
```

causes the shell to start a time-consuming sort in the background and prompt you for another command.

     The shell executes a background command in a subshell (see Section 6.14), displaying the subshell's process number in brackets. Some uses of background execution are described in Section 6.9.2.

|&   The |& operator specifies that the preceding command is to be run as a coprocess (see Section 6.9.3). The coprocess executes

in the background, but its standard input and output can be accessed at any time. This operator is not included in POSIX.

When two commands are combined with an operator, the exit status of the combination is that of the second command. A command executed in the background returns exit status 0 when it is initiated. You can invert the exit status of a pipeline (including a pipeline consisting of a single command) with the ! operator:

!   The ! (negation) operator precedes a pipeline and inverts the exit status of the entire pipeline. If the last command cmd_k in a pipeline

$$!cmd_1 \mid cmd_2 \mid \ldots \mid cmd_k$$

has an exit status of 0, the exit status of the entire pipeline is 1; if the last command has a nonzero exit status, the exit status of the entire pipeline is 0.

6.9.1
Combinations of Operators

The order of precedence of the operators listed above, from high to low, is

(1)   ! |
(2) || &&
(3)   ;   & |&

In particular, commands are first grouped with '!' and '|' to form pipelines. A pipeline can and often does consist of just one command.

The pipelines are then grouped with '||' and '&&' into "conditional lists" (our term). When you connect several pipelines with '||' and '&&', the pipelines are executed in sequence until one of them returns a zero exit status and is followed by '||' or one of them returns a nonzero exit status and is followed by '&&'. If and when that happens, the rest of the pipelines are ignored.

Finally, the conditional lists are grouped with ';' and '&' to form *lists*. A list must be ended with a semicolon, ampersand, or ⟨newline⟩ if its last command is a simple command (see the example under if in Section 6.13).

For example, the command line

```
tryit | feed && ls -l ; sleep 20 && echo hi &
```

is interpreted as follows:

(1)   Execute 'tryit' and 'feed' as a pipeline, with the standard output of tryit becoming the standard input of feed.
(2)   If that succeeds, execute 'ls -l'.
(3)   Then, in any case, start a new background process.
(4)   In that background process, execute 'sleep 20'.
(5)   If that execution succeeds (which it does unless it is interrupted), execute 'echo hi' within the same background process.

6.9.2
Uses of Background Execution

Some uses of background execution are the following:

• Suppose you wish to execute some commands that take a long time and your other work doesn't depend on the results of those commands. If you execute the time-consuming commands in the background, you can do your other work without having to wait for them to finish.

- You can schedule a command execution for a later time by preceding the command with a delay and executing the combination in the background. For example, the command list

    ```
    (sleep 600; retry) &
    ```

    sets up a background process that waits for 10 minutes (600 seconds) and then executes `retry`.

    If you use `sleep` to produce the delay and log out before the command has finished executing, the process goes away and the command is aborted (or never starts). You can ensure that the command is executed in any case by scheduling it for a specific time with `at` (see Section 5.3.3). Alternatively, you can use `nohup` to execute the command with hangups ignored (see Section 5.3.2). For each of these methods, the combination must be set up as a background process.

- In a windowing system such as X (see Chapter 13), you may wish to have several terminal emulations (some of which may be remote logins) active simultaneously. Each emulated terminal has its own window, thereby enabling you to switch back and forth among the emulations. If you start a new terminal emulation as a foreground process, you are blocked from using your current window until the terminal emulation has exited. For instance, if you type

    ```
    xterm
    ```

    to create a new terminal, your current window sits on this command until the new terminal has gone away. But if you make the new terminal a background process by typing

    ```
    xterm &
    ```

    you can switch back and forth freely between the new terminal and the old one.

6.9.3
Coprocesses

A *coprocess* is a process that executes in the background, but with its standard input and standard output accessible at any time from within the foreground process. The '`print -p`' command sends text to the standard input of a coprocess; the '`read -p`' command retrieves text from the standard output of a coprocess. Coprocesses are not included in POSIX.

Once you've created a coprocess, you can't create another one until the first one has terminated or its standard input has been redirected. You don't need to redirect the first coprocess's standard output since the standard output of multiple coprocesses is merged. You can redirect standard input of a coprocess to file descriptor n with the form 'n<&p' and redirect standard output to file descriptor m with the form 'm>&p' (see Section 6.10). To make the redirections persist for the duration of the coprocess, you need to specify them in an **exec** command (see p. 363). For example, the command

```
exec 3>&p 4<&p
```

redirects standard output of the coprocess to file descriptor 3 and standard input of the coprocess from file descriptor 4.

Coprocesses provide a useful form of parallel execution. You can communicate with a coprocess without having to suspend communication with the primary process, and by astute use of redirected file descriptors you can maintain communication with several coprocesses at once. In that respect, a coprocess differs from an ordinary background process initiated with **&**.

6.10   Redirection

Using redirection, you can cause a program to take its input from a specified file instead of from the terminal or send its output to a specified file instead of to a terminal. The principal forms of redirection are explained in Section 2.10. The descriptions that follow include these forms as well as more general forms, such as redirection for arbitrary file descriptors (see Section 2.10.2). In these forms, the whitespace preceding *file*, *n*, or '−' is optional.

< *file*   Take standard input from the file *file*; that is, make the file associated with file descriptor 0 be *file*. See Section 2.10 for a further description of this form of redirection.

<< [−] *word*

Take standard input from the following here-document, delimited by *word* (see Section 6.11). If '−' is present, leading tabs are removed as each line is read; otherwise, tabs are not treated specially.

> *file*
>| *file*   Send standard output to the file *file*; that is, make the file associated with file descriptor 1 be *file*.

- If *file* does not already exist, it is created.

- Otherwise:

    ○ If the > form is used and the **noclobber** option (see p. 376) is set, the shell generates an error message.
    ○ Otherwise, the file is forced to be empty before any output is sent to it.[12]

---

12. If you redirect output to an existing file but don't actually send any output there, the original contents of the file are still lost.

>> *file*   This form of redirection is like '> *file*', except that the new output is appended to *file* if it already exists. The previous contents of the file are not lost.

<&*n*   Cause the file now associated with file descriptor *n* to be associated with standard input as well, thus creating another way to read that file.[13] This form and the following ones must be written without whitespace between the '<' or '>' and the '&'.

>&*n*   Cause the file now associated with file descriptor *n* to be associated with standard output as well, thus creating another way to write to standard output.

<&-   Close standard input; that is, disassociate file descriptor 0 from its file. Note that it is the descriptor, not the file itself, that is closed.

>&-   Close standard output; that is, disassociate file descriptor 1 from its file. Note that it is the descriptor, not the file itself, that is closed.

n< *file*
n<< *file*
n> *file*
n>> *file*
n<&*m*
n>&*m*
n<&-
n>&-   These forms are like the ones listed above, except that they use file descriptor *n* instead of file descriptor 0 or 1. There must not be any whitespace between *n* and '<' or '>', nor between these characters and '&'. For example,

```
exper 3>&1    1>&2    2>&3    3>&-
```

executes the program `exper`, interchanging the role of standard output (file descriptor 1) and standard error (file descriptor 2). The second redirection could be written as '>&2'. The purpose of the last redirection is to avoid leaving behind an extra file descriptor.

n<&p
n>&p   These forms redirect the standard input or standard output of the coprocess (see Section 6.9.3) to file descriptor *n*, much as the previous forms do. They are not included in POSIX.

[*n*]<> *file*   Open the file *file* for both reading and writing on file descriptor *n*, or standard input (file descriptor 0) if *n* is omitted. Usually

---

13. More precisely, file descriptor *n* is duplicated and the new copy assigned to file descriptor 1. The other forms are analogous.

file is a terminal since both reading from and writing to any other kind of file is unlikely to make sense.

As this example illustrates, the shell acts on file redirections in the order it encounters them, from left to right.

Usually the numbers m and n in the forms above are given as integers. However, they can be given by any word that yields an integer (or, where appropriate, a hyphen) after quotation and substitution are applied.

A redirection applied to a compound command affects all the command's components. For example, the command

```
for f in *.data; do analyze $f; done > gigo
```

causes the `analyze` program to be executed for every file in the current directory whose name matches '`*.data`' and causes the output of all these executions to be sent to the file `gigo`.

The `exec` command (see p. 363) has a special interpretation when its arguments consist entirely of redirections: the redirections are made effective for the rest of the execution of the shell (or its subshell), and execution then continues with the next command. For example,

```
exec < newinput
```

causes standard input for subsequently executed commands to be taken from the file `newinput`.

6.11   Here-Documents

A *here-document* provides a way to include lines of text in a shell script. You can include a here-document in interactive input, but it is rarely useful to do so.

You introduce a here-document with a redirection operator of the form '`<<[-] word`', where *word* is a delimiter that indicates the end of the here-document. When the shell interprets a command containing this redirection operator, it reads input from the lines following the command until it encounters either a line consisting exactly of *word* or an end-of-file. This input becomes the standard input of the command. The string *word* thus serves as a delimiter to indicate the end of the here-document. The here-document should appear after the ⟨newline⟩ ending the command. If a line contains more than one sequentially executed command, it can utilize more than one here-document; in this case, the here-documents should appear one after the other.

If '`-`' is present in the operator, leading tabs are removed as each line is read; otherwise, tabs are not treated specially. The tab-stripping happens after any applicable substitutions are performed.

Within the here-document, the shell normally performs certain limited transformations. It applies parameter expansion (see Section 6.16) and command substitution (see Section 6.18.1). It deletes the sequence

\⟨newline⟩ and treats a backslash as a quoting character when it precedes one of the characters '\ $ ''. (Any other backslash is taken literally and left alone.) However, if any portion of *word* is quoted (according to any of the quoting conventions), the shell takes the here-document literally and does not perform any of these transformations (although tab-stripping can still occur).

Example.   The following shell script produces a long-form listing of a directory, labelling it with the directory and the time:

```
cat << "*EOF*"
Listing of $1 as of $(date)
$(ls -l $1)
*** End of listing ***
```

Since the shell script ends with the last line of the here-document, the *EOF* delimiter isn't needed.

6.12   The test, true, and false Commands

The test command, which is intrinsic to the shell, can be used to compare numbers and strings and to test the existence and properties of files. It has two forms:

```
test expr
[ expr ]
```

A test returns a zero exit status if it succeeds and a nonzero exit status if it fails. The elements in a test, *including the square brackets*, must be distinct words, separated by spaces or other separators.

An example of test is

```
[ -x buildit -a "$action" = cons ]
```

This test succeeds (is true) if buildit is an executable file in the current directory and the value of the variable action is the string 'cons'.

6.12.1
String Comparisons

Test provides the following string comparisons:

s_1 = s_2	True if strings s_1 and s_2 are identical.
s_1 != s_2	True if strings s_1 and s_2 are not identical.
s_1	True if s_1 has at least one character (i.e., is not the empty string).
-n s_1	True if s_1 has at least one character (i.e., is not the empty string).
-z s_1	True if s_1 has no characters (i.e., is the empty string).

Note that a nonempty string appearing by itself (the third form) tests true. Be careful—the comparisons don't work properly if either string is a null string or contains whitespace unless you enclose the string in double quotes. Such strings can result from a parameter expansion. To test the variable var for equality with Q, use something like

```
[ "$var" = Q ]
```

Another way to write the same test is

```
[ ${var}0 = Q0 ]
```

as long as you're sure the value of `var` doesn't contain any whitespace. The 0 after the first comparand ensures that the comparand can't be empty.

6.12.2 Numerical Comparisons

Test provides the following numerical comparisons. In these comparisons, n_1 and n_2 are integers; that is, sequences of digits possibly preceded by '+' or '-'.

n_1 `-eq` n_2
> True if $n_1 = n_2$.

n_1 `-ne` n_2
> True if $n_1 \neq n_2$.

n_1 `-lt` n_2
> True if $n_1 < n_2$.

n_1 `-le` n_2
> True if $n_1 \leq n_2$.

n_1 `-gt` n_2
> True if $n_1 > n_2$.

n_1 `-ge` n_2
> True if $n_1 \geq n_2$.

6.12.3 File Tests

Test provides the following tests for the existence and attributes of files:

`-s` *file* True if *file* exists and its size is greater than zero.

`-f` *file* True if *file* exists and is an ordinary file (neither a directory nor a device).

`-r` *file* True if *file* exists and is readable.

`-w` *file* True if *file* exists and is writable.

`-x` *file* True if *file* exists and is executable.

`-d` *file* True if *file* exists and is a directory.

`-L` *file* True if *file* exists and is a symbolic link. This test is not supported by POSIX.

`-p` *file* True if *file* exists and is a FIFO special file (named pipe).

`-c` *file* True if *file* exists and is a character device file.

`-b` *file* True if *file* exists and is a block device file.

`-S` *file* True if *file* exists and is a socket special file. This test is not supported by POSIX.

`-u` *file* True if *file* exists and its set-uid bit is set.

`-g` *file* True if *file* exists and its set-gid bit is set.

`-k` *file* True if *file* exists and its sticky bit is set. This test is not supported by POSIX.

`-O` *file* True if *file* exists and its owner is the effective user ID. This test is not supported by POSIX.

`-G` *file* True if *file* exists and its group is the effective group ID. This test is not supported by POSIX.

The following binary tests compare properties of files:

file$_1$ `-nt` *file*$_2$
> True if *file*$_1$ is newer than *file*$_2$.

file$_1$ `-ot` *file*$_2$
> True if *file*$_1$ is older than *file*$_2$.

file$_1$ `-ef` *file*$_2$
> True if *file*$_1$ is another name for *file*$_2$.

The following test applies to file descriptors:

`-t` [*n*]
> True if the file associated with file descriptor *n* is a terminal.[14] If *n* is omitted, it is taken to be 1.

**6.12.4
Option Test**

The following test for options is provided by `ksh` but not, in general, by other implementations of `test` nor by POSIX:

`-o` *opt*
> True if the option *opt* is turned on.

**6.12.5
Combinations of
Tests**

The following operators can be used to combine tests:

`!` *expr*
> True if *expr* is false and false otherwise.

expr$_1$ `-a` *expr*$_2$
> True if *expr*$_1$ and *expr*$_2$ are both true.

expr$_1$ `-o` *expr*$_2$
> True if either *expr*$_1$ or *expr*$_2$ is true.

`(` *expr* `)`
> True if *expr* is true. The parentheses provide a way of grouping subexpressions.

The [...] construct is less convenient for combinations of tests than the [[...]] construct (see p. 336) provided by `ksh`, but the latter is not included in POSIX.

**6.12.6
The `true` and `false`
Commands**

The `true` and `false` commands do nothing and have no options or arguments. The only reason for executing them is to produce their exit status: zero for `true` and nonzero for `false`.

6.13   Compound Commands

A *compound command* is one that contains other commands. Compound commands provide conditional execution, iteration, case testing, grouped execution, and function definition.

The following keywords are used in compound commands:

```
if   then   else   elif   fi   case   esac
for   while   until   do   done
```

---

14. In this context a "terminal" is a character special file that has an appropriate device driver associated with it. The *isatty* system call is the usual method by which a C program can test whether a file descriptor corresponds to a terminal.

The shell recognizes them only in a context where a command name can appear, such as at the beginning of a line, following ';', or following '||'. Because these keywords have special meaning to the shell, you can't use them as the names of shell scripts or compiled programs.

You can follow a compound command with one or more redirection operators. Redirection applied to a compound command affects the input and output of all contained commands (see p. 332).

6.13.1 Conditional Commands

The compound commands for conditional execution are the following:

if   The `if` command has the form

```
if list
    then list
[elif list
    then list]
...
[else list]
fi
```

Each of the keywords in this command ('`if`', '`then`', '`elif`', '`else`', and '`fi`') must appear either as the first word on a line or as the first word following a semicolon. Each *list* represents a list of commands as defined on page 328.

The command lists following '`if`' and '`elif`' act as tests and are tried in turn until one succeeds. Then the *list* following the '`then`' after the successful test is executed. If none of the tests succeed, the *list* following '`else`' (if '`else`' is present) is executed. If all tests fail and no '`else`' is present, the execution of the entire command is complete. In this case, the entire '`if ... fi`' construct returns an exit code of 0; in all other cases, the entire construct returns the exit code of the last executed *list*. The `test` command (see Section 6.12) is particularly useful as a test in an `if` command.

Be sure that each *list* in this command and the others below are properly terminated. For example, the command

```
if true then echo egad!;fi      # Wrong!
```

produces an error diagnostic because '`true`' is a simple command and therefore requires a semicolon after it. However, the command

```
if { true;} then echo egad!;fi
```

correctly produces the output '`egad!`' (see the description of '`{...}`' later in this section).

[[*test*]]

   This construct tests an expression, returning an exit status of failure or success. It is typically used as the first operand of

&& or in an `if`, `while`, or `until` command. It performs much the same function as the `test` command (see Section 6.12) but offers the additional amenities of comparison of a string with a pattern, more transparent notation for combinations of tests, and simplified handling of comparisons with variables whose value is the null string. This construct is not supported by POSIX.

The test *test* is built from primitive tests. A primitive test is one of the elementary tests provided by the `test` command; that is, any of the tests listed there other than one of those for a combination of tests. However, the = and != tests are given a more general interpretation and two new primitive tests are provided:

str = *pat*   True if the string *str* matches the pattern *pat* (see Section 6.7).

str != *pat*

True if the string *str* doesn't match the pattern *pat* (see Section 6.7).

s_1 < s_2 True if the string s_1 is lexically less than (sorts before) the string s_2.

s_1 > s_2 True if the string s_1 is lexically greater than (sorts after) the string s_2.

Each test yields *true* or *false*, corresponding to success or failure.

Combinations of tests are built up using these logical operators:

(*test-expr*)

The result of evaluating *text-expr*. (Within '[[...]]', parentheses signify grouping, not execution in a subshell.)

! *test-expr*

The logical negation of the result of *text-expr*; that is, *true* if *test-expr* yields *false* and *false* if *test-expr* yields *true*.

test-expr$_1$ && *test-expr*$_2$

True if both *test-expr*$_1$ and *test-expr*$_2$ yield *true*. If *test-expr*$_1$ yields *false*, *test-expr*$_2$ is not evaluated.

test-expr$_1$ || *test-expr*$_2$

True if either *test-expr*$_1$ or *test-expr*$_2$ yields *true*. If *test-expr*$_1$ yields *true*, *test-expr*$_2$ is not evaluated.

case   The `case` command has the form

```
case word in
    casetest
    ...
esac
```

where each *casetest* has the form

> *pattern* [| *pattern...*]) *list*;;

You may omit the '; ;' at the end of the last case test, but we recommend you include it as a safeguard in case the script is modified later.

Each *pattern* in turn is matched against the *word* that precedes it until a match succeeds according to the rules given in Section 6.7. The *list* in the *casetest* containing the matching pair is then executed. If no match succeeds, none of the *list*s are executed and the entire command returns an exit status of zero.

Here is an example of a `case` command:

```
case $fn in
    *.c | *.cpp ) cppcompile $fn;;
    *.pas       ) pascompile $fn;;
    *           ) echo "Unclassified function $fn!";;
esac
```

The appropriate compilation procedure is selected for the file `$fn`, depending on the form of its name. Using '*' as the last case is a general method of catching anything that can't be recognized.

6.13.2 Iteration

The compound commands for iteration are the following:

for   The `for` command has the form

> for *name* [in *word* ... ;] do *list*
> done

The commands in *list* are executed repeatedly, once for each *word* following 'in'. Each time these commands are executed, the variable *name* (whose value is obtained from $*name*) takes on the value of the next *word*. (See Section 6.15 for a discussion of variables.) For example, executing the command

```
for nbr in one two three
do
    echo [$nbr]
done
```

produces the output

```
[one]
[two]
[three]
```

Note that the ⟨newline⟩ at the end of the first line obviates putting a semicolon there.

If you omit 'in', the shell uses the positional parameters starting with $1 as the *word*s. The number of *word*s in this case is the number of parameters that actually have values.

See Section 6.22.4 for ways to break out of the middle of an iteration.

while   The `while` command has the form

> while *list*
> do *list*
> done

The first *list* represents a test, just as in the `if` command. The shell repeatedly tests this *list*. If the test succeeds (zero exit status), the second *list* is executed and the cycle continues. If it fails (nonzero exit status), the `while` command terminates.

until   The `until` command has the form

> until *list*
> do *list*
> done

It behaves just like the `while` command except that the sense of the test is reversed: success means "terminate" and failure means "continue". Unlike the `until` construct in some programming languages, the iteration here can exit immediately without executing the second *list*.

6.13.3
Execution of
Command Lists

The following constructs execute a list of commands:

(*list*)   This construct causes the commands of *list* to be executed in a subshell (see Section 6.14). A separator (space or tab) is not required between *list* and either one of its surrounding parentheses, and a terminator (';' or '&') is not required at the end of *list*.

{ *list* ; }
{ *list* & }

These constructs cause the commands of *list* to be executed directly (see Section 6.14). The only effect of the braces is to create a kind of grouping, similar to that created by parentheses in mathematical expressions. A separator (space or tab) *is* required between the left brace and *list*, but not between the semicolon or ampersand and the right brace.[15] Braces differ in this respect from parentheses.

---

15. The space is required because braces don't act as separators between words.

**6.13.4
Function Definitions**

The following construct defines a function:

```
function name { list; }
name () { list; }
name () compound-cmd [redir]
```

Unlike the previous constructs, this one does not cause any commands to be executed. The first two forms are the ones recognized by ksh; the third is a generalization of the second accepted by a POSIX shell.[16] The third form takes advantage of the fact that a compound command, here indicated by *compound-cmd*, is self-delimiting. Since the form '{ *list*; }' is a particular compound command, the third form includes the second. Each of the indicated semicolons can be replaced by a ⟨newline⟩.

A function definition defines *name* as a function; thereafter, the command *name* is equivalent to the sequence

```
{ list; }
```

For example, the function definition

```
backdate()  { cd ../old;}
```

in effect creates a command `backdate` that changes the current directory to the parallel one `old`. Note that this function would not work correctly if function definitions were not executed directly (see Section 6.14), since the effect of the `cd` command would be lost. The space after the left brace cannot be omitted.

POSIX enables you to attach redirections to a function definition (see Section 6.10), although many ksh implementations don't yet support that capability. These redirections then apply to all commands within the function definition. For example, the function `vlog` defined by

```
vlog () { echo $@; } >> $LOGFILE
```

records its arguments in the log file `$LOGFILE`. If you redefine `$LOGFILE`, the command redirects its arguments to a new log file.

It's often useful to load function definitions into your shell when you start it. To do this, include in your `ENV` initialization file a command such as

```
. funcdefs
```

where `funcdefs` is a file containing a list of function definitions (see Section 6.25). Function definitions load quickly and execute efficiently since the shell can execute them without

---

16. The POSIX shells available to us haven't implemented this form in its full generality, however.

reading any files. Function definitions are also useful in shell scripts as local definitions (definitions needed within that script but not elsewhere). You can postpone reading function definitions until they are actually needed by using the autoload feature of ksh (see "Autoloading Function Definitions in ksh" on p. 324).

If you use a variable within a function without defining it, it becomes global (i.e., known throughout the shell). Sometimes it's useful to create local variables, particularly when you're defining a recursive function. You can create such local variables in ksh with the typeset command (see p. 365), but POSIX does not provide any mechanism for it.[17]

Function definitions are not inherited by subshells unless you export them explicitly. You can arrange to export functions $fn_1, fn_2, \ldots, fn_k$ by issuing the command

   typeset -fx fn_1 fn_2 ... fn_k

Usually you'd put this command in one of your initialization files.

6.13.5
Menu Selection

The following construct, not supported by POSIX, enables you to define a menu for user interaction:

select   The select command has the form

           select *name* [in *word* ... ;] do *list*
           done

Ksh expands each *word* and then produces the resulting items in one or more columns on standard error, followed by the PS3 prompt. Each item is preceded by a number. The number of columns is determined by the values of the LINES and COLUMNS variables.

Next, ksh reads a line from standard input, saving its value *reply* in the REPLY variable.

- If *reply* is the number of one of the displayed items, ksh sets *name* to the text of that item.
- If *reply* is empty, ksh produces the list of items and the PS3 prompt again.
- In all other cases, ksh sets *name* to the null string.

Finally, ksh executes the commands in *list*, which usually consists of a case compound statement that makes a selection according to the value of *name*.

Figure 6-3 shows an example of the use of select to choose an appropriate set of options for sort.

---

17. The rationale of the POSIX standard hints that some such mechanism might eventually be introduced, most likely under the name typeset or local.

```
opts=""
PS3="Enter the number of your choice:"
select i in "Forward" "Forward, case-folded" \
    "Reverse" "Reverse, case-folded"
do  case $i in
    Forward) opts="";    break;;
    Fo*lded) opts="-f";  break;;
    Rev*rse) opts="-r";  break;;
    Rev*ded) opts="-rf"; break;;
    *)           printf "Please try again.\n" ;;
    esac
done
sort $opts $1
```

Fig. 6-3. Using the `select` command.

6.14   How Commands Are Executed

The shell has three methods of executing commands: direct execution, direct execution in a subshell, and indirect execution in a subshell:[18]

- For *direct execution*, the shell executes commands as it encounters them. Any changes that the commands make to the shell's state (e.g., changing the values of variables) remain in effect until the shell terminates. Intrinsic shell commands and user-defined functions (see Section 6.13.4) are always executed directly.

- For *direct execution in a subshell*, the shell uses the *fork* system function to create a subshell; that is, a child process that is a copy of itself. The subshell then executes the commands.[19] The parent process either waits for the child to complete or just continues, depending on whether the child is executing in the foreground or the background. The child process executes the commands and then terminates.[20]

---

18. Most published descriptions fail to distinguish clearly between the two kinds of subshell execution. Recognizing the distinction is essential to understanding when variables are visible in subshells and when they aren't. These terms are our invention.

19. The mechanism for doing that is interesting. The *fork* function actually creates a copy of the current process. Each process is then in the state of just having completed the call on *fork*. The only difference between the states of the two processes—parent and child—is in the value returned by that call. But that difference is sufficient for each process to know what to do next, since the next action can be made to depend on it.

20. A background grandchild process started by the child process continues when the child terminates and becomes a child of process #1, the system process named 'init'.

The subshell inherits a copy of all the variables of the parent shell. Any changes of state within the subshell—in particular, assignments to variables—do not affect the parent shell.

The following constructs are directly executed in a subshell:

- ○   A list of commands in parentheses
- ○   A list of commands executed as a background process
- ○   A command in a command substitution
- ○   All commands but the last in a pipeline

- For *indirect execution in a subshell*, the shell creates a subshell as for direct execution and then calls on the *exec* system function to execute the commands in that subshell (see Section 6.14.2). Exported variables are inherited by the subshell but other local variables are not (see Section 6.15.3). Commands not intrinsic to the shell, including both shell scripts and commands implemented as compiled programs, are handled by indirect execution in a subshell.

**6.14.1
Example of
Execution Methods**

The implications of the differences among the three methods are shown by the following example. Suppose that your user name is `abigail` and you issue the commands

```
cd ~/one
X=1 Y=2 Z=3
export X
```

All of these commands are directly executed. Next, suppose you issue

```
(cd ../two; pwd; Y=7; echo $X $Y $Z)
pwd
echo $X $Y $Z
```

The commands in parentheses are directly executed in a subshell, resulting in the following behavior:

(1)   The first `pwd` produces '/home/abigail/two'.
(2)   The first `echo` produces '1 7 3'.
(3)   The second `pwd` produces '/home/abigail/one', since the state of the parent shell remains untouched and that state includes the current directory.
(4)   The second `echo` produces '1 2 3'.

Next, suppose you put the line

```
cd ../two; pwd; Y=7; echo $X $Y $Z
```

in an executable file `tryit` (in the current directory) and issue the commands

```
tryit
pwd
echo $X $Y $Z
```

This time the shell indirectly executes the commands of `tryit` in a sub-shell, resulting in the following behavior:

(1)   The first `pwd` produces '/home/abigail/two', as before.
(2)   The first `echo` produces '1 7'. Z appears not to be set because it was not exported.
(3)   The second `pwd` produces '/home/abigail/one', as before.
(4)   The second `echo` produces '1 2 3', as before.

**6.14.2
Indirectly Executing
Commands in
a Subshell**

When the shell encounters a non-intrinsic command *cmd*, it indirectly executes *cmd* in a subshell, using the *fork* system function to create a subshell. The subshell then calls the *exec* system function. The *exec* function in turn searches the path as given in the PATH environment variable (see Section 2.9.2), looking for an executable file whose name is *cmd*. The *exec* function then executes the file, either as a shell script or as a compiled program.

- If the file is a compiled program, *exec* loads it into memory and executes it, passing it the list of arguments following the name *cmd*. When the compiled program exits, the subshell terminates.

- If the file is a shell script, *exec* calls a shell to execute it (see Section 6.5). If the first line of the shell script has the form

    `#!` *shell*

  where *shell* is the name of a shell (or any executable file, in fact), *exec* uses *shell* to interpret the script; otherwise, *exec* uses `ksh` or a shell compatible with it. The precise rules for the choice of shell may vary from one system to another.

In the first case, the compiled program can use a system subroutine to retrieve the argument list. In the second case, the shell makes the arguments available within the script by assigning them to shell parameters (as described in Section 6.15).

6.15   Parameters

A *parameter* is a named entity whose value you can retrieve. There are three kinds of parameters: positional parameters, special parameters, and variables (named parameters). The notation '$*param*' or a variation of it is used to retrieve the value of a parameter.

**6.15.1
Positional
Parameters**

When you call a shell script as a command, the shell assigns the command name to $0[21] and each argument of the command to a positional parameter: the first to $1, the second to $2, and so forth. You can then refer to

---

21. A shell script can have several names, each being a distinct link to the script. The script can test $0 to determine the name by which it was called. Through this device, a single script can implement several different commands.

these parameters within the script. To reference a positional parameter after $9, you need to enclose the digits in braces (e.g., '${13}').[22]

For example, if you call the command `whoopee` using the command line

    whoopee food drink merriment

the parameter $0 receives the value `whoopee` and the parameters $1 through $3 receive the values 'food', 'drink', and 'merriment', respectively. The quotation conventions described in Section 6.17 apply, so for the command line

    whoopee "food drink merriment"

the value of $1 is 'food drink merriment'. Sections 6.14.2 and 6.5 explain in greater detail what happens when a shell script is called.

The assignment construct *'variable=value'* (see Section 6.15.6) does not apply to positional parameters. However, you can assign a value to a positional parameter with the `set` command (see p. 367).

**6.15.2
Variables**

Variables are used to store information within a shell script. They can also be used at the level of the shell itself; in particular, certain predefined variables have special meanings to the shell (see Section 6.23). To make a variable visible to a program you call from a shell script or from the shell directly, you have to export it as explained below. Some variables are exported automatically, but others must be exported explicitly.

The name of a variable starts with a letter or an underscore. Unlike variables in most modern programming languages, variables need not be declared. They come into existence when the shell starts executing or when you assign values to them, though under `ksh` you can also declare a variable explicitly with the `typeset` command (see p. 365). See Section 2.13 for a general discussion of variables.

When the shell starts to execute, it receives a set of environment variables from its parent process (see Section 2.6.5) and copies them into its own set of local variables, adding some predefined variables of its own. When the shell terminates, both these local variables and the environment variables of the parent process disappear.

The values of local variables are visible to commands executed in a subshell only if that subshell is executed directly or if the variables are exported (see Section 6.14). The values of environment variables, on the other hand, are always visible to commands executed in a subshell. Export of variables is discussed next.

**6.15.3
Exporting Variables
to a Subshell**

Exporting a variable to a subshell places it in the environment of the subshell and makes its value available to the subshell (see Section 2.6.5). A variable *var* is marked for export with the `export` attribute, which you can set with '`typeset -x` *var*' or '`export` *var*', or unset with '`typeset +x` *var*'.

---

22. Older shells did not allow multidigit parameters, so you had to use the `shift` command (see p. 367) to retrieve positional parameters after $9.

When the shell creates a subshell in order to execute a compiled program or a shell script (see Section 6.14), it creates a set E of environment variables for that subshell. The shell constructs E by placing all exported variables in E, giving them their current values. If any assignments precede the command that initiated the subshell, the shell then adds to E the variables specified by those assignments. As a special case, however, ksh (but not a POSIX shell) reinitializes the IFS variable (see p. 372) to its default value even if you've exported it.

When the shell begins execution, it inherits the environment variables of its parent process. Copies of these variables are assigned to identically named shell local variables, which are automatically given the export attribute. Later on, you can assign the export attribute to any other variable or remove it from an inherited variable.

The following dialogue shows how exported and inherited variables behave:

```
$ X=1 Y=2 Z=3 ksh
$ typeset +x Y # Remove export attribute
$ unset Z
$ T=4 U=5 X=6
$ export T
$ V=7 ksh
$ echo "X=$X Y=$Y Z=$Z T=$T U=$U V=$V"
X=6 Y= Z= T=4 U= V=7
```

The first line starts a copy of ksh and provides it with three environment variables X, Y, and Z, with the indicated values. The sixth line starts another inner copy of ksh. The variables and their values as seen by this inner copy appear on the last line and are as follows:

X (6)   Modified by the outer ksh; inherited by the inner ksh.

Y (no value)
             Modified by the outer ksh but not exported; not inherited by the inner ksh.

Z (no value)
             Modified by the outer ksh but unset; not inherited by the inner ksh.

T (4)   Created and set by the outer ksh and then exported; inherited by the inner ksh.

U (no value)
             Created and set by the outer ksh but not exported; not inherited by the inner ksh.

V (7)   Added to the environment of the inner ksh by the outer ksh.

6.15.4
Array Variables

A variable name can designate an integer-indexed array of elements, each of which behaves like a variable in its own right. All elements of an array have the same attributes, which are those declared for the array itself.

You refer to element k of array A as $A[k]$, where k is the subscript of the array reference. Historically, arrays have been limited to 512 elements, but some implementations may let them be much larger. Array variables are not included in POSIX.

You can declare an array with `typeset` (see p. 365), but you don't have to declare it. When you first reference an array variable, the array is created. The size of the array is determined by the largest subscript in use. The mininum subscript is zero. You can still reference the array without a subscript; if you do, you'll get element number zero.

You can reference all of the elements of an array A at once as $A[*]$ or $A[@]$. Within double quotes, these constructs behave like the analogous `$*` and `$@` constructs (see "Special Parameters Derived from Arguments" on p. 349), with undefined elements omitted and the remaining elements separated either by a single space or (for `"A[*]"`) by the first character of the value of `IFS` (see p. 372) if that variable is defined.

**6.15.5
Attributes of
Variables**

Under `ksh`, a variable can have various *attributes*. When `ksh` retrieves the value of a variable, the variable's attributes affect how the retrieved value is formatted. Attributes also affect the read-only status and export of a variable. POSIX, however, regards the value of a variable as being just a string and does not support attributes for variables. You specify the attributes of a variable with the `typeset` command (see p. 365).

Formatting Attributes. Ksh supports the following formatting attributes:

u   Convert the retrieved value to uppercase. (Only letters in the value are affected.)

l   Convert the retrieved value to lowercase.

i[*base*]   Convert the retrieved value to a base *base* integer ($2 \leq base \leq 36$). If *base* isn't specified, it defaults to 10. Ksh predefines `integer` as an alias for '`typeset -i`', so you can use the command

            integer minyan=10

            to create the integer variable `minyan` and give it the value 10.

L[*width*] Left-justify the retrieved value within a field of size *width*. Excess characters are truncated on the right. If you don't specify *width*, it defaults to the width of the first value assigned to the variable.

LZ[*width*] Like L, except that leading zeroes are stripped from the retrieved value.

R[*width*] Like L, except that the retrieved value is right-justified and excess characters are truncated on the left.

[R]Z[*width*]

            Like R, except that if the leading non-space character of the value is a digit, any leading spaces are replaced by zeroes.

If you specify conflicting attributes such as L and R, the last attribute prevails.

Other Attributes.   The following additional attributes are supported:

r   Make the variable read-only, so any subsequent attempt to change its value or unset it will generate an error message. You can also use the `readonly` command to make a variable read-only.

x   Export the value of this variable to any child process initiated by `ksh` (see Section 6.15.3).

t   Tag this variable. The only semantics of this attribute are its presence or absence.

**6.15.6
Assignments to
Variables**

You can assign values to one or more variables with an assignment (single or multiple) of the form

> *variable=value* [*variable=value* ...]

in any context where the shell expects a command. You must quote the value if it contains any blanks or other characters that have special meaning to the shell (see Section 6.17). The assignment sets each *variable* to the corresponding *value* (treated as a string). For example, the assignment

```
CAT=tabby GOAT='the chomper'
```

causes the variable CAT to acquire the value 'tabby' and the variable GOAT to acquire the value 'the chomper'. You can also use `typeset` (see p. 365) to assign values to variables, though `typeset` performs other functions as well.

You can also precede a call on a program with one or more assignments to variables (see Section 6.8). The values of the variables specified in the assignment are available to the called program in its environment but don't affect the calling environment. The following dialogue illustrates this behavior:

```
$ var=one
$ var=two ksh
$ echo $var
two
$ exit
$ echo $var
one
```

The assignment on the second line makes the value of var available to the called program, which in this case is another copy of ksh. When the called program exits, var still has its original value within the outer copy of ksh.

**6.15.7
Special Parameters**

When you call a shell script, the shell sets a number of special parameters along with the positional parameters.

Special Parameters Derived from Arguments. The following special parameters are derived from the arguments passed to the script:

$@   The positional parameters in sequence, starting with $1, with each separator character replaced by a single space. The result is given by the string

$1␣$2␣ ... ␣$n

where n is the number of arguments, or by a null string if no arguments are passed to the script. If you include this parameter in double quotes, it expands to n separate words rather than a single word with the separator characters left unchanged.

    This special parameter is particularly useful within a shell script when the script can be called with a variable number of arguments.

$*   Like $@ except that if the construct occurs within double quotes, (a) the separator character is the first character of the IFS variable (see p. 372) or a space if IFS is undefined, and (b) the entire sequence is treated as a single word. The result of "$*" is given by the string

"$1s$2s ... s$n"

where n is the number of arguments and s is the first character in IFS, or by a null string if no arguments are passed to the script.

$#   The number of arguments, as a decimal number.

Other Special Parameters. The following special parameters are also set:

$-   The flags supplied to the shell when it was called. Modifying the command line options with set (see p. 367) causes the value of $- to be updated.

$$ The process number of the current shell invocation.

$?   The exit code returned by the most recent executed foreground command.

$!   The process number of the most recent asynchronously executed command.

6.16 Parameter Expansions

A *parameter expansion* refers to the value of a parameter. When a parameter expansion occurs within a command line, the expansion is evaluated to produce text that is then substituted for the expansion. Several forms of parameter expansion, as a side effect, set the value of a variable. You can conveniently evaluate a parameter expansion for its side effect by writing it after a null command (see Section 6.22.5). For example,

```
: ${bumbles=7}
```

sets `$bumbles` to 7 if it does not exist and leaves it undisturbed otherwise.

   Each parameter expansion begins with '$'. If you wish a '$' to be taken literally, you need to escape it by writing it as '\$'. However, a '$' followed by whitespace is taken literally whether or not it is escaped.

   In the following descriptions of parameter expansions, *param* signifies a parameter (either positional, special, or named). Where braces are not shown, they are still permitted around the character following the '$'. They are needed for a positional parameter numbered 10 or higher.

Basic Expansions.   The following construct provided the basic form of parameter expansion:

$*param*

${*param*}   Replace this construct by the value of *param*. The braces are required if the construct is not followed by a separator. The following dialogue illustrates the replacement:

```
$ book=Decameron
$ echo $book
Decameron
```

As another example, suppose that the shell script in the file `vfy` consists of the text

```
diff ~/screed1/$1.tex ~/screed2/$1.tex
```

and you issue the command

```
vfy oink
```

Then the shell compares two versions of the TeX file `oink.tex` by executing the command

```
diff ~/screed1/oink.tex ~/screed2/oink.tex
```

Conditional Expansions.   The following forms provide expansions that depend on the current value of the parameter involved:

${*param-word*}

${*param*:-*word*}

   These constructs provide a form of conditional substitution as follows:

- If $*param* exists and has a non-null value, its value is substituted into the text.
- If $*param* does not exist, *word* is substituted into the text.
- If $*param* exists but has a null value, then
  - the '-' form produces an empty string;
  - the ':-' form produces *word*.

The braces are required.

For example, suppose the command `toast` is defined as

```
echo ${1:-skoal}
```

Then the command line

```
toast prosit
```

produces the output

```
prosit
```

while the command line

```
toast
```

produces the output

```
skoal
```

${*param*?[*word*]}
${*param*:?[*word*]}

These constructs are like `:-` and `-`, except that if *param* does not exist, the shell exits and sends *word* to the standard error file. If *word* is omitted, it defaults to the message 'parameter null or not set'. The braces are required.

${*param*+*word*}
${*param*:+*word*}

These constructs work like '-' and ':-', but in a nearly opposite sense:

- If $*param* exists and has a non-null value, *word* is substituted into the text.
- If $*param* does not exist, nothing is substituted into the text.
- If $*param* exists but has a null value, then
  - the '+' form produces *word*;
  - the ':+' form produces nothing.

The braces are required.

Expansions with Assignment. The following construct provides conditional expansion for variables that also performs an assignment as a side effect:

${*param*=*word*}
${*param*:=*word*}

These constructs are valid for variables but not for other kinds of parameters. They are like '-' and ':-', except that they have a side effect: if *word* is inserted into the text, it is also assigned to *param*. The braces are required. In effect, these constructs make *word* a default value for *param*.

Length and Count Expansion.   The following constructs produce parameter lengths and counts:

${#*param*}

>   If *param* is * or @, substitutes the number of positional parameters, and otherwise substitutes the length of $*param*.

${#*var*[@|*]}

>   Substitutes the number of elements of the array variable *var* that have been set. If *var* is not an array variable, the result is 0. This construct is not supported by POSIX.

Pattern-Matching Expansion.   The following constructs provide for extracting substrings from a parameter when retrieving its value:

${*param*#*pat*}

>   Removes the smallest prefix matching the pattern *pat* from the value of $*param*, then substitutes the resulting value.

${*param*##*pat*}

>   Like #, but removes the largest matching prefix.

${*param*%*pat*}

>   Like #, but removes the smallest matching suffix.

${*param*%%*pat*}

>   Like #, but removes the largest matching suffix.

The following table illustrates the expansion of the pattern-extracting constructs, assuming $1 has the value 'entrepot.tar.gz':

Construct	*Value*
${1#*.}	tar.gz
${1##*.}	gz
${1%.*}	entrepot.tar
${1%%.*}	entrepot

6.17   Quotation

You can use quotation to cause characters, normally meaningful to the shell, to be treated as ordinary characters with no special meaning (see Section 2.12.2). The shell provides three forms of quotation:

(1)   **Backslash quotation.** The form '*c*' quotes the single character *c*, depriving *c* of any special meaning it might have as an operator, separator, or other special character. A backslash at the end of a

line acts as a line continuation; the backslash and ⟨newline⟩ both disappear.[23] For example, if you type

```
echo On a sin\
gle line.
```

you obtain the output

```
On a single line.
```

Without the backslash, you'd receive a complaint about the 'gle' command not being found. **Note:** A backslash must itself be quoted if it is to be treated as an ordinary character.

(2) **Single quotation.** The form '*text*' quotes *text* literally. Every character between the apostrophes, even a backslash or a ⟨newline⟩, is treated as an ordinary character. A ⟨newline⟩ within a single quotation does *not* disappear, even if preceded by a backslash. The quoted text obviously cannot include an apostrophe, but you can produce an apostrophe with '"'"'.

(3) **Double quotation.** The form "*text*" provides a weaker form of quotation in which most characters within *text* are treated as ordinary characters, but the four characters '"', '$', '`', and '\' are interpreted as follows:

- The double quote character (unless quoted with a backslash) marks the end of the quoted text.

- The characters '$' and '`' are given their normal interpretations, so variable and command substitutions are performed even within double quotes.

- A backslash preceding a ⟨newline⟩ disappears together with the ⟨newline⟩.

- A backslash escapes the four special characters listed above and therefore quotes them.

- A backslash preceding any other character is taken literally.

Unquoted ⟨newline⟩s are taken literally, just as they are in a single quotation. For parsing purposes, a null string, which you can write as '""' or ''', counts as a word.

Examples.   An example showing how the three forms of quotation interact is

```
X='this & that'
echo 'He said, "Why isn'"'"'"""t my cat
doing $X?\""
```

---

23. Be careful: If a backslash is followed by some spaces and a ⟨newline⟩, the backslash quotes the first space and the ⟨newline⟩ does not disappear, yet the line is visually indistinguishable from one without the trailing spaces.

These commands produce the output

```
He said, "Why isn't my cat
doing this & that?"
```

And here is an example that shows the difference among the three forms of quotation:

```
echo ele\
phant "ze\
bra" "gir
affe" 'ti\
ger'
```

This input produces

```
elephant zebra gir
affe ti\
ger
```

6.18   Substitutions

The shell provides three forms of substitution: command substitution (using either of two notations), parameter expansion, and arithmetic evaluation. Parameter expansion is described in Section 6.16; we describe the other two forms below. We also explain how the shell interprets nested substitutions and quotations.

6.18.1 Command Substitution

Using *command substitution*, you can execute a list of commands and use the output as all or part of the text of some other command (see Section 2.12.3) using either of the forms

> $(*text*)
> '*text*'

The first form is much more straightforward to use, particularly when nested substitutions and quotations are involved. The second form was retained in the POSIX shell and `ksh` primarily for compatibility with the Bourne shell, though it sometimes is more convenient for simple applications. When the shell encounters a command substitution of the form '$(*list*)', it executes the commands in *list*. It then replaces the command substitution by the standard output that results from executing those commands.

The output of command substitution, unlike the input, is *always* treated as a single simple command, either intrinsic or externally defined. The first word on the line is taken as the name of the command. The rest of the line is parsed into words, with the separator characters taken from the

IFS variable (see p. 372) if that variable has a value. During this parse, all characters other than the separator characters are treated as ordinary characters—even operator characters such as '|' or ';'. For example, the command line

```
$(echo "echo one;echo    two")
```

or its equivalent

```
`echo "echo one;echo    two"`
```

produces the output

```
one;echo two
```

The shell treats the sequence of characters 'one;echo' as a single word despite the semicolon. The several spaces following this sequence act as a single separator and therefore produce a single space in the output.

If IFS is not defined or has its default value '␣⟨tab⟩⟨newline⟩', any sequence of separator characters turns into a single space. Furthermore, a ⟨newline⟩ within the text produced by command substitution acts as an argument separator rather than as a command separator (i.e., like a space rather than like a semicolon). This behavior can be useful when the text has been produced by a command having ⟨newline⟩s in its output. For instance, suppose that the file junque contains a list of files, one per line, that you wish to remove. (This is the most convenient format for creating such a list.) If you then type

```
rm -i $(cat junque)
```

you remove all the files in the list (with confirmation queries).[24] This method works even when some of the file names contain wildcards.

If IFS is defined and its value is anything other than the default value precisely, a sequence of separator characters in the result of the substitution is transformed into a sequence containing the same number of spaces. For instance, if IFS includes the colon as a separator character, two colons in a row in the substitution's result turn into two spaces.

6.18.2 Arithmetic Evaluation

You can evaluate an arithmetic expression using the construct[25]

```
$((expr))
```

---

24. As a special case, ksh recognizes the command

```
rm -i $(< junque)
```

as equivalent; it uses the contents of junque as the tail of the rm command.

25. Ksh also provides the form '((*expr*))' (no '$') for arithmetic evaluation, which returns *true* for nonzero values and *false* otherwise. This construct is not supported by POSIX and is better avoided.

```
( ... )                  grouping
~                        one's complement (−(n + 1))
!                        negation (0 yields 1, anything else yields 0)
*   /   %                multiplication, division, remainder
+   −                    binary addition, binary subtraction
<<   >>                  left shift, right shift
<   >   <=   >=          less, greater, less or equal, greater or equal
==   !=   =~   !~        equal, not equal, matches, does not match
&                        logical "and"
^                        logical difference
|                        logical "or"
&&                       conditional "and"
||                       conditional "or"
```

Fig. 6-4.   Precedence of shell arithmetic operators.

The parentheses in each pair must be adjacent. The resulting sequence of digits, possibly prefixed by '−', is then treated as text. The characters of *expr* are treated just as though they were written between double quotes, so an operator character such as '<' is interpreted as an arithmetic comparison rather than as a redirection operator.

An arithmetic expression has nearly the same form as it does in C. The lowest-level operators of the expression are integer constants and variables.

- An integer constant has the form '[*base*#]*number*', where *base* is a number between 2 and 36 that defines the numerical base (assumed to be 10 if omitted). Thus '49' represents the ordinary decimal number 49, while '8#61' and '16#31' represent that number in octal and hexadecimal, respectively.

- A variable has either integer type or string type. If its type is integer, then its value is used. Otherwise, the string must have the form of an arithmetic expression, and that expression is recursively evaluated to yield an integer. For example, the command line

      a=b+9; b=−2; echo $((a*5))

  produces the output '35'.

Figure 6-4 lists the operators recognized by the shell in decreasing order of precedence.

**6.18.3
Nested
Substitutions and
Quotations**

When substitutions are nested with each other or with quotations, it may not be obvious how the shell interprets the combination of constructs. Here is how the interpretation works.

The shell processes a command line from left to right. When it encounters one of the characters

      "   '   \ $ `

it begins parsing the corresponding construct. If an inner construct is encountered, that construct is analyzed recursively. As soon as the shell sees the end of a construct, it interprets that construct and replaces it by its result. The effect is that inner constructs are always processed before outer ones. In particular, a single quotation ''*text*'' is always replaced by *text*, treated as a single word, before any outer construct sees it, and an escape '*c*' is always replaced by the character *c* deprived of any special meaning it would otherwise have. For example, the output of each of the command lines

```
echo $(echo \))
echo $(echo ')')
echo $(echo ")")
```

is a single right parenthesis. Note how the backslash in the first line quotes the right parenthesis before it has a chance to be interpreted as closing off the left parenthesis. And if you type

```
echo "There are $(who | wc -l) users logged in."
```

you obtain an output such as

```
There are     17 users logged in.
```

The '|', being within the command substitution, is treated as part of that (inner) construct rather than as part of the (outer) double quotation.

Special Rule for Backquotes. A special rule applies to backslashes within a command substitution written using the older ''`*cmd*`'' notation—which is one reason we recommend avoiding that form whenever possible. A back-slash preceding a backquote, a dollar sign, or another backslash quotes that character and then disappears, but any other backslash is treated literally, even one within a nested construct.[26] After the shell has processed all backslash quotation within such a command substitution, it treats the resulting string just as though you had typed it as an input line. The following sample output shows some effects of this special rule:

```
$ echo `echo \$\$ "\\\\"`
208 \
$ echo $(echo \$\$ "\\\\")
$$ \\
$ echo `echo \$\$ \`echo "\\\\\\\\"`\``
208 \
```

---

26. Quoting a dollar sign with a backslash turns out to have no effect because, in either case, the dollar sign is interpreted later as introducing a substitution.

6.19   Aliases

You can define an *alias* as an abbreviation for a command that you commonly use. The `alias` and `unalias` commands create, display, and destroy aliases. The shell keeps a list of your aliases; each alias in the list associates a command word with the text of its definition. Section 6.8.1 describes how the shell interprets alias definitions. Aliases, unlike variables, are not (and can't be) exported to shell scripts that are executed indirectly in a subshell.

**6.19.1
Defining or
Displaying Aliases
with** `alias`

The `alias` utility either defines a set of aliases or lists all current aliases (see Section 6.19). The form of the `alias` command line is

    alias [name[=str] ...]

For each assignment indicated by '=', the `alias` utility assigns the specified value *value* to the alias name *name*. If a name *name* is specified without an assignment, the name and its alias value are produced on standard output. For example, the command

    alias grn="grep -n"

defines the name `grn` as an alias for 'grep -n'.

  If no names are specified, all alias names and their values are produced on standard output. If you capture that output and provide it as input to the shell, those alias definitions will be restored.

Options for `ksh`.   Ksh provides two options, not included in POSIX and considered obsolete, that apply to the `alias` command:

`-t`   Define each *name* as a tracked alias.

`-x`   Export each *name* to any shell script that is directly (but not indirectly) executed in a subshell.

With no *name*s, these options cause the tracked or exported aliases to be listed.

**6.19.2
Removing Aliases
with** `unalias`

The `unalias` utility removes a specified set of alias definitions (see Section 6.19.1). The forms of the `unalias` command line are

    unalias name ...
    unalias -a

With the first form, the aliases for the names *name* ... are removed. For example, the command

    unalias grippe grn

removes the alias definitions of the names `grippe` and `grn`. With the second form, specifying the `-a` option, all aliases are removed.

6.19.3
Examples

Here are some examples of the use of aliases:

- If you issue the command

      alias ls="ls -CF"

  then the command 'ls subdir' is transformed into 'ls -CF subdir' but the command '\ls subdir' is executed without change.

- If you issue the command

      alias locate="who | fgrep"

  then the command 'locate igor' is transformed into 'who | fgrep igor', which shows you any terminal where 'igor' is logged in.

6.19.4
Tracked Aliases

Ksh includes a feature called *tracked aliases* for rapid lookup of command names. If a name is defined as a tracked alias, ksh substitutes the alias value for the name at the same time it processes other aliases. You activate this feature by turning on the **trackall** option with the command 'set -h' or 'set -o trackall' (see p. 367). Tracked aliases are not used if you don't activate them. Tracked aliases are not included in POSIX.

Ksh defines a tracked alias when it encounters a command name *cmd* that turns out to refer to an executable program or shell script found in a file. It then defines *cmd* as an alias for the absolute pathname of the file where the program or shell script was found.

If you change the value of PATH (see Section 2.9.2), all existing tracked aliases become undefined but still remain known to ksh as tracked aliases. If you reference an undefined tracked alias, ksh looks it up using the current value of PATH. Note that alias processing, including the processing of tracked aliases, takes place at a very early stage in the interpretation of command names (see Section 6.8.1).

6.20   Commands for Job Control

The **fg** and **bg** commands move a job to the foreground or background, respectively. The **jobs** command displays the status of your jobs. In addition, the **kill** command (see Section 5.3.1) can be used to kill a job. See Section 2.6.3 for a discussion of job control concepts.

6.20.1
Activating Jobs with
fg and bg

The forms of the **fg** and **bg** command lines are

    fg [job]
    bg [job ...]

For `fg`, the specified job *job* is run in the foreground. For `bg`, the specified jobs *job* ... are run in the background. If no jobs are specified, the most recently suspended job is run in the foreground or background, respectively. The job identifiers are described in "Job Identifiers" on page 34.

6.20.2
Listing Jobs
with `jobs`

The `jobs` command lists the status of a set of jobs. The form of the `jobs` command line is

```
jobs [-l | -p] [ job ... ]
```

In this form, each *job* is a job identifier (see "Job Identifiers" on p. 34). If any jobs *job* ... are specified, the status of those jobs is shown. Otherwise the status of all stopped and background jobs is shown, together with the status of any job whose status has changed but for which the status change has not yet been reported. The command-line options are as follows:

`-l` Provide additional information about each job, including at least the process group ID. Further information may include the status of each process within the job.

`-p` Display only the process IDs for the process group leaders of each job.

6.20.3
Form of the `jobs`
Output

The default output from `jobs` looks like this:

```
[1]    Running              grinder
[2]    Done                 grep oboe hobo |
       Running              sort > lobo
[4]  - Stopped              emacs scrimp.c
[5]  + Stopped (tty input)  collect
```

The `jobs` command itself is the foreground job and is not shown. The number in brackets is the job number. The *current job* is the job most recently stopped, or started in the background; it is indicated by '+'. The *previous job* is the job that was current when this one became the current job; it is indicated by '-'. The third column shows the status of each job. Note that a job can be stopped either because it is expecting input from the terminal or because it was stopped explicitly. The last column shows the command associated with each process of a job. If you specify the `-l` option to `jobs`, it shows you the process numbers as well. The numbers shown in the `jobs` output are the same ones you use in job identifiers.

6.21   The Command History and the `fc` Command

Whenever you execute a command, the shell keeps a record of that command in a *history list*. Using the `fc` command, you can retrieve previous commands and execute them again without having to retype them. Most shells enable you to retrieve commands from previous shell invocations and previous logins; to activate this feature, set the `HISTSIZE` variable to the number of commands to be preserved from the previous invocation. The record of that past history is kept in a file whose pathname is given by the value of the `HISTFILE` variable (default `~/.sh_history`).

Each command in the history list is numbered, although the numbers act only as labels. The most recent portion of a history list might look like this:

```
...
14  ls -l
15  mailx
16  cd ~/bin
17  ls -l | tee longlist
18  rm miasma*
```

You can refer to a command in the history list in three ways: (a) by its number, optionally with a preceding '+'; (b) by *-n*, designating the *n*th most recently executed command; or (c) by a string *str*, indicating the most recently executed command that begins with *str*. For example, you could refer to command 17 in the example above as '17', '+17', '-2', 'ls', or 'l'.

The forms of the `fc` command line are[27]

> `fc` [`-r`] [`-e` *editor*] [*first* [*last*]]
> `fc -l` [`-nr`] [*first* [*last*]]
> `fc  -s` [*old=new*] [*first*]

The first form is used to edit a sequence of commands and then re-execute the edited version of those commands. The second form is used to list all or part of the command history. The third form provides a simpler kind of re-execution of a single command. The variables *first* and *last* in these forms are history list references in one of the three forms just described.

Ksh provides a convenient predefined alias `r` whose definition is '`fc -s`'. Called without an argument, it re-executes the previous command; called with an argument *n*, it re-executes command *n*. The predefined alias `history`, defined as '`fc -l`', displays the command history.

**6.21.1
Editing and
Executing
Commands**

If neither `-l` nor `-s` is specified as in the first form, then the commands in the range from *first* to *last* are edited. If you omit *last*, then just *first* is edited; if you omit both *first* and *last*, then '`-1`' (the most recently executed command) is edited. The editor used is given by *editor* if you specify the `-e` option; otherwise, it is given by the value of the `FCEDIT` environment variable, if `FCEDIT` is set and has a non-null value; and finally, as a last resort, the `ed` editor (see Section 8.4) is used. The `-r` option causes the

---

27. Older versions of `ksh` don't recognize the `-s` option but do recognize an '`-e -`' option for re-executing a previously entered command.

text to be edited to consist of the commands in reverse order rather than in forward order.

When you exit from the editor, the lines of the edited text are executed as commands and the newly executed commands are added as a single command to the end of the history list.[28] For example, with the history in the previous example, the command

```
fc 16 -1
```

presents the text

```
cd ~/bin
ls -l | tee longlist
rm miasma*
```

in an editor buffer. Suppose you change the contents of the buffer to

```
cd ~/bin
rm effluent*
```

and exit from the editor. Then the `cd` and `rm` commands just above will be executed and added as a single item to the end of the history list, leaving the history list as

```
...
14   ls -l
15   mailx
16   cd ~/bin
17   ls -l | tee longlist
18   rm miasma*
19   cd ~/bin
     rm effluent*
```

6.21.2
Listing Commands

If the `-l` option is specified as in the second form, the commands from *first* to *last* are listed (i.e., are produced on standard output). The `-n` option suppresses the command numbers and the `-r` option reverses the order of the listing. No commands are executed and the command history is unaffected except that the `fc` command itself is added to the history.

6.21.3
Modifying and Executing a Single Command

If the `-s` option is specified as in the third form, a single command is executed, namely, the one specified by *first*. If *first* is not specified, it defaults to the most recent command. If a substitution '*old*=*new*' is specified, the string *new* is substituted for the first occurrence of *old* in the command before it is executed. Using the history above, executing the command

```
fc -s miasma=outflow rm
```

causes the command

```
rm outflow*
```

to be executed.

---

28. Some shells such as Bash assign a distinct line number to each newly executed command.

6.21.4 **Command-Line** **Options**	In summary, these are the command-line options for `fc`:

`-l`	List the specified commands from the history list.
`-s`	Substitute *old* for *new* in the command identified by *first* and execute the revised command.
`-e` *editor*	Use the editor *editor* to edit commands rather than the default editor.
`-r`	Reverse the order of the commands to be edited or listed.
`-n`	Suppress the command numbers for an `-l` listing.

6.22   Intrinsic Commands and Predefined Aliases

Most of the commands listed in this section are intrinsic to the shell; the shell interprets them directly rather than executing them indirectly in a subshell. A couple of them, which we note, are predefined aliases.

6.22.1 **Special Forms of** **Command** **Execution**	The following commands provide special forms of command execution: `exec` *cmd* [*arg*...] `exec` *redir* ...

> For the first form of `exec`, executes *cmd* with the specified arguments (if any). The execution of *cmd* replaces the execution of the shell as the activity of the current process; when *cmd* terminates, the process terminates also.
>
> The second form of `exec` specifies one or more redirections (see Section 6.10). These redirections cause the associations between file descriptors and files to be changed for the rest of the time that the shell is in control (unless further redirections change the associations again). This form of `exec` does not cause any commands to be executed; command interpretation continues as usual afterwards.

`.` *file* ("dot")

> Executes the contents of *file* directly (not in a subshell). It is useful when *file* contains commands that are intended to affect the state of the shell; for example, by modifying variables or changing the current directory. The space after the dot is required. The shell uses `PATH` to locate *file* just as it does to locate commands (see Section 2.9.2).

6.22.2 **Exiting from** **the Shell**	The following command terminates execution of the shell: `exit` [*n*] Terminates the shell with an exit status of *n*. If *n* is omitted, the exit status is that of the last command executed within the shell. An end-of-file has the same effect as `exit`.

6.22.3
Exiting from Shell Functions

The following command terminates execution of a shell function (see Section 6.13.4):

return [*n*]

> Returns from a defined shell function with an exit status of *n*. If *n* is omitted, the exit status is that of the last command executed within the function.

6.22.4
Exiting from an Iteration

The following commands enable you to break out of an iteration before control has reached the end of it:

break [*n*]   Exits from *n* enclosing `while` or `for` iterations. If *n* is omitted, it is taken as 1.

continue [*n*]

> Exits from *n* − 1 enclosing `while` or `for` iterations and continues execution at the beginning of the *n*th enclosing iteration. If *n* is omitted, it is taken as 1.

6.22.5
Null Command

The following command acts as a null command:

: [*text*]   Does nothing but parses *text* as usual. You can use this command to execute constructs solely for their side effects by including those constructs in *text*. For example, the command

```
: ${TEA_TEMP:=HOT}
```

conditionally sets the value of `TEA_TEMP`.

> **Note:** In some systems, a colon at the beginning of a shell script specifies that the script is to be interpreted by the Bourne shell.

6.22.6
Catching Signals

The following command enables you to intercept signals that occur during the execution of a command and take appropriate action:

trap [[*cmdtext*] *signal* ...]

> Associates an action with one or more signals. The signal names are given by the list *signal* ... and the action by *cmdtext*. Thereafter, when the shell receives one of these signals it executes the commands in *cmdtext*. The signal names are written without the 'SIG' (e.g., 'TERM' or 'HUP'). Alternatively you can specify signals by their numbers, a historically common but murkier practice.
>
> The shell actually interprets *cmdtext* twice: once when it processes the `trap` command and once when it takes the actions, so *cmdtext* is usually quoted. The result of the first interpretation can include compound commands and operators.
>
> If *cmdtext* is '−', the listed traps are reset to their original values. If no arguments are given, `trap` lists the commands associated with each signal number. Signal 0 is associated with

exit from the shell. (The kernel does not use 0 as a signal number.)

The default actions for the various signals are those inherited from the parent process of the shell, except that the shell ignores SIGINT and SIGQUIT when received from a background process. The latter condition rarely occurs, since these signals by their nature are supposed to originate from a terminal.

If *cmdtext* is the null string, the specified signals are ignored. For example, the command

```
trap '' 1 2 15
```

causes the shell to ignore signals 1, 2, and 15.

See Section 2.6.1 for an explanation of signals and a list of signal numbers. In addition to the signals listed there, the shell recognizes the ERR, EXIT, and DEBUG signals:

- The ERR signal is raised when a command at the end of a pipeline returns a nonzero exit status, provided that the errexit option (see p. 374) is turned on. This signal is not supported by POSIX.

- The EXIT signal is raised when a function completes after executing a trap within the function, or when the shell itself attempts to exit.

- The DEBUG signal is raised after the execution of each simple command. This signal is not supported by POSIX.

The ERR and DEBUG traps are not inherited by functions. In other words, if you set one of these traps and then call a function, the action you've specified has no effect within the function.

6.22.7 Operations Pertaining to Variables

The following commands affect the status of variables:

typeset [{+|-}fLRZilrtux [*n*]] [*name*[=*value*]] ...

Sets (with '-') or unsets (with '+') the specified attributes of one or more variables or functions given by *name* ... .] The meanings of the attributes are given in Section 6.15.5.

- If f is not specified, then each *name* must be a variable. If an assignment (with '=') is included, *value* is assigned to *name*; otherwise, the value of *name* is left alone. The specification of *n*, if present, specifies the length of the value of *name*. When you use typeset within a function definition, it creates a new instance of each variable *name*, which disappears when the function exits. You can also use typeset without any *name*s to produce information on standard output:

  typeset   Displays the names and values of all variables.

typeset −*attrs*
> Displays the names and values of all variables with the specified attributes *attrs*.

typeset +*attrs*
> Displays the names but not the values of all variables with the specified attributes *attrs*.

- If f is specified, then each *name* must be a function, no assignments are permitted, and the only valid attributes are t, u, and x. In this case, x specifies that the named function definitions are to be in effect for any shell script executed directly with the '. *func*' form. By omitting specifications from the typeset command, you can cause it to produce several kinds of information:

  ○ If you specify only −f or +f, typeset produces the names (with +f) or the names and definitions (with −f) of all functions.
  ○ If you specify names but no attributes, typeset produces the names (with +f) or the names and definitions (with −f) of the specified functions.
  ○ If you specify attributes but no names, typeset produces the names (with +f) or the names and definitions (with −f) of all functions with the specified attributes.

The typeset command is not supported by POSIX.

export [*name*[=*val*] ...]
> Exports the variables *name* ... if specified. An exported variable can be assigned a value *val* at the same time. Exporting a variable places it in the environment of any subshell executed by the shell (see Section 6.15.3). For instance, the command

> ```
> export olives hides pottery
> ```

> marks the variables olives, hides, and pottery for export. The export command used by itself lists the variables currently being exported. Under POSIX, the only way to undo the effect of export is to remove the variable altogether with unset.

unset *name* ...
> Deletes ("unsets") one or more variables or shell functions (see Section 6.13.4).

readonly [*name*[=*val*] ...]
> Marks the listed variables as read-only. You can assign a value *val* to a variable when you make it read-only, but thereafter the shell treats an assignment to the variable as an error. If no variables are given in the command, the current read-only variables are listed. Once you've made a variable read-only,

you can't undo this action—not only can't you assign to the variable, you can't remove it with unset either.

integer [*name*[=*val*] ...]

Defines the listed variables and assigns them integer type. This command is a predefined alias whose definition is 'typeset -i'.

shift [*n*]   Renumbers the parameters so that parameter $n + 1$ becomes parameter 1, parameter $n + 2$ becomes parameter 2, and so on. The first n parameters become inaccessible. If n is omitted, it is taken as 1. This command is rarely useful outside of shell scripts. At one time it was the only way to retrieve parameters beyond $9.

**6.22.8
Setting Options and
Parameters**

The following command can be used to set options and parameters for the shell:

set [*options*] [*word*...]

Enables or disables the indicated options, or sets the positional parameters, starting with $1, to the indicated words. The detailed syntax is

set [{+|-}aefhmnopstuvx] [{+|-}o *option*]
    [+|-A *name*] [*arg*...]

The options and their meanings are listed in Section 6.24. The usual conventions for the interpretation of options apply (see Section 2.12), except that '-' enables options and '+' disables them. You can specify several '+' and '-' groups in a single command. For example, the command

set -en +fhv -- - nguyen

enables the e and n options, disables the f, h, and v options, and assigns '-' to $1 and 'nguyen' to $2. The '--' separates the options from the actual arguments.

If no arguments follow '--', the shell unsets all positional parameters. As usual, $- contains the flag settings following execution of set (see p. 349). Turning on the s option causes the words generated by the expansion of the arguments to be sorted, which is useful when those words are eventually to appear in a listing.

Executing set without any options or words shows the names and values of all variables; the form 'set +' shows the names but not the values. If you redirect the output of set called by itself to a file *setvals*, you can later restore the values of the variables by executing that file with the command '. *setvals*'.

**6.22.9
Evaluations**

The following command evaluates the words of a command before executing it, thereby causing those words to be evaluated twice:

eval [*word*...]

Evaluates each word by applying the usual substitutions, then treats the sequence of words that results as a command (or list of commands) and executes that command. For example, suppose that a shell script contains the single command

```
eval echo \$$#
```

If the script is called with three arguments (not counting the command name itself), eval yields the command line

```
echo $3
```

Thus the shell script echoes its last argument, an effect that would be difficult to obtain otherwise.

let *arg* ...

Evaluates each argument *arg* as an arithmetic expression (see Section 6.18.2), returning *true* if the last expression has a nonzero value and *false* otherwise. Since the results are otherwise discarded, the main purpose of this command is to use the arithmetic assignment operator to perform multiple assignments, as in the following example:

```
let flea_count=$2-$1 midge_count=$4-$3
```

Of course, you could also do the same thing with the statements

```
flea_count=$(($2-$1)) midge_count=$(($4-$3))
```

so let isn't all that useful.

**6.22.10
Process Monitoring and Control**

The following commands monitor the resources used by ksh and its child processes and wait for child processes to terminate:

times   Produces the user time and system time used so far by child processes. For instance, an output of

```
2m47s 0m19s
```

indicates that child processes have so far used 2 minutes, 47 seconds of user time and 19 seconds of system time. The listed times don't include any time used by the invocation of ksh itself. This command is not included in POSIX.

ulimit [*n*]

Limits the size of files written by ksh and its child processes to *n* blocks. You can lower the limit with ulimit but not raise it. If *n* is omitted, the command shows the current size limit. This command is not included in POSIX.

wait [*n*]   Waits for the process with process ID *n* to finish, then returns the exit status of that process. If *n* is omitted, the shell waits for all background processes that it has spawned to complete. It then returns an exit code of zero.

**6.22.11
Utility Commands**

The following utility commands are described elsewhere in the book. Some of them are intrinsic to the shell because they affect the state of the shell itself. For example, the alias command is intrinsic because the shell needs to know at all times what aliases are defined. The others are intrinsic for the sake of efficiency.

`alias` [*name*[=*str*] ...]
> Defines one or more aliases (see Section 6.19.1).

`cd` [*path*]   Changes the current directory (see Section 3.1.1).[29]

`echo` [*word*...]
> Echoes back the arguments (see Section 5.8.1).

`getopts` *text name* [*word*...]
> Parses the command line for a shell script (see Section 6.26).

`newgrp` [*arg*...]
> Changes the group identification (see Section 5.4.3).

`print` [-Rnprs] [-u[*n*]] [*arg* ...]
> Produces ("prints") the arguments *arg* ... (see Section 5.8.3).

`pwd`   Shows ("prints") the name of the current (working) directory (see Section 3.1.2).

`r` [*first* [*last*]]
> Re-executes commands *first* through *last* from the command history (see Section 6.21). If *last* is omitted, just *first* is re-executed; if both are omitted, the previous command is re-executed. This command is a predefined alias.

`history`   Displays the command history. This command is a predefined alias for '`fc -l`' and accepts the additional options associated with that form..

`read` [-r] *var* ...
> Reads an input line into a set of variables (see Section 5.8.4).

`[...]`
`test`   Performs a test (see Section 6.12).

`umask`   Reduces the default permissions used for file creation (see Section 3.11.2).

`unalias` *name* ...
> Removes one or more aliases (see Section 6.19.2).

6.23   Predefined Variables Used by the Shell

In the following subsections, we describe the predefined variables of the shell and their effects.

---

29. Were `cd` to be implemented by executing a child process, its effects would be lost when the child process terminated. Thus `cd` must be executed by the shell itself.

6.23.1
Predefined Variables
Set by the Shell

The variables described below are set by the shell itself. Ordinarily, you should not change their values.

POSIX Variables.   The following variables are supported by POSIX:

PPID   This variable contains the process ID of the process that called this invocation of the shell (the parent process).

LINENO   As the shell interprets a script or shell function, it sets LINENO to the sequential line number of the line it is interpreting.

OPTARG   After executing getopts (see Section 6.26), the shell sets OPTARG to the value of the requested option.

OPTIND   After executing getopts, the shell sets OPTIND to the index of the next unprocessed option.

Non-POSIX Variables.   The following variables are not supported by POSIX:

_   The value of the underscore variable depends on the context in which you examine it:

 • After executing a shell command, it contains the last argument of the previous simple command.
 • After the shell notifies you of mail, it contains the file where the mail was found.
 • Within the environment of an invoked program, it contains the pathname of the program.

OLDPWD   After a cd command, this variable contains the pathname of the previous working directory.

RANDOM   This variable contains a random integer k ($0 \leq k \leq 32767$) that changes with each reference to $RANDOM. You can set the seed of the random number generator by assigning a value to RANDOM, but you should never unset RANDOM.

REPLY   This variable contains the string typed in response to select (see p. 341).

ERRNO   If a system call fails, this variable contains the (system-dependent) error number of the failure.

SECONDS   This variable contains the elapsed time in seconds since ksh was invoked.

6.23.2
Directory
Operations

The following variables determine how the shell interprets the cd command and how it searches through directories:

HOME   HOME normally designates your home directory; for example, /home/hagar for user hagar (see Section 2.7.3). Many UNIX commands look for files in your home directory and use HOME to find that directory. If you issue the `cd` command without an argument, the shell uses the value of HOME as its argument.

PATH   When the shell encounters a command that is not intrinsic, it searches the directories in PATH for a file with the same name as the command. PATH is inherited from the environment; see Section 2.9.2 for further explanation of how it works.

CDPATH   The value of CDPATH is a list of directories used by the `cd` command when it searches for its argument. This value should have the form

> *path*[: *path*...]

where each *path* specifies a directory. An empty *path* is legitimate and specifies the current directory. For example, suppose that the value of CDPATH is

```
:~:/usr/lib:..
```

and that you execute the command

```
cd dates
```

while the current directory is `~/imports/new`. Then `cd` checks the following directories in turn until it finds one that exists and changes the current directory to that one:

```
~/imports/new/dates
~/dates
/usr/lib/dates
~/imports/dates
```

FPATH   The value of FPATH is the search path that `ksh` uses to locate the definitions of autoloaded functions; that is, functions that have not yet been defined (see "Autoloading Function Definitions in `ksh`" on p. 324). You specify that a function is to be autoloaded with the `autoload` alias, which in turn makes use of the `-fu` option combination of `typeset` (see p. 365). FPATH is not included in POSIX since POSIX does not include autoloading.

6.23.3
Prompts and
Separators

The following variables pertain to prompts and separators:

PS1   This variable contains the primary command prompt; that is, the prompt that the shell issues when it expects a new command. It defaults to '$'.

PS2   This variable contains the secondary command prompt; that is, the prompt that the shell issues when it expects the continuation of a command on a new line. It defaults to '>'.

PS3   This variable contains the prompt produced by the `select` command (see p. 341). PS3 is not included in POSIX since POSIX does not support `select`.

PS4 This variable contains the prompt that the shell produces during an execution trace when it is ready to execute the command just displayed.

IFS This variable contains the characters that act as input field separators (i.e., that mark the end of a word). The default value of IFS is a string containing the three characters ⟨space⟩, ⟨tab⟩, and ⟨newline⟩, which is also the value used if IFS is unset. The separators in IFS are used by the read command (see Section 5.8.4) and during certain expansions such as command substitutions, but the value of IFS does *not* affect how direct shell command-line input is parsed. It's rarely useful to change IFS except to modify the behavior of the read command. Note that awk has an FS variable (see p. 220) with virtually the same meaning.

An input field separator can have another meaning as well. For example, you could include '|' in IFS—although it wouldn't make any difference since '|', being an operator character, already terminates a word.

6.23.4 Mail Notification

Ksh can automatically notify you when mail arrives (or is waiting for you when you log in). The following variables, which are not included in POSIX, control this notification:

MAILPATH This variable contains a list of the files that the shell checks to see if mail has arrived (indicated by a change to a file's modification time). The list of files has the form

filespec [: *filespec*...]

Each *filespec* has the form

filename [%*message*]

The indicated *message* is sent to your terminal whenever mail arrives in the file named *filename*. If *message* is omitted, the default message 'you have mail' is used.[30] For example, setting MAILPATH to

~/mail:~/bills%you are being dunned

causes the message 'you have mail' to appear whenever mail arrives in the mail subdirectory of your home directory and the message 'you are being dunned' whenever mail arrives in the bills subdirectory of your home directory.

MAIL This variable exists primarily for compatibility with programs that don't recognize MAILPATH. It is equivalent to MAILPATH

---

30. To include a colon as part of *message*, define $COLON as ':' and use '\$COLON' within *message* wherever you want a colon.

except that it accepts only a single file name and no alternate *message*. Ksh ignores MAIL if MAILPATH is set. The value of MAIL is inherited from the environment, where it is set to the file name of your primary mailbox when you log in (see Section 11.3).

MAILCHECK

This variable, which should have an integer value, specifies how often ksh checks whether mail has arrived. A value of n greater than 0 specifies a check every n seconds; a value of 0 indicates that ksh should check for mail after *every* prompt. If MAILCHECK is not set, it defaults to 600 (check every 10 minutes).

6.23.5
Other Variables

The shell also provides the additional variables described below.

Execution Environment. The following variables affect the execution environment:

ENV
The pathname of the script that the shell executes when it starts up. This script is executed both on login (when it is executed after ~/.profile) and when the shell is called as a subshell. It is a good place for defining aliases and functions and for setting options with the set command (see p. 367).

TMOUT
Timeout period in seconds for entering commands at the shell level. If you're at a shell prompt and don't enter a command within the timeout period, ksh automatically logs you out. Timeout doesn't affect idle time when you're in a called program. This variable is not included in POSIX.

SHELL
When you call ksh in a simple command, the value of SHELL is checked to see if it is a pathname whose filename is rsh, rksh, or krsh. If it is, ksh runs in restricted mode (see Section 6.2.2). You might expect that other values of SHELL would have some effect on ksh, but they don't. The default value of SHELL is the pathname of your login shell. Although several POSIX commands use SHELL, the POSIX shell itself ignores it.

Choice of Editor. The following variables affect the command-line editor that ksh uses and the editor that the fc command uses to edit command histories:

EDITOR
VISUAL
A pathname that determines the command-line editor unless you override it with an explicit option. If you define both VISUAL and EDITOR, VISUAL takes precedence. Only the filename part of the pathname matters, and the only significant values are emacs, gmacs, and vi.

FCEDIT
The editor that fc uses when you edit a sequence of commands (see Section 6.21). Any editor at all will do.

None of these variables affect the behavior of a POSIX shell, although EDITOR and VISUAL are used by other POSIX utilities.

Terminal Properties.   The following variables specify the screen dimensions of your terminal:

LINES   The number of lines on your terminal's screen.

COLUMNS   The number of columns on your terminal's screen.

These variables are used by a number of commands such as select, ls, and more. It is sometimes useful to set them to a value that differs from the actual number of lines or columns on your screen.

History Maintenance.   The following variables affect the history file that saves the history list over shell invocations:

HISTFILE The pathname of the history file (see Section 6.21).

HISTSIZE The number of commands from the previous invocation of the shell saved in the history file.

6.24   Execution Options

You can modify the way that the shell executes by specifying various execution options, either on the shell command line or with the set command (see p. 367). The options given on the command line are in effect initially; you can modify them later with set. The options described in Section 6.4 are available only on the command line since it would not generally make sense to change them while the shell is running.

The options described below can be used in either place. Most options have both a name and a letter. You use the letter in the usual way; you use the name as an argument to the o option. Options without a letter can be used only with o. Both notations have the same meaning. We indicate options letters without the usual hyphen since they can be used either with a hyphen to turn them on or with a plus to turn them off.

**6.24.1
Process-Related
Options**

The following options relate to process execution:

t   Exit after executing the first command list; that is, at the point where the shell would otherwise issue the primary command prompt.

monitor (m)
           Run background jobs in a separate process group. This option is enabled by default for interactive systems that support job control and must be enabled if job control is to be recognized.

errexit (e)
           If a command at the end of a pipeline returns a nonzero exit

status, execute the ERR trap and then exit the shell. POSIX does not support the ERR trap.

bgnice Run all background jobs at lower priority. This option is not included in POSIX.

privileged (p)

Restore the effective user/group IDs to the values in effect when ksh was invoked. This option is automatically turned on if the real and effective IDs are different when ksh is invoked. If this option is on initially, the ~/.profile file is not processed and the file /etc/suid_profile is processed instead of the file specified by the ENV variable. The purpose of these changes is to run a program or a shell script on behalf of a user in an environment that the user cannot corrupt. This option is not included in POSIX.

6.24.2
Debugging Options

The following options relate to debugging:

verbose (v)

Show each input line as it is read; that is, be "verbose".

noexec (n)

Don't execute commands, just read them. This option, which is ignored if the shell is running interactively, is useful for checking shell scripts for syntax errors.

xtrace (x)

Show each simple command and its arguments as it is executed.

6.24.3
Options Affecting Names

The following options relate to variables, substitutions, and aliases:

allexport (a)

Cause any variable that is assigned a value to be exported automatically.

nounset (u)

When substituting for variables, treat an unset variable as an error and issue a complaint.

markdirs Append a trailing slash to directory names that result from pathname expansion. This option is not included in POSIX.

noglob (f)

Turn off the pattern expansion of pathnames.

trackall (h)

Make tracked aliases when possible (see Section 6.19.4). This option is not included in POSIX.

6.24.4
Editor-Related Options

The following options affect the choice of built-in editor and the editor's behavior:

emacs Use emacs as the command-line editor.

gmacs Use gmacs variant of emacs as the command-line editor.

vi   Use vi as the command-line editor.

viraw   When vi is the command-line editor, have it use character-mode input rather than line-mode input.

Of these options, only vi is included in POSIX.

**6.24.5
Miscellaneous
Options**

The following options have other functions:

ignoreeof

Don't exit the shell when an ⌈EOF⌉ is typed; instead, warn the user.

noclobber (C)

Don't overwrite a file with output that has been redirected by >. You can force the overwrite by using the >| redirection operator. Some versions of ksh don't recognize the C single-letter form.

nolog   Don't store function definitions in the history list. This option is not included in POSIX.

s   Sort the positional parameters created by set. This option is useful when the argument of set is given as a pattern that expands to a list of pathnames that will eventually appear in a listing. It has a different meaning when given on the shell invocation line.

6.25   Initialization Files for the Shell

When the shell is called as a login shell, it first executes the commands in the /etc/profile, ~/.profile, and ENV files (if they exist) in that order. It then prompts you for a command. The commands in /etc/profile are intended to apply to all users of the shell (not all systems provide this file). The commands in ~/.profile are intended to be modified to taste by each user. When your account is set up, a canned version of this file is usually installed in your home directory. Typically, ~/.profile includes commands to set PATH to a preassigned search path and to set TERM to the type of your terminal.

When the shell is called as a subshell through an explicit invocation of its name, it first executes the commands in the ENV file but not the commands in any of the profile files. Thus the ENV file contains commands that are executed whenever the shell is called, either as a login shell or as a subshell. The location of this file is given by the ENV variable. If the value of ENV is not the pathname of a readable file, ENV is ignored. The ENV file is useful as a place for defining aliases and functions and for setting options with the set command (see p. 367).

Ksh determines if it was called as a login shell by looking at the first character of $0 (i.e., the first character of the name by which it was called). If that character is '-', ksh assumes it was called as a login shell.[31],[32]

The login command on some systems enables you to specify values for certain environment variables on the login line (see Section 5.4.1). On such systems you can set up your .profile file to test these variables, which provides a handy way to control what .profile does when you log in. For instance, some systems set L0 to the first word after your name on the command line if there is such a word. On these systems you can set up .profile to execute the C shell whenever you put CS after your login name by including the following line at the end of .profile:

```
if [ "$L0" = CS ]; then exec csh; fi
```

6.26   Parsing Command Lines with getopts

The getopts ("get options") command, intrinsic to the shell, parses options and arguments on a command line according to the standard syntax described in Section 2.12. You can analyze the contents of a command line using ordinary shell programming facilities rather than getopts, but it isn't easy.

The form of the getopts command is

getopts *optstring name* [*arg...*]

Here *optstring* describes the allowable options, *name* specifies a variable for receiving notification of each option that is present, and the *args* specify arguments to be used in place of the arguments appearing in the command line. To distinguish the arguments of options from those of the command itself, we refer to these as "option arguments" and "arguments", respectively.

The option string *optstring* contains a single letter for each allowable option. If the option takes an argument, the letter is followed by a colon. For example, the option string 'ah:q' used in the example below signifies that the command in question expects options 'a' and 'q' without arguments and option 'h' with an argument.

Note: Arguments to options are never optional. An option either always takes an argument or never does.

---

31. Should you need to, you can "fake" a login shell by creating a link from '-*shell*' to *shell* within your home directory with a command such as

```
ln -- ksh ~/-ksh
```

However, the extra link you've created may worry some system administrators for highly secure systems. If that's the case, ask the administrator either to change your login shell or to create the '-ksh' link in the same directory where ksh resides.

32. There's no guarantee that this convention will apply to a POSIX shell in general.

6.26.1
Using getopts

To use getopts, you call it repeatedly until it has parsed all the options. Each time you call it, getopts absorbs either one argument or two, starting with the leftmost argument. It returns a zero exit status if one or more options remain and a nonzero exit status if none do. In addition, it sets three variables: *name*, OPTIND ("options index"), and OPTARG ("option argument"). It sets them as follows:

- The variable *name* contains the name of the option just found, or '?' for an option not in *optstring*.

- The variable contains the index of the next unprocessed argument. When getopts returns, it sets OPTIND to the index of the first argument that is not part of the options. The value of OPTIND is ordinarily uninteresting until all the options have been processed. The command

      shift $((OPTIND - 1))

  is often used after the options have been processed in order to renumber the arguments. Before the renumbering, the first argument ($1) is the first option to the command. After the renumbering, the first argument becomes the one that previously was the first command argument (after the options).

- The variable contains the option argument provided for the option in *name*. That argument may contain commas or, if it was quoted, blanks. The presence of commas or blanks indicates that the option argument is really a list of arguments such as file names.

6.26.2
Example of getopts

The following shell script, while not useful in itself, shows how getopts works:

```
while getopts ah:q opt; do
   case $opt in
   a | q)   printf "$opt, OPTIND=$OPTIND\n" ;;
   h)       printf "$opt: \"$OPTARG\", OPTIND=$OPTIND\n" ;;
   *)       printf "other: \"$opt\"\n" ;;
   esac
done
for arg do printf "[$arg] "; done; printf "\n"
shift $(( OPTIND - 1 ))
for arg do printf "[$arg] "; done; printf "\n"
```

If you name this script doit and issue the command line

```
doit -h one,two -qa three four >out
```

you obtain the output

```
h: "one,two", OPTIND=3
q, OPTIND=3
a, OPTIND=4
[-h] [one,two] [-qa] [three] [four]
[three] [four]
```

```
#!/bin/posix/sh
# tolower - replace files by their lowercase equivalents
#
# Example:   tolower file1 file2 ... filen

YESEXPR="$(locale yesexpr)"

function yes_response
{
   if [ $# -ne 1 ]
   then
      printf Response should be just one word\\n
      return 1
   fi

   # Return true if $1 matches $YESEXPR.
   printf $1 | grep -E "$YESEXPR" >/dev/null 2>&1
   return $?  # Not needed, but clearer
}

for file; do
   # if $file is not a regular file, then continue
   if [ ! -f $file ]; then continue; fi

   # Convert $file to lower case, save it as $lfile
   lfile=$(printf $file | tr "[:upper:]" "[:lower:]")

   # Continue if $file and $lfile are the same,
   # that is, if $file is already in lower case
   if [ $file = $lfile ]; then continue; fi
```

Fig. 6-5, Part 1.   A sample shell script.

6.27   A Sample Shell Script

The sample shell script in Figure 6-5 effectively changes the name of each file in a file list to lowercase if the name contains any uppercase characters. It asks the user to confirm each replacement and asks for further confirmation if the corresponding file with a lowercase name already exists. The script illustrates a number of features of the shell's programming language and is also useful in its own right.

```
# If we are here then $file must be a legitimate
# candidate for conversion to lower case.
# Prompt the user and read the response:
printf "change $file to ${lfile}? "
read ans
yes_response $ans ||
{
    printf "$file will not be changed\n"
    continue
}

# If you are here then the user answered Yes!
if [ -f $lfile ]
then
    printf "$lfile already exists.  Overwrite? "
    read ans
    yes_response $ans ||
    {
        printf "$file will not be changed\n"
        continue
    }
fi

mv -f $file $lfile

if [ $? -ne 0 ]; then
    printf "mv failed, $file is unchanged\n"
fi
done
```

Fig. 6-5, Part 2. A sample shell script.

7

Other Shells

In this chapter we discuss two other important shells, the C shell and Bash. The C shell is a BSD derivative of an early version of the Bourne shell that had a strong influence on the KornShell. It is still in wide use on older BSD-based systems such as Solaris 1. Bash, the "Bourne-again shell", was developed as part of the GNU project.

7.1 The C Shell `csh`

The C shell, known under the name `csh`, was developed by Bill Joy early in the BSD project as an improvement on the Bourne shell. Despite its name, the C shell is not significantly more C-like than the Bourne shell. These are some of the features introduced by `csh`:

- The ability to recall previous commands in whole or in part via a "history" mechanism.
- The ability to switch back and forth among several processes and control their progress ("job control").
- More flexible forms of parameter expansion.
- Additional operators as they appear in C.
- Aliases for frequently used commands without using shell scripts.

All these features have been included in subsequent shells, the KornShell in particular. However, `csh` lacks two important capabilities found in most

381

other shells: selective trapping of signals and redirection for arbitrary file descriptors. These were not in the early version of the Bourne shell from which `csh` evolved.

Since most `csh` constructs behave identically to their `ksh` counterparts, we describe `csh` by describing only those features that are different from `ksh`. If you are using `csh`, the best way to learn about it is first to review the list of differences below and then to use the `ksh` description, bearing in mind those features of `ksh` that are not in `csh` or take a different form in `csh`.

The `tcsh` shell is a popular enhanced version of the C shell. These are some of the facilities that `tcsh` adds:

- Ability to edit the command line interactively.
- Easy call-up of previously executed commands, which can then be edited.
- Interactive completion of file names and command names.
- Lookup of documentation of a command as you're typing it.
- Ability to schedule periodic execution of a command.
- Time stamps in the history list.

On some systems `csh` is a synonym for `tcsh`. You can find `tcsh` in most BSD distributions, including the ones on CD-ROM, or obtain it by anonymous FTP from `tesla.ee.cornell.edu`, file `/pub/tcsh/ tcsh-`*m*`.`*nn*`.tar.gz`.

**7.1.1
Summary of
Differences**

These are the features of `ksh` that `csh` does not include:

- General interactive command-line editing.
- A `trap` command or other way to specify the response to interrupts.
- Coprocesses.
- The use of file descriptors as well as pathnames in redirection operators (e.g., the redirection '2<&4').
- Use of `$( ... )` for command substitutions.
- Ability to run as a restricted shell.
- In-line function definitions.
- Autoloading of function definitions from files.
- The `env`, `print`, and `read` intrinsic utilities.
- The `!` operator for negating the result of a pipeline.
- Menu selection and related facilities.
- Array variables.
- Formatting attributes for variables.
- Ability to modify execution options dynamically.

These are the other principal differences from `ksh` you'll need to be aware of if you're using `csh`:

- You can exit from `csh` by typing `logout` as well as by typing `exit`.

- An escaped ⟨newline⟩ (i.e., a backslash at the end of a line) continues a command but acts as a separator between words.

- The default command prompt is '%' (which makes it easy to tell you're in csh).

- Csh recognizes comments only in shell scripts.

- The |& operator has a different interpretation: in the form 'cmd_1|&cmd_2', the standard error and the standard output from the command cmd_1 are both sent to the standard input of the command cmd_2.

- The order of precedence of the linking operators is as follows:

  (1) |
  (2) || &&
  (3) ;
  (4) &

  Note that csh assigns the ';' operator a higher precedence than '&', while ksh assigns the ';' and '&' operators the same precedence.[1]

- The csh construct 'source *file*' directly executes the commands in *file*, just as the ksh construct '. *file*' does. The ksh "dot file" syntax is not in csh.

- Command lookup (see Section 7.1.3) uses a variable path, initialized from the PATH environment variable. It also uses a hash table that can affect the results of the lookup.

- Aliases interact with history substitutions and are not fully protected against looping (see Section 7.1.4).[2]

- The <> redirection operator is not provided, and the >| redirection operator from ksh is written as '>!'. An ampersand on an output redirection operator specifies that standard error as well as standard output should be redirected, and has nothing to do with redirecting file descriptors. For example, '>& junque' redirects both standard output and standard error to the file junque.

- Although csh does not provide general interactive editing of the command line, it does include a facility for completing file names interactively (see Section 7.1.5).

---

1. This subtle difference can be demonstrated by the command

    ```
    echo one; sleep 3; echo two & echo three
    ```

    For ksh the output is in the order 'one', 'two', 'three', but for csh it is in the order 'one', 'three', 'two'.

2. Csh cannot detect the loop created by a sequence of commands such as

    ```
    alias abc ''def''
    alias def ''abc''
    echo 'abc'
    ```

    Executing these commands causes csh to run out of memory and produce a "core dump".

- Of the patterns for pathname expansion provided by ksh, csh provides only the basic '*', '?', and '[...]' wildcards. Csh does, however, have a special notation for lists that is not included in the ksh forms (see Section 7.1.6).

- Csh provides a powerful if baroque syntax for retrieving previous commands or portions of them from the history list (see Section 7.1.2). It does not, however, support the fc command.

- Csh, unlike ksh, explicitly distinguishes between environment variables and local variables and has different commands that apply to them (see Section 7.1.7).

- The parameter expansions provide for extracting portions of the value of a parameter. Most of the special forms of parameter expansion (e.g., conditional expansion) are not provided by csh (see Section 7.1.8).

- Csh has somewhat different rules for handling nested quotations. In particular, the bang character must be quoted with a backslash and most backslashes are taken literally even within double quotes (see Section 7.1.9).

- Csh does not use the IFS variable when parsing the output of a command substitution (see Section 7.1.10).

- Csh does not recognize arithmetic expansions, but a number of intrinsic commands accept C-like expressions (see Section 7.1.11). File tests are written as in ksh, but include tests for fewer attributes (see "Tests" on p. 393); other tests are incorporated within the expression language.

- The names of csh predefined variables are in lowercase, not uppercase. The csh predefined variables are somewhat different from the ksh predefined variables (see Section 7.1.12).

- Both the intrinsic commands (see Section 7.1.13) and the compound commands (see Section 7.1.14) differ from those of ksh.

- Csh looks for its initialization commands in a file named ~/.cshrc and for additional login initialization commands in ~/.login. When you log out, csh executes the commands in ~/.logout.

- The command-line syntax and options are somewhat different (see Section 7.1.15).

In the following subsections we describe those aspects of csh that either differ markedly from ksh or are not provided in ksh at all.

**7.1.2
History
Substitutions**

A history substitution enables you to reuse a portion of a previous command as you type the current command. History substitutions save typing and also help reduce typing errors.

A history substitution normally starts with '!'. A history substitution has three parts: an *event* that specifies a previous command, a *selector* that selects one or more words of the event, and some *modifiers* that modify the selected words. The selector and modifiers are optional. A history substitution has the form

> ![*event*][[:]*selector*[:*modifier*...]]

The event is required unless it is followed by a selector that does not start with a digit (see "Special Conventions" on p. 387). The ':' can be omitted before *selector* if *selector* does not begin with a digit. You can change the character '!' used in history substitutions to another character by changing the value of `histchars` (see p. 394).

History substitutions are interpreted by `csh` before anything else—even before quotations and command substitutions. The only way to quote the '!' of a history substitution is to escape it with a preceding backslash. Be particularly careful to escape the '!' when you call a mailer with a UUCP network address on the command line (see Section 12.1.2).[3] A '!' need not be escaped, however, if it is followed by whitespace, '=', or '('.

See "History-Related Variables" on page 394 for information about intrinsic variables that affect history substitutions.

Events and Their Specifications.   Csh saves each command that you type on a history list provided that the command contains at least one word. The commands on the history list are called *events*. The events are numbered, with the first command that you issue when you enter `csh` being number one. For complex commands, such as `foreach`, that consist of more than one line, only the first line makes its way to the history list. The `history` variable (see p. 394) specifies how many events are retained on the history list. You can view the history list with the `history` command (see p. 398).

These are the forms of an event in a history substitution:

`!!`	The preceding event. Typing '!!' is an easy way to reissue the previous command.
`!n`	Event number *n*.
`!-n`	The *n*th previous event. For example, '! 1' refers to the immediately preceding event and is equivalent to '!!'.
`!str`	The unique previous event whose name starts with *str*.
`!?str?`	The unique previous event containing the string *str*. The closing '?' can be omitted if it is followed by a ⟨newline⟩.

Selectors.   You can select a subset of the words of an event by attaching a *selector* to the event. A history substitution without a selector includes all the words of the event. These are the possible selectors for selecting words of the event:

`:0`	The command name
`[:]^`	The first argument

---

3. This inconvenience might not exist had UUCP-style addressing been used more heavily in the original BSD environment.

[:]$	The last argument
:n	The nth argument ($n \geq 1$)
:n_1-n_2	Words n_1 through n_2
[:]*	Words 1 through $
:x*	Words x through $
:x-	Words x through ($ - 1$)
[:]-x	Words 0 through x
[:]%	The word matched by the preceding '?str?' search

The colon preceding a selector can be omitted if the selector does not start with a digit.

Modifiers.   You can modify the words of an event by attaching one or more modifiers. Each modifier must be preceded by a colon.

The following modifiers assume that the first selected word is a pathname:

:r	Removes a trailing '.str' component from the first selected word.
:h	Removes a trailing pathname component from the first selected word.
:t	Removes all leading pathname components from the first selected word.

For example, if the command

```
ls -l /home/elsa/toys.text
```

has just been executed, then the command

```
echo !!^:r !!^:h !!^:t !!^:t:r
```

produces the output

```
/home/elsa/toys /home/elsa toys.text toys
```

The following modifiers enable you to substitute within the selected words of an event. If the modifier includes 'g', the substitution applies to the entire event; otherwise, it applies only to the first modifiable word.

:[g]s/l/r/

> Substitutes the string r for the string l. The delimiter '/' may be replaced by any other delimiting character. Within the substitution, the delimiter can be quoted by escaping it with '\'. If l is empty, the most recently used string takes its place—either a previous l or the string str in an event selector of the form '!?str?'. The closing delimiter can be omitted if it is followed by a ⟨newline⟩.

| :[g]& | Repeats the previous substitution. |

The following modifiers quote the selected words, possibly after earlier substitutions:

| :q | Quotes the selected words, preventing further substitutions. |

:x   Quotes the selected words but breaks the selected text into words at whitespace.

The following modifier enables you to see the result of a substitution without executing the resulting command:

:p   Shows ("prints") the new command but doesn't execute it.

Special Conventions.   The following additional special conventions provide abbreviations for commonly used forms of history substitutions:

- An event specification can be omitted from a history substitution if it is followed by a selector that does not start with a digit. In this case, the event is taken to be the event used in the most recent history reference on the same line if there is one, or the preceding event otherwise. For example, the command

      echo !?quetzal?∧ !$

  echoes the first and last arguments of the most recent command containing the string 'quetzal'.

- If the first nonblank character of an input line is '∧', the '∧' is taken as an abbreviation for '!:s∧'. This form provides a convenient way to correct a simple spelling error in the previous line. For example, if by mistake you typed the command

      cat /etc/lasswd

  you could re-execute the command with 'lasswd' changed to 'passwd' by typing

      ∧l∧p

  You can replace '∧' with a different character by changing the value of `histchars` (see p. 394).

- You can enclose a history substitution in braces to prevent it from absorbing the following characters. In this case, the entire substitution except for the starting '!' must be within the braces. For example, suppose that you previously issued the command

      cp accounts ../money

  Then the command '!cps' looks for a previous command starting with 'cps', while the command '!{cp}s' turns into the command

      cp accounts ../moneys

**7.1.3
Command Lookup**

When `csh` encounters a non-intrinsic command, either a compiled program or a shell script, it searches for that command in a sequence of directories specified by the variable `path`. Csh derives the initial value of `path` from the environment variable `PATH`, obtained from the environment within which `csh` was called. The `path` variable uses whitespace rather than colons to separate path components, but otherwise has the same meaning as PATH (see Section 2.9.2).

Csh accelerates the command search by means of a *hash table*. The hash table records the names of the executable files in the directories listed in path. Beware: when you create a new executable file, either a shell script or a compiled program, csh will not be able to find it unless you instruct csh to recreate the hash table, which you can do with the rehash command (see p. 398).

7.1.4
Interpretation of Aliases

When csh reads a command line, it tests whether the first word of the line has an alias. If it does, csh replaces the word by the definition of the alias as follows:

- If the definition contains no history substitutions (see Section 7.1.2), the command name is directly replaced by its definition.

- If the definition contains any history substitutions, the substitutions are applied as though the entire text of the command were the previous input line. The result replaces the *entire* command line. Such history substitutions enable the alias definition to utilize the arguments on the command line.

An alias for 'shell' is treated specially: csh uses its value as the shell to call when it executes a command in a subshell. The alias definition must consist of the full pathname of that shell.

7.1.5
Command Completion

Most versions of csh have a feature for completing file names interactively. To enable this feature, you must set the variable filec (see p. 395). The following conventions then apply:

- If you type a file name at the end of a command followed by ⎡Esc⎤, csh completes the file name if it has a unique completion. For example, if you type the command

      fgrep roc av ⎡Esc⎤

and the only file in the current directory that starts with 'av' is 'aviary', csh changes the input line to

      fgrep roc aviary

If the variable fignore contains a list of suffixes, files with those suffixes are not eligible candidates for file name completion unless they are the only candidates. If no unique completion exists, csh completes the file name as far as possible and then sounds the terminal bell.

- If you type a file name followed by ⎡EOF⎤, csh provides a list of all possible completions of the file name and then echoes your input again so that you can complete the file name.

**7.1.6
File Name
Expansions**

In csh parlance, the process of file name expansion is called *globbing*. A csh file name can include the usual wildcards (see Section 2.9.1), though not the other pattern forms provided by ksh. In addition, a string within a file name of the form

$$a\{x_1,x_2,\ \ldots\ ,x_n\}b$$

stands for the list of file names

$$ax_1b\ ax_2b\ \ldots\ ax_nb$$

Either *a*, *b*, or both can be empty. However, an occurrence of '{', '}', or '{}' surrounded by whitespace is taken literally and is not treated by csh as an abbreviation. For example, the command

```
echo {} a{bb,caci,rmad}a
```

produces the output

```
{} abba acacia armada
```

More usefully, the command

```
cp ~noah/fauna/{terns,gerbils,lemurs,zebras} .
```

copies four files from user noah's directory fauna to your current directory. Lacking the '{}' notation, you would have to repeat the reference to '~noah/fauna' four times.

**7.1.7
Variables**

Csh variables include both predefined variables (see Section 7.1.12) and user-defined variables. You can retrieve the values of these variables and set them to new values. You can also retrieve or set the individual words within a variable.

In addition, csh enables you to retrieve and set environment variables. Different commands apply to ordinary local variables and to environment variables:

- The set and @ commands set variables and also display them.
- The unset command removes variables.
- The setenv command sets environment variables.
- The env command displays environment variables.
- The unsetenv command removes environment variables.

If a variable and an environment variable have the same name, the variable takes precedence over the environment variable in any parameter expansions.

**7.1.8
Parameter
Expansions**

A csh parameter expansion, like its ksh counterpart, begins with '$'. If you wish a '$' to be taken literally, you must escape it by writing it as '\$'. However, a '$' followed by whitespace need not be escaped.

Named Variables. The following parameter expansions pertain to named variables:

${*name*} Produces the words of the variable *name*.

${*name*[*sel*]}

> Produces the words of the variable `${name}` that are selected by *sel*. The selector *sel* selects either a single word or a sequence of words. It has one of the following forms:
>
> | | |
> |---|---|
> | n | Selects the nth word. |
> | n_1–n_2 | Selects the sequence of words from the n_1th word through the n_2th word. |
> | n_1– | Selects the sequence of words from the n_1th word through the last word. |
> | –n_2 | Selects the sequence of words from the first word through the n_2th word. |
> | * | Selects all the words. |
>
> The first word of a variable is numbered as 1. The selectors can themselves be the result of parameter expansion.

${#*name*}

> Produces the number of words in the variable *name* as a decimal number.

${?*name*}

> Produces 1 if the variable *name* is set and 0 if it isn't.

Command-Line Arguments.   The following substitutions pertain to the words of the command line:

${*n*}   Produces the nth command-line argument. The predefined variable `argv` (see p. 394) contains the words of the command-line arguments, so this form is equivalent to `$argv[`*n*`]`.

$*   Produces the list of arguments on the command line.

Other Parameter Expansions.   The following substitutions provide other kinds of information:

$0   Produces the name of the current input file.

$?0   Produces 1 if the current input file name is known and 0 if it isn't.

$$ Produces the process number of the copy of `csh` now in control.

$<   Reads a line from standard input and produces it without making any substitutions within it or otherwise interpreting it in any way. This construct is particularly useful for retrieving answers to queries in interactive shell scripts.

Modifiers for Parameter Expansions.   The result of a parameter expansion can be edited by attaching a modifier to it. If the substitution is written using braces, the modifier must appear within the braces. No more than one modifier can be attached.

The following modifiers have the same meanings as the corresponding modifiers for events (see p. 386) except that the `:e` modifier applies only to parameter expansions. If a modifier includes 'g', the substitution applies to the entire result; otherwise it applies only to the first modifiable word of the result.

:[g]r   Removes a trailing '.*str*' component.

:[g]e   Removes everything preceding a trailing '.*str*' component.

:[g]h   Removes a trailing pathname component.

:[g]t   Removes all leading pathname components.

:q   Quotes the substituted words, preventing further substitutions.

:x   Quotes the substituted words but breaks the text into words at whitespace.

7.1.9 Quotation

You can use *quotation* to prevent metacharacters, including whitespace, from being given their normal interpretation (see Section 2.12.2 for a general discussion of quotation). These are the forms of quotation that csh recognizes:

c   Quotes the character *c*. This form of quotation is the only way to quote the history substitution character, normally '!'.

"*text*"   Quotes *text*, except that the characters '$', '`', and '!' within *text* are still recognized as metacharacters. Parameter expansions, command substitutions, and history substitutions are therefore honored. A backslash preceding a bang or a ⟨newline⟩ escapes and quotes the bang or ⟨newline⟩; a backslash in any other context is treated as an ordinary character, even when it precedes another backslash. Since whitespace is taken literally, the entire quoted text acts as a single word. The only exception is that a ⟨newline⟩ produced by an embedded command substitution acts as a separator between words.

'*text*'   Like '"*text*"', except that '!' is the only character recognized as a metacharacter within text. As with '"*text*"', bangs and ⟨newline⟩s are the only characters that can be escaped with a backslash.

For example, the commands

```
set terrier=rufus
echo \! "[\$terrier; `echo vera`;\\]"\
    '[\$terrier; `echo vera`;\\]'
```

produce the output

```
! [\rufus; vera;\\] [\$terrier; `echo vera`;\\]
```

and each bracketed portion of this output is treated as a single word despite its embedded spaces.

7.1.10 Command Substitutions

A command substitution executes a command and then uses its output immediately as part of another command (see Section 2.12.3). Csh recognizes only the backquote form of command substitution.

If the output of a command substitution ends with a ⟨newline⟩, that ⟨newline⟩ is discarded. Whitespace within the output separates words of the resulting command line, although no whitespace is implied at the beginning and end of the command substitution.

If a command substitution occurs within a quotation formed using double quotes, spaces and tabs within its output do not act as word separators but ⟨newline⟩s within its output do. Such ⟨newline⟩s are the only way that the material between double quotes can consist of more than one word. For example, the commands

```
set v1 = (X'echo a b c'Y)
set v2 = ("X'echo a b c'Y")
echo \[$v1\] \[$v2\] \[$#v1\] \[$#v2\]
```

produce the output

```
[Xa b cY] [Xa b cY] [3] [1]
```

7.1.11
Expressions

A number of `csh` intrinsic commands accept expressions having nearly the same form as expressions in C. The operands of these expressions are either decimal numbers, octal numbers, strings, or tests. A sequence of digits beginning with zero is taken as an octal number. Tests are described in "Tests" on page 393. The operands can be obtained as the result of parameter expansion.

These are the operators recognized by `csh`, in decreasing order of precedence:

(...)	grouping
~	one's complement $(-(n + 1))$
!	negation (0 yields 1, anything else yields 0)
* / %	multiplication, division, remainder
+ −	binary addition, binary subtraction
<< >>	left shift, right shift
< > <= >=	less, greater, less or equal, greater or equal
== != =~ !~	equal, not equal, matches, does not match
&	logical "and"
^	logical difference
|	logical "or"
&&	conditional "and"
||	conditional "or"

Since these operators are intended primarily for use by C programmers, we explain only those that are peculiar to `csh`:

- The '==' and '!=' operators compare strings exactly.

- The '=~' operator matches its left operand against the pattern given by its right operand. The pattern can contain any of the wildcards recognized by file name substitution. The match succeeds if the left operand can be derived from the right operand by making substitutions for the wildcards. The '!~' operator is the negation of '=~'.

The following rules apply to expressions:

- Any two adjacent components, either operators or operands, must be separated by whitespace.

- If an expression uses any of the characters (< > & |), these characters must be made part of a subexpression enclosed in parentheses. That subexpression may be the entire expression.

- Empty operands are permitted. An empty operand of a string comparison is taken as the null string; any other empty operand is taken as 0.

Tests.   Each of the tests described below is an expression that returns 1 if it succeeds and returns 0 if it fails. These tests are chiefly useful in shell scripts.

The following test executes a command and tests if it terminated successfully.

{*cmd*}   Executes *cmd* in a subshell, tests if its exit status is zero.

The following tests provide information about a file's status.

-r *file*	Tests if *file* has read access.
-w *file*	Tests if *file* has write access.
-x *file*	Tests if *file* has execute access.
-e *file*	Tests if *file* exists.
-o *file*	Tests if *file* is owned by the user who called `csh`.
-z *file*	Tests if *file* has zero size.
-f *file*	Tests if *file* is an ordinary file.
-d *file*	Tests if *file* is a directory.

**7.1.12
Predefined Variables**

The variables listed below have predefined meanings for `csh`. Many of them have the same meanings as they do for `ksh`; see Section 6.23 for further details about them.

Directories and Files.   The following variables indicate where certain files and directories are to be found:

home	The home directory of the user who called this shell. It is initialized to the value of the HOME environment variable.
cwd	The full pathname of the current working directory. Csh updates this variable whenever you change directories. Not all versions of `csh` provide this variable.
path	The list of directories to search for commands. It is initialized to the value of the PATH environment variable (see Section 2.9.2).
cdpath	The list of directories that the `cd` command uses when it searches for its argument. Csh does not use the CDPATH environment variable.

mail The list of files where mail might be found. Csh checks these files after each command completion to see if the file has been accessed since it was last modified. If not, csh notifies you that new mail has arrived. If the first word of mail is a number n, csh checks for mail every n seconds. The default interval is 600 (10 minutes).

shell The file in which the shell resides. It is initialized to the location of csh itself.

The values of HOME and PATH in csh's inherited environment are updated whenever you change home and path, so any programs that you call from csh see the updated values. However, any changes to these environment variables are lost when csh terminates.

Command Interpretation. The following variables affect the way that csh interprets commands:

ignoreeof

  If set, ignore an end-of-file received from the terminal. If ignoreeof is not set, an end-of-file causes csh to exit.

noclobber

  If set, inhibit redirections specified by '>' from sending output to a file that already exists.

noglob If set, inhibit expansion of wildcards in file names ("globbing"). See Section 7.1.6.

nonomatch

  If set, allow file name expansions that don't match any files. If nonomatch is not set, a file name expansion that does not match any files is treated as an error.

Command-Line Arguments. The following variable provides access to the arguments on the command line:

argv List of the command-line arguments (as a sequence of words).

History-Related Variables. The following variables affect history substitutions:

histchars

  The pair of characters used in history substitutions. The first character, '!' by default, is the one that introduces a history substitution. The second character, '∧' by default, is the one that you can use at the beginning of a command line as an abbreviation for a substitution into the previous command.

history The size of the history list; that is, the number of commands that csh remembers. By default, savehist is not set and csh remembers just the last command.

savehist The number of history entries that csh saves when you log out. (Invocations of csh other than as a login shell are unaffected.)

These entries are restored when you log in again. By default, `savehist` is not set and no history is saved.

Terminal Interaction.   The following variables affect how `csh` interacts with your terminal:

`prompt`   The string that `csh` sends to your terminal before reading a command interactively. If the prompt string includes the character '!', that character is replaced by the current event number, which you can refer to in later history substitutions.

`echo`   If set, show each command and its arguments before executing the command.

`verbose`   If set, show the words of each command after history substitutions.

`notify`   If set, send a notice of any change in the status of a background job immediately instead of waiting for the next command completion.

`time`   If set to a value n, any command that requires more than n seconds of processor time to execute causes `csh` to produce a line of timing information when the command terminates.

`filec`   If set, perform file name completion.

`fignore`   A list of suffixes to be ignored during file name completion.

Exit Status.   The following variable provides information on the exit status of the most recently executed command:

`status`   The exit status of the most recently executed command.

**7.1.13
Simple Intrinsic
Commands**

The commands described below are intrinsic to the shell and do not contain other commands.

Variables.   The following commands pertain to the definitions of variables:

`@ [name[[n]] = expr]`
> Used by itself, '`@`' shows the values of all the local variables. Used with a name but no index n, it sets *name* to the value of *expr*. Used with an index n, it sets the nth word of the variable *name* to *expr*. The expression *expr* is interpreted as described in Section 7.1.11. You must leave whitespace between '`@`' and *name*.
>
> You can increment or decrement *name* by 1 using the form '`@ name++`' or '`@ name--`'. You can also use operators such as '`+=`' in place of '`=`'. The effect of
>
> `@ name += expr`

is to increase *name* by the value of *expr* (taking *name* as 0 if it is not a number). More generally, any binary operator can be used in place of '+' and *name* can have an index attached to it.

```
set
set name
set name[n]=word
set name=(wordlist)
```
Used by itself, 'set' shows the values of all the local variables and is equivalent to '@'. Used with a name only, it sets *name* to the null string. Used with a name but no index *n*, it sets *name* to the indicated word *word* or list of words *wordlist*. Used with an index *n*, it sets the *n*th word of *name* to the word *word*. The difference between '@' and 'set' is that '@' treats the right side of the assignment as a number, eventually converting it to a string, while 'set' treats the right side as a string to begin with.

unset *pat*

Deletes all local variables whose names match the pattern *pat*. The pattern *pat* can contain the same wildcards that are used in file name expansions.

setenv *name val*

Sets the environment variable *name* to *val*. Note that this command does not include an '='.

unsetenv *pat*

Deletes all environment variables whose names match *pat*. The pattern *pat* can contain the same wildcards that are used in file name expansions.

shift [*var*]

Shifts the words of *var* one word left by deleting the first word. If *var* is omitted, it is taken to be argv (see p. 394).

Control Flow.   The following commands provide exits from certain compound commands and otherwise affect the flow of control within a shell script:

break   Resumes execution after the nearest enclosing foreach or while.

breaksw   Resumes execution after the nearest enclosing switch.

continue   Continues execution of the nearest enclosing while or foreach.

[*label*]:   Does nothing, but labels this statement with *label* (if present) for use in goto and onintr commands.

goto *word*

Executes commands starting with the first available one following the label *word*. The goto command is generally useful only in shell scripts.

The Directory Stack.   In order to make it easy to return to directories that you've previously visited, csh provides a stack of directories. You can think of the stack as a list; *popping* the stack removes the first element of the list, while *pushing* a directory onto the stack places that directory at the head of the list. The first element of the stack is numbered 0. The following commands change or display the current directory or the directory stack:

cd [*dir*]
chdir [*dir*]
> Changes the working directory to *dir*. If *dir* is not specified, changes it to the home directory.

dirs
> Shows the directory stack.

popd
> Pops the directory stack, making the popped directory the current directory.

popd +*n*
> Discards the *n*th element in the stack, leaving the current directory unchanged.

pushd
> Exchanges the top two elements of the directory stack, then makes the directory at the top of the stack the current directory. Pushd by itself is a convenient way to switch back and forth between two directories.

pushd *dir*
> Pushes the current directory onto the stack, then makes *dir* the new current directory.

pushd +*n*
> Promotes the *n*th element of the stack to the top of the stack by rotating the preceding elements to the bottom of the stack, then makes the directory at the top of the stack the current directory.

Exiting from csh. The following commands provide ways of exiting from csh:

logout
> Terminates this shell if it is a login shell.

login
> Terminates this shell if it is a login shell, then invites a new login.

exit [(*expr*)]
> Exits from the shell with *expr* as the exit status. If you call exit from within parentheses, csh does not exit since the exit is only from a subshell.

exec *cmd*
> Executes *cmd* in place of the current shell. This command is the usual way to switch to a different shell.

Echoing Arguments. The following command echoes its arguments:

glob [*word*...]
> Echoes *word* .... Unlike the echo command (see Section 5.8.1), it ignores '\' quotation.

Status Information. The following commands provide status information and enable you to change certain parameters:

notify [%*job*]
> Provides immediate notice when the status of a job changes

instead of waiting until the next command completion. If a job *job* is specified (see "Job Identifiers" on p. 34), only the status of that job is reported; otherwise all changes in job status are reported.

history [-r] [-h] [*n*]

Displays the *n* most recent events in the history list. If -r is specified, the events are displayed in reverse order with the most recent events first. If -h is specified, the leading numbers are omitted from the history list, thus making it suitable for saving in a file that can later be re-executed. Each of these options must be surrounded by whitespace.

limit [*resource* [*max*]]

Used by itself, this command lists the limits on the consumption of certain resources. If *resource* is also specified, it lists the limit on the consumption of that resource. If *max* is also given, it limits the consumption of that resource by this process and its children to *max*. The particular resources depend on the system.

unlimit [*resource*]

If *resource* is specified, removes the limitation on that resource; otherwise, removes the limitations on all resources. Only the superuser may execute this command.

Job and Process Control. The following command provides control over interrupt handling:

onintr
onintr -
onintr *label*

Used by itself, this command restores the default interrupt actions. Used with '-', it causes all interrupts to be ignored. Used with a label *label*, it causes csh to transfer control to the command labelled with *label* when an interrupt is received or a child process terminates because it was interrupted.

Miscellaneous Commands. Here are the remaining csh intrinsic commands:

rehash   Recalculates the lookup table for command names. Executing this command causes csh to recognize recently created executable files.

unhash   Disables use of the hashed lookup table for commands.

source [-h] *file*

Reads commands from the file *file* and executes them without creating a subshell. If the commands set any local variables, these settings are retained. The commands are not placed on the history list, except that if -h is specified, they are placed on the history list but not executed.

eval *arg* ...

Performs textual substitutions in *arg* ... , then executes the resulting command. You can sometimes use eval to construct commands that would be difficult to specify otherwise (see p. 368 for an example).

time [*cmd*]

If *cmd* is specified, executes it and shows how much time it used. Otherwise, shows how much time this shell has used. See Section 5.12.2 for further discussion.

**7.1.14
Compound
Commands
(Statements)**

The following compound commands, also called *statements*, provide conditional tests, case testing, and iterations. A compound command can occupy several lines and can include other compound commands within it. It's customary to place the parts of a compound command on separate lines as shown in the form of the command. Doing that also makes your shell script more readable. If you execute a compound command interactively, csh prompts you for the continuation lines. Only the first line of a compound command appears in the history list.

if (*expr*) *cmd*

Executes *cmd* if *expr* is nonzero (*true*).

if (*expr*) then ...

This variant of the if statement has the form

```
if (expr₁) then
    cmdlist₁
[else if (expr₂) then
    cmdlist₂]
...
[else
    cmdlistₙ]
endif
```

It tests each *expr* in turn until one is found whose value is nonzero (*true*), then executes the corresponding command list *cmdlist_i*. If no nonzero *expr* is found and an 'else' part is present, it executes its command list.

switch

The switch statement enables you to select commands to be executed according to the form of a string. It corresponds to the ksh case command. The form of the switch statement is

```
switch(string)
case str: ...
    cmdlist
[default:
    cmdlist]
endsw
```

The statement can contain any number of cases. The string *string* at the top is expanded using all applicable substitutions. Each case label is then examined in turn. The string *str* is treated as a pattern and compared with *string*. If *string* can be obtained from *str* by file name expansion (i.e., by expanding wildcards), then that case is selected. Its command list *cmdlist* and any following command lists associated with other cases are executed until either the 'endsw' is reached or a 'breaksw' command is encountered. Normally each case should be ended with 'breaksw' so that control does not pass to the next case.

If none of the cases match and a default statement is present, its command list is executed. If none of the cases match and no default case is present, execution of the entire statement is considered to be complete.

foreach   The foreach statement corresponds to the ksh for command. It has the form

        foreach *name* (*word* ...)
            cmdlist
        end

The command list *cmdlist* is executed once for each word in the list *word* ... , with *name* being set to the current word. Typically, *word* ... is gotten as the result of a file name expansion involving wildcards.

repeat *n cmd*
Executes the command *cmd* *n* times. The count *n* must be given by a decimal integer, although that integer can be the result of a substitution.

while   The while statement has the form

        while (*expr*)
            cmdlist
        end

The commands in *cmdlist* are executed repeatedly while the value of the expression *expr* is nonzero (*true*). The expression *expr* is tested before each execution of *cmdlist*, including the first one.

7.1.15
Calling csh

The form of the csh command line is

    csh [-VXefinstvx] [-c *file*] [*arg*...]

The arguments *arg* ... are made available through the argv shell variable (see p. 394).

Command-Line Options.   The following options specify the source from which csh obtains its input:

-c *file*   Read commands from the file *file*.

`-s`	Read commands from standard input.
`-t`	Read and execute a single line of input. You can continue the input onto additional lines by ending each line with a backslash.
`-i`	Issue a prompt whenever a line of input is expected. This is the default if input is from a terminal.

The following options control echoing of commands as they are executed:

`-v`	Set the `verbose` variable (see p. 395) so that command input is echoed after history substitutions.
`-V`	Like `-v`, except that `verbose` is set before the initialization file `.cshrc` is executed.
`-x`	Set the `echo` variable (see p. 395) so that commands are echoed before they are executed.
`-X`	Like `-x`, except that `echo` is set before the initialization file `.cshrc` is executed.

The following options serve other purposes:

`-e`	Exit if any invoked command terminates abnormally. This option is most useful for executing shell scripts.
`-f`	Don't look for a `.cshrc` initialization file.
`-n`	Parse commands but don't execute them.

7.2   Bash, the "Bourne-again Shell"

Bash, the "Bourne-again Shell", is a shell developed as part of the GNU project. In essence, it is a POSIX-conforming shell that includes some extra features taken either from the KornShell or from the C shell, as well as a few of its own. We summarize its features below, providing more detail on those features that are not found in either of these other shells. You can usually assume that for those aspects of Bash we don't mention, Bash behaves in the same way as `ksh`.

7.2.1
Invoking Bash

The form of a call on Bash is

    bash [*long-option*] [`-is`] [`-aefhknoptuvxldCH`] [`-o` *option*] ...
        [`-c` *cmds*] ... [*cmdname* [*arg* ...]]

The options and arguments *arg* are interpreted much as they are for a POSIX shell (see Section 6.4.2). There are two differences:

- Bash recognizes a number of multicharacter options. A multi-character option is indicated here as *long-option*. If you provide any of these options, they must come first.
- The single-letter options include a few that are not in POSIX. Note that the `-i` and `-s` options apply only to invocation; the others have the same meaning as for `set`.

Long-Form Options.   Bash recognizes the following long-form options:

-rcfile *file*

>   If Bash is interactive, take initialization commands from *file* rather than from ~/.bashrc.

-norc   If Bash is interactive, don't load ~/.bashrc.

-noprofile

>   Don't read any profile files for a login shell.

-posix   Follow the POSIX standard where it differs from what Bash normally does.

-version   Produce the version number of this version of Bash when start-ing up.

-quiet   Don't produce any messages when starting up.

-login   Behave as though this invocation was for a login shell.

-nobraceexpansion

>   Don't expand braces in pathname lists (see "Brace Expansion" on p. 404).

-nolineediting

>   Don't use the *readline* line-editing library (see Section 7.2.2).

7.2.2 Command-Line Editing

Bash is able to use the GNU *readline* library for editing each command line as you type it. The *readline* library is also aware of the command history. The conventions are very close to those of the emacs mode of ksh (see Section 6.3.2), except that they usually correspond to true Emacs where directives differ. You select this editing mode with the command

```
set -o emacs
```

See the bash manual pages for further details on emacs-mode command-line editing. Further documentation for *readline* is available in the form of an Info file. You can read it either with an Info reader that's part of the GNU distribution or with the Info mode of Emacs.

Bash also supports the vi editing mode of ksh (see Section 6.3.3), which you can select with the command

```
set -o vi
```

7.2.3 Syntax of Bash Input

Bash input follows virtually the same syntactic conventions as ksh (see Section 6.6). The list of reserved words is the same. A comment, as usual, starts with a word that begins with '#'. When Bash is running inter-actively, however, comments are not recognized unless you turn on the interactive-comments option. Quotation also follows the ksh conven-tions (see Section 6.17).

History Expansion.   Bash supports a history expansion feature similar to the one provided by csh (see Section 7.1.2). History substitutions are triggered by the bang character occurring in a command. This character introduces an event designator such as '`!`*string*', which refers to the most recent command starting with *string*, or '`!!`', which refers to the previous command. History expansion takes place before any other interpretation of an input command, even before the input is broken into words. See the `csh` description for further details.

Other aspects of the history are handled as they are in any POSIX shell (see Section 6.21).

7.2.4
Commands, Redirections, and Parameters

Simple commands are interpreted as they are for `ksh`. Compound commands are as in POSIX (see Section 6.13). Bash supports neither the `|&` operator that initiates a coprocess nor the '`[[` *test* `]]`' form that tests the value of an expression; these are `ksh` extensions not included in POSIX.

All the POSIX redirection forms (see Section 6.10) are included in Bash. Since Bash does not support coprocesses, Bash does not recognize the `ksh` redirection operators *n*`<&p` and *n*`>&p`. Bash also supports the `csh` operator `>&`*file*, which redirects both standard output and standard error to *file*. (Ksh only supports this redirection operator when the output is a file descriptor.) You can also write this operator as `&>`*file*, but the first form is preferable. The effect is equivalent to

> `>`*file* `2>&1`

Positional and named parameters (variables) generally follow the `ksh` rules. The `$_` special parameter behaves almost like the `ksh` variable '`_`'. It expands to the last argument of the previous command. Within the environment of an invoked program, it contains the pathname of the program. It differs from the `ksh` variable in that (a) you can't assign anything to it explicitly (not that you'd want to), and (b) it isn't involved in notifying you of incoming mail.

Function Definitions.   Function definitions have the form

> `[function]` *name* `() {` *cmdlist*`; }`

which is not precisely like either of the `ksh` forms but generalizes the POSIX form (see Section 6.13.4). You can use the `local`, `typeset`, or `declare` intrinsic commands (see p. 408) to create variables that are local to a function definition and invisible outside it.

Hashed Lookup of Commands.   Bash does not include the tracked aliases provided by `ksh`. Instead it has a different mechanism, carried over from the Bourne shell, for remembering the absolute pathnames of commands so that they don't have to be looked up repeatedly. Whenever you execute a command that requires a search through the directories specified by `PATH` (see Section 2.9.2), Bash remembers where it found the command and stores that information in a *hash table*. Later, when the command is called for again, Bash simply uses the absolute pathname it found earlier.

This scheme speeds up command execution, but it has a drawback: if the searched-for command has moved, Bash will find it in the wrong place or not at all. To remedy that, you have to use the `hash` command (see p. 408) to tell Bash either to forget the old location or to recalculate the location whenever you take an action that would invalidate the current location. For instance, if you create a new definition of a command in your current directory and '`.`' appears at the end of your `PATH`, you'll have to rehash the command name in order to ensure that Bash finds the new definition.

7.2.5
Substitutions and Expansions

Bash, like `ksh`, provides command substitution, parameter expansion, and arithmetic evaluation (see Section 6.18). An arithmetic evaluation can be written using either the POSIX form '`$(( ... ))`' or the slightly more convenient form '`$[ ... ]`'. Evaluating a variable with the *integer* attribute (attached with '`declare -i`') retrieves its numerical value even outside of an arithmetic evaluation. Bash also expands braces much as `csh` does. It also provides a form of expansion called process substitution that provides the functionality of coprocesses in `ksh` (see Section 6.9.3).

Brace Expansion. Bash generalizes the brace expansion mechanism that `csh` uses for expanding filenames, applying it to a word in any context at all where it's legitimate to replace the word by several words. A string of the form

$$a\{x_1, x_2, \ldots, x_n\}b$$

within a word is expanded to the sequence of words

$$ax_1b \ ax_2b \ldots ax_nb$$

Either *a*, *b*, or both can be empty. However, an occurrence of '`{`', '`}`', or '`{}`' surrounded by whitespace is taken literally since these constructs are used as parts of compound commands. For example, the command

```
echo {} re{tir,,fri}ed
```

produces the output

```
{} retired reed refried
```

You can disable brace expansion with the `-nobrace-expansion` to avoid a minor incompatibility with the way the Bourne shell treats a construct such as '`file{1,2}`'. Bash will expand that construct to '`file1 file2`', but the Bourne shell will treat it as a single word.

Pathname Expansion. Pathnames are expanded as in `csh` (see Section 7.1.6). The usual wildcards ('`?`', '`*`', and '`[ ... ]`') are recognized, as well as the brace expansion described previously. Bash does not recognize the more general pattern operators provided by `ksh`, which are also not in POSIX. Two variables affect the expansion:

- The `allow_null_glob_expansion` variable, if set, causes pathname expansions that don't match anything to be removed altogether. If it is unset, Bash simply retains the unexpanded form (which is what shells generally do).

- The `glob_dot_filenames` variable, if set, relaxes the requirement that a dot at the start of a pathname or immediately after a slash must be matched explicitly (i.e., cannot be matched by a wildcard). For instance, setting this variable enables '`*`' to match filenames that start with a dot, which it wouldn't otherwise.

Process Substitution.   Bash provides a method of piping the output of any number of processes to a command, provided that your system supports FIFO special files (see Section 2.11.1).[4] When Bash encounters the construct '`<(`*cmdlist*`)`', which superficially looks like a redirection, it expands the construct to the pathname of an automatically generated FIFO special file *fifo*. Bash then initiates *cmdlist* in a subshell, with standard output redirected to *fifo*. The effect is that when the outermost command reads from `<(`*cmdlist*`)`, it reads the output generated by *cmdlist*. In a similar way, '`>(`*cmdlist*`)`' expands to the pathname of a file that passes whatever is written to it to the standard input of *cmdlist*.

The advantage of these constructs over ordinary pipes is that they enable a program to read its input from several output-producing processes at once, all operating in parallel. An ordinary pipe only allows a program to read from one such process. The same is true on the output side.

7.2.6
Predefined Variables Used by Bash

Below we enumerate the predefined variables of Bash.

Variables Set by Bash.   The following variables are set by Bash and have the same meaning they do for `ksh`:

CDPATH	IFS	MAILPATH	PPID	REPLY
ENV	IGNOREEOF	OLDPWD	PS1	SECONDS
HISTFILE	LINENO	OPTARG	PS2	
HISTSIZE	MAIL	OPTIND	PS4	
HOME	MAILCHECK	PATH	PWD	

The following variables are not part of `ksh`, though a few of them are part of `csh`:

FIGNORE   A colon-separated list of suffixes to be ignored when Bash is doing filename completion on the command line.

HOSTTYPE A string specifying the hardware Bash is running on.

UID   The (numerical) real user ID of the current user.

EUID   The effective user ID of the current user.

BASH   The pathname used to invoke this copy of Bash.

BASH_VERSION
          The version number of this copy of Bash.

---

4. Process substitution also works on systems that support the `/dev/fd` method of naming open files.

SHLVL The number of nested invocations of Bash.

MAIL_WARNING

If set, causes Bash to issue a message if a mail file has been accessed since the last time that file was checked.

NO_PROMPT_VARS

If set, inhibits expansion of parameters and other constructs within a prompt when the prompt is issued.

HISTFILESIZE

The maximum number of lines kept in the stored history file (as distinct from the history list).

OPTERR If set to 1 (the default), causes Bash to issue error messages generated by `getopts`.

PROMPT_COMMAND

Contains a command to be executed before Bash issues a primary prompt.

ignoreeof

Has the same effect as IGNOREEOF when set or unset.

notify If set, causes Bash to report terminated background jobs immediately rather than waiting for the next primary prompt.

history_control

If set to '`ignorespace`', inhibits entry on the history list of lines starting with a space; if set to '`ignoredups`', inhibits entry of a line matching the last history line.

command_oriented_history

If set, causes Bash to save all lines of a multiple-line command in a single history entry.

glob_dot_filenames

If set, causes Bash to include filenames beginning with a dot in the results of a pathname expansion.

allow_null_glob_expansion

If set, causes Bash to remove pathname expansions that don't match anything.

histchars

Contains two or three characters '$c_1 c_2 c_3$' that are significant for history expansions. The character c_1 (normally '!') signifies the start of a history expansion; c_2 signifies quick substitution (rerunning the previous command); and c_3, if present, signifies that the rest of the line is a comment.

nolinks If set, inhibits Bash from following symbolic links when changing the current directory.

hostname_completion_file

Contains the name of a file in the same format as /etc/hosts

(see Section 12.6.1) that Bash should read when completing a
hostname.

noclobber

> If set, prevents output redirections other than >| from over-
> writing files.

auto_resume

> If set, allows single-word simple commands without redirec-
> tions to be used in job identifiers to identify stopped jobs.

no_exit_on_failed_exec

> If set, inhibits a noninteractive copy of Bash from exiting if an
> exec command fails.

cdable_vars

> If set, causes an argument to cd that doesn't name a directory
> to be checked to see if it is a variable whose value names a
> directory.

7.2.7
Intrinsic Commands

The intrinsic commands are those that Bash interprets directly and does
not execute in a subshell.

Commands Also in ksh.   The following commands are intrinsic to Bash
and have the same meaning as they do for ksh:

: (null)	continue	getopts	readonly	trap
. *file*	echo	jobs	return	type
alias	eval	kill	set	ulimit
bg	exec	let	shift	umask
break	exit	logout	test	unalias
cd	fc	pwd	[...]	unset
command	fg	read	times	wait

Directory Stack Operations.   In order to make it easy to return to directories that you've previously visited, Bash provides a stack of directories
like the one provided by csh (see "The Directory Stack" on p. 396). You
can think of the stack as a list; *popping* the stack removes the first (leftmost) element of the list, while *pushing* a directory onto the stack placed
that directory at the head of the list. The first element of the stack is
numbered 0 and contains the directory most recently placed on the stack.
The following commands change or display the current directory or the
directory stack:

dirs [-l] Displays the current stack of remembered directories, using a
long form if −l is specified.

popd [+*n* |−*n*]

> With no arguments, removes the first directory from the stack.
> Otherwise, removes the *n*th directory from the left for '+*n*'
> and the *n*th directory from the right for '−*n*'. For example,

'popd -0' removes the rightmost (and usually the oldest) directory on the stack.

pushd [*dir* | +*n* | -*n*]

> With no arguments, pushd exchanges the top two entries of the
> directory stack. With a *dir* argument, it adds *dir* at the top of
> the directory stack. Otherwise, it rotates the stack *n* positions
> to the left for '+*n*' and *n* positions to the right for '-*n*'.

Operations on Names. The following commands operate on names or
affect the interpretation of names:

declare [-frxi] [*name*[=*value*]]
typeset [-frxi] [*name*[=*value*]]

> These synonymous commands work just like typeset in ksh
> (see p. 365), except that only the indicated attributes are rec-
> ognized.

local [*name*[=*value*]]

> Creates a local variable named *name* and assigns it the value
> *value*, much as typeset and declare do. With no arguments,
> local lists all local variables. You can only use local within a
> function.

export [[-nf] [*name*[=*word*]] ... | -p]

> With no arguments or with -p, export lists all exported names.
> With a list of names but no -n, it marks all the names for export
> and assigns each name the corresponding value, if any. With
> -n, it unmarks the names so that they are no longer exported.
> With -f, all the names are assumed to refer to functions (and
> no assignments are permitted).

builtin *name* [*arg* ...]

> Executes *name* with the given arguments as a shell intrinsic
> (built-in) function even if a function of the same name exists.

enable [-n | -all] [*name* ...]

> With -n, enable disables each *name* as an intrinsic command
> so that a reference to it will search for an executable program
> or shell script. With no arguments, it lists all (enabled) intrinsic
> commands. With -all, it lists all intrinsic commands and their
> enablement status.

hash [-r] [*name* ...]

> Remembers in the hash table the full pathname of the com-
> mands *name* ... to speed up future lookups (see "Hashed
> Lookup of Commands" on p. 403). If -r is specified, all names
> other than those listed are erased from the hash table, which
> will cause Bash to recalculate them when they are next needed.
> The command 'hash' by itself lists the contents of the hash table.

Synonyms. The following Bash intrinsic commands are synonyms for others:

bye   Synonymous with `exit`.

source *file*
      Synonymous with '. *file*', the "dot" command.

Other Intrinsic Commands. Bash also provides the following intrinsic commands:

help [*pfx*] With no argument, `help` displays a list of the built-in commands and their syntax. With a string argument *pfx*, `help` provides somewhat more detailed information on each command whose name begins with the prefix *pfx*.

history [*n*]
history [-anrw] [*file*]
      With no options, `history` lists the command history (see Section 6.21) with line numbers. An argument *n* restricts the listing to the *n* most recent lines. For the second form, *file* is used as the pathname of the history file; if it's omitted, the value of `HISTFILE` is used. The options for the second form are as follows:

    -a   Append to the history file all lines generated since the beginning of this Bash session.

    -n   Add to the history list any lines in the history file that were not previously read.

    -r   Make the contents of the history file be the current history list.

    -w   Copy the current history list into the history file.

suspend [-f]
      Suspends the execution of this shell, provided it isn't a login shell, until it receives a `SIGCONT` signal. With `-f`, even a login shell is suspended.

**7.2.8
Execution Options**

Most of the execution options are the same as those for `ksh`. The following single-letter options have the same meaning for Bash as for `ksh`: a e f m n o p t u v x C . So do the following long-form options:

allexport	noclobber	verbose
emacs	noexec	vi
errexit	noglob	xtrace
ignoreeof	nounset	
monitor	privileged	

These are the long-form options that are different:

braceexpand
      Expand braces in pathnames and other patterns (on by default).

`histexpand (H)`
>   Enable history substitutions (see "History Expansion" on p. 402).

`nohash (d)`
>   Disable use of the hash table for command lookup (see "Hashed Lookup of Commands" on p. 403).

`interactive-comments`
>   Recognize command-line comments when Bash is running interactively.

These are the single-letter options that are different:

`b`
>   Report terminated background jobs immediately (like the `notify` variable).

`h`
>   Locate and remember function commands as functions are defined.

`l`
>   When executing a `for` compound command, save the binding of the iteration variable before executing the command and restore it after executing the command.

`C`
>   Activate the `noclobber` option.

Options Controlled by Variables.   When an option is controlled both by a variable and by a setting via `set`, Bash monitors changes to the variable's state. A change of state has the same effect as a setting via `set`.

7.2.9
Initialization Files

When Bash is called as a login shell, it first executes the commands in the system-wide initialization file in `/etc/profile`, if it exists. Bash then looks for the following initialization files in order and executes the commands in the first one it finds:

```
~/.bash_profile
~/.bash_login
~/.profile
```

When a Bash login shell exits, it executes the commands in the file `~/.bash_logout` if it exists. These procedures are entirely analogous to those used by `csh`.

When Bash is called as a non-login shell, it executes the commands in `~/.bashrc`, if that file exists. Note that `~/.bashrc` is not executed for a login shell, though you can cause it to be executed by including the command '. `~/.bashrc`' at the end of your `~/.bash_profile` or other login initialization file.

A third case is when Bash is called noninteractively. In this case, it executes the file whose pathname is found in the `ENV` environment variable (but without using `PATH` to locate the file). This use of `ENV` follows the practice of `ksh` rather than `csh`.

8

Standard Editors

An editor is a program for creating, modifying, or viewing a file of text. UNIX editors come in two varieties: full-screen editors and line editors.

- A full-screen editor assumes that your terminal has a display screen and is at least capable of moving the cursor to a specified screen position. It maintains a model of what the screen should look like and updates the screen in response to your typed commands. Usually the commands you type are not shown on the screen. If your terminal is a "smart" terminal that allows lines and characters to be added and deleted, the editor updates the screen by modifying only that portion of it whose contents have changed. On the other hand, if your terminal is a "dumb" terminal that lacks these facilities, the editor updates the screen by rewriting it completely.

- A line editor is a "lines in, lines out" editor. It expects you to type some lines; it then types some lines back at you and awaits your next command. Each line, whether typed by you or the editor, appears underneath the previous typed line. Most line editors were developed in the days when computer terminals could only display output by printing it.

Line editors have largely been eclipsed by full-screen editors, which are far easier to use. Nevertheless, you may find a line editor useful or even essential when you're communicating over a slow or noisy phone line or when you're working with a crippled system in a maintenance mode for which most of the usual UNIX facilities are not available.

In this chapter we describe one full-screen editor and two line editors that come with nearly every UNIX system:

- The full-screen editor `vi`, sometimes called the Visual Editor, was developed as part of the BSD project. It was the first popular UNIX full-screen editor and is still very widely used.

- The line editor `ed` is the oldest UNIX editor; under some circumstances, it may be the only editor you have. We recommend against using it if you have an alternative, but many people still use `ed` just because they don't want to bother learning a new editor.

- The line editor `ex` is an extended and improved form of `ed`. `Vi` and `ex` are actually the two faces of a single editor. Our main reason for describing `ex` is that you sometimes need to use `ex` commands from within `vi`.

Historically, `ed` led to `ex` and `ex` led to `vi`, but our order of presentation is the reverse since `vi` is likely to be the most useful of the three editors and `ed` the least.

In the next two chapters we describe the GNU Emacs editor. Although in our opinion Emacs is far more powerful than `vi`, more flexible, and easier to use, many people still prefer `vi` because it is part of the standard UNIX package.

8.1   The `vi` Visual Editor

The visual editor `vi`, pronounced "vee-eye" by Berkeley people, was developed by Bill Joy as part of the BSD project. It has since been adopted as a standard System V feature. `Vi` is a full-screen editor; it always maintains an image on your screen of a portion of the file that you're editing. It requires a terminal that enables it to control the position of the cursor and place text at an arbitrary position on the screen. In particular, you may not be able to use `vi` if your terminal can only receive and transmit text a line at a time, or if `vi` is unable to access information about your terminal because your system is not fully operational.

`Vi` is an extension to the `ex` line-oriented editor described in Section 8.3 and depends on `ex` for many of its facilities. In fact, `vi` is just `ex` working in *visual mode*. An unfortunate result of that arrangement is that you need to learn certain parts of `ex` in order to use `vi`. For instance, in order to insert another file into the one you're editing, you need to use the `ex` command `r` (which you call from `vi` by typing ':r'). In our description of `vi` we include those `ex` commands that are most likely to be useful; if you need others, you'll have to learn about `ex`.

When you edit a file, `vi` acts on a working copy of the file called the *main buffer*. All of your editing actions apply to the main buffer; the file is not modified until you request it. Vi also provides some other buffers that contain text, but when we refer to "the buffer" without qualification, we mean the main buffer. The *current file* is the file that you most recently asked vi to edit.

8.1.1
Organization of the Screen

As you edit, the screen displays a portion of the buffer. The visual cursor indicates vi's position in the buffer. The *current line* is the line containing the cursor.

If a line of text is longer than the screen width, the part that runs over is placed on one or more additional lines. Commands that move the cursor down or up by lines move by logical lines, not screen lines, so a command that moves down by one logical line may well move down by several screen lines if the logical lines are oversized.

If the portion of the buffer being displayed is too short to fill the screen, vi fills the rest of the screen with lines that contain '~' in the first column and are otherwise blank. When you start to edit an empty buffer, the entire screen is filled with such lines.

The Status Line.   The bottom line of your screen is the *status line*, which vi uses for the following purposes:

- Error messages appear on the status line.

- When vi generates status information such as the name of the current file in response to a command, this information appears on the status line.

- As you type a search pattern or an ex command, vi echoes what you're typing to the status line.

8.1.2
Meanings of Keys

Vi assigns specific meanings to many keys on your keyboard. In addition, it recognizes and uses certain assignments of control keys made via stty (see Section 5.5.2):

(Intr)	The interrupt key, which interrupts and cancels whatever you're doing.
(Kill)	The kill key, which erases all the characters you've typed on the current line.
(Erase)	The erase key, which erases the character to the left of the cursor. (If you didn't type the character as part of the current input operation, however, (Erase) won't erase it.)

The (Erase) key is often set to (Ctrl)H; vi treats (Ctrl)H as an additional erase key if you set your (Erase) key to something else. The (Ctrl)D command works as described here whether or not you set your (EOF) key to (Ctrl)D. When vi uses a control key for a particular purpose, that purpose preempts any other vi meaning that the key might have. For instance, if your (Kill) key is set to '@' (the default for printing terminals), the vi commands that use '@' to operate on registers are not available.

Vi is usually configured so that the cursor arrow keys perform the indicated motions. Other directional keys such as Home may also work in some systems.[1]

8.1.3 Modes

At any moment, vi is in one of three modes: *command mode, input mode,* or *status-line mode* (called *last-line mode* in most vi documentation). Of these, command mode is the most fundamental since the other two are really excursions from command mode.

- Command mode is the mode for issuing short commands. In command mode, vi treats each character you type as a command to do something or as part of such a command; the character is not echoed to your terminal. The typing conventions for command mode are described in Sections 8.1.4 and 8.1.5.

- Input mode is the mode for inserting text into the buffer. In input mode, vi treats each character you type as data and echoes it to the terminal, adding it at the cursor position and moving the cursor one position to the right. The typing conventions for input mode are described in Section 8.1.6.

- Status-line mode is the mode for issuing long commands. As you type characters in status-line mode, vi echoes them to the status line. When you finish typing the command, vi executes it. The typing conventions for status-line mode are described in Section 8.1.7.

The treatments of control characters in input mode and in status mode are similar but not identical.

8.1.4 Commands

When vi is in command mode, it interprets every character you type as a command or part of a command. Characters that you type in command mode are not echoed to the screen, so you need to type them carefully. Although most commands are short, you can easily lose track of where you are. If you do, you can always cancel the current command by typing Intr.

Nearly all the characters on your keyboard are meaningful commands. If you start typing what you think is input text when vi is in command mode, you'll get a useless and often destructive sequence of actions as a result. This is an easy mistake to make if you're accustomed to using a "modeless" editor in which all the commands are summoned by control characters that are never used in text. If you enable the showmode variable (see p. 437), vi will place an indicator on the status line whenever it's in input mode. If the indicator is absent and the cursor is in the buffer rather than on the last line, vi is in command mode.

The effects of most commands are limited to the current line. The exceptions are those commands that search for text, explicitly move across line boundaries, or move the cursor in units of words.

---

1. Vi uses the database of terminal descriptions (see Section 2.15) to establish these meanings.

Form of Commands.   Each vi command consists of one or two characters, optionally preceded by a count and possibly followed by various modifiers. In most but not all cases the count specifies a number of repetitions; what is repeated depends on the command. For example, the command '3j' moves the cursor down three lines, while the command '8dd' deletes eight lines starting with the current one.

A command named by a capital letter is usually related to the command named by the corresponding small letter, although the nature of the relationship depends on the command:

- The 'f', 'o', 'p', 't', and 'x' commands act at or after the cursor (i.e., forward); the 'F', 'O', 'P', 'T', and 'X' commands act before the cursor (i.e., backward).
- The 'i' and 'a' commands act at the cursor position; the 'I' and 'A' commands act at the beginning and end of the current line.
- The 'e', 'w', and 'b' commands act on words; the 'E', 'W', and 'B' commands act on blank-delimited words, also known as *bigwords*. The difference is that a word contains only letters, digits, and underscores, while a bigword can contain special characters such as hyphens.

Objects.   Some commands take *objects*. An object is specified by a command that moves the cursor; the object denotes the region of text passed over by the command. A command that takes an object acts on the region it denotes. For instance, the 'w' command moves to the start of the next word, so the 'w' object denotes the text between the cursor and the start of the next word. The 'd' command deletes its object, so the command 'dw' deletes the text preceding the next word.

For a motion command that moves the cursor to a different line, the corresponding object is the set of lines containing the new and old cursor positions. For example, the 'j' command moves to the next line, so the object it specifies consists of all of the current line and all of the next line— even though both the old and new cursor positions may be in the middle of the line. The 'dj' command thus deletes two lines: the current line and the next line. This behavior can be surprising until you get used to it.

Commands That Change the Mode.   Certain commands initiate other modes:

- Commands that expect input text, such as 'i', 'A', and 'o', initiate input mode.

- The ':' command, which introduces an ex command, initiates status-line mode. The searching commands '/' and '?' also initiate status-line mode.

8.1.5
Cancelling and
Interrupting
Commands

The following keys cancel and interrupt commands:

(Esc)   Cancels the command you're currently typing. Typing (Esc) is useful when you're not sure what you've typed, since it lets you start over.

(Intr)   Cancels the command you're currently typing; if a command is already executing, interrupts it. The cursor returns to where it was before the command was executed. Vi beeps whenever you interrupt it.

Interrupting is a stronger action than cancelling because it works even in input mode and while vi is in the middle of searching for a pattern.

8.1.6
Typing Text in
Input Mode

Several commands expect you to type some text in input mode. The text appears on the screen as you type it. The following keys have special meaning in input mode:

(Enter)   Ends the current line and starts another one.

(Intr)
(Esc)   Terminates this insertion and returns to command mode. The only difference between (Intr) and (Esc) is that (Intr) beeps at you while (Esc) does not.

(Erase)
(Ctrl)H   Erases the character preceding the cursor.

(Kill)   Erases all the characters typed on the current line. Typing (Kill) does not affect any characters that were present before you entered input mode, nor does it affect any previously typed lines.

(Ctrl)W   Erases the previous word that you typed.

(Ctrl)Q
(Ctrl)V   Quotes the next character; that is, inserts the next character into the text verbatim, even if it is a control character such as (Esc).

When you back up over characters with (Ctrl)H or (Ctrl)W, the characters you back up over remain on the screen even though they have effectively been deleted. This effect can be confusing at first.

Insert mode is affected by whether vi is in autoindent mode (see Section 8.1.9).

8.1.7
Typing Text in
Status-Line Mode

The ':', '/', and '?' commands initiate status-line mode. The following keys have special meaning in status-line mode:

(Esc)
(Enter)   Terminates the command you're typing and executes it.

(Intr)   Cancels the command you're typing and returns vi to command mode. If you type (Intr) after issuing a command but before it finishes executing, the execution is interrupted.

⟨Erase⟩

⟨Ctrl⟩ H   Erases the character preceding the cursor. If you erase the first character on the line, vi returns you to command mode.

⟨Kill⟩   Erases all the characters of the command (but not the first character on the line).

⟨Ctrl⟩ W   Erases the previous word that you typed.

⟨Ctrl⟩ Q

⟨Ctrl⟩ V   Quotes the next character; that is, inserts the next character into the text verbatim, even if it is a control character such as ⟨Esc⟩.

Note the following differences between insert mode and status-line mode in what these keys do:

- In input mode, ⟨Intr⟩ ends the input but does not erase anything. In status-line mode, ⟨Intr⟩ cancels the command you're typing.

- In input mode, ⟨Enter⟩ starts a new line but does not end the input. In status-line mode, ⟨Enter⟩ ends the command you're typing and executes it.

**8.1.8
Using** ex
Commands

You can issue an ex command from vi by preceding it with a colon. The command is displayed on the status line as you type it. Vi itself doesn't provide commands for file actions such as reading a file or for global actions such as replacing all occurrences of a certain pattern within the buffer; instead it relies on ex for these functions. The descriptions of vi commands below include descriptions of some particularly useful ex commands (see the description of the :s command on p. 428 and in Section 8.1.27). The only ex commands that you can't issue from vi are those that insert lines of text: 'i', 'I', 'a', 'A', and 'R'.

**8.1.9
Autoindent Mode**

Autoindent mode is a vi mode of operation that makes it easier to create and modify indented text. Autoindent mode is particularly useful for typing programs. It only affects what you type in input mode. You can activate autoindent mode by typing ':set ai' and deactivate it by typing ':set noai'.

In autoindent mode, vi automatically lines up the beginnings of lines as you type them. It indents each new line by the same amount as the previous line. You can increase the indentation by typing one or more tabs or spaces at the beginning of a line. Vi provides several commands for reducing the indentation either temporarily or permanently. All of them use ⟨Ctrl⟩ D and all of them must be typed at the very beginning of an input line.

⟨Ctrl⟩ D   Decreases the indentation by backing up to the previous shift width interval. The shift-width intervals behave like tab stops, so that if the shift width is 3, you back up to the previous column in the set 1, 4, 7, etc. (see the description of the shiftwidth variable on p. 438).[2] The shift-width interval need not be the same as the tab stop setting, although it ought to be. The (Erase) key won't back up to a shift-width interval because it only affects characters that you type explicitly.

0 (Ctrl)D   Moves to the left margin, cancelling all indentation. The '0' appears on the line when you type it but disappears along with the indentation when you type the (Ctrl)D.

∧ (Ctrl)D   Moves to the left margin but remembers the indentation. The next line you type that does not start with '∧(Ctrl)D' resumes the previous indentation unless you start it with one of the other (Ctrl)D commands. The '∧' appears on the line when you type it but disappears along with the indentation when you type the (Ctrl)D. This facility is useful for putting comments in programs.

8.1.10
The Screen Window

As you edit, vi displays a portion of the main buffer called the *window*. The window occupies the lower part of your screen. Usually the size of the window is the number of lines on the screen minus one or a smaller number of lines if you're using a slow terminal, but you can change its initial value with the window variable (see p. 440).

You can change the window size as you edit by using the 'z' commands (see p. 421). If you move the cursor to a line not in the window but vi can display that line by enlarging the window, it does so. The next time that vi needs to redraw the window entirely, it reduces the window to the specified size. Reducing the window size is generally not useful on terminals where the time it takes to display a full-screen window is negligible.

8.1.11
Regular Expressions
in vi and ex

The search and substitution commands of vi and ex search for patterns defined by regular expressions. Regular expressions are as defined in Section 2.17, but with certain extensions:

- In a pattern, the sequence '\<' matches the beginning of a word and the sequence '\>' matches the end of a word. For the purpose of this construct, a word is a sequence of letters, digits, underscores, and hyphens.

- In a replacement string, '\u' causes the next character to be converted to uppercase, and '\l' causes the next character to be converted to lowercase. Similarly, '\U' causes subsequent characters of the replacement string to be converted to all uppercase, and '\L' causes them to be converted to all lowercase. The affected characters are ended by '\E', '\e', or the end of the replacement string.

---

2. Because vi automatically converts leading spaces to tabs, this command may produce unexpected effects if you use it when you're not positioned at a shift-width interval.

**8.1.12
Calling** vi

The call on vi has the form

>   vi [-rR] [-c *cmd*] [-t *tag*] [-w *size*] [*file...*]

An obsolescent variant uses + in place of -c. The files *file ...* can contain wildcards. If you don't specify any files, vi initiates the editing of an unnamed empty file. Within vi you can call for the next file to be edited using the ':n' command or return to the first file in the list with the ':rew' command. Some older versions of vi recognize the view command for editing in read-only mode and the vedit command for editing in a "novice" mode.

**8.1.13
Command-Line
Options**

These are the options for the vi command line:

-t *tag*   Edit the file containing *tag* (see Section 8.5). The cursor is initially positioned at the tag. If you also specify a file list, the file containing *tag* is edited first and then the files in the file list are edited. The relevant tag file, usually the file in the current directory named tags, must be available (see the tags variable, p. 436).

-r   Attempt to recover the specified files after an editor or system crash. As vi works, it periodically saves the state of the buffer in a recovery file. Some older versions of vi send you a mail message containing the name of the recovery file when the editor crashes. If you later call vi and specify this recovery file with the -r option, vi resumes in whatever state it was when it saved the recovery file. Note that for these versions, *file* is *not* the name of the file to be recovered.

-R   Edit these files in read-only mode (the readonly variable is enabled). Setting this flag helps to protect the files from accidental overwriting by inhibiting vi from writing to them unless special commands such as ':w!' are used. This flag is irrelevant for view since view sets it anyway.

-c *cmd*
+*cmd*   Execute the ex command *cmd* before starting to edit the first (or only) file in the file list. For example, the command line

>   vi -c:122 krumhorn

starts editing the file krumhorn at line 122 since the ex command ':122' jumps to line 122. The + form is obsolescent, though some older versions of vi may not recognize -c.

-w *size*   Set the default size of a screenful, as recorded in the window variable (see p. 440), to *size*. There is no necessary relation between the size of a screenful and the actual screen size; the screenful size only affects scrolling commands such as z.

8.1.14
Quick Exit

If you're stuck and need to get out of vi quickly, there are two sure ways to do it:

- If you want to save the file you're working on, type '[Esc]ZZ'. If that fails to work, type '[Intr]ZZ'. The [Intr] may cause your most recent changes to be lost.

- If you don't care about saving the file, type '[Intr]:q![Enter]'. Any changes you've made since the file was last written are discarded.

Under unusual circumstances you may need more than one [Intr] to get these to work.

   If your shell provides job control (see Section 2.6.3), you can suspend vi by typing [Ctrl]Z. See Section 8.1.27 for more information about exiting from vi.

8.1.15
Initializing vi or ex

You can provide a set of initialization commands that the editor, be it vi or ex, executes whenever it starts up. Initialization commands are useful for setting variables and for defining macros that you want to have available whenever you use the editor. You can provide these commands in either of two ways:

- You can record the commands in the environment variable EXINIT (see Section 2.6.5).

- You can store the commands in an .exrc file.

   Here's how the editor looks for preset variables:

(1)   It checks the environment variable EXINIT. If EXINIT is nonempty, the editor executes the commands in it.

(2)   If EXINIT is empty but a file named .exrc exists in your home directory, the editor executes the commands in that file.

(3)   If the commands thus executed cause the exrc variable to be enabled (it's disabled by default), the editor then executes the commands in the .exrc file in the current directory (if it exists).

By placing different .exrc files in different directories, you can adjust the editor's behavior to the nature of the files in the directory.

8.1.16
Adjusting the Screen

The following commands adjust what is displayed on the screen.

Scrolling Commands.   The scrolling commands change what is displayed on the screen while changing your position in the file as little as possible. The cursor usually doesn't appear to move.

[Ctrl]F   Scrolls down (forward) one screen.

[Ctrl]B   Scrolls up (backward) one screen.

[Ctrl]D   Scrolls down (forward) by half a screen. If you specify a count *n*, vi scrolls down by *n* lines. Subsequent [Ctrl]D's and [Ctrl]U's then scroll by the same amount.

Ctrl U   Scrolls up (backward) by half a screen. If you specify a count n, vi scrolls up by n lines. Subsequent Ctrl D's and Ctrl U's then scroll by the same amount.

Ctrl E   Scrolls down (forward) by one line. The form n Ctrl E scrolls down by n lines. It differs from n Ctrl D in that it does not affect subsequent commands.

Ctrl Y   Scrolls up (backward) by one line. The form n Ctrl Y scrolls up by n lines. It differs from n Ctrl U in that it does not affect subsequent commands.

Orienting the Screen.   The following commands are useful for placing the current line or a line containing a particular pattern at a specified position on the screen:

z Enter
z+   Regenerates the screen with the current line as the top line of the screen and the cursor positioned at the beginning of that line.

z-   Regenerates the screen with the current line as the bottom line of the screen and the cursor positioned at the beginning of that line.

z.   Regenerates the screen with the current line as the middle line of the screen and the cursor positioned at the beginning of that line.

/*pat*/z Enter
         Regenerates the screen with the next line containing the pattern *pat* as the top line of the screen and the cursor positioned at the beginning of that line. Other forms of '/*pat*/z' (e.g., '/*pat*/z-') behave analogously.

zn Enter   Uses a window of n lines and positions the cursor at the top of that window. Combinations using 'zn' (e.g., '/*pat*/zn-') behave analogously. A 'zn' command sets the default value of n; subsequent 'z' commands without n gives you a window size of that default value.

Restoring the Screen.   The following commands for restoring your screen are useful when your screen has become scrambled. This can happen if you interrupt vi with Intr, if some other program writes to your screen in the middle of editing, or if you're using vi over a noisy line.

Ctrl L   Regenerates the screen.

Ctrl R   Regenerates the screen, eliminating any lines that have no characters at all, not even spaces. Normally this command is equivalent to Ctrl L, except for dumb terminals.

**8.1.17
Moving by Direction**

The following commands move the cursor horizontally or vertically:

[Space]
l
Moves right one character, but not past the end of the line.

[Erase]
h
[Ctrl] H
Moves left one character, but not past the beginning of the line. Note that h works only when you're in command mode.

[Ctrl] N
[Ctrl] J
j
Moves directly down one line. Vi tries to maintain your horizontal position. [Ctrl] N is a mnemonic for "next".

[Ctrl] P
k
Moves directly up one line. Vi tries to maintain your horizontal position. [Ctrl] P is a mnemonic for "previous".

0
Moves to the first character on the current line. This command is unaffected by a repetition count.

^
Moves to the first *nonwhite* character on the current line. (The "white" characters are space, end of line, tab, and formfeed.) This command is unaffected by a repetition count.

$
Moves to the last character on the current line. This command is unaffected by a repetition count.

[Enter]
+
Moves to the first nonwhite character on the following line.

−
Moves to the first nonwhite character on the previous line.

$n|$
Moves to column n of the current line. The first column is numbered 1. You can omit the count; it defaults to 1.

H
Moves to the beginning of the first line on the screen. If you precede this command with a count n, you move to the nth line from the top of the screen.

M
Moves to the beginning of the middle line on the screen. A count with this command has no effect.

L
Moves to the beginning of the last line on the screen. If you precede this command with a count n, you move to the nth line from the bottom of the screen.

G
Moves to the first character on line n, where n is the count preceding 'G'. If you omit n, vi moves to the last line of the buffer. The '1G' command is the simplest way to move to the beginning of the buffer. You may find it convenient to use the ':map' command (see p. 434) to define the otherwise unassigned 'g' command as '1G'.

**8.1.18
Moving by
Syntactic Units**

For the purposes of the commands that follow, a *word* is either (a) a sequence of letters, digits, and underscores, or (b) a sequence of characters none of which are either whitespace or word characters. A *blank-delimited word* is a sequence of characters surrounded by whitespace. *Whitespace* is a sequence of the following "white" characters: space, end of line, tab, formfeed. Generally speaking, a word doesn't include punctuation but a blank-delimited word does.

Moving by Words.   The following commands move the cursor by words:

e   Moves to the last character of the current word (or the next word, if the cursor is on whitespace).

E   Moves to the last character of the current blank-delimited word (or the next word, if the cursor is on whitespace).

w   Moves forward to the start of the next word.

W   Moves forward to the start of the next blank-delimited word.

b   Moves back to the start of the current word (or to the start of the previous word, if the cursor is on whitespace).

B   Moves back to the start of the current blank-delimited word (or to the start of the previous blank-delimited word, if the cursor is on whitespace).

Moving by Sentences.   The following commands move the cursor by sentences:

)   Moves forward to the end of the current sentence and then to the first nonwhite character of the next sentence. If the cursor is within the last sentence in the buffer, this command moves the cursor to the end of the buffer. Vi considers a sentence to be ended by any of the following:

  • An end-of-sentence character (. ! ?) followed by two spaces
  • An end-of-sentence character followed by a blank line
  • A blank line

Vi also treats the characters ( )] ') following punctuation at the end of a sentence as part of the sentence. A repetition count causes vi to move forward several sentences.

(Moves backward to the first character of the current sentence as defined just above. A repetition count causes vi to move backward several sentences.

Moving by Paragraphs and Sections.   The following commands move the cursor by paragraphs and sections:

}   Moves forward to the next paragraph boundary. Vi considers a paragraph boundary to be (a) a blank line, (b) one of the nroff requests listed in the paragraphs variable (see Section 8.2), or

(c) the end of the buffer. A repetition count causes `vi` to move forward several paragraphs.

{   Moves backward to the previous paragraph boundary as defined previously (the beginning of the buffer acts as a paragraph boundary). A repetition count causes `vi` to move backward several paragraphs.

]]   Moves forward to the next line that marks a section boundary. The following lines mark section boundaries:

- An `nroff` section command, namely, one of the `nroff` requests listed in the `sections` variable (see Section 8.2)

- A line that starts with a left brace at the left margin (e.g., the beginning of a C function definition)

      When this command is combined with a command for deleting, altering, or copying text (see Section 8.1.22), it treats a line starting with '}' as a section boundary. You can't use a repetition count with this command.

[[Moves backward to the nearest previous line that marks a section boundary as defined just above. You can't use a repetition count with this command.

8.1.19
Searching

The commands below search for specified textual items.

Searching for Characters. The following commands search for particular characters. None of them move beyond the current line.

f*c*   Moves to the next occurrence of the character *c* on the current line.

F*c*   Moves to the previous occurrence of the character *c* on the current line.

t*c*   Moves to the character just before the next occurrence of the character *c* on the current line.

T*c*   Moves to the character just after the previous occurrence of the character *c* on the current line.

;   Repeats the last 'f', 'F', 't', or 'T' command. Note that if the last command was 't' or 'T', the ';' command has no effect unless you precede it with a count (since the cursor is already positioned just before or just after a *c*).

,   Repeat the last 'f', 'F', 't', or 'T' command, but reverse the direction.

The following command finds the mate to a delimiter:

%   Moves the cursor to the delimiter that matches the character under the cursor. The delimiters are (( ) [ ] { }). For example, if the cursor is on a '(', this command moves it to the

matching ‘)’; if the cursor is on a ‘}’, this command moves it to
the matching ‘{’. If the cursor is not on a delimiter, you receive
an error warning. This command can move to another line.

Searching for Patterns.   The following commands search for patterns:

/*pat* (Enter)
/*pat*/
/*pat*/+*n*
/*pat*/-*n*   Moves forward to the first character of the next portion of text
that matches the pattern *pat*. The pattern appears on the status
line as you type it.

The pattern is given as a regular expression (see Section 8.1.11). If you've enabled the `wrapscan` variable and the
pattern isn't found in the rest of the buffer, `vi` continues the
search at the beginning of the buffer. You must quote any use
of the character ‘/’ within the pattern by typing it as ‘\/’. You
can disable the special interpretation of regular expression
characters by turning off the `magic` variable.

The forms ‘/*pat*/+*n*’ and ‘/*pat*/-*n*’ indicate the first nonwhite
character on the *n*th line after or before the place where *pat* is
found, or the end of that line if it contains only whitespace. The
form ‘/*pat*/+0’ works and is sometimes useful since it forces the
object specified by the motion to be line-oriented.

Note: You cannot use a count with this command.

?*pat* (Enter)
?*pat*?
?*pat*?+*n*
?*pat*?-*n*   These commands are like the corresponding ‘/pat/’ commands except that they search backward rather than forward.
The new cursor position is at the first character of the
matching text.

/   Searches again for the pattern you most recently searched for
in the forward direction (no matter what the direction of the
previous search). In other words, an empty search pattern
means "repeat the search".

?   Searches again for the pattern you most recently searched for
in the backward direction (no matter what the direction of the
previous search).

n   Searches again for the pattern you most recently searched for,
in the same direction as the most recent ‘/’ or ‘?’ command.
For the purpose of determining the direction, a search with
an empty pattern still counts. The advantage of this command
and the next one over ‘/’ and ‘?’ is that they are just single
keystrokes.

N   Searches again for the pattern you most recently searched for,
but in the opposite direction from the most recent “/’ or ‘?’

command. For the purpose of determining the direction, a search with an empty pattern still counts.

**8.1.20
Setting and Moving
to Placemarks**

The following commands enable you to put *placemarks* in the buffer and to move the cursor to those placemarks. The placemarks are denoted by a letter or digit, indicated as *c* in the descriptions below. Uppercase and lowercase letters are equivalent.

m*c*   Attaches placemark *c* to the current cursor position.

'*c*   Moves the cursor to placemark *c*.

'*c*   Moves the cursor to the beginning of the line containing placemark *c*.

' '   Moves to the previous *context*, determined as follows:

- Initially, the context is at the top of the buffer.
- An insertion sets the context to the beginning of the insertion.
- A pattern search sets the context to the beginning of the text that matches the pattern.
- A deletion sets the context to the cursor position after the deletion.
- A ' ' or ' ' command sets the context to the cursor position.

You can conveniently use this command to move back and forth between two places in the buffer.

' '   Moves to the beginning of the line containing the previous context.

**8.1.21
Inserting Text**

Whenever you type one of the commands in this group, vi enters input mode and expects you to type the text to be inserted.

a   Inserts (appends) text after the cursor.

A   Inserts (appends) text at the end of the current line.

i   Inserts text before the cursor.

I   Inserts text before the first non-white character at the start of the line (or at the start of the line if the line is empty).

o   Opens up a blank line under the current line, then starts inserting text there.

O   Opens up a blank line above the current line, then starts inserting text there.

You can put a count in front of 'a', 'A', 'i', or 'I'; a count of *n* causes *n* copies of the text to be inserted. (Vi silently ignores a count in front of 'o' or 'O'.[3]) But beware of this anomaly in some versions of vi: if the text

3. In early versions of vi, a count *n* in front of 'o' or 'O' caused *n* lines to be opened up. This was useful only for slow terminals.

includes an (Enter), only the text preceding the (Enter) is repeated; the text on the following lines appears only once.

8.1.22
Deleting and
Altering Text

The commands in this section delete or alter text. You can think of altering text as consisting of two operations: deleting the text and then inserting some new text. Some commands take objects, an object being a motion command that defines the range of action of another command. For example, the 'dG' command deletes all lines from the current line down to the end of the buffer, 'G' being the line-oriented motion that moves to the end of the buffer. We first describe the commands that don't take objects and then the commands that do.

Commands That Don't Take Objects.   The commands below for deleting and altering text don't take objects. A number of them are single-letter abbreviations for often-used commands that do take objects.

   The following commands replace existing text. For each of them, the replacement text is typed in input mode. You can type beyond the end of the current line and even start new lines; the effect is as though the additional text was appended at the end of the current line. In particular, new lines are *inserted* after the current line and do not overwrite lines below the current line.

s   Substitutes for the character under the cursor by erasing the cursor character and then inserting new text. With a count of *n*, substitutes for *n* characters starting with the character under the cursor (or the rest of the line if fewer than *n* characters remain). This command is equivalent to 'cl'.

S   Substitutes for the current line by erasing the current line and then inserting new text. With a count of *n*, substitutes for *n* lines starting with the current line. This command is equivalent to 'cc'.

C   Changes the rest of the line. A count given with this command is ignored. The 'C' command is equivalent to 'c$'.

R   Overwrites ("replaces") characters with input text starting with the character under the cursor. The overwritten characters are *not* copied to the anonymous buffer. You can't use a count with this command.

Note that there's no single-letter command for deleting an entire line; use the dd command to do that.

   The following commands delete or replace characters within a line:

x   Deletes the character under the cursor. Used with a count of *n*, this command deletes *n* characters starting with the character under the cursor and going to the right. It is equivalent to 'dl'.

X   Deletes the character preceding the cursor. Used with a count of *n*, this command deletes *n* characters starting with the character before the cursor and going to the left. It is equivalent to 'dh'.

r*c*   Replaces the character under the cursor with the character *c*.
              If you give a count *n* with this command, the next *n* characters
              on the line are replaced with copies of *c*. The count must not
              exceed the number of characters remaining on the line.

D   Deletes the rest of the line. A count given with this command
              is ignored. The 'D' command is equivalent to 'd$'.

The following commands reinsert yanked or deleted text:

p   Puts the contents of the anonymous buffer (the one that 'y' and
              'd' write to) just after the cursor character. If the anonymous
              buffer contains whole lines, it is put just after the current line.
              The anonymous buffer is lost when you change files, so you
              should use named buffers when you're transferring text from
              one file to another.

P   Puts the contents of the anonymous buffer (the one that 'y' and
              'd' write to) just before the cursor character. If the anonymous
              buffer contains whole lines, it is put just before the current line.

The following commands perform other operations:

Y   Yanks the current line into the anonymous buffer. With a count
              of *n*, this command yanks *n* lines starting with the current line.
              The 'Y' command is equivalent to 'yy'.

J   Joins the current line with the next line. With a count of *n*,
              joins *n* lines; that is, joins the current line with the next ($n - 1$)
              lines. When two lines are joined, the junction is created as
              follows:

              (1) If the first character of the second line is ')', all whitespace
                   at the junction is eliminated.
              (2) If the first line ends with a period, question mark, or bang,
                   the junction and any adjacent whitespace are replaced by
                   two spaces.
              (3) In all other cases, the junction and any adjacent white-
                   space are replaced by a single space.

:g /*pat*/s//*repl*/g
              Replaces *pat* by *repl* throughout the buffer. The 's' in this form
              invokes the ex command substitute; the preceding ':g /*pat*/'
              causes the substitution to take place globally (i.e., throughout
              the buffer) on all lines containing *pat*. The trailing 'g' indi-
              cates that the command applies to all occurrences within the
              line rather than just to the first occurrence. The substitute
              command is explained in Section 8.3.17; global execution of
              commands is explained in Section 8.3.23. See those explana-
              tions for variations on this form.

&   Repeats the previous replacement command (applied to the
              first occurrence only).

~   Changes the case of the letter under the cursor and moves to
           the next character. Nonalphabetic characters are unaffected.

See Section 8.1.24 for additional commands that delete, alter, or copy text,
and the '.' command for repeating actions (see p. 432).

Conventions for Commands That Take Objects.   The following conventions apply to commands that take objects:

- An object is specified by a motion command, which can be any
  command that moves the cursor other than one that scrolls the
  screen or inserts text. The commands in Sections 8.1.17 through
  8.1.20 all qualify as motion commands. The action of a command
  taking an object applies to the region denoted by the object (see
  "Objects" on p. 415). For example, 'dW' deletes the next blank-
  delimited word.

- If the command is preceded by a count n, its motion is performed n
  times. For example, '4yt; [Enter]' yanks the text from the cursor up
  to but not including the fourth following semicolon on the current
  line. (You receive an error warning if there aren't four more semicolons on the line.) The forms '4yt;' and 'y4t;' are equivalent, as
  are other analogous pairs of forms.

- A line-oriented motion command defines a region that consists of
  whole lines. The region includes the line containing the starting
  cursor position, the line containing the ending cursor position, and
  all lines in between. For example, the 'j' command defines a region
  consisting of the line containing the cursor and the next line. The
  line-oriented motion commands are

      j k + - H M L G

  A command using line-oriented motions may operate on a region
  bigger than you'd expect. For instance, 'dj' deletes the current line
  and the next one, while '3yk' yanks *four* lines, the current line being
  the last of them.

- If you double the command character, the command applies to all
  of the current line (and does not take an object). For example, 'dd'
  deletes the current line, while '3dd' deletes the current line and the
  next two lines.

Commands That Take Objects.   Each of the following commands takes an
object m:

dm Deletes the region of text from the cursor to m and puts it into
           the anonymous buffer.

cm Changes the region of text from the cursor to m by deleting
           it and then inserting new text. The replacement text is typed
           in input mode and can include ⟨newline⟩s. The deleted text is
           placed in the anonymous buffer.

y*m*   Yanks the region of text into the anonymous buffer (see Section 8.1.24), leaving it undisturbed.[4]   The contents of the anonymous buffer can then be put somewhere else, giving you the effect of a copy action.

>*m*   Indents the region from the current line to the line containing *m* by one shift width (see p. 438). Note that a preceding count affects the search for *m* and does not produce multiple indenting. A convenient way to get multiple indenting is to follow this command by the '.' (dot) command.

<*m*   Outdents the region from the current line to the line containing *m* by one shift width. If the line is already at the left margin, it is unaffected. Note that a preceding count affects the search for *m* and does not produce multiple outdenting. A convenient way to get multiple outdenting is to follow this command by the '.' (dot) command.

!*m-cmd*   Executes *cmd*, transmitting the region of text from the cursor to *m* as the standard input for *cmd*. The standard output of *cmd* then replaces the text in this region. For example, if `fmt` is a program for formatting a paragraph, the command '!}fmt' causes the lines of the next paragraph to be formatted.

8.1.23
Moving and
Copying Text

Vi does not have any explicit commands for moving and copying text. Instead, you move text in two steps: deleting it from its original location and putting the deleted text in the new location. Similarly, you copy text by "yanking" it from its original location and putting it in its new location. Here are two examples:

- To move the next two lines to another place, type '2dd', move to the place you want to put the lines, and type 'p'.

- To copy an arbitrary block of text to an arbitrary place, go to one end of it, type '`a' (to mark that end), go to the other end, and type 'y`a'. Then go to the place you want to put the text and type 'p'.

8.1.24
Named Buffers

Vi has a set of 26 named buffers for holding text, named by the letters of the alphabet. You can transfer text between these buffers and the main buffer. When you transfer text *to* a named buffer, the nature of the transfer depends on whether you specify the buffer with a lowercase letter or with an uppercase letter. For a lowercase letter, the transferred text replaces the previous buffer contents; for an uppercase letter, the transferred text, preceded by a newline, is appended to the previous buffer contents. When you transfer text *from* a named buffer, however, lowercase and uppercase buffer names are equivalent.

---

4. The term "yank" is misleading since it suggests that the yanked text no longer remains where it was; but the use of the term has a long tradition among people who write editors—probably because 'y' doesn't naturally stand for anything else.

A named buffer contains either lines or characters, depending on whether it was filled by a line-oriented command or a character-oriented command. This distinction affects the behavior of commands that insert the contents of a named buffer into the main buffer. Appending text to a named buffer makes it a line-oriented buffer.

With the exception of the @*b* command, each of the named-buffer commands is gotten from a corresponding command for the anonymous buffer by prefixing the corresponding command with '"*b*'. These are the commands for operating on named buffers:

"*b*d*m*   Deletes the region of text from the cursor to *m* and stores it in buffer *b*. In this command, 'd*m*' has the same meaning as it does in the deletion commands of Section 8.1.22. For example, '"xdw' deletes the next word and stores it in buffer X. The '"*b*dd' command deletes the current line and stores it in *b*, while the '"*b*D' command deletes the rest of the current line and stores it in *b*. You can also precede 'd' with a count; the conventions of Section 8.1.22 apply. An example of such a command is '"R3dj', which deletes the next three lines and appends them to buffer R.

"*b*y*m*   Yanks the region of text from the cursor to *m* and stores it in buffer *b*. In this command, 'y*m*' has the same meaning as it does in the deletion commands of Section 8.1.22. For example, '"Ay0' copies the text from the beginning of the line up to and including the character under the cursor into buffer A. The '"*b*yy' command deletes the current line and stores it in *b*. You can also precede 'y' with a count; the conventions of Section 8.1.22 apply.

"*b*p   If buffer *b* contains characters, inserts those characters after the cursor. If it contains lines, inserts those lines just after the current line. Usually this *isn't* what you want; for inserting lines, the '"*b*P' command just below is more likely to give you the right result. If you provide a count with this command, vi ignores it.

"*b*P   If buffer *b* contains characters, inserts those characters before the cursor. If it contains lines, inserts those lines just before the current line. If you provide a count with this command, vi ignores it.

@*b*   Treats the contents of buffer *b* as a sequence of vi commands and executes them. If *b* is specified as '@', then the commands in the most recently executed buffer are executed again. This command usually won't work if '@' is your ⌜Kill⌝ character.

Vi provides two commands for recovering from a mistake:

8.1.25
Undoing or
Repeating Actions

u   Undoes the most recent change, insertion, or macro-defined command. Two 'u's in a row cancel each other. If you undo a command defined by a macro (see Section 8.1.29), *all* the actions of the macro are undone.

U   Restores the current line to the state it was in when you most recently started editing it. The restoration may undo several individual changes.

"*n*p   Retrieves the *n*th most recently deleted block of text and inserts it into the buffer following the cursor. Up to 10 blocks can be retrieved. This command is useful for recovering from accidental large deletions.

"*n*P   Like p, except that the text is inserted preceding the cursor.

.   Repeats the last action that modified the buffer. As a special case, vi increments the deletion number if the action was '"*n*p' or '"*n*P'. Thus the sequence '"1pu.u.u.', continued as long as necessary, causes vi to insert successively older deletions. If you're not sure which deletion you want to retrieve, this sequence is a good way to find the right one.

8.1.26
Checking the Status

The following command reveals vi's status:

Ctrl G   Displays on the status line the name of the current file, the number of the current line, and how far down in the buffer the current position is (as a percentage).

8.1.27
Reading Files,
Writing Files,
and Exiting

We discuss reading and writing files along with exiting from vi because the actions of writing the buffer to a file and exiting are often combined.

Vi has only one file command, 'ZZ', of its own. It relies on ex for all other operations on files. We list the most useful such ex commands below, writing them with the preceding colon that you need in order to use them from vi.

:wq
ZZ   Saves the buffer you're editing and exits from vi. The buffer is saved in the current file.

:[*r*]w [*file*] Here *r* is a range as defined by ex (see Section 8.3.5). If *r* is omitted, the command writes the buffer to *file*, then continues editing it. If you specify *r*, just those lines are written to *file*. If you omit *file*, it is taken to be the current file. By using ':w' with both *r* and *file*, you can write a portion of the buffer to a different file than the one you're editing. The portion must consist of entire lines. Here is the method:

(1) Type 'ma' to mark the beginning of the region you want to write out (see the 'm' command in Section 8.1.20).

(2) Move to the end of the region (i.e., to the beginning of the next line).

      (3)   Type ':'a,.w *file*' to write out the region.

      There are many variations on this method.

:q   Quits vi, abandoning the buffer. Vi rejects this command if you've changed the current file since the last time you wrote it and the warn variable is enabled.

:q!   Quits vi, abandoning the buffer even if you've changed the current file. Vi rejects this command if you've changed the current file since the last time you wrote it and the warn variable is enabled.

:x[it][!] [*file*]

      Exits from vi after writing the current buffer to *file*, or to the current file if *file* is not specified. If *file* already exists but is not the current file, the write fails and vi does not exit. The bang overrides this behavior and forces an unconditional write.

:e *file*   Abandons the buffer and starts editing *file*.

:r *file*   Reads in (inserts) the file *file*, inserting it just after the current line.

:ta *tag*   Opens the file containing the tag file entry *tag* and moves the cursor to that tag within the file. The tags are searched for in the list of tag files given by the tags variable (see p. 436). By default, the file named tags in the current directory is searched first. See Section 8.5 for more information about tag files.

8.1.28
Setting Local
Variables

You can use the following ex command to set the values of the local variables that modify vi's behavior. The local variables are enumerated and explained in Section 8.2.

:set   Specifies or queries a variable using the set command of ex (see Section 8.3.21).

8.1.29
Defining Macros

Vi includes a very useful facility for defining *macros*. Although the commands for defining and undefining macros are all ex commands, they are of no use in ex since macros are recognized only in visual mode. You issue them in vi by preceding them with a colon.

A macro definition has two parts: a left side and a right side. Both parts are sequences of keystrokes. When you type the keystrokes on the left-hand side, vi translates them into the keystrokes on the right-hand side. The left-hand side consists of a sequence of one or more characters. If the sequence contains more than one character, the first character must be a nonprinting character.[5]

Macros are most often used to create definitions for special keys such as function keys and arrow keys on your keyboard, but you can also use them to associate commands with single characters that don't already

---

5. This restriction is a safeguard against defining macros that you are likely to type unintentionally.

have a meaning. You can override a built-in `vi` command with a macro definition; that is sometimes convenient when you've run out of command letters and there are some `vi` commands you never use. You can make a collection of macro definitions available whenever you use `vi` by including the definitions in your initialization commands (see Section 8.1.15).

`Vi` starts out with a set of precompiled macro definitions for the arrow keys and possibly a few others if your keyboard has them. `Vi` extracts the key definitions from the database of terminal descriptions (see Section 2.15). You can see them by issuing the `map` command by itself.[6]

The way that `vi` responds to a multicharacter macro can be affected by the `timeout` variable (see p. 439). It usually makes no difference for macros that you call by pressing just one special key, but it may affect macros that you call by explicitly pressing several keys in sequence.

The following commands enable you to create and remove macro definitions:

`:map` [*lhs rhs*] (Enter)

> The `map` command defines a macro as a "map" of one sequence of keystrokes into another sequence. Macros defined using `:map` only affect command mode; `vi` ignores them when it is in input mode. In the `map` command, *lhs* is the sequence you want to type and *rhs* is the sequence you want `vi` to execute. For example, typing
>
> `:map v :%subst /∧/>  / ` (Ctrl) V (Enter) (Enter)
>
> defines the 'v' key, which is otherwise unused, to mean the same thing as
>
> `:%subst /∧/>  / ` (Enter)
>
> Typing 'v' then puts the sequence '>   ' in front of each line in the buffer—a handy thing to do when the buffer contains a mail message that you wish to respond to. (See Section 8.3.17 for an explanation of the `substitute` command). The (Ctrl) V quotes the (Enter) following it; it is needed because otherwise the first (Enter) would appear to end *lhs* instead of being part of it. The final (Enter) ends the map command itself. In general, you need to put a (Ctrl) V in front of any whitespace character (space, tab, (Enter)) that is part of *lhs* or *rhs*. The left-hand side *lhs* is limited to 10 characters and the right-hand side *rhs* is limited to 100 characters. Contrary to the information in many `vi` documents, one (Ctrl) V always suffices except for one peculiar case: a '|' in a macro definition needs two (Ctrl) V's in front of it (so that the definition contains the sequence '(Ctrl) V |').

---

6. The `map` listing shows three columns: a key name, the characters transmitted by the key, and the definition. Although the first and second columns are different for the precompiled definitions, you can't create such named definitions yourself; any definition you create will have the same information in the first two columns.

Unless the remap variable has been disabled, the editor attempts to map the result of a macro mapping repeatedly until there are no more changes. For example, if you map 'q' to '#' and '#' to 'a', 'q1' maps to 'a1'. With remap off you can, for example, map [Ctrl]L to 'l' and [Ctrl]R to [Ctrl]L without having [Ctrl]R map to 'l'.

Vi has a special notation for associating macros with the function keys on your terminal. If *lhs* has the form '#*n*', where *n* is a digit between 0 and 9, the definition is associated with function key *n*. (The notation '#0' generally refers to function key 10, not function key 0.)

If you type map without *lhs* and *rhs*, you get a listing of all the existing macros.

map! *lhs rhs* [Enter]

This form of map is like the previous one, except that the macro thus defined is interpreted in input mode rather than in command mode.

unm[ap][!] *lhs*

Deletes the mapping you've defined for *lhs*. This command affects input-mode macros if the '!' is present and command-mode macros if the '!' is not present.

**8.1.30
Switching to** ex

The following command enables you to switch from vi to ex:

Q   Switches from vi to ex and enters line-editing mode.

8.2   Local Variables for vi and ex

The local variables listed here affect the behavior of both vi and ex. You can set or query their values from vi with :set and from ex with set (see Section 8.3.21). Some of them are either enabled or disabled; others have numbers or strings as their values. It is often useful to include commands for setting these variables among your initialization commands (see Section 8.1.15).

**8.2.1
Search Control**

The following variables affect the way that search and motion commands work:

magic   If this variable is enabled, the editor gives special meaning to the regular expression characters (. \ [*) in patterns. If this variable is disabled, those characters are treated as ordinary data characters when left unquoted but are treated as meta-characters when quoted with a preceding backslash—just the opposite of the usual convention for regular expressions. The

'∧' and '$' characters represent the beginning and end of the line as usual whether `magic` is enabled or disabled.

Default: `magic` (for most systems)

wrapscan
ws   This variable indicates that when the editor is searching for a pattern and reaches the end of the buffer, it should continue the search at the beginning of the file; that is, it should "wrap around" the end of the buffer.

Default: `nowrapscan`

ignorecase
ic   If this variable is enabled, the editor ignores the case of the letters in a search pattern so that, for example, the string 'digital' matches the string 'Digital' (no matter which one is the pattern and which one is in the file text).

Default: `noignorecase`

paragraphs
para   This variable contains a string giving the names of the `troff` or `nroff` macros that are assumed to start a paragraph (see the '{' and '}' commands in `vi`).

Default: `IPLPPPQPbpP LI`

sections
sect   This variable contains a string giving the names of the `troff` or `nroff` macros that are assumed to start a section (see the '[[' and ']]' commands in `vi`).

Default: `NHSHH HU`

tags   This variable contains a sequence of files to be used as tag files by the `ta` (or `:ta`) command. The files in the sequence are separated by spaces.

Default: `tags /usr/lib/tags`

taglength
tl   If this variable has a nonzero value n, the tags processed by the `:ta` command are significant only to n characters. If n is zero, all characters in a tag are significant.

Default: `0`

**8.2.2
Read-Only Mode
and Automatic
Writing**

readonly   Enter read-only mode, inhibiting modifications to the buffer. In this mode, writing to a file other than the current file is permitted provided you haven't modified the file since you last wrote it. You can still force a write to another file with `write!`.

Default: `noreadonly`, unless `-R` option specified or the file lacks write permission

autowrite

aw   If this variable is enabled and you've changed the buffer since
            you last saved it, the editor writes out the current file before
            executing a command (!, n, or ta) that switches to another file.

Default: noautowrite

8.2.3
Warnings and Status
Information

The following variables control what the editor does in order to protect
you from losing your work:

writeany

wa   When this variable is enabled, the editor does not make any
            safety checks before writing to a file.

Default: nowriteany

warn   If this variable is enabled, the editor prevents you from leaving
            the editor or switching files if you have not saved your latest
            changes. It issues a warning when you attempt such an action.

Default: warn

report   If the value of this variable is *n*, the editor tells you whenever it
            modifies, removes, or yanks more than *n* lines as the result of
            a single operation. The message, which appears on the status
            line, tells you the number of lines affected.

Default: 5

The following variables control how the editor warns you of a potential
problem:

errorbells

ob   If this variable is enabled, the editor sounds the bell (Ctrl G)
            before every error message.

Default: noerrorbells

terse   If this variable is enabled, the editor's error diagnostics are
            given in their terse, shortened form.

Default: terse

The following variable tells the editor to put an indicator on the status
line whenever you are in input mode:

showmode   If this variable is enabled, vi places an indicator on the sta-
            tus line whenever you are in input mode. The indicators are
            'INSERT MODE', 'APPEND MODE', 'OPEN MODE', and 'CHANGE MODE'.
            This variable has no effect in ex.

Default: noshowmode

**8.2.4
Tabbing and
Word Wrap**

The following variable enables or disables autoindent mode, described in Section 8.1.9:

`autoindent`

`ai`   If this variable is enabled, the editor indents each line by the same amount as the previous nonempty line. Enabling this variable is particularly useful for editing computer programs.

Default: `noautoindent`

The following variables affect the number of columns that tabbing commands move backward or forward:

`shiftwidth`

`sw`   The value of this variable specifies the shift width, which defines the number of spaces in the shifts produced by the '<' and '>' commands and the tab stops used by Ctrl D when backing up during textual input in autoindent mode.

Default: `8`

`tabstop`

`ts`   The value of this variable is an integer n. The editor assumes that there is a tab stop every n spaces across the line. When it prints or displays a ⟨tab⟩ character, it converts that character to the number of spaces needed to position the cursor at the next tab stop. (The variable has no effect on the buffer itself—only on the way that it is displayed.) Note that although `shiftwidth` and `tabstop` should usually be set to the same value, the editor does not require that they be.

Default: `8`

The following command affects the treatment of long input lines:

`wrapmargin`

`wm`   If this variable has a nonzero value n, the editor automatically starts a new line when you're in input mode and fewer than n characters remain on the line that you're typing (not when the length of the line exceeds n characters, as you might expect). This feature is called "wordwrap" in many editors. Wordwrap is disabled if the value of `wrapmargin` is zero.

Default: `0`

**8.2.5
Input Interpretation**

The following variables affect how the editor interprets your input:

`beautify`

`bf`   If this variable is enabled, the editor discards any nonprinting characters that you type in input mode, except for Ctrl I (⟨tab⟩), Ctrl J (⟨linefeed⟩), and Ctrl L (⟨formfeed⟩). This variable is not included in POSIX.

Default: `nobeautify`

8.2.6
Macro Expansion
and Definition

The following variables affect macro expansion and definition:

remap   If this variable is enabled, the editor repeats the macro mapping process until no more characters are mapped (see Section 8.1.29). If it is disabled, the editor does not apply macros to the result of a macro expansion.

    Default: remap

timeout   This variable affects how vi behaves when you type a character that begins a multicharacter macro. If it is enabled, vi assumes that any further characters you type after about a second has elapsed are *not* part of a macro call. If timeout is disabled, vi waits indefinitely for more characters to see if they are part of a macro call. See Section 8.1.29 for a discussion of macros. The timeout variable is not included in POSIX since POSIX requires the timeout behavior always to be enabled.

    The purpose of this variable is to ensure that macros associated with special keys on your keyboard work properly. These keys usually transmit a sequence of characters starting with (Esc) when you type them. You can associate an action with a special key by defining its sequence as a macro. Ordinarily, the character sequence for a special key is transmitted very quickly—well within the timeout interval—so vi recognizes the sequence in any case. But if you're working with vi over a network, the network may impose arbitrary delays between the characters in the sequence, preventing vi from recognizing it. By disabling timeout, you enable vi to recognize the sequence in any case.

    For example, some keyboards have a (Meta) or (Alt) shift key. Typing '(Meta)*c*' for any key *c* usually produces the sequence '(Esc)*c*'. Suppose you define the (Meta)W key as a macro that searches for the next occurrence of the string '*/' using the command

        :map (Ctrl)V (Meta)W /*\/\ctl-v (Enter) (Enter)

Typing (Meta)W produces the sequence '(Esc)w'. You can now observe the following behavior, assuming no line delays:

- If you type '(Esc)w' quickly, the search is performed in any case.

- If you type '(Esc)w' slowly and timeout is disabled, the search is still performed.

- If you type '(Esc)w' slowly and timeout is enabled, the current command is terminated in response to the (Esc) and the cursor moves forward one word in response to the 'w'.

The timeout interval is system-dependent but is usually about a second. A few versions of `vi` provide a separate command for changing it. The value of `timeout` has no effect on anything you type when you're not in visual mode.

Default: `timeout`

8.2.7
Display Control

The following variables affect how the editor displays or types lines:

`list`   If this variable is enabled, the editor prints or displays each line with tabs shown explicitly as '∧I' and the end of each line shown explicitly as '$'.

Default: `nolist`

`number`
`nu`   If this variable is enabled, the editor places a line number in front of each line that it prints or displays.

Default: `nonumber`

`autoprint`
`ap`   If this variable is enabled, the current line is shown after each `ex` command that modifies text. This variable has no effect on `vi`.

Default: `autoprint`

`prompt` This variable tells `ex` to display the prompt character ':' when it's waiting for a command. This variable has no effect on `vi`.

Default: `noprompt`

The following variables affect the distance that scrolling commands move:

`scroll` This variable specifies the number of lines that Ctrl U and Ctrl D initially scroll up or down. Using these commands with a count changes the scroll amount thereafter.

Default: half the number of lines on the screen, or 11

`window` This variable sets the number of lines in a screenful as understood by scrolling commands such as `z`. It has no necessary relation to the actual number of lines shown on the screen.

Default: the number of lines on the screen minus one

When you type a ')' or '}' character, you can have the editor show you the matching '(' or '{' by enabling the following variable:

`showmatch`
`sm`   If this variable is enabled, `vi` shows you the corresponding '(' or '{' whenever you type a ')' or '}', provided that the matching symbol is on the current screen. This variable has no effect on `ex`.

Default: `noshowmatch`

8.2.8 **Editor Commands** **in Documents**	The following command enables the editor to recognize and execute editor commands that appear in a document that you're editing:

modelines

> If this variable is enabled, you can embed commands in the first five lines and/or the last five lines of a file, and the editor executes them whenever it starts editing that file. The command lines must have one of the forms
>
> > ex:*cmd*:
> > vi:*cmd*:
>
> You should leave this option disabled unless you are editing a specific file that requires it. The modelines variable is not included in POSIX, though historically it has been part of vi.[7]
>
> **Default:** nomodelines

8.2.9 **Inhibiting Messages**	The following variable enables you to control whether your terminal can receive messages from other users:

mesg

> If this variable is enabled, other programs can send messages to your screen while you're editing. If it's disabled, messages from other programs are rejected. If you disable mesg, enabling it again has no effect.
>
> **Default:** mesg

8.2.10 **Environmental** **Information**	The following variables tell the editor about your environment:

directory
dir

> This variable contains the name of the directory where vi puts its temporary file. It is not included in POSIX.
>
> **Default:** /tmp

exrc

> If this variable is enabled, the editor looks for an .exrc file in the current directory before starting to edit your file. Since exrc is disabled by default, exrc can only have an effect if it is enabled by commands in the environment variable EXINIT or by commands in an .exrc file in your home directory. Not all systems provide this variable—if your system doesn't, you should assume that it behaves as though exrc is enabled.
>
> **Default:** noexrc

---

7. POSIX does require that if this variable or a similar one is provided as an extension, it must be disabled by default. This requirement is intended to deal with the security hazards posed by possibly unintended execution of commands at the beginning of a file.

shell   This variable gives the name of the shell that the editor uses for commands such as those in Section 8.3.24 that either execute a command in a subshell or call a subshell interactively.

Default: the value of the SHELL environment variable

term   This variable contains the name of your terminal type. You cannot set it from within vi.

Default: the value of the TERM environment variable

slowopen   If this variable is enabled, vi does not update your screen when you're in insert mode. Instead, it delays the update until you've finished the insertion. Vi still shows you what you're typing, but it overwrites lines on the screen that will later be restored. This mode is useful if you're working with a slow terminal.

Default: slowopen

8.3 The Extended Editor ex

The ex line editor is so named because it extends the ed editor. The ex line editor and the vi visual editor (see Section 8.1) are integrated into a single program.

**8.3.1
Calling ex**

The call to ex has the form

> ex [-rR] [-s | -v] [-c *cmd*] [-t *tag*] [-w *size*] [*file*...]

An obsolescent form uses '-' in place of -s and '+*cmd*' in place of '-c *cmd*'. The items in the list of files can contain wildcards. Within ex you can call for the next file to be edited using the next command. When you call ex, it prompts you for commands. The possible commands are described below. You can have ex take its input from a file by redirecting standard input from that file.

The following are the options for the ex command line. You can give them in any order.

-s
-    Configure ex for batch use by suppressing all prompts and informational messages, ignoring the value of TERM, assuming the terminal is incapable of supporting visual mode, and suppressing the reading of any .exrc file. This option is intended for processing editor scripts provided on stdin. The - form is obsolescent.

-v   Invoke ex in *visual mode*. The call 'ex -v' is equivalent to calling vi and accepts the same additional options that vi does.

-t *tag*   Edit the file containing *tag* (see Section 8.5). The cursor is initially positioned at the tag. If you also specify a file list, the file containing *tag* is edited first and then the files in the file list. The relevant tag file, usually the file in the current directory named `tags`, must be available (see the `tags` variable, p. 436).

-r   Attempt to recover the specified files after the editor or the system crashes. As `ex` works, it periodically saves the state of the buffer in a recovery file. Some older versions of `ex` send you a mail message containing the name of the recovery file when the editor crashes. If you later call `ex` and specify this recovery file with the `-r` option, `ex` resumes in whatever state it was when it saved the recovery file. Note that for these versions, *file* is *not* the name of the file to be recovered.

-R   Edit these files in read-only mode (the `readonly` flag is set). Setting this flag helps to protect the files from accidental over-writing by inhibiting `ex` from writing to them unless special commands such as `w!` are used.

+*cmd*
-c *cmd*   Execute the `ex` command *cmd* before starting to edit the first (or only) file in the file list. The +*cmd* form is obsolescent.

-w *size*   Set the default size of a screenful, as recorded in the `window` variable (see p. 440), to *size*. There is no necessary relation between the size of a screenful and the actual screen size; the screenful size only affects scrolling commands such as `z`.

8.3.2
Initializing ex

When `ex` starts up it executes a set of initialization commands before reading any input from your terminal. These commands are gotten just as they are for `vi`. The procedure is described in Section 8.1.15.

8.3.3
The Main Buffer

The material you're editing is kept in a place called the *main buffer*. The same main buffer is used for `ex` and `vi`. All editing commands apply to the main buffer, sometimes just called "the buffer". A typical editing cycle consists of reading a file into the main buffer, editing it, and writing it back to the same file.

The focus of editing is a particular line in the main buffer called the *current line*. An empty file has, in effect, a single current line numbered zero. Whenever you operate on a line, say by finding some text in that line or changing that line, that line becomes the current line. If you operate on a sequence of lines as a group, for example by showing them, the last line in the sequence becomes the current line.

The main buffer has a file associated with it called the *current file*. When you start editing a file, that file becomes the current file. A number of `ex` commands change the current file (see Section 8.3.19).

8.3.4
Form of a Command

An `ex` command has one of the following forms:

> [*lineset*] *cmd* [`!`] [*params*] [*count*] [*flags*]
> *lineset*
> Enter

In the first form, the allowable components depend on the command. The second form is equivalent to

> *lineset* `print`

The third form is equivalent to '+print'. It advances the current line to the next line and prints that line.

Here is what the items in the first form mean:

lineset   The address of a single line or a range of consecutive lines (see Section 8.3.5). Most commands, if given an extra address, ignore it.

cmd   The name of the command to be executed.

!   A modifier that changes the meaning of the command. For commands such as `quit` that may cause editing changes to be lost, the bang allows the command to proceed; without it, `ex` issues a warning and aborts the command. For commands such as `insert` that put `ex` into input mode, the bang temporarily reverses the state of the `autoindent` flag. For other commands, the bang has a variety of meanings. For the `write` command, it matters whether you put a space between '`write`' and '`!`'; *the forms '`write!`' and '`write`␣`!`' have entirely different meanings.* For other commands it doesn't matter; '`read!`' and '`read`␣`!`' are equivalent.

params   The parameters expected by the command. File names and regular expressions are examples of such parameters.

count   The number of lines that the command displays or operates on. An omitted count defaults to 1.

flags   A set of flags that affect the operation of the command (see Section 8.3.7).

For example, the command

```
3 join 2 #
```

joins two lines beginning with line #3 and produces the resulting line. The # flag causes the displayed line to be preceded by a line number.

Except for '`write!`' and for commands where the command name is followed by something that starts with a letter, spaces between the components of a command are optional. For example, the `join` command above could also be written more compactly as

```
3j2#
```

The j here is an abbreviation of `join`.

Multiple Commands on a Line. You can put several commands on a single line by separating them with '`|`'. Commands prefixed by `global` and commands that use '`!`' to call a UNIX program must appear last on a line.

8.3.5
Line Addresses and
Line Ranges

Some ex commands operate on a line or on a range of lines. You can specify a line in a number of ways:

.   The current line.

$ The last line of the file.

n The nth line of the file, where n is a decimal number.

$'c$ The line marked with the letter c (see the ma command below).

$''$ The line that you most recently moved to with a non-relative motion of any kind. A relative motion is one that you obtain with a count such as '+5'. A motion with ''' itself is non-relative, so you can switch between two locations by using this form of address.

$/pat/$ The next line containing the pattern *pat*. The pattern is given by a regular expression. See Section 8.1.11 for a description of the particular kinds of regular expressions accepted by ex and vi.

$?pat?$ The nearest previous line containing the pattern *pat*.

$a+n$
$a-n$
$a\ n$ The address a plus or minus n lines, where n is a decimal number. You can omit the '+ 'as shown in the third line. For example, '/reg/+4' denotes the fourth line after the next line containing the string 'reg'.

$+n$
$-n$ The nth line relative to the current line either forward ('+') or backward ('-'). For example, if the current line is line 27, '-5' denotes line 22.

$a+$
$a-$
$+$
$-$ The line after ('+') or before ('-') the line with address a. If a is omitted, it is taken as the current line. Note that you can generate addresses such as '--', which means the second previous line, by using '+' and '-' repeatedly.

An address of zero, whether computed or given explicitly, refers to the very beginning of the main buffer. Such an address is valid only for commands that append text *after* a given line. For example, the command '0 append' is valid but the command '0 insert' is not.

A line range can have one of three forms:

a_1, a_2 The group of lines starting with a_1 and ending with a_2. For example, '/whit/,$' designates the range starting with the next line containing 'whit' and continuing to the end of the file.

$a_1 ; a_2$ Like a_1 , a_2 except that the current line is set to a_1 before a_2 is evaluated. For example, the command '+,+p' produces the next line, while the command '+;+p' produces the next two lines.

%   Equivalent to '1,$' (the entire file). This abbreviation is particularly useful.

If a line range is used in a context where only a single address is expected, the second address of the range is used. If a single address is used in a context where a line range is expected, the line range consists of the single line specified by the address.

8.3.6
Specifying Groups of Lines

Many ex commands operate on groups of lines. All of these commands let you specify a line range r, a count n, or both. The lines affected by the command are determined as follows:

(1) If r is missing, it is taken as the address of the current line.
(2) If n is given, r is interpreted as a line address and the command affects n lines starting with line r.
(3) If n is not given, the lines in r are shown.

Here are a few examples:

p3   Produce ("print") three lines starting with the current line.

/fault/d2   Delete two lines starting with the next line containing 'fault'.

-,+j   Join the preceding line, the current line, and the next line.

8.3.7
Command Flags

Certain commands can have the following *print flags* attached to them. The following flags cause a line to be shown ("printed") after the command is executed:

p   Produce ("print") the last line affected by the command. Used by itself, this flag usually makes no difference since the last line affected would be shown anyway.

l   Produce the last line affected by the command, showing tabs and the end of line as they would be shown with the list option (see p. 440) enabled.

\#   Produce the last affected line, preceded by a line number as it would be with the number option (see p. 440) enabled.

\+   Increase the line number by 1 before showing a line. Multiple uses of '+' increase the line number by 1 for each use. For example, '++' increases the line number by 2.

\-   Decrease the line number by 1 before showing a line. Multiple uses of '-' decrease the line number by 1 for each use.

These flags can be used in any combination and in any order. The effect of the 'l' and '#' flags persists until the next command that changes text. If you use '+' or '-' without any other flags, the last line affected by the command is still printed.

**8.3.8
Abbreviations**

You can abbreviate the names of most of the ex commands. The description of each command indicates the shortest abbreviation that ex recognizes, but you can use longer abbreviations too. For instance, the so[urce] command can be written as 'so', 'sour', or 'source'. You'll almost always want to use the shortest abbreviation you can, although the longer forms are sometimes helpful when you're writing an editing script.

You can also create your own abbreviations for useful phrases using the abbreviate command (see Section 8.3.22). These abbreviations are only recognized in input text.

**8.3.9
Comments**

When you have a prepackaged file of editor commands, it's often useful to include comments in it. A comment begins with '"'. It can be on a line by itself or come at the end of a command line. The editor ignores everything from the comment character to the end of the line.

**8.3.10
Typing Conventions**

The following keys have special meanings as you type commands:

Enter	When you're typing a command, ends the command and issues it. When you're typing input text, ends the current line and starts another one.
Intr	Terminates this command and prompts for another one. If you press Intr while typing textual input for a command such as insert, the current line is discarded but previously typed lines are retained.
Erase Ctrl H	Erases the character preceding the cursor.
Kill	Erases all the characters typed on the current line.
Ctrl Q Ctrl V	Quotes the next character; that is, inserts it into the text verbatim even if it is a control character such as Esc. In addition, if autoindent is enabled, the Tab and Ctrl D characters behave as they do in vi (see Section 8.1.9).

**8.3.11
Special Buffers**

In addition to the main buffer, ex keeps 26 named buffers, one for each letter of the alphabet, and an anonymous buffer. You can use these special buffers to move text from one place to another using the yank, delete, and put commands.

Each of these commands accepts a buffer name as a parameter. If you omit the buffer name, the command uses the anonymous buffer. For yank and delete, the command replaces the contents of a named buffer if you specify the buffer name with a lowercase letter. If you specify a buffer name to yank or delete with an uppercase letter, the command appends to the existing contents of that named buffer. For example, the command

        .,+y A

appends the current and next lines to named buffer A, while the command

    d

deletes the current line and places it in the anonymous buffer.

    The @ command also operates on a buffer, executing its contents as a sequence of ex commands.

8.3.12
Producing Lines

The following commands produce one or more lines on your terminal:

CR   Produces the next line and sets the current line to that line.

r [*flags*]
[*r*] p[rint] [*n*] [*flags*]

> Produces ("prints") a group of lines, specified as described in Section 8.3.6. As particularly simple cases, typing '.' produces the current line and typing '+' produces the next line. Typing a line range by itself produces that range. The command can include print flags, indicated as *flags*. These behave as described in Section 8.3.7. After the lines are produced, the current line is set to the last line produced.

r l[ist] [*n*] [*flags*]

> Like print, except that tab characters are shown as '∧I' and the actual end of the line is indicated by '$'. The effect is equivalent to print with the 'l' flag.

r # [*n*] [*flags*]
r nu[mber] [*n*] [*flags*]

> Like print, except that a line number is displayed in front of the text of each line. The effect is equivalent to print with the '#' flag.

[*a*] Ctrl D Scrolls down the file to line *a*, then produces a sequence of lines. The number of lines produced is given by the scroll variable (see p. 440). The default for *a* is the current line.

[*a*] z [*t*] [*n*]

> Produces a window of *n* lines with the line at *a* placed in the window according to *t*:
>
> +   Produces a window starting with line *a*. Successive 'z+' commands display successive windows of text.
> −   Produces a window ending with line *a*.
> ∧   Produces a window ending with the line two windows back from line *a*. Successive 'z∧' commands back up through the buffer.
> .   Produces a window with line *a* at its center.
> =   Like '.', except that the indicated line is surrounded by lines of hyphens and is made the current line.
>
> The default for *a* is the current line. The default for *n* is twice the value of the scroll variable (see p. 440).

8.3.13 **Status Information**	The following commands provide various kinds of status information:

[*a*]=   Produces the address of the line at *a*, but doesn't change the current line. The default for *a* is the current line.

ar[gs]   Produces the file arguments that were on the command line. These are the files that you can access using the next command. It is chiefly useful when these files were specified using wildcards.

ve[rsion] Shows the version number of the editor.

8.3.14 **Inserting Text**	The following commands insert text into the buffer. The inserted text is ended by a line containing a period and nothing else. If you want the text to include a line that appears to contain a period and nothing else, you can put a blank after the period—or if that is unacceptable, insert some other text and change it to a period later.[8]

[*a*] a[ppend][!]

> Appends input text after line *a*. If you omit *a*, it defaults to the current line. The current line becomes the last line appended.
>
> If '!' is present, the autoindent variable (see p. 438) is toggled from its current state to the opposite state for the duration of the input. The next command that reads input will revert to the old state.

[*a*] i[nsert][!]

> Inserts input text before line *a*. If you omit *a*, it defaults to the current line. If *a* is 1, the text is inserted at the beginning of the buffer. The current line becomes the last line inserted. The '!' modifier does the same thing as for append.

8.3.15 **Modifying Text**	The following commands enable you to delete or change text by groups of lines:

[*r*] d[elete] [*buf*][*n*][*flags*]

> Deletes a group of lines, specified as described in Section 8.3.6. The deleted lines are sent to a special buffer according to the rules described in Section 8.3.11. If you specify a named buffer *buf*, you need to put a space in front of its name.
>
> The command can include print flags, indicated as *flags*. These behave as described in Section 8.3.7. After executing this command, the editor produces the line following the last line it deleted.
>
> For example, the command '/rug/d e3#' deletes three lines starting with the next line containing the string 'rug'. The

---

8. This situation isn't entirely theoretical—it comes up all the time in writing documentation for programs such as ex, ed, and mail.

deleted lines replace the contents of buffer **e**. After the deletion, the editor produces the next line preceded by a line number (because of the '#' flag).

$[r]$ c[hange][!][n]

> Deletes a group of lines, then inserts input text in their place. The lines in the group are specified as described in Section 8.3.6. The replacement text is ended by a dot on a line by itself as it is for the **insert** and **append** commands.

The following command enables you to join two or more lines into one:

r j[oin][!][n]

> Joins a group of lines. The group is specified as described in Section 8.3.6, except that if both r and n are missing the current line is joined with the next line. When two lines are joined, the junction is created as follows:

> (1) If the first character of the second line is ')', all whitespace at the junction is eliminated.
> (2) If the first line ends with a period, question mark, or bang, the junction and any adjacent whitespace are replaced by two spaces.
> (3) In all other cases, the junction and any adjacent whitespace are replaced by a single space.

The following commands enable you to shift groups of lines right or left:

$[r]$ > [n] [*flags*]

> Shifts a group of lines right by one shift width (see p. 438). The group is specified as described in Section 8.3.6. Typing '>>' shifts by two shift widths, typing '>>>' shifts by three, etc. The current line is set to the last line in the affected region.
>
> The command can include print flags, indicated as *flags*. These behave as described in Section 8.3.7.

$[r]$ < [n] [*flags*]

> Like '>', except that leading indentation is deleted rather than inserted. A line with no leading indentation is unaffected.

8.3.16
Moving and
Copying Text

The following commands enable you to move and copy text:

r m[ove] [a]

> Moves the lines in region r to the location after address a. If a is zero, the lines are moved to the beginning of the file. If you omit r, it defaults to the current line. After **ex** moves the lines, it sets the current line to the last line it moved. Line a must not fall within r.

$[r]$t a
$[r]$co[py] a [*flags*]

> Copies ("transfers") the lines in range r to address a. If a is

zero, the lines are copied to the beginning of the file. If you omit r, it defaults to the current line. After ex copies the lines, it sets the current line to the last line it copied.

The command can include print flags, indicated as *flags*. These behave as described in Section 8.3.7.

$[r]$ ya[nk][*buf*][*n*]

Copies ("yanks") a group of lines into a special buffer. The group is specified as described in Section 8.3.6. The lines are copied into or appended to a special buffer according to the rules described in Section 8.3.11. If you specify a named buffer *buf*, you must put a space in front of its name. If you omit r, it defaults to the current line. After ex copies the lines, it sets the current line to the last line it copied.

You can use this command, together with pu, as an alternate way of copying lines. It is particularly convenient when you want to copy the lines to several places.

$[a]$ pu[t][*buf*]

Copies ("puts") the lines from a special buffer into the main buffer following address a. The special buffer can be either the anonymous buffer or a named buffer (see Section 8.3.11). If you omit a, it defaults to the current line.

8.3.17
Substitutions

The following commands enable you to perform substitutions, also known as "search and replace" operations:

$[r]$ s [/*pat*/*repl*/ [*opts*] [*n*] [*flags*]]

Substitutes the replacement text *repl* for the pattern *pat* in each line of a specified group of lines. Unless the g option described below is specified, only the first occurrence of the pattern on a particular line is affected. The group of lines eligible for substitution are determined as described in Section 8.3.6. The pattern is given by a regular expression (see Section 8.1.11 for an explanation of the particular regular expressions accepted by ex and vi). The s command by itself repeats the previous substitution.

The following options can be specified individually or in combination as *opts*:

c   Ask for confirmation of each substitution. If you type 'y', the substitution is made; if you type anything else, it is not.

g   Perform the substitution throughout the line.

Following the substitutions, the current line becomes the last line where a substitution took place. If you omit r, it defaults to the current line. If you specify any flags, the editor shows you the last line where it made a substitution (see Section 8.3.7).

A replacement consisting only of '~' or '%' denotes the replacement that was used in the most recent s command. An '&' within the replacement is replaced by the entire search pattern. An occurrence of '\n' in the replacement, n being a single digit, is replaced by the nth such subexpression (see p. 84). You can cancel the special meanings of '%', '&', or '~' by escaping these characters with a preceding backslash. Within the replacement text, a newline escaped by '\' turns into a real newline, causing the replacement text to be split into two lines at that place.

Note that there isn't a "search" command corresponding to the "replace" command, but you can search for a pattern *pat* by using the command '/*pat*/p'.

[*r*] & [*opts*] [*n*] [*flags*]

Repeats the most recent substitution; that is, performs the command

[*r*] s /*p_pat*/*p_repl*/ [*opts*] [*n*] [*flags*]

where *p_pat* and *p_repl* are the pattern and replacement used in the most recent substitution. An '&' by itself is equivalent to an 's' by itself—but '&', unlike 's', lets you change *opt*, *n*, or *flags* without respecifying *pat* or *repl*.

[*r*] ~ [*opts*] [*n*] [*flags*]

Repeats the most recent substitution using the most recent pattern; that is, performs the command

[*r*] s /*p_pat*/*p_repl*/ [*opts*] [*n*] [*flags*]

where *p_pat* is the regular expression most recently used in any context, and *p_repl* are the pattern and replacement used in the most recent substitution.

8.3.18
Marking Lines

The following command attaches a mark to a line so that you can go back to that line later:

[*a*] k *c*
[*a*] ma[rk] *c*

Marks the line at *a* with the letter *c*, which you can later use in the address ''*x*' to refer to this line. This command does not change the current line.

8.3.19
File Operations

The commands that follow enable you to read from a file, write to a file, or start editing a different file.

Reading a File.   The following commands enable you to read a file:

ex[!] +*linefile*
e[dit][!] +*line file*

Discards what is in the buffer, then starts editing *file*. The file *file* must already exist; you cannot edit an empty nonexistent file. If autowrite is enabled (see p. 437), the buffer is saved automatically before the new file is edited. If you attempt to execute this command and the current file has been modified but not saved (either explicitly or automatically), the editor issues an error message and aborts the command. If '!' is present, the editor executes the command without complaint in any case.

If '+*line*' is present, editing starts at line *line*. You can specify *line* as a line number ($ is a permissible line number) or as a search pattern. The pattern /*pat* specifies a forward search for *pat*, the pattern ?*pat* a backward search.

Note that this and the following commands require a blank between the command and the file name that follows it.

a r[ead] *file*

Reads the contents of *file* into the buffer, inserting them after line *a* in the manner of append. If you omit *file*, it defaults to the current file. You can also use a variant of the read command, 'read!', to execute a shell command and insert its output into the buffer (see p. 457).

ta[g][!] *tag*

Opens the file containing the tag file entry *tag* and moves the cursor to that tag within the file. If the tag is not in the current file but the current buffer has been modified since the last write, ex issues a warning and aborts the command. Specifying the '!' option in the command overrides this protection. The relevant tag file, usually the file in the current directory named tags, must be available (see the tags variable, p. 436). See Section 8.5 for more information about tag files.

Writing to a File.   The following commands enable you to write to a file:

[*r*] w[rite][!] [>>] *file*

Writes the lines in region *r* to *file*. The following rules apply:

- If you omit *r*, it defaults to the entire buffer.

- If you omit *file*, ex writes the contents of the buffer to the current file.

- If *file* already exists but its name does not match the name of the file being edited, the editor gives you an error message and aborts the command. If '!' is present, however, the command is executed without complaint in any case. For this use of '!', you *must not* leave a space between the 'write' and the '!'.

- If '>>' is present, the text is appended to the file instead of replacing its contents.

- If the current buffer has no current file associated with it, the write fails.

This command does not change the current line.

[*r*] wq[!] [>>] *file*

> Writes the buffer to *file*, then quits. This command behaves exactly like the corresponding form of write followed by quit.

You can also use a variant of the write command, 'write␣!', to execute a shell command with the lines of the region as input (see p. 457).

Editing Another File.   The following commands enable you to start editing a different file:

n[ext][!] [+*cmd*] [*file*...]

> If the files *file*...are omitted, discards the buffer and edits the next file in the current file list. Otherwise, replaces the current file list by *file*... and edits the first file in the new file list. If the current file has not been written out, the editor behaves as it does with the edit command.
>
> If '+*cmd*' is present, the editor executes the command *cmd* immediately upon starting to edit the first file in the file list. In particular, if *cmd* is a line address such as a number or pattern, the editor starts editing at that line address. The command *cmd* must not contain any spaces. If the current buffer has been modified since the last write, ex issues a warning and aborts the command. The '!' option overrides this protection. This command is useful when the file list is specified with wildcards and contains more than one file, since otherwise edit would be the natural way to switch files.

rew[ind][!]

> Resets the list of files to be edited to its beginning and edits the first file as you would with the next command. If the current buffer has been modified since the last write, ex issues a warning and aborts the command. The '!' option overrides this protection.

f[ile] *file*   Changes the name of the current file to *file* and marks it as "not edited", indicating that this file was not the original one edited. If you omit *file*, ex tells you the name of the current file and its status.

Changing Directories.   The following command enables you to change to another directory:

chd[ir][!] [*dir*]

cd [*dir*]   Changes the current directory to *dir*, or to ~ if *dir* is not specified. Executing '!cd *dir*' does not have this effect because the change is lost when the subshell exits. If the current buffer has been modified since the last write, ex issues a warning and aborts the command. The '!' option overrides this protection.

**8.3.20
Exiting from
the Editor**

The following commands enable you to exit from the editor:

q[uit][!]   Quits the editor without writing out the buffer. If the buffer
has been modified since it last was written or initialized, the
editor issues an error message and aborts the command. The
behavior in this case is similar to the edit command; the '!'
modifier silences the error message.

x[it][!][*file*]
Exits from the editor, writing out the buffer if it contains any
unsaved changes by issuing a write command with the same
'!' modifier and optional *file* as this command. If the write
command fails (which can't happen if '!' is specified), ex does
not exit, but even xit! can fail with an error message if the
buffer has been modified but has no associated pathname.

st[op][!]
su[spend][!]
Stops the editor and suspends the process under which it's
running, returning to the shell from which it was initiated.
The editing process can be resumed later on. If the buffer
has been modified and the autowrite variable is enabled, the
buffer is saved before the editor is stopped. The '!' modifier
inhibits the action of saving the buffer. If job control is either
disabled or unsupported in the shell you used to invoke ex,
you'll get a warning message and the command will have no
effect.

**8.3.21
Setting Local
Variables**

The set command enables you to set the value of a local variable. The
local variables are described in Section 8.2. These are the forms of the
set command:

set x Enables variable x (i.e., turns it on).

set no$x$ Disables variable x (i.e., turns it off). For example, 'set
nomagic' disables the magic variable, thus disabling the
interpretation of certain characters in regular expressions.

set x=*val*
Sets the value of variable x to *val*.

set   Shows those variables that have been changed from their
default values.

set all   Shows the values of all the variables. An important use for this
command is finding out what variables are available on your
system.

set x?   Shows the value of variable x.

You can include several settings in a single command such as

    set ai wm=6 nomesg

You can preset the variables to suit your taste by putting them in initialization files (see Section 8.1.15).

8.3.22 Abbreviations and Macros

The following commands enable you to create and remove abbreviations:

ab[breviate] *lhs rhs*
> Makes the single word *lhs* an abbreviation for the keystroke sequence *rhs*. The abbreviation *lhs* can contain digits as well as letters, but it must start with a letter. Thereafter when you type *lhs* in input mode, vi replaces it by *rhs*. If *lhs* isn't surrounded by spaces or punctuation, vi won't recognize it. For example, suppose you type the command
>
> > ab clm the Computer Liberation Movement ⏎Enter
>
> Thereafter whenever you type 'clm' as a word in input mode, vi replaces it by 'the Computer Liberation Movement'. The replacement would not apply to 'clm1', however, since in this case 'clm' isn't surrounded by blanks or punctuation.

una[bbreviate] *lhs*
> Removes the abbreviation *lhs*.

Macros. Ex also includes map and unmap commands for creating and removing macro definitions (see Section 8.1.29). However, these commands are of no use within ex since ex never recognizes macros.

8.3.23 Performing Commands Globally

The following commands enable you to perform some other command for each line in the buffer that matches a pattern:

[*r*] g[lobal] /*pat*/ *cmds*
> Performs the list of commands *cmds* globally for each line containing text that matches the pattern *pat*, where *pat* is given by a regular expression (see Section 2.17). Any '/' in *pat* must be quoted by writing it as '\/'. If a region *r* is specified, only the lines in *r* are examined; otherwise, all lines in the buffer are examined.
>
> Each command of *cmds* must appear on a line by itself. Each line in turn must be ended by a backslash except for the line containing the last command in the list. The insert, append, and change commands are permitted and should be followed by their input, ending with a line containing only a dot and a backslash (.\). An empty line ends both the input and the command list (the dot isn't needed in this case). The command list can be empty; in this case, ex simply produces the lines containing text that matches the pattern.
>
> For example, here is a command that gets rid of 'cholesterol' by deleting each line containing it:
>
> > g /cholesterol/d

[r] g/*pat*/*cmds*
[r] v/*pat*/*cmds*

> The two forms of this command are like the g command, except that the editor performs the indicated commands on those lines in the region *r* that *don't* meet the search criterion.

8.3.24
Calling Programs
from Within
the Editor

The following commands enable you to execute UNIX commands in a subshell and to apply them to portions of text in the buffer:

sh[ell]   Runs an interactive subshell, with control returning to the editor when the shell exits.

[r] ! *cmd*   Executes the command *cmd* in a subshell, taking the standard input for *cmd* from the lines specified by the range *r* and replacing those lines by the standard output of *r*. If *r* is omitted, both standard input and standard output are taken from your terminal; the editor waits for you to provide the input. For example, the command '%!sort' sorts the contents of the entire buffer.

[a] r[ead] ! *cmd*
> Executes *cmd* in a subshell, inserting its standard output after line *a*. The default for *a* is the current line.

[r] w[rite] ! *cmd*
> Executes *cmd* in a subshell, passing the lines in region *r* to *cmd* as its standard input. If *r* is omitted, it is taken to be the entire buffer. This command does not change or produce the current line.

!!   Executes the most recent '!' command again.

8.3.25
Saving and
Recovering

The editor periodically saves its state so that you can recover if the editor or the system crashes. The following commands recover the state and save the state explicitly:

rec[over] *file*
> Recovers the state of ex from *file* after a crash. In the event of a crash, you receive a mail message giving you the name of the recovery file to use with this command.

pre[serve]
> Saves a copy of the buffer to a special "preserve" area for use by the editor's recovery procedure. This command can be useful when a write command has failed and you don't know how else to save your work. You can later recover the buffer using the -r command-line option.

8.3.26
Entering Visual
Mode

The following commands enable you to enter visual mode or its variant, open mode:

[*line*] vi[sual] [*type*] [*n*] [*flags*]
> Enters visual mode and enables full-screen editing according to

the `vi` conventions (see Section 8.1). The current line indicator is set to *line*. The type *type* can be '+', '−', or '∧' and indicates the position of the current line on the screen as in the `vi` commands `z+`, `z−`, or `z∧`. The count *n* specifies the initial window size. The *flags* have the meaning described in Section 8.3.7. Typing '`Q`' from within `vi` returns you to `ex`.

[*line*] o [pen] [*/pat/*] [*flags*]
> Enters *open mode* with the current line reset to *line* if specified. If *pat* is specified, the cursor is moved to the beginning of *pat* within the line. The *flags* have the meaning described in Section 8.3.7. Open mode is like visual mode except that only one line is displayed at a time. It is sometimes useful when you're running `ex` on a terminal of an unknown type. A `vi` command that would move you to another line under `vi` causes that line to be displayed. For example, typing '`j`' causes the next line to be displayed. Just as with visual mode, the '`Q`' command returns to `ex`.

8.3.27 Undoing the Previous Action

The following command enables you to undo a previous action:

u[ndo]
> Undoes the most recent change or insertion. If the previous action was carried out with the `global` command, all the consequent changes are undone. Two u's in a row cancel each other.

8.3.28 Executing Commands from a File

The following command enables you to execute commands that are in a file:

so[urce] *file*
> Reads the lines in the file *file* and executes them as though they had been typed at the terminal.

8.3.29 Executing Commands in a Buffer

The following command enables you to execute commands from a named buffer:

@*buf*
*buf
> Interprets the text in named buffer *buf* as a sequence of commands and executes those commands. If *buf* is '*' or '@', then the commands in the most recently executed buffer are executed again. It is an error if no such buffer exists.

8.4 The `ed` Line Editor

The `ed` line editor is the oldest and simplest of the UNIX editors. It was originally designed when UNIX was mostly used with slow teletypewriters and its design reflects that fact. At one time ed was widely imitated; for example, the old MS-DOS edlin editor is based on ed. Despite ed's age, a few people still prefer it, and some shell scripts depend on it.

8.4.1
The Command Line

The form of the ed command line is

> ed [-s] [-p *string*] [*file*]

where *file* is a file to be edited. If you omit *file*, ed starts editing an unnamed empty file.

When you call ed, it first shows you the number of characters in the file you're editing. It then expects you to type a sequence of commands. The possible commands are described below. Ed does not explicitly prompt you unless you ask it to with the P command or by specifying the -p option on the command line. You can also provide the input to ed from a file by redirecting standard input from that file.

There are two possible options for ed:

-p *string*   Use *string* as the interactive prompt string.

-s   Suppress the messages that give information about character counts, and also suppress the '!' prompt after a subshell call. If this option is set, ed does not produce any output that you do not request explicitly. Setting this option is usually desirable when you are providing an editing script as the standard input to ed. An example of such a script might be the output of diff (see Section 3.10.2).

By default, ed merely issues a '?' when you type an illegal command. To get more revealing error messages, issue the H command before you start editing (see Section 8.4.16). You can also use the h command to get an explanation of an error.

8.4.2
The Buffer

The material you're editing is kept in a place called the *buffer*. All editing commands apply to the buffer. A typical editing cycle consists of reading a file into the buffer, editing it, and writing it back to the same file.

The focus of editing is a particular line in the buffer called the *current line*. The buffer has a file associated with it called the *current file*. When you start editing a file, that file becomes the current file. Two ed commands change the current file: the e command, which starts editing a different file, and the f command, which explicitly changes the current file. The r (read) command sets the current file if it was undefined, as it would be if you called ed without a file name.

8.4.3
Form of a Command

A command has one of the forms

> [*lineset*] *cmd* [!] [*params*] [*sfx*]
> *address*
> [Enter]

All command names consist of a single character, usually a letter. For example, the command '2,5p' produces ("prints") lines 2 through 5 of the buffer on your terminal. Spaces between the parts of a command are optional, except that a space is required between an alphabetical command and a bang or parameter that follows it.

- The *lineset* or *address* part specifies the group of lines or single line affected by the command. In the form above, *lineset* is a line address or a line range, as described below, and *address* is a line address.

- The *params* part contains any addresses, file names, commands, or other information required by the command.

- The suffix *sfx* is one of the command names (l n p). A suffix can be attached to any command that does not expect a file name or UNIX command as a parameter. A suffix causes the current line to be produced after the command to which it is attached has been executed. The line is shown as it would be by the command appearing in the suffix. For example, the command 'dn' deletes the current line and produces the following line with a line number. Here 'd' is the command and 'n' is the suffix.

Line Addresses and Line Ranges. The notations for specifying a line address are as follows:

$	The last line of the file.
.	The current line.
n	The *n*th line of the file.
'*c*	The line marked with the letter *c* (see the k command below).
/*pat*/	The next line containing the pattern *pat*. The pattern is given by a BRE (see Section 2.17.1).
?*pat*?	The nearest previous line containing the pattern *pat*.
a n	The address *a* plus or minus *n* lines, where *n* is a decimal number. You can omit the '+' as shown in the third line. For example, '/mao/-3' denotes the third line before the next line containing the string 'mao'.
+*n* -*n*	The *n*th line relative to the current line either forward ('+') or backward ('-'). For example, if the current line is line 103, '+7' denotes line 110.
a+ *a*- + -	The line after ('+') or before ('-') the line with address *a*. If *a* is omitted, it is taken as the current line. Note that you can generate addresses such as '++', which means the second line after the current line, by using '+' and '-' repeatedly.

An address of zero, whether computed or given explicitly, refers to the very beginning of the buffer. Such an address is valid only for commands that append text *after* a given line. For example, the command '0a' is valid but the command '0i' is not.

A line range can have one of the following forms:

a_1, a_2 The group of lines starting with a_1 and ending with a_2. For example, '1,/catafalque/' designates the range starting with line 1 and continuing to the first line containing 'catafalque'.

$a_1; a_2$ Like a_1, a_2 except that the current line is set to a_1 before a_2 is evaluated. For example, the command '+,+p' produces the next line, while the command '+;+p' produces the next two lines.

,   The entire file.

;   The pair '.,$'.

If a line range is used in a context where only a single address is expected, the second address of the range is used. If a single address is used in a context where a line range is expected, the line range consists of the single line specified by the address.

Producing Lines Implicitly.   You can omit the closing delimiter of a pattern or of a replacement string when that delimiter is the last character before the ⟨newline⟩ in a g, G, s, v, or V command. In that event, the line addressed by the command is produced on standard output just as it would be by the p suffix. For example, the following pairs of commands are equivalent:

```
s/vole/mole          s/vole/mole/p
g?blazes             g?blazes?p
```

8.4.4
Producing Lines

The following commands produce one or more lines on your terminal:

[*r*]p   Produces ("prints") the group of lines in the line range *r*. The current line is set to the last line produced. The default for *r* is the current line.

⟨CR⟩   Produces the next line.

a   Produces the line at address *a*.

[*r*]n   Produces the group of lines in the line range *r*, putting a line number at the beginning of each line. The current line is set to the last line produced. The default for *r* is the current line.

[*r*]l   Produces the group of lines in the line range *r* in a visually unambiguous form. Nonprinting characters are represented as escape sequences such as \t (tab) or *nnn* (*nnn* being an octal number); long lines are split into shorter ones, with each break indicated by a trailing backslash; and the end of each output line is marked with a '$' (to show whether trailing spaces are present). The current line is set to the last line produced.

8.4.5
Showing the
Line Number

The following command shows you the line number of a specified line.

[*a*]=   Produces the address of the line at *a*. If *a* is omitted, it is taken to be the last line of the buffer, so typing '=' is a convenient way to see how many lines are in the buffer. The form '/*pat*/=' shows you the address of the next line containing the pattern *pat*. This command does not change the current line.

8.4.6
Inserting Text

The following commands insert text into the buffer. The inserted text is ended by a line containing a period and nothing else. If you want the text to include such a line, you can put a blank after the period—or if that is unacceptable, you can insert some other text and change that text to a period later.

[*a*]a   Appends input text after line *a*. If you omit *a*, it defaults to the current line. The current line becomes the last line appended.

[*a*]i   Inserts input text before line *a*. If *a* is 1, the text is inserted at the beginning of the buffer. If you omit *a*, it defaults to the current line. The current line becomes the last line inserted.

8.4.7
Modifying Text

The following commands delete or change text by groups of lines:

[*r*]d   Deletes the lines in range *r*.

[*r*]c   Changes the lines in range *r* by deleting them and then inserting input text. The input text is ended by a line containing just a dot, as it is for the a and i commands.

[*r*]j   Joins the lines in *r* into a single line by deleting the ⟨newline⟩s between them. Any whitespace at the beginning or end of a joined line is unaffected, and no additional whitespace is added. The default for *r* is '.,.+1'; that is, the current line and the next one.

8.4.8
Moving and
Copying Text

The following commands move and copy text:

[*r*]m*a*   Moves the lines in range *r* to the location after *a*. The default for *r* is the current line.

[*r*]t*a*   Copies ("transfers") the lines in range *r* to address *a*. The default for *r* is the current line.

8.4.9
Substitutions

The following command performs substitutions, also known as "search and replace" operations:

[*r*]s/*pat*/*repl*/[*opts*]
[*r*]s*c pat c repl c* [*opts*]
          Replaces the pattern *pat* by the text *repl* within each line in the line range *r*, which defaults to the current line. The pattern is given by a regular expression (see Section 2.17). Although

the pattern and replacement are customarily delimited by '/' as shown in the first form, you can use any character other than space or tab as the delimiter, as shown in the second form.

The options *opts*, if specified, consist of one or more letters, an integer, or both. They determine which occurrences of *pat* are replaced and what output, if any, is produced:[9]

n	Replace just the *n*th occurrence, where *n* is an integer between 1 and 512.
g	Replace all occurrences.
l	Produce the last line where a substitution was made, using the same format as the l command.
n	Produce the last line where a substitution was made, using the same format as the n command.
p	Produce the last line where a substitution was made, using the same format as the p command.

If neither *n* nor g is specified, the first occurrence is replaced.

An '&' character appearing in the replacement stands for the text matched by the pattern unless the '&' is quoted with '\'. The '\(... \)' notation described in Section 2.17.1 can also be used. A replacement consisting of the single character '%' stands for the most recent previous replacement. An escaped newline (i.e., a newline preceded by '\') can appear in the replacement provided that this command is not part of a global execution specified by a g or v command.

8.4.10 Marking Lines

The following command attaches a mark to a line so that you can go back to that line later:

[*a*]k*c*	Marks the line at *a* with the letter *c*, which you can later use in the address ''*x*' to refer to this line. This command does not change the current line.

8.4.11 File Operations

The following commands enable you to read from a file, write to a file, or change the name of the current file:

[*a*]r [*file*]	Reads the file *file* into buffer after line *a*. The default for *file* is the current file; the default for *a* is the end of the buffer. After reading a file, ed shows you the number of characters that it read. This command does not change the current file unless the current file is undefined, as it is when you start editing the empty file.

The 'r !' command (see p. 465) also provides a form of reading.

---

9. The BSD version of ed uses different conventions for *opts*.

[*r*]w [*file*] Writes the lines in the line range *r* to *file*. If *file* does not exist, it is created. The default for *file* is the current file; the default for *r* is the entire buffer. After writing a file, ed shows you the number of characters that it wrote. If *file* is omitted, ed writes to the current file. This command does not change the current file unless the current file is undefined, as it is when you start editing the empty file.

   The 'w !' command (see p. 466) also provides a form of writing.

e [*file*] Discards the contents of the buffer, reads *file* into the buffer, makes it the current file, and starts editing it. When ed reads *file*, it shows you how many characters it read. If the buffer has not been written out since it was last modified, ed warns you and leaves the buffer unchanged. If you type 'e' a second time, however, the command is executed. The default for *file* is the current file.

   The 'e !' command (see p. 465) enables you to edit the standard output of a UNIX command.

E [*file*] Like e, except that ed unconditionally executes the command without complaint.

f [*file*] Changes the name of the current file to *file*. If you omit *file*, ed shows you the name of the current file.

8.4.12
Exiting from
the Editor

The following commands enable you to exit from the editor:

q   Quits the editor. If the buffer has not been written out since it was last modified, ed warns you and lets you continue editing. A second q at this point does take effect.

Q   Like q, except that ed unconditionally quits without complaint.

8.4.13
Performing
Commands
Globally

The following commands enable you to perform some other command for each line in the buffer that matches a pattern:

[*r*]g/*pat*/[*cmds*]

   Performs the commands in *cmds* for those lines in *r* that match the regular expression *pat* (i.e., performs them "globally"). The default for *r* is the entire buffer. The command list *cmds* can contain multiple commands, provided that each command except the last one is on a line by itself ended with a backslash. The a, i, and c commands are permitted, with their input becoming part of the command list. The input lines must also be ended by a backslash.

   As usual, the input for one of these commands is ended by a line containing just a dot (and its backslash). If the last command in the list is an input command, however, the dot line ending its input can be omitted. An empty command list is equivalent to a command list containing just p. The command list cannot contain any g, G, v, or V commands.

Ed executes this command by looking for the next line l in r that contains *pat*. It then executes *cmds* with the current line set to l. It continues this cycle until no more lines containing *pat* remain in r. For example, the command

```
g /loser/ s//winner/g\
a\
Hooray!
```

causes ed to go through the buffer replacing each occurrence of 'loser' by 'winner'. (The implicit substitution pattern for the s command is 'loser'.) At each line where ed makes a replacement, it adds a line containing 'Hooray!'.

You can terminate this command with (Intr) if it starts to run away.

[*r*]G/*pat*/ Like g, except that the commands are gotten interactively. For each matching line in r, ed shows you the line and then awaits a *single* command. The command cannot be an a, c, i, g, G, v, or V command. It then executes the command that you type. Typing just (Enter) acts as a null command; typing '&' executes the previously entered command for this line.

[*r*]v/*pat*/*cmds*

Like g, except that the selected lines are those in r that do *not* contain a match for *pat*.

[*r*]V/*pat*/ Like G, except that the selected lines are those in r that do *not* contain a match for *pat*.

8.4.14
Calling Programs from Within the Editor

The following commands execute UNIX commands in a subshell and apply them to portions of text in the buffer:

!*cmds* Executes the UNIX commands *cmds* in a subshell. Any unquoted occurrence of '%' within *cmds* is replaced by the name of the current file. If the first character of *cmds* is itself a bang, that bang is replaced by the text of the most recently executed subshell commands. Thus '!!' provides an easy way of executing one command several times.

e !*cmds* Executes the UNIX commands *cmds* in a subshell and edits their standard output as though that output were a file brought in with the e command. Ed shows you the number of characters that it read into the buffer. The 'e !' command does not change the current file.

[*a*]r !*cmds*

Executes the UNIX commands *cmds* in a subshell and inserts their standard output after line *a*, which defaults to the end of the buffer. Ed shows you the number of characters that it read into the buffer.

[*r*]w !*cmds*

> Executes the UNIX commands *cmds* in a subshell, using the lines in range *r* as the standard input to *cmds*. The default for *r* is the entire buffer. Ed shows you the number of characters that it passed to *cmds*.

**8.4.15
Undoing the
Previous Action**

The following command enables you to undo a previous action:

u

> Undoes the most recent change or insertion. If the previous action was carried out with the global command, all the consequent changes are undone. Two u's in a row cancel each other.

**8.4.16
Prompts and Error
Messages**

The following commands control the prompts and error messages that you get from ed:

P

> Toggles prompting for subsequent commands.

h

> Gives help on the most recent error diagnostic.

H

> Toggles the display of explanatory error messages for '?' diagnostics.

8.5   Tag Files

A *tag file* is a kind of index file that gives the location of each definition appearing in a set of files. An example of such a definition is a C function definition. Each line of a tag file specifies the name of a definition, the file containing that definition, and the line within that file where the definition is to be found. The vi and ex editors use the information in a tag file to enable you to edit files containing C programs and similar text conveniently.

The ctags program reads a collection of C source programs and constructs a tag file from them. For example, the command

```
ctags *.c
```

creates a tag file named tags in the current directory that you can use to conveniently edit all the '.c' files (which presumably contain C programs) in that directory. We don't discuss the ctags program further in this book.

The Emacs editor can create and use tag files (see Section 10.3), but Emacs tag files are in a format incompatible with that of the tag files created by ctags and utilized by vi.

9

The GNU Emacs Editor

The GNU Emacs editor is an extensible, customizable, self-documenting, full-screen editor written by Richard Stallman as part of the GNU project and made available through the Free Software Foundation.[1] You can obtain the latest version of Emacs over the Internet via anonymous FTP from `prep.ai.mit.edu`, directory `/pub/gnu` (see Section 12.8).

Emacs is a working environment by itself—besides its document editing facilities, it provides a file manager (called a "directory editor"), a mailer, an appointment calendar, a LISP debugger, and many other services. It also provides modes for handling several classes of specialized text, including TeX documents, outlines, programs in any of several programming languages, and pictures made out of text characters. Its operations are integrated with those of other widely used programs such as the revision control system RCS (see Section 5.15).

Emacs is able to handle the ISO Latin-1 character set (see Section 2.16.1). If the environment variable `LC_CTYPE` is set to `iso_8859_1` or `iso-8859-1`, Emacs displays the ISO characters properly and recognizes their syntactic roles.

Unlike `vi`, Emacs is a *modeless* editor. Commands for operations such as moving the cursor or deleting some text are all assigned to special keys; when you type an ordinary printable character, it is inserted into the text of your document. Since Version 19, Emacs has been able to use the

---

1. In our references to Emacs we follow the convention of the Emacs manual in calling the editor "Emacs" rather than "`emacs`".

facilities of the X Window System, including independent windows at the X level, mouse support, and configurable fonts and window colorings.

Emacs is written in a dialect of LISP called Elisp. You can customize Emacs in simple ways without becoming involved in LISP programming or customize it more extensively by modifying its source code. Modifying the source code, which is freely available from the same sources as Emacs itself, requires specialized knowledge and usually is not a small project.

The material in this chapter should suffice for most editing tasks, but Emacs has too many specialized commands and facilities and too many details for us to cover it completely here. We don't describe the commands and modes associated with specific programming languages, nor do we explain every aspect of each command's behavior. Moreover, we describe but a few of the many variables that you can use to customize Emacs. You'll find these details in the Emacs manual, which you can view on-line in hypertext form with the Ctrl H Ctrl I command (see Section 9.6).

9.1 Calling and Terminating Emacs

The simplest way to call Emacs is just to type 'emacs'. Calling Emacs without options causes it to display a screen of introductory information; typing any key makes that information go away. Once within Emacs, you can choose a file to edit. Alternatively, to specify the file you wish to edit when you first call Emacs, type

    emacs *file*

where *file* is the pathname of that file.

9.1.1 Command-Line Options

The Emacs command-line options don't follow the standard UNIX conventions described in Section 2.12.4. Options can be specified either with single letters or with full words as indicated below, but options cannot be combined. A blank is needed between the name of an option and its argument. A file name on the command line is treated as a particular type of option rather than as a separate argument following the options.

The general form of the Emacs command line is

    emacs [*init-options*] [*options-and-files*] [*X-options*]

where the *init-options* have the form

    [-t *dev*] [-d *disp*] [-nw] [-batch] [-q | -no-init-file] [-u[ser] *user*]

and must appear in the order shown, the *options-and-args* have the form

    [[+*n*] *file*] [-l[oad] *file*] [-f[unction] *func*] [-i[nsert] *file*] [-kill]

and the *X-options*, which apply only to operation under X, are the X Toolkit options such as `-bg`, which sets the background color (see Section 13.7). The *options-and-args* and *X-options* can appear in any order but are honored in order of appearance. The *init-options* must precede the *options-and-args*; the *X-options* can be intermixed with either or both groups.

Initial Options.   The options in *init-options* are as follows:

`-t` *dev*   Use *dev* as the terminal device.

`-batch`   Run Emacs in batch mode. The text being edited is not displayed; the standard interrupt characters have their usual meanings. This option is normally used only with the `-l` or `-f` options.

`-q`
`-no-init-file`
        Don't load the Emacs initialization file (the file `.emacs` in your home directory).

`-u[ser]` *user*
        Load the Emacs initialization file `.emacs` from *user*'s home directory.

`-d` *disp*   Use *disp* as the display under X.

`-nw`   Don't communicate directly with the X Window System even if it is active; instead, assume that communication is with an ordinary terminal.

Other Options and Files.   The options and files in *options-and-files* may appear more than once and are honored in the order they appear. Here they are:

`[+n]` *file*   Visit *file* using `file-find`, loading it into an Emacs buffer (see Section 9.4.1). If *n* is specified, move the cursor to line *n* of that buffer. If you specify several files, each file will be loaded into a different buffer. The last file you load is the one whose buffer will appear on your screen.

`-l[oad]` *file*
        Load LISP code from *file* with `load`.

`-f[uncall]` *func*
        Call LISP function *func* with no arguments.

`-i[nsert]` *file*
        Insert *file* into the current buffer. This option is useful only when the buffer has already been loaded by specifying a file to be visited. It provides a way of concatenating files in the buffer.

`-kill`   Perform all initialization actions, then exit from Emacs without asking for further confirmation.

9.1.2
Quick Exit

If you're stuck within a command, you usually can get out of it by typing Ⓒtrl G one or two times. If you're stuck within a recursive edit (indicated by square brackets on the mode line at the bottom of your screen), you can get out of it by typing ⒨eta Ⓒtrl C several times or ⒨eta X top-level once. The sequence ⒨eta X top-level Ⓒtrl G should get you out of anything.

The sequence Ⓒtrl X Ⓒtrl C causes Emacs to exit immediately. Before exiting, it gives you an opportunity to save your work. If you're not running under X, you can also suspend Emacs without actually killing it by typing Ⓒtrl Z. Under X, you can merely move the focus away from the Emacs window.

9.2   Conventions for Typing Input

Emacs is a modeless editor; unlike editors such as vi, it does not have distinct command and input modes. When you type an ordinary printable character such as the letter 'U', it is inserted into your document; when you type a control character such as 'Ⓒtrl C' or 'Ⓔsc', it is taken as a command (or the beginning of a command) to perform an operation such as deleting the previous character, moving to the next line, or saving the file you're editing. For example, to erase the next character, you type 'Ⓒtrl D'; to start editing a new file named fiddleheads, you type 'Ⓒtrl X Ⓒtrl F fiddleheads'. Ordinary printable characters are commands also; typing a 'U' summons the self-insert command whose effect is to insert a 'U'.[2]

Emacs uses the capabilities of your keyboard more intensively than any other program we describe in this book. It recognizes three kinds of shift keys: ordinary, control, and meta. Most commands start with either a control-shifted key such as Ⓒtrl C or a meta-shifted key such as ⒨eta X. Many of these shifted keys are commands by themselves. The three shift keys can be used individually or in combination.

- The ordinary shift key is the one that changes 'a' to 'A'.

- The control shift key is the one that produces control characters.

- How you produce a meta shift depends on your particular keyboard; on some keyboards it's not possible at all.[3] For those keyboards that don't have a meta shift, you can obtain the same effect by preceding

2. The vi emulation provided by Emacs redefines the printable characters so that, for example, 'j' becomes a command to move down by one line.

3. On the PC-type keyboards that we work with ourselves, the Ⓐlt key acts as a meta shift—but only under X.

the meta-shifted character with $\boxed{\text{Esc}}$; for example, typing '$\boxed{\text{Esc}}$ x' is one way to produce the $\boxed{\text{Meta}}$ X character. On keyboards that do have a meta shift, you can still use $\boxed{\text{Esc}}$ to "meta"-ize a character.

In the following description, we use $\boxed{\text{Meta}}$ C to indicate the letter 'c' with meta shift and $\boxed{\text{Meta}}$ $\boxed{\text{Ctrl}}$ C to indicate the letter 'c' with both meta and control shift. ($\boxed{\text{Meta}}$ c is equivalent to $\boxed{\text{Meta}}$ C and $\boxed{\text{Ctrl}}$ c is equivalent to $\boxed{\text{Ctrl}}$ C, and similarly for the other letters.) For some other characters, the ordinary shift can modify the other shifts. For instance, the $\boxed{\text{Ctrl}}$ _ character (control underscore) is usually generated by holding down the ordinary shift and the control shift at the same time while pressing the '-' key. That's because the standard typewriter keyboard has the '_' character on the same key as the '-' character.

Unlike most UNIX programs, Emacs assigns the $\boxed{\text{LnFd}}$ (linefeed) key a different meaning than the $\boxed{\text{Enter}}$ key; $\boxed{\text{LnFd}}$ starts a new line but also, under some circumstances, indents that new line. If your terminal doesn't have a $\boxed{\text{LnFd}}$ key (most don't), you can obtain its effect by typing '$\boxed{\text{Ctrl}}$ J'.

The Emacs key bindings specify the action caused by a particular key, key sequence, or mouse action. You can modify the key bindings or define new ones (see Section 9.25.1). Emacs will update the help information where it can to account for the change. A disadvantage of altering the normal key bindings is that much of the Emacs documentation (including the description in this book) won't reflect your alterations.

9.3   Getting Acquainted with Emacs

Emacs offers an extensive help system—in fact, the screen you first see when you call Emacs tells you how to start the Emacs tutorial. The $\boxed{\text{Ctrl}}$ H key activates the help menu (see Section 9.6); in particular, typing '$\boxed{\text{Ctrl}}$ H t' starts the tutorial at any time.

The tutorial provides an excellent guided tour of the most important Emacs features and concepts, but it isn't of much use for retrieving information on how to do something in particular. The other options of the help system can be difficult to use until you've already gained some familiarity with Emacs. The hints that follow are intended to aid you in using the help system before you've gained that familiarity.

To display the help options, type $\boxed{\text{Ctrl}}$ H three times. Emacs displays a window that lists the options and provides a brief explanation of each one. Some options replace the window by a window of help information; some others split the screen into two windows. The screen always contains at least one window; the window containing the cursor is called the *selected window*.

The following commands provide the window operations that you'll need in order to use the help system and escape from it when you're done:

- To switch windows when the screen contains more than one window, type '⟨Ctrl⟩ X o'.
- To scroll the selected window forward (down), type either '⟨Ctrl⟩ V' or ⟨PgDn⟩.
- To scroll the selected window backward (up), type either '⟨Meta⟩ V' or ⟨PgUp⟩.
- To scroll the other window forward, type either '⟨Meta⟩ ⟨PgDn⟩' or ⟨Meta⟩ ⟨Ctrl⟩ V'. To scroll it backward, type '⟨Meta⟩ ⟨PgUp⟩'.
- To make all windows disappear except for the selected window, type '⟨Ctrl⟩ X 1'.
- To remove help information from the selected window, type '⟨Ctrl⟩ X k ⟨Enter⟩'.

All these commands are described again later in this chapter.

Probably the most useful form of help when you're first starting out is "apropos" help, which you can use to find out all the commands relating to a particular topic. You can get "apropos" help by typing '⟨Ctrl⟩ H a'. Emacs then asks you for some text that might appear in the names of the commands you are interested in. For instance, if you respond with 'delete', Emacs lists all the commands that have 'delete' in their names along with their explanations. If the listing is too long to fit in the window, you can use the scrolling and window-switching commands listed previously to view the entire list and to make the help window go away when you're done with it. Some of the keywords commonly used in command names are the following:

```
char line word sentence paragraph region page sexp
list defun buffer screen window file dir register mode
beginning end forward backward next previous up down
search goto kill delete mark insert yank fill indent
case change set what list find view describe
```

9.4   Emacs Concepts

In the following subsections we explain some of the concepts that are used in the explanations of the Emacs commands.

9.4.1
Buffers

All editing takes place in a *buffer*—a region of computer memory that holds a body of text. The usual way to edit is to read a file into a buffer, modify the buffer, and write the modified buffer back to the file. There are many other ways to use buffers, however. For instance, you can start with an empty buffer and create a file in it, or use a buffer as a scratchpad that you abandon when you're done with it. Emacs often creates buffers for you that hold specialized text. For example, Emacs puts the help information in a buffer when you use the help system and puts the directory list in a buffer when you use the directory editor Dired. See Section 9.16 for a discussion of the commands that apply to buffers.

Read-Only Buffers.   A buffer can have read-only status. When a buffer is read-only, Emacs refuses to execute any command that would modify the buffer's text. If you issue such a command, Emacs warns you that the buffer is read-only. Many Emacs special-purpose buffers such as an Info buffer or a Dired buffer are normally read-only. In addition, when you visit a file for which you don't have write permission in order to edit it, Emacs automatically makes the editing buffer read-only. You can toggle a buffer's read-only status by typing '(Ctrl) X (Ctrl) Q' (see p. 516). It's sometimes useful to make a writable buffer read-only in order to protect it from being modified by accident, but it's rarely useful to make a buffer writable when Emacs initially gave it read-only status.

9.4.2
Treatment of Newlines

Emacs treats a ⟨newline⟩ like any other character:

- If the cursor is at the end of a line and you move right by one position, the cursor moves to the first character of the next line.
- If you delete a ⟨newline⟩, the line that you're on is joined with the next line. (Pressing (Ctrl) D at the end of a line deletes the following ⟨newline⟩; pressing (Del) at the beginning of a line deletes the preceding ⟨newline⟩.)
- If you insert a ⟨newline⟩ in the middle of a line (which you can do by typing (Enter)), the line is split in two.

See Section 9.10.5 for a description of the commands that insert ⟨newline⟩s.

9.4.3
Typing Special Characters

You can insert a control character into your document by preceding it with (Ctrl) Q, which calls the `quoted-insert` command. For instance, typing (Ctrl) Q (Ctrl) X inserts a (Ctrl) X character.

9.4.4
Major and Minor Modes

Each buffer has a set of *modes* associated with it: one major mode and any number of minor modes. These modes serve to adapt Emacs's behavior to the nature of the information in the buffer and to your preferences. The modes in effect at any moment are those of the buffer in the current window.

Major Modes.   A *major mode* defines a set of local key bindings that override the global key bindings—the ones that are in effect by default. A major mode usually redefines other aspects of Emacs's behavior as well. The mode line at the bottom of a window indicates the major mode of the buffer in that window. The major mode appears in parentheses near the middle of the line.

Emacs has different major modes for different kinds of information that can appear in a buffer. The major modes fall into three groups:

- **Document modes.** These include modes for ordinary text, outlines, TEX, LATEX, and `nroff`.
- **Programming language modes.** These include modes for several varieties of LISP, Fortran, C, and many other programming languages.
- **Internal modes.** These modes are for specialized buffers such as those associated with the directory editor, the buffer list, subshells, and help screens.

The command for entering a mode usually has the form '*mode*-`mode`', where *mode* is the name of the mode. For example, the command Meta X `fortran-mode` turns on the Fortran major mode.

In this book we don't discuss the modes associated with particular formatters and programming languages. Major modes are mutually exclusive—only one major mode can be in effect for a given buffer at a time. The least specialized major mode is "Fundamental Mode", which gives each key its most general meaning and sets each option to its default value.

When you visit a file in order to edit it, Emacs tries to choose a major mode according to the filename. For instance, if you edit a file whose name ends in '`.c`', Emacs assumes you're editing a C program and automatically activates C mode.

Ordinary characters have special meanings in many of the internal modes. For instance, if you type '?' when you're in an internal mode, Emacs usually provides a help screen that shows your alternatives. Typing '?' in an ordinary document or in a computer program merely inserts a question mark into the edited text.

Minor Modes. A *minor mode* defines a variation in behavior that you can either turn on or turn off. Minor modes, unlike major modes, are independent of each other. Each minor mode has a command associated with it for turning the mode on or off in the current buffer. For example, the Auto Fill minor mode is controlled by the `auto-fill-mode` command. With a negative or zero argument, these commands turn off the mode; with a positive argument, they turn it on (see Section 9.5.4 for a discussion of arguments to commands). Called without an argument, they toggle the mode; that is, they turn it off if it was on and on if it was off.

Emacs provides the following minor modes and commands for turning them on or off:

- **Auto Fill mode.** In Auto Fill mode, which is controlled by the Meta X `auto-fill-mode` command, Emacs inserts ⟨newline⟩s as needed in order to prevent lines from becoming too long (see Section 9.10.2).

- **Overwrite mode.** In Overwrite mode, which is controlled by the `Meta` X `overwrite-mode` command, characters you type replace characters on the screen instead of pushing those characters to the right.

- **Auto Save mode.** In Auto Save mode, which is controlled by the `Meta` X `auto-save-mode` command, Emacs periodically saves the buffer by writing a copy of it in its associated file.

- **Abbrev mode.** In Abbrev mode, which is controlled by the `Meta` X `abbrev-mode` command, abbreviations are activated (see Section 9.25.3).

- **Line Number mode.** In Line Number mode, controlled by the `Meta` X `line-number-mode` command, the number of the line containing the cursor is displayed on the mode line.

- **Transient Mark mode.** In Transient Mark mode, usually useful only under X, the mark is activated by certain commands but is deactivated by any change to the buffer. This mode is controlled by the `Meta` X `transient-mark-mode` command.

- **Font Lock mode.** In Font Lock mode, useful only under X, syntax highlighting is activated. This mode is controlled by the `Meta` X `font-lock-mode` command.

These minor modes are meaningful in all major modes that allow general editing; that is, in all major modes other than internal ones such as directory editing mode.

Emacs could have been set up to provide minor modes that are meaningful only in certain major modes, but it wasn't. However, nothing prevents you from defining such minor modes in your own customized version of Emacs.

9.4.5 Windows

As you edit, your screen is divided into *windows*, each containing a buffer. The same buffer can appear in more than one window. Any changes you make to the text in one window are reflected in all the other windows containing the same buffer. The window containing the cursor is called the *selected window*.

At the bottom of each window is a status line called the *mode line* that looks something like this:

```
--**-Emacs: diary.txt     (Text Abbrev Fill)--18%----------
```

It contains the following information:

- The name of the buffer in the window (here, `diary.txt`).
- The major and minor modes for that buffer (here, major mode Text and minor modes Abbrev and Fill).
- The position of the window relative to the rest of the buffer ('`Top`', '`Bottom`', or some percentage in between such as '`18%`').
- Two characters near the left end of the status line that indicate the buffer's modification status: '`%%`' for "read-only", '`--`' for "unmodified", and '`**`' for "modified".

In addition, if Line Number mode has been activated (see Section 9.16.7), the mode line shows the line number of the line containing the cursor. See Section 9.13 for a discussion of the commands that apply to windows.

Sometimes a window contains a text line longer than the window's width. In this case, Emacs splits the text line into two or more screen lines, putting a backslash at the end of all but the last one. When you move to the end of such a text line, you also move down one or more lines on the screen.

The last line of your screen is shared by the *minibuffer*, which displays commands as you enter them (see Section 9.5.1), and the *echo line*, which shows the results of executing commands and also displays error messages. See Section 9.5.1 for a discussion of the commands pertaining to the minibuffer.

9.4.6
Frames

If you are running Emacs under X, something we recommend highly, you can use the X windowing facilities with Emacs (see Chapter 13). Each X window that belongs to Emacs is called a *frame* to distinguish it from the Emacs windows discussed earlier. A frame can contain several windows in the Emacs sense. Each window in an Emacs frame has its own scrollbar, which you can use to move around the buffer displayed in that window.

Some frame operations are provided by Emacs, others by your X window manager, and a few by both. You use Emacs to create a frame or to control the appearance of a frame (see Section 9.14). You use the window manager to move the cursor from one frame to another, to move a frame around the screen, or to change the size of a frame. You can use either Emacs or the window manager to delete a frame, to reduce a frame to an icon, or to expand a frame from an icon.

9.4.7
The Point, the Cursor, the Mark, and the Region

The *point* is the position in the selected window where editing commands take effect. Each window has its own point. The point lies *between* characters, not *on* them.[4] The point can also be at the very beginning or the very end of the buffer. The cursor is always on the character just to the right of the point in the window that's currently active.[5]

The *mark* is a position in a buffer that, like the point, is either between two characters or at one end. Each buffer has exactly one mark, although it may have more than one point (since it may appear in several windows).

The *region* of the selected window is the area between the point and the mark. Each window has a region, although the region might include some text that isn't visible in the window (since the mark need not be in the window). When you remove a buffer from a window, Emacs remembers the point position from that window. When you next restore that buffer

---

4. This convention makes it much easier to describe precisely what commands do, particularly in the cases where the point is at the very beginning or the very end of the buffer.

5. If the point is at the end of the buffer, the cursor is on a character that doesn't actually exist in the buffer.

to a window, the point position in the window is set to the remembered position.[6]

By default, the mark is always active. Since a terminal ordinarily has only one cursor, the mark is not directly visible. Unless you are operating under X, the region is not directly visible either since Emacs has no way of highlighting text. The best way to see where the mark is is to execute the command 'Ctrl X Ctrl X' (see p. 493), which exchanges the point and the mark and thus puts the cursor where the mark just was.

Transient Mark Mode.   Emacs has a minor mode called Transient Mark mode that is particularly useful under X and not particularly useful otherwise. Enabling Transient Mark mode has two effects: (a) the mark can be made inactive, and (b) under X, when the the mark is active, the region is visibly highlighted. You enable Transient Mark mode by executing the command 'Meta X transient-mark-mode' (see p. 475).

In Transient Mark mode, the mark can be activated in several ways:

- By setting it explicitly with 'Ctrl Space' (set-mark-command) (see p. 493) or with a mouse command under X that sets it (see Section 9.9).
- By executing a keyboard command such as Meta @ (mark-word) or 'Ctrl X h' (mark-whole-region) that defines a region and thus implicitly redefines the mark.
- By exchanging the point and the mark with the 'Ctrl X Ctrl X' command (exchange-point-and-mark) (see p. 493).

It can also be deactivated in two ways:

- By making a change to the buffer such as inserting or deleting a character.
- By executing the 'Ctrl G' (keyboard-quit) command.

Under X you can see the region before you execute a command such as 'Ctrl W' (kill-region) that operates on the region. You can modify the region by moving the cursor and see the effect of what you are doing. If you try to execute a region command when the mark is inactive and no region is defined, Emacs will just beep at you.

**9.4.8
Variables**

In Emacs, a variable is a LISP symbol that has a value associated with it. Emacs uses some variables for recordkeeping; the variables of interest to users are those that customize Emacs's behavior, called *options*. The Ctrl H v command (see p. 485) provides documentation on any variable.

The name of a variable usually consists of a sequence of words separated by hyphens, although the syntax for variable names is more permissive. Section 9.21 describes the operations on variables, including how to set and retrieve their values. You can create your own variables with the LISP defvar function (type 'Ctrl H f defvar Enter' to get documentation on it).

---

6. The situation is really more complicated since the buffer could have been changed in the meantime by actions in another window.

9.4.9
Faces, Fonts, and Colors

Under X, Emacs uses different *faces* to display different portions of the information in a frame. For instance, normal text uses the `default` face and the mode line uses the `modeline` face. The definition of each face specifies the appearance of the characters that use that face: the font, the foreground color, the background color, and the presence or absence of underlining. Customizing the use of faces is a complex task in general, but customization of faces in the standard set is not difficult. The standard faces are as follows:

- `default`, for ordinary text
- `modeline`, for the mode line
- `highlight`, for highlighted text
- `region`, for the region, under Transient Mark mode
- `secondary-selection`, for the secondary selection
- `bold`, a boldface variant of the `default` face
- `italic`, an italic variant of the `default` face
- `bold-italic`, a bold italic variant of the `default` face
- `underline`, an underlined variant of the `default` face

You can see what the available faces look like in the current frame (they may be different for other frames) by issuing the command '[Meta] X `list-faces-display`'. See Section 9.25.4 for a discussion of how to customize faces.

Syntax Highlighting with Font Lock Mode.   Emacs modes associated with particular programming languages use the face mechanism for syntax highlighting. Emacs provides a minor mode called Font Lock mode (see p. 475) that activates such highlighting. In Font Lock mode, recognized portions of the text are displayed in one of the variant modes: `bold`, `italic`, or `bold-italic`. These portions include comments and strings in all major modes, as well as other syntactic elements such as keywords for some particular major modes. By customizing these variant modes, you can change the appearance of the highlighting.

9.4.10
The Syntax Table

Each major mode has a *syntax table* associated with it that specifies the syntactic role of each character. The syntax table entry for a character specifies the character's syntactic class together with other information about it. The syntactic class is recorded as a single character, chosen in most cases to be a representative of the class. These are the syntactic classes for text:

(space)	Whitespace (e.g., space, tab, ⟨newline⟩)
w	Word-constituent characters
_	Characters that are part of symbol names but not part of words
.	Punctuation characters that don't belong to any other class
(	Opening delimiters
)	Closing delimiters

The syntax table for a program mode usually has additional syntactic classes. The (Ctrl) H s command displays the syntax table for the current mode. See the Emacs documentation for further information about the syntax table.

9.5   How to Issue Commands

Many commands, including nearly all the commonly used ones, have key bindings. A command's key binding consists of a sequence of one or more keys and provides a shortcut for executing the command. In addition, every Emacs command has a full name, namely, the name of the LISP function that does its work. You can call a command either by typing the keys bound to it (if it has a key binding) or by typing its full name preceded by (Meta) X .[7] For example, the command for leaving Emacs can be typed either as (Ctrl) X (Ctrl) C or as

(Meta) X `save-buffers-kill-emacs`

In the rest of our discussion we assume that you're using the key bindings that come with Emacs. You can modify these bindings using the methods described in Section 9.25.1.

In our descriptions of the commands we denote a command by its key binding if it has one, since that's how you'll usually summon it. In most cases we also show the full name of the command, enclosing it in parentheses and setting it in typewriter type. In the alphabetic summary of the commands (Appendix A) we list the commands according to their default key bindings.

9.5.1
The Minibuffer

The *minibuffer* is a line at the bottom of the screen that displays commands as you type them, as well as other status information. When you type a command consisting of more than one key, each key is displayed in the minibuffer as you type it. A one-key command isn't shown in the minbuffer; since the command is executed as soon as you type it, there's nothing to show.

When you enter a command starting with (Meta) X , you may edit the command as you type it. The (Del) command, which erases the character you last typed, is particularly useful. You may also use any of the other editing commands, including those described in "Moving Short Distances" on page 487 and "Erasing Text" on page 490. When you finish typing the command, execute it by pressing (Enter) .

---

7. The (Meta) X key is itself bound to the command `execute-extended-command`.

**9.5.2
Cancelling
Commands**

The usual way to cancel a command before you've finished typing it (or if you started typing it by accident) is to type Ctrl G, the `keyboard-quit` command. If you don't know what state Emacs is in, typing two Ctrl G's halts any ongoing commands. (You need two of them to cancel an interactive search.)

If you're in the middle of a recursive edit (see Section 9.5.6), Ctrl G still cancels commands but does not get you out of the recursive edit. The Ctrl] command (`abort-recursive-edit`) gets you out of the recursive edit and also cancels the command that caused the recursive edit.

**9.5.3
Command
Completion**

To make it easier to fill in the information needed to execute a command, Emacs provides a completion feature for the minibuffer. You can type parts of the command's name and use the completion feature to fill in the rest. The following keys support command completion:

Tab   Extends the text in the minibuffer as far as possible. A character is added if it is the only possible character. For example, if the text in the minibuffer is a command and you type 'fil Tab', Emacs extends it to 'fill-' since all the commands whose names start with 'fil' have 'l-' as their next two characters.

Space   Extends the last word in the minibuffer as far as possible. This command is like the previous one, except that Emacs ends the completion at a word boundary. If you type Space repeatedly, Emacs continues to add words one at a time as long as it can.

Enter   Completes the text and acts on it:

- If the text in the minibuffer is a valid value, Emacs uses it and executes the command.
- If the text in the minibuffer has a unique completion, Emacs completes it. For command names or for names of output files, Emacs then executes the command; for names of input files that must exist, Emacs then asks for confirmation.

If you type a buffer name or the name of a visited file followed by Enter, Emacs always accepts it without attempting further completion. If the buffer or file does not exist, Emacs creates an empty buffer for it.

**9.5.4
Arguments to
Commands**

Most Emacs commands accept arguments. The argument to a command is always a number or something that denotes a number. You type an argument by meta-shifting its digits and its sign, if any. For instance,

Meta 1 Meta 3 Ctrl F

executes the command Ctrl F with an argument of 13, while

Meta – Ctrl F

executes the command Ctrl F with an argument of '-', equivalent to −1.

For most commands, an argument of n specifies that the command should be repeated n times. For example, typing

Meta 1 Meta 3 Ctrl F

executes the Ctrl F command 13 times, moving the point forward by 13 positions. Negative arguments usually specify repetition in the opposite sense, so

Meta − Meta 4 Ctrl F

moves the point backward by four positions. Since an ordinary printable character acts as a command, typing

Meta 5 y

inserts 'yyyyy' into the buffer.

Not all commands follow these conventions, however:

- For some commands, the very presence of an argument changes the command's meaning; it doesn't matter what the argument is. For example, the command Meta Q with no argument fills out the text of a paragraph; given an argument, it also justifies the text.

- Some commands use an argument as a repeat count but behave differently when called without an argument. For instance, the Ctrl K command with an argument of n kills the text up to and including the nth following ⟨newline⟩. If you type Ctrl K without an argument when the point is before the end of the line, however, it kills the rest of the line but not the ⟨newline⟩ at the end of it.

- Although Meta − is usually equivalent to Meta − Meta 1, a few commands treat it differently.

In the descriptions of the commands below, we mention arguments only when they modify the command's meaning in an unconventional way.

There's another way to specify arguments that's often more convenient. If you type Ctrl U (universal-argument) in front of a command, that command is repeated four times. You can apply Ctrl U to Ctrl U itself, giving you 16 repetitions. You can also follow Ctrl U by a sequence of digits that specifies an explicit repetition count. For example, 'Ctrl U 20 Ctrl N' repeats the Ctrl N command 20 times and moves the point down 20 lines. A few commands give a preceding Ctrl U an entirely different meaning, however. For example, Space by itself sets the mark while Ctrl U Space moves to the previous mark.

**9.5.5
Recalling Complex
Commands**

Emacs keeps a history of the complex commands (those starting with Meta X) that you've recently executed. You can save some typing by recalling these commands, editing them if necessary, and then re-executing them. The following commands recall, execute, and display previous complex commands:

Ctrl X Esc

Recalls the complex command you most recently executed

(repeat-complex-command).   The command appears in the minibuffer in its LISP form; an example is

```
Redo: (query-replace "Queeg" "Ahab" nil)
```

Meta P   Brings the previous command of the command history into the minibuffer (previous-complex-command).

Meta N   Brings the next command of the command history into the minibuffer (next-complex-command). This command is useful when you want to look at a recent command again.

Enter   Executes the complex command in the minibuffer.

Meta X list-command-history
        Displays the command history in a window. The commands are listed in their LISP form, with the most recent one at the top of the list.

You may only issue the Meta P, Meta N, and Enter commands when the minibuffer contains a recalled command.

9.5.6
Recursive Editing

Sometimes it's useful to interrupt what you're doing in the minibuffer in order to work in another buffer. The most common instance arises during a query-replace operation (see "Replacement with Querying" on p. 526) when you want to edit the area around a replacement before going on to the next replacement. Typing Ctrl R in response to a query executes the recursive-edit command (the Ctrl R key is bound to that command in the context of a query-replace). You can now do any editing you wish, using the Meta Ctrl C command described below to resume the query-replace.

The following commands terminate a recursive edit:

Meta Ctrl C
        Terminates the recursive edit and returns to the activity underway before you started it (exit-recursive-edit).

Ctrl]   Terminates this recursive edit as well as the command that invoked it (abort-recursive-edit).   This command is stronger than Ctrl G (see Section 9.5.2).

Meta X top-level
        Terminates all currently active recursive edits and returns to the activity underway before you started the outermost one.

As you might guess, recursive edits can be very confusing; generally, you should avoid them.

9.5.7
Disabling
Commands

A disabled command requires confirmation before it can be executed. By marking a command as disabled, you can prevent it from being executed by accident. The following commands enable and disable other commands:

Meta X disable-command

> This command asks you interactively for the name of the command *cmd* to be disabled. It then edits your .emacs initialization file to include a LISP command that will disable *cmd* in future Emacs sessions.
>
> **Note:** This command does not affect the current Emacs session.

Meta X enable-command

> This command asks you interactively for the name of the command *cmd* to be enabled. You can choose to have the command enabled for the current Emacs session or permanently. If you choose permanent enablement, Emacs inserts an appropriate LISP command in your .emacs file.

9.5.8 Undoing Changes

The Emacs undo facility enables you to correct your mistakes by undoing your actions.

Ctrl _

Ctrl X u

> Undoes the most recent group of actions that changed the text in the current buffer (undo). If you enter a sequence of characters without doing anything in between, the sequence is removed by a single undo. Some other sequences of simple actions are also grouped. **Note:** On some keyboards you can type Ctrl _ by pressing the '_/~' key while holding down the control and shift keys.

Each buffer has its own undo history. By repeating the undo command you can undo any number of actions up to the capacity of the undo history kept by Emacs (about 8000 characters). One way to revert a buffer to its original state is to issue an undo command with a very large argument. You'll know you've succeeded if the stars disappear from the status line.

   You can undo an undo if you first perform some simple but irrelevant action such as moving the point forward by a character. That breaks the sequence of undo's, making the previous undo's the most recent actions to be undone. The following experiment illustrates how this works:

(1)   Start with an empty buffer.
(2)   Type 'abcx'. The buffer now contains 'abcx'.
(3)   Type ' Del '. The buffer now contains 'abc'.
(4)   Type ' Ctrl B def'. The buffer now contains 'abdefc'.
(5)   Type ' Ctrl _'. The insertion of 'def' is undone and the buffer now contains 'abc'.
(6)   Type ' Ctrl _' again. The deletion of 'x' is undone and the buffer now contains 'abcx'.
(7)   Type ' Ctrl B'. The buffer is unchanged but the point moves left by one position.

(8) Type '$\boxed{\text{Ctrl}}$ _'. The previous undo is undone and the buffer again contains 'abc'.

(9) Another undo yields 'abdefc'.

After you save a file, Emacs marks the file as unmodified. Nevertheless you can undo changes that you made before you saved it (causing the file to be marked as modified again).

9.6 Getting Help

Emacs has an extensive help system, which you can activate by typing $\boxed{\text{Ctrl}}$ H or $\boxed{\text{Erase}}$.[8] A second $\boxed{\text{Ctrl}}$ H (or a '?') causes Emacs to list the help options; a third $\boxed{\text{Ctrl}}$ H causes Emacs to pop up a window explaining the options. You can also type an option immediately after $\boxed{\text{Ctrl}}$ H. For example, typing $\boxed{\text{Ctrl}}$ H k causes Emacs to bring up the describe-key help option.

Most of the help commands create a window to display the help information. You can make this window go away by typing $\boxed{\text{Ctrl}}$ X 1 from the original window or $\boxed{\text{Ctrl}}$ X 0 from the help window.

The help options that you can specify after $\boxed{\text{Ctrl}}$ H are described below.

9.6.1 Information About Commands and Key Bindings

The following help options provide information about commands and key bindings.

a *str*   Lists and explains all commands whose names contain the string *str* (command-apropos). See page 472 for a list of words that are useful to include in *str*. The $\boxed{\text{Meta}}$ X apropos command described below provides a useful extension to this command.

c   Asks you to type a key, then indicates which key you typed and what command is bound to it (describe-key-briefly). You can use this command to explore the effects of typing odd key combinations on your keyboard.[9]

k   Asks you to type a key, then indicates which key you typed and what command is bound to it; in addition, it provides an explanation of that command (describe-key).

b   Lists all key bindings currently in effect (describe-bindings). Since the bindings are mode-dependent, you may get different results when you execute this command in different windows.

---

8. The use of $\boxed{\text{Erase}}$ as a help key may seem strange. The reason for it is that $\boxed{\text{Ctrl}}$ H is a natural choice for the help key, and on most keyboards $\boxed{\text{Erase}}$ and $\boxed{\text{Ctrl}}$ H generate the same code.

9. For example, we discovered that typing $\boxed{\text{Ctrl}}$ 7 on our keyboard produced the same effect as $\boxed{\text{Ctrl}}$ _, providing a particularly convenient way to call the undo command.

w   Asks you to type a command, then indicates which keys (if any) are bound to it (`where-is`).

m   Describes the current mode, indicating those keys that are redefined in this mode (`describe-mode`).

9.6.2
Information About
LISP Symbols

The following help options provide information about LISP symbols that support Emacs.

f   Asks you to type the name of a LISP function, then describes it (`describe-function`). Since all commands are LISP functions, this help option is one way to get information about a particular command. The 'a' option is usually more convenient than the 'f' option but provides fewer details. The 'f' option can query LISP functions that are not Emacs commands.

v   Asks you to type a LISP variable, then describes it (`describe-variable`). See Section 9.4.8 for more information about variables.

s   Displays the syntax table (see Section 9.4.10) that indicates the role of each character in the current mode (`describe-syntax`).

9.6.3
Information About
Recently Executed
Commands

The following help option shows recently executed commands:

l   Displays the last 100 command characters you typed (`view-lossage`). This command is useful when something has gone wrong and you don't know what you've done.

9.6.4
Tutorial and
On-Line Manual

The following help options provide access to more extended information about Emacs:

t   Starts the Emacs tutorial (`help-with-tutorial`).

i   Runs the `info` program, which provides hypertext-like access to the complete Emacs manual on line (`info`). Typing 'h' when you start `info` leads you to a tutorial on `info`.

Ctrl F   Asks you to type the name of a LISP function, then takes you to the Info node that describes the function (`info-goto-emacs-command-node`).

Ctrl K   Asks you to type a key, then takes you to the Info node for the command bound to that key (`info-goto-emacs-key-command-node`).

9.6.5
Information About
Emacs Itself

The following commands display information about Emacs itself and policies relating to it:

n
Ctrl N   Displays documentation on changes to Emacs in chronological order (`view-emacs-news`).

[Ctrl] C   Displays the conditions pertaining to distributing copies of Emacs (`describe-copying`).

[Ctrl] D   Displays information on how to obtain the latest copy of Emacs (`describe-distribution`).

[Ctrl] W   Displays information about the lack of warranty for Emacs (`describe-no-warranty`).

9.6.6
Other Help
Commands

The following commands provide help information but are *not* preceded by [Ctrl] H :

[Meta] X `apropos`
     Like `command-apropos`, except that it lists *all* LISP symbols that match the regular expression.

[Meta] X `manual-entry`
     Displays the on-line manual page that describes a specified UNIX command.

9.6.7
Command
Continuations

For multikey sequences, you can use the [Ctrl] H key to see what the possible continuations of a key are. For example, if you press the key sequence '[Ctrl] X 5 [Ctrl] H', Emacs will open another window and show you all the key sequences that start with '[Ctrl] X 5' together with the command each sequence is bound to both locally and globally.

9.7   Exiting from or Suspending Emacs

The following command gets you out of Emacs altogether:

[Ctrl] X [Ctrl] C
     Offers to save any modified buffers that are associated with files (so you don't lose your changes), then terminates Emacs (`save-buffers-kill-emacs`). An argument to this command causes immediate termination.

A less drastic alternative is to suspend Emacs, giving you the opportunity to resume it where you left off. The following command suspends Emacs:

[Ctrl] Z   Suspends Emacs, returning to the shell (`suspend-emacs`). This command is disabled under X because it makes no sense there; under X, [Ctrl] Z turns the selected frame into an icon instead. If your shell supports job control (see Section 2.6.3), you can resume Emacs again by typing 'fg %emacs'. For shells that don't support job control, this command creates a subshell that communicates directly with your terminal. The only way to get back to Emacs from this subshell is to terminate the subshell.

9.8   Basic Editing Commands

In the following subsections we describe the editing commands that you're likely to use most often. In Section 9.9 we describe how to edit using a mouse, and in Section 9.10 we describe some additional editing commands.

9.8.1
Moving the Point

The commands described below move the point.

Moving Short Distances.   The following commands move the point by short distances.

Right	
Ctrl F	Moves forward (right) one character (`forward-char`).
Left	
Ctrl B	Moves backward (left) one character (`backward-char`).
Down	
Ctrl N	Moves to the next line (`next-line`). This command and the next one attempt to keep the horizontal position unchanged. Their behavior is also affected by the Ctrl X Ctrl N command described below.
Up	
Ctrl P	Moves to the previous line (`previous-line`).
Ctrl E	Moves to the end of the line (`end-of-line`).
Ctrl A	Moves to the beginning of the line (`beginning-of-line`).
Meta M	Moves to the first nonblank character on the line (`back-to-indentation`).
Meta F	Moves forward (right) one word (`forward-word`).
Meta B	Moves backward (left) one word (`backward-word`).
Meta R	Moves to the beginning of the line at the center of the window (`move-to-window-line`). With a positive argument n, this command moves to the nth line from the top; with a negative argument $-n$, it moves to the nth line from the bottom.

You can arrange to have the Ctrl N and Ctrl P commands always move to the same column whenever possible. The following command enables and disables this behavior:

Ctrl X Ctrl N

Sets the current column as the goal column, so that Ctrl N and Ctrl P attempt to move the point as close as possible to this column (`set-goal-column`). Issuing this command with an argument cancels the use of the goal column.

Moving by Larger Units.   The following commands move the point by larger units. Emacs assumes that a sentence ends, as in English, with a '.',

'?', or '!' followed by an end of line or two spaces, with closing parentheses and quotes accounted for properly. A paragraph boundary also ends a sentence. Paragraphs are usually demarcated by blank lines and, for text, by indented lines and formatter commands (but see "Paragraphs" below). Pages are demarcated by ⟨formfeed⟩ characters, which you can produce by typing Ctrl Q Ctrl L.

Meta E   Moves forward to the character following the end of the current sentence (`forward-sentence`).

Meta A   Moves backward to the first character of the current sentence (`backward-sentence`).

Meta }   Moves forward to the character following the end of the current paragraph (`forward-paragraph`).

Meta {   Moves backward to the first character of the current paragraph (`backward-paragraph`).

Ctrl X]   Moves forward to the character following the next page marker (`forward-page`).

Ctrl X [Moves backward to the character *following* the previous page marker (`backward-page`). If the point is currently just after a page marker, this command moves back over that page marker and looks for the one before that. Thus two Ctrl X [commands in a row move the point back two pages.

Paragraphs. In Text mode, the definition of a paragraph is controlled by two variables: `paragraph-separate` and `paragraph-start`, both given by regular expressions (see "Regular Expressions in Emacs" on p. 524):

- `Paragraph-separate` matches any line that cannot occur within a paragraph and therefore always separates paragraphs.
- `Paragraph-start` matches any line that either starts a paragraph or separates paragraphs.

By default, `paragraph-separate` matches any line containing only spaces, ⟨tab⟩s and ⟨formfeed⟩s; `paragraph-start` matches any line that starts with a space, ⟨tab⟩, ⟨formfeed⟩, or ⟨newline⟩. (A line that starts with a ⟨newline⟩ is empty.) Some text modes have values for `paragraph-separate` and `paragraph-start` that match additional patterns; for example, in Nroff mode, these variables match certain `nroff` commands.

Moving to One End of the Buffer. The following commands move the point to the beginning or the end of the entire buffer. With an argument, they move part way.

Home
Meta <   Moves to the beginning of the entire buffer (`beginning-of-buffer`). With an argument of n, moves to a point $n/10$ of the way toward the end of the buffer.

End Meta >	Moves to the end of the entire buffer (`end-of-buffer`). With an argument of n, moves to a point $n/10$ of the way toward the beginning of the buffer.

Moving to a Character or Line.   The following commands move the point to a specified character position or line:

Meta X `goto-char`	Moves the point to the left of the nth character in the buffer. Emacs prompts you for the number n.
Meta X `goto-line`	Moves the point to the left end of the nth line in the buffer. The first line is numbered 1. Emacs prompts you for n.

**9.8.2
Positioning and
Scrolling the
Window**

The following command repositions the selected window around the point:

Ctrl L	Repaints the screen and repositions the current window so that the point is at its middle line (`recenter`). With an argument of n, this command positions the point at line n from the top (or line $-n$ from the bottom if n is negative).

The following commands scroll the text in the window either horizontally or vertically. The horizontal scrolling commands are useful when some of the lines are longer than the width of the window, as often happens when you split a window into two side-by-side windows.

PgDn Ctrl V	Scrolls the text up (i.e., forward) by one page (`scroll-up`).[10] With an argument n, scrolls up by n lines.
PgUp Meta V	Scrolls the text down (i.e., backward) by one page (`scroll-down`). With an argument n, scrolls down by n lines.
Ctrl X <	Scrolls the text left by a little less than the width of the screen (`scroll-left`). With an argument, scrolls left by n columns.
Ctrl X >	Scrolls the text right by a little less than the width of the screen (`scroll-right`). With an argument, scrolls right by n columns.

**9.8.3
Erasing, Moving,
and Copying Text**

You can erase text either by deleting it or by killing it. Deleted text is not explicitly saved, although you can get it back by undoing the deletion. Killed text is saved in a kill ring from which you can retrieve it later by yanking it (see "Retrieving Killed Text" on p. 491). You can also retrieve

---

10. The PgDn key on a PC keyboard corresponds to the Next key on some workstation keyboards. That PgDn should scroll up seems perverse when you read about it but very natural when you're typing.

killed text by undoing the kill, although the capacity of Emacs's undo buffer is smaller than that of its kill buffer; as a result, some kills cannot be undone but can still be yanked (reinserted).

Deletion applies to small units of text such as a single character or a blank line that aren't worth saving; killing applies to larger units of text. The name of a command implies whether it kills or deletes.

The usual way to move text ("cut and paste") is to kill the text, move the point to the place where the text should go, and yank the text. The usual way to copy text is to kill it, reinsert it immediately by yanking it, move the point to the place where the text should go, and yank it again. Since yanking leaves the kill ring unchanged, you can use this method to copy text to several places. You can also copy text by using the (Meta) (Ctrl) W command to move the text to the kill ring without erasing it.

In "Moving Text Between Buffers" on page 492, we describe commands for moving text between buffers.

Erasing Text. The following commands erase small amounts of text by deleting it:

(Ctrl) D   Deletes the character to the right of the point (i.e., the character under the cursor) (`delete-char`).

(Del)   Deletes the character to the left of the point (i.e., the character to the left of the cursor) (`delete-backward-char`).

The following commands erase larger amounts of text by killing it:

(Ctrl) W   Kills the text in the region (`kill-region`). This is the most general kill command because you can get it to kill any sequence of text by putting the point at one end of the text and the mark at the other end.

(Ctrl) K   Kills the text up to the end of the line, but doesn't kill the ⟨newline⟩ unless the point is already at the end of the line (`kill-line`). Two (Ctrl) K's in a row kill the rest of the current line and join the beginning of the current line with the beginning of the next line. With an argument of n, (Ctrl) K kills the text up to and including the nth following ⟨newline⟩. The usual way to kill a line entirely is to type (Ctrl) A (Ctrl) K (Ctrl) K .

(Meta) D   Kills the word to the right of the point (`kill-word`). The erased text includes any spaces between the point and the word.

(Meta) (Del)   Kills the word to the left of the point (`backward-kill-word`). The erasure includes any spaces between the point and the word—note that these are the spaces *after* the word.

(Meta) K   Kills the sentence to the right of the point (`kill-sentence`). The erasure includes any spaces between the point and the first word of the sentence.

(Ctrl) X (Del)   Kills the text between the point and the end of the previous sentence (`backward-kill-sentence`). Spaces following the end of the previous sentence aren't erased.

Meta Z   Kills all characters up to and including the character *c* (`zap-to-char`). The command prompts you for *c*.

The following commands do other kinds of erasures (as deletions):

Meta \   Deletes any spaces and tabs surrounding the point (`delete-horizontal-space`).

Meta Space

Replaces all the spaces and tabs around the point by a single space (`just-one-space`). If there are no spaces adjacent to the point, this command inserts a single space.

Meta ^   Joins the current line with the preceding one by deleting the ⟨newline⟩ at the end of the preceding line along with any spaces or tabs after it (`delete-indentation`). This command works even if you type it in the middle of a line. If you have a fill prefix (see p. 497) and it appears after the deleted ⟨newline⟩, the fill prefix is deleted too. The deleted text is replaced by a space unless that space would come after a '(' or before a ')'.

Ctrl X Ctrl O

Deletes blank lines (`delete-blank-lines`) as follows:

- If the point is on an isolated blank line, deletes that line.

- If the point is on a nonblank line followed by one or more blank lines, deletes those blank lines.

- If the point is currently on one of several adjacent blank lines, deletes all but one of those blank lines.

Retrieving Killed Text. Retrieving killed text is called "yanking" it.[11] Whenever you kill some text, Emacs saves that text in the *kill ring*, from which you can later retrieve it.

You can cycle through the kill ring, examining each fragment of previously killed text, by typing ' Ctrl Y ' and then typing ' Meta Y ' repeatedly. The cycle always starts with the most recently killed text and proceeds to the oldest text in the ring, then returns to the newest text again. Typing ' Ctrl W ' erases the yanked text. Note that retrieving text from the kill ring does not change the information in the kill ring, so you can make several copies of text by yanking it repeatedly.

Ctrl Y   Copies the most recently killed text into the buffer starting at the point, leaving the cursor at the end of the copied text (`yank`). If you type Ctrl U Ctrl Y , the cursor is left at the beginning of

---

11. Note that Emacs and `vi` use the word "yank" in opposite senses—in `vi`, yanking text copies it *from* the working buffer, while in Emacs, yanking text copies it *to* the working buffer. Neither usage reflects the meaning of the word in English—to yank something ordinarily implies that the thing yanked is no longer where it was.

the text instead. An argument *n* of any other form retrieves the *n*th most recently killed text. (If *n* is negative, Emacs moves through the kill ring in oldest-to-newest order.)

[Meta] Y   Replaces the most recently yanked text by the previous text in the kill ring (yank-pop). Executing this command repeatedly enables you to retrieve text that is several kills old, since it circulates through the kill ring. An argument has the same effect as it does with [Ctrl] Y, except that [Ctrl] U by itself has no special meaning. This command is only meaningful after a [Ctrl] Y or another [Meta] Y.

A few other commands besides the ones listed here also do yanking. Note that the commands for killing and yanking rectangles (see Section 9.12) do not use the kill ring.

Copying Text.   One way to copy text is to kill it, reinsert it in its previous place with [Ctrl] Y, move to the destination, and insert another copy with a second [Ctrl] Y. You can avoid the reinsertion by using the [Meta] W command.

[Meta] W   Copies the text from the region to the kill ring without erasing it (copy-region-as-kill). The effect is like that of [Ctrl] W except that the buffer is not modified and the point does not move.

[Meta] [Ctrl] W

If the next command is a kill command (not necessarily [Ctrl] W), forces it to append the killed text to the last killed text instead of making that text a separate entry in the kill ring (append-next-kill). This command enables you to collect and accumulate text from several locations. It has no effect if the following command is not a kill command.

You can also copy text by copying it into a register and then yanking the contents of the register (see Section 9.19.3).

Moving Text Between Buffers.   The following commands move text directly from one buffer to another. One of the buffers is the current buffer; the command prompts you for the name of the other buffer (see p. 514).

[Meta] X copy-to-buffer

Copies the text in the region to the specified buffer, erasing the previous contents of the destination buffer.

[Meta] X append-to-buffer

Copies the text in the region to just after the position of the point in the specified buffer, leaving the point at the end of the appended text. Successive uses of this command cause the successive text fragments to appear in the *same* order that they were copied.

Meta X `prepend-to-buffer`

> Copies the text in the region to just before the position of the point in the specified buffer, leaving the point at the beginning of the appended text. Successive uses of this command cause the successive text fragments to appear in the *reverse* order that they were copied.

Meta X `insert-buffer`

> Inserts the contents of a selected buffer into the current buffer at the point.

9.8.4 Setting the Mark

The commands below provide for setting the mark.

Setting the Mark Explicitly.   The following commands explicitly set the mark to the point:

Ctrl - Space
Ctrl @   Sets the mark to the place where the point is (`set-mark-command`). The actual key binding is to Ctrl @ ; Ctrl - Space is merely a convenient way of producing this key on most keyboards. If you execute this command with an argument of Ctrl U , it doesn't set the mark; instead, it moves the mark to the previous mark.

Ctrl X Ctrl X

> Exchanges the point and the mark (`exchange-point-and-mark`). Executing this command twice is a convenient way of seeing where the mark is.

The Mark Ring.   Each time you set the mark, Emacs saves its location in a *mark ring*. There is one mark ring for each buffer; by default it contains 16 marks. Repeatedly executing Ctrl U Ctrl Space circulates the point around the mark ring, from the newest mark to the oldest and back again to the newest.

In addition, there's a global mark ring that stores a (*buffer*, *position*) pair. Setting the mark also sets the global mark, provided the current buffer is not the same one where the mark was last set. The command Ctrl X Ctrl Space (`pop-global-mark`) circulates the point around the global mark ring, switching to the appropriate buffer each time it is executed.

Marking Text.   The following commands set the mark at the end of a unit of text, thereby making that unit the region. The Meta @ command sets only the mark; the other commands set both the point and the mark.

Meta @   Puts the mark at the end of the next word (`mark-word`).

Meta H   Puts the point at the beginning of the paragraph that surrounds or follows the point and puts the mark at the end of it (`mark-paragraph`).

[Ctrl] X [Ctrl] P
> Puts the point at the beginning of the page that surrounds or follows the point and puts the mark at the end of it (`mark-page`).

[Ctrl] X h   Puts the point at the beginning of the buffer and puts the mark at the end of it (`mark-whole-buffer`).

See also the `mark-sexp` command (p. 500).

9.9   Mouse Operations on Text

9.9.1 Operations on the Mark and the Region

Under X you can use the mouse to set the mark, define a primary or secondary region, kill text, or insert killed text.

There are two operations you can perform with the mouse whether or not Transient Mark mode is enabled:

[Mouse-1]   Moves the point to where you click.

[Mouse-2]   Copies ("yanks") the most recently killed text to the location where you click.

These operations don't depend on where the region is.

The next group of operations define the region. They all require that Transient Mark mode be enabled. The [Double-Mouse-1] action consists of two rapid clicks of Button 1 in the same place; the [Double-Drag-Mouse-1] action consists of a click of Button 1 followed rapidly by pressing Button 1, dragging the mouse to another location, and releasing Button 1.

[Double-Mouse-1]
> Sets the region to the word containing the place where you click.

[Triple-Mouse-1]
> Sets the region to the line containing the place where you click.

[Drag-Mouse-1]
> Sets the region to the text that you drag over.

[Double-Drag-Mouse-1]
> Like [Drag-Mouse-1], but operates on entire words.

[Triple-Drag-Mouse-1]
> Like [Drag-Mouse-1], but operates on entire lines.

[Mouse-3]   If a region is already selected, modifies the region by moving its nearer end to the location where you click. Otherwise, it sets the mark where you click. If you press [Mouse-3] twice in a row in the same place, the region you selected is killed.

The simplest way to kill text using the mouse is to click [Mouse-1] at one end, then click [Mouse-3] twice (not necessarily rapidly) at the other end.

If you click ⟨Mouse-3⟩ only once, the text will be copied into the kill ring but not removed. You can also copy text into the kill ring by doing a ⟨Drag-Mouse-1⟩ over the region you wish to copy. Once you've copied the text, you can put it somewhere else by clicking ⟨Mouse-2⟩ on the place you wish to put it, possibly in a different buffer.

Moving Text to or from Other Programs. You can copy text to or from an X window that is not controlled by Emacs (including one controlled by a different invocation of Emacs). To copy text from another program, use that program's 'cut' or 'copy' command on the text you want, then click ⟨Mouse-2⟩ on the place you want that text in an Emacs buffer. To copy to another program, mark the region of an Emacs buffer you wish to copy with the mouse, then go to the other program and use its 'paste' command.

9.9.2
Operations on the Secondary Selection

You can also define a secondary selection using the mouse and use that selection to kill text, in order to either copy it or delete it. The secondary selection, which is accessible only under X, is entirely independent of the point, the mark, and the region. It is highlighted using the `highlight` face (see Section 9.4.9) rather than the `region` face and is available regardless of the setting of Transient Mark mode.

The mouse commands for operating on the secondary selection are very similar to those affecting the primary selection (i.e., the region):

⟨Meta⟩ ⟨Mouse-1⟩
> Sets one endpoint of the secondary selection to the place where you click.

⟨Meta⟩ ⟨Mouse-2⟩
> Inserts the secondary selection at the place where you click. The secondary selection must be active; if you deactivate or kill it, Emacs does not remember it. Therefore you cannot use the secondary selection to *move* text unless you go back and delete the selection after copying it.

⟨Meta⟩ ⟨Double-Mouse-1⟩
> Sets the secondary selection to the word containing the place where you click.

⟨Meta⟩ ⟨Triple-Mouse-1⟩
> Sets the secondary selection to the line containing the place where you click.

⟨Meta⟩ ⟨Drag-Mouse-1⟩
> Sets the secondary selection to the text that you drag over.

⟨Meta⟩ ⟨Double-Drag-Mouse-1⟩
> Like ⟨Meta⟩ ⟨Drag-Mouse-1⟩, but operates on entire words.

⟨Meta⟩ ⟨Triple-Drag-Mouse-1⟩
> Like ⟨Meta⟩ ⟨Drag-Mouse-1⟩, but operates on entire lines.

(Meta) (Mouse-3)

> Sets or modifies the secondary selection by moving its nearer end to the location where you click. If no secondary selection is visible, the command takes one endpoint of the secondary selection as the place where (Meta) (Mouse-1) was last clicked and sets the other endpoint to the place where you have just clicked (Meta) (Mouse-3). If you press (Meta) (Mouse-3) twice in a row in the same place, the secondary selection is killed.

9.10   Additional Editing Commands

The commands described below provide additional editing facilities that are convenient but less essential than the ones described previously.

9.10.1
Filling Regions

Filling text consists of breaking it up into lines that are as long as possible but still don't exceed a specified length, given by the *fill column*. The fill column is used by Auto Fill mode (see Section 9.10.2). The following commands enable you to specify the fill column, to fill portions of the buffer, and to center one or more lines. See "Paragraphs" on page 488 for the definition of a paragraph.

(Ctrl) X f   Sets the fill column to the column to the right of the point (set-fill-column). With an argument n, this command sets the fill column to n.

(Meta) Q   Fills the paragraph containing the point (fill-paragraph).

(Meta) X fill-region-as-paragraph
> Fills the region, treating it as a single paragraph.

(Meta) X fill-individual-paragraphs
> Fills the paragraphs in the region, treating blank lines as paragraph separators and giving each line of a paragraph the same indentation as its first line.

(Meta) X fill-region
> Fills all the lines of the region, honoring paragraph boundaries.

(Meta) X center-line
> Centers the current line within the line length as given by the fill column. With an argument of n, this command centers n lines.

Suppose that you have a paragraph in which each line starts with the same text, such as a few spaces (for an indented paragraph) or the text '# ' (for a comment that starts a shell script). You can fill the paragraph while excluding that common text from filling by making that common text a *fill prefix* using the following command:

Ctrl X .   Sets the fill prefix to the portion of the current line preceding the point (set-fill-prefix). You can make the fill prefix empty by moving to the beginning of a line and issuing this command again.

The fill commands remove the fill prefix from each line before filling and put it back after filling. A line that does not start with the fill prefix is considered to start a paragraph, as does a line that is blank or indented once the prefix is removed.

9.10.2 Auto Fill Mode

Auto Fill mode is a minor mode in which lines are broken at spaces when they exceed a certain width. The Meta X auto-fill-mode command toggles the mode on or off. The width is given by the fill column, which you can set with the Ctrl X f (set-fill-column) command (see p. 496). Line breaking is triggered when you type Space, Enter, or LnFd. When you type one of these keys, Emacs checks to see if the line is too long; if it is, Emacs breaks it into two or more lines that don't exceed the allowable width, choosing breaks that are as far to the right as possible. You can deliberately create a long line by quoting the triggering character with Ctrl Q. For some major modes, Emacs indents the line after an inserted ⟨newline⟩ if the previous line was indented, or adjusts the indentation in some other way to suit the mode.

Note that turning on Auto Fill mode does not guarantee that all lines will lie within the specified width. If you make a line too long by inserting material in the middle, Emacs doesn't do anything about it. If a paragraph contains lines that are too long, usually the easiest way to fix it is to use one of the fill commands described previously.

9.10.3 Transposing Textual Units

The following commands transpose textual units:

Ctrl T   Transposes the character under the cursor with the character preceding it; that is, interchanges the two characters surrounding the point (transpose-chars). The point moves one character to the right, so you can use this command to move a character across several others.

Meta T   Transposes the word following the point with the word preceding it (transpose-words). If the point is between words, the two words around the point are affected; if the point is within a word, that one and the next one are affected. The point moves to the beginning of the next unaffected word. With an argument of zero, this command interchanges the word around or after the point with the word around or after the mark.

Ctrl X Ctrl T
          Transposes the line containing the point with the line above it (transpose-lines). The point moves to the beginning of the

next unaffected line. With an argument of zero, this command interchanges the line around or after the point with the line around or after the mark.

9.10.4 Changing the Case of Text

The following commands change a sequence of words to all uppercase or to all lowercase, or capitalize a sequence of words:

[Meta] U   Converts the word to the right of the point to uppercase and advances the point to the next word (`upcase-word`).

[Meta] L   Converts the word to the right of the point to lowercase and advances the point to the next word (`downcase-word`).

[Meta] C   Capitalizes the letter to the right of the point (i.e., the letter under the cursor) and advances the point to the next word (`capitalize-word`).

Since these commands advance the point to the next word, you can easily use them to modify a sequence of words. If you provide a negative argument to one of these commands by preceding it with '[Meta] –', the command applies to the preceding word and the point does not move.

The following commands are similar to the previous ones except that they apply to the region and do not move the point:

[Ctrl] X [Ctrl] U

    Converts all the letters in the region to uppercase (`upcase-region`).

[Ctrl] X [Ctrl] L

    Converts all the letters in the region to lowercase (`downcase-region`).

[Meta] X `capitalize-region`

    Capitalizes the first letter of each word in the region. If the region begins in the middle of a word, the first letter of the region rather than the first letter of the word is capitalized.

9.10.5 Commands for Inserting Newlines

The following commands insert ⟨newline⟩s and may have other effects as well:

[Enter]   Inserts a ⟨newline⟩ (`newline`). If Auto Fill mode is on (see Section 9.10.2), inserting a ⟨newline⟩ causes the preceding line to be broken if it is too long.

[LnFd]   Inserts a ⟨newline⟩ and indents the next line according to the indentation conventions that are currently in effect (`newline-and-indent`).

[Ctrl] O   Opens up a new line (`open-line`). This command acts like [Enter] except that it leaves the point before the newly inserted ⟨newline⟩ rather than after it.

[Meta] [Ctrl] O

    Starts a new line at the point, indenting the new line to the position of the point (`split-line`). For example, if the point is at the indicated position in the line

```
Exit,. pursued by a bear.
```

and you execute this command, the result is

```
Exit, .
       pursued by a bear.
```

9.10.6 Operations on Lists

The following commands move the point around parenthesis-balanced lists. The units of motion are called *sexps*. A sexp is either a word (or similar syntactic unit) or a parenthesis-balanced portion of text that begins with a left parenthesis and ends with a right parenthesis.[12] These commands are useful for nearly all programming languages and sometimes even for ordinary text. For most languages they treat '[' and '{' as equivalent to '(' and ']' and '}' as equivalent to ')'.

Meta Ctrl F
> Moves the point forward (to the right) to just after the next sexp (`forward-sexp`).

Meta Ctrl B
> Moves the point backward (to the left) to just before the previous sexp (`backward-sexp`).

Meta Ctrl N
> Moves the point forward (to the right) until it's just after the next *parenthesized* sexp (`forward-list`).

Meta Ctrl P
> Moves the point backward (to the left) until it's just before the parenthesis that starts the previous *parenthesized* sexp (`backward-list`).

Meta Ctrl D
> Moves the point forward (to the right) to just before the next parenthesis that starts a sexp (`down-list`).

Meta Ctrl U
> Moves the point backward (to the left) until it's just before the parenthesis that starts the sexp containing the point (`backward-up-list`). A negative argument moves the point to the right in an analogous way.

The following example shows how these commands work. Suppose that the point is just before the 'o' of 'four' in the following text:

```
(one (two) three f.our five (six) seven)
```

---

12. The term "sexp" is derived from the LISP term "S-expression", which stands for "symbolic expression". More formally, a sexp can be defined as follows:

   (1)   A single word is a sexp.
   (2)   A sequence of sexps enclosed in parentheses is a sexp.

Whitespace and punctuation are permitted between components of a sexp and are required between adjacent words.

Then the following table shows the effect of the various commands, with the final position of the point underlined:

Meta	Ctrl	F	(one (two) three four. five (six) seven)
Meta	Ctrl	B	(one (two) three .four five (six) seven)
Meta	Ctrl	N	(one (two) three four five (six). seven)
Meta	Ctrl	P	(one (two) three four five .(six) seven)
Meta	Ctrl	D	(one (two) three four five (.six) seven)
Meta	Ctrl	U	(one (two) three four five .(six) seven)

The following commands kill, mark, and transpose sexps:

Meta Ctrl K

> Kills the sexp following the point (kill-sexp).

Meta Ctrl T

> Transposes the sexp preceding the point and the sexp following the point by dragging the previous one across the next one (transpose-sexps).

Meta Ctrl @

> Places the mark just after the next sexp, which is the place where forward-sexp would move to (mark-sexp). The point is unchanged.

9.10.7
Sorting

The following commands enable you to sort a portion of the buffer in different ways. All of them apply to the region.

Meta X sort-lines

> Rearranges the lines of the region into sorted order. If the command has a prefix, the sort is in reverse order.

Meta X sort-paragraphs

> Rearranges the paragraphs of the region into sorted order, comparing the entire text of each paragraph except for leading blank lines. See "Paragraphs" on page 488 for the definition of a paragraph. If the command has a prefix, the sort is in reverse order.

Meta X sort-pages

> Rearranges the pages of the region into sorted order, comparing the entire text of each page. Pages are considered to be separated by ⟨formfeed⟩s. If the command has a prefix, the sort is in reverse order.

Meta X sort-fields

> Rearranges the lines of the region, sorting them according to the contents of the nth field of each line where n is the argument to the command. If no argument is given, n defaults to 1. A negative argument indicates a decreasing sort of the specified field.

Consecutive fields consist of runs of non-whitespace characters, with whitespace separating the fields. The fields are sorted using the ASCII values of the characters; for example, the field '23' comes before the field '7'. The order of records having the same sort key is preserved, so you can sort on several fields by sorting on the individual fields in *decreasing* (right-to-left) order.

[Meta] X `sort-numeric-fields`
Like `sort-fields`, except that the fields are converted to unsigned integers if possible before sorting and these integers are used to determine the ordering. Fields not containing unsigned integers compare equal.

[Meta] X `sort-columns`
Sorts the lines that include the region according to the contents of certain columns of each line. The columns that affect the sort are those between the column containing the point and the column containing the mark. The comparison is done by comparing the strings in those columns of each line. As usual, an argument to the command causes the sort to be in decreasing order.

Another way to sort a region, not using these commands at all, is to apply the UNIX `sort` command (see Section 4.1) to the region with the [Meta] | (`shell-command-on-region`) command (see p. 530).

9.10.8 Checking and Correcting Spelling

You can check and optionally correct the spelling of words in a document of English text. Emacs uses the UNIX `spell` program to do the checking. When it finds a misspelled word, it asks you to correct the spelling by editing the word in the minibuffer. It then does a `query-replace` over the entire buffer, giving you the opportunity to make the correction wherever the misspelled word appears. You can accept a correction by typing 'y' or reject it by typing 'n'.

The following commands check and correct spelling over portions of a buffer:

[Meta] $
Checks and corrects the spelling of the word containing the point (`spell-word`).

[Meta] X `spell-region`
Checks and corrects the spelling of every word in the region.

[Meta] X `spell-buffer`
Checks and corrects the spelling of every word in the buffer.

[Meta] X `spell-string`
Prompts for a word, then checks its spelling.

[Meta] [Tab]
Completes the word at point, using the spelling dictionary (`ispell-complete-word`).

**9.10.9
Working with
Outlines**

Emacs has a special mode called Outline mode for working with outlines. You activate Outline mode with the command Meta X outline-mode. Facilities in Outline mode include the following:

- Marking heading lines to distinguish them from body lines.

- Moving among heading lines at the same level or to heading lines at adjacent levels.

- Hiding or revealing body lines and heading lines at lower levels.

See the Emacs manual for instructions on how to use Outline mode.

9.11 Indentation

Different major modes have different indentation conventions. For instance, when in Lisp mode, Emacs indents code lines according to their parenthesis depth; when in C mode, it indents according to the nesting of language constructs such as '{ ... }', conditional statements, and for loops.

Emacs has two text modes: ordinary Text mode and Indented Text mode. You switch back and forth with the Meta X text-mode and Meta X indented-text-mode commands. Indented Text mode is intended for editing text in which most lines are indented. In Indented Text mode, Tab is defined to perform relative indentation (see below).

Inserting Single Indentations. The following commands insert single indentations:

Tab Inserts indentation according to the mode:

- In Text mode, inserts enough spaces and tabs to advance the point to the next tab stop.[13]

- In Indented Text mode, performs a relative indentation (see indent-relative below).

- In major modes for programming languages, indents the entire line according to the conventions of the particular language.

If you really want to insert a tab character, type 'Ctrl Q Tab'.

---

13. In general, Emacs uses tabs in preference to sequences of more than three spaces. You can force Emacs to use just spaces by setting the variable indent-tabs-mode to nil.

Meta I   Inserts enough spaces and tabs to advance the point to the next
             tab stop, no matter what the mode (`tab-to-tab-stop`). In Text
             mode, Tab and Meta I are equivalent.

Meta X `indent-relative`
             Performs a relative indentation, in which the point is advanced
             until it is under an *indentation point*, namely, the end of a
             sequence of whitespace or the end of the line, in the following
             manner:

- If the point is to the left of or under the last indentation
  point of the previous line, Emacs advances it to be under
  the next indentation point.
- If the point is to the right of the last indentation point
  of the previous line, Emacs tries deleting any whitespace
  before the point and then uses the next indentation point
  of the previous line.
- If that doesn't work, Emacs simply advances the point to
  the next tab stop.

Relative indentation is particularly useful for tabular material,
since a relative tab at the end of an item usually causes that
item to line up with the item in the same column of the table
in the previous row.

Following an empty line, absolute and relative indentation are equivalent.   In Indented Text mode, Tab and
Meta X `indent-relative` are equivalent.

Indenting Lines of a Region.   The following commands indent all the lines
in the region. A line is considered to be in the region if it begins in the
region.

Meta Ctrl \
             Indents each line as it would be indented by Tab typed at the
             beginning of the line (`indent-region`). With an argument n,
             this command causes the first nonblank character of each line
             to be positioned at column n.

Ctrl X Tab
             Indents each line in the region by one column (`indent-`
             `rigidly`). With an argument n, this command indents each
             line by n columns. This command, unlike the previous one,
             preserves relative indentation.

Tab Stops.   The tab stops are stored in the variable `tab-stop-list`. For
text, the default tab stops are in columns 1, 9, 17, ... Changes to
the tab stops affect all buffers unless you've made a local copy of the
`tab-stop-list` variable. The following command sets the tab stops.

Meta X `edit-tab-stops`
             Creates and selects a buffer containing a description of the tab

stop settings. Assuming tab stops every three spaces, the buffer looks like this:

```
:  :  :  :  :  :  :  :  :  :  :  :  :
0          1          2          3          4  ...
01234567890123456789012345678901234567890 1
To install changes, type C-c C-c
```

You can then set the colons to the positions you want. While editing this buffer, the key sequence '⌃Ctrl C ⌃Ctrl C' is bound to the command `edit-tab-stops-note-changes`, which kills the buffer and saves your changes.

The positions of the tab stops are independent of the way that Emacs actually displays a tab character embedded in the text. For display purposes, Emacs assumes that tab stops are in columns $1, n + 1, 2n + 1, \ldots$, where n is the value of the variable `tab-width`. The default value of `tab-width` is 8. When Emacs is deciding how to translate a [Tab] that you type into a combination of spaces and recorded ⟨tab⟩ characters, it takes the value of `tab-width` into account. If you change `tab-width`, the appearance of the buffer is likely to change if the buffer contains any actual tab characters.

Converting Between Tabs and Spaces.   The following commands convert tabs to spaces and vice versa:

[Meta] X untabify
> Converts each tab within the region to a sequence of spaces, preserving the appearance of the text.

[Meta] X tabify
> Converts each sequence of three or more spaces within the region to a tab, preserving the appearance of the text.

9.12   Operations on Rectangles

The Emacs rectangle commands operate on a rectangular region of a buffer. They are particularly useful for working with multicolumn or tabular information.

You define a rectangle by placing the point at one corner of it and the mark at the other corner. For instance, if the point is to the left of line 3, column 7, and the mark is to the left of line 26, column 17, the rectangle consists of columns 7–16 of lines 3–26. If any lines within the rectangle don't already extend to the right edge of the rectangle, they are extended as necessary with spaces.

The following commands operate on rectangles:

[Ctrl] X r d Deletes the text in the rectangle (`delete-rectangle`), moving the text that was to the right of the rectangle leftward so that it occupies the vacated space.

Ctrl X r k   Kills the text in a rectangle (`kill-rectangle`). This command is like the previous one, except that the rectangle is saved as the "last killed rectangle". Emacs remembers only a single killed rectangle.

Ctrl X r y   Inserts the last killed rectangle into the text with its upper left corner at the point (`yank-rectangle`). Existing text in the area occupied by the rectangle is moved rightward so that it starts just to the right of the newly inserted rectangle.

Ctrl X r c   Replaces all the text in the rectangle by spaces (`clear-rectangle`).

Ctrl X r o   Opens a rectangle (`open-rectangle`). This command is like the previous one, except that the text in the region occupied by the rectangle is moved rightward rather than blanked out.

Ctrl X r t   Inserts a specified string on each line of a rectangle (`string-rectangle`).

In addition there are commands for copying a rectangle to or from a register (see Section 9.19.3).

9.13   Operations on Windows

This section describes commands that operate on windows. See Section 9.4.5 for a general discussion of windows.

9.13.1 Splitting Windows

The following commands split the selected window into two windows. Initially, each of the windows contains the same material as the parent window.

Ctrl X 2   Splits the selected window vertically into two windows (`split-window-vertically`). The new windows are one above the other and have the same width as the old one.

Ctrl X 3   Splits the selected window horizontally into two side-by-side windows (`split-window-horizontally`). The new windows have the same height as the old one and are separated by a column of vertical bars. It's usually better to force the text in a narrow window to be truncated rather than wrapped. You can get this effect by setting the variable `truncate-partial-width-windows` to 't' (see Section 9.21.1). The horizontal scrolling commands (see Section 9.8.2) are often useful with narrow windows.

9.13.2
Operations on
Other Windows

The windows on your screen have a particular order, generally from top to bottom and from left to right. By default, a window command applies to the next window; with an argument *n*, it applies to the *n*th window. For example, an argument of '-2' causes a next-window command to apply to the second previous window.

The following command enables you to select the next window:

(Ctrl) X o   Makes the next window the selected window (`other-window`). In the common case when there are just two windows, this command switches to the other window.

The following commands start a particular activity in the next window. If there is only one window, they create another one. The commands all start with '(Ctrl) X 4'—without the '4', they start the same activity in the selected window.

(Ctrl) X 4 (Ctrl) F
(Ctrl) X 4 f   Visits a file in the next window (see p. 510).

(Ctrl) X 4 r   Visits a file in the next window, but in read-only mode.

(Ctrl) X 4 b   Brings a particular buffer to the next window (see p. 514).

(Ctrl) X 4 d   Starts Dired in the next window (see p. 551).

(Ctrl) X 4 m   Starts composing a mail message in the next window (see p. 563).

(Ctrl) X 4 .   Starts searching for a tag in another window (see p. 562).

There is a similar group of commands for starting an activity in a new frame (see Section 9.14). Those commands start with '(Ctrl) X 5'.

The following commands perform scrolling and comparison operations on the next window.

(Meta) (PgDn)
(Meta) (Ctrl) V
              Scrolls the next window down by one page; that is, does a (Ctrl) V in that window (`scroll-other-window`).

(Meta) (PgUp)
              Scrolls the next window up by one page (`scroll-other-window-down`).

(Meta) (Home)
              Moves to the beginning of the buffer in the next window (`beginning-of-buffer-other-window`).

(Meta) (End)
              Moves to the end of the buffer in the next window (`end-of-buffer-other-window`).

(Meta) X compare-windows
              Compares the selected window with the next window, starting at the point. After the comparison, the point in each window is positioned at the first differing character.

**9.13.3
Deleting and
Resizing Windows**

The following commands remove a window or change its size:

[Ctrl] X 0   Deletes the selected window, redistributing the space that it occupies among the other windows (`delete-window`). Deleting a window does not kill the buffer associated with the window; the buffer remains available to be recalled to a window later.

[Ctrl] X 1   Deletes all windows other than the selected one (`delete-other-windows`).

[Ctrl] X ^   Makes the selected window taller by one line (`enlarge-window`). With an argument of n (n positive), enlarges the window by n lines; with an argument of n (n negative), reduces the window by n lines.

[Ctrl] X }   Makes the selected window wider by one column (`enlarge-window-horizontally`). With an argument of n (n positive), widens the window by n columns; with an argument of n (n negative), narrows the window by n columns.

**9.13.4
Mouse Actions for
Rearranging
Windows**

Under X you can also use the mouse to resize, delete, or split windows with the following actions:

[Mouse-1] *on mode line*
Selects the window above the mode line. You can move the mode line, thus changing the boundary between windows, by clicking [Mouse-1] on the mode line and dragging it to the new location.

[Mouse-2] *on mode line*
Expands the window above the mode line to fill the entire frame.

[Mouse-3] *on mode line*
Deletes the window above the mode line.

[Ctrl] [Mouse-2] *on mode line*
Splits the window above the mode line into two vertical windows, with the boundary aligned with where you clicked.

[Ctrl] [Mouse-2] *on scrollbar*
Splits the window to the left of the scrollbar into two horizontal windows, with the boundary aligned with where you clicked.

9.14   Operations on Frames

When operating under X, Emacs provides commands for operating on frames that are analogous to the commands for operating on windows.

**9.14.1
Opening a
New Frame**

The following commands start an activity in another frame. Unlike the corresponding window commands, they *always* do so in a newly created frame.

⌈Ctrl⌉ X 5 2   Creates a new frame (`make-frame`) containing a copy of the current window, but doesn't move the cursor there.

⌈Ctrl⌉ X 5 f   Creates a new frame containing the buffer that results from visiting a particular file (`find-file-other-frame`).

⌈Ctrl⌉ X 5 r   Creates a new frame containing the buffer that results from visiting a particular file in read-only mode (`find-file-read-only-other-frame`).

⌈Ctrl⌉ X 5 b   Creates a new frame containing a particular buffer (`switch-to-buffer-other-frame`).

⌈Ctrl⌉ X 5 d   Creates a new frame and starts the Dired directory editor in it (`dired-other-frame`).

⌈Ctrl⌉ X 5 m   Creates a new frame and starts composing a mail message in it (`mail-other-frame`).

⌈Ctrl⌉ X 5 .   Creates a new frame and starts searching for a tag in it (`find-tag-other-frame`).

**9.14.2
Other Operations
on Frames**

The following commands perform other useful operations on frames:

⌈Ctrl⌉ X 5 o   Goes to the next frame (`other-frame`). Frames that have been reduced to icons aren't candidates.

⌈Ctrl⌉ X 5 0   Deletes the frame containing the cursor.

⌈Ctrl⌉ Z   Reduces the current frame to an icon, or if invoked when the cursor is on the icon for an Emacs frame, expands that icon back to a full frame (`iconify-or-deiconify-frame`).

In addition to these operations, Emacs includes operations for customizing frames. See your Emacs documentation for details.

9.15   Operations on Files

To edit a file, you must bring it into a buffer by *visiting* it. You can visit a file that doesn't exist in order to create it. When you've finished editing the copy of a file in a buffer, you can update the file by saving the buffer.

**9.15.1
Specifying File
Names**

When you issue an Emacs command that requires a file name (really a pathname), Emacs displays a default directory in the minibuffer and prompts you for the rest of the name. If the file you want is in that directory, you can specify it by completing the name. If not, you can specify a different directory by editing the pathname of the default directory. Often the simplest way to do that is to type the full pathname of the file you want. Emacs will not be confused if the edited pathname contains '//' or '~' somewhere in the middle, as in

```
/home/genghis//etc/passwd
```

or

```
/home/mikhail/~boris/comrades
```

The first pathname refers to /etc/passwd, the second to ~boris/comrades. These pathnames would not be accepted by the usual UNIX shells.

You can type Enter in response to a request for a file name, asking Emacs to use the default file name. If the current buffer is associated with a file, Emacs uses the name of that file as the default. Otherwise, it uses the current directory and either gives you a Dired (directory editor) buffer for that directory or complains.

Environment Variables in Pathnames. You can insert the value of an environment variable *var* into a pathname by typing '$*var*'. To refer to a file whose name includes '$', replace the '$' with '$$'.

Files on Other Machines. You can refer to a file on another machine by using the syntax

/[*user*@]*host* : *pathname*

If you don't specify *user*, Emacs assumes the user is you. Emacs then uses ftp (see Section 12.8) to read or write the file at location *pathname* on the machine *host*. If a password is needed, Emacs will prompt you for it.

Default Directory. Each buffer has a default directory, which you can set or query with the following commands:

Meta X cd Sets the current directory to the pathname *dir*. Emacs prompts you for *dir*. You can use '~' to start the pathname with your home directory.

Meta X pwd
Shows the pathname of the current (working) directory.

Whenever Emacs prompts you for a pathname, it takes the default directory from the current buffer. If the current buffer happens to be, say, a help window, the current directory will be somewhere in the middle of the system Emacs files, not in your own files—a nuisance but not a disaster.

**9.15.2
Visiting Files**

The following commands visit a file:

Ctrl X Ctrl F
Visits a file, loading it into the selected window (find-file). Emacs prompts you for the pathname of the file. If a buffer doesn't already exist for the file, Emacs creates one and names

it after the file, appending '<2>', '<3>', etc., to the name if necessary to make it unique. If you visit a directory, Emacs starts the directory editor Dired for that directory in the selected window (see Section 10.1). Emacs tries to choose a major mode according to the filename part of the pathname (see Section 9.4.4) (e.g., C mode for a file whose name ends in '.c').

⌨Ctrl X 4 ⌨Ctrl F
⌨Ctrl X 4 f   Visits a file and brings its buffer to the next window (`find-file-other-window`). Emacs prompts you for the pathname.

⌨Ctrl X ⌨Ctrl R
             Visits a file in read-only mode, loading it into the selected window (`find-file-read-only`).   Changes to the window are inhibited.   You can turn off the read-only status with ⌨Ctrl X ⌨Ctrl Q, the `toggle-read-only` command (see p. 516).

⌨Ctrl X 4 r   Visits a file in read-only mode and brings its buffer to the next window (`find-file-read-only-other-window`). Emacs prompts you for the pathname.

⌨Ctrl X ⌨Ctrl V
             Kills the current buffer, then visits a file as with `find-file` (`find-alternate-file`).   If the current buffer contains unsaved modifications to a file, Emacs asks you for confirmation before killing the buffer. This command is useful when you've just visited the wrong file by accident.

In addition, the `find-file-other-window` command visits a file in the next window.

9.15.3
Saving Regions and Buffers to Files

The following commands save part or all of a buffer in a file and perform related operations:

⌨Ctrl X ⌨Ctrl S
             Saves the contents of the current buffer in the file associated with that buffer (`save-buffer`). If no file is associated with the buffer, Emacs prompts you for one.

⌨Ctrl X s   Goes through the list of buffers that have been modified but not saved, asking you for each one if you want to save it (`save-some-buffers`).

⌨Meta X `set-visited-file-name`
             Associates the current buffer with a specified file, usually different from the one it's currently associated with. Emacs prompts you for the pathname of the new file. The buffer need not currently be associated with any file.

⌨Ctrl X ⌨Ctrl W
             Saves the current buffer to a specified file and associates the

current buffer with that file from now on just as with the `set-visited-file-name` command (`write-file`). Emacs prompts you for the pathname of the new file.

Meta X `write-region`
Writes the region to a specified file. Emacs prompts you for the pathname of the file. The file associated with the buffer is not affected.

Meta X `append-to-file`
Like `write-region`, except that the region is appended to the specified file instead of replacing it.

Meta ~
Marks the current buffer as "not modified", thus inhibiting Emacs from saving it automatically or complaining if you abandon it (`not-modified`). This command is useful when you've modified a file but don't want to save the modifications.

9.15.4
Inserting a File

The following command enables you to insert the contents of a file into a buffer:

Ctrl X i
Inserts the contents of a specified file into the current buffer following the point (`insert-file`). Emacs prompts you for the name of the file.

9.15.5
Miscellaneous
File Operations

The following command provides a listing of a directory or a set of files:

Ctrl X Ctrl D
Creates a buffer containing a brief listing of a directory or a set of files (`list-directory`). Emacs prompts you for the name of a directory or a pathname possibly containing wildcards. With an argument, this command gives you a verbose listing, by default the same one you obtain from '`ls -l`' (see Section 3.2.2).

Generally, only the brief listing form is useful since you can obtain the verbose form just as easily with Dired (see Section 10.1).

The following commands provide various operations on files, unrelated to the contents of the Emacs buffers (although `view-file` uses a buffer temporarily). All these commands are also available through Dired (see Section 10.1).

Meta X `view-file`
Scans a file without modifying it. The file is brought to a temporary buffer whose major mode is View. In View mode, certain keys are rebound as follows:

Space
Moves down by one screenful. If you press **Space** when the last line of the file is visible, you'll exit from viewing.

Del
Moves up by one screenful.

Ctrl C
Exits from viewing, kills the view buffer.

Most other keys have their usual meanings, except that you can't modify the view buffer.

Meta X `copy-file`
> Copies the contents of a specified file to another file. Emacs prompts you for the names of both files.

Meta X `delete-file`
> Deletes a specified link to a file, just as you would with `rm` (see Section 3.5.1).

Meta X `rename-file`
> Renames a specified file, just as you would with `mv` (see Section 3.4.2). Emacs prompts you for the names of both files.

Meta X `add-name-to-file`
> Provides an additional name for a specified file, just as you would with `ln` (see Section 3.4.1). Emacs prompts you for the names of both files.

Meta X `make-symbolic-link`
> Provides an additional symbolic link to a specified file, provided that your system supports symbolic links (see p. 41). Emacs prompts you for the names of both files.

9.15.6 Automatically Saving, Recovering, and Backing Up Files

Emacs has two mechanisms for protecting you from accidentally losing files that you're working on: automatic backup and auto-saving.

- When you save a file and an older copy of that file already exists, Emacs saves the older copy in a backup file. You can create a series of numbered backup files if you wish.
- Periodically, Emacs saves all of the files you've visited in Auto Save files, distinct from the backup files.

Either of these mechanisms may be disabled.

Backup Files. By default, Emacs makes a single backup file whenever you save a file and discards the previous backup file. If you save a buffer more than once, however, only the first save causes the backup file to be made—though if you kill the buffer and reread the file, you'll get a new backup. The backup file is named by adding a '~' to the name of the original file, so the backup file for `stilton` would be `stilton~`. Setting the variable `make-backup-files` to `nil` inhibits the creation of backup files (see Section 9.21.1).

You can also arrange to back up files more extensively by using numbered backup files. The backup files for the file `ricotta` would be named `ricotta.~1~`, `ricotta.~2~`, etc. You can activate numbered backups by setting the `version-control` variable (see Section 9.21.1). Its possible values are as follows:

`t`	Make numbered backups.
`nil`	Make numbered backups only for files that already have them; make single backups for all other files. (This is the default.)
`'never`	Never make numbered backups, but always make single backups.

Emacs does not reuse version numbers for backup files—the newest numbered backup always has a version number one higher than the highest existing one.

When Emacs creates a new numbered backup, it normally keeps the oldest two versions (usually '.~1~' and '.~2~') and the newest two, deleting any in the middle after asking you. The following variables affect which versions Emacs keeps:

`kept-old-versions`
> How many of the oldest versions to keep (default 2).

`kept-new-versions`
> How many of the newest versions to keep (default 2).

`trim-versions-without-asking`
> If non-`nil`, middle versions are deleted without a confirmation query.

You can restore a file from one of its backups either by renaming the backup to the original filename using the `rename-file` command or by visiting the backup file with the Ctrl X Ctrl F command and saving it under the original name.

Auto-Saving.   Auto-saving provides protection against disasters such as killing Emacs by mistake and power failures. Periodically, Emacs saves the contents of each file you edit in an Auto Save file. The auto-save file is independent of any backup files. The name of the auto-save file for `camembert` is `#camembert#`.

By default, auto-save takes place every 300 keystrokes or when you stop typing for 30 seconds. The keystroke count and timeout interval are recorded in the variables `auto-save-interval` and `auto-save-timeout`. You can also auto-save a file explicitly with the Meta X `do-auto-save` command.

You can recover an auto-save file with the `recover-file` command (type Meta X `recover-file`), which visits a file and then restores it (after confirmation) from its auto-saved version. Saving the current buffer with Ctrl X Ctrl S then causes the recovered file to become the current version of the file in question. In addition, the `revert-buffer` command (see p. 516) offers to revert to the auto-save file rather than the original file if the auto-save file is newer than the original file.

Auto-saving is a minor mode, controlled by the `auto-save-mode` command (see p. 475).

9.16   Explicit Operations on Buffers

Nearly all Emacs operations affect buffers in one way or another. In this section we describe Emacs operations that explicitly relate to buffers.

Section 9.17 describes the buffer menu, a facility for operating on a list of buffers in a window.

9.16.1
Specifying a Buffer Name

When Emacs prompts you for a buffer name, the default is the buffer that was previously in the selected window. If you specify a buffer that doesn't already exist, Emacs creates a new empty buffer by that name (in Fundamental mode). You can type a prefix of a buffer name followed by a tab or space to get Emacs to complete the name automatically (see Section 9.5.3). But if you just type the prefix of a name and then press (Enter), Emacs takes the prefix as the entire name of the buffer—usually not what you want.

9.16.2
Bringing a Buffer into a Window

The following commands bring a specified buffer into a window:

(Ctrl) X b   Brings a specified buffer into the current window (`switch-to-buffer`). Emacs prompts you for the name of the buffer.

(Ctrl) X 4 b   Brings a specified buffer into the next window (`switch-to-buffer-other-window`). Emacs prompts you for the name of the buffer.

(Ctrl) X 4 (Ctrl) O
   Brings a specified buffer into the next window, but without selecting it (`display-buffer`). Emacs prompts you for the name of the buffer.

9.16.3
Killing Buffers

The following command kills a specified buffer:

(Ctrl) X k   Kills a specified buffer (`kill-buffer`). Emacs prompts you for the buffer name; the default is the current buffer. If the current buffer is associated with a file and has been modified, Emacs asks you for confirmation before performing the kill.

The following command provides a convenient way of getting rid of buffers you don't want, as an alternative to calling up a buffer menu.

(Meta) X `kill-some-buffers`
   Goes through the list of buffers, asking you for each one if you want to kill it. Emacs tells you if a buffer has been modified; if you kill it anyway, your changes will be lost (although you still may be able to recover most of them from an auto-save file).

9.16.4
Positions and Counts

The following commands enable you to find your position in the buffer:

(Ctrl) X =   Shows the position of the point (as a character number) on the echo line (`what-cursor-position`).

(Meta) X `what-line`
   Shows the current line number on the echo line.

(Meta) X `what-page`
   Shows the current page number, and line number within the

page, on the echo line. For the purposes of this command, pages are considered to be delimited by ⟨formfeed⟩ characters.

The following related commands count the lines in the region or in the current page:

(Meta) =   Counts the number of lines in the region (count-lines-region).

(Ctrl) X l   Counts the number of lines in the current page, which is delimited by ⟨formfeed⟩s (count-lines-page). This command also shows the number of lines before and after the point.

9.16.5 Selective Display

You can hide lines indented by more than a certain number of columns with Emacs's *selective display* feature. The following command turns it on:

(Ctrl) X $ With argument *n*, hides all lines indented by at least *n* columns (set-selective-display). With no argument, reveals all the hidden lines again.

The hidden lines are indicated by '...' at the end of each visible line preceding one or more invisible ones. The (Ctrl) N and (Ctrl) P commands move over invisible lines as though they weren't there, but most other editing commands see them as usual. When the point is on an invisible line, the cursor appears at the end of the previous line after the three dots.

9.16.6 Narrowing a Buffer

Narrowing a buffer is useful when you want to work with only a portion of it (e.g., for restricting the scope of a search-and-replace operation). When you narrow a buffer, only the narrowed portion is visible and motion commands are restricted to that portion. However, the invisible portion is not lost; if you ask to save a buffer when it's narrowed, Emacs saves the entire buffer, not just the visible part.

(Ctrl) X n n   Narrows the buffer to the region between the point and the mark (narrow-to-region).

(Ctrl) X n p   Narrows the buffer to the current page (narrow-to-page). See page 488 for the definition of a page.

(Ctrl) X n w   Widens the buffer to its full extent (widen).

The narrow-to-region command is normally disabled (see Section 9.5.7). If you try to use it, you're given the opportunity to enable it either temporarily or permanently.

9.16.7 Displaying Line Numbers

You can cause Emacs to include the line number in the mode line by activating Line Number mode, which is a minor mode. That causes the line number of the line containing the cursor to be displayed in the mode line. The (Meta) X line-number-mode command toggles the mode. With a positive argument, it turns the mode on; with a negative argument, it turns the mode off.

**9.16.8
Modifying
Read-Only Status**

You can toggle the read-only status of a buffer (see "Read-Only Buffers" on p. 473), changing it from read-only to writable or vice versa, with the following command:

Ctrl X Ctrl Q

> Toggles the read-only status of the current buffer. In addition, if the buffer is associated with a file that is registered under version control (see Section 10.8), checks the file in or out.[14]

**9.16.9
Other Operations**

The following commands provide other operations on buffers:

Meta X revert-buffer

> Restores the contents of the buffer from its associated file, discarding all changes. If an auto-save file newer than the associated file exists, Emacs asks you if you want to revert to the auto-save file instead, thereby keeping all but your most recent changes.

Meta X rename-buffer

> Gives the current buffer a new name. Emacs prompts you for the new name. Renaming a buffer does not change the name of the file associated with the buffer, so saving the buffer saves to the same file as before.

Meta X rename-uniquely

> Gives the current buffer a new, unique name by adding a numerical suffix.

Meta X view-buffer

> Changes the major mode of the current buffer to View mode. In View mode, the buffer becomes read-only, but a few keys are rebound to make it easier to scan through the buffer:

Space	Moves down one page.
Del	Moves up one page.
Ctrl C	Reverts to the previous major mode, preserving the position of the point.
?	Displays a list of available commands.

9.17 The Buffer Menu

A buffer menu lists all the buffers and enables you to perform operations on them. Here is an example of what a buffer menu looks like:

---

14. In earlier versions of Emacs, the keystrokes ' Ctrl X Ctrl Q ' were bound to a different command, `toggle-read-only`. The two commands behave similarly but not identically when version control is not involved. If you provide an argument to `toggle-read-only`, the buffer is made read-only if and only if the argument is nonnegative. The `vc-toggle-read-only` command ignores its argument and always toggles the status.

```
MR Buffer          Size  Mode               File
-- ------          ----  ----               ----
.  % shrink.c      1974  C                  /home/alice/shrink.c
   % *info*         50661 Info
*    cheshire.tex  109585 Text              /home/alice/cheshire.tex
     *scratch*     0     Lisp Interaction
*    *Buffer List* 351   Buffer Menu
```

Here is what the indications in the first three columns mean:

.   The buffer selected before the buffer menu itself.

*   File has been modified.

%   File is read-only.

A buffer containing a buffer menu is in the Buffer Menu major mode and is named '`*Buffer List*`' unless you forcibly change its name. Ordinarily, at most one buffer contains a buffer menu.

9.17.1 Creating or Selecting a Buffer Menu

The following commands create a buffer menu and select a buffer menu if it already exists:

(Meta) X `buffer-menu`

Displays a buffer menu in another window and selects it. The buffer menu is created if it doesn't already exist.

(Ctrl) X (Ctrl) B

Displays a buffer menu in another window but doesn't select it. The buffer menu is created if it doesn't already exist.

9.17.2 Operations on a Buffer Menu

When you select a buffer menu, Emacs puts you into Buffer Menu mode in which certain ordinary keys are bound to commands. Typing '?' causes Emacs to display explanations of the buffer menu commands in another window. The window goes away when you type a command.

Vertical Motions.   The following keys provide vertical motions:

(Space)   Moves down one line.

(Del)   Moves up one line.

Deleting and Saving Buffers.   The following commands enable you to flag buffers for deletion or saving, to remove the flags, and to carry out the operations specified by the flags. A buffer flagged for deletion is marked with 'D', while one flagged for saving is marked with 'S'. Flagging a buffer does not cause Emacs to delete or save it immediately; Emacs postpones these actions until you call for them with an 'x' command.

The following commands are available from a buffer menu:

(Ctrl) K

d

k   Flags this buffer for deletion and moves down one line.

(Ctrl) D   Flags this buffer for deletion and moves up one line.

s   Flags this buffer for saving.

u   Removes all deletion and save requests from this line and moves down one line.

x   Performs all outstanding deletion and save requests.

~   Marks this buffer as unmodified. This marking is not a request for action; its effect is to prevent the buffer from being saved in its current state (since Emacs doesn't carry out a save action on an unmodified buffer).

Assigning Buffers to Windows. The following commands enable you to choose which buffers occupy windows. All of them except 'm' cause the buffer menu to be deselected. In each case, the buffer referred to as "this buffer" is the one on the line containing the cursor.

1   Selects this buffer in a full-screen window.

2   Sets up two windows, one containing this buffer and the other containing the buffer that was replaced by the buffer list (so the buffer displaced by the buffer list returns to the screen).

f   Replaces the buffer list by this buffer.

o   Selects this buffer in another window, leaving the buffer list visible.

q   Selects this buffer and displays any buffers marked with 'm' in other windows. If no other buffers are marked with 'm', this buffer is displayed in a full-size window.

m   Marks this buffer so that the 'q' command will display it. The mark appears as an 'm' in the buffer list.

9.17.3
The Electric Buffer List

A particularly handy way to select a buffer is with the electric buffer list, which you can bring up in another window with the command [Meta] X electric-buffer-list. The electric buffer displays a list very similar to the one produced by the buffer menu, but less typing is needed and fewer actions are available:

- You can press [Space] or [Enter] to select the buffer the cursor is on and make the buffer list go away. Since the cursor is initially on the buffer you were in when you selected, pressing [Space] right away is a good way to see what buffers are around without changing the current buffer.

- You can move around the menu as usual with cursor keys, n (next), or p (previous).

- You can mark buffers with m; when you exit, each marked buffer will be in its own window.

- You can delete and save buffers with d and s; these actions become effective when you leave the buffer menu.

- You can view a small piece of a buffer with v; exiting the view with [Ctrl] C brings back the buffer list.

9.18   Printing

The following commands print either a buffer or a region. You can attach page headings to the printed output or print it as is.

(Meta) X `print-buffer`
>   Prints the entire buffer with page headings.

(Meta) X `print-region`
>   Prints the region with page headings.

(Meta) X `lpr-buffer`
>   Prints the entire buffer as is, without automatically attaching page headings.

(Meta) X `lpr-region`
>   Prints the region as is.

Printing is done with the '`lpr -p`' command if you ask for page headings and with the '`lpr`' command otherwise. The command doesn't actually cause the printing to happen—it merely places the output on the print queue. You can add other options to the '`lpr`' command by assigning them to the variable `lpr-switches` (see Section 9.21.1). The '`lpr`' commands work on almost any system, but the '`print`' commands may not work on systems that use '`lp`' as their print spooler.[15]

9.19   Registers and Their Operations

A *register* is a place where you can store a position, a portion of text, or a rectangle. A particular register can hold only one of these at a time. Each register has a name, which can be any printable character. Retrieving the contents of a register does not disturb the register's contents.

**9.19.1
Viewing Register
Contents**

The following command shows you what is in a register:

(Meta) X `view-register` (Enter) *r*
>   Displays the contents and type of register *r*.

---

15. The reason for this strange state of affairs is that the Emacs implementation translates '`lpr`' to '`lp`' when necessary, but it doesn't account properly for the '`-p`' option, which '`lp`' doesn't recognize.

**9.19.2
Saving and
Retrieving Positions**

The following commands save a position in a register or move to a position specified by a register. The position includes both a buffer and a point location within that buffer.

Ctrl X r Space *r*
> Saves the location of the point from the selected window in register *r* (point-to-register).

Ctrl X r j*r*
> Restores the location that's recorded in register *r* (jump-to-register). If the stored location is from a different buffer, that buffer is brought to the selected window.

**9.19.3
Saving and
Retrieving Text
Using Registers**

The following commands save text in a register or restore text from a register. The text can be either ordinary text or a rectangle (see Section 9.12).

Ctrl X r x*r*
> Copies the text contained in the region into register *r* (copy-to-register). If you provide an argument, the copied text is deleted from the buffer.

Ctrl X r r*r*
> Copies the rectangle defined by the point and the mark into register *r* (copy-region-to-rectangle). If you provide an argument, the copied rectangle is deleted from the buffer.

Ctrl X r i*r*
> Inserts the text or rectangle stored in register *r* into the text (insert-register). The type of the register's contents determine the nature of the insertion. The effect is the same as yank or Meta X yank-rectangle.

**9.19.4
Quick File Access
with Registers**

You can visit a file quickly if you put its name in a register. If you evaluate the LISP expression

```
(set-register ?r '(file . pathname))
```

then executing the command Ctrl X r j *r* will visit the file at *pathname*. This method is useful when you need to visit a file often but you don't want to keep it in a buffer all the time.

9.20 Searching and Replacing

Emacs has two types of search commands: incremental and nonincremental. Incremental search is usually more convenient, although you can't use it in conjunction with replacement. You can search for a regular expression as well as for a specific string. You can also use a regular expression when you're doing a replacement. You can perform a replacement with or without querying each occurrence of the string you're replacing; you have this option both when replacing strings and when replacing regular expressions.

Searches are normally case-insensitive; for example, the search string 'hermes' matches 'Hermes', 'HERMES', and 'HerMes'. You can make searches case-sensitive by setting the variable `case-fold-search` to `nil` (see Section 9.21.1). Setting this variable in one buffer does not affect any other buffer.

The search commands all start at the point and continue to the end of the buffer. They don't provide any method of restricting the search to just a portion of the rest of the buffer. However, you can get that effect easily enough with the `Ctrl`X n n (`narrow-to-region`) command (see Section 9.16.6).

9.20.1 Incremental Search

In an incremental search, Emacs starts searching as soon as you type even a single character in the search string. These are the commands for ordinary incremental search:

`Ctrl`S   Searches forward incrementally (`isearch-forward`).

`Ctrl`R   Searches backward incrementally (`isearch-backward`).

As soon as you type one of these commands, Emacs prompts you for the search string. Typing `Meta`P or `Meta`N will cycle you through a ring of previously used search strings. You can also search incrementally for a regular expression (see Section 9.20.4).

The most striking property of incremental search is that you often find the string you're searching for before you've typed the entire search string. Suppose you are searching for the next occurrence of the string 'schlock.' You start the search by typing '`Ctrl`S s'. Emacs immediately positions you just after the next 's'. You now type 'c', and Emacs positions you just after the next 'sc'. If the first 's' was immediately followed by a 'c', the point moves by just one character. Typing 'h' causes Emacs to look for the next 'sch', and so forth. When you've typed enough letters to locate the next 'schlock', you end the search by typing `Esc`.

The effects of typing various characters in the search string are as follows:

(*any printable or other non-command character*)
          Adds this character to the search string and looks for the next occurrence of the search string.

`Meta`Y   Adds the most recent kill to the search string.

`Enter`   Terminates the search. The mark is set to the point, which is at the end of the matched string.

`Esc`   Like `Enter`, except that the `Esc` remains active, causing the next key you press to be meta-shifted.

Ctrl S   Searches for the next occurrence of the search string so far. If your search finds a different occurrence than the one you're looking for, Ctrl S enables you to get to the right one. If you type Ctrl S after a failed search, Emacs performs a wrapped search, starting at the beginning of the buffer.

If you type Ctrl S as the very first character of the search string, Emacs searches for the string from the previous search. In this case, you can't edit the search string.

Ctrl R   Searches for the previous occurrence of the search string (as typed so far).

Del   Deletes the last character of the search string. Emacs moves the point back to the previous string that it found. When you repeat a search using the previous search string, however, attempting to delete part of that search string deletes all of it.

Ctrl G   The effect of Ctrl G depends on the context:

- If you've just found the search string, it cancels the search.
- If the search string has not been found, it deletes all characters in the search string that you've typed since the last successful match—or all characters in the search string if there hasn't yet been a successful match. There are two reasons why the search string might not have been found: it doesn't exist, or it exists but Emacs is still looking for it. Ctrl G produces the same effect in either case.

It follows from the previous description that Ctrl G Ctrl G always cancels the search. A cancelled search reverts the point to where it was before the search.

Ctrl W   Adds the word (or the rest of the word) following the point to the search string.

Ctrl Y   Adds the rest of the line following the point to the search string.

Control Characters in Search Strings. You can include any character in a search string, not just printable ones. To include a character such as Ctrl S or Del, quote it with Ctrl Q. That convention doesn't work for ⟨newline⟩, though; to include a ⟨newline⟩ in a search string, type it as Ctrl J or Ctrl Q Ctrl J. The same conventions work for replacement strings, except that in a replacement string, Ctrl J has to be quoted.

9.20.2 Nonincremental Search

The following commands perform nonincremental searches:

Ctrl S Enter

Performs a forward nonincremental search for a specified string (`search-forward`). Emacs prompts you for the string.

Ctrl R Enter

Performs a backward nonincremental search for a specified string (`search-backward`). Emacs prompts you for the string.

In either case, if you type ⌈Ctrl⌉ W as the first character of the search string, you get a word search (see Section 9.20.3).

The nonincremental search commands don't include a feature for repeating a search, but you can conveniently repeat a search with the ⌈Ctrl⌉ X ⌈Esc⌉ ⌈Esc⌉ (`repeat-complex-command`) command.

9.20.3 Word Search

A word search searches for a sequence of words. The words may be separated by single spaces, ⟨newline⟩s, tabs, punctuation, or sequences of these characters. For instance, the command

⌈Ctrl⌉ S ⌈Enter⌉ ⌈Ctrl⌉ W `fat.cat` ⌈Enter⌉

finds any of the following:

```
fat cat
fat    cat
fat-cat
Fat, Cat
```

These are the word search commands:

⌈Ctrl⌉ S ⌈Enter⌉ ⌈Ctrl⌉ W
> Searches forward nonincrementally for a specified sequence of words (`word-search-forward`). Emacs prompts you for the string.

⌈Ctrl⌉ R ⌈Enter⌉ ⌈Ctrl⌉ W
> Searches backward nonincrementally for a specified sequence of words (`word-search-backward`). Emacs prompts you for the string.

9.20.4 Regular Expression Search

The following commands perform a search for a regular expression (see "Regular Expressions in Emacs" on p. 524). You can search either incrementally or nonincrementally

⌈Meta⌉ ⌈Ctrl⌉ S
> Searches incrementally in the forward direction for a regular expression (`isearch-forward-regexp`).

⌈Meta⌉ ⌈Ctrl⌉ R
> Searches incrementally in the backward direction for a regular expression (`isearch-backward-regexp`).

⌈Meta⌉ X `re-search-forward`
> Searches forward nonincrementally for a regular expression.

⌈Meta⌉ X `re-search-backward`
> Searches backward nonincrementally for a regular expression.

Emacs prompts you for the characters of an incremental search expression or for the entire expression string of a nonincremental search in the same way that it does for the versions of these commands that work with plain strings. Adding characters to the regular expression of an incremental search does not cause the cursor to move in the opposite direction, even though a match might be found earlier (since adding characters to a regular expression can enlarge the set of matching strings).

You can repeat an incremental search for a regular expression. Having found one occurrence, you can find another one by typing '[Ctrl]S' (not '[Meta] [Ctrl]S'). To repeat an earlier incremental search for a regular expression, type '[Meta] [Ctrl]S [Ctrl]S'.

When you're typing the regular expression for an incremental search, [Space] represents a match for *one or more* spaces. To match just a single space, type '[Ctrl]Q [Space]'.

Regular Expressions in Emacs. Regular expressions in Emacs are an extension of the basic UNIX set (see Section 2.17), although the Emacs regular expressions don't include the '\{...\}' notation described there. The following characters act as metacharacters with special meanings when they appear unquoted in a regular expression:

.   Matches any single character.

*   Matches the preceding regular expression repeated zero or more times.

\+   Matches the preceding regular expression repeated one or more times.

?   Matches the preceding regular expression zero or one times.

[*str*]   Matches any character in the set of characters specified by *str* according to the usual conventions (see p. 82).

∧   At the beginning of a regular expression, matches an empty string at the beginning of a line; in any other context, matches a '∧' character.[16]

$ At the end of a regular expression, matches an empty string at the end of a line; in any other context, matches a '$' character.

c   Matches the character *c* unless it is one of the special constructs listed below. The characters that need to be quoted with '\\' are (. * + ? [\\ ).

A regular expression can also include the following "quoted" constructs:

a\\|*b*   Matches either *a* or *b*. '\\|' applies to the largest possible expressions *a* and *b*.

\\(*expr* \\)

       Matches the regular expression *expr*. The parentheses provide grouping. Parenthesized expressions can be referred to later using the '*n*' notation.

n   Matches the *n*th parenthesized expression, which must come earlier in the regular expression. The variable *n* must be a single decimal digit.

\\'   Matches an empty string at the beginning of the buffer.

\\'   Matches an empty string at the end of the buffer.

---

16. A regular expression such as 'a?∧Q' does not match a 'Q' at the beginning of a line.

\b	Matches an empty string at the beginning or end of a word. For example, the regular expression '\bfa\(cts|x\)' matches either of the words 'facts' and 'fax'.
\B	Matches an empty string that is *not* at the beginning or end of a word.
\<	Matches an empty string at the beginning of a word.
\>	Matches an empty string at the end of a word.
\w	Matches any character that can be part of a word.
\W	Matches any character that cannot be part of a word.
\x*code*	Matches any character whose syntax code is *code* (see Section 9.4.10).
\X*code*	Matches any character whose syntax code differs from *code*.

9.20.5 Replacement

The replacement commands search for a string and replace it with another string. The replacement starts at the point and continues to the end of the buffer. You can carry out the replacement unconditionally or with querying. The narrowing commands, Ctrl X n n and Ctrl X n p, are often very convenient in conjunction with the replacement commands in order to restrict the search and replacement to a particular part of the buffer (see Section 9.16.6).

If the replacement string for a replacement command is entirely in lowercase, the replacement preserves case. That is, if a word is entirely in uppercase, its replacement is translated to full uppercase; if a word starts with an uppercase letter, its replacement also starts with an uppercase letter. For instance, if the search string is 'cheddar' and the replacement string is 'tilsit', then 'CHEDDAR' is replaced by 'TILSIT' and 'Cheddar' or 'ChedDar' is replaced by 'Tilsit'. Setting the variable case-replace to nil inhibits the case conversion (see Section 9.21.1).

Unconditional Replacement.   These are the commands for an unconditional replacement:

Meta X replace-string
  Replaces each occurrence of a specified string with another specified string. Emacs prompts you for both strings. The search for occurrences begins at the point and continues to the end of the buffer.

Meta X replace-regexp
  Like replace-string, except that it searches for a regular expression rather than for a string. Within the replacement expression you can use the following notations:

\&	The entire string matching the regular expression.
\n	The string matching the nth parenthesized expression in the regular expression.
\\	The character '\'.

Replacement with Querying.   These are the commands for replacement with querying:

(Meta) %   Replaces each occurrence of a specified string with another specified string, querying each replacement (query-replace).

(Meta) X query-replace-regexp
                Like the previous command, except that this one searches for a regular expression rather than for a string. The notations described for replace-regexp apply to this command also.

These are the possible responses to the query:

(Ctrl) H
?   Displays a list of the possible responses.

y
(Space)   Performs the replacement.

n
(Del)   Skips this occurrence.

,   Replaces this occurrence and displays the result. If you now type (Ctrl) R, you can edit the replacement. After this command, (Space) and (Del), respectively, accept and reject the replacement.

(Enter)   Exits without doing any more replacements.

(Esc)   Exits without doing any more replacements, but acts as a Meta shift for the next typed key.

.   Performs this replacement, then exits.

!   Replaces all remaining occurrences without asking.

^   Returns to the previous occurrence (but doesn't undo it). You can then edit that occurrence with (Ctrl) R. This command only remembers the immediately preceding occurrence, so you cannot issue it twice in a row.

(Ctrl) R   Enters a recursive edit, enabling you to edit the text in the neighborhood of the text that matched the search string. (see Section 9.5.6). You can exit from the recursive edit with (Meta) (Ctrl) C.

(Ctrl) W   Like (Ctrl) R, except that the replacement string is not inserted before the recursive edit starts.

(Ctrl) L   Redisplays the screen, then asks again.

Typing an unrecognized key ends the replacement and causes the command bound to the key to be executed.

**9.20.6
Searching for
Matching Lines**

The following commands search from the point to the end of the buffer, looking for lines that match a specified regular expression. Emacs prompts you for the regular expression.

(Meta) X occur
(Meta) X list-matching-lines

> Opens an Occur buffer and lists in it each line in the current buffer matching a specified regular expression. Each line in the listing is preceded by its line number. The search for matching lines starts at the point and runs to the end of the buffer.

(Meta) X count-matches

> Counts the number of lines following the point that include a string matching a specified regular expression.

(Meta) X delete-matching-lines

> Deletes each line between the point and the end of the buffer that contains a match for a specified regular expression.

(Meta) X delete-non-matching-lines

> Deletes each line between the point and the end of the buffer that does *not* contain a match for a specified regular expression.

Note: The two deletion commands do *not* ask for confirmation of each deletion!

9.21   Operations on Variables

A variable can be either local (particular to a single buffer) or global (common to all buffers). A reference to a variable looks first for a local copy and then for a global one. A variable may have different values in different buffers and may be local to some buffers but not to others. Option variables provide adjustments to Emacs's behavior; other variables are used for internal recordkeeping (see Section 9.4.8).

**9.21.1
Examining and
Setting Variables**

You can use the following commands to examine or set the value of a variable. You can also use the (Esc) (Esc) command for these purposes (see p. 529) and the help command (Ctrl) H v (see p. 485) to see the value and documentation of a variable.

(Meta) X set-variable

> Sets a specified variable to a specified value. Emacs prompts you for both the variable and the value. The effect is local if the current buffer has a local variable by that name, global otherwise.
>
> You can use the LISP operator setq-default to set the global value of a variable independently of its local value. For example, typing
>
> (Esc) (Esc) (setq-default fill-column 60)

sets the fill column to 60 globally, leaving the local value undisturbed. Section 9.22 discusses the evaluation of LISP expressions such as this one.

(Meta) X `list-options`
> Displays a buffer giving the name, value, and documentation of each option variable (see Section 9.21).

(Meta) X `edit-options`
> Creates a List Options buffer and edits it in Options mode. The editing commands make it easy to change and set values. The "nearby" variable is the one that the point is in or near.
>
> | | |
> |---|---|
> | n | Moves to the next variable. |
> | p | Moves to the previous value. |
> | s | Sets the nearby variable to a specified value, which Emacs prompts you for. |
> | 0 | Sets the nearby variable to `nil`. |
> | 1 | Sets the nearby variable to `t` (the canonical non-`nil` value). |
> | x | Toggles the nearby variable between `nil` and `t`. |

**9.21.2
Creating and
Removing Local
Variables**

The following operations relate to creating and removing local variables in the current buffer:

(Meta) X `make-local-variable`
> Reads the name of a variable and makes that variable local to the current buffer.

(Meta) X `kill-local-variable`
> Reads the name of a variable and removes its local copy so that references to the variable within the current buffer become references to the global variable.

(Meta) X `make-variable-buffer-local`
> Reads the name of a variable and arranges for it to become local when it is next set. Until then, Emacs uses the value of the global variable. If the variable is already local, this command has no effect.

9.22   Evaluating LISP Expressions

In this section we explain a few basic aspects of LISP. A full discussion of LISP is outside the scope of this book.

**9.22.1
LISP Expressions**

A LISP expression, also called a *sexp*, is either an *atom* or a parenthesized list. An apostrophe (') in front of an expression quotes that expression; the value of a quoted expression is the expression itself.

Certain atoms stand for themselves. Evaluating such an atom yields the atom again. The following kinds of atoms stand for themselves:

- String literals in double quotes (e.g., `"rock 'n roll"`).
- Numbers.
- The special atoms 't' (true) and 'nil' (false).

Evaluating a quoted atom such as `'never'` yields that atom, unquoted. Other atoms are *symbols*; a variable is one kind of symbol.

A parenthesized list contains a function name or other LISP operator followed by the arguments of the function. Since the arithmetic operators are functions, the value of the LISP expression

```
(+ (* 8 4) (* 3 5) 5)
```

is 52. A particularly useful operator is `setq`; evaluating the form '`(setq var expr)`' evaluates the expression *expr* and assigns its value to the variable *var*. For example, evaluating

```
(setq case-fold-search nil)
```

sets the variable `case-fold-search` to `nil` and causes string searches to be case-sensitive (see p. 521).

You can quote a parenthesized list as well as an atom. The value of the quoted list is the unquoted list. A quoted list is data and thus need not start with the name of an operation.

9.22.2
Commands for
Evaluating
LISP Expressions

The following commands evaluate one or more LISP expressions:

Esc Esc Interactively evaluates a LISP expression (`eval-expression`). Emacs prompts you for the expression. This command provides an easy way to retrieve or set the value of an Emacs variable. If you respond to the prompt with a variable, you see its value; if you respond with a '`setq`' expression as described above, you assign a value to a variable.

Ctrl X Ctrl E
Evaluates the LISP expression preceding the point (`eval-last-sexp`). That expression is either an atom or a parenthesis-balanced portion of text.

LnFd In Lisp Interaction mode, evaluates the LISP expression preceding the point and inserts its value in front of the point (`eval-print-last-sexp`).

Meta X `eval-region`
Evaluates all the expressions in the region, discarding the results.

Meta X `eval-current-buffer`
Evaluates all the expressions in the current buffer, discarding the results.

9.23   Executing UNIX Commands from Emacs

You can execute UNIX commands from within Emacs, either singly or in a subshell. Many Emacs users find the Emacs command execution facilities so convenient that they issue all their UNIX commands from within Emacs. When you're not working under X, another way to execute UNIX commands from Emacs is to suspend Emacs with (Ctrl) Z (see p. 486), execute the commands, and resume Emacs again. Under X, of course, you can just move the mouse to another window that has xterm running (see Section 13.14).

9.23.1
Executing a Single Command

The following commands execute a single UNIX command *cmd* in a subshell. Emacs chooses the shell to use by looking in the variable shell-file-name, which it initializes from the SHELL environment variable. In each case Emacs prompts you for *cmd*.

(Meta) !   Executes a specified UNIX command *cmd* in a subshell with standard input taken from the null device \dev\null (shell-command). If *cmd* produces any output, Emacs creates a buffer called '*Shell Command Output*' for it. If *cmd* ends in '&', Emacs runs it asynchronously just as the shell would.

(Meta) | Executes a specified UNIX command *cmd* in a subshell with standard input taken from the region (shell-command-on-region).

- If (Meta) | is called without an argument, any output *cmd* produces is placed in a '*Shell Command Output*' buffer as it is with (Meta) ! .
- If (Meta) | is called with an argument, the old region is deleted and any output produced by *cmd* replaces the old region. In effect, the text in the region is transformed by *cmd*.

9.23.2
Running a Subshell in a Buffer

Emacs provides some very powerful facilities for working within a subshell, while at the same time disabling some of the facilities built into your native shell. For example, the Emacs-like editing facilities of the KornShell don't work well within Emacs itself. Emacs looks in the variable explicit-shell-file-name for the name of the shell to use. If that variable contains nil, Emacs then first looks in the environment variable ESHELL and finally in the environment variable SHELL.

An Emacs subshell runs in a major mode called Shell mode. Shell mode is a specialization of Comint mode, a general mode Emacs uses to communicate with interactive processes. That's why many of the commands we now describe have 'comint' in their names.

9.23.3
Initiating a
Subshell

The following command initiates a subshell and creates a buffer to hold its input and output:

(Meta) X shell

> Creates a buffer called '*Shell*' in Shell mode and initiates a subshell in that buffer, which then becomes the current buffer. If you execute this command a second time, you are returned to the same buffer. To create a second shell buffer, rename the first one to something else such as 'shell1' and then issue this command. A convenient way to do the renaming is with the (Meta) X rename-uniquely command.

When you issue a command in a shell buffer, you don't have to wait for it to finish—you can switch to another buffer and edit that buffer while the command is executing.

9.23.4
Executing and
Editing Subshell
Commands

You can freely edit the contents of the shell buffer, so it's easy to construct new commands from fragments of old ones or even from the output of commands.

Executing a Command.   The (Enter) key has a special binding in a shell buffer:

(Enter)

> Sends the current line as input to the shell (send-shell-input). If the point is on the last line in the buffer, that line is sent; otherwise, the current line is copied to the end of the buffer and then sent. In either case, any text at the beginning of the line that matches the shell prompt is removed from the line that is sent to the shell. Positioning yourself at a previously executed command and pressing (Enter) is therefore an easy way to execute that command again, possibly after editing it. To insert a ⟨newline⟩ into the edited text, use the (Ctrl) O command.

Editing a Command.   The following key combinations are also bound to shell commands and provide convenient editing facilities for input:

(Tab)

> Completes the command or pathname before the point (comint-dynamic-complete).

(Meta) ?

> Temporarily displays a list of possible completions of the pathname before the point (comint-dynamic-list-filename-completions).

(Ctrl) C (Ctrl) A

> If the current line begins with a prompt, moves to after the prompt; otherwise, moves to the beginning of the line (comint-bol).

(Ctrl) D

> Sends an end-of-file to the shell if the point is at the end of the buffer; otherwise, deletes the next character (comint-delchar-or-maybe-eof).

(Ctrl) C (Ctrl) W

> Kills the word preceding the point (backward-kill-word).

[Ctrl] C [Ctrl] U

> Kills the text between the end of the most recent shell output and the point (`comint-kill-input`).

[Ctrl] C [Ctrl] F

> Moves forward across one shell command, but not past the end of line (`shell-forward-command`).

[Ctrl] C [Ctrl] B

> Moves backward across one shell command, but not past the end of line (`shell-backward-command`).

Multiline Commands.   Sometimes you may want to execute a command that occupies several lines. In order to have it entered properly in the command history, you should type it by ending each line other than the last with [LnFd] or the equivalent, [Ctrl] J. The entire sequence of lines will then appear in the command history as a single command, from which you can retrieve it for re-editing and re-execution.

Scrolling the Shell Buffer.   The following commands provide scrolling effects for the shell buffer:

[Ctrl] C [Ctrl] E

> Scrolls the buffer so that the end of the buffer is at the bottom of the window (`comint-show-maximum-output`).

[Meta] [Ctrl] L
[Ctrl] C [Ctrl] R

> Scrolls the shell window so that the first line of output from the most recently executed command is the first line of the window (`comint-show-output`).

9.23.5
Using the
Command History

Emacs keeps a history of the commands you execute in a shell buffer, enabling you to retrieve previous commands and execute them. The commands form a ring, so the command previous to the first one is the last one.

Searching the Command History.   The following Emacs commands operate on the command history:

[Meta] P   Fetches the previous shell command from the command history (`comint-previous-input`). You need to be at the shell prompt for this command to work. Executing this command repeatedly retrieves successively older shell commands.

[Meta] N   Fetches the next shell command from the command history (`comint-next-input`). This command is like the previous one, except that it moves in the opposite direction.

[Meta] R   Searches in the backward direction through the command history for a command that matches a regular expression (`comint-previous-matching-input`). Emacs prompts you for the regular expression.

[Meta] S   Searches in the forward direction through the command history for a command that matches a regular expression (`comint-next-matching-input`). Emacs prompts you for the regular expression.

[Ctrl] C [Ctrl] L

Shows the command history in a separate help buffer (`comint-dynamic-list-input-ring`). You can then select a command from that buffer. The selected command is copied to the end of the shell buffer, from where you can then either execute it as is or edit it and execute it.

Searching through Prompts.   The following commands search the buffer by shell prompts or copy a command from a previous prompt:

[Ctrl] C [Ctrl] P

Moves the point to the previous prompt (`comint-previous-prompt`).

[Ctrl] C [Ctrl] N

Moves the point to the next prompt (`comint-next-prompt`).

[Ctrl] C [Enter]

Copies the input command containing the point (or the line containing the point if the point isn't within an input command) to the end of the buffer (`comint-copy-old-input`). After executing this command, you can edit the copied shell command and then execute the edited command with [Enter]. Note the difference between [Ctrl] C [Enter] and [Enter] when the point is within an old input command: [Ctrl] C [Enter] merely copies the command; [Enter] copies it and then executes it.

9.23.6
Subshell Control Characters

The following key combinations consist of [Ctrl] C followed by the key that usually produces the desired effect as a control character outside of Emacs.

[Ctrl] C [Ctrl] D

Sends an end-of-file to the shell (`comint-send-eof`).

[Ctrl] C [Ctrl] C

Interrupts the shell or the command that the shell is currently executing (`comint-interrupt-subjob`).

[Ctrl] C [Ctrl] O

Discards any further output from the command that the shell is currently executing, but allows the command to finish executing (`kill-output-from-shell`). This command may not work in some environments.

[Ctrl] C [Ctrl] \

Sends a quit signal to the shell or the command that it is currently executing (`comint-quit-subjob`). This command, unlike the previous one, produces a memory dump (in a file named `core` in the current directory.)

Ctrl C Ctrl Z

> Sends a stop ("suspend") signal to the shell or the command that it is currently executing (`comint-stop-subjob`). It only works if executed under a shell that supports BSD job control (see Section 2.6.3).

**9.23.7
Other Subshell
Operations**

The following commands provide other subshell operations:

Meta X `dirs`

> Asks the shell what the current directory is and resynchronizes Emacs to that directory. This command is useful when Emacs loses track of the current directory.

Meta X `send-invisible`

> Prompts you for some text, then sends that text as input to the shell without displaying it. This command is useful for typing passwords.

Meta X `comint-continue-subjob`

> Resumes the shell process if you've accidentally suspended it.

Meta X `shell-strip-ctrl-m`

> Removes trailing '^M' characters (the ASCII ⟨return⟩ character) from the most recent output group. This command is useful for cleaning up output from programs that end lines with the ⟨return⟩⟨newline⟩ sequence (the convention used under MS-DOS).

9.24   Environmental Inquiries

Emacs has two commands for inquiring about your environment:

Meta X `display-time`

> Causes the time and (on some systems) the system load to be displayed on each mode line.

Meta X `version`
Meta X `emacs-version`

> Displays the current version of Emacs on the echo line.

9.25   Customizing Emacs

In this section we discuss several methods of customizing Emacs: changing key bindings, defining macros and abbreviations, and setting up a `.emacs` initialization file in your home directory.

9.25.1
Key Bindings

In Emacs, a *key sequence* is a sequence of input events (keys pressed on your keyboard or mouse actions) that has a meaning as a unit. A *key binding*—that is, the binding of a key sequence—determines the command that Emacs runs when you press the keys of the sequence or perform its mouse actions. You can redefine the binding for any key sequence either locally or globally, and either interactively or by evaluating an appropriate LISP expression. A local definition applies only to the current mode. If you want a key binding to be in effect whenever you run Emacs, you should place the LISP expression for it in your `.emacs` initialization file (see Section 9.25.5).

Keymaps.   Emacs keeps the information about key bindings in LISP data structures called *keymaps*. There's a global keymap, stored in the variable `global-map`, that defines the default mappings for all the single-character commands. In addition, each major mode has its own local keymap for single-character commands. For the major mode *mode*, the local keymap is stored in the variable *mode*-`mode-map`; thus `text-mode-map` contains the keymap for Text mode. When you rebind a key, either locally or globally, Emacs effects the rebinding by modifying one of these keymaps.

   A keymap can have either of two LISP forms: an array of length 128 that lists the binding for each key, or a list of pairs, each containing an ASCII code and its associated binding. If you know the name of a keymap, you can examine it by typing (Ctrl) H v followed by the name.

Prefix Keys and Their Keymaps.   A *prefix key* is a key sequence that has no meaning by itself as a command but can be followed by other keys to form a command. For example, (Ctrl) X and (Ctrl) X 4 are both prefix keys. Prefix keys also have keymaps. The entry in a keymap for a prefix key is a LISP symbol that denotes another keymap; the second keymap gives the bindings of the keys that can follow the prefix key. These bindings can in turn denote further key maps. For example, the entry in `global-map` for (Ctrl) X 4 is a LISP symbol, `ctl-x-4-map`, that contains the key bindings for keys that can follow (Ctrl) X 4. Note that (Ctrl) X 4 is not a valid key sequence by itself, and couldn't be; you have to type something else after it.[17]

   To create a new prefix key, you need to (a) create a keymap for it, (b) give the keymap a name, and (c) create an entry for it in *its* prefix. The following bit of LISP shows how you would make the sequence (Ctrl) X 9 a prefix key:

```
(defvar ctl-x-9-map (make-keymap) "Keymap for ctl-x 9")
(fset 'ctl-x-9-prefix ctl-x-9-map)
(define-key ctl-x-map "9" 'ctl-x-9-prefix)
```

---

17.   That's because all Emacs commands are required to be self-delimiting—when you've typed the last character of the command, Emacs knows it.

To write this code you have to know the name of the keymap for the prefix key's predecessor, in this case `ctl-x-map`. You can get this information from the Emacs documentation, or (more painfully) from the value of the variable `global-map`.

Binding a Key Sequence Interactively.   The following commands enable you to bind a key sequence to a command either globally or for the current major mode (including all buffers in that mode). If the key sequence consists of more than one key, the prefix part (all keys but the last) must be a valid key prefix.

(Meta) X `global-set-key`
> Globally binds a key sequence to a specified command.

(Meta) X `local-set-key`
> Binds a key sequence to a specified command, but for the current mode only.

For each of these commands, Emacs prompts you for the key sequence to bind and for the command to bind it to.

If you rebind a key sequence that already has a standard binding, remember that the explanations in this book and in the Emacs documentation assume the standard key bindings. However, the Emacs help system is quite clever about this—if you rebind a key sequence, the information displayed by help commands such as '`w`' and '`k`' reflect the new binding (see Section 9.6).

Binding a Key Sequence Noninteractively.   You can bind a key sequence to a command noninteractively by evaluating an appropriate LISP expression. To customize your key bindings for all your Emacs sessions, you include such LISP expressions in your `.emacs` file. For a global binding, the expression is

```
(global-set-key keyseq 'cmd)
```

where *keyseq* is the key sequence in a notation described below and *cmd* is the command to which the key sequence is to be bound. For example, the expression

```
(global-set-key [?\C-z] 'shell)
```

binds the (Ctrl) Z key to the `shell` command.

For a local binding that applies to a particular mode *mode*, the procedure is more complicated (and not well documented). An appropriate entry needs to be made in the keymap belonging to *mode*, but for some modes such as Dired mode, that keymap is created only when Dired mode is first entered. Here the magical expression is

```
(add-hook 'mode-mode-hook (function (lambda ()
    (define-key mode-mode-map keyseq 'cmd)
    ...
)))
```

For example, evaluating the following expression causes the Meta-arrow keys to perform various directory motions in Dired mode:

```
(add-hook 'dired-mode-hook (function (lambda ()
    (define-key dired-mode-map [M-up] 'dired-tree-up)
    (define-key dired-mode-map [M-down] 'dired-tree-down)
    (define-key dired-mode-map [M-right] 'dired-next-subdir)
    (define-key dired-mode-map [M-left] 'dired-prev-subdir)
)))
```

Some modes for special facilities have different hook names. For example, the calendar mode (see Section 10.6) has a hook whose name is `calendar-load-hook` that plays the role of *mode*-mode-hook. The Shell mode (see Section 9.23.2) first performs the actions associated with `comint-mode-hook` (for command interpreters in general) and then those associated with `shell-mode-hook`.

Names of Keys and Key Sequences. The LISP functions for binding a key sequence noninteractively require that you specify the sequence as a LISP constant composed from characters and other key names. If the sequence contains only characters, you can write it either as a string or as a vector; if it contains keys such as function keys that are not characters, you must write it as a vector. A vector has the form '[*key* ...]', where the *key*s are separated by spaces and each key *key* is one of the following:

- An ordinary character *c*, written as '?*c*'.
- The symbol for a key name, written as itself.
- A shifted key symbol, written as 'C-*key*' for a control-shifted key, 'M-*key*' for a meta-shifted key, 'S-*key*' for a case-shifted key, 'S-C-*key*' for a key both case-shifted and control-shifted, and so forth.
- A shifted character, written as '?\C-*c*' for a control-shifted character, and so forth.

For example, '[right]' denotes the key sequence ⟨Right⟩ (the right arrow on most keyboards) and '[?\C-x S-tab]' denotes the key sequence ⟨Ctrl⟩ X ⟨Shift⟩ ⟨Tab⟩. The string '"\C-x4"' denotes the key sequence ⟨Ctrl⟩ X 4.

   To write such LISP constants, you need to know what characters or key symbols are generated when you type a key sequence and what Emacs thinks their names are. For function keys and for keys pressed with various shift combinations, that may not be obvious. One way to find out is to type ⟨Ctrl⟩ H c followed by the key sequence. Emacs shows you both the name of the keys in the key sequence and the binding of the key sequence. Another way is to select a scratch buffer, type ⟨Ctrl⟩ Q followed by the key, and then type ⟨Ctrl⟩ H l (`view-lossage`). That displays the characters most recently received by Emacs and is the best way to see what a function key generates when Emacs is not running under X (usually ⟨escape⟩ followed by several other characters).

Named Control Characters. On older terminals, certain control keys generate control characters from which they are indistinguishable. For

Function Key Name	Control Key Name	Typed Function Key	Control Character Constant
tab	TAB	(Tab)	?\C-i
return	RET	(Enter)	?\C-m
backspace	BS	(Backspace)	?\C-h
linefeed	LFD	(LnFd)	?\C-j
escape	ESC	(Esc)	?\C-[
delete	DEL	(Del)	?\C-?

Fig. 9-1.   Named control characters for Emacs.

example, the (Tab) key generates the ASCII code for (Ctrl) I and is indistinguishable from typing (Ctrl) I. Under X, however, the result of pressing a control key can be distinguished from the result of pressing a control-shifted character key. In this case, 'TAB' and '?\C-i' both denote the (Ctrl) I key while 'tab' denotes the actual (Tab) key. If you define a binding for tab, it is recognized as distinct from the binding for ?\C-i. If you don't, the binding for tab defaults to the binding for ?\C-i. Figure 9-1 shows the named control characters.

Names of Mouse Actions.   Just as you can name key sequences, you can name mouse actions. The symbol mouse-1 stands for clicking the leftmost mouse button, mouse-2 for clicking the next mouse button, and so forth. Other mouse events for the leftmost button are drag-mouse-1 for dragging the mouse while holding down that button, double-mouse-1 for double-clicking that button, triple-mouse-1 for triple-clicking that button, and double-drag-mouse-1 for double-clicking the button and then dragging the mouse. You can also apply various shifts to mouse actions. For example, S-double-mouse-2 corresponds to double-clicking Button 2 while holding down the case-shift key. An example of a mouse binding is

```
(global-set-key [mouse-2] 'split-window-vertically)
```

You can make the effect of a mouse click dependent on where the mouse cursor is when you click the mouse by specifying a special area (mode-line, vertical-line, vertical-scroll-bar, horizontal-scroll-bar) as a dummy prefix key in a key binding. For example, the binding

```
(global-set-key [mode-line mouse-1] 'scroll-up)
```

specifies that if you click Button 1 while the mouse cursor is on the mode line, the command scroll-up will be executed.

9.25.2
Keyboard Macros

A *keyboard macro* is an abbreviation for a sequence of keystrokes. Emacs enables you to define your own keyboard macros. Once you've defined a keyboard macro, you can either use it without naming it or give it a name, making it available even after you've defined other keyboard macros.

Emacs's macro-defining facilities are simple and convenient, but they aren't adequate for defining complex commands. To define a command that isn't expressible as a macro, you'll have to write a LISP program.

Defining Keyboard Macros.   These are the commands for defining keyboard macros:

Ctrl X (Starts defining a keyboard macro (`start-kbd-macro`). If you precede this command with Ctrl U, it re-executes the most recently defined macro and then adds the keys you type to its definition.

Ctrl X)   Ends the definition of a keyboard macro (`end-kbd-macro`).

These are the steps in defining a keyboard macro:

(1)   Type 'Ctrl X (' to start the definition.
(2)   Type the sequence of commands that you want to define as a keyboard macro. These commands are executed as you type them. If you make a mistake, you can correct it as long as the mistake combined with the correction still leaves you with a workable definition.
(3)   Type 'Ctrl X)' to end the definition.

The keyboard macro has now been defined, although it does not have a name. For example, to define a keyboard macro that replaces the current line by the text '`*Deleted*`' no matter where you are within the line, leaving you positioned at the beginning of the next line, type

Ctrl X (Ctrl A Ctrl K Deleted* Ctrl F Ctrl X)

Calling the Most Recently Defined Keyboard Macro.   After you've defined a keyboard macro, you can call it with the following command:

Ctrl X e   Calls the keyboard macro that you've most recently defined (`call-last-kbd-macro`). Calling a keyboard macro causes the commands associated with it to be executed. Preceding the macro call by an argument n causes the macro to be repeated n times.

Only one macro at a time is available to be called by this command, since defining a new macro causes the new one to replace the previous one as the most recently defined macro.

Naming and Saving Keyboard Macros.   In order to save the definition of a keyboard macro, even within a single Emacs session, you must name it using the following command:

Meta X `name-last-kbd-macro`

Assigns a name to the most recently defined keyboard macro. Assigning a name makes the macro available to be called as a command under that name. Emacs prompts you for the name. For example, if you define a keyboard macro as above for deleting and labelling a line, you can call it `label-deleted-line` by typing

---

(Meta) X `name-last-keyboard-macro` (Enter) `label-deleted-line` (Enter)

Command completion works for commands defined by macros just as it does for predefined commands. You can also bind a macro-defined command to a key using the methods described in Section 9.25.1.

To make a macro-defined command available in subsequent sessions, you must save its definition in your initialization file, `.emacs` (see Section 9.25.5). The usual way to do that is to visit the `.emacs` file and execute the following command:

(Meta) X `insert-kbd-macro`

> Inserts some LISP code into the buffer to define a specified keyboard macro. Emacs prompts you for the name of the macro. The code, which starts with '`(fset` ...', is inserted at the point. This command is primarily useful for inserting macro-defining commands in your initialization file.

Note that you must name a macro before you can save it for later sessions.

Executing a Keyboard Macro with Variations. By including the following query command in a macro definition, you can have the macro ask you whether to make a particular change:

(Ctrl) X q

> Inserts a query into the ongoing macro definition (`kbd-macro-query`). If you execute this command with an argument, it behaves differently:
>
> - During definition, it initiates a recursive edit (see Section 9.5.6) that enables you to do editing that does not become part of the definition.
> - During execution, it enters a recursive edit that enables you to make arbitrary changes.
>
> You can get out of these recursive edits with (Meta) (Ctrl) C, the same command you use to get out of a recursive edit during an incremental search-and-replace operation. This command is only meaningful when you're defining or executing a keyboard macro.

When Emacs is executing a macro definition and it encounters a (Ctrl) X q command, it offers you five responses:

(Space) Continues execution.

(Del) Aborts this execution.

(Esc) If the macro call had no argument, aborts this execution as with (Del). If it had an argument, aborts this execution and all remaining executions.

(Ctrl) L Redraws the screen and asks again.

(Ctrl) R Enters a recursive edit that gives you the opportunity to make arbitrary changes. You can abort the edit with (Meta) (Ctrl) C. The effect of executing (Ctrl) U (Ctrl) X q in a macro definition is equivalent to executing Ctrl X q and generating an automatic Ctrl R response.

Typing anything else aborts the execution of the macro.

9.25.3
Abbreviations

An *abbreviation* is a word that expands into some different text when you insert it. For instance, if you define 'phd' as an abbreviation for 'piled higher and deeper', then whenever you type 'phd', Emacs automatically replaces it by 'piled higher and deeper'. Expansion is triggered by typing a word terminator, so if you create an abbreviation by editing existing text, the abbreviation is never expanded (unless you later type a space, period, etc., after it).

The expansion of an abbreviation is capitalized if you capitalize the abbreviation itself when you type it, so typing 'PhD' (or 'Phd') yields 'Piled higher and deeper'. Fully capitalized abbreviations produce fully capitalized expansions. You can turn off the capitalization by setting the variable `abbrev-all-caps` to `nil`.

Emacs expands abbreviations only when the minor mode Abbrev is enabled.

Defining Abbreviations. You can define an abbreviation either globally or for the current major mode. **Note:** A mode abbreviation applies to all buffers having that mode for the rest of your editing session.

When you define an abbreviation, the word before the point becomes the expansion of the abbreviation; Emacs prompts you for the abbreviation itself. You can also define an abbreviation inversely; in this case, the abbreviation is taken from the buffer and Emacs prompts you for the expansion.

The following commands define abbreviations and remove the definitions:

Ctrl X a g Defines a global abbreviation (`add-global-abbrev`). With argument *n*, takes the *n* words preceding the point as the expansion. For example, typing ' Meta 4 Ctrl X agphd' defines 'phd' as an abbreviation for the preceding four words.

Ctrl X a l Defines an abbreviation for the current mode only (`add-mode-abbrev`).

Ctrl X a i g
    Inversely defines a global abbreviation (`inverse-add-global-abbrev`). The abbreviation is taken from the buffer and Emacs prompts you for the expansion. An argument of *n* indicates the *n*th preceding word.

Ctrl X a i l
    Inversely defines an abbreviation for the current mode only (`inverse-add-mode-abbrev`).

Meta X kill-all-abbrevs
    Removes all abbreviations, whether mode-specific or global.

Further Expansion of Abbreviations. The following commands enable you to expand abbreviations even under circumstances when they would not ordinarily be expanded:

[Meta] ‘ Indicates the beginning of a possible abbreviation (`abbrev-prefix-mark`). For instance, if ‘`sgl`’ abbreviates ‘`signal`’ and you type ‘`re` [Meta] ‘ `sgl`’, what you typed turns into ‘`resignal`’. This command provides a convenient way of expanding an abbreviation with an attached prefix.

[Ctrl] X a e Expands the abbreviation, if any, that precedes the point (`expand-abbrev`). This command is effective even if Abbrev mode is off.

[Meta] X `unexpand-abbrev`
Undoes the most recent abbreviation.

[Meta] X `expand-region-abbrevs`
Expands all unexpanded abbreviations in the region. This command is useful when you've typed some text that uses abbreviations but you've forgotten to turn Abbrev mode on.

Editing Abbreviations. You can change or even add abbreviations by editing the list of abbreviations. A typical entry in this list looks like this:

```
    "rtb"    7     "rock the boat"
```

Here ‘`rtb`’ is the abbreviation, ‘`rock the boat`’ is its expansion, and the ‘7’ indicates that the abbreviation has been expanded seven times during the current editing session. These are the commands for editing abbreviations:

[Meta] X `edit-abbrevs`
Creates a buffer listing the current abbreviations. The buffer's name is ‘`*Abbrevs*`’ and its major mode is Edit Abbrevs.

[Meta] X `list-abbrevs`
Creates a buffer listing the current abbreviations as `edit-abbrevs` does, but without making it the current buffer.

[Meta] X `edit-abbrevs-redefine`
Redefines the current set of abbreviations according to the `*Abbrevs*` buffer. In Edit Abbrevs mode, this command is bound to [Ctrl] C [Ctrl] C.

Saving and Restoring Abbreviations. The following commands save the current set of abbreviations in a file and read them back in. The default pathname for each of these commands is `~/.abbrev_defs`.

[Meta] X `write-abbrev-file`
Saves the current set of abbreviations in a file. Emacs prompts you for the pathname of the file.

[Meta] X `read-abbrev-file`
Reads a file containing a set of abbreviation definitions and makes those definitions effective.

(Meta) X `quietly-read-abbrev-file`

> Like the previous command, except that no message is displayed. This command is mainly useful in your initialization file.

The following commands enable you to save and restore abbreviations using a buffer:

(Meta) X `insert-abbrevs`

> Inserts a description of all current abbreviations into the current buffer at the point.

(Meta) X `define-abbrevs`

> Treats all of the current buffer as a set of abbreviation definitions and makes those definitions effective.

Dynamic Abbreviations. Emacs's *dynamic abbreviation* facility enables you to type part of a word you've typed before and have it completed automatically. The following command indicates a dynamic abbreviation:

(Meta) /   Expands the word in the buffer preceding the point as a dynamic abbreviation (`dabbrev-expand`). For instance, if you type the word 'Millard' and later type 'Mil (Meta) /', Emacs replaces what you typed with 'Millard'.

> The search order is backward from the point to the beginning of the buffer and then forward from the point to the end of the buffer. An argument *n* with this command specifies that the *n*th expansion found should be used; a positive value indicates backward search and a negative value indicates forward search.

9.25.4 Customizations for X Operations

There are three ways to customize the appearance of Emacs frames under X: (a) modifying the definition of the various faces used in a frame, (b) setting the value of X resources, and (c) calling Emacs with X toolkit options (see Section 9.1.1). Some aspects of the appearance can be set several ways. You should use X resources or Emacs command-line options to set the default background color. If you try to do that by setting the background color of the default face, portions of a frame that don't contain characters may show up in a different color. (When a character is displayed, the color used for the "ink" is the foreground color and the color used for the surrounding pixels is the background color.) See Section 13.12 for a discussion of X colors and their names, and Section 13.11 for a discussion of X's font-naming conventions.

X Resources for Emacs. You can set a number of properties of Emacs frames by placing appropriate entries in the X resource database (see Section 13.9), ordinarily your `~/.Xdefaults` file. Of those, the most important are the following:

`background`

> The background color.

`foreground`
> The foreground color.

`geometry` The window size and position (see Section 13.10).

`bitmapIcon`
> A flag that, if *on*, represents an iconified window as a bitmapped picture of a gnu.

`font`   The font name for text.

You can also set attributes of particular faces as resources:

face.`attributeFont`
> The font for face *face*.

face.`attributeForeground`
> The foreground color for face *face*.

face.`attributeBackground`
> The background color for face *face*.

face.`attributeUnderline`
> The underline flag for face *face*.

Here is an example of entries in the X resource database for Emacs:[18]

```
Emacs.font:    6x13
Emacs.geometry:   89x68-16+27
Emacs.background: OliveDrab1
Emacs.bitmapIcon: Off
```

Changing Properties of Faces.   An Emacs frame may contain text in several different faces: `default`, `modeline`, `highlight`, and so forth (see Section 9.4.9). You can customize each face by inserting the LISP commands given below into your `.emacs` file (see Section 9.25.5). Each of the commands also has an interactive form, though that form is not as useful. Changes to face definitions are global and affect all frames. There's no way to modify the appearance of a single window within a frame.

The following LISP commands set or modify the font used for a face:

`(set-face-font `*face font*`)`
> Changes face *face* to use font *font*.

`(make-face-bold `*face*`)`
> Converts face *face* to use a bold version of its current font.

`(make-face-italic `*face*`)`
> Converts face *face* to use an italic version of its current font.

`(make-face-bold-italic `*face*`)`
> Converts face *face* to use a bold-italic version of its current font.

`(make-face-unbold `*face*`)`
> Converts face *face* to use a non-bold version of its current font.

---

18. If you use the X toolkit option '`-name` *name*' to call Emacs under another name, you should replace '`Emacs`' in the example by that name.

(make-face-unitalic *face*)
> Converts face *face* to use a non-italic version of its current font.

The following commands set the colors and underline flag of a face:

(set-face-foreground *face color*)
> Sets the foreground color of face *face* to *color*.

(set-face-background *face color*)
> Sets the background color of face *face* to *color*.

(set-face-underline *face color*)
> Specifies that characters in face *face* should be underlined.

(invert-face *face*)
> Swaps the foreground and background colors of face *face*.

For example, the following two lines of LISP set the background color of the region to Thistle and the background color of highlighted text to PaleTurquoise:

```
(set-face-background 'region "thistle")
(set-face-background 'highlight "paleturquoise")
```

Activating Transient Mark Mode.   Operating under X, it's usually desirable to turn on Transient Mark mode. To do that, insert the following line in your .emacs file:

```
(transient-mark-mode 1)
```

Changing the Appearance of One Frame.   You can change the appearance of a single frame by setting the font or colors for that frame. For example, the command '(Meta) X set-foreground-color' sets the foreground color of the current frame to a specified color. Other commands are similar. However, these commands aren't very useful for customization since there's no obvious way to achieve effects such as giving all Dired buffers a different background color.

Special Frame Buffers.   Special frame buffers have the property that when they are created, they are placed in frames of their own rather than in one window of a split frame. Several Emacs variables relate to them:

- The variable special-display-regexps lists a set of regular expressions. If the name of a buffer matches one of those expressions, the buffer is special and gets its own frame. A similar variable, special-display-buffer-names, contains specific buffer names to match.

- The variable special-display-frame-alist specifies frame parameters for special frame buffers.

**9.25.5
The .emacs
Initialization File**

When Emacs is called, it looks for a file named .emacs in your home directory and executes the LISP commands in it. The principal method of customizing Emacs is placing appropriate LISP commands in this file. You can inhibit Emacs from executing .emacs or have it execute someone else's .emacs file with the -q and -u command-line options (see p. 469).

Although any serious discussion of LISP is beyond the scope of this book, we can point out a few of the most common cases of LISP commands in the initialization file:

- To define a key globally, use the `global-set-key` command. For example, the command

    ```
    (global-set-key "\C-x\C-y" 'buffer-menu)
    ```

    globally binds the key combination ' Ctrl X Ctrl Y ' to the `buffer-menu` command.

- To define a key for a particular mode, use the `define-key` command. For example, the command

    ```
    (define-key text-mode-map "\C-xz" 'lpr-region)
    ```

    binds the key combination ' Ctrl X z ' to the `lpr-region` command in Text mode only.

- To set the global variable *var* to the value *val*, use the command

    ```
    (setq-default var val)
    ```

- To use a LISP symbol as a value, prefix it with an apostrophe. Thus the command

    ```
    (setq default-major-mode 'text-mode)
    ```

    causes the default major mode of a newly created buffer to be Text mode. To use a string *str* as a value, enclose it in double quotes.

- To include a macro definition in an initialization file, use the `insert-keyboard-macro` command (see p. 540).

- To include a set of abbreviations, save them to a file and read them with the command

    ```
    (quietly-read-abbrev-file file)
    ```

    where *file* is the file containing the abbreviations (see "Saving and Restoring Abbreviations" on p. 542), written as a string enclosed in double quotes.

- To set a variable *var* to the value *val* in the mode *mode*, use the command

    ```
    (setq mode-hook
          '(lambda () (setq var val)))
    ```

    If you want to set several variables or execute other commands whenever you enter a mode, you must collect them in a sequence following the '`lambda ()`', as a given mode can have only one listing hook.

An easy way to see the LISP form of a command is to execute it and then bring the LISP form to the echo line with the Ctrl X Esc Esc command (see `repeat-complex-command`, p. 481).

Example of an Initialization File. Figure 9-2 contains an example of an initialization file, heavily stripped down. Part of it is designed to work

```
;; Provide for non-unique key combinations starting with
;; ESC by extending 'esc-map'.  These are needed for
;; operations outside of X

(defvar cursor-map-1 (make-keymap)
  "Keymap for cursor commands with ESC-O")
(fset 'Cursor-Map-1 cursor-map-1)
(define-key esc-map "O" 'Cursor-Map-1)

(defvar cursor-map-2 (make-keymap)
  "Keymap for cursor commands with ESC-[")
(fset 'Cursor-Map-2 cursor-map-2)
(define-key esc-map "[" 'Cursor-Map-2)

;; Now define keys whose representations start with ESC.
;; For example, typing Right generates ESC OC on this
;; keyboard.  These definitions don't apply within X.

(define-key esc-map "OC" 'forward-char)          ; Right
(define-key esc-map "OD" 'backward-char)         ; Left
(define-key esc-map "OA" 'previous-line)         ; Up
(define-key esc-map "OB" 'next-line)             ; Down
(define-key esc-map "O\0" 'beginning-of-line)    ; Home
(define-key esc-map "O$" 'end-of-line)           ; End
(define-key esc-map "[5~" 'scroll-down)          ; PgUp
(define-key esc-map "[6~" 'scroll-up)            ; PgDn
(define-key esc-map "[[" 'backward-paragraph)

;; Map 'help' to function key 1, backward delete
;; to backspace, forward delete to DEL.

(define-key esc-map "[11~" 'help-command) ; Function key 1
(define-key esc-map "[20~" 'undo)         ; Function key 9
(define-key esc-map "[21~" 'other-window) ; Function key 10
(global-set-key "\C-h" 'backward-delete-char-untabify)
(global-set-key "\177" 'delete-char)
```

Fig. 9-2, Part 1.   Sample initialization file for Emacs.

---

with a PC keyboard in a particular environment, so you should take it
as an example of method rather than as a piece of code that you can
transcribe and use without modification. You'll need to consult the Emacs
documentation to understand how some of it works.

```
;; The following commands are needed so that changes to the
;; global map to redefine DEL don't get overridden locally.

(define-key lisp-interaction-mode-map "\177" nil)
(define-key emacs-lisp-mode-map "\177" nil)
(define-key c-mode-map "\177" nil)


;; Now reset the backspace to do what DEL used to do

(define-key lisp-interaction-mode-map
   "\C-h" 'backward-delete-char-untabify)
(define-key emacs-lisp-mode-map "\C-h"
   'backward-delete-char-untabify)
(define-key c-mode-map "\C-h"
   'backward-delete-char-untabify)
(setq search-delete-char ?\b)


;; Other useful key bindings

(global-set-key "\eG" 'goto-line)

; Set the tab stops every 3 columns

(setq-default tab-stop-list
   '(3 6 9 12 15 18 21 24 27 30 33 36 39 42 45 48 51 54
      57 60 63 66 69 72 75 78 81))
(setq-default tab-width 3)


;; Calendar settings

(setq calendar-latitude 42.4)
(setq calendar-longitude -72.1)
(setq calendar-location-name "Greenfield, MA")


;; The following keybindings only work under X since
;; otherwise the function keys aren't recognized.

;; Use Meta for the Lisp motion keys

(global-set-key [M-up] 'backward-up-list)
(global-set-key [M-down] 'down-list)
```

Fig. 9-2, Part 2. Sample initialization file for Emacs.

```
(global-set-key [M-left] 'backward-sexp)
(global-set-key [M-right] 'forward-sexp)
(global-set-key [S-M-right] 'forward-list)
(global-set-key [S-M-left] 'backward-list)


;; Dired enhancements

(add-hook 'dired-mode-hook (function (lambda ()
   (define-key dired-mode-map [M-up] 'dired-tree-up)
   (define-key dired-mode-map [M-down] 'dired-tree-down)
   (define-key dired-mode-map [M-right] 'dired-next-subdir)
   (define-key dired-mode-map [M-left] 'dired-prev-subdir)
)))


;; We don't want colorization in listings produced by
;; find-grep-dired or find-name-dired.
(setq find-ls-option "-exec ls -ldo {} \\;")
(setq find-grep-options "-q")

; We don't want to disable narrowing
(put 'narrow-to-region 'disabled nil)


;; Disable automatic loading of TeX mode

(setq auto-mode-alist
   (cons '("\\.tex\\'" . text-mode) auto-mode-alist))


;; These settings set colors, etc. for X

(set-face-background 'region "thistle")
(set-face-background 'highlight "paleturquoise")
(set-face-foreground 'modeline "ivory")
(set-face-background 'modeline "firebrick4")


;; Very important for X: enable Transient Mark Mode

(transient-mark-mode 1)
```

Fig. 9-2, Part 3.   Sample initialization file for Emacs.

10

Emacs Utilities

In this chapter we discuss a number of special-purpose utilities and other facilities provided by Emacs that are not integral to ordinary text editing.

10.1 Directory Operations with Dired

The Emacs directory editor Dired enables you to view directories and entire directory trees in a directory buffer, to select individual files or sets of files, and to perform a variety of operations on each selected file. The available operations include editing, viewing, deleting, copying, renaming, modifying permissions, linking, printing, and compressing. The copying, renaming, and linking operations permit you to specify a substitution, so you can change the names of the targets systematically. You can also execute a shell command on a file or set of files and create a subdirectory of any directory. Dired provides several ways of navigating among the files in the directory, of marking files for later processing, and of hiding or unhiding files within the directory tree.

You can open one or more Dired buffers when you first start Emacs and then carry out nearly all of your file operations from those buffers. For example, selecting files for editing from a Dired buffer is usually more convenient than visiting them explicitly with the Ctrl X Ctrl F command,

and common file operations are easily performed with Dired single-letter commands.

When you start Dired, it asks you to specify the directory you wish to edit according to the usual conventions for specifying file names (see Section 9.15.1). You may provide a file name instead of a directory name; the file name may contain wildcards. Once started, Dired lists the files in that directory or set of files, using the same "long" format as the 'ls -l' command (see Section 3.2.2). You can then operate on one or more listed files, selecting a single file by moving the cursor to the line where it appears or a set of files by marking them.

Several Dired buffers can be active at the same time. Visiting a directory with the Dired f command creates a new Dired buffer for that directory; you cannot, however, switch an existing Dired buffer to a different directory.

A Dired buffer, like any other Emacs buffer, has a point and a mark. The current file, if any, is the file shown on the line where the point is.

Note: If you change the contents of the directory tree in a Dired buffer from outside Emacs, the information in the buffer will not reflect the change. To update the buffer, issue the g, l, or (Meta) X revert-buffer command.

10.1.1
Starting Dired

The following commands start Dired, either in the selected window or in another window:

(Ctrl) X d   Creates a Dired buffer in the selected window (`dired`).

(Ctrl) X 4 d Creates a Dired buffer in the next window (`dired-other-window`).

For each of these commands, Emacs prompts you for the directory name.

In addition, visiting a directory causes Emacs to start up Dired for that directory.

10.1.2
Getting Help

The following command provides help on Dired:

?   Provides a listing of several important Dired commands on the echo line.

h   Shows an extended description of Dired mode in a window, including all the keybindings.

10.1.3
Marks and Flags

You can mark a set of files appearing in a Dired buffer. A mark appears as a single character at the left of the file line. The most common marks are '*' (general marking) and 'D' (deletion), but a mark can be any printable character at all. For historical reasons the 'D' mark is also called a flag. The C (copy) operation marks each file it copies with 'C'. In addition, you can attach a different mark by changing an existing one. An unmarked file is effectively marked with a space. Commands that operate on "marked files" operate only on those lines marked with '*'.

The general marking commands are these:

m	Marks the current file with '*'. If you issue this command when the point is on a subdirectory heading, it marks all the files in that subdirectory.
%m	Marks files satisfying a regular expression with '*'. With a prefix argument, it unmarks them. The command prompts you for the regular expression.
@	Marks all symbolic links with '*'. With a prefix argument, it unmarks them.
/	Marks all directories other than '.' and '..' with '*'. With a prefix argument, it unmarks them.
*	Marks all executable files with '*'. With a prefix argument, it unmarks them.

The following command changes a mark throughout the Dired buffer:

c c_1 c_2	Changes mark c_1 to mark c_2. The command prompts you for c_1 and c_2. By specifying c_1 as '␣', you can mark all unmarked files, and by specifying c_2 as '␣', you can unmark all files with a particular mark.

The following commands remove marks selectively:

u	Removes the mark on this line and moves down one line.
Del	Moves up one line and then removes any mark on the current line.

If you issue either of these commands when the point is on a subdirectory heading, all files in that subdirectory are unmarked. These commands can also be used as motion commands since they don't complain if you attempt to unmark an unmarked line.

The following command removes marks globally:

Meta Del	Removes marks from all files in the buffer. The command prompts you for the mark to be removed (Enter for all marks). With a prefix argument, the command asks you to confirm each removal.

In addition, the commands described in Section 10.1.6 provide for flagging files for deletion.

10.1.4
Moving Around the Listing

The following commands move you to the next or previous line in the listing:

Space	
Ctrl N	
n	Moves to the beginning of the file name on the next line if there is one; otherwise, to the beginning of the line.
Ctrl P	
p	Moves to the beginning of the file name on the previous line, if there is one; otherwise, to the beginning of the line.

The following commands move you to the next or previous marked file:

(Meta) }   Moves to the next marked file, wrapping around if necessary.

(Meta) {   Moves to the previous marked file, wrapping around if necessary.

The following commands move you to a subdirectory that you have inserted into the Dired listing with the i command:

(Ctrl) X]
(Meta) (Ctrl) N

> Goes to the next subdirectory in the directory tree.[1]

(Ctrl) X [
(Meta) (Ctrl) P

> Goes to the previous subdirectory in the directory tree.

(Meta) (Ctrl) D

> Goes down in the directory tree to the first subdirectory of the current directory.

(Meta) (Ctrl) U

> Goes up in the directory tree to the parent directory of the current directory. With an argument n, it goes up n levels.

The following commands move you to lines containing filenames that name directories (unlike the commands in the previous group, which move you to directory header lines):

>   Goes to the next filename that names a directory.

<   Goes to the previous filename that names a directory.

You can also use any of the usual commands for buffer navigation, including search commands.

**10.1.5
Visiting and
Viewing Files**

The following commands enable you to visit a file for editing or to view a file:

f   Visits this file. If you visit a directory, Emacs creates another Dired buffer for it. For instance, if you visit the '..' file, Emacs creates a Dired buffer for the parent directory of the one you're now examining.

(Mouse-2)
o   Visits this file in another window and moves the cursor to that window.

(Ctrl) O   Like o, but doesn't move the cursor.

v   Views this file using the view-file command (see p. 511).

---

1. The (Ctrl) X] command is really a "next page" command, but it has nearly the same effect. The (Ctrl) X [command behaves analogously.

**10.1.6
Deleting Files**

You can delete a file directly with the D command:

D   Deletes the current file, querying you first. With an argument n, it deletes the files on the next n lines.

Alternately, you can use the following commands to flag files for deletion. Each flagged file is marked with a 'D'.

d   Flags this file for deletion.

%d   Flags files satisfying a regular expression for deletion. With a prefix argument, it unflags them. The command prompts you for the regular expression.

\#   Flags all auto-save files for deletion. An autosave file has a name that starts and ends with '#' (see "Auto-Saving" on p. 513).

~   Flags all backup files for deletion. A backup file has a name that ends with '~' (see "Backup Files" on p. 512).

.   Flags excess numbered backup files (see "Backup Files" on p. 512) for deletion. The excess files are those that are neither oldest nor newest.

The following command does the actual deletion:

x   Asks for comfirmation, then deletes all flagged files.

**10.1.7
Other Operations
on Files**

The commands in this subsection provide other operations on files. If any files are marked with '*' (other marks don't matter), the command operates on those files; otherwise, it operates on the current file or on the next n files if a prefix argument n is given.

Simple Operations. The following commands provide copying, renaming, and similar operations:

C   Copies a single file to another file or copies a set of files to a directory. Emacs prompts you for the destination file or directory.

R   Moves (renames) a single file to another file or moves a set of files to a directory.

H   Constructs a hard link from one or more files.

S   Constructs a symbolic link from one or more files.

P   Prints one or more files.

X

!   Runs a shell command on one or more files. Emacs prompts you for the command to be executed. Standard output from the command is shown on the echo line if it occupies just one line; otherwise, it appears in a buffer entitled '`*Shell Command Output*`'.

- If the command string *cmd* doesn't contain a '`*`', Emacs runs the command '*cmd fn*' for each selected filename *fn*.
- If *cmd* does contain a '`*`', a list of the selected filenames (separated by spaces) is substituted for the '`*`'. For example,

> `! cat * > amalgam` (Enter)

concatenates all the selected files into a single file named `amalgam`.

Note: The working directory for the shell command is the top-level directory of the Dired buffer.

Z   Compresses or uncompresses one or more files using `gzip` if it's available, otherwise `compress`.

Operations That Transform Filenames.   The following commands provide operations on files that transform a source filename to a target filename. Each command prompts you for a "from" regular expression and a "to" regular expression. The selected filenames are transformed just as they are by the `query-replace-regexp` command (see p. 526).

%C   Copies one or more files, transforming each source filename to a target filename through regular expression substitution.

%R   Renames one or more files, transforming each source filename to a target filename through regular expression substitution.

%H   Creates a hard link from one or more files, transforming each source filename to a target filename through regular expression substitution.

%S   Creates a symbolic link from one or more files, transforming each source filename to a target filename through regular expression substitution.

Modifying Permissions and Ownership.   The following commands provide operations that relate to file permissions and ownership:

M   Modifies the file permissions of one or more files. You specify the modification using the usual notation for permissions (see Section 2.8) as used by the `chmod` program.

O   Changes the owner of one or more files.

G   Changes the group of one or more files.

Comparing Files.   The following commands compare a single file:

=   Compares this file with file at the mark, producing a `diff` listing (see Section 3.10.2). With a prefix argument, it prompts you for `diff` switches.

(Meta)=   Like '`=`', but compares this file with its latest backup.

Changing the Case of Filenames.   The following commands change the case of filenames:

%l   Changes the name of one or more files to lowercase.

%u   Changes the name of one or more files to uppercase.

Loading Lisp Code.   The following commands compile or load files of Lisp code:

B   Byte-compiles one or more files.

L   Loads this Emacs Lisp file.

**10.1.8
Directory
Operations**

The following command creates a subdirectory of the current directory (the one with the nearest preceding directory header line):

+   Creates a subdirectory.

The following commands cause new directories to be displayed if they aren't displayed already:

i   If the current file is a directory, this command inserts its contents into the Dired buffer as a subdirectory if that subdirectory isn't already in the buffer. The command then moves the cursor to the header line of that subdirectory.

^   Moves to the parent directory of the directory containing the point. If that parent directory isn't in the current Dired buffer, Dired creates a new Dired buffer and moves to it.

See also the commands in Section 10.1.4 that provide directory-oriented motions.

**10.1.9
Modifying the
Display**

The following commands update either the entire display or the display of the current subdirectory:

g   Updates the entire contents of the Dired buffer.   The (Meta) X revert-buffer command is an alternative to this command.

l   Updates the file containing the point—or if any files are marked, the marked files. If the point is on a subdirectory header, the entire subdirectory is updated.

The following command undoes a change to the display:

(Ctrl) X u   Undoes the most recent Dired change. This command does *not* have any effect on the files themselves. Its purpose is to recover marks, killed lines, or subdirectories.

The following commands hide or reveal subdirectories:

$ Hides or reveals the subdirectory where the point is.

(Meta) $ Hides or reveals all subdirectories.

The following commands produce other effects on the display:

s   Toggles the sort order between alphabetical order and chronological order. With a prefix, this command regenerates the display by prompting you for a set of ls switches (see Section 3.2), calling `ls` with those switches, and using the `ls` output as the Dired display.

k   Deletes all file lines marked with '`*`' (but not the files them-
         selves).

q   Buries this Dired buffer by switching to the next buffer, but
         doesn't kill this Dired buffer.

10.1.10
Finding Files

You can search for files using several types of criteria and create a Dired buffer containing the files you find. The following search commands, which do *not* use or affect the current buffer, use various forms of `find`:[2]

`find-name-dired`
         Searches for files in a directory tree whose names match a
         particular pattern, given by a shell wildcard expression (not
         a regular expression). A Dired buffer is created that contains
         those files.

`find-grep-dired`
         Searches for files in a directory tree that contain text matching
         a specified regular expression. A Dired buffer is created that
         contains those files.

`find-dired`
         Calls `find` (see Section 3.8) on a directory and creates a Dired
         buffer containing the files whose pathnames are produced as
         `find`'s output. You can specify any valid `find` criterion; that is,
         any combination of tests that `find` would recognize.

10.2   Composing and Editing Pictures

Emacs has a special major mode, Picture mode, for editing pictures made out of text characters. In Picture mode, the buffer is treated as an area with its upper left corner at the beginning of the document, extending indefinitely to the right and downward. Lines are extended by adding spaces at the right end whenever they are needed. In Picture mode, you cannot tell where the right end of a line is; you only know where its rightmost nonblank character is.

To fit this model, Picture mode rebinds a number of keys to commands appropriate to the mode. For instance, Ctrl F always moves one position to the right—if you move past the actual end of the line, Emacs assumes

---

2. These commands may not work correctly if you're using a fancy version of `ls`, such as the one provided with Linux, that produces "colorized" directory listings. To cure the problem, set the variable `find-ls-option` as shown in Figure 9-2.

that the positions you pass over contain spaces. In contrast, in an ordinary mode (Ctrl) F moves to the beginning of the next line when you reach the end of a line. In Picture mode, tab characters within the text are treated as though they were expanded to spaces.

Picture mode is designed so that you can edit a picture as part of a larger document, leaving the rest of the document undisturbed. You can restrict the effects of Picture mode, however, by using the (Ctrl) X n command to narrow the document to the region of interest (see Section 9.16.6).

10.2.1 Entering and Leaving Picture Mode

The following commands enable you to enter and leave Picture mode:

(Meta) X edit-picture
> Enters Picture mode, remembering the mode that you were previously in.

(Ctrl) C (Ctrl) C
> Leaves Picture mode, restoring the major mode previously in effect (`picture-mode-exit`). This command also strips trailing spaces from the end of each line, even if the spaces were there before you entered Picture mode.

10.2.2 Moving Around a Picture

The following commands have very similar effects to the corresponding commands in non-Picture modes. Whenever a horizontal motion command encounters a tab character, it converts the tab to a sequence of spaces.

(Ctrl) F
> Moves one column to the right (`picture-forward-column`). This command never moves to a new line.

(Ctrl) B
> Moves one column to the left (`picture-backward-column`). If the left end of the line is reached, the point moves to the end of the previous line.

(Ctrl) N
> Moves down one line (`picture-move-down`). This command preserves the columnar position no matter what the actual length of the line that it moves to.

(Ctrl) P
> Moves up one line (`picture-move-up`). This command preserves the columnar position no matter what the actual length of the line that it moves to.

(Enter)
> Moves to the beginning of the next line (`picture-newline`).

10.2.3 Inserting New Lines

The following commands insert new lines into the picture.

(Ctrl) J
(LnFd)
> Makes a copy of the current line underneath the current line and moves down to the same columnar position on that line (`picture-duplicate-line`).[3] This command is not affected by arguments.

---

3. Or at least it's supposed to.

<kbd>Ctrl</kbd> O Inserts an empty line immediately below the current line (`picture-open-line`).

10.2.4
Erasing Parts of a Picture

<kbd>Del</kbd> Replaces the preceding character with a space (`picture-backward-clear-column`). The point moves left by one position.

<kbd>Ctrl</kbd> D Replaces the character under the cursor with a space (`picture-clear-column`). Unlike the previous command, *the point does not move*. With an argument of n, this command clears out n characters—but the point still remains in the same place.

<kbd>Ctrl</kbd> K Erases the portion of the current line to the right of the point (`picture-clear-line`). Unlike the usual `clear-line` command, this one never erases newlines.

<kbd>Ctrl</kbd> C <kbd>Ctrl</kbd> D
Deletes the character under the cursor (`delete-char`). This command has the same meaning as usual; it's just bound to a different key sequence.

In addition to these commands, the <kbd>Ctrl</kbd> W (`delete-region`) command works as usual.

10.2.5
Linear Motions

The following commands set the direction of motion after an insertion. For instance, if you type '<kbd>Ctrl</kbd> C ***', you produce a sequence of stars moving diagonally down and right. Note that motion to the right or down is unbounded.

<kbd>Ctrl</kbd> C < Moves left after each insertion (`picture-movement-left`).

<kbd>Ctrl</kbd> C > Moves right after each insertion (`picture-movement-right`).

<kbd>Ctrl</kbd> C ∧ Moves up after each insertion (`picture-movement-up`).

<kbd>Ctrl</kbd> C . Moves down after each insertion (`picture-movement-down`).

<kbd>Ctrl</kbd> C ' Moves up and to the right after each insertion (`picture-movement-ne`).

<kbd>Ctrl</kbd> C `  Moves up and to the left after each insertion (`picture-movement-nw`).

<kbd>Ctrl</kbd> C \ Moves down and to the right after each insertion (`picture-movement-se`).

<kbd>Ctrl</kbd> C / Moves down and to the left after each insertion (`picture-movement-sw`).

The following commands move in the current direction of motion without changing anything. They provide a convenient way of moving along a line drawn with the commands above.

<kbd>Ctrl</kbd> C <kbd>Ctrl</kbd> F
Moves by one unit along the direction of motion (`picture-motion`).

Ctrl C Ctrl B

> Moves by one unit backwards along the direction of motion (`picture-motion-reverse`).

10.2.6
Tab-Based
Operations

In Picture mode, Emacs recognizes a context-based form of tabbing in which tab stops are assumed at each position occupied by an "interesting" character. By default the interesting characters are the nonblank printing characters, but you can change this set by assigning a character string containing the desired characters to the variable `picture-tab-chars` (see Section 9.21.1). You must be in Picture mode when you make the assignment.

These are the tab-based operations:

Tab

> Moves to the next tab stop (`picture-tab`). With an argument, blanks out the text that it moves over. The value of the argument is irrelevant. Initially the tab stops are at the positions that they had when you entered Picture mode, but you can reset them with the Ctrl C Tab command below.

Ctrl C Tab

> Sets a tab stop at each position occupied by an "interesting" character on the current line (`picture-set-tab-stops`). These tab stops remain in effect even when you move to a different line.

Meta Tab

> Moves to the position underneath the next "interesting" character that follows whitespace in the previous nonblank line (`picture-tab-search`). With an argument, moves to the next "interesting" character in the current line. The value of the argument is irrelevant. This command never modifies the buffer.

10.2.7
Rectangle-Based
Operations

The following commands that operate on rectangles are analogous to their non-rectangle counterparts, which are also available and sometimes useful (see Section 9.12):

Ctrl C Ctrl K

> Kills and clears the rectangle defined by the region, leaving the rest of the picture undisturbed (`picture-clear-rectangle`). With an argument, deletes the rectangle and moves the material to its right leftward.

Ctrl C Ctrl W *r*

> Clears the rectangle defined by the region as in the previous command, but saves its contents in register *r* (`picture-clear-rectangle-to-register`).

Ctrl C Ctrl Y

> Copies the last killed rectangle into the picture, aligning its upper left corner with the point and overwriting whatever was previously in the picture (`picture-yank-rectangle`). With an

argument, moves the material previously in the area occupied by the rectangle to the right so that it isn't lost.

(Ctrl) C (Ctrl) X *r*
> Copies the rectangle from register *r* as in the previous command (`picture-yank-rectangle-from-register`).

10.3   Tags and Tag Tables

A *tag table* is a file that describes and locates definitions of textual units within a set of files. The nature of the definitions depends on what is in the files. For example, for C or LISP programs, the definitions include C or LISP functions; for LATEX text, they are LATEX commands such as \section or \cite. Emacs has at most one tag table selected at a time. All the tag table commands work with the selected tag table.

You can create an Emacs tag table with the UNIX command

>   `etags` *file* ...

where *file* ... is a list of files to be analyzed. This command creates a file named `TAGS` in the current directory that contains the tag table.

Note: Tag tables produced by Emacs do not have the same form as those produced by `ctags` (see Section 8.5) even though they serve the same purpose. Emacs cannot handle `ctags` tag tables; the `vi` editor, which understands `ctags` tag tables, cannot handle Emacs tag tables.

10.3.1
Selecting a Tag Table

The following command selects a tag table you created with `etags`:

(Meta) X `visit-tags-table`
> Adds a specified file to the list of selected tag tables. Emacs prompts you for the pathname of the tags file to be added. When you search for a tag, all files in the list are searched.

10.3.2
Finding a Definition

Once a tag table has been selected, you can use the following commands to find any definition named in that table. You can specify a tag by giving just the beginning of its name. If the first tag you find isn't the one you want, you can look for another one.

(Meta) .
> Locates the nearest definition matched by the specified tag, then visits the file containing that definition and positions the point at the definition (`find-tag`). Emacs prompts you for the tag to match. With an argument of (Ctrl) U, this command searches for another match to the specified tag. With an argument of (Ctrl) U -, it goes back to places you've recently found matching tags.

(Meta) (Ctrl) .
> Like (Meta) ., but searches for a regular expression rather than a fixed string.

⌈Ctrl⌉ X 4.   Locates the definition named by the specified tag as with
⌈Meta⌉ ., but visits the file in another window (find-tag-
other-window).

10.3.3
Regular Expression
Search and Replace

The following commands enable you to search for a regular expression
(see "Regular Expressions in Emacs" on p. 524) in the files listed in the
selected tag table. You can replace the regular expression once you've
found it. For these commands, only the files matter; they pay no attention
to the tags themselves.

⌈Meta⌉ X tags-search
Searches for a regular expression within the files listed in the
tag table. Emacs prompts you for the regular expression.

⌈Meta⌉ X tags-query-replace
Performs a query-replace on each file listed in the tags
table. Emacs prompts you for the search expression and the
replacement.

⌈Meta⌉ ,   Restarts one of the commands above, beginning the search at
the point (tags-loop-continue). You can use this command
to continue a search without having to respecify the regular
expression.

10.3.4
Visiting Files
Containing
Definitions

You can advance through the files explicitly with the following command:

⌈Meta⌉ X next-file
Given an argument, this command visits the first file listed
in the selected tag table. Without an argument, it visits the
next file.

10.3.5
Information
About Tags

The following commands provide information about the tags in the
selected tag table:

⌈Meta⌉ X list-tags
Lists all the tags in one of the files named in the selected tag
table. Emacs prompts you for the file name.

⌈Meta⌉ X tags-apropos
Lists all the tags in the selected tag table that match a specified regular expression. Emacs prompts you for the regular
expression.

10.4   The Emacs Mailer

Emacs has a rich set of commands for handling mail. Rmail is the Emacs
subsystem for reading mail. Emacs doesn't have a name for the group of

commands that handle outgoing mail, so we call them "Smail". See Chapter 11 for a discussion of mail in general and the relevant terminology.

Emacs uses its own format, called "Rmail format", for mail files. Although Rmail format is incompatible with the standard UNIX format for mail files, Emacs provides commands for converting between Rmail format and UNIX format.

10.4.1 Sending Mail with Smail

These are the Smail commands for composing an outgoing mail message:

Ctrl X m   Prepares to accept a mail message in the current window (`mail`). If you provide an argument to this command and a `*mail*` buffer already exists, Smail selects that buffer.

Ctrl X 4m   Prepares to accept a mail message in the next window (`mail-other-window`). If you provide an argument to this command and a `*mail*` buffer already exists, Smail selects that buffer.

These commands create a `*mail*` buffer for your message if one doesn't already exist, fill it with a skeletal message, and put you into Mail mode (an internal mode), ready to compose the message. If you use one of these commands without an argument and a `*mail*` buffer does already exist, Smail gives you the option of discarding it or returning to it.

After composing a message, you can send it with the Ctrl C Ctrl S or the Ctrl C Ctrl C command. These commands are described below. If you edit a message and then decide not to send it, you can kill or simply abandon the mail buffer.

Form of a Mail Message.   An outgoing mail message has the following form:

> *headers*
> `--text follows this line--`
> *message text*

You can edit a message freely before you send it, but if you attempt to send a message that doesn't contain the 'text follows this line' line exactly, Smail complains about an unsuccessful search and proceeds no further.

Smail knows about the following header fields:

To	The recipients of the message.
Subject	The subject of the message.
CC	Additional "carbon copy" recipients to whom the message is not primarily addressed.[4]
BCC	Additional "blind carbon copy" recipients who should receive the message but who should not be listed in the header.
FCC	The name of a file (in UNIX mail format) to which the message should be appended after it has been sent.

---

4. According to bureaucratic tradition, however, it matters less to whom you send a memo than to whom you send the carbon copies.

From   Your own mailing address, if you're sending the message from
             someone else's account.

Reply-To The sender of the message, if the automatically generated
             return address for the message is not usable as a reply address.
             From and Reply-To differ only in what they mean to a person
             reading the message.

In-Reply-To

             Text describing a message you're replying to. Normally Rmail
             fills in this field automatically when you're replying to mail.

The following rules apply to the header fields:

- The name of each field ends with a colon and is followed by optional
  whitespace and the contents of the field.

- Field names are case-insensitive.

- Recipient names in fields are separated by commas. The commas
  can be preceded or followed by whitespace.

- A field can be continued on additional lines. The continuation lines
  must start with whitespace.

- If recipients are listed in two fields of the same type, the lists are
  combined.

- There must be at least one To field.

- If you have a .mailrc initialization file for mailx in your home
  directory (see Section 11.5.7), any aliases contained in it are used
  when the names of recipients are interpreted.

You can also include other header fields that Smail doesn't know about.
Smail passes them to the mail transport agent unmodified.

Commands for Mail Mode. The following commands are available in
Mail mode (the mode you're in when Smail is active):

Ctrl C Ctrl S

             Sends the message in the buffer but leaves the buffer selected
             (mail-send).

Ctrl C Ctrl C

             Sends the message in the buffer and reverts to the previously
             selected buffer in this window (mail-send-and-exit).

Ctrl C Ctrl F Ctrl T

             Moves to the first To field, creating one if it doesn't exist
             (mail-to).

Ctrl C Ctrl F Ctrl S

             Moves to the first Subject field, creating one if it doesn't
             exist (mail-subject).

Ctrl C Ctrl F Ctrl C

             Moves to the first CC field, creating one if it doesn't exist
             (mail-cc).

<kbd>Ctrl</kbd> C <kbd>Ctrl</kbd> W

> Inserts the file `.signature` from your home directory at the end of the message text (`mail-signature`).

<kbd>Ctrl</kbd> C <kbd>Ctrl</kbd> Y

> When sending mail as a result of the Rmail commands for composing responses (see "Creating Responses to Messages" on p. 568), inserts the original message into the outgoing message at the point (`mail-yank-original`). The original message is the one that was current in Rmail. Most header fields are deleted.
>
> - With no argument, the command indents the inserted message by four spaces.
>
> - With an argument of n, it indents by n spaces.
>
> - With an argument of <kbd>Ctrl</kbd> U alone, it doesn't indent at all and doesn't remove any of the header fields from the original.

<kbd>Ctrl</kbd> C <kbd>Ctrl</kbd> Q

> Fills all the paragraphs of the inserted message (`mail-fill-yanked-message`).

10.4.2
Receiving Mail
with Rmail

Rmail is the Emacs subsystem for reading and processing mail. The following command starts Rmail:

<kbd>Meta</kbd> X rmail

> Create or select a buffer for reading mail and enter Rmail mode, an internal mode. The name of the buffer is 'RMAIL'.

When you start up Rmail, it reads any new mail that has arrived in your primary mailbox (see Section 11.3), appends it to the mail that you've already received, and positions you at the first new message. You can operate on the messages either directly or via a message summary (see Section 10.4.3). As you process your mail, you can mark messages for deletion. Deleted messages remain in the buffer until you expunge them or until you quit Rmail—but if you merely save the buffer with the <kbd>Ctrl</kbd> X <kbd>Ctrl</kbd> S (`save-buffer`) command, the deleted messages are saved along with the others.

Rmail Files. Rmail keeps your mail in mailboxes called "Rmail files". Your secondary mailbox—the one that Rmail uses by default—is the file `RMAIL` in your home directory.[5] You can also store mail in other auxiliary mailboxes. Rmail uses its own format for these mailboxes, different from the UNIX mailbox format. Within an Rmail file, messages are arranged in order of receipt, oldest first.

---

5. The Emacs manual calls this file your "primary mail file", a usage that conflicts with the terminology we use elsewhere in this book.

When you call Rmail, it automatically saves newly arrived messages in your secondary mailbox. Furthermore, if you're exiting from Emacs and you've abandoned an Rmail buffer, Emacs asks you if you want to save it. You can check for new mail while you're within Rmail with the 'g' command (see p. 569).

Arguments to Rmail Commands.   When you're in Rmail, the buffer is normally in a read-only state in which ordinary characters that you type are not inserted into the text. Therefore you don't need to "meta"-ize an argument to a command when you type it. For example, you can supply the argument '3' to the 'j' command by typing '3j' (although '(Meta)3 j' still works). If you explicitly make the buffer modifiable with the 'w' command, however, the meta shift is necessary (see "Editing Received Messages" on p. 568).

Exiting from Rmail or Saving the Buffer.   The following commands enable you to exit from Rmail or save the Rmail buffer without exiting. Executing either of them expunges deleted messages.

q   Saves the Rmail buffer in the secondary mailbox, then exits from Rmail (`rmail-quit`).

s   Saves the Rmail buffer in the secondary mailbox (`rmail-expunge-and-save`). Use the (Ctrl)X (Ctrl)S (`save-buffer`) command to save the buffer without expunging deleted messages.

Burying the Rmail Buffers.   The following command buries (hides) the Rmail buffers:

b   Buries the Rmail buffers, eliminating them from the screen but not killing them (`rmail-bury`).

Creating a Message Summary.   The following commands create either a complete or a selective summary of the messages in the buffer. The summary appears in another window and has its own set of key bindings defined for it (see Section 10.4.3).

h
(Meta)(Ctrl)H
             Makes a summary of all messages (`rmail-summary`).

l
(Meta)(Ctrl)L *labels*
             Makes a summary of the messages with a label from the set of labels *labels* (`rmail-summary-by-labels`).

(Meta)(Ctrl)R *names*
             Makes a summary of all messages with a recipient in *names* (`rmail-summary-by-recipients`). The recipient's name can appear in any header field, so you can use this command to select messages by author—although you'll also get those sent to you by other people with copies to that author.

[Meta] [Ctrl] T *topic*
> Makes a summary of all messages with topic *topic*, where *topic* is given by a regular expression (`rmail-summary-by-topic`).

Selecting a Message to Read.   The message that you're reading at any moment is the *current message*. The following commands enable you to select a particular message as the current message:

n
> Selects the next nondeleted message (`rmail-next-undeleted-message`).

p
> Selects the preceding nondeleted message (`rmail-previous-undeleted-message`).

[Meta] N
> Selects the next message whether or not it has been deleted (`rmail-next-message`).

[Meta] P
> Selects the preceding message whether or not it has been deleted (`rmail-previous-message`).

j
> Selects the first message (`rmail-show-message`). With an argument *n*, selects the *n*th message (whether deleted or not).

<
> Selects the first message (`rmail-first-message`).

>
> Selects the last message (`rmail-last-message`).

[Meta] S
> Selects the next message matching a specified regular expression (`rmail-search`). Preceded by '-', this command moves to the preceding message matching a specified regular expression. Emacs prompts you for the regular expression.

Scrolling Within a Message.   The following commands enable you to scroll through the current message:

[Space]
> Scrolls the current message forward (`scroll-up`).

[Del]
> Scrolls the current message backward (`scroll-down`).

.
> Scrolls to the beginning of the current message (`rmail-beginning-of-message`).

Deleting and Undeleting Messages.   The following commands enable you to delete or undelete a specified message.

d
> Deletes the current message (`rmail-delete-forward`).

[Ctrl] D
> Deletes the current message and moves to the nearest preceding undeleted message (`rmail-delete-backward`).

u
> If the current message was deleted, undeletes it; if not, undeletes the nearest preceding deleted message (`rmail-undelete-previous-message`).

x
> Expunges the Rmail buffer by removing all deleted messages (`rmail-expunge`). Unlike 's', this command does not save the buffer; if you kill the buffer without saving it, the expunged messages remain in the mailbox.

Creating Responses to Messages. After reading a message, you may wish to respond to it by replying to the person who sent it, by sending a message to someone else, or by forwarding the message to some other recipients. The following commands provide these facilities, calling Smail for you so that you can create the response. Within Smail, you can use the (Ctrl) C (Ctrl) Y (`mail-yank-original`) command (see p. 565) to copy the original message into the one you're composing.

r   Prepares for a reply to the current message (`rmail-reply`) by activating Smail in another buffer and filling in the header fields of the reply message, using the information in the header of the message you're replying to.

m   Starts editing a new message (not a reply) with Smail in another buffer (`rmail-mail`). The difference between using this command and using (Ctrl) X 4m is that if you use this command, you can insert the current (received) message with (Ctrl) C (Ctrl) Y.

c   Resumes editing an outgoing message (`rmail-continue`). This command is useful when you were creating a reply but switched back to Rmail to look at, and possibly copy, another message. You need this command to create a reply that incorporates two different messages from your Rmail buffer.

f   Forwards the current message to other recipients (`rmail-forward`). This command activates Smail in another buffer and initializes that buffer with the text of the current message and appropriate header information. You can then fill in the new recipients and send the message.

Editing Received Messages. Normally the Rmail buffer is read-only and cannot be modified. The following two commands enable you to modify it:

t   Toggles the full header display (`rmail-toggle-header`). Normally this toggle is off, and header fields that Rmail presumes to be uninteresting are not shown. With this toggle on, all fields are shown.

e   Enables you to edit the current message (`rmail-edit-current-message`). Executing this command disables all the other Rmail commands, since ordinary characters now become self-inserting. The following key combinations have special meaning in this mode, called Rmail Edit mode:

         (Ctrl) C (Ctrl) C
             Returns to Rmail, making the buffer read-only again and re-enabling the usual key bindings.

         (Ctrl) C (Ctrl)]
             Like (Ctrl) C (Ctrl) C, except that the editing changes you made are discarded.

Some messages have the form of a message digest (a sequence of messages collected into a single message). The following command decomposes a message digest:

[Meta] X undigestify-rmail-message

> If the current message is a message digest, separates it into its component messages.

Reading Mail from Other Mailboxes.   You can use Rmail to read and process mail in auxiliary mailboxes as well as in your primary mailbox. The mail in these mailboxes can be in UNIX mail format. The following commands enable you to read mail from other mail files:

i *file*   Runs Rmail on the messages in *file*, treating it as an auxiliary mailbox (rmail-input). When you exit from Rmail with 'q' or a similar command, the current buffer is saved to *file*. Other mailboxes are unaffected by anything you do to the mailbox in *file*.

[Meta] X set-rmail-inbox-list

> Specifies a list of input mailboxes for the current Rmail file. The file names in this list should be separated by commas. If the list is empty, this Rmail file will have no input mailboxes. The list is stored in the Rmail file when you save it; when you next process the Rmail file, these input mailboxes will be checked for new mail.

g   Checks the input mailboxes of the current Rmail file for new mail and appends it to the mail in the buffer (rmail-get-new-mail). This command works both for secondary mailboxes and for auxiliary mailboxes.

Copying Messages to Other Mailboxes.   The following commands enable you to copy a message from the current Rmail buffer to a specified file:

o *file*   Appends a copy of the current message in Rmail format to *file* (rmail-output-to-rmail-file).

[Ctrl] O *file*   Appends a copy of the current message in UNIX format to *file* (rmail-output).

Labelling Messages.   A message can have a set of labels attached to it. You can make up your own labels and attach or remove them. In addition, Rmail attaches and removes certain predefined labels, called *attributes*, automatically. Attributes are not displayed either as part of the message or as part of the message summary, but user-defined labels do appear in the message summary. These are the Rmail attributes:

unseen   This message has never been current.
deleted   This message has been deleted (indicated by the 'D' flag).
filed   This message has been copied to a file.
answered This message has been answered using the r command.
forwarded
          This message has been forwarded to other recipients.

`edited`   This message has been edited.

These are the commands for attaching and removing labels:

a *label*   Assigns the label *label* to the current message (`rmail-add-label`).

k *label*   Removes the label *label* from the current message (`rmail-kill-label`).

These are the commands for selecting labelled messages:

(Meta) (Ctrl) N *labels*
          Moves to the next message with a label from the set of labels *labels* (`rmail-next-labeled-message`).

(Meta) (Ctrl) P *labels*
          Moves to the preceding message with a label from the set of labels *labels* (`rmail-previous-labeled-message`).

For each of these commands, the labels are separated by commas. You can also use the l (`rmail-summary-by-labels`) command to locate those messages that have a particular label. Message selection commands can be used with attributes as well as with user-defined labels.

10.4.3
Rmail Summary
Commands

You can operate on a message either by working with the message itself or by working with the header summary. The following key bindings are available when you select the buffer containing the header summary. When you select a message using the header summary, the Rmail buffer is selected and the message you've chosen is displayed in that buffer.

j   Selects the current message (`rmail-summary-goto-msg`).

(Meta) N   Moves to the next line and selects its message (`rmail-summary-next-all`).

(Meta) P   Moves to the preceding line and selects its message (`rmail-summary-previous-all`).

n   Moves to the next line containing a nondeleted message and selects its message (`rmail-summary-next-msg`).

p   Moves to the preceding line containing a nondeleted message and selects its message (`rmail-summary-previous-msg`).

d   Deletes the current message, then moves to the next line containing a nondeleted message (`rmail-summary-delete-forward`).

u   Undeletes and selects this message or the nearest preceding deleted message (`rmail-summary-undelete`).

(Space)   Scrolls the message window forward (down) (`rmail-summary-scroll-msg-up`).

(Del)   Scrolls the message window backward (up) (`rmail-summary-scroll-msg-down`).

x   Removes the summary from its window (`rmail-summary-`
            `expunge`). The Rmail buffer is reselected.

q   Exits from Rmail (`rmail-summary-quit`). The Rmail buffer is
            saved and both the summary window and the Rmail window
            are killed. (The buffers themselves still remain.)

10.5   The GNUS Newsreader

GNUS is an Emacs subsystem for browsing network newsgroups, reading
articles of interest, creating summaries of articles in particular groups,
and submitting your own items to newsgroups. You start GNUS by typing
'⟨Meta⟩ X `gnus`'. In response, GNUS reads your `.newsrc` news initialization
file and establishes communication with your local news server. When it's
active, GNUS has three buffers:

- The Newsgroup buffer, which contains a list of newsgroups.
- The Summary buffer, which lists articles in a single newsgroup.
- The Article buffer, which displays the text of a selected article.

You exit from GNUS with the q command; upon exit, GNUS records all
relevant status changes in your `.newsrc` file.

To read news, you choose a newsgroup from the Newsgroups buffer.
That causes articles from that newsgroup to be displayed in the Summary
buffer. You then select articles to read; these show up in the Article buffer.
When you are finished with the newsgroup, you can choose another one
or exit from GNUS.

The meaning of a GNUS command depends on what buffer you're in
when you execute it, but the meanings are generally analogous. The
GNUS commands are the following:

z   In the Newsgroup buffer, suspends GNUS.

q   In the Newsgroup buffer, exits from GNUS; in the Summary
            buffer, exits from the current newsgroup.

L   In the Newsgroup buffer, lists all available newsgroups.

l   In the Newsgroup buffer, lists only newsgroups to which you
            subscribe that contain unread articles.

u   In the Newsgroup buffer, toggles the subscribed/unsubscribed
            status of the newsgroup on the current line.

⟨Ctrl⟩ K   In the Newsgroup buffer, kills the newsgroup on the current
            line so that it won't be listed in `.newsrc` from now on.

⟨Space⟩   In the Newsgroup buffer, selects the newsgroup on the current
            line and displays its first unread article. In the Summary buffer:

            - Selects the article on the current line if no article is
              selected.

- Scrolls the text of the selected article if it isn't at the end of that article.
- Selects the next unread article otherwise.

The effect of repeatedly typing (Space) is to move through all unread articles in the newsgroup.

(Del)   In the Newsgroup buffer, moves the point to the nearest previous newsgroup containing unread articles. In the Summary buffer, scrolls the text of the article backwards.

n

p   In the Newsgroup buffer, moves to the next or previous unread newsgroup; in the Summary buffer, selects the next or previous unread article.

(Ctrl) N

(Ctrl) P   In the Newsgroup or Summary buffer, moves to (but doesn't select) the next or previous item (newsgroup or article), whether or not you've read it.

s   In the Summary buffer, does an incremental search of the current text in the Article buffer (the same search that (Ctrl) S does).

(Ctrl) C (Ctrl) S (Ctrl) N
(Ctrl) C (Ctrl) S (Ctrl) S
(Ctrl) C (Ctrl) S (Ctrl) D
(Ctrl) C (Ctrl) S (Ctrl) A

    In the Summary buffer, sorts the articles by number (N), by subject (S), by date (D), or by author (A).

(Meta) (Ctrl) N
(Meta) (Ctrl) P

    In the Summary buffer, reads the next or previous article having the same subject as the current article.

10.6 The Calendar

The Emacs calendar facility displays a three-month calendar in a buffer of its own. Calendar facilities include scrolling to other months, computing the number of days between two dates, displaying dates of holidays, showing the time of sunrise and sunset, showing the phases of the moon, converting dates to other calendar systems, and carrying out operations on the diary (see Section 10.7).

You bring up the calendar with the command (Meta) X calendar. The initial calendar is centered around the current month; if you issue the command with a prefix argument, it prompts you for a year and month to use instead of the current month. The calendar buffer has a major mode of its own, Calendar mode. The q command in Calendar mode exits from the calendar and removes the buffer.

Many operations pertain to the selected date. That is the date where the point is (i.e., the date under the cursor). The three months shown in the window are the three months surrounding the selected date.

Under X you can use mouse buttons 1, 2, and 3 for common operations. Clicking Button 1 on a day selects that day; clicking Button 2 brings up a menu of date-specific actions; and clicking Button 3 brings up a menu of more general actions such as scrolling the calendar.

10.6.1
Moving Around the Calendar

The following commands scroll the selected date ahead or back in time:

`Right`	
`Ctrl` F	Moves the selected date a day forward.
`Left`	
`Ctrl` B	Moves the selected date a day backward.
`Down`	
`Ctrl` N	Moves the selected date a week forward.
`Up`	
`Ctrl` P	Moves the selected date a week backward.
`Meta` }	Moves the selected date a month forward.
`Meta` {	Moves the selected date a month backward.
`Ctrl` X]	Moves the selected date a year forward.
`Ctrl` X [	Moves the selected date a year backward.

With a numeric argument n, each of these commands scrolls by n units of time.

The following commands set the selected date to the beginning or end of a time period:

`Ctrl` A	Sets the selected date to the start of the week.
`Ctrl` E	Sets the selected date to the end of the week.
`Meta` A	Sets the selected date to the start of the month.
`Meta` E	Sets the selected date to the end of the month.
`Meta` <	Sets the selected date to the start of the year.
`Meta` >	Sets the selected date to the end of the year.

The following commands move to a particular date:

.	Moves the selected date to today's date.
g d	Moves the selected date to a specified date. Emacs prompts you for the date.
o	Centers the calendar around a specified month. Emacs prompts you for the year and month.

**10.6.2
Other Calendar
Operations**

The commands described below perform operations that don't involve changing the selected date.

Operations for Holidays.   The Emacs calendar knows about all major holidays and many minor ones. The following commands perform holiday-related operations:

h   Displays any holidays that occur on the selected date.

x   Visibly marks each day in the calendar window that is a holiday.

u   Unmarks all holidays in the calendar window.

a   Lists in another window each holiday that occurs in the displayed three months.

(Meta) X holidays
               Lists in another window each holiday that occurs in a three-month window around today's date.

Sunrise, Sunset, and Phases of the Moon.   The following commands show you information about sunrise and sunset:

S   Displays sunrise and sunset times for the selected date.

(Meta) X sunrise-sunset
               Displays sunrise and sunset times for today. With an argument, this command displays the times for a specified date, which Emacs prompts you for.

For these operations to work correctly, you need to tell Emacs where on earth you are. You do so by setting three variables, as in the following example:

```
(setq calendar-latitude 42.4)
(setq calendar-longitude -72.1)
(setq calendar-location-name "Deerfield, MA")
```

You should use one decimal place in the values of the latitude and longitude. The location is used only for display purposes.

   The following commands show you the dates and times of the phases of the moon:

M   Displays the dates and times for all quarters of the moon within the three-month period in the window.

(Meta) X phases-of-moon
               Displays the dates and times for all quarters of the moon within the three-month period around today's date. With an argument, this command displays the information for a three-month period around a specified date, which Emacs prompts you for.

Other Calendar Systems.   The Emacs calendar facility knows about several other calendars: the ISO commercial calendar, the Julian calendar, the Hebrew calendar, the Islamic calendar, the French Revolutionary calendar, and the Mayan calandar. The `p c` command displays ("prints") the ISO commercial calendar equivalent for the selected day, and similarly for other `p` commands and calendars. The `g c` command moves to a date in the ISO commercial calendar, which Emacs prompts you for. See your Emacs documentation for further details on these and other related commands.

Miscellaneous Operations.   The following commands perform miscellaneous useful operations:

Meta =   Displays the number of days in the current region; that is, between the point and the mark. To count the number of days between two dates, set the mark at one of them and the point to the other one.

p d   Displays the number of days elapsed since the start of the year.

Ctrl C Ctrl L
      Regenerates the calendar window.

Space   Scrolls the next window (useful, for instance, for scrolling through holidays or diary entries in another window).

q   Exits from the calendar. This command does *not* save the diary implicitly.

10.7   The Diary

The Emacs diary keeps track of your appointments and other events of interest. You access the diary through commands issued in a calendar window (see Section 10.6). Emacs can pick out and display the events for a particular day or group of days.

10.7.1
The Diary File

Diary information is kept in a diary file, by default `~/diary`. You can initialize this file simply by touching it (see Section 3.12.2) or by inserting actual diary entries into it. Later on you can use calendar commands to add entries, or (with caution) edit the diary file explicitly. if you've modified the diary file, be sure to save it before you exit from Emacs.

Figure 10-1 shows some sample diary entries. Each entry starts at the left margin and can be continued with additional lines that start with whitespace. Entries containing times can be used by the appointment scheduler. Entries starting with '&', called *nonmarking entries*, are not considered when Emacs is highlighting days of the calendar that have diary entries. The entry on the second and third lines indicates a block of days to which the entry applies. The entry on the fourth line indicates

```
11/17       Paul's birthday
%%(diary-block 3 12 1996 3 15 1996)
            ASQF symposium, Ulan Bator
&Fri 12:15pm   Crocodile Collector's Club lunch
Dec 3, 1995 2:45pm Checkup, Dr. Snuppnagle
&*/3        Mortgage payment due
Apr 15      Income tax due
&Wed        Put out the trash
```

Fig. 10-1. A sample diary file.

that a mortgage payment is due on the third day of every month; that on the fifth line that income taxes are due on April 15 of every year. The `Wed` entry applies to all Wednesdays.

You can edit the diary entries, but use caution. Portions of the diary file may not be visible. It is always safe to add lines or to make changes in the visible part of a line, but editing at the end of a line or deleting a line may not do what you expect. If you wish to edit the diary safely, display the entire diary with the `s` command (or edit it independently of the calendar facility). The only way to delete a diary entry is through manual editing.

10.7.2
Diary Operations

You perform diary operations from the calendar window. Most of these operations cause Emacs to create a Diary window that shows all or part of the diary file. You can enable "fancy diary display" by including the line

```
(add-hook 'diary-display-hook 'fancy-diary-display)
```

in your `.emacs` file. The fancy display prettifies the diary buffer in a number of ways.

Displaying Entries. The following operations display diary entries in a Diary window:

d   Displays all diary entries for the selected date.

s   Displays the entire diary. You can then edit the diary safely.

m   Marks all visible dates that have diary entries.

u   Removes all diary and holiday marks from the calendar window.

Meta X `print-diary-entries`
         Sends the contents of the Diary window to the printer.

Meta X `diary`
         Displays all diary entries for today.

If you put the LISP expression '`(diary)`' in your `.emacs` file and activate fancy diary display as described earlier, Emacs will display a window with today's diary entries whenever you start it. The mode line of the window will also show the date and any holidays that fall on the date.

Simple Diary Entries.   The following calendar commands create simple diary entries (ones that don't require the '%%' notation). Each command displays the end of your diary file in another window and inserts an appropriate date. You can then type the actual diary entry. A prefix argument makes the entry nonmarking.

i d   Adds a diary entry for the selected date.

i w   Adds a diary entry for all weekdays that correspond to the selected date. For instance, if the selected date is a Monday, the command adds a diary entry for all Mondays.

i m   Adds a diary entry for all days of the month that correspond to the selected date.

i d   Adds a diary entry for all days of the year that correspond to the selected date.

Complex Diary Entries.   The following calendar commands create more complex diary entries. Just as for the previous ones, a prefix argument makes the entry nonmarking.

i b   Adds a block diary entry for the current region. The diary entry applies to all dates within the block.

i a   Adds an anniversary diary entry for the current region. The difference in effect between this command and the i d command is that the diary entry can contain the format code '%d' or the format code '%d%s'. If the fancy diary display is enabled, the former code is replaced by the number of years since the anniversary event, the latter by the number of years followed by an appropriate ordinal ending: 'st', 'nd', 'rd', or 'th'.

i c   Adds a cyclic diary entry starting at the selected date. The entry applies to every nth day starting with the selected date. The command prompts you for n and the starting date. You can use the same format codes described above.

Appointment Alerts.   You can have Emacs remind you of any appointment 10 minutes in advance by including the following lines in your .emacs file:

```
(load "appt")
(display-time)
(add-hook 'diary-hook 'appt-make-list)
```

The notifications are based on the dates and times in your diary and appear as messages in the Emacs mode line.

You can add appointments to the appointment list independently of the diary with the command [Meta] X appt-add and delete them with the command [Meta] X appt-delete.

10.8   The Version Control Interface

Emacs provides a convenient interface to the GNU version control system, RCS (see Section 5.15). The same interface works with SCCS. The interface is not complete; some RCS commands and options produce effects you can't reproduce using Emacs's version control commands. For example, the interface provides no way of checking out a specific version or of merging two versions. For actions such as these, you have to issue RCS commands directly (perhaps from an Emacs shell). Most of the Emacs commands for version control begin with the sequence '⎡Ctrl⎤ X v'.

10.8.1
Checking Files In and Out

Emacs is able to tell if a working file corresponds to an RCS file—in Emacs terminology, such a working file is *registered*. When a buffer contains a registered file, the buffer's mode line displays the indicator RCS or SCCS and the version number of the head version (the newest version on the trunk), which is usually the version you're editing.[6]

The usual way of using RCS with a file under Emacs is to register the file with RCS using the ⎡Ctrl⎤ X v i command. Later, you check the file out with the ⎡Ctrl⎤ X ⎡Ctrl⎤ Q command, edit it, and check it in again by issuing another ⎡Ctrl⎤ X ⎡Ctrl⎤ Q command. If the file is not marked as read-only, you know it is checked out and in a locked state.

The following commands provide for checking files in and out. They all assume the current buffer is the working file for an RCS file.

⎡Ctrl⎤ X v i   Registers the file in the buffer as an RCS file. After issuing this command, the RCS file is unlocked and the buffer is read-only. If you issue this command with an argument, Emacs prompts you for the initial version number, which otherwise defaults to 1.1.

⎡Ctrl⎤ X ⎡Ctrl⎤ Q
Checks out the file if it is not already checked out with locking; otherwise, checks the file in (vc-toggle-read-only). When you check a file in, Emacs prompts you for a log entry, which you terminated by typing ⎡Ctrl⎤ C ⎡Ctrl⎤ C. You can retrieve previous log entries using the same ⎡Meta⎤ N, ⎡Meta⎤ P, ⎡Meta⎤ S, and ⎡Meta⎤ R commands you use for retrieving previous minibuffer entries. If the third and fourth characters of the mode line are '%%', the file is not locked and the buffer is in a read-only state; otherwise, the file is locked and you can edit the copy of it in the buffer.

---

6. As of this writing, Emacs behaves erratically when confronted with version numbers not on the trunk. The next version (19.29) is supposed to support general version numbers.

[Ctrl] X v v   Checks the file in (vc-next-action). Issued by itself, this command is rarely useful; but issued with an argument, it prompts you for the version number to be assigned to the checked-in version.

The following commands provide for discarding and cancelling changes:

[Ctrl] X v u   Discards any changes you've made since you last checked in a version, and reverts the buffer to the last checked-in version (vc-revert-buffer). The file is left unlocked, so if you want to make a different set of changes, you have to check the file out again.

[Ctrl] X v c   Discards the version you've most recently checked in, removing the record of it from the RCS file (vc-cancel-version). Use this command cautiously, since it can lead you to throw away a lot of work accidentally.

**10.8.2
Other Version
Control Commands**

The following commands perform a variety of version control functions:

[Ctrl] X v a   Visits the current directory's Emacs change log file and creates new entries for versions checked in since the most recent entry in the change log file (vc-update-change-log), thus keeping the Emacs change log in sync with the RCS change log.

[Ctrl] X v ~   Examines a specific version of the current file in another window ('vc-version-other-window'). Emacs prompts you for the version. You can use this command to view two different versions at once.

[Ctrl] X v =   Compares the current buffer contents with the latest checked-in version of the file (vc-diff). With an argument, compares two specified versions and prompts you for both of them.

[Ctrl] X v l   Displays the log for the RCS file, including the history of changes (vc-print-log).

[Ctrl] X v d   Lists all locked files in or beneath the current directory (vc-directory). With an argument, it lists all files in or beneath the current directory that are maintained under version control. The files are listed in a Dired-like buffer. Within that buffer, the [Ctrl] X v d command operates on all marked files if any files are marked; otherwise, on the file on the current line.

[Meta] X vc-rename-file
Renames a file under RCS control, making the necessary corresponding changes to the RCS file and other snapshot files that mention the file.

[Ctrl] X v h   Inserts a version control header (marker such as 'Id') into the working file (vc-insert-headers).

```
      1 6   2 7     3
  7 - - - - - - - - -
    - - - - - O - - 3
  R - - - - - - O - H
    - - - - - - O - -
  4 - - - - - - - - -
    - - - - - - - O H
  5 - - - - - - - - -
    - - - - - - - - -
      1 6   2 4   5
```

Fig. 10-2. The `blackbox` game.

Snapshots.   A snapshot is a picture of the version status of a collection of RCS files. The snapshot records the number of the latest revision in each of the files. Snapshot files are very small, so you can make snapshots freely. The following commands pertain to snapshots:

Ctrl X v s Defines a release called *name* containing the most recently saved version of every RCS file in or under the current directory (`vc-create-snapshot`). Emacs prompts you for *name*.

Ctrl X v r Checks out each of the RCS files belonging to release *name* (`vc-retrieve-snapshot`). Emacs prompts you for *name*.

10.9   Amusements

The following commands call for one of Emacs's amusements:

Meta X doctor

Executes the Eliza program. You end each input line by typing Enter twice.

Meta X yow

Displays an amusing maxim or quotation.

Meta X hanoi

Runs the towers of Hanoi. An argument, if present, specifies the number of discs.

Meta X gomoku

Plays a game of gomoku ("five-in-a-row") with you.

Meta X blackbox

Challenges you to determine the location of four hidden balls inside a black box by tomography—shooting rays into the box. When you issue the command, a grid of hyphens is displayed

in a game buffer. You move around the grid and its perimeter using the arrow keys or their equivalents (Ctrl N , Ctrl P ,
Ctrl F , and Ctrl B). Pressing Space on a grid location toggles
a guess that a ball is at that location. Pressing Space from
a perimeter position shoots a ray from there with one of the
following outcomes:

- The ray exits the box, possibly after being deflected by a
  ball. The entry and exit points are shown with a number.
  A ray is deflected by 90° if it would otherwise pass next
  to a ball. For example, in the figure ray 1 passes straight
  through, ray 7 is deflected by the ball on the second line,
  and ray 3 is deflected by the ball on the third line.

- The ray hits a ball directly, possibly after one or more
  deflections, and is absorbed. Each H indicates an
  absorbed ray.

- The ray is returned because it can neither pass, be
  deflected, nor be absorbed. A returned ray is indicated
  by R. The ray sent from the left on the third line is
  returned because, when it reaches the fifth column, it
  cannot be deflected both up and down at the same time.
  A ray sent from the left might also be returned because
  of a ball in the first column, one row above or below the
  launch position, and similarly for rays sent from other
  sides.

Pressing Enter when all balls have been guessed shows you
the answer. Figure 10-2 shows the playing grid after shooting
a number of rays and (correctly) guessing the location of the
balls. The only way to start a new game is to issue the command
again.

  If you have the Emacs LISP source files, you can get further
information about this game by looking at the comments near
the beginning of the file `blackbox.el`.

Meta X `mpuz`

Displays a multiplication puzzle with letters standing for digits.
To guess a value for a letter, type the letter followed by the digit
you think it stands for.

Meta X `dissociated-press`

Scrambles a buffer of text in an amusing way. Killing the Dis-
sociated Press buffer restores the previous buffer, so you can
try this command without destroying what you're working on.

11

Mailers and Newsreaders

Sending and receiving messages by electronic mail is a major activity on most UNIX systems. You can use electronic mail to communicate with users at your own site as well as at other sites. Electronic mail is also the medium for participating in certain newsgroups and bulletin boards.

A *mailer* is a program for sending and receiving electronic mail. In this chapter we focus on mailers and how to use them. In the next chapter we discuss remote addressing and also discuss other forms of communication with remote sites.

Several mailers are likely to be available on your system. The original Seventh Edition mailer, naturally enough called `mail`, has largely been superseded by the BSD Mail program, standardized by POSIX under the name `mailx`. That is the name we use for it here. On most modern systems, the name `mail` is a link to `mailx`, so calling `mail` is likely to get you the POSIX/BSD mailer. Some older systems may use `mail` to designate the Seventh Edition mailer, however, or may provide that mailer under the name `binmail`.

In this chapter we cover mail conventions in general and discuss the `mailx` mailer in detail. We also cover briefly the MH and `elm` mailers. The `emacs` editor also includes its own mailer, which we discuss in Section 10.4.

Technically, the mailers you work with as a user are *mail user agents*. Most of them use other, more primitive, mailers to handle the actual transmission of mail. These other mailers, known as *mail transport agents*, go by names such as `smail`, `rmail`, `delivermail`, and `sendmail`. You'll probably never need to deal with a mail transport agent directly.

11.1 What's in a Message?

Here is an example of a message, sent using `mailx`:

```
From gkc  Wed Sep 27 21:35:13 1995
Received: by booker (8.6.12/8.6.12)
    id AA00406; Wed, 27 Sep 95 21:35:13 -0500
Date: Wed, 27 Sep 95 21:35:13 -0500
From: gkc (Gilbert K. Chesterton)
Message-Id: <9509280235.AA00406@booker>
To: gbs
Subject: A shocking observation
Status: RO

To look at you, Shaw, one would think
there was a famine in England.
```

And here is the reply to it:

```
From gbs  Wed Sep 27 21:36:01 1995
Received: by booker (8.6.12/8.6.12)
    id AA00413; Wed, 27 Sep 95 21:36:01 -0500
Date: Wed, 27 Sep 95 21:36:01 -0500
From: gbs (George Bernard Shaw)
Message-Id: <9509280236.AA00413@booker>
To: gkc
Subject: Re:  A shocking observation
Status: RO

To look at you, Chesterton, one would think
you were the cause of it.
```

As these examples show, a message consists of a *header* that contains information about the message followed by the text of the message. The header starts with a *postmark* that says who sent the message and when it was delivered to you. The postmark for the first message above is

```
From gkc  Wed Sep 27 21:35:13 1995
```

The postmark is attached as part of local mail delivery and is not part of the header. A postmark is not attached to messages sent to remote systems such as those sent over the Internet.

The rest of the header consists of a sequence of *fields*. (Observe that the 'From' in a postmark is followed by a space, not a colon; the lack of a colon distinguishes it from the 'From' field below it.) Each field starts with a field name followed by a colon. Which fields are present in a message header depends in part on which mailer first sent the message and which other mailers have processed it afterwards. It should be obvious what most of the header information means, but a few points are worth explaining:

- The (8.6.12/8.6.12) in the 'Received' field indicates the version of the mail transport agent—sendmail in this case—that handled this message.

- The date indicates when the message was sent. The '-0500' in the 'Date' field indicates that the time at the receiving machine is five hours ahead of Greenwich Mean Time.

- The 'Re:' in the subject of the second message indicates that this message is a response to the previous one. Most mailers automatically create the subject of a response by putting 'Re:' in front of the subject of the original message.

- The 'RO' in the 'Status' field indicates that you have read this message and that it is an "old" one (see Section 11.5.10). A message can be old even if you haven't read it. This use of the 'Status' field is peculiar to mailx.

Some messages have other fields in their headers in addition to the ones shown here; for example, a message from a newsgroup may have an 'Article-Id' field.

When a mailer processes a message, it places the message in an *envelope* that bears a description of the message for routing purposes. Any mailer can then process the message just by looking at its envelope—even if the message itself has been encrypted.

11.2   Recipients

A *recipient* of a message is the person or entity to whom the message is sent. You can send a message to any number of recipients. A recipient can be a user in your own system or a user at a remote computer linked to your system over a network or telephone line (see Section 12.1). Most newer mailers and mail facilities also allow a recipient to be a file or a program. Mail sent to a file is appended to that file; mail sent to a program is used as the standard input of that program.

Most mailers enable you to denote a set of recipients by a single name called an *alias*—for example, using the alias command of mailx (see p. 601). The aliases you define are augmented by whatever system-wide aliases have been defined on your system. The system-wide aliases are listed in /etc/aliases or /usr/lib/aliases.

Although a message has only one sender, it may have many recipients. The primary recipients are listed in the 'To' field. You can send "carbon copies" of a message to other recipients. These recipients are listed in a 'Cc' field. You can also send "blind carbon copies", which are listed in a

'Bcc' field that does not show up on the copies of the message received by any of its other recipients.

Comments in Recipient Names.   Most mailers enable you to attach a comment to a recipient's name. That's helpful when the name is cryptic, e.g., `U12834.7`. You can either put the comment in parentheses or put the actual name in angle brackets. For example, either of

```
gbs (George Bernard Shaw)
<gbs> George Bernard Shaw
```

designates the user `gbs` with the identifying comment 'George Bernard Shaw' attached.

11.3   Mailboxes

A *mailbox* is a place where messages are stored. Each UNIX user has at least two mailboxes, a *primary mailbox* for new mail and a *secondary mailbox* for old mail:

- When a mailer receives a message addressed to you, it stores the message in your primary mailbox, also known as your *system mailbox*. If your user name is `zog`,[1] your primary mailbox is a file named `/usr/mail/zog`, `/usr/spool/mail/zog`, `/var/spool/mail/zog`, or a similar name assigned by your system. You can locate it by typing

  ```
  echo $MAIL
  ```

  Although you have write permission for your primary mailbox, you have no control over its location; it isn't even in a subdirectory of your home directory.

- Once you've read a message, the mailer normally puts it into your default secondary mailbox, a file named `mbox` in your home directory (and sometimes referred to as your *mbox*). Thus if your user name is `zog`, your default secondary mailbox is `/home/zog/mbox`. You can have the mailer put your mail in a different file if you choose.

In addition to your primary and secondary mailboxes, you can have other mailboxes, which we call *auxiliary mailboxes*. Auxiliary mailboxes are useful for sorting mail by category or according to the person who sent it.

When you read your mail, the mailer by default shows you each message in your primary mailbox and adds it to your secondary mailbox after you've read it. These are some of the alternative dispositions you can request:

- Leave the message in your primary mailbox.
- Delete the message altogether.
- Save the message in a mailbox other than the usual one.

---

1. Zog was the last king of Albania.

11.4   Forwarding Mail

You can arrange to have your mail forwarded to one or more recipients. Forwarding your mail to yourself under another name or at a different site can be particularly useful when you're away. To have your mail forwarded, you place a file named `.forward` in your home directory.[2] The `.forward` file lists the recipients to whom your forwarded mail should be sent. A recipient can be a user name (local or remote), a file, or a program:

- A file name must be specified using an absolute pathname. Each forwarded message is appended to the specified file.

- A program is written in the form '"|*cmd*"'. Whenever a message is forwarded, the command *cmd* is called with the message as its standard input. The double quotes are usually needed to prevent the shell from misinterpreting the '|'.

You can keep a local copy of forwarded mail by employing this undocumented trick: include yourself as one of the recipients in `.forward` but put a backslash in front of your name. You'll continue to receive a copy of your mail in your primary mailbox as usual. Another method is to forward your mail to a file, where it will accumulate.

The recipients listed in the `.forward` file are separated by commas, optionally followed by whitespace. Assuming your user name is `duchess`, you can set up a `.forward` file by typing something like

```
cat > .forward
mhare, dodo, dormouse@tparty, \duchess
[EOF]
```

See Section 3.3 for an explanation of this use of `cat`. Your mail will be forwarded to the specified people and also will be saved in your own mailbox.

If you don't know whether your system supports `.forward` files, you can find out by typing

```
cd
cat > .forward
"|cat >> ~/junque"
[EOF]
```

and sending yourself a message. If the message appears in the file `junque` in your home directory, `.forward` works in your system. Don't forget to delete `.forward` after you've done this experiment!

---

2. BSD systems have a `vacation` program for notifying people who send you mail that you are away. The `vacation` program makes use of your `.forward` file.

11.5   The `mailx` (Berkeley `Mail`) Mailer

The `mailx` mailer is the System V adaptation of the `Mail` mailer developed at Berkeley. You can use `mailx` either to send mail or to read it. `Mailx` is a mail user agent that acts as a "front" for the mail transport agents that actually deliver mail. It moves mail among your mailboxes and mail files, shows you your incoming messages and their headers, and passes your outgoing mail to the transport agents. It has nothing to do with putting mail into your primary mailbox—it just handles your mail once it arrives there.

11.5.1
Sending a Message

The command for sending a mail message has the form

        `mailx` [-FinU] [-h *n*] [-r *addr*] [-s *string*] *name* ...

where *name* ... is a list of recipients. The names of the recipients are separated by whitespace or commas. After you've given the command, `mailx` asks you for the subject of your message. It then puts you into *input mode* (see Section 11.5.21), expecting you to type the text of your message followed by an end-of-message indicator, usually EOF. You can interrupt the composition of your message to give any of the input mode commands described in the subsections following Section 11.5.21. An input mode command starts with a tilde (~) and appears on a line by itself. You can use input mode commands for such tasks as including a message you've received in the text of the message you're sending or adding "carbon copy" recipients to an outgoing message.

   Note: If you're reading messages, you can switch over to sending a message by using the `mail` command (see Section 11.5.14).

Sending Messages Noninteractively. It's often useful to send a canned message noninteractively, perhaps as part of a shell script. You can do that by redirecting `mailx`'s input from a file or a here-document (see Section 6.11). For example, the following lines might be included in a shell script that periodically sends a message from `mabel` to `ebenezer`:

```
mailx ebenezer << -end-
Ebenezer, just remember: I love you greatly! - Mabel
-end-
```

11.5.2
Reading Your Mail

The command for reading your mail has the form

        `mailx` [-eHInN] [-f *file*] [-T *file*] [-u *user*]

`Mailx` first gives you a summary of the headers of the messages you've received (unless you tell it to do something else) and then puts you into *command mode*. In command mode, you can give any of the commands listed in the subsections following Section 11.5.11, including commands that let you switch over to sending mail. It would be convenient if you could call `mailx` in a way that would put you into command mode even when you don't have any mail, but unfortunately `mailx` doesn't provide for that.

When you exit from `mailx` after reading some messages in your primary mailbox, it transfers those messages to your secondary mailbox. The messages you haven't read remain in your primary mailbox. When `mailx` transfers a message to your secondary mailbox, it puts that message at the beginning, not the end, of the secondary mailbox. The secondary mailbox therefore has the newest messages first if they were put there by `mailx` itself. However, some of the commands also transfer messages to mailboxes; these commands always append the messages to the *end* of the mailbox.

The simplest way to retrieve messages with `mailx` is to type (Enter) in response to every query and to type 'q' when `mailx` tells you that it's reached the end of the file. `Mailx` shows you all of your incoming messages and transfers each one to your secondary mailbox after you've read it. You can review the messages in your secondary mailbox by typing

```
mailx -f
```

and then typing (Enter) after each one. To delete a message from any mailbox, type 'dp' after you've read it. That deletes the message and shows you the next one.

11.5.3
Quick Exit

You can exit from `mailx` when you're at a `mailx` prompt by typing 'q' or 'x' (see Section 11.5.18). If `mailx` is showing you a long message and you don't want to see any more of it, you can get back to the `mailx` prompt by typing (Intr).

11.5.4
Recipients for
`mailx` Messages

A recipient of a `mailx` message may be any of the following:

- A user registered in your system.
- A user at a remote site (see Section 12.1).
- A file for which you have write permission. You need a '/' somewhere in the file name so that the mailer knows you're referring to a file rather than a user. You can designate a file in your current directory by putting './' in front of its name.
- A shell-level command with the message used as standard input, denoted by '|*cmd*'. You should quote this form to prevent the shell from interpreting the '|' as a pipe symbol; for example, writing it as '"| noteit"'. Most versions of `mailx` cannot interpret *cmd* properly if it contains any spaces, even if you quote them.

The recipients you can specify to `mailx` are nearly the same as those you can specify in a `.forward` file (see Section 11.4). There are two differences:

- A file name in `.forward` must be absolute but a file name as a recipient for `mailx` can be relative, either to your current directory or to your home directory, as long as it contains a slash.
- The syntax in a `.forward` file is a little more permissive; spaces are acceptable in an address that's a shell-level command.

Aliases for Recipients.   You can use the `alias` command (see p. 601) to define an alias for a single recipient or for a group of recipients. Aliases are particularly useful as nicknames for people you often send mail to, or for mailing lists. You can then use the alias name to specify that recipient or group of recipients. Since you don't ordinarily want to recreate aliases each time you send mail, you should place `alias` or `group` commands (the two are equivalent) in your `.mailrc` file (see Section 11.5.7). For example, the commands

```
alias superman clark-kent@comix.com
group reporters clark-kent@comix.com lois-lane@comix.com
```

create aliases for `superman` and `reporters`.   Whenever you use `superman` as a recipient name for a message, the message will be sent to `clark-kent@comix.com`. Whenever you use `reporters` as a recipient name for a message, the message will be sent to `clark-kent@comix.com` and also to `lois-lane@comix.com`.

11.5.5
Naming Files After Recipients

Certain commands such as `Save` save a message in a file named after the message's sender, providing a convenient way of sorting your mail. When `mailx` stores a message in a file named after its sender, it derives the actual file name by stripping off all network addressing from the sender's name and prefixing it by '+' if the `outfolder` variable (see p. 609) is enabled. The treatment of '+' is in turn determined by whether the `folder` variable (see p. 609) is enabled; if `folder` isn't enabled, the '+' simply becomes part of the file name.

   To illustrate, suppose that the current directory is `~/stash` and that `mailx` is saving a message sent by `amherst!emily` (user `emily` at remote computer `amherst`) in a file named after her. The file where `mailx` stores the message is determined by `folder` and `outfolder` as follows:

```
outfolder disabled                    ~/stash/emily
outfolder enabled, folder disabled    ~/stash/+emily
outfolder enabled, folder=mail        ~/mail/emily
```

The same rules apply when a message is saved in a file named after the first recipient of the message, an effect you can obtain with the `-F` command-line option.

11.5.6
Command-Line Options

The command-line options for `mailx` depend on whether you're sending a message or reading your mail.

Options for Sending a Message.   When you call `mailx` to send a message, the options on the command line are as follows:

`-s` *string* Set the subject of the message to *string*. If you specify this option, you don't get a 'Subject' prompt.

`-i`   Ignore any interrupts that occur while you're composing mail. This option is often useful when you're working with a noisy phone line that can generate spurious interrupts.

-F   Save each message of your mail in a file named after the first
            recipient of that message rather than in your secondary mail-
            box (see Section 11.5.5). This option overrides any setting of
            the `record` variable (see p. 608). It's useful for sorting mail
            according to whom you've sent it to.

The following options are, to quote the Berkeley manual, "not for human
use". They are intended to support scripts and programs that employ
`mailx` to transmit mail over networks. They affect only the envelopes of
messages, not the messages themselves, and their effects are not visible to
ordinary users of `mailx`.

-h *n*   Set the number of network hops so far to *n*. This option would
            be used by a script that retransmits messages to another site.
            The hop count is used by mail transport agents to prevent mes-
            sages with defective addresses from cycling endlessly around a
            network; messages whose hop count exceeds a certain maxi-
            mum (usually 17) are returned to the sender or, if that isn't
            possible, to a postmaster.

-r *addr* Cause *addr* to appear to network delivery software as the sender
            of the message, and disable '~' commands. Such a substitute
            address is rejected by `sendmail`, the underlying mail transport
            agent, unless the sender is known to be trustworthy.

-U   Convert path-style UUCP addresses to domain-style Internet
            addresses (see Section 12.1). Uses of '!' are removed where
            possible and '`.UUCP`' is appended to the address.

Options for Reading Your Mail.   When you call `mailx` to read your mail,
the options on the command line are as follows:

-e   Test for presence of mail and exit immediately. The status code
            on exit is 1 if you have mail and 0 if you don't.[3] You can use
            this option in initialization files such as `.profile` and `.login`
            to test for the existence of mail without actually processing it.

-H   Just show a summary of the headers and exit.

-N   Go into command mode immediately without showing a sum-
            mary of the headers.

-f [*file*] Read mail from *file* instead of from your primary mailbox. If
            file is omitted, read the mail from your secondary mailbox.

-u *user* Read mail from *user*'s mailbox instead of from your own. This
            option will work only if you have read access to that mailbox.

---

3. The usual convention for status codes is that 0 indicates success and any other value
indicates failure. You can think of these status codes as indicating success or failure in testing
for the *absence* of mail.

The following options are sometimes useful for reading messages sent by newsgroups:

-I   In the header summary, treat the first newsgroup in the 'Newsgroups' field as the sender of the message. This option can only be used if the -f option is also present. It's useful for scanning mail that comes from several newsgroups at once.

-T *file* Extract the 'Article-Id' field of each message containing such a field and list these fields in *file*, one per line. This option is intended for use in shell scripts that use mailx to read mail sent by newsgroups. Mailx does not accept the -T option unless you also specify an explicit input file with the -f option.

Option for Suppressing Initialization. The following option can be applied either when you're sending mail or when you're receiving it:

-n   Don't execute the commands in the initialization file for this mailer (see Section 11.5.7). The commands in this file are intended to be appropriate for all users. Mailx executes these commands, if at all, before it does anything else. Specifying -n does not stop mailx from executing the commands in your local initialization file.

11.5.7
Initialization Files
for mailx

When mailx is called, it executes the commands in two initialization files before it does anything else—in particular, before it asks you for any input. It executes these commands whether you're sending mail or reading it.

- The first initialization file is global (common to all users). It is named either /usr/lib/mailx/mailx.rc or /usr/lib/Mail.rc, depending on your system. This file contains commands that are expected to be useful to anyone. You can suppress its execution with the -n option described above.

- The second initialization file is local (particular to each user). By default it is named .mailrc and resides in each user's home directory. You can specify a different local initialization file by putting its file name into the environment variable MAILRC (see p. 606). You can tailor the initialization file to suit your own needs.

When mailx is called, it first executes the global initialization file and then the local initialization file of the user who called it if these files exist.

Here is an example of an initialization file:

```
set PAGER=less
set crt=24
alias jekyll cellar!hyde
group mates wynken blynken nod
```

The settings for PAGER and crt cause long messages (those of at least 24 lines) to be shown using the less paging program. The alias lets you substitute the short name jekyll for the longer network address `cellar!hyde`. The `group` lets you give a name to a set of people so that you can easily send a message to all of them at once. Initialization files often contain long lists of aliases and groups. The `set`, `alias`, and `group` commands are explained in the following subsections.

11.5.8
Using a Folder Directory

You can keep your secondary and auxiliary mailboxes in a separate directory that you use for all your saved mail. The mailboxes in that directory are called *folders*, and the directory itself is called your *folder directory*.[4]

When you specify a file name to `mailx` and that name starts with '+', `mailx` takes that name to be relative to your folder directory (if you have one). For instance, if your folder directory is `~/mymail`, `mailx` takes the file name `+aaron` to mean `~/mymail/aaron`. You can use this convention for file names that you specify for `mailx` internal commands. You can also use it on the `mailx` command line provided that `folder` is set in your `mailx` initialization file. If you haven't specified a folder directory, a '+' at the start of a file name is not treated specially by `mailx`.

You can set up a folder directory by including commands in your initialization file that take the following actions:

(1) Set the `folder` variable to your mail directory (which must already exist).
(2) Enable the `outfolder` variable.
(3) Set the `MBOX` variable to `+mbox`.
(4) Optionally, set the `DEAD` variable to '`+dead.letter`' (see p. 608).

See Section 11.5.33 for a description of these variables and "Setting the Values of Variables" on page 601 for the commands that set variables..

The `followup`, `Followup`, `Save`, and `Copy` commands save a message in a file named after the sender of the message. The first two steps above cause `mailx` to keep these files in your folder directory. The third step ensures that your secondary mailbox is in your folder directory rather than in your home directory.

11.5.9
Message Lists

Many commands use *message lists* to designate a subset of the messages you've retrieved. The numbers in a message list are those that appear in the header summary. The notation for message lists is as follows:

n	Message number *n*.
.	The current message. Whenever you read a message, that message becomes the current message.
^	The first (undeleted) message.
$	The last (undeleted) message.
m-n	The messages numbered from *m* to *n*, where *m* and *n* are any of the single message specifiers given above.

---

4. The `mailx` documentation from Berkeley is inconsistent in its use of the term "folder", sometimes taking it to mean a single mailbox and sometimes taking it to mean the directory that contains your mailboxes.

*	All the messages in the message list.
name	All messages from the user *name*.
/*string*	All messages with *string* in the subject. For the purposes of this test, the case of the letters in *string* is ignored.
:*c*	All messages of type *c*, where *c* is given as follows:

	d	deleted messages
	n	new messages (from your primary mailbox)
	o	old messages
	r	messages that you've read
	u	messages that are unread

In the commands below, an omitted *msglist* or *msg* is taken as referring to the current message. The ':d' message specifier works only with the undelete command described below.

**11.5.10
Header Summary
and Status Codes**

When mailx is called, it gives you a summary of the headers in your primary mailbox. You can get an updated header summary at any time when you're in command mode.

Here is an example of what a header summary looks like:

	1	empor!slick	Mon Apr 29	15:18	56/2257	What a deal!
	3	curie@pasteur.fr	Sat May 18	14:20	90/3595	Glowing reports
U	4	empor!slick	Wed May 22	9:07	44/1786	Sales analysis
N	5	dvorak	Wed May 22	16:32	17/452	Re: Keyboard layout
N	6	hst	Thu May 23	10:31	21/496	Election results
N	7	To gorgon	Thu May 23	15:19	10/302	Dinner invitation

Here is how to interpret it:

- The first column gives the status code for each message.
- The second column gives the message number. In this case, message 2 is missing because it's been deleted.
- The third column gives the sender of the message. Generally, a name with '!' in it indicates a UUCP network address, while a name with '@' in it indicates an Internet address (see Section 12.1). The sender information is obtained from the 'From' line in the header (the one with the colon) rather than from the postmark. A 'To' in this column indicates a message that you've sent; for such messages, the recipient rather than the sender (you) is shown if you've enabled the showto variable (see p. 606).
- The next four columns give the date and time when the message was received.
- The next column gives the number of lines and number of characters in each message.
- The last column gives the subject of the message.

These are the status codes that can appear in a header summary:

N   A new unread message; that is, one that has arrived since you last called the mailer but that you haven't read.

U   An old unread message, one that was in your primary mailbox when you last called the mailer.

P   A preserved message, one that you've explicitly requested `mailx` to leave in your primary mailbox.

M   A message that `mailx` will move to your secondary mailbox when you exit even if you haven't read it.

*   A message that `mailx` has copied to an auxiliary mailbox. Such a message won't be saved when you leave `mailx` (since it's already saved in the auxiliary mailbox).

A blank code indicates a message that you've read.

   The status codes stored in a message within a mailbox appear in the `Status` field of a message header and are different from those that appear in the header summary. There are just two of them:

O   An old message; that is, one that isn't new. A new message is one that arrived in your primary mailbox since you last called `mailx`.

R   A message that you've read but haven't yet moved out of your primary mailbox.

'R' and 'O' can appear either separately or together. A message with no 'Status' field is new and unread, but `mailx` never shows you a message without an 'R' status since the very act of showing it to you gives it 'R' status. (You can verify this by reading your primary mailbox as a file.)

**11.5.11
Command Mode**

Command mode is the mode you're in when reading mail. The commands you can issue from command mode are listed below. `Mailx` prompts you for a command when it first starts up (after showing you the list of message headers) and after it's finished executing the most recent command. Pressing ⌈Enter⌉ in response to a prompt is equivalent to giving the `next` command—it tells `mailx` to show the next message.

   Most commands can be abbreviated by typing just the first letter or so of the command. The part that can be omitted is shown in brackets. Thus the `copy` command, indicated as 'c[opy]', can be typed as 'c', 'co', 'cop', or 'copy'.

**11.5.12
Commands for
General Information**

The following commands give you information about `mailx` itself and enable you to control the content and form of the visible part of the header summary.

Information About `mailx`.   The following commands give you information about `mailx` itself.

?

hel[p]   Shows a summary of the most commonly used commands. Not all commands are included in this summary.

l[ist]   Shows the available commands but omits their explanations.

ve[rsion] Shows the version number and release date of the version of
                `mailx` you're using.

Controlling the Header Display.   The following commands control the
header display (see Section 11.5.10).

.
=   Shows the current message number.

h[eaders] *msg*
                Shows the page of the header summary that includes *msg*.

f[rom] [*msglist*]
                Shows the header summary for *msglist*. This command is help-
                ful when you want to select the messages that were sent by
                a particular person or that refer to a particular subject. You
                can select these messages using the *name* or '/*string*' forms of
                message specifier (see Section 11.5.9).

to[p] [*msglist*]
                Shows the top few lines of the messages of *msglist*.

z
z+
z−   Scrolls the header display. The z and z+ commands scroll
                it one screen forward; the z− command scrolls it one screen
                backward.

di[scard] *header-field-list*
ig[nore] *header-field-list*
                Causes the specified header fields to be omitted from now
                on when messages are being shown. For example, 'ignore
                Path' causes `mailx` to omit the 'Path' field whenever it shows a
                message—convenient if the routing information given in that
                field is just visual clutter to you.

Listing Your Mail Folders.   The following command is useful for keeping
track of your mailboxes if you keep them in a folder directory:

folders   Shows the names of the files in the directory specified by the
                folder variable (see p. 609).

**11.5.13
Showing Messages**

The commands in this group enable you to read your messages, check
their sizes, or mark them as though you've read them. If the `crt` variable
is enabled (see p. 606), long messages are sent to the pager specified by
the `PAGER` variable (see p. 606) instead of being shown directly.

[Enter]   Shows the next message.

n   Shows message number *n*.

−[*n*]   Shows the *n*th previous message. If you omit *n* (the usual case),
                this command shows the previous message.

p[rint] [*msglist*]
t[ype] [*msglist*]

> Shows the messages of *msglist*.

P[rint] [*msglist*]
T[ype] [*msglist*]

> Shows the messages of *msglist*, including all header fields—
> even those that you earlier asked to have ignored by using the
> `ignore` command described earlier.

si[ze] [*msglist*]

> Shows the length in characters of each message in *msglist*. This
> command is redundant since the `headers` command also gives
> you this information.

n[ext] *msg*

> Goes to the next message matching *msg* and shows it. Unlike
> `Type`, `next` shows only a single message even if you give it a
> message list. It's useful, for example, if you want to retrieve
> the next message from a particular user.

tou[ch] [*msglist*]

> "Touches" the messages of *msglist* so that they appear to have
> been read. This command is useful when you want some mes-
> sages to be moved to your secondary mailbox even though you
> haven't read them, perhaps because you already know what
> they say. Touching a message does not affect its status as shown
> in the header summary.

11.5.14 Responding to Messages

The following commands enable you to send responses to mail you've
received. Each of them places you into input mode.

m[ail] *namelist*

> Enters input mode to compose a message, then mails that mes-
> sage to the people in *namelist*.

M[ail] *name*

> Enters input mode to compose a message, then mails that mes-
> sage to *name* and records a copy of the message in a file named
> for that person.

r[espond] [*msglist*]
r[eply] [*msglist*]

> Enters input mode to compose a response to the messages in
> *msglist*, then sends the response to the sender of each message
> in *msglist*. The subject line is obtained by putting 'Re:' in front
> of the subject of the first message in *msglist* (if 'Re:' isn't there
> already).

R[espond] [*msg*]
R[eply] [*msg*]

> Enters input mode to compose a response to *msg*, then mails

that response to the sender of *msg* and to all other recipients of *msg* other than yourself. The subject line is gotten by putting 'Re:' in front of the subject of the first message in *msglist* (if 'Re:' isn't there already).

The difference between `respond` and `Respond` is that `respond` responds to a *set* of messages, sending copies of your response to the senders of all messages in the set but *not to the recipients* of those messages; `Respond` responds to a *single* message, sending copies of your response to the sender *and all recipients* of that message. You can reverse the meanings of these commands by setting the `flipr` variable (see p. 607).

fo[llowup] [*msg*]
:   Like `respond`, except that a copy of the message is saved in a file named after the sender of *msg* (see Section 11.5.5).

F[ollowup] [*msglist*]
:   Like `Respond`, except that a copy of the message is saved in a file named after the sender of the first message (see Section 11.5.5).

Forwarding Messages.   Suppose you've received a message from `miller` and want to forward that message to `monroe`. Mailx doesn't have an explicit command for this, but you can do it in three steps:

(1)   Use the `mail` command described earlier to compose a message to `monroe`.

(2)   Within that message, use the ~f input-mode command (see p. 604) to include the message from `miller` in the message you're composing.

(3)   Send the message you've just composed to `monroe`.

Including Messages in Responses.   When you respond to a message, you can include parts of that message, distinctively marked, in your response. Use the `reply` command or one of its variants, immediately inserting the text of the current message into your response with ~f or ~m (see Section 11.5.21). Then enter your editor with the ~e or ~v command. If, for instance, you want to put '>␣' in front of each line of the original message, use the editor to replace the beginning of each line with '>␣'.

Your response now consists of the original message with each line preceded by '>␣'. By further editing, you can delete the parts you don't want to respond to and put your own comments after the other parts. Now exit from the editor. Your response is ready to send—just transmit it by typing ⎡EOF⎤ or '~.' (or '.' if the `dot` variable has been enabled).

Newer POSIX-conforming versions of `mailx` provide the `indent-prefix` variable for specifying a prefix to be inserted at the beginning of each line of a message included with the ~m command (see p. 608).

**11.5.15
Saving and Deleting
Messages**

Ordinarily, messages are saved in your secondary mailbox after you've read them. The commands in this group let you save messages in other files as well.

mb[ox] [*msglist*]

> Marks the messages of *msglist* for saving in the secondary mailbox. Whenever you issue a quit or file command, all messages so marked are then saved there. A message marked by this command is indicated by an 'M' status in the header summary. If mailx is terminated by an interruption or by exit, all messages have the same status as when mailx started and the special saving indicated by 'M' does not take place.

ho[ld] [*msglist*]
pre[serve] [*msglist*]

> Causes the messages of *msglist* to be left in your primary mailbox when mailx terminates or when you switch files with the file command.

s[ave] [*file*]
s[ave] *msglist file*

> Saves the messages of *msglist* in *file*. When mailx terminates or when you switch files, a second copy of these messages will not be saved to your secondary mailbox. You can force that second copy to be saved by enabling the keepsave variable (see p. 608). The default for *file* is your secondary mailbox.
>
> **Note:** If you specify a message list but fail to specify a file, mailx will misinterpret the message list as a file name.

S[ave] [*msglist*]

> Saves each message of *msglist* in a file named for the sender of the first message (see Section 11.5.5). This command is useful for filing messages according to who sent them to you. It behaves like save except that it puts the messages in a different place.

c[opy] [*file*]
c[opy] *msglist file*

> Copies the messages of *msglist* to *file* without marking them as saved. If you save a message with copy, it appears in your secondary mailbox as well as in the file that you specify with copy. If you don't specify *file*, *file* defaults to your secondary mailbox.
>
> **Note:** If you specify a message list but fail to specify a file, mailx will misinterpret the message list as a file name.

C[opy] [*msglist*]

> Saves each message in *msglist* in a file named for the sender of the first message in *msglist* (see Section 11.5.5). The messages are not marked as saved. Copy behaves like copy except that it

puts the messages in a different place. Alternatively, you can think of `Copy` as behaving like `Save` except for the fact that `Copy` doesn't mark the messages as saved.

`w[rite]` [*msglist*] *file*

> Writes the messages of *msglist* to *file*, omitting headers and the trailing blank line. This command is otherwise equivalent to `save`.

When these commands save messages to a file, they always put those messages at the end of the file. In contrast, when messages are implicitly transferred from your primary mailbox to your secondary mailbox, those messages go at the beginning of the secondary mailbox (so the newest mail is first).

The files named in the `save` and `copy` commands are taken to be in the current directory unless you explicitly designate another directory. A common way to designate another directory is to use the '+' notation described in connection with the `file` command (see p. 600). Note that the current directory is the one from which you called `mailx` and isn't necessarily your home directory.

Deleting and Undeleting Messages. The following commands delete messages and recover deleted messages:

`d[elete]` [*msglist*]

> Deletes the messages of *msglist* from the mailbox. If the `auto-print` variable is set, the message following the deleted one is shown.

`dp` [*msglist*]
`dt` [*msglist*]

> Deletes the messages in *msglist* from the mailbox and shows the message after the last one deleted. This command produces the same effect as `delete` with `autoprint` set.

`u[ndelete]` [*msglist*]

> Undeletes the messages of *msglist*. You can only undelete messages that you've deleted in the same `mailx` session. When you undelete a message, it is marked as having been read even if you did not read it before you deleted it.

**11.5.16
Editing Messages**

The following commands enable you to edit or otherwise manipulate the messages in a set of messages. When you edit a message that is later saved, the edited version is saved.

`e[dit]` [*msglist*]

> Edits the messages in *msglist* using the editor specified in the `mailx` variable `EDITOR` (see p. 609). The default value of `EDITOR` is the line editor `ed`.

`v[isual]` [*msglist*]

> Edits the messages in *msglist* using the editor specified in the

mailx variable `VISUAL` (see p. 610). The default value of `VISUAL` is the visual editor `vi`.

Note: There is no *requirement* that `edit` call a line editor and `visual` call a visual (full-screen) editor. You can, for instance, define one of these "editors" to be a shell script that reformats the messages so that you can easily reply to them. Whatever editor you specify is called with a single argument that names a temporary file containing the messages in *msglist*. `Mailx` puts the text of the messages into this file before it calls the editor and expects to find edited messages in this file when the editor returns.

**11.5.17
Switching Files and Directories**

The following commands pertain to switching files and directories:

ch[dir]*dir*
cd *dir*   Changes the current directory to *dir*.

fold[er] *file*
fi[le] *file* Stops processing the current set of messages and takes a new set from *file*. You can specify *file* by name or by using one of the following notations:

%	Your primary mailbox
%*user*	The primary mailbox of *user*
#	The previous file
&	Your secondary mailbox (as specified by the `MBOX` variable)
+*file*	The file in your folder directory (see p. 609) whose filename is *file*

When you issue this command, the files in your current mailbox are saved just as though you had given the `quit` command. Note that `mailx` understands these notations (except for +*file*) *only* in the context of the `file` command.

so[urce] *file*
              Reads and executes the commands in *file*. Afterwards, `mailx` returns you to command mode.

**11.5.18
Quitting** `mailx`

The following commands let you get out of `mailx`:

q[uit]   Quits `mailx`, saving all the messages you've read in the secondary mailbox. This is the usual way to exit from `mailx`.

x[it]
ex[it]   Exits from `mailx`, leaving your primary mailbox unchanged. The messages there retain the status they had before you called `mailx`. In particular, any messages you deleted will still be there.

**11.5.19
Shells and Pipes**

The following commands enable you to call shells and other programs from within `mailx`, possibly using those other programs to process a set of messages. `Mailx` chooses the shell to use for executing these commands as follows:

(1)   If the `SHELL` variable (see p. 609) has a value, `mailx` uses that value.

(2)   Otherwise, if the environment contains a `SHELL` variable, `mailx` uses the value of that variable.

(3)   Otherwise, `mailx` uses your login shell.

| [[*msglist*] *cmd*]
pi[pe] [[*msglist* [*cmd*]

> Passes the messages in *msglist* as standard input to *cmd*. For example, if *cmd* is `lp` or `lpr`, the messages are printed on your system's printer. You can omit *cmd* if you've given it a default value with the `cmd` variable (see p. 607).

! *cmd*   Executes *cmd* in a subshell.

sh[ell]
> Starts a subshell. You can use this subshell just as you would your login shell. You'll probably find job control or some other form of process switching more convenient than using the `shell` command if your environment provides it (see Section 2.6).

11.5.20
Commands Useful for Initialization

The commands below are primarily useful for adapting `mailx` to your requirements and tastes. To have them executed each time you start `mailx`, put them in your initialization file (see Section 11.5.7).

Defining Alternate Names.   The following commands let you introduce alternate names for people you send mail to and for your own login name:

a[lias] *name namelist*
g[roup] *name namelist*

> Treats *name* as an alias for each name in *namelist*. This command is particularly useful for naming groups of people you send mail to and for providing shortened forms of long addresses. If you issue more than one `alias` or `group` command for a single *name*, the *namelist*s you specify are concatenated. Thus the commands

        group heroes batman@comix.com wonderwoman@comix.com

> and

        group heroes batman@comix.com
        alias heroes wonderwoman@comix.com

> are equivalent.

alt[ernates] *namelist*
> Treats the names in *namelist* as alternates for your login name. This command is useful when you have accounts on more than one system to avoid having automatically generated mail sent to another system.

Setting the Values of Variables.   The following commands let you control the internal variables of `mailx` (see Section 11.5.29). These variables and the commands that set them generally follow the conventions described in Section 2.13.

se[t]   Shows all `mailx` variables and their values.

se[t] *name*
          Enables the `mailx` variable *name*.

se[t] no*name*
          Disables the variable *name*. This form has the same meaning as 'unset *name*'.

se[t] *name*=*string*
          Sets the variable *name* to the value *string*.

se[t] *name*=*n*
          Sets the variable *name* to the numerical value *n*.

uns[et] *namelist*
          Disables (erases) the `mailx` variables in *namelist*.

You can combine settings of several variables in a single `set` command. Here is an example:

```
set metoo crt=24 noignore
```

Conditional Execution.   The following command executes another command conditionally, depending on whether `mailx` was called to send messages or to receive them:

if s *action₁* [el[se] *action₂*] en[dif]
if r *action₁* [el[se] *action₂*] en[dif]
          Executes *action₁* or *action₂* depending on whether `mailx` is sending mail (s) or receiving mail (r). The 'if', 'else', and 'endif' must all appear on separate lines. The items *action₁* and *action₂* are sequences of commands, one per line. As the syntax indicates, the 'else' is optional.

Comments and Messages.   The following commands enable you to put comments in an initialization file and send messages to the terminal:

Treats the rest of the line as a comment.

ec[ho] *string*
          Echoes the string *string* to your terminal.

11.5.21
Input Mode

When you specify one or more mail recipients on the `mailx` command line, `mailx` assumes that you're sending a message, first prompting you for a subject and then putting you into input mode. You then compose your message, ending it with EOF or '~.'. If you've enabled the `dot` variable (see p. 607), you can also end the message with a dot on a line by itself. `Mailx` also puts you into input mode when you use one of the command-mode commands such as `Followup` to reply to a message.

Input mode has a peculiarity of which you should be aware. Because mailx usually calls mail indirectly for local delivery of messages, a line containing just a dot is likely to cause the rest of the message to be lost. Mailx itself, however, processes such a line without comment. If you really want such a line in your message, put a space or two after the dot. This behavior is a good reason for enabling the dot variable.

In input mode, a line starting with '~' is taken as an input-mode command. These lines are sometimes called *tilde escapes*. To include a text line that starts with '~' in a message, double the '~'. You can change the escape character by assigning a different variable to the mailx variable escape (see p. 607). The input-mode commands are described below.

Interrupting Input.   You can break out of input mode without completing the message you're working on by pressing (Intr). Mailx then returns you to command mode or to your shell, depending on how you entered input mode in the first place. Your incomplete message won't be lost, however—mailx stores it in a dead-letter file. By default, that file is ~/dead.letter, but you can choose a different default by setting the DEAD variable (see p. 608). The dead-letter file is *not* cumulative—each interrupted message obliterates the previous one.

11.5.22
Getting Help

The following command provides help for the input-mode commands:

~?   Shows a summary of the input-mode commands.

11.5.23
Showing or Saving the Message

The next two commands let you show or save the text of a partially composed message:

~p   Shows the text of the message composed so far, omitting the header.

~w *file*   Writes the text of the message composed so far to *file*, omitting the header.

11.5.24
Editing the Message

The next two commands let you edit the message you're composing. Because you can't go back to a previous line while composing a message in input mode, these commands provide the best way to construct a message of more than a few lines.

~e   Edits the message text using the editor specified in the mailx variable EDITOR (see p. 609). The default value of EDITOR is the line editor ed.

~v   Edits the message text using the editor specified in the mailx variable VISUAL (see p. 610). The default value of VISUAL is the visual editor vi.

Note that there's no requirement that ~e call a line editor and ~v call a visual editor. For instance, in systems that don't support the ~a and ~A commands for generating signatures, ~e is often used to call a shell script or other program that adds a signature to a message.

**11.5.25
Inserting Text**

The following commands enable you to insert text into a message. The inserted text is always placed at the end of the message you've composed so far.

Inserting the Output of a Command. The following commands execute a command in a subshell and insert the standard output of that command in the message:

~<! *cmd* Executes *cmd* in a subshell and appends its standard output to the message text.

~| *cmd* Pipes the text of the message composed so far through *cmd*, then replaces the message text with the standard output of *cmd*.

Inserting Files and Messages. The following commands include the text of a file or of a received message in a message that you're composing:

~r *file*
~< *file* Appends the contents of *file* to the message text.

~d Appends the contents of the dead-letter file to the message text (see "Interrupting Input" on p. 603).

~f [*msglist*]

    Forwards the messages from *msglist* by inserting them into the message text. You can only use this command when you're replying to a message. Note that the default for *msglist* is the first message you're replying to.

~m [*msglist*]

    Inserts the messages of *msglist* into the message text, shifting them to the right by one tab stop. You can only use this command when you're replying to a message. Note that the default for *msglist* is the first message you're replying to.

The following commands enable you to insert your favorite sequence of signature lines into a message:

~a   Inserts the signature ("autograph") given by the `mailx` variable `sign` into the message text.

~A   Inserts the signature given by the `mailx` variable `Sign` into the message text.

Customarily, ~a is used for an informal signature attached to local mail, while ~A is used for a more formal signature attached to mail sent to other sites. These commands don't exist in some versions of `mailx`.

Inserting the Value of a Variable. The following command inserts the value of a variable into the message:

~i *var* Inserts the value of the `mailx` variable *var* (see Section 11.5.29) into the text. If the value of the variable is empty, you just get a newline.

Inserting a Line Starting with a Tilde. The following command includes in a message a line that starts with a tilde:

~~*text*   Appends the line '~*text*' to the message.

11.5.26
Specifying Header Fields

The following commands enable you to specify or modify the header fields of the message you're composing. In each case, *namelist* is a list of recipients separated by whitespace. If you type one of these commands without a *string* or *namelist*, `mailx` prompts you for the information.

~s *string* Sets the subject line to *string*, discarding the current subject.

~t *namelist*
>   Adds the names in *namelist* to the 'To' (recipient) list of the message.

~c *namelist*
>   Adds the names in *namelist* to the 'Cc' (carbon copy) list of the message.

~b *namelist*
>   Adds the names in *namelist* to the Bcc (blind carbon copy) list of the message.

~h
>   Prompts for the header fields ('Subject', 'To', 'Cc', and 'Bcc') of the message. You can interactively edit the previous contents of these fields.

11.5.27
Issuing Other Commands

You can issue a command-mode command from input mode with the following input-mode command, which you can only use if you originally called `mailx` in receive mode.

~: *cmd*
~_ *cmd*   Performs the command-mode command *cmd*.

The following command calls a subshell from input mode:

~! [*cmd*]   Performs the command *cmd* in a subshell. The shell that is used is the one given in the SHELL variable (see p. 609). The default is the shell named `sh`. If *cmd* is absent, the subshell is given control of your terminal so that you can issue a sequence of UNIX commands.

11.5.28
Quitting `mailx`

The following commands provide alternative ways of leaving `mailx`. You can also leave it, abandoning the message you're composing, by pressing [Intr] twice.

~.
>   Terminates the message you're composing, sends it, and exits from `mailx`.

~q
>   Quits, saving the message text in the dead-letter file (see "Interrupting Input" on p. 603).

~x
>   Quits, abandoning the message text.

If you use these commands in send mode, they terminate the message you're composing but don't terminate `mailx` itself.

**11.5.29
Local and Imported
Variables**

Mailx has a collection of local variables that you can enable, disable, or set (see Section 2.13 and "Setting the Values of Variables" on p. 601). Mailx lets you set and erase any variable, not just those it recognizes. An extra variable can be useful, for example, if you set it to some canned text and later use the ~i input-mode command to insert the text into a message (see p. 604).

Mailx imports the following two variables from its environment:

HOME   Your home directory.

MAILRC   The name of the file of commands that mailx executes when it starts up (see Section 11.5.7).

You cannot modify the values of these variables from within mailx.

**11.5.30
Controlling What
mailx Shows You**

The following variables affect the information that mailx shows you and the format of that information:

header   Show the header summary when starting up. (Enabled by default.)

quiet   Don't show the opening identification line (the one that contains the version number) when starting up in send mode. (Disabled by default.)

toplines=n
          Cause the top command (see p. 595) to show n lines of the header summary. (The default value is 5.)

showto   When mailx is showing a message in the header summary and you're its sender, show the first recipient's name rather than yours. The recipient's name is preceded by 'To'. (Disabled by default.)

autoprint
          Whenever messages are deleted, show the text of the message following the last one that was deleted. Similarly, after messages are restored by undelete, show the last of the restored messages. (Disabled by default.)

screen=n Set the number of lines in a full screen of headers to n. (The default is 20 if your transmission rate is 2400 baud or greater, 10 if your transmission rate is 1200 baud, and 5 otherwise.)

crt=n Send messages of more than n lines to your pager (as selected by PAGER) instead of simply showing them on your screen. The message text is the standard input to the pager. (Disabled by default; that is, don't use a pager.)

PAGER=cmd
          Use cmd as the pager for showing long messages. (The default is usually more [see Section 3.6.1], though on some systems it may be different.)

prompt=*string*
> Set the command-mode prompt to *string*. (The default is '?'.)

debug
> Turn on verbose diagnostics, but suppress the actual delivery of messages. (Disabled by default.)

sendwait
> Wait for the background mailer to finish before returning from `mailx`. (Disabled by default.)

11.5.31
Input Interpretation

The following variables affect the way that `mailx` interprets what you type.

asksub
> In send mode, prompt for a subject if a subject isn't given by the `-s` option on the command line. (Enabled by default.)

bang
> Enable the special casing of '!' in shell escape commands so that typing '!!' causes the previously executed command to be repeated. With this variable disabled, '!!' executes '!' as an ordinary shell command. (Disabled by default.)

escape=*c*
> Use *c* as the escape character when in input mode. (The default is '~'.)

cmd=*cmd*
> If a `pipe` command (see p. 601) is given without an explicit command, use *cmd* as the default. (Disabled by default.)

dot
> When you're composing a message, cause a dot on a line by itself to end the message. Although this option is disabled by default, we strongly recommend enabling it—see page 602 for the reasons.

ignore
> Ignore interrupts while entering messages.[5] Setting this variable can be helpful when you're working with a noisy telephone line, since the line noise can generate spurious interrupts. (Disabled by default.)

ignoreeof
> Ignore end-of-file during message input. If this variable is enabled, you need to end your message either with '~.' or, if you've enabled `dot`, with a dot on a line by itself. (Disabled by default.)

metoo
> Prevent your name from being deleted from an automatically generated list of recipients for a message that you're sending. Normally your name *is* deleted from such a list. (Disabled by default.)

flipr
> Reverse the senses of the `Reply`/`Respond` and `reply`/`respond` commands (see p. 596) so that `Reply` and `Respond` respond to a set of messages, while `reply` and `respond` respond to all recipients of a single message. The original BSD version of `mailx` used the name `Replyall` for this variable, and some versions still use that name instead of `flipr`.

---

5. Don't confuse the `ignore` variable with the `ignore` command.

**11.5.32
Message Processing**

The following variables affect the way that `mailx` processes messages after you've created or saved them.

`append` Append rather than prepend messages sent to the secondary mailbox when you quit; that is, put them at the end rather than at the beginning. (Disabled by default.)

`keep` Don't remove a mailbox when it becomes empty. Normally a mailbox is deleted when `mailx` removes all the messages in it. (Disabled by default.)

`keepsave` When a message is saved to a specific file using a command such as `save`, save it to your secondary mailbox as well. Normally such a message isn't saved to your secondary mailbox when you quit. `Keepsave` has no effect if you're reading messages from any mailbox other than your primary one. (Disabled by default.)

`hold` Preserve messages that you've read in your primary mailbox rather than in your secondary mailbox. (Disabled by default.)

`save` Cause interrupted messages to be saved in the dead-letter file (see "Interrupting Input" on p. 603). If `save` is disabled, such messages are discarded. (Enabled by default.)

`indentprefix=`*string*

Insert *string* at the start of each line included in a response by the `~m` command. The default value is ⟨tab⟩.

`sign=`*string*

Use *string* as the "signature" for the `~a` command. (Empty by default.)

`Sign=`*string*

Use *string* as the "signature" for the `~A` command. (Empty by default.)

`page` Put a ⟨formfeed⟩ after each message passed through the `pipe` command (see p. 601). When the collected messages are displayed on a screen, the ⟨formfeed⟩s make them easier to read. (Disabled by default.)

`record=`*file*

Record all outgoing mail in *file*. If `outfolder` is enabled, *file* is taken as relative to your folder; otherwise, it is taken as relative to your home directory (see the following explanations of `folder` and `outfolder`). (Disabled by default.)

`allnet` Treat network names as identical if their last components match (e.g., treat `mars!alien`, `lune!alien`, and `alien` as all referring to the same person). Enabling this variable avoids having a message sent to the same person at several locations. (Disabled by default.)

**11.5.33
Mailbox Locations**

Using the `followup`, `Followup`, `Save`, and `Copy` commands, you can save a message in a mailbox named after its sender or first recipient. You can also save a message in a mailbox named after its sender by specifying the `-F` option on the command line. Normally `mailx` looks for these mailboxes in your current directory, (the directory you were in when you called `mailx`), but you can have `mailx` look for them in a folder directory instead (see Section 11.5.8). The following commands enable you to define a folder directory:

`folder=`*dir*

> Define the directory for your mail folders to be `~/`*dir*. Enabling `folder` causes the '+' notation for file names to be defined. If `folder` is disabled, no substitution is made for a '+' at the beginning of a file name. You need to create the folder directory yourself; `mailx` won't make it for you. (Disabled by default.)

`outfolder`

> Keep outgoing messages in the directory specified by `folder`. Outgoing messages that you create explicitly are saved in the file designated by the `record` variable; those saved in files named after message senders or recipients follow the rules below. (Disabled by default.)

The following variables specify the location of your secondary mailbox and of the mailbox where `mailx` puts partially completed messages:

`MBOX=`*file*   Use *file* as your secondary mailbox. The location of your secondary mailbox is unaffected by `folder` and `outfolder`, but you can place it in your mail folder by setting `MBOX` to '+mbox'. (The default value of `MBOX` is 'mbox'.)

`DEAD=`*file*   Save partial messages that were interrupted in the dead-letter file *file* (see "Interrupting Input" on p. 603). (The default is `dead.letter`.)

**11.5.34
Command
Interpreters**

The following variables determine the executable UNIX commands that `mailx` calls upon for certain services:

`LISTER=`*cmd*

> Use *cmd* to list the contents of the folder directory. (The default is `ls`.)

`SHELL=`*cmd*

> Use *cmd* as your shell. (The default is the value of the `SHELL` environment variable in effect when `mailx` was called or from your login shell if that environment variable doesn't exist.)

`EDITOR=`*cmd*

> Use *cmd* as the editor for the `~e` command. (The default is the line editor `ed`.)

VISUAL=*cmd*
> Use *cmd* as the editor for the ~v command. (The default is the visual editor vi.)

sendmail=*cmd*
> Use *cmd* as the mail transport agent that actually delivers the messages you send. (The default is usually either /usr/lib/sendmail or /bin/rmail.)

**11.5.35
Network Addressing**

The following variables affect how mailx interprets network addresses (see Section 12.1):

onehop
> Disable alterations to remote recipients' addresses in the case where you're responding to a message that was sent to several remote recipients. If onehop is disabled, mailx adds additional components to the addresses of these recipients so as to get your response from your machine to the machine from which the original message was sent.[6] Enabling onehop may improve efficiency in a network where any node can send messages directly to any other node, but it may also cause messages not to be delivered. (Enabled by default.)

conv=*style*
> Convert UUCP network addresses to the form of *style*. The only value of *style* that mailx currently recognizes is 'internet'. If you set 'conv=internet', an address such as vienna!freud will be recast to freud@vienna.UUCP. (Disabled by default.)

11.6   Other Mailers

We briefly discuss two other popular mailers, MH and elm.

**11.6.1
The MH Message
Handling System**

The MH message handling system is a collection of programs originally developed at the Rand Corporation and subsequently adapted as part of BSD. As the MH manual states, "the list of 'MH immortals' is too long to list here." We briefly summarize the major features of MH.

The approach of MH is very different from that of mailx. Instead of providing a single program for all mail functions, it provides a set of independent programs for particular functions that you can call from an ordinary shell prompt. MH keeps track of the mail context in a context file in your home directory, so a sequence of calls on different MH programs maintains the same continuity that is found in unitary programs

---

6. If you think this explanation is complicated and hard to understand, you're right.

such as `mailx`. For example, after you've read a message, you can read the next one with a simple `next` command at the shell level; no further specification is needed. MH also maintains profile information in a file named `.mh_profile` in your home directory containing the name of the directory where folders and special files are kept, default arguments for each MH program, and other information for customizing MH to your tastes.

Viewing New Mail.   The principal command for viewing new mail is `inc`. It transfers newly arrived messages from your primary mailbox to your secondary mailbox and provides a summary of those messages.

Folders.   MH keeps messages in UNIX directories called *folders*. Each message is kept in its own file; the files within a folder are named by the message numbers. Using the UNIX directory structure, you can have folders within folders. You can also include a message in several folders by creating a link to that message from each folder. This arrangement makes the full power of UNIX available for working with messages, but it has the disadvantage that the messages kept in MH folders cannot be read by other mailers.

Operations on Folders and Messages.   There are four commands for examining the messages in a folder:

`show`	Displays a message or a set of messages.
`prev`	Shows the message preceding the current message.
`next`	Shows the message following the current message.
`scan`	Provides a summary of the messages in the folder.

You can rearrange and examine the messages in folders with the following commands:

`rmm`	Removes a message from a folder.
`pick`	Selects a set of messages based on their contents and assigns that set a sequence name.
`mark`	Modifies a message sequence by adding or deleting messages.
`refile`	Moves a message from one folder to another.
`folder`	Optionally changes to a different folder. It then shows the name of the current folder and summarizes its contents.
`folders`	Summarizes the contents of all the folders.
`rmf`	Removes a message folder.
`anno`	Adds an annotation to a message in a folder. It can also be used to add an annotation to a message after you create it.
`burst`	Breaks up a digest of messages into its individual messages.

Creating and Sending Messages.   The following commands provide for creating and sending messages:

`comp`	Enables you to compose a new message.
`dist`	Redistributes a message to other people.
`forw`	Forwards a message to other people.

`repl`	Enables you to compose and send a reply to a message.
`send`	Retransmits a message or sends the contents of a file as a message.

Aliases.   You can create one or more files of aliases for MH. Each alias associates a name with a group of addresses. A message sent to an alias is sent to all the addresses in its associated group. The `ali` command shows the addresses associated with a particular alias or, alternatively, shows the aliases associated with a particular address.

11.6.2
The `elm` Mailer

The `elm` mailer was written by Dave Taylor and is available in the public domain. Unlike the other mailers discussed in this chapter, `elm` is screen-oriented rather than line-oriented. It is designed to be used with little or no need for auxiliary documentation since it lists the alternative actions available at any point and provides on-line help on all of its facilities. Like other modern mailers, `elm` enables you to forward or reply to a message, to group messages into folders, to delete and move messages, and to create aliases for mail addresses or groups of addresses that you often use. Its interactive nature provides additional conveniences. For example, you can move up and down a message summary with cursor motions and then choose a message to read by pressing (Enter). You can also easily create an alias for the sender of a message after you've received the message.

The primary location for retrieving the `elm` mailer by FTP is `ftp .dsi.com`, directory `/pub/elm`. You can get a list of other sites where `elm` is available by sending the message 'send elm elm.ftp' to `archive-server@dsi.com`.

11.7   Archiving Files for Mailing with `shar`

The widely used `shar` archiver, written by Bill Davidsen, enables you to create an archive in text form that you can include in a mail message. The contents of the archive are self-extracting, so the recipient only has to extract the correct portion of the mail message and execute it as a shell script. The `shar` archiver is not included in POSIX.

The form of the `shar` command line is

```
shar [-bcDflMsvx] [-d delim] [-o ofile] [-lsize] file ...
```

A shell archive containing the specified files is sent to standard output.

Command-Line Options.   The following options determine what `shar` assumes about the input files. By default, `shar` assumes that all input files are text files (and doesn't check that assumption).

`-b`	Assume all input files are binary and convert them to text with `uuencode`.

-M   Assume the input files are a mixture of text files and binary files. Check each one to see if it is a binary file and if it is, convert it to text with `uuencode`.

The following options for `shar` specify how to break up a long input file into shorter output files:

-o *file*   Send the output to file *ofile* rather than to standard output.

-l *size*   Limit each output file to *size* kilobytes. If an output file would be longer than that, it is broken up into segments *ofile*00, *ofile*01, etc. The extraction code included in the archive checks that the files are put together in the right sequence when the archive is unpacked. If you specify -l, you must also specify an output file with -o earlier in the command line. The value *size* must be a two-digit decimal number and must follow '-l with no intervening whitespace.

-s   Check files for damage in transit by applying the `sum` utility to them.[7]

The following options affect whether and where the file is unpacked:

-f   Use only the filename part of each pathname as the output file recorded in the archive. With this option, each file in the archive is unpacked into the current directory.

-x   If a file to be unpacked already exists in the file system, don't overwrite the existing file.

The following options specify additional material to be put into the archive or otherwise modify its form:

-D   Add details to the archive as comments. The details describe the date, user, and working directory when the archive was built.

-c   Produce a line with the text 'cut here' at the beginning of each output file. If you happen to have the `unshar` utility, you can use it to unpack a `shar` archive without extracting the archive from the mail message containing it. `Unshar` reads from standard input or from a file, ignoring everything up to the beginning of an archive, and then applies `sh` to what's left.

-d *delim*   Use *delim* as the delimiter between output files. The default delimiter is `SHAR_EOF`. You should rarely need to change it.

The following option affects the informative messages produced by `shar`:

-v   Produce verbose messages in the form of a running commentary as an archive is being created or unpacked.

---

7. The `sum` utility, which we don't describe in this book, is an older and less robust version of the `cksum` utility.

Unpacking `shar` Archives.   If a `shar` archive consists of a single file *file*, the procedure for unpacking it is simple once you've extracted it from its mail message: execute the command '`sh` *file*'. That will write the file back into its original location or into the current directory if it was packed using the `-f` option. If the archive consists of a sequence of files named *file*01, *file*02, etc., the following command line will do the job:

```
ls -1 file* | xargs -n 1 sh
```

11.8   Newsgroups and Newsreaders

A *newsgroup* is a kind of electronic forum. Participants can post articles on the newsgroup's subject, read the articles posted by others, and reply to articles. Subjects of discussion include nearly any topic you can think of and range from UNIX esoterica (newsgroup `comp.unix.wizards`) to sexual esoterica (newsgroup `alt.sex.bondage`). Some newsgroups are moderated, which means that articles are not actually posted until they have been approved by the newsgroup's moderator. Others are unmoderated; anyone can post to them without restriction.

A particularly useful if not very interesting newsgroup is `alt.test`. Its purpose is to provide a location where you can experiment with posting and retrieving articles, so no one will mind if you place long sequences of '`This is a test`' posts there. More generally, you can post test messages freely to any group whose name ends in '`.test`'.

The Internet has become the major means of distribution of newsgroups, but it isn't the only one. Newsgroups were distributed over the UUCP network long before the Internet gained its current prominence. The largest collection of newsgroups is found in Usenet, a worldwide distributed discussion system.

The programs you use to read newsgroups and post articles to newsgroups are called *newsreaders*, and UNIX includes several of them. A newsreader will do you no good, however, unless you have access to a *news server* it can communicate with. A news server is a program that transmits articles and administrative information such as lists of newsgroups to your newsreader and accepts articles to be posted. The news server, in turn, exchanges articles and other information with other news servers; the information that flows from another server is often called a *news feed*. Most news servers are network nodes dedicated to that one task; the news server you use might well reside on a different machine than your newsreader. Under most circumstances, you'll rely on a network administrator to provide you with access to a news server.

Most newsreaders these days are able to use NNTP (Network News Transport Protocol) to communicate directly with a news server. To connect your newsreader to the server, you need to inform the newsreader of the server's hostname or IP address (see Section 12.1.1) and record that information in the `NNTPSERVER` environment variable. If you're using a local newsreader connected to a remote system, you should be able to get the news server's address from the remote system's administrator.

A very similar kind of electronic forum is the automated mailing list. You join the list by sending a mail message to an appropriate address, usually with the keyword '`Subscribe`' as the message body. Customarily the address is '*list*-`request@`*node*', where *list* is the name of the list and *node* is the location where the list is maintained. Thereafter, every message that's sent to the list is automatically forwarded to you and every message you send to the list is forwarded to all the other subscribers. Such mailing lists take very little maintenance, but they have the disadvantage for a subscriber that there's no good way to sort through the posted messages. They are often used for specialized groups with a relatively small number of participants.

11.9   UNIX Newsreaders

The earliest useful newsreader for UNIX was `rn` (read news), written by Larry Wall and freely distributed. It is no longer widely used, having been replaced by its threaded version, `trn`. The other principal UNIX newsreaders nowadays are `nn` and `tin`. Although the three newsreaders differ in detail and are still being improved, they all share certain concepts and modes of operation. Since they are all about equally capable and easy to use, which one you choose is a matter of taste. The Emacs editor provides a simpler newsreader called GNUS (see Section 10.5). You can also use a Web explorer as a newsreader (see Section 12.4.1).

Since there are thousands of newsgroups available, each newsreader provides a way of subscribing or unsubscribing to particular newsgroups and of listing all the newsgroups provided by your news server (which may not be all those available). A configuration file, usually `~/.newsrc`, keeps track of which newsgroups are available and which ones you've subscribed to. There are three types of information that the newsreader displays for you: the newsgroups, the articles within a newsgroup, and the text of the articles. Usually the articles are grouped by topics, so article selection operates on two levels: selecting the topic and selecting the article within the topic. How this information is displayed and how you select the newsgroups and articles you wish to see depends, of course, on the particular newsreader.

Modern newsreaders also provide a way automatically to designate articles as particularly interesting (you always want to see them) or particularly uninteresting (you never want to see them). The selection can be made on the author or subject of the article. When you call the newsreader to check for new articles, the interesting ones are always marked for showing to you and the uninteresting ones are not even listed in the list of new articles.

When you examine a newsgroup, two kinds of articles might be available: articles left over from when you last looked at the newsgroup and new articles that have arrived since you last invoked the newsreader. One activity is selecting articles you wish to read; another is actually reading them. Generally, the newsreader can keep track of which articles you've read. In addition, having read an article, you might want to keep it around, kill it, save it, reply to it, or reply to its author by mail.

Conventionally, the reply to an article on a subject has the same subject but with the title preceded by 'Re:␣'. Most newsreaders group articles on the same subject together to make it easier to select them. The information in an article's header indicates the other article, if any, to which it was replying. That information enables a newsreader to reconstruct the tree of replies. A threaded newsreader is able to display and navigate the reply tree. `Tin` and `trn` are threaded newsreaders, while `nn` is not.

12

Communicating with Remote Computers

Using the power of your own computer to communicate with remote computers provides important benefits:

- You can send mail or files to remote users and receive mail or files from them.

- You can log in on a remote computer and use its facilities.

- You can retrieve information over the Internet using different tools such as gophers, newsreaders, and World Wide Web explorers.

- Under a windowing system such as X, you can switch back and forth among several remote computers, even using the windowing system to transfer text from one to another (see Chapter 13).

- You can use remote logins as a mechanism for distributing a task among several computers, with the different parts communicating with each other by means of remote procedure calls and similar methods. (A discussion of remote procedure calls is beyond the scope of this book.)

In the first part of this chapter we discuss network addresses, which apply both to sending mail and to other forms of communication with remote computers. In the second part we discuss the programs that you can use to log into remote computers—even ones not running UNIX—and to transfer files to and from those computers.

12.1   Network Addresses

To send a message or a file to someone at another site, you must provide
that person's network address to the program that handles the communication.   In this section we talk about network addresses in terms of
sending messages via mailers—or more precisely, mail transport agents
(see p. 582). See Section 12.1.5 for a discussion of sending files rather
than messages.

UNIX communications software understands two kinds of network
addresses: *path-style addresses* and *domain-style addresses.*[1] A path-style
address specifies the transmission route that the message is to take; a
domain-style address specifies the destination of the message as though
it were a postal address, with each part of the address narrowing down
the location. If someone gives you an electronic mail address, you can
easily tell which kind it is—if it contains '!'s, it's a path-style address, but
if it contains '@'s and dots, it's a domain-style address. Mixed addresses
containing both '!' and '@' are possible but are best avoided.

The two major networks used with UNIX systems are the Internet and
the UUCP network:

- The Internet, successor to the Arpanet, is an internetwork (i.e.,
  a "network of networks") that interconnects most major networks
  sponsored by U.S. organizations in the public sector. It also provides
  connections to the major networks of other countries. Although the
  networks in the Internet are independently managed, the Internet
  appears to its users to be a single network. Individual organizations
  can also belong to the Internet—the Internet structure is indifferent
  to how big its components are or how much substructure they have.

- The UUCP network is entirely composed of computers running
  UNIX or UNIX-like systems such as the MKS system for MS-DOS and
  OS/2. It is named for the uucp program (UNIX to UNIX copy) that
  supports communication from one such computer to another (see
  Section 12.9.3). The UUCP network originally used point-to-point
  telephone connections for all its communication, though modern
  versions of the supporting software can handle other forms of connection as well.

---

1. These are the two kinds of addresses understood by *generic* UNIX software. Particular
network handlers may understand other kinds as well. Moreover, an address for a network
other than the UUCP network or the Internet can almost always be cast into a path-style or
domain-style address. The computer that acts as a gateway for the other network can then
reparse the address as necessary.

As a rule, domain-style addresses are used within the Internet[2] while path-style addresses are used within the UUCP network, though the UUCP network is slowly converting to domain-style addresses.

The World Wide Web (see Section 12.4.1) uses addresses called Universal Resource Locators (URLs). One component of a URL is a domain-style Internet address. Sometimes you may see network addresses given in URL form (e.g., `ftp://prep.ai.mit.edu`).

When you send mail to a domain-style address, your mailer translates that address into a communication path. A path-style address does not require such a translation since it specifies a route explicitly—the mailer has only to know how to send the message one hop further. However, a smart mailer may revise a path-style address in order to provide a better routing or may recognize aliases for sites that are several links away.

We've spoken of messages being sent to people, but the recipient of a message is really a mailbox rather than a person. A mailbox can belong to any entity that handles mail—a specific individual, someone with a particular responsibility (e.g., `Postmaster`), a mailing list, or even a program.

12.1.1 Domain-Style (Internet) Addresses

Domain-style addresses are the standard addressing form for communication over the Internet. Many local-area networks and uucp-based computers also recognize them. A domain-style address specifies the recipient of a message in the form '$p@l_n. \ldots .l_2.l_1$'. Here p is the person you're sending the message to and l_n through l_1 together form a *domain name* that serves as the person's electronic mail address and identifies a computer where the person can receive mail. The l_i (i.e., the components of the domain name) are called *labels*. The domain name is like a postal address—reading from right to left, it narrows down the destination of the message. The names you obtain by deleting labels from left to right are also domain names, although they usually designate groups of computers rather than individual computers—just as "Montana" contains many towns and cities, "Kalispell, Montana" contains a number of streets, and so forth. To send someone a message, you must specify a domain narrow enough to identify a computer where that person is known.

For instance, the address dduck@orlando.disney.com[3] would be interpreted as follows: Within the domain of commercial institutions (`com`), look for a particular commercial institution (`disney.com`); within that institution, look for the site `orlando.disney.com`. Send the message to the person `dduck` who receives mail via that site.

---

2. A number of networks, such as Telemail and SPAN, use other kinds of addresses but are connected to the Internet through one or more gateway computers. The usual convention for sending mail to a location on a network such as Telemail is to treat the entire Telemail address as though it referred to a single individual at the gateway site. It may be necessary to transform the Telemail address somewhat in order to get it to work; the rules are network-specific and beyond the scope of this book.

3. After inventing this example, we were intrigued to discover that Walt Disney International does indeed have an Internet connection under the domain name `walt.disney.com`.

The rightmost label in an Internet address is a three-letter code for most addresses within the United States ('com', 'gov', 'edu', 'org', etc.). For addresses outside of the United States and for some United States addresses as well, it is a two-letter country code ('.uk', '.jp', '.fr', '.us', etc.). These labels are called *top-level domains* or *administrative domains*.

Hosts and Name Servers.   The term *host* is often used in the computing literature but rarely defined. We take it to mean a computer that renders services to other computers. In the Internet world, the hosts are just the computers that are connected to the Internet. Often any computer connected to a network is called a host, even one connected only to a local-area network. Most Internet hosts act as mail delivery agents for a domain or a group of domains. A few hosts provide other specialized services such as looking up addresses. When a host handles mail delivery for a domain, it usually handles mail delivery for the subdomains of that domain as well. However, some subdomains have their own Internet connections; mail addressed to them usually goes to them directly rather than through the host responsible for an outer domain.[4] A few hosts also handle mail for destinations such as computers on other networks that are not part of the Internet.

When a mailer connected to the Internet is given a message to deliver, the mailer sends a query to one or more *name servers* to find out where to send the message. The query specifies the domain appearing in the message's address. The name servers respond with the IP address of the Internet host that handles mail for that domain;[5] the IP address is a physical address that acts like a telephone number (see "IP Addresses" on p. 621). The originating mailer then ships the message to the IP address.

A host that receives a message sent via the Internet may in turn need to forward it to some other computer, particularly if the host is responsible for a number of domains. When you see a very long computer-generated domain name, the chances are that the name servers use only the rightmost few components of it to select an Internet host—the rest of the components are used by the host itself to effect delivery. Mailers often generate origination addresses that include the label of every domain containing the point of origin, even when many of those labels aren't needed. So if someone gives you a short mail address, use it—even if the return address in the mail you receive from that person is longer.

---

4.   The relation between hosts and domain names is one-to-many; that is, every domain has a single host responsible for it, but a single host may be responsible for many domains. If the domain is very broad, the responsibility probably won't include actual mail delivery but will include services such as looking up addresses of subdomains.

5.   What actually happens is that if the name server for the outermost domain doesn't know the IP address of the appropriate host, it returns the IP address of a more specialized name server that might know it. A mailer thus calls upon a sequence of name servers, each responsible for a narrower domain than the one before, until it finds a name server that does know the IP address.

For instance, suppose that you receive a message from

```
dduck@fantasy.orlando.disney.com
```

but the sender advises you to use the return address `dduck@orlando.`
`disney.com`. It's possible that `fantasy` is a host that's not always connected
to the Internet, or that for some other reason, `fantasy` is not the best place
to send `dduck`'s mail. In this case, the host that handles mail for `orlando.`
`disney.com` should know how to deliver `dduck`'s mail.

Note the following:

- Internet domain names are case-insensitive, unlike UUCP addresses.

- A valid domain may be a subdomain of some other domain; that
  is, it may have the same name but with additional labels. The user
  names associated with the domain and the subdomain have no necessary relation. For instance, `walt@orlando.disney.com` and `walt@`
  `disney.com` might be two different people, or one of those users
  might exist even though the other one doesn't.[6]

- You may be able to omit extra labels in the domain name, but
  don't count on it. For instance, you might be able to shorten the
  address `dduck@fantasy.orlando.disney.com` to `dduck@orlando.`
  `disney.com`—or you might not. It all depends on how much
  the responsible host knows about the users in the domains that it
  handles. If the `orlando` host knows that `dduck` receives mail from
  the computer at the `fantasy` domain, the `fantasy` label probably
  isn't needed.

IP Addresses.   An *IP address* (Internet protocol address) specifies the
exact routing to an Internet host. When a name server is given a domain
name, it resolves that name to an IP address. Two programs, `telnet` and
`ftp`, accept IP addresses as alternatives to domain names (see Sections
12.7 and 12.8). If you need to communicate with an Internet site but
the programs you are using cannot communicate with a name server, you
can use the IP address of the site instead. A disadvantage of using IP
addresses is that they sometimes change.

An IP address consists of four numbers (e.g., '`126.6.40.93`'). The structure is similar to that of a telephone number, with the first number acting
as an area code, the second as an exchange, etc. Just as a telephone number tells the telephone switching equipment how to reach the telephones
that bear that number, an IP address tells the network software how to
reach the host that has that address. The structure of an IP address is
more complicated because it accounts for several classes of networks, each
with the capacity for a different number of nodes.

---

6. If you have accounts on several machines, it's a good idea to use the same name for all of
them if you can. This may not always be possible—if you have a user name `morris` on your
local machine, you may well find that there's already another `morris` on a remote machine
where you're establishing an account.

Use of Percents. You may encounter a domain-style address with extra components for local addressing, marked off by '%'. These components are ignored by Internet mailers, but are used by local hosts for mail delivery. For example, the address

```
minnie%fantasy@orlando.disney.com
```

indicates that `fantasy` is the name of the computer where Minnie receives her mail (and that the `orlando.disney.com` host knows how to deliver mail to `fantasy`). You might also sometimes see this address as

```
minnie%fantasy@fantasy.orlando.disney.com
```

There's a chance this form won't work even if it was generated by a mailer. You can often repair it by omitting the '`%fantasy`' after '`minnie`'.

Looking Up Internet Domains. You can get information about Internet domains with the `whois`, `nslookup`, `dig`, and `host` programs if they are available on your system:

- The `whois` program provides administrative information about a domain such as its full name, location, and the names of the site administrators, but does not list all the lowest-level domains.

- The `nslookup` program provides the IP address of any domain, even one at the lowest level. It also provides other information about the domain chiefly of interest to network administrators.

- The `dig` program is similar to `nslookup` but has a better interface and is easier to program in shell scripts. You can get `dig` via anonymous FTP from `venera.isi.edu` or from `ftp.uu.net`, directory `networking/ip/dns`.

- The `host` program called without options simply converts between the domain name of a host and its Internet address. With the `-a` option, it provides exhaustive information about the domain. `Host` is particularly easy to use from the command line.

**12.1.2
Path-Style
(UUCP Network)
Addresses**

In a path-style address—the kind that's used within the UUCP network—you specify the explicit routing that the message is to take in the form '$a_1!a_2!\ldots!a_n!p$'. This notation indicates that the message is first to be sent from your computer to the site a_1, from there to the site a_2, and so on. The final destination is the person p at the site a_n. For example, the address

```
tinker!evers!chance!ruth
```

indicates that the message is to be passed first to the site `tinker`, then to the site `evers`, then to the site `chance`, and finally to the person `ruth` at that site.

Suppose you want to send a message to a remote site but don't know of a path to that site. You may be able to get your message there by sending it to a site that has a smart mailer containing a table giving the layout of the

UUCP network. The smart mailer can then fill in the rest of the path. For instance, suppose you want to send a message to moby at the site whales. You don't know of a path to whales, but you know that the site benezra has a smart mailer. You might be able to get your message to moby by sending it to

```
benezra!whales!moby
```

possibly with some other path components preceding benezra. Benezra will then supply the routing needed to get your message to whales (assuming that whales is a registered UUCP site).[7] A set of maps showing the connections among UUCP computers is currently available by FTP from ftp.uu.net, directory networking/uumap.

Sometimes someone will give you a UUCP address like

```
...{jupiter, saturn, mars}!earth!peoria!oldlady
```

or possibly

```
...{jupiter|saturn|mars}!earth!peoria!oldlady
```

Such an address means that you can reach the person oldlady at any of the addresses

```
...!jupiter!earth!peoria!oldlady
...!saturn!earth!peoria!oldlady
...!mars!earth!peoria!oldlady
```

where the ... indicates some sequence of sites that will get you to jupiter, saturn, or mars (which presumably are registered UUCP sites).

Be careful when writing path-style addresses on a command line under the C shell. The '!' character has a special meaning to that shell. If you write something like

```
mailx athens!timon
```

it won't work; the shell will interpret the '!' as referring to the previous command line. Instead you must quote the '!', like this:

```
mailx athens\!timon
```

Double quotes aren't sufficient here to prevent the misinterpretation of the '!'.

The path-style addresses used within the UUCP network, like nearly everything else in UNIX, are case-sensitive.

---

7. When a message is sent over a path with intermediate nodes, the intermediate nodes bear the cost of the transmission but gain none of its benefits. UNIX system managers may grumble about it but generally have been willing to tolerate it as long as their hospitality is not abused, on the assumption that the externally imposed costs and the benefits to their own users will eventually even out.

12.1.3
Addresses Involving More Than One Network

It's almost always better to send a message using just a single network, be it the UUCP network or the Internet. But when you're on one network and you need to send a message to someone who's only on another, you can't avoid crossing network boundaries. Sending a message over a path involving both the Internet and the UUCP network requires that you route your message through a *gateway*—a computer connected to both networks. You often can send such as message without using a mixed address, but you can use a mixed address if all else fails.

Internet to UUCP. To send a message from the Internet to the UUCP network, put the UUCP routing from the gateway at the left of the '@'. For instance, suppose that `mandelbaum.il` is the Internet domain name for a gateway to the UUCP network.[8] Then the message address

>   amman!hussein@mandelbaum.il

specifies that the message should first be sent to the Internet node `mandelbaum.il`. The host in charge of that node forwards the message to the UUCP node `amman`, which in turn delivers the message to the user `hussein`. A safer form of the same address—if it works—is

>   mandelbaum.il!amman!hussein

Another example of a UUCP address acceptable to an Internet mailer is

>   heehaw%barn3.uucp@agri.com

This address tells the host responsible for the domain `agri.com` to send the message to the person `heehaw` at the UUCP site `barn3` known to the `agri.com` host. Observe carefully the inversion of order here: with the '%' notation, the UUCP site comes after rather than before the user name. As before, an alternate form is

>   agri.com!barn3!heehaw

UUCP to Internet. To send a message from the UUCP network to the Internet, construct a path-style address in which the next to the last component is the Internet domain name for the gateway and the last component is the person you want to send the message to. Assume as above that `mandelbaum` is a UUCP node that serves as a gateway to the Internet. Then an example of such an address is

>   amman!mandelbaum!knesset.il!sharon

A message with this address is passed by the UUCP node `amman` to the UUCP node `mandelbaum`, which in turn passes the message to the user `sharon` at the Internet node `knesset.il`.

You may also be able to send the message using the address

>   amman!mandelbaum!sharon%knesset.il

---

8. The Internet country code for Israel is '`il`'; the Mandelbaum Gate was the only crossing point between East and West Jerusalem during the period 1948–1967.

An up-to-date UUCP mailer turns the '%' into an '@' and treats `sharon@knesset.il` as a conventional Internet address. A '%' is supposed to be treated as belonging to the local part of an address, not to be interpreted if the address includes any routing information. In this example, `mandelbaum` is the only host entitled to interpret `sharon%knesset.il`.

More on Mixed Addresses. A hazard of using mixed addresses—and one of the reasons for staying within one network whenever you can—is that different mailers may interpret them differently. The Internet conventions specify that '@' has precedence over everything else, but some older UUCP mailers may not follow them. Thus the address

> `garden!alice@wonderland.uk`

ought to be interpreted by routing the message first to `wonderland` and then to `garden`, where `alice` is. But an older UUCP mailer might instead send the message to `garden`, expecting the mailer there to send it to `alice@wonderland.uk`.

Occasionally you may see an address such as `zeus@olympus.uucp`, a domain-style version of the UUCP address `olympus!zeus` (`olympus` being a registered UUCP site). This address won't work from an Internet site unless your Internet mailer understands the UUCP network. Two possible alternatives are the following:

> `zeus%olympus.uucp@uunet.uu.net`
> `uunet.uu.net!olympus!zeus`

In these addresses, `uunet` is the name of a specific host that is responsible for relaying messages between the Internet and the UUCP net.

Domain-style addresses are also sometimes used for sending mail to other networks such as Bitnet that are connected to the Internet but are not part of it. The addresses have the same form as Internet addresses. An example of such an address is

> `cindy@castle.bitnet`

The '`bitnet`' label is not the name of an Internet domain, but many mailers will recognize it as a "fake domain" and handle it properly. An Internet mailer may also recognize direct Bitnet addresses such as

> `cindy@castle`

Another example is

> `60173.542@compuserve.com`

which refers to user [60173,542] on the Compuserve network.

<table>
<tr><td>

**12.1.4
When Messages
Go Astray**

</td><td>

A message you send to a remote site is handled by at least two mailers, the one at your site and the one at the destination site, and often by several more.[9] The header information on a message that you receive should tell you which mailers have handled it.

</td></tr>
</table>

---

9. We emphasize what we mentioned earlier: the mailers involved here are mail transport agents, not mail user agents.

A message can go astray in either of two ways: it can be rejected by some mailer on the way or it can be lost entirely. It's unusual for a message to be lost entirely, but it does happen. *Very* rarely, a message will be sent to an inappropriate destination such as an unrelated newsgroup and accepted there. If a message is rejected, a copy of it is sent back to you accompanied by a log of the mailers that handled it. But alas, if a message is lost, you may never know it unless you've asked for a return receipt, and very few mailers are able to provide one. You can insert a `Return-Receipt-To:` field into a header with a mailer such as the one in Emacs that allows you to construct your own headers (see Section 10.4). Whether or not a return receipt is actually generated depends on the receiving mailer. A mailer that conforms to the Internet rules generates the return receipt, but some mailers on the UUCP network do not.

Problems with Automatic Replying. When you respond to a message using an automatic reply mechanism such as the `reply` command of `mailx` (see p. 596), your response may go astray if the apparent source of the message is not the right address or is not an address acceptable to *your* mailer. Mixed addresses are particularly vulnerable to being mangled, especially by some older mailers. In some cases the apparent source will be in a 'Reply-To' component of the message header; if the header doesn't have such a component, your mailer will probably look for the source in the 'From' component (the one with the colon). If it finds more than one address there, an address enclosed in '< ... >' takes precedence. Most modern mailers can recognize 'Reply-To'.

A return address will be wrong if the message you're responding to was forwarded and the return address is that of the forwarder rather than that of the original author. Usually a topical forum sends out messages under its own name rather than under the names of the contributors to the forum, so a reply to such a message reaches the original contributor either indirectly or not at all. If you get one of your own messages back from `MAILER-DAEMON` or `Postmaster`, there's little point in using the `reply` mechanism—especially to `MAILER-DAEMON`.

Addressing Convention Conflicts. Messages that pass through both the UUCP network and the Internet may be misdirected because UUCP network addresses are case-sensitive ('a' and 'A' are different), while Internet addresses are case-insensitive ('a' and 'A' are the same). Some Bitnet mailers convert addresses to all lowercase or all uppercase; when such an address reaches the UUCP network via the Internet, it is likely to be incorrect. You may be able to cure this problem by replacing the first component *a* of the UUCP address by '`a.uucp`', which tells the mailers how *a* is to be interpreted.

Other Problems. If a message is lost, you may be the victim of an overzealous mailer somewhere on its path. For instance, some mailers attempt to eliminate duplicate addresses and messages that appear to be caught in an endless cycle of retransmissions. If your message appears to be one of those but isn't, it may vanish.

Finally, if you're having a problem getting mail through to a particular location and nothing seems to work, you can send mail to `Postmaster` at that address—or, if that doesn't work, to your local `Postmaster` if you have one. Every Internet site has a person—not just some clever program—who is responsible for handling mail problems involving that site.[10]

**12.1.5
Addressing
Considerations for
File Transmission**

Sending a file via the UUCP network is similar to sending a message—a file is always sent to a particular person. Instead of using a mailer, you use `uucp` or one of its relatives. These programs are described later in this chapter. The address you use for sending a file is the same as the one you use for sending a message.

Sending a file via the Internet or another network using the TCP/IP protocols (see "TCP/IP" on p. 628) is fundamentally different from sending a message. These networks don't provide methods of sending files to individuals.[11] Instead, they provide programs for explicitly copying a file from one machine to another (see the descriptions of `ftp` and `rcp` later in this chapter). The implication for addressing is that when you transmit a file, you provide the address of a computer, not a person. In terms of domain addresses, you use only the text to the right of the '@'. However, the considerations for resolving such addresses are the same as they are for mail messages.

12.2 Local-Area Networks

Perhaps the most common type of UNIX system today is a collection of workstations and servers connected by an Ethernet using the TCP/IP protocols. The servers provide administrative services and network connections and also act as repositories for files, both those shared among users and those private to individual users.

Ethernets. An Ethernet is a kind of local area network in which the nodes can be connected by simple direct wiring and can communicate with one another just by sending a properly addressed message over the network. The key to the Ethernet technology is its ability to resolve collisions among messages sent at the same time. The Ethernet idea was invented by Robert Metcalf at the Xerox Corporation Palo Alto Research Center.

---

10. Of course, if the program is clever enough, no one will ever know that it isn't a person.

11. People sometimes get around this limitation by putting files into mail messages. That's not a good practice since it tends to overload both mailers and people's mailboxes.

TCP/IP. TCP/IP, which stands for "Transmission Control Protocol/ Internet Protocol", is a set of rules governing transmission of information between computers (including the case of transmission between a server and a workstation):

- TCP deals with the assembly and disassembly of data packets, which are the units of information sent over the network. It is responsible for guaranteeing the integrity of the data and will request that a packet be re-sent if necessary.
- IP deals with the assembly of data packets into *datagrams* and the delivery of datagrams to a specified IP address (see "IP Addresses" on p. 621), and provides network-level services such as choosing a routing for a datagram.

Users rarely deal with TCP or IP directly, but it's useful to know what they are because references to them appear so frequently in UNIX literature.

12.3   Distributing Files Over Networks

All modern UNIX systems provide facilities for distributing various kinds of files over networks. These facilities are designed to be nearly transparent to the operations that you might perform on files. In other words, as a user you rarely either know or care whether the files you're using reside on your own workstation or on a file server. The only time you're likely to be concerned with the location of files is when you want to make files local for efficiency reasons or when something goes wrong. With most modern systems, the issue of efficiency rarely arises, since file servers transmit files almost as rapidly as you could access them locally.

Nonetheless, it's helpful to be familiar with the two major facilities for distributed files because references to them crop up so frequently in UNIX literature and documentation:

- NIS, the Network Information Service, is a database of system administration information, earlier known as the Sun Yellow Pages. An example of information often provided through NIS is the password file. The NIS database is ordinarily kept on one or more servers, where it can be accessed by any host with the right permissions. This arrangement makes it much easier to maintain the database than it would be if copies of the database were kept in several locations, since it avoids the problem of inconsistent updating.
- NFS, the Network File System, is a facility that allows a file system to be on a different computer than its mount point (see p. 40). Since mount points are the points of connection among file systems, this facility is the key to distributing files over several computers in a

way that allows the files to be accessed as though they were local. NFS uses IP, the Internet Protocol, for data transmission. NFS has been implemented under other operating systems besides UNIX, so NFS can even be used to share files among computers that are not running the same operating system.

12.4   Internet Resources

The Internet is a rich source of information about UNIX and UNIX software, as well as information about practically any other area of interest you can think of. In Section 11.8 we discuss newsgroups; in this section we discuss other Internet resources. Using the Internet is a major subject in itself and a rapidly changing one, so our goal in this section is merely to describe some of the important resources that are available. A good source of further information is the book by LaQuey and Ryer (reference [B16]).

12.4.1
Exploring the
World Wide Web

The World Wide Web, first developed at CERN, provides a way of exploring information resources distributed throughout the Internet. The resources include not just text files but also graphics and audio. The most popular Web exploration program is Mosaic, which provides a graphical interface. You can also use programs such as `lynx` to explore the Web using a text-based interface. Although a graphical interface might at first seem the better way to go, it does have the disadvantage of requiring a high-speed connection to the source of its data. At speeds less than 14,400 bps, a text-based interface is likely to be much more pleasant to use. Just about all Web explorers are very intuitive and easy to use.

A Web explorer can access many different kinds of resources through different protocols. The protocols include traditional Internet services such as `ftp` and `telnet` (see Sections 12.8 and 12.7), but by far the most common protocol used with Web explorers is the `http` protocol (Hypertext Transport Protocol). The resources accessed through this protocol are called *home pages*. A *home page* is simply a file written in HTML, the Hypertext Markup Language. This language provides a way of designating further resources from within an HTML document. A Web explorer, accessing the document, can then proceed to explore any of the resources it references. The resources can be located anywhere on the Internet, which is why the Web is such a powerful concept.

Web resources are located via an address called a *universal resource locator*, or URL. The general form of a URL is

$$protocol\!:\!/\!/hostname[\,:port][\,/path/filename]$$

Each protocol corresponds to a server that is able to locate a type of resource. Some commonly accepted protocols and the resources they access are the following:

`http`	Files written in HTML
`ftp`	Directories accessible via FTP
`telnet`	Ports that accept `telnet` logins, including `archie` sites
`gopher`	Gopher clients

You can use a Web server to explore the directories of an FTP site, and it may even be more convenient to do that than to use the `ftp` program. For example, the Web server makes it easy to view text files that you find as you're exploring the site or to move around the directory structure there. You can also use a Web server to access a newsgroup, but the URL syntax for that is a special case, namely

> `news:`*newsgroup*

A port that accepts accesses using the `http` protocol must be running an `http` server, also called an `http` dæmon. At some sites, any user can create his or her own home page. The server then routes incoming Web traffic to the appropriate home page.

12.4.2 Browsing Menus with a Gopher

Gopher is a menu-based system for exploring Internet resources that is a predecessor of the World Wide Web. It consists of a network of clients, each capable of transferring to other clients. Many systems already have a Gopher client, which you can access just by typing `gopher`. You'll be given a list of choices, most of which will pertain to the first gopher you started at. Some choices will be directories, others documents. If you choose a document, you'll get to view it and, if you wish, retrieve it. If you choose a directory, you'll see a similar list of choices. For example, many gophers are located at universities; a typical menu might look like this:

```
  -->  1.  About the University/
       2.  University Services/
       3.  Using Computers on Campus/
       4.  Academic Department Information/
       5.  Administrative Department Information/
       6.  Governance Bodies/
            . . .
```

Items ending with a slash are directories; other items are viewable files.

There should always be a choice labelled "Other Gophers" or something like that. That choice is your key to getting to other gophers.

12.4.3 Locating Files with Archie

The Archie program performs an interactive search for files available via FTP from Internet sites. To access `archie`, use `telnet` to call an Archie server and log in under the name `archie`. No password is required. A short help screen will come up explaining how to use the system.

Archie can search for files either by their names or by their descriptors. Several kinds of file searches are available: exact matching, regular expression matching, case-sensitive substring matching, and case-insensitive substring matching. Descriptor searches yield the names of files whose descriptors contain the search string as a substring. Descriptor searches depend on a database that may not be as complete or as current as the file lists.

Generally, you should try to use an Archie server that's near you geographically. To do that, call any Archie server at all and issue the `servers` command. You'll get a list of all the servers, from which you can choose the one to use next time. To get started you can use the server at `archie.internic.net`, which happens to be located in New Jersey.

12.5   Programs for Remote Communications

In the rest of this chapter, we describe a number of programs for remote communications. They fall into several groups, reflecting the different forms of connection to remote computers as well as UNIX history—for a long time, the AT&T tradition was to connect computers via dial-up telephone lines or direct wires, while the Berkeley tradition was to connect computers via packet-switched networks. The following table shows how the different programs relate:

Operation	Dial-up Connections	Local Network Connections	Remote Network Connections
Logging in	`cu`	`rlogin,` `tolnot`	`rlogin,` `tolnot`
Copying files	`uucp, uuto,` `uupick`	`rcp, ftp`	`ftp`
Other operations	`uuname`	`rsh, rwho`	—

Generally, the goal of the programs that work over local network connections is to make the connection between the local computer and the remote one as transparent as possible. The programs for local network connections assume that all the computers involved are running UNIX and that the computers are aware of each other. Most of the programs that work over dial-up lines and over remote network connections do not make that assumption.

Two programs are particularly useful when you need to send a binary file to another computer in the form of a mail message: `uuencode` and `uudecode` (see Section 3.13.3). The `uuencode` program transforms a binary file into a sequence of printable ASCII characters; the `uudecode` program undoes the transformation.

A popular program for transmitting files to and from remote computers is `kermit`, a public-domain contribution from Columbia University. Kermit was designed to work over phone lines but has been extended to work over TCP/IP and X25 networks as well. Like `ftp`, it is supported by many different kinds of systems. You can obtain `kermit` over the Internet via anonymous `ftp` from `watsun.cc.columbia.edu`.

12.6   Remote Operations on "Nearby" Computers

The commands described below provide operations on remote computers that are very similar to operations on your own computer. They have names such as `rlogin` that start with 'r', indicating that they are remote versions of local commands. Except for `rlogin`, they all require that the remote computer be "nearby" in the sense that it recognizes and trusts your local computer—and even `rlogin` works more conveniently if the remote computer is nearby. The notion of a computer being recognized and trusted is quite specific: when data is transmitted to such a computer on a local-area network, the computer can verify that the sending computer is on its own list of trusted computers. That list, in turn, is prepared by a system administrator and ordinarily consists of a group of computers that share account names. Computer systems that share account names are sometimes said to be *equivalent*.

12.6.1
Files Used for
Remote Operations

The remote operations described below make use of certain files, both in system-wide directories and in the directories of individual users. Understanding these files is helpful in understanding how the commands work.

`/etc/hosts`

> This file contains a list of other computers (not necessarily trusted ones) known to your computer. A sample line in the `hosts` file might be

---
```
158.121.104.3 head.god.net zeus bigshot  # from Olympus
```

> Here the first item is an Ethernet or Internet address, the second item is the full domain name of the remote computer, and the remaining items are nicknames, or alternate names, of that computer. In this case, the network address is `158.121.104` and the full domain name of the computer there is '`head.god.net`', with nicknames '`zeus`' and '`bigshot`'. The material after the '`#`' is a comment. You can use an alternate name whenever you need to refer to a remote computer in a command.

`/etc/hosts.equiv`

> This file contains a list of other computers equivalent to your

local computer (i.e., that share account names). Computers that are not part of a local-area network usually do not have this file. Each line in the file contains an entry of the form

> [-]*host* [[-]*user*]

where *host* is the official name of an equivalent computer and *user* is a user on that computer. An entry without a '-' indicates that access is allowed. A '-' in an entry indicates that access is denied, either to the computer entirely or to a particular user (e.g., `guest` or `root`) on that computer. Negative entries are intended to override other equivalences that would otherwise be in effect.

`/usr/hosts`

> This directory contains links to the remote shell program `rsh` (see Section 12.6.3). Each link has the name of a remote computer and serves as a command to execute `rsh` on that computer. For instance, if `/usr/hosts` contains a file `hammarfest`, then the command `hammarfest` is equivalent to `rsh hammarfest`. `Rsh` is clever enough to know the name under which it was called.

`~/.rhosts`

> This file, unlike the others listed above, is in *your* home directory and under your control. It enables you to permit a user located on another computer (most likely yourself using an account there) to log in as you on your local computer without providing a password. This permission is essential to using the `rcp` and `rsh` programs from a remote computer.[12]
>
> Each line in the file contains the name of a remote computer and a user name. For example, the line
>
> > `hammarfest gynt`
>
> specifies that user `gynt` on the computer `hammarfest` can log in and assume your identity without providing a password. In addition, you can log in as yourself from a trusted remote computer listed in `/etc/hosts.equiv`.
>
> The name that you use in your `.rhosts` file must be the full domain-style name of the remote computer, which may be longer than the name that you ordinarily use to refer to

---

12. Careless use of this file can create security hazards, since it enables an intruder who has captured your password on one computer to penetrate all the other computers where you have access. In particular, `.rhosts` should not be used for the `root` user at all except on a system that is isolated from the rest of the world.

that computer. Here are three ways to find out what the full name is:

(1) If you can connect to the remote computer using `telnet` (by any name), you'll find its full name on the banner line that appears when you make the connection.

(2) Look for the name of the remote computer in `/etc/hosts` on your own computer. The name to use in `.rhosts` is the first one listed on the relevant line of `/etc/hosts` (after the network address).

(3) Look at the first `Received` header line on mail you've received from that computer.

If you have an account on a remote computer that isn't equivalent to your local computer, you can set yourself up to log onto it without a password by making an appropriate entry in your `.rhosts` file under your own user name.[13]

12.6.2 Remote Login with `rlogin`

The `rlogin` command enables you to log in at a remote computer via a network. The form of the `rlogin` command line is

        rlogin *rhost* [-8] [-e*c*] [-l *user*]

For some systems, the order is reversed:

        rlogin [-8] [-e*c*] [-l *user*] *rhost*

In either case, *rhost* is the name of the remote computer. If you don't provide a user name with the -l option, you are logged in under your own name. If the remote computer is equivalent (see Section 12.6.1), you don't need to provide a password. You'll be disconnected from the remote computer when you log out; alternatively, you can disconnect by typing '~.' (or '*c*.' if you've changed your escape character to *c* with the -e option).

When you log in at a remote computer, your terminal type is the same on the remote computer as on your local computer; in most respects, you can use the remote computer as you would your local computer.

Command-Line Options. The `rlogin` command has the following options:

-l *user*   Log in as *user* rather than as yourself. You need not provide a password if you are listed in the `.rhosts` file located in the home directory of the account you are trying to access on the remote computer (see Section 12.6.1).

-e*c*   Use *c* as the escape character. There must not be any space between the 'e' and *c*.

-8   Use an eight-bit data path.

---

13. Although many people use this shortcut, a number of experts advise against it for security reasons.

**12.6.3
Executing a Shell
Command Remotely
with** rsh

The rsh command enables you to execute a command on a remote computer. To use it, the remote computer must be one that you can log onto using rlogin without a password. The form of the rsh command line is

rsh *rhost* [-ln] [*cmd*]

where *rhost* is the name of a remote computer and *cmd* is a command to be executed on that computer. If you omit *cmd*, rsh becomes equivalent to rlogin. In this context it supports the -l option but not the -e or -8 option.

If the remote computer is listed in /usr/hosts, you can execute a command on it by typing its name and the name of the command. For instance, if fakir is listed there and you type

fakir make believe

the command make believe is executed on fakir. The result is the same as if you had logged in on fakir under your own name (or the name specified with -l) and executed the command there.

Remember that shell metacharacters such as '<' are interpreted on the local computer, not on the remote one, unless you quote them. For example, the command

rsh fakir make believe \> belfile

is the proper way to execute the command make believe on the remote computer, redirecting its output to the file belfile there.

Rsh is not ordinarily able to execute in the background even if *cmd* expects no input, since rsh itself tries to read input in order to pass it to *cmd* and thereby becomes blocked. You can enable rsh to execute in the background by using the -n option, explicitly indicating that *cmd* expects no input.

Unfortunately, another UNIX program, the restricted Bourne shell, also has the name rsh on some systems. If your system includes both programs, the one you get when you type 'rsh' depends on the value of your $PATH environment variable. The restricted Bourne shell is usually stored as /bin/rsh; the remote shell program is usually stored as /usr/ucb/rsh. The authors of the remote shell program recommend that you provide another link to it under a name such as remsh, and some System V systems come with that link already installed.

Command-Line Options. The rsh command line has the following options:

-l *user*   Log in as *user* rather than as yourself. If you're listed in the ~*user*/.rhosts file on the remote computer (see Section 12.6.1), you need not provide a password.

-n   Take input from /dev/null, thus enabling rsh to execute in the background.

12.6.4 Remote Copying with `rcp`

The `rcp` command enables you to copy files from one computer to another. For this command to work, you must be able to log onto each remote computer involved in the copy without providing a password (see Section 12.6.2). The form of the `rcp` command line is

> `rcp [-pr]` *source ... dest*

where each *source* is a source file or directory and *dest* is a destination file or directory. Each source and destination has the form

> [*rhost*:]*path*

where *rhost* is the name of a remote computer and *path* is the pathname of the file or directory you wish to use as a source or destination. If you omit *rhost*, `rcp` assumes that the computer is your local computer. For the purposes of the copy, the current directory on a remote computer is assumed to be your home directory there. The copy applies both to directories and files.

Note: You can use `rcp` to copy files from one remote computer to another as well as to copy files to or from your local computer.

By default, the login implied by `rcp` takes place under your own user name. You can copy files stored under another user name provided that you can log in at the remote computer under that name without a password. To do this, replace *rhost* by '*ruser@rhost*', where *ruser* is the user name on the remote computer *rhost*. For example, the file name

> `rajiv@fakir:items/ropes`

refers to the file `ropes` in the `items` subdirectory of `rajiv`'s home directory on the computer `fakir`.

Command-Line Options. The `rcp` command line has the following options:

`-p`   Preserve modification times and permissions of source files instead of using the default permissions and the current time.

`-r`   Recursively copy the subtree rooted at each *source*.

12.6.5 Listing Users on the Local Network with `rwho`

The `rwho` command lists all users currently on the local network—or more precisely, all such users whose machines are broadcasting `rwho` data. The form of the command line is

> `rwho [-a]`

Unless you specify the `-a` option, users who have not typed anything in the last hour are not shown. The form of the listing is similar to the one you get from `who` (see Section 5.1.2).

Since this command requires querying every computer on your local network, you generally should avoid using it unless your network is small or very lightly loaded. In fact, some systems administrators disable `rwho` because it is known to be a resource hog.

You can also get information about users on another computer with the `finger` command (see Section 5.1.3).

12.7   Calling a Remote Computer with `telnet`

The `telnet` program enables you to conduct a dialog with another computer via a network. It is analogous to `cu`, which provides connections to other computers over telephone lines. Communications via `telnet` follow a set of conventions known as the TELNET protocol.

Compared with `rlogin` (see Section 12.6.2), `telnet` provides more control and flexibility but less convenience; in particular, `rlogin` does not work for communicating with computers that are not running UNIX. With `telnet`, you must log into the remote computer explicitly; with `rlogin`, you are usually logged in automatically.

The form of the `telnet` command line is

    telnet [*host* [*port*]]

where *host* is the name of the remote computer to which you wish to connect and *port* is a particular port on that computer. In this command, *host* can be either a domain name or an IP address (see "IP Addresses" on p. 621). If you omit *host*, `telnet` enters its command mode immediately without attempting to connect you to a particular computer. Once you've made the connection, whatever you type is sent to the remote computer and whatever the remote computer sends back is shown on your screen. If the remote computer breaks the connection, `telnet` exits and returns you to your shell.

You can issue a command to `telnet` by typing the command on a line by itself, preceded by the `telnet` escape character (by default, Ctrl]). Telnet issues a 'telnet>' prompt when it's expecting you to type something. You can abbreviate any `telnet` command, variable, etc., to its shortest unique prefix. In the command descriptions in the rest of this section, the unique prefix of each command is indicated. The shortest unique prefix may be different from the one given here if your system has a larger set of commands.

Telnet ordinarily translates your interrupt character, kill character, etc., to TELNET signals that are recognized by the remote computer and given the same meaning. The `localchars` toggle (see p. 640) activates or deactivates this translation. You can send these signals explicitly with the `telnet` command `send`. You can also arrange to use different special characters for remote communication than you use for your own computer (see Section 12.7.3).

`Telnet` can operate either in character mode or line mode, although some remote computers may support only one of these modes:

- In character mode, each character is sent to the remote computer as you type it.

- In line mode, only completed lines are sent to the remote computer. Each character that you type is echoed locally, although you can turn off local echo by typing the echo-toggle character (by default Ctrl E). Turning off local echo is useful for typing passwords.

UNIX systems usually operate in character mode by default but also are able to operate in line mode. The initial mode is determined by the remote computer. You can change modes with the `mode` command if the remote computer supports both modes. It's a good idea to use line mode rather than character mode when communicating with a distant computer since fewer packets need to be sent across the network.

`Telnet` does not have file transfer capability. If you're using `telnet` and wish to transfer a file, you must exit from `telnet` and call a program such as `ftp` that can perform the transfer.

12.7.1 Quick Exit

To exit from `telnet` quickly, first log out from the remote computer if you can, then type ' Ctrl] q Enter ' to close the remote connection and exit from `telnet` itself. If you've set your `telnet` escape character to something other than Ctrl] , use that other character instead. See "Connecting and Disconnecting" below for more information about exiting from `telnet`.

12.7.2 Commands

The following commands provide a variety of functions for `telnet` communications. You can issue any of them by preceding the command with the `telnet` escape character.

Getting Help.   The following command provides help information:

? [*cmd*]   Displays help on *cmd*. If you omit *cmd*, you get a help summary.

Connecting and Disconnecting.   The following commands connect you to a remote computer or disconnect you from it:

o[pen] [*host* [*port*]]
          Opens a connection to *host* at the specified port. If you don't specify a port, `telnet` uses *host*'s default port.

c[lose]   Disconnects from the remote computer but remains in `telnet`.

q[uit]   Disconnects from the remote computer and exits from `telnet`.

z   Suspends `telnet` and returns to the local computer. In some systems that support job control, the `telnet` job is suspended and you are returned to the command line. Other systems treat z as a command to enter a subshell on the local computer.

Showing telnet's **Status.**   The following commands provide information about telnet's state and the values of its variables and toggles:

st[atus]   Shows the current status of telnet.

d[isplay] [*var...*]
> Shows the value of each variable *var*.

Setting Variables and Toggles.   The following commands affect the state of telnet:

m[ode] *type*
> Enters the specified mode (l[ine] or c[haracter]).   Some remote computers are able to work in only one mode and therefore cannot honor this request.

set *var val*
> Sets the telnet variable *var* to the value *val*.   An example of what you'd type to issue this command is
>
>   Ctrl] set brk Ctrl C Enter
>
> Note that when you type the Ctrl C, you don't see it on your screen.

t[oggle] *var ...*
> Toggles each variable *var*, changing its state from true to false, or vice versa.   The command 'toggle ?' shows a list of the toggles.

See Section 12.7.3 for a list of the variables.

Sending Specific Signals.   The following command provides a way of sending specific signals to the remote computer:

sen[d] *tseq ...*
> Sends the specified TELNET sequences to the remote computer. The command 'send ?', instead of sending anything, shows a list of the available sequences. The sequences are

es[cape]	The current character for escaping to command mode
s[ynch]	The TELNET ⟨SYNCH⟩ (Synchronize) sequence
b[rk]	The TELNET ⟨BRK⟩ (Break) sequence
i[p]	The TELNET ⟨IP⟩ (Interrupt Process) sequence
ao	The TELNET ⟨AO⟩ (Abort Output) sequence
ay[t]	The TELNET ⟨AYT⟩ (Are You There) sequence
ec	The TELNET ⟨EC⟩ (Erase Character) sequence
el	The TELNET ⟨EL⟩ (Erase Line) sequence
g[a]	The TELNET ⟨GA⟩ (Go Ahead) sequence
n[op]	The TELNET ⟨NOP⟩ (No Operation) sequence

> Usually you can send most of these signals more easily by typing the appropriate control characters (see Section 12.7.3).

<table>
<tr><td>

**12.7.3
Variables with
Values**

</td><td>

The variables listed below contain the characters you can type to send various signals to the remote computer. They generally correspond to characters you would specify for your local computer with `stty` (see Section 5.5.2).

Characters with Special Meaning to `telnet`. The following variables define characters that have special meaning to `telnet`:

</td></tr>
</table>

ec[ho]   The character that toggles echoing of locally typed characters in line mode. Its default value is Ctrl E.

es[cape]   The character that returns you to command mode. Its default value is Ctrl] .

Characters for Sending Control Signals. The following variables specify characters that are intended to send control signals to the remote computer. Typing one of these characters causes the TELNET sequence with the specified meaning to be sent to the remote computer. For instance, if you set the `erase` character to Ctrl B , typing Ctrl B causes the TELNET sequence ⟨EC⟩ (Erase Character) to be sent to the remote computer. The default value of each of these characters is the local character with the same meaning. For example, the default value of the remote interrupt character is your local interrupt character (as listed by `stty`). If the `localchars` toggle is off, the characters are not given any special interpretation.

i[nterrupt]
        The remote interrupt character.

q[uit]   The remote quit character.

f[lushoutput]
        The character for flushing remote output. Not all systems support this function, which enables you to discard the output of a command without halting its execution. What matters here is whether the remote computer supports the function; it's irrelevant whether your local computer supports it. The default value of this character is the flush character on your local computer; if the local computer doesn't have a flush character, it's usually set to a null character.

er[ase]   The remote erase character.

k[ill]   The remote kill character.

eo[f]   The remote end-of-file character.

**12.7.4
Toggles**

The `telnet` toggles are either off or on; the command `toggle` *t* reverses the state of the toggle *t*.

Interpretation of Control Characters. The following toggles affect the interpretation of control characters that you type at your terminal:

l[ocalchars]
        If on, transform local control characters to TELNET control

sequences that produce the specified effect. If off, local control characters are not given any special interpretation. See "Characters for Sending Control Signals" on page 640 above for a list of the characters affected by `localchars`. The default value of `localchars` is off for character mode and on for line mode.

For instance, if `localchars` is on, typing the interrupt character causes `telnet` to send the TELNET ⟨IP⟩ sequence, which is supposed to cause a process interrupt on the remote computer. With `localchars` off, the local interrupt character (as defined by the `interrupt` variable) is not interpreted by `telnet`—it is treated as an ordinary data character and doesn't interrupt `telnet` itself.

Note: The setting of `localchars` has no effect on the interpretation of characters sent back by the remote computer. Those characters are interpreted according to your `stty` settings, which is why you need to tell the remote computer your terminal type.

`autof[lush]`

If on, don't show typed data if an interrupt signal (flush, interrupt, or quit) has been sent to the remote computer but the remote computer has not yet acknowledged it. The initial value is on unless you've issued an 'stty -noflsh' command locally.[14] Autoflushing is deactivated in any case if `localchars` is off.

`autos[ynch]`

If `autosynch` and `localchars` are both on, typing an interrupt or quit character instructs the remote computer to discard any unprocessed input. `Telnet` achieves that effect by sending a TELNET synch signal to the remote computer before sending an interrupt or quit character. Since it may take the remote computer a while to act on this signal, you usually cannot predict how much input, if any, will be discarded.

Treatment of ⟨return⟩ Characters. The following toggles are useful when communicating with a remote computer that indicates end-of-line by ⟨return⟩ alone:

`crm[od]`

If on, map ⟨return⟩ characters received from the remote computer to ⟨return⟩ ⟨linefeed⟩. Turning on this toggle does not affect ⟨return⟩ characters sent from the local computer. By default, `crmod` is off.

`crl[f]`

If on, map outgoing ⟨return⟩ characters to ⟨return⟩ ⟨linefeed⟩. This toggle is rarely useful since the UNIX newline character

---

14. `Telnet` can detect the change of state that results from this command, since it's part of the information yielded by `stty`.

is ⟨linefeed⟩, not ⟨return⟩; in any event, many systems do not implement the `crlf` toggle. By default, `crlf` is off.

Flow Control.   The following toggle affects the use of the flow control characters ⟨DC1⟩/⟨DC3⟩:

`f[lowcontrol]`

If on, use flow control signals (⟨DC1⟩/⟨DC3⟩) to regulate communication between your computer and the remote computer. The state of the `flowcontrol` toggle determines what happens when you type Ctrl Q (⟨DC1⟩) or Ctrl S (⟨DC3⟩) as follows:

- If on, `telnet` interprets each of these characters immediately and translates it into a signal that it passes to the remote computer (provided that the remote computer is also prepared to interpret these signals).

- If off, `telnet` passes each of these characters to the remote computer as typed.

If you're using a program such as the Emacs editor that assigns meanings to Ctrl S and Ctrl Q, you should turn `flowcontrol` off. By default, `flowcontrol` is on.

Debugging Control.   Turning on the following toggles causes debugging information to be generated. These toggles are unlikely to be useful unless you're familiar with the details of the TELNET protocol. All are off by default.

`d[ebug]`   If on, enable socket-level debugging. This toggle is useful only if you have superuser privileges.

`o[ptions]` If on, show how `telnet` is processing the TELNET options.

`n[etdata]` If on, enable display of network data.

12.8   Transferring Files Between Computers with `ftp`

The `ftp` program enables you to transmit files to and from a remote computer that understands FTP ("File Transfer Protocol") and to operate on files and directories there. FTP is understood by many different operating systems, not just UNIX. It is built on top of the TELNET protocol—the same protocol used by the `telnet` program (see Section 12.7). `Ftp` is particularly effective at coping with the variety of conventions used to store files on different computers. Compared with `uucp`, `ftp` is far more general but also far more complex (see Section 12.9.3). Historically, `ftp` is part of the Berkeley heritage, while `uucp` is part of the AT&T heritage.[15]

---

15. FTP was actually designed at Bolt, Beranek, and Newman—the Berkeley contribution was to integrate it into UNIX.

Ftp is a command interpreter—it processes commands that you provide either interactively or from a file and translates them into instructions to the server that handles the lower-level FTP commands. Ftp issues an 'ftp>' prompt when it's expecting you to type something. The form of the ftp command line is

ftp [-dgintv] [*host*]

See Section 12.8.16 for a list of the available options.

In this command, *host* can be either a domain name or an IP address (see "IP Addresses" on p. 621). If *host* is specified, ftp immediately attempts to connect to that computer. Once the connection is completed, ftp enters its command interpreter, ready to interpret the commands described later in this section. If *host* is not specified, ftp enters its command interpreter immediately.

In either case, once you enter the command interpreter, you can issue commands to log in or out, send or receive files from the remote computer, do file maintenance on the remote computer, and carry out several other useful operations. You can abbreviate the name of a command to its shortest unique prefix as indicated for each command.

Note: The shortest unique prefix may be different if your version of ftp has a different or larger command set than the one we list here.

To use ftp you must log into the remote computer. As a security measure, ftp does not allow you to log into a user account on a remote computer that has no password. If you try, you're prompted for a password anyway—and the login is then rejected (so the fact that the account requires no password is not revealed).

Some of the commands and features described below may not work in your system, particularly if it's running an older version of ftp. However, if a given command is implemented at all, it should work as we describe.

Remember—ftp is a *program* while FTP is a *protocol*—a set of conventions that govern file transmissions. Usually the programs that actually transmit the files are the only ones that care about these conventions. An alternative way of accessing Internet sites via FTP is a Web explorer (see Section 12.4.1).

**12.8.1
Anonymous ftp**

A particularly important application of ftp—and the only one that many people ever use—is the so-called "anonymous ftp". Several computers, repositories of publicly available files, accept logins under the name anonymous. Use your net address as the password when logging in. Available files are typically found in a directory named pub. You can use the dir command to explore the directory structure of the remote computer and locate the files you're looking for. Having found them, you can retrieve them using the get or mget command.

**12.8.2
Quick Exit**

If ftp is in the middle of an activity such as transmitting a file or showing a directory, typing (Intr) halts that activity and returns you to the ftp prompt. You can then exit from ftp by typing 'bye (Enter)' (see "Closing Connections" on p. 644).

**12.8.3
Auto-Login**

Ftp provides a facility called *auto-login* for automatically logging in at a remote computer. Auto-login uses the .netrc file in your home directory (if that file exists) to provide the information that the remote computer requires. When you connect to a remote computer, ftp provides the required user name and passwords as long as .netrc exists and auto-login has not been disabled. You can make the connection either by specifying a host name on the command line or by using the open command described below. See Section 12.8.14 for a description of the information in the .netrc file. You can disable auto-login with the -n option (see p. 658).

**12.8.4
Opening, Closing,
and Controlling
Remote
Connections**

The commands in this group open a connection with a remote computer, terminate a connection, or control how the connection operates.

Opening Connections. The following commands enable you to open a connection to a remote computer, identify yourself to that computer, or gain access to its resources:

o[pen] *host* [*port*]

> Opens a connection to the computer named *host*. You can use *port* to specify a port number on the remote computer. If you don't specify *port*, ftp chooses a port by default. If your information about the remote computer doesn't include specific port numbers (the usual case), then the default port is almost certain to be the one you want. Auto-login always uses the default port.

us[er] *usrname* [*passwd1* [*passwd2*]]

> Identifies a user to the remote computer. This command expects a user name and optionally, one or two passwords. The first password is associated with the user name, the second with an account that provides access to particular resources on the remote computer. Not all computers make use of accounts; in particular, most UNIX systems don't. If you fail to specify a password that the remote computer requires, you are prompted for it.

ac[count] [*passwd*]

> Verifies a supplemental password that the remote computer requires in order to grant you access to particular resources on that computer. If you don't specify a password, you're prompted for one.

Closing Connections. The following commands enable you to break the connection to a remote computer. After breaking the connection, you can either terminate ftp or continue running it.

(EOF)
by[e]
qui[t]   Breaks the connection with the remote computer and terminates ftp.

`cl[ose]`
`dis[connect]`
> Breaks the connection with the remote computer without leaving `ftp`. A side effect of this command is that all current macro definitions are erased.

Controlling Connections.   The following commands enable you to control the communications link to the remote computer:

`rese[t]`   Resynchronizes communication with the remote computer by clearing the reply queue. This command is useful when the link has gotten into a state where neither computer can understand the other one.

`rest[art]` *marker*
> Restarts the immediately following `get` or `put` at the position given by *marker*. Generally, *marker* is a byte offset into the file. This command provides for transmitting just the last part of a file and is useful when a long file transfer has aborted part way through.

`id[le]` [*n*] Sets the inactivity timer of the remote computer to *n* seconds. If you omit *n*, `ftp` shows the current value of the inactivity timer. If the remote computer uses an inactivity timer and no activity takes place under your `ftp` login within the inactivity interval, the remote computer automatically logs you out.

`sendp[ort]`
> Toggles the use of `PORT` commands. `PORT` commands are part of the FTP protocol. Allowing `ftp` to use these commands can speed up transfers of multiple files, but may cause problems if the remote computer does not interpret the `PORT` command correctly.

`quo[te]` *arg* ...
> Sends the specified arguments to the remote computer. This command provides a method of sending specific communications instructions if you know what you're doing and understand the FTP protocol.

`sit[e]` *arg* ...
> Sends the command 'SITE *arg* ...' to the remote computer.

**12.8.5
Getting Help**

Because the `ftp` facilities on the remote computer may not be the same as those on your local computer, `ftp` provides two forms of help, one for each computer:

`?` [*cmd*]
`he[lp]` [*cmd*]
> Provides local help information on *cmd*. If you omit *cmd*, you obtain a list of available commands.

`remoteh[elp]` [*cmd*]

> Requests help information on *cmd* from the remote computer. What happens if you omit *cmd* depends on the help facility on that computer, although you're likely to get a list of commands just as you would from your own computer.

12.8.6 Remote File Operations

The operations in this group enable you to operate on files and directories residing on the remote computer, but they do not in themselves transmit the contents of those files. You can specify a remote file by using an absolute pathname if the remote computer understands absolute pathnames. However, some computers reinterpret such paths so as to start them at a special directory such as `~ftp` rather than at the true root when you log in using anonymous `ftp`.

Directory Operations. The following operations show you what the current directory is on the remote computer and change it:

`pw[d]`   Shows the name of the current (working) directory on the remote computer.

`cd` *rdir*   Changes the current directory on the remote computer to *rdir*.

`cdu[p]`   Changes the current directory on the remote computer to its parent. `Cdup` is equivalent to 'cd ..' for systems with UNIX-like file structures, but not all systems recognize the '..' convention—not even all that have tree-structured directories.

The following operations perform various kinds of directory maintenance on the remote computer. Normally, you apply them only to directories that belong to you or over which you have some administrative control.

`mk[dir]` *dir*

> Makes directory *dir* on the remote computer. You can specify *dir* as a pathname; thus you can use this command to make directories in places other than the current directory (on most computers).

`rm[dir]` *dir*

> Deletes directory *dir* on the remote computer.

`del[ete]` *rfile*

> Deletes file *rfile* on the remote computer.

`mde[lete]` [*rfile...*]

> Deletes the specified remote files. If prompting is on (see the `prompt` command on p. 653), you're given the opportunity to confirm or reject each deletion. If you don't provide any files, you're prompted for the list.

`ren[ame]` *name₁* *name₂*

> Renames file *name₁* on the remote computer to *name₂*.

ch[mod] *mode rfile*

> Changes the permissions of remote file *rfile* to *mode*. The variable *mode* must be given as an octal number. In effect, this command does a `chmod` (see Section 3.11.1) on the remote computer. The remote computer must be running UNIX.

um[ask] [*mask*]

> Sets the default file permission mask on the remote computer to *mask*. In effect, this command does a `umask` on the remote computer, which must be running UNIX (see Section 3.11.2).

Information About Directories and Files.   The following operations enable you to retrieve information about directories and files from the remote computer and store those listings locally. Note that in all cases, using '-' for the local file name causes the listing to be sent to standard output.

dir [*rdir* [*lfile*]]

> Sends a listing of remote directory *rdir* to the local file *lfile*. The listing is a "long" listing in the style produced by '`ls -l`' (see Section 3.2). If you omit *rdir*, `ftp` takes it to be the current directory on the remote computer. If you omit *lfile*, `ftp` sends the listing to standard output. If a directory listing is too long to fit on a single screen, you can use the command

> > `dir |more`

> to view it a screenful at a time (see p. 657).

ls [*rdir* [*lfile*]]

> Like `dir`, except that on some systems you may get an abbreviated listing. The difference between an abbreviated and an unabbreviated listing depends on the implementation.

nl[ist] [*rdir* [*lfile*]]

> Like `dir`, except that the listing is usually in the style of '`ls -a`'; it shows just the names of the files, not their attributes, but includes files whose names start with a dot.

mdi[r] *rfile* ... *lfile*

> Like `dir`, except that you can provide a list of files instead of a directory. Normally, the point of doing so would be to use wildcards in the specification of *rfile*. If *rfile* is a directory, you get a list of its files.

ml[s] *rfile* ... *lfile*

> Like `mdir`, except that on some systems you obtain an abbreviated listing even if the listing you obtain with `ls` is not abbreviated.

modt[ime] *rfile*

> Shows the time when remote file *rfile* was last modified.

siz[e] *rfile*

> Shows the size of remote file *rfile*.

If the directory listing produced by one of these commands runs off the end of your screen, you can read it more easily by piping it to a pager with a command like 'dir |more'.

12.8.7 Transmitting Files

The commands in this group enable you to transmit either a single file or a group of files from the remote computer to your computer or conversely. The file-naming conventions for the remote computer need not correspond to those on your computer (presumably the UNIX conventions). Ftp therefore enables you to specify a translation from each remote file name to the name of the corresponding local file and vice versa. It also provides a mechanism for creating unique names for received files when those files would otherwise have the same name (see Section 12.8.8).

Transmitting From the Remote Computer. The following commands are used to transmit files from the remote computer to your computer. File names apply to the current directory on each computer unless that directory is overridden by an absolute pathname.

ge[t] *rfile* [*lfile*]
rec[v] *rfile* [*lfile*]

> Retrieves remote file *rfile* and stores it in local file *lfile*. If *lfile* is not given, it is obtained by translating the remote file name as described below. Wildcard substitution is not applied to *rfile* since it must be a single file. For example, the command

        get scoundrels cads

> retrieves the remote file scoundrels and copies it into your local file cads.

reg[et] *rfile* [*lfile*]

> Retrieves the portion of remote file *rfile* that has not already been transferred and stores it in local file *lfile*. The transfer takes place only if *lfile* does not exist or is shorter than *rfile*. If *lfile* is not given, it is obtained by translating the remote file name as described below. The purpose of this command is to complete a transfer of a large file that may have been interrupted by a dropped connection.

ne[wer] *rfile* [*lfile*]

> Retrieves remote file *rfile* and copies it into the local file *lfile* provided that *rfile* is newer than *lfile* or *lfile* doesn't exist. If you don't specify *lfile*, it is assumed to have the same name as *rfile*.

mg[et] *rfile* ...

> Retrieves the specified remote files. First, wildcards in the *rfile*s are expanded. Then the file names specified by the *rfile*s are translated into local names as described in Section 12.8.8. Finally, each remote file is transmitted to the corresponding

local file, with a prompt preceding each transfer if prompting is turned on.

Transmitting to the Remote Computer.   The following commands are used to transmit files from your computer to the remote computer. File names apply to the current directory on each computer unless the current directory is overridden by an absolute pathname.

`send` *lfile* [*rfile*]
`pu[t]` *lfile* [*rfile*]

> Transmits local file *lfile* to the remote computer, naming it *rfile*. If *rfile* is not given, it is obtained by translating the local file name as described below. The file name *lfile* should not contain any wildcards.[16]

`ap[pend]` *lfile* [*rfile*]

> Appends local file *lfile* to remote file *rfile*. The file naming and translation conventions are the same as for `put`.

`mp[ut]` *lfile* ...

> Transmits the specified local files to the remote computer. First, wildcards in the *lfiles* are expanded. Then the file names specified by the *lfiles* are translated into remote names as described below. Finally, each local file is transmitted to the corresponding remote file, with a prompt preceding each transfer if prompting is turned on.

Aborting a Transfer.   If anything goes wrong with a transfer, you can abort it by pressing (Intr). An outgoing transfer is halted immediately, but an incoming transfer may not be. For an incoming transfer, `ftp` sends an FTP `ABOR` sequence to the remote computer—but the remote computer may take a while to respond to it or, in the worst case, may not recognize the `ABOR` command at all. It all depends on what support the remote computer provides for FTP. If the remote computer does not recognize `ABOR`, you won't see the next '`ftp>`' prompt until the file has been entirely transmitted.

**12.8.8
Translating
File Names**

The following commands provide translation from remote file names to local file names and vice versa. Note that a single translation is almost certainly not correct for both directions, so if you are transmitting files in both directions during a single use of `ftp`, you must change the translations in between. The following commands are listed in the order in which their translations are applied, so that `case`, for example, is done before `nmap`.

`gl[ob]`

> Toggles wildcard expansion, called *globbing* in the C shell, for file names. If it is off, no wildcard expansion is done for file

---

16. If *lfile* contains wildcards, the first file in the expansion is used and the others are ignored.

names appearing in `mget`, `mput`, or `mdelete`. By default, wild-card expansion is turned on.

ca[se]   Toggles case mapping for remote file names. Case mapping causes remote file names consisting of all uppercase characters to be translated to all lowercase characters. By default, case mapping is turned off.

nm[ap] *inpat outpat*

Maps file names according to the input pattern *inpat* and the output pattern *outpat*. Each pattern acts as a template, with up to nine variable parts $1, $2, ... , $9. The entire input file name is available as $0. Each input file name is matched against the input pattern in order to determine the variable parts, which are then substituted into the output pattern. For `get` and `mget`, the input file name is the remote name and the output file name is the local name; for `put` and `mput`, the relationship is reversed. The pattern need not match completely. Any parts of the input pattern that cannot be matched reading from left to right are simply deleted; the corresponding variable parts are made empty.

Both the input pattern and the output pattern can use '\' as a quoting character. In the output pattern, the construct '[seq_1,seq_2]' is replaced by seq_1 if seq_1 is not empty, and by seq_2 otherwise.

An example showing the transformation is

```
nmap $1:$2.$3 [$2,FILE].[$3,EXT]:[$1,x]
```

Some input file names and the corresponding output file names are the following:

Input	Output
c:grackle.b	grackle.b:c
starling	FILE.EXT:starling
m:wren	wren.EXT:m

nt[rans] [*inchars* [*outchars*]]

Sets or unsets a translation table for characters in file names. If `ntrans` is issued by itself, it turns off translation. Otherwise, a character in the file name that occurs as the *n*th character of *inchars* is translated to the *n*th character of *outchars*. If *n* is greater than the length of *outchars*, the character is deleted from the file name. In particular, if *outchars* is absent, all characters appearing in *inchars* are deleted. For example, if you issue the command

```
ntrans %![] ..
```

and then transfer a remote file whose name is `x1%Y!q[T]`, the corresponding local file is `x1.Y.qT`.

The variable *inchars* should not have any repeated characters.

ru[nique] Toggles the generation of unique names for files obtained from the remote computer. Suppose that generation of unique names is turned on and a file is received whose (local) name *name* is the name of a file that already exists. Then the new file is stored under the name '*name*`.1`'. Further duplicates are stored under the names '*name*`.2`', '*name*`.3`', etc,, with a maximum of 99. By default, unique name generation is turned off.

su[nique] Toggles the generation of unique names for files sent to the remote computer. Unique generation of remote names works only if the remote server supports it. You receive a report of any files that are renamed as a result of remote generation of unique names. Remotely generated unique names are not necessarily generated by the same rule as local ones.

12.8.9 Interpretation of Transmitted Files

Although UNIX views a file as a stream of bytes, not all operating systems do. Even among operating systems that take that view of what a file is, conventions differ for representing the end of a line. In order to support file transfer between computers that view files differently, the `ftp` program provides several parameters that specify the nature of the transfer. In effect, these parameters determine a common language for the sending computer and the receiving computer. Each computer does whatever translation is needed to convert the transmitted stream of data to or from that common language.

The following parameters affect file transfers:

- **Representation type.** The representation type defines how the information content of a file relates to the bits in the file. The two principal representations supported by `ftp` are seven-bit ASCII and image. The former views each group of eight bits as representing a character as defined by the ASCII encoding (with the highest bit ignored); the latter views a file as an uninterpreted sequence of bits that could mean anything at all. You *must* use the image mode (which you can get with `image`) for transferring eight-bit files. Ftp also supports the representation used on TENEX computers.

- **Form.** The form applies only to files having a character set (ASCII or EBCDIC) as representation type. It determines whether vertical format controls (e.g., ⟨newline⟩s and ⟨formfeed⟩s) are to be left uninterpreted, translated to conform to TELNET conventions, or translated to conform to Fortran conventions. Ftp currently supports only the uninterpreted form.

- **File structure.** The file structure is either `file` (no internal substructure), `record` (the file is viewed as a sequence of records), or page (the file is viewed as a sequence of pages separated by form-feeds). Ftp currently supports only `file`.

- **Transfer mode.** The transfer mode is either `stream` (a sequence of bits ended by an end-of-file), `block` (a sequence of fixed-length blocks of bits), or `compressed` (data compressed by the sender and decompressed by the receiver). Ftp currently supports only `stream`.

Setting the Representation.   The following commands choose the representation for subsequent transfers. As a rule, you should use `ascii` for any file that isn't explicitly binary. An example of an explicitly binary file would be a compiled C program.

as[cii]   Selects seven-bit ASCII as the representation type.

im[age]
bi[nary]   Selects image as the representation type.

te[nex]   Selects the representation type that is appropriate to TENEX computers.

ty[pe] [*name*]
           Uses *name* as the representation type. This command merely provides an alternate syntax for the preceding ones.

The following command is meaningful only when the representation type is `ascii`.

cr   Toggles stripping of carriage returns for ASCII file transfers from remote computers. This facility is needed because the standard for ASCII file transfers uses the ⟨return⟩⟨linefeed⟩ sequence to represent a newline, while UNIX expects the ⟨linefeed⟩ alone. If this stripping is on, carriage returns are removed from the file as it is received. Some files received from non-UNIX computers may contain single ⟨linefeed⟩s; to use such files, you must turn off carriage return stripping and do some local interpretation. By default, carriage return stripping is turned on.

Setting Other Transfer Parameters.   The following commands set other transfer parameters—but since in each case ftp recognizes only one possible value, you should never need to use them. They are included only for the sake of future extensions.

f[orm] [*fmt*]
           Selects 'non-print' for interpreting vertical format controls.

mode [*name*]
           Sets the transfer mode to *name*.

str[uct] [*name*]
           Sets the file structure to *name*.

**12.8.10
Local Operations**

The following commands enable you to execute commands on your own computer without leaving `ftp`.

`! [cmd]`   Runs *cmd* locally in a subshell. If you omit *cmd*, you obtain an interactive shell. `Ftp` looks in the `SHELL` environment variable to see which shell to use; if `SHELL` does not exist, `ftp` uses the shell named `sh`.

`lc[d] [dir]` Changes the current local directory to *dir*.
> **Note:** It does no good to execute `cd` in a subshell because the effect of the change disappears when the subshell terminates.

**12.8.11
Controlling
Feedback from `ftp`**

The following commands affect the feedback that you get during a file transfer:

`prom[pt]`   Toggles interactive prompting during multiple file transfers and deletions. By default, prompting is turned on, giving you the opportunity to accept or reject any transfer or deletion. If prompting is turned off, all transfers or deletions are performed.

`ha[sh]`   Toggles use of a hash mark (#) to indicate that a data block is being transferred. By default, the hash marks do not appear.

`be[ll]`   Toggles the sounding of a bell after each file transfer. By default, the bell is not sounded.

The following commands provide information about the status of `ftp` and what it is doing.

`sta[tus]`   Shows the current status of `ftp`, including which toggles are on and which ones are off. The display looks something like this:

```
Connected to miasma.com.
No proxy connection.
Mode: stream; Type: ascii; Form: non-print
Structure: file; Verbose: on; Bell: off
Prompting: on; Globbing: on
Store unique: off; Receive unique: off
Case: off; CR stripping: on
Ntrans: off
Nmap: off
Hash mark printing: off; Use of PORT cmds: on
Macros:
        ready
        groupsend
```

`remotes[tatus] [rfile]`
> Shows the current status of remote file *rfile*, or of the remote computer if *rfile* is omitted.

`sy[stem]`   Shows the type of operating system running on the remote computer.

deb[ug] [*n*]

> Sets the debugging level to *n* (an integer). If you don't specify *n*, this command toggles debugging on (with a default level) or off. With debugging on, each FTP command sent to the remote computer is shown, preceded by '-->'. Most implementations of ftp ignore the value of *n*.

v[erbose] Toggles verbose mode for showing ftp responses. In verbose mode, ftp shows all responses from the FTP server and reports statistics on the efficiency of each file transfer. By default, verbose mode is turned on if ftp is getting its input from a terminal, and turned off otherwise.

tr[ace] Toggles packet tracing. This facility is unimplemented; the command exists only for compatibility with future enhancements.

12.8.12
Linking Two Remote Computers

You can use ftp for *third-party transfers* in which you transfer files from one remote computer to another, using your own computer to control the transfer. The following command makes such transfers possible:

prox[y] *cmd*

> Executes *cmd* as an ftp command on the remote computer. Ordinarily, the first proxy command is an open that connects the remote computer to another remote computer. The command 'proxy ?' executes '?' on the remote computer, producing a list of the commands that the version of ftp on the secondary computer can execute.

12.8.13
Defining and Using Macros

You can name a sequence of commands by defining a *macro*. Calling the macro then causes those commands to be executed. For instance, typing

```
macdef xfc
mget *.c
cdup
cd lib
mget *.h
Enter
```

defines a macro xfc that you can use as a new command; typing $xfc becomes equivalent to typing the sequence of four commands following the macdef line. The principal use of macros is in the .netrc file; it is rarely worthwhile to type macro definitions as direct commands.

ma[cdef] *mac*

> Defines a macro named *mac*. The definition appears on the lines following the macdef and is ended by an empty line.
>
> A macro can have parameters, indicated by $*n* where *n* is a digit. Arguments (which are delimited by whitespace) are substituted for the corresponding parameters: the first argument

for '`$1`', the second for '`$2`', and so forth. The special parameter '`$i`' indicates repetition of the macro; its entire sequence of commands is executed once for each argument, with successive arguments substituted for '`$i`' on successive repetitions.

The '`\`' character quotes the following character. It's needed in order to be able to include a literal '`$`' in a macro definition. A '`\`' must itself be quoted; that is, it must be written as '`\\`'.

$ *mac* [*arg...*]

Executes macro *mac* with arguments *arg* ...

When you execute a `close` command, all macro definitions are erased. Executing an '`open` *rhost*' command can cause macros to be defined (or redefined) if the entry in `.netrc` for the computer *rhost* includes macro definitions.

**12.8.14
The `.netrc` File**

You can provide information in an initialization file, `.netrc`, that enables `ftp` to perform auto-login (see Section 12.8.3). The `.netrc` file is a collection of definitions rather than an initialization file in the usual sense of a file containing more or less arbitrary commands to be executed when a program starts up. It consists of a sequence of machine definitions.

Each machine definition either describes a particular remote computer or provides a default in case no earlier machine definition applies. A machine definition consists of a sequence of items; each item in turn consists of one or more words (called *tokens* in the `ftp` manual pages). Words are separated by whitespace (including newlines), except that special rules apply to a `macdef` item (see below).

The first word in each machine definition is either a `machine` item or a `default` item. When you use `ftp`'s auto-login facility to log into a remote computer named *name*, `ftp` searches for the first machine definition that begins with either '`machine` *name*' or '`default`'. The definition consists of the words up to the next definition or the end of the file. Ftp then uses the information supplied in the machine definition to execute the login. If the information is insufficient, `ftp` prompts you for the missing items.

A machine definition may contain the following items:

machine *name*

Begins the definition of a machine whose name is *name*. The variable *name* must be a valid network address.

default   Begins a machine definition to be used in case none of the preceding definitions matches the name of the specified remote computer. Since `default` matches any computer, it should follow all other definitions. Some systems do not yet support `default`.

login *name*

Provides the user name *name* when logging in at the remote computer.

password *string*

> Provides the password *string* when logging in at the remote computer.

account *string*

> Uses *string* as the account password if the remote computer requires it. If the remote computer does not request an account password when you log in at it but the machine description includes an `account` item, `ftp` executes an `account` command, thus making the account password available later when the remote computer asks for it.

macdef *mac*

> Defines a macro using the same conventions as the `macdef` command (see Section 12.8.13). The macro definition is given by a sequence of lines; consequently, the next word seen by `ftp` after scanning a macro definition in `.netrc` is the one following the empty line that terminates the macro definition. If you define a macro named `init`, `ftp` executes it immediately after a successful login.
>
> Macro definitions are part of a machine definition and have no effect if auto-login is disabled. If you execute a `close` command followed by an `open` for a new machine, the macros for the old machine are erased and the macros for the new machine are installed as a consequence of the fact that `close` erases macros and auto-login defines them.

An example of a short `.netrc` file is

```
machine family.org login grandma
    account kNitting
macdef inmap
nmap $1.$2 $1.[$2,EXT]


default login anonymous password timon@athens
```

If you log into any remote computer other than `family.org`, you'll be set up to do an anonymous `ftp` from that computer.

Security Considerations for `.netrc`.   Since the `.netrc` file contains passwords, no one but you should have permission to read it. Many versions of `ftp` refuse to use a `.netrc` file unless its group and other read and write permissions are turned off.

You should also avoid putting real passwords in your `.netrc` file. The reason is that anyone who illegitimately gains access to this file then gains access to the remote computers listed there as well—thus turning a local break-in into a network-wide one. On the other hand, putting a default line for anonymous `ftp` into `.netrc` as shown above is both convenient and innocuous.

12.8.15
Special Forms of File Names

Ftp recognizes certain special file names:

- A file name of '-' specifies standard input in a context that calls for reading a file and standard output in a context that calls for writing a file.

- A file name of the form '|*cmd*' can be used in place of a local file name. It indicates that the command *cmd* is to be executed in a subshell by calling the shell named sh with the -c option.

  - If the '|*cmd*' construct appears in the context of a local file name specifying the *output* of an ftp command such as get or dir, then the actual output of the ftp command becomes the standard input of *cmd* and the standard output of *cmd* is sent to your terminal. The actual output of the ftp command can be either a file or a directory listing. For example,

    ```
    dir * |more
    ```

    gives you a paged listing of a remote directory.

  - If the '|*cmd*' construct appears in the context of a local file name specifying the *input* of an ftp command such as put, then *cmd* is executed with an empty file as its standard input and its standard output is used as the data source for the ftp command. For example,

    ```
    put |who herefolks
    ```

    places a listing of the logged-in users on your computer into the remote file herefolks. You should avoid allowing the remote file name to be defaulted when you use '|' in that way, since ftp treats '|' in a remote file name as an ordinary character— almost certainly not what you want. If you allow the remote file name to be defaulted, it becomes something like '|who'.

  You must either surround the '|*cmd*' construct by double quotes or make sure that it doesn't contain any internal spaces. The first command above could also be written as

  ```
  dir * "| more"
  ```

In addition to these forms, wildcard substitution according to the usual conventions applies unless you've disabled it with the -g option or the glob command.

12.8.16
Command-Line Options

The following options are available on the command line:

-d   Enable debugging.

-g   Disable wildcard substitution (globbing) in file names.

-i   Turn off interactive prompting during multiple file transfers .

-n   Don't do auto-login when initially connecting to another computer (see Section 12.8.3). With auto-login turned off, `ftp` establishes the connection and then waits for you to issue commands. You aren't logged in at the remote computer until you issue a `user` command.

-v   Show all responses from the remote server and provide statistics on all data transfers. This option is turned on automatically if `ftp` is receiving its input from a terminal.

-t   Enable packet tracing. This option is as yet unimplemented.

12.9   File Transfers Based on `uucp`

The easiest way to transfer files between computers running UNIX is to send the files with `uuto` and retrieve them with `uupick`. Both of these programs use `uucp` (UNIX to UNIX copy) to carry out the actual transfer; the UUCP network gets its name from this program. Other useful programs in this group are `uustat` for checking the status of outgoing files and deleting them if necessary, `uuname` for finding out which other UNIX systems your computer knows about, and `cu` for connecting directly to another computer.

The `uucp` program is part of a group of programs called the "Basic Networking Utilities" (BNU).[17] These utilities were written for store-and-forward communications networks in which messages are held until they can be transmitted and then are sent over direct lines to another station. `Ftp` and related programs, in contrast, were written under the assumption that they would be used with packet-switching networks in which messages are broken up into packets that are transmitted individually and reassembled at the destination (see Section 12.8).

Although `uucp` has been extended to work with packet-switching networks and `ftp` can work with direct connections,[18] they are usually used in these ways only when no alternative exists. Which program you should use depends on the nature of your connection with the remote computer. For a direct connection over a phone line, you'll usually need to use `uucp`; for a network connection, you'll usually need to use `ftp`. Most of the time you won't have a choice, since a particular remote computer is likely to be conveniently accessible only via one type of connection. If you do have the choice, `uucp` is probably better because you can just issue the request and forget about it—your system will transmit the file at the next opportunity.

---

17. These utilities are also sometimes referred to as HoneyDanBer `uucp`, after their authors Peter Honeyman, Dan Nowitz, and Brian Redman.

18. These connections are constructed using SLIP (Serial Line Internet Protocol).

The uucp program must be configured before you can use it. A discussion of how to do that is beyond the scope of this book; should you need to do the job yourself, your system manuals together with reference [B24] are your best guide.

12.9.1
Sending Files
with uuto

The uuto command sends a set of files or directories to a specified user at a specified computer by generating a request to uucp to send the files. The actual transmission occurs later. Uucp usually transmits the files going to a particular computer in batches, with the uucp scheduling parameters determining when the transmissions take place.

The form of the uuto command is

uuto [-pm] *source* ... *path*!*person*

where *path* is a uucp-style path address of the destination computer and *person* is a user known to that computer. If you're calling this command from the C shell, you must quote the '!' character by writing it as '\!'. The first computer name in *path* must be listed in the Systems file on your own computer (see Section 12.9.5), but the remaining computer names need not be. Each source can be either an ordinary file or a directory; if you specify a directory, all files contained in that directory and its subdirectories are sent and the structural information is retained in the transmission. For example, the command

uuto grammar/adjs grammar/advs handoff!editors!fowler

sends the files grammar/adjs and grammar/advs to the person fowler at the site editors via the site handoff.[19] Only handoff need be known to your computer. Normally, uucp transmits the files from where they reside on your computer rather than making its own copy of them. If a file to be transmitted is deleted before the transmission takes place, it will be lost; if it is modified before the transmission takes place, the modified version will be transmitted. You can change this behavior with the -p option described below.

Command-Line Options.   Uuto recognizes two options on the command line:

-p   Copy each file to be transmitted to a spooling directory when the transmission is requested. The copied file will be transmitted later; any changes to the original will not affect what is transmitted.

-m   Send mail to the sender indicating when the transmission has been accomplished.

12.9.2
Retrieving Files
with uupick

The uupick command retrieves files or directories that were sent to you via uucp by a user on a remote computer. When the files arrive, uucp stores them in a special directory, usually

/usr/spool/uucppublic/receive/*user*/*rsys*

---

19. Many systems disable file transfers that involve multiple computers, however.

where *user* is your user name and *rsys* is the name of the remote computer from which the files were received. You can then examine them, discard them, or move them to a more convenient place using uupick.

The form of the uupick command line is:

    uupick [-s *system*]

If you specify *system*, the retrieval is limited to files sent from the remote computer *system*. When you call uupick, it goes through the files and directories sent to you, one by one. For each one, it sends the appropriate message to standard output:

    from *system*: file *file*?
    from *system*: dir *dir*?

Your response to the message determines what uupick does with the item. These are the possible responses:

?
*   Shows a summary of the commands.

[Enter]   Goes on to the next item.

d   Discards this item.

m [*dir*]   Moves this item to the directory *dir*. If the item is a directory, it and all its subdirectories are moved.

a [*dir*]   Moves all the items received from the computer that sent the current item. If *dir* is not specified, the current directory is assumed.

p   Shows the item; that is, sends the item to standard output. This option does not apply to directories.

[EOF]
q   Quits, exiting from uupick.

! *cmd*   Executes *cmd* in a subshell.

12.9.3
UNIX to UNIX
Copying with uucp

The UNIX to UNIX copy program, uucp, copies files from one UNIX system to another. You can use it not just to send files but to fetch them as well, as long as you have the necessary permissions.

The uucp command line has the form:

    uucp [-cCdfgjmnrsx] *sfile* ... *dfile*

where each *sfile* is a source file and *dfile* is a destination file. Both *sfile* and *dfile* have the form

    [*system*!] ... *path*

For each source file, the sequence of *systems* is a path-style route to the computer where the file is to be found (see Section 12.1.2). The first computer name in *path* must be listed in the Systems file on your own computer (see Section 12.9.5), but the remaining computer names need not be. Similarly, for the destination file, the sequence of *system*s is a path-style address of the computer where the files are to be put. For example, the command

```
uucp igloo!~/huskies/* .
```

copies all the files from the publicly accessible huskies directory on the remote system igloo to your current directory.[20] Here the '~' indicates a directory that contains the publicly accessible files on igloo (see below).

Note the following points:

- A file name that does not specify a system is taken relative to the current directory unless it is an absolute pathname.

- For a transfer to work, the following conditions must hold:
  - Each intermediate computer must be willing to perform the transfer.
  - Each source file must have r permission for everyone.
  - Each directory enroute to the source files must have rx permission for everyone.
  - Each destination directory must have wx permission for everyone.
  - Each directory enroute to the destination files (except for the destination directories themselves) must have x permission for everyone.

  If a transfer fails for any reason, you're sent a mail message telling you of the failure.

- A source file must not be a directory. Although you can transfer all the files in a directory, you cannot transfer the directory itself.

- A source file name can contain wildcards, although the destination file name cannot. If a source file specifies a computer and contains any wildcard characters (* ? [ ]), you must quote them to prevent them from being interpreted as shell metacharacters.

- If there is more than one source file after any wildcards have been expanded, the destination is taken to be a directory and the source files are then placed within that directory, using just the last component of each source file's pathname.

- To create a destination file, it may be necessary to construct additional directories. By default, uucp constructs these directories, provided that the necessary permissions are turned on. You can stop uucp from constructing these directories with the -f option.

---

20. If you're using the C shell, you'll need to write the command as

```
uucp igloo\!~/huskies/* .
```

to prevent the C shell from misinterpreting the bang.

- The notation '~*user*' designates the home directory of *user*, either on your own computer or on a remote computer. A pathname starting with '\~/' refers to the directory containing those files that are publicly available for remote access. (The backslash prevents the shell from misinterpreting the tilde.) Usually this directory is /usr/spool/uucppublic.

- You can specify your own computer explicitly just as if it were a remote computer. For example, if the name of your computer is chutzpah, a possible source or destination file on your own computer would be chutzpah!hush.

- If the destination file name does not include any '!'s, the transfer is treated as a request that the source files be sent to you. No external communication is involved. You can also use uucp to move files from one remote computer to another.

- When you ask uucp to transfer a local file, uucp normally doesn't make a copy of that file; instead, it transmits the file directly when the time comes. You can force a local copy with the -C option; in this case, changing or deleting the original file will not affect what is transmitted.

- For security reasons, many system administrators only allow files to be transferred to or from the public directory /usr/spool/ uucppublic.

For example, the command

        uucp ~/pooch/* mongrels!~hound/infiles

sends the files in your pooch directory to the directory infiles belonging to user hound at remote computer mongrels. The infiles directory must have x permission available to others. The command

        uucp mongrels!~hound/pup \~/

requests that the file pup belonging to user hound at computer mongrels be sent to you and stored in your system's public UUCP directory under the name pup.

Each request for a file transmission is called a *job*—not to be confused with jobs as sets of processes in the sense of job control.

Command-Line Options. The following options determine whether uucp makes copies of local files and whether it constructs directories at the destination:

-C   Make a copy of each local file when transmission is requested.

-c   Don't make copies of local files.

-d   Make subdirectories at the destination as needed.

-f   Don't make subdirectories at the destination.

The following options affect the messages that result from the job:

-j   Show the job identifier when the job is requested.

-m   Send a mail message to the requestor when the job is done.

-n *user*   Notify *user* on the remote computer that a file was sent.

-s *file*   Send a status report to *file*. You must specify *file* as a full path-
              name because the report is not sent until the uucp command
              has already terminated.

-x *n*   Turn on debugging at level *n*, where *n* ranges from 0 (no
              debugging information) to 9 (maximum debugging informa-
              tion).

The following options affect when the files are actually transmitted:

-r   Queue the job without starting the transfer.

-g *c*   Assign the job a priority of *c*, where *c* is a single letter or
              digit. The priorities are taken in order of the ASCII values of
              the characters—first the digits, then the uppercase letters, and
              finally the lowercase letters.

**12.9.4
Controlling and
Querying** uucp
with uustat

The uustat command enables you to see the status of jobs awaiting transmission by uucp and the status of uucp's communications with other computers. It also enables you to kill the transmission of one of your files.

The uustat command line has the form

uustat [-ampq] [-k *id*] [-r *id*] [-s *sys*] [-u *user*]

Generally, you can use only a single option, although the -s and -u options
can be used together. If you call uustat without any options, you obtain
a list of your files and messages awaiting transmission. The list looks
like this:

```
gastonC1b68    06/15-17:29   S   gaston   uriah 285 D.booke7c71290
               06/15-17:29   S   gaston   uriah  rmail uriah
gastonN1b69    06/15-17:41   S   gaston   uriah 21 /home/uriah/td/osh
liederC00b1    06/15-18:03   S   lieder   uriah 285 D.booke7c72456
               06/15-18:03   S   lieder   uriah  rmail uriah
```

Each job occupies one or more lines. Here is what the items in the first
row for each job mean:

- The first item contains an identifier for each file awaiting transmission.

- The second item contains the date and time when the file was queued
  for transmission.

- The third item contains 'S' for a message to be sent and 'R' for a
  request for an arriving file. It is almost always 'S'.

- The fourth item contains the destination computer.

- The fifth item contains the user ID of the sender of the file.

- The sixth item contains the length of the file to be transmitted.

- The seventh item contains the full pathname of a file to be transmitted or a message identifier (for the first row of a message item).

The job identifier is essential for killing an outgoing transmission.

Command-Line Options.   The following command-line options are the most useful ones:

-a   Output the names of all jobs awaiting transmission.

-k *id*   Kill the job whose identifier is *id*. In order to use this command, you must run uustat without options.

-s *sys*   Only report jobs destined for remote computer *sys*.

-u *user* Only report jobs originated by user *user*.

The -s and -u options can be used together; all other options can only be used by themselves. The following short shell script provides an easy way of killing all your outstanding uucp jobs:

```
for jn in $(uustat | cut -f1 -d" "); do
    if [ -n "$jn" ]; then uustat -k $jn; fi
done
```

See Section 4.3.2 for information on what cut is doing here.

   The following options are intended for system administrators. Understanding what they do requires an understanding of uucp and the files that it uses. We list them only for the sake of completeness.

-m   Report the status of all remote computers known to uucp.

-p   Execute the command ps -flp for all processes that are in lock files.

-q   List the jobs queued for each remote computer.

-r *id*   Rejuvenate job *id* by resetting its modification time to the current time, thus preventing the cleanup dæmon from deleting it.

Obtaining uucp Status Information with uulog.   The uulog command sends a portion of the log of uucp transfers to standard output. Normally, it is useful only to system administrators; we mention it only for the sake of completeness. It has the following three options:

-s *system*

            Show only information on transfers involving *system*.

-f *system*

            Do a tail -f command on the log of transfers involving *system* (see Section 4.4.2).

-x   Look in the uuxqt log rather than the uucico log.

-n   Use a tail command with *n* lines.

If you use one of the tail options, you must press (Intr) to terminate the output.

**12.9.5
The `Systems` File**

The `Systems` file contains the information needed by `uucp` and its supporting programs to establish a link to a remote computer. Each remote system referenced by `uucp` or one of its relatives must have an entry in this file. For System V, the full pathname of the file is usually `/usr/lib/uucp/Systems` or `/etc/uucp/Systems`. On BSD systems, the `Systems` file is named `L.sys`; the format is nearly the same. Usually this file is only of concern to system administrators; superuser privileges are required to modify it or even to read it. You can determine which systems are known to your system by typing '`uuname`'.

Whenever you wish to establish direct `uucp` communication with a UNIX system not already listed in `Systems`, you must add an entry to `Systems` or have your system administrator do it for you. For example, an entry for the UUCP gateway at `ixl.net` might be

```
ixluu1 Any ACU 38400 1-508-647-0747 ogin--ogin--ogin: mylogin sword: mypasswd
```

The parts of this entry are as follows:

- '`ixluu1`'. The name of the remote system (to be used on the `uucp` command line).

- '`Any`'. The time when the remote computer can be called.

- '`ACU 38400`'. The type of communications device used to call the remote system (in this case, an autodialing modem [Automatic Calling Unit] operating at 38400 baud).

- '`1-508-647-0747`'. The telephone number of the remote system.[21]

- '`ogin:--ogin:--ogin: mylogin`'. A sequence of *expect-send* pairs that define the dialog needed to log into the remote computer and establish the connection. The *expect* items are sent by the remote computer; the *send* items are sent by your computer in response. The '`ogin:`' in this example is the end of the string '`login:`'; it is repeated several times to allow for the possibility of an initial failure in the communication. Similarly, '`sword:`' is the end of '`Password:`'.

A full discussion of the form of this entry is beyond the scope of this book; see your system manuals for more information about the `Systems` file.

**12.9.6
Identifying Remote
Computers
with `uuname`**

The `uuname` command lists the names of computers known to `uucp`. It has the following options:

`-l`	List the name of the computer you're on.
`-c`	List the names of computers known to the `cu` program (see Section 12.10).

Normally, you get the same list with or without `-c`.

---

21. The hyphens are only for readability; omitting them will speed up the dialing slightly.

12.10   Connecting to Remote Computers with cu

Although cu stands for "connect to UNIX", you can use the cu program to connect to any remote computer over a direct line. Once you've made the connection, your terminal behaves as though it were a terminal on the remote computer. Whatever you type is sent to the remote computer; whatever output the remote computer produces is sent to your terminal. You can still communicate with your local computer by issuing the tilde commands described below, which resemble the input mode commands of mailx (see Section 11.5.21). Because cu is essentially oblivious to the nature of the remote computer (except for a couple of the commands discussed below), you can even use it for tasks such as explicit control of a modem. Cu is analogous to telnet, which provides connections to other computers via a network.

The cu command line has the form

        cu [-dehlnost] [*dest*]

where *dest* is either the name of a remote computer, a telephone number, or dir (for "direct"). Some versions of cu require that you specify *dest*; others don't recognize dir but instead assume dir if you omit *dest*.

- If you use a computer name, it must be a computer known to your own computer. You can find a list of such computers by using the 'uuname -c' command (see Section 12.9.6).

- If you use a telephone number, then your computer must have auto-dialers available. Within the telephone number, '=' indicates a wait for a secondary dial tone and '-' indicates a four-second delay.

  - If you specify a speed with the -s option, then the call is made at that speed or not at all.
  - If you specify a particular line with the -l option, then the call is made using the calling unit attached to that line.
  - If you specify a speed but not a line, the call is made on the first available line that operates at that speed.
  - If you specify neither a speed nor a line, the call is made on the first available line, no matter what its speed.

- If you specify dir (or omit *dest*, depending on your version of cu), then you must either

  - indicate a device name to use as the communication line with the -l option; or
  - indicate with the -n option that cu should prompt you for a telephone number.

You can communicate directly with a modem on a particular line by using the -l option without a computer or telephone number.

The -l, -s, and -n options are described below.

12.10.1 Quick Exit

You can exit from cu by typing '~.' on a line by itself. Before exiting, you should log out from the remote computer if you can. See "Terminating cu" below for further details.

12.10.2 Command-Line Options

The following options determine the communications line and the speed at which it operates:

-l *dev*   Use the device *dev* as the communication line. Usually the device is a directly connected asynchronous line whose name has the form '/dev/tty*nn*' or simply 'tty*nn*'; cu assumes a prefix of '/dev/' if necessary.

-s *speed*   Cause the communication line to operate at *speed*. The recognized values of *speed* are 300, 1200, 2400, 4800, 9600, and sometimes higher values, such as 19200 and 38400.

You should not use either of these options if you specify a remote computer as the destination of cu since the computer already has a line and speed associated with it.

The following option provides an alternative to specifying a telephone number on the command line:

-n   Prompt the user for the telephone number. Using this option provides a little more security than putting the telephone number on the command line. You should use this option only if you specify neither a telephone number nor a computer name.

The following options specify characteristics of the data transmission:

-e   Send data using even parity.

-o   Send data using odd parity.

-h   Provide local echoing of typed lines (half-duplex mode).

-t   Map ⟨linefeed⟩ on the local computer to ⟨return⟩ ⟨linefeed⟩ on the remote computer and vice versa. This option may be necessary for communicating with non-UNIX systems such as MS-DOS.

The following option causes cu to produce debugging information:

-d   Show diagnostic traces.

12.10.3 Tilde Commands for cu

You can issue commands to cu itself while you're running it. These commands, called *tilde commands* or *local commands*, all appear on a line that starts with a tilde (~).

Terminating cu. The following command provides the mechanism for terminating cu:

~.   Terminates the conversation with the remote computer and exits from cu. You should log out from that computer before you issue this command so that you get a clean termination on the remote end. If the remote computer drops the line carrier signal after you log out, cu exits of its own accord and you don't need to issue this command.

The following commands enable you to execute commands on your local computer:

~![*cmd*] Executes *cmd* in a subshell on the local computer. If you omit *cmd*, you obtain an interactive shell.

~%cd [*dir*] Changes the current directory on the local computer. You must use this command to change directories because issuing a cd command within a subshell has no external effect. If you omit *dir*, your home directory becomes the current directory as usual.

~$*cmd* Executes *cmd* in a subshell on the local computer and sends its output to the remote computer.

Controlling the Communication Channel. The following commands provide control over the communication channel:

~%b
~%break Sends a break signal to the remote computer.

~%nostop Toggles DC3/DC1 input control. Normally the ⟨DC3⟩ (Ctrl S) signal tells the receiver to stop sending output while the ⟨DC1⟩ (Ctrl Q) signal tells the receiver to start sending output again. These signals can be used to prevent the remote computer from sending output faster than the local computer can accept it or vice versa. If ⟨DC1⟩/⟨DC3⟩ input control doesn't work, you can turn it off with this command.

Sending Lines That Start with a Tilde. The following command provides an escape mechanism for sending a line of text that actually begins with a tilde:

~~*line* Sends ~*line* to the remote computer.

This command is particularly useful when the remote computer is running cu to communicate with a third computer, since it enables you to issue tilde commands on the remote computer (by starting them with '~~'). It's also useful for running mailx on the remote computer.

Transferring Files. The following commands enable you to transfer files to or from the remote computer:

~%put *rfile* [*lfile*]
Copies remote file *rfile* to local file *lfile*. If you omit *lfile*, cu takes it to be the same as *rfile*.

~%take *lfile* [*rfile*]
Copies local file *lfile* to remote file *rfile*. If you omit *rfile*, cu takes it to be the same as *lfile*.

These commands require the remote computer to be a UNIX system that supports the cat and stty commands. If the erase and kill characters are not the same on the local computer as on the remote one, the transfer may not work. These commands don't work for transferring binary files—the arbitrary control characters that can appear in such files won't be transmitted correctly and are likely to wreak havoc. The uuencode and uudecode programs mentioned in Section 12.5 can be used to transform binary files to files containing only printable characters and back again.

We recommend that you avoid using ~%put and ~%take if you can. They can leave dead processes on the remote computer or even hang that computer if anything goes wrong. Unfortunately, most versions of UNIX don't provide any other way of transferring files to or from a remote UNIX system that you've dialed into—uucp only works if your computer and the remote computer know each other. The kermit program (see p. 632) is often a good alternative; whatever communications package you use must be supported on both ends.

Commands for Debugging. The following commands enable you to examine line and terminal characteristics for debugging purposes and to turn debugging output off or on. Using them presumes some knowledge of UNIX internals as they make use of a particular data structure called termio. You can usually find a specification of termio in the file /usr/include/sys/termio.h.

~l   Shows the values of the termio variables for the communication line.

~t   Shows the values of the termio variables for your terminal.

~%d
~%debug   Toggles diagnostic tracing. Using this command produces the same output that you'd get with the -d option described earlier.

**12.10.4
Output Diversions**

Ordinarily, each line received from the remote computer is sent directly to your terminal. You can use an *output diversion* to send these lines to a file instead. An output diversion begins with a line having one of the forms

> ~>:*file*
> ~>>:*file*

and ends with a line containing just '~>'. Cu then copies all of the lines between the beginning and end of the diversion to the file *file*. The difference between '~>' and '~>>' is that '~>' erases *file* first, while '~>>' appends the diversion to *file*.

13

The X Window System

The X Window System, usually referred to simply as X, is a graphically oriented working environment originally developed at MIT. X has become popular in the UNIX world because it helps to overcome the limitations of the traditional UNIX character-oriented model of computing. It runs under several operating systems besides UNIX and supports the distribution of different parts of a task over a network. Using the `xterm` terminal emulator running under X, you can run any UNIX program under X that you could run otherwise. You can also use X running under UNIX to execute X programs running under non-UNIX operating systems on remote computers.

X is a large and complex system—a system of the same order of complexity as UNIX itself. In this chapter we present the basic concepts and vocabulary of X and describe some of the most useful client programs that run under it; however, space does not permit us to cover X completely. Fortunately, many of the X clients are easy to use even without instructions.

You can obtain the X files over the Internet via anonymous FTP from `ftp.x.org` or on CD-ROM (reference [C9]).

13.1   The X Screen

The X screen consists of a set of rectangular *windows* displayed within a background area called the *root window*. Each window contains an application program called a *client*. The computational effect of running several processes at once is reflected in the visual effect of having several windows on the screen. The screen also contains a cursor whose appearance depends on how the cursor is currently being used. The window that contains the cursor is called the *focus* of the cursor; if the cursor is on the background, then the focus is the root window.

The `xterm` terminal emulator (see Section 13.14) is a particularly important client. An `xterm` window appears to be a terminal from which you can run either ordinary UNIX programs such as `ls` or special X programs such as `xclock`. You can run several terminal sessions in parallel by creating several `xterm` windows.

13.2 Getting Started and Quitting

Many systems are set up to start X automatically at your terminal. For these systems, you log in under X as you would at a character-oriented terminal. Normally the `xdm` program, which handles logins and manages X sessions, is called as part of the procedures for initializing your system. Only the superuser can run it. If X has not been started automatically, you can start it with the `xinit` program (see Section 13.17.1). In either case, you can set up files that tailor X to your preferences (see Section 13.13).

If X was started automatically, you exit from it by logging out, just as you would from an ordinary shell. If you started it using `xinit`, it will terminate when the last foreground program that you started via `xinit` (usually a window manager) has terminated.

13.3 Window Managers

A window manager is a special client that controls the layout of windows on your machine. A window manager usually provides at least these operations:

- Creating and removing windows.

- Moving windows from one place to another and changing their sizes.

- Converting windows into *icons* and back again. An icon is a small symbol that stands for a particular window that is currently not being displayed.

- Selecting the apparent relative depth of overlapping windows, the top window being completely visible.

A window manager is not logically necessary in order to run X, but without one you would lose most of X's convenience.

The original X window manager `uwm` (universal window manager) is still in common use. An improved version known as `twm` (Tab window manager[1]) is also widely used in the X world. Two commercially important window managers are Motif from the Open Software Foundation and Open Look from AT&T.[2] Many clients can run under any window manager, but some depend on the facilities provided by a particular window manager (see Section 13.5). Because of the variety of window managers in use, we do not attempt to describe them here.

13.4 Servers, Displays, and Display Specifications

When you use X, your interaction with your computer (or a computer at a remote site) is handled by a program called a *server*. The server controls your screen (or screens, if you have more than one), your keyboard, and your mouse or other pointing device. These are collectively called your *display*. Each server is specialized to the hardware that it controls. For example, different types of video adapters require different servers.

A display specification informs a client how to connect to the display where the client is running. Display specifications can be given to most clients with the `-display` command-line option. The specification of a display has the form

> [*host*]: *display*[. *screen*]

The parts of the specification are as follows:

- The host name *host* specifies the computer to which the display is physically connected. It is needed because the client can be running on a different computer than the server. For stand-alone machines, it should be the string '`unix`'. If *host* is not specified, the server is assumed to be on the same computer.

- The display number *display* is the number of the display with respect to the computer where the server is running. It cannot be omitted. The first (or only) display on a computer is display #0.

- The screen number *screen* is the number of the screen within the display. You can omit it in the usual case where the display has only one screen. For multiscreen displays, the first screen is screen #0.

---

1. This window manager was originally called "Tom's Window Manager" after its author, Tom LaStrange.

2. The Sun Microsystems version of Open Look is called Open Windows.

The default display name is stored in the DISPLAY environment variable; for stand-alone systems, it is usually 'unix:0.0' (same computer, first display, first screen). When you log onto another computer over a network, you must either (a) set DISPLAY on that computer to point back to your own computer, or (b) use the -display option on the command line to specify the display explicitly to each client program that you call.

13.5   Widgets

X clients are programmed to use predefined software components called *widgets*. The collection of widgets available with the standard version of X is called the X Toolkit. Other widgets may be provided by particular window managers.

Widgets are intended to be used by X application programmers, not by users. Even so, you can customize certain aspects of X clients by customizing the widgets that they use. That's why widgets are significant to users as well as to programmers. When you customize a widget, you affect all the clients that use that widget. Thus, customizing widgets provides a method of customizing clients in a uniform way. If this kind of customization is possible, the client's documentation should tell you about it.

13.6   Properties

A window has a set of *properties* associated with it. A property is a packet of information associated with the window. The properties of a window are available to all clients running under the same server and provide a way for different clients to communicate with each other. In particular, they enable a client to communicate with the window manager. Each kind of property is named by a label called an *atom*. An atom has the form of an ASCII string. The *standard properties* are a minimum set that a client should specify; particular clients may have other properties as well.

13.7   Command-Line Options for X Applications

The command-line options for X applications usually have multicharacter names and often begin with '+' rather than '-', so they do *not* follow the command-line conventions given in Section 2.12.4. Usually '-' turns an option on and '+' turns it off—just the opposite of what you'd expect. Most recently written applications let you abbreviate an option to its shortest unique form (e.g., to write '-g' for '-geometry' if no other option starts with '-g').

Certain command-line options are supported by the X Toolkit and therefore are available in those X applications that use the Toolkit. Most of these specify characteristics of the window in which the application will run once it is started.

`-display` *display*

> Use the display specified by *display* (see Section 13.4).

`-geometry` *geometry*

> Take the size and placement of the window from *geometry*. See Section 13.10 for the form and meaning of *geometry*.

`-fg` *color*
`-foreground` *color*

> Use *color* as the foreground color for the window. See Section 13.12 for more information about colors.

`-bg` *color*
`-background` *color*

> Use *color* as the background color for the window.

`-bd` *color*
`-bordercolor` *color*

> Use *color* to form a border around the window.

`-bw` *n*
`-borderwidth` *n*

> Use a border *n* pixels wide.

`-fn` *font*
`-font` *font*

> Use *font* when displaying text (see Section 13.11). The font *font* can contain the wildcards '*' and '?' with their usual meanings. Wildcards are particularly useful when you specify fonts whose names are given by X Logical Font Descriptions (XLFD's) because these names are very long. You need to quote *font* if it contains any wildcards to ensure that the wildcards are interpreted by the X client rather than by your shell.

`-title` *string*

> Use *title* as the title for this window if the window manager wants a title.

`-iconic`   When starting up this application, display it as an icon rather than as a full window.

`-rv`
`-reverse` Simulate reverse video if possible, usually by swapping the foreground and background colors. Usually this option is used only on monochrome displays.

+rv   Don't simulate reverse video. This option would be specified only if one of the defaults specifies -rv and that is not what you want.

-name *name*

        Use *name* as the name of the client in determining which resource specifications apply. See page 676 for information on how -name is used.

-rxm *resource-spec*

        Use the resource specification *resource-spec* to override any defaults. This option can appear any number of times.

In addition to the Toolkit options, most clients accept this one:

-help   Produce a list of the options for this command on standard output.

13.8   Resources and Their Specifications

You can adjust the behavior of an X client by providing options on the command line when you call it. These options specify the values of certain attributes of clients and widgets called *resources*.[3] In addition, you can place specifications that establish defaults for resources in *resource files*. The resource specifications available from different sources are interpreted and combined by a program called the *resource manager*.

A resource specification specifies a set of resources and assigns a value to each resource in the set. In the simplest case, the resource specification has the form

     client[. *widget...*] . *resource* : *value*

Here the client uses the first widget, the first widget uses the second, and so on. For example, a resource specification

     xbrowse.scrollbar.foreground : green

indicates that the hypothetical client 'xbrowse' uses a widget 'scrollbar' that in turn uses a resource 'foreground'. The value of 'foreground' should be the color 'green'. If several widgets appear, each one makes use of the one to its right.

This notation has several extensions:

- You can use stars to indicate a sequence of zero or more unspecified widgets. This notation is useful when you don't know what the needed widgets might be. For example, you could write the preceding example either as

     xbrowse*scrollbar*foreground : green

---

3. The term "resource" reflects a programmer's view of what a resource is, not a user's view.

or as

```
xbrowse*foreground : green
```

The second specification would affect all widgets that use a 'foreground' resource.

- You can omit the client, causing the specification to apply to all clients for which it is meaningful. For example, the specification

```
*foreground : green
```

sets the foreground of all clients and widgets that have a foreground resource to green.

- You can replace the reference to an individual resource, referred to in this context as an *instance*, by a reference to a set of resources, called a *class*. The specification then sets all the resources in the class. By convention, instance names start with lowercase letters and class names start with uppercase letters. Most class names are uppercase forms of their most conspicuous instances. For example, the class 'Foreground' contains instances 'foreground', 'cursorColor', and 'pointerColor'. Thus the three specifications

```
xterm*foreground : orchid
xterm*cursorColor : orchid
xterm*pointerColor : orchid
```

are encompassed by the single specification

```
xterm*Foreground : orchid
```

- If a '-name *name*' option has been specified (see p. 675), the name *name* is used as the client name instead of the actual name. You can use this facility to modify the attributes of a client when you call it. For example, if there is an applicable specification

```
greenterm*background : green
```

then the call

```
xterm -name greenterm &
```

will cause the xterm client to have a green background.

Several resource specifications may apply to the same resource of the same widget or client. In that case, a specific citation of a resource takes precedence over a more general citation, regardless of order. For example, an instance takes precedence over a class and a specification with '.' takes precedence over a specification with '*'. In a case such as

```
myxterm.vt100.Background : green
myxterm.vt100*background : orange
```

the dot specification ('green') takes precedence over the instance specification ('orange'). When two conflicting specifications have the same precedence, the later one wins.

13.9   The Resource Database

You can provide resource specifications to X clients by placing the specifications in a resource database. By default, that database is the file `.Xdefaults` in your home directory. That file is available to clients running on your computer but not to clients running on other computers. However, you can specify the resource database in other ways too:

- You can store resource specifications for particular clients in files within a directory of application defaults, typically named `/usr/lib/X11/app-defaults`. The file for a particular client has the name of that client.

- You can create a global resource database with the `xrdb` program (see Section 13.17.2). That database, unlike `.Xdefaults`, is visible to a client that is using your server even if that client is running on a different computer.[4]

- You can create a set of resource databases in files with names of the form

    `.Xdefaults-`*hostname*

  where *hostname* is the name of a remote computer. Any clients running on that computer will use this database. By this mechanism, you can specify the behavior of clients running on a particular remote computer. For example, you could use these databases to cause windows on different remote computers to have different border colors.

Application-specific resource specifications are loaded before the resource databases and thus can be overridden by the databases. If a computer-specific resource database and a global resource database both exist, they are both used. Computer-specific specifications take precedence in case of conflict; in any event, specifications provided via the `-xrm` command-line option take precedence over all others.

13.10   Geometry Specifications

The *geometry* of a window specifies its size and its placement on the screen. The geometry, specified with the `geometry` resource, has the form

   *w*x*h*+*xoff*+*yoff*

---

4. The `xrdb` program stores the database in the `RESOURCE_MANAGER` property of the root window.

Here w and h give the width and height of the window, measured in either pixels or characters according to the application. (The `xterm` client in particular uses characters.) The values *xoff* and *yoff* give the offset in pixels from the screen's left edge and top edge, respectively. Many clients allow the '+' preceding *xoff* or *yoff* to be replaced by a '–'; in this case, *xoff* and *yoff* give the offset of the screen's right edge or bottom edge, respectively. In addition, either *xoff* or *yoff* can be negative (indicated by two signs in a row), causing the indicated edge to be off the screen. For example, the command

```
xclock -g 75x75-0+0
```

creates a clock that is 75 pixels square, positioned at the upper right corner of your screen.

You can omit any of the elements in the geometry specification. The window manager will use default values for the missing elements.

13.11   Fonts

X provides a collection of fonts that you can use in almost any text-oriented client. The available fonts fall into two groups: miscellaneous fonts that are useful on all systems and contributed fonts provided by several font vendors. Most of the fonts have names given as X Logical Font Descriptions, or XLFDs. Here is an example of one:

```
-bitstream-charter-medium-r-normal--15-140-75-75-p-84-iso8859-1
```

You could specify this font as '`*chart*med*-r-*-140-*`' in an `-fn` option, or in a resource specification since this pattern is sufficient to identify the font uniquely. You would need to quote the pattern if it appeared in an option to a command so as to prevent the shell from interpreting the stars.

The description consists of the following fields:

foundry	bitstream
family	charter
weight	medium
slant	r (upright)
set width	normal
additional style	(none)
pixel size	15
point size	140
resolutionX	75
resolutionY	75
spacing	p (proportional)
average width	84

registry   iso8859
encoding   1

We forego further discussion of the meanings of most of these fields. Normally, you need not be concerned with them, particularly since your only concern is likely to be to select a font that you like.

A number of the fonts have aliases, notably the fixed-width fonts in the miscellaneous group. For instance, the font

```
-misc-fixed-bold-r-semicondensed--13-120-75-75-c-60-iso8859-1
```

has an alias '6x13'; this font is a fixed-width font six pixels wide and 13 pixels high. You can refer to a font either by its alias or by its full name. Wildcards work with aliases as well as with full names.

Several programs exist for seeing what fonts are available (see Section 13.16). In addition, you can look directly at certain files that list all the fonts. The command 'xset q' reveals, among other things, the locations of the directories containing the font files. These directories also contain files `fonts.dir` and `fonts.alias`. The `fonts.dir` file lists the font files and their names (you usually care only about the names). The `fonts.alias` file lists a set of aliases and the font name corresponding to each.

13.12   Colors

Several resources such as `foreground` and `background` require you to specify a color, either with a name or with a number that provides intensity values for its red, green, and blue components.

**13.12.1
Color Names**

X keeps a database that defines a set of color names in a file named `rgb.txt`. A typical location for this file is `/usr/lib/X11/rgb.txt`. In any event, you can usually find it by retrieving the font path with 'xset q' and then looking in the X11 directory shown in that path. The colors themselves include the ordinary ones such as `green` and `white`, as well as more picturesquely named ones such as `khaki`, `orchid`, and `mediumForestGreen`. The names are case-insensitive. The numbers associated with each color give its red, green, and blue intensities on a scale from 0 to 255. The appearance of the colors varies greatly from one type of color monitor to another. Unfortunately, there is no way for you to assign names to your own color choices.

**13.12.2
Color Numbers**

A color number consists of three hexadecimal numbers that specify the intensity of the red, green, and blue components of the color. The numbers can have up to four hexadecimal digits per color, but most often they have two hexadecimal digits per color. The intensities range from 00 to FF (hexadecimal) or 0 to 255 (decimal), with 0 meaning this color is absent and 255 meaning it has maximum intensity. Encodings for one, two, or four digits are analogous. To illustrate, here are some color values as they appear in `rgb.txt`:

```
000 000 000  black
252 252 252  white
255 000 000  red
000 255 000  green
000 000 255  blue
255 255 000  yellow
000 255 255  cyan
255 000 255  magenta
```

You can specify a two-digit color value by writing it as '#*rrggbb*', where *rr*, *gg*, and *bb* are the hexadecimal values for the three colors. Using this notation, a magenta background would be produced by '`-bg "#ff00ff"`'. If that's the color you really want, you're better off writing it as '`-bg magenta`'; however, the numerical notation enables you to create the subtlest shades of color that your monitor can generate.

13.13   Initialization Files for X

You can provide an initialization file containing commands that are executed when X starts up. The name and location of the file depend on whether X has been started automatically or manually.

- If X is in control when you log in, startup is automatic. The arrangements for executing an initialization file are a local option, but the usual convention is that they are found in a file named `.xsession` in your home directory. The contents of `.xsession` will be executed *before* the login initialization file associated with your shell (`.profile` or `.login`, see Section 2.14).

- If X is not in control when you log in, you must start it manually with the `xinit` program (see Section 13.17.1). In this case, the initialization file is `~/.xinitrc`. At a minimum, it should contain commands to call `xterm` in the background and a window manager in the foreground.

13.14   The `xterm` Terminal Emulator

The `xterm` terminal emulator provides a window that acts like a terminal. The terminal associated with the window is sometimes called a *virtual terminal*; the associated device is called a *pseudo-terminal device*. When xterm creates a virtual terminal, it places that terminal under control of a shell specified by the value of the SHELL environment variable, with /bin/sh as the default. You can use this shell to issue the same commands that you would issue from an ordinary terminal, including calling the various X clients.

The form of the xterm command line is

> xterm [*options*]

See Section 13.7 for a list of the Toolkit options and your system manual for those not discussed below.

13.14.1 Emulations

The xterm client emulates two ancient terminals, the DEC VT102 text-oriented terminal and the Tektronix 4015 graphics terminal.[5] You are unlikely to have either of them, of course. However, the purpose of the emulation is to establish a common language between xterm and the application programs you run under it. That language need not concern you under most circumstances. The nature of the emulation is discussed in Section 2.15.6.

The VT102 provides many sequences for operating on a screenful of characters, while the 4015 provides hardly any. The 4015, on the other hand, provides sequences for drawing lines and plotting collections of points that are not understood by the VT102. By default, xterm starts in VT102 mode, but you can use the -t option on the command line to start it in 4015 mode instead. A single incarnation of xterm has two windows, one for the VT102 and one for the 4015; by default, the 4015 window is not displayed.

13.14.2 Using the Mouse

The mouse or other pointing device serves several purposes in xterm: copying text, moving within the recently displayed text, and selecting items from menus. Note that there are two independent cursors in the window: the mouse cursor and the text cursor.

Copying Text.   You can select text in one window and copy it to elsewhere in the same window or to another window. For example, you can use the mouse to retrieve a command that you recently executed and execute that command again. The default key and button use described here can be changed by including appropriate specifications in the resource database. Here is what the buttons do:

- The left button saves text into a *cut buffer*. You select the text by moving the mouse cursor to the beginning of the text and holding the button down while moving the mouse cursor to the end of the text. By double-clicking at the beginning of the selection, you can select text a word at a time; by triple-clicking, you can select

---

5. The widgets within xterm for the emulations are called vt100 and tek4014, an anachronism from when xterm was first written.

text a line at a time. The text is highlighted as you select it and remains highlighted after you release the button. To remove the highlighting, click the left button again.

- The right button extends or contracts the selected text at whichever end it is closest to. When you first press the right button, the boundary of the selected (highlighted) text moves to the position of the mouse cursor. If you hold down the button and move the mouse cursor, the text boundary follows it.

- The middle button inserts the text in the cut buffer at the position of the *text* cursor. The position of the mouse cursor is irrelevant except to determine which window receives the text.

Moving Within Recently Displayed Text.   You also can use the mouse in the scrollbar at the left edge of the window to move within the recently displayed text:

- The left button moves the text backward.

- The right button moves the text forward.

- The middle button repositions the text, centering it about a position proportional to the position of the cursor within the scrollbar when you release the button. By moving the cursor off the top or bottom of the scrollbar while holding down the middle button, you can move to the bottom or the top of the displayable region.

For the left and right buttons, the lower the position of the cursor within the scrollbar, the greater the movement. You can create a scrollbar with the `-sb` option and specify the number of extra lines of text to save with the `-sl` option. These extra lines define the region that you can view by using the scrollbar (64 by default).

Selecting Items from Menus.   You can select one of three menus by holding down the Ctrl shift and pressing a mouse button:

- The left button selects the `xterm` menu. Items on this menu enable you to initiate logging and to send various signals to the current foreground process. When logging is on, all your input and output are captured to a logging file, by default named `XtermLog.`*n*, where *n* is a five-digit decimal number that represents `xterm`'s process number. The log file is kept in the directory from which `xterm` was started or in your home directory if `xterm` was started as a login shell.

- The middle button sets various modes in the VT102 or 4105 emulation, depending on which window the mouse cursor is in. Among other things, you can use the middle button to establish or remove a scrollbar for the VT102 window.

The right button is not used with the Ctrl key.

13.15   Informational Displays for X

The `xclock` program displays a clock and the `xbiff` program alerts you to incoming mail. These popular clients are almost always run in the background so that their windows are always on the screen.

**13.15.1
Displaying a Clock
with** `xclock`

The `xclock` command displays a clock on your screen. The form of the `xclock` command line is

> xclock [*options*] **&**

The '**&**', while not actually part of the command, indicates that the command should be run in the background. The only way to get rid of the clock is to kill its process (see Section 5.3.1).

Command-Line Options.   The following options determine the nature of the clock:

`-analog`   Display a conventional 12-hour clock face. This is the default.

`-digital`   Display a 24-hour digital clock.

The following options apply to any clock:

`-chime`   Chime once on the half hour, twice on the hour.

`-update` *n*

> Update the clock every *n* seconds. A value of *n* less than 60 will cause an analog clock to show a second hand. The default is 60.

`-padding` *n*

> Use *n* pixels of padding between the window border and the text or picture of the clock. The default is 10 for a digital clock, 8 for an analog clock.

The following options affect the appearance of the hands of an analog clock:

`-hd` *color*   Use *color* as the color of the hands.

`-hl` *color*   Use *color* as the color of the edges of the hands.

`Xclock` also supports the Toolkit options (see Section 13.7).

**13.15.2
Flagging Mail
with** `xbiff`

The `xbiff` client notifies you when new mail arrives.[6] It displays a picture of a mailbox with a flag. The flag is raised when mail arrives and lowered

---

6. One legend has it that `biff`, the ancestor of `xbiff`, was named by Ken Thompson for his dog Biff, who barked whenever the letter carrier arrived. According to Heidi Stettner, as quoted by Peter Salus, however, John Foderero, the author of `biff`, named the program after *her* dog Biff when she was a graduate student at Berkeley, and the legend is a scurrilous canard.

when the mail has been retrieved. You can also lower the flag explicitly by moving the mouse cursor to the mailbox and clicking the left button.

The form of the `xbiff` command line is

    xbiff [*options*] &

The '&', while not actually part of the command, indicates that the command should be run in the background. See Section 13.7 for a list of the Toolkit options and your system manual for the others.

13.16 Color and Font Information for X

The `xcolors` program displays a color chart, while the `xfd`, `xlsfonts`, and `xfontsel` programs provide information about fonts.

13.16.1 Displaying Colors with `xcolors`

The `xcolors` client displays a color chart that shows you what the different named colors look like. The form of the `xcolors` command line is

    xcolors [*options*]

See Section 13.7 for a list of the Toolkit options and your system manual for the others.

13.16.2 Displaying a Font with `xfd`

The `xfd` client displays the characters in a specified font. The form of the `xfd` command line is

    xfd [*options*]

The options must include '-font *font*' (or '-fn *font*'), where *font* specifies the font to be displayed. See Section 13.7 for a list of the Toolkit options and your system manual for the others.

13.16.3 Listing Fonts with `xlsfonts`

The `xlsfonts` program lists the available fonts. The form of the `xlsfonts` command line is

    xlsfonts [*options*]

The '-font *font*' (or '-fn *font*') option specifies a font name with wildcards that is matched against the available fonts (see Section 13.11). If you omit the option, all fonts are listed. See your system manual for the other options. This program uses none of the X facilities; it merely sends its listing to standard output.

13.16.4 Selecting and Displaying Fonts with `xfontsel`

The `xfontsel` program lists and displays fonts. It works only for fonts named by XLFDs (see p. 678). You can use it interactively to try alternatives for the font fields, seeing which fonts match, and to view any of those fonts. The form of the `xfontsel` command line is

    xfontsel [*options*]

See Section 13.7 for a list of the Toolkit options and your system manual for the others.

13.17   Clients for Initializing and Customizing X

The clients described in the following subsections enable you to start X and to customize the appearance of its root window.

**13.17.1
Initiating X
with** `xinit`

The `xinit` program starts an X server and a first client program. If your system is not configured to start X automatically, you should start it with `xinit`.

The form of the `xinit` command line is

> `xinit` [[*client*] *options*] [-- [*server*] [:*display*] [*options*]]

The information on the command line determines a command or script to be initially executed and a server to be employed. In most cases, `xinit` is called without any command-line information and its behavior is determined entirely by default.

The Initial Commands.   When `xinit` is called, it starts the server and then executes a sequence of commands. When these commands have finished executing, the server terminates and X ends. Usually the last command in the sequence is `xterm`, so X remains in control until you exit from your `xterm` shell.

If the command line has no arguments or has '--' as its first argument, then all client information is determined by default. In this case, `xinit` executes the commands in the `.xinitrc` file of your home directory. This is the simplest and most common case. Usually the `.xinitrc` file includes, at a minimum, commands to start a window manager in the foreground and `xterm` in the background or vice versa. It also often includes commands to start other programs such as `xclock` and `xbiff` in the background.

If client information is specified, the client can either be given by *client* or defaulted. If the first argument of the client information starts with '.' or '/', indicating a pathname, then it is taken as the name of a client program. Otherwise *client* defaults to

> `xterm -geometry +1+1 -n login -display :0`

which sets up a virtual terminal with the string '`login`' used to select resources (see p. 675). Any options included in the client information are appended to the client, whether given explicitly or defaulted.

The Server.   Server information is indicated by '--' on the command line. The server program, like the client program, must start with '.' or '/' if it is given explicitly. If the first server argument is not such a program or there is no server information, xinit looks for a file .xserverrc in your home directory and executes its commands. If no such file exists, xinit executes the command 'X :0', which calls the default server for the default display. Any other arguments on the command line following '--' are passed as arguments to the server, whether given explicitly or defaulted.

13.17.2 Specifying Global Resources with xrdb

The xrdb program creates and displays a collection of global resources available to all clients that are using your server, even if they are running on other computers (see Section 13.9). The form of the xrdb command line is

> xrdb [*options*] [*file*]

where *file* specifies a file containing a set of resource specifications that replaces standard input in the options described below.

Command-Line Options.   Here are the most important options for xrdb:

-query   Send the current contents of the global resource database to standard output.

-load   Load the global resource database from standard input.

-merge   Merge standard input with the global resource database.

-remove   Make the global resource database empty.

See your system manual for descriptions of the remaining options.

13.17.3 Setting User Preferences for X

The xset command sets a number of user preferences, including the pathname of the font directories, the mouse acceleration, the keyboard autorepeat adjustments, and the screen-saver parameters. The screen-saver blanks your screen or displays a moving pattern if your keyboard has been inactive for a while. The form of the xset command line is

> xset [*options*]

The q option (no '-') lists the current settings. See your system manual for descriptions of the remaining options.

13.17.4 Setting the Root Window Appearance with xsetroot

The xsetroot client adjusts the appearance of the root window. The root window is the background of all the other windows. Using this client, you can specify a one- or two-color pattern for the window and specify what the colors will be. You can also control the appearance of the cursor when it is in the root window.

The form of the xsetroot command line is

> xsetroot [*options*]

The option '-solid *color*' sets the color of the background to *color*. Other options can be used to fill the background with a two-color pattern. See your system manual for a list of the options.

13.18   Killing an X Client with xkill

The xkill program forces the X server to close its connection to a client. It is useful for getting rid of unwanted windows, although the clients that it kills may not terminate cleanly. You select the client to be killed by clicking the left mouse button on its window. The form of the xkill command line is

xkill [*options*]

See Section 13.7 for a list of the Toolkit options and your system manual for the others.

13.19   Viewing Manual Pages with xman

The xman command enables you to view manual pages in an X window. The form of the xman command line is

xman [*options*]

See Section 13.7 for a list of the Toolkit options and your system manual for the others.

When you start xman, it displays a small window with three mouse-selectable buttons: "Help", "Quit", and "Manual Page". The 'Manual Page' button brings up a window with full instructions on using the program. At the top of the window, you'll find two selectable boxes, "Options" and "Sections". After choosing one of those boxes with a mouse button, you drag the mouse to a selection and release it. The "Options" selections determine what you do next, while the "Sections" selections choose a category of manual pages such as "(1) User Commands". What the selections mean should mostly be obvious. To get to a particular manual page, you either display its directory (the one for the chosen section) or search for it.

You can scan the pages for a command or other entity using the X scrollbars. Alternatively, you can use the keyboard scrolling commands within the manual pages:

b   Moves one page back.

Space
f   Moves one page forward.

1   Moves one line forward.

2   Moves two lines forward.

3   Moves three lines forward.

4   Moves four lines forward.

You can quickly switch back and forth between manual pages and directories with (Ctrl)M and (Ctrl)D or search for a topic or manual page with (Ctrl)S. A number of other keyboard and mouse actions are provided; see the help screen for details.

14

Managing Your System

In this chapter we discuss what is involved in managing a UNIX system, primarily from the perspective of running a system such as Linux on a personal computer when the system has only one real user. Managing the system on a workstation attached to a network is often very similar. The activities involved in managing a UNIX system are usually called *system administration*.

The task of managing a large UNIX system is a major subject in its own right and not one we attempt to cover in this book. However, much of the material presented here also applies to large multi-user systems since many of the programs and files involved are the same in either case. A number of excellent books on system administration, such as the one by Nemeth, Snyder, Seebass, and Hein (see reference [B20]) are available; we also list several others in Appendix C. Your chief source of information should be the manuals that come with your system.

14.1 Running with Superuser Privileges

For the sake of both security and safety, all UNIX systems restrict certain operations to users running with superuser privileges, also called root privileges. You gain these privileges by logging in as root or by using the su command (see Section 5.4.2) to become root temporarily. On some high-security systems, the privileges normally accorded to `root` are partitioned into subsets, allowing system administrators to exercise some privileges but not others.

With superuser privileges, you can carry out nearly any operation you wish. For example, you can write to a file even if the file does not have write permission. Even with superuser privileges, though, you can't do things that don't make sense. For example, you can't execute a file that lacks execute permission since presumably such a file was never meant to be executed.

It's obvious that a rogue user with superuser privileges can utterly destroy a UNIX system, which is why security is such a concern for multi-user systems or for single-user systems that are not physically secure. What's less obvious is that even when security is not a concern at all, superuser privileges should be used as sparingly as possible. The inter-locks built into UNIX protect not just against predators but also against careless actions. It's all too easy to remove or overwrite a critical system file if you're not paying careful attention. Therefore, we strongly advise that you always operate with the minimum privileges that you actually need and that when you do become `root`, you go back to being an ordinary user as soon as possible.

In one respect, though, operating in a system where security is not at issue does give you certain conveniences. For instance, it's convenient and even customary on such systems not to use passwords at all, even for `root`. You can remove password protection for any user, `root` included, by editing the `/etc/passwd` file (or, on some systems, `/etc/shadow` instead) to remove the password field. The password field is the second field on each line of `/etc/passwd`; just replace it by a null string.[1] Once you've done that, an easy way to execute a particular command with superuser privileges is with the form

    su -c "*cmd*"

where *cmd* is the command, together with its arguments, that you wish to execute. You can also become superuser just by typing 'su', but the single-command method is a little safer since you won't accidentally retain the superuser privileges. The `su` command gives you a new subshell; to relinquish the privileges, exit the subshell by typing 'exit'. While you're in the subshell, the prompt has a different form (it ends with '#', usually) to remind you of your powerful but dangerous privileges.

---

1. To edit the file, copy it to your own directory, edit it, and then, as superuser, copy the edited version back to where it belongs, being sure to save a backup first. On some systems, there is an easier alternative: as superuser, type '`passwd -d` *user*' to nullify *user*'s password.

14.2   System Administration Programs

All commercial UNIX systems come supplied with a system administration program whose functions typically include the following:

- Assigning passwords
- Setting the date, time, and machine identification
- Adding and deleting users and groups
- Installing and removing software packages
- Backing up the data on your disks and restoring it when necessary
- Configuring modems and other serial devices
- Configuring printers and managing printer queues
- Mounting and unmounting file systems
- Formatting diskettes
- Tuning the performance of your disk and your memory allocations

Usually the system administration program is menu-driven and easy to use without any special instruction. System administration programs include `sysadm` for System V-based systems, `admintool` for Solaris, `SMIT` for AIX, `sysadmsh` for SCO Open Server Release 5, and `SAM` for HP-UX.

Noncommercial systems usually have administration programs also, but with fewer functions. Often these systems have different tools for different purposes. For example, Linux has a `setup` program for installing system components and an `adduser` program for adding users.

14.3   Explicit System Administration

If your system doesn't provide a program for handling the aspects of system administration listed in Section 14.2, you'll need to deal with them yourself. Below we describe the issues you're most likely to encounter.

14.3.1
User and Group Information

Information about users is recorded in the file `/etc/passwd`, with password information often kept in `/etc/shadow`.[2] In systems that use `/etc/shadow`, the password field of `/etc/password` is always just 'x' and the encoded password is in the shadow file, which is readable only by `root`.

---

2. It may seem odd that `/etc/passwd` doesn't contain password information, but its historical use as the repository for information about users and the convention that it's world-readable are firmly established. For those systems where `/etc/passwd` does contain password information, the passwords are encoded using a one-way algorithm that enables them to be checked but not discovered.

A list of groups is recorded in the file /etc/groups (or sometimes /etc/group).

You can add a user manually by inserting a line in /etc/passwd for that user, following the format of the other lines and specifying an empty password (second field). You may also need to insert a line in /etc/shadow. You can delete a user by deleting that user's line in the file. However, it's always better to use a system utility such as adduser to add a user since that utility sets up the user's home directory and performs a number of other functions. Having extra user names and group names is sometimes handy even if you're the only real user of the system, particularly for running experiments.

14.3.2
Printers

Under System V, the main programs for correcting printer problems are lpsched, lpshut, and lpmove, which operate on the queue of files to be printed. More permanent adjustments to the printer arrangements should be done using sysadm. The corresponding BSD program is lpc ("line printer control"). Consult your system manual for instructions on using these programs.

Under BSD-style systems (and Linux as well), information about printers is contained in the file /etc/printcap (see Section 2.15). You may need to modify this file to get your printer to work properly. In particular, you should make sure the printer named lp in /etc/printcap (the default assumed by lpr) is your default printer, even though you can override the choice of a printer with the PRINTER variable.

14.3.3
Terminals

Traditionally, UNIX systems use the getty ("get TTY") program to handle terminals. The System V /etc/inittab file normally contains an entry that activates a copy of getty for each port to which a terminal can be connected. Configuration information is usually in the file /etc/gettydefs. Under BSD systems, terminal setup is handled by init, which uses the /etc/ttys file to get its configuration information. Recent UNIX systems eschew the use of separate gettys for each terminal altogether and replace them with a unitary program called ttymon.

A different aspect of terminal configuration relates to configuring a display for use under X. To set up the display properly, you need to set up the Xconfig file that provides the hardware characteristics of the display. Each user can have an Xconfig file in his or her home directory; if that file isn't found, X uses a system-wide version of Xconfig, often stored in /usr/lib/X11/Xconfig or /etc/Xconfig.

14.3.4
Reconfiguring
the Kernel

Usually the kernel takes care of itself and you don't need to do anything to maintain it. The kernel of many modern systems includes code for sensing what devices are attached to the computer, loading the necessary drivers, and checking other relevant properties of the hardware.

Nevertheless, there are reasons you might want to modify the kernel: you have hardware that the kernel isn't sensing properly, you want to reduce the size of the kernel, or you want to install a new version of it. On some systems, you can create an empty file named `reconfigure` and place it in your root directory; on the next reboot, the kernel will automatically reconfigure itself to the current hardware and remove the file. On other systems, you may need to recompile the kernel in whole or in part.

Partial recompilation occurs when your kernel is divided into two parts: configuration files you can modify and object files you can't. Reconfiguring your kernel involves modifying the configuration files and relinking them with the object files to obtain a new kernel image. Full recompilation occurs when you recompile the entire kernel.

In the case of Linux, you call the command

```
make config
```

from the directory `/usr/src/linux`. The Makefile found there will ask you questions about your system and use your answers to modify the kernel it builds. The entire kernel will be recompiled. You then type

```
make depend
```

to build the system dependencies that enable `make` to recompile only the files that have to be recompiled. Next, you type

```
make zImage
```

to build a compressed (and therefore small) kernel named `zImage`. You install the new kernel by moving it to the root directory, modifying the configuration files used by the LILO boot loader, and calling LILO to install the kernel. See the LILO documentation for further details. Procedures on other systems are likely to follow very similar steps, although some of these steps may be automated.

14.4   Software Installation

One task of system administration you may face even if you aren't in charge of your own system is installing new or updated software. As long as you aren't trying to make the software publicly available, you don't need any special privileges to do that; you can install all the necessary files in directories you control. The only difference between installing software for public consumption and software for private consumption is where the software is put and what privileges are required to put it there.

Some software, particularly commercial software, comes with complete instructions on how to install it. If the software is in the form of a compiled binary program, then you need to place it in one of the directories listed in your `PATH` variable and make it executable with 'chmod +x' (see Section 3.11.1).

Free software such as that obtained from the GNU project or found at various `ftp` sites often is in the form of a file whose name ends in '`.tar.gz`'. In that case, you should decide where you want to install it, move the file to that directory, and execute the command

```
gunzip -c file.tar.gz | tar -xvf -
```

That will create all the necessary subdirectories. Look for a file whose name is something like '`INSTALL`' or '`README`' for installation instructions.

14.4.1 Using `make` and Makefiles

Noncommercial UNIX software is traditionally distributed in the form of source code. To install it, you need to compile and load the source code and then place the resulting binary programs in an appropriate location. The distribution also customarily includes a file called `Makefile` that serves as input to the `make` program. Using the Makefile, `make` does everything necessary to install the software.

To apply the Makefile, set the current directory to the directory containing the Makefile and call `make` with the name of a target. The installation instructions will probably tell you what the possible targets are, but there probably is also a default target that does most of what you want. For example, calling `make` by itself might generate the executable programs, while '`make install`' would put the programs in the right places and '`make man`' would put the documentation in the right places. The Makefile may need to be modified so that `make` can find the right places if its assumptions about the naming structure of your directories are wrong; a well-constructed Makefile should have instructions on how to make the necessary changes. A common target is `clean`; calling '`make clean`' removes all the intermediate files created during the installation process.

To install programs for X, you need to go through another level by calling the program `xmkmf`. The installation directory in this case should include a file named `Imakefile`. The `xmkmf` program will build a Makefile from the Imakefile and then execute `make` appropriately with the newly constructed Makefile as its input.

These methods of installing software are nearly automatic—provided nothing goes wrong. The Makefiles and Imakefiles make a lot of assumptions about where files are located, which compilers and other tools are available, and so forth. If the installation fails, you have no choice but to try to figure out what is going on in greater detail than we can possibly cover here.

14.4.2 Manual Pages

Part of the task of installing new UNIX software is installing the manual pages for it. Manual pages come in several forms and can be installed in several places. The places where your system expects to find them are given by the value of the `MANPATH` environment variable.

The `man` command and its X counterpart, `xman` (see Sections 5.1.1 and 13.19) can work with either preformatted or unformatted documents. An unformatted document is in the form of input to the `nroff` formatting program (see Section 5.14.1), using the an collection of macros.[3] If the manual pages are unformatted, man formats them before presenting them to you. In addition, manual pages may be stored in compressed form, indicated by a suffix on the file such as '.Z' or '.gz'. Again, man can decompress these pages before presenting them to you.

The manual pages are stored in subdirectories of the directories listed in MANPATH. The convention for naming the subdirectories is quite specific: formatted manual pages for section *s* are stored in subdirectory cat*s*, while unformatted manual pages are stored in subdirectory man*s*. Though *s* is usually a single digit, it can also be a sequence such as '1c'. As an example, the formatted manual page for grep (Section 1) might be found in directory /usr/man/cat1 as file grep.1. Usually the different directories in MANPATH contain manual pages for different parts of the system (e.g., /usr/TeX/man for manual pages relating to TeX and its supporting programs).

Putting the manual pages in the right place isn't sufficient; for 'man -k' and apropos to work properly, you also have to enter descriptions of them in a database of manual pages. Here are some sample lines from that database:

```
grep, egrep, fgrep (1V) - search a file for a string or regular expression
group (5)     - group file
groups (1)    - display a user's group memberships
hack (6)      - replacement for rogue
halt (8)      - stop the processor
hangman (6) - computer version of the game hangman
head (1)      - display first few lines of specified files
help (5)      - help file format
```

There can be several such databases, each in one of the directories listed in MANPATH (not its subdirectories). The database is in a file named whatis or, on Solaris and some other systems, windex. For example, one of the databases might be in /usr/man/whatis. The database lists manual pages, their sections, and their titles (not necessarily all from within the directory where whatis is found). Your system probably includes a program makewhatis for building the database. Some systems use the command 'catman -w' to call makewhatis. However, you may sometimes find it more convenient to add items to the database manually.

GNU software often comes with Info files like the ones that come with Emacs. You can read them with the GNU Info reader info or with the Info reader built into Emacs. To install them, you need to make an appropriate entry in the top node of the Info tree. The Emacs variable Info-directory-list contains the list of directories that Emacs searches

3. Why an? Nroff has an -m option for specifying a macro set, so calling 'nroff -man' invokes the manual macros.

for Info files, so you should be sure to put your Info files in one of the places on that list.

14.5   File System Maintenance

In this section we discuss what's needed to maintain your file systems: how to mount them to make them accessible, how to create them in the first place, how to check them to see if they have been corrupted, and how to back them up as a protection against disaster. We also discuss the `/etc/fstab` and `/etc/mtab` files, which record information about mountable systems and about which file systems have actually been mounted.

14.5.1
Mounting a File System with `mount`

In order to make a file system accessible, you need to *mount* it at a *mount point* with the `mount` command. The mount point is simply a directory, often kept either as a subdirectory of the root directory or as a subdirectory of `/mnt`. In order to mount a file there, that directory should be empty since any files in it will become inaccessible after the mount. Once the file system has been mounted, its root becomes identified with the directory at the mount point. Superuser privileges are ordinarily required in order to mount a file system, but it's possible and sometimes useful to allow certain file systems such as those on removable media to be mounted by anyone.[4] You can mount file systems at another network node as well as at your own node. The operation reciprocal to mounting a file system is unmounting it. When a file system is unmounted, its mount point reverts to being an ordinary directory. A file system cannot be unmounted if it is currently in use.

Usually the `mount` commands that mount filesystems are included in the `rc` scripts that are executed as part of system startup. Corresponding `umount` commands are included in the procedures for shutting down the system.

The form of the `mount` command under Linux is

    mount [-afrwvn] [-o *options*] [-t *fstype*] [*dev*] [*mountdir*]

Forms for other systems are similar. In this form, *options* is a comma-separated list of mounting options, *dev* is the name of the device to be mounted, and *mountdir* is the absolute pathname of the directory that is to serve as the mount point. A device name of the form '*node*:*dir*' designated the directory *dir* at network node *node*. If either *dev* or *node* is omitted, mounting information is taken from the `/etc/fstab` file (see

---

4. If file systems on diskettes, say, are mountable by anyone, then it isn't necessary to grant superuser privileges to someone who needs to mount a diskette. In this case, granting a privilege actually enhances system security.

Section 14.5.3). A successful mount is recorded in the `/etc/mtab` file. If neither *dev* nor *node* is specified and `-a` isn't specified either, a list of all mounted file systems is produced. You can restrict this list to file systems of a particular type with the `-t` option.

Command-Line Options.   These are the command-line options for `mount`:

`-t` *fstype* Assume the file system is of type *fstype*. The default type is the one typically used for hard disk partitions, but other types are usually available. On Linux, the other types include `msdos` for MS-DOS-style FAT file systems, `iso9660` for CD-ROMs, `hfps` for OS/2 HPFS-style file systems, and `nfs` for file systems accessed over a network. Where it makes sense, *fstype* can be given as a comma-separated list of types or a type can be prefixed by 'no' to negate it.

`-o` *options*

Use the options specified by *options*, which is a comma-separated list of specific options (see "Mounting Options" on p. 699). Options specified in the `mount` command override those derived from the `/etc/fstab` table.

`-r`   Mount the file system read-only.

`-w`   Mount the file system for writing as well as reading.

`-a`   Mount all the file systems listed in `/etc/fstab` except for those with the `noauto` option.

`-f`   Do everything except the actual mount.

`-n`   Don't make any entries in `/etc/mtab` for this mount.

`-v`   Report verbosely on the mount.

Examples.   Here are some examples of the use of `mount`:

- The command

      mount -av -t iso9660

  causes all file systems listed in `/etc/fstab` that are of type `iso9660` to be mounted, with verbose messages produced.

- The command

      mount -t nfs -o noexec lactarius:/usr /net/lactarius/usr

  causes the directory `/usr` on the remote system `lactarius` to be mounted with execution of binary programs inhibited.

- The command

      mount -t msdos /dev/fd0 /mnt/floppy

  causes the floppy disk in drive 0, presumed to be in MS-DOS format, to be mounted as a file system attached at the directory `/mnt/floppy`.

```
/dev/sda2    /          ext2      defaults
/dev/sda5    /dos_e     msdos     user,rw,gid=1,uid=1
/dev/sdb5    /aux       ext2      defaults
/dev/sr0     /cdrom     iso9660   user,noauto,ro
/dev/fd0     /dos35fd   msdos     user,noauto,rw
r:/          /russ      nfs       noauto,rw
none         /proc      proc      defaults
```

Fig. 14-1. Sample lines from /etc/fstab.

14.5.2 Unmounting a File System with umount

You can unmount one or more file systems with the umount command. The forms of the umount command line are

> umount -a [-t *fstype*]
> umount { *dev* | *mountdir* }

where the device to be unmounted is specified by its device name *dev* or its mount point *mountdir*. These are the command-line options:

-a   Unmount all mounted file systems listed in /etc/fstab.

-t *fstype*   Unmount file systems of the specified type or types. The conventions are the same as for -t with mount.

-v   Unmount the file systems verbosely.

14.5.3 The Mounting Tables

UNIX systems generally use two tables to assist in mounting and unmounting file systems: /etc/fstab and /etc/mtab (or on some systems, /etc/vfstab and /etc/mnttab). The /etc/fstab table records file systems that are or might be available for mounting, while the /etc/mtab table records those that are actually mounted. Figure 14-1 shows a sample portion of /etc/fstab as it might look under Linux.

- The first column shows the device or file system to be mounted.

- The second column shows the directory where it is to be attached.

- The third column shows the type of the file system (ext2 being the usual type for Linux).

- The fourth column shows the options that apply to the mount.

The command 'mount -a' is issued as part of system initialization and causes all file systems other than those with the noauto option to be mounted. The contents of /etc/mtab after the mount would be as follows:

```
/dev/sda2 / ext2 rw 0 0
/dev/sda5 /dos_e msdos rw,noexec,nosuid,nodev,gid=1,uid=1 0 0
/dev/sdb5 /aux ext2 rw 0 0
none /proc proc rw 0 0
```

The two zeroes at the end of each line relate to dumping and checking file systems. You can see the same information in a slightly more readable form by calling `mount` with no options or arguments (superuser privileges not required).

Mounting Options.   These are some of the more common and important options used in `/etc/fstab` and with the `mount` command:

`remount`   Attempt to remount a file system that's already mounted. The usual reason for using this option is to change the status of the file system and in particular to make a read-only file system writable.

`ro`   Mount this file system read-only.

`rw`   Mount this file system with writing enabled.

`user`   Allow an ordinary user to mount this file system.

`nouser`   Only allow `root` to mount this file system.

`auto`   Mount this file system whenever the `-a` option is used with `mount`.

`noauto`   Mount this file system only if it is called for explicitly by a `mount` command.

`exec`   Allow binary programs on this file system to be executed.

`noexec`   Don't allow binary programs on this file system to be executed. This option is useful when the file system to be mounted is on a networked machine with an incompatible architecture.

`defaults` Use the default options when mounting this file system.

Some options such as `auto` are only useful in `/etc/fstab`. Options specified explicitly on a `mount` command always override options specified in `/etc/fstab`.

**14.5.4
Creating a File
System**

You can create a file system on a hard disk, a floppy disk, a magneto-optical disk, or any other random-access device supported by the kernel of your UNIX system. The process has two steps: formatting or otherwise preparing the device, and building the actual file system.

The most common case is creating a file system on a hard disk. On most computer systems, each hard disk is divided into regions of storage called *partitions*.[5] A file system occupies a single partition. You can store more than one operating system on a hard disk; each operating system occupies its own partition but can use file systems in other partitions. For example, you might have your system set up to run UNIX, MS-DOS, and OS/2.

On Intel machines, the standard program across operating systems for creating and modifying partitions is `fdisk`. Functions provided by `fdisk`

---

5. Systems based on OSF/1 use the term *physical volume* to refer to a partition.

include displaying the available partitions, creating a new partition from empty space, deleting a partition, and setting a partition's type. You can usually use one operating system's `fdisk` to create partitions that can be used by a different operating system. For example, the Linux `fdisk` is capable of creating an MS-DOS partition, while Linux is itself capable of using a partition created by the MS-DOS `fdisk`. Some operating systems are fussier, however, and can only work in partitions that they themselves created. In order to make a partition usable as a file system, you first have to allocate its space and then set its type.

The program for creating a file system is `mkfs` (replaced on 4.4BSD by `newfs`). The form of the Linux `mkfs` command is

> `mkfs` [`-V`] [`-t` *fstype*] [*fs-options*] *filesys* [*blocks*]

where *filesys* is the name of the device or disk partition where the file system is to be created. The `mkfs` program on other systems should be similar. The device name `/dev/hda1` indicates all of disk drive 1, `/dev/hdb1` indicates all of disk drive 2, etc., while the partitions of disk drive 1 are `/dev/hda2`, `/dev/hda3`, etc. SCSI disk drives are named `/dev/sda1`, `/dev/sdb1`, etc., with analogous names for their partitions. You can use `mkfs` to create file systems on diskettes or other devices as well.

The `-V` option instructs `mkfs` to produce verbose output, while the `-t` option instructs `mkfs` to create a file system of type *fstype*. The types are those of the `mount` command (see Section 14.5.1). The default is a normal Linux partition. The options *fs-options* are specific to the type of file system being created, while the *blocks* specification tells `mkfs` how many blocks should be used for the file system.

To create a file system on a diskette, you need to format the diskette if it isn't already formatted. The program for doing that is usually called `fdformat`.

14.5.5 Checking a File System with `fsck`

Each time your system restarts, the normal initialization procedures include calls on the `fsck` program to ensure that each file system to be mounted is in a consistent state. Under Linux and some other systems, the check is bypassed if a `clean` flag has been set on the previous shutdown, but after a certain number of restarts, the file system is checked anyway. The check precedes the actual mounting, although the root file system has to be mounted read-only so that the initialization files and the `fsck` program itself can be retrieved. Following the check, the root file system is remounted as writable and the other files systems are initially mounted as writable.

If the check fails, you'll have to run `fsck` manually to repair the defective file systems. If `fsck` is located in `/sbin`, the appropriate command for an inconsistent file system on device *dev* is simply

> `/sbin/fsck` *dev*

As it runs, `fsck` will ask you to confirm each corrective change to the file system. A change may well lead to loss of data, but unless you have a very good understanding of the internal structure of your file systems, you have little choice but to say yes to everything. You can avoid all the confirmation queries by calling `fsck` with the `-y` option. Another useful option is `-f`, which forces a file system to be checked even if the clean flag is on. If one file system is corrupted, it's often a good idea to check the others as well after repairing it.

When `mkfs` builds a UNIX file system, on some systems it automatically creates a directory called `lost+found` that serves as a home for orphan files. When `fsck` tries to recover a file system and encounters files that are at least partially intact but have corrupted links, it creates new links to them in `lost+found`. If you don't have enough slots in your `lost+found` directory, `fsck` will not be able to relink all your files in case it finds errors in the file system.

14.5.6 Backup

Backing up your file systems consists of copying their contents to an external medium or possibly to another network node. Backups serve two purposes: they provide you with a means of recovery if the file systems or their supporting hardware become damaged; and they provide a way of retrieving old files that have been accidentally deleted or overwritten (provided you still have the backups, of course). We won't attempt to advise you on how often to back up your file systems or, more generally, what your backup strategy should be, but we will describe some backup methods.

There are three varieties of backups: full, incremental, and differential.

- A full backup is what the name implies: it includes every file on the file system you're backing up (except, perhaps, for spooling files and others you know to be transient).

- An incremental backup contains all files since the previous incremental backup or, if you haven't yet made any incremental backups, all files since the last full backup.

- A differential backup contains all files since the last full backup.

The advantage of incremental backups over differential backups is that they are less bulky; the disadvantage is that you may have to search through many of them to find a particular lost file. If you use differential backups, you can always find a file by looking in just two places: the full backup and the differential backup.

To back up a file system, you need to be running with superuser privileges so that you can access any file no matter who owns it. For a full backup, you need only use one of the archivers discussed in Section 3.14. If you choose to use `cpio` on a System V system, you may prefer to do the actual backup with `find` and its `-cpio` criterion (see Section 3.8), since `cpio`, unlike the other archivers, does not descend into subdirectories but needs to be provided with a full file list.

For a differential or incremental backup, you need to use `find` or the equivalent to select the files to be included. `Find` has a criterion

'-newer *file*' that tests a candidate file to see if it was modified more recently than *file*. A useful technique is to create an empty "marker" file, accessible only to `root`, and modify that file with `touch` (see Section 3.12.2) just before doing any full or incremental backup. For an incremental or differential backup, you then include just those files that are newer than the marker file. For example, you could call `pax` to do an incremental backup of `/usr` with the command line

```
find /usr -newer /etc/marker | pax -wfX archive
```

Opinions vary on the wisdom of using compressed backups. Compressed backups are faster, since less information needs to be written, and occupy less storage. On the other hand, if the data in a compressed backup becomes corrupted at all, the entire backup is likely to be unusable.

14.6 Startup and Shutdown

In this section we discuss how to start up your system or shut it down and what happens when you go through these processes.

14.6.1
Boot and Recovery Procedures

Here is what typically happens when you start up your UNIX system, beginning with the moment when you reboot your computer or turn on the power:

(1) The ROM (read-only memory) built into the hardware starts a loader or a sequence of loaders that ultimately brings the UNIX kernel into memory. It's usually possible to interrupt this process at one or more points to do additional hardware checking, to specify a location for the kernel other than the default location, to reconfigure the system, or to do certain kinds of low-level debugging. It may also be possible at this point to load a different operating system altogether.

(2) The kernel investigates and records your hardware configuration and also carries out some preliminary structuring of the root file system. It then creates two processes: one for swapping pages in and out of memory and another for executing the `init` program.

(3) The `init` program executes an appropriate `rc` file, which initiates actions for mounting other file systems, starting dæmons, making network connections, and other similar activities (see Section 14.6.2). When these activities are complete, the system is ready to accept logins from the local terminal and from any remote sources to which it is connected.

Alternate Boot Sources. Most systems boot by default from your hard disk or, if you have a diskless workstation, from the network connection.

Most systems also provide some way of altering the bootup sequence to enable you to boot from a different source or from a different version of the kernel. For Linux, you can turn on `CapsLock` or `ScrollLock` before the LILO boot loader starts to load the kernel, or hold down `Shift`, `Ctrl`, or `Alt`; for other systems, the procedure is similar. When LILO starts up, it then issues a prompt and enables you to specify various loading options, including a different kernel. One reason for loading from a different kernel is that you might have recompiled the kernel and gotten a defective one. You can recover the situation by loading an older kernel. On a Sun workstation, you can get to the low-level monitor, which provides similar options, by holding down the `L1` or `Stop` key and pressing the 'A' key.

Recovery Boot.   If your file systems are corrupted or you've lost your `root` password, you can start the recovery process by booting from a diskette or other removable medium. On Intel machines the boot process will naturally start from a diskette if there's one in the primary diskette drive. The boot diskette then creates a minimal UNIX system in your computer's memory and logs you onto that system as `root`. This is the same system you use for initial installation.

The minimal system does not use any hard disks or other external storage devices since it can't assume that any usable file systems exist on those devices. If you're recovering from a corrupted file system, you can use the facilities of the minimal system to repair that file system if you can and to recreate it if you can't.

If you've lost the `root` password, your best bet is to mount the root file system and then to edit the `/etc/passwd` file (or on some systems, `/etc/shadow`) to remove the password information from the entry for `root`. That way `root` can log in without a password and later define one with the `passwd` program or by some other means.

We strongly advise you to learn about these procedures *before* you need them. It's often helpful to have a written list of any file systems you've previously created and their associated device names, since you won't be able to extract that information from the file systems themselves very easily when your system is crippled. Printing the contents of `/etc/fstab` will give you this information.

Selecting an Operating System.   On Intel machines, a hard disk may contain several operating systems. When the machine is powered up, reset, or rebooted, the operating system that is started is the one residing in the boot partition. One way to switch operating systems is to call the `fdisk` program just before shutting down and use it to designate a different boot partition. An alternative is to use a loader such as Linux's LILO loader or OS/2's Boot Manager that gives you an opportunity as the system is starting up to select the boot partition.

**14.6.2
Initializing the
System**

After the kernel has finished its tasks in initializing the system, it calls init to complete the job. Init in turn calls upon the various rc scripts to do the actual work. The way that init and the rc scripts are organized is different in System V-style systems (including Linux) than in BSD-style systems.

Initialization in System V-Style Systems. Under System V, the init program is guided by a table in /etc/inittab. The table specifies the actions to be taken when the system is initialized at a particular run level. The run levels, which in principle are arbitrary single characters, always include the digits 1–7 and the letter s. Run level s designates single-user mode, while run levels 3 or 5 are the ones most often used for normal startup in multi-user mode. Here are a few typical entries in /etc/inittab:

```
# System initialization (runs when system boots).
si:S:sysinit:/etc/rc.d/rc.S
# Script to run when going multi user.
rc:123456:wait:/etc/rc.d/rc.M
# What to do at the "Three Finger Salute".
ca::ctrlaltdel:/sbin/shutdown -t3 -rf now
# A getty in multi-user mode on a serial line.
c1:12345:respawn:/sbin/agetty 38400 tty1
```

Comment lines start with a hash mark. The other lines have the form

id : *runlevels* : *action* : *process*

In these lines:

- The label *id* serves to identify the inittab entry.

- The run levels *runlevels* indicate all run levels to which this line applies.

- The process *process* specifies a program to be run.

- The action *action* specifies when and how *process* should be run; for example, during system boot ('sysinit') or when the specified run level is entered by init ('wait').

The initialization scripts are kept in the directory /etc/rc.d. As the inittab entries show, the rc.S script is the one called for single-user operation. The configuration utilities that come with your system usually customize these scripts on your behalf. You may sometimes find it useful to modify them yourself, but do so with caution.

Initialization in BSD-Style Systems. On BSD-style systems, the init program runs the rc files directly. It is also capable of setting the system to run at different levels of security. At the highest level, for example, disks are always read-only whether or not they are mounted. The BSD init program does not use /etc/inittab at all. It knows about two rc files: /etc/rc, which contains the standard initialization procedures, and

/etc/rc.local, which contains initialization procedures specific to the local site.

Both rc and rc.local are executed implicitly by init. When rc is called during the first part of a reboot or initial boot, it is passed the argument 'autoboot'. If it is called subsequently, that argument is omitted. The usual rc procedures check the disks with fsck only if the 'autoboot' argument was present in the call.

14.6.3
Shutting Down

Most systems provide several commands you can invoke as superuser to shut down your system in an orderly way: halt, reboot, and shutdown. The halt command shuts down the system in preparation for turning off the power; the reboot command shuts down the system and then immediately restarts it. The shutdown command provides more flexible ways of shutting down. We describe the Linux forms of these commands, but the forms for other systems are very similar. Under Linux, you need to call halt as /sbin/halt since the /sbin directory is not on the default path, and similarly for the other two commands.

When you shut down the system with any of these commands, all logged-in users are sent a warning that the system is about to shut down and the SIGTERM signal is sent to all running processes. After a grace period (default is about 30 seconds), all running processes, including user logins, are terminated with a SIGKILL signal and the file systems are cleaned up with the sync command. At that point, there is nothing left in the system state that needs to be saved and the computer can safely be rebooted or powered off.

Linux and possibly other Intel-based systems honor the convention that the "three-finger salute", Ctrl Alt Del , causes a reboot. It doesn't work under X, however, since X catches the keypresses before the rest of Linux sees them.

The halt and reboot Commands. The Linux forms of the halt and reboot commands are

    halt [-t *sec*] [-nq]
    reboot [-t *sec*] [-nq]

The options are as follows:

-t *sec*   Allow *sec* seconds after sending the warning message before SIGKILL is sent.

-n   Don't synchronize the file systems before shutting down.

-q   Shut down quickly by sending SIGKILL to all processes immediately and without warning.

The best way to shut down a system immediately is to type one of these:

    /sbin/reboot -t0
    /sbin/halt -t0

The `shutdown` **Command.**   The forms of the `shutdown` command under Linux are

```
shutdown [-h|-r|-k] [-t sec] [-fn] time [msg]
shutdown -c
```

where *time* is the time when shutdown should commence ('now' for immediately, '+*m*' for *m* minutes from now, and '*hh*:*mm*' for hour *hh*, minute *mm*). The warning message *msg*, if provided, is sent to all logged-in users.

Command-Line Options for `shutdown`.   The following options determine the shutdown action:

-h   Halt after shutdown. You can then power down the computer.

-r   Reboot the system again after the shutdown is finished.

-k   Send warning messages to all users but don't actually shut down.

-c   Cancel a shutdown that's already been started.

The following option determines the delay:

-t *sec*   Allow *sec* seconds after sending the warning message before SIGKILL is sent.

The following options cause file system checks to be bypassed and shouldn't ordinarily be used:

-n   Don't synchronize the file systems before shutting down.

-f   Do a fast reboot without checking the file systems on restart.

Synchronizing the File Systems.   An important action that takes place as your system shuts down is synchronizing the file systems by flushing their memory buffers. This action ensures that any information that belongs in the file systems but hasn't yet been stored there is transferred to the file system, particularly including cached disk blocks that need to be written. On modern hardware, the process is usually so fast as to be barely visible, but for older systems or very large disks it may take longer. It's vital that the shutdown process not be interrupted nor the machine powered down until all synchronizations are complete. You can perform an explicit synchronization on all devices by calling `sync` by itself (no arguments or options needed). To be safe, call `sync` twice and wait for a few seconds to make sure that everything has settled down.

Powering Down.   The simplest way to shut down your system, of course, is just to turn off the power—but it's not a good idea to do that. Most UNIX systems will recover perfectly from a loss of power almost every time, but there's always a chance that some work will be lost by accident or that some damage will be done to a file system whose state has not been fully updated. Shutting down by powering down doesn't save time, either, since the system will need to go through recovery steps when it comes back up that you could have avoided. The proper procedure is first to do a `shutdown` and then to turn off the power. But occasionally a system may be so badly hung—for example, when it pays no attention to the keyboard—that your only choice for recovery is to power it down or reset it.[6]

14.6.4
Single-User Mode

For debugging your system, it's often useful to operate in single-user mode. When you enter this mode, the kernel automatically logs you in as `root` and provides you with a shell environment. In single-user mode, all multi-user services are turned off and only the root file system is mounted—and that file system is mounted read-only.

Under Linux and under System V-style systems more generally, you can enter single-user mode by typing 'init s' (superuser privileges required). You can also arrange to enter single-user mode as the kernel is loading. Under BSD-style systems, you enter single-user mode by sending a SIGTERM signal to the `init` process (always #1) with the command

```
kill -s TERM 1
```

You return to (or initiate) multi-user mode by exiting from the shell. That causes the normal `rc` startup scripts to be executed. However, these scripts may bypass remounting the file systems as writable if they were mounted that way once before. In that case, you'll need to reboot to get a usable system.

---

6. If your keyboard is hung, you still may be able to gain access to your system through a serial port or over a network.

A

Alphabetical Summary of Commands

In this appendix we provide, in alphabetical order, capsule summaries of the UNIX commands discussed in this book. The purpose of these summaries is to remind you of what each command does and to point you to its full explanation. The first group of summaries lists the commands. The second group of summaries lists the command-line options, flags, and subcommands of each command. The page references are to the full discussions earlier in the book.

Subcommands named by special characters are alphabetized according to their English names (see p. 16).

A.1 List of Commands

The first page number listed for each command refers to its description in the main text. The second page number refers to the summary of its syntax, options, and subcommands (if any).

`alias`   Define or display aliases (p. 358, p. 711).
`at`   Schedule a job at a future time (p. 243, p. 711).
`awk`   Programming language for data manipulation (p. 199, p. 712).
`basename`   Extract base of pathname (p. 294, p. 714).
`batch`   Schedule a batch job (p. 243, p. 715).
`bc`   Arbitrary-precision calculator (p. 280, p. 715).
`bg`   Run jobs in background (p. 359, p. 716).

`cal`   Show a calendar (p. 234, p. 716).
`cancel`   Cancel printer requests (p. 118, p. 716).
`cat`   Concatenate files (p. 98, p. 716).
`cd`   Change directory (p. 92, p. 717).
`chgrp`   Change file's group (p. 136, p. 717).
`chmod`   Change file permissions (p. 134, p. 717).
`chown`   Change file's owner (p. 136, p. 717).
`chsh`   Change your login shell (p. 254, p. 717).
`cksum`   Calculate checksums of files (p. 129, p. 718).
`cmp`   Compare files (p. 130, p. 718).
`comm`   List lines common to two sorted files (p. 184, p. 718).
`command`   Execute a simple command (p. 288, p. 718).
`compress`   Compress a file (p. 140, p. 718).
`cp`   Copy files (p. 103, p. 718).
`cpio`   Copy file archives (p. 154, p. 719).
`crontab`   Define schedule of background jobs (p. 246, p. 719).
`csplit`   Split file by context (p. 186, p. 720).
`cu`   Connect to a UNIX system (p. 666, p. 720).
`cut`   Extract fields from lines (p. 179, p. 721).
`date`   Display the date and time (p. 232, p. 721).
`dd`   Convert and copy a file (p. 160, p. 722).
`df`   Report free disk space (p. 271, p. 722).
`diff`   Find file differences (p. 130, p. 723).
`dirname`   Extract directory from pathname (p. 294, p. 723).
`du`   Report disk space in use (p. 271, p. 723).
`echo`   Echo arguments (p. 272, p. 723).
`ed`   Line editor (p. 458, p. 723).
`egrep`   Find regular expression, extended version (p. 175, p. 725).
`emacs`   Emacs extensible text editor (p. 467, p. 725).
`env`   Set environment for command invocation (p. 326, p. 736).
`ex`   Line editor, extended version of `ed` (p. 442, p. 736).
`expand`   Convert tabs to spaces (p. 181, p. 738).
`expr`   Evaluate an expression (p. 286, p. 739).
`false`   Return false (p. 333, p. 739).
`fc`   Process command history list (p. 360, p. 739).
`fg`   Run job in foreground (p. 359, p. 739).
`fgrep`   Find regular expression, fast version (p. 175, p. 739).
`file`   Classify files (p. 128, p. 739).
`find`   Find files (p. 121, p. 740).
`finger`   Look up information about a user (p. 230, p. 741).
`fold`   Fold input lines (p. 181, p. 741).
`ftp`   Transfer files with File Transfer Protocol (p. 642, p. 741).
`getconf`   Get configuration values (p. 291, p. 743).
`grep`   Find regular expression (p. 175, p. 743).
`gunzip`   Expand zip-encoded files (p. 141, p. 743).
`gzcat`   Expand and concatenate zip-encoded files (p. 141, p. 743).
`gzip`   Compress files using zip encoding (p. 141, p. 744).
`halt`   Shut down the system and halt (p. 705, p. 744).
`head`   Copy beginning of files (p. 184, p. 744).
`id`   Show user and group IDs (p. 255, p. 744).
`jobs`   Show job status (p. 360, p. 745).
`join`   Database join on two files (p. 190, p. 745).
`kill`   Signal a process (p. 242, p. 745).
`ksh`   The KornShell (p. 307, p. 745).
`ln`   Link pathnames (p. 101, p. 749).
`locale`   Get locale information (p. 296, p. 750).
`localedef`   Define a new locale (p. 297, p. 750).
`logger`   Save message for administrator (p. 295, p. 750).
`login`   Log in (p. 250, p. 750).
`logname`   Return user's login name (p. 255, p. 750).
`lp`   Send files to a printer (p. 114, p. 751).
`lpr`   Berkeley print spooler (p. 115, p. 751).

`lpstat`   Show printer status (p. 117, p. 751).
`ls`   File lister (p. 94, p. 752).
`mailx`   Send and receive mail (p. 586, p. 752).
`man`   Display manual pages (p. 226, p. 755).
`mesg`   Lock out messages (p. 270, p. 756).
`mkdir`   Make a directory (p. 93, p. 756).
`mkfifo`   Make a FIFO special file (p. 168, p. 756).
`mknod`   Make a special file (p. 169, p. 756).
`more`   Page through files interactively (p. 108, p. 756).
`mount`   Mount a file system (p. 696, p. 757).
`mv`   Move files (p. 102, p. 758).
`newgrp`   Change your current group (p. 253, p. 758).
`nice`   Run a command at low priority (p. 248, p. 758).
`nohup`   Ignore hangups (p. 243, p. 758).
`od`   Octal dump (p. 158, p. 758).
`paste`   Paste input fields (p. 189, p. 759).
`patch`   Apply changes to files (p. 164, p. 759).
`pathchk`   Check validity of pathnames (p. 129, p. 760).
`pax`   Portable archive interchange (p. 145, p. 760).
`pr`   Format files for printing (p. 118, p. 761).
`print`   Write output arguments under `ksh` (p. 278, p. 761).
`printf`   Write formatted output (p. 274, p. 761).
`ps`   List processes, System V version (p. 235, p. 763).
`ps`   List processes, BSD version (p. 237, p. 762).
`ps`   List processes, POSIX version (p. 240, p. 763).
`pwd`   Show working directory (p. 93, p. 763).
`rcp`   Remote copy (p. 636, p. 763).
`read`   Read an input line (p. 279, p. 763).
`reboot`   Shutdown the system and reboot (p. 705, p. 764).
`renice`   Set priorities of processes (p. 248, p. 764).
`rlogin`   Remote login (p. 634, p. 764).
`rm`   Remove files or directories (p. 105, p. 764).
`rmdir`   Remove directories (p. 106, p. 765).
`rsh`   Remote shell (p. 635, p. 765).
`rwho`   List users on the local network (p. 636, p. 765).
`sed`   Edit from a script (p. 192, p. 765).
`sh`   POSIX shell (p. 308, p. 766).
`shar`   Create a shell archive (p. 612, p. 766).
`shutdown`   Shut down the system (p. 706, p. 767).
`sleep`   Suspend execution (p. 249, p. 767).
`sort`   Sort files (p. 170, p. 767).
`split`   Split files into pieces (p. 188, p. 767).
`strings`   Find printable strings in files (p. 293, p. 768).
`stty`   Set terminal characteristics (p. 260, p. 768).
`su`   Substitute user (p. 252, p. 769).
`tabs`   Set tabs on your terminal (p. 267, p. 769).
`tail`   Extract the end of a file (p. 184, p. 769).
`talk`   Talk to another user (p. 269, p. 770).
`tar`   Tape archiver (p. 151, p. 770).
`tee`   Duplicate input (p. 139, p. 770).
`telnet`   Call a remote system over a network (p. 637, p. 770).
`test`   Compare values, test file properties (p. 333, p. 771).
`time`   Time a command (p. 292, p. 772).
`touch`   Touch a file (p. 138, p. 773).
`tput`   Send setup instructions to a terminal (p. 265, p. 773).
`tr`   Translate or delete characters (p. 177, p. 773).
`true`   Return true (p. 333, p. 773).
`tset`   Set terminal information (p. 256, p. 773).
`tty`   Get the terminal name (p. 232, p. 774).
`type`   Show interpretation of a command (p. 292, p. 774).
`umask`   Mask default file permissions (p. 135, p. 774).
`umount`   Unmount a file system (p. 698, p. 774).

unalias   Remove alias definitions (p. 358, p. 774).
uname   Produce system information (p. 291, p. 775).
uncompress   Uncompress a file (p. 140, p. 775).
unexpand   Convert spaces to tabs (p. 181, p. 775).
uniq   Eliminate adjacent repeated lines (p. 183, p. 775).
uucp   UNIX to UNIX copy (p. 660, p. 775).
uudecode   Decode a binary file (p. 143, p. 776).
uuencode   Encode a binary file (p. 143, p. 776).
uuname   Get names of remote UNIX systems (p. 665, p. 776).
uupick   Pick up files from UNIX to UNIX transfer (p. 659, p. 776).
uustat   Check uucp status (p. 663, p. 776).
uuto   Send files UNIX to UNIX (p. 659, p. 777).
vi   Visual editor (p. 412, p. 777).
wait   Wait for a process to finish (p. 249, p. 781).
wc   Count words, lines, or characters (p. 137, p. 781).
which   Show pathname of command (p. 128, p. 781).
who   List users and processes (p. 228, p. 781).
write   Write message to terminal (p. 270, p. 781).
xargs   Call a utility with constructed arguments (p. 289, p. 782).
xbiff   Mailbox flag for X (p. 683, p. 782).
xclock   Analog/digital clock for X (p. 683, p. 782).
xcolors   Display the X colors (p. 684, p. 782).
xfd   Display an X font (p. 684, p. 782).
xfontsel   Select and display X fonts (p. 684, p. 782).
xinit   Start the X server (p. 685, p. 782).
xkill   Kill an X client (p. 687, p. 782).
xlsfonts   Display a list of X fonts (p. 684, p. 783).
xman   Display manual pages under X (p. 687, p. 783).
xrdb   Resource database utility for X (p. 686, p. 783).
xset   Set user preferences for X (p. 686, p. 783).
xsetroot   Set root window appearance for X (p. 686, p. 783).
xterm   Terminal emulator for X (p. 680, p. 783).
zcat   Uncompress and concatenate files (p. 140, p. 783).

A.2   Summary of Commands and Features

A.2.1
alias (Define or Display Aliases)

The form of the **alias** command line (p. 358) is

    alias [*name*[=*str*] ...]

The indicates aliases are defined, or all the aliases are listed.

Command-Line Options Under ksh.   Under ksh, alias recognizes these command-line options:

-t Define each *name* as a tracked alias (p. 358)
-x Export each *name* to any shell script directly executed in a subshell (p. 358)

A.2.2
at (Schedule a Job at a Future Time)

The forms of the **at** command line (p. 244) are

    at [-m] [-f *file*] [-q *queue*] *atime* [*adate*] [+ *increment*]
    at [-m] [-f *file*] [-q *queue*] -t *time*
    at -l [*job* ...]
    at -lq *queue*
    at -r *job* ...

A job is read from standard input and scheduled for execution at a later time.

Command-Line Options.

-f *file*   Read the job from file *file* (p. 244)
-l   List invoking user's scheduled jobs (p. 245)
-m   Send mail when a scheduled job has finished (p. 244)
-q *queue*   Place job in queue *queue* or list that queue (p. 244)
-r   Remove the indicated *job*s (p. 245)

Syntax for Time and Date (First Form).   The forms for *atime* are the following:

- A one-digit or two-digit number specifying an hour
- A four-digit number specifying an hour and minute
- Two numbers (hour and minute) separated by a colon
- One of these followed by 'am', 'pm', or 'zulu'
- 'noon', 'midnight', or 'now'

The forms for *adate* are

- A month name followed by a day number, an optional comma, and an optional year number
- A day of the week
- 'today' or 'tomorrow'

In the command, *increment* is a number followed by 'minutes', 'hours', 'days', 'weeks', 'months', or 'years', or their singular forms.

Month names and day names can be written in full or with three-letter abbreviations. An omitted *date* defaults to 'today'.

Case is ignored, as are blanks between components.

A.2.3
awk (Programming Language for Data Manipulation)

The forms of the awk command line (p. 199) are

> awk [-F *regexpr*] [-v *asst*] ... *prog* [*arg* ...]
> awk [-F *regexpr*] -f *progfile* [-v *asst*] [*arg* ...]

The program must be provided either on the command line or via the -f option. If given on the command line, it is almost always enclosed in apostrophes. The arguments *arg* ... are a mixture of (a) pathnames denoting files to be read by the program, and (b) assignments to be performed before reading each file.

Command-Line Options.

-F*s*   Set the field separator to *s* (p. 199)
-f *progfile*   Read the program from the file *progfile* (p. 200)
-v *asst*   Perform the assignment *asst* before executing the program (p. 200)

Pattern-Action Statements.   A pattern-action statement (p. 201) has one of the following forms:

BEGIN { *action* }   Executes *action* before reading any data (p. 201)
END { *action* }   Executes *action* after reading all data (p. 201)
{ *action* }   Executes *action* for each line of input data (p. 201)
pattern [{ *action* }]   Executes *action* for each line of input data matching *pattern* (p. 201)
*pattern*₁,*pattern*₂ [{ *action* }]   Executes *action* for lines of input data from the first one
matching *pattern*₁ through the next one matching *pattern*₂ (p. 202)

In these forms, *action* has the form

> [*statement*...]

In the last two forms the default action is 'print $0'.

A *pattern* is one of the following:

> *expr*
> /*regexpr*/

Here *expr* is an expression and *regexpr* is a generalized regular expression.

Expressions.   An expression (see Section 5.9.2) is formed from the following primary elements:

- Numeric constants
- String constants
- Variables
- Function calls of the form $f(a_1, a_2, \ldots, a_n)$
- Array elements of the form `a[i]`.

These elements can be combined using the following operators, listed in order of increasing precedence:

`= += -= *= /= %= ^=`   Assignment operators
`? ... :`   Conditional expression operator
`||`   Logical "or" operator
`&&`   Logical "and" operator
`in`   Array membership operator
`~ !~`   Pattern-matching operators (used with `/regexpr/`)
`< <= == != > >=`   Relational operators
(juxtaposition)   Concatenation operator
`+ -`   Additive operators
`* / %`   Multiplicative operators
`+ -`   Unary arithmetic operators
`!`   Logical "not" operator
`^`   Exponentiation operator
`++ --`   Increment and decrement operators
`$`   Field selection operator
`( ... )`   Grouping operators

Predefined Variables.

`ARGC`   Number of command-line arguments (p. 220)
`ARGV`   Array of command-line arguments (p. 220)
`CONVFMT`   Format for `printf` conversions of numbers other than during output (p. 221)
`ENVIRON`   Array giving names and values of environment variables (p. 221)
`FILENAME`   Name of current input file (p. 220)
`FNR`   Record number in current file (p. 220)
`FS`   Input field separator specification (p. 220)
`NF`   Number of fields in current record (p. 220)
`NR`   Number of records read so far (p. 220)
`OFMT`   Format used for showing numbers in output (p. 221)
`OFS`   Output field separator (p. 217)
`ORS`   Output record separator (p. 217)
`RLENGTH`   Length of string matched by `match` (p. 213)
`RS`   Input record separator specification (p. 220)
`RSTART`   Start of string matched by `match` (p. 214)
`SUBSEP`   Subscript separator (p. 208)

Predefined Numerical Functions.   All of the following functions return floating-point values, except for `int`:

`atan2(y,x)`   Arctangent of y/x, result r satisfies $-\pi \leq r \leq \pi$ (p. 215)
`cos(x)`   Cosine of x radians (p. 215)
`exp(x)`   Exponential e^x (p. 215)
`int(x)`   Integer part of x (p. 215)
`log(x)`   Natural logarithm of x (p. 215)
`rand()`   Random number r, $0 \leq r < 1$ (p. 215)
`sin(x)`   Sine of x radians (p. 215)
`sqrt(x)`   Square root of x (p. 215)
`srand([x])`   Set new seed for `rand` (p. 215)

Predefined String Functions.

`gsub(r,s[,t])`   Substitutes s for r globally in `$0` or t (p. 214)
`index(s,t)`   Returns first position of string t within string s (p. 213)

`length(`*s*`)`   Returns number of characters in string *s* (p. 213)
`match(`*s*`,`*r*`)`   Tests whether string *s* contains a match for regular expression *r* (p. 213)
`split(`*s*`,`*a*`[,`*fs*`])`   Splits *s* into array *a* using separator *fs* (p. 214)
`sprintf(`*fmt*`,`*expr*`, ... )`   Formats *expr* ... according to *fmt* (p. 215)
`sub(`*r*`,`*s*`[,`*t*`])`   Substitutes *s* for *r* once in `$0` or *t* (p. 214)
`substr(`*s*`,`*p*`[,`*n*`])`   Returns substring of *s*, or rest of string, starting at position *p* (p. 213)
`tolower(`*s*`)`   Returns *s* converted to lowercase (p. 214)
`toupper(`*s*`)`   Returns *s* converted to uppercase (p. 215)

Other Predefined Functions.
`getline` [*var*] [`<` *file*]   Reads a line into *var* or `$0` from *file* or standard input (p. 216)
cmd `|` `getline` [*var*]   Reads a line from the standard output of *cmd* into *var* or `$0` (p. 216)
`system(`*cmd*`)`   Executes the UNIX command *cmd*, returns its exit value (p. 220)

Statements.   In the `print` and `printf` statements, *redir* has one of the following forms (p. 218):

`>` *file*   Sends the output to *file*.
`>>` *file*   Appends the output to *file*.
`|` *cmd*   Pipes the output through the UNIX command *cmd*.

These are the `awk` statements:

expr   Evaluates *expr* and discards its value (p. 221)
`{ `*stmt* `... }`   Executes a group of statements (p. 222)
`;`   Does nothing (empty statement) (p. 222)
`break`   Leaves innermost `while`, `for`, or `do` (p. 223)
`close(`*cmd*`)`   Breaks the connection between `print` and *cmd* (p. 219)
`close(`*file*`)`   Breaks the connection between `print` and *file* (p. 219)
`continue`   Starts next iteration of innermost `while`, `for`, or `do` (p. 223)
`delete `*a*`[`*sub*`]`   Deletes the element with subscript *sub* from the array *a* (p. 207)
`do` *stmt* `while (`*expr*`)`   Executes *stmt* once, then repeatedly while *expr* is true (p. 222)
`for (`*expr*$_1$`; `*expr*$_2$`; `*expr*$_3$`)` *stmt*   Executes *expr*$_1$, then executes *stmt* and *expr*$_3$ while *expr*$_2$ is true (p. 222)
`for (`*var* `in` *array*`)` *stmt*   Executes *stmt* with *var* set to each subscript of *array* in turn (p. 223)
`if (`*expr*`)` *stmt*$_1$ `[; else` *stmt*$_2$ `]`   Executes *stmt*$_1$ if *expr* is true, *stmt*$_2$ otherwise (p. 222)
`next`   Starts next iteration of main input loop (p. 223)
`exit` [*expr*]   Goes to the `END` action, returns *expr* or 0 as program status if within that action (p. 223)
`print`   Sends `$0` to standard output (p. 217)
`print` *expr* `[,` *expr*`...` `]` [*redir*]   Sends *expr* ... to standard output, separated by `OFS` (p. 217)
`print(`*expr* `[,` *expr*`...` `]` `)` [*redir*]   Sends *expr* ... to standard output, separated by `OFS` (p. 217)
`printf(`*format*`,` *expr* `[,` *expr*`...` `]` `)` [*redir*]   Sends *expr* ... to standard output, formatted using *format* (p. 217)
`return` [*expr*]   Returns from a function with value *expr* (p. 224)
`while (`*expr*`)` *stmt*   Executes *stmt* while *expr* is true (p. 222)

User-Defined Functions.   A user-defined function (p. 223) has the following form:

> `function` *name*(*param* `[,` *param*... `] )` `{`
>   `[` *stmt*... `]`
> `}`

A user-defined function can appear wherever a pattern-action statement can.

A.2.4

`basename`

(Extract Base of Pathname)

The form of the `basename` command line (p. 295) is

> `basename` *string*$_1$ `[` *string*$_2$ `]`

where *string*$_1$ is a string that represents a pathname and *string*$_2$ is a suffix of *string*$_1$.

A.2.5
batch **(Schedule a Batch Job)**

The form of the `batch` command line (p. 244) is

    batch
    command file

The command file can be taken from a file if redirection is used.

A.2.6
bc **(Arbitrary Precision Calculator)**

The form of the `bc` command line (p. 280) is

    bc [-l] [*file* ...]

where *file* ... are files containing definitions to be processed before `bc` requests user input.

Command-Line Argument.

-l   Predefine math functions, set *scale* to 20 (p. 285)

Arithmetic Operators.

+   Addition (p. 282)
−   Subtraction (p. 282)
*   Multiplication (p. 282)
/   Division (p. 282)
%   Remainder (p. 283)
^   Power (p. 283)

Each of these operators may be turned into an assignment operator such as +=. There is also a direct assignment operator:

=   Assign a value to a named expression (p. 283)

There are two modifying operators for named expressions:

++   Increment by 1 (prefix or postfix) (p. 283)
−−   Decrement by 1 (prefix or postfix) (p. 283)

Operands.   An operand within an expression can be any of the following:

- A number (signed integer or decimal fraction) (p. 282)
- A named expression (p. 282)
- A parenthesized expression (p. 282)
- A function call (p. 282)
- The form '`length`(*expr*)' (p. 282)
- The form '`scale`(*expr*)' (p. 282)
- The form '`sqrt`(*expr*)' (p. 282)

Named Expressions.   The three kinds of named expressions are the following:

- Simple variables (single letters) (p. 282)
- Array references (single letters, subscripted) (p. 282)
- Internal registers (p. 282)

Internal Registers.

ibase   Base for interpreting input (p. 281)
obase   Base for producing output (p. 281)
scale   Digits to right of radix point for certain operations (p. 282)

Relational Operators.

==   Equal
!=   Not equal
<   Less than
>   Greater than
<=   Less than or equal to
>=   Greater than or equal to

Statements.   In the following statement forms, *expr* represents an expression with a value, *relexpr* represents a relational expression, and *stmt* represents a statement.

- *expr* (p. 284)
- *string* (a character string enclosed in double quotes) (p. 284)
- {*stmt*; ... ; *stmt*} (p. 284)
- break (p. 284)
- for (*expr*; *relexpr*; *expr*) *stmt* (p. 284)
- if (*relexpr*) *stmt* (p. 284)
- quit (p. 284)
- return [(*expr*)] (p. 284)
- while (*relexpr*) *stmt* (p. 284)

Function Definitions.   A function definition has the form (p. 285)

```
define fn ([arg [, arg] ... ]) {
    [auto var [, var] ... ]
    stmt ...
}
```

where *fn*, *arg*, and *var* are single letters denoting the function name, the argument names, and the automatic variables, respectively, and *stmt* denotes a statement.

Library Math Functions.   These functions are activated by −l (p. 285)

a(*x*)   Arctangent
c(*x*)   Cosine
e(*x*)   Exponential
j(*n*, *x*)   Bessel function
l(*x*)   Natural logarithm
s(*x*)   Sine

**A.2.7
bg (Run Jobs in Background)**

The form of the bg command line (p. 359) is

```
bg [job ... ]
```

The specified jobs *job* ... are run in the background. If no jobs are specified, the most recently suspended job is run in the background.

**A.2.8
cal (Show a Calendar)**

The form of the cal command line (p. 234) is

```
cal [[\thsmonth] year]
```

**A.2.9
cancel (Cancel Printer Requests)**

The forms of the cancel command line (p. 118) are

```
cancel [id... ] [printer... ]
cancel -u login-names [printer... ]
```

In the first form, each *id* identifies a printer request and each *printer* identifies a particular printer. In the second form, the *login-names* specify users whose print jobs are to be cancelled.

**A.2.10
cat (Concatenate Files)**

The form of the cat command line (p. 98) is

```
cat [-estuv] [file] ...
```

The files in *filelist* are concatenated and copied to standard output (p. 98) A '-' in *filelist* denotes standard input.

Command-Line Options.

-e   Put '$' at the end of each line (p. 100)
-s   Don't complain about nonexistent source files (p. 99)
-t   Show tabs as '∧I' (p. 100)
-u   Don't buffer the output (p. 99)
-v   Represent nonprinting characters with printable ones (p. 100)

A.2.11
cd (Change Directory)

The form of the `cd` command line (p. 92) is

    cd [\ths*dir*]

dir becomes the current directory; if *dir* is omitted, it is taken as your home directory.

A.2.12
chgrp
(Change File Group)

The form of the `chgrp` command line (p. 136) is

    chgrp ["-R"] *group* *file* . . .

Command-Line Option.
-R   Descend recursively through directories (p. 137)

A.2.13
chmod
(Change File Permissions)

The form of the `chmod` command line (p. 134) is

    chmod [-Rf] *perms* *file* . . .

where *file* . . . is a sequence of pathnames, and *perms* is either of the following:
- a comma-separated list of symbolic modes
- an octal number of up to four digits

Each symbolic mode has three parts: one or more "who" letters, an operator, and either one or more permission letters, a "who" letter, or nothing.

The "Who" Letters.   The "who" letters (p. 48) are as follows:

g   Group
o   Others
u   User (owner)
a   Everyone (all)

Operators.   The operators (p. 49) are as follows:
-   Take away these permissions
=   Set these permissions and no others
+   Add these permissions

Permission Letters.   The permission letters (p. 49) are as follows:

l   Lock during access
r   Read
s   Set user or group ID
t   Sticky bit
w   Write
X   Execute only if file is a directory or some x permission is already set
x   Execute

A "who" letter after an operator indicates the permissions associated with that letter.

Command-Line Options.
-R   Descend recursively through directories (p. 134)
-f   Suppress complaints (p. 134)

A.2.14
chown
(Change File Owner)

The form of the `chown` command line (p. 136) is

    chown ["-R"] *owner* [":"*group*] *file* . . .

Command-Line Option.
-R   Descend recursively through directories (p. 137)

A.2.15
chsh (Change Your Login Shell)

The form of the `chsh` command line (p. 254) is

    chsh [*user*]

where *user* is the name of the user whose login shell is to be changed. The command prompts you for your password and the new shell.

A.2.16
cksum **(Calculate Checksums of Files)**

The form of the cksum command line (p. 129) is

> cksum [*file* . . .]

The checksum and octet count of each specified file is calculated.

A.2.17
cmp **(Compare Files)**

The form of the cmp command line (p. 130) is

> cmp [-l | -s] *file₁* *file₂*

The return code is 0 if the files are the same, 1 if the files differ, and 2 if one or both files could not be accessed.

Command-Line Options.

-l Show the byte number and the differing characters for each difference (p. 130)
-s Show nothing (p. 130)

A.2.18
comm **(List Lines Common to Two Sorted Files)**

The form of the comm command line (p. 184) is

> comm [-*flags*] *file₁* *file₂*

where *flags* consists of one or more of the digits 123. Each digit in *flags* indicates that the corresponding column of the listing should be suppressed. You can use '-' for *file₁* or *file₂* to denote standard input.

A.2.19
command **(Execute a Simple Command)**

The forms of the command command line (p. 288) are

> command [-p] *cmd* [*arg* . . .]
> command -v *cmd* [*arg* . . .]
> command -V *cmd* [*arg* . . .]

Using the first form, the command *cmd* is executed with arguments *arg* . . . , giving shell intrinsic commands preference over function definitions in command lookup. Using the second form, information is produced about how the shell interprets the command name *cmd*.

Command-Line Options.

-p Use a value of PATH guaranteed to find all standard utilities (p. 288)
-v Produce the pathname where *cmd* is found, the name *cmd* (for shell built-ins), or the alias definition of *cmd* (p. 288)
-V Produce the pathname where *cmd* is found, the name *cmd* (for shell built-ins), or the alias definition of *cmd*, as well as an indication of how *cmd* is interpreted (p. 288)

A.2.20
compress **(Compress a File)**

The form of the compress command line (p. 140) is

> compress [-cfv] [-b *n*] [*file*. . .]

where *file* . . . is a list of files to be compressed. By default, each file is replaced by its compressed version *file*.Z.

Command-Line Options.

-b *n* Use *n* bits in the compression algorithm ($9 \leq n \leq 16$) (p. 140)
-c Write the compressed files to standard output (p. 140)
-f Force compression of a file even if nothing is gained (p. 140)
-v Show the percentage of reduction for each file compressed (p. 140)

A.2.21
cp **(Copy Files)**

The forms of the command line (p. 103) are

> cp [-fip] *ifile ofile*
> cp [-fiprR] *iname* . . . *odir*

where *ifile* is an input file, *ofile* is an output file, each *iname* is an input file or directory, and *odir* is an output directory.

Command-Line Options.   These options vary from one system to another.

-f   Force copying if necessary by unlinking the destination file (p. 104)
-i   Ask interactively for confirmation of each copy (p. 104)
-p   Preserve the permission modes and modification time of the original file (p. 104)
-r   Copy subdirectories recursively (p. 104)
-R   Copy subdirectories recursively (preferred form) (p. 104)

A.2.22
cpio
(Copy File Archives)

The forms of the cpio command line (p. 154) are

cpio -o [-acBLvV] [-C *size*] [-H *hdr*] [-O *file*]
cpio -i [-BcdkmrtuvVbsS6] [-C *size*] [-H *hdr*] [-I *file*] [[-f] *pattern*]
cpio -p [-adlLmuvV] *directory*

Here *pat* specifies files to be extracted from an archive and is used only with the -i option, while *dir* specifies a destination directory and is used only with the -p option.

Command-Line Options.

-6   Read archive in Sixth Edition format (p. 157)
-a   Leave the access times of input files unchanged (p. 156)
-b   Reverse byte order within each word (p. 157)
-B   Use 5120-byte blocks for data transfer (p. 157)
-c   Write header information in ASCII character form (p. 156)
-C *n*   Use *n*-byte blocks for data transfer (p. 157)
-d   Create directories as needed (p. 156)
-f   Copy in those files *not* matching the patterns (p. 155)
-i   Copy archive in (p. 154)
-H *format*   Read or write headers in format *format* (crc, ustar, tar, or odc) (p. 156)
-I *file*   Read the archive from *file* (p. 155)
-k   Attempt to get past bad headers and i/o errors (p. 157)
-l   Link files when possible rather than copying them (p. 156)
-L   Follow symbolic links (p. 156)
-m   Retain previous file modification time (p. 156)
-M *msg*   Issue *msg* when switching media (p. 156)
-o   Copy archive out (p. 155)
-O *file*   Write the archive to *file* (p. 155)
-p   Pass archive to another directory (p. 155)
-r   Interactively rename files (p. 155)
-s   Reverse byte order within each halfword (p. 157)
-S   Reverse halfword order within each word (p. 157)
-t   Show a table of contents of the input, create no files (p. 155)
-u   Copy unconditionally, replacing newer files (p. 156)
-v   List all file names (p. 156)
-V   Show a dot for each file transferred (p. 156)

A.2.23
crontab (Define Schedule of Background Jobs)

The form of the crontab command line (p. 246) is

crontab [*file* | -e | -l | -r]

The user's crontab file is listed, edited, removed, or replaced. By default, it is replaced by the contents of standard input. The crontab file lists jobs to be executed periodically.

Command-Line Options.

file   Read a new crontab entry from *file* (p. 246)
-e   Edit a copy of your crontab entry (p. 246)
-l   List your crontab entry (p. 246)
-r   Remove your crontab entry (p. 246)

Contents of the crontab File.

The crontab file consists of lines with the following fields:

(1)   Minute (0–59)
(2)   Hour (0–23)

(3)   Day of month (1–31)
(4)   Month of year (1–12)
(5)   Day of week (0–6, 0=Sunday)
(6)   Command to execute

Each of the items 1–5 is either a star (all valid values), an element, or a list of elements separated by commas. Each element is either a number *n* or a range '*n-m*'. The interpretation of crontab in a locale other than the POSIX locale may be different.

A.2.24 csplit (Split File by Context)

The form of the csplit command line (p. 186) is

csplit [-ks] [-f *pfx*] [-n *digs*] *file crit* ...

The file *file* is split into subfiles using the criteria in *crit* ... to define the splits (see below).

Command-Line Options.

-f *pfx*   Name the created file *pfx*00, etc. (p. 186)
-k   Leave previously created files intact (p. 187)
-n *digs*   Use *digs* digits in created filenames (p. 186)
-s   Suppress output of file size messages (p. 187)

Forms of Criteria.   Each criterion has the form

locator [{*num*}]

where *num* is a repetition count. The possible locators *locator* are these:

/*regexpr*/[*offset*]   Split at a line matching the BRE *regexpr* plus *offset* lines (p. 187)
%*regexpr*%[*offset*]   Split at a line matching the BRE *regexpr* plus *offset* lines, but don't create corresponding file (p. 187)
linenbr   Split at line number *linenbr* (p. 187)

A.2.25 cu (Connect to a UNIX System)

The form of the cu command line (p. 666) is

cu [-dehlnost] [*dest*]

where *dest* is either the name of a remote system or a telephone number.

Command-Line Options.

-d   Show diagnostic traces (p. 667)
-e   Send data using even parity (p. 667)
-h   Provide local echoing of typed lines (half-duplex mode) (p. 667)
-l *dev*   Use the device *dev* as the communication line (p. 667)
-n   Prompt the user for the telephone number (p. 667)
-o   Send data using odd parity (p. 667)
-s *speed*   Cause the communication line to operate at *speed* (p. 667)
-t   Map carriage return to carriage return plus line feed (p. 667)

Tilde Commands.

~![*cmd*]   Executes *cmd* in a subshell on the local system (p. 668)
~$*cmd*   Executes *cmd* in a subshell on the local system and sends its output to the remote system (p. 668)
~%b   Sends a break signal to the remote system (p. 668)
~%break   Sends a break signal to the remote system (p. 668)
~%cd [*dir*]   Changes the current directory on the local system (p. 668)
~%d   Toggles debugging output (p. 669)
~%debug   Toggles debugging output (p. 669)
~%nostop   Toggles DC3/DC1 input control (p. 668)
~%put *rfile* [*lfile*]   Copies remote file *rfile* to local file *lfile* (p. 668)
~%take *lfile* [*rfile*]   Copies local file *lfile* to remote file *rfile* (p. 668)
~.   Terminates the conversation (p. 667)
~~*line*   Sends '~*line*' to the remote system (p. 668)
~l   Shows the values of the termio variables for the communication line (p. 669)
~t   Shows the values of the termio variables for your terminal (p. 669)

A.2.26
cut (Extract Fields from Lines)

The forms of the cut command line (p. 179) are

    cut -b *list* [-n] [*file...*]
    cut -c *list* [*file...*]
    cut -f *list* [-d *delim*] [-s] [*file...*]

where the *files* provide the input.

Command-Line Options.   In the following commands, *list* indicates a list of field numbers, with commas separating the fields and – indicating ranges.

-b *list*   Extract the bytes specified in *list* (p. 180)
-c *list*   Extract the characters specified in *list* (p. 180)
-d *c*   Use the character *c* as the field delimiter (p. 180)
-f *list*   Extract the fields specified in *list* (p. 180)
-n   Don't split multibyte characters (p. 180)
-s   Suppress lines containing no delimiter characters (p. 180)

A.2.27
date (Display the Date and Time)

The form of the date command line (p. 232) is

    date [-u] [+*format*]

where *format* specifies the format in which the date and time are displayed.

Command-Line Option.

-u   Calculate the date and time using Greenwich Mean Time.

Format Descriptors.

A   Day of week spelled in full ('Sunday'–'Saturday') (p. 233)
a   Day of week as three letters ('Sun'–'Sat') (p. 233)
B   Month spelled in full ('January'–'December') (p. 233)
b   Month as three letters ('Jan'–'Dec') (p. 233)
C   Century (e.g., '19') (p. 233)
c   Date and time in the default format (as above) (p. 233)
D   Date in the form '*mm/dd/yy*' (e.g., '07/04/96') (p. 233)
d   Day of month as two digits ('01'–'31') (p. 233)
e   Day of month as one or two digits with leading ⟨space⟩ for 1–9 (p. 233)
H   Hour as two digits in a 24-hour clock ('00'–'23') (p. 234)
h   Month as three letters ('Jan'–'Dec') (p. 233)
I   Hour as two digits in a 12-hour clock ('01'–'12') (p. 234)
j   Day of year as three digits ('001'–'366') (p. 233)
M   Minute as two digits ('00'–'59') (p. 234)
m   Month as two digits ('01'–'12') (p. 233)
n   ⟨newline⟩ character (p. 234)
p   Either 'AM' or 'PM' for forenoon or afternoon (p. 234)
r   Time in AM/PM notation (p. 234)
S   Second as two digits ('00'–'59') (p. 234)
T   Time in the form '*hh*:*mm*:*ss*' (p. 234)
t   ⟨tab⟩ character (p. 234)
U   Week of the year ('00'–'53') with Sunday as the first day of the week (p. 233)
u   Day of week as one digit ('1' for Monday, '7' for Sunday) (p. 233)
V   Week of the year ('01'–'53') with Monday as the first day of the week according to standard ISO 8601 (p. 234)
W   Week of the year ('00'–'53') with Monday as the first day of the week (p. 233)
w   Day of week as one digit ('0' for Sunday, '6' for Saturday) (p. 233)
X   Time in the default format (p. 234)
x   Date in the default format (p. 233)
Y   Four-digit year (p. 233)
y   Last two digits of the year (p. 233)
Z   Time zone (e.g., 'EDT') (p. 234)

A.2.28
dd (Convert and Copy a File)

The form of the dd command line (p. 160) is

> dd [*operand* ...]

By default, standard input is copied and converted to standard output, with the conversion specified by the *operand*s.

Operands.

bs=*size*   Use *size* as both input and output block size (p. 162)
cbs=*size*   Use *size* as conversion block size (p. 162)
conv=*value-list*   Perform the conversions specified in *value-list* (p. 162)
count=*n*   Copy only *n* input blocks (p. 162)
ibs=*size*   Use *size* as input block size (p. 162)
if=*file*   Read input from *file* (p. 161)
obs=*size*   Use *size* as output block size (p. 162)
of=*file*   Write output to *file* (p. 161)
seek=*n*   Initially skip *n* output blocks (p. 162)
skip=*n*   Initially skip *n* input blocks (p. 162)

In these operands, *size* is one of the following:
- A decimal constant possibly suffixed by k or b
- The product of two such decimal constants, written with an x between them

In this notation, k stands for units of 1024 bytes and b for units of 512 bytes.

Keywords for Data Transformation.   The following keywords are used with the conv operand:

ascii   Convert EBCDIC to ASCII (p. 163)
block   Convert variable-length records to fixed length (p. 162)
ebcdic   Convert ASCII to standard EBCDIC (p. 163)
ibm   Convert ASCII to IBM EBCDIC (p. 163)
lcase   Map uppercase characters to lowercase (p. 163)
noerror   Continue processing when errors occur (p. 163)
notrunc   Don't truncate the output file (p. 163)
swab   Swap pairs of input bytes (p. 163)
sync   Pad input blocks to specified size (p. 163)
ucase   Map lowercase characters to uppercase (p. 163)
unblock   Convert fixed-length records to variable length (p. 163)

A.2.29
df
(Report Free Disk Space)

The main variants of the df command line (p. 271) are

df [-kP] [*name* ...]	(POSIX)
df [-lt] [*name*...]	(System V)
df [-in] [-t *type*] [*name* ...]	(4.4BSD, SunOS)

where each *name* refers to a mounted file system or a directory.

Command-Line Options for POSIX.

-k   Use units of 1024 bytes rather than 512 bytes (p. 271)
-P   Produce one line of output for each file system in a POSIX standard format (p. 271)

Command-Line Options for System V and Solaris.

-l   Report only on local file systems (p. 271)
-t   Report the total number of allocated blocks and i-nodes on the device (p. 271)

Command-Line Options for SunOS and BSD.

-i   Report the number of free i-nodes (p. 271)
-t *type*   Report only on file systems of type *type* (p. 271)
-n   Use previously available statistics without recalculating new ones (BSD only) (p. 271)

A.2.30
diff **(Find File Differences)**

The form of the `diff` command line (p. 130) is

     diff [-bcefhr] [-C n] $file_1$ $file_2$

The return code is 0 if the files are the same, 1 if the files differ, and 2 if the differences could not be computed.

Command-Line Options.

-b   Ignore trailing whitespace, condense other whitespace to a single blank (p. 132)
-c   Show three lines of context before and after differences (p. 131)
-C n Show n lines of context before and after differences (p. 131)
-e   Produce an editor script (p. 132)
-f   Produce a pseudo-editor script that reads forward (p. 132)
-h   Do a fast but not as effective (i.e., half-hearted) job (p. 132)
-r   Compare subdirectories recursively (p. 131)

A.2.31
dirname
(Extract Directory from Pathname)

The form of the `dirname` command line (p. 294) is

     dirname *string*

where *string* is a string that represents a pathname.

A.2.32
du **(Report Disk Space in Use)**

The form of the `du` command line (p. 271) is

     du [-ars] [*name...*]

where each *name* is a directory or a file.

Command-Line Options.

-a   Produce an output line for each file (p. 272)
-r   Report directories that can't be read and files that can't be opened (p. 272)
-s   Report only the total usage for each *name* (p. 272)

A.2.33
echo **(Echo Arguments)**

The form of the `echo` command line (p. 272) is

     echo ["-n"] *string*

The *string* is echoed to standard output followed by a trailing ⟨newline⟩. Under some systems the trailing ⟨newline⟩ is suppressed if -n is specified. The 4.4BSD echo recognizes the usual escape sequences in *string* provided that -e is specified. The System V version of `echo` does not recognize -n.

A.2.34
ed **(Line Editor)**

The form of the `ed` command line (p. 459) is

     ed [-s] [-p *string*] [*file*]

where *file* is a file to be edited.

Command-Line Options.

-p *string*   Use *string* as the interactive prompt string (p. 459)
-s   Suppress informational messages (p. 459)

Line Addresses and Line Ranges.   The notations for specifying a line address are as follows:

$ The last line of the file (p. 460)
.   The current line (p. 460)
n   The *n*th line of the file (p. 460)
'*c*   The line marked with the letter *c* (p. 460)
/*pat*/   The next line containing the pattern *pat* (p. 460)
?*pat*?   The nearest previous line containing the pattern *pat* (p. 460)
[*a*]*n*   The address *a* plus *n* lines (p. 460)
[*a*]+[*n*]   The address *a* plus *n* lines (p. 460)
[*a*]-[*n*]   The address *a* minus *n* lines (p. 460)

The notations for specifying a line range are as follows:

a_1,a_2 Lines a_1 through a_2 (p. 461)
$a_1;a_2$ Like the previous form, but the current line is set to a_1 before a_2 is evaluated
     (p. 461)
,   The entire file (p. 461)
;   The pair '.,$' (p. 461)

Commands.   The text before the brackets indicates the shortest recognized abbreviation. A line address is indicated by *a* and a line range is indicated by *r*.

a   Shows the line at address *a* (p. 461)
CR   Shows the next line (p. 461)
!*cmds*   Executes the UNIX commands *cmds* in a subshell (p. 465)
[*a*]=   Shows the address of the line at *a* (p. 462)
[*a*]a   Appends input text after line *a* (p. 462)
[*r*]c   Deletes the lines in range *r*, then inserts input text (p. 462)
[*r*]d   Deletes the lines in range *r* (p. 462)
e [*file*]   Starts editing *file*, discards the current buffer (p. 464)
e !*cmds*   Edits the standard output of *cmds* (p. 465)
E [*file*]   Starts editing *file*, discards the current buffer without checking (p. 464)
f [*file*]   Changes name of current file to *file* (p. 464)
[*r*]g/*pat*/ [*cmds*]   Performs *cmds* for those lines in *r* that match *pat* (p. 465)
[*r*]G/*pat*/   Interactively performs commands for those lines in *r* that match *pat* (p. 465)
h   Gives help on the most recent error diagnostic (p. 466)
H   Toggles error messages for '?' diagnostics (p. 466)
[*a*]i   Inserts input text after line *a* (p. 462)
[*r*]j   Joins the lines in *r* (p. 462)
[*a*]k*c*   Marks the line at *a* with the letter *c* (p. 463)
[*r*] l   Shows a group of lines, showing nonprinting characters explicitly (p. 461)
[*r*]m *a*   Moves a group of lines to the location after *a* (p. 462)
[*r*]n   Shows a group of lines with line numbers (p. 461)
[*r*]p   Shows a group of lines (p. 461)
P   Toggles prompting for subsequent commands (p. 466)
q   Quits the editor without writing the buffer (p. 464)
Q   Quits the editor without checking or writing the buffer (p. 464)
[*a*]r [*file*]   Reads *file* into buffer after line *a* (p. 463)
[*a*]r !*cmds*   Puts output of *cmds* into buffer after line *a* (p. 465)
[*r*]s/*pat*/*repl*/[*opts*]   Replaces the pattern *pat* by the text *repl* (p. 462)
[*r*]s*c pat c repl c*[*opts*]   Replaces the pattern *pat* by the text *repl* (p. 462)
[*r*]t*a*   Copies the lines in range *r* to address *a* (p. 462)
u   Undoes the most recent change or insertion (p. 466)
[*r*]v/*pat*/ [*cmds*]   Performs *cmds* for those lines in *r* that do *not* match *pat* (p. 465)
[*r*]V/*pat*/   Interactively performs commands for those lines in *r* that do *not* match *pat*
     (p. 465)
[*r*]w [*file*]   Writes the lines in region *r* to *file* (p. 464)
[*r*]w !*cmds*   Executes *cmds* as a shell command, *r* is input (p. 466)

A.2.35
`egrep`
(Find Regular Expression, Extended Version)

This command is an obsolescent equivalent of 'grep -E' (p. 175).

A.2.36
`emacs` **(Emacs Extensible Text Editor)**

The form of the Emacs command line (p. 468) is

emacs [*init-options*] [*options-and-args*] [*X-options*]

where the *init-options* have the form

[-t *dev*] [-d *disp*] [-nw] [-batch] [-q | -no-init-file] [-u[ser] *user*]

and must appear in the order shown, the *options-and-args* have the form

[[+ *linenum*] *file*] [-l[oad] *file*] [-f[unction] *func*] [-i[nsert] *file*] [-kill]

and the *X-options*, which apply only to operation under X, are the X Toolkit options (see Section 13.7). The *options-and-args* and *X-options* can appear in any order but are honored in order of appearance. The *init-options* must precede the *options-and-args*; the *X-options* can be intermixed with either or both groups.

Command-Line Options and Arguments.

[+*n*]*file*   Initially visit *file* using `file-find`, move cursor to line *n* if specified (p. 469)
-batch   Run Emacs in batch mode (p. 469)
-d *disp*   Use *disp* as the display (X only) (p. 469)
-f[uncall] *func*   Call LISP function *func* with no arguments (p. 469)
-i[nsert] *file*   Insert *file* into the current buffer (p. 469)
-kill   Exit from Emacs without asking for confirmation (p. 469)
-l[oad] *file*   Load LISP code from *file* with `load` (p. 469)
-no-init-file   Don't load the Emacs initialization file ~/.emacs (p. 469)
-nw   Don't communicate directly with X (p. 469)
-q   Don't load the Emacs initialization file ~/.emacs (p. 469)
-t *dev*   Use *dev* as the terminal device (p. 469)
-u[ser] *name*   Load *name*'s initialization file ~*name*/.emacs (p. 469)

Commands.   Commands are listed according to their default global key bindings.

Del	`delete-backward-char` (p. 490)
End	`end-of-buffer` (p. 489)
Enter	`newline` (p. 498)
Home	`beginning-of-buffer` (p. 488)
Tab	`comint-dynamic-complete` (p. 531)
LnFd	`newline-and-indent` (p. 498)
LnFd	(in Lisp Interaction mode) `eval-print-last-sexp` (p. 529)
Ctrl @	`set-mark-command` (p. 493)
Ctrl _	`undo` (p. 483)
Ctrl]	`abort-recursive-edit` (p. 482)
Ctrl A	`beginning-of-line` (p. 487)
Ctrl B	`backward-char` (p. 487)
Ctrl C Ctrl \	`comint-quit-subjob` (p. 533)
Ctrl C Ctrl A	`comint-bol` (p. 531)
Ctrl C Ctrl B	`shell-backward-command` (p. 532)
Ctrl C Ctrl C	`comint-interrupt-subjob` (p. 533)
Ctrl C Ctrl D	`comint-send-eof` (p. 533)
Ctrl C Ctrl E	`comint-show-maximum-output` (p. 532)
Ctrl C Ctrl F	`shell-forward-command` (p. 532)
Ctrl C Ctrl L	`comint-dynamic-list-input-ring` (p. 533)

`Ctrl` C `Ctrl` N   `comint-next-prompt` (p. 533)
`Ctrl` C `Ctrl` P   `comint-previous-prompt` (p. 533)
`Ctrl` C `Ctrl` U   `comint-kill-input` (p. 532)
`Ctrl` C `Ctrl` Z   `comint-stop-subjob` (p. 534)
`Ctrl` C `Enter`   `comint-copy-old-input` (p. 533)
`Ctrl` D   `delete-char` (p. 490)
`Ctrl` E   `end-of-line` (p. 487)
`Ctrl` F   `forward-char` (p. 487)
`Ctrl` G   `keyboard-quit` (p. 480)
`Ctrl` H a   `command-apropos` (p. 484)
`Ctrl` H b   `describe-bindings` (p. 484)
`Ctrl` H c   `describe-key-briefly` (p. 484)
`Ctrl` H f   `describe-function` (p. 485)
`Ctrl` H i   `info` (p. 485)
`Ctrl` H k   `describe-key` (p. 484)
`Ctrl` H l   `view-lossage` (p. 485)
`Ctrl` H m   `describe-mode` (p. 485)
`Ctrl` H s   `describe-syntax` (p. 485)
`Ctrl` H t   `help-with-tutorial` (p. 485)
`Ctrl` H v   `describe-variable` (p. 485)
`Ctrl` H w   `where-is` (p. 485)
`Ctrl` H `Ctrl` C   `describe-copying` (p. 486)
`Ctrl` H `Ctrl` D   `describe-distribution` (p. 486)
`Ctrl` H `Ctrl` F   `info-goto-emacs-command-node` (p. 485)
`Ctrl` H `Ctrl` K   `info-goto-emacs-key-command-node` (p. 485)
`Ctrl` H `Ctrl` N   `view-emacs-news` (p. 485)
`Ctrl` H `Ctrl` W   `describe-no-warranty` (p. 486)
`Ctrl` L   `recenter` (p. 489)
`Ctrl` N   `next-line` (p. 487)
`Ctrl` O   `open-line` (p. 498)
`Ctrl` P   `previous-line` (p. 487)
`Ctrl` Q   `quoted-insert` (p. 473)
`Ctrl` R   `isearch-backward` (p. 521)
`Ctrl` R `Enter` `Ctrl` W   `word-search-backward` (p. 523)
`Ctrl` S   `isearch-forward` (p. 521)
`Ctrl` S `Enter` `Ctrl` W   `word-search-forward` (p. 523)
`Ctrl` T   `transpose-chars` (p. 497)
`Ctrl` U   `universal-argument` (p. 481)
`Ctrl` V   `scroll-up` (p. 489)
`Ctrl` W   `kill-region` (p. 490)
`Ctrl` X (`start-kbd-macro` (p. 539)
`Ctrl` X)   `end-kbd-macro` (p. 539)
`Ctrl` X .   `set-fill-prefix` (p. 497)
`Ctrl` X 0   `delete-window` (p. 507)
`Ctrl` X 1   `delete-other-windows` (p. 507)
`Ctrl` X 2   `split-window-vertically` (p. 505)
`Ctrl` X 3   `split-window-horizontally` (p. 505)
`Ctrl` X 4 .   `find-tag-other-window` (p. 562)
`Ctrl` X 4 b   `switch-to-buffer-other-window` (p. 514)
`Ctrl` X 4 d   `dired-other-window` (p. 551)
`Ctrl` X 4 f   `find-file-other-window` (p. 510)
`Ctrl` X 4 m   `mail-other-window` (p. 563)
`Ctrl` X 4 r   `find-file-read-only-other-window` (p. 506, p. 510)
`Ctrl` X 4 `Ctrl` O   `display-buffer` (p. 514)
`Ctrl` X 5 .   `find-tag-other-frame` (p. 508)
`Ctrl` X 5 0   `delete-frame` (p. 508)
`Ctrl` X 5 b   `switch-to-buffer-other-frame` (p. 508)
`Ctrl` X 5 d   `dired-other-frame` (p. 508)
`Ctrl` X 5 f   `find-file-other-frame` (p. 508)
`Ctrl` X 5 m   `mail-other-frame` (p. 508)
`Ctrl` X 5 o   `other-frame` (p. 508)

`Ctrl` X 5 r   `find-file-read-only-other-frame` (p. 508)
`Ctrl` X <   `scroll-left` (p. 489)
`Ctrl` X =   `what-cursor-position` (p. 514)
`Ctrl` X >   `scroll-right` (p. 489)
`Ctrl` X [`backward-page` (p. 488)
`Ctrl` X]   `forward-page` (p. 488)
`Ctrl` X a e   `expand-abbrev` (p. 542)
`Ctrl` X a g   `add-global-abbrev` (p. 541)
`Ctrl` X a i g   `inverse-add-global-abbrev` (p. 541)
`Ctrl` X a i l   `inverse-add-mode-abbrev` (p. 541)
`Ctrl` X a l   `add-mode-abbrev` (p. 541)
`Ctrl` X b   `switch-to-buffer` (p. 514)
`Ctrl` X d   `dired` (p. 551)
`Ctrl` X e   `call-last-kbd-macro` (p. 539)
`Ctrl` X f   `set-fill-column` (p. 496)
`Ctrl` X h   `mark-whole-buffer` (p. 494)
`Ctrl` X i   `insert-file` (p. 511)
`Ctrl` X k   `kill-buffer` (p. 514)
`Ctrl` X l   `count-lines-page` (p. 515)
`Ctrl` X m   `mail` (p. 563)
`Ctrl` X n n   `narrow-to-region` (p. 515)
`Ctrl` X n p   `narrow-to-page` (p. 515)
`Ctrl` X n w   `widen` (p. 515)
`Ctrl` X o   `other-window` (p. 506)
`Ctrl` X q   `kbd-macro-query` (p. 540)
`Ctrl` X r c   `clear-rectangle` (p. 505)
`Ctrl` X r d   `delete-rectangle` (p. 504)
`Ctrl` X r i *r*   `insert-register` (p. 520)
`Ctrl` X r j *r*   `jump-to-register` (p. 520)
`Ctrl` X r k   `kill-rectangle` (p. 505)
`Ctrl` X r o   `open-rectangle` (p. 505)
`Ctrl` X r r *r*   `copy-region-to-rectangle` (p. 520)
`Ctrl` X r t   `string-rectangle` (p. 505)
`Ctrl` X r x *r*   `copy-to-register` (p. 520)
`Ctrl` X r y   `yank-rectangle` (p. 505)
`Ctrl` X r `Space` *r*   `point-to-register` (p. 520)
`Ctrl` X s   `save-some-buffers` (p. 510)
`Ctrl` X v =   `vc-diff` (p. 579)
`Ctrl` X v c   `vc-cancel-version` (p. 579)
`Ctrl` X v d   `vc-directory` (p. 579)
`Ctrl` X v h   `vc-insert-headers` (p. 579)
`Ctrl` X v i   `vc-register` (p. 578)
`Ctrl` X v r   `vc-retrieve-snapshot` (p. 580)
`Ctrl` X v s   `vc-create-snapshot` (p. 580)
`Ctrl` X v u   `vc-revert-buffer` (p. 579)
`Ctrl` X v v   `vc-next-action` (p. 579)
`Ctrl` X v ~   `vc-version-other-window` (p. 579)
`Ctrl` X }   `enlarge-window-horizontally` (p. 507)
`Ctrl` X $ `set-selective-display` (p. 515)
`Ctrl` X ^   `enlarge-window` (p. 507)
`Ctrl` X `Ctrl` B   `list-buffers` (p. 517)
`Ctrl` X `Ctrl` C   `save-buffers-kill-emacs` (p. 486)
`Ctrl` X `Ctrl` D   `list-directory` (p. 511)
`Ctrl` X `Ctrl` E   `eval-last-sexp` (p. 529)
`Ctrl` X `Ctrl` F   `find-file` (p. 509)
`Ctrl` X `Ctrl` L   `downcase-region` (p. 498)
`Ctrl` X `Ctrl` N   `set-goal-column` (p. 487)
`Ctrl` X `Ctrl` O   `delete-blank-lines` (p. 491)
`Ctrl` X `Ctrl` P   `mark-page` (p. 494)
`Ctrl` X `Ctrl` Q   `vc-toggle-read-only` (p. 516, p. 578)
`Ctrl` X `Ctrl` R   `find-file-read-only` (p. 510)

Ctrl X	Ctrl S	save-buffer (p. 510)	
Ctrl X	Ctrl T	transpose-lines (p. 497)	
Ctrl X	Ctrl U	upcase-region (p. 498)	
Ctrl X	Ctrl V	find-alternate-file (p. 510)	
Ctrl X	Ctrl W	write-file (p. 510)	
Ctrl X	Ctrl X	exchange-point-and-mark (p. 493)	
Ctrl X	Ctrl Space	pop-global-mark (p. 493)	
Ctrl X	Esc Esc	repeat-complex-command (p. 481)	
Ctrl X	DEL	backward-kill-sentence (p. 490)	
Ctrl X	TAB	indent-rigidly (p. 503)	
Ctrl Y	yank (p. 491)		
Ctrl Z	iconify-or-deiconify-frame (under X) (p. 508)		
Ctrl Z	suspend-emacs (not under X) (p. 486)		
Meta Del	backward-kill-word (p. 490)		
Meta End	end-of-buffer-other-window (p. 506)		
Meta Esc	eval-expression (p. 529)		
Meta Home	beginning-of-buffer-other-window (p. 506)		
Meta PgDn	scroll-other-window (p. 506)		
Meta PgUp	scroll-other-window-down (p. 506)		
Meta Space	just-one-space (p. 491)		
Meta Tab	ispell-complete-word (p. 501)		
Meta !	shell-command (p. 530)		
Meta '	abbrev-prefix-mark (p. 542)		
Meta ,	tags-loop-continue (p. 562)		
Meta -	negative-argument (p. 481)		
Meta .	find-tag (p. 561)		
Meta /	dabbrev-expand (p. 543)		
Meta <	beginning-of-buffer (p. 488)		
Meta =	count-lines-region (p. 515)		
Meta >	end-of-buffer (p. 489)		
Meta ?	comint-dynamic-list-filename-completions (p. 531)		
Meta @	mark-word (p. 493)		
Meta $	spell-word (p. 501)		
Meta %	query-replace (p. 526)		
Meta \	delete-horizontal-space (p. 491)		
Meta ^	delete-indentation (p. 491)		
Meta {	backward-paragraph (p. 488)		
Meta }	forward-paragraph (p. 488)		
Meta ~	not-modified (p. 511)		
Meta A	backward-sentence (p. 488)		
Meta B	backward-word (p. 487)		
Meta C	capitalize-word (p. 498)		
Meta D	kill-word (p. 490)		
Meta E	forward-sentence (p. 488)		
Meta F	forward-word (p. 487)		
Meta H	mark-paragraph (p. 493)		
Meta I	tab-to-tab-stop (p. 503)		
Meta K	kill-sentence (p. 490)		
Meta L	downcase-word (p. 498)		
Meta M	back-to-indentation (p. 487)		
Meta N	comint-next-input (p. 532)		
Meta P	comint-previous-input (p. 532)		
Meta Q	fill-paragraph (p. 496)		
Meta R	comint-previous-matching-input (p. 532)		
Meta R	move-to-window-line (p. 487)		
Meta S	comint-next-matching-input (p. 533)		
Meta T	transpose-words (p. 497)		
Meta U	upcase-word (p. 498)		
Meta V	scroll-down (p. 489)		
Meta W	copy-region-as-kill (p. 492)		
Meta X	execute-extended-command (p. 479)		

[Meta] Y   `yank-pop` (p. 492)
[Meta] Z   `zap-to-char` (p. 491)
[Meta] | `shell-command-on-region` (p. 530)
[Meta] [Ctrl] @   `mark-sexp` (p. 500)
[Meta] [Ctrl] \   `indent-region` (p. 503)
[Meta] [Ctrl] B   `backward-sexp` (p. 499)
[Meta] [Ctrl] C   `exit-recursive-edit` (p. 482)
[Meta] [Ctrl] D   `down-list` (p. 499)
[Meta] [Ctrl] F   `forward-sexp` (p. 499)
[Meta] [Ctrl] K   `kill-sexp` (p. 500)
[Meta] [Ctrl] L   `comint-show-output` (p. 532)
[Meta] [Ctrl] N   `forward-list` (p. 499)
[Meta] [Ctrl] O   `split-line` (p. 498)
[Meta] [Ctrl] P   `backward-list` (p. 499)
[Meta] [Ctrl] R   `isearch-backward-regexp` (p. 523)
[Meta] [Ctrl] S   `isearch-forward-regexp` (p. 523)
[Meta] [Ctrl] T   `transpose-sexps` (p. 500)
[Meta] [Ctrl] U   `backward-up-list` (p. 499)
[Meta] [Ctrl] W   `append-next-kill` (p. 492)
[Meta] X `abbrev-mode` (p. 475)
[Meta] X `add-name-to-file` (p. 512)
[Meta] X `append-to-buffer` (p. 492)
[Meta] X `append-to-file` (p. 511)
[Meta] X `appt-add` (p. 577)
[Meta] X `appt-del` (p. 577)
[Meta] X `apropos` (p. 486)
[Meta] X `auto-fill-mode` (p. 474)
[Meta] X `auto-save-mode` (p. 475)
[Meta] X `blackbox` (p. 580)
[Meta] X `buffer-menu` (p. 517)
[Meta] X `calendar` (p. 572)
[Meta] X `capitalize-region` (p. 498)
[Meta] X `cd` (p. 509)
[Meta] X `center-line` (p. 496)
[Meta] X `comint-continue-subjob` (p. 534)
[Meta] X `comint-delchar-or-maybe-eof` [Ctrl] D
[Meta] X `compare-windows` (p. 506)
[Meta] X `copy-file` (p. 512)
[Meta] X `copy-to-buffer` (p. 492)
[Meta] X `count-matches` (p. 527)
[Meta] X `define-abbrev` (p. 543)
[Meta] X `delete-file` (p. 512)
[Meta] X `delete-matching-lines` (p. 527)
[Meta] X `delete-non-matching-lines` (p. 527)
[Meta] X `dirs` (p. 534)
[Meta] X `disable-command` (p. 483)
[Meta] X `display-time` (p. 534)
[Meta] X `dissociated-press` (p. 581)
[Meta] X `do-auto-save` (p. 513)
[Meta] X `doctor` (p. 580)
[Meta] X `edit-abbrevs` (p. 542)
[Meta] X `edit-abbrevs-redefine` (p. 542)
[Meta] X `edit-options` (p. 528)
[Meta] X `edit-picture` (p. 558)
[Meta] X `edit-tab-stops` (p. 503)
[Meta] X `edit-tab-stops-note-changes` (p. 504)
[Meta] X `emacs-version` (p. 534)
[Meta] X `enable-command` (p. 483)
[Meta] X `eval-current-buffer` (p. 529)
[Meta] X `eval-region` (p. 529)
[Meta] X `expand-region-abbrevs` (p. 542)

Meta X `fill-individual-paragraphs` (p. 496)
Meta X `fill-region` (p. 496)
Meta X `fill-region-as-paragraph` (p. 496)
Meta X `find-dired` (p. 557)
Meta X `find-grep-dired` (p. 557)
Meta X `find-name-dired` (p. 557)
Meta X `font-lock-mode` (p. 475)
Meta X `global-set-key` (p. 536)
Meta X `gnus` (p. 571)
Meta X `goto-char` (p. 489)
Meta X `goto-line` (p. 489)
Meta X `hanoi` (p. 580)
Meta X `indent-relative` (p. 503)
Meta X `indented-text-mode` (p. 502)
Meta X `insert-abbrevs` (p. 543)
Meta X `insert-buffer` (p. 493)
Meta X `insert-kbd-macro` (p. 540)
Meta X `interrupt-shell-subjob` (p. 533)
Meta X `kill-all-abbrevs` (p. 541)
Meta X `kill-line` (p. 490)
Meta X `kill-local-variable` (p. 528)
Meta X `kill-output-from-shell` (p. 533)
Meta X `kill-some-buffers` (p. 514)
Meta X `line-number-mode` (p. 475)
Meta X `list-abbrevs` (p. 542)
Meta X `list-command-history` (p. 482)
Meta X `list-faces` (p. 478)
Meta X `list-matching-lines` (p. 527)
Meta X `list-options` (p. 528)
Meta X `list-tags` (p. 562)
Meta X `local-set-key` (p. 536)
Meta X `lpr-buffer` (p. 519)
Meta X `lpr-region` (p. 519)
Meta X `mail-cc` (p. 564)
Meta X `mail-fill-yanked-message` (p. 565)
Meta X `mail-send` (p. 564)
Meta X `mail-send-and-exit` (p. 564)
Meta X `mail-signature` (p. 565)
Meta X `mail-subject` (p. 564)
Meta X `mail-to` (p. 564)
Meta X `mail-yank-original` (p. 565)
Meta X `make-frame` (p. 508)
Meta X `make-local-variable` (p. 528)
Meta X `make-symbolic-link` (p. 512)
Meta X `make-variable-buffer-local` (p. 528)
Meta X `manual-entry` (p. 486)
Meta X `mpuz` (p. 581)
Meta X `name-last-kbd-macro` (p. 539)
Meta X `next-complex-command` (p. 482)
Meta X `next-file` (p. 562)
Meta X `occur` (p. 527)
Meta X `overwrite-mode` (p. 475)
Meta X `picture-backward-clear-column` (p. 559)
Meta X `picture-backward-column` (p. 558)
Meta X `picture-clear-column` (p. 559)
Meta X `picture-clear-line` (p. 559)
Meta X `picture-clear-rectangle` (p. 560)
Meta X `picture-clear-rectangle-to-register` (p. 560)
Meta X `picture-duplicate-line` (p. 558)
Meta X `picture-forward-column` (p. 558)
Meta X `picture-mode-exit` (p. 558)

(Meta) X picture-motion   (p. 559)
(Meta) X picture-motion-reverse   (p. 559)
(Meta) X picture-move-down   (p. 558)
(Meta) X picture-move-up   (p. 558)
(Meta) X picture-movement-down   (p. 559)
(Meta) X picture-movement-left   (p. 559)
(Meta) X picture-movement-ne   (p. 559)
(Meta) X picture-movement-nw   (p. 559)
(Meta) X picture-movement-right   (p. 559)
(Meta) X picture-movement-se   (p. 559)
(Meta) X picture-movement-sw   (p. 559)
(Meta) X picture-movement-up   (p. 559)
(Meta) X picture-newline   (p. 558)
(Meta) X picture-open-line   (p. 559)
(Meta) X picture-set-tab-stops   (p. 560)
(Meta) X picture-tab   (p. 560)
(Meta) X picture-tab-search   (p. 560)
(Meta) X picture-yank-rectangle   (p. 560)
(Meta) X picture-yank-rectangle-from-register   (p. 561)
(Meta) X prepend-to-buffer   (p. 493)
(Meta) X previous-complex-command   (p. 482)
(Meta) X print-buffer   (p. 519)
(Meta) X print-region   (p. 519)
(Meta) X pwd   (p. 509)
(Meta) X query-replace-regexp   (p. 526)
(Meta) X quietly-read-abbrev-file   (p. 543)
(Meta) X quit-shell-subjob   (p. 533)
(Meta) X re-search-backward   (p. 523)
(Meta) X re-search-forward   (p. 523)
(Meta) X read-abbrev-file   (p. 542)
(Meta) X recover-file   (p. 513)
(Meta) X rename-buffer   (p. 516)
(Meta) X rename-file   (p. 512)
(Meta) X rename-uniquely   (p. 516)
(Meta) X replace-regexp   (p. 525)
(Meta) X replace-string   (p. 525)
(Meta) X revert-buffer   (p. 516)
(Meta) X rmail   (p. 565)
(Meta) X search-backward   (p. 522)
(Meta) X search-forward   (p. 522)
(Meta) X self-insert   (p. 470)
(Meta) X send-invisible   (p. 534)
(Meta) X send-shell-input   (p. 531)
(Meta) X set-rmail-inbox-list   (p. 569)
(Meta) X set-variable   (p. 527)
(Meta) X set-visited-file-name   (p. 510)
(Meta) X shell   (p. 531)
(Meta) X shell-send-eof   (p. 533)
(Meta) X shell-strip-ctrl-m (p. 534)
(Meta) X show-output-from-shell   (p. 532)
(Meta) X sort-columns   (p. 501)
(Meta) X sort-fields   (p. 500)
(Meta) X sort-lines   (p. 500)
(Meta) X sort-numeric-fields   (p. 501)
(Meta) X sort-pages   (p. 500)
(Meta) X sort-paragraphs   (p. 500)
(Meta) X spell-buffer   (p. 501)
(Meta) X spell-region   (p. 501)
(Meta) X spell-string   (p. 501)
(Meta) X stop-shell-subjob   (p. 534)
(Meta) X tabify   (p. 504)

[Meta] X `tags-apropos` (p. 562)
[Meta] X `tags-query-replace` (p. 562)
[Meta] X `tags-search` (p. 562)
[Meta] X `text-mode` (p. 502)
[Meta] X `toggle-read-only` `toggle-read-only` (p. 516)
[Meta] X `top-level` (p. 482)
[Meta] X `transient-mark-mode` `transient-mark-mode` (p. 475)
[Meta] X `undigestify-rmail-message` (p. 569)
[Meta] X `unexpand-abbrev` (p. 542)
[Meta] X `untabify` (p. 504)
[Meta] X `vc-rename-file` (p. 579)
[Meta] X `version` (p. 534)
[Meta] X `view-buffer` (p. 516)
[Meta] X `view-file` (p. 511)
[Meta] X `view-register` (p. 519)
[Meta] X `visit-tags-table` (p. 561)
[Meta] X `what-line` (p. 514)
[Meta] X `what-page` (p. 514)
[Meta] X `write-abbrev-file` (p. 542)
[Meta] X `write-region` (p. 511)
[Meta] X `yow` (p. 580)

Mouse Commands for Marking Text.

[Mouse-1]   Moves point to where you click (p. 494)
[Double-Mouse-1]   Sets region to word containing the place where you click (p. 494)
[Triple-Mouse-1]   Sets region to line containing the place where you click (p. 494)
[Drag-Mouse-1]   Sets region to dragged-over text (p. 494)
[Double-Drag-Mouse-1]   Sets region to words of dragged-over text (p. 494)
[Triple-Drag-Mouse-1]   Sets region to lines of dragged-over text (p. 494)
[Mouse-2]   Copies most recently killed text to click location (p. 494)
[Mouse-3]   Adjusts region boundary, or sets mark, or if used twice in a row, kills region (p. 494)
[Meta] [Mouse-1]   Inserts secondary selection where you click (p. 495)
[Meta] [Double-Mouse-1]   Sets secondary selection to word containing the place where you click (p. 495)
[Meta] [Triple-Mouse-1]   Sets secondary selection to line containing the place where you click (p. 495)
[Meta] [Drag-Mouse-1]   Sets secondary selection to dragged-over text (p. 495)
[Meta] [Double-Drag-Mouse-1]   Sets secondary selection to words of dragged-over text (p. 495)
[Meta] [Triple-Drag-Mouse-1]   Sets secondary selection to lines of dragged-over text (p. 495)
[Meta] [Mouse-2]   Inserts the secondary selection to where you click (p. 495)
[Meta] [Mouse-3]   Adjusts secondary selection boundary, or if used twice in a row, kills secondary selection (p. 496)

Mouse Actions for Rearranging Windows.

[Mouse-1] *on mode line*   Selects window above, changes window boundary if dragged (p. 507)
[Mouse-2] *on mode line*   Expands window to fill frame (p. 507)
[Ctrl] [Mouse-2] *on mode line*   Splits window above into two vertical windows (p. 507)
[Ctrl] [Mouse-2] *on scrollbar*   Splits window to left into two horizontal windows (p. 507)
[Mouse-3] *on mode line*   Deletes window above (p. 507)

Dired Commands.

[Del]   Removes the deletion flag on this line, moves up one line (p. 552)
[Space]   Moves to the beginning of the file name on the next line (p. 552)
[Ctrl] N   Moves to the beginning of the file name on the next line (p. 552)
[Ctrl] O   Visits this file in another window but doesn't go to that window (p. 553)

Ctrl P   Moves to the beginning of the file name on the previous line (p. 553)
Ctrl X u   Undoes the most recent Dired change (p. 556)
Ctrl X [Goes to the previous directory in the directory tree (p. 553)
Ctrl X]   Goes to the next directory in the directory tree (p. 553)
Meta Del   Removes marks from all files in the buffer (p. 552)
Meta $ Hides or reveals all subdirectories (p. 556)
Meta =   Compares this file with its latest backup (p. 555)
Meta {   Moves to previous marked file (p. 553)
Meta }   Moves to next marked file (p. 553)
Meta Ctrl D   Goes down in the directory tree (p. 553)
Meta Ctrl N   Goes to the next directory in the directory tree (p. 553)
Meta Ctrl P   Goes to the previous directory in the directory tree (p. 553)
Meta Ctrl U   Goes up in the directory tree (p. 553)
Mouse-2   Visits this file in another window (p. 553)
@   Marks all symbolic links with '*' (p. 552)
!   Runs shell command on this file (p. 554)
$ Hides or reveals subdirectory where point is (p. 556)
.   Flags excess numeric backup files for deletion (p. 554)
=   Compares this file with file at the mark (p. 555)
>   Goes to next directory line (p. 553)
Flags all auto-save files (p. 554)
^   Runs Dired on parent of directory containing the point (p. 556)
<   Goes to previous directory line (p. 553)
%C   Copies matching files through regular expression substitution (p. 555)
%d   Marks files satisfying a regular expression for deletion (p. 554)
%H   Hard-links matching files through regular expression substitution (p. 555)
%l   Changes this file's name to lowercase (p. 556)
%m   Marks files satisfying a regular expression with '*' (p. 552)
%R   Renames matching files through regular expression substitution (p. 555)
%S   Symbolically links matching files through regular expression substitution (p. 555)
%u   Changes this file's name to uppercase (p. 556)
+   Creates a subdirectory (p. 556)
?   Provides brief help on Dired (p. 551)
/   Marks all directories other than '.' and '..' with '*' (p. 552)
*   Marks all executable files with '*' (p. 552)
~   Flags all backup files (p. 554)
B   Byte-compiles this file (p. 556)
c c_1 c_2 Changes mark c_1 to mark c_2 (p. 552)
C   Copies this file to another file (p. 555)
d   Marks this file for deletion (p. 554)
D   Deletes this file (p. 554)
f   Visits this file (p. 553)
g   Updates the entire contents of the Dired buffer (p. 556)
G   Changes the group of this file (p. 555)
h   Shows description of Dired mode in a window (p. 551)
H   Constructs a hard link from this file (p. 555)
i   Inserts contents of this subdirectory if necessary, then moves to it (p. 556)
k   Deletes marked file lines (but not the files themselves) (p. 557)
l   Updates the subdirectory containing the point (p. 556)
L   Loads this Emacs Lisp file (p. 556)
m   Marks this file with '*' (p. 552)
M   Modifies the file permissions of this file (p. 555)
n   Moves to the beginning of the file name on the next line (p. 552)
o   Visits this file in another window (p. 553)
O   Changes the owner of this file (p. 555)
p   Moves to the beginning of the file name on the previous line (p. 553)
P   Prints this file (p. 554)
q   Buries this Dired buffer but doesn't kill it (p. 557)
R   Renames this file (p. 554)
s   Toggles sort order or, with Ctrl U, does nonstandard `ls` (p. 556)
S   Constructs a symbolic link from this file (p. 555)
u   Removes the deletion flag on this line (p. 556)

v   Views this file (p. 553)
x   Deletes all flagged files (p. 554)
X   Runs shell command on this file (p. 554)
Z   Compresses or uncompresses this file (p. 555)

Buffer Menu Commands.
(Ctrl) D   Marks this buffer for deletion, moves up one line (p. 517)
(Ctrl) K   Marks this buffer for deletion, moves down one line (p. 517)
(Del)   Moves up one line (p. 517)
(Space)   Moves down one line (p. 517)
?   Displays explanations of the buffer menu commands (p. 517)
~   Marks this buffer as unmodified (p. 518)
1   Selects this buffer in a full-screen window (p. 518)
2   Sets up two windows with this buffer and the previously selected one (p. 518)
d   Marks this buffer for deletion, moves down one line (p. 517)
f   Replaces the Buffer List buffer by this buffer (p. 518)
k   Marks this buffer for deletion, moves down one line (p. 517)
m   Marks this buffer for display with q (p. 518)
o   Selects this buffer in another window, leaving the buffer list visible (p. 518)
q   Selects this buffer, displays any buffers marked with m in other windows (p. 518)
s   Marks this buffer for saving (p. 518)
u   Removes all requests from this line, moves down one line (p. 518)
x   Performs all deletions and saves requested so far (p. 518)

Rmail Commands.
(Space)   Scrolls the current message forward (p. 567)
(Ctrl) D   Deletes the current message, moves to the previous nondeleted message (p. 567)
(Ctrl) O *file*   Appends a copy of the current message in UNIX format to *file* (p. 569)
(Del)   Scrolls the current message backward (p. 567)
(Meta) N   Moves to the next message, deleted or not (p. 567)
(Meta) P   Moves to the previous message, deleted or not (p. 567)
(Meta) S   Moves to the next message matching a specified regular expression (p. 567)
(Meta) X set-rmail-inbox-list   Specifies input mailboxes for Rmail (p. 569)
(Meta) (Ctrl) H   Makes a summary of all messages (p. 566)
(Meta) (Ctrl) L *labels*   Makes a summary of the messages with a label from *labels* (p. 566)
(Meta) (Ctrl) N *labels*   Moves to the next message with a label from *labels* (p. 570)
(Meta) (Ctrl) P *labels*   Moves to the previous message with a label from *labels* (p. 570)
(Meta) (Ctrl) R *names*   Makes a summary of all messages with a recipient in *names* (p. 566)
(Meta) (Ctrl) T *topic*   Makes a summary of all messages with topic *topic* (p. 567)
– (Meta) S   Moves to the previous message matching a specified regular expression (p. 567)
n j   Moves to the *n*th message (p. 567)
.   Scrolls to the beginning of the current message (p. 567)
>   Moves to the last message (p. 567)
<   Moves to the first message (p. 567)
a *label*   Assigns the label *label* to the current message (p. 570)
b   Buries the Rmail buffer and its summary buffer (p. 566)
d   Deletes the current message (p. 567)
e   Enables editing of the current message (p. 568)
g   Merges new mail from input mailboxes (p. 569)
h   Makes a summary of all messages (p. 566)
i *file*   Runs Rmail on the messages in *file* (p. 569)
k *label*   Removes the label *label* from the current message (p. 570)
l *labels*   Makes a summary of the messages with a label from *labels* (p. 566)
n   Moves to the next nondeleted message (p. 567)
o *file*   Appends a copy of the current message in Rmail format to *file* (p. 569)
p   Moves to the previous nondeleted message (p. 567)
q   Exits from Rmail (p. 566)
s   Saves the Rmail file (p. 566)
t   Toggles the full header display (p. 568)
u   Undeletes the current message or the nearest previous deleted message (p. 567)
x   Expunges the Rmail file (p. 567)

Rmail Summary Commands.

[Del]   Scrolls the other window backward (p. 570)
[Space]   Scrolls the other window forward (p. 570)
[Meta] N   Moves to the next line and selects its message (p. 570)
[Meta] P   Moves to the previous line and selects its message (p. 570)
d   Deletes the current message, then moves to the next line containing a nondeleted message (p. 570)
j   Selects the current message (p. 570)
n   Moves to the next line containing a nondeleted message and selects its message (p. 570)
p   Moves to the previous line containing a nondeleted message and selects its message (p. 570)
q   Exits from Rmail (p. 571)
u   Undeletes and selects this message or the nearest previous deleted message (p. 570)
x   Kills the summary window (p. 571)

Calendar Commands.

[Down]   Moves the selected date a week forward (p. 573).
[Left]   Moves the selected date a day backward (p. 573).
[Right]   Moves the selected date a day forward (p. 573).
[Up]   Moves the selected date a week backward (p. 573).
[Ctrl] A   Sets the selected date to the start of the week (p. 573).
[Ctrl] B   Moves the selected date a day backward (p. 573).
[Ctrl] C [Ctrl] L   Regenerates the calendar window (p. 575).
[Ctrl] E   Sets the selected date to the end of the week (p. 573).
[Ctrl] F   Moves the selected date a day forward (p. 573).
[Ctrl] N   Moves the selected date a week forward (p. 573).
[Ctrl] P   Moves the selected date a week backward (p. 573).
[Ctrl] X [Moves the selected date a year backward (p. 573).
[Ctrl] X]   Moves the selected date a year forward (p. 573).
[Meta] <   Sets the selected date to the start of the year (p. 573).
[Meta] =   Displays the number of days in the current region (p. 575).
[Meta] >   Sets the selected date to the end of the year (p. 573).
[Meta] A   Sets the selected date to the start of the month (p. 573).
[Meta] E   Sets the selected date to the end of the month (p. 573).
[Meta] X diary   Displays all diary entries for today (p. 576).
[Meta] X holidays   Displays all holidays occurring in a three-month window around today's date (p. 574).
[Meta] X phases-of-moon   Displays quarters of the moon within the three-month period around today's date (p. 574).
[Meta] X print-diary-entries   Sends the contents of the Diary window to the printer (p. 576).
[Meta] X sunrise-sunset   Displays sunrise and sunset times for today (p. 574).
[Meta] {   Moves the selected date a month backward (p. 573).
[Meta] }   Moves the selected date a month forward (p. 573).
[Space]   Scrolls the next window (p. 575).
.   Moves the selected date to today's date (p. 573).
a   Displays all holidays occurring in the displayed three months (p. 574).
d   Displays all diary entries for the selected date (p. 576).
g d   Moves the selected date to a specified date (p. 573).
h   Displays any holidays that occur on the selected date (p. 574).
i c   Adds a cyclic diary entry starting at the selected date (p. 577).
i a   Adds an anniversary diary entry for the current region (p. 577).
i b   Adds a block diary entry for the current region (p. 577).
i d   Adds a diary entry for days of the year corresponding to the selected date (p. 577).
i d   Adds a diary entry for the selected date (p. 577).
i m   Adds a diary entry for days of the month corresponding to the selected date (p. 577).
i w   Adds a diary entry for weekdays corresponding to the selected date (p. 577).
m   Marks all visible dates that have diary entries (p. 576).
M   Displays quarters of the moon within the three-month period in the window (p. 574).

o   Centers the calendar around a specified month (p. 573).
p d   Displays the number of days elapsed since the start of the year (p. 575).
q   Exits from the calendar (p. 575).
s   Displays the entire diary (p. 576).
S   Displays sunrise and sunset times for the selected date (p. 574).
u   Removes all diary and holiday marks (p. 574, p. 576).
x   Visibly marks each day in the calendar window that is a holiday (p. 574).

GNUS Newsreader Commands.

[Del]   Moves to the nearest previous newsgroup containing unread articles, or scrolls the article backwards (p. 572).
[Ctrl] C [Ctrl] S [Ctrl] A   Sorts articles by author (p. 572).
[Ctrl] C [Ctrl] S [Ctrl] D   Sorts articles by date (p. 572).
[Ctrl] C [Ctrl] S [Ctrl] N   Sorts articles by number (p. 572).
[Ctrl] C [Ctrl] S [Ctrl] S   Sorts articles by subject (p. 572).
[Ctrl] K   Kills the newsgroup on the current line (p. 571).
[Ctrl] N   Moves to the next item whether or not you've read it (p. 572).
[Ctrl] P   Moves to the previous item whether or not you've read it (p. 572).
[Meta] [Ctrl] N   Reads the next article having the same subject as the current article (p. 572).
[Meta] [Ctrl] P   Reads the previous article having the same subject as the current article (p. 572).
[Space]   Selects the newsgroup on the current line or scrolls through all unread articles in a newsgroup (p. 571).
L   Lists all available newsgroups (p. 571).
l   Lists only newsgroups to which you subscribe that contain unread articles (p. 571).
n   Moves to the next unread newsgroup or selects the next unread article (p. 572).
p   Moves to the previous unread newsgroup or selects the previous unread article (p. 572).
q   Exits from GNUS or from the current newsgroup (p. 571).
s   Does an incremental search of the current text in the Article buffer (p. 572).
u   Toggles the subscribed/unsubscribed status of the newsgroup on the current line (p. 571).
z   Suspends GNUS (p. 571).

A.2.37
env (Set Environment for Command Invocation)

The form of the **env** command line (p. 326) is

env [-i] [*name=value*] ... [*cmd* [*arg* ...]]

In the obsolescent form, the -i is written as '-'. The specified environment variables are set to the indicated values and the utility *cmd* is executed in the resulting environment.

Command-Line Option.

-i   Ignore the inherited environment (p. 326)

A.2.38
ex (Extended Editor)

The form of the command line (p. 442) is

ex [-rR] [-s | -v] [-c *cmd*] [-t *tag*] [-w *size*] [*file*...]

An obsolescent form uses '-' in place of -s and '+*cmd*' in place of '-c *cmd*'.

Command-Line Options.

-c *cmd*   Execute *cmd* before editing (p. 443)
-s   Configure **ex** for batch use (p. 442)
-v   Invoke the visual editor **vi** (p. 442)
-t *tag*   Edit the file containing *tag* (p. 442)
-r *file*   Recover from file *file* (p. 443)
-R   Edit in read-only mode (p. 443)
-w *size*   Set **window**, the default screenful size, to *size* (p. 443)

Line Addresses and Line Ranges.   The notations for specifying a line address are as follows:

$ The last line of the file (p. 445)
. The current line (p. 445)
n The *n*th line of the file (p. 445)
'*c* The line marked with the letter *c* (p. 445)
' ' The line you most recently went to with a non-relative move (p. 445)
/*pat*/ The next line containing the pattern *pat* (p. 445)
?*pat*? The nearest previous line containing the pattern *pat* (p. 445)
[*a*]*n* The address *a* plus *n* lines (p. 445)
[*a*]+[*n*] The address *a* plus *n* lines (p. 445)
[*a*]-[*n*] The address *a* minus *n* lines (p. 445)

The notations for specifying a line range are as follows:

a_1,a_2 Lines a_1 through a_2 (p. 445)
$a_1;a_2$ Like the previous form, but the current line is set to a_1 before a_2 is evaluated (p. 446)
% The entire file (p. 446)

Flags on Commands.

\# Show the last affected line with a line number (p. 446)
- Decrease the line number by 1 before showing a line (p. 446)
+ Increase the line number by 1 before showing a line (p. 446)
l Show the last affected line, showing tabs and end-of-line explicitly (p. 446)
p Show (print) the last affected line (p. 446)

Commands.   The text before the brackets indicates the shortest recognized abbreviation. A line address is indicated by *a* and a line range by *r*. A count is indicated by *n*.

r [*flags*]   Shows the lines in range *r* (p. 448)
%   Begins a comment.
[CR]   Shows the next line (p. 448)
a [Ctrl] D   Shows a window of lines starting at line *a* (p. 448)
[*r*] & [*opts*] [*n*] [*flags*]   Repeats the most recent substitution command (p. 452)
@ *buf*   Executes the commands in named buffer *buf* (p. 458)
[*r*] ! *cmd*   Executes the command *cmd* in a subshell, inserts its output just after *a* (p. 457)
! !   Re-executes the most recently executed shell escape (p. 457)
[*a*]=   Shows the address of the line at *a* (p. 449)
[*r*] > [*n*] [*flags*]   Shifts the lines in region *r* right by one tab (p. 450)
\#   Shows lines with line numbers (p. 448)
[*r*] < [*n*] [*flags*]   Shifts the lines in region *r* left by one tab (p. 450)
* *buf*   Executes the commands in named buffer *buf* (p. 458)
[*r*] ~ [*opts*] [*n*] [*flags*]   Repeats the most recent substitution command with the most recently used regular expression (p. 452)
ab[breviate] *lhs rhs*   Makes *lhs* an abbreviation for *rhs* (p. 456)
[*a*] a[ppend][!]   Appends input text after line *a* (p. 449)
ar[gs]   Shows the arguments that were on the command line (p. 449)
[*r*] c[hange][!][*n*]   Deletes the lines in range *r*, then inserts input text (p. 451)
cd[!]   Changes the current directory to *dir* (p. 454)
chd[ir][!]   Changes the current directory to *dir* (p. 454)
[*r*]co[py] *a* [*flags*]   Copies the lines in range *r* to address *a* (p. 450)
[*r*] d[elete][*buf*][*n*][*flags*]   Deletes the lines in range *r*, saving them to an anonymous or named buffer (p. 449)
e[dit][!] [+*line*] *file*   Starts editing *file* at line *line*, discards the current buffer (p. 452)
ex[!] [+*line*] *file*   Starts editing *file* at line *line*, discards the current buffer (p. 452)
f[ile] *file*   Changes the name of the current file to *file* (p. 454)
[*r*] g[lobal]/*pat*/*commands*   Performs *commands* globally for those lines matching *pat* (p. 456)
[*a*] i[nsert][!]   Inserts input text after line *a* (p. 449)
[*r*] j[oin][!][*n*]   Joins the lines in *r* (p. 450)

[*a*] k *c*   Marks the line at *a* with the letter *c* (p. 452)

[*r*] l[ist] [*n*] [*flags*]   Shows a group of lines, showing tabs and end-of-line explicitly (p. 448)

map[!] [*lhs rhs*] (Enter)   Defines a macro; that is, maps a sequence of keystrokes into another sequence (p. 434)

[*a*] ma[rk] *c*   Marks the line at *a* with the letter *c* (p. 452)

[*r*] m[ove] [*a*]   Moves a group of lines to the location after *a* (p. 450)

n[ext][!] [+*cmd*] [*files*]   Edits the next file, optionally replacing the argument list with *files* and executing *cmd* (p. 454)

[*r*] nu[mber] [*n*] [*flags*]   Shows a group of lines with line numbers (p. 448)

[*line*] o [pen] [*pat*] [*flags*]   Enters open mode at the current line or at the next line matching *pat* (p. 458)

pre[serve] Saves copy of buffer to "preserve" area (p. 457)

[*r*] p[rint] [*n*] [*flags*]   Shows a group of lines (p. 448)

[*a*] pu[t][*buf*]   Puts the lines from the anonymous buffer or from a named buffer after address *a* in the main buffer (p. 451)

q[uit][!]   Quits the editor without writing the buffer (p. 455)

[*a*] r[ead] *file*   Reads *file* into buffer after line *a* (p. 453)

[*a*] r[ead] ! *cmd*   Puts output of *cmd* into buffer after line *a* (p. 457)

rec[over] *file*   Recovers ex from *file* after a crash (p. 457)

rew[ind]   Resets list of files to be edited to its beginning (p. 454)

[*r*] s [/*pat*/*repl*/ [*opts*] [*n*] [*flags*]]   Replaces the pattern *pat* by the text *repl* (p. 455)

se[t]   Lists all variables and their values (p. 455)

se[t] *x*[=*val*]   Enables variable *x*, sets its value to *val* (p. 455)

se[t] no*x*   Disables variable *x* (p. 455)

sh[ell]   Runs a subshell, then returns to the editor (p. 457)

so[urce]\ *file*   Reads and executes the lines in *file* (p. 458)

st[op][!]   Stops the editor, suspends its process (p. 455)

su[spend][!]   Stops the editor, suspends its process (p. 455)

[*r*]t *a*   Copies the lines in range *r* to address *a* (p. 450)

ta[g][!] *tag*   Opens the tag file containing *tag*, moves the cursor to *tag* (p. 453)

una[breviate] *lhs*   Removes an abbreviation (p. 456)

u[ndo]   Undoes the most recent change or insertion (p. 458)

unm[ap][!] *lhs*   Removes a macro definition (p. 435)

[*r*] v/*pat*/*commands*   Performs *commands* globally for those lines *not* matching *pat* (p. 457)

ve[rsion]   Show the editor's version number (p. 449)

[*line*] vi[sual] [*type*] [*n*] [*flags*]   Enters "visual mode" (p. 457)

[*r*] w[rite][!] [>>] *file*   Writes the lines in region *r* to *file* or appends them (p. 453)

[*r*] w[rite] ! *cmd*   Executes *cmd* as shell command, *r* is input (p. 457)

wq[!][>>][*file*]   Writes the buffer to *file*, then quits (p. 454)

x[it][!][*file*]   Exits from the editor, writes the buffer to *file* if it's been modified (p. 455)

[*r*] ya[nk][*buf*][*n*]   Copies ("yanks") the lines in *r* into an anonymous or named buffer (p. 451)

[*a*] z *t n*   Shows a window of *n* lines with the line at *a* placed in the window according to *t* (+, -, ., ∧, =) (p. 448)

Variables.   Both ex and vi have the same set of variables; see "Environment Variables" on page 780 for a list of them.

A.2.39
expand (Convert Tabs to Spaces)

The form of the expand command line (p. 181) is

    expand [-t *tablist*] [*file* . . .]

An obsolescent form is

    expand [-*tab₁*, *tab₂*, . . . , *tabₙ*] [*file* . . .]

The files are transformed by replacing each tab character by an appropriate number of spaces.

Command-Line Options.

-t *tablist*   Assume tab stops at positions given by *tablist* (or at multiples of *tablist* if *tablist* is just a single number) (p. 183)

**A.2.40
expr (Evaluate an
Expression)**

The form of the `expr` command line (p. 286) is

>   `expr` *expr*

where *expr* is composed from the following operators:

>   `&   |   =   !=   >   >=   <   <=`
>   `+   -   *   /   %   :   ( ... )`

The `:` operator denotes matching of a string by a regular expression.

**A.2.41
false (Return False)**

The form of the `false` command line (p. 335) is

>   `false`

It does nothing and returns a nonzero exit code.

**A.2.42
fc (Processing the
Command History
with `fc`)**

The forms of the `fc` command line (p. 361) are

>   `fc [-r] [-e` *editor*`] [`*first* `[`*last*`]]`
>   `fc -l [-nr] [`*first* `[`*last*`]]`
>   `fc -s [`*old=new*`] [`*first*`]`

Commands from the history list are listed or re-executed, possibly after being edited.

Command-Line Options.

`-e` *editor*   Use the editor *editor* to edit commands (p. 363)
`-l`   List the commands in the history list (p. 363)
`-n`   Suppress command numbers for `-l` listing (p. 363)
`-r`   Reverse the order of the commands (p. 363)
`-s`   Re-execute the command without invoking an editor (p. 363)

**A.2.43
fg (Run a Job in
Foreground)**

The form of the `fg` command line (p. 359) is

>   `fg [`*job*`]`

The specified job *job* is run in the foreground. If *job* is not specified, the most recently suspended job is run in the foreground.

**A.2.44
fgrep
(Find Regular
Expression,
Fast Version)**

This command is an obsolescent equivalent of '`grep -F`' (p. 175).

**A.2.45
file (Classify Files)**

The form of the command line (p. 128) is

>   `file [-cL] [-f` *file*`] [-m` *file*`]` *file* `...`

where *file* ... is a list of files to be classified.

Command-Line Options.

`-c` Check the magic file (p. 128)
`-f` *file* Read files to be classified from *file* (p. 128)
`-L` If a file is a symbolic link, test the file
that the link references rather than the link itself (p. 128)
`-m` *file* Use *file* as the magic file (p. 128)

A.2.46
`find` **(Find Files)**

The form of the command line (p. 121) is

> `find` *pathlist* [*criterion*]

where *pathlist* specifies a set of files and directories to be searched recursively and *criterion* specifies tests applied to each file in the set. If *criterion* is absent, it is taken to be `-print`.

Components of the Criterion. A numerical value *n* in a criterion is interpreted as follows:

- *n* by itself indicates exactly the value *n*
- `-`*n* indicates a value less than *n*
- `+`*n* indicates a value greater than *n*

`\(` Begin grouped criterion (p. 126)
`\)` End grouped criterion (p. 126)
`!` Negate criterion (p. 126)
`-a` Take logical "and" of criteria (p. 127)
`-atime` *n* True if the current file was accessed within the past *n* days (p. 124)
`-cpio` *archive* Always true; adds the current file to a `cpio`-format archive in *archive* (p. 125)
`-ctime` *n* True if the i-node information of the current file was modified within the past *n* days (p. 124)
`-depth` Always true; processes directory entries before the directory itself (p. 125)
`-exec` *cmd* Execute *cmd*, return true if the exit status is 0 (p. 124)
`-follow` Always true; cause symbolic links to be followed (p. 126)
`-group` *gname* True if *gname* is the group of the current file (p. 123)
`-inum` *n* True if the current file starts with i-node *n* (p. 124)
`-links` *n* True if the current file has *n* links (p. 123)
`-local` True if the current file resides on the local system (p. 124)
`-mount` Always true; restricts the search to the file system containing the current pathname from *pathlist* (p. 126)
`-mtime` *n* True if the current file was modified within the past *n* days (p. 124)
`-name` *file* True if the current file matches *file* (p. 122)
`-newer` *file* True if the current file has been modified more recently than *file* (p. 124)
`-nogroup` True if the current file belongs to a group not listed in the `/etc/group` file (p. 126)
`-nouser` True if the current file belongs to a user not listed in the `/etc/user` file (p. 126)
`-o` Take logical "or" of criteria (p. 127)
`-ok` *cmd* Like `-exec` but ask for confirmation (p. 125)
`-perm` [`-`] *mode* True if the permissions of the current file agree with the permissions calculated from *mode* (p. 123)
`-perm` [`-`] *octnum* True if the permissions of the current file agree with the permissions specified by the octal number *octnum* (p. 123)
`-print` Always true, send file name to standard output (p. 125)
`-prune` Prevent `find` from looking at members of a directory (p. 126)
`-size` *n* True if the current file is *n* blocks long (p. 124)
`-size` *n*c True if the current file is *n* characters long (p. 124)
`-type` *c* True if the type of the current file is *c*, where *c* is `-`, `b`, `c`, `d`, `f`, `l`, `p`, or `s` (p. 122)
`-user` *uname* True if *uname* is the owner of the current file (p. 123)
`-xdev` Always true; restricts the search to the file system containing the current pathname from *pathlist* (p. 126)

A.2.47
finger
(Look Up Information About a User)

The form of the `finger` command line (p. 230) is

> `finger` [`-lmps`] [*name...*]

where each *name* is a case-insensitive substring of the name of a user.

Command-Line Options.

`-l` Use long output format (p. 232)
`-m` Match arguments against exact user names (p. 232)
`-p` Don't show `.plan` files (p. 232)
`-s` Force short output format (p. 232)

A.2.48
fold (Fold Input Lines)

The form of the `fold` command line (p. 181) is

> `fold` [`-bs`] [`-w` *width*] [*file ...*]

Lines are read from the input files and folded so as to have a maximum length.

Command-Line Options.

`-b` Count column positions in bytes rather than characters (p. 181)
`-s` Break line at last whitespace before *width* columns (or bytes) (p. 181)
`-w` *width* Take *width* as the maximum line length (p. 181)

A.2.49
ftp (Transfer Files with File Transfer Protocol)

The form of the `ftp` command line (p. 643) is

> `ftp` [`-dgintv`] [*host*]

If *host* is specified, `ftp` immediately attempts to connect to that host.

Command-Line Options.

`-d` Enable debugging (p. 657)
`-g` Disable wildcard substitution (globbing) in file names (p. 657)
`-i` Turn off interactive prompting during multiple file transfers (p. 657)
`-n` Don't do auto-login on initial connection (p. 658)
`-t` Enable packet tracing (unimplemented) (p. 658)
`-v` Show responses from remote server and statistics (p. 658)

Commands.

`EOF` Terminates `ftp` (p. 644)
`!` [*cmd*] Runs *cmd* locally in a subshell (p. 653)
`$` *mac* [*arg...*] Executes macro *mac* with arguments *arg ...* (p. 655)
`?` [*cmd*] Provides help information on *cmd* (p. 645)
`ac`[`count`] [*passwd*] Supplies a supplemental remote password (p. 644)
`ap`[`pend`] *lfile* [*rfile*] Appends local file *lfile* to remote file *rfile* (p. 649)
`as`[`cii`] Uses network ASCII as the representation type (p. 652)
`be`[`ll`] Sounds a bell after each file transfer (p. 653)
`bi`[`nary`] Uses image as the representation type (p. 652)
`by`[`e`] Terminates `ftp` (p. 644)
`ca`[`se`] Toggles case-mapping for remote file names (p. 650)
`cd` *rdir* Changes the remote directory to *rdir* (p. 646)
`cdu`[`p`] Changes the remote directory to its parent (p. 646)
`ch`[`mod`] *mode rfile* Changes the permissions of remote file *rfile* to *mode* (p. 647)
`cl`[`ose`] Terminates the remote connection but remains in `ftp` (p. 645)
`cr` Toggles stripping of carriage returns for ASCII file transfers (p. 652)
`del`[`ete`] *rfile* Deletes remote file *rfile* (p. 646)
`deb`[`ug`] [*n*] Sets the debugging level to *n* or toggle debugging (p. 654)
`dir` [*rdir* [*lfile*]] Sends listing of remote directory *rdir* to local file *lfile* (p. 647)
`dis`[`connect`] Terminates the remote connection, remains in `ftp` (p. 645)
`f`[`orm`] [*fmt*] Uses 'non-print' for interpreting vertical format controls (p. 652)

ge[t] *rfile* [*lfile*]   Retrieves remote file *rfile*, stores it in local file *lfile* (p. 648)

gl[ob]   Toggles wildcard expansion, called "globbing", for file names (p. 649)

ha[sh]   Toggles use of '#' to indicate when a data block is transferred (p. 653)

he[lp] [*cmd*]   Provides help information on *cmd* (p. 645)

id[le] [*n*]   Sets the inactivity timer of the remote machine to *n* seconds (p. 645)

im[age]   Uses image as the representation type (p. 652)

lc[d] [*dir*]   Changes the current local directory to *dir* (p. 653)

ls [*rdir* [*lfile*]]   Sends short listing of remote directory *rdir* to local file *lfile* (p. 647)

ma[cdef] *mac*   Defines a macro named *mac* (p. 654)

mde[lete] [*rfile...*]   Deletes the remote file *rfile ...* (p. 646)

mdi[r] *rfile ... lfile*   Sends listing of remote files *rfile ...* to *lfile* (p. 647)

mg[et] *rfile ...*   Gets the specified remote files (p. 648)

mk[dir] *dir*   Makes directory *dir* on the remote machine (p. 646)

ml[s] *rfile ... lfile*   Sends short listing of specified remote files to local file *lfile* (p. 647)

mode [*name*]   Sets the transfer mode to *name* (p. 652)

modt[ime] *rfile*   Shows the time when remote file *rfile* was last modified (p. 647)

mp[ut] *lfile ...*   Transmits the specified local files to the remote machine (p. 649)

ne[wer] *rfile* [*lfile*]   Retrieves remote file *rfile* and copies it to *lfile*, but only if it's newer (p. 648)

nl[ist] [*rdir* [*lfile*]]   Sends listing of remote directory *rdir* to local file *lfile* (p. 647)

nm[ap] *inpat outpat*   Maps file names according to *inpat* and *outpat* (p. 650)

nt[rans] [*inchars* [*outchars*]]   Sets translation for characters in file names (p. 650)

o[pen] *host* [*port*]   Connects to *host* at the specified port or the default port (p. 644)

prom[pt]   Toggles interactive prompting during multiple file transfers (p. 653)

prox[y] *cmd*   Executes *cmd* on a remote machine (p. 654)

pu[t] *lfile* [*rfile*]   Transmits local file *lfile* to the remote machine (p. 649)

pw[d]   Shows the name of the working directory on the remote machine (p. 646)

qui[t]   Terminates `ftp` (p. 644)

quo[te] *arg ...*   Sends the specified arguments to the remote machine (p. 645)

rec[v] *rfile* [*lfile*]   Retrieves remote file *rfile*, stores it in local file *lfile* (p. 648)

reg[et] *rfile* [*lfile*]   Retrieves remote file *rfile*, but only if it's longer than the corresponding local file (p. 648)

remoteh[elp] [*cmd*]   Requests help information on *cmd* from the remote machine (p. 646)

remotes[tatus] [*rfile*]   Shows the current status of remote file *rfile* or of the remote machine (p. 653)

ren[ame] *name₁ name₂*   Renames file *name₁* on the remote machine to *name₂* (p. 646)

rese[t]   Resynchronizes communication with the remote machine (p. 645)

rest[art] *marker*   Restarts the immediately following `get` or `put` at the position given by *marker* (p. 645)

rm[dir] *dir*   Deletes directory *dir* on the remote machine.

ru[nique]   Toggles creation of unique names for files gotten from the remote machine (p. 651)

send *lfile* [*rfile*]   Transmits local file *lfile* to the remote machine (p. 649)

sendp[ort]   Toggles the use of PORT commands (p. 645)

sit[e] *arg ...*   Sends the command SITE *arg ...* to the remote machine (p. 645)

siz[e] *rfile*   Shows the size of remote file *rfile* (p. 647)

sta[tus]   Shows the current status of `ftp` (p. 653)

str[uct] [*name*]   Sets the file structure to *name* (p. 652)

su[nique]   Toggles generation of unique names for files sent to the remote machine (p. 651)

sy[stem]   Shows the type of operating system running on the remote machine (p. 653)

te[nex]   Uses the representation type appropriate to TENEX machines (p. 652)

tr[ace]   Toggles packet tracing (unimplemented) (p. 654)

ty[pe] [*name*]   Uses *name* as the representation type (p. 652)

um[ask] [*mask*]   Sets the default file permission mask on the remote machine to *mask* (p. 647)

us[er] *usrname* [*passwd₁* [*passwd₂*]]   Identifies yourself to the remote machine (p. 644)

v[erbose]   Toggles verbose mode for showing `ftp` responses (p. 654)

**A.2.50
getconf (Get
Configuration Values)**

The forms of the `getconf` command line (p. 291) are

    `getconf` *sysvar*
    `getconf` *pathvar pathname*

Information about configuration values for your version of UNIX is produced on standard output.

**A.2.51
grep
(Find Regular
Expression)**

The forms of the `grep` command line are (p. 175)

    `grep` [`-E` | `-F`] [`-c` | `-l` | `-q`] [`-insvx`] `-e` *patlist* ...
      [`-f` *patfile*] ... [*file* ...]
    `grep` [`-E` | `-F`] [`-c` | `-l` | `-q`] [`-insvx`] [`-e` *patlist*] ...
      `-f` *patfile* ... [*file* ...]
    `grep` [`-E` | `-F`] [`-c` | `-l` | `-q`] *patlist* [*file* ...]

The obsolescent commands `egrep` and `fgrep` are equivalent to '`grep -E`' and '`grep -F`', respectively. In these forms, *patlist* is a list of patterns to be searched for, *patfile* is a file containing a list of patterns, and *file* ... is a list of files to be searched. The default form of pattern is a basic regular expression.

Command-Line Options.

`-b` Precede each line by its disk block number (p. 176)
`-c` Only show a count of matching lines (p. 176)
`-E` Assume patterns are extended regular expressions (p. 177)
`-F` Assume patterns are fixed strings (p. 176)
`-i` Ignore case of letters in making comparisons (p. 177)
`-l` Only show the names of files containing matching strings (p. 176)
`-n` Precede each line by its file name and line number (p. 176)
`-q` Run quietly, producing no output (p. 176)
`-s` Show only error messages (p. 176)
`-v` Show all lines that *don't* match (p. 177)
`-w` Search for the pattern as a word (p. 177)
`-x` Accept a match only if the pattern matches the entire line (p. 177)

**A.2.52
gunzip (Expand
Zip-Encoded Files)**

The form of the `gunzip` command line (p. 141) is

    `gunzip` [`-cfhlLnNrtvV`] [`-S` *suffix*] [*name* ...]

The files designated by *name* ... , with assumed extensions `.gz`, `-gz`, `.z`, `-z`, `_z`, or `.Z`, are expanded.

Command-Line Options.

`-c` Send output to standard output (p. 142)
`-f` Force decompression even if it causes overwriting (p. 142)
`-h` Display a help screen and quit (p. 142)
`-l` List information about compressed files (p. 142)
`-L` Display the GNU license (p. 143)
`-n` Don't restore original pathname and timestamp (p. 142)
`-N` Restore original pathname and timestamp (p. 142)
`-r` Traverse the directory structure recursively (p. 142)
`-S` *suffix* Use *suffix* in place of `.gz` (p. 142)
`-t` Test the compressed file for integrity (p. 142)
`-v` Display name and percentage reduction for each file (p. 142)
`-V` Display the version number and compilation options (p. 143)

**A.2.53
gzcat (Expand and
Concatenate
Zip-Encoded Files)**

The form of the `gzcat` command line (p. 141) is

    `gzcat` [`-fhLV`] [*name* ...]

The files designated by *name* ... , with assumed extensions `.gz`, `-gz`, `.z`, `-z`, `_z`, or `.Z`, are expanded and concatenated. This command is often provided under the name `zcat`.

Command-Line Options.

`-f` Force expansion even if it causes overwriting (p. 142)
`-h` Display a help screen and quit (p. 142)

-L   Display the GNU license (p. 143)
-V   Display the version number and compilation options (p. 143)

A.2.54
gzip (Compress Files Using Zip Encoding)

The form of the gzip command line (p. 141) is

gzip [-cdfhlLnNrtvV] [*digit*] [-S *suffix*] [*name* ...]

The files designated by *name* ... are compressed using Lempel-Ziv coding.

Command-Line Options.

digit   Favor speed (1) or compactness (9) (p. 142)
-c   Send output to standard output (p. 142)
-d   Do decompression rather than compression (p. 142)
-f   Force compression even if it causes overwriting (p. 142)
-h   Display a help screen and quit (p. 142)
-l   List information about compressed files (with -d only) (p. 142)
-L   Display the GNU license (p. 143)
-n   Don't save original pathname and timestamp (p. 142)
-N   Save original pathname and timestamp (p. 142)
-r   Traverse the directory structure recursively (p. 142)
-t   Test the compressed file for integrity (with -d only) (p. 142)
-S *suffix*   Use *suffix* in place of .gz (p. 142)
-v   Display name and percentage reduction for each file (p. 142)
-V   Display the version number and compilation options (p. 143)

A.2.55
halt (Shut Down the System and Halt)

The form of the halt command line (p. 705) is

halt [-t *sec*] [-nq]

Command-Line Options.

-t *sec*   Allow *sec* seconds before sending SIGKILL (p. 705)
-n   Don't synchronize the file systems before shutting down
-q   Send SIGKILL immediately, without warning

A.2.56
head (Copy Beginning of Files)

The form of the head command line (p. 184) is

head [-n *num*] [*files* ...]

The first *num* lines (default is 10) of each of *files* ... are copied to standard output. In an obsolescent form of the command, the -n is omitted.

Command-Line Option.

-n *num*   Copy *num* lines from each file (p. 184)

A.2.57
id (Show User and Group IDs)

The forms of the id command line (p. 255) are

id [*user*]
id -G [-n] [*user*]
id -g [-nr] [*user*]
id -u [-nr] [*user*]

User and group information about the invoking process is produced, or about *user* if *user* has been specified.

Command-Line Options.

-G   Produce real, effective, and supplementary IDs (p. 255)
-g   Produce only the effective group ID (p. 255)
-n   Produce the user or group name, not the number (p. 255)
-r   Produce the real ID, not the effective one (p. 255)
-u   Produce only the effective user ID (p. 255)

A.2.58
jobs (Show Job Status)

The form of the jobs command line (p. 360) is

    jobs [-l | -p] [*job* ...]

The status of all jobs, or of the jobs *job* ... , is shown.

Command-Line Options.

-l   Provide more information about each job (p. 360)
-p   Display only the process IDs for the process group leaders of each job (p. 360)

A.2.59
join (Database Join on Two Files)

The form of the join command line (p. 190) is

    join [-a *fnum* | -v *fnum*] [-e *str*] [-o *list*] [-t *char*]
         [-1 *fdnum*] [-2 *fdnum*] *file₁ file₂*

An obsolescent form is

    join [-a *fnum*] [-e *str*] [-j *fdnum*] [-j1 *fdnum*] [-j2 *fdnum*]
         [-o *list* ...] [-t *char*] *file₁ file₂*

A database join is performed on *file₁* and *file₂*. The obsolescent options -j1 and -j2 are equivalent to -1 and -2, respectively; -j is equivalent to both of them together.

Command-Line Options.

-1 *field*   Join on field *fdnum* of file 1 (p. 191)
-2 *field*   Join on field *fdnum* of file 2 (p. 191)
-a *fnum*   Produce a line for each unpairable line in file *fnum* (p. 191)
-e *str*   Replace empty output fields with *str* (p. 191)
-o *list*   Construct output line from fields in *list* (p. 191)
-t *char*   Use *char* as field separator for both input and output (p. 191)
-v *fnum*   Produce lines only for unpairable lines in file *fnum* (p. 191)

A.2.60
kill (Signal a Process)

The POSIX forms of the kill command are (p. 242)

    kill -s *signame pid* ...
    kill -l [*signum*]

Two obsolescent forms are also recognized:

    kill [-*signame*] *pid* ...
    kill [-*signum*] *pid* ...

The signal designated by the symbolic name *signame* or by the signal number *signum* is sent to the processes numbered *pid* ... .

Command-Line Options.

-l   Produce the name of *signum*, or all signal names (p. 242)
-s   Send signal *signame* to process *pid* (p. 242)

A.2.61
ksh (The KornShell)

The form of the ksh command line (p. 317) is

    ksh [{+|-}Caefhimnoprstuvx] [{+|-}o *option*] ...
        [-c *cmds*] [*arg* ...]

where the options *options* are the single-letter execution-time options described next (turned on by -, turned off by +) and *arg* ... are positional parameters.

Execution Options. The following options can appear in a `set` command. If no letter is shown for an option, it can only be specified with `-o` and cannot be given on the command line.

`allexport` (a)   Automatically export modified or created variables (p. 375)
`bgnice`   Run all background jobs at lower priority (p. 375)
`emacs`   Use `emacs` as the command-line editor (p. 375)
`errexit` (e)   Exit `ksh` on nonzero exit status of command (p. 374)
`f`   *See* `noglob`.
`gmacs`   Use `gmacs` variant of `emacs` as the command-line editor (p. 375)
`h`   *See* `trackall`.
`ignoreeof`   Don't exit the shell when $\boxed{\text{EOF}}$ typed (p. 376)
`markdirs`   Append a trailing slash to directory names (p. 375)
`monitor` (m)   Run background jobs in a separate process group (p. 374)
`noclobber` (C)   Don't overwrite files with output redirected by `>` (p. 376)
`noexec` (n)   Don't execute commands, just read them (p. 375)
`noglob` (f)   Turn off the pattern expansion of pathnames (p. 375)
`s`   Sort the arguments (p. 376)
`t`   Exit `ksh` after executing just one command list (p. 374)
`nolog`   Don't store function definitions in history file (p. 376)
`nounset` (u)   Treat unset variables as erroneous (p. 375)
`privileged` (p)   Restore effective user/group IDs to values at time of invocation (p. 375)
`trackall` (h)   Make tracked aliases when possible (p. 375)
`verbose` (v)   Show each input line as it is read (p. 375)
`vi`   Use `vi` as the command-line editor (p. 376)
`viraw`   Always use character input for `vi` built-in editor (p. 376)
`xtrace` (x)   Show each simple command and its arguments as it is executed (p. 375)

The following options can only be given on the command line:

`-c` *cmds*   Use *string* as input to `ksh` (p. 317)
`-i`   Expect interactive input (p. 318)
`-r`   Make this shell restricted (p. 318)
`-s`   Read input from standard input, write output to standard error (p. 318)

Operators.

c`&`   Executes c in the background, then continues (p. 327)
c_1 `&&` c_2 Executes c_1, then c_2 if the exit status of c_1 is zero (p. 327)
c_1 `|` c_2 Connects the standard output of c_1 to the standard input of c_2 through a pipe (p. 326)
`!`c_1 `|` c_2 `|` ... `|` c_k Makes the exit status of the entire pipeline be the negation of c_k (p. 328)
c`|&`   Executes c in the background, but with its standard input and standard output connected to the `ksh` coprocess (p. 327)
c_1 `||` c_2 Executes c_1, then c_2 if the exit status of c_1 is nonzero (p. 327)
c`;`   Executes c and waits for it to finish, then continues (p. 327)

Attributes of Variables.

`i`[*base*]   Convert the retrieved value to a base *base* integer (default 10) (p. 347)
`l`   Convert the retrieved value to lowercase (p. 347)
`L`[*width*]   Left-justify the retrieved value within a field of size *width* (p. 347)
`LZ`[*width*]   Left-justify the retrieved value within a field of size *width*, stripping leading zeroes (p. 347)
`r`   Make the variable read-only (p. 348)
`R`[*width*]   Right-justify the retrieved value within a field of size *width* (p. 347)
`[R]Z`[*width*]   Right-justify the retrieved value within a field of size *width*, replacing leading spaces by zeroes (p. 347)
`t`   Tag this variable (p. 348)
`u`   Convert the retrieved value to uppercase (p. 347)
`x`   Export the value of this variable (p. 348)

Attributes of Functions.

t   Turn tracing (`xtrace` attribute) on or off (p. 325)
u   Autoload this function on first use (p. 325)
x   Export this function to directly executed shell scripts (p. 325)

Patterns for Pathname Expansion.

[...]   A single character matching a bracket expression (p. 322)
?   An arbitrary single character (p. 322)
*   (p. 322) An arbitrary, possibly empty sequence of characters.
@(*pat*[|*pat* ...])   A single occurrence of one of the patterns *pat* (p. 322)
!(*pat*[|*pat* ...])   Any string not matched by one of the patterns *pat* (p. 322)
+(*pat*[|*pat* ...])   One or more occurrences of any of the patterns *pat* (p. 322)
?(*pat*[|*pat* ...])   Zero or one occurrence of any of the patterns *pat* (p. 322)
*(*pat*[|*pat* ...])   Zero or more occurrences of any of the patterns *pat* (p. 322)

Parameter Expansions.

$*param*   Substitutes value of $*param* (p. 350)
${*param*}   Substitutes value of $*param* (p. 350)
${#*param*}   Substitutes the length of $*param* (p. 352)
${#*var*[@|*]}   Substitutes the number of elements of the array *var* that have been set (p. 352)
$*param*−*word*   Substitutes for $*param* if it exists, otherwise uses *word* (p. 350)
$*param*:−*word*   Substitutes for $*param* if its value is non-null, otherwise uses *word* (p. 350)
$*param*=*word*   Substitutes for $*param* if it exists and assigns *word* to *param*, otherwise uses *word* (p. 351)
$*param*:=*word*   Substitutes for $*param* if its value is non-null and assigns *word* to *param*, otherwise uses *word* (p. 351)
${*param*#*pat*}   Substitutes for $*param* with the smallest suffix matching *pat* deleted (p. 352)
${*param*##*pat*}   Substitutes for $*param* with the largest suffix matching *pat* deleted (p. 352)
${*param*%*pat*}   Substitutes for $*param* with the smallest prefix matching *pat* deleted (p. 352)
${*param*%%*pat*}   Substitutes for $*param* with the largest prefix matching *pat* deleted (p. 352)
$*param*+*word*   Substitutes *word* for $*param* if $*param* exists, otherwise substitutes nothing (p. 351)
$*param*+:*word*   Substitutes *word* for $*param* if $*param* is non-null, otherwise substitutes nothing (p. 351)
$*param*?[*word*]   Substitutes for $*param* if it exists and assigns *word* to *param*, otherwise issues error message *word* (p. 351)
$*param*:?[*word*]   Substitutes for $*param* if its value is non-null and assigns *word* to *param*, otherwise issues error message *word* (p. 351)

Special Parameters.

$@   Substitutes entire argument list, spaces are not quoted (p. 349)
$!   The process number of the most recent asynchronously executed command (p. 349)
$−   The flags supplied to `ksh` when it was called (p. 349)
$$ The process number of the current shell invocation (p. 349)
$#   The number of arguments, as a decimal number (p. 349)
$?   The exit code of the most recent synchronously executed command (p. 349)
$*   Substitutes entire argument list, spaces are quoted (p. 349)

Quotation and Command Substitution.

c   Quotes the character *c* (p. 352)
"*text*"   Quotes *text*, allows substitutions within it (p. 353)
'*text*'   Quotes *text*, allows no substitutions within it (p. 353)
`*text*`   Executes *text*, substitutes its standard output (p. 354)

Redirection.

< *file*   Takes standard input from *file* (p. 330)
n<&p   Takes standard input of the coprocess from file descriptor *n* (p. 331)

`<<[-]`*word*   Takes standard input from following text (p. 331)
`<>` *file*   Opens *file* for both reading and writing on file descriptor 1 (standard input) (p. 331)
`>` *file*   Sends standard output to *file* (p. 330)
`>|` *file*   Sends standard output to *file* unconditionally (p. 330)
`>>` *file*   Appends standard output to *file* (p. 331)
n`>&p`   Sends standard output of the coprocess to file descriptor *n* (p. 331)
`<&`*n*   Copies file descriptor *n* to standard input descriptor (p. 331)
`>&`*n*   Copies file descriptor *n* to standard output descriptor (p. 331)
`<&-`   Closes standard input (p. 331)
`>&-`   Closes standard output (p. 331)

These forms can be preceded by *m* to make them apply to file descriptor *m* rather than to standard input or output.

Intrinsic Commands and Predefined Aliases.   These are the `ksh` intrinsic commands and predefined aliases. Not all of them are intrinsic for a POSIX shell.

`EOF`   Exits the shell with exit status 0 (p. 363)
`[` *test* `]`   Performs the indicated test (p. 369)
`:` `[` *text* `]`   Does nothing; *text* is ignored (p. 364)
`.` *file*   Executes commands in *file* directly (p. 363)
`alias` [*name*[`=`*str*] ...]   Defines one or more aliases (p. 369)
`break` [*n*]   Breaks out of *n* enclosing loops (p. 364)
`cd` [*path*]   Changes the current directory to *path* (p. 369)
`continue` [*n*]   Restarts the *n*th enclosing loop (p. 364)
`echo` [*word...*]   Echoes the arguments (p. 369)
`eval` [*word...*]   Evaluates words, then uses their values (p. 367)
`exec` *cmd* [*arg...*]   Executes *cmd*, replacing this shell (p. 363)
`exec` *redir ...*   Uses the redirections *redir* from now on (p. 366)
`exit` [*n*]   Exits the shell with exit status *n* (p. 363)
`export` [*name*[`=`*val*] ...]   Exports named variables (p. 366)
`getopts` *text name* [*word...*]   Parses options of a command (p. 369)
`history` [`-nr`] [*first* [*last*]]   Displays the command history (p. 369)
`integer` *var*[`=`*val*]   Defines *var* as an integer variable, sets it to *val* (p. 367)
`let` *arg ...*   Evaluates *arg ...* as arithmetic expressions (p. 368)
`newgrp` [*arg...*]   Changes group identification (p. 369)
`pwd`   Shows the current (working) directory (p. 369)
`print` [`-Rnprsu` [*n*]] [*arg ...*]   Produces ("prints") arguments (p. 369)
`r` [*first* [*last*]]   Re-executes commands *first* through *last* (p. 369)
`read` [`-r`] *var ...*   Reads an input line into variables (p. 369)
`readonly` [*name*[`=`*val*] ...]   Makes named variables read-only (p. 366)
`return` [*n*]   Returns from function with exit status *n* (p. 364)
`set` [*options*] [*word...*]   Enables or disables options and sets numbered parameters (p. 367)
`shift` [*n*]   Renumbers parameters by shifting them left by *n* (p. 367)
`test` *test*   Performs the indicated test (p. 369)
`times`   Shows time usage (p. 368)
`trap` [[*cmdtext*] *signal ...*]   Associates commands with signals (p. 364)
`typeset` [*attrs*] [*name*[`=`*value*]] ...   Sets, unsets, or lists attributes, values, or definitions of variables and functions (p. 365)
`ulimit` [*n*]   Limits child processes to *n* disk blocks (p. 368)
`umask` *n*   Reduces the default permissions for file creation by subtracting *n* (p. 369)
`unalias` *name ...*   Removes one or more aliases (p. 369)
`unset` *name ...*   Deletes named variables (p. 366)
`wait` [*n*]   Waits for process *n*, or all processes, to finish (p. 368)

Compound Commands.

`{` *list*`;}`   Executes foreground commands in-line (p. 339)
`{` *list*`&}`   Executes background commands in-line (p. 339)
`(` *list* `)`   Executes commands in a subshell (p. 339)
name `() {` *list*`; }` [*redir*]   Defines a shell function (p. 340)

case *word* in *casetest* [*casetest*...] esac
where each *casetest* has the form
pattern [| *pattern*...]) *list*; ;
    Selects commands by matching a word against patterns (p. 337)

for *name* [in *word* ... ;] do *list* done
    Executes commands once for each word in a list (p. 338)

if *list* then *list* [elif *list* then *list*...]
    [else *list*] fi
    Executes commands conditionally (p. 336)

select *name* [in *word* ... ;] do *list* done
    Selects an item from a menu (p. 341)

until *list* do *list* done
    Executes commands until a command returns nonzero exit status (p. 339)

while *list* do *list* done
    Executes commands while a command returns zero exit status (p. 339)

Predefined Variables.

_   Last argument of previous simple command, etc. (p. 370)
CDPATH The sequence of directories searched by the cd command (p. 371)
COLUMNS   Number of columns on your terminal (p. 374)
EDITOR   Pathname for your editor (p. 373)
ENV   Pathname of script executed when ksh starts up (p. 373)
ERRNO   System error number (p. 370)
FCEDIT   Editor that fc uses to edit a sequence of commands (p. 373)
FPATH   Search path for autoload functions (p. 373)
HISTFILE   Pathname of history file (p. 374)
HISTSIZE   Size of history saved from previous invocation (p. 374)
HOME   Your home directory (p. 370)
IFS   The input field separators (p. 372)
LINENO   Current line within script or function (p. 370)
LINES   Number of lines on your terminal (p. 374)
MAIL   File checked for mail (p. 372)
MAILCHECK   Value of *n*, mail checked every *n* seconds (p. 373)
MAILPATH   Sequence of files checked for mail (p. 372)
OLDPWD   Previous working directory (p. 370)
OPTARG   Value of next option for getargs (p. 370)
OPTIND   Index of next option for getargs (p. 370)
PATH   The sequence of directories searched for commands (p. 371)
PPID   Process ID of this shell's parent (p. 370)
PS1   Primary command prompt (p. 371)
PS2   Secondary command prompt (p. 371)
PS3   Prompt for select command (p. 371)
PS4   Prompt for execution trace (p. 372)
RANDOM   Random integer, changes with each reference (p. 370)
REPLY   String typed in response to select (p. 370)
SECONDS   Elapsed time in seconds since ksh was invoked (p. 370)
SHELL   Location of command for child shells (p. 373)
TMOUT   Timeout period in seconds for entering commands (p. 373)
VISUAL   Pathname for your editor (p. 373)

A.2.62
ln (Link Pathnames)

The forms of the `ln` command (p. 101) are

    ln [-fs] *file pathname*
    ln [-fs] *file* ... *dir*

In the first form, a link is created from *pathname* to the file named by *file*. In the second form, a link is created from *dir* to each file in *file* ....

Command-Line Options.

-f   Force confirmation even when overwriting a link lacking write permission (p. 101)
-s   Make a symbolic link (not all systems) (p. 101)

A.2.63
locale
(Get Locale
Information)

The forms of the `locale` command (p. 296) are

```
locale [-a | -m]
locale [-ck] name ...
```

where *name* is the name of a locale category, a keyword in a locale category, or `charmap`.

Command-Line Options.

-a   Produce the names of all publicly known locales (p. 296)
-c   Include the category name in the output line (p. 296)
-k   Include the keyword name in the output line (p. 296)
-m   Produce the names of all known charmaps (p. 296)

A.2.64
localedef
(Define a New Locale)

The form of the `localedef` command (p. 297) is

```
localedef [-c] [-f charmap] [-i source] name
```

where *name* identifies a locale to be defined.

Command-Line Options.

-c   Create the locale even if there were warnings (p. 298)
-f *charmap*   Get the charmap from file *charmap* (p. 298)
-i *source*   Get the source definitions from file *source* (p. 298)

A.2.65
logger (Save Message
for Administrator)

The form of the `logger` command line (p. 295) is

```
logger string ...
```

A message derived from *string* . . . is sent to the system administrator.

A.2.66
login (Log In)

The form of the an initial login (p. 250) is

name [*var-setting. . .*]

The form of a replacement login is

`exec login` [*name* [*var-settings . . .*]]

Each *var-setting* has the form

[*name* =] *value*

A.2.67
logname (Return
User's Login Name)

The form of the `logname` command line (p. 255) is

```
logname
```

The user's login name is produced on standard output.

A.2.68
`lp`
(Send Files to a Printer)

The form of the `lp` command line (p. 114) is

> `lp` [`-cmsw`] [`-d` *dest*] [`-n` *n*] [`-t` *title*] [`-o` *prinopt*] [*file . . .*]

where each *file* is a file to be printed. Some versions of `lp` allow options and files to be intermixed.

Command-Line Options.

`-c`　Make copies of the files when the command is executed (p. 115)
`-d` *dest*　Send the job to the specific printer or class of printers named by *dest* (p. 115)
`-m`　Send a mail message when the job is completed (p. 115)
`-n` *n*　Make *n* copies of the output (p. 114)
`-o` *printopt*　Specify a printer option (p. 115)
`-s`　Suppress messages (p. 115)
`-t` *title*　Put *title* on the banner page of the output (p. 114)
`-w`　Write a message to your terminal when all files have been printed (p. 115)

A.2.69
`lpr`
(Berkeley Print Spooler)

The form of the `lpr` command line (p. 115) is

> `lpr` [`-flpsrmh`] [`-i` [*n*]] [`-T` *text*] [`-w` *n*] [`-P` *printer*]
> 　　　 [`-#`*n*] [`-J` *text*] [`-C` *text*] [*file . . .*]

where the *files* are the files to be printed.

Command-Line Options.

`-#`*n*　Print *n* copies (p. 116)
`-C` *text*　Use *text* as the system name on the header page (p. 116)
`-f`　Interpret the first character of each line as Fortran carriage control (p. 116)
`-h`　Suppress the header page (p. 116)
`-i` [*n*]　Indent the output by *n* columns (p. 116)
`-J` *text*　Use *text* as the job name on the header page (p. 116)
`-l`　Print control characters, suppress page breaks (p. 116)
`-m`　Send a mail message upon completion (p. 116)
`-p`　Pass the files through `pr` (p. 116)
`-P` *printer*　Print the job on the printer named *printer* (p. 116)
`-r`　Remove the file after printing it (p. 116)
`-s`　Use symbolic links for the files to be printed (p. 116)
`-T` *text*　Use *text* as the title passed to `pr` (p. 116)
`-w` *n*　Pass *n* to `pr` as the page width (p. 116)

In addition to these options, `lpr` has options for filtering the output of specific programs. These options depend on the installation.

A.2.70
`lpstat` **(Show Printer Status)**

The form of the `lpstat` command line (p. 117) is

> `lpstat` [`-drst`] [`-o` [*list*]] [`-u` [*list*]] [`-p` [*list*]]
> 　　　　 [`-a` [*list*]] [`-c` [*list*]] [`-v` [*list*]]

Command-Line Options.　In the following commands, *list* is a list of names of printers and classes of printers.

`-a` [*list*]　Show the acceptance status of each item in *list* (p. 117)
`-c` [*list*]　Show the names of the printer classes and their members (p. 117)
`-d`　Show the name of the default printer (p. 117)
`-o` [*list*]　Show the status of each output request in *list* (p. 117)
`-p` [*list*]　Show the status of each printer in *list* (p. 117)
`-r`　Show the status of the request scheduler (p. 117)
`-s`　Show a summary of the printers known to your system (p. 117)
`-t`　Show all status information (p. 117)
`-u` [*ulist*]　Show the status of each output request for each user in *ulist* (p. 117)
`-v` [*list*]　Show the pathnames associated with the printers in *list* (p. 118)

A.2.71
ls (File Lister)

The form of the `ls` command (p. 94) is

   `ls [-1CFRabcdfgilmnopqrstux]` [*pathname* ...]

where *pathname* ... specifies the directories and files to be listed (the current directory if no *pathname*s given).

Command-Line Options.

`-1` List exactly one file per line (p. 96)
`-a` List all files, including those whose names begin with a dot (p. 95)
`-b` Show nonprinting characters in octal (p. 97)
`-c` Use time of last i-node modification (p. 97)
`-C` Produce multicolumn output, sorted down columns (p. 96)
`-d` List directory names only, not contents (p. 95)
`-f` List files in directories, not the directories themselves (p. 95)
`-F` Put '/' after listed directories and '*' after executable files (p. 96)
`-g` List the files in long format, omitting the owner (p. 96)
`-i` For each file, print the number of its i-node (p. 96)
`-l` List the files in long format (p. 96)
`-m` List the files separated by commas (p. 96)
`-n` List the files in long format, with user and group numbers (p. 96)
`-o` List the files in long format, omitting the group (p. 96)
`-p` Put '/' after listed directories (p. 95)
`-q` Show nonprinting characters as '?' (p. 97)
`-r` List the files in reverse order (p. 96)
`-R` List subdirectories recursively (p. 95)
`-s` Give the size of each file in blocks (p. 96)
`-t` List the files in chronological order (p. 96)
`-u` Use time of last access (p. 96)
`-x` Produce multicolumn output, sorted across rows (p. 96)

A.2.72
mailx (Send and Receive Mail)

The form of the `mailx` command line for sending mail (p. 587) is

   `mailx [-FinU] [-h` *n*`] [-r` *addr*`] [-s` *string*`]` *name* ...

The form for retrieving mail (p. 587) is

   `mailx [-eHInN] [-f` *file*`] [-T` *file*`] [-u` *user*`]`

Command-Line Options. The command-line options for sending mail are as follows:

`-F` Save mail in a file named after the first recipient (p. 590)
`-i` Ignore interrupts (p. 589)
`-n` Don't initialize from `mailx.rc` (p. 591)
`-s` *string* Set message subject to *string* (p. 589)

The command-line options for retrieving mail are as follows:

`-e` Just test for presence of mail (p. 590)
`-f` *file* Read mail from *file* (p. 590)
`-h` *n* Set number of network hops so far to *n* (p. 590)
`-H` Show header summary only (p. 590)
`-I` Take message authors to be newsgroups, not individuals (p. 591)
`-n` Don't initialize from `mailx.rc` (p. 591)
`-N` Don't show initial header summary (p. 590)
`-r` *addr* Pass the address *addr* to network delivery software, disable '~' commands (p. 590)
`-T` *file* Save list of `Article-Id` fields in *file* (p. 591)
`-u` *user* Read mail from *user*'s mailbox (p. 590)
`-U` Convert `uucp` addresses to Internet addresses (p. 590)

Notation for Message Lists.

n Message number *n* (p. 592)
`^` The first message that you haven't deleted (p. 592)
`$` The last message (whether deleted or not) (p. 592)

  .   The current message (p. 592)

  *   All the messages in the message list (p. 593)

Commands for Command Mode. An optional *msglist* is taken as referring to all messages in the current message set. An optional *msg* is taken as referring to the current message.

(Enter) Shows the next message (p. 595)

n Shows message number *n* (p. 595)

!*cmd* Executes *cmd* in a subshell (p. 601)

| [[*msglist*] *cmd*] Passes the messages in *msglist* as standard input to *cmd* (p. 601)

-[*n*] Shows the *n*th previous message (p. 595)

. Shows the current message number (p. 595)

= Shows the current message number (p. 595)

Treats the rest of the line as a comment (p. 602)

? Shows a summary of commands (p. 594)

a[lias] *name namelist* Treats *name* as an alias for each name in *namelist* (p. 601)

alt[ernates] *namelist* Treats the names in *namelist* as alternates for your login name (p. 601)

cd *dir* Changes the current directory to *dir* (p. 600)

ch[dir] *dir* Changes the current directory to *dir* (p. 600)

c[opy] [*msglist*] [*file*] Copies messages in *msglist* to *file* without marking them as saved (p. 598)

C[opy] [*msglist*] Saves each message in *msglist* in a file named by the message's author (p. 598)

d[elete] [*msglist*] Deletes messages in *msglist* from the mailbox (p. 599)

di[scard] *header-field-list* Doesn't show the specified header fields when showing messages (p. 595)

dp [*msglist*] Deletes messages in *msglist* from the mailbox, shows the message after the last one deleted (p. 599)

dt [*msglist*] Deletes messages in *msglist* from the mailbox, shows the message after the last one deleted (p. 599)

ec[ho] *string* Echoes the string *string* (p. 602)

e[dit] [*msglist*] Edits the messages in *msglist* (p. 599)

ex[it] Exits from `mailx`, leaving the mailbox unchanged (p. 600)

fi[le] *file* Stops processing the current set of messages, takes a new set from *file* (p. 600)

fold[er] *file* Stops processing the current set of messages, takes a new set from *file* (p. 600)

folders Shows the names of the files in the directory specified by the **folder** variable (p. 595)

fo[llowup] [*msg*] Responds to the message *msg* and records the response in a file named for the message's author (p. 597)

F[ollowup] *msglist* Responds to the first message in *msglist*, sends the response to the author of each message in *msglist* (p. 597)

f[rom] [*msglist*] Shows the header summary for *msglist* (p. 595)

g[roup] *name namelist* Treats *name* as an alias for each name in *namelist* (p. 601)

h[eaders] *msg* Shows the page of the header summary that includes *msg* (p. 595)

hel[p] Shows a summary of commands (p. 594)

ho[ld] [*msglist*] Leaves the messages of *msglist* in the mailbox (p. 598)

if (s or r) *action₁* else *action₂* endif Executes *action₁* or *action₂* depending on send or receive mode (p. 602)

ig[nore] *header-field-list* Doesn't show the specified header fields when showing messages (p. 595)

l[ist] Lists available commands without explanations (p. 595)

m[ail] *namelist* Composes and mails a message to the people in *namelist* (p. 596)

Mail *name* Composes a message to *name* and saves a copy of it in a file named for that person (p. 596)

mb[ox] [*msglist*] Causes the messages in *msglist* to be saved in the secondary mailbox when `mailx` terminates (p. 598)

n[ext] *msg* Goes to the next message matching *msg* (p. 596)

pi[pe] [*msglist*] [*cmd*] Passes the messages in *msglist* as standard input to *cmd* (p. 601)

pre[serve] [*msglist*] Leaves the messages of *msglist* in the mailbox (p. 598)

P[rint] [*msglist*] Shows the messages of *msglist*, including all header fields (p. 596)

p[rint] [*msglist*] Shows the messages of *msglist* (p. 596) q[uit   Quits `mailx`, saving messages you've read in the secondary mailbox (p. 600)

R[eply] [*msg*]   Composes a response to *msg* and sends it to the author and to all other recipients of *msg* (p. 596)

r[eply] [*msglist*]   Composes a response to the author of each message in *msglist* (p. 596)

R[espond] [*msg*]   Composes a response to *msg* and sends it to the author and to all other recipients of *msg* (p. 596)

r[espond] [*msglist*]   Composes a response to the author of each message in *msglist* (p. 596)

S[ave] [*msglist*]   Saves messages of *msglist* in a file named for the author of the first message in *msglist* (p. 598)

s[ave] [*msglist*] [*file*]   Saves the messages of *msglist* in *file* (p. 598)

se[t]   Shows all `mailx` variables and their values (p. 602)

se[t] *name*   Sets the `mailx` variable *name* (p. 602)

se[t] *name=string*   Sets the `mailx` variable *name* to *string* (p. 602)

se[t] *name=n*   Sets the `mailx` variable *name* to the number *n* (p. 602)

se[t] no*name*   Disables the variable *name* (p. 602)

sh[ell]   Calls a subshell (p. 601)

si[ze] [*msglist*]   Shows the size, in characters, of the messages in *msglist* (p. 596)

so[urce] *file*   Reads and executes commands from *file* (p. 600)

to[p] [*msglist*]   Shows the top few lines of the messages of *msglist* (p. 595)

tou[ch] [*msglist*]   "Touches" the messages of *msglist* so they appear to have been read (p. 596)

T[ype] [*msglist*]   Shows the messages of *msglist*, including all header fields (p. 596)

t[ype] [*msglist*]   Shows the messages of *msglist* (p. 596)

u[ndelete] [*msglist*]   Undeletes the messages of *msglist* (p. 599)

un[set] *namelist*   Erases the `mailx` variables in *namelist* (p. 602)

ve[rsion]   Shows the version number and release date of this `.mailx` (p. 595)

v[isual] [*msglist*]   Edits the messages in *msglist* using your visual editor (p. 599)

write [*msglist*] *file*   Writes the messages of *msglist* to *file*, omitting headers and the trailing blank line (p. 599)

x[it]   Exits from `mailx`, leaving the mailbox unchanged (p. 600)

z   Scrolls the header summary one screen forward (p. 595)

z+   Scrolls the header summary one screen forward (p. 595)

z-   Scrolls the header summary one screen backward (p. 595)

Commands for Input Mode.   The commands for input mode all start with '~'.

~!   Calls a subshell (p. 605)

~.   Terminates message input (p. 605)

~: *cmd*   Performs the command *cmd* (p. 605)

~_ *cmd*   Performs the command *cmd* (p. 605)

~?   Shows summary of '~' commands (p. 603)

~< *file*   Inserts the contents of *file* into the message text (p. 604)

~<! *cmd*   Executes *cmd*, inserts its standard output into the message text (p. 604)

~~*text*   Appends '~*text*' to the message (p. 605)

~| *cmd*   Pipes the message text through *cmd*, replacing the text with the standard output of *cmd* (p. 604)

~a   Inserts autograph '`sign`' into the message text (p. 604)

~A   Inserts autograph '`Sign`' into the message text (p. 604)

~b *namelist*   Adds names in *namelist* to '`Bcc`' (blind carbon copy) list (p. 605)

~c *namelist*   Adds names in *namelist* to '`Cc`' (carbon copy) list (p. 605)

~d   Inserts the contents of the `dead.letter` file (p. 604)

~e   Edits the message text using your designated editor (p. 603)

~f [*msglist*]   Forwards the messages from *msglist* by inserting them into the message text (p. 604)

~h   Prompts for header fields (p. 605)

~i *var*   Inserts value of *var* into the text (p. 604)

~m [*msglist*]   Inserts the messages of *msglist* into the text of the message you're composing (p. 604)

~p   Shows the message text (p. 603)

~q   Quits, saving the message text in `dead.letter` (p. 605)

~r *file*   Inserts the contents of *file* into the message text (p. 604)

~s *string*   Sets the subject line to *string* (p. 605)

~t *namelist*   Adds names in *namelist* to '`To`' (recipient) list (p. 605)

~v   Edits the message text using your designated visual editor (p. 603)
~w *file*   Writes the message text to *file* (without the header) (p. 603)
~x   Quits, abandoning the message text (p. 605)

Environment Variables.

allnet   Treat network names as identical if their last components match (p. 608)
append   Append rather than prepend messages to mbox file (p. 608)
asksub   Prompt for a subject if one isn't given on the command line (p. 607)
autoprint   Enable automatic showing of messages after delete, undelete (p. 606)
bang   Enable '!!' for repeating the previous shell command (p. 607)
cmd=*cmd*   Set default for | (pipe) to *cmd* (p. 607)
conv=*style*   Convert UUCP addresses to form of *style* (normally *style* is internet) (p. 610)
crt=*nbr*   Pipe messages of more than *nbr* lines through your pager (p. 606)
DEAD=*file*   Save partial messages that were interrupted in *file* (p. 609)
debug   Turn on verbose diagnostics, don't deliver messages (p. 607)
dot   Take a dot on a line by itself as end of message (p. 607)
EDITOR=*cmd*   Use *cmd* as editor for the ~e command (p. 609)
escape=*c*   Use *c* as the escape character (p. 607)
flipr   Reverse the sense of Reply and reply (p. 607)
folder=*dir*   Save standard mail files in directory *dir* (p. 609)
header   Show the header summary when starting mailx (p. 606)
hold   Preserve messages that you've read in your primary mailbox, not the secondary
   mailbox (p. 608)
HOME=*dir*   Use *dir* as your home directory (p. 606)
ignore   Ignore interrupts while entering messages (p. 607)
ignoreeof   Ignore end-of-file during message input (p. 607)
indentprefix=*string*   Use *string* as prefix for each line of a quoted message (p. 608)
keep   Don't remove an empty mailbox (p. 608)
keepsave   Keep messages saved to specific files in mbox as well (p. 608)
MAILRC=*file*   Use *file* as the mailx startup file (p. 606)
MBOX=*file*   Put messages you've read in *file* (p. 609)
metoo   Delete your login from recipient lists (p. 607)
LISTER=*cmd*   Use *cmd* to list contents of the folder directory (p. 609)
onehop   Disable alterations to remote recipients' addresses (p. 610)
outfolder   Keep outgoing messages in the directory specified by folder (p. 609)
page   Put formfeed after each message sent through a pipe (p. 608)
PAGER=*cmd*   Use *cmd* as the pager for showing long messages (p. 606)
prompt=*string*   Set command mode prompt to *string* (p. 607)
quiet   Don't show the opening message when starting mailx (p. 606)
record=*file*   Record all outgoing mail in *file* (p. 608)
save   Enable saving of interrupted messages (p. 608)
screen=*n*   Set the number of lines in a screenful of the header summary to *n* (p. 606)
sendmail=*cmd*   Use *cmd* to deliver messages (p. 610)
sendwait   Don't return until background mailer is finished (p. 607)
SHELL=*cmd*   Use *cmd* as your shell (p. 609)
showto   Show the recipient's name for messages from you when showing the header
   summary (p. 606)
sign=*string*   Use *string* as signature for *a* command (p. 608)
Sign=*string*   Use *string* as signature for *A* command (p. 608)
toplines=*n*   Show *n* lines for the top command (p. 606)
VISUAL=*cmd*   Use *cmd* as editor for the ~v command (p. 610)

A.2.73
man (Display Manual
Pages)

A typical form of the man command line (p. 226) is

   man [-ahkw] [-M *path*] [-P *pager*] [*section*] *name* ...

Information about the manual pages named *name* ... from section *section* is displayed. The
POSIX version of man recognizes only -k and does not recognize *section*. The apropos
command is often a synonym for 'man -k'.

Command-Line Options.

-a   Display all matching manual pages, not just the first (p. 227)
-h   Produce help message and exit (p. 227)
-k   Produce descriptions that match topic *name* instead (p. 227)
-M *path*   Search for manual pages using the path *path* (p. 227)
-P *pager*   Use pager *pager* for viewing (p. 227)
-w   Show locations of man pages, not the pages themselves (p. 227)

A.2.74
mesg (Lock Out
Messages)

The form of the `mesg` command line (p. 270) is

        mesg [n | y]

If no options are specified, `mesg` reports the message status.

Command-Line Options.

n   Don't allow others to write to your terminal (p. 270)
y   Allow others to write to your terminal (p. 270)

A.2.75
mkdir (Make a
Directory)

The form of the `mkdir` command line (p. 93) is

        mkdir [-p] [-m *mode*] *dir* . . .

Here each *dir* is the absolute pathname of a directory you want to create.

Command-Line Options.   The following options apply to `mkdir`:

-m *n*   Set the permissions of each created directory to *n* (p. 94)
-p   Create intermediate empty directories if necessary (p. 94)

A.2.76
mkfifo (Make a
FIFO Special File)

The form of the `mkfifo` command line (p. 168) is

        mkfifo [-m *mode*] *pathname* . . .

where *pathname* . . . are the names of the FIFO special files to be created.

Command-Line Option.

-m *mode*   Modify the default permissions by *mode* (p. 168)

A.2.77
mknod (Make a
Special File)

The forms of the `mknod` command line (p. 169) are

        mknod [-m *mode*] *pathname* b *major minor*
        mknod [-m *mode*] *pathname* c *major minor*
        mknod [-m *mode*] *pathname* p

where *pathname* is the pathname of the file to be constructed and the letters b, c, and p specify its type to be a block special file, character special file, or FIFO special file (named pipe), respectively.

A.2.78
more (Page Through
Files Interactively)

The form of the `more` command line (p. 108) is

        more [-ceisu] [-n *number*] [-t *tag*] [-p *cmd*] [*file*. . .]

Interactive Commands. In the following commands, *n* represents a count of a number of lines that overrides the indicated number of lines.

[*n*] (Enter) Move forward one line (p. 110)
[*n*] (Space)   Move forward one screenful (p. 110)
[*n*] (Ctrl) B Scroll backward one screenful (p. 110)
[*n*] (Ctrl) D Scroll forward (down) half a screenful (p. 110)
[*n*] (Ctrl) F Scroll forward one screenful (p. 110)
(Ctrl) G Show status information (p. 112)
(Ctrl) L Redisplay the current page (p. 111)
[*n*] (Ctrl) U Scroll backward (up) half a screenful (p. 110)
'*letter* Go to mark *letter* (p. 110)
'' Return to the position before the last large movement (p. 111)
:e[*file*] (Enter) Examine the file whose pathname is *file* (p. 112)
[*k*]:n Examine the *k*th next file (p. 111)
[*k*]:p Examine the *k*th previous file (p. 111)
:q Quit the program (p. 109)
:t *tag* (Enter) Go to the tag *tag* (p. 111)
! *cmd* (Enter) Execute the command *cmd* in a subshell (p. 112)
= Show status information (p. 112)
[*k*]?[!]*pat* (Enter) Search backward for the *k*th occurrence of pattern *pat* (p. 111)
[*k*]/[!]*pat* (Enter) Search forward for the *k*th occurrence of pattern *pat* (p. 111)
[*n*]b Scroll backward one screenful (p. 110)
[*n*]d Scroll forward (down) half a screenful (p. 110)
[*n*]f Scroll forward one screenful (p. 110)
[*n*]g Move to the first line of the file (p. 110)
[*n*]G Move to the last line of the file (p. 110)
h Display a help list (p. 109)
[*n*]j Move forward one line (p. 110)
[*n*]k Move backward one line (p. 110)
m*letter* Mark the current position with *letter* (p. 110)
[*k*]n Search for the previous pattern in the same direction as before (p. 111)
[*k*]N Search for the previous pattern in the opposite direction as before (p. 111)
q Quit the program (p. 109)
r Redisplay the current page (p. 111)
R Reread the file, redisplay the current page (p. 111)
[*n*]s Skip forward one line (p. 110)
[*n*]u Scroll backward (up) half a screenful (p. 110)
v Invoke an editor to edit the file being examined (p. 112)
ZZ Quit the program (p. 109)

Command-Line Options.

-c Bypass scrolling if a screen has no lines in common with the previous one (p. 113)
-e Don't always exit immediately at end-of-file (p. 113)
-i Ignore case when doing a pattern match (p. 112)
-n *number* Assume *number* lines per screenful (p. 112)
-s Replace consecutive empty lines with a single empty line (p. 113)
-t *tag* Start viewing with tag *tag* (p. 113)
-u Treat ⟨backspace⟩ as a printable control character (p. 113)

A.2.79
mount (Mount a
File System)

The form of the `mount` command line (p. 696) is

mount [-afrwvn] [-o *options*] [-t *fstype*] [*dev*] [*mountdir*]

This is the form under Linux; forms for other systems are similar.

Command-Line Options.

-a Mount all file systems in `fstab` (p. 697)
-f Do everything except the actual mount (p. 697)
-n Don't make an entry in `mtab` (p. 697)
-o *options* Use the specified mounting options (p. 697)

-r　Mount the file system read-only (p. 697)
-t *fstype*　Assume the file system is of type *fstype* (p. 697)
-v"　Report verbosely on the mount (p. 697)
-w　Mount the file system for writing as well as reading (p. 697)

A.2.80
mv (Move Files)

The forms of the mv command (p. 102) are

> mv [-if] *file pathname*
> mv [-if] *file ... dir*

In the first form, *file* is renamed to *pathname*. In the second form, each file in *file ...* is renamed to a file in *dir* having the same file identifier.

Command-Line Options.

-f　Don't ask for confirmation even when overwriting a link lacking write permission (p. 103)
-i　Ask for confirmation when overwriting any link (p. 102)

A.2.81
newgrp (Change Your Current Group)

The form of the newgrp command line (p. 253) is

> newgrp [-l] [*group*]

where *group* is the name of the group that you want to join. In the obsolescent syntax, the '-l' is written as '-'.

Command-Line Option.

-l　Simulate logging in as a member of *group* (p. 254)

A.2.82
nice
(Run a Command at Low Priority)

The form of the nice command line (p. 248) is

> nice [-n *n*] *cmd* [*arg...*]

where *n* is a decrease in priority and the *arg*s are the arguments of *cmd*. In the obsolescent syntax, the '-n *n*' is written as '-*n*'.

A.2.83
nohup (Ignore Hangups)

The form of the nohup command line (p. 243) is

> nohup *command* [*argument ...*]

A.2.84
od (Octal Dump)

The form of the od command (p. 158) line is

> od [-v] [-A *base*] [-j *skip*] [-N *count*] [-t *type-spec ...*] [*file ...*]

Type Specifications.　A type specification *type-spec* consists of a type character and an optional byte count or input type descriptor. The type character is one of the following:

d Decimal number
u Unsigned decimal number
o Octal number
x Hexadecimal number
f Floating point number
c Character
a Named character (nonprintable characters shown symbolically)

Any of the numerical type characters (`d`, `u`, `o`, `x`, or `f`) can be followed by a decimal count indicating how many bytes are to be represented. Instead of a count, you can use one of the following letters, corresponding to types in C:

`F` *float* (for `f` only)
`D` *double* (for `f` only)
`L` *long double* (for `f` only)
`C` *char* (for `d`, `u`, `o`, or `x`)
`S` *short* (for `d`, `u`, `o`, or `x`)
`I` *int* (for `d`, `u`, `o`, or `x`)
`L` *long* (for `d`, `u`, `o`, or `x`)

Command-Line Options.

`-A` *base*   Express the offset using base *base* (`o`, `d`, `x`, or `n`) (p. 159)
`-j` *skip*   Skip over *skip* bytes (p. 159)
`-N` *count*   Produce output for at most *count* bytes (p. 159)
`-t` *type-spec*   Format output according to type specification *type-spec* (p. 159)
`-v`   Show repeated data explicitly (p. 159)

Older Form.   An older form of the `od` command line (p. 158) is

  od [-bcdox] [*file*] [*offset*]

where *options*, *file*, and *offset* are all optional. *offset*, the starting byte, has the form (p. 160)

  [+] *n* [.] [b]

n   Offset value
.   Take offset value in decimal, not octal
+   Optional separator from *file*
b   Take offset in 512-byte blocks, not single bytes

Command-Line Options for Older Form.   The options indicate the display modes and units:

`-b`   Show bytes in octal (p. 160)
`-c`   Show bytes as ASCII characters (p. 160)
`-d`   Show words in signed decimal (p. 160)
`-o`   Show words in octal (p. 160)
`-x`   Show words in hexadecimal (p. 160)

A.2.85
paste
(Paste Input Fields)

The form of the `paste` command line (p. 189) is

  paste [-d *list*] [-s] [*file*...]

If *file* is given as '`-`', input is taken from standard input.

Command-Line Options.

`-d` *list*   Use the characters in *list* circularly as separators (p. 190)
`-s`   Merge lines serially from one file (p. 190)

A.2.86
patch (Apply Changes
to Files)

The form of the `patch` command line (p. 165) is

  patch [-bflNRs] [-c | -e | -n] [-d *dir*] [-D *def*] [-F *ff*] [-i *pfile*]
      [-o *ofile*] [-p *num*] [-r *rfile*] [*file*]

where *file* is a file to be patched according to the patches in *pfile*, a differences file generated by `diff`, or by the patches in standard input if `-i` is not specified.

Command-Line Options.

-b   Save original file in *file*.`orig` (p. 166)
-c   Interpret the patches as if generated by '`diff -c`' (p. 166)
-d *dir*   Change to directory *dir* before processing (p. 166)
-D *def*   Mark changes with C `#ifdef` ... `#endif` (p. 167)
-e   Interpret the patches as if generated by '`diff -e`' (p. 166)
-F   Ignore *ff* (fuzz factor) lines of context (p. 167)
-f   Force processing; don't ask for user input (p. 167)
-i *pfile*   Read patches from file *pfile* (p. 166)
-l   Treat sequences of spaces as equivalent (p. 167)
-n   Interpret patches as if from `diff` without options (p. 166)
-N   Ignore patches already applied (p. 167)
-o *ofile*   Write patched file to *ofile* (p. 166)
-p *num*   Delete *num* pathname components from names of files to be patched (p. 166)
-R   Reverse patch, going from new version to old one (p. 167)
-r *rfile*   Send rejected hunks of patches to *rfile* (p. 166)
-s   Work silently (p. 167)

A.2.87
pathchk (Check Validity of Pathnames)

The form of the `pathchk` command line (p. 129) is

> `pathchk` [`-p`] *pathname* ...

where *pathname* ... are the pathnames to be checked for validity.

Command-Line Option.

-p   POSIX conformance check only (p. 129)

A.2.88
pax (Portable Archive Interchange)

The forms of the `pax` command line (p. 145) are

> `pax` [`-cdnv`] [`-f` *archive*] [`-s` *repl*] ...
> [*pattern* ...]
>
> `pax -r` [`-cdiknuv`] [`-f` *archive*] [`-o` *options*] ... [`-p` *privs*] ... [`-s` *repl*] ... [*pattern* ...]
>
> `pax -w` [`-dituvX`] [`-b` *blksize*] [`-f` *archive* [`-a`]] [`-o` *options*] ...
> [`-s` *repl*] ... [`-x` *fmt*] [*file* ...]
>
> `pax -rw` [`-dikltuvX`] [`-p` *privs*] ... [`-s` *repl*] ... [*file* ...] *dir*

where *pattern* ... describes files to be included or excluded on reading and *file* ... describes files to be written.

Command-Line Options.

-a   Append files to the end of the archive (p. 146)
-b *blksize*   Write blocks of *blksize* bytes (p. 149)
-c   Don't restore files specified by *pattern* (p. 146)
-d   Don't process the hierarchy under a directory (p. 147)
-f *archive*   Use *archive* as the archive file (p. 146)
-i   Interactively rename files or archive members (p. 147)
-k   Don't overwrite existing files (p. 148)
-l   When copying, link new and old files whenever possible (p. 148)
-n   Match only one archive member for each *pattern* (p. 147)
-o *options*   Provide implementation-dependent format information (p. 149)
-p *privs*   Specify privilege data to be preserved (a, e, m, o, or p) (p. 148)
-r   Read an archive (p. 145)
-s *repl*   Modify file names according to the substitution *repl* (p. 147)
-t   Don't let `pax` affect file access times (p. 149)
-u   Don't replace files with older ones (p. 148)
-v   Produce verbose table of contents (p. 147)
-w   Write an archive (p. 145)

-x *fmt* Specify the output format (`cpio`, `ustar`, or an implementation-defined format) (p. 149)

-X Don't cross file system boundaries (p. 148)

A.2.89
pr
(Format Files for Printing)

The form of the `pr` command line (p. 118) is

pr [+*bgn*] [-*col*] [-adfFmrt] [-e[*tc*][*k*]] [-h *hdr*] [-i[*tc*][*k*]]
[-l *lines*] [-n[*tc*][*k*]] [-o *offset*] [-s[*tc*]] [-w *width*] [*file* ...]

Command-Line Options.

+*bgn* Start formatted output at page *bgn* (p. 120)
-*col* Format using *col* columns (p. 119)
-a Format columns across the page (p. 119)
-d Format with double spacing (p. 120)
-e[*tc*[*k*]] Replace tabs by spaces up to every *k*th position, with *tc* as tab character (p. 120)
-f End pages with formfeeds rather than linefeeds (non-POSIX version) (p. 120)
-F End pages with formfeeds rather than linefeeds (POSIX version) (p. 120)
-h *hdr* Use *hdr* as the page header text (p. 120)
-i[*tc*[*k*]] Replace spaces by tabs to every *k*th position, with *tc* as tab character (p. 120)
-l *n* Set the page length to *n* lines (p. 119)
-m Merge and format files, one file per column (p. 119)
-n[*tc*[*k*]] Provide *k*-digit line numbers followed by tab character *tc* (p. 120)
-o *offset* Offset each line by *offset* spaces (p. 119)
-p Pause before starting each page (p. 121)
-r Don't issue messages about files that can't be opened (p. 121)
-s[*tc*] Use *tc* as the separator character between columns (p. 120)
-t Don't set aside space for top and bottom margins (p. 120)
-w *width* Set the line width to *widthn* characters (p. 119)

A.2.90
print (Write Output Arguments under `ksh`**)**

The form of the `print` command line (p. 278) is

print [-Rnprs [-u *n*]] [*arg* ...]

where *arg* ... are the arguments to be sent to standard output.

Command-Line Options.

-R Treat backslashes and hyphens literally (p. 278)
-n Don't add a trailing ⟨newline⟩ to the output (p. 278)
-p Redirect the arguments to the coprocess (p. 278)
-r Treat backslashes literally, not as escapes (p. 278)
-s Redirect the arguments to the history file (p. 278)
-u [*n*] Redirect the arguments to file descriptor *n* (default 1) (p. 278)

A.2.91
printf (Write Formatted Output)

The form of the `printf` command line (p. 274) is

printf *format* [*argument* ...]

The *argument*s are formatted according to *format*. Within *format*, conversions may appear. They have the form

% [*flag* ...] [*width* . *precision*] *convchar*

where *convchar* is a character specifying the type of conversion, *width* and *precision* are integers giving subfield widths, and each *flag* modifies the meaning of the conversion.

Conversion Characters.

%	Literal percent (p. 277)
b	echo-style string conversion (p. 277)
c	Unsigned character conversion (p. 277)
d	Signed decimal conversion (p. 276)
E	Floating-point to fixed conversion (p. 277)
e	Floating-point to fixed conversion (p. 277)
f	Floating-point conversion (p. 277)
G	Floating-point conversion, value-dependent (p. 277)
g	Floating-point conversion, value-dependent (p. 277)
i	Signed decimal conversion (p. 276)
o	Octal conversion (p. 276)
s	String conversion (p. 277)
u	Unsigned decimal conversion (p. 276)
X	Hexadecimal conversion (p. 277)
x	Hexadecimal conversion (p. 277)

Flag Characters.

⟨space⟩	Prefix a space (p. 276)
#	Use alternate form (p. 276)
-	Left-justify the converted string (p. 275)
+	Start converted string with a sign (p. 276)
0	Pad with leading zeroes (p. 276)

Escape Sequences.　These escape sequences can appear in *format*:

\\	Backslash (p. 278)
\a	Alert (p. 278)
\b	Backspace (p. 278)
\c	Ignore remaining characters (p. 278)
\f	Formfeed (p. 278)
\n	Newline (p. 278)
\r	Carriage return (p. 278)
\t	Tab (p. 278)
\v	Vertical tab (p. 278)
\0*nnn*	Octal character *nnn* (p. 278)

A.2.92
ps (List Processes, BSD Version)

The form of the BSD ps command line (p. 237) is

    ps [-][acegklnsuvwx][t *term*] [*pid*]

where *pid* is a process ID. See your system manual for other information that can appear on the command line.

Command-Line Options.

a	Produce information about all processes with terminals (p. 238)
c	Show the internally stored command name (p. 239)
e	Show the environment as well as the command (p. 239)
g	Produce information about all processes (p. 238)
k	Use the /vmcore file (p. 240)
l	Produce a long listing (p. 238)
n	Show information numerically rather than symbolically (p. 240)
-o *items*	Include items listed in *items* in the output (p. 239)
s	Show the kernel stack size of each process (p. 240)
t*term*	Show only processes running on terminal *term* (p. 238)
u	Produce information in a user-oriented format (p. 238)
v	Show virtual memory statistics (p. 239)
w	Use a wide output format (p. 239)
x	Show information about processes not associated with a terminal (p. 238)
U	Update the private database of system information (p. 240)

A.2.93
ps (List Processes, POSIX Version)

The form of the POSIX `ps` command line (p. 240) is

> `ps` [`-aA`] [`-G` *grouplist*] [`-o` *items*] ... [`-p` *proclist*] [`-t` *termlist*] [`-U` *userlist*]

Command-Line Options. In the following options, a list such as *grouplist* is a sequence of items separated by spaces or commas.

`-a`   Produce information about every process associated with a terminal (p. 240)
`-A`   Produce information about every process (p. 240)
`-G` *grouplist*   Produce only output pertaining to processes whose real group IDs are in *grouplist* (p. 241)
`-o` *items*   Include items listed in *items* in the output (p. 241)
`-p` *proclist*   Produce only output pertaining to the specified processes (p. 241)
`-t` *termlist*   Produce only output pertaining to the specified terminals (p. 241)
`-U` *userlist*   Produce only output pertaining to processes whose real group IDs are in *userlist* (p. 241)

A.2.94
ps (List Processes, System V Version)

The form of the System V `ps` command line (p. 235) is

> `ps` [`-adefl`] [`-g` *grouplist*] [`-n` *name*] [`-p` *proclist*] [`-t` *termlist*] [`-u` *userlist*]

Command-Line Options. In the following options, a *list* is a sequence of items separated by spaces or commas.

`-a`   Produce information about every process except for process group leaders and processes not associated with a terminal (p. 236)
`-d`   Produce information about every process except for process group leaders (p. 236)
`-e`   Produce information about every process (p. 236)
`-f`   Produce a full listing (p. 237)
`-g` *grouplist*   Produce only output pertaining to the specified process groups (p. 236)
`-l`   Produce an extended (long) listing (p. 237)
`-n` *name*   Produce output for the processes running on system *name* (p. 236)
`-p` *proclist*   Produce only output pertaining to the specified processes (p. 236)
`-t` *termlist*   Produce only output pertaining to the specified terminals (p. 236)
`-u` *userlist*   Produce only output pertaining to the specified users (p. 236)

A.2.95
pwd (Show Working Directory)

The form of the `pwd` command line (p. 93) is

> `pwd`

A.2.96
rcp (Remote Copy)

The form of the `rcp` command line (p. 636) is

> `rcp` [`-pr`] *source* ... *dest*

where each *source* is a source file or directory and *dest* is a destination file or directory.

Command-Line Options.
`-p`   Preserve modification times and permissions of source files (p. 636)
`-r`   Recursively copy the subtree rooted at each *source* (p. 636)

A.2.97
read (Read an Input Line)

The form of the `read` command line (p. 279) is

> `read` [`-r`] *var* ...

The **read** command reads a line from standard input and assigns successive fields on the line to the shell variables *var* ....

Command-Line Option.

-r   Treat backslashes as ordinary characters (p. 279)

Additional ksh Command-Line Options.

-p   Read the input line from the coprocess (p. 279)
-s   Save a copy of the input line in the history file (p. 279)
-u [*n*]   Read from file descriptor *n* (default 0) (p. 279)

A.2.98
reboot (Shut Down the System and Reboot)

The form of the reboot command line (p. 705) is

   reboot [-t *sec*] [-nq]

Command-Line Options.

-t *sec*   Allow *sec* seconds before sending SIGKILL (p. 705)
-n   Don't synchronize the file systems before shutting down
-q   Send SIGKILL immediately, without warning

A.2.99
renice (Set Priorities of Processes)

The form of the renice command line (p. 249) is

   renice [-n *incr*] [-g | -p | -u] *id* ...

It also has these obsolescent forms:

   renice *niceval* [-p] *id* ... [-g *id* ...] [-p *id* ...] [-u *id* ...]
   renice *niceval* -g *id* ... [-g *id* ...] [-p *id* ...] [-u *id* ...]
   renice *niceval* -u *id* ... [-g *id* ...] [-p *id* ...] [-u *id* ...]

The designated processes have their priorities adjusted by *incr* or, for the obsolescent forms, set to *niceval*. The change is made only if the requesting user has appropriate privileges.

Command-Line Options.

-g   Interpret *id* ... as group IDs (p. 249)
-g *gid* ...   Adjust priorities of processes for group *gid* ... (p. 249)
-n *incr*   Adjust priorities up or down by *incr* (p. 249)
-p   Interpret *id* ... as process IDs (p. 249)
-p *pid* ...   Adjust priorities of processes *pid* ... (p. 249)
-u   Interpret *id* ... as user IDs (p. 249)
-u *gid* ...   Adjust priorities of processes for user *uid* ... (p. 249)

A.2.100
rlogin (Remote Login)

The form of the rlogin command line (p. 634) is

   rlogin *rhost* [-8] [-e*c*] [-l *user*]

For some systems, the order is reversed:

   rlogin [-8] [-e*c*] [-l *user*] *rhost*

In either case, *rhost* is the name of a remote system.

Command-Line Options.

-8   Use an eight-bit data path (p. 634)
-e*c*   Use *c* as the escape character (p. 634)
-l *user*   Log in as *user* rather than as yourself (p. 634)

A.2.101
rm (Remove Files or Directories)

The form of the rm command line (p. 105) is

   rm [-firR] *file* ...

where the files in *file* ... can include directories if the -r option is present.

Command-Line Options.

-f Don't ask for confirmation of files lacking write permission (p. 106)
-i Ask interactively for confirmation of each removal (p. 105)

-r Remove directories and all indirectly contained files and subdirectories (p. 105)
-R Remove directories and all indirectly contained files and subdirectories (p. 105)

A.2.102
rmdir (Remove Directories)

The form of the **rmdir** command line (p. 105) is

      rmdir [-ps] *dir* ...

where *dir* ... is a list of directories.

Command-Line Options.
-p Remove empty parent directories (p. 106)
-s Suppress messages (p. 106)

A.2.103
rsh (Remote Execution of a Shell Command)

The form of the **rsh** command line (p. 635) is

      rsh *rhost* [-ln] [*cmd*]

where *rhost* is the name of a remote system and *cmd* is a command to be executed on that system.

Command-Line Options.
-l *user*   Log in as *user* rather than as yourself (p. 635)
-n   Take input from /dev/null (p. 635)

A.2.104
rwho (List Users on the Local Network)

The form of the **rwho** command line (p. 636) is

      rwho [-a]

The -a option indicates that users who have not typed anything in the last hour are also to be included.

A.2.105
sed (Edit from a Script)

The forms of the **sed** command line (p. 192) are

      sed [-n] *script* [*file*...]
      sed [-n] [-e *script*] ... [-f *sfile*] [*file*...]

where *script* is a script of editing commands and *file* ... is a list of files to be edited.

Command-Line Options.
-e *script*   Edit the files according to *script* (p. 193)
-f *sfile*   Edit the files according to the script found in *sfile* (p. 193)
-n   Don't produce the input buffer after processing a line (p. 193)

Addresses.
/*regexpr*/   Any line that matches the regular expression *regexpr* (p. 194)
c regexpr c   Any line that matches the regular expression *regexpr* (p. 194)
n   Line number *n* (p. 194)
a_1,a_2 Lines a_1 through a_2, where a_1 and a_2 are any of the forms above (p. 194)

Commands.
In the following list of commands, *r* indicates an address range and *a* indicates a single address. A range can be replaced by an address or omitted; a single address can also be omitted. A command is executed only if the range or address applies, or if it has no range or address.

empty   Does nothing (p. 198)
r!*cmd*   Applies the command to all lines not selected by *r* (p. 199)
r{ [*cmd*...] }   Executes the commands *cmd* ... (p. 199)
: *label*   Places the label *label* (p. 198)
a=   Produces a line containing the current line number (p. 198)

   #   Indicates a comment (first line only) (p. 198)
a a*text*   Produces *text* before reading the next line (p. 197)
r b [*label*]   Branches to *label* (p. 198)
r c\\ *text*   Changes the lines in *r* to *text* (p. 197)
r d   Deletes the input buffer, recycle (p. 196)
r D   Deletes the first line of the input buffer, recycle (p. 196)
r g   Replaces the input buffer by the hold buffer (p. 197)
r G   Appends the hold buffer to the input buffer (p. 197)
r h   Replaces the hold buffer by the input buffer (p. 197)
r H   Appends the input buffer to the hold buffer (p. 197)
a i*text*   Produces *text* immediately (p. 196)
r l   Produces the input buffer in a representation that folds long lines and shows non-printing characters (p. 198)
r n   Produces the input buffer, then replaces it with the next input line (p. 197)
r N   Appends the next input line to the input buffer (p. 197)
r p   Produces the input buffer (p. 197)
r P   Produces the first line of the input buffer (p. 198)
a q   Quits editing (p. 198)
r r *file*   Produces the contents of *file* before reading the next line (p. 198)
r s/*pat*/*repl*/[*flags*]   Substitutes *repl* for the pattern *pat*, applying the flags listed below (p. 195)
r t [*label*]   Branches to *label* if any substitutions have been made (p. 198)
r w *file*   Appends the input buffer to *file* (p. 198)
r x   Exchanges the input buffer with the hold buffer (p. 197)
r y /*string*$_1$/*string*$_2$/   Substitutes characters in *string*$_2$ for the corresponding characters of *string*$_1$ (p. 196)

Flags for the s Command.

n   Substitute for the *n*th occurrence (p. 195)
g   Substitute for all occurrences (p. 195)
p   Produce the input buffer if any substitutions were made.
w file   Append the input buffer to *file* if any substitutions were made (p. 195)

A.2.106
sh (**POSIX Shell**)

The form of the sh command line (p. 318) is

    sh [-Cabefimnuvx] [-o *option*] ... [*cmdfile* [*arg* ...]]
    sh -c [-Cabefimnuvx] [-o *option*] ... *cmdlist* [*cmdname* [*arg* ...]]
    sh -s [-Cabefimnuvx] [-o *option*] ... [*arg* ...]

See the description of ksh (p. 745) for further details.

A.2.107
shar (**Create a Shell Archive**)

The form of the shar command line (p. 612) is

    shar [-bcDflMsvx] [-d *delim*] [-o *ofile*] [-l*size*] *file* ...

A shell archive containing the specified files is sent to standard output.

Command-Line Options.

-b   Assume all files are binary (p. 612)
-c   Produce "cut here" line for each output file (p. 613)
-D   Include details in the resulting archive (p. 613)
-d *delim*   Use *delim* as the file delimiter (p. 613)
-f   Use filename only as the pathname (p. 613)
-l *size*   Limit output files to *size* kilobytes (p. 613)
-M   Assume files are a mixture of text and binary (p. 613)
-o *file*   Send output to file *ofile* (p. 613)
-s   Check files for damage (p. 613)
-v   Produce verbose messages (p. 613)
-x   Don't overwrite existing files (p. 613)

A.2.108
`shutdown` **(Shut Down the System)**

The form of the Linux `shutdown` command line (p. 706) is

> `shutdown [-t` *sec*`] [-cfhknr]` *time* [*msg*]

The system shuts down at time *time* (`now` for immediately).

Command-Line Options.

- `-c`   Cancel a shutdown that's already been started (p. 706)
- `-f`   Do a fast reboot without checking file systems (p. 706)
- `-h`   Halt after shutdown (p. 706)
- `-k`   Send warning messages but don't actually shut down (p. 706)
- `-n`   Don't synchronize file systems before shutting down (p. 706)
- `-r`   Reboot after shutdown (p. 706)

A.2.109
`sleep` **(Suspend Execution)**

The form of the `sleep` command line (p. 249) is

> `sleep` *n*

where *n* is the number of seconds for which execution is to be suspended.

A.2.110
`sort` **(Sort Files)**

The forms of the `sort` command line (p. 171) are

> `sort [-m] [-o` *ofile*`] [-bdfinru] [-t` *char*`] [-k` *keydef*`]` ... [*file* ...]
> `sort -c [-bdfinru] [-t` *char*`] [-k` *keydef*`]` ... [*file*]

The obsolescent forms are

> `sort [-mu] [-o` *ofile*`] [-bdfinr] [-t` *char*`] [+`*pos*₁ `[-`*pos*₂`]]` ... [*file* ...]
> `sort -c [-u] [-bdfinr] [-t` *char*`] [+`*pos*₁ `[-`*pos*₂`]]` ... [*file*]

where the *files* are the files to be concatenated and sorted. Each *keydef* has the form

> *pos*₁[,*pos*₂]

where *pos*₁ indicates where a key starts and *pos*₂ where it ends. Each *pos* in turn has the form

> *f*[.*c*][*flags*]

Here *f* specifies a field number and *c* a character position within the field, with fields and characters numbered starting with zero. The flags are specified as letters only (no hyphens). In the obsolete forms, *pos*₁ and *pos*₂ have the same meanings as they do within a *keydef*.

Options Applying to All Keys.

- `-c`   Check that the input is already sorted, returning exit status 0 if it is, 1 if it isn't (p. 173)
- `-m`   Merge the input files, assuming them already sorted (p. 173)
- `-u`   For sets of lines having equal keys, produce only one of them; with `-c`, check for duplicate keys (p. 173)
- `-o` *outfile*   Send the output to *outfile* (p. 173)
- `-t` *char*   Use *char* as the field delimiter (p. 173)

The flags applying to individual keys can also be applied to all keys by indicating them as options.

Flags Applying to Individual Keys.

- `-b`   Ignore leading whitespace in determining character positions within a key (p. 174)
- `-d`   Use "dictionary order", ignoring characters other than letters, digits, and whitespace (p. 174)
- `-f`   Fold lowercase letters to uppercase (p. 174)
- `-i`   Ignore nonprinting ASCII characters (p. 174)
- `-n`   Treat the key as a number (p. 174)
- `-r`   Reverse the sense of comparisons (p. 174)

A.2.111
`split` **(Split Files into Pieces)**

The forms of the `split` command line (p. 188) are

> `split [-l` *lines*`] [-a` *len*`] [`*file* [*name*]]
> `split -b` *n*[`k` | `m`] `[-a` *len*`] [`*file* [*name*]]

An obsolescent form is

> `split [-`*lines*`] [-a` *len*`] [`*file* [*name*]]

The specified *file*, or standard input, is split into subfiles.

Command-Line Options.

-a *len*   Use *len* letters to form the suffixes of the split portions (p. 188)
-b *n*   Split the file into chunks of *n* bytes (p. 188)
-l *lines*   Split the file into chunks of *lines* lines (p. 188)

A.2.112
strings (Find Printable Strings in Files)

The form of the strings command line (p. 293) is

> strings [-a] [-t *fchar*] [-n *len*] [*file* . . .]

The files named by the pathnames *file* . . . are searched for printable strings. An obsolescent form is

> strings [-] [-t *fchar*] [-*len*] [*file* . . .]

where the '-' has the same meaning as -a.

Command-Line Options.

-a   Scan files in their entirety (p. 293)
-n *len*   Assume minimum string length of *len* (p. 293)
-t *fchar*   Write byte offset for each string using format *fchar* (d for decimal, o for octal,
    x for hexadecimal) (p. 294)

A.2.113
stty (Set Terminal Characteristics)

The form of the stty command line (p. 260) is

> stty [-ag] [*setting*. . .]

Command-Line Options.   These are the POSIX options; in general, the options and settings vary considerably among systems.

-a   List all settings (p. 261)
-g   List current settings in a form that can be used as input to stty later (p. 261)

Settings for Control Characters.

eof *c*   Set the eof (end-of-file) character to *c* (p. 262)
erase *c*   Set the erase character to *c* (p. 262)
flush *c*   Set the flush character to *c* (p. 262)
intr *c*   Set the interrupt character to *c* (p. 262)
kill *c*   Set the kill character to *c* (p. 262)
quit *c*   Set the quit character to *c* (p. 262)
start *c*   Set the start character to *c* (p. 262)
stop *c*   Set the stop character to *c* (p. 262)
susp *c*   Set the job suspension character to *c* (p. 262)
swtch *c*   Set the job switch character to *c* (p. 262)
werase *c*   Set the "erase last word" character to *c* (p. 262)

Other Settings.   These are some of the more commonly used settings.   This is not an exhaustive list. A '-' in front of a setting negates it.

speed   Set the line to the indicated speed (baud rate) (p. 263)
term   Set all settings to values appropriate for the terminal *term* (p. 265)
0   Hang up the phone line (p. 263)
[-]clocal   Disable modem control signals (p. 263)
columns *n*   Specify that your terminal has *n* columns (p. 265)
cols *n*   Specify that your terminal has *n* columns (p. 265)
cooked   Enable processing of special characters (p. 265)
[-]cread   Allow the terminal to receive input (p. 263)
cs5 cs6 cs7 cs8   Set the character size to 5, 6, 7, or 8 bits (p. 263)
[-]cstopb   Use two stop bits per character (one with -) (p. 263)
[-]echo   Echo each typed character (p. 264)
[-]echoe   Echo erase characters as ⟨backspace⟩⟨space⟩⟨backspace⟩ (p. 264)

[-]echok   Send a newline after each kill character (p. 264)
ek   Set the erase and kill characters to # and @ (p. 265)
[-]evenp   Enable even parity and seven-bit characters (p. 265)
[-]hup   Hang up the phone line upon logout (p. 263)
[-]icanon   Enable the erase and kill characters (p. 263)
[-]icrnl   Map ⟨return⟩ to ⟨newline⟩ on input (p. 263)
[-]igncr   Ignore ⟨return⟩ on input (p. 263)
[-]inlcr   Map ⟨newline⟩ to ⟨return⟩ on input (p. 263)
[-]isig   Enable the interrupt, quit, switch, and flush characters (p. 263)
[-]istrip Force the high (eighth) bit of each input character to zero (p. 263)
[-]iuclc   Map uppercase alphabetic characters to lowercase on input (p. 263)
[-]ixon   Enable the start and stop characters (p. 263)
[-]lcase   Enable conversion of lowercase alphabetic characters to uppercase ones (p. 265)
[-]litout   Transmit eight-bit characters literally for both input and output (p. 265)
[-]nl   Disable special processing of ⟨newline⟩ and ⟨return⟩ (p. 265)
[-]ocrnl   Map ⟨return⟩ to ⟨newline⟩ on output (p. 264)
[-]oddp   Enable odd parity and seven-bit characters (p. 265)
[-]olcuc   Map lowercase alphabetic characters to uppercase on output (p. 264)
[-]onlcr   Map ⟨newline⟩ to ⟨return⟩ on output (p. 264)
[-]opost   Post-process the output (p. 264)
[-]parenb   Enable parity generation and detection (p. 263)
[-]parity   Enable even parity and seven-bit characters (p. 265)
[-]parodd   Enable odd parity (even with -) (p. 263)
[-]pass8   Transmit eight-bit input characters literally (p. 265)
[-]raw   Disable processing of special characters (p. 265)
rows *n*   Specify that your terminal has *n* rows (p. 265)
[-]rtscts   Enable RTS/CTS handshaking as a method of modem control (p. 263)
sane   Set all settings to reasonable values (p. 264)
[-]tabs   Replace tabs by spaces when showing text (p. 264)
[-]tostop   Inhibit output from background jobs (p. 264)
[-]xcase   Indicate uppercase characters with backslash (p. 264)

A.2.114
su **(Substitute User)**

The form of the `su` command line (p. 252) is

$$\text{su } [-\text{fl}]\ [-\text{c } cmd]\ [-]\ [\,user\ [arg \ldots\,]\,]$$

The arguments are as follows:

-   Install login environment if present, preserve current environment if absent (p. 253)
-c *cmd*   Pass the command line *cmd* to the new shell (p. 253)
-f   Don't execute the login initialization file (p. 253)
-l   Produce login environment if present, preserve current environment if absent (p. 253)
user   Name of new user
arg . . .   Arguments passed to the newly created shell

A.2.115
tabs **(Set Tabs on Your Terminal)**

The POSIX forms of the `tabs` command line (p. 267) are

$$\text{tabs } [-n]\ [-\text{T } term]$$
$$\text{tabs } [-\text{T } term]\ n_1\ [\,,\ n_2,\ \ldots\,]$$

Command-Line Options.

$n_1, n_2, \ldots$ Set tab stops at positions n_1, n_2, etc. (p. 267)
-code   Use the correct tabs for the programming language designated by *code* (p. 267)
-n   Set tab stops every *n* spaces (p. 267)
+m[*n*]   Use a left margin of *n* (p. 268)
-T *term*   Send the tab-setting sequence for a terminal of type *term* (p. 268)

A.2.116
tail **(Extract the End of a File)**

The form of the `tail` command (p. 184) is

$$\text{tail } [-\text{f}][-\text{c } number\ |\ -\text{n } number]\ [file]$$

where *number* is an integer *n* optionally preceded by '+' or '-'.

Command-Line Options.

-c *number*   Start *n* bytes from the beginning (+*n*) or *n* bytes from the end (*n* or -*n*) (p. 185)

-f   Monitor *file* (or standard input) continuously (p. 185)
-n *number*   Start *n* lines from the beginning (+*n*) or *n* lines from the end (*n* or -*n*) (p. 185)

Obsolescent Form.   An obsolescent form of the `tail` command line (p. 186) is

> `tail` *sign*[*n*][*unit*][f] [*file*]

The components of the first argument are as follows:

sign   Start from beginning of file if +, from end if -
n   Number of units to extract
unit   Lines (`1`), 1024-byte blocks (`b`), or single bytes (`c`)
f   Continuous monitoring of *file*

A.2.117
`talk` (Talk to Another User)

The form of the `talk` command line (p. 269) is

> `talk` *user* [*term*]

An on-line conversation is initiated with the user *user*. If the user is logged on at more than one terminal, the terminal *term* is selected.

A.2.118
`tar` (Tape Archiver)

The form of the `tar` command line (p. 151) is

> `tar` *key* [*arg*...] [*file*...]

The *key* consists of a sequence of key letters. The number of *arg*s is equal to the number of letters in *key* that require arguments. The *file*s are the files to be written to the archive or extracted. The form and key letters for this program vary greatly, even among System V–style or Berkeley-style systems.

Key Letters.   The key letters that follow are the most common ones:

n   Use drive #*n* for the archive (p. 153)
b   Take the blocking factor for raw magnetic tape from the next argument (p. 153)
c   Create a new archive containing the files (p. 152)
-C *dir*   Change directory to *dir* before writing more files (p. 152)
f   Take archive device name from the next argument (p. 153)
k   Take the capacity of the archive device (in kilobytes) from the next argument (p. 153)
l   Don't complain about files that can't be found (p. 153)
m   Don't restore modification times (p. 153)
o   Disregard ownership information when reading a file (p. 153)
p   Assign original permissions to extracted files (p. 153)
r   Write the files at the end of the archive (p. 152)
t   List the contents of the archive (p. 152)
u   Add the files to the archive if they are newer (p. 152)
v   Show the name of each file processed (p. 153)
w   Wait for confirmation of each action (p. 153)
x   Extract the files from the archive (p. 152)
z   Compress and expand the archive using `gzip` and `gunzip` (p. 153)
Z   Compress and expand the archive using `compress` and `uncompress` (p. 153)

A.2.119
`tee` (Duplicate Input)

The form of the `tee` command line (p. 139) is

> `tee` [-ai] [*file* ...]

Command-Line Options.

-i   Ignore interrupts (p. 139)
-a   Append the output to each file instead of overwriting the file (p. 139)

A.2.120
`telnet` (Call a Remote System Over a Network)

The form of the `telnet` command line (p. 637) is

> `telnet` [*host* [*port*]]

Commands.

? [*cmd*]   Gets help on *cmd* (p. 638)

c[lose]   Disconnects from the remote host but remains in `telnet` (p. 638)

d[isplay] [*var*...]   Shows the value of each variable *var* (p. 639)

m[ode] *type*   Enters the specified mode (`line` or `character`) (p. 639)

o[pen] [*host* [*port*]]   Opens a connection to *host* at the specified port (p. 638)

q[uit]   Disconnects from the remote host and exit from `telnet` (p. 638)

sen[d] *tseq* ...   Sends the specified TELNET sequences to the remote host (p. 639)

set *var val*   Sets the `telnet` variable *var* to the value *val* (p. 639)

st[atus]   Shows the current status of `telnet` (p. 639)

t[oggle] *var* ...   Toggles each variable *var* (p. 639)

z   Suspends `telnet`, returns to the local system (p. 638)

TELNET Sequences.

?   Show help information for `send` (p. 639)

ao   The TELNET ⟨AO⟩ (Abort Output) sequence (p. 639)

ay[t]   The TELNET ⟨AYT⟩ (Are You There) sequence (p. 639)

b[rk]   The TELNET ⟨BRK⟩ (Break) sequence (p. 639)

ec   The TELNET ⟨EC⟩ (Erase Character) sequence (p. 639)

el   The TELNET ⟨EL⟩ (Erase Line) sequence (p. 639)

es[cape]   The current character for escaping to command mode (p. 639)

g[a]   The TELNET ⟨GA⟩ (Go Ahead) sequence (p. 639)

i[p]   The TELNET ⟨IP⟩ (Interrupt Process) sequence (p. 639)

n[op]   The TELNET ⟨NOP⟩ (No Operation) sequence (p. 639)

s[ynch]   The TELNET ⟨SYNCH⟩ (Synchronize) sequence (p. 639)

Variables with Values.

ec[ho]   The character that toggles echoing of locally typed characters (p. 640)

eo[f]   The remote end-of-file character (p. 640)

er[ase]   The remote erase character (p. 640)

es[cape]   The character that returns you to command mode (p. 640)

f[lushoutput]   The character for flushing remote output (p. 640)

i[nterrupt]   The remote interrupt character (p. 640)

k[ill]   The remote kill character (p. 640)

q[uit]   The remote quit character (p. 640)

Toggles.

?   Show the names of the available toggles (p. 639)

autof[lush]   Don't show typed data until remote interrupt is acknowledged (p. 641)

autos[ynch]   Cause the remote system to discard input preceding an interrupt (p. 641)

crl[f]   Map ⟨return⟩ sent by local system to ⟨return⟩ ⟨linefeed⟩ (p. 641)

crm[od]   Map ⟨return⟩ received from remote system to ⟨return⟩ ⟨linefeed⟩ (p. 641)

d[ebug]   Enable socket-level debugging (for superuser only) (p. 642)

f[lowcontrol]   Use flow-control signals to regulate communications (p. 642)

l[ocalchars]   Transform local control characters to TELNET control sequences (p. 640)

n[etdata]   Enable showing of network data (p. 642)

o[ptions]   Show internal protocol processing (p. 642)

A.2.121

test (Compare Values, Test File Properties)

The `test` command line (p. 333) has two forms:

     test *expr*

     [*expr*]

The tests listed here are provided by `ksh`, but not necessarily by other implementations of `test`.

String Comparisons.

s_1 True if s_1 is nonempty (p. 333)

$s_1 = s_2$ True if strings s_1 and s_2 are identical (p. 333)
s_1 != s_2 True if strings s_1 and s_2 are not identical (p. 333)
-n s_1 True if s_1 is nonempty (p. 333)
-z s_1 True if s_1 is empty (p. 333)

Numerical Comparisons.

n_1 -eq n_2 True if $n_1 = n_2$ (p. 334)
n_1 -ge n_2 True if $n_1 \geq n_2$ (p. 334)
n_1 -gt n_2 True if $n_1 > n_2$ (p. 334)
n_1 -le n_2 True if $n_1 \leq n_2$ (p. 334)
n_1 -lt n_2 True if $n_1 < n_2$ (p. 334)
n_1 -ne n_2 True if $n_1 \neq n_2$ (p. 334)

File Tests.

-b *file*   True if *file* exists and is a block device file (p. 334)
-c *file*   True if *file* exists and is a character device file (p. 334)
-d *file*   True if *file* exists and is a directory (p. 334)
-f *file*   True if *file* exists and is an ordinary file (neither a directory nor a device) (p. 334)
-g *file*   True if *file* exists and its set-gid bit is set (p. 334)
-G *file*   True if *file* exists and its group is the effective group ID (p. 334).
-k *file*   True if *file* exists and its sticky bit is set (p. 334)
-L *file*   True if *file* exists and is a symbolic link (p. 334)
-O *file*   True if *file* exists and its owner is the effective user ID (p. 334).
-p *file*   True if *file* exists and is a FIFO special file (p. 334)
-r *file*   True if *file* exists and is readable (p. 334)
-s *file*   True if *file* exists and its size is greater than zero (p. 334)
-S *file*   True if *file* exists and is a socket special file (p. 334)
-t [*n*]   True if the file associated with file descriptor *n* is a terminal (p. 335)
-u *file*   True if *file* exists and its set-uid bit is set (p. 334)
-w *file*   True if *file* exists and is writable (p. 334)
-x *file*   True if *file* exists and is executable (p. 334)
file$_1$ -eft *file$_2$*   True if *file$_1$* is another name for *file$_2$* (p. 335)
file$_1$ -nt *file$_2$*   True if *file$_1$* is newer than *file$_2$* (p. 335)
file$_1$ -nt *file$_2$*   True if *file$_1$* is older than *file$_2$* (p. 335)

Option Test.

-o *opt* True if the option *opt* is turned on

Combinations of Tests.

! *expr* True if *expr* is false and false otherwise (p. 335)
(*expr*)   True if *expr* is true (p. 335)
expr$_1$ -a *expr$_2$*   True if *expr$_1$* and *expr$_2$* are both true (p. 335)
expr$_1$ -o *expr$_2$*   True if either *expr$_1$* or *expr$_2$* is true (p. 335)

**A.2.122
time (Time a
Command)**

The form of the `time` command line (p. 292) is

> `time [-p]` *cmd*

where *cmd* is the command to be timed.

Command-Line Option.

-p   Force output to appear in a standardized format (p. 292)

**A.2.123
touch (Touch a File)**

The form of the `touch` command line (p. 138) is

   touch [-acm] [-r *ref-file* | -t *time*] *file* ...

where *time* is a sequence of digits of the form

   [[*CC*]*YY*]*MMDDhhmm*[.*ss*]

The pairs of digits represent the century, year, month, day, hour, minute, and second.

Command-Line Options.

-a   Change the access time (p. 139)
-c   Don't create the file if it doesn't already exist (p. 139)
-f   Force the touch no matter what the file permissions (p. 139)
-m   Change the modification time (p. 139)
-r *ref-file*   Use the times of the pathname *ref-file* (p. 138)
-t *time*   Set the times to *time* (p. 138)

Obsolescent Form of `touch`.   The following form of `touch` is obsolescent:

   touch [-acm] [*time*] *file* ...

The time in this case has the form *MMDDhhmm*[*YY*].

**A.2.124
tput (Send Setup
Instructions to a
Terminal)**

The form of the `tput` command line (p. 266) is

   tput [-T *term*] *cmd*

where *term* is your terminal type and *cmd* is one of the following:

name [*param*...]   Set the `terminfo` capability *name* as indicated by the *params* (p. 266)
`clear`   Send the string that clears the screen (p. 266)
`init`   Send the terminal initialization string (p. 266)
`longname`   Produce the full name of the terminal on standard output (p. 266)
`reset`   Send the terminal reset string (p. 266)

**A.2.125
tr (Translate or
Delete Characters)**

The form of the `tr` command line (p. 177) is

   tr [-cds] *str*$_1$ [*str*$_2$]

where *str*$_1$ contains characters to be replaced or deleted and *str*$_2$ contains characters to be substituted or squeezed.

Command-Line Options.

-c   Use the complement of *str*$_1$ rather than *str*$_1$ (p. 178)
-d   Delete the characters in *str*$_1$ (p. 178)
-s   Squeeze repetitions of characters in *str*$_2$ to single characters (p. 178)

**A.2.126
true (Return True)**

The form of the `true` command line (p. 335) is

   true

It does nothing and returns a zero exit code.

**A.2.127
tset (Set Terminal
Information)**

The form of the `tset` command line (p. 256) is

   tset [-IQrs] [-] [-e[*c*]] [-i[*c*]] [-k[*c*]] [-m [*itype*][*test speed*]:[?] *type*] [*term*]

where *term* is the name of a terminal type.

Command-Line Options.

- Produce the terminal type on standard output (p. 259)
-e[*c*]   Set the erase character to *c* (p. 259)
-E[*c*]   Set the erase character to *c* if the terminal can backspace (p. 259)
-h   Use the terminal type found in the /etc/ttytype table (p. 257)
-i[*c*]   Set the interrupt character to *c* (p. 259)
-I   Don't initialize the terminal, just reset it (p. 258)
-k[*c*]   Set the kill character to *c* (p. 259)
-m[*itype*][*test speed*]:[?]*type*   Match terminal type *itype* according to *speed*, conditionally set it
    to *type* (p. 257)
-Q   Suppress "Erase set to" and "Kill set to" messages (p. 260)
-r   Produce a message identifying the terminal type on standard error (p. 260)
-s   Produce commands for setting TERM on standard output (p. 259)
-S   Produce value for setting TERM on standard output (p. 260)

A.2.128
tty (Get the Terminal Name)

The form of the tty command line (p. 232) is:

    tty [-ls]

Command-Line Options.

-l   Show the line number of the terminal if it's a synchronous line (p. 232)
-s   Suppress the printing of the terminal's pathname (p. 232)

A.2.129
type (Show Interpretation of a Command)

The form of the type command line (p. 292) is

    type [*name* ...]

The interpretation as a command of each specified *name* is produced.

A.2.130
umask (Mask Default File Permissions)

The form of the umask command line (p. 135) is

    umask [-S] [*perm*]

where *perm* is a symbolic mode to be applied to the current file creation mask to obtain a new one.

Command-Line Option.

-S   Produce the permissions symbolically on standard output (p. 136)

A.2.131
umount (Unmount a File System)

The forms of the umount command line (p. 698) are

    umount -a [-v] [-t *fstype*]
    umount [-v] { *dev* | *mountdir* }

where the device to be unmounted is specified by its device name *dev* or its mount point *mountdir*.

Command-Line Options.

-a   Unmount all mounted file systems (p. 698)
-t *fstype*   Unmount file systems of the specified type(s) (p. 698)
-v   Unmount the file systems verbosely (p. 698)

A.2.132
unalias (Remove Alias Definitions)

The forms of the unalias command line (p. 358) are

    unalias *name* ...
    unalias -a

The indicated alias definitions are removed.

Command-Line Option.
-a   Remove all alias definitions (p. 358)

A.2.133
uname (Produce System Information)

The form of the uname command line (p. 291) is

        uname [-amnrsv]

Information about your system is produced on standard output. The default output is the same as with -s.

Command-Line Options.
-a   Produce the information for all the other options (p. 291)
-m   Produce the name of the hardware type of your machine (p. 291)
-n   Produce the name of your network node (p. 291)
-r   Produce the release level of your operating system (p. 291)
-s   Produce the name of the implementation of your operating system (p. 291)
-v   Produce the version level of the current release of your operating system (p. 291)

A.2.134
uncompress (Uncompress a File)

The form of the uncompress command line (p. 140) is

        uncompress [-cv] [*file*...]

where *file* ... is a list of files to be uncompressed. By default, each file, whose name must have the form '*file*.Z', is replaced by its uncompressed version.

Command-Line Option.
-c   Write the uncompressed files to standard output (p. 140)

A.2.135
unexpand (Convert Spaces to Tabs)

The form of the unexpand command line (p. 181) is

        unexpand [-a | -t *tablist*] [*file* ...]

The files are transformed by replacing leading whitespace by a sequence of tabs and spaces.

Command-Line Options.
-a   Also transform whitespace within a line to tabs (p. 183)
-t *tablist*   Assume tab stops at positions given by *tablist* (or at multiples of *tablist* if *tablist* is just a single number) (p. 183)

A.2.136
uniq (Eliminate Adjacent Repeated Lines)

The form of the uniq command line (p. 183) is

        uniq [-c | -d | -u] [-f *nf*] [-s *nc*] [*infile* [*outfile*]]

where the input comes from *infile* and is written to *outfile*. An obsolescent form is

        uniq [-c | -d | -u] [-*nf*] [+*nc*] [*infile* [*outfile*]]

Command-Line Options.
-*nf*   Ignore the first *n* fields, and any blanks preceding them (p. 183)
+*nc*   Ignore the first *n* characters (p. 183)
-c   Precede each output line by a count of how many times it occurs (p. 183)
-d   Produce just one copy of each repeated line (p. 183)
-f *nf*   Ignore the first *nf* fields, and any blanks preceding them (p. 183)
-s *nc*   Ignore the first *nc* characters (p. 183)
-u   Produce just the lines that are not repeated (p. 183)

A.2.137
uucp (UNIX to UNIX Copy)

The form of the uucp command line (p. 660) is

        uucp [-cCdfgjmnrsx] *sfile* ... *dfile*

where each *sfile* is a source file and *dfile* is a destination file of the form $system_1 !system_2! ... !system_n !path$.

Command-Line Options.

-c Don't make a copy of local files (p. 662)
-C Make a copy of local files (p. 662)
-d Make subdirectories as needed (p. 662)
-f Don't make subdirectories (p. 662)
-g *c* Assign the job a priority of *c* (p. 663)
-j Show the job identifier (p. 662)
-m Send a mail message to the requestor when the job is done (p. 663)
-n *user* Notify *user* on remote system that a file was sent (p. 663)
-r Queue the job without starting the transfer (p. 663)
-s *file* Send a status report to *file* (p. 663)
-x *n* Turn on debugging at level *n* (p. 663)

A.2.138
uudecode (Decode a Binary File)

The form of the uudecode command line (p. 143) is

    uudecode [*file*]

The specified *file*, or standard input, is read and the pathname specified by the input data is overwritten with the decoded version of the file found in the input data.

A.2.139
uuencode (Encode a Binary File)

The form of the uuencode command line (p. 143) is

    uuencode [*file*] *tpath*

The specified *file*, or standard input, is read and encoded. The pathname *tpath* specifies where the file should be placed when it is decoded.

A.2.140
**uuname
(Get Names of Remote UNIX Systems)**

The form of the uuname command line (p. 665) is

    uuname [-cl]

Command-Line Options.

-l List the name of the machine you're on (p. 665)
-c List the names of systems known to the cu program (p. 665)

A.2.141
uupick (Pick Up Files from UNIX to UNIX Transfer)

The form of the uupick command line (p. 660) is

    uupick [-s *system*]

If you specify *system*, then you'll only get to retrieve files sent from that remote system.

Responses for Each Item. For each item retrieved, uupick asks for a response. The possible responses are as follows:

[Enter] Go on to the next item (p. 660)
[EOF] Quit, exit from uupick (p. 660)
!*cmd* Execute *cmd* in a subshell (p. 660)
* Show a summary of the commands (p. 660)
a [*dir*] Move all the items received from the system that sent the current item (p. 660)
d Discard this item (p. 660)
m [*dir*] Move this item to the directory *dir* (p. 660)
p Show the item; that is, send it to standard output (p. 660)
q Quit, exit from uupick (p. 660)

A.2.142
uustat (Check uucp Status)

The form of the uustat command line (p. 663) is

    uustat [-ampq] [-k *id*] [-r *id*] [-s *sys*] [-u *user*]

Command-Line Options.

-a   Output the names of all items awaiting transmission (p. 664)
-k *id*   Kill the item whose identifier is *id* (p. 664)
-m   Report the status of all machines known to uucp (p. 664)
-p   Execute the command ps -flp for all processes that are in lock files (p. 664)
-q   List the items queued for each remote machine (p. 664)
-r *id*   Rejuvenate item *id* by resetting its modification time (p. 664)
-s *sys*   Only report items destined for remote system *sys* (p. 664)
-u *user*   Only report items originated by user *user* (p. 664)

Except for -s and -u, only one option can be used at a time.

A.2.143
uuto **(Send Files UNIX to UNIX)**

The form of the uuto command line (p. 659) is

    uuto [-pm] *source* ... *path*!*person*

Command-Line Options.

-p   Copy each file to be transmitted to a spooling directory (p. 659)
-m   Send mail notification to the sender (p. 659)

A.2.144
vi **(Visual Editor)**

The form of the vi command line (p. 419) is

    vi [-rR] [-c *cmd*] [-t *tag*] [-w *size*] [*file*...]

Input Mode Commands.

(Erase)   Erases the previous character (p. 416)
(Enter)   Ends the input line, starts a new one (p. 416)
(Esc)   Ends the insertion, returns to command mode (p. 416)
(Intr)   Ends the insertion, returns to command mode (p. 416)
(Kill)   Deletes all characters typed on the current line (p. 416)
(Ctrl) D   Backs up over a tab at the start of a line (p. 417)
(Ctrl) Q   Takes the next character literally (p. 416)
(Ctrl) V   Takes the next character literally (p. 416)
(Ctrl) W   Erases the word just typed (p. 416)
∧ (Ctrl) D   Starts this line at the left margin in autoindent mode (p. 418)
0 (Ctrl) D   Cancels all indentation in autoindent mode (p. 418)

Status-Line Mode Commands.

(Erase)   Erases the previous character (p. 417)
(Enter)   Executes the command, then returns to command mode (p. 416)
(Esc)   Executes the command, then returns to command mode (p. 416)
(Intr)   Interrupts whatever is happening, returns to command mode (p. 416)
(Kill)   Deletes all but the first character of the status line (p. 417)
(Ctrl) Q   Takes the next character literally (p. 417)
(Ctrl) V   Takes the next character literally (p. 417)
(Ctrl) W   Erases the word just typed (p. 417)

Cancelling and Interrupting Commands.

(Esc)   Cancels the command you're typing (p. 416)
(Intr)   Interrupts the command that's executing (p. 416)

Command-Line Options.

+*command* Execute *command* before editing (p. 419)
-c *command* Execute *command* before editing (p. 419)
-r   Recover *file* ... after an editor crash (p. 419)

-R   Edit in read-only mode (p. 419)
-t *tag*   Edit the file containing *tag* (p. 419)
-w *size*   Set `window`, the default screenful size, to *size* (p. 419)

Commands for Command Mode.   Most commands can be preceded by an integer *n*, which indicates a repetition count. In the list of commands that follows, *n* is shown only when it is explicitly mentioned in the command's description.

(Erase)   Moves left one character (p. 422)
(Enter)   Moves to the first nonwhite character on the following line (p. 422)
(SPACE)   Move right one character (p. 422)
(Ctrl) B   Scrolls up (backward) one screen (p. 420)
(Ctrl) D   Scrolls down (forward) by half a screen or *n* lines (p. 420)
(Ctrl) E   Scrolls down (forward) by one line (p. 421)
(Ctrl) F   Scrolls down (forward) one screen (p. 420)
(Ctrl) G   Shows status information (p. 432)
(Ctrl) J   Moves directly down one line (p. 422)
(Ctrl) H   Moves left one character (p. 422)
(Ctrl) L   Regenerates the screen (p. 421)
(Ctrl) N   Moves directly down one line (p. 422)
(Ctrl) P   Moves directly up one line (p. 422)
(Ctrl) R   Regenerates the screen, eliminating null lines (p. 421)
(Ctrl) U   Scrolls up (backward) by half a screen or *n* lines (p. 421)
(Ctrl) Y   Scrolls up (backward) by one line (p. 421)
&   Repeats the previous global replacement command (p. 428)
'*c*   Moves to the beginning of the line containing mark *c* (p. 426)
''   Moves to the beginning of the line containing the previous context (p. 426)
@*b*   Executes commands in buffer *b* (p. 431)
'*c*   Moves to mark *c* (p. 426)
''   Moves to the previous context (p. 426)
!*m cmd*   Executes *cmd* with the region to *m* as standard input, replaces that region by standard output (p. 430)
n| Moves to column *n* of the current line (p. 422)
{   Moves backward to the previous paragraph boundary or non-atomic LISP S-expression (p. 424)
}   Moves forward to the next paragraph boundary or non-atomic LISP S-expression (p. 423)
[[Moves backward to the previous section boundary (p. 424)
]]   Moves forward to the next section boundary (p. 424)
∧ Moves to the first nonwhite character on the current line (p. 422)
:*cmd*   Executes the **ex** command *cmd* (p. 417)
, Repeats the last **f**, **F**, **t**, or **T** command in the reverse direction (p. 424)
−   Moves to the first nonwhite character on the previous line (p. 422)
$ Moves to the last character on the current line (p. 422)
.   Repeats the last action that modified the buffer (p. 432)
"*b*d*m*   Deletes the region of text from the cursor to *m* and stores it in buffer *b* (p. 431)
"*b*p   Inserts contents of buffer *b* after the current character or line (p. 432)
"*n*p   Puts the *n*th most recently deleted block of text after the cursor (p. 432)
"*b*P   Inserts contents of buffer *b* before the current character or line (p. 432)
"*n*P   Puts the *n*th most recently deleted block of text before the cursor (p. 432)
"*b*y*m*   Yanks the region of text from the cursor to *m* and stores it in buffer *b* (p. 431)
>*m*   Indents the region from the current line to the line containing *m* (p. 430)
<*m*   Outdents the region from the current line to the line containing *m* (p. 430)
(Moves backward to the first character of the current sentence or the previous LISP S-expression (p. 423)
)   Moves forward to the first nonwhite character of the next sentence or the next LISP S-expression (p. 423)
%   Moves to the matching delimiter (p. 424)
+   Moves to the first nonwhite character on the following line (p. 422)
?   Searches backward for the most recent search pattern (p. 425)
?*pat* (Enter)   Moves backward to the next text matching *pat* (p. 425)
?*pat*?   Moves backward to the next text matching *pat* (p. 425)

?*pat*?+*n*   Moves backward to the beginning of the *n*th line before the next text matching
    pat (p. 425)

;   Repeats the last f, F, t, or T command (p. 424)

/   Searches forward for the most recent search pattern (p. 425)

/*pat* (Enter)   Moves forward to the next text matching *pat* (p. 425)

/*pat*/   Moves forward to the next text matching *pat* (p. 425)

/*pat*/+*n*   Moves forward to the beginning of the *n*th line after the next text matching *pat*
    (p. 425)

/*pat*/z (Enter)   Regenerates the screen with the next line containing *pat* at the top (p. 421)

~   Changes the case of the letter under the cursor (p. 429)

0   Moves to the first character on the current line (p. 422)

a   Appends text after the cursor (p. 426)

A   Appends text at the end of the current line (p. 426)

b   Moves back to the beginning of the current word (p. 423)

B   Moves back to the beginning of the current blank-delimited word (p. 423)

c*m*   Changes the text from the cursor to *m* (p. 429)

cc   Changes the current line (p. 429)

C   Changes the rest of the current line (p. 427)

d*m*   Deletes the text from the cursor to *m* (p. 429)

dd   Deletes the current line (p. 429)

D   Deletes the rest of the current line (p. 428)

e   Moves to the last character of the current word (p. 423)

E   Moves to the last character of the current blank-delimited word (p. 423)

f*c*   Moves to the next occurrence of *c* (p. 424)

F*c*   Moves to the previous occurrence of *c* (p. 424)

*n*G   Moves to the first character on line *n* (p. 422)

h   Moves left one character (p. 422)

H   Moves to the beginning of the first line on the screen (p. 422)

i   Inserts text before the cursor (p. 426)

I   Inserts text before the first non-white character on the line (p. 426)

j   Moves directly down one line (p. 422)

J   Joins the current line with the next line (p. 428)

k   Moves directly up one line (p. 422)

l   Moves right one character (p. 422)

L   Moves to the beginning of the last line on the screen (p. 422)

m*c*   Places mark *c* at the current cursor position (p. 426)

M   Moves to the beginning of the middle line on the screen (p. 422)

n   Searches in the same direction for the most recent search pattern (p. 425)

N   Searches in the opposite direction for the most recent search pattern (p. 425)

o   Opens a line under the current line (p. 426)

O   Opens a line above the current line (p. 426)

p   Puts the contents of the anonymous buffer just after the cursor (p. 428)

P   Puts the contents of the anonymous buffer just before the cursor (p. 428)

Q   Switches over to ex (p. 435)

r*c*   Replaces the character under the cursor with *c* (p. 428)

R   Replaces characters with input text (p. 427)

s   Substitutes for the character under the cursor (p. 427)

S   Substitutes for the current line (p. 427)

t*c*   Moves to the character just before the next occurrence of *c* (p. 424)

T*c*   Moves to the character just after the next occurrence of *c* (p. 424)

u   Undoes the most recent change or insertion (p. 432)

U   Restores the current line (p. 432)

w   Moves forward to the beginning of the next word (p. 423)

W   Moves forward to the beginning of the next blank-delimited word (p. 423)

x   Deletes the character under the cursor (p. 427)

X   Deletes the character before the cursor (p. 427)

y*m*   Yanks the text from the cursor to *m* (p. 430)

yy   Yanks the current line (p. 429)

Y   Yanks the current line (p. 428)

z (Enter)   Regenerates the screen with the current line at the top (p. 421)

z*n* (Enter)   Regenerates the screen with an *n*-line window and the current line at the top
    (p. 421)

z-   Regenerates the screen with the current line at the bottom (p. 421)
z.   Regenerates the screen with the current line in the middle (p. 421)
z+   Regenerates the screen with the current line at the top (p. 421)
ZZ   Saves the buffer you're editing and exits (p. 432)

ex Commands Commonly Used in vi.

:e *file*   Abandons the buffer and starts editing *file* (p. 433)
:q   Quits vi, abandoning the buffer (p. 433)
:q!   Quits vi unconditionally, abandoning the buffer (p. 433)
:r *file*   Reads and inserts the file *file* (p. 433)
:s/*pat*/*repl*/g   Globally replaces the pattern *pat* by *repl* (p. 428)
:set   Specifies or queries a variable (p. 433)
:ta *tag*   Opens the file containing *tag*, moves the cursor to *tag* (p. 433)
:[*r*]w [*file*]   Writes region *r* of the buffer to *file*, continues editing (p. 432)
:wq   Writes the buffer to the current file and quits (p. 432)
:x[it][!] [*file*]   Writes the buffer to *file* and exits (p. 433)

Environment Variables.   The bracketed commands indicate abbreviations.

autoindent [ai]   Enable automatic indentation (p. 438)
autoprint [ap]   Show line whenever modified (p. 440)
autowrite [aw]   Write changed file before switching to another file (p. 437)
beautify [bf]   Discard nonprinting characters from input (p. 438)
errorbells [eb]   Sound bell before every error message (p. 437)
exrc   Look for .exrc file before editing (p. 441)
ignorecase [ic]   Ignore case of letters in search pattern (p. 436)
list   Show tabs as '∧I', newlines as '$' (p. 440)
magic   Recognize regular expression characters (.\ [*) in patterns (p. 435)
mesg   Accept messages from other programs (p. 441)
modelines   Recognize editor commands in the first five lines and/or the last five lines of a
     file to be edited (p. 441)
number [nu]   Prefix each output line with a line number (p. 440)
paragraphs [para]   Specify nroff macros that start a paragraph (p. 436)
prompt   Show the prompt character ':' when waiting for a command (p. 440)
readonly   Inhibit changes to the buffer (p. 436)
remap   Repeat macro mapping until no more characters are mapped (p. 439)
report   Specify *n* for reporting changes of more than *n* lines resulting from a single
     operation (p. 437)
scroll   Specify number of lines that Ctrl U and Ctrl D initially scroll up or down
     (p. 440)
sections   Specify nroff macros that start a section (p. 436)
shell   Specify shell for "escaped" commands (p. 442)
shiftwidth [sw]   Specify tab spacing for < and > commands and for Ctrl D in input
     (p. 438)
showmatch [sm]   Show '(' or '\{' matching typed ')' or '\}' (p. 440)
showmode   Put insert indicator on status line (p. 437)
slowopen   Delay updating the screen until an insert is finished (p. 442)
tabstop [ts]   Specify tab stop interval for showing text (p. 438)
tags   Specify list of files to be searched for tags (p. 436)
term   Specify terminal type (p. 442)
terse   Give error diagnostics in terse form (p. 437)
timeout   Allow one second for typing left-hand side of macro definitions (p. 439)
warn   Issue warning when leaving editor or switching files when current file is unsaved
     (p. 437)
window   Set number of lines in a screenful (p. 440)
wrapscan [ws]   "Wrap around" the end of the buffer during a search (p. 436)
wrapmargin [wm]   Specify input line length for wrapping to a new line (p. 438)
writeany [wa]   Inhibit safety checks before writing to a file (p. 437)

A.2.145
`wait` **(Wait for a Process to Finish)**

The form of the `wait` command line (p. 249) is

    `wait [ n ]`

where *n* is the number of the process being waited for.

A.2.146
`wc` **(Count Words, Lines, or Characters)**

The form of the `wc` command line (p. 137) is

    `wc [-clw]` [*file* ...]

Command-Line Options.

`-c` Count characters (p. 138)
`-l` Count lines (p. 138)
`-w` Count words (p. 138)

A.2.147
`which` **(Show Pathname of Command)**

The form of the `which` command line (p. 128) is

    `which` *progname* ...

where *progname* ... is a series of programs to be located.

A.2.148
`who` **(List Users and Processes)**

The POSIX form of the `who` command line (p. 228) is

    `who [-mTu]`

The non-POSIX forms of the `who` command line (p. 228) are

    `who ["-abdHlprqstTu"]` *file*
    `who am i`
    `who am I`

The file *file* is optional; if it is given, `who` looks for its data there. The second and third forms produce your login name and the name of the terminal you're currently using.

Command-Line Options for POSIX Versions.

`-m` Show only information about your own terminal (p. 228)
`-T` Show information in a standard form (p. 229)
`-u` Show idle time for each user (p. 229)

Command-Line Options for Non-POSIX Versions.

`-a` Turn on all other options except `-T` (p. 230)
`-b` Indicate when the system was last rebooted (p. 229)
`-d` List dead processes started by `init` (p. 230)
`-H` Put a heading above each column.
`-l` List only those terminals currently not in use (p. 229)
`-p` List all active processes started by `init` (p. 230)
`-r` Indicate the current run level of `init` (p. 229)
`-q` Show only the names and count of logged-on users (p. 229)
`-s` List only the name, terminal, and login time of each user (p. 229)
`-t` Indicate when the system clock was last changed (p. 229)
`-T` Indicate the "write state" of each terminal (p. 229)
`-u` List only those users currently logged in (p. 229)

A.2.149
`write` **(Write to Terminal)**

The usage of the `write` command (p. 270) is

    `write` *user* [*line*]
    ... *text of the message*
    `EOF`

The message is sent to *user*. The terminal name *line* is necessary only if *user* is logged in at more than one terminal.

A.2.150
xargs (Call a Utility with Constructed Arguments)

The form of the `xargs` command line (p. 289) is

> xargs [-t] [-n *nargs* [-x]] [-s *size*] [*cmd* [*arg* ...]]

Command-Line Options.

-n *nargs*   Call *cmd* with up to *nargs* arguments (p. 289)
-s *size*   Call *cmd*, limiting length of command line to *size* (p. 289)
-t   Enable trace mode (p. 289)
-x   Terminate if *nargs* arguments won't fit in command length (p. 289)

A.2.151
xbiff (Mailbox Flag for X)

The form of the `xbiff` command line (p. 684) is

> xbiff [*options*]

See Section 13.7 for a list of the Toolkit options and your system manual for the others.

A.2.152
xclock (Analog/Digital Clock for X)

The form of the `xclock` command line (p. 683) is

> xclock [*options*]

Command-Line Options.

-analog   Display a conventional 12-hour clock face (p. 683)
-chime   Chime once on the half hour, twice on the hour (p. 683)
-digital   Display a 24-hour digital clock (p. 683)
-hd *color*   Use *color* as the color of the hands on an analog clock (p. 683)
-hl *color*   Use *color* as the color of the edges of the hands on an analog clock (p. 683)
-padding *n*   Pad the edges of the clock with *n* pixels (p. 683)
-update *n*   Update the clock every *n* seconds (p. 683)

See Section 13.7 for a list of the Toolkit options for `xclock`.

A.2.153
xcolors (Display the X Colors)

The form of the `xcolors` command line (p. 684) is

> xcolors [*options*]

See Section 13.7 for a list of the Toolkit options and your system manual for the others.

A.2.154
xfd (Display an X Font)

The form of the `xfd` command line (p. 684) is

> xfd [*options*]

The options must include **-fn** *font*, where *font* specifies the font to be displayed. See Section 13.7 for a list of the Toolkit options and your system manual for the others.

A.2.155
xfontsel (Select and Display X Fonts)

The form of the `xfontsel` command line (p. 684) is

> xfontsel [*options*]

See Section 13.7 for a list of the Toolkit options and your system manual for the others.

A.2.156
xinit (Start the X Server)

The form of the `xinit` command line (p. 685) is

> xinit [[*client*] *options*] [-- [*server*] [:*display*] [*options*]]

Here *client* is a program to be started initially, *server* is the server program to be used, ':*display*' is the display to be used, and the second set of *options* are appended to the command line for *server*.

A.2.157
xkill (Kill an X Client)

The form of the `xkill` command line (p. 687) is

> xkill [*options*]

See Section 13.7 for a list of the Toolkit options and your system manual for the others.

**A.2.158
xlsfonts (Display
a List of X Fonts)**

The form of the xlsfonts command line (p. 684) is

>   xlsfonts [*options*]

The -fn *font* option specifies a font name with wildcards that is matched against the available fonts. See your system manual for the other options.

**A.2.159
xman (Display Manual
Pages Under X)**

The form of the xman command line (p. 687) is

>   xman [*options*]

See Section 13.7 for a list of the Toolkit options and your system manual for the others.

**A.2.160
xrdb (Resource
Database Utility
for X)**

The form of the xrdb command line (p. 686) is

>   xrdb [*options*] [*file*]

where *file* specifies a file containing a set of resource specifications.

Command-Line Options.

-load   Load the global resource database from standard input (p. 686)
-merge   Merge standard input with the global resource database (p. 686)
-query   Send the current contents of the global resource database to standard output (p. 686)
-remove   Make the global resource database empty (p. 686)

See your system manual for a description of the remaining options.

**A.2.161
xset (Set User
Preferences for X)**

The form of the xset command line (p. 686) is

>   xset [*options*]

The q option (no '-') lists the current settings. See your system manual for a list of the remaining options.

**A.2.162
xsetroot (Set Root
Window Appearance
for X)**

The form of the xsetroot command line (p. 686) is

>   xsetroot [*options*]

See your system manual for a list of the options.

**A.2.163
xterm (Terminal
Emulator for X)**

The form of the xterm command line (p. 681) is

>   xterm [*options*]

See Section 13.7 for a list of the Toolkit options and your system manual for the others.

**A.2.164
zcat
(Uncompress and
Concatenate Files)**

The form of the zcat command line (p. 140) is

>   zcat [*file . . .*]

where *file . . .* is a list of files to be uncompressed by uncompress. By default, each file, whose name must have the form '*file*.Z', is replaced by its uncompressed version. The uncompressed files are written to standard output.

On systems that provide the GNU utilities, zcat may refer to gzcat rather than to the version described here.

B

Comparison of MS-DOS and UNIX

If you're accustomed to working with the MS-DOS operating system for the IBM PC family of computers, you'll find a lot of resemblance between MS-DOS and UNIX; in fact, much of the structure of MS-DOS is derived from UNIX. In this appendix we correlate features of MS-DOS with similar features of UNIX.

B.1 Treatment of Files

These are some of the differences between the treatment of files in MS-DOS and in UNIX:

- The directories in an MS-DOS path are separated by '\'; those in a UNIX path are separated by '/'.

- In MS-DOS, file names are case-insensitive; in UNIX they are case-sensitive.

- The dot in an MS-DOS file name separates the name part from the extension. Every MS-DOS file name has an eight-character name and a three-character extension, even though the extension may be blank. In UNIX, a dot is like any other character in a file name, so a UNIX file name can have any number of dots or none at all. Some UNIX programs, however, do adopt the convention of suffixing file names with an extension such as '.c'. The division of a name into a name part and an extension is a convention adopted by particular programs, not a property of UNIX itself. A UNIX file name may have any length up to the maximum permitted by the implementation you're using (at least 14 characters).

- In MS-DOS, each file system resides on its own drive, designated by 'd:' where d is the drive letter. In UNIX, all file systems are part of a single hierarchical tree descending from the root directory '/'.

- In MS-DOS, an executable file is one with an extension of .exe, .com, or .bat. In UNIX, any file whose execute permission is turned on is executable, regardless of its name.

- In MS-DOS, a sequence of commands may be collected into a batch file with an extension of .bat. In UNIX, such a sequence of commands is treated as a shell script. The file containing the script must have execute permission but need not have any special name.

- An MS-DOS file has only one name; a UNIX file may have several names, each represented by a different link.

- Both in MS-DOS and in UNIX, a file name can include the wildcards '?' and '*'. The '?' stands for any single character and the '*' for an arbitrary sequence of characters.

  - In MS-DOS, a file name to be matched against a name with wildcards is first padded with blanks to extend the name part to eight characters and the extension to three characters. Wildcards are matched independently within the name part and within the extension. A star matches everything up to the end of the part containing it, so characters after a star have no effect. The construct '*.*' matches all files, while the construct '*' matches just those files with an empty or blank extension.

  - In UNIX, a file name to be matched against a name with wildcards is treated as a single string.[1] Characters after a star are considered in the match and can affect the result. UNIX file names can also include wildcards of the form '[*cset*]' (see Section 2.9.1). The construct '*.*' matches file names containing one or more dots, while the construct '*' matches all file names (except those whose names start with a dot).

As another example, a file name 'agley.c' would be matched by the constructs 'agl*z.c*' and 'agley.c??' under MS-DOS but not under UNIX. It would be matched by the construct 'agl*c' under UNIX but not under MS-DOS.

---

1. Wildcard matching, also called "file substitution", is done by the various UNIX shells, not by the kernel. Nevertheless, all shells follow essentially the same conventions for wildcard matching. In MS-DOS, wildcard matching is handled by MS-DOS itself in response to low-level system requests.

- In an MS-DOS text file, the end of a line is indicated by the two-character sequence ⟨linefeed⟩ ⟨return⟩ (ASCII 13 followed by ASCII 10). In a UNIX text file, the end of a line is indicated by a single newline character, represented as ⟨linefeed⟩. Some MS-DOS and UNIX programs are affected by this difference, while others are not. When you need to use a file created under one system within the other one, you may need to do a format conversion. The utility programs for this conversion vary from system to system, but typical names for them are `dtou` (MS-DOS to UNIX) and `utod` (UNIX to MS-DOS).

- The information about a file kept by MS-DOS differs somewhat from that kept by UNIX. For instance, there is nothing in a UNIX directory entry corresponding to the MS-DOS archive bit, which MS-DOS uses to keep track of whether a file has been backed up. On the other hand, UNIX has a more extensive set of file permissions.

- In MS-DOS, you can make a file read-only by setting its read-only attribute or make it invisible to most programs by setting its system or hidden attribute. These permissions apply to any program that accesses the file. In UNIX, a file has independent sets of "read", "write", and "execute" permissions for its owner, the other members of its owner's group, and the rest of the world. The only way to make a file invisible is to deny read permission for the directory containing the file.

- When you create a pipeline under MS-DOS, the operating system creates a temporary file to contain the output of the first program. The second program then reads that file. The second program cannot start until the first one has finished. Under UNIX, no file is created; the data passed through the pipeline is passed through memory and the two programs run in parallel.

B.2   MS-DOS Commands and Their UNIX Equivalents

These are some of the most common MS-DOS commands and the UNIX commands that perform approximately the same functions:

MS-DOS	UNIX	*Function*
`attrib`	`chmod, ls -l`	Sets or displays file attributes.
`cd, chdir`	`cd, chdir, pwd`	Sets or displays current directory.
`command`	`sh, csh, ksh, bash`	Calls a subshell.
`comp`	`cmp`	Compares files byte by byte.
`copy`	`cp,cat`	Copies files.
`date`	`date`	Shows or set the date.
`del, erase`	`rm`	Removes files.

dir	ls	Lists files in a directory.
exit	exit	Exits from the command processor.
fc	cmp,diff	Compares files.
find	fgrep	Searches for a string in a set of files.
md, mkdir	mkdir	Makes a directory.
more	more, less	Displays output by screenfuls.
path	set PATH	Sets search path for commands.
print	lp,lpr	Prints files.
prompt	set PS1, set prompt	Sets shell prompt.
rem	echo	Displays a comment.
ren	mv	Renames files.
rd,rmdir	rmdir,rm -r	Removes directories.
set	set,setenv	Sets or displays environment strings.
sort	sort	Sorts data in files.
time	date	Shows or sets the time.
type	cat	Displays the contents of a file.
xcopy	cp,cpio -p	Copies files and subdirectories.

B.3   Other Related Features

These are some other correspondences between MS-DOS and UNIX:

- In MS-DOS, you are automatically connected to your system when you turn on the computer; in UNIX, you must log in and provide a password (unless explicit provision has been made to the contrary).

- In MS-DOS, the autoexec.bat file contains commands that are executed when you start the system. The corresponding UNIX file is .profile or .login, depending on which shell you're using. The MS-DOS config.sys file has no direct analogue in UNIX.

- In both MS-DOS and UNIX, your interaction with the system is controlled by a shell. In MS-DOS, your primary shell is specified as part of the config.sys file or defaulted to command.com. In UNIX, it is set by the system administrator and recorded in /etc/passwd or defaulted. The UNIX default is a local option; usually it is chosen to be either /bin/sh or /bin/csh.

- In MS-DOS, you can turn a sequence of commands into a command *name* by placing the commands in a file '*name*.bat'. In UNIX, you would place such a sequence of commands in an executable file '*name*', making it into a shell script with the command

    chmod +x *file*

- Both MS-DOS and UNIX provide for a set of environment variables to be associated with a shell. In UNIX, the variables are associated with a process, which need not be a shell; in MS-DOS, there are no processes other than shells in execution. Environment variables are referenced as '%*name*%' in MS-DOS but as '$*name*' in UNIX.

C

Resources

In this appendix we list a number of books on UNIX as well as collections of software on CD-ROM. The Internet is a rich source of UNIX resources as well; see Section 12.4 for a discussion of these resources.

C.1 Books

While in our more sanguine moments we may believe we've written the most useful book about UNIX, we certainly wouldn't claim that we've written the only useful book about UNIX. Here are some of the others that we recommend:

[B1] Abrahams, Paul; Berry, Karl; and Hargreaves, Kathy. *TEX for the Impatient*. Reading, Mass.: Addison-Wesley, 1990.

A TEX handbook for technically oriented users who are not TEX experts.

[B2] Aho, Alfred V.; Kernighan, Brian W.; and Weinberger, Peter J. *The AWK Programming Language*. Reading, Mass.: Addison-Wesley, 1988.

The definitive book on `awk`, written by `awk`'s authors. It includes a tutorial, many examples, and a reference manual.

[B3]   Andleigh, Prabhat K. *UNIX System Architecture.* Englewood Cliffs, N.J.: Prentice-Hall, 1990.

A book whose coverage is similar to [B4] but whose organization makes it easier to find quick answers to difficult questions about UNIX subsystems and internals.

[B4]   Bach, Maurice J. *The Design of the UNIX Operating System.* Englewood Cliffs, N.J.: Prentice-Hall, 1986.

An excellent reference source on UNIX internals. Topics include the buffer cache, internal representation of files, process scheduling, memory management (swapping and paging), and the I/O subsystem.

[B5]   Bolsky, Morris I., and Korn, David G. *The New KornShell: Command and Programming Language.* Englewood Cliffs, N.J.: Prentice-Hall, 1995.

The definitive guide to the Korn shell, including both a tutorial and a reference manual.

[B6]   Computer Systems Research Group, University of California, Berkeley, Cal. *4.4 Berkeley Software Distribution Manual Set: 4.4BSD User's Reference Manual, 4.4BSD User's Supplementary Documents, 4.4BSD User's Reference Manual, 4.4BSD Programmer's Supplementary Documents, 4.4BSD Programmer's Reference Manual, 4.4BSD System Manager's Manual.* Newton, Mass.: O'Reilly & Associates, 1994.

An exceedingly useful collection of documents even for those who are not using BSD, updated from an earlier version published by USENIX. The Supplementary Documents include nearly all the classic UNIX papers from Bell Telephone Laboratories, tutorials on many UNIX programs, and information on the internals of BSD. Much of this information is very difficult to locate elsewhere.

[B7]   Dougherty, Dale, and O'Reilly, Tim. *UNIX Text Processing.* Indianapolis, Ind.: Hayden, 1987.

A tutorial on UNIX editors and formatters. Its coverage includes `nroff`, `troff`, `tbl`, `eqn`, `pic`, `vi`, `ex`, `sed`, and `awk`.

[B8]   Griswold, Ralph E., and Griswold, Madge T. *The Icon Programming Language.* 2nd ed. Englewood Cliffs, N.J.: Prentice-Hall, 1990.

The authoritative tutorial and reference manual for Icon, written by Icon's authors.

[B9]   Hewlett-Packard. *The Ultimate Guide to the VI and EX Text Editors.* Redwood City, Cal.: Benjamin/Cummings, 1990.

A guide to `vi` and `ex` that includes many details not found elsewhere.

[B10]   IEEE Computer Society, Technical Committee on Operating Systems and Application Environments. *Portable Operating System Interface (POSIX). Part 2: Shell and Utilities, Vols. 1-2.* New York, N.Y.: Institute of Electrical and Electronics Engineers, 1993.

The text of the POSIX standard. Vol. 1 contains the requirements of the standard; Vol. 2 contains the rationale. The rationale is very helpful in understanding the requirements.

[B11]   Kernighan, Brian, and Pike, Rob. *The UNIX Programming Environment.* Englewood Cliffs, N.J.: Prentice-Hall, 1984.

The classic overview of Seventh Edition UNIX by two of its major contributors. It covers both the user's view and the essentials of the implementation.

[B12]   Kernighan, Brian W., and Ritchie, Dennis M. *The C Programming Language.* 2nd ed. Englewood Cliffs, N.J.: Prentice-Hall, 1988.

The classic book on the C programming language. The second edition has been updated to describe the ANSI standard version of C.

[B13]   Knuth, Donald E. *The TEXbook.* Reading, Mass.: Addison-Wesley, 1986.

The ultimate source of information on TEX, written by TEX's designer and implementor.

[B14]   Krol, Ed. *The Whole Internet: User's Guide & Catalog.* 2nd ed. Newton, Mass.: O'Reilly & Associates, 1994.

A comprehensive guide from the user's standpoint to what the Internet is and how to use it. The book covers most of the activities an Internet user is likely to undertake. Krol also wrote *Hitchhiker's Guide to the Internet.*

[B15]   Lamport, Leslie. 2nd ed. *LATEX: A Document Preparation System.* Reading, Mass.: Addison-Wesley, 1994.

The authoritative user's guide and reference manual for LATEX, updated to LATEX2$_\varepsilon$.

[B16]   LaQuey, Tracy, and Ryer, Jeanne C. *Internet Companion.* 2nd ed. Reading, Mass.: Addison-Wesley, 1994.

A lively and entertaining walking tour of the Internet. It includes pointers to many interesting places and services and introductions to Archie, `gopher`, WAIS, and the World Wide Web.

[B17]   Leffler, Samuel J.; McKusick, Marshall Kirk; Karels, Michael J.; and Quarterman, John S. *The Design and Implementation of the 4.3 BSD UNIX Operating System.* Reading, Mass.: Addison-Wesley, 1989.

The authoritative description of the design of BSD.

[B18]   Libes, Don, and Ressler, Sandy. *Life with UNIX: A Guide for Everyone.* Englewood Cliffs, N.J.: Prentice-Hall, 1989.

An excellent source for material on the history and culture of UNIX. It includes a lot of information about the USENET.

[B19]   Linux Documentation Project. *The Linux Documentation Project.* Chesterfield, Mich.: Linux System Labs, 1994.

A collection of guides to using and installing Linux, including Matthew Welsh's "Linux Installation and Getting Started", the Yggdrasil Linux manual, Olaf Kirch's "Linux Network Administrator's Guide", Michael Johnson's "Kernel Hacker's Guide", and a series of "how-to"s on various topics. Though all this information is available electronically, this book is a very useful centralized source of it in printed form. The book is updated regularly.

[B20]   Nemeth, Evi; Snyder, Garth; Seebass, Scott; and Hein, Trent R. *UNIX System Administration Handbook.* Englewood Cliffs, N.J.: Prentice-Hall, 1995.

A wide-ranging handbook that covers all major UNIX variants and provides practical details and useful tips about every aspect of system administration. The book includes a CD-ROM with many useful tools.

[B21]   O'Donnell, Sandra Martin. *Programming for the World, A Guide to Internationalization.* Englewood Cliffs, N.J.: Prentice-Hall, 1994.

A fine description of the linguistic and cultural differences that internationalized versions of UNIX must cope with. It describes the POSIX locale facilities and character-set issues in great and revealing detail and has lots of pragmatic advice.

[B22]   Olczack, Anatole. *The Korn Shell: User and Programming Manual.* Reading, Mass.: Addison-Wesley, 1992.

Complete coverage of the 1988 Korn shell for both shell programmers and interactive users. This tutorial-style book is well organized and has many examples.

[B23]   O'Reilly, Tim; Quercia, Valerie; and Lamb, Linda. *X Window System User's Guide, Vol. 3.* 3rd ed. Newton, Mass.: O'Reilly & Associates, 1990.

A guide to X from the user's viewpoint, including the structure of the system, major X clients, the `twm` window manager, and the procedures for configuring X on your system. Other volumes in this series deal with programming conventions for X.

[B24]   O'Reilly, Tim, and Todino, Grace. *Managing UUCP and USENET.* 10th ed. Newton, Mass.: O'Reilly & Associates, 1992.

One of the few books to completely explain how to set up `uucp`. It even explains how to wire a null modem. Particularly useful to new system administrators.

[B25]   Salus, Peter. *A Quarter Century of* UNIX. Reading, Mass.: Addison-Wesley, 1994.

A valuable source of information on the history of UNIX as told to the author by many of the participants. The book contains transcripts of many fascinating interviews.

[B26]   Stevens, W. Richard. *TCP/IP Illustrated, Volume 1: The Protocols.* Reading, Mass.: Addison-Wesley, 1994.

A thoroughly modern and detailed technical discussion of the architecture of the Internet and its protocols. Stevens demonstrates these protocols in action with the aid of freely available diagnostic tools.

[B27]   UNIX Systems Laboratory. *UNIX SVR4.2: System Manuals.* Englewood Cliffs, N.J.: Prentice-Hall, 1992.

A collection of several volumes containing all the manual pages for System V Release 4.2 and some tutorials as well. The User's Reference Manual is particularly useful.

[B28]   Wall, Larry, and Schwartz, Randal L. *Programming Perl.* Newton, Mass.: O'Reilly & Associates, 1991.

The authoritative description of Perl, written by Perl's authors.

[B29]   X/Open Company Limited. *X/Open Single UNIX Specification: X/Open CAE Specification, Commands and Utilities, Issue 4,*

Version 2; X/Open CAE Specification, System Interface Definitions, Issue 4, Version 2; X/Open CAE Specification, System Interfaces and Headers, Issue 4, Version 2; X/Open CAE Specification, Networking Services, Issue 4, Version 2. X/Open Company Limited, U.K., 1994.

These documents define the meaning of the X/Open UNIX brand.

[B30]   Zlotnick, Fred. *The POSIX.1 Standard: A Programmer's Guide.* Redwood City, Cal.: Benjamin/Cummings, 1991.

A guide to the conventions for writing C programs that will work on nearly all UNIX systems.

C.2 CD-ROMs

A great deal of software, including most free UNIX systems, is now available on CD-ROM. We have not given publication dates since most CD-ROMs are updated regularly and newer versions are likely to be available.

[C1]   *4.4BSD-Lite CD-ROM Companion.* Newton, Mass.: O'Reilly & Associates.

Source code for the BSD Lite release, derived from 4.4BSD.

[C2]   *BSDisc.* Flagstaff, Ariz.: InfoMagic, Inc.

Complete sources for both NetBSD and FreeBSD.

[C3]   *FreeBSD CDROM.* Walnut Creek, Cal.: Walnut Creek CD-ROM.

Source and executable code for FreeBSD Berkeley Software Distributions//FreeBSD on the i386 architecture, along with XFree86, networking support, and GNU development tools.

[C4]   *Linux Developer's Resource.* Flagstaff, Ariz.: InfoMagic, Inc.

Complete materials to install and run Linux. The CD-ROM includes all the official Linux archives, the Slackware and Debian distributions as well as several others, and the complete GNU archives. As of mid-1995, a notable bargain—four disks for $25!

[C5]   *Perl & Tcl/Tk CD-ROM.* Flagstaff, Ariz.: InfoMagic, Inc.

Source and binary files for both Perl and Tcl/Tk.

[C6]   *Prime Time Freeware for* UNIX. Sunnyvale, Cal.: Prime Time
Freeware.

A periodically published collection of UNIX archives, including
X11R6 and 4.4BSD-Lite, as well as "interesting source code for
adventurous programmers".

[C7]   *Prime Time TEXcetera.* Sunnyvale, Cal.: Prime Time Freeware.

An annotated, indexed copy of the Comprehensive TeX Archive
Network (CTAN) collection.   It contains more than 2000
megabytes (after decompression) of TEX-related materials,
including documentation, filters, fonts, graphics tools, language
support, and macros.

[C8]   *USENET CD Set.* Flagstaff, Ariz.: InfoMagic, Inc.

Assorted archives of the USENET newsgroups, including source
code and FAQ (Frequently Asked Questions) lists.

[C9]   *X11R6 CDROM.* Walnut Creek, Cal.: Walnut Creek CD-ROM.

Source code and precompiled Solaris 1, Solaris 2 binaries for X
Consortium Release X11R6 of the X Window System.

[C10]   *Yggdrasil Plug-and-Play Linux.* Walnut Creek, Cal.: Walnut
Creek CD-ROM.

The popular Yggdrasil version of Linux.

D

Glossary

absolute pathname	A pathname given relative to the root of the file system. An absolute pathname starts with '/'.
archive	A file containing the contents of a collection of other files, chiefly used for backup.
argument	A word following the name of a command in a call on that command that specifies input information to the command. When a shell script is called, the arguments of the call become available as parameters within the script.
array	An indexed collection of variables. In most cases, the indices must be integers, but some languages such as `awk` and Icon allow them to be other kinds of values.
ASCII	A standard character set whose full name is "American Standard Code for Information Interchange".
attribute	A property of a `ksh` variable that affects how the variable's value is formatted when it is retrieved by a parameter expansion, as well as its read-only status and export.
autoloading	A feature of the KornShell that provides for loading a function definition when the function is first called, thus saving the computational resources needed to load and store function definitions that are never used.
basename	The last filename in a pathname.
background color	The color used for the pixels surrounding the "ink" when a character is displayed under X.

796

background job	A job whose processes are running in the background.
background process	A process initiated by a shell as a background activity. When a shell executes a command as a background process, the shell does not wait for that command to complete but continues to execute commands from the command list it is working on.
backup	An archive of a file system made in order to preserve the files in the file system in case they are later lost or damaged.
basic regular expression	The form of regular expression that is used in older UNIX programs such as ed, grep, and sed.
block	A unit of storage allocation, particularly used with respect to disk storage.
buffer	(a) A region of computer memory that holds a portion of the data in a file after that portion has been read from the file or before that portion is written to the file. (b) A place where an editor stores text that is being edited.
byte	A unit of data, usually but not necessarily consisting of eight bits. For locales based on Latin characters, a byte ordinarily corresponds to a character; for some locales, such as those for Asian countries, a character may consist of multiple bytes.
cache	A set of buffers, usually in main memory, that is used to hold data from a block device or from another source, such as a name server, so that the data does not need to be read again when a program asks for it.
character	A sequence of one or more bytes that represents a printed or displayed symbol. An ASCII character contains just one byte.
child process	With respect to a parent process, one of the processes it has spawned.
client	(a) A terminal or workstation connected to a server. (b) A program run under the auspices of a server, as in the X system.
code set	A mapping or table that specifies a set of glyphs (written representations of characters) and the numerical representation of each glyph in computerized text.
collating element	A sequence of one or more characters that acts as a single character for sorting and collation purposes.
collating sequence	The ordering of collating elements for the purpose of sorting text comprised of those elements.
command mode	A mode of interpretation in which a program expects its input to consist of executable commands, such as to delete a range of lines (in an editor) or to respond to a message (in a mailer).
command substitution	A construct that enables you to execute a command *cmd* and then use its output as part of another command. The substitution has the form '$(*cmd*)' or ''*cmd*''.
concatenate	To combine two or more sequences of characters into a single sequence. For example, the concatenation of 'fat' and 'her' is 'father'.

control character	A character that when typed at the terminal performs a control function such as interrupting a program or erasing the previously typed character.
control sequence	A sequence of characters sent to a terminal that does not cause a graphic character to be displayed but instead changes the state of the terminal, for example by moving the cursor to the beginning of the next line or causing the following characters to appear in a different color.
cooked mode	The mode of reading from or writing to a terminal in which the incoming and outgoing streams of characters are preprocessed in order to put them into the form convenient for most programs. The opposite of *raw mode*.
copyleft	A term, analogous to copyright, for the requirements imposed by the GNU General Program License. Copylefted software can be modified and redistributed freely, but distributors must allow recipients to modify and redistribute it in turn and must make the source form of the software available at nominal cost.
core dump	A listing showing the contents of memory and other aspects of the state of the machine, produced by the kernel in cases of errors that might indicate program or machine malfunctions. The name is quaint, since magnetic cores have not been used as memory devices in computers for more than two decades.
current directory	The directory that is used as the starting point for pathnames that do not begin with '/'. In particular, a pathname consisting of a single filename is assumed to refer to a file in the current directory. The current directory is also called the *working directory*.
dæmon	A process that resides in a running UNIX system more or less permanently and performs some ongoing task, such as collecting files to be printed and routing them to printers.
device	A piece of equipment used to store or communicate data.
device driver	A program associated with a special file that performs input and output for its associated device. A device driver is also called an *interface* to the device.
directory	A file that contains links to other files.
disabled	Not in existence, with respect to a local variable.
dump	A listing of the contents of a file or a region of memory, usually showing each byte in octal or hexadecimal notation.
editor	A program for creating, modifying, or viewing a file of text.
effective group ID	A group ID associated with a process that determines the group privileges accorded to that process.
effective user ID	A user ID associated with a process that determines the user privileges accorded to that process.
enabled	In existence, with respect to a local variable.

envelope An electronic container for a message that contains a description of the message for routing purposes.

environment The set of environment variables associated with a process.

environment variable A variable associated with a process that can be queried or set by any program running within the process. Environment variables are inherited by child processes.

erase character The character that, when typed, erases the previously typed character.

escape A character, most often a backslash but sometimes a tilde, that gives a special meaning to the character or characters after it. Also, the ASCII ⟨escape⟩ character.

escaped character A character following an escape character that is effectively quoted by the escape character.

escape sequence A sequence of characters, starting with a backslash, that represents a single character, usually a nonprinting one. The standard escape sequences are \b (⟨backspace⟩), \f (⟨formfeed⟩), \n (⟨newline⟩), \r (⟨return⟩), \t (⟨tab⟩), \v (⟨vertical tab⟩), and \\ (backslash). In most contexts the sequence \\nnn is recognizes as an escape sequence denoting the character whose numerical code, in octal, is the three-digit octal number nnn.

exit status A number returned by a process to its parent process that indicates whether or not it succeeded at its task. Conventionally, zero indicates success and nonzero indicates failure.

extended regular expression The form of regular expression that is used in newer UNIX programs such as awk and 'grep -E'.

face The display style used by Emacs for the characters in a portion of the screen, such as normal text, the modeline, and the region.

field An identifiable portion of a line of text, record of data, header of a message, etc.

FIFO special file A kind of file that behaves much like a pipe but exists independently of any process, so named because reading and writing take place in first-in/first-out order. Any number of different processes can read from or write to a FIFO special file. Also called a *named pipe*.

file A sequence of bytes that can be accessed using the file operations provided by UNIX. A UNIX file can be a regular file (a collection of data stored on a disk or similar storage medium), a special file, or a directory.

file descriptor An entity provided by the kernel that enables a program to refer to a file. Each file descriptor has a number; the first three file descriptors are standard input, standard output, and standard error.

filename The name of a file within a directory.

file permissions A binary number associated with a file that specifies who can do what to the file.

file serial number The identifying number of an i-node, also called an i-node number.

file substitution   The process of substituting for wildcards in filenames. See *wildcard*.

filter   A program that modifies or transforms its input in order to obtain its output.

folder   A directory designated for containing mailboxes and files of messages.

foreground color   The color used for the pixels of the "ink" when a character is displayed under X.

foreground job   A job whose processes are running in the foreground.

foreground process   The process that currently has control of your terminal.

gateway   A computer that is connected to two or more networks and is willing and able to relay messages and other communications from one network to another.

globbing   The BSD term for *file substitution*.

glyph   The visual representation of a character, either on a display or on a printed page.

group   A set of users recognized by the file system. Each file in the file system has a group ID associated with it; members of the group can be given permissions to operate on the file that are not given to other users.

header   (a) A block of information at the beginning of a message that gives information about the message, such as who its sender is and when it was delivered. (b) A descriptive block of information at the beginning of an archive file.

here-document   A sequence of input lines following a command that is redirected to the command's standard input by the redirection operator '<<[-]*word*', with *word* delimiting the end of the input.

hexadecimal number   A number in base-16 notation. The hexadecimal digits are either `0123456789abcdef` or `0123456789ABCDEF`, with the letters representing the digits from (decimal) 10 to 15. Each hexadecimal digit consists of four bits, so the hexadecimal number `1a` would be `0001_1010` in the binary number system (and 26 in the decimal number system).

history file   A file containing the history of commands you've previously typed as input to the shell.

`HOME`   The environment variable containing the full pathname of your home directory.

home directory   The directory that is the starting point for a user's directory structure.

home page   A file written in the HTML (Hypertext Markup Language) that is accessible using the `http` protocol over the World Wide Web.

host   A computer that renders services to other computers. A computer connected to a network, particularly a network using the TCP/IP communications protocols, is often called a host.

initialization file	A file containing commands that a program executes before it does anything else. Most initialization files reside in a user's home directory and therefore can be constructed to meet the user's requirements and preferences.
initialization string	A string sent to your terminal to make it behave as expected when you start using it.
i-node	A data structure that stores the essential information about a file—where the actual contents of the file are stored, how long it is, how many links there are to it, when it was created, and so forth. Each i-node in a file system has a unique identifying number. The term *i-node* stands for *information node*.
input mode	A mode of interpretation in which a program expects its input to be general text; for example, the contents of a document (for an editor) or of a message (for a mailer).
interface	See *device driver*.
internationalization	The process of generalizing UNIX programs to adapt them to national linguistic and cultural conventions.
interrupt	An external event that interrupts the normal execution of a program, such as the signal generated when a user presses the (Intr) key.
IP address	A set of four numbers that specifies the exact routing to an Internet host.
job	A group of processes that behaves as a unit with respect to job control.
job control	A facility that allows jobs to be started, stopped, killed, or moved between the foreground and the background.
job identifier	A construct beginning with '%' that can be used in one of the job control commands to refer to a particular job.
kernel	The program at the heart of the operating system that controls access to the computer and its files, allocates resources among the various activities taking place within the computer, maintains the file system, and manages the computer's memory.
key	A portion of a record of data used either to retrieve the record or to sort the record within a file of similar records. A record may contain several keys.
kill character	The character that, when typed, causes the contents of the current line to be deleted.
lightweight process	A thread of control that shares its execution environment with other lightweight processes.
link	An entry in a directory. The entry consists of a filename that designates a file within the directory and an i-node number.
local variable	A variable in a program that is capable of holding a value and is not visible outside that program.

locale	A collection of definitions that record those aspects of the UNIX environment that depend on national language and cultural conventions.
logging in	The process of establishing a connection to a UNIX system.
login name	The name that you use when logging into a UNIX system.
login shell	The shell that is called on your behalf when you log in.
macro	A named sequence of commands, possibly containing parameters. A macro definition associates the sequence with the name; a macro call causes the commands to be executed, with macro arguments substituted for macro parameters.
magic number	A number appearing at the beginning of a file that helps to identify what kind of file it is.
mail transport agent	A program that handles the transportation and delivery of mail.
mail user agent	A program that provides a user interface for sending and receiving mail.
mailbox	A file where messages are stored by a mailer.
mailer	A program for sending and receiving electronic mail.
major number	A number that characterizes the type of a device. Devices with the same major number all use the same device driver.
mask	A binary number (usually written in octal notation) used to remove bits from another binary number, such as a set of file permissions.
mbox	See *secondary mailbox*.
message of the day	A message that is sent to all users when they log in, containing information such as the status of the system and announcements of newly installed software.
metacharacter	A character used in a regular expression or in a shell command that has a special meaning rather than standing for itself. For example, '.' is a metacharacter in a regular expression that stands for an arbitrary character and '>' is a metacharacter in a shell command that stands for output redirection.
minor number	A number that identifies a particular device within a group of devices of the same type (e.g., the number of a particular tape drive).
mount point	A directory in a file system that corresponds to the root directory of some other file system.
named pipe	See *FIFO special file*.
newsgroup	An electronic forum on a particular subject, with posted messages distributed over the Internet or a similar network.
newline	The character that marks the end of a line. It corresponds to the ASCII ⟨linefeed⟩ character (code 10). You can usually produce a newline at your terminal by typing either (Enter) or (Ctrl) J , although a few programs (such as Emacs) differentiate between the two in certain contexts.

null character	The character whose binary representation is all zeros. By UNIX convention, it is used to mark the end of a string.
null string	A string with no characters in it, synonymous with the empty string.
octal number	A number in base-8 notation. The octal digits are 01234567. Each octal digit consists of three bits, so the octal number 175 would be 001_111_101 in the binary number system (and 125 in the decimal number system). Octal numbers are used throughout UNIX, but they must be regarded as an anachronism.
option	An indicator that can be attached to a command in order to modify or control what the command does. Options are ordinarily indicated by single letters.
packet	A portion of a message that is transmitted as a unit over a network such as an Ethernet or the Internet.
pager	A program that breaks up its input into screen-size chunks and sends these chunks to your terminal, waiting for confirmation after each one. Modern pagers such as the POSIX version of more allow you to move around a file as you view it.
parameter	A variable within a shell script that corresponds to an argument passed to the script.
parent directory	The directory that lies above a given directory in the file system.
parent process	With respect to a child process, the process that spawned it.
partition	A region of storage on a hard disk that is capable of holding a file system.
password	A sequence of characters that you type when you log in in order to verify your identity.
pathname	A sequence of directories that indicates how to locate a particular file.
path prefix	The portion of a pathname preceding the last filename.
pipe	A connection between two processes that passes the output of the first to the input of the second.
pipeline	A sequence of two or more processes connected by pipes.
pixel	A picture element, namely, a dot on a screen.
platform	The hardware configuration on which a UNIX operating system is running. With respect to particular application programs, the platform is sometimes taken to include the particular version of UNIX.
port	A connection between a machine and the outside world, usually identified by a port number.
POSIX locale	The default locale, which corresponds to the traditional use of the ASCII character set in the UNIX environment.
postmark	An item in the header of a message that says who sent the message and when it was delivered to you.

primary mailbox	The mailbox where mailers put your mail originally, before you have looked at it. Also called *system mailbox*.
process	An activity or thread of execution taking place within UNIX that is recognized as such by the kernel. The state of a process contains all the information that the kernel needs to know about it.
process group	A group of processes that behaves as a unit for certain purposes, such as control of the terminal. Under job control, each job forms a process group; without job control, the processes associated with a terminal form a process group.
process group leader	A process in a group whose process number serves as an identifier for the entire group, typically the first process in a pipeline.
produce	To send to standard output. Also, vegetables.
quotation	A collection of syntactic devices for marking single characters or sequences of characters so that the characters are taken literally and their meanings as metacharacters are ignored.
raw interface	An interface to a block device that transfers data between the device and memory without using a cache (another name for *character interface*).
raw mode	The mode of reading or writing a terminal in which input/output operations transfer data directly between the terminal and memory without interpreting the data in any way.
real group ID	A group ID associated with a process that ordinarily specifies the group of the user who initiated the process.
real user ID	A user ID associated with a process that ordinarily specifies the user who initiated the process.
recipient	The person or entity to whom a message is sent.
recursive	Pertaining to a process or action that is applied to an entity and its directly or indirectly contained subparts.[1]
redirection	A shell construct for causing a program to take its standard input from a specified file or to send its standard output to a specified file. Other file descriptors can also be redirected in some shells.
regular expression	An expression used to specify a set of strings being searched for. Regular expressions use metacharacters to specify variable parts of the expression.
regular file	A file that contains stored data.
relative pathname	A pathname taken relative to your current directory. A relative pathname does not start with '/'.
reset string	A string that can be sent to your terminal when it is in an unknown mixed-up state in order to restore it to sanity.

---

1. The mathematical definition of a recursive process is more general than this definition.

restricted shell	A shell that restricts its user to a limited, well-understood set of facilities; for example, by preventing that user from changing the current directory.
root	(a) The directory in the file system that is at the top of the tree and of which all files are descendents. (b) The name of the superuser (`root`).
secondary mailbox	A mailbox where your mailer puts messages after you've read them. Also called the *mbox*.
server	A computer in a local-area network that provides administrative services and network connections, and also acts as a file repository.
set-uid bit	A bit within the permissions of an executable file that gives the file the permissions of its owner rather than the permissions of the user who called it.
shell	A program that controls your interaction with UNIX by reading input from your terminal and sending output to it. It is also possible to provide input to a shell from a source other than a terminal or to send the output of the shell to another destination.
shell script	A sequence of commands to a shell, written in the form of an input file for that shell, that can be called as though it were a command in its own right. A shell executes a shell script by passing it to a subshell; the subshell need not use the same shell program as the outer shell.
signal	An indication sent to a program of an unusual event such as disconnection of the terminal, timeout, or forced termination of the program by the user.
special file	A file that is neither a regular file nor a directory.
standard error	The file descriptor, normally associated with the terminal, to which programs usually send error messages.
standard input	The file descriptor, normally associated with the terminal, from which programs usually read their input.
standard output	The file descriptor, normally associated with the terminal, to which programs usually write their output.
sticky bit	A bit within the permissions of a file that enables a program to be retained in memory so that many users can share a single copy of it.
string	A sequence of zero or more characters.
subcommand	A command that provides a particular facility of a program; that is, a specialized command that you call from within that program. Subcommands are often referred to as commands—occasionally a source of confusion.
subshell	A process, constructed as a child of the current process, that starts up a shell and executes a specified command or list of commands within that shell.
superuser	A person logged in under the special name `root` who is automatically granted permission to access any file and to carry out other operations not permitted to ordinary users. The purpose of having a superuser is

to provide a mechanism for carrying out essential maintenance activities that ordinary users are not permitted to carry out for security reasons.

symbolic mode A set of instructions for creating or modifying file permissions (e.g., 'u=rwx').

system administration A collection of tasks whose purpose is to make the UNIX system available to its users in an orderly and secure manner.

system mailbox See *primary mailbox*.

tag file A file that acts as an index for a set of textual definitions, such as C function definitions, by giving the location of each definition in the set. Each line of the tag file specifies the definition's name, the file containing that definition, and the line within that file where the definition is to be found.

TCP/IP Transmission Control Protocol/Internet Protocol, the communications protocol developed at Berkeley that serves as the basis for BSD communications software and is used for most communications over the Internet.

terminal A device, including a keyboard and a screen (or printer), used to send data to and receive data from a computer.

thread The sequence of actions that takes place as a process executes. A process running on a multiprocessing system can support several threads, each of which has access to the process's environment.

toggle To turn on a switch or flag that is turned off, and vice versa.

tree A data structure that visually looks like an upside-down arboreal tree and consists of nodes. The top node of the tree is the root, and the nodes under any node are its branches. The UNIX file system is organized as a tree.

umask value An octal number that specifies the permissions to be masked out when a file is created.

UNIX The operating system that is the subject of this book.

user A person or entity registered within a system and permitted to use that system. Ordinarily a user is able to log onto the system and send and receive mail.

virtual terminal A simulated terminal that behaves logically as an independent connection to your computer but physically shares the same keyboard and screen.

visible space The character '␣', used to represent a space character explicitly in samples of input and output.

whitespace A sequence of characters that produce only empty space: spaces and ⟨tab⟩s. In some contexts, vertical tabs and newlines are also treated as whitespace. Whitespace is used to separate parts of commands and other syntactic entities. The POSIX standard uses the symbol ⟨blank⟩ to designate whitespace; it is defined in the LC_TYPE category of the current locale. In the POSIX locale, ⟨blank⟩ consists of spaces and ⟨tab⟩s.

wildcard   A character or sequence of characters appearing in a filename that stands for a set of possible characters or sequences of characters. The wildcards are '?' (any single character), '*' (any sequence of characters), and '[...]' (any character from a specified set of characters). The process of substituting for wildcards is called *file substitution* or, in BSD-derived programs, *globbing*.

window   An area on a display screen devoted to an activity or process.

window manager   A program that controls windows and provides services such as creating and destroying windows, moving windows around the screen, and changing the appearance of windows.

word   A syntactic unit, typically forming the argument of a command. A word consists of a sequence of characters; the successive words of a command are separated by whitespace.

working directory   See *current directory*.

Index

Within this index, special characters are ordered according to their English names (see p. 16). Terms such as `.profile` are listed under 'p' rather than under '.'. Page references in *italics* are places where the index term is defined. (Some index terms are defined in several places.)

Subcommands and options for the various commands are generally not listed in this index, since you can easily look them up in Appendix A. Including them in the index would have been redundant and would have made the index more cluttered and difficult to use.

⊔, *16*
&, 327
&&, 327
', 63, 391
@, 395, 619
`, 63
\, 63, 391
!, 384, 430, 622
|, 57, 326
||, 327
[...], 51
    See also test
:, 364, 407
-, 62
--, 62
$, 389
., *39*, 93, 363, 407
.., *39*, 93
", 63, 391
>, 56, 330
>|, 330

>&, 331
>>, 331
#, 321
<, 56, 330
<&, 331
<<, 330
%, 34
?, 51
;, 327
/, 38
*, 51
~, 40, 587, 667

absolute pathnames, *38*, 796
adduser, 692
adm directory, 55
administrative domains, *620*
Aho, Alfred, 199
AIX, 3
Albania, 585
alias, *358*, 407, *711*

aliases
    defining, 358
    listing, 358
    removing, 358
ALRM, 31
Amdahl, 3
anonymous ftp, 643
ANSI, 9
ansi, 72
apropos, 26, 227, 755
ARC, 144
Archie, 630–631
archives, *144–158*, 612–614, 796
arguments, *61*, 796
arithmetic
    arbitrary precision, 280
Arpanet, 4, 618
arrays, 796
ASCII, 796
at, *243–246*, 329, *711–712*
Athena, 5
AT&T, 1, 2, 3, 5, 6
attributes, *347*, 796
autoloading, *324*, 796
auxiliary mailboxes, *585*
awk, *199–224*, 280, *712–714*
    actions, *202*
    ARGC, 220
    ARGV, 200, 220
    array membership, 210–211
    arrays, *207–208*
        multidimensional, 208
    assignments, *211–212*
    case conversion, 214
    closing files and pipes, 219–220
    coercing numbers to strings, 204
    coercing strings to numbers, 204
    command line, 199–200
        arguments, 200, 220–221
        options, 199
    comparison operators, 209–210
    concatenation, 209
    conditional expressions, 211
    conditional statements, 222
    CONVFMT, 204, 219, 221
    empty statement, 222
    ENVIRON, 221
    environment variables, accessing, 221
    escape sequences, 205
    expressions, *203–220*
        as statements, 221
        type of, 206, 210
    field variables, *205*
    fields, *200, 206–207*, 211
    FILENAME, 220
    FNR, 220
    form of programs, 201
    formatting, 215
    FS, 220, 372
    function calls, *212–213*
    functions, 223–224
    group of statements, 222

awk *(Continued)*
    input field separators, *206–207*
    input record separators, *207*
    input records, *200*
    iteration statements, 222–223
    iterations, breaking out of, 223
    NF, 220
    NR, 220
    numeric constants, *205*
    numerical functions, 215–216
    OFMT, 205, 221
    OFS, 221
    operators, 208–212
        precedence of, 212
    ORS, 221
    output formats, *218–219*
    pattern matching, 213–214
    pattern-action statements, *201–202*
    pattern-matching operators, 210
    patterns, *202*
    predefined variables, 220–221
    producing output, 217–219
    program format, 203
    random number generation, 215–216
    reading input, 216–217
    RLENGTH, 213, 221
    RS, 220
    RSTART, 214, 221
    statements, *202*
    string constants, *205*
    subscripts, *207*
    SUBSEP, 221
    substitution, 213–214
    truth values, *204*
    type of expressions, *206*, 210
    user-defined variables, 205
    values, 203
    variables
        command-line arguments, 220
        input-related, 220
        output-related, 221
        pattern-matching, 221

background colors, 796
background jobs, *33*, 797
    output from, 264
    starting, 327
background processes, 327
backreferences, *84*
backups, *701–702*, 797
barking dogs, 683
basename, *295, 714*
basenames, *38*, 796
Bash, 308, 381, *401–410*
    brace expansion, 404, 409
    commands, simple and compound, 403
    comments, 402
    default login shell, 250
    directory stack, 407–408
    editors, built-in, 402
    function definitions, 403
    hashing command names, 403–404, 410

Bash   (*Continued*)
  help information,   409
  history expansion,   402–403, 410
  initialization files,   410
  intrinsic commands,   407–409
  invoking,   401–402
  options,   402, 409–410
  parameters,   403
  pathname expansion,   404–405
  process substitution,   405
  redirection,   403
  syntax,   402
  variables, predefined,   405–407
bash,   786
Basic Networking Utilities,   658
basic regular expressions,   *81*, 797
  searching for,   176
batch,   *243–244, 715*
bc,   *280–286, 715–716*
bdiff,   129
Bell Laboratories,   1, 2
Berkeley Software Distributions,   2, *3–4*
  386BSD,   4, 7, 8
  3BSD,   4
  4.1BSD,   4
  4.2BSD,   4
  4.3BSD,   4
  4.4BSD,   4, 7, 794
  4.4BSD Lite,   4, 6, 7, 8
  4BSD,   4
  BSD Lite,   794
  BSD/386,   4
  BSD/OS,   4, 6
  FreeBSD,   4, 7–8
  Net/1,   4, 5
  Net/2,   4, 8
  NetBSD,   4, 7, 8
Berkeley Software Design, Inc.,   4
Berry, Karl,   302
bg,   *359–360*, 407, *716*
BIBTEX,   301
Biff,   683
big-endian form,   163
bigwords,   *415*
bin directories,   53
binary files
  encoding and decoding,   143
binmail,   582
  See also mail, Seventh Edition version
bit bucket,   91
⟨blank⟩,   806
block devices,   *87–88*
block size,   87
block special files,   *88, 89*
blocks,   *87*, 797
BNU,   658
booting up,   702–703
Bourne shell,   307–308
  KornShell, relation to,   309
  predecessor of csh,   382
  script interpreter, default for,   319
Bourne, Steve,   307

bracket expressions,   *82*
BRE.   *See* basic regular expressions
break,   364, 396, 407
breaksw,   396
BSD.   *See* Berkeley Software Distributions
buffered input,   *43*
buffered output,   *44*
buffers,   *43–44*, 797
builtin,   408
bye,   409
bytes,   797

C,   791
  Emacs editing,   474
  libraries, directory for,   54
  library, manual pages for,   24
  RCS identification for,   304
  role in UNIX,   11
C shell.   *See* csh
C locale,   73
caches,   *88*, 797
cal,   *234–235, 716*
calendar systems,   80
calendars, displaying,   234, 572
cancel,   *118, 716*
cat,   22, *98–100*, 103, *716*, 786, 787
cd,   22, *92–93*, 369, 371, 397, 407, *717*, 786
CDPATH,   93, 393
character classification,   82
character devices,   *87*
  testing for,   334
character interface,   *88*
character maps,   *74–75*
character special files,   *88*, 89
character translation,   177–179
characters,   797
charmaps,   296
  See also character maps
  in locale definitions,   298
checksums,   129
Cherry, Lorinda,   280, 300
chgrp,   *136–137, 717*
child processes,   *30*
chmod,   48, 50, 91, *134–135*, 136, 555, *717*
chown,   *136–137*, 717
chpass,   28, 254
chsh,   28, *254–255, 717*
ci,   303, 306
cksum,   *129*, 613, *718*
Clark, James,   299
clients,   *671*, 797
cmp,   129, *130, 718*, 786, 787
co,   303, 304, 305
code sets,   *73–74*, 797
coded character sets.   *See* code sets
Coherent,   6
collating elements,   77, 83, 797
collating sequence,   797
columns, number on screen,   265
comm,   *184, 718*
command,   128, 287, *288*, 292, 324, 407, *718*
command history,   360–363

command interpreters, *28, 307*
command mode, *587,* 797
command substitution, *63–64, 354,* 797
commands, *60–65*
   arguments, 61
   operands, 61
   options, 61–62
   pathname of, showing, 128
   specialized invocations, 287–290
   standard syntax, 60–62
   timing, *292–293*
Common Application Environment, 10
compact disks, 87
components, *38*
compound commands, 335–341
compress, 55, *140,* 144, 153, *718*
Compuserve, 625
concatenation, 98, 797
conditional lists, 328
configuring the kernel, 29, 692–693
CONT, 32
continue, 364, 396, 407
control characters, *19,* 798
control key, 19
control keys, 16
   setting with stty, 261, *262*
control sequences, *68,* 798
cooked mode, *89,* 798
coprocesses, *329*
copyleft, *8,* 798
core, 20, 262
core dump, 262
core dumps, 20, 31, 798
counting words, lines, characters, 137
cp, 22, 103–104, *718–719,* 786, 787
   command-line options, 104
   recursive copying, 104
cpio, 103, 127, 144, 149, 151, *154–158, 719,* 787
cron, 247
crontab, *246–248, 719–720*
crontab entries, 246
csh, 4, 308, 309, *381–401,* 786
   aliases, interpretation of, 388
   catching interrupts, 398
   command completion, 388
   command lookup, 387–388
   command substitutions, 391–392
   .cshrc, 384
   directory stack, *396*
   echoing arguments, 397
   events, *385*
   exiting from, 397
   expressions, *392–393*
   features not in ksh, 381
   file name expansion, *389*
   globbing, 394
   history substitutions, 384–387
   intrinsic commands, 395–400
   job control, 381
   .login, 384
   .logout, 384
   modifiers, 386–387

csh (*Continued*)
   parameter expansions, *389–391*
   path, 53
   predefined variables, 393–395
   quotation, 391
   rehashing, 53
   statements, 399–400
   subshell, executing commands in, 388
   tests, *393*
   variables, 389
   variables, setting, 395–396
.cshrc, 67
csplit, *186–188, 720*
CSRG, 3, 4
ctags, 466, 561
CTAN, 302
cu, 631, 658, *666–669, 720*
   compared to telnet, 637
   exiting from, 667
   output diversions, 669
   tilde commands, 667–669
current directory, *39,* 93, 798
current file, *443, 459*
current job, *33*
curses, 10, 70
cut, *179–181,* 664, *721*

dæmons, *30,* 54, 798
DARPA, 3
datagrams, *628*
date, 72, 79, *232–234, 721,* 786, 787
Davidsen, Bill, 612
dc, 280
dd, *160–164,* 188, *722*
dead-letter file, 609
DEC VT100, 71
DEC VT102, 681
declare, 408
deleting files with unusual names, 106–107
desk calculator, 280
dev directory, 54
device drivers, 25, *87,* 90, 798
device names, 90–91
device numbers, 90
device special files, 169
devices, *86–91,* 798
df, *271, 722*
   reported blocks in use, 272
diff, 129, *130–132, 723,* 787
   context of differences, 131
   directories as arguments, 131
   exit status, 132
   generating patches, 164
   whitespace, ignoring, 132
diff3, 129
dig, 622
Digital Equipment Corporation, 3, 4, 6
Digital UNIX, 4, 10
direct execution, *342*
directories, 798
   creating, 93, 756
   naming conventions, 53–55

directories   (*Continued*)
   permissions for,   45–46
   removing,   106
directory stack,   93, 396–397
Dired,   511
dirname,   *294, 723*
dirs,   397, 407
disabled,   *65*, 798
disk partitions,   90, 699–700
disk usage information,   270–272
disk usage, limiting,   368
diskettes, device names for,   90
disks as block devices,   87
DISPLAY,   673
displays,   *672*
ditroff,   298
document processing,   298–302
documentation,   24–26
Documenter's Workbench,   299
domain-style addresses,   *618*
MS-DOS,   8
dosemu,   7
du,   *271–272, 723*
dumps,   798

echo,   *272–274*, 278, 369, 407, *723*, 787
  printf differences,   274
  simulating with printf,   273, 277
ed,   *458–466*, 609, *723–725*
  buffer,   459
  copying text,   462
  current file,   *459*
  current line,   *459*
  error messages,   466
  exiting,   464
  file operations,   463–464
  global execution,   464–465
  inserting text,   462
  marking lines,   463
  producing lines,   461
  producing the line number,   462
  prompting,   466
  regular expressions,   81
  relation to sed,   192
  scripts produced by diff,   132
  search and replace,   462–463
  subshell execution,   465–466
  substitutions,   462–463
  undoing commands,   466
editing scripts.   *See* sed
EDITOR,   112, 246, 312
editors,   411–466, 467–581, 798
  use of buffers,   44
  viewing files with,   107
edlin,   459
effective group ID,   *36*, 47, 334, 798
  restored by ksh,   375
effective user ID,   *36*, 46, 334, 798
  restored by ksh,   375
egrep,   *175–177, 725*
Elisp,   468
elm,   612

Emacs,   8, 16, *467–581, 725–736*
  Abbrev mode,   475
  abbreviations,   541–543
    dynamic,   543
  accumulating text,   492–493
  aliases,   584
  amusements,   580–581
  appointments,   577
  arguments,   480–481
  atoms,   *528*
  Auto Fill mode,   474, *497*
  Auto Save mode,   475
  auto-saving,   513
  backup files,   512–513
  buffer menu,   516–518, 734
  buffers,   472–473
    electric,   518
    narrowing,   515
  calendar,   572–575
    holidays,   574
    sunrise and sunset,   574
  centering lines,   496
  character position,   514
  checking and correcting spelling,   501
  colors for faces under X,   545
  Comint mode,   530
  command completion,   480
  command continuations, help on,   486
  command-line options,   468–469
  commands, cancelling,   470, 480
  copying text,   492
  cursor position,   476
  customizing,   534–547
  defvar,   477
  diary,   572, 575–577
  Dired,   92, 508, 510, *550–557*, 732–734
  disabling commands,   482–483
  disabling control-S and control-Q,   263
  echo line,   476
  electric buffer list,   518
  .emacs initialization file,   545–547
  erasing text,   490–491
  executing UNIX commands,   530–534
  exiting,   470
  faces,   478
  file names, specifying,   508–509
  files
    operations on,   508–512
    visiting,   508, 520
  fill column,   *496*
  filling text,   496–497
  finding files,   557
  Font Lock mode,   478
  fonts under X,   544–545
  frames,   *476*
    changing appearance of,   545
    commands for,   507–508
  getting started,   471–472
  global mark ring,   493
  GNUS,   571–572
  help information,   484–486
  indentation,   502–504

Emacs *(Continued)*
  indented text mode, 502
  Info files, 695–696
  Info on-line manual, 485
  joining lines, 491
  key bindings, 471, 479, 535–538
    listing, 484–485
  keyboard conventions, 470–471
  keyboard macros, 538–541
    in initialization files, 546
  keymaps, 535–536
  keys, names of, 537–538
  LFD key, 471
  Line Number mode, 475, 476
  line numbers, 514
  line numbers, displaying, 475, 476, 515
  LISP expressions, 528–529
  mailer, 562–571
    message attributes, 569
    message digests, 569
    receiving mail, 565–571
    sending mail, 563–565
  mark, *476*, 477
    setting, 493, 494
  mark ring, 493
  marking text, 493–494
  meta keys, 470
  minibuffer, 476, *479–482*
  mode line, *475*
  modes, 473–475
    information about, 485
    major, 473–474
    minor, 474–475
  mouse actions, 494–496
    bindings for, 538
    resizing windows, 507
  moving the point, 487–489
  newlines, 473
  newsreader, 571–572
  on-line manual, 485
  options, *177*
  outlines, 502
  overwrite mode, 475
  page numbers, 515
  pages, 488
  paragraphs, *488*
  pictures, 557–561
  point, *476*
  prefix key, *535*
  printing, 519
  quick exit, 470
  recalling complex commands, 481–482
  rectangle commands, 504–505
  recursive editing, 482
  region, *476*
  registers, 519–520
  regular expressions, 81, 524–525
  replacement, 525–526
  restoring text, 491–492
  Rmail files, *565*
  Rmail format, 563
  searching, 521–525

Emacs *(Continued)*
  searching for matching lines, 527
  secondary selection, 495–496
  selected window, *475*
  selective display, 515
  `setq`, 529
  `setq-default`, 527
  sexps, *528*
  Shell mode, 530
  shell operations, 531–534
  sorting, 500–501
  special characters, typing, 473
  subshell buffers, 530–534
  syntax highlighting, 478
  syntax table, *478–479*, 485
  tab stops, 503–504
  tag files, 466
  tag tables, 561–562
  Transient Mark mode, 475, *477*, 478, 494, 545
  transposing text, 497–498
  tutorial, 471, 485
  undo, 483–484
  use of flow control characters, 642
  variables, *477*
    listing, 485
  version control interface, 578–580
  viewing earlier commands, 485
  windows, *475–476*, 505–507
  word search, 523
  X, operating under
    command-line options, 469
    customization, 543–545
    faces, 478
    frames, 476
    mouse operations, 494
    Transient Mark mode, 475, 477
emTeX, 9
emulation, *71–72*
  under `xterm`, 681
emx, 8–9
`enable`, 408
enabled, *65*, 798
end-of-file key, 20
enter key. *See* newline key
env, 35, *326*, *736*
ENV, 67
  function definitions in, 340
envelopes, *584*, 799
environment variables, *35–36*, 799
  inheriting, 346
environments, 799
eof character, 262
eqn, *300*
equivalence classes, 77, 83
equivalent systems, *632*
erase character, 20, 262, 799
ERE. *See* extended regular expressions
error notification
  `logger` used for, 295
escape, *63*, 799
escape character, *63*
escape sequences, 799

escaped character, *63*, 799
etc directory, 54
/etc/fstab, 696, 698
/etc/groups, 692
/etc/hosts.equiv, 632
/etc/hosts, 632
/etc/inittab, 230, 704
/etc/mtab, 697
/etc/passwd, 28, 231, 250, 251–252, 254, 691
/etc/printcap, 692
/etc/shadow, 691, 692
/etc/ttytype, 257
Ethernet, 627
eval, 367, 399, 407
ex, 67, *442–458, 736–738*
   abbreviations, 456
   changing directories, 454
   changing groups of lines, 450
   copying text, 450–451
   deleting groups of lines, 449
   executing commands from a buffer, 458
   executing commands from a file, 458
   exiting, 455
   extended to vi, 412
   file operations, 452–454
   flags, 446
   form of commands, 443–444
   global execution, 456–457
   initializing, 443
   inserting text, 449
   joining lines, 450
   local variables, 435–442
   macro definitions, 456
   main buffer, 443
   marking lines, 452
   moving text, 450
   multiple commands on a line, 444
   open mode, *458*
   producing lines, 448
   recovering from crashes, 457
   regular expressions, 81, 418
   screenful size, 443
   search and replace, 451–452
   shifting lines, 450
   special buffers, 447–448
   status information, 449
   subshell execution, 457
   substitutions, 451–452
   undoing commands, 458
   visual mode, 457–458
   windows of lines, 448
exec, 332, 363, 397, 407
exec system function, 343
EXINIT, 67
exit, 19, 363, 397, 407, 787
exit status, *32–33*, 799
expand, *181–183, 738*
export, 366, 408
expr, 280, *286–287, 739*
expressions, evaluating, 280–287
extended regular expressions, *81*, 799
   searching for, 177

Fabry, Robert, 3
faces, *478*, 799
false, *739*
FAQs, 26
fc, *360–363*, 407, *739*
FCEDIT, 361
fdformat, 700
fdisk, 699–700
fg, *359–360*, 407, *739*
fgrep, *175–177, 739*, 787
fields, *583*, 799
   cutting, 179–181
   pasting, 189–190
FIFO special files, *37, 59*, 96, 98, 104, 168, 169, 799
   process substitution in Bash, 405
   testing for, 334
file, *128, 739–740*
file creation mask, *50*
file descriptors, *58*, 330–332, 799
file group classes, 45
file names, *36*
file other classes, 45
file owner classes, 45
file permissions, 799
   See also files (permissions)
file serial numbers, *41*, 799
file substitution, 800
file systems, *40–41*
   archiving, 151
   backing up, 701–702
   checking, 700–701
   creating, 699–700
   maintenance, 696–702
   mounting, 696–697
   mounting options, 699
   repairing, 700–701
   synchronizing, 706
File Transfer Protocol. *See* FTP
filenames, *37–38*, 799
files, *36–58*, 799
   access, 134–135
   character count, 137–138
   checksum calculation, 129
   classifying, *128, 739–740*
   common lines in, 184
   comparing, 129–134
   comparing modification dates, 335
   compressed, 55–56
   compressing, 139–143
   concatenating, 98–100
   converting, *160–164*
   copying, 99, 103–104
   deleting, 105–106
   differences, finding, 130–134
   directories, *36*
   displaying, 98–100
   distributed over networks, *628–629*
   dumping, 158–160
   erasing, 105–106
   examining, 158–160
   existence, testing for, 334
   extracting fields, 179–181

files (*Continued*)
  extracting head of, 184
  extracting tail of, 184–186
  finding, 121
  formatting for printing, 118–121
  joining, 190–192
  line count, 137–138
  linking, 101
  listing contents of, 99
  listing information about, 94–98
  long format listing, 97
  moving, 102–103
  ownership, 136–137
  pasting fields, 189–190
  patching, *164–168*
  permissions, *44–48,* 134–137
    default on creation, 50
    octal notation for, 50
    testing for, 334
    umask value, 135–136
  printing, 113–121
  quotas, 43
  reblocking, *160–164*
  regular, *36*
  remote copying, 636
  removing, 105–107
  renaming, 102–103
  repeated lines in, 183–184
  searching for strings in, 293–294
  sorting, 170–175
  space limitations, 43
  special, *805*
    See also special files
  splitting, 186–189
  storage conventions, 42–43
  touching, 138–139
  translating characters in, 177–179
  transmitting, 627, 642–664
  updating, *164–168*
  viewing, 107–113
  word count, 137–138
filters, *58, 170–225,* 800
find, 48, 107, *121–127, 740*
finger, *230–232, 741*
flush key, 20
Foderero, John, 683
fold, 177, *181, 741*
folders, *592, 609, 611,* 800
Font Lock mode, 475
foreground colors, 800
foreground job, *33,* 800
fork system function, *342,* 344
formatted output, *274–278*
formatters, 298–302
.**forward**, 585–586
Free Software Foundation, 467
FreeBSD, 8
FS, 206
fsck, 700–701
ftp, 621, 627, 631, *642–658, 741–742*
  auto-login, 644
  closing remote connections, 644–645

ftp (*Continued*)
  command abbreviations, 643
  controlling remote connections, 645
  debugging, 654
  directory listings, 647–648
  exiting from, 643
  file name translation, 649–651
  help facility, 645–646
  linking remote computers, 654
  local operations, 653
  macros, *654–655*
  opening remote connections, 644
  options on command line, 657–658
  prompt, 643
  remote directory operations, 646–647
  status information, 653–654
  tokens, 655
  transmitting files, 648–649
  verbose mode, 654
FTP, 642
fundamental mode, 474

gateways, *624,* 800
gcc, 8
gdb, 8
geqn, 300
getconf, *291–292, 743*
getopts, 369, *377 378,* 407
getty, 250, 692
glob, 397
globbing, *52, 389,* 800, *807*
glyphs, 800
GNU, 8, 467
GNU General Public License, 7, 8
GNUS, *571–572,* 615
gomoku, 580
gophers, 630
goto, 396
gpic, 300
grep, 23, *175–177, 743*
  regular expressions, 81
Griswold, Ralph, 224
groff, 299
groups, *27–28,* 47, 800
  changing, 253
  showing ID, 255
groups, 28
gtbl, 300
gtroff, 299
gunzip, 140, *141–143,* 153, *743*
gzcat, *141–143, 743–744*
gzip, 55, 140, *141–143,* 144, 153, *744*

halt, *705, 744*
hangups
  ignoring, 243
  signalling, 31
hard links, *41*
hash, 408
head, *184, 744*
header files, 54
headers, 800

here-documents, *332*, 800
Hewlett-Packard, 3, 6
hexadecimal numbers, 800
hidden files, *95*
`history`, 398, 409
history files, 800
history lists, *360*
`HOME`, 251, 371, 800
home directory, *39–40*, 54, 252, 800
home pages, *629*, 800
`/home`, 54
HoneyDanBer uucp, 658
Honeyman, Peter, 658
`host`, 622
hosts, *620*, 800
HP-UX, 3
HTML, 629
`http`, 629
HUP, 31
Hypertext Markup Language. *See* HTML
Hypertext Transport Protocol, 629

i-nodes, *42*, 107, 801
i-numbers, *42*
i386 architecture, 4, 7, 8, 35
IBM, 3, 6
IBM 3270, 87
Icon, 207, 224–225, 280
icons, *671*
`id`, 28, *255*, *744*
`ident`, 304, 306
IDRIS, 6
IEEE, 9
`include` directory, 54
indirect blocks, *43*
`info`, 485, 695
`infocmp`, 69, 70
information nodes, *801*
`init`, 702, 704
`init` process, 229
initialization files, *66–67*, 801
initialization string, *70*, 257, 801
input mode, *587*, 801
INT, 31
Interactive Systems Corporation, 3
Interdata 8/32, 2
interfaces, *87*, *88–89*, *798*, 801
internationalization, *72–81*, 801
Internet, 4, *618*, 619–622, 624, 806
    domain information, 622
    gophers, 630
    locating files, 630–631
    resources, 629–631
interrupt key, 20, 31
interrupts, 801
interval expressions, *84*
IP addresses, *621*, 628, 637, 643, 801
IRIX, 3

Jerusalem, 624
job control, *30*, *33–35*, 359–360, 601, 801
job identifiers, *34*, 360, 801

jobs, *33*, *662*, 801
    scheduling, 243–248
`jobs`, 359, *360*, 407, *745*
Johnson, Michael K., 792
`join`, 189, *190–192*, *745*
Jolitz, Bill, 4
Joy, Bill, 3, 381, 412

`kermit`, 632, 669
kernel, *29*, 55, 801
    reconfiguring, 692–693
`kernel` directory, 55
Kernighan, Brian, 6, 199, 300
keyboards
    names of keys, 15
keys, 801
`kill`, 31, 60, *242–243*, 359, 407, *745*
KILL, 31, 32
kill character, 20, 262, 801
Kirch, Olaf, 792
Knuth, Donald E., 301
Korn, David, 308
KornShell. *See* ksh
ksh, *307–379*, *745–749*, 786
    aliases, 323, *358–359*
        cancelling effect of, 323
    arithmetic evaluation, 355–356
    arithmetic expressions, 356
    array variables, 346–347
    case testing, 335, 337
    command history, 360–363
    command line, form of, 318
    command substitution, 354–355
    compound commands, redirected, 336
    conditional execution, 335, 336
    coprocesses, 278, 279
    DEBUG signal, 365
    debugging, 317
        DEBUG signal, 365
        line number display, 370
        syntax checking, 375
        tracing, 325, 375
        verbose execution, 375
    editors, built-in, 311–317
    `emacs` built-in editor, 312–314
    end of file in, 363
    ENV file, 311, 376
    ERR signal, 365, 375
    execution of commands, 342–344
    EXIT signal, 365
    exiting from, 310, 363
    exporting variables, 345–346
        automatic, 375
    FPATH, 325
    function definitions, 324, 340–341
        autoloading, 324–325, 371
        returning from, 364
    here-documents, 330, 332–333
    HISTFILE, 361
    HISTSIZE, 361
    IFS, 207, 349, 355, 372
    initializing, 376–377

`ksh` (*Continued*)
  input line
      editing, 311–317
      parsing, 320–321
  interaction with, 310–311
  intrinsic commands, 363–369
  iteration, 335, 338–339
      exiting from, 364
  job control, 359–360
      `monitor` needed for, 374
  limiting disk usage, 368
  loops. *See* iteration
  menu selection, 341
      prompt for, 371
  operators, *320,* 326–330
  options, 317–318, 374–376
      testing for, 335
  other shells, relation to, 309
  parameter expansions, 349–352
  parameters, 344–352
      length of, 352
      pattern matching for, 352
  parsing command lines, 377–378
  patterns, *322*
  pipelines, *326,* 328
  positional parameters, *344*
      sorting, 376
  POSIX.2, role in, 12
  quotation, 321, 352–354
  read-only variables, 366
  redirection, 330–333
      for function definitions, 340
  renumbering parameters, 367
  restricted mode, 310–311, 318, 373
  sample script, 379
  separators, *320*
      redefining, 372
  shell scripts, 318–320
  signals, catching, 364–365
  simple commands, 322–323
  subshell, executing commands in, 339
  substitutions, 354–357
      nested, 356–357
      unset variables, 375
  syntax, 320–321
  `trackall`, 359, 375
  tracked aliases, 323, 359
  unsetting variables, 366
  variables, *345–348*
      assignment to, 351
      attributes of, 347–348
      predefined, 369–374
  verbose execution, 375
  `vi` built-in editor, 314–317
  `viraw`, 314

labels, *619*
Lamport, Leslie, 301
`LANG`, 73, 80, 296
LaStrange, Tom, 672
L𝗪T_EX, 301–302
`LC_*`, *80–81,* 296

`LC_ALL`, 80
`LC_COLLATE`, 76, 80
`LC_CTYPE`, 75, 80, 467
`LC_MESSAGES`, 80
`LC_MONETARY`, 78, 80
`LC_NUMERIC`, 78, 80
`LC_TIME`, 79, 80
`LC_TYPE`, 174, 214, 215, 806
      `sort`, effect on, 174
      `tr`, effect on, 178
Lempel-Ziv compression, 55, 140, 141
Lesk, Michael, 300
`less`, 107, 787
`let`, 407
`lib` directory, 54
libraries, 54
lightweight processes, *30,* 801
LILO, 693, 703
`limit`, 398
lines, folding, 181
links, *41–42,* 801
      counting, 98
      symbolic, *41–42*
Linux, 7, 8, 35, 792, 795
      CD-ROM distribution, 794, 795
      documentation, 792
      File System Standard, 55
      LILO, 693, 703
      rebuilding the kernel, 693
list, *57*
lists, *328*
little-endian form, 163
`ln`, 41, 101, *749–750*
`local`, 408
local variables, *65,* 801
`local` directory, 54
`locale`, *296, 297, 750*
`localedef`, 75, 296, *297–298, 750*
locales, *72–81,* 295–298, 802
      categories, *75–80*
      character classification, *75–76*
      collating rules, *76–78*
      confirmations, *80*
      dates and times, *79–80*
      defining, 297–298
      displaying information about, 296
      environment variables for, *80–81*
      monetary quantities, *78*
      numeric quantities, *78–79*
      regular expressions, effects on, 81
`locate`, 122
locking bit, *48*
`logger`, *295, 750*
logging in, 18, 19–21, 250–255, 802
      on remote computer, 634
logging out, 19
logical font descriptions, 678
`login`, *250–252, 397, 750*
login initialization file, 67, 376–377
      setting variables in, 377
login names, 802
login shells, *28,* 252, 376, 377, 802

.login, 67, 250, 787
logname, *255, 750–751*
logout, 397, 407
lp, 113, *114–115*, 118, *751*, 787
    Berkeley version. *See* lpr
LPDEST, 114
lpmove, 692
lpq, 113, 115, 117
lpr, 113, *115–116*, *751*, 787
lprm, 113, 115, 118
lpsched, 692
lpshut, 692
lpstat, 113, *117–118*, *751*
ls, 22, *94–98*, *752*, 787

Mach, 6
macros, *433*, 802
magic file, 128
magic numbers, 128, 802
magnetic tape archives, 151–152
magnetic tapes, 91
mail. *See* messages
    encoding binary files for, 143
    notice of arrival, 372
    notification of, 683
    sending and receiving, 582–612
mail
    Seventh Edition version, 582
Mail. *See* mailx
MAIL, 251
mail transport agents, *582*, 802
mail user agents, *582*, 802
mailboxes, *585*, 802
mailers, 562–571, *582–612*, 802
    archiving files for, 612–614
mailing lists, 615
MAILRC, 591
.mailrc, 67, *591–592*
mailx, 67, 168, *587–610*, *752–755*
    abbreviating commands, 594
    aliases, 601
    command mode, 594–602
    command-line options, 589–591
    comments, 602
    conditional execution of commands, 602
    dead-letter file, *603*, 604, 605, 608
    deleting messages, 598–599
    editing messages, 599–600
    exiting from, 588, 600
    folder directory, 592
    folders, 595
    general information commands, 594–595
    getting help, 594
    header summary, 593–594, 595
    initializing, 591–592, 601–602
    input mode, 602–605
        calling an editor, 603
        command-mode escape, 605
        exiting from, 605
        getting help, 603
        inserting a file, 604
        inserting a message, 604

mailx (*Continued*)
    input mode (*Continued*)
        inserting a signature, 604
        inserting a variable's value, 604
        inserting output of a command, 604
        inserting tilde lines, 605
        interrupting, 603
        saving messages, 603
        shell escape, 605
        showing messages, 603
        specifying header fields, 605
    local variables, 606–610
        setting and unsetting, 601–602
    message lists, *592–593*
    messages, 602
    quitting, 600
    reading mail, 587–588
    recipients for messages, 588–589
    Replyall, 607
    responding to messages, 596–597
        prefix for quoted lines, 608
    running on remote computer, 668
    saving messages, 598–599
    sending mail, 587
    shell commands from, 600–601
    showing messages, 595–596
    suppressing initialization, 591
    switching directories, 600
    switching message files, 600
    tilde escapes, 603
major mode, *473*
major numbers, *90*, 802
make, 694
man, *226–228*, *755–756*
Mandelbaum Gate, 624
MANPATH, 227, 694
MANSEC, 228
manual pages, 24–26, 299
    compressed storage, 141
    installing, 694–696
    viewing, 226–228
    viewing under X, 687–688
    whatis file, 695
Mark Williams Company, 6
masks, 802
Mattes, Eberhard, 8
mbox, *585*, 802, *805*
me, 299
Memorandum Macros, 299
mesg, 91, *270*, *756*
message of the day, 18, 802
messages
    forwarding, 586
    header, *583*
    recipients, *584–585*
    sending, 270
    turning off, 270
metacharacters, *63*, 802
Metcalf, Robert, 627
MH message handling system, 610–612
MINIX, 7
minor mode, *474*

minor numbers, *90*, 802
mkdir, *93–94, 756,* 787
mkfifo, 59, *168,* 756
mkfs, 700
mknod, *169, 756*
MKS. *See* Mortice Kern Systems
    running UUCP, 618
mm, 299
modems, controlling, 666
modes, *473*
more, *108–113,* 227, 606, *756–757,* 787, 803
Morris, Robert, 280
Mortice Kern Systems, 6
Motif, 5, 6, 672
mount, 40, *696–697, 757–758*
mount points, *40, 696,* 802
mouse clicks, 16
ms, 299
mt, 91, 152
Multics, 1
mv, 23, 102–103, *758,* 787

name servers, *620*
named pipes, *37, 59, 799,* 802
.netrc, *655–656*
    security considerations, 656
NetWare, 3
network addresses
    across networks, 624–625
    domain-style, 618, *619–622*
    lost messages, 625–627
    path-style, 618, *622–623*
Network File System, 628
Network Information Service, 628
networked file systems, 696
newform, 268
newfs, 700
newgrp, 28, *253–254,* 369, *758*
newlines, *37,* 786, 802
NeWS, 3
news feeds, *614*
news servers, *614*
newsgroups, 591, *614–616,* 802
newsreaders, *614,* 615–616
NFS. *See* Network File System
nice, *248, 758*
Ninth Edition, 2
NIS. *See* Network Information Service
NNTP, 614
NNTPSERVER, 615
nohup, *243,* 329, *758*
notify, 397
Novell, 2, 10
Nowitz, Dan, 658
nroff, *298–301,* 488
nslookup, 622
null character, *37,* 803
null signal, 242
null string, 803

O'Donnell, Sandra Martin, 72
octal numbers, 803

od, *158–160, 758–759*
on-line conversation, 269–270
onintr, 398
Open Look, 672
OPEN LOOK, 5
Open Server Release 5, 3, 10
Open Software Foundation, 6
open systems, 10
Open Windows, 672
operands, *61*
OPTARG, 370, 378
OPTIND, 370, 378
options, *61,* 803
    GNU utilities, 63
OS/2, 8, 697, 699
Osanna, Joseph, 298
output monitoring, 185

pack, 55, 141
packets, 803
PAGER, 228
pagers, *107–113,* 803
parameter expansions, *349*
parameters, *344,* 803
parent, *39*
parent directories, 803
parent process, *30*
partitions, *699,* 803
passwd, 47, *254*
passwords, 21, 251, 803
    changing, 254
    lost superuser, 703
paste, *189–190, 759*
patch, 130, *164–168, 759–760*
PATH, *52–53,* 128, 251, 288, 291, 324, 344, 376, 718, 787
path prefixes, *38,* 803
path-style addresses, *618*
pathchk, *129, 760*
pathname expansion, *52*
pathnames, *38–39,* 803
    parsing, 294–295
    validity checking, *129*
patterns
    searching for, 175–177
pax, 103, 144, *145–151,* 154, *760–761*
PDP-11, 2
Perl, 794
perl, 225
permissions. *See* files (permissions)
pg, 108
physical volumes, *699*
pic, *300–301*
PIPE, 31
pipelines, 22, 35, *57, 326,* 803
pipes, *57–58, 326,* 803
    named, *802*
        See also FIFO files
pixels, 803
PKZIP, 141, 144
PL/I, 199
.plan, 231
platforms, 803

Plauger, P.J. (Bill), 6
popd, 397, 407
PORT commands, 645
portable character set, 75
ports, 803
POSIX, *9–10*
POSIX.1, 9
POSIX.2, 9, 11–13
POSIX locale, 73, 803
postmarks, *583*, 803
pr, 113, *118–121, 761*
primary groups, 28
primary mailbox, 251, *585*, 804
print, *278*, 369, *761*
print requests, 113–118
   cancelling, 118
   displaying, 117–118
   issuing, 114–116
printcap, 69
printenv, 35
PRINTER, 114, 692
printer status, 117–118
printers, 114
printf, 272, *274–278, 761–762*
priorities, adjusting, 248–249
proc directory, 55
process group leaders, *35*, 804
process groups, *35*, 360, 804
process ID, 30
processes, *30–36*, 804
   abnormal termination, 32
   adjusting priorities, 248–249
   background, *797*
   child, *797*
   foreground, *800*
   killing, 242–243
   listing, 235–241
   monitoring, 185
   parent, *803*
   real and effective IDs, 36
   sending signals to, 242
   waiting for completion, 249, 368
produce, *57*, 804
.profile, 67, 250, 311, 376–377, 787
programs
   locating, 128
.project, 231
prompts, 787
protection modes, *44*
ps, 235, 242
   BSD version, 237–240, 762
   POSIX version, 240–241, 763
   System V version, 235–237, 763
pushd, 397, 408
pwd, 22, *93*, 369, 407, *763*, 786

QUIT, 31
quit key, 31
quitting. *See* logging out
quotation, *63–64*, 804

Rand Corporation, 610

random numbers, 370
raw interfaces, 89, 804
raw mode, *89*, 804
rcp, 627, 631, *636, 763*
RCS, 302–306, 578
rcs, 304, 306
rcsdiff, 304, 306
rcsfile, 306
rcsfreeze, 306
rcslog, 306
rcsmerge, 304, 306
read, 272, *279*, 369, 407, *763–764*
   input separators for, 372
readline, 402
readonly, 366, 407
real group ID, *36*, 47, 804
real user ID, *36*, 46, 804
reboot, *705, 764*
recipients, *584*, 804
recursion, 820
recursive, 804
redirection, 22, *56*, 330–333, 804
Redman, Brian, 658
regular expressions, *81–86*, 804
   basic, *81–84*
   defined in ed, 81
   extended, *84–85*
   interval expressions, 84
   replacements for, 85–86
   searching for, 175–177
   subexpressions, 84
regular files, 804
rehash, 398
relative pathnames, *39*, 804
remote computers
   names of, 632
remote operations, 632–636
   common files, 632–634
   copying files, 636
   executing commands, 635
   listing users, 636–637
   logging in, 634
remote procedure calls, 617
remsh, 635
renice, *248–249, 764*
repeated lines, eliminating, 183–184
request ID, 114, 118
reset, 72, *257*, 258
reset string, *70*, 804
resources, *675*
respawning, 230
restarting output, 21
restricted shells, 805
return, 364, 407
.rhosts, 633
Ritchie, Dennis, 2
rlogin, 60, 631, *634*, 637, *764*
rm, 23, *105–106, 764–765*, 786, 787
rmdir, 105, *106*, 765, 787
rn, 615
root, 805
root, 21, 27, 703

rows, number on screen, 265
rsh (remote shell), 631, *635, 765*
run levels, 704
    shown by who, 229
rusers, 228
rwho, 631, *636–637, 765*

Saltzer, Jerry, 298
Salus, Peter, 683
sbin directory, 53, 54
SCCS, 302, 578
scheduling jobs, 243–248
scheduling tasks, 30
Schwartz, Randal L., 225
SCO, 3, 10
Script formatter, 298
secondary mailbox, *585,* 805
sed, 81, *192–199, 765–766*
    addresses, 194–195
    form of a script, 194–195
    hold buffer, *193*
    hold space, 193
    input buffer, *193*
    pattern space, 193
    regular expressions, 81
sendmail, 584
servers, 627, *672,* 805
set, 65, 367, 407, 787
set-gid bit, *47,* 48, 255, 334, 772
    testing for, 334
set-uid bit, *46–47,* 255, 334, 772, 805
    testing for, 334
setenv, 396, 787
setlocale, 73
Seventh Edition, 2, 4
sexps, *499*
sh, *318, 766,* 786
    exiting with eof character, 262
    variables, 66
shadow files, 251
shar, *612–614, 766*
share directory, 54
shell, *18,* 805
    cd handled by, 93
SHELL, 251, 310
shell procedures, *29*
    See also shell scripts
shell scripts, *29, 318–320,* 805
    choice of interpreter, 320, 364
    debugging, 317, 320
    execute permission for, 44
    use of expr in, 287
shells, *28–29, 307–379, 381–410*
    See also ksh
    scripts, 29
shift, 367, 396, 407
shutdown, 705, *706, 767*
shutting down, 705–707
signals, *31–32,* 805
    codes for, 31–32
    sending, 242
    sent on shutdown, 705

Silicon Graphics, 3
simple command, *322*
single-user mode, 707
Sixth Edition, 2
Slackware, 7
sleep, *249,* 329, *767*
SLIP, 658
Snobol, 199, 207
sockets, *59–60,* 122, 225
    testing for, 334
soft links. *See* symbolic links
software installation, 693–696
    Makefiles, using, 694
    manual pages, 694–696
Solaris 1, 4, 795
Solaris 2, 3, 4, 795
sort, 60, 72, *170–175, 767,* 787
source, 398, 409
source files, 54
space, visible, 16
special files, 25, *86, 88–89,* 805
    See also block special files, character special files
    creating, 168–169
spell, 501
split, 184, 186, *188–189,* 290, *767–768*
spreadsheets, 78
src directory, 54
Stallman, Richard, 8, 467
stand directory, 55
standard error, *56,* 805
standard input, *56,* 62, 64, 805
    duplicating, 139
standard output, *56,* 64, 805
start key, 21
status check, 432
Stettner, Heidi, 683
sticky bit, *48,* 49, 135, 334, 772, 805
    testing for, 334
STOP, 32, 34
stop key, 21
stopped job, 33
stopping output, 21
Streams, *60*
strings, 805
    locating within files, 293–294
    producing, *274–278*
strings, *293–294, 768*
stty, 19, 89, 256, *260–265, 768–769*
    form of command, 260
    negated settings, 261
    setting control characters, 262
    setting control modes, 263
    settings for interpreting input, 263–264
    settings for interpreting output, 264
su, *252–253, 769*
subcommands, 805
subexpressions, *84*
subshells, *342,* 805
    direct execution, *342–343*
    indirect execution, *343,* 344
sum, 129, 613
Sun Microsystems, 3

Sun Yellow Pages,   628
SunOS,   4
SunOS 5.x,   3
superuser,   *27*, 805
   lost password,   703
superuser privileges,   689–690
   acquiring,   252–253
supplementary groups,   *28*
`suspend`,   409
suspend key,   20
suspending execution,   249
SVID,   10, 12
SVR4,   2
symbolic links,   *41–42*, 98, 101, 122
   testing for,   334
symbolic modes,   *48–49*, 806
   group,   48
   locking,   49
   permissions,   49
   who letters,   48
`sync`,   705, 706
`sysadm`,   253
system administration,   *26–27*, *689–707*, 806
   error notification,   295
   printers,   692
   software installation,   693–696
   terminals,   692
   users and groups,   691–692
   utilities,   691
system date,   234
system information, producing,   291
system initialization,   704–705
system mailbox,   *585*, 806
`Systems`,   *665*
System V,   2–3
   releases of,   2
   Streams,   60
   System V Interface Definition,   10
System V/386,   3

tabs
   expanding and unexpanding,   181–183
   setting positions,   267–268
`tabs`,   256, *267–268*, 769
tag files,   433, 436, *466*, 806
   `more`, used with,   111
tag tables,   561
`tail`,   *184–186*, *769–770*
`talk`,   *269*, 270, *770*
Tanenbaum, Andrew,   7
tapes as block devices,   87
`tar`,   103, 149, *151–154*, *770*
Taylor, Dave,   612
`.taz` files,   141
`tbl`,   *300*
TCP/IP,   4, 627, *628*, 806
`tcsh`,   382
`tee`,   *139*, *770*
Tektronix 4015,   681
Telemail,   619
telephone dialing,   666
TELNET,   637

TELNET   (*Continued*)
   FTP, basis for,   642
`telnet`,   60, 621, 631, 634, *637–642*, *770–771*
   commands,   638–639
   compared to `cu`,   666
   exiting from,   638
   flow control,   642
   line mode versus character mode,   638
   prompt,   637
   TELNET sequences,   639
   toggles,   640–642
   typing passwords,   638
   variables,   640
TELNET protocol,   639
TELNET protocol,   771
TENEX,   651, 652
Tenth Edition,   2
`TERM`,   31, 68, 72, 256, 257, 259
terminal descriptions,   68–72, 265
terminal driver,   260
terminals,   806
   displaying the pathname,   232
   emulation under X,   680–682
   initializing,   266
   interfaces for,   89
   names for,   90
   resetting,   266
   restoring to sanity,   257
   retrieving descriptions,   70
   setting,   72
   setting tab stops,   267–268
   setting up,   256–260
`terminfo`,   68–72
`termio`,   669
`test`,   *333–335*, 369, 407, *771–772*
TEX,   9, 301–302
third-party transfers,   *654*
Thompson, Kenneth,   1
threads,   *30*, 806
three-finger salute,   705
`tic`,   69
Tichy, Walter,   302
`time`,   *292–293*, 399, *772*
time usage, displaying,   368
`times`,   368, 407
timing a command,   *292–293*
tmp directory,   54
toggles,   806
`tolower`,   76, 179
top-level domains,   *620*
Torvalds, Linus,   7
`tostop`,   33, 264
`touch`,   *138–139*, 244, *773*
`toupper`,   76, 179
`tput`,   70, 256, 257, *265–267*, *773*
`tr`,   *177–179*, *773*
`trap`,   31, 407
trees,   *37*, 806
`troff`,   116, *298–301*
`true`,   *773*
`tset`,   70, 71, 72, *256–260*, *773–774*
`TSTP`,   32

TTIN, 32, 34
TTOU, 32, 34, 264
tty, *232, 774*
ttymon, 250, 692
twm, 793
type, 128, 288, *292*, 407, *774*
typeset, 365, 408
TZ, 251

ulimit, 368, 407
ULIMIT, 43
Ultrix, 4
umask, 48, 50, 93, *135–136*, 407, *774*
umask value, *50–51*, 806
umount, *698, 774*
unalias, *358*, 407, *774–775*
uname, *291, 775*
uncompress, *140*, 153, *775*
unexpand, *181–183, 775*
unhash, 398
Unics, 1
uniq, *183–184, 775*
universal resource locators, *629*
UNIX, 1–807
  early history, *1–2*
  file system, 36–56
  free systems, 7–9
  licensing, 5–6
  managing a system, 689–707
  standards, 9–10
UNIX Systems Laboratories, 2
UNIX 32V, 3
UNIX International, 3
UnixWare, 3, 35
unset, 366, 396, 407
unsetenv, 396
unshar, 613
untic, 69, 70
unzip, 144
URL, 619
Usenet, 26
user names, 18, 39, 692
  changing, 252–253
users, 26, *27–28*, 45, 46, 806
  finding, 230–232
  listing, 228–230
  showing ID, 255
usr directory, 53
/usr/hosts, 633
ustar format, 149
utilities, built-in, 324
UTS, 3
uucp, 631, 658, *660–663*, 669, *775–776*
  command-line options, 662–663
  configuring, 659, 793
  local copies, 662
  permissions required, 661
  requesting remote files, 662
UUCP network, 618, 619, 624, 658
uudecode, *143*, 631, 669, *776*
uuencode, 140, *143*, 631, 669, *776*
uulog, *664*
uuname, 631, *665, 776*

uupick, 631, *659–660, 776*
uustat, 658, *663–664*, 776–777
uuto, 631, *659*, 777
uwm, 672

vacation, 586
var directory, 55
variables, *65–66*
  displaying with echo, 272
  set and unset, 65
VAX, 2, 3, 4
vedit, 419
version control, 130, 302–306
  Emacs interface, 578–580
vi, 4, 67, 109, 112, *412–442*, 610, *777–780*
  adjusting the screen, 420–421
  altering text, 427–430
  as extension of ex, 412
  autoindent mode, 417–418
  cancelling commands, 416
  command line, 419
  commands in general, 414–415
  context, *426*
  control characters, quoting, 417
  copying text, 430
  current file, *413*
  current line, *413*
  deleting text, 427–430
  executing ex commands from, 417
  exiting from, 420
  file commands, 432–433
  indentation, 417–418, 430
  input mode, 416
  inserting text, 426–427
  local variables, 435–442
  macros, 433–435
  main buffer, *412*
  meanings of keys, 413–414
  modes, 414
  moving by direction, 422
  moving by syntactic units, 423–424
  moving text, 430
  named buffers, 430–431
  objects, *415*
  regular expressions, 81, 418
  repeating actions, 432
  repetition count, *415*
  restoring the screen, 421
  screen organization, 413
  screenful size, 419, 440
  scrolling the screen, 420
  searching, 424–426
  setting local variables, 433
  setting placemarks, 426
  shift width, 417, 438
  status line, 413
  status-line mode, 416–417
  substitution, 428
  switching to ex, 435
  tilde lines, 413
  undo, 432
  visual mode, *412*
  windows, *418*

vi *(Continued)*
  wordwrap, 438
  yanking, 491
view, 419
virtual terminals, *35, 806*
visible space, *16*
visible spaces, 806
VISUAL, 312

w, 228
wait, *249,* 368, 407, *781*
Wall, Larry, 164, 225, 615
wc, *137–138, 781*
Weinberger, Peter, 199
Welsh, Matthew, 792
whatis, 695
which, *128,* 288, *781*
Whitesmiths Ltd., 6
whitespace, *61,* 76, 806
who, 9, *228–230,* 255, *781*
whoami, 230
whodo, 228
whois, 622
widgets, *673*
wildcards, 22, *51,* 389, 807
WINCH, 32
windex, 695
window managers, 671–672, 807
windows, *670,* 807
word-erase key, 20
words, *61,* 807
words (in commands), *61*
working directory, *39,* 93, 763, 807
workstations, 627
World Wide Web, 629–630
write, 91, 229, *270, 781*

X, 5, 35, *670–688,* 795
  colors, 679–680
  display specifications, 672–673
  displays under, 692
  Emacs under, 468
  focus, *671*
  fonts, 678–679
  geometry, *677–678*
  getting started, 671
  initialization files, 680
  initializing, 685–686
  installing software, 694
  instance, *676*
  logical font descriptions, 674
  properties, *673*

X *(Continued)*
  pseudo-terminals, 90
  resource database, 677
  resource files, *675*
  resource manager, *675*
  resources, *675–676*
  root window, *670,* 686
  servers, *672*
  Toolkit options, 674–675
  widgets, *673*
  with remote logins, 617
X Consortium, 5, 8
X Toolkit, 673
X Window System. *See* X
X11R6, 5, 795
xargs, 288, *289–290, 782*
xbiff, *683–684, 782*
xclock, *683, 782*
xcolors, *684, 782*
Xconfig, 692
.Xdefaults, 677
xdm, 671
Xenix, 3
xfd, *684, 782*
xfontsel, *684–685, 782*
XFree86, 7, 8, 794
XFree86 Project, Inc., 8
xinit, *685–686, 782*
.xinitrc, 685
xkill, *687, 782*
XLFD, 678
xlsfonts, *684, 783*
xman, 26, *687–688,* 694, *783*
xmkmf, 694
X/Open, 2, 10
XPG, 10
xrdb, 677, *686, 783*
xset, *686, 783*
xsetroot, *686–687, 783*
xterm, 71, 671, *680–682, 783*
  screen saver, 686
  using the mouse, 681–682

yank, *491*
Yggdrasil, 7, 792, 795

zcat, *140, 783*
zip, 144
zipped files, 141–143
Zog, 585
zulu, 712

About the Authors

Paul W. Abrahams, Sc.D., CCP, is the author of *T$_E$X for the Impatient*, a book whose success inspired *UNIX for the Impatient*. A consulting computer scientist and past president of the Association for Computing Machinery, he specializes in programming languages, design and implementation of software systems, and technical writing. He received his bachelor's degree in mathematics from the Massachusetts Institute of Technology in 1956 and his doctorate in mathematics there in 1963, studying artificial intelligence under Marvin Minsky and John McCarthy and writing his dissertation on "Machine Verification of Mathematical Proof". He is one of the designers of the first LISP system and also the designer of the CIMS PL/I system, which he developed while a professor at New York University. He also participated in the design of the Software Engineering Design Language (SEDL), developed at the IBM T.J. Watson Laboratories. Currently he is working on the design of SPLASH, a Systems Programming LAnguage for Software Hackers and on a new book, *OS/2 for the Impatient*. In 1995 he was honored as a Fellow of the ACM. Paul resides in Deerfield, Massachusetts, where he writes, hacks, hikes, hunts wild mushrooms, and listens to classical music. His Internet address is `abrahams@acm.org`.

Bruce R. Larson is the founder of Integral Resources, a systems integration and UNIX consulting firm, a co-founder of BRInet (1995), which provides Internet connection and consulting services, and a partner in Internet Exchange Limited (1994), which provides dialup and ISDN connectivity in the Boston area. His specialties are shell tools, systems programming, IP and X.25 networks, performance monitoring, software integration, mail systems, and security. He has worked with Solaris, AIX, HPUX, IRIX, SCO UNIX, and other Intel-based UNIX systems. His experience includes configuring and administering Internet domains and connecting UNIX systems to X.25 networks, as well as designing and implementing custom installation scripts, kernel-level data extraction tools, shell tools, a software message switch, and IP-based utilities. From 1979 to 1981, he did software modelling for the Federal Aviation Authority under a grant from the U.S. Department of Transportation; in 1988 he received his bachelor's degree in pure mathematics from the University of Massachusetts at Boston. A member of UniForum, the IEEE Computer Society, and the American Mathematical Society, Bruce resides in Milton, Massachusetts. His Internet address is `blarson@ires.com`.

Other Books from Addison-Wesley

BUGS in Writing
Lyn Dupré

If you are a scientist, engineer, or other person who writes and who works with computers, Dupré's *BUGS in Writing* will show you how to rid your prose of the most common problems that writers face. With simple principles for lucid writing conveyed by numerous, intriguing, and frequently hilarious examples, BUGS may also be the first book on English grammar that you will read for sheer fun. Whether you have a paper, proposal, research study, thesis, software manual, conference talk, business report, or any other document to prepare, if you want to communicate your ideas effectively, first browse through a copy of BUGS. ISBN 0-201-60019-6

On to C   On to C++
Patrick Henry Winston   Patrick Henry Winston

A best-selling author has written two books of interest if you already know how to program and want quickly to add C or C++ to your programming-language repertoire. Designed to be brief—about 300 pp each—the books nevertheless contain everything you need to know to get up and running in one or both of these languages. ISBN 0-201-58042-X; ISBN 0-201-58043-8

Scientific and Engineering C++
An Introduction with Advanced Techniques and Examples
John J. Barton and Lee R. Nackman

Building on knowledge of FORTRAN and C, this 671–pp book shows how you can use C++ and the object-oriented programming style to produce better-quality scientific and engineering programs. Moving quickly beyond the syntax and rules of the language, it illustrates the application of more interesting and important concepts and techniques in solving substantial problems. ISBN 0-201-53393-6

The LaTeX Companion
Michel Goossens, Frank Mittelbach, Alexander Samarin

This book is an advanced guide to the current LaTeX standard for typesetting technical documents, and to more than 150 packages that can be used at any site to provide additional features. A useful companion to Lamport's authoritative user's guide and reference manual, it answers the questions most frequently posed to the authors during years of LaTeX support and application development.
ISBN 0-201-54199-8

Up-to-date information about Addison-Wesley books is available from our Internet site, World Wide Web address `http://www.aw.com`. For Gopher access, type gopher `aw.com`. You will find these books wherever technical books are sold, or you may call Addison-Wesley at 1-800-822-6339.